ELEVENTH EDITION

Principles of
Macroeconomics

ELEVENTH EDITION

Principles of
Macroeconomics

Karl E. Case
Wellesley College

Ray C. Fair
Yale University

Sharon M. Oster
Yale University

PEARSON

Boston   Columbus   Indianapolis   New York   San Francisco   Upper Saddle River
Amsterdam   Cape Town   Dubai   London   Madrid   Milan   Munich   Paris   Montréal   Toronto
Delhi   Mexico City   São Paulo   Sydney   Hong Kong   Seoul   Singapore   Taipei   Tokyo

Dedicated To
Professor Richard A. Musgrave
and
Professor Robert M. Solow
and
Professor Richard Caves

Editor in Chief: Donna Battista
AVP/Executive Editor: David Alexander
Senior Editorial Project Manager: Lindsey Sloan
AVP/Executive Marketing Manager: Lori DeShazo
Marketing Assistant: Kimberly Lovato
Managing Editor: Jeff Holcomb
Senior Production Project Manager: Roberta Sherman
Senior Manufacturing Buyer: Carol Melville
Senior Art Director: Jonathan Boylan
Cover Design: Jonathan Boylan
Cover Image: Pressmaster/Fotolia

Image Manager: Rachel Youdelman
Photo Researcher: Integra PDY-IN
Full-Service Project Management/Composition:
  GEX Publishing Services
Typeface: 10/12 Minion
Text Permission Project Manager: Samantha Graham
Director of Media: Susan Schoenberg
Content Lead, MyEconLab: Noel Lotz
Senior Media Producer: Melissa Honig
Printer/Binder: Courier, Kendallville
Cover Printer: Lehigh Phoenix

Credits and acknowledgments borrowed from other sources and reproduced, with permission, in this textbook appear on appropriate page within text.

FRED® is a registered trademark and the FRED® Logo and ST. LOUIS FED are trademarks of the Federal Reserve Bank of St. Louis. http://research.stlouisfed.org/fred2/

Case, Karl E.
  Principles of macroeconomics / Karl E. Case, Wellesley College, Ray C. Fair, Yale University, Sharon M. Oster, Yale University. —Eleventh edition.
    pages cm
  Includes index.
  ISBN 978-0-13-302367-1 (pbk.)
  1. Macroeconomics. I. Fair, Ray C. II. Oster, Sharon M. III. Title.
  HB172.5.C375 2014
  339—dc23
              2013012313

10 9 8 7 6 5 4 3 2 1

ISBN 13: 978-0-13-302367-1
ISBN 10: 0-13-302367-2

About the Authors

Karl E. Case is Professor of Economics Emeritus at Wellesley College where he has taught for 34 years and served several tours of duty as Department Chair. He is a Senior Fellow at the Joint Center for Housing Studies at Harvard University and a founding partner in the real estate research firm of Fiserv Case Shiller Weiss, which produces the S&P Case-Shiller Index of home prices. He serves as a member of the Index Advisory Committee of Standard and Poor's, and along with Ray Fair he serves on the Academic Advisory Board of the Federal Reserve Bank of Boston.

Before coming to Wellesley, he served as Head Tutor in Economics (director of undergraduate studies) at Harvard, where he won the Allyn Young Teaching Prize. He was Associate Editor of the *Journal of Economic Perspectives* and the *Journal of Economic Education,* and he was a member of the AEA's Committee on Economic Education.

Professor Case received his B.A. from Miami University in 1968; spent three years on active duty in the Army, and received his Ph.D. in Economics from Harvard University in 1976.

Professor Case's research has been in the areas of real estate, housing, and public finance. He is author or coauthor of five books, including *Principles of Economics, Economics and Tax Policy*, and *Property Taxation: The Need for Reform*, and he has published numerous articles in professional journals.

For the last 25 years, his research has focused on real estate markets and prices. He has authored numerous professional articles, many of which attempt to isolate the causes and consequences of boom and bust cycles and their relationship to regional and national economic performance.

Ray C. Fair is Professor of Economics at Yale University. He is a member of the Cowles Foundation at Yale and a Fellow of the Econometric Society. He received a B.A. in Economics from Fresno State College in 1964 and a Ph.D. in Economics from MIT in 1968. He taught at Princeton University from 1968 to 1974 and has been at Yale since 1974.

Professor Fair's research has primarily been in the areas of macroeconomics and econometrics, with particular emphasis on macroeconometric model building. He also has done work in the areas of finance, voting behavior, and aging in sports. His publications include *Specification, Estimation, and Analysis of Macroeconometric Models* (Harvard Press, 1984); *Testing Macroeconometric Models* (Harvard Press, 1994); and *Estimating How the Macroeconomy Works* (Harvard Press, 2004).

Professor Fair has taught introductory and intermediate macroeconomics at Yale. He has also taught graduate courses in macroeconomic theory and macroeconometrics.

Professor Fair's U.S. and multicountry models are available for use on the Internet free of charge. The address is http://fairmodel.econ.yale.edu. Many teachers have found that having students work with the U.S. model on the Internet is a useful complement to an introductory macroeconomics course.

Sharon M. Oster is the Frederic Wolfe Professor of Economics and Management and former Dean of the Yale School of Management. Professor Oster joined Case and Fair as a coauthor in the ninth edition of this book. Professor Oster has a B.A. in Economics from Hofstra University and a Ph.D. in Economics from Harvard University.

Professor Oster's research is in the area of industrial organization. She has worked on problems of diffusion of innovation in a number of different industries, on the effect of regulations on business, and on competitive strategy. She has published a number of articles in these areas and is the author of several books, including *Modern Competitive Analysis* and *The Strategic Management of Nonprofits*.

Prior to joining the School of Management at Yale, Professor Oster taught for a number of years in Yale's Department of Economics. In the department, Professor Oster taught introductory and intermediate microeconomics to undergraduates as well as several graduate courses in industrial organization. Since 1982, Professor Oster has taught primarily in the Management School, where she teaches the core microeconomics class for MBA students and a course in the area of competitive strategy. Professor Oster also consults widely for businesses and nonprofit organizations and has served on the boards of several publicly traded companies and nonprofit organizations.

Brief Contents

Contents

17 Long-Run Growth 321

18 Alternative Views in Macroeconomics 337

Preface

Our goal in the 11th edition, as it was in the first edition, is to instill in students a fascination with both the functioning of the economy and the power and breadth of economics. The first line of every edition of our book has been "The study of economics should begin with a sense of wonder." We hope that readers come away from our book with a basic understanding of how market economies function, an appreciation for the things they do well, and a sense of the things they do poorly. We also hope that readers begin to learn the art and science of economic thinking and begin to look at some policy and even personal decisions in a different way.

What's New in This Edition?

- The 11th edition has continued the changes in the *Economics in Practice* boxes that we began several editions ago. In these boxes, we try to bring economic thinking to the concerns of the typical student. In many cases, we do this by spotlighting recent research, much of it by young scholars.
  - Chapter 6 looks at recent work on "green" national income accounting, a topic likely to excite many environmentally conscious undergraduates.
  - Chapter 7 describes research on the long-term effects on wages and job prospects of new college graduates who begin their careers in a recession.

  In other cases, we use recent events to show the power and breadth of economic models and principles.
  - When Hurricane Sandy struck the east coast of the United States, why did most of the subsequent charges of price-gouging involve gas and hotel rooms? Chapter 4 uses principles of elasticity to answer this question.
  - Several of the new boxes in the macroeconomics chapters focus on the debates we have had in the United States in the last year on tax and spending policy. Finally, more of the boxes are global, with examples on the move from tea to coffee drinking in China, or roads in India, or the relative productivity of American versus Indian managers.

  It is our hope that students will come to see both how broad the tools of economics are and how exciting is much of the new research in the field. For each box, we have also added questions to take students back from the box to the analytics of the textbook to reinforce the underlying economic principles of the illustrations.

- As in the previous edition, we have reworked some of the chapters to streamline them and to improve readability. In this edition, Chapters 2 and 3, have been substantially reworked, while many of the other chapters have been tightened and made more current.

- A major change has been made in macro: We have replaced the LM curve with a Fed interest rate rule. Chapters 12 and 13 have been completely rewritten to incorporate this change. There is no IS/LM model, and no longer does the money supply play any exogenous role in the AS/AD model. This change simplifies the analysis and makes the model more realistic. The Fed does in practice target the interest rate and not the money supply! The supply of money and demand for money chapters (Chapters 10 and 11) have been retained because they deal with many basic questions in macro. The main point of these two chapters going forward is to show how the Fed controls the interest rate. This then allows us to use the Fed rule in Chapters 12 and 13. Without Chapters 10 and 11, students would not understand what is behind the Fed rule and would not understand quantitative easing and the like.

- U.S. short-term interest rates have been roughly zero since the 10th edition, and we have added discussion on what a zero interest rate bound means. This discussion is now framed around the Fed rule. We have also updated and expanded our discussion of the Fed's balance sheet (Chapter 10). Also, federal government deficits have been high since the 10th edition, and we have expanded our discussion of this (Chapters 9 and 15).
- All of the macro data have been updated through 2012. The slow recovery from the 2008–2009 recession is evident in these data. This gives students a good idea of what has been happening to the economy since they left high school.
- Many new questions and problems at the end of the chapters have been added.

The Foundation

The themes of *Principles of Macroeconomics*, 11th edition, are the same themes of the first ten editions. The purposes of this book are to introduce the discipline of economics and to provide a basic understanding of how economies function. This requires a blend of economic theory, institutional material, and real-world applications. We have maintained a balance between these ingredients in every chapter. The hallmark features of our book are as follows:

1. Three-tiered explanations of key concepts (*stories-graphs-equations*)
2. Intuitive and accessible structure
3. International coverage

Three-Tiered Explanations: Stories-Graphs-Equations

Professors who teach principles of economics are faced with a classroom of students with different abilities, backgrounds, and learning styles. For some students, analytical material is difficult no matter how it is presented; for others, graphs and equations seem to come naturally. The problem facing instructors and textbook authors is how to convey the core principles of the discipline to as many students as possible without selling the better students short. Our approach to this problem is to present most core concepts in the following three ways.

First, we present each concept in the context of a simple intuitive *story* or example in words often followed by a table. Second, we use a *graph* in most cases to illustrate the story or example. And finally, in many cases where appropriate, we use an *equation* to present the concept with a mathematical formula.

Macroeconomic Structure

We remain committed to the view that it is a mistake simply to throw aggregate demand and aggregate supply curves at students in the first few chapters of a principles book. To understand the *AS* and *AD* curves, students need to know about the functioning of both the goods market and the money market. The logic behind the simple demand curve is wrong when it is applied to the relationship between aggregate demand and the price level. Similarly, the logic behind the simple supply curve is wrong when it is applied to the relationship between aggregate supply and the price level. We thus build up to the AS/AD model slowly.

The goods market is discussed in Chapters 8 and 9 (the IS curve). The money market is discussed in Chapters 10 and 11 (material behind the Fed rule). Everything comes together in Chapter 12, which derives the AD and AS curves and determines the equilibrium values of aggregate output, the price level, and the interest rate. This is the core chapter and where the Fed rule plays a major role. Chapter 13 then uses the model in Chapter 12 to analyze policy effects and cost shocks. Chapter 14 then brings in the labor market. The figure at the top of the next page (Figure III.1 on page 145) gives you an overview of this structure.

One of the big issues in the organization of the macroeconomic material is whether long-run growth issues should be taught before short-run chapters on the determination of national income and countercyclical policy. In the last four editions, we moved a significant discussion of growth to Chapter 7, "Unemployment, Inflation, and Long-Run Growth," and

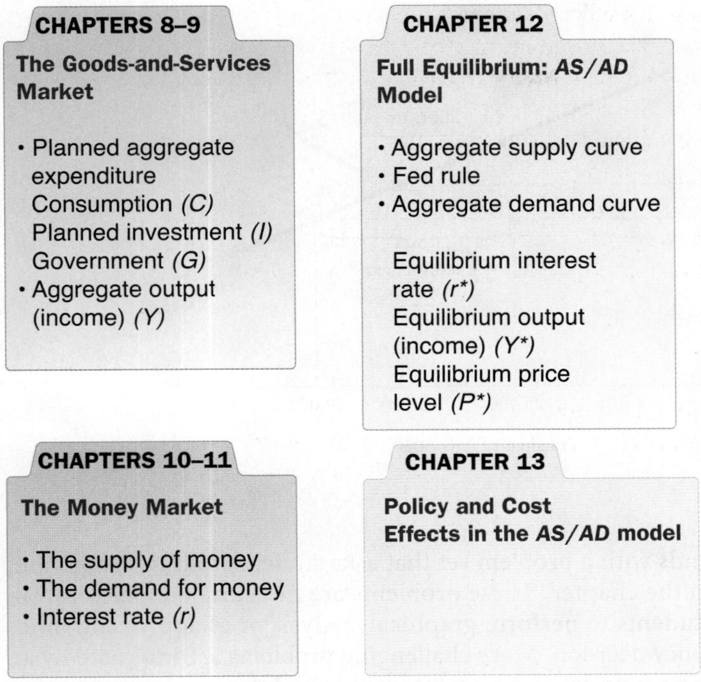

CHAPTERS 8–9

The Goods-and-Services Market

- Planned aggregate expenditure
  Consumption (C)
  Planned investment (I)
  Government (G)
- Aggregate output (income) (Y)

CHAPTER 12

Full Equilibrium: AS/AD Model

- Aggregate supply curve
- Fed rule
- Aggregate demand curve

  Equilibrium interest rate (r*)
  Equilibrium output (income) (Y*)
  Equilibrium price level (P*)

CHAPTER 14

The Labor Market

- The supply of labor
- The demand for labor
- Employment and unemployment

CHAPTERS 10–11

The Money Market

- The supply of money
- The demand for money
- Interest rate (r)

CHAPTER 13

Policy and Cost Effects in the AS/AD model

▲ FIGURE III.1 **The Core of Macroeconomic Theory**

highlighted it. However, while we wrote Chapter 17, the major chapter on long-run growth, so that it can be taught before or after the short-run chapters, we remain convinced that it is easier for students to understand the growth issue once they have come to grips with the logic and controversies of short-run cycles, inflation, and unemployment.

International Coverage

As in previous editions, we continue to integrate international examples and applications throughout the text. This probably goes without saying: The days in which an introductory economics text could be written with a closed economy in mind have long since gone.

Tools for Learning

As authors and teachers, we understand the challenges of the principles of economics course. Our pedagogical features are designed to illustrate and reinforce key economic concepts through real-world examples and applications.

Economics in Practice

As described earlier, the *Economics in Practice* feature focuses on recent research or events that support a key concept in the chapter and help students think about the broad and exciting applications of economics to their lives and the world around them. Each box contains a question or two to further connect the material they are learning with their lives.

Graphs

Reading and interpreting graphs is a key part of understanding economic concepts. The Chapter 1 Appendix, "How to Read and Understand Graphs," shows readers how to interpret the 200-plus graphs featured in this book. We use red curves to illustrate the behavior of firms and blue curves to show the behavior of households. We use a different shade of red and blue to signify a shift in a curve.

◀ **FIGURE 3.9 Excess Demand, or Shortage**
At a price of $1.75 per bushel, quantity demanded exceeds quantity supplied. When excess *demand* exists, there is a tendency for price to rise. When quantity demanded equals quantity supplied, excess demand is eliminated and the market is in equilibrium. Here the equilibrium price is $2.50 and the equilibrium quantity is 35,000 bushels.

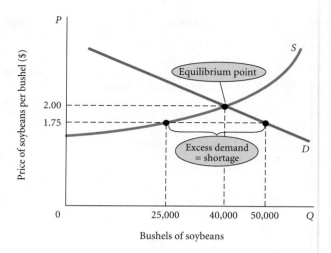

Problems and Solutions

Each chapter and appendix ends with a problem set that asks students to think about and apply what they've learned in the chapter. These problems are not simple memorization questions. Rather, they ask students to perform graphical analysis or to apply economics to a real-world situation or policy decision. More challenging problems are indicated by an asterisk. Many problems have been updated. The solutions to all of the problems are available in the *Instructor's Manuals*. Instructors can provide the solutions to their students so they can check their understanding and progress.

MyEconLab   MyEconLab Real-time data

MyEconLab is a powerful assessment and tutorial system that works hand-in-hand with *Microeconomics*, *Macroeconomics*, and *Economics*. MyEconLab includes comprehensive homework, quiz, test, and tutorial options, allowing instructors to manage all assessment needs in one program. Key innovations in the MyEconLab course for the eleventh edition, include the following:

- Real-time *Data Analysis Exercises*, marked with ⊕, allow students and instructors to use the absolute latest data from FRED, the online macroeconomic data bank from the Federal Reserve Bank of St. Louis. By completing the exercises, students become familiar with a key data source, learn how to locate data, and develop skills to interpret data.

- In the eText available in MyEconLab, select figures labeled MyEconLab Real-time data allow students to display a popup graph updated with real-time data from FRED.

- Current News Exercises, new to this edition of the MyEconLab course, provide a turnkey way to assign gradable news-based exercises in MyEconLab. Every week, Pearson scours the news, finds a current article appropriate for the course, creates an exercise around this news article, and then automatically adds it to MyEconLab. Assigning and grading current news-based exercises that deal with the latest macro events and policy issues and has never been more convenient.

Both the text and supplement package provide ways for instructors and students to assess their knowledge and progress through the course. MyEconLab, the new standard in personalized online learning, is a key part of Case, Fair, and Oster's integrated learning package for the 11th edition.

For the Instructor

MyEconLab is an online course management, testing, and tutorial resource. Instructors can choose how much or how little time to spend setting up and using MyEconLab. Each chapter contains two Sample Tests, Study Plan Exercises, and Tutorial Resources. Student use of these materials requires no initial setup by their instructor. The online Gradebook records each student's performance and time spent on the Tests and Study Plan and generates reports by student or by chapter. Instructors can assign tests, quizzes, and homework in MyEconLab using four resources:

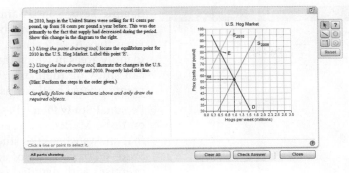

- Preloaded Sample Tests
- Problems similar to the end-of-chapter problems
- Test Item File questions
- Self-authored questions using Econ Exercise Builder

Exercises use multiple-choice, graph drawing, and free-response items, many of which are generated algorithmically so that each time a student works them, a different variation is presented. MyEconLab grades every problem, even those with graphs. When working homework exercises, students receive immediate feedback with links to additional learning tools.

Customization and Communication MyEconLab in CourseCompass™ provides additional optional customization and communication tools. Instructors who teach distance learning courses or very large lecture sections find the CourseCompass format useful because they can upload course documents and assignments, customize the order of chapters, and use communication features such as Digital Drop Box and Discussion Board.

Experiments in MyEconLab

Experiments are a fun and engaging way to promote active learning and mastery of important economic concepts. Pearson's experiments program is flexible and easy for instructors and students to use.

- Single-player experiments allow your students to play an experiment against virtual players from anywhere at any time with an Internet connection.
- Multiplayer experiments allow you to assign and manage a real-time experiment with your class. In both cases, pre- and post-questions for each experiment are available for assignment in MyEconLab.

For the Student

MyEconLab puts students in control of their learning through a collection of tests, practice, and study tools tied to the online interactive version of the textbook, as well as other media resources. Within MyEconLab's structured environment, students practice what they learn, test their understanding, and pursue a personalized Study Plan generated from their performance on Sample Tests and tests set by their instructors. At the core of MyEconLab are the following features:

- Sample Tests, two per chapter
- Personal Study Plan
- Tutorial Instruction
- Graphing Tool

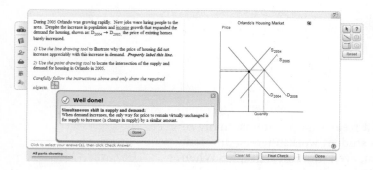

Sample Tests   Two Sample Tests for each chapter are preloaded in MyEconLab, enabling students to practice what they have learned, test their understanding, and identify areas in which they need further work. Students can study on their own, or they can complete assignments created by their instructor.

Personal Study Plan   Based on a student's performance on tests, MyEconLab generates a personal Study Plan that shows where the student needs further study. The Study Plan consists of a series of additional practice exercises with detailed feedback and guided solutions that are keyed to other tutorial resources.

Tutorial Instruction   Launched from many of the exercises in the Study Plan, MyEconLab provides tutorial instruction in the form of step-by-step solutions and other media-based explanations.

Graphing Tool   A graphing tool is integrated into the Tests and Study Plan exercises to enable students to make and manipulate graphs. This feature helps students understand how concepts, numbers, and graphs connect.

Additional MyEconLab Tools   MyEconLab includes the following additional features:

1. **Economics in the News**—This feature provides weekly updates during the school year of news items with links to sources for further reading and discussion questions.

2. **eText**—While students are working in the Study Plan or completing homework assignments, one of the tutorial resources available is a direct link to the relevant page of the text so that students can review the appropriate material to help them complete the exercise.

3. **Glossary**—This searchable version of the textbook glossary provides additional examples and links to related terms.

4. **Glossary Flashcards**—Every key term is available as a flashcard, allowing students to quiz themselves on vocabulary from one or more chapters at a time.

MyEconLab content has been created through the efforts of the following individuals:

Charles Baum, Middle Tennessee State University; Sarah Ghosh, University of Scranton; Russell Kellogg, University of Colorado–Denver; Bert G. Wheeler, Cedarville University; and Noel Lotz and Douglas A. Ruby, Pearson Education.

Resources for the Instructor

The following supplements are designed to make teaching and testing flexible and easy and are available for *Micro*, *Macro*, and *Economics* volumes.

Instructor's Manuals

Two *Instructor's Manuals*, one for *Principles of Microeconomics* and one for *Principles of Macroeconomics*, were prepared by Tony Lima of California State University, East Bay (Hayward, California). The *Instructor's Manuals* are designed to provide the utmost teaching support for instructors. They include the following content:

- Detailed *Chapter Outlines* include key terminology, teaching notes, and lecture suggestions.

- *Topics for Class Discussion* provide topics and real-world situations that help ensure that economic concepts resonate with students.

- Unique *Economics in Practice* features that are not in the main text provide extra real-world examples to present and discuss in class.

- *Teaching Tips* provide tips for alternative ways to cover the material and brief reminders on additional help to provide students. These tips include suggestions for exercises and experiments to complete in class.
- *Extended Applications* include exercises, activities, and experiments to help make economics relevant to students.
- *Excel Workbooks*, available for many chapters, make it easy to customize numerical examples and produce graphs.
- *Solutions* are provided for all problems in the book.

Six Test Item Files

We have tailored the Test Item Files to help instructors easily and efficiently assess student understanding of economic concepts and analyses. Test questions are annotated with the following information:

- **Difficulty:** 1 for straight recall, 2 for some analysis, 3 for complex analysis
- **Type:** Multiple-choice, true/false, short-answer, essay
- **Topic:** The term or concept the question supports
- **Skill:** Fact, definition, analytical, conceptual
- **AACSB:** See description in the next section.

The Test Item Files include questions with tables that students must analyze to solve for numerical answers. The Test Item Files also contain questions based on the graphs that appear in the book. The questions ask students to interpret the information presented in the graph. Many questions require students to sketch a graph on their own and interpret curve movements.

Microeconomics Test Item File 1, by Randy Methenitis of Richland College: Test Item File 1 (TIF1) includes over 2,700 questions. All questions are machine gradable and are either multiple-choice or true/false. This Test Item File is for use with the 11th edition of *Principles of Microeconomics* in the first year of publication. TIF1 is available in a computerized format using TestGen EQ test-generating software and is included in MyEconLab.

Microeconomics Test Item File 2, by Randy Methenitis of Richland College: This additional Test Item File contains another 2,700 machine-gradable questions based on the TIF1 but regenerated to provide instructors with fresh questions when using the book the second year. This Test Item File is available in a computerized format using TestGen EQ test-generating software.

Microeconomics Test Item File 3, by Richard Gosselin of Houston Community College: This third Test Item File includes 1,000 conceptual problems, essay questions, and short-answer questions. Application-type problems ask students to draw graphs and analyze tables. The Word files are available on the Instructor's Resource Center (**www.pearson highered.com/educator**).

Macroeconomics Test Item File 1, by Randy Methenitis of Richland College: Test Item File 1 (TIF1) includes over 2,900 questions. All questions are machine gradable and are either multiple-choice or true/false. This Test Item File is for use with the 11th edition of *Principles of Macroeconomics* in the first year of publication. This Test Item File is available in a computerized format using TestGen EQ test-generating software and included in MyEconLab.

Macroeconomics Test Item File 2, by Randy Methenitis of Richland College: This additional Test Item File contains another 2,900 machine-gradable questions based on the TIF1 but regenerated to provide instructors with fresh questions when using the book the second year. This Test Item File is available in a computerized format using TestGen EQ test-generating software.

Macroeconomics Test Item File 3, by Richard Gosselin of Houston Community College: This third Test Item File includes 1,000 conceptual problems, essay questions, and short-answer questions. Application-type problems ask students to draw graphs and analyze tables. The Word files are available on the Instructor's Resource Center (**www.pearson highered.com/educator**).

The Test Item Files were checked for accuracy by the following professors:

Leon J. Battista, Bronx Community College; Margaret Brooks, Bridgewater State College; Mike Cohick, Collin County Community College; Dennis Debrecht, Carroll College; Amrik Dua, California State Polytechnic University, Pomona; Mitchell Dudley, The College of William & Mary; Ann Eike, University of Kentucky; Connel Fullencamp, Duke University; Craig Gallet, California State University, Sacramento; Michael Goode, Central Piedmont Community College; Steve Hamilton, California State Polytechnic University; James R. Irwin, Central Michigan University; Aaron Jackson, Bentley College; Rus Janis, University of Massachusetts, Amherst; Jonatan Jelen, The City College of New York; Kathy A. Kelly, University of Texas, Arlington; Kate Krause, University of New Mexico; Gary F. Langer, Roosevelt University; Leonard Lardaro, University of Rhode Island; Ross LaRoe, Denison University; Melissa Lind, University of Texas, Arlington; Solina Lindahl, California State Polytechnic University; Pete Mavrokordatos, Tarrant County College; Roberto Mazzoleni, Hofstra University; Kimberly Mencken, Baylor University; Ida Mirzaie, Ohio State University; Shahruz Mohtadi, Suffolk University; Mary Pranzo, California State University, Fresno; Ed Price, Oklahoma State University; Robert Shoffner, Central Piedmont Community College; James Swofford, University of South Alabama; Helen Tauchen, University of North Carolina, Chapel Hill; Eric Taylor, Central Piedmont Community College; Henry Terrell, University of Maryland; John Tommasi, Bentley College; Mukti Upadhyay, Eastern Illinois University; Robert Whaples, Wake Forest University; and Timothy Wunder, University of Texas, Arlington.

The Association to Advance Collegiate Schools of Business (AACSB) The authors of the Test Item File have connected select Test Item File questions to the general knowledge and skill guidelines found in the AACSB assurance of learning standards.

What Is the AACSB? AACSB is a not-for-profit corporation of educational institutions, corporations, and other organizations devoted to the promotion and improvement of higher education in business administration and accounting. A collegiate institution offering degrees in business administration or accounting may volunteer for AACSB accreditation review. The AACSB makes initial accreditation decisions and conducts periodic reviews to promote continuous quality improvement in management education. Pearson Education is a proud member of the AACSB and is pleased to provide advice to help you apply AACSB assurance of learning standards.

What Are AACSB Assurance of Learning Standards? One of the criteria for AACSB accreditation is quality of the curricula. Although no specific courses are required, the AACSB expects a curriculum to include learning experiences in areas such as the following:

- Communication
- Ethical Reasoning
- Analytic Skills
- Use of Information Technology
- Multicultural and Diversity
- Reflective Thinking

Questions that test skills relevant to these guidelines are appropriately tagged. For example, a question testing the moral questions associated with externalities would receive the Ethical Reasoning tag.

How Can Instructors Use the AACSB Tags? Tagged questions help you measure whether students are grasping the course content that aligns with the AACSB guidelines noted. In addition, the tagged questions may help instructors identify potential applications of these skills. This in turn may suggest enrichment activities or other educational experiences to help students achieve these skills.

TestGen

The computerized TestGen package allows instructors to customize, save, and generate classroom tests. The test program permits instructors to edit, add, or delete questions from the Test Item Files; create new graphics; analyze test results; and organize a database of tests and student results. This software allows for extensive flexibility and ease of use. It provides many options for organizing and displaying tests, along with search and sort features. The software and the Test Item Files can be downloaded from the Instructor's Resource Center (**www.pearsonhighered.com/educator**).

PowerPoint® Lecture Presentations

Six sets of PowerPoint slides, three for *Principles of Microeconomics* and three for *Principles of Macroeconomics*, prepared by Fernando Quijano of Dickinson State University, are available:

- A comprehensive set of PowerPoint slides that can be used by instructors for class presentations or by students for lecture preview or review. The presentation includes all the figures, photos, tables, key terms, and equations in the textbook. Two versions are available—the first is in step-by-step mode so that you can build graphs as you would on a blackboard, and the second is in automated mode, using a single click per slide.
- A comprehensive set of PowerPoint slides with Classroom Response Systems (CRS) questions built in so that instructors can incorporate CRS "clickers" into their classroom lectures. For more information on Pearson's partnership with CRS, see the description below. Instructors may download these PowerPoint presentations from the Instructor's Resource Center (**www.pearsonhighered.com/educator**).
- Student versions of the PowerPoint presentations are available as .pdf files from the book's MyEconLab course. This version allows students to print the slides and bring them to class for note taking.

Classroom Response Systems

Classroom Response Systems (CRS) is an exciting new wireless polling technology that makes large and small classrooms even more interactive because it enables instructors to pose questions to their students, record results, and display the results instantly. Students can answer questions easily by using compact remote-control transmitters. Pearson has partnerships with leading providers of classroom response systems and can show you everything you need to know about setting up and using a CRS system. We provide the classroom hardware, text-specific PowerPoint® slides, software, and support; and we show you how your students can benefit. Learn more at **www.pearsonhighered.com/crs**.

Resources for the Student

The following supplements are designed to help students understand and retain the key concepts of each chapter.

MyEconLab

MyEconLab allows students to practice what they learn, test their understanding, and pursue a personalized Study Plan generated from their performance on Sample Tests and tests set by their instructors. Here are MyEconLab's key features. (See page xx of this preface for more details on MyEconLab.)

- Sample Tests, two per chapter
- Personal Study Plan
- Tutorial Instruction
- Graphing Tool

CourseSmart

CourseSmart is an exciting new *choice* for students looking to save money. As an alternative to purchasing the print textbook, students can purchase an electronic version of the same content and save up to 50 percent off the suggested list price of the print text. With a CourseSmart eTextbook, students can search the text, make notes online, print out reading assignments that incorporate lecture notes, and bookmark important passages for later review. For more information or to purchase access to the CourseSmart eTextbook, visit www.coursesmart.com.

Acknowledgments

We are grateful to the many people who helped us prepare the 11th edition. We thank David Alexander, our editor, and Lindsey Sloan, our project manager, for their help and enthusiasm.

Lori DeShazo, Executive Marketing Manager, carefully crafted the marketing message. Roberta Sherman, production editor, and Jeffrey Holcomb, our production managing editor, ensured that the production process of the book went smoothly. In addition, we also want to thank Michelle Durgerian and Marisa Taylor of GEX Publishing Services, who kept us on schedule, and Rachel Youdelman, who managed the research of the many photographs that appear in the book.

We want to give special thanks to Patsy Balin, Murielle Dawdy, and Tracy Waldman for their research assistance.

We also owe a debt of gratitude to those who reviewed and checked the 11th edition for accuracy. They provided us with valuable insight as we prepared this edition and its supplement package.

Reviewers of the Current Edition

Mannie Bloemen, Houston Community College
George Bowling, St. Charles Community College
Scott Cunningham, Baylor University
Leslie Doss, University of Texas San Antonio
Ali Faegh, Houston Community College
William Ganley, Buffalo State, SUNY
Rus Janis, University of Massachusetts
Tony Lima, California State University, East Bay
Ronnie McGinness, University of Mississippi
Todd McFall, Wake Forest University
Charlie Pearson, Southern Maine Community College
Travis Roach, Texas Tech University
Kenneth Slaysman, York College of Pennsylvania
Boone Turchi, University of North Carolina

Reviewers of Previous Editions

The following individuals were of immense help in reviewing all or part of previous editions of this book and the teaching/learning package in various stages of development:

Cynthia Abadie, Southwest Tennessee Community College
Shawn Abbott, College of the Siskiyous
Fatma Abdel-Raouf, Goldey-Beacom College
Lew Abernathy, University of North Texas
Rebecca Abraham, Nova Southeastern University
Basil Adams, Notre Dame de Namur University
Jack Adams, University of Maryland
Douglas K. Adie, Ohio University
Douglas Agbetsiafa, Indiana University, South Bend
Sheri Aggarwal, University of Virginia
Carlos Aguilar, El Paso Community College
Ehsan Ahmed, James Madison University
Ferhat Akbas, Texas A&M University
Sam Alapati, Rutgers University
Terence Alexander, Iowa State University
John W. Allen, Texas A&M University
Polly Allen, University of Connecticut
Stuart Allen, University of North Carolina at Greensboro
Hassan Aly, Ohio State University
Alex Anas, University at Buffalo, The State University of New York
David Anderson, Centre College
Joan Anderssen, Arapahoe Community College
Jim Angresano, Hampton-Sydney College
Kenneth S. Arakelian, University of Rhode Island

Harvey Arnold, Indian River Community College
Nick Apergis, Fordham University
Bevin Ashenmiller, Occidental College
Richard Ashley, Virginia Technical University
Birjees Ashraf, Houston Community College Southwest
Kidane Asmeron, Pennsylvania State University
Musa Ayar, University of Texas, Austin
James Aylesworth, Lakeland Community College
Moshen Bahmani, University of Wisconsin—Milwaukee
Asatar Bair, City College of San Francisco
Diana Bajrami, College of Alameda
Mohammad Bajwa, Northampton Community College
Rita Balaban, University of North Carolina, Chapel Hill
A. Paul Ballantyne, University of Colorado, Colorado Springs
Richard J. Ballman, Jr., Augustana College
King Banaian, St. Cloud State University
Nick Barcia, Baruch College
Henry Barker, Tiffin University
Robin Bartlett, Denison University
Laurie Bates, Bryant University
Kari Battaglia, University of North Texas
Leon Battista, Bronx Community College
Amanda Bayer, Swarthmore College
Klaus Becker, Texas Tech University
Richard Beil, Auburn University

Clive Belfield, Queens College

Willie J. Belton, Jr., Georgia Institute of Technology

Daniel K. Benjamin, Clemson University

Charles A. Bennett, Gannon University

Emil Berendt, Siena Heights University

Daniel Berkowitz, University of Pittsburgh

Kurt Beron, University of Texas, Dallas

Derek Berry, Calhoun Community College

Tibor Besedes, Georgia Institute of Technology

Thomas Beveridge, Durham Technical Community College

Anoop Bhargava, Finger Lakes CC

Eugenie Bietry, Pace University

Kelly Blanchard, Purdue University

Mark Bock, Loyola College in Maryland

Howard Bodenhorn, Lafayette College

Bruce Bolnick, Northeastern University

Frank Bonello, University of Notre Dame

Jeffrey Bookwalter, University of Montana

Antonio Bos, Tusculum College

Maristella Botticini, Boston University

G. E. Breger, University of South Carolina

Dennis Brennan, William Rainey Harper Junior College

Anne E. Bresnock, California State Polytechnic University, Pomona, and the University of California, Los Angeles

Barry Brown, Murray State University

Bruce Brown, California State Polytechnic University, Pomona

Jennifer Brown, Eastern Connecticut State University

David Brownstone, University of California, Irvine

Don Brunner, Spokane Falls Community College

Jeff Bruns, Bacone College

David Bunting, Eastern Washington University

Barbara Burnell, College of Wooster

Alison Butler, Willamette University

Charles Callahan, III, State University of New York at Brockport

Fred Campano, Fordham University

Douglas Campbell, University of Memphis

Beth Cantrell, Central Baptist College

Kevin Carlson, University of Massachusetts, Boston

Leonard Carlson, Emory University

Arthur Schiller Casimir, Western New England College

Lindsay Caulkins, John Carroll University

Atreya Chakraborty, Boston College

Suparna Chakraborty, Baruch College of the City University of New York

Winston W. Chang, University at Buffalo, The State University of New York

Janie Chermak, University of New Mexico

David Ching, University of Hawaii – Honolulu

Harold Christensen, Centenary College

Daniel Christiansen, Albion College

Susan Christoffersen, Philadelphia University

Samuel Kim-Liang Chuah, Walla Walla College

Dmitriy Chulkov, Indiana University, Kokomo

David Colander, Middlebury College

Daniel Condon, University of Illinois at Chicago; Moraine Valley Community College

Karen Conway, University of New Hampshire

Cesar Corredor, Texas A&M University

David Cowen, University of Texas, Austin

Tyler Cowen, George Mason University

Amy Cramer, Pima Community College, West Campus

Peggy Crane, Southwestern College

Barbara Craig, Oberlin College

Jerry Crawford, Arkansas State University

James Cunningham, Chapman University

Scott Cunningham, Baylor University

Elisabeth Curtis, Dartmouth

James D'Angelo, University of Cincinnati

David Dahl, University of St. Thomas

Sheryll Dahlke, Lees-McRae College

Joseph Dahms, Hood College

Sonia Dalmia, Grand Valley State University

Rosa Lea Danielson, College of DuPage

David Danning, University of Massachusetts, Boston

Minh Quang Dao, Eastern Illinois University

Amlan Datta, Cisco Junior College

David Davenport, McLennan Community College

Stephen Davis, Southwest Minnesota State University

Dale DeBoer, Colorado University, Colorado Springs

Dennis Debrecht, Carroll College

Juan J. DelaCruz, Fashion Institute of Technology and Lehman College

Greg Delemeester, Marietta College

Yanan Di, State University of New York, Stony Brook

Amy Diduch, Mary Baldwin College

Timothy Diette, Washington and Lee University

Vernon J. Dixon, Haverford College

Alan Dobrowolksi, Manchester Community College

Eric Dodge, Hanover College

Carol Dole, Jacksonville University

Michael Donihue, Colby College

Shahpour Dowlatshahi, Fayetteville Technical Community College

Joanne M. Doyle, James Madison University

Robert Driskill, Ohio State University

James Dulgeroff, San Bernardino Valley College

Kevin Duncan, Colorado State University

Yvonne Durham, Western Washington University

Debra Sabatini Dwyer, State University of New York, Stony Brook

Gary Dymski, University of Southern California

David Eaton, Murray State University

Jay Egger, Towson State University

Erwin Ehrhardt, University of Cincinnati

Ann Eike, University of Kentucky

Eugene Elander, Plymouth State University

Ronald D. Elkins, Central Washington University

Tisha Emerson, Baylor University

Michael Enz, Western New England College

Erwin Erhardt III, University of Cincinnati

William Even, Miami University

Dr. Ali Faegh, Houston Community College, Northwest

Noel J. J. Farley, Bryn Mawr College

Mosin Farminesh, Temple University

Dan Feaster, Miami University of Ohio

Susan Feiner, Virginia Commonwealth University

Getachew Felleke, Albright College

Lois Fenske, South Puget Sound Community College

William Field, DePauw University

Deborah Figart, Richard Stockton College

Barbara Fischer, Cardinal Stritch University

Mary Flannery, Santa Clara University

Bill Foeller, State University of New York, Fredonia

Fred Foldvary, Santa Clara University

Roger Nils Folsom, San Jose State University

Mathew Forstater, University of Missouri-Kansas City

Kevin Foster, The City College of New York

Richard Fowles, University of Utah

Sean Fraley, College of Mount Saint Joseph

Johanna Francis, Fordham University

Roger Frantz, San Diego State University

Mark Frascatore, Clarkson University

Amanda Freeman, Kansas State University

Morris Frommer, Owens Community College

Brandon Fuller, University of Montana

David Fuller, University of Iowa

Mark Funk, University of Arkansas, Little Rock

Alejandro Gallegos, Winona State University

Craig Gallet, California State University, Sacramento

N. Galloro, Chabot College

Bill Galose, Drake University

Bill Ganley, Buffalo State College

Martin A. Garrett, Jr., College of William and Mary

Tom Gausman, Northern Illinois University

Shirley J. Gedeon, University of Vermont

Jeff Gerlach, Sungkyunkwan Graduate School of Business

Lisa Giddings, University of Wisconsin, La Crosse

Gary Gigliotti, Rutgers University

Lynn Gillette, Spalding University

Donna Ginther, University of Kansas

James N. Giordano, Villanova University

Amy Glass, Texas A&M University

Sarah L. Glavin, Boston College

Roy Gobin, Loyola University, Chicago

Bill Godair, Landmark College

Bill Goffe, University of Mississippi

Devra Golbe, Hunter College

Roger Goldberg, Ohio Northern University

Joshua Goodman, New York University

Ophelia Goma, DePauw University

John Gonzales, University of San Francisco

David Gordon, Illinois Valley College

Richard Gosselin, Houston Community College

Eugene Gotwalt, Sweet Briar College

John W. Graham, Rutgers University

Douglas Greenley, Morehead State University

Thomas A. Gresik, University of Notre Dame

Lisa M. Grobar, California State University, Long Beach

Wayne A. Grove, Le Moyne College

Daryl Gruver, Mount Vernon Nazarene University

Osman Gulseven, North Carolina State University

Mike Gumpper, Millersville University

Benjamin Gutierrez, Indiana University, Bloomington

A. R. Gutowsky, California State University, Sacramento

Anthony Gyapong, Penn State University, Abington

David R. Hakes, University of Missouri, St. Louis

Bradley Hansen, University of Mary Washington

Stephen Happel, Arizona State University

Mehdi Haririan, Bloomsburg University of Pennsylvania

David Harris, Benedictine College

David Harris, San Diego State University

James Hartley, Mount Holyoke College

Bruce Hartman, California Maritime Academy of California State University

Mitchell Harwitz, University at Buffalo, The State University of New York

Dewey Heinsma, Mt. San Jacinto College

Sara Helms, University of Alabama, Birmingham

Brian Hill, Salisbury University

David Hoaas, Centenary College

Arleen Hoag, Owens Community College

Carol Hogan, University of Michigan, Dearborn

Harry Holzer, Michigan State University

Ward Hooker, Orangeburg-Calhoun Technical College

Bobbie Horn, University of Tulsa

John Horowitz, Ball State University

Daniel Horton, Cleveland State University

Ying Huang, Manhattan College

Janet Hunt, University of Georgia

E. Bruce Hutchinson, University of Tennessee, Chattanooga

Creed Hyatt, Lehigh Carbon Community College

Ana Ichim, Louisiana State University

Aaron Iffland, Rocky Mountain College

Fred Inaba, Washington State University

Richard Inman, Boston College

Aaron Jackson, Bentley College

Brian Jacobsen, Wisconsin Lutheran College

Russell A. Janis, University of Massachusetts, Amherst

Jonatan Jelen, The City College of New York

Eric Jensen, The College of William & Mary

Aaron Johnson, Missouri State University

Donn Johnson, Quinnipiac University

Paul Johnson, University of Alaska, Anchorage

Shirley Johnson, Vassar College

Farhoud Kafi, Babson College

R. Kallen, Roosevelt University

Arthur E. Kartman, San Diego State University

Hirshel Kasper, Oberlin College

Brett Katzman, Kennesaw State University

Bruce Kaufman, Georgia State University

Dennis Kaufman, University of Wisconsin, Parkside

Pavel Kapinos, Carleton College

Russell Kashian, University of Wisconsin, Whitewater

Amoz Kats, Virginia Technical University

David Kaun, University of California, Santa Cruz

Brett Katzman, Kennesaw State University

Fred Keast, Portland State University

Stephanie Kelton, University of Missouri, Kansas City

Deborah Kelly, Palomar College

Erasmus Kersting, Texas A&M University

Randall Kesselring, Arkansas State University

Alan Kessler, Providence College

Dominique Khactu, The University of North Dakota

Gary Kikuchi, University of Hawaii, Manoa

Hwagyun Kim, State University of New York, Buffalo

Keon-Ho Kim, University of Utah

Kil-Joong Kim, Austin Peay State University

Sang W. Kim, Hood College

Phillip King, San Francisco State University

Barbara Kneeshaw, Wayne County Community College

Inderjit Kohli, Santa Clara University

Heather Kohls, Marquette University

Janet Koscianski, Shippensburg University

Vani Kotcherlakota, University of Nebraska, Kearney

Barry Kotlove, Edmonds Community College

Kate Krause, University of New Mexico

David Kraybill, University of Georgia

David Kroeker, Tabor College

Stephan Kroll, California State University, Sacramento

Joseph Kubec, Park University

Jacob Kurien, Helzberg School of Management

Rosung Kwak, University of Texas at Austin

Sally Kwak, University of Hawaii- Manoa

Steven Kyle, Cornell University

Anil K. Lal, Pittsburg State University

Melissa Lam, Wellesley College

David Lang, California State University, Sacramento

Gary Langer, Roosevelt University

Anthony Laramie, Merrimack College

Leonard Lardaro, University of Rhode Island

Ross LaRoe, Denison University

Michael Lawlor, Wake Forest University

Pareena Lawrence, University of Minnesota, Morris

Daniel Lawson, Drew University

Mary Rose Leacy, Wagner College

Margaret D. Ledyard, University of Texas, Austin

Jim Lee, Fort Hays State University

Judy Lee, Leeward Community College

Sang H. Lee, Southeastern Louisiana University

Don Leet, California State University, Fresno

Robert J. Lemke, Lake Forest College

Gary Lemon, DePauw University

Alan Leonard, Wilson Technical Community College

Mary Lesser, Iona College

Ding Li, Northern State University

Zhe Li, Stony Brook University

Larry Lichtenstein, Canisius College

Benjamin Liebman, Saint Joseph's University

Jesse Liebman, Kennesaw State University

George Lieu, Tuskegee University

Stephen E. Lile, Western Kentucky University

Jane Lillydahl, University of Colorado at Boulder

Tony Lima,California State University, East Bay, Hayward, CA

Melissa Lind, University of Texas, Arlington

Al Link, University of North Carolina Greensboro

Charles R. Link, University of Delaware

Robert Litro, U.S. Air Force Academy

Samuel Liu, West Valley College

Jeffrey Livingston, Bentley College

Ming Chien Lo, St. Cloud State University

Burl F. Long, University of Florida

Alina Luca, Drexel University

Adrienne Lucas, Wellesley College

Nancy Lutz, Virginia Technical University

Kristina Lybecker, Colorado College

Gerald Lynch, Purdue University

Karla Lynch, University of North Texas

Ann E. Lyon, University of Alaska, Anchorage

Bruce Madariaga, Montgomery College

Michael Magura, University of Toledo

Marvin S. Margolis, Millersville University of Pennsylvania

Tim Mason, Eastern Illinois University

Don Mathews, Coastal Georgia Community College

Don Maxwell, Central State University

Nan Maxwell, California State University at Hayward

Roberto Mazzoleni, Hofstra University

Cynthia S. McCarty, Jacksonville State University

J. Harold McClure, Jr., Villanova University

Patrick McEwan, Wellesley College

Rick McIntyre, University of Rhode Island

James J. McLain, University of New Orleans

Dawn McLaren, Mesa Community College

B. Starr McMullen, Oregon State University

K. Mehtaboin, College of St. Rose

Martin Melkonian, Hofstra University

Alice Melkumian, Western Illinois University

William Mertens, University of Colorado, Boulder

Randy Methenitis, Richland College

Art Meyer, Lincoln Land Community College

Carrie Meyer, George Mason University

Meghan Millea, Mississippi State University

Jenny Minier, University of Miami

Ida Mirzaie, The Ohio State University

David Mitchell, Missouri State University

Bijan Moeinian, Osceola Campus

Robert Mohr, University of New Hampshire

Shahruz Mohtadi, Suffolk University

Amyaz Moledina, College of Wooster

Gary Mongiovi, St. John's University

Terry D. Monson, Michigan Technological University

Barbara A. Moore, University of Central Florida

Joe L. Moore, Arkansas Technical University

Myra Moore, University of Georgia

Robert Moore, Occidental College

Norma C. Morgan, Curry College

W. Douglas Morgan, University of California, Santa Barbara

David Murphy, Boston College

John Murphy, North Shore Community College, Massachusetts

Ellen Mutari, Richard Stockton College of New Jersey

Steven C. Myers, University of Akron

Veena Nayak, University at Buffalo, The State University of New York

Ron Necoechea, Robert Wesleyan College

Doug Nelson, Spokane Community College

Randy Nelson, Colby College

David Nickerson, University of British Columbia

Sung No, Southern University and A&M College

Rachel Nugent, Pacific Lutheran University

Akorlie A. Nyatepe-Coo, University of Wisconsin LaCrosse

Norman P. Obst, Michigan State University

William C. O'Connor, Western Montana College

Constantin Ogloblin, Georgia Southern University

David O'Hara, Metropolitan State University

Albert Okunade, University of Memphis

Ronald Olive, University of Massachusetts, Lowell

Martha L. Olney, University of California, Berkeley

Kent Olson, Oklahoma State University

Jaime Ortiz, Florida Atlantic University

Theresa Osborne, Hunter College

Donald J. Oswald, California State University, Bakersfield

Mete Ozcan, Brooklyn College

Alexandre Padilla, Metropolitan State College of Denver

Aaron Pankratz, Fresno City College

Niki Papadopoulou, University of Cyprus

Walter Park, American University

Carl Parker, Fort Hays State University

Spiro Patton, Rasmussen College

Andrew Pearlman, Bard College

Richard Peck, University of Illinois at Chicago

Don Peppard, Connecticut College

Elizabeth Perry, Randolph College

Nathan Perry, University of Utah

Joe Petry, University of Illinois-Urbana-Champaign

Joseph A. Petry, University of Illinois

Mary Ann Pevas, Winona State University

Chris Phillips, Somerset Community College

Jeff Phillips, Morrisville Community College

Frankie Pircher, University of Missouri, Kansas City

Tony Pizelo, Spokane Community College

Dennis Placone, Clemson University

Mike Pogodzinski, San Jose State University

Linnea Polgreen, University of Iowa

Elizabeth Porter, University of North Florida

Bob Potter, University of Central Florida

Ed Price, Oklahoma State University

Abe Qastin, Lakeland College

Kevin Quinn, St. Norbert College

Ramkishen S. Rajan, George Mason University

James Rakowski, University of Notre Dame

Amy Ramirez-Gay, Eastern Michigan University

Paul Rappoport, Temple University

Artatrana Ratha, St. Cloud State University

Michael Rendich, Westchester Community College

Lynn Rittenoure, University of Tulsa

Brian Roberson, Miami University

Michael Robinson, Mount Holyoke College

Juliette Roddy, University of Michigan, Dearborn

Michael Rolleigh, University of Minnesota

Belinda Roman, Palo Alto College

S. Scanlon Romer, Delta College

Brian Rosario, University of California, Davis

Paul Roscelli, Canada College

David C. Rose, University of Missouri-St. Louis

Greg Rose, Sacramento City College

Richard Rosenberg, Pennsylvania State University

Robert Rosenman, Washington State University

Robert Rosenthal, Stonehill College

Howard Ross, Baruch College

Paul Rothstein, Washington University

Charles Roussel, Louisiana State University

Jeff Rubin, Rutgers University

Mark Rush, University of Florida

Dereka Rushbrook, Ripon College

Jerard Russo, University of Hawaii

Luz A. Saavedra, University of St. Thomas

William Samuelson, Boston University School of Management

Allen Sanderson, University of Chicago

David Saner, Springfield College – Benedictine University

Ahmad Saranjam, Bridgewater State College

David L. Schaffer, Haverford College

Eric Schansberg, Indiana University – Southeast

Robert Schenk, Saint Joseph's College

Ramon Schreffler, Houston Community College System (retired)

Adina Schwartz, Lakeland College

Jerry Schwartz, Broward Community College

Amy Scott, DeSales University

Gary Sellers, University of Akron

Atindra Sen, Miami University

Chad Settle, University of Tulsa

Jean Shackleford, Bucknell University

Ronald Shadbegian, University of Massachusetts, Dartmouth

Linda Shaffer, California State University, Fresno

Dennis Shannon, Southwestern Illinois College

Stephen L. Shapiro, University of North Florida

Paul Shea, University of Oregon

Geoff Shepherd, University of Massachusetts Amherst

Bih-Hay Sheu, University of Texas at Austin

David Shideler, Murray State University

Alden Shiers, California Polytechnic State University

Gerald Shilling, Eastfield College

Dongsoo Shin, Santa Clara University

Elias Shukralla, St. Louis Community College, Meramec

Anne Shugars, Harford Community College

Richard Sicotte, University of Vermont

William Simeone, Providence College

Scott Simkins, North Carolina Agricultural and Technical State University

Larry Singell, University of Oregon

Priyanka Singh, University of Texas, Dallas

Sue Skeath, Wellesley College

Edward Skelton, Southern Methodist University

Ken Slaysman, York College

John Smith, New York University

Paula Smith, Central State University, Oklahoma

Donald Snyder, Utah State University

Marcia Snyder, College of Charleston

David Sobiechowski, Wayne State University

John Solow, University of Iowa

Angela Sparkman, Itawamba Community College

Martin Spechler, Indiana University

David Spigelman, University of Miami

Arun Srinivasa, Indiana University, Southeast

David J. St. Clair, California State University at Hayward

Sarah Stafford, College of William & Mary

Richard Stahl, Louisiana State University

Rebecca Stein, University of Pennsylvania

Mary Stevenson, University of Massachusetts, Boston

Susan Stojanovic, Washington University, St. Louis

Courtenay Stone, Ball State University

Ernst W. Stromsdorfer, Washington State University

Edward Stuart, Northeastern Illinois University

Chris Stufflebean, Southwestern Oklahoma State University

Chuck Stull, Kalamazoo College

Della Sue, Marist College

Abdulhamid Sukar, Cameron University

Christopher Surfield, Saginaw Valley State University

Rodney B. Swanson, University of California, Los Angeles

James Swofford, University of Alabama

Bernica Tackett, Pulaski Technical College

Michael Taussig, Rutgers University

Samia Tavares, Rochester Institute of Technology

Timothy Taylor, Stanford University

William Taylor, New Mexico Highlands University

Sister Beth Anne Tercek, SND, Notre Dame College of Ohio

Henry Terrell, University of Maryland

Jennifer Thacher, University of New Mexico

Donna Thompson, Brookdale Community College

Robert Tokle, Idaho State University

David Tolman, Boise State University

Susanne Toney, Hampton University

Karen M. Travis, Pacific Lutheran University

Jack Trierweler, Northern State University

Brian M. Trinque, University of Texas at Austin

HuiKuan Tseng, University of North Carolina at Charlotte

Boone Turchi, University of North Carolina, Chapel Hill

Kristin Van Gaasbeck, California State University, Sacramento

Amy Vander Laan, Hastings College

Ann Velenchik, Wellesley College

Lawrence Waldman, University of New Mexico

Chris Waller, Indiana University, Bloomington

William Walsh, University of St. Thomas

Chunbei Wang, University of St. Thomas

John Watkins, Westminster

Janice Weaver, Drake University

Bruce Webb, Gordon College

Ross Weiner, The City College of New York

Elaine Wendt, Milwaukee Area Technical College

Walter Wessels, North Carolina State University

Christopher Westley, Jacksonville State University

Joan Whalen-Ayyappan, DeVry Institute of Technology

Robert Whaples, Wake Forest University

Leonard A. White, University of Arkansas

Alex Wilson, Rhode Island College

Wayne Winegarden, Marymount University

Jennifer Wissink, Cornell University

Arthur Woolf, University of Vermont

Paula Worthington, Northwestern University

Bill Yang, Georgia Southern University

Ben Young, University of Missouri, Kansas City

Darrel Young, University of Texas

Michael Youngblood, Rock Valley College

Jay Zagorsky, Boston University

Alexander Zampieron, Bentley College

Sourushe Zandvakili, University of Cincinnati

Walter J. Zeiler, University of Michigan

Abera Zeyege, Ball State University

James Ziliak, Indiana University, Bloomington

Jason Zimmerman, South Dakota State University

We welcome comments about the 11th edition. Please write to us care of David Alexander, Executive Editor, Pearson Economics, 75 Arlington Suite 300, Boston, MA 02116.

Karl E. Case

Ray C. Fair

Sharon M. Oster

Save a Tree!

Many of the components of the teaching and learning package are available online. Online supplements conserve paper and allow you to select and print only the material you plan to use. For more information, please contact your Pearson Prentice Hall sales representative.

The Scope and Method of Economics

1

The study of economics should begin with a sense of wonder. Pause for a moment and consider a typical day in your life. It might start with a bagel made in a local bakery with flour produced in Minnesota from wheat grown in Kansas and bacon from pigs raised in Ohio packaged in plastic made in New Jersey. You spill coffee from Colombia on your shirt made in Texas from textiles shipped from South Carolina.

After class you drive with a friend on an interstate highway that is part of a system that took 20 years and billions of dollars to build. You stop for gasoline refined in Louisiana from Saudi Arabian crude oil brought to the United States on a supertanker that took 3 years to build at a shipyard in Maine.

Later, you log onto the Web with a laptop assembled in Indonesia from parts made in China and Skype with your brother in Mexico City, and you call a buddy on your iPhone with parts from a dozen countries. You use or consume tens of thousands of things. Somebody organized men and women and materials to produce and distribute them. Thousands of decisions went into their completion. Somehow they got to you.

In the United States, over 143 million people—almost half the total population—work at hundreds of thousands of different jobs producing over $16 trillion worth of goods and services every year. Some cannot find work; some choose not to work. Some are rich; others are poor.

The United States imports over $250 billion worth of automobiles and parts and over $450 billion worth of petroleum and petroleum products each year; it exports around $125 billion worth of agricultural products, including food. Every month, the United States buys around $35 billion worth of goods and services from China, while China buys about $9 billion worth from the United States.

Some countries are wealthy. Others are impoverished. Some are growing. Some are not. Some businesses are doing well. Others are going bankrupt. As the 11th edition of our text goes to press, the world is beginning to recover from a period during which many people felt the pain of a major economic downturn. In the United States, at the beginning of 2013, there were about 11 million people who wanted to work but could not find a job.

LEARNING OBJECTIVES

Identify three key reasons to study economics

Describe microeconomics, macroeconomics, and the diverse fields of economics

Discuss the fundamentals of economic methods, theories, and models

Identify the criteria for evaluating economic policies and outcomes

economics The study of how individuals and societies choose to use the scarce resources that nature and previous generations have provided.

Economics is the study of how individuals and societies choose to use the scarce resources that nature and previous generations have provided. The key word in this definition is *choose*. Economics is a behavioral, or social, science. In large measure, it is the study of how people make choices. The choices that people make, when added up, translate into societal choices.

The purpose of this chapter and the next is to elaborate on this definition and to introduce the subject matter of economics. What is produced? How is it produced? Who gets it? Why? Is the result good or bad? Can it be improved?

Why Study Economics?

There are three main reasons to study economics: to learn a way of thinking, to understand society, and to be an informed citizen.

To Learn a Way of Thinking

Probably the most important reason for studying economics is to learn a way of thinking. Economics has three fundamental concepts that, once absorbed, can change the way you look at everyday choices: opportunity cost, marginalism, and the working of efficient markets.

opportunity cost The best alternative that we forgo, or give up, when we make a choice or a decision.

Opportunity Cost   What happens in an economy is the outcome of thousands of individual decisions. People must decide how to divide their incomes among all the goods and services available in the marketplace. They must decide whether to work, whether to go to school, and how much to save. Businesses must decide what to produce, how much to produce, how much to charge, and where to locate. It is not surprising that economic analysis focuses on the process of decision making.

Nearly all decisions involve trade-offs. A key concept that recurs in analyzing the decision-making process is the notion of *opportunity cost*. The full "cost" of making a specific choice includes what we give up by not making the best alternative choice. The best alternative that we forgo, or give up, when we make a choice or a decision is called the **opportunity cost** of that decision.

When asked how much a movie costs, most people cite the ticket price. For an economist, this is only part of the answer: to see a movie takes not only a ticket but also time. The opportunity cost of going to a movie is the value of the other things you could have done with the same money and time. If you decide to take time off from work, the opportunity cost of your leisure is the pay that you would have earned had you worked. Part of the cost of a college education is the income you could have earned by working full-time instead of going to school.

scarce Limited.

Opportunity costs arise because resources are scarce. **Scarce** simply means limited. Consider one of our most important resources—time. There are only 24 hours in a day, and we must live our lives under this constraint. A farmer in rural Brazil must decide whether it is better to continue to farm or to go to the city and look for a job. A hockey player at the University of Vermont must decide whether to play on the varsity team or spend more time studying.

marginalism The process of analyzing the additional or incremental costs or benefits arising from a choice or decision.

Marginalism   A second key concept used in analyzing choices is the notion of **marginalism**. In weighing the costs and benefits of a decision, it is important to weigh only the costs and benefits that arise from the decision. Suppose, for example, that you live in New Orleans and that you are weighing the costs and benefits of visiting your mother in Iowa. If business required that you travel to Kansas City, the cost of visiting Mom would be only the additional, or *marginal*, time and money cost of getting to Iowa from Kansas City.

There are numerous examples in which the concept of marginal cost is useful. For an airplane that is about to take off with empty seats, the marginal cost of an extra passenger is essentially zero; the total cost of the trip is roughly unchanged by the addition of an extra passenger. Thus, setting aside a few seats to be sold at big discounts through www.priceline.com or other Web sites can be profitable even if the fare for those seats is far below the average cost per seat of making the trip. As long as the airline succeeds in filling seats that would otherwise have been empty, doing so is profitable.

Efficient Markets—No Free Lunch   Suppose you are ready to check out of a busy grocery store on the day before a storm and seven checkout registers are open with several people in each line. Which line should you choose? Usually, the waiting time is approximately the same no matter which register you choose (assuming you have more than 12 items). If one line is much shorter than the others, people will quickly move into it until the lines are equalized again.

As you will see later, the term *profit* in economics has a very precise meaning. Economists, however, often loosely refer to "good deals" or risk-free ventures as *profit opportunities*. Using the term loosely, a profit opportunity exists at the checkout lines when one line is shorter than the others. In general, such profit opportunities are rare. At any time, many people are searching for them; as a consequence, few exist. Markets like this, where any profit opportunities are eliminated almost instantaneously, are said to be **efficient markets**. (We discuss *markets*, the institutions through which buyers and sellers interact and engage in exchange, in detail in Chapter 2.)

efficient market   A market in which profit opportunities are eliminated almost instantaneously.

The common way of expressing the efficient markets concept is "there's no such thing as a free lunch." How should you react when a stockbroker calls with a hot tip on the stock market? With skepticism. Thousands of individuals each day are looking for hot tips in the market. If a particular tip about a stock is valid, there will be an immediate rush to buy the stock, which will quickly drive up its price. This view that very few profit opportunities exist can, of course, be carried too far. There is a story about two people walking along, one an economist and one not. The non-economist sees a $20 bill on the sidewalk and says, "There's a $20 bill on the sidewalk." The economist replies, "That is not possible. If there were, somebody would already have picked it up."

There are clearly times when profit opportunities exist. Someone has to be first to get the news, and some people have quicker insights than others. Nevertheless, news travels fast, and there are thousands of people with quick insights. The general view that large profit opportunities are rare is close to the mark.

> The study of economics teaches us a way of thinking and helps us make decisions.

To Understand Society

Another reason for studying economics is to understand society better. Past and present economic decisions have an enormous influence on the character of life in a society. The current state of the physical environment, the level of material well-being, and the nature and number of jobs are all products of the economic system.

At no time has the impact of economic change on a society been more evident than in England during the late eighteenth and early nineteenth centuries, a period that we now call the **Industrial Revolution**. Increases in the productivity of agriculture, new manufacturing technologies, and development of more efficient forms of transportation led to a massive movement of the British population from the countryside to the city. At the beginning of the eighteenth century, approximately 2 out of 3 people in Great Britain worked in agriculture. By 1812, only 1 in 3 remained in agriculture; by 1900, the figure was fewer than 1 in 10. People jammed into overcrowded cities and worked long hours in factories. England had changed completely in two centuries—a period that in the run of history was nothing more than the blink of an eye.

Industrial Revolution   The period in England during the late eighteenth and early nineteenth centuries in which new manufacturing technologies and improved transportation gave rise to the modern factory system and a massive movement of the population from the countryside to the cities.

It is not surprising that the discipline of economics began to take shape during this period. Social critics and philosophers looked around and knew that their philosophies must expand to accommodate the changes. Adam Smith's *Wealth of Nations* appeared in 1776. It was followed by the writings of David Ricardo, Karl Marx, Thomas Malthus, and others. Each tried to make sense out of what was happening. Who was building the factories? Why? What determined the level of wages paid to workers or the price of food? What would happen in the future, and what *should* happen? The people who asked these questions were the first economists.

Similar changes continue to affect the character of life in more recent times. In fact, many argue that the late 1990s marked the beginning of a new Industrial Revolution. As we turned the corner into the new millennium, the "e" revolution was clearly having an impact on virtually every aspect of our lives: the way we buy and sell products, the way we get news, the way we plan vacations, the way we communicate with each other, the way we teach and take classes, and on and on. These changes have had and will clearly continue to have profound impacts on societies across the globe, from Beijing to Calcutta to New York.

These changes have been driven by economics. Although the government was involved in the early years of the World Wide Web, private firms that exist to make a profit (such as Facebook, YouTube, Yahoo!, Microsoft, Google, Monster.com, Amazon.com, and E-Trade) created almost all the new innovations and products. How does one make sense of all this? What will the effects of these innovations be on the number of jobs, the character of those jobs, the family incomes, the structure of our cities, and the political process both in the United States and in other countries?

> The study of economics is an essential part of the study of society.

To Be an Informed Citizen

A knowledge of economics is essential to being an informed citizen. Between 2009 and 2013 much of the world struggled with a major recession and very slow recovery, leaving millions of people around the world out of work. Understanding what happens in a recession and what the government can and cannot do to help in a recovery is an essential part of being an informed citizen.

Economics is also essential in understanding a range of other everyday government decisions at the local and federal levels. Why do governments pay for public schools and roads, but not cell phones? In 2010, the federal government under President Obama moved toward universal health care for U.S. citizens. How do you understand the debate of whether this is or is not a good idea? In some states, scalping tickets to a ball game is illegal. Is this a good policy or not? Every day, across the globe, people engage in political decision making around questions like these, questions that depend on an understanding of economics.

> To be an informed citizen requires a basic understanding of economics.

The Scope of Economics

Most students taking economics for the first time are surprised by the breadth of what they study. Some think that economics will teach them about the stock market or what to do with their money. Others think that economics deals exclusively with problems such as inflation and unemployment. In fact, it deals with all those subjects, but they are pieces of a much larger puzzle.

Economics has deep roots in and close ties to social philosophy. An issue of great importance to philosophers, for example, is distributional justice. Why are some people rich and others poor? And whatever the answer, is this fair? A number of nineteenth-century social philosophers wrestled with these questions, and out of their musings, economics as a separate discipline was born.

The easiest way to get a feel for the breadth and depth of what you will be studying is to explore briefly the way economics is organized. First of all, there are two major divisions of economics: microeconomics and macroeconomics.

Microeconomics and Macroeconomics

microeconomics The branch of economics that examines the functioning of individual industries and the behavior of individual decision-making units—that is, firms and households.

Microeconomics deals with the functioning of individual industries and the behavior of individual economic decision-making units: firms and households. Firms' choices about what to produce and how much to charge and households' choices about what and how much to buy help to explain why the economy produces the goods and services it does.

ECONOMICS IN PRACTICE

iPod and the World

It is impossible to understand the workings of an economy without first understanding the ways in which economies are connected across borders. The United States was importing goods and services at a rate of over $2.7 trillion per year in 2012 and was exporting at a rate of over $2.1 trillion per year.

For literally hundreds of years, the virtues of free trade have been the subject of heated debate. Opponents have argued that buying foreign-produced goods costs Americans jobs and hurts American producers. Proponents argue that there are gains from trade—that all countries can gain from specializing in the production of the goods and services they produce best.

In the modern world, it is not always easy to track where products are made. A sticker that says "Made in China" can often be misleading. Recent studies of two iconic U.S. products, the iPod and the Barbie doll, make this complexity clear.

The Barbie doll is one of Mattel's best and longest selling products. The Barbie was designed in the United States. It is made of plastic fashioned in Taiwan, which came originally from the Mideast in the form of petroleum. Barbie's hair comes from Japan, while the cloth for her clothes mostly comes from China. Most of the assembly of the Barbie is also done in China, using, as we see, pieces from across the globe. A doll that sells for $10 in the United States carries an export value when leaving Hong Kong of $2, of which only 35 cents is for Chinese labor, with most of the rest covering transportation and raw materials. Because the Barbie comes to the United States from assembly in China and transport from Hong Kong, some would count it as being produced in China. Yet, for this Barbie, $8 of its retail value of $10 is captured by the United States![1]

The iPod is similar. A recent study by three economists, Greg Linden, Kenneth Kraemer, and Jason Dedrick, found that once one includes Apple's payment for its intellectual property, distribution costs, and production costs for some components, almost 80% of the retail price of the iPod is captured by the United States.[2] Moreover, for some of the other parts of the iPod, it is not easy to tell exactly where they are produced. The hard drive, a relatively expensive component, was produced in Japan by Toshiba, but

some of the components of that hard drive were actually produced elsewhere in Asia. Indeed, for the iPod, which is composed of many small parts, it is almost impossible to accurately tell exactly where each piece was produced without pulling it apart.

So, next time you see a label saying "Made in China" keep in mind that from an economics point of view, one often has to dig a little deeper to see what is really going on.

THINKING PRACTICALLY

1. What do you think accounts for *where* components of the iPod and Barbie are made?

[1] For a discussion of the Barbie see Robert Feenstra, "Integration of Trade and Disintegration of Production in the Global Economy," *Journal of Economic Perspectives*, Fall 1998, 31–50.
[2] Greg Linden, Kenneth Kraemer, and Jason Dedrick, "Who Profits from Innovation in Global Value Chains?" *Industrial and Corporate Change*, 2010: 81–116.

Another big question addressed by microeconomics is who gets the goods and services that are produced? Wealthy households get more than poor households, and the forces that determine this distribution of output are the province of microeconomics. Why does poverty exist? Who is poor? Why do some jobs pay more than others?

Macroeconomics looks at the economy as a whole. Instead of trying to understand what determines the output of a single firm or industry or what the consumption patterns are of a single household or group of households, macroeconomics examines the factors that determine national output, or national product. Microeconomics is concerned with *household* income; macroeconomics deals with *national* income.

macroeconomics The branch of economics that examines the economic behavior of aggregates—income, employment, output, and so on—on a national scale.

Whereas microeconomics focuses on individual product prices and relative prices, macroeconomics looks at the overall price level and how quickly (or slowly) it is rising (or falling). Microeconomics questions how many people will be hired (or fired) this year in a particular industry or in a certain geographic area and focuses on the factors that determine how much labor a firm or an industry will hire. Macroeconomics deals with *aggregate* employment and unemployment: how many jobs exist in the economy as a whole and how many people who are willing to work are not able to find work.

To summarize:

> Microeconomics looks at the individual unit—the household, the firm, the industry. It sees and examines the "trees." Macroeconomics looks at the whole, the aggregate. It sees and analyzes the "forest."

Table 1.1 summarizes these divisions of economics and some of the subjects with which they are concerned.

The Diverse Fields of Economics

Individual economists focus their research and study in many different areas. Many of these specialized fields are reflected in the advanced courses offered at most colleges and universities. Some are concerned with economic history or the history of economic thought. Others focus on international economics or growth in less developed countries. These fields are summarized in Table 1.2.

Economists also differ in the emphasis they place on theory. Some economists specialize in developing new theories, whereas other economists spend their time testing the theories of others. Some economists hope to expand the frontiers of knowledge, whereas other economists are more interested in applying what is already known to the formulation of public policies.

As you begin your study of economics, look through your school's course catalog and talk to the faculty about their interests. You will discover that economics encompasses a broad range of inquiry and is linked to many other disciplines.

TABLE 1.1 Examples of Microeconomic and Macroeconomic Concerns

Division of Economics	Production	Prices	Income	Employment
Microeconomics	*Production/output in individual industries and businesses*	*Prices of individual goods and services*	*Distribution of income and wealth*	*Employment by individual businesses and industries*
	How much steel	Price of medical care	Wages in the auto industry	Jobs in the steel industry
	How much office space	Price of gasoline	Minimum wage	Number of employees in a firm
	How many cars	Food prices	Executive salaries	Number of accountants
		Apartment rents	Poverty	
Macroeconomics	*National production/output*	*Aggregate price level*	*National income*	*Employment and unemployment in the economy*
	Total industrial output	Consumer prices	Total wages and salaries	Total number of jobs
	Gross domestic product	Producer prices	Total corporate profits	Unemployment rate
	Growth of output	Rate of inflation		

TABLE 1.2 The Fields of Economics	
Behavioral economics	uses psychological theories relating to emotions and social context to help understand economic decision making and policy. Much of the work in behavioral economics focuses on the biases that individuals have that affect the decisions they make.
Comparative economic systems	examines the ways alternative economic systems function. What are the advantages and disadvantages of different systems?
Econometrics	applies statistical techniques and data to economic problems in an effort to test hypotheses and theories. Most schools require economics majors to take at least one course in statistics or econometrics.
Economic development	focuses on the problems of low-income countries. What can be done to promote development in these nations? Important concerns of development for economists include population growth and control, provision for basic needs, and strategies for international trade.
Economic history	traces the development of the modern economy. What economic and political events and scientific advances caused the Industrial Revolution? What explains the tremendous growth and progress of post–World War II Japan? What caused the Great Depression of the 1930s?
Environmental economics	studies the potential failure of the market system to account fully for the impacts of production and consumption on the environment and on natural resource depletion. Have alternative public policies and new economic institutions been effective in correcting these potential failures?
Finance	examines the ways in which households and firms actually pay for, or finance, their purchases. It involves the study of capital markets (including the stock and bond markets), futures and options, capital budgeting, and asset valuation.
Health economics	analyzes the health care system and its players: government, insurers, health care providers, and patients. It provides insight into the demand for medical care, health insurance markets, cost-controlling insurance plans (HMOs, PPOs, IPAs), government health care programs (Medicare and Medicaid), variations in medical practice, medical malpractice, competition versus regulation, and national health care reform.
The history of economic thought,	which is grounded in philosophy, studies the development of economic ideas and theories over time, from Adam Smith in the eighteenth century to the works of economists such as Thomas Malthus, Karl Marx, and John Maynard Keynes. Because economic theory is constantly developing and changing, studying the history of ideas helps give meaning to modern theory and puts it in perspective.
Industrial organization	looks carefully at the structure and performance of industries and firms within an economy. How do businesses compete? Who gains and who loses?
International economics	studies trade flows among countries and international financial institutions. What are the advantages and disadvantages for a country that allows its citizens to buy and sell freely in world markets? Why is the dollar strong or weak?
Labor economics	deals with the factors that determine wage rates, employment, and unemployment. How do people decide whether to work, how much to work, and at what kind of job? How have the roles of unions and management changed in recent years?
Law and economics	analyzes the economic function of legal rules and institutions. How does the law change the behavior of individuals and businesses? Do different liability rules make accidents and injuries more or less likely? What are the economic costs of crime?
Public economics	examines the role of government in the economy. What are the economic functions of government, and what should they be? How should the government finance the services that it provides? What kinds of government programs should confront the problems of poverty, unemployment, and pollution? What problems does government involvement create?
Urban and regional economics	studies the spatial arrangement of economic activity. Why do we have cities? Why are manufacturing firms locating farther and farther from the centers of urban areas?

The Method of Economics

positive economics An approach to economics that seeks to understand behavior and the operation of systems without making judgments. It describes what exists and how it works.

Economics asks and attempts to answer two kinds of questions: positive and normative. **Positive economics** attempts to understand behavior and the operation of economic systems *without making judgments* about whether the outcomes are good or bad. It strives to describe what exists and how it works. What determines the wage rate for unskilled workers? What would happen if we abolished the corporate income tax? The answers to such questions are the subject of positive economics.

normative economics An approach to economics that analyzes outcomes of economic behavior, evaluates them as good or bad, and may prescribe courses of action. Also called *policy economics*.

In contrast, **normative economics** looks at the outcomes of economic behavior and asks whether they are good or bad and whether they can be made better. Normative economics involves judgments and prescriptions for courses of action. Should the government subsidize or regulate the cost of higher education? Should medical benefits to the elderly under Medicare be available only to those with incomes below some threshold? Should the United States allow importers to sell foreign-produced goods that compete with U.S.-made products? Should we reduce or eliminate inheritance taxes? Normative economics is often called *policy economics*.

Of course, most normative questions involve positive questions. To know whether the government *should* take a particular action, we must know first if it *can* and second what the consequences are likely to be. (For example, if we lower import fees, will there be more competition and lower prices?)

Theories and Models

In many disciplines, including physics, chemistry, meteorology, political science, and economics, theorists build formal models of behavior. A **model** is a formal statement of a theory. It is usually a mathematical statement of a presumed relationship between two or more variables.

model A formal statement of a theory, usually a mathematical statement of a presumed relationship between two or more variables.

A **variable** is a measure that can change from time to time or from observation to observation. Income is a variable—it has different values for different people and different values for the same person at different times. The price of a quart of milk is a variable; it has different values at different stores and at different times. There are countless other examples.

variable A measure that can change from time to time or from observation to observation.

Because all models simplify reality by stripping part of it away, they are abstractions. Critics of economics often point to abstraction as a weakness. Most economists, however, see abstraction as a real strength.

The easiest way to see how abstraction can be helpful is to think of a map. A map is a representation of reality that is simplified and abstract. A city or state appears on a piece of paper as a series of lines and colors. The amount of reality that the mapmaker can strip away before the map loses something essential depends on what the map will be used for. If you want to drive from St. Louis to Phoenix, you need to know only the major interstate highways and roads. You lose absolutely nothing and gain clarity by cutting out the local streets and roads. However, if you need to get around Phoenix, you may need to see every street and alley.

Ockham's razor The principle that irrelevant detail should be cut away.

Like maps, economic models are abstractions that strip away detail to expose only those aspects of behavior that are important to the question being asked. The principle that irrelevant detail should be cut away is called the principle of **Ockham's razor** after the fourteenth-century philosopher William of Ockham.

Be careful—although abstraction is a powerful tool for exposing and analyzing specific aspects of behavior, it is possible to oversimplify. Economic models often strip away a good deal of social and political reality to get at underlying concepts. When an economic theory is used to help formulate actual government or institutional policy, political and social reality must often be reintroduced if the policy is to have a chance of working.

The appropriate amount of simplification and abstraction depends on the use to which the model will be put. To return to the map example: You do not want to walk around San Francisco with a map made for drivers—there are too many very steep hills.

All Else Equal: *Ceteris Paribus*   It is usually true that whatever you want to explain with a model depends on more than one factor. Suppose, for example, that you want to explain the total number of miles driven by automobile owners in the United States. Obviously, many things might affect total miles driven. First, more or fewer people may be driving. This number, in turn, can be affected by changes in the driving age, by population growth, or by changes in state laws. Other factors might include the price of gasoline, the household's income, the number and age of children in the household, the distance from home to work, the location of shopping facilities, and the availability and quality of public transport. When any of these variables change, the members of the household may drive more or less. If changes in any of these variables affect large numbers of households across the country, the total number of miles driven will change.

Very often we need to isolate or separate these effects. For example, suppose we want to know the impact on driving of a higher tax on gasoline. This increased tax would raise the price of gasoline at the pump, and this could reduce driving.

To isolate the impact of one single factor, we use the device of *ceteris paribus, or* **all else equal**. We ask, "What is the impact of a change in gasoline price on driving behavior, *ceteris paribus*, or assuming that nothing else changes?" If gasoline prices rise by 10 percent, how much less driving will there be, assuming no simultaneous change in anything else—that is, assuming that income, number of children, population, laws, and so on, all remain constant? Using the device of *ceteris paribus* is one part of the process of abstraction. In formulating economic theory, the concept helps us simplify reality to focus on the relationships that interest us.

> ***ceteris paribus,*** *or* **all else equal**   A device used to analyze the relationship between two variables while the values of other variables are held unchanged.

Expressing Models in Words, Graphs, and Equations   Consider the following statements: Lower airline ticket prices cause people to fly more frequently. Higher gasoline prices cause people to drive less and to buy more fuel-efficient cars. By themselves, these observations are of some interest. But for a firm, government, or an individual to make good decisions, oftentimes they need to know more. How much does driving fall when prices rise? Quantitative analysis is an important part of economics as well. Throughout this book, we will use both graphs and equations to capture the quantitative side of our economic observations and predictions. The appendix to this chapter reviews some graphing techniques.

Cautions and Pitfalls   In formulating theories and models, it is especially important to avoid two pitfalls: the *post hoc* fallacy and the fallacy of composition.

What Is Really Causal?   In much of economics, we are interested in cause and effect. But cause and effect are often very hard to figure out. Recently, many people in the United States have begun to worry about consumption of soda and obesity. Some areas have begun taxing soda, trying to raise the price so that people will drink less of it. Is this working? Answering this question turns out to be very hard. Suppose we see that one city raises the tax and at more or less the same time, soda consumption falls. Did the increased tax and price really *cause* all or most of the change in behavior? Or perhaps the city that voted the soda tax increase is more health conscious than its neighbors and it is that health consciousness that accounts for both the town's decision to raise taxes *and* its reduction in soda purchases. In this case, raising taxes on the neighboring towns will not necessarily reduce soda consumption. Sorting out causality is not always easy, particularly when one wants a quantitative answer to a question.

In our everyday lives, we often confuse causality. When two events occur in a sequence, it is natural to think A caused B. I walked under a ladder and subsequently stubbed my toe. Did the ladder cause my bad luck? Most of us would laugh at this. But everyday we hear stock market analysts make a similar causal jump. "Today the Dow Jones industrial average rose 100 points on heavy trading due to progress in talks between Israel and Syria." How do they know this? Investors respond to many news events on any given day. Figuring out which one, if any, causes the stock market to rise is not easy. The error of inferring causality from two events happening

ECONOMICS IN PRACTICE

Does Your Roommate Matter for Your Grades?

Most parents are very concerned about their children's friends. Often they worry that if one of their children has a misbehaving friend, their own child will be led astray. And, in fact, in many areas of life, there are strong indications that *peer effects* matter. The likelihood that a child will be obese, have difficulties in school, or engage in criminal activity all seem to be higher if their friends also have these issues. And yet, in looking at peer effects, it is not hard to see the problem of causality we described in the text. At least to some extent, children choose their own friends. The father worried about the bad influence of his son's friends on his own son should perhaps be equally worried about what his son's choice of friends says about that son's inclinations. Did the friends cause the misbehavior or did an inclination toward mischief cause the son's choice of friends?

Sorting out causality in peer effects, given that peer groups are oftentimes partially a matter of choice, is difficult. But several recent economics studies of the effect of roommates on college grades do a nice job of sorting out the causality puzzle. Dartmouth college, in common with many other schools, randomly assigns roommates to freshmen. In this case, part of a student's peer group—his or her roommate—is not a matter of choice, but a matter of chance. Bruce Sacerdote, a professor at Dartmouth, used data on freshmen academic and social performance, combined with their background data, to test the peer effects from different types of roommates.[1]

Sacerdote found that after taking into account many background characteristics, there were strong roommate effects both on grade point average, effort in school, and fraternity membership.

Of course, a roommate is only part of one's peer group. At the U.S. Air Force Academy, students are assigned to thirty-person squadrons with whom they eat, study, live, and do intramural sports. Again, these groups were randomly assigned, so one did not have the problem of similarly inclined people choosing one another. Scott Carrell, Richard Fullerton, and James West found that for this very intense peer group, there were very strong peer effects on academic effort and performance.[2] The bottom line: Choose your friends wisely!

THINKING PRACTICALLY

1. Would you expect college seniors who choose their own roommates to have more or less similar grades than college freshmen who are assigned as roommates? Why or why not?

[1] Bruce Sacerdote, "Peer Effects with Random Assignment: Results for Dartmouth Roommates," *Quarterly Journal of Economics,* 2001, 681–704.

[2] Scott E. Carrell, Richard L. Fullerton, and James E. West, "Does Your Cohort Matter? Measuring Peer Effects in College Achievement," *Journal of Labor Economics,* 2009, 439–464.

---

post hoc, ergo propter hoc Literally, "after this (in time), therefore because of this." A common error made in thinking about causation: If Event A happens before Event B, it is not necessarily true that A caused B.

fallacy of composition The erroneous belief that what is true for a part is necessarily true for the whole.

empirical economics The collection and use of data to test economic theories.

one after the other is called the **post hoc, ergo propter hoc** fallacy ("after this, therefore because of this"). The *Economics in Practice* box describes a causality confusion in looking at peer effects.

The Fallacy of Composition To conclude that what is true for a part is necessarily true for the whole is to fall into the **fallacy of composition**. Suppose that a large group of cattle ranchers graze their cattle on the same range. To an individual rancher, more cattle and more grazing mean a higher income. However, because its capacity is limited, the land can support only so many cattle. If every cattle rancher increased the number of cattle sent out to graze, the land would become overgrazed and barren; as a result, everyone's income would fall. In short, theories that seem to work well when applied to individuals or households often break down when they are applied to the whole.

Testing Theories and Models: Empirical Economics
In science, a theory is rejected when it fails to explain what is observed or when another theory better explains what is observed. The collection and use of data to test economic theories is called **empirical economics**.

Numerous large data sets are available to facilitate economic research. For example, economists studying the labor market can now test behavioral theories against the actual working experiences of thousands of randomly selected people who have been surveyed continuously since the 1960s. Macroeconomists continuously monitoring and studying the behavior of the national economy at the National Bureau of Economic Research (NBER) pass thousands of items of data, collected by both government agencies and private companies, over the Internet. Firms like Google and Amazon have an enormous amount of data about individual consumers that they analyze with the help of PhD economists to understand consumers' buying behavior and improve the profitability of their businesses.

In the natural sciences, controlled experiments, typically done in the lab, are a standard way of testing theories. In recent years, economics has seen an increase in the use of experiments, both in the field and in the lab, as a tool to test its theories. One economist, John List of Chicago, tested the effect on prices of changing the way auctions for rare baseball cards were run by sports memorabilia dealers in trade shows. (The experiment used a standard Cal Ripkin Jr. card.) Another economist, Keith Chen of Yale, has used experiments with monkeys to investigate the deeper biological roots of human decision making.

Economic Policy

Economic theory helps us understand how the world works, but the formulation of *economic policy* requires a second step. We must have objectives. What do we want to change? Why? What is good and what is bad about the way the system is operating? Can we make it better?

Such questions force us to be specific about the grounds for judging one outcome superior to another. What does it mean to be better? Four criteria are frequently applied in judging economic outcomes:

1. Efficiency
2. Equity
3. Growth
4. Stability

Efficiency   In physics, "efficiency" refers to the ratio of useful energy delivered by a system to the energy supplied to it. An efficient automobile engine, for example, is one that uses a small amount of fuel per mile for a given level of power.

In economics, **efficiency** means *allocative efficiency*. An efficient economy is one that produces what people want at the least possible cost. If the system allocates resources to the production of goods and services that nobody wants, it is inefficient. If all members of a particular society were vegetarians and somehow half of all that society's resources were used to produce meat, the result would be inefficient. It is inefficient when steel beams lie in the rain and rust because somebody fouled up a shipping schedule. If a firm could produce its product using 25 percent less labor and energy without sacrificing quality, it too is inefficient.

> **efficiency** In economics, allocative efficiency. An efficient economy is one that produces what people want at the least possible cost.

The clearest example of an efficient change is a voluntary exchange. If you and I each want something that the other has and we agree to exchange, we are both better off and no one loses. When a company reorganizes its production or adopts a new technology that enables it to produce more of its product with fewer resources, without sacrificing quality, it has made an efficient change. At least potentially, the resources saved could be used to produce more of something.

Inefficiencies can arise in numerous ways. Sometimes they are caused by government regulations or tax laws that distort otherwise sound economic decisions. Suppose that land in Ohio is best suited for corn production and that land in Kansas is best suited for wheat production. A law that requires Kansas to produce only corn and Ohio to produce only wheat would be inefficient. If firms that cause environmental damage are not held accountable for their actions, the incentive to minimize those damages is lost and the result is inefficient.

equity Fairness.

Equity   While efficiency has a fairly precise definition that can be applied with some degree of rigor, **equity** (fairness) lies in the eye of the beholder. To many, fairness implies a more equal distribution of income and wealth. Fairness may imply alleviating poverty, but the extent to which the poor should receive cash benefits from the government is the subject of enormous disagreement. For thousands of years, philosophers have wrestled with the principles of justice that should guide social decisions. They will probably wrestle with such questions for thousands of years to come.

Despite the impossibility of defining equity or fairness universally, public policy makers judge the fairness of economic outcomes all the time. Certainly, most social welfare programs are created in the name of equity.

Growth   As the result of technological change, the building of machinery, and the acquisition of knowledge, societies learn to produce new goods and services and to produce old ones better. In the early days of the U.S. economy, it took nearly half the population to produce the required food supply. Today less than 2.0 percent of the country's population works in agriculture.

economic growth An increase in the total output of an economy.

When we devise new and better ways of producing the goods and services we use now and when we develop new goods and services, the total amount of production in the economy increases. **Economic growth** is an increase in the total output of an economy. If output grows faster than the population, output per person rises and standards of living increase. Presumably, when an economy grows, it produces more of what people want. Rural and agrarian societies become modern industrial societies as a result of economic growth and rising per capita output.

Some policies discourage economic growth, and others encourage it. Tax laws, for example, can be designed to encourage the development and application of new production techniques. Research and development in some societies are subsidized by the government. Building roads, highways, bridges, and transport systems in developing countries may speed up the process of economic growth. If businesses and wealthy people invest their wealth outside their country rather than in their country's industries, growth in their home country may be slowed.

stability A condition in which national output is growing steadily, with low inflation and full employment of resources.

Stability   Economic **stability** refers to the condition in which national output is growing steadily, with low inflation and full employment of resources. During the 1950s and 1960s, the U.S. economy experienced a long period of relatively steady growth, stable prices, and low unemployment. Between 1951 and 1969, consumer prices never rose more than 5 percent in a single year, and in only 2 years did the number of unemployed exceed 6 percent of the labor force. From the end of the Gulf War in 1991 to the beginning of 2001, the U.S. economy enjoyed price stability and strong economic growth with rising employment. It was the longest expansion in American history.

The decades of the 1970s and 1980s, however, were not as stable. The United States experienced two periods of rapid price inflation (over 10 percent) and two periods of severe unemployment. In 1982, for example, 12 million people (10.8 percent of the workforce) were looking for work. The beginning of the 1990s was another period of instability, with a recession occurring in 1990–1991. In 2008–2009, much of the world, including the United States, experienced a large contraction in output and rise in unemployment. This was clearly an unstable period.

The causes of instability and the ways in which governments have attempted to stabilize the economy are the subject matter of macroeconomics.

An Invitation

This chapter has prepared you for your study of economics. The first part of the chapter invited you into an exciting discipline that deals with important issues and questions. You cannot begin to understand how a society functions without knowing something about its economic history and its economic system.

The second part of the chapter introduced the method of reasoning that economics requires and some of the tools that economics uses. We believe that learning to think in this very powerful way will help you better understand the world.

As you proceed, it is important that you keep track of what you have learned in earlier chapters. This book has a plan; it proceeds step-by-step, each section building on the last. It would be a good idea to read each chapter's table of contents at the start of each chapter and scan each chapter before you read it to make sure you understand where it fits in the big picture.

SUMMARY

1. *Economics* is the study of how individuals and societies choose to use the scarce resources that nature and previous generations have provided.

WHY STUDY ECONOMICS? *p. 2*

2. There are many reasons to study economics, including (a) to learn a way of thinking, (b) to understand society, and (c) to be an informed citizen.

3. The best alternative that we forgo when we make a choice or a decision is the *opportunity cost* of that decision.

THE SCOPE OF ECONOMICS *p. 4*

4. *Microeconomics* deals with the functioning of individual markets and industries and with the behavior of individual decision-making units: business firms and households.

5. *Macroeconomics* looks at the economy as a whole. It deals with the economic behavior of aggregates—national output, national income, the overall price level, and the general rate of inflation.

6. Economics is a broad and diverse discipline with many special fields of inquiry. These include economic history, international economics, and urban economics.

THE METHOD OF ECONOMICS *p. 8*

7. Economics asks and attempts to answer two kinds of questions: positive and normative. *Positive economics* attempts to understand behavior and the operation of

economies without making judgments about whether the outcomes are good or bad. *Normative economics* looks at the results of economic behavior and asks whether they are good or bad and whether they can be improved.

8. An economic *model* is a formal statement of an economic theory. Models simplify and abstract from reality.

9. It is often useful to isolate the effects of one variable on another while holding "all else constant." This is the device of *ceteris paribus*.

10. Models and theories can be expressed in many ways. The most common ways are in words, in graphs, and in equations.

11. Figuring out causality is often difficult in economics. Because one event happens before another, the second event does not necessarily happen as a result of the first. To assume that "after" implies "because" is to commit the fallacy of *post hoc, ergo propter hoc*. The erroneous belief that what is true for a part is necessarily true for the whole is the *fallacy of composition*.

12. *Empirical economics* involves the collection and use of data to test economic theories. In principle, the best model is the one that yields the most accurate predictions.

13. To make policy, one must be careful to specify criteria for making judgments. Four specific criteria are used most often in economics: *efficiency, equity, growth,* and *stability*.

REVIEW TERMS AND CONCEPTS

ceteris paribus, or all else equal, *p. 9*

economic growth, *p. 12*

economics, *p. 2*

efficiency, *p. 11*

efficient market, *p. 3*

empirical economics, *p. 10*

equity, *p. 12*

fallacy of composition, *p. 10*

Industrial Revolution, *p. 3*

macroeconomics, *p. 5*

marginalism, *p. 2*

microeconomics, *p. 4*

model, *p. 8*

normative economics, *p. 8*

Ockham's razor, *p. 8*

opportunity cost, *p. 2*

positive economics, *p. 8*

post hoc, ergo propter hoc, *p. 10*

scarce, *p. 2*

stability, *p. 12*

variable, *p. 8*

PROBLEMS

All problems are available on MyEconLab.

1. One of the scarce resources that constrain our behavior is time. Each of us has only 24 hours in a day. How do you go about allocating your time in a given day among competing alternatives? How do you go about weighing the alternatives? Once you choose a most important use of time, why do you not spend all your time on it? Use the notion of opportunity cost in your answer.

2. In the summer of 2007, the housing market and the mortgage market were both in decline. Housing prices in most U.S. cities began to decline in mid-2006. With prices falling and the inventory of unsold houses rising, the production of new homes fell to around 1.5 million in 2007 from 2.3 million in 2005. With new construction falling dramatically, it was expected that construction *employment* would fall and that this would have the potential of slowing the national economy and increasing the general unemployment rate. Go to www.bls.gov and check out the recent data on total employment and construction employment. Have they gone up or down from their levels in August 2007? What has happened to the unemployment rate? Go to www.fhfa.gov and look at the housing price index. Have home prices risen or fallen since August 2007? Finally, look at the latest GDP release at www.bea.gov. Look at residential and nonresidential investment (Table 1.1.5) during the last 2 years. Do you see a pattern? Does it explain the employment numbers? Explain your answer

3. Which of the following statements are examples of positive economic analysis? Which are examples of normative analysis?
   a. The inheritance tax should be repealed because it is unfair.
   b. Allowing Chile to join NAFTA would cause wine prices in the United States to drop.
   c. The first priorities of the new regime in the Republic of South Sudan should be to rebuild schools and highways and to provide basic health care.

4. Sarita signed up with Netflix for a fixed fee of $15.98 per month. For this fee, she can receive up to 1 DVD at a time in the mail and exchange each DVD as often as she likes. She also receives unlimited instant access to movies being streamed from Netflix to her computer or TV. During the average month in 2012, Sarita received and watched 6 movies sent to her through the mail and she watched an additional 13 movies that were streamed to her computer. What is the average cost of a movie to Sarita? What is the marginal cost of an additional movie?

5. A question facing many U.S. states is whether to allow casino gambling. States with casino gambling have seen a substantial increase in tax revenue flowing to state government. This revenue can be used to finance schools, repair roads, maintain social programs, or reduce other taxes.
   a. Recall that efficiency means producing what people want at the least cost. Can you make an efficiency argument in favor of allowing casinos to operate?
   b. What nonmonetary costs might be associated with gambling? Would these costs have an impact on the efficiency argument you presented in part a?
   c. Using the concept of equity, argue for or against the legalization of casino gambling.

   d. What do you think would happen to the flow of tax revenue to state governments if all 50 states legalized casino gambling?

6. For each of the following situations, identify the full cost (opportunity cost) involved:
   a. A worker earning an hourly wage of $8.50 decides to cut back to part-time to attend Houston Community College.
   b. Sue decides to drive to Los Angeles from San Francisco to visit her son, who attends UCLA.
   c. Tom decides to go to a wild fraternity party and stays out all night before his physics exam.
   d. Annie spends $200 on a new dress.
   e. The Confab Company spends $1 million to build a new branch plant that will probably be in operation for at least 10 years.
   f. Alex's father owns a small grocery store in town. Alex works 40 hours a week in the store but receives no compensation.

7. [Related to the *Economics in Practice* on *p. 5*] Log onto www. census.gov/foreign-trade/statistics/state/. In the State Trade by Commodity and Country section, click on "Exports and Imports", then click on "Exports" for your state. There you will find a list of the top 25 commodities produced in your state which are exported around the world. In looking over that list, are you surprised by anything? Do you know any of the firms that produce these items? Search the Internet to find a company that does. Do some research and write a paragraph about this company: what it produces, how many people it employs, and whatever else you can learn about the firm. You might even call the company to obtain the information.

8. [Related to the *Economics in Practice* on *p. 10*] Most college students either currently have, or at one time have had, roommates or housemates. Think about a time when you have shared your living space with one or more students, and describe the effect this person (or people) had on your college experience, such as your study habits, the classes you took, your grade point average, and the way you spent time away from the classroom. Now describe the effect you think you had on your roommate(s). Were these roommates or housemates people you chose to live with, or were they assigned randomly? Explain if you think this made a difference in your or their behavior?

9. Explain the pitfalls in the following statements.
   a. Whenever Jeremy decides to wash his car, the next day it usually rains. Since Jeremy's town is suffering from a severe drought, he decided to wash his car and, just as he expected, the next day, the thunderstorms rolled in. Obviously it rained because Jeremy washed his car.
   b. The principal of Hamilton High School found that requiring those students who were failing algebra to attend an after-school tutoring program resulted in a 30 percent average increase in their algebra grades. Based on this success, the principal decided to hire more tutors and require that all students must attend after-school tutoring, so everyone's algebra grades would improve.

c. People who drive hybrid automobiles recycle their trash more than people who do not drive hybrids. Therefore, recycling trash causes people to drive hybrid automobiles.

10. Explain whether each of the following is an example of a macroeconomic concern or a microeconomic concern.
   a. Ford Motor Company is contemplating increasing the production of full-size SUVs based on projected future consumer demand.
   b. Congress is debating the option of implementing a value-added tax as a means to cut the federal deficit.

c. The Federal Reserve announces it is increasing the discount rate in an attempt to slow the rate of inflation.
   d. The Bureau of Labor Statistics projects a 33 percent increase in the number of workers in the healthcare industry from 2010–2020.

11. On the *Forbes* 2013 list of the World's Billionaires, Mexico's Carlos Slim Helu ranks at the top with a net worth of U.S. $73 billion. Does this "richest man in the world" face scarcity, or does scarcity only affect those with more limited incomes and lower net worth?
   Source: "The World's Billionaires," *Forbes,* March, 4, 2013.

CHAPTER 1 APPENDIX

How to Read and Understand Graphs

Economics is the most quantitative of the social sciences. If you flip through the pages of this or any other economics text, you will see countless tables and graphs. These serve a number of purposes. First, they illustrate important economic relationships. Second, they make difficult problems easier to understand and analyze. Finally, they can show patterns and regularities that may not be discernible in simple lists of numbers.

A **graph** is a two-dimensional representation of a set of numbers, or data. There are many ways that numbers can be illustrated by a graph.

Time Series Graphs

It is often useful to see how a single measure or variable changes over time. One way to present this information is to plot the values of the variable on a graph, with each value corresponding to a different time period. A graph of this kind is called a **time series graph**. On a time series graph, time is measured along the horizontal scale and the variable being graphed is measured along the vertical scale. Figure 1A.1 is a time series graph that presents the total disposable personal income in the U.S. economy for each year between 1975 and 2012.[1] This graph is based on the data found in Table 1A.1. By displaying these data graphically, we can see that (1) total disposable personal income has increased steadily since 1975 and (2) during certain periods, income has increased at a faster rate than during other periods.

Graphing Two Variables

More important than simple graphs of one variable are graphs that contain information on two variables at the same time. The most common method of graphing two variables is a graph constructed by drawing two perpendicular lines: a horizontal line, or **X-axis**, and a vertical line, or

Y-axis. The axes contain measurement scales that intersect at 0 (zero). This point is called the **origin**. On the vertical scale, positive numbers lie above the horizontal axis (that is, above the origin) and negative numbers lie below it. On the horizontal scale, positive numbers lie to the right of the vertical axis (to the right of the origin) and negative numbers lie to the left of it. The point at which the graph intersects the Y-axis is called the **Y-intercept**. The point at which the graph intersects the X-axis is called the **X-intercept**. When two variables are plotted on a single graph, each point represents a pair of numbers. The first number is measured on the X-axis, and the second number is measured on the Y-axis.

Plotting Income and Consumption Data for Households

Table 1A.2 presents data collected by the Bureau of Labor Statistics (BLS). In a recent survey, 5,000 households were asked to keep track of all of their expenditures. This table shows average income and average spending for those households, ranked by income. For example, the average income for the top fifth (20 percent) of the households was $158,652. The average spending for the top 20 percent was $97,003.

Figure 1A.2 presents the numbers from Table 1A.2 graphically. Along the horizontal scale, the X-axis, we measure average income. Along the vertical scale, the Y-axis, we measure average consumption spending. Each of the five pairs of numbers from the table is represented by a point on the graph. Because all numbers are positive numbers, we need to show only the upper right quadrant of the coordinate system.

---

[1] The measure of income presented in Table 1A.1 and in Figure 1A.1 is disposable personal income in billions of dollars. It is the total personal income received by all households in the United States minus the taxes that they pay.

▶ FIGURE 1A.1 **Total Disposable Personal Income in the United States: 1975–2012 (in billions of dollars)**

Source: See Table 1A.1.

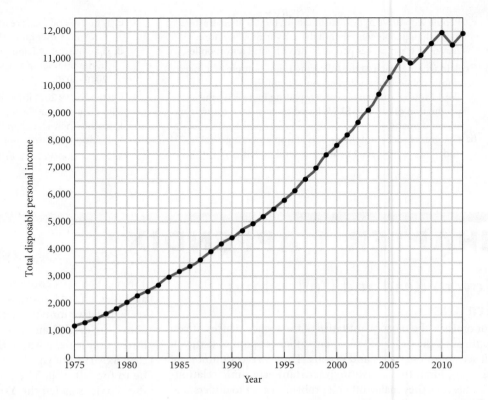

TABLE 1A.1 Total Disposable Personal Income in the United States, 1975–2012 (in billions of dollars)

Year	Total Disposable Personal Income	Year	Total Disposable Personal Income
1975	1,187.3	1994	5,184.3
1976	1,302.3	1995	5,457.0
1977	1,435.0	1996	5,759.6
1978	1,607.3	1997	6,074.6
1979	1,790.8	1998	6,498.9
1980	2,002.7	1999	6,803.3
1981	2,237.1	2000	7,327.2
1982	2,412.7	2001	7,648.5
1983	2,599.8	2002	8,009.7
1984	2,891.5	2003	8,377.8
1985	3,079.3	2004	8,889.4
1986	3,258.8	2005	9,277.3
1987	3,435.3	2006	9,915.7
1988	3,726.3	2007	10,423.6
1989	3,991.4	2008	11,024.5
1990	4,254.0	2009	10,772.4
1991	4,444.9	2010	11,127.1
1992	4,736.7	2011	11,549.3
1993	4,921.6	2012	11,930.6

Source: U.S. Department of Commerce, Bureau of Economic Analysis.

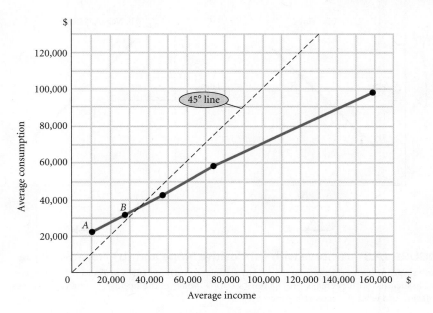

Household Consumption and Income
A graph is a simple two-dimensional geometric representation of data. This graph displays the data from Table 1A.2. Along the horizontal scale (*X*-axis), we measure household income. Along the vertical scale (*Y*-axis), we measure household consumption.

Note: At point *A*, consumption equals $22,304 and income equals $10,263. At point *B*, consumption equals $31,751 and income equals $27,442.

Source: See Table 1A.2.

TABLE 1A.2 Consumption Expenditures and Income, 2008		
	Average Income Before Taxes	Average Consumption Expenditures
Bottom fifth	$ 10,263	$22,304
2nd fifth	27,442	31,751
3rd fifth	47,196	42,659
4th fifth	74,090	58,632
Top fifth	158,652	97,003

Source: Consumer Expenditures in 2008, U.S. Bureau of Labor Statistics.

To help you read this graph, we have drawn a dotted line connecting all the points where consumption and income would be equal. *This 45° line does not represent any data.* Instead, it represents the line along which all variables on the *X*-axis correspond exactly to the variables on the *Y*-axis, for example, (10,000, 10,000), (20,000, 20,000), and (37,000, 37,000). The heavy blue line traces the data; the purpose of the dotted line is to help you read the graph.

There are several things to look for when reading a graph. The first thing you should notice is whether the line slopes upward or downward as you move from left to right. The blue line in Figure 1A.2 slopes upward, indicating that there seems to be a **positive relationship** between income and spending: The higher a household's income, the more a household tends to consume. If we had graphed the percentage of each group receiving welfare payments along the *Y*-axis, the line would presumably slope downward, indicating that welfare payments are lower at higher income levels. The income level/welfare payment relationship is thus a **negative relationship**.

Slope

The **slope** of a line or curve is a measure that indicates whether the relationship between the variables is positive or negative and how much of a response there is in *Y* (the variable on the vertical axis) when *X* (the variable on the horizontal axis) changes. The slope of a line between two points is the change in the quantity measured on the *Y*-axis divided by the change in the quantity measured on the *X*-axis. We will normally use Δ (the Greek letter *delta*) to refer to a change in a variable. In Figure 1A.3, the slope

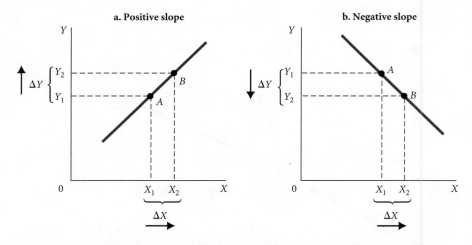

a. Positive slope   **b. Negative slope**

▲ **FIGURE 1A.3   A Curve with (a) Positive Slope and (b) Negative Slope**
A *positive* slope indicates that increases in X are associated with increases in Y and that decreases in X are associated with decreases in Y. A *negative* slope indicates the opposite—when X increases, Y decreases; and when X decreases, Y increases.

of the line between points A and B is ΔY divided by ΔX. Sometimes it is easy to remember slope as "the rise over the run," indicating the vertical change over the horizontal change.

To be precise, ΔX between two points on a graph is simply X_2 minus X_1, where X_2 is the X value for the second point and X_1 is the X value for the first point. Similarly, ΔY is defined as Y_2 minus Y_1, where Y_2 is the Y value for the second point and Y_1 is the Y value for the first point. Slope is equal to

$$\frac{\Delta Y}{\Delta X} = \frac{Y_2 - Y_1}{X_2 - X_1}$$

As we move from A to B in Figure 1A.3(a), both X and Y increase; the slope is thus a positive number. However, as we move from A to B in Figure 1A.3(b), X increases [$(X_2 - X_1)$ is a positive number], but Y decreases [$(Y_2 - Y_1)$ is a negative number]. The slope in Figure 1A.3(b) is thus a negative number because a negative number divided by a positive number results in a negative quotient.

To calculate the numerical value of the slope between points A and B in Figure 1A.2, we need to calculate ΔY and ΔX. Because consumption is measured on the Y-axis, ΔY is 9,447 [$(Y_2 - Y_1) = (31,751 - 22,304)$]. Because income

is measured along the X-axis, ΔX is 17,179 [$(X_2 - X_1) = (27,442 - 10,263)$]. The slope between A and B is

$$\frac{\Delta Y}{\Delta X} = \frac{9,447}{17,179} = +0.55.$$

Another interesting thing to note about the data graphed in Figure 1A.2 is that all the points lie roughly along a straight line. (If you look very closely, however, you can see that the slope declines as you move from left to right; the line becomes slightly less steep.) A straight line has a constant slope. That is, if you pick any two points along it and calculate the slope, you will always get the same number. A horizontal line has a zero slope (ΔY is zero); a vertical line has an "infinite" slope because ΔY is too big to be measured.

Unlike the slope of a straight line, the slope of a *curve* is continually changing. Consider, for example, the curves in Figure 1A.4. Figure 1A.4(a) shows a curve with a positive slope that decreases as you move from left to right. The easiest way to think about the concept of increasing or decreasing slope is to imagine what it is like walking up a hill from left to right. If the hill is steep, as it is in the first part of Figure 1A.4(a), you are moving more in the Y direction for each step you take in the X direction. If the hill is less

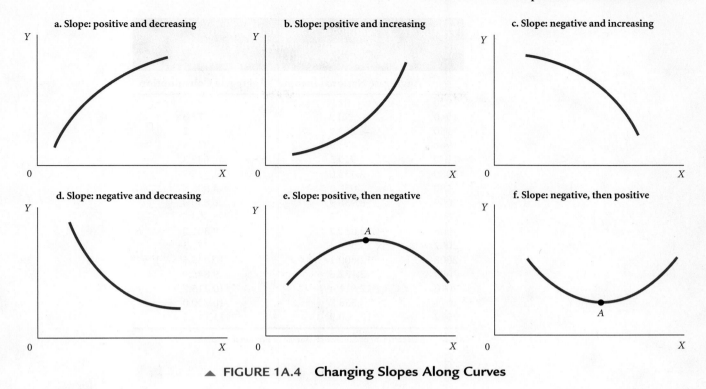

▲ **FIGURE 1A.4   Changing Slopes Along Curves**

steep, as it is further along in Figure 1A.4(a), you are moving less in the *Y* direction for every step you take in the *X* direction. Thus, when the hill is steep, slope $(\Delta Y/\Delta X)$ is a larger number than it is when the hill is flatter. The curve in Figure 1A.4(b) has a positive slope, but its slope *increases* as you move from left to right.

The same analogy holds for curves that have a negative slope. Figure 1A.4(c) shows a curve with a negative slope that increases (in absolute value) as you move from left to right. This time think about skiing down a hill. At first, the descent in Figure 1A.4(c) is gradual (low slope), but as you proceed down the hill (to the right), you descend more quickly (high slope). Figure 1A.4(d) shows a curve with a negative slope that *decreases* (in absolute value) as you move from left to right.

In Figure 1A.4(e), the slope goes from positive to negative as *X* increases. In Figure 1A.4(f), the slope goes from negative to positive. At point *A* in both, the slope is zero. [Remember, slope is defined as $\Delta Y/\Delta X$. At point *A*, *Y* is not changing $(\Delta Y = 0)$. Therefore, the slope at point *A* is zero.]

Some Precautions

When you read a graph, it is important to think carefully about what the points in the space defined by the axes represent. Table 1A.3 and Figure 1A.5 present a graph of consumption and income that is very different from the one in Table 1A.2 and Figure 1A.2. First, each point in Figure 1A.5 represents a different year; in Figure 1A.2, each point represented a different group of households at the *same* point in time (2008). Second, the points in Figure 1A.5 represent *aggregate* consumption and income for the whole nation measured in *billions* of dollars; in Figure 1A.2, the points represented average *household* income and consumption measured in dollars.

It is interesting to compare these two graphs. All points on the aggregate consumption curve in Figure 1A.5 lie below the 45° line, which means that aggregate consumption is always less than aggregate income. However, the graph of average household income and consumption in Figure 1A.2 crosses the 45° line, implying that for some households, consumption is larger than income.

TABLE 1A.3 Aggregate National Income and Consumption for the United States, 1930–2012 (in billions of dollars)

	Aggregate National Income	Aggregate Consumption
1930	82.9	70.1
1940	90.9	71.3
1950	263.9	192.2
1960	473.9	331.8
1970	929.5	648.3
1980	2,433.0	1,755.8
1990	5,059.8	3,835.5
2000	8,938.9	6,830.4
2005	11,273.8	8,803.5
2006	12,031.2	9,301.0
2007	12,396.4	9,772.3
2008	12,609.1	10,035.5
2009	12,132.6	9,845.9
2010	12,811.4	10,215.7
2011	13,358.9	10,729.0
2012	13,720.9	11,119.5

Source: U.S. Department of Commerce, Bureau of Economic Analysis.

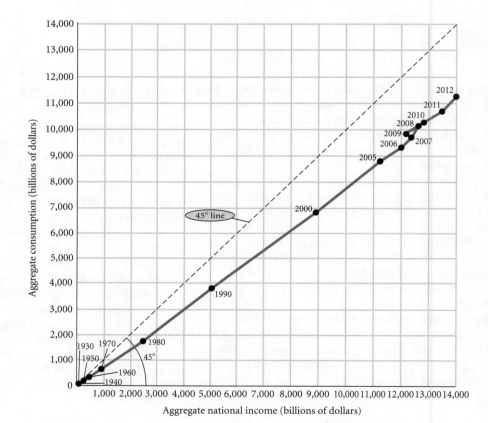

▲ **FIGURE 1A.5** **National Income and Consumption**

It is important to think carefully about what is represented by points in the space defined by the axes of a graph. In this graph, we have graphed income with consumption, as in Figure 1A.2, but here each observation point is national income and aggregate consumption in *different years*, measured in billions of dollars.

Source: See Table 1A.3.

APPENDIX SUMMARY

1. A *graph* is a two-dimensional representation of a set of numbers, or data. A *time series graph* illustrates how a single variable changes over time.

2. A graph of two variables includes an *X* (horizontal)-*axis* and a *Y* (vertical)-*axis*. The points at which the two axes intersect is called the *origin*. The point at which a graph intersects the *Y*-axis is called the *Y-intercept*. The point at which a graph intersects the *X*-axis is called the *X-intercept*.

3. The *slope* of a line or curve indicates whether the relationship between the two variables graphed is positive or negative and how much of a response there is in *Y* (the variable on the vertical axis) when *X* (the variable on the horizontal axis) changes. The slope of a line between two points is the change in the quantity measured on the *Y*-axis divided by the change in the quantity measured on the *X*-axis.

APPENDIX REVIEW TERMS AND CONCEPTS

graph   A two-dimensional representation of a set of numbers or data. *p. 15*

negative relationship   A relationship between two variables, *X* and *Y*, in which a decrease in *X* is associated with an increase in *Y* and an increase in *X* is associated with a decrease in *Y*. *p. 17*

origin   The point at which the horizontal and vertical axes intersect. *p. 15*

positive relationship   A relationship between two variables, *X* and *Y*, in which a decrease in *X* is associated with a decrease in *Y*, and an increase in *X* is associated with an increase in *Y*. *p. 17*

slope   A measurement that indicates whether the relationship between variables is positive or negative and how much of a response there is in *Y* (the variable on the vertical axis) when *X* (the variable on the horizontal axis) changes. *p. 17*

time series graph   A graph illustrating how a variable changes over time. *p. 15*

X-axis   The horizontal line against which a variable is plotted. *p. 15*

X-intercept   The point at which a graph intersects the *X*-axis. *p. 15*

Y-axis   The vertical line against which a variable is plotted. *p. 15*

Y-intercept   The point at which a graph intersects the *Y*-axis. *p. 15*

APPENDIX PROBLEMS

All problems are available on MyEconLab.

1. Graph each of the following sets of numbers. Draw a line through the points and calculate the slope of each line.

1		2		3		4		5		6	
X	Y	X	Y	X	Y	X	Y	X	Y	X	Y
1	5	1	25	0	0	0	40	0	0	0.1	100
2	10	2	20	10	10	10	30	10	10	0.2	75
3	15	3	15	20	20	20	20	20	20	0.3	50
4	20	4	10	30	30	30	10	30	10	0.4	25
5	25	5	5	40	40	40	0	40	0	0.5	0

2. For each of the graphs in Figure 1, determine whether the curve has a positive or negative slope. Give an intuitive explanation for what is happening with the slope of each curve.

3. For each of the following equations, graph the line and calculate its slope.
   a. $P = 10 - 2q_D$ (Put q_D on the X-axis.)
   b. $P = 100 - 4q_D$ (Put q_D on the X-axis.)
   c. $P = 50 + 6q_S$ (Put q_S on the X-axis.)
   d. $I = 10,000 - 500r$ (Put I on the X-axis.)

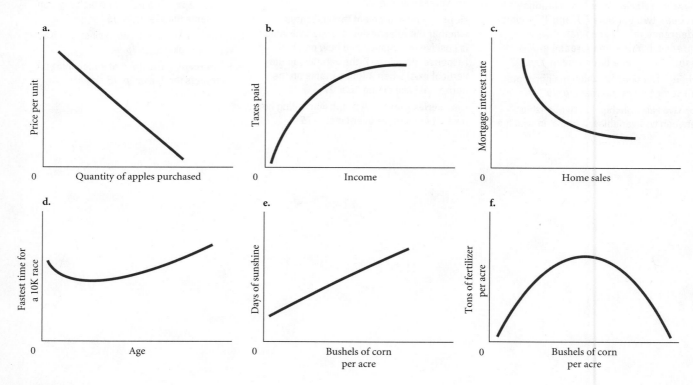

▲ FIGURE 1

4. The following table shows the relationship between the price of a dozen roses and the number of roses sold by Fiona's Flowers.
   a. Is the relationship between the price of roses and the number of roses sold by Fiona's Flowers a positive relationship or a negative relationship? Explain.
   b. Plot the data from the table on a graph, draw a line through the points, and calculate the slope of the line.

PRICE PER DOZEN	QUANTITY OF ROSES (DOZENS)	MONTH
$20	30	January
50	90	February
25	40	March
30	50	April
40	70	May

5. Calculate the slope of the demand curve at point *A* and at point *B* in the following figure.

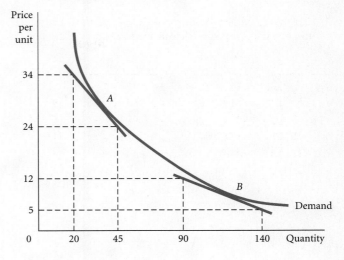

The Economic Problem: Scarcity and Choice

2

In the last chapter we provided you with some sense of the questions asked by economists and the broad methods that they use. As you read that chapter, some of you may have been surprised by the range of topics covered by economics. A look at the work done by the economists teaching at your own university will

likely reveal a similarly broad range of interests. Some of your faculty will study how Apple and Samsung compete in smart phones. Others will look at discrimination in labor markets. Still others may be exploring the effects of microfinance in India. On the surface, these issues seem quite different from one another. But fundamental to each of these inquiries is the concern with choice in a world of scarcity. Economics explores how individuals make choices in a world of scarce resources and how those individual's choices come together to determine three key features of their society:

- What gets produced?
- How is it produced?
- Who gets what is produced?

This chapter explores these questions in detail. In a sense, this entire chapter *is* the definition of economics. It lays out the central problems addressed by the discipline and presents a framework that will guide you through the rest of the book. The starting point is the presumption that *human wants are unlimited but resources are not.* Limited or scarce resources force individuals and societies to choose among competing uses of resources—alternative combinations of produced goods and services—and among alternative final distributions of what is produced among households.

These questions are *positive* or *descriptive.* Understanding how a system functions is important before we can ask the normative questions of whether the system produces good or bad outcomes and how we might make improvements.

LEARNING OBJECTIVES

Discuss scarcity, choice, and opportunity cost in a one-person economy

Discuss specialization, exchange, and comparative advantage in an economy of two or more

Explain the implications of the production possibility frontier

Describe the role of government in economic systems

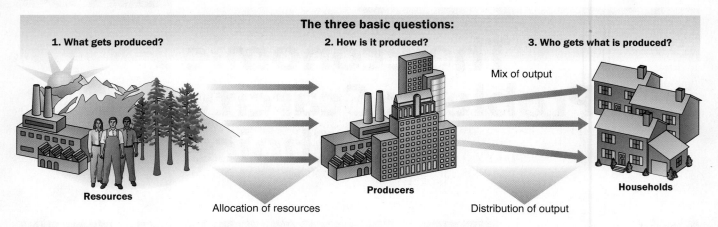

The three basic questions:

1. What gets produced?　　　2. How is it produced?　　　3. Who gets what is produced?

Mix of output

Resources

Allocation of resources

Producers

Distribution of output

Households

▲ **FIGURE 2.1　The Three Basic Questions**
Every society has some system or process that transforms its scarce resources into useful goods and services. In doing so, it must decide what gets produced, how it is produced, and to whom it is distributed. The primary resources that must be allocated are land, labor, and capital.

capital　Things that are produced and then used in the production of other goods and services.

factors of production (*or* factors)　The inputs into the process of production. Another term for resources.

production　The process that transforms scarce resources into useful goods and services.

inputs *or* resources　Anything provided by nature or previous generations that can be used directly or indirectly to satisfy human wants.

outputs　Goods and services of value to households.

Economists study choices in a world of scarce resources. What do we mean by resources? If you look at Figure 2.1, you will see that resources are very broadly defined. They include products of nature like minerals and timber, but also the products of past generations like buildings and factories. Perhaps most importantly, resources include the time and talents of the human population.

Things that are produced and then used in the production of other goods and services are called capital resources, or simply **capital**. Buildings, equipment, desks, chairs, software, roads, bridges, and highways are a part of the nation's stock of capital.

The basic resources available to a society are often referred to as **factors of production**, or simply **factors**. The three key factors of production are land, labor, and capital. The process that transforms scarce resources into useful goods and services is called **production**. In many societies, most of the production of goods and services is done by private firms. Private airlines in the United States use land (runways), labor (pilots and mechanics), and capital (airplanes) to produce transportation services. But in all societies, some production is done by the public sector, or government. Examples of government-produced or government-provided goods and services include national defense, public education, police protection, and fire protection.

Resources or factors of production are the **inputs** into the process of production; goods and services of value to households are the **outputs** of the process of production.

Scarcity, Choice, and Opportunity Cost

In the second half of this chapter we discuss the global economic landscape. Before you can understand the different types of economic systems, it is important to master the basic economic concepts of scarcity, choice, and opportunity cost.

Scarcity and Choice in a One-Person Economy

The simplest economy is one in which a single person lives alone on an island. Consider Bill, the survivor of a plane crash, who finds himself cast ashore in such a place. Here individual and society are one; there is no distinction between social and private. *Nonetheless, nearly all the same basic decisions that characterize complex economies must also be made in a simple economy.* That is, although Bill will get whatever he produces, he still must decide how to allocate the island's resources, what to produce, and how and when to produce it.

First, Bill must decide *what* he wants to produce. Notice that the word *needs* does not appear here. Needs are absolute requirements; but beyond just enough water, basic nutrition, and shelter to survive, needs are very difficult to define. What is an "absolute necessity" for one person may not be for another person. In any case, Bill must put his wants in some order of priority and make some choices.

Next, he must look at the *possibilities*. What can he do to satisfy his wants given the limits of the island? In every society, no matter how simple or complex, people are constrained in what they can do. In this society of one, Bill is constrained by time, his physical condition, his knowledge, his skills, and the resources and climate of the island.

Given that resources are limited, Bill must decide *how* to best use them to satisfy his hierarchy of wants. Food would probably come close to the top of his list. Should he spend his time gathering fruits and berries? Should he hunt for game? Should he clear a field and plant seeds? The answers to those questions depend on the character of the island, its climate, its flora and fauna (*are* there any fruits and berries?), the extent of his skills and knowledge (does he know anything about farming?), and his preferences (he may be a vegetarian).

Opportunity Cost   The concepts of *constrained choice* and *scarcity* are central to the discipline of economics. They can be applied when discussing the behavior of individuals such as Bill and when analyzing the behavior of large groups of people in complex societies.

Given the scarcity of time and resources, if Bill decides to hunt, he will have less time to gather fruits and berries. He faces a trade-off between meat and fruit. There is a trade-off between food and shelter too. If Bill likes to be comfortable, he may work on building a nice place to live, but that may require giving up the food he might have produced. As we noted in Chapter 1, the best alternative that we give up, or forgo, when we make a choice is the **opportunity cost** of that choice.

> **opportunity cost**   The best alternative that we give up, or forgo, when we make a choice or decision.

Bill may occasionally decide to rest, to lie on the beach, and to enjoy the sun. In one sense, that benefit is free—he does not have to buy a ticket to lie on the beach. In reality, however, relaxing does have an opportunity cost. The true cost of that leisure is the value of the other things Bill could have produced, but did not, during the time he spent on the beach.

The trade-offs that are made in this kind of society are vividly and often comically portrayed in the reality television shows that show groups of strangers competing on some deserted island, all trying to choose whether it is better to fish, hunt for berries, build a hut, or build an alliance. Making one of these choices involves giving up an opportunity to do another, and in many episodes we can see the consequences of those choices.

In making everyday decisions, it is often helpful to think about opportunity costs. Should you go to the dorm party or not? First, it costs $4 to attend. When you pay money for anything, you give up the other things you could have bought with that money. Second, it costs 2 or 3 hours. Time is a valuable commodity for a college student. You have exams next week, and you need to study. You could go to a movie instead of the party. You could go to another party. You could sleep. Just as Bill must weigh the value of sunning on the beach against more food or better housing, so you must weigh the value of the fun you may have at the party against everything else you might otherwise do with the time and money.

Scarcity and Choice in an Economy of Two or More

Now suppose that another survivor of the crash, Colleen, appears on the island. Now that Bill is not alone, things are more complex and some new decisions must be made. Bill's and Colleen's preferences about what things to produce are likely to be different. They will probably not have the same knowledge or skills. Perhaps Colleen is very good at tracking animals and Bill has a knack for building things. How should they split the work that needs to be done? Once things are produced, the two castaways must decide how to divide them. How should their products be distributed?

The mechanism for answering these fundamental questions is clear when Bill is alone on the island. The "central plan" is his; he simply decides what he wants and what to do about it. The minute someone else appears, however, a number of decision-making arrangements immediately become possible. One or the other may take charge, in which case that person will decide for both of them. The two may agree to cooperate, with each having an equal say, and come up

ECONOMICS IN PRACTICE

Frozen Foods and Opportunity Costs

In 2012, $44 billion of frozen foods were sold in U.S. grocery stores, one quarter of it in the form of frozen dinners and entrées. In the mid-1950s, sales of frozen foods amounted to only $1 billion, a tiny fraction of the overall grocery store sales. One industry observer attributes this growth to the fact that frozen food tastes much better than it did in the past. Can you think of anything else that might be occurring?

The growth of the frozen dinner entrée market in the last 50 years is a good example of the role of opportunity costs in our lives. One of the most significant social changes in the U.S. economy in this period has been the increased participation of women in the labor force. In 1950, only 24 percent of married women worked; by 2013, that fraction had risen to 58 percent. Producing a meal takes two basic ingredients: food and time. When both husbands and wives work, the opportunity cost of time for housework—including making meals—goes up. This tells us that making a home-cooked meal became more expensive in the last 50 years. A natural result is to shift people toward labor-saving ways to make meals. Frozen foods are an obvious solution to the problem of increased opportunity costs.

Another, somewhat more subtle, opportunity cost story is at work encouraging the consumption of frozen foods. In 1960, the first microwave oven was introduced. The spread of this device into America's kitchens was rapid. The microwave turned out to be a quick way to defrost and cook those frozen entrées. So this technology lowered the opportunity cost of making frozen dinners, reinforcing the advantage these meals had over home-cooked meals. Microwaves made cooking with frozen foods cheaper once opportunity cost was considered while home-cooked meals were becoming more expensive.

The entrepreneurs among you also might recognize that the rise we described in the opportunity cost of the home-cooked meal *contributed* in part to the spread of the microwave, creating a reinforcing cycle. In fact, many entrepreneurs find that

the simple tools of economics—like the idea of opportunity costs—help them anticipate what products will be profitable for them to produce in the future. The growth of the two-worker family has stimulated many entrepreneurs to search for labor-saving solutions to family tasks.

The public policy students among you might be interested to know that some researchers attribute part of the growth in obesity in the United States to the lower opportunity costs of making meals associated with the growth of the markets for frozen foods and the microwave. (See David M.Cutler, Edward L. Glaeser, and Jesse M. Shapiro, "Why Have Americans Become More Obese?" *Journal of Economic Perspectives*, Summer 2003, 93–118.)

THINKING PRACTICALLY

1. Many people think that soda consumption also leads to increased obesity. Many schools have banned the sale of soda in vending machines. Use the idea of opportunity costs to explain why some people think these bans will reduce consumption. Do you agree?

---

with a joint plan; or they may agree to split the planning as well as the production duties. Finally, they may go off to live alone at opposite ends of the island. Even if they live apart, however, they may take advantage of each other's presence by specializing and trading.

Modern industrial societies must answer the same questions that Colleen and Bill must answer, but the mechanics of larger economies are more complex. Instead of two people living together, the United States has over 300 million people. Still, decisions must be made about what to produce, how to produce it, and who gets it.

theory of comparative advantage Ricardo's theory that specialization and free trade will benefit all trading parties, even those that may be "absolutely" more efficient producers.

Specialization, Exchange, and Comparative Advantage　　The idea that members of society benefit by specializing in what they do best has a long history and is one of the most important and powerful ideas in all of economics. David Ricardo, a major nineteenth-century British economist, formalized the point precisely. According to Ricardo's **theory of comparative advantage**, specialization and free trade will benefit all trading parties, even when some are "absolutely" more efficient producers than others. Ricardo's basic point applies just as much to Colleen and Bill as it does to different nations.

To keep things simple, suppose that Colleen and Bill have only two tasks to accomplish each week: gathering food to eat and cutting logs to burn. If Colleen could cut more logs than Bill in one day and Bill could gather more nuts and berries than Colleen could, specialization would clearly lead to more total production. Both would benefit if Colleen only cuts logs and Bill only gathers nuts and berries, as long as they can trade.

Suppose that Bill is slow and somewhat clumsy in his nut gathering and that Colleen is better at cutting logs *and* gathering food. At first, it might seem that since Colleen is better at everything, she should do everything. But that cannot be right. Colleen's time is limited after all, and even though Bill is clumsy and not very clever, he must be able to contribute something.

One of Ricardo's lasting contributions to economics has been his analysis of exactly this situation. His analysis, which is illustrated in Figure 2.2, shows both how Colleen and Bill should divide the work of the island and how much they will gain from specializing and exchanging even if, as in this example, one party is absolutely better at everything than the other party.

Suppose Colleen can cut 10 logs per day and Bill can cut only 4. Also suppose Colleen can gather 10 bushels of food per day and Bill can gather only 8. A producer has an **absolute advantage** over another in the production of a good or service if he or she can produce the good or service using fewer resources, including time. Since Colleen can cut more logs per day than Bill, we say that she has an absolute advantage in the production of logs. Similarly, Colleen has an absolute advantage over Bill in the production of food.

Thinking just about productivity and the output of food and logs, you might conclude that it would benefit Colleen to move to the other side of the island and be by herself. Since she is more productive in cutting logs and gathering food, would she not be better off on her own? How could she benefit by hanging out with Bill and sharing what they produce?

To answer that question we must remember that Colleen's time is limited: This limit creates opportunity cost. A producer has a **comparative advantage** over another in the production of a good or service if he or she can produce the good or service at a lower opportunity cost. First, think about Bill. He can produce 8 bushels of food per day, or he can cut 4 logs. To get 8 additional bushels of food, he must give up cutting 4 logs. Thus, *for Bill, the opportunity cost of 8 bushels of food is 4 logs.* Think next about Colleen. She can produce 10 bushels of food per day, or she can cut 10 logs. She thus gives up 1 log for each additional bushel; so *for Colleen, the opportunity cost of 8 bushels of food is 8 logs.* Bill has a comparative advantage over Colleen in the production of food because he gives up only 4 logs for an additional 8 bushels, whereas Colleen gives up 8 logs.

Think now about what Colleen must give up in terms of food to get 10 logs. To produce 10 logs she must work a whole day. If she spends a day cutting 10 logs, she gives up a day of gathering 10 bushels of food. Thus, *for Colleen, the opportunity cost of 10 logs is 10 bushels of food.* What must Bill give up to get 10 logs? To produce 4 logs, he must work 1 day. For each day he cuts logs, he gives up 8 bushels of food. He thus gives up 2 bushels of food for each log; so *for Bill, the opportunity cost of 10 logs is 20 bushels of food.* Colleen has a comparative advantage over Bill in the production of logs since she gives up only 10 bushels of food for an additional 10 logs, whereas Bill gives up 20 bushels.

Ricardo argued that two parties can benefit from specialization and trade even if one party has an absolute advantage in the production of both goods. Let us see how this works in the current example.

Suppose Colleen and Bill both want equal numbers of logs and bushels of food. If Colleen goes off on her own and splits her time equally, in one day she can produce 5 logs and 5 bushels of food. Bill, to produce equal amounts of logs and food, will have to spend more time on the wood than the food, given his talents. By spending one third of his day producing food and two thirds chopping wood, he can produce $2\frac{2}{3}$ units of each. In sum, when acting alone $7\frac{2}{3}$ logs and bushels of food are produced by our pair of castaways, most of them by Colleen. Clearly Colleen is a better producer than Bill. Why should she ever want to join forces with clumsy, slow Bill?

The answer lies in the gains from specialization, as we can see in Figure 2.2. In block a, we show the results of having Bill and Colleen each working alone chopping logs and gathering food: $7\frac{2}{3}$ logs and an equal number of food bushels. Now, recalling our calculations indicating that Colleen has a comparative advantage in wood chopping, let's see what happens if we assign Colleen to the wood task and have Bill spend all day gathering food. This system is described

absolute advantage
A producer has an absolute advantage over another in the production of a good or service if he or she can produce that product using fewer resources (a lower absolute cost per unit).

comparative advantage
A producer has a comparative advantage over another in the production of a good or service if he or she can produce that product at a lower *opportunity cost*.

▶ **FIGURE 2.2**

Comparative Advantage and the Gains from Trade

Panel (a) shows the best Colleen and Bill can do each day, given their talents and assuming they each wish to consume an equal amount of food and wood. Notice Colleen produces by splitting her time equally during the day, while Bill must devote two thirds of his time to wood production if he wishes to equalize his amount produced of the two goods. Panel (b) shows what happens when both parties specialize. Notice more units are produced of each good.

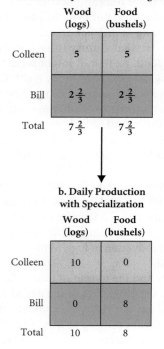

a. Daily production with no specialization, assuming Colleen and Bill each want to consume an equal number of logs and food

	Wood (logs)	Food (bushels)
Colleen	5	5
Bill	$2\frac{2}{3}$	$2\frac{2}{3}$
Total	$7\frac{2}{3}$	$7\frac{2}{3}$

b. Daily Production with Specialization

	Wood (logs)	Food (bushels)
Colleen	10	0
Bill	0	8
Total	10	8

in block b of Figure 2.2. At the end of the day, the two end up with 10 logs, all gathered by Colleen and 8 bushels of food, all produced by Bill. By joining forces and specializing, the two have increased their production of both goods. This increased production provides an incentive for Colleen and Bill to work together. United, each can receive a bonus over what he or she could produce separately. This bonus—here $2\frac{1}{3}$ extra logs and $\frac{1}{3}$ bushel of food—represent the gains from specialization.

The simple example of Bill and Colleen should begin to give you some insight into why most economists see value in free trade. Even if one country is absolutely better than another country at producing everything, our example has shown that there are gains to specializing and trading.

A Graphical Presentation of the Production Possibilities and Gains from Specialization

Graphs can also be used to illustrate the production possibilities open to Colleen and Bill and the gains they could achieve from specialization and trade.

Figure 2.3(a) shows all of the possible combinations of food and wood Colleen can produce given her skills and the conditions on the island, acting alone. Panel (b) does the same for Bill. If Colleen spends all of her time producing wood, the best she can do is 10 logs, which we show where the line crosses the vertical axis. Similarly, the line crosses the horizontal axis at 10 bushels of food, because that is what Colleen could produce spending full time producing food. We have also marked on the graph possibility C, where she divides her time equally, generating 5 bushels of food and 5 logs of wood.

Bill in panel (b) can get as many as 4 logs of wood or 8 bushels of food by devoting himself full time to either wood or food production. Again, we have marked on his graph a point F, where he produces $2\frac{2}{3}$ bushels of food and $2\frac{2}{3}$ logs of wood. Notice that Bill's production line is lower down than is Colleen's. The further to the right is the production line, the more productive is the individual; that is, the more he or she can produce of the two goods. Also notice that the slope of the two lines is not the same. Colleen trades off one bushel of food for one log of wood, while Bill gives up 2 bushels of food for one log of wood. These differing slopes show the differing opportunity costs faced by Colleen and Bill. They also open up the possibility of gains from specialization. Try working through an example in which the slopes are the same to convince yourself of the importance of differing slopes.

a. Colleen's production possibilities

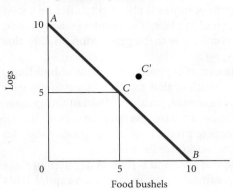

b. Bill's production possibilities

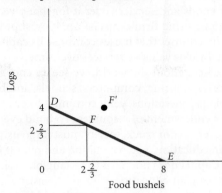

▲ **FIGURE 2.3 Production Possibilities with and without Trade**
This figure shows the combinations of food and wood that Colleen and Bill can each generate in one day of labor, working by themselves. Colleen can achieve independently any point along line ACB, while Bill can generate any combination of food and wood along line DFE. Specialization and trade would allow both Bill and Colleen to move to the right of their original lines, to points like C′ and F′. In other words, specialization and trade allow both people to be better off than they were acting alone.

What happens when the possibility of working together and specializing in either wood or food comes up? In Figure 2.2 we have already seen that specialization would allow the pair to go from production of $7\frac{2}{3}$ units of food and wood to 10 logs and 8 bushels of food. Colleen and Bill can split the $2\frac{1}{3}$ extra logs and the $\frac{1}{3}$ extra bushel of food to move to points like C′ and F′ in Figure 2.3, which were unachievable without cooperation. In this analysis we do not know how Bill and Colleen will divide the surplus food and wood they have created. But because there is a surplus means that both of them can do better than either would alone.

Weighing Present and Expected Future Costs and Benefits Very often we find ourselves weighing benefits available today against benefits available tomorrow. Here, too, the notion of opportunity cost is helpful.

While alone on the island, Bill had to choose between cultivating a field and just gathering wild nuts and berries. Gathering nuts and berries provides food now; gathering seeds and clearing a field for planting will yield food tomorrow if all goes well. Using today's time to farm may well be worth the effort if doing so will yield more food than Bill would otherwise have in the future. By planting, Bill is trading present value for future value.

The simplest example of trading present for future benefits is the act of saving. When you put income aside today for use in the future, you give up some things that you could have had today in exchange for something tomorrow. Because nothing is certain, some judgment about future events and expected values must be made. What will your income be in 10 years? How long are you likely to live?

We trade off present and future benefits in small ways all the time. If you decide to study instead of going to the dorm party, you are trading present fun for the expected future benefits of higher grades. If you decide to go outside on a very cold day and run 5 miles, you are trading discomfort in the present for being in better shape later.

Capital Goods and Consumer Goods A society trades present for expected future benefits when it devotes a portion of its resources to research and development or to investment in capital. As we said earlier in this chapter, *capital* in its broadest definition is anything that has already been produced that will be used to produce other valuable goods or services over time.

Building capital means trading present benefits for future ones. Bill and Colleen might trade gathering berries or lying in the sun for cutting logs to build a nicer house in the future. In a modern society, resources used to produce capital goods could have been used to produce **consumer goods**—that is, goods for present consumption. Heavy industrial machinery does not directly satisfy the wants of anyone, but producing it requires resources that could instead have gone into producing things that do satisfy wants directly—for example, food, clothing, toys, or golf clubs.

consumer goods Goods produced for present consumption.

Capital is everywhere. A road is capital. Once a road is built, we can drive on it or transport goods and services over it for many years to come. A house is also capital. Before a new manufacturing firm can start up, it must put some capital in place. The buildings, equipment, and inventories that it uses comprise its capital. As it contributes to the production process, this capital yields valuable services over time.

Throughout the world, we see an enormous amount of capital, in the form of buildings, factories, housing, computers, schools, and highways. Much of that capital was put in place by previous generations, yet it continues to provide valuable services today; it is part of this generation's endowment of resources. To build every building, every road, every factory, every house, and every car or truck, society must forgo using resources to produce consumer goods today. To get an education, you pay tuition and put off joining the workforce for a while.

Capital does not need to be tangible. When you spend time and resources developing skills or getting an education, you are investing in human capital—your own human capital. This capital will continue to exist and yield benefits to you for years to come. A computer program produced by a software company and available online may cost nothing to distribute, but its true intangible value comes from the ideas embodied in the program itself. It too is capital.

investment The process of using resources to produce new capital.

The process of using resources to produce new capital is called **investment**. (In everyday language, the term *investment* often refers to the act of buying a share of stock or a bond, as in "I invested in some Treasury bonds." In economics, however, investment *always* refers to the creation of capital: the purchase or putting in place of buildings, equipment, roads, houses, and the like.) A wise investment in capital is one that yields future benefits that are more valuable than the present cost. When you spend money for a house, for example, presumably you value its future benefits. That is, you expect to gain more in shelter services than you would from the things you could buy today with the same money. One also invests in intangible capital like education. Clearly education can yield decades of future "benefits" including higher wages while costing something today. Because resources are scarce, the opportunity cost of every investment in capital is forgone present consumption.

The Production Possibility Frontier

production possibility frontier (ppf) A graph that shows all the combinations of goods and services that can be produced if all of society's resources are used efficiently.

A simple graphic device called the **production possibility frontier (ppf)** illustrates the principles of constrained choice, opportunity cost, and scarcity. The ppf is a graph that shows all the combinations of goods and services that can be produced if all of a society's resources are used efficiently. Figure 2.4 shows a ppf for a hypothetical economy. We have already seen a simplified version of a ppf in looking at the choices of Colleen and Bill in Figure 2.3. Here we will look more generally at the ppf.

On the *Y*-axis, we measure the quantity of capital goods produced. On the *X*-axis, we measure the quantity of consumer goods. All points below and to the left of the curve (the shaded area) represent combinations of capital and consumer goods that are possible for the society given the resources available and existing technology. Points above and to the right of the curve, such as point *G*, represent combinations that cannot be reached. You will recall in our example of Colleen and Bill that new trade and specialization possibilities allowed them to expand their production possibilities and move to a point like *G*. If an economy were to end up at point *A* on the graph, it would be producing no consumer goods at all; all resources would be used for the production of capital. If an economy were to end up at point *B*, it would be devoting all its resources to the production of consumer goods and none of its resources to the formation of capital.

While all economies produce some of each kind of good, different economies emphasize different things. About 13 percent of gross output in the United States in 2012 was new capital. In Japan, capital has historically accounted for a much higher percent of gross output, while in the Congo, the figure is about 7 percent. Japan is closer to point *A* on its ppf, the Congo is closer to *B*, and the United States is somewhere in between.

Points that are actually on the ppf are points of both full resource employment and production efficiency. (Recall from Chapter 1 that an efficient economy is one that produces the things that people want at the least cost. *Production efficiency* is a state in which a given mix of outputs is produced at the least cost.) Resources are not going unused, and there is no waste. Points that

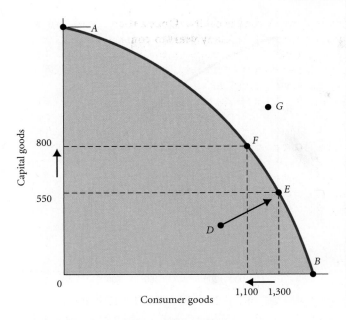

▲ **FIGURE 2.4 Production Possibility Frontier**
The ppf illustrates a number of economic concepts. One of the most important is *opportunity cost*. The opportunity cost of producing more capital goods is fewer consumer goods. Moving from *E* to *F*, the number of capital goods increases from 550 to 800, but the number of consumer goods decreases from 1,300 to 1,100.

lie within the shaded area but that are not on the frontier represent either unemployment of resources or production inefficiency. An economy producing at point *D* in Figure 2.4 can produce more capital goods and more consumer goods, for example, by moving to point *E*. This is possible because resources are not fully employed at point *D* or are not being used efficiently.

Negative Slope and Opportunity Cost   Just as we saw with Colleen and Bill, the slope of the ppf is negative. Because a society's choices are constrained by available resources and existing technology, when those resources are fully and efficiently employed, it can produce more capital goods only by reducing production of consumer goods. The opportunity cost of the additional capital is the forgone production of consumer goods.

The fact that scarcity exists is illustrated by the negative slope of the ppf. (If you need a review of slope, see the Appendix to Chapter 1.) In moving from point *E* to point *F* in Figure 2.4, capital production *increases* by 800 − 550 = 250 units (a positive change), but that increase in capital can be achieved only by shifting resources out of the production of consumer goods. Thus, in moving from point *E* to point *F* in Figure 2.4, consumer goods production *decreases* by 1,300 − 1,100 = 200 units (a negative change). The slope of the curve, the ratio of the change in capital goods to the change in consumer goods, is negative.

The value of the slope of a society's ppf is called the **marginal rate of transformation (MRT)**. In Figure 2.4, the MRT between points *E* and *F* is simply the ratio of the change in capital goods (a positive number) to the change in consumer goods (a negative number).

marginal rate of transformation (MRT)
The slope of the production possibility frontier (ppf).

The Law of Increasing Opportunity Cost   The negative slope of the ppf indicates the trade-off that a society faces between two goods. In the example of Colleen and Bill, we showed the ppf as a straight line. What does it mean that the ppf here is bowed out?

In our simple example, Bill gave up two bushels of food for every one log of wood he produced. Bill's per hour ability to harvest wood or produce food didn't depend on how many hours he spent on that activity. Similarly Colleen faced the same trade off of food for wood regardless of how much of either she was producing. In the language we have just introduced, the marginal rate of transformation was constant for Bill and Colleen; hence the straight line ppf. But that is not always true. Perhaps the first bushel of food is easy to produce, low-hanging fruit for example. Perhaps it is harder to get the second log than the first because the trees are farther away. The bowed out ppf tells us that the more society tries to increase production of one good

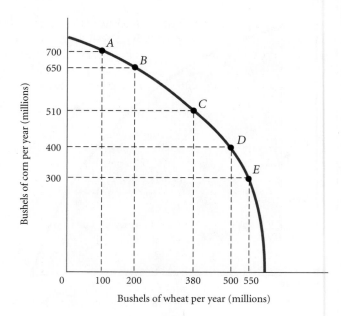

TABLE 2.1	Production Possibility Schedule for Total Corn and Wheat Production in Ohio and Kansas	
Point on ppf	Total Corn Production (Millions of Bushels per Year)	Total Wheat Production (Millions of Bushels per Year)
A	700	100
B	650	200
C	510	380
D	400	500
E	300	550

rather than another, the harder it is. In the example in Figure 2.4 the opportunity cost of using society's resources to make capital goods rather than consumer goods increases as we devote more and more resources to capital goods. Why might that be? A common explanation is that when society tries to produce only a small amount of a product, it can use resources—people, land and so on—most well-suited to those goods. As a society spends a larger portion of its resources on one good versus all others, getting more production of that good often becomes increasingly hard.

Let's look at the trade-off between corn and wheat production in Ohio and Kansas as an example. In a recent year, Ohio and Kansas together produced 510 million bushels of corn and 380 million bushels of wheat. Table 2.1 presents these two numbers, plus some hypothetical combinations of corn and wheat production that might exist for Ohio and Kansas together. Figure 2.5 graphs the data from Table 2.1.

Suppose that society's demand for corn dramatically increases. If this happens, farmers would probably shift some of their acreage from wheat production to corn production. Such a shift is represented by a move from point *C* (where corn = 510 and wheat = 380) up and to the left along the ppf toward points *A* and *B* in Figure 2.5. As this happens, it becomes more difficult to produce additional corn. The best land for corn production was presumably already in corn, and the best land for wheat production was already in wheat. As we try to produce more corn, the land is less well-suited to that crop. As we take more land out of wheat production, we are taking increasingly better wheat-producing land. In other words, the opportunity cost of more corn, measured in terms of wheat, increases.

Moving from point *E* to *D*, Table 2.1 shows that we can get 100 million bushels of corn (400 − 300) by sacrificing only 50 million bushels of wheat (550 – 500)—that is, we get 2 bushels of corn for every bushel of wheat. However, when we are already stretching the ability of the land to produce corn, it becomes harder to produce more and the opportunity cost increases.

Moving from point *B* to *A*, we can get only 50 million bushels of corn (700 – 650) by sacrificing 100 million bushels of wheat (200 – 100). For every bushel of wheat, we now get only half a bushel of corn. However, if the demand for *wheat* were to increase substantially and we were to move down and to the right along the ppf, it would become increasingly difficult to produce wheat and the opportunity cost of wheat, in terms of corn, would increase. This is the *law of increasing opportunity cost*.

Unemployment   During the Great Depression of the 1930s, the U.S. economy experienced prolonged unemployment. Millions of workers found themselves without jobs. In 1933, 25 percent of the civilian labor force was unemployed. This figure stayed above 14 percent until 1940. More recently, between the end of 2007 and 2010, the United States lost over 8 million payroll jobs and unemployment rose to over 15 million.

In addition to the hardship that falls on the unemployed, unemployment of labor means unemployment of capital. During economic downturns or recessions, industrial plants run at less than their total capacity. When there is unemployment of labor and capital, we are not producing all that we can.

Periods of unemployment correspond to points inside the ppf, points such as *D* in Figure 2.4. Moving onto the frontier from a point such as *D* means achieving full employment of resources.

Inefficiency   Although an economy may be operating with full employment of its land, labor, and capital resources, it may still be operating inside its ppf (at a point such as *D* in Figure 2.4). It could be using those resources *inefficiently*.

Waste and mismanagement are the results of a firm operating below its potential. If you are the owner of a bakery and you forget to order flour, your workers and ovens stand idle while you figure out what to do.

Sometimes inefficiency results from mismanagement of the economy instead of mismanagement of individual private firms. Suppose, for example, that the land and climate in Ohio are best-suited for corn production and that the land and climate in Kansas are best-suited for wheat production. If Congress passes a law forcing Ohio farmers to plant 50 percent of their acreage with wheat and Kansas farmers to plant 50 percent with corn, neither corn nor wheat production will be up to potential. The economy will be at a point such as *A* in Figure 2.6—inside the ppf. Allowing each state to specialize in producing the crop that it produces best increases the production of both crops and moves the economy to a point such as *B* in Figure 2.6.

The Efficient Mix of Output   To be efficient, an economy must produce what people want. This means that in addition to operating *on* the ppf, the economy must be operating at the *right point* on the ppf. This is referred to as *output efficiency*, in contrast to production efficiency.

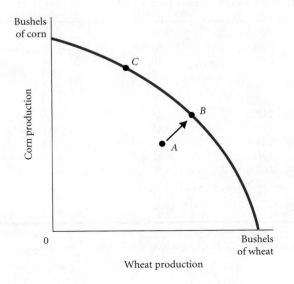

◀ **FIGURE 2.6**
Inefficiency from Misallocation of Land in Farming
Society can end up inside its ppf at a point such as *A* by using its resources inefficiently. If, for example, Ohio's climate and soil were best-suited for corn production and those of Kansas were best suited for wheat production, a law forcing Kansas farmers to produce corn and Ohio farmers to produce wheat would result in less of both. In such a case, society might be at point *A* instead of point *B*.

Suppose that an economy devotes 100 percent of its resources to beef production and that the beef industry runs efficiently using the most modern techniques. Also suppose that everyone in the society is a vegetarian. The result is a total waste of resources (assuming that the society cannot trade its beef for vegetables produced in another country).

Points *B* and *C* in Figure 2.6 are points of production efficiency and full employment. Whether *B* is more or less efficient than *C*, however, depends on the preferences of members of society and is not shown in the ppf graph.

It is important to remember that the ppf represents choices available within the constraints imposed by the current state of agricultural technology. In the long run, technology may improve, and when that happens, we have *growth*.

economic growth An increase in the total output of an economy. Growth occurs when a society acquires new resources or when it learns to produce more using existing resources.

Economic Growth   **Economic growth** is characterized by an increase in the total output of an economy. It occurs when a society acquires new resources or learns to produce more with existing resources. New resources may mean a larger labor force or an increased capital stock. The production and use of new machinery and equipment (capital) increase workers' productivity. (Give a man a shovel, and he can dig a bigger hole; give him a steam shovel, and wow!) Improved productivity also comes from technological change and *innovation*, the discovery and application of new, more efficient production techniques.

In the past few decades, the productivity of U.S. agriculture has increased dramatically. Based on data compiled by the Department of Agriculture, Table 2.2 shows that yield per acre in corn production has increased sixfold since the late 1930s, while the labor required to produce it has dropped significantly. Productivity in wheat production has also increased, at only a slightly less remarkable rate: Output per acre has more than tripled, while labor requirements are down nearly 90 percent. These increases are the result of more efficient farming techniques, more and better capital (tractors, combines, and other equipment), and advances in scientific knowledge and technological change (hybrid seeds, fertilizers, and so on). As you can see in Figure 2.7, changes such as these shift the ppf up and to the right.

Sources of Growth and the Dilemma of Poor Countries   Economic growth arises from many sources. The two most important over the years have been the accumulation of capital and technological advances. For poor countries, capital is essential; they must build the communication networks and transportation systems necessary to develop industries that function efficiently. They also need capital goods to develop their agricultural sectors.

Recall that capital goods are produced only at a sacrifice of consumer goods. The same can be said for technological advances. Technological advances come from research and

TABLE 2.2   Increasing Productivity in Corn and Wheat Production in the United States, 1935–2009

	Corn		Wheat	
	Yield per Acre (Bushels)	Labor Hours per 100 Bushels	Yield per Acre (Bushels)	Labor Hours per 100 Bushels
1935–1939	26.1	108	13.2	67
1945–1949	36.1	53	16.9	34
1955–1959	48.7	20	22.3	17
1965–1969	78.5	7	27.5	11
1975–1979	95.3	4	31.3	9
1981–1985	107.2	3	36.9	7
1985–1990	112.8	NA[a]	38.0	NA[a]
1990–1995	120.6	NA[a]	38.1	NA[a]
1998	134.4	NA[a]	43.2	NA[a]
2001	138.2	NA[a]	43.5	NA[a]
2006	145.6	NA[a]	42.3	NA[a]
2007	152.8	NA[a]	40.6	NA[a]
2008	153.9	NA[a]	44.9	NA[a]
2009	164.9	NA[a]	44.3	NA[a]

[a]Data not available.

Source: U.S. Department of Agriculture, Economic Research Service, Agricultural Statistics, Crop Summary.

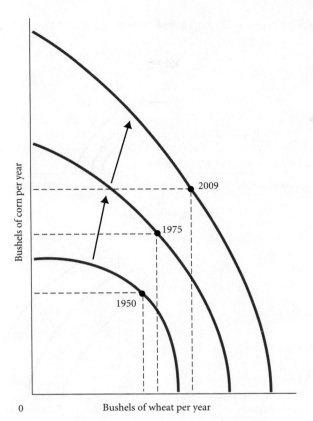

Bushels of corn per year

2009

1975

1950

0   Bushels of wheat per year

◀ FIGURE 2.7 **Economic Growth Shifts the PPF Up and to the Right**
Productivity increases have enhanced the ability of the United States to produce both corn and wheat. As Table 2.2 shows, productivity increases were more dramatic for corn than for wheat. Thus, the shifts in the ppf were not parallel.

Note: The ppf also shifts if the amount of land or labor in corn and wheat production changes. Although we emphasize productivity increases here, the actual shifts between years were due in part to land and labor changes.

development that use resources; thus, they too must be paid for. The resources used to produce capital goods—to build a road, a tractor, or a manufacturing plant—*and* to develop new technologies could have been used to produce consumer goods.

When a large part of a country's population is very poor, taking resources out of the production of consumer goods (such as food and clothing) is very difficult. In addition, in some countries, people wealthy enough to invest in domestic industries choose instead to invest abroad because of political turmoil at home. As a result, it often falls to the governments of poor countries to generate revenues for capital production and research out of tax collections.

All these factors have contributed to the growing gap between some poor and rich nations. Figure 2.8 shows the result using ppfs. On the bottom left, the rich country devotes a larger portion of its production to capital while the poor country on the top left produces mostly consumer goods. On the right, you see the results: The ppf of the rich country shifts up and out further and faster.

The importance of capital goods and technological developments to the position of workers in less developed countries is well illustrated by Robert Jensen's study of South India's industry. Conventional telephones require huge investments in wires and towers and, as a result, many less developed areas are without landlines. Mobile phones, on the other hand, require a less expensive investment; thus, in many areas, people upgraded from no phones directly to cell phones. Jensen found that in small fishing villages, the advent of cell phones allowed fishermen to determine on any given day where to take their catch to sell, resulting in a large decrease in fish wasted and an increase in fishing profits. The ability of newer communication technology to aid development is one of the exciting features of our times. (See Robert Jensen, "The Digital Provide: Information Technology, Market Performance, and Welfare in the South Indian Fisheries Sector," *Quarterly Journal of Economics*, 2007, 879–924.)

Although it exists only as an abstraction, the ppf illustrates a number of very important concepts that we will use throughout the rest of this book: scarcity, unemployment, inefficiency, opportunity cost, the law of increasing opportunity cost, economic growth, and the gains from trade.

▶ FIGURE 2.8 **Capital Goods and Growth in Poor and Rich Countries**
Rich countries find it easier than poor countries to devote resources to the production of capital, and the more resources that flow into capital production, the faster the rate of economic growth. Thus, the gap between poor and rich countries has grown over time.

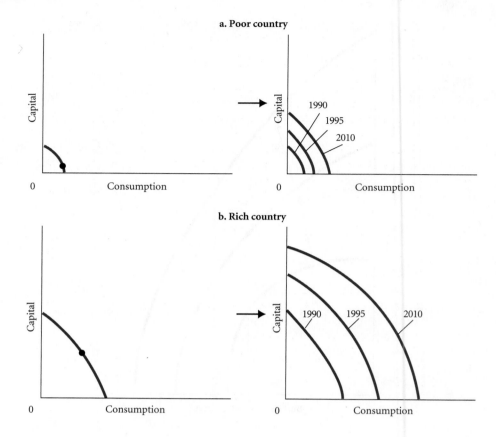

The Economic Problem

Recall the three basic questions facing all economic systems: (1) What gets produced? (2) How is it produced? and (3) Who gets it?

When Bill was alone on the island, the mechanism for answering those questions was simple: He thought about his own wants and preferences, looked at the constraints imposed by the resources of the island and his own skills and time, and made his decisions. As Bill set about his work, he allocated available resources quite simply, more or less by dividing up his available time. Distribution of the output was irrelevant. Because Bill was the society, he got it all.

Introducing even one more person into the economy—in this case, Colleen—changed all that. With Colleen on the island, resource allocation involves deciding not only how each person spends his or her time but also who does what; now there are two sets of wants and preferences. If Bill and Colleen go off on their own and form two separate self-sufficient economies, there will be lost potential. Two people can do more things together than each person can do alone. They may use their comparative advantages in different skills to specialize. Cooperation and coordination may give rise to gains that would otherwise not be possible.

When a society consists of millions of people, the problem of coordination and cooperation becomes enormous, but so does the potential for gain. In large, complex economies, specialization can go wild, with people working in jobs as different in their detail as an impressionist painting is from a blank page. The range of products available in a modern industrial society is beyond anything that could have been imagined a hundred years ago, and so is the range of jobs.

The amount of coordination and cooperation in a modern industrial society is almost impossible to imagine. Yet something seems to drive economic systems, if sometimes clumsily and inefficiently, toward producing the goods and services that people want. Given scarce resources, how do large, complex societies go about answering the three basic economic questions? This is the economic problem, which is what this text is about.

ECONOMICS IN PRACTICE

Trade-Offs among the Rich and Poor

In all societies, for all people, resources are limited relative to people's demands. There are, however, quite large differences in the kinds of trade-offs individuals face in rich versus poor countries.

In 1990, the World Bank defined the extremely poor people of the world as those earning less than $1 a day. Among development economists and policy makers, this figure continues to be used as a rough rule of thumb. In a recent survey, Abhijit Banerjee and Esther Duflo, two MIT economists, surveyed individuals living at this level in 13 countries across the world.[1] What did they learn about the consumption trade-offs faced by these individuals versus consumers in the United States?

It should not surprise you to learn that for the extremely poor, food is a much larger component of the budget. On average over the 13 countries, between 56 percent and 78 percent of consumption was spent on food. In the United States, just under 10 percent of the average budget goes to food. Even for the poorest consumers, however, biological need is not all determining. The Banerjee and Duflo study finds that in Udaipur, India, almost 10 percent of the typical food budget goes to sugar and processed foods rather than more nutritionally valuable grains. So even at these very low levels of income, some choice remains. Perhaps more interestingly, almost 10 percent of the budget of those surveyed goes to weddings, funerals, and other festivals. In societies with very few entertainment outlets, Banerjee and Duflo suggest we may see more demand for festivals, indicating

that even in extremely poor societies, household choice plays a role.

THINKING PRACTICALLY

1. Why might we see a greater demand for festivals in poor countries than in rich ones? How might this be affected by choices available?

[1] Abhijit Banerjee and Esther Duflo, "The Economic Lives of the Poor," *Journal of Economic Perspective*, Winter 2007, 141–167.

Economic Systems and the Role of Government

Thus far we have described the questions that the economic system must answer. Now we turn to the mechanics of the system. Here the basic debate concerns the role of government.

On the one hand, many favor leaving the economy alone and keeping the government at bay while others believe that there are many circumstances in which the government may be able to improve the functioning of the market.

Command Economies

During the long struggle between the United States and the Soviet Union, the choice between a market economy and one centrally controlled was an all or nothing proposition. The Soviet Union had a planned economy run by the government. In a pure **command economy**, the basic economic questions are answered by a central government. Through a combination of government ownership of state enterprises and central planning, the government, either directly or indirectly, sets output targets, incomes, and prices.

At present, for most countries in the world, the debate is not about whether we have government at all, it is about the extent and the character of government's role in the economy. Government involvement, in theory, may improve the efficiency and fairness of the allocation of

command economy An economy in which a central government either directly or indirectly sets output targets, incomes, and prices.

a nation's resources. At the same time, a poorly functioning government can destroy incentives, lead to corruption, and result in the waste of a society's resources.

Laissez-Faire Economies: The Free Market

laissez-faire economy
Literally from the French: "allow [them] to do." An economy in which individual people and firms pursue their own self-interest without any central direction or regulation.

market The institution through which buyers and sellers interact and engage in exchange.

At the opposite end of the spectrum from the command economy is the **laissez-faire economy**. The term *laissez-faire*, which translated literally from French means "allow [them] to do," implies a complete lack of government involvement in the economy. In this type of economy, individuals and firms pursue their own self-interest without any central direction or regulation; the sum total of millions of individual decisions ultimately determines all basic economic outcomes. The central institution through which a laissez-faire system answers the basic questions is the **market**, a term that is used in economics to mean an institution through which buyers and sellers interact and engage in exchange.

The interactions between buyers and sellers in any market range from simple to complex. Early explorers of the North American Midwest who wanted to exchange with Native Americans did so simply by bringing their goods to a central place and trading them. Today, the Internet dominates exchange. A jewelry maker in upstate Maine can exhibit wares through digital photographs on the Web. Buyers can enter orders or make bids and pay by credit card.

In short:

> Some markets are simple and others are complex, but they all involve buyers and sellers engaging in exchange. The behavior of buyers and sellers in a laissez-faire economy determines what gets produced, how it is produced, and who gets it.

The following chapters explore market systems in great depth. A quick preview is worthwhile here, however.

consumer sovereignty The idea that consumers ultimately dictate what will be produced (or not produced) by choosing what to purchase (and what not to purchase).

Consumer Sovereignty   In a free, unregulated market, goods and services are produced and sold only if the supplier can make a profit. In simple terms, making a *profit* means selling goods or services for more than it costs to produce them. You cannot make a profit unless someone wants the product that you are selling. This logic leads to the notion of **consumer sovereignty**: The mix of output found in any free market system is dictated ultimately by the tastes and preferences of consumers who "vote" by buying or not buying. Businesses rise and fall in response to consumer demands. No central directive or plan is necessary.

free enterprise The freedom of individuals to start and operate private businesses in search of profits.

Individual Production Decisions: Free Enterprise   Under a free market system, individual producers must also determine how to organize and coordinate the actual production of their products or services. The owner of a small shoe repair shop must alone buy the needed equipment and tools, hang signs, and set prices. In a big corporation, so many people are involved in planning the production process that in many ways, corporate planning resembles the planning in a command economy. In a free market economy, producers may be small or large. One person who hand-paints eggshells may start to sell them as a business; a person good with computers may start a business designing Web sites. On a larger scale, a group of furniture designers may put together a large portfolio of sketches, raise several million dollars, and start a bigger business. At the extreme are huge corporations such as Microsoft, Mitsubishi, Apple, and Intel, each of which sells tens of billions of dollars' worth of products every year. Whether the firms are large or small, however, production decisions in a market economy are made by separate private organizations acting in what they perceive to be their own interests.

Often the market system is called a free enterprise system. **Free enterprise** means the freedom of individuals to start private businesses in search of profits. Because new businesses require capital investment before they can begin operation, starting a new business involves risk. A well-run business that produces a product for which demand exists is likely to succeed; a poorly run business or one that produces a product for which little demand exists now or in the future is likely to fail. It is through free enterprise that new products and new production techniques find their way into use.

Proponents of free market systems argue that free enterprise leads to more efficient production and better response to diverse and changing consumer preferences. If a producer produces inefficiently, competitors will come along, fight for the business, and eventually take it away. Thus, in a free market economy, competition forces producers to use efficient techniques of production. It is competition, then, that ultimately dictates how output is produced.

Distribution of Output   In a free market system, the distribution of output—who gets what—is also determined in a decentralized way. The amount that any one household gets depends on its income and wealth. *Income* is the amount that a household earns each year. It comes in a number of forms: wages, salaries, interest, and the like. *Wealth* is the amount that households have accumulated out of past income through saving or inheritance.

To the extent that income comes from working for a wage, it is at least in part determined by individual choice. You will work for the wages available in the market only if these wages (and the products and services they can buy) are sufficient to compensate you for what you give up by working. Your leisure certainly has a value also. You may discover that you can increase your income by getting more education or training. You *cannot* increase your income, however, if you acquire a skill that no one wants.

Price Theory   The basic coordinating mechanism in a free market system is price. A price is the amount that a product sells for per unit, and it reflects what society is willing to pay. Prices of inputs—labor, land, and capital—determine how much it costs to produce a product. Prices of various kinds of labor, or *wage rates*, determine the rewards for working in different jobs and professions. Many of the independent decisions made in a market economy involve the weighing of prices and costs, so it is not surprising that much of economic theory focuses on the factors that influence and determine prices. This is why microeconomic theory is often simply called *price theory*.

In sum:

In a free market system, the basic economic questions are answered without the help of a central government plan or directives. This is what the "free" in free market means— the system is left to operate on its own with no outside interference. Individuals pursuing their own self-interest will go into business and produce the products and services that people want. Other individuals will decide whether to acquire skills; whether to work; and whether to buy, sell, invest, or save the income that they earn. The basic coordinating mechanism is price.

Mixed Systems, Markets, and Governments

The differences between command economies and laissez-faire economies in their pure forms are enormous. In fact, these pure forms do not exist in the world; all real systems are in some sense "mixed." That is, individual enterprise exists and independent choice is exercised even in economies in which the government plays a major role.

Conversely, no market economies exist without government involvement and government regulation. The United States has basically a free market economy, but government purchases accounted for just over 20 percent of the country's total production in 2010. Governments in the United States (local, state, and federal) directly employ about 14 percent of all workers (15 percent including active duty military). They also redistribute income by means of taxation and social welfare expenditures, and they regulate many economic activities.

One of the major themes in this book, and indeed in economics, is the tension between the advantages of free, unregulated markets and the desire for government involvement. Advocates of free markets argue that such markets work best when left to themselves. They produce only what people want; without buyers, sellers go out of business. Competition forces firms to adopt efficient production techniques. Wage differentials lead people to acquire needed skills. Competition also leads to innovation in both production techniques and products. The result is quality and variety, but market systems have problems too.

Even staunch defenders of the free enterprise system recognize that market systems are not perfect. First, they do not always produce what people want at the lowest cost—there are inefficiencies. Second, rewards (income) may be unfairly distributed and some groups may be left out. Third, periods of unemployment and inflation recur with some regularity.

Many people point to these problems as reasons for government involvement. Indeed, for some problems, government involvement may be the only solution. However, government decisions are made by people who presumably, like the rest of us, act in their own self-interest. While governments may be called on to improve the functioning of the economy, there is no guarantee that they will do so. Just as markets may fail to produce an allocation of resources that is perfectly efficient and fair, governments may fail to improve matters. We return to this debate many times throughout this text.

Looking Ahead

This chapter described the economic problem in broad terms. We outlined the questions that all economic systems must answer. We also discussed very broadly the two kinds of economic systems. In the next chapter, we analyze the way market systems work.

--- S U M M A R Y ---

1. Every society has some system or process for transforming into useful form what nature and previous generations have provided. Economics is the study of that process and its outcomes.

2. *Producers* are those who take resources and transform them into usable products, or *outputs*. Private firms, households, and governments all produce something.

SCARCITY, CHOICE, AND OPPORTUNITY COST *p. 26*

3. All societies must answer *three basic questions*: What gets produced? How is it produced? Who gets what is produced? These three questions make up the *economic problem*.

4. One person alone on an island must make the same basic decisions that complex societies make. When a society consists of more than one person, questions of distribution, cooperation, and specialization arise.

5. Because resources are scarce relative to human wants in all societies, using resources to produce one good or service implies *not* using them to produce something else. This concept of *opportunity cost* is central to understanding economics.

6. Using resources to produce *capital* that will in turn produce benefits in the future implies *not* using those resources to produce consumer goods in the present.

7. Even if one individual or nation is absolutely more efficient at producing goods than another, all parties will gain if

they specialize in producing goods in which they have a *comparative advantage*.

8. A *production possibility frontier* (ppf) is a graph that shows all the combinations of goods and services that can be produced if all of society's resources are used efficiently. The ppf illustrates a number of important economic concepts: scarcity, unemployment, inefficiency, increasing opportunity cost, and economic growth.

9. *Economic growth* occurs when society produces more, either by acquiring more resources or by learning to produce more with existing resources. Improved productivity may come from additional capital or from the discovery and application of new, more efficient techniques of production.

ECONOMIC SYSTEMS AND THE ROLE OF GOVERNMENT *p. 39*

10. In some modern societies, government plays a big role in answering the three basic questions. In pure *command economies*, a central authority directly or indirectly sets output targets, incomes, and prices.

11. A *laissez-faire economy* is one in which individuals independently pursue their own self-interest, without any central direction or regulation, and ultimately determine all basic economic outcomes.

12. A *market* is an institution through which buyers and sellers interact and engage in exchange. Some markets involve

simple face-to-face exchange; others involve a complex series of transactions, often over great distances or through electronic means.

13. There are no purely planned economies and no pure laissez-faire economies; all economies are mixed. Individual enterprise, independent choice, and relatively free markets exist in centrally planned economies; there is significant government involvement in market economies such as that of the United States.

14. One of the great debates in economics revolves around the tension between the advantages of free, unregulated markets and the desire for government involvement in the economy. Free markets produce what people want, and competition forces firms to adopt efficient production techniques. The need for government intervention arises because free markets are characterized by inefficiencies and an unequal distribution of income and experience regular periods of inflation and unemployment.

REVIEW TERMS AND CONCEPTS

absolute advantage, *p. 29*

capital, *p. 26*

command economy, *p. 39*

comparative advantage, *p. 29*

consumer goods, *p. 31*

consumer sovereignty, *p. 40*

economic growth, *p. 36*

factors of production (*or* factors), *p. 26*

free enterprise, *p. 40*

inputs *or* resources, *p. 26*

investment, *p. 32*

laissez-faire economy, *p. 40*

marginal rate of transformation (MRT), *p. 33*

market, *p. 40*

opportunity cost, *p. 27*

outputs, *p. 26*

production, *p. 26*

production possibility frontier (ppf), *p. 32*

theory of comparative advantage, *p. 28*

PROBLEMS

All problems are available on MyEconLab.

1. For each of the following, describe some of the potential opportunity costs:
   a. Studying for your economics test
   b. Spending 2 hours playing computer games
   c. Buying a new car instead of keeping the old one
   d. A local community voting to raise property taxes to increase school expenditures and to reduce class size
   e. A number of countries working together to build a space station
   f. Going to graduate school

2. "As long as all resources are fully employed and every firm in the economy is producing its output using the best available technology, the result will be efficient." Do you agree or disagree with this statement? Explain your answer.

3. You are an intern to the editor of a small-town newspaper in Mallsburg, Pennsylvania. Your boss, the editor, asks you to write the first draft of an editorial for this week's paper. Your assignment is to describe the costs and the benefits of building a new bridge across the railroad tracks in the center of town. Currently, most people who live in this town must drive 2 miles through thickly congested traffic to the existing bridge to get to the main shopping and employment center. The bridge will cost the citizens of Mallsburg $25 million, which will be paid for with a tax on their incomes over the next 20 years. What are the opportunity costs of building this bridge? What are the benefits that citizens will likely receive if the bridge is built? What other factors might you consider in writing this editorial?

4. Kristen and Anna live in the beach town of Santa Monica. They own a small business in which they make wristbands and pot holders and sell them to people on the beach. As shown in the table, Kristen can make 15 wristbands per hour but only 3 pot holders. Anna is a bit slower and can make only 12 wristbands or 2 pot holders in an hour.

	OUTPUT PER HOUR	
	WRISTBANDS	POT HOLDERS
Kristen	15	3
Anna	12	2

   a. For Kristen and for Anna, what is the opportunity cost of a pot holder? Who has a comparative advantage in the production of pot holders? Explain your answer.
   b. Who has a comparative advantage in the production of wristbands? Explain your answer.
   c. Assume that Kristen works 20 hours per week in the business. Assuming Kristen is in business on her own, graph the possible combinations of pot holders and wristbands that she could produce in a week. Do the same for Anna.
   d. If Kristen devoted half of her time (10 out of 20 hours) to wristbands and half of her time to pot holders, how many of each would she produce in a week? If Anna did the same, how many of each would she produce? How many wristbands and pot holders would be produced in total?
   e. Suppose that Anna spent all 20 hours of her time on wristbands and Kristen spent 17 hours on pot holders and 3 hours on wristbands. How many of each item would be produced?
   f. Suppose that Kristen and Anna can sell all their wristbands for $1 each and all their pot holders for $5.50 each. If each of them worked 20 hours per week, how should they split their time between wristbands and pot holders? What is their maximum joint revenue?

5. Briefly describe the trade-offs involved in each of the following decisions. Specifically, list some of the opportunity costs associated with each decision, paying particular attention to the trade-offs between present and future consumption.

MyEconLab Visit **www.myeconlab.com** to complete these exercises online and get instant feedback. Exercises that update with real-time data are marked with 🌐.

a. After a stressful senior year in high school, Sherice decides to take the summer off instead of working before going to college.

b. Frank is overweight and decides to work out every day and to go on a diet.

c. Mei is diligent about taking her car in for routine maintenance even though it takes 2 hours of her time and costs $100 four times each year.

d. Jim is in a hurry. He runs a red light on the way to work.

*6. The countries of Figistan and Blah are small island countries in the South Pacific. Both produce fruit and timber. Each island has a labor force of 1,200. The following table gives production per month for each worker in each country. Assume productivity is constant and identical for each worker in each country.

	BASKETS OF FRUIT	BOARD FEET OF TIMBER
Figistan workers	10	5
Blah workers	30	10

Productivity of one worker for one month

a. Which country has an absolute advantage in the production of fruit? Which country has an absolute advantage in the production of timber?

b. Which country has a comparative advantage in the production of fruit? of timber?

c. Sketch the ppf's for both countries.

d. Assuming no trading between the two, if both countries wanted to have equal numbers of feet of timber and baskets of fruit, how would they allocate workers to the two sectors?

e. Show that specialization and trade can move both countries beyond their ppf's.

7. Suppose that a simple society has an economy with only one resource, labor. Labor can be used to produce only two commodities—X, a necessity good (food), and Y, a luxury good (music and merriment). Suppose that the labor force consists of 100 workers. One laborer can produce either 5 units of necessity per month (by hunting and gathering) or 10 units of luxury per month (by writing songs, playing the guitar, dancing, and so on).

a. On a graph, draw the economy's ppf. Where does the ppf intersect the Y-axis? Where does it intersect the X-axis? What meaning do those points have?

b. Suppose the economy produced at a point *inside* the ppf. Give at least two reasons why this could occur. What could be done to move the economy to a point *on* the ppf?

c. Suppose you succeeded in lifting your economy to a point on its ppf. What point would you choose? How might your small society decide the point at which it wanted to be?

d. Once you have chosen a point on the ppf, you still need to decide how your society's production will be divided. If you were a dictator, how would you decide? What would happen if you left product distribution to the free market?

*8. Match each diagram in Figure 1 with its description here. Assume that the economy is producing or attempting to produce at point *A* and that most members of society like meat and not fish. Some descriptions apply to more than one diagram, and some diagrams have more than one description.

a. Inefficient production of meat and fish
b. Productive efficiency
c. An inefficient mix of output
d. Technological advances in the production of meat and fish
e. The law of increasing opportunity cost
f. An impossible combination of meat and fish

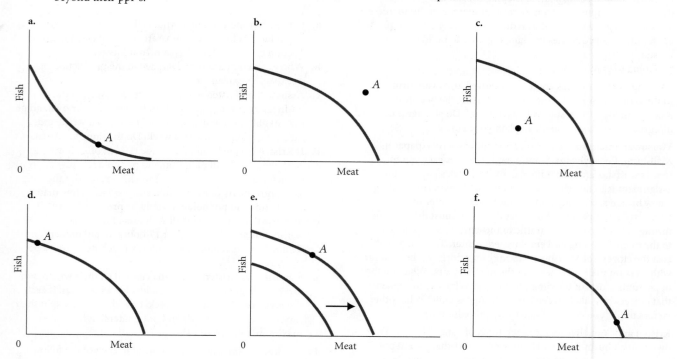

▲ **FIGURE 1**

*Note: Problems marked with an asterisk are more challenging.

9. A nation with fixed quantities of resources is able to produce any of the following combinations of bread and ovens:

LOAVES OF BREAD (MILLIONS)	OVENS (THOUSANDS)
75	0
60	12
45	22
30	30
15	36
0	40

These figures assume that a certain number of previously produced ovens are available in the current period for baking bread.

   a. Using the data in the table, graph the ppf (with ovens on the vertical axis).
   b. Does the principle of "increasing opportunity cost" hold in this nation? Explain briefly. (*Hint:* What happens to the opportunity cost of bread—measured in number of ovens—as bread production increases?)
   c. If this country chooses to produce both ovens and bread, what will happen to the ppf over time? Why?

Now suppose that a new technology is discovered that allows twice as many loaves of bread to be baked in each existing oven.

   d. Illustrate (on your original graph) the effect of this new technology on the ppf.
   e. Suppose that before the new technology is introduced, the nation produces 22 ovens. After the new technology is introduced, the nation produces 30 ovens. What is the effect of the new technology on the production of bread? (Give the number of loaves before and after the change.)

10. [Related to the *Economics in Practice* on *p. 28*] An analysis of a large-scale survey of consumer food purchases by Mark Aguiar and Erik Hurst indicates that retired people spend less for the same market basket of food than working people do. Use the concept of opportunity cost to explain this fact.

*11. Dr. Falk is a dentist who performs two basic procedures: filling cavities and whitening teeth. Falk charges $50 per cavity filled, a process that takes him 15 minutes per tooth and requires no help or materials. For tooth whitening, a process requiring 30 minutes, Falk charges $150 net of materials. Again, no help is required. Is anything puzzling about Falk's pricing pattern? Explain your answer.

12. Following the Baltimore Raven's victory in the 2013 Super Bowl, the Maryland Lottery increased the number of available prizes in the Ravens Cash Fantasy scratch-off ticket second chance drawings. Prizes in this contest included cash, gameday packages, trips with the team, and Ravens' season tickets. Suppose you entered this second chance drawing and won free season tickets for the Ravens' 2013 season. Would there be a cost to you to attend the Ravens' games during the 2013 season?

13. [Related to the *Economics in Practice* on *p. 39*] High school football is arguably more popular in West Texas than in any other region of the country. During football season, small towns seem to shut down on Friday nights as local high school teams take to the field, and for the following week the results of the games are the talk of each town. Taking into consideration that many of these towns are one hundred or more miles away from any medium-sized or large cities, what might be an economic explanation for the extreme popularity of high school football in these small West Texas towns?

14. Describe a command economy and a laissez-faire economy. Do any economic systems in the world reflect the purest forms of command or laissez-faire economies? Explain.

15. The nation of Rougarou is able to produce turnips and potatoes in combinations represented by the data in the following table. Each number represents thousands of bushels.
    Plot this data on a production possibilities graph and explain why the data shows that Rougarou experiences increasing opportunity costs.

	A	B	C	D	E
Turnips	100	90	70	40	0
Potatoes	0	10	20	30	40

16. Explain how each of the following situations would affect a nation's production possibilities curve.
   a. A technological innovation allows the nation to more efficiently convert solar energy into electricity.
   b. A prolonged recession increases the number of unemployed workers in the nation.
   c. A category 5 hurricane destroys over 40 percent of the nation's productive capacity.
   d. The quality of education in the nation's colleges and universities improves greatly.
   e. The nation passes a law requiring all employers to give their employees 16 weeks of paid vacation each year. Prior to this law, employers were not legally required to give employees any paid vacation time.

Demand, Supply, and Market Equilibrium

3

Chapters 1 and 2 introduced the discipline, methodology, and subject matter of economics. We now begin the task of analyzing how a market economy actually works. This chapter and the next present an overview of the way individual markets work. They introduce some of the concepts needed to understand both microeconomics and macroeconomics.

As we proceed to define terms and make assumptions, it is important to keep in mind what we are doing. In Chapter 1

we explained what economic theory attempts to do. Theories are abstract representations of reality, like a map that represents a city. We believe that the models presented here will help you understand the workings of the economy. Just as a map presents one view of the world, so too does any given theory of the economy. Alternatives exist to the theory that we present. We believe, however, that the basic model presented here, while sometimes abstract, is useful in gaining an understanding of how the economy works.

In the simple island society discussed in Chapter 2, Bill and Colleen solved the economic problem directly. They allocated their time and used the island's resources to satisfy their wants. Bill might be a farmer, Colleen a hunter and carpenter. Exchange occurred, but complex markets were not necessary.

In societies of many people, however, production must satisfy wide-ranging tastes and preferences. Producers therefore specialize. Farmers produce more food than they can eat so they can sell it to buy manufactured goods. Physicians are paid for specialized services, as are attorneys, construction workers, and editors. When there is specialization, there must be exchange, and *markets* are the institutions through which exchange takes place.

This chapter begins to explore the basic forces at work in market systems. The purpose of our discussion is to explain how the individual decisions of households and firms together, without any central planning or direction, answer the three basic questions: What gets produced? How is it produced? Who gets what is produced? We begin with some definitions.

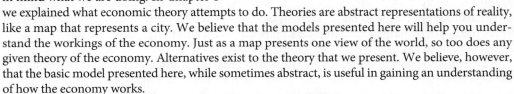

LEARNING OBJECTIVES

Describe the economic functions and roles of firms and households

Explain the circular flow of economic activity

Discuss factors that affect demand and the demand curve

Discuss the variables that influence supply

Explain the principles of market equilibrium

Firms and Households: The Basic Decision-Making Units

Throughout this book, we discuss and analyze the behavior of two fundamental decision-making units: *firms*—the primary producing units in an economy—and *households*—the consuming units in an economy. Both are made up of people performing different functions and playing different roles. Economics is concerned with how those people behave, and the interaction among them.

firm An organization that transforms resources (inputs) into products (outputs). Firms are the primary producing units in a market economy.

A **firm** exists when a person or a group of people decides to produce a product or products by transforming *inputs*—that is, resources in the broadest sense—into *outputs*, the products that are sold in the market. Some firms produce goods; others produce services. Some are large, many are small, and some are in between. All firms exist to transform resources into goods and services that people want. The Colorado Symphony Orchestra takes labor, land, a building, musically talented people, instruments, and other inputs and combines them to produce concerts. The production process can be extremely complicated. For example, the first flautist in the orchestra combines training, talent, previous performance experience, score, instrument, conductor's interpretation, and personal feelings about the music to produce just one contribution to an overall performance.

Most firms exist to make a profit for their owners, but some do not. Columbia University, for example, fits the description of a firm: It takes inputs in the form of labor, land, skills, books, and buildings and produces a service that we call *education*. Although the university sells that service for a price, it does not exist to make a profit; instead, it exists to provide education and research of the highest quality possible.

Still, most firms exist to make a profit. They engage in production because they can sell their product for more than it costs to produce it. The analysis of a firm's behavior that follows rests on the assumption that *firms make decisions in order to maximize profits*. Sometimes firms suffer losses instead of earning profits. In recent years this has occurred frequently. When firms suffer losses, we will assume that they act to minimize those losses.

entrepreneur A person who organizes, manages, and assumes the risks of a firm, taking a new idea or a new product and turning it into a successful business.

An **entrepreneur** is someone who organizes, manages, and assumes the risks of a firm. When a new firm is created, someone must organize the new firm, arrange financing, hire employees, and take risks. That person is an entrepreneur. Sometimes existing firms introduce new products, and sometimes new firms develop or improve on an old idea, but at the root of it all is entrepreneurship, which some see as the core of the free enterprise system.

households The consuming units in an economy.

The consuming units in an economy are **households**. A household may consist of any number of people: a single person living alone, a married couple with four children, or 15 unrelated people sharing a house. Household decisions are presumably based on individual tastes and preferences. The household buys what it wants and can afford. In a large, heterogeneous, and open society such as the United States, wildly different tastes find expression in the marketplace. A six-block walk in any direction on any street in Manhattan or a drive from the Chicago Loop south into rural Illinois should be enough to convince anyone that it is difficult to generalize about what people do and do not like.

Even though households have wide-ranging preferences, they also have some things in common. All—even the very rich—have ultimately limited incomes, and all must pay in some way for the goods and services they consume. Although households may have some control over their incomes—they can work more hours or fewer hours—they are also constrained by the availability of jobs, current wages, their own abilities, and their accumulated and inherited wealth (or lack thereof).

Input Markets and Output Markets: The Circular Flow

product *or* output markets The markets in which goods and services are exchanged.

Households and firms interact in two basic kinds of markets: product (or output) markets and input (or factor) markets. Goods and services that are intended for use by households are exchanged in **product *or* output markets**. In output markets, firms *supply* and households *demand*.

input *or* factor markets The markets in which the resources used to produce goods and services are exchanged.

To produce goods and services, firms must buy resources in **input *or* factor markets**. Firms buy inputs from households, which supply these inputs. When a firm decides how much to produce (supply) in output markets, it must simultaneously decide how much of each input it needs to produce the desired level of output. To produce automobiles, Ford

Motor Company must use many inputs, including tires, steel, complicated machinery, and many different kinds of labor.

Figure 3.1 shows the *circular flow* of economic activity through a simple market economy. Note that the flow reflects the direction in which goods and services flow through input and output markets. For example, real goods and services flow from firms to households through output—or product—markets. Labor services flow from households to firms through input markets. Payment (most often in money form) for goods and services flows in the opposite direction.

In input markets, households *supply* resources. Most households earn their incomes by working—they supply their labor in the **labor market** to firms that demand labor and pay workers for their time and skills. Households may also loan their accumulated or inherited savings to firms for interest or exchange those savings for claims to future profits, as when a household buys shares of stock in a corporation. In the **capital market**, households supply the funds that firms use to buy capital goods. Households may also supply land or other real property in exchange for rent in the **land market**.

Inputs into the production process are also called **factors of production**. Land, labor, and capital are the three key factors of production. Throughout this text, we use the terms *input* and *factor of production* interchangeably. Thus, input markets and factor markets mean the same thing.

Early economics texts included entrepreneurship as a type of input, just like land, labor, and capital. Treating entrepreneurship as a separate factor of production has fallen out of favor, however, partially because it is unmeasurable. Most economists today implicitly assume

labor market The input/factor market in which households supply work for wages to firms that demand labor.

capital market The input/factor market in which households supply their savings, for interest or for claims to future profits, to firms that demand funds to buy capital goods.

land market The input/factor market in which households supply land or other real property in exchange for rent.

factors of production The inputs into the production process. Land, labor, and capital are the three key factors of production.

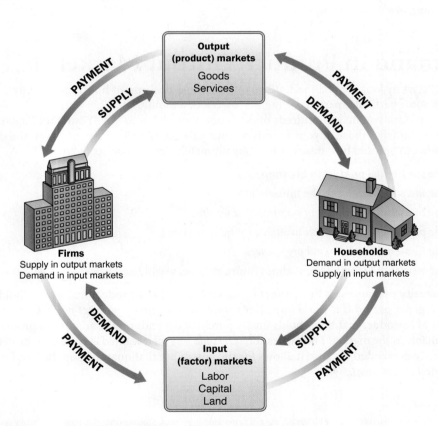

▲ **FIGURE 3.1 The Circular Flow of Economic Activity**
Diagrams like this one show the circular flow of economic activity, hence the name *circular flow diagram*. Here goods and services flow clockwise: Labor services supplied by households flow to firms, and goods and services produced by firms flow to households. Payment (usually money) flows in the opposite (counter-clockwise) direction: Payment for goods and services flows from households to firms, and payment for labor services flows from firms to households.

Note: Color Guide–In Figure 3.1 households are depicted in *blue* and firms are depicted in *red*. From now on all diagrams relating to the behavior of households will be blue or shades of blue and all diagrams relating to the behavior of firms will be red or shades of red. The green color indicates a monetary flow.

that entrepreneurship is in plentiful supply. That is, if profit opportunities exist, it is likely that entrepreneurs will crop up to take advantage of them. This assumption has turned out to be a good predictor of actual economic behavior and performance.

The supply of inputs and their prices ultimately determine household income. Thus, the amount of income a household earns depends on the decisions it makes concerning what types of inputs it chooses to supply. Whether to stay in school, how much and what kind of training to get, whether to start a business, how many hours to work, whether to work at all, and how to invest savings are all household decisions that affect income.

As you can see:

> Input and output markets are connected through the behavior of both firms and households. Firms determine the quantities and character of outputs produced and the types and quantities of inputs demanded. Households determine the types and quantities of products demanded and the quantities and types of inputs supplied.[1]

In 2013 a 12-pack of 12 oz. soda costs about $5, and many of you likely have one somewhere in your dormitory room. What determines the price of that soda? How can I explain how much soda you will buy in a given month or year? By the end of this chapter you will see the way in which prices in the market are determined by the interaction of buyers like you and suppliers like soda manufacturers. The model of supply and demand covered in this chapter is the most powerful tool of economics. By the time you finish this chapter we hope you will look at shopping in a different way.

Demand in Product/Output Markets

We will start by looking at an individual or household decision of how much to buy of something in some particular period of time, say a week or a month.

Every week you make hundreds of decisions about what to buy. Your choices likely look a lot different from those of your friends or your parents. For all of you, however, the decision about what to buy and how much of it to buy ultimately depends on six factors:

- The *price of the product* in question.
- The *income available* to the household.
- The household's *amount of accumulated wealth*.
- The *prices of other products* available to the household.
- The household's *tastes and preferences*.
- The household's *expectations* about future income, wealth, and prices.

quantity demanded The amount (number of units) of a product that a household would buy in a given period if it could buy all it wanted at the current market price.

Quantity demanded is the amount (number of units) of a product that a household would buy in a given period *if it could buy all it wanted at the current market price*. Of course, the amount of a product that households finally purchase depends on the amount of product actually available in the market. The expression *if it could buy all it wanted* is critical to the definition of quantity demanded because it allows for the possibility that quantity supplied and quantity demanded are unequal.

---

[1] Our description of markets begins with the behavior of firms and households. Modern orthodox economic theory essentially combines two distinct but closely related theories of behavior. The "theory of household behavior," or "consumer behavior," has its roots in the works of nineteenth-century utilitarians such as Jeremy Bentham, William Jevons, Carl Menger, Leon Walras, Vilfredo Parcto, and F. Y. Edgeworth. The "theory of the firm" developed out of the earlier classical political economy of Adam Smith, David Ricardo, and Thomas Malthus. In 1890, Alfred Marshall published the first of many editions of his *Principles of Economics*. That volume pulled together the main themes of both the classical economists and the utilitarians into what is now called *neoclassical economics*. While there have been many changes over the years, the basic structure of the model that we build can be found in Marshall's work.

Changes in Quantity Demanded versus Changes in Demand

In our list of what determines how much you buy of a product the price of that product comes first. This is no accident. The most important relationship in individual markets is between market price and quantity demanded. So that is where we will start our work. In fact, we begin by looking at what happens to the quantity a typical individual demands of a product when all that changes is its price. Economists refer to this device as *ceteris paribus*, or "all else equal." We will be looking at the relationship between quantity demanded of a good by an individual or household when its price changes, holding income, wealth, other prices, tastes, and expectations constant. If the price of that 12-pack of soda were cut in half, how many more cases would you buy in a given week?

In thinking about this question it is very important to focus on the price change alone and to maintain the all else equal assumption. If next week you suddenly found yourself with more money than you expected (perhaps a windfall from an aunt), you might well find yourself buying an extra 12-pack of soda even if the price did not change at all. To be sure that we distinguish clearly between changes in price and other changes that affect demand, throughout the rest of the text we will be very precise about terminology. Specifically:

> Changes in the price of a product affect the *quantity demanded* per period. Changes in any other factor, such as income or preferences, affect *demand*. Thus, we say that an increase in the price of Coca-Cola is likely to cause a decrease in the *quantity of Coca-Cola demanded*. However, we say that an increase in income is likely to cause an increase in the *demand* for most goods.

Price and Quantity Demanded: The Law of Demand

A **demand schedule** shows how much of a product a person or household is willing to purchase per time period (each week or each month) at different prices. Clearly that decision is based on numerous interacting factors. Consider Alex who just graduated from college with an entry-level job at a local bank. During her senior year, Alex got a car loan and bought a used Mini Cooper. The Mini gets 25 miles per gallon of gasoline. Alex lives with several friends in a house 10 miles from her workplace and enjoys visiting her parents 50 miles away.

How often Alex will decide to drive herself to work and parties, visit her family, or even go joy riding depends on many things, including her income and whether she likes to drive. But the price of gasoline also plays an important role, and it is this relationship between price and quantity demanded that we focus on in the law of demand. With a gasoline price of $3.00 a gallon, Alex might decide to drive herself to work every day, visit her parents once a week, and drive another 50 miles a week for other activities. This driving pattern would add up to 250 miles a week, which would use 10 gallons of gasoline in her Mini. The demand schedule in Table 3.1 thus shows that at a price of $3.00 per gallon, Alex is willing to buy 10 gallons of gasoline. We can see that this demand schedule reflects a lot of information about Alex including where she lives and works and what she likes to do in her spare time.

Now suppose an international crisis in the Middle East causes the price of gasoline at the pump to rise to $5.00 per gallon. How does this affect Alex's demand for gasoline, assuming that everything else remains the same? Driving is now more expensive, and we would not be surprised if Alex decided to take the bus some mornings or share a ride with friends. She might visit her parents less frequently as well. On the demand schedule given in Table 3.1, Alex cuts her desired consumption of gasoline by half to 5 gallons when the price goes to $5.00. If, instead, the price of gasoline fell substantially, Alex might spend more time driving, and that is in fact the pattern we see in the table. This same information presented graphically is called a **demand curve**. Alex's demand curve is presented in Figure 3.2. You will note in Figure 3.2 that *quantity* (*q*) is measured along the horizontal axis and *price* (*P*) is measured along the vertical axis. This is the convention we follow throughout this book.

demand schedule Shows how much of a given product a household would be willing to buy at different prices for a given time period.

demand curve A graph illustrating how much of a given product a household would be willing to buy at different prices.

TABLE 3.1	Alex's Demand Schedule for Gasoline
Price (per Gallon)	Quantity Demanded (Gallons per Week)
$8.00	0
7.00	2
6.00	3
5.00	5
4.00	7
3.00	10
2.00	14
1.00	20
0.00	26

Demand Curves Slope Downward   The data in Table 3.1 show that at lower prices, Alex buys more gasoline; at higher prices, she buys less. Thus, there is a *negative, or inverse, relationship between quantity demanded and price.* When price rises, quantity demanded falls, and when price falls, quantity demanded rises. Thus, demand curves always slope downward. This negative relationship between price and quantity demanded is often referred to as the **law of demand**, a term first used by economist Alfred Marshall in his 1890 textbook.

law of demand   The negative relationship between price and quantity demanded: *Ceteris paribus*, as price rises, quantity demanded decreases; as price falls, quantity demanded increases.

Some people are put off by the abstraction of demand curves. Of course, we do not actually draw our own demand curves for products. When we want to make a purchase, we usually face only a single price and how much we would buy at other prices is irrelevant. However, demand curves help analysts understand the kind of behavior that households are *likely* to exhibit if they are actually faced with a higher or lower price. We know, for example, that if the price of a good rises enough, the quantity demanded must ultimately drop to zero. The demand curve is thus a tool that helps us explain economic behavior and predict reactions to possible price changes.

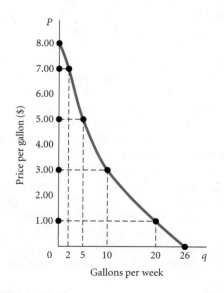

▲ FIGURE 3.2   **Alex's Demand Curve**
The relationship between price (*P*) and quantity demanded (*q*) presented graphically is called a demand curve. Demand curves have a negative slope, indicating that lower prices cause quantity demanded to increase. Note that Alex's demand curve is blue; demand in product markets is determined by household choice.

Marshall's definition of a social "law" captures the idea:

> The term "law" means nothing more than a general proposition or statement of tendencies, more or less certain, more or less definite . . . a *social law* is a statement of social tendencies; that is, that a certain course of action may be expected from the members of a social group under certain conditions.[2]

It seems reasonable to expect that consumers will demand more of a product at a lower price and less of it at a higher price. Households must divide their incomes over a wide range of goods and services. At \$3.00 per gallon and 25 miles to a gallon, driving the 20 miles round trip to work costs Alex \$2.40. At \$5.00 per gallon, the trip now costs \$4.00. With the higher prices, Alex may have to give up her morning latte if she drives, and that may turn out to be too big a sacrifice for her. As the price of gasoline rises, the opportunity cost of driving in terms of other types of consumption also rises and that is why Alex ends up driving less as the price of gasoline rises. Goods compete with one another for our spending.

Economists use the concept of *utility* to explain the slope of the demand curve. Presumably, we consume goods and services because they give us utility or satisfaction. As we consume more of a product within a given period of time, it is likely that each additional unit consumed will yield successively less satisfaction. The utility you gain from a second ice cream cone is likely to be less than the utility you gained from the first, the third is worth even less, and so on. This *law of diminishing marginal utility* is an important concept in economics. If each successive unit of a good is worth less to you, you are not going to be willing to pay as much for it. Thus, it is reasonable to expect a downward slope in the demand curve for that good.

Thinking about the ways that people are affected by price changes also helps us see what is behind the law of demand. Consider this example: Luis lives and works in Mexico City. His elderly mother lives in Santiago, Chile. Last year the airlines servicing South America got into a price war, and the price of flying between Mexico City and Santiago dropped from 20,000 pesos to 10,000 pesos. How might Luis's behavior change?

First, he is better off. Last year he flew home to Chile three times at a total cost of 60,000 pesos. This year he can fly to Chile the same number of times, buy exactly the same combination of other goods and services that he bought last year, and have 30,000 pesos left over. Because he is better off—his income can buy more—he may fly home more frequently. Second, the opportunity cost of flying home has changed. Before the price war, Luis had to sacrifice 20,000 pesos worth of other goods and services each time he flew to Chile. After the price war, he must sacrifice only 10,000 pesos worth of other goods and services for each trip. The trade-off has changed. Both of these effects are likely to lead to a higher quantity demanded in response to the lower price.

In sum:

> It is reasonable to expect quantity demanded to fall when price rises, *ceteris paribus*, and to expect quantity demanded to rise when price falls, *ceteris paribus*. Demand curves have a negative slope.

Other Properties of Demand Curves   Two additional things are notable about Alex's demand curve. First, it intersects the *Y*, or price, axis. This means that there is a price above which she buys no gasoline. In this case, Alex simply stops driving when the price reaches \$8 per gallon. As long as households have limited incomes and wealth, all demand curves will intersect the price axis. For any commodity, there is always a price above which a household will not or cannot pay. Even if the good or service is very important, all households are ultimately constrained, or limited, by income and wealth.

---

[2] Alfred Marshall, *Principles of Economics*, 8th ed. (New York: Macmillan, 1948), p. 33. (The first edition was published in 1890.)

Second, Alex's demand curve intersects the X, or quantity, axis. Even at a zero price, there is a limit to how much she will drive. If gasoline were free, she would use 26 gallons, but not more. That demand curves intersect the quantity axis is a matter of common sense. Demand in a given period of time is limited, if only by time, even at a zero price.

To summarize what we know about the shape of demand curves:

1. They have a negative slope. An increase in price is likely to lead to a decrease in quantity demanded, and a decrease in price is likely to lead to an increase in quantity demanded.
2. They intersect the quantity (X) axis, a result of time limitations and diminishing marginal utility.
3. They intersect the price (Y) axis, a result of limited income and wealth.

That is all we can say; it is not possible to generalize further. The actual shape of an individual household demand curve—whether it is steep or flat, whether it is bowed in or bowed out—depends on the unique tastes and preferences of the household and other factors. Some households may be very sensitive to price changes; other households may respond little to a change in price. In some cases, plentiful substitutes are available; in other cases, they are not. Thus, to fully understand the shape and position of demand curves, we must turn to the other determinants of household demand.

Other Determinants of Household Demand

Of the many factors likely to influence a household's demand for a specific product, we have considered only the price of the product. But household income and wealth, the prices of other goods and services, tastes and preferences, and expectations also matter to demand.

income The sum of all a household's wages, salaries, profits, interest payments, rents, and other forms of earnings in a given period of time. It is a flow measure.

wealth *or* **net worth** The total value of what a household owns minus what it owes. It is a stock measure.

Income and Wealth Before we proceed, we need to define two terms that are often confused, *income* and *wealth*. A household's **income** is the sum of all the wages, salaries, profits, interest payments, rents, and other forms of earnings received by the household *in a given period of time*. Income is thus a *flow* measure: We must specify a time period for it—income *per month* or *per year*. You can spend or consume more or less than your income in any given period. If you consume less than your income, you save. To consume more than your income in a period, you must either borrow or draw on savings accumulated from previous periods.

Wealth is the total value of what a household owns minus what it owes. Another word for wealth is **net worth**—the amount a household would have left if it sold all of its possessions and paid all of its debts. Wealth is a *stock* measure: It is measured at a given point in time. If, in a given period, you spend less than your income, you save; the amount that you save is added to your wealth. Saving is the flow that affects the stock of wealth. When you spend more than your income, you *dissave*—you reduce your wealth.

Households with higher incomes and higher accumulated savings or inherited wealth can afford to buy more goods and services. In general, we would expect higher demand at higher levels of income/wealth and lower demand at lower levels of income/wealth. Goods for which demand goes up when income is higher and for which demand goes down when income is lower are called **normal goods**. Movie tickets, restaurant meals, telephone calls, and shirts are all normal goods.

normal goods Goods for which demand goes up when income is higher and for which demand goes down when income is lower.

However, generalization in economics can be hazardous. Sometimes demand for a good falls when household income rises. Consider, for example, the various qualities of meat available. When a household's income rises, it is likely to buy higher-quality meats—its demand for filet mignon is likely to rise—but its demand for lower-quality meats—chuck steak, for example—is likely to fall. Transportation is another example. At higher incomes, people can afford to fly. People who can afford to fly are less likely to take the bus long distances. Thus, higher income may *reduce* the number of times someone takes a bus. Goods for which demand tends to fall when income rises are called **inferior goods**.

inferior goods Goods for which demand tends to fall when income rises.

Prices of Other Goods and Services No consumer decides in isolation on the amount of any one commodity to buy. Instead, each decision is part of a larger set of decisions that are made simultaneously. Households must apportion their incomes over many different goods and services. As a result, the price of any one good can and does affect the demand for other goods. This is most obviously the case when goods are substitutes for one another. For Alex the bus is an alternative that she uses when gasoline gets expensive.

ECONOMICS IN PRACTICE

Have You Bought This Textbook?

As all of you know full well, college textbooks are expensive. And, at first, it may seem as though there are few substitutes available for the cash-strapped undergraduate. After *all*, if your professor assigns Smith's *Principles of Biology* to you, you cannot go out and see if Jones' *Principles of Chemistry* is perhaps cheaper and buy it instead. As it turns out, as some recent work by Judy Chevalier and Austan Goolsbee[1] discovered, even when instructors require particular texts, when prices are high students have found substitutes. Even in the textbook market student demand does slope down!

Chevalier and Goolsbee collected data on textbooks from over 1600 colleges for the years 1997–2001 to do their research. For that period, the lion's share of both new and used college textbooks was sold in college bookstores. Next, they looked at class enrollments for each college in the large majors, economics, biology, and psychology. In each of those classes they were able to learn which textbook had been assigned. At first, one might think that the total number of textbooks, used plus new, should match the class enrollment. After all, the text is required! In fact, what they found was the higher the textbook price, the more text sales fell below class enrollments.

So what substitutes did students find for the required text? While the paper has no hard evidence on this, students themselves gave them lots of suggestions. Many decide to share books with roommates. Others use the library more. These solutions are not perfect, but when the price is high enough, students find it worth their while to walk to the library!

THINKING PRACTICALLY

1. If you were to construct a demand curve for a required text in a course, where would that demand curve intersect the horizontal axis?

2. And this much harder question: In the year before a new edition of a text is published, many college bookstores will not buy the older edition. Given this *fact*, what do you think happens to the gap between enrollments and new plus used book sales in the year before a new edition of a text is expected?

[1] Judith Chevalier and Austan Goolsbee, "Are Durable Goods Consumers Forward Looking? Evidence From College Textbooks," *Quarterly Journal of Economics*, 2009, 1853–1884.

When an *increase* in the price of one good causes demand for another good to *increase* (a positive relationship), we say that the goods are **substitutes**. A *fall* in the price of a good causes a *decline* in demand for its substitutes. Substitutes are goods that can serve as replacements for one another.

To be substitutes, two products do not need to be identical. Identical products are called **perfect substitutes**. Japanese cars are not identical to American cars. Nonetheless, all have four wheels, are capable of carrying people, and run on gasoline. Thus, significant changes in the price of one country's cars can be expected to influence demand for the other country's cars. Restaurant meals are substitutes for meals eaten at home, and flying from New York to Washington, D.C., is a substitute for taking the train. The *Economics in Practice* box describes substitution in the textbook market.

Often two products "go together"—that is, they complement each other. Bacon and eggs are **complementary goods**, as are cars and gasoline. When two goods are **complements**, a *decrease* in the price of one results in an *increase* in demand for the other and vice versa. The makers of Guitar Hero and Rock Band, two popular and competitive video games, understand that there is a strong connection between how many songs can be played on their operating platforms and how strong the demand is for their games. For iPods and Kindles as well, the availability of content at low prices stimulates demand for the devices.

substitutes Goods that can serve as replacements for one another; when the price of one increases, demand for the other increases.

perfect substitutes Identical products.

complements, complementary goods Goods that "go together"; a decrease in the price of one results in an increase in demand for the other and vice versa.

Tastes and Preferences   Income, wealth, and prices of goods available are the three factors that determine the combinations of goods and services that a household is *able* to buy. You know that you cannot afford to rent an apartment at $1,200 per month if your monthly income is only $400, but within these constraints, you are more or less free to choose what to buy. Your final choice depends on your individual tastes and preferences.

Changes in preferences can and do manifest themselves in market behavior. Thirty years ago the major big-city marathons drew only a few hundred runners. Now tens of thousands enter and run. The demand for running shoes, running suits, stopwatches, and other running items has greatly increased. For many years, people drank soda for refreshment. Today convenience stores are filled with a dizzying array of iced teas, fruit juices, natural beverages, and mineral waters.

Within the constraints of prices and incomes, preference shapes the demand curve, but it is difficult to generalize about tastes and preferences. First, they are volatile: Five years ago more people smoked cigarettes and fewer people had Smartphones. Second, tastes are idiosyncratic: Some people like to text, whereas others still prefer to use e-mail; some people prefer dogs, whereas others are crazy about cats. Some eat fried cockroaches. The diversity of individual demands is almost infinite.

One of the interesting questions in economics is why, in some markets, diverse consumer tastes give rise to a variety of styles, while in other markets, despite a seeming diversity in tastes, we find only one or two varieties. All sidewalks in the United States are a similar gray color, yet houses are painted a rainbow of colors. Yet it is not obvious on the face of it that people would not prefer as much variety in their sidewalks as in their houses. To answer this type of question, we need to move beyond the demand curve. We will revisit this question in a later chapter.

Expectations What you decide to buy today certainly depends on today's prices and your current income and wealth. You also have expectations about what your position will be in the future. You may have expectations about future changes in prices too, and these may affect your decisions today.

There are many examples of the ways expectations affect demand. When people buy a house or a car, they often must borrow part of the purchase price and repay it over a number of years. In deciding what kind of house or car to buy, they presumably must think about their income today, as well as what their income is likely to be in the future.

As another example, consider a student in the final year of medical school living on a scholarship of $25,000. Compare that student with another person earning $12 an hour at a full-time job, with no expectation of a significant change in income in the future. The two have virtually identical incomes. But even if they have the same tastes, the medical student is likely to demand different goods and services, simply because of the expectation of a major increase in income later on.

Increasingly, economic theory has come to recognize the importance of expectations. We will devote a good deal of time to discussing how expectations affect more than just demand. For the time being, however, it is important to understand that demand depends on more than just *current* incomes, prices, and tastes.

Shift of Demand versus Movement Along a Demand Curve

Recall that a demand curve shows the relationship between quantity demanded and the price of a good. Demand curves are constructed while holding income, tastes, and other prices constant. If income, tastes, or other prices change, we would have to derive an entirely new relationship between price and quantity.

Let us return once again to Alex. (See Table 3.1 and Figure 3.2 on p. 52.) Suppose that when we derived the demand curve in Figure 3.2 Alex was receiving a salary of $500 per week after taxes. If Alex faces a price of $3.00 per gallon and chooses to drive 250 miles per week, her total weekly expenditure works out to be $3.00 per gallon times 10 gallons or $30 per week. That amounts to 6.0 percent of her income.

Suppose now she were to receive a raise to $700 per week after taxes. Alex's higher income may well raise the amount of gasoline being used by Alex *regardless* of what she was using before. The new situation is listed in Table 3.2 and graphed in Figure 3.3. Notice in Figure 3.3 that Alex's entire curve has shifted to the right—at $3.00 a gallon the curve shows an increase in the quantity demanded from 10 to 15 gallons. At $5.00, the quantity demanded by Alex increases from 5 gallons to 10 gallons.

The fact that demand *increased* when income increased implies that gasoline is a *normal good* to Alex.

TABLE 3.2 Shift of Alex's Demand Schedule Due to an Increase in Income

Price (per Gallon)	Schedule D_0 Quantity Demanded (Gallons per Week at an Income of $500 per Week)	Schedule D_1 Quantity Demanded (Gallons per Week at an Income of $700 per Week)
$ 8.00	0	3
7.00	2	5
6.00	3	7
5.00	5	10
4.00	7	12
3.00	10	15
2.00	14	19
1.00	20	24
0.00	26	30

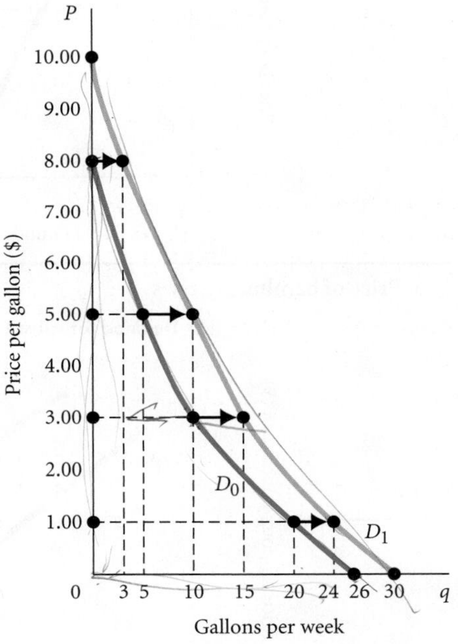

▲ **FIGURE 3.3 Shift of a Demand Curve Following a Rise in Income**
When the price of a good changes, we move *along* the demand curve for that good. When any other factor that influences demand changes (income, tastes, and so on), the relationship between price and quantity is different; there is a *shift* of the demand curve, in this case from D_0 to D_1. Gasoline is a normal good.

The conditions that were in place at the time we drew Alex's original demand curve have now changed. In other words, a factor that affects Alex's demand for gasoline (in this case, her income) has changed, and there is now a new relationship between price and quantity demanded. Such a change is referred to as a **shift of a demand curve**.

It is very important to distinguish between a change in quantity demanded—that is, some movement *along* a demand curve—and a shift of demand. Demand schedules and demand curves show the relationship between the price of a good or service and the quantity demanded per period, *ceteris paribus*. If price changes, quantity demanded will change—this is a **movement along a demand curve**. When any of the *other* factors that influence demand change, however, a new relationship between price and quantity demanded is established—this is

shift of a demand curve The change that takes place in a demand curve corresponding to a new relationship between quantity demanded of a good and price of that good. The shift is brought about by a change in the original conditions.

movement along a demand curve The change in quantity demanded brought about by a change in price.

a *shift of a demand curve*. The result, then, is a *new* demand curve. Changes in income, preferences, or prices of other goods cause a demand curve to shift:

> Change in price of a good or service leads to
> └──────➤ change in *quantity demanded* (**movement along a demand curve**).

> Change in income, preferences, or prices of other goods or services leads to
> └──────➤ change in *demand* (**shift of a demand curve**).

Figure 3.4 illustrates the differences between movement along a demand curve and shifting demand curves. In Figure 3.4(a), an increase in household income causes demand for hamburger

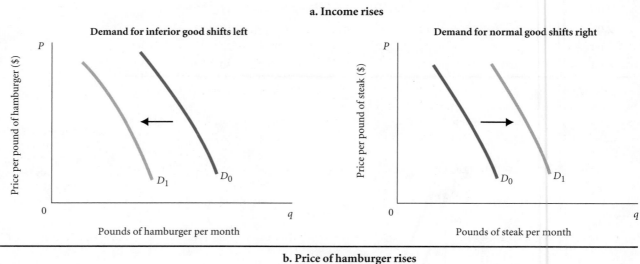

a. Income rises

Demand for inferior good shifts left

Demand for normal good shifts right

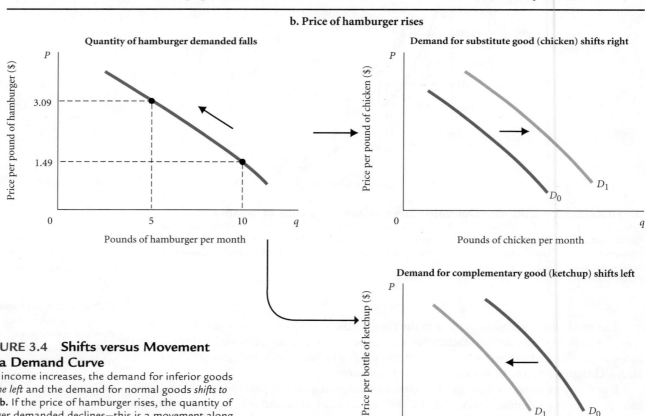

b. Price of hamburger rises

Quantity of hamburger demanded falls

Demand for substitute good (chicken) shifts right

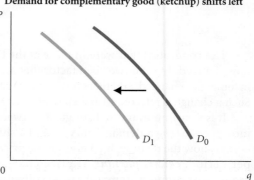

Demand for complementary good (ketchup) shifts left

▲ **FIGURE 3.4** **Shifts versus Movement Along a Demand Curve**

a. When income increases, the demand for inferior goods *shifts to the left* and the demand for normal goods *shifts to the right*. **b.** If the price of hamburger rises, the quantity of hamburger demanded declines—this is a movement along the demand curve. The same price rise for hamburger would shift the demand for chicken (a substitute for hamburger) to the right and the demand for ketchup (a complement to hamburger) to the left.

(an inferior good) to decline, or shift to the left from D_0 to D_1. (Because quantity is measured on the horizontal axis, a decrease means a *shift to the left*.) In contrast, demand for steak (a normal good) increases, or *shifts to the right*, when income rises.

In Figure 3.4(b), an increase in the price of hamburger from $1.49 to $3.09 a pound causes a household to buy less hamburger each month. In other words, the higher price causes the *quantity demanded* to decline from 10 pounds to 5 pounds per month. This change represents a movement *along* the demand curve for hamburger. In place of hamburger, the household buys more chicken. The household's demand for chicken (a substitute for hamburger) rises—the demand curve shifts to the right. At the same time, the demand for ketchup (a good that complements hamburger) declines—its demand curve shifts to the left.

From Household Demand to Market Demand

So far we have been talking about what determines an individual's demand for a product. We ask the question: How many 12-packs of soda are you willing to buy per week when the price of that 12-pack is $5. This is a question you answer often in your life, whenever you go to the local store. We see the answer depends on how much money you have, how much you like soda, and what else is available to you at what price. Next time you go to the store and see a price change, we hope you think a bit more about your buying reaction.

Individual reactions to price changes are interesting, especially to the individual. But for us to be able to say something more general about prices in the market, we need to know about market demand.

Market demand is simply the sum of all the quantities of a good or service demanded per period by all the households buying in the market for that good or service. Figure 3.5 shows the derivation of a market demand curve from three individual demand curves.

market demand The sum of all the quantities of a good or service demanded per period by all the households buying in the market for that good or service.

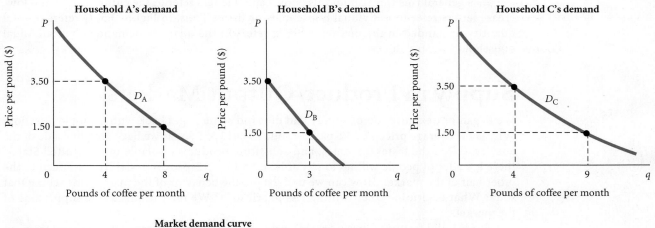

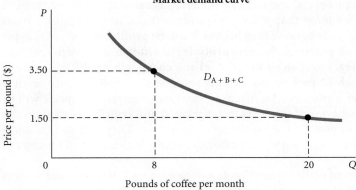

Price	Quantity (q) Demanded by			Total Quantity Demanded in the Market (Q)
	A	B	C	
$3.50	4 +	0 +	4	= 8
1.50	8 +	3 +	9	= 20

▲ **FIGURE 3.5   Deriving Market Demand from Individual Demand Curves**
Total demand in the marketplace is simply the sum of the demands of all the households shopping in a particular market. It is the sum of all the individual demand curves—that is, the sum of all the individual quantities demanded at each price.

(Although this market demand curve is derived from the behavior of only three people, most markets have thousands, or even millions of demanders.) As the table in Figure 3.5 shows, when the price of a pound of coffee is $3.50, both household A and household C would purchase 4 pounds per month, while household B would buy none. At that price, presumably, B drinks tea. Market demand at $3.50 would thus be a total of 4 + 4, or 8 pounds. At a price of $1.50 per pound, however, A would purchase 8 pounds per month; B, 3 pounds; and C, 9 pounds. Thus, at $1.50 per pound, market demand would be 8 + 3 + 9, or 20 pounds of coffee per month.

The total quantity demanded in the marketplace at a given price is simply the sum of all the quantities demanded by all the individual households shopping in the market *at that price*. A market demand curve shows the total amount of a product that would be sold at each price if households could buy all they wanted at that price. As Figure 3.5 shows, the market demand curve is the sum of all the individual demand curves—that is, the sum of all the individual quantities demanded at each price. Thus, the market demand curve takes its shape and position from the shapes, positions, and number of individual demand curves. If more people decide to shop in a market, more demand curves must be added and the market demand curve will shift to the right. Market demand curves may also shift as a result of preference changes, income changes, or changes in the number of demanders.

An interesting fact about the market demand curve in Figure 3.5 is that at different prices, not only the number of people demanding the product may change but also the *type* of people demanding the product. When Apple halved the price of its iPhone in fall 2007, it announced that it wanted to make the iPhone available to a broader group of people. When prices fall, people like those in household B in Figure 3.5 move into markets that are otherwise out of their reach. When Apple introduced a new, improved, but much more expensive iPhone 5 in the fall of 2012, its first sales were likely made to people who both had more resources and were more tech-savvy than the average old model iPhone user.

As a general rule throughout this book, capital letters refer to the entire market and lowercase letters refer to individual households or firms. Thus, in Figure 3.5, Q refers to total quantity demanded in the market, while q refers to the quantity demanded by individual households.

Supply in Product/Output Markets

We began our exploration of supply and demand some pages back with a simple question: Why is the average price of a 12-pack of soda in 2013 $5? So far we have seen one side of the answer: Given the tastes, incomes, and substitute products available in the United States, there are a lot of people willing to pay at least $5 for a 12-pack of soda! Now we turn to the other half of the market: How can we understand the behavior of the many firms selling that soda? What determines their willingness to sell soda? We refer to this as the supply side of the market.

Firms build factories, hire workers, and buy raw materials because they believe they can sell the products they make for more than it costs to produce them. In other words, firms supply goods and services like soda because they believe it will be profitable to do so. Supply decisions thus depend on profit potential. Because **profit** is the difference between revenues and costs, supply is likely to react to changes in revenues and changes in production costs. If the prices of soda are high, each 12-pack produces more revenue for suppliers, since revenue is simply price per unit times units sold. So, just as in the case of buyers, the price will be important in explaining the behavior of suppliers in a market. It also typically costs suppliers something to produce whatever product they are bringing to market. They have to hire workers, build factories, buy inputs. So the supply behavior of firms will also depend on costs of production.

profit The difference between revenues and costs.

In later chapters, we will focus on how firms decide *how* to produce their goods and services and explore the cost side of the picture more formally. For now, we will begin our examination of firm behavior by focusing on the output supply decision and the relationship between quantity supplied and output price, *ceteris paribus*.

production into soybeans. Thus, an increase in soybean prices actually affects the amount of corn supplied.

Similarly, if beef prices rise, producers may respond by raising more cattle. However, leather comes from cowhide. Thus, an increase in beef prices may actually increase the supply of leather.

To summarize:

> Assuming that its objective is to maximize profits, a firm's decision about what quantity of output, or product, to supply depends on:
>
> 1. The price of the good or service.
> 2. The cost of producing the product, which in turn depends on:
>   - the price of required inputs (labor, capital, and land), and
>   - the technologies that can be used to produce the product.
> 3. The prices of related products.

Shift of Supply versus Movement Along a Supply Curve

A supply curve shows the relationship between the quantity of a good or service supplied by a firm and the price that good or service brings in the market. Higher prices are likely to lead to an increase in quantity supplied, *ceteris paribus*. Remember: The supply curve is derived holding everything constant except price. When the price of a product changes *ceteris paribus*, a change in the quantity supplied follows—that is, a **movement along a supply curve** takes place. As you have seen, supply decisions are also influenced by factors other than price. New relationships between price and quantity supplied come about when factors other than price change, and the result is a **shift of a supply curve**. When factors other than price cause supply curves to shift, we say that there has been a *change in supply*.

Recall that the cost of production depends on the price of inputs and the technologies of production available. Now suppose that a major breakthrough in the production of soybeans has occurred: Genetic engineering has produced a superstrain of disease- and pest-resistant seed. Such a technological change would enable individual farmers to supply more soybeans at *any* market price. Table 3.4 and Figure 3.7 describe this change. At $3 a bushel, farmers would have produced 30,000 bushels from the old seed (schedule S_0 in Table 3.4); with the lower cost of production and higher yield resulting from the new seed, they produce 40,000 bushels (schedule S_1 in Table 3.4). At $1.75 per bushel, they would have produced 10,000 bushels from the old seed; but with the lower costs and higher yields, output rises to 23,000 bushels.

Increases in input prices may also cause supply curves to shift. If Farmer Brown faces higher fuel costs, for example, his supply curve will shift to the left—that is, he will produce less at any given market price. If Brown's soybean supply curve shifted far enough to the left, it would intersect the price axis at a higher point, meaning that it would take a higher market price to induce Brown to produce any soybeans at all.

movement along a supply curve The change in quantity supplied brought about by a change in price.

shift of a supply curve The change that takes place in a supply curve corresponding to a new relationship between quantity supplied of a good and the price of that good. The shift is brought about by a change in the original conditions.

TABLE 3.4 Shift of Supply Schedule for Soybeans Following Development of a New Disease-Resistant Seed Strain

	Schedule S_0	Schedule S_1
Price (per Bushel)	Quantity Supplied (Bushels per Year Using Old Seed)	Quantity Supplied (Bushels per Year Using New Seed)
$1.50	0	5,000
1.75	10,000	23,000
2.25	20,000	33,000
3.00	30,000	40,000
4.00	45,000	54,000
5.00	45,000	54,000

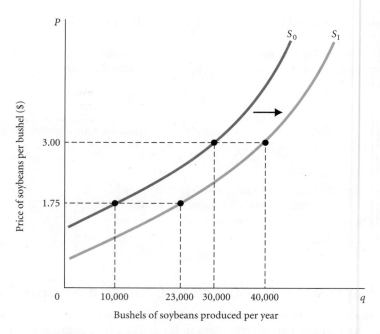

▲ **FIGURE 3.7** **Shift of the Supply Curve for Soybeans Following Development of a New Seed Strain**
When the price of a product changes, we move *along* the supply curve for that product; the quantity supplied rises or falls. When any other factor affecting supply changes, the supply curve *shifts*.

As with demand, it is very important to distinguish between *movements along* supply curves (changes in quantity supplied) and *shifts in* supply curves (changes in supply):

Change in price of a good or service leads to
└──→ change in *quantity supplied* (**movement along a supply curve**).

Change in costs, input prices, technology, or prices of related goods and services leads to
└──→ change in *supply* (**shift of a supply curve**).

From Individual Supply to Market Supply

So far we have focused on the supply behavior of a single farmer. For most markets many, many suppliers bring product to the consumer, and it is the behavior of all of those producers together that determines supply.

market supply The sum of all that is supplied each period by all producers of a single product.

Market supply is determined in the same fashion as market demand. It is simply the sum of all that is supplied each period by all producers of a single product. Figure 3.8 derives a market supply curve from the supply curves of three individual firms. (In a market with more firms, total market supply would be the sum of the amounts produced by each of the firms in that market.) As the table in Figure 3.8 shows, at a price of $3, farm A supplies 30,000 bushels of soybeans, farm B supplies 10,000 bushels, and farm C supplies 25,000 bushels. At this price, the total amount supplied in the market is 30,000 + 10,000 + 25,000, or 65,000 bushels. At a price of $1.75, however, the total amount supplied is only 25,000 bushels (10,000 + 5,000 + 10,000). Thus, the market supply curve is the simple addition of the individual supply curves of all the firms in a particular market—that is, the sum of all the individual quantities supplied at each price.

The position and shape of the market supply curve depends on the positions and shapes of the individual firms' supply curves from which it is derived. The market supply curve also depends on the number of firms that produce in that market. If firms that produce for a particular market are earning high profits, other firms may be tempted to go into that line of business. When the technology to produce computers for home use became available, literally hundreds of new firms got into the act. The popularity and profitability of professional football

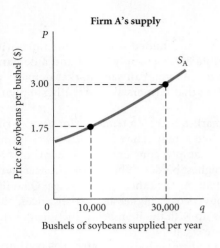

Firm A's supply

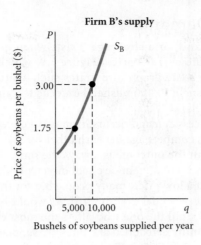

Firm B's supply

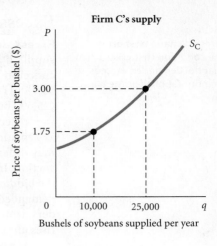

Firm C's supply

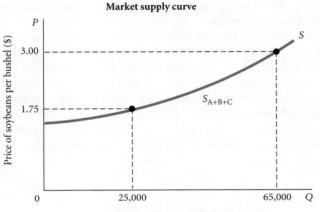

Market supply curve

	Quantity (q) Supplied by			Total Quantity Supplied in the Market (Q)
Price	A	B	C	
$3.00	30,000 +	10,000 +	25,000	= 65,000
1.75	10,000 +	5,000 +	10,000	= 25,000

▲ **FIGURE 3.8 Deriving Market Supply from Individual Firm Supply Curves**
Total supply in the marketplace is the sum of all the amounts supplied by all the firms selling in the market. It is the sum of all the individual quantities supplied at each price.

has, three times, led to the formation of new leagues. When new firms enter an industry, the supply curve shifts to the right. When firms go out of business, or "exit" the market, the supply curve shifts to the left.

Market Equilibrium

So far, we have identified a number of factors that influence the amount that households demand and the amount that firms supply in product (output) markets. The discussion has emphasized the role of market price as a determinant of both quantity demanded and quantity supplied. We are now ready to see how supply and demand in the market interact to determine the final market price.

We have been very careful in our discussions thus far to separate household decisions about how much to demand from firm decisions about how much to supply. The operation of the market, however, clearly depends on the interaction between suppliers and demanders. At any moment, one of three conditions prevails in every market: (1) The quantity demanded exceeds the quantity supplied at the current price, a situation called *excess demand*; (2) the quantity supplied exceeds the quantity demanded at the current price, a situation called *excess supply*; or (3) the quantity supplied equals the quantity demanded at the current price, a situation called **equilibrium**. At equilibrium, no tendency for price to change exists.

equilibrium The condition that exists when quantity supplied and quantity demanded are equal. At equilibrium, there is no tendency for price to change.

Excess Demand

Excess demand, or a **shortage**, exists when quantity demanded is greater than quantity supplied at the current price. Figure 3.9, which plots both a supply curve and a demand curve on the same graph, illustrates such a situation. As you can see, market demand at $1.75 per bushel (50,000 bushels) exceeds the amount that farmers are currently supplying (25,000 bushels).

When excess demand occurs in an unregulated market, there is a tendency for price to rise as demanders compete against each other for the limited supply. The adjustment mechanisms may differ, but the outcome is always the same. For example, consider the mechanism of an auction. In an auction, items are sold directly to the highest bidder. When the auctioneer starts the bidding at a low price, many people bid for the item. At first, there is a shortage: Quantity demanded exceeds quantity supplied. As would-be buyers offer higher and higher prices, bidders drop out until the one who offers the most ends up with the item being auctioned. Price rises until quantity demanded and quantity supplied are equal.

At a price of $1.75 (see Figure 3.9 again), farmers produce soybeans at a rate of 25,000 bushels per year, but at that price, the demand is for 50,000 bushels. Most farm products are sold to local dealers who in turn sell large quantities in major market centers, where bidding would push prices up if quantity demanded exceeded quantity supplied. As price rises above $1.75, two things happen: (1) The quantity demanded falls as buyers drop out of the market and perhaps choose a substitute, and (2) the quantity supplied increases as farmers find themselves receiving a higher price for their product and shift additional acres into soybean production.[3]

This process continues until the shortage is eliminated. In Figure 3.9, this occurs at $2.00, where quantity demanded has fallen from 50,000 to 40,000 bushels per year and quantity supplied has increased from 25,000 to 40,000 bushels per year. When quantity demanded and quantity supplied are equal and there is no further bidding, the process has achieved an equilibrium, a situation in which *there is no natural tendency for further adjustment*. Graphically, the point of equilibrium is the point at which the supply curve and the demand curve intersect.

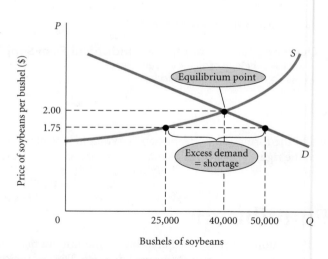

▲ **FIGURE 3.9** **Excess Demand, or Shortage**
At a price of $1.75 per bushel, quantity demanded exceeds quantity supplied. When *excess demand* exists, there is a tendency for price to rise. When quantity demanded equals quantity supplied, excess demand is eliminated and the market is in equilibrium. Here the equilibrium price is $2.00 and the equilibrium quantity is 40,000 bushels.

---

[3] Once farmers have produced in any given season, they cannot change their minds and produce more, of course. When we derived Clarence Brown's supply schedule in Table 3.3, we imagined him reacting to prices that existed at the time he decided how much land to plant in soybeans. In Figure 3.9, the upward slope shows that higher prices justify shifting land from other crops. Final price may not be determined until final production figures are in. For our purposes here, however, we have ignored this timing problem. The best way to think about it is that demand and supply are *flows*, or *rates*, of production—that is, we are talking about the number of bushels produced *per production period*. Adjustments in the rate of production may take place over a number of production periods.

Increasingly, items are auctioned over the Internet. Companies such as eBay connect buyers and sellers of everything from automobiles to wine and from computers to airline tickets. Auctions are occurring simultaneously with participants located across the globe. The principles through which prices are determined in these auctions are the same: When excess demand exists, prices rise.

While the principles are the same, the process through which excess demand leads to higher prices is different in different markets. Consider the market for houses in the hypothetical town of Boomville with a population of 25,000 people, most of whom live in single-family homes. Normally, about 75 homes are sold in the Boomville market each year. However, last year a major business opened a plant in town, creating 1,500 new jobs that pay good wages. This attracted new residents to the area, and real estate agents now have more buyers than there are properties for sale. Quantity demanded now exceeds quantity supplied. In other words, there is a shortage.

Properties are sold very quickly, and housing prices begin to rise. Boomville sellers soon learn that there are more buyers than usual, and they begin to hold out for higher offers. As prices for Boomville houses rise, quantity demanded eventually drops off and quantity supplied increases: (1) Encouraged by the high prices, builders begin constructing new houses, and (2) some people, attracted by the higher prices their homes will fetch, put their houses on the market. Discouraged by higher prices, however, some potential buyers (demanders) may begin to look for housing in neighboring towns and settle on commuting. Eventually, equilibrium will be reestablished, with the quantity of houses demanded just equal to the quantity of houses supplied.

Although the mechanics of price adjustment in the housing market differ from the mechanics of an auction, the outcome is the same:

> When quantity demanded exceeds quantity supplied, price tends to rise. When the price in a market rises, quantity demanded falls and quantity supplied rises until an equilibrium is reached at which quantity demanded and quantity supplied are equal.

This process is called *price rationing*. When a shortage exists, some people will be satisfied and some will not. When the market operates without interference, price increases will distribute what is available to those who are willing and able to pay the most. As long as there is a way for buyers and sellers to interact, those who are willing to pay more will make that fact known somehow. (We discuss the nature of the price system as a rationing device in detail in Chapter 4.)

Excess Supply

Excess supply, or a **surplus**, exists when the quantity supplied exceeds the quantity demanded at the current price. As with a shortage, the mechanics of price adjustment in the face of a surplus can differ from market to market. For example, if automobile dealers find themselves with unsold cars in the fall when the new models are coming in, you can expect to see price cuts. Sometimes dealers offer discounts to encourage buyers; sometimes buyers themselves simply offer less than the price initially asked. In any event, products do no one any good sitting in dealers' lots or on warehouse shelves. The auction metaphor introduced earlier can also be applied here: If the initial asking price is too high, no one bids and the auctioneer tries a lower price. It is almost always true that certain items do not sell as well as anticipated during the Christmas holidays. After Christmas, most stores have big sales during which they lower the prices of overstocked items. Quantities supplied exceeded quantities demanded at the current prices, so stores cut prices. Many Web sites exist that do little more than sell at a discount clothing and other goods that failed to sell at full price during the past season.

Figure 3.10 illustrates another excess supply/surplus situation. At a price of $3 per bushel, suppose farmers are supplying soybeans at a rate of 65,000 bushels per year, but buyers are demanding only 25,000. With 40,000 bushels of soybeans going unsold, the market price falls. As price falls from $3.00 to $2.00, quantity supplied decreases from 65,000 bushels per year to 40,000. The lower price causes quantity demanded to rise from 25,000 to 40,000. At $2.00, quantity demanded and quantity supplied are equal. For the data shown here, $2.00 and 40,000 bushels are the equilibrium price and quantity, respectively.

excess supply *or* surplus
The condition that exists when quantity supplied exceeds quantity demanded at the current price.

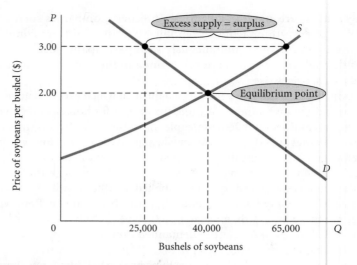

▲ **FIGURE 3.10** **Excess Supply or Surplus**
At a price of $3.00, quantity supplied exceeds quantity demanded by 40,000 bushels. This excess supply will cause the price to fall.

Although the mechanism by which price is adjusted is different for automobiles, housing, soybeans, and crude oil, the outcome is the same:

> When quantity supplied exceeds quantity demanded at the current price, the price tends to fall. When price falls, quantity supplied is likely to decrease and quantity demanded is likely to increase until an equilibrium price is reached where quantity supplied and quantity demanded are equal.

Changes in Equilibrium

When supply and demand curves shift, the equilibrium price and quantity change. The following example will help to illustrate this point.

South America is a major producer of coffee beans. A cold snap there can reduce the coffee harvest enough to affect the world price of coffee beans. In the mid-1990s, a major freeze hit Brazil and Colombia and drove up the price of coffee on world markets to a record $2.40 per pound. Bad weather in Colombia in 2005 and more recently in 2012 caused similar shifts in supply.

Figure 3.11 illustrates how the freeze pushed up coffee prices. Initially, the market was in equilibrium at a price of $1.20. At that price, the quantity demanded was equal to quantity supplied (13.2 billion pounds). At a price of $1.20 and a quantity of 13.2 billion pounds, the demand curve (labeled D) intersected the initial supply curve (labeled S_0). (Remember that equilibrium exists when quantity demanded equals quantity supplied—the point at which the supply and demand curves intersect.)

The freeze caused a decrease in the supply of coffee beans. That is, the freeze caused the supply curve to shift to the left. In Figure 3.11, the new supply curve (the supply curve that shows the relationship between price and quantity supplied after the freeze) is labeled S_1.

At the initial equilibrium price, $1.20, there is now a shortage of coffee. If the price were to remain at $1.20, quantity demanded would not change; it would remain at 13.2 billion pounds. However, at that price, quantity supplied would drop to 6.6 billion pounds. At a price of $1.20, quantity demanded is greater than quantity supplied.

When excess demand exists in a market, price can be expected to rise, and rise it did. As the figure shows, price rose to a new equilibrium at $2.40. At $2.40, quantity demanded is again equal to quantity supplied, this time at 9.9 billion pounds—the point at which the new supply curve (S_1) intersects the demand curve.

Notice that as the price of coffee rose from $1.20 to $2.40, two things happened. First, the quantity demanded declined (a movement along the demand curve) as people shifted to

ECONOMICS IN PRACTICE

Coffee or Tea?

China has a history of more than five thousand years of devotion to tea drinking. Virtually every Chinese city has multiple tea houses, in which many varieties of teas are carefully brewed and served, often in elaborate ceremonies. But, as we all know, China is rapidly changing, and tea-drinking habits are no exception. Chinese consumers have discovered coffee!

Ten years ago many visitors to China came with their own envelopes of instant coffee. Today, Starbucks has more than 600 stores throughout urban China. By 2015 Starbucks expects China to be its largest market. Similar trends are seen throughout emerging markets in Vietnam and India, for example. Some observers suggest that the fast pace of current day China is more compatible with coffee drinking than tea. Perhaps coffee drinking is a complement to economic growth?

The growth of coffee drinking in places like China has left many investors enthusiastic about coffee. With new and large populations now interested in coffee, the world demand for coffee shifts rightward. This is good news for coffee growers. As you already know from this chapter, however, how good that news really is from the point of view of coffee prices depends on the supply side as well!

THINKING PRACTICALLY

1. Show in a graph the effect that the growth in China's interest in coffee will likely have on coffee prices? What features of supply determine how big the price increase will be?

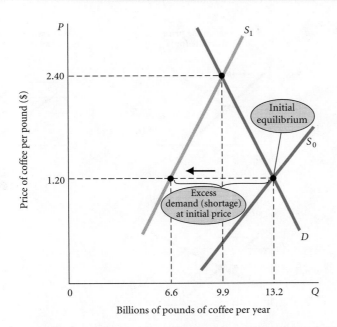

▲ **FIGURE 3.11   The Coffee Market: A Shift of Supply and Subsequent Price Adjustment**
Before the freeze, the coffee market was in equilibrium at a price of $1.20 per pound. At that price, quantity demanded equaled quantity supplied. The freeze shifted the supply curve to the left (from S_0 to S_1), increasing the equilibrium price to $2.40.

substitutes such as tea and hot cocoa. Second, the quantity supplied began to rise, but within the limits imposed by the damage from the freeze. (It might also be that some countries or areas with high costs of production, previously unprofitable, came into production and shipped to the world market at the higher price.) That is, the quantity supplied increased in response to the higher price *along* the new supply curve, which lies to the left of the old supply curve. The final result was a higher price ($2.40), a smaller quantity finally exchanged in the market (9.9 billion pounds), and coffee bought only by those willing to pay $2.40 per pound.

Since many market prices are driven by the interaction of millions of buyers and sellers, it is often difficult to predict how they will change. A series of events in the mid-1990s led to the leftward shift in supply, thus driving up the price of coffee, but the opposite occurred more recently. Today coffee beans are exported by over 50 countries, with Brazil being the largest producer with about 30 percent of the market. Large increases in production have kept prices low. In May 2013, the average price per pound was $1.58.

Figure 3.12 summarizes the possible supply and demand shifts that have been discussed and the resulting changes in equilibrium price and quantity. Study the graphs carefully to ensure that you understand them.

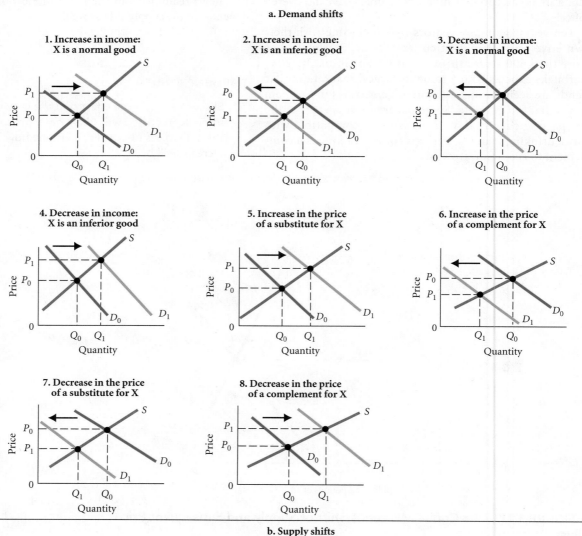

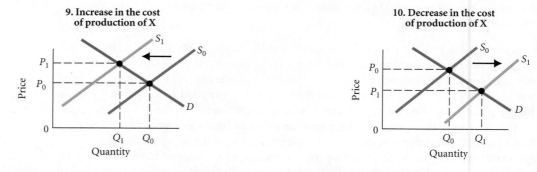

▲ **FIGURE 3.12**   **Examples of Supply and Demand Shifts for Product X**

Demand and Supply in Product Markets: A Review

As you continue your study of economics, you will discover that it is a discipline full of controversy and debate. There is, however, little disagreement about the basic way that the forces of supply and demand operate in free markets. If you hear that a freeze in Florida has destroyed a good portion of the citrus crop, you can bet that the price of oranges will rise. If you read that the weather in the Midwest has been good and a record corn crop is expected, you can bet that corn prices will fall. When fishermen in Massachusetts go on strike and stop bringing in the daily catch, you can bet that the price of local fish will go up.

Here are some important points to remember about the mechanics of supply and demand in product markets:

1. A demand curve shows how much of a product a household would buy if it could buy all it wanted at the given price. A supply curve shows how much of a product a firm would supply if it could sell all it wanted at the given price.
2. Quantity demanded and quantity supplied are always per time period—that is, per day, per month, or per year.
3. The demand for a good is determined by price, household income and wealth, prices of other goods and services, tastes and preferences, and expectations.
4. The supply of a good is determined by price, costs of production, and prices of related products. Costs of production are determined by available technologies of production and input prices.
5. Be careful to distinguish between movements along supply and demand curves and shifts of these curves. When the price of a good changes, the quantity of that good demanded or supplied changes—that is, a movement occurs along the curve. When any other factor that affects supply or demand changes, the curve shifts, or changes position.
6. Market equilibrium exists only when quantity supplied equals quantity demanded at the current price.

Looking Ahead: Markets and the Allocation of Resources

You can already begin to see how markets answer the basic economic questions of what is produced, how it is produced, and who gets what is produced. A firm will produce what is profitable to produce. If the firm can sell a product at a price that is sufficient to ensure a profit after production costs are paid, it will in all likelihood produce that product. Resources will flow in the direction of profit opportunities.

■ Demand curves reflect what people are willing and able to pay for products; demand curves are influenced by incomes, wealth, preferences, prices of other goods, and expectations. Because product prices are determined by the interaction of supply and demand, prices reflect what people are willing to pay. If people's preferences or incomes change, resources will be allocated differently. Consider, for example, an increase in demand—a shift in the market demand curve. Beginning at an equilibrium, households simply begin buying more. At the equilibrium price, quantity demanded becomes greater than quantity supplied. When there is excess demand, prices will rise, and higher prices mean higher profits for firms in the industry. Higher profits, in turn, provide existing firms with an incentive to expand and new firms with an incentive to enter the industry. Thus, the decisions of independent private firms responding to prices and profit opportunities determine *what* will be produced. No central direction is necessary.

Adam Smith saw this self-regulating feature of markets more than 200 years ago:

> Every individual ... by pursuing his own interest ... promotes that of society. He is led ... by an invisible hand to promote an end which was no part of his intention.[4]

---

[4] Adam Smith, *The Wealth of Nations*, Modern Library Edition (New York: Random House, 1937), p. 456 (1st ed., 1776).

ECONOMICS IN PRACTICE

Why Do the Prices of Newspapers Rise?

In 2006, the average price for a daily edition of a Baltimore newspaper was $0.50. In 2007, the average price had risen to $0.75. Three different analysts have three different explanations for the higher equilibrium price.

Analyst 1: The higher price for Baltimore newspapers is good news because it means the population is better informed about public issues. These data clearly show that the citizens of Baltimore have a new, increased regard for newspapers.

Analyst 2: The higher price for Baltimore newspapers is bad news for the citizens of Baltimore. The higher cost of paper, ink, and distribution reflected in these higher prices will further diminish the population's awareness of public issues.

Analyst 3: The higher price for Baltimore newspapers is an unfortunate result of newspapers trying to make money as many consumers have turned to the Internet to access news coverage for free.

As economists, we are faced with two tasks in looking at these explanations: Do they make sense based on what we know about economic principles? And if they do make sense, can we figure out which explanation applies to the case of rising newspaper prices in Baltmore?

What is Analyst 1 saying? Her observation about consumers' new increased regard for newspapers tells us something about the demand curve. Analyst 1 seems to be arguing that tastes have changed in favor of newspapers, which would mean a shift in the demand curve to the right. With upward-sloping supply, such a shift would produce a price increase. So Analyst 1's story is plausible.

Analyst 2 refers to an increased cost of newsprint. This would cause production costs of newspapers to rise, shifting the supply curve to the left. A downward-sloping demand curve also results in increased prices. So Analyst 2 also has a plausible story.

Since Analyst 1 and Analyst 2 have plausible stories based on economic principles, we can look at evidence to see who is in fact right. If you go back to the graphs in Figure 3.12 on p. 70, you will find a clue. When demand shifts to the right (as in Analyst 1's story) the price rises, but so does the quantity as shown in Figure (a). When supply shifts to the left (as in Analyst 2's story) the price rises, but the quantity falls as shown in Figure (b). So we would look at what happened to newspaper circulation during this period to see whether the price increase is from the demand side or the supply side. In fact, in most markets, including Baltimore, quantities of newspapers bought have been falling, so Analyst 2 is most likely correct.

But be careful. Both analysts may be correct. If demand shifts to the right and supply shifts to the left by a greater amount, the price will rise and the quantity sold will fall.

What about Analyst 3? Analyst 3 clearly never had an economics course! Free Internet access to news is a substitute for print media. A decrease in the price of this substitute should shift the demand for newspapers to the left. The result should be a lower price, not a price increase. The fact that the newspaper publishers are "trying to make money" faced with this new competition does not change the laws of supply and demand.

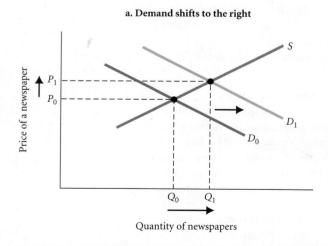

a. Demand shifts to the right

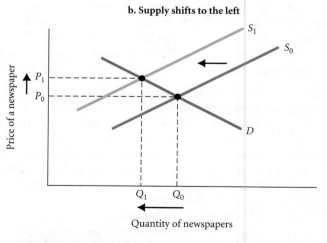

b. Supply shifts to the left

The term Smith coined, the *invisible hand*, has passed into common parlance and is still used by economists to refer to the self-regulation of markets.

■ Firms in business to make a profit have a good reason to choose the best available technology—lower costs mean higher profits. Thus, individual firms determine *how* to produce their products, again with no central direction.

■ So far, we have barely touched on the question of distribution—*who* gets what is produced? You can see part of the answer in the simple supply and demand diagrams. When a good is in short supply, price rises. As they do, those who are willing and able to continue buying do so; others stop buying.

The next chapter begins with a more detailed discussion of these topics. How, exactly, is the final allocation of resources (the mix of output and the distribution of output) determined in a market system?

SUMMARY

1. In societies with many people, production must satisfy wide-ranging tastes and preferences, and producers must therefore specialize.

FIRMS AND HOUSEHOLDS: THE BASIC DECISION-MAKING UNITS *p. 48*

2. A *firm* exists when a person or a group of people decides to produce a product or products by transforming resources, or *inputs*, into *outputs*—the products that are sold in the market. Firms are the primary producing units in a market economy. We assume that firms make decisions to try to maximize profits.

3. *Households* are the primary consuming units in an economy. All households' incomes are subject to constraints.

INPUT MARKETS AND OUTPUT MARKETS: THE CIRCULAR FLOW *p. 48*

4. Households and firms interact in two basic kinds of markets: *product* or *output markets* and *input* or *factor markets*. Goods and services intended for use by households are exchanged in output markets. In output markets, competing firms supply and competing households demand. In input markets, competing firms demand and competing households supply.

5. Ultimately, firms choose the quantities and character of outputs produced, the types and quantities of inputs demanded, and the technologies used in production. Households choose the types and quantities of products demanded and the types and quantities of inputs supplied.

DEMAND IN PRODUCT/OUTPUT MARKETS *p. 50*

6. The quantity demanded of an individual product by an individual household depends on (1) price, (2) income, (3) wealth, (4) prices of other products, (5) tastes and preferences, and (6) expectations about the future.

7. *Quantity demanded* is the amount of a product that an individual household would buy in a given period if it could buy all that it wanted at the current price.

8. A *demand schedule* shows the quantities of a product that a household would buy at different prices. The same information can be presented graphically in a *demand curve*.

9. The *law of demand* states that there is a negative relationship between price and quantity demanded: As price rises, quantity demanded decreases and vice versa. Demand curves slope downward.

10. All demand curves eventually intersect the price axis because there is always a price above which a household cannot or will not pay. Also, all demand curves eventually intersect the quantity axis because demand for most goods is limited, if only by time, even at a zero price.

11. When an increase in income causes demand for a good to rise, that good is a *normal good*. When an increase in income causes demand for a good to fall, that good is an *inferior good*.

12. If a rise in the price of good X causes demand for good Y to increase, the goods are *substitutes*. If a rise in the price of X causes demand for Y to fall, the goods are *complements*.

13. *Market demand* is simply the sum of all the quantities of a good or service demanded per period by all the households buying in the market for that good or service. It is the sum of all the individual quantities demanded at each price.

SUPPLY IN PRODUCT/OUTPUT MARKETS *p. 60*

14. *Quantity supplied* by a firm depends on (1) the price of the good or service; (2) the cost of producing the product, which includes the prices of required inputs and the technologies that can be used to produce the product; and (3) the prices of related products.

15. *Market supply* is the sum of all that is supplied in each period by all producers of a single product. It is the sum of all the individual quantities supplied at each price.

16. It is very important to distinguish between *movements* along demand and supply curves and *shifts* of demand and supply curves. The demand curve shows the relationship between price and quantity demanded. The supply curve shows the relationship between price and quantity supplied. A change

in price is a movement along the curve. Changes in tastes, income, wealth, expectations, or prices of other goods and services cause demand curves to shift; changes in costs, input prices, technology, or prices of related goods and services cause supply curves to shift.

MARKET EQUILIBRIUM *p. 65*

17. When quantity demanded exceeds quantity supplied at the current price, *excess demand* (or a *shortage*) exists and the price tends to rise. When prices in a market rise, quantity demanded falls and quantity supplied rises until an equilibrium is reached at which quantity supplied and quantity demanded are equal. At *equilibrium*, there is no further tendency for price to change.

18. When quantity supplied exceeds quantity demanded at the current price, *excess supply* (or a *surplus*) exists and the price tends to fall. When price falls, quantity supplied decreases and quantity demanded increases until an equilibrium price is reached where quantity supplied and quantity demanded are equal.

--- **REVIEW TERMS AND CONCEPTS** ---

capital market, *p. 49*
complements, complementary goods, *p. 55*
demand curve, *p. 51*
demand schedule, *p. 51*
entrepreneur, *p. 48*
equilibrium, *p. 65*
excess demand *or* shortage, *p. 66*
excess supply *or* surplus, *p. 67*
factors of production, *p. 49*
firm, *p. 48*
households, *p. 48*
income, *p. 54*

inferior goods, *p. 54*
input *or* factor markets, *p. 48*
labor market, *p. 49*
land market, *p. 49*
law of demand, *p. 52*
law of supply, *p. 61*
market demand, *p. 59*
market supply, *p. 64*
movement along a demand curve, *p. 57*
movement along a supply curve, *p. 63*
normal goods, *p. 54*
perfect substitutes, *p. 55*

product *or* output markets, *p. 48*
profit, *p. 60*
quantity demanded, *p. 50*
quantity supplied, *p. 61*
shift of a demand curve, *p. 57*
shift of a supply curve, *p. 63*
substitutes, *p. 55*
supply curve, *p. 61*
supply schedule, *p. 61*
wealth *or* net worth, *p. 54*

--- **PROBLEMS** ---

All problems are available on **MyEconLab**.

1. Illustrate the following with supply and demand curves:
   a. With increased access to wireless technology and lighter weight, the demand for tablet computers has increased substantially. Tablets have also become easier and cheaper to produce as new technology has come online. Despite the shift of demand, prices have fallen.

   b. Cranberry production in Massachusetts totaled 2.35 million barrels in 2011, a 24 percent increase from the 1.89 million barrels produced in 2010. Demand increased by even more than supply, pushing 2011 prices to $44.20 per barrel from $41.90 in 2010.

c. During the high-tech boom in the late 1990s, San Jose office space was in very high demand and rents were very high. With the national recession that began in March 2001, however, the market for office space in San Jose (Silicon Valley) was hit very hard, with rents per square foot falling. In 2005, the employment numbers from San Jose were rising slowly and rents began to rise again. Assume for simplicity that no new office space was built during the period.

d. Before economic reforms were implemented in the countries of Eastern Europe, regulation held the price of bread substantially below equilibrium. When reforms were implemented, prices were deregulated and the price of bread rose dramatically. As a result, the quantity of bread demanded fell and the quantity of bread supplied rose sharply.

e. The steel industry has been lobbying for high taxes on imported steel. Russia, Brazil, and Japan have been producing and selling steel on world markets at $610 per metric ton, well below what equilibrium would be in the United States with no imports. If no imported steel was permitted into the country, the equilibrium price would be $970 per metric ton. Show supply and demand curves for the United States, assuming no imports; then show what the graph would look like if U.S. buyers could purchase all the steel that they wanted from world markets at $610 per metric ton; label the portion of the graph that represents the quantity of imported steel.

2. On Sunday, September 30, the Los Angeles Angels and the Texas Rangers played baseball at Rangers Ballpark in Arlington. Both teams were in pursuit of league championships. Tickets to the game were sold out, and many more fans would have attended if additional tickets had been available. On that same day, the Kansas City Royals and the Cleveland Indians played each other and sold tickets to only 18,099 people in Cleveland.

The Indians stadium, Progressive Field, holds 43,545. Rangers Ballpark in Arlington holds 49,170. Assume for simplicity that tickets to all regular-season games are priced at $40.

a. Draw supply and demand curves for the tickets to each of the two games. (*Hint:* Supply is fixed. It does not change with price.) Draw one graph for each game.

b. Is there a pricing policy that would have filled the ballpark for the Cleveland game?

c. The price system was not allowed to work to ration the Texas tickets when they were initially sold to the public. How do you know? How do you suppose the tickets were rationed?

3. During the last 10 years, Orlando, Florida, grew rapidly, with new jobs luring young people into the area. Despite increases in population and income growth that expanded demand for housing, the price of existing houses barely increased. Why? Illustrate your answer with supply and demand curves.

4. Do you agree or disagree with each of the following statements? Briefly explain your answers and illustrate each with supply and demand curves.

a. The price of a good rises, causing the demand for another good to fall. Therefore, the two goods are substitutes.

b. A shift in supply causes the price of a good to fall. The shift must have been an increase in supply.

c. During 2009, incomes fell sharply for many Americans. This change would likely lead to a decrease in the prices of both normal and inferior goods.

d. Two normal goods cannot be substitutes for each other.

e. If demand increases and supply increases at the same time, price will clearly rise.

f. The price of good A falls. This causes an increase in the price of good B. Therefore, goods A and B are complements.

5. [Related to the *Economics in Practice* on *p. 55*] Merchandise sales for professional sports leagues is a multibillion dollar business, and leagues such as the NBA, NFL, and MLB have very strict licensing rules for official league merchandise. Suppose you are a huge NBA fan and wish to purchase an authentic NBA jersey, size-large. Go to the NBA Store's Website at store.nba.com and click on "Jerseys". Select a team and then click on "Authentic" and find the price of the jerseys. Do the same for two other teams. Would the jerseys you found be considered perfect substitutes or just substitutes? Why? Do you think there are other products available that would be considered substitute products for the authentic jerseys you looked up? Briefly explain.

6. The U.S. government administers two programs that affect the market for cigarettes. Media campaigns and labeling requirements are aimed at making the public aware of the health dangers of cigarettes. At the same time, the Department of Agriculture maintains price supports for tobacco. Under this program, the supported price is above the market equilibrium price and the government limits the amount of land that can be devoted to tobacco production. Are these two programs at odds with the goal of reducing cigarette consumption? As part of your answer, illustrate graphically the effects of both policies on the market for cigarettes.

7. During the period 2006 through 2010, housing production in the United States fell from a rate of over 2.27 million housing starts per year to a rate of under 500,000, a decrease of over 80 percent. At the same time, the number of new households slowed to a trickle. Students without a job moved in with their parents, fewer immigrants came to the United States, and more of those already here went home. If there are fewer households, it is a decline in demand. If fewer new units are built, it is a decline in supply.

a. Draw a standard supply and demand diagram which shows the demand for new housing units that are purchased each month, and the supply of new units built and put on the market each month. Assume that the quantity supplied and quantity demanded are equal at 45,000 units and at a price of $200,000.

b. On the same diagram show a decline in demand. What would happen if this market behaved like most markets?

c. Now suppose that prices did not change immediately. Sellers decided not to adjust price even though demand is below supply. What would happen to the number of homes for sale (the inventory of unsold new homes) if prices stayed the same following the drop in demand?

d. Now supposed that the supply of new homes put on the market dropped, but price still stayed the same at $200,000. Can you tell a story that brings the market back to equilibrium without a drop in price?

e. Go to www.census.gov/newhomesales. Look at the current press release, which contains data for the most recent month and the past year. What trends can you observe?

8. The following sets of statements contain common errors. Identify and explain each error:

   a. Demand increases, causing prices to rise. Higher prices cause demand to fall. Therefore, prices fall back to their original levels.

   b. The supply of meat in Russia increases, causing meat prices to fall. Lower prices mean that the demand for meat in Russian households will increase

9. For each of the following statements, draw a diagram that illustrates the likely effect on the market for eggs. Indicate in each case the impact on equilibrium price and equilibrium quantity.

   a. The surgeon general warns that high-cholesterol foods cause heart attacks.

   b. The price of bacon, a complementary product, decreases.

   c. The price of chicken feed increases.

   d. Caesar salads become trendy at dinner parties. (The dressing is made with raw eggs.)

   e. A technological innovation reduces egg breakage during packing.

*10. Suppose the demand and supply curves for eggs in the United States are given by the following equations:

$$Q_d = 100 - 20P$$

$$Q_s = 10 + 40P$$

where Q_d = millions of dozens of eggs Americans would like to buy each year; Q_s = millions of dozens of eggs U.S. farms would like to sell each year; and P = price per dozen eggs.

   a. Fill in the following table:

PRICE (PER DOZEN)	QUANTITY DEMANDED (Q_d)	QUANTITY SUPPLIED (Q_s)
$ .50	____	____
$ 1.00	____	____
$ 1.50	____	____
$ 2.00	____	____
$ 2.50	____	____

   b. Use the information in the table to find the equilibrium price and quantity.

   c. Graph the demand and supply curves and identify the equilibrium price and quantity.

11. Housing policy analysts debate the best way to increase the number of housing units available to low-income households. One strategy—the demand-side strategy—is to provide people with housing vouchers, paid for by the government, that can be used to rent housing supplied by the private market. Another—a supply-side strategy—is to have the government subsidize housing suppliers or to build public housing.

   a. Illustrate supply- and demand-side strategies using supply and demand curves. Which results in higher rents?

   b. Critics of housing vouchers (the demand-side strategy) argue that because the supply of housing to low-income households is limited and does not respond to higher rents, demand vouchers will serve only to drive up rents and make landlords better off. Illustrate their point with supply and demand curves.

*12. Suppose the market demand for pizza is given by $Q_d = 300 - 20P$ and the market supply for pizza is given by $Q_s = 20P - 100$, where P = price (per pizza).

   a. Graph the supply and demand schedules for pizza using $5 through $15 as the value of P.

   b. In equilibrium, how many pizzas would be sold and at what price?

   c. What would happen if suppliers set the price of pizza at $15? Explain the market adjustment process.

   d. Suppose the price of hamburgers, a substitute for pizza, doubles. This leads to a doubling of the demand for pizza. (At each price, consumers demand twice as much pizza as before.) Write the equation for the new market demand for pizza.

   e. Find the new equilibrium price and quantity of pizza.

13. [Related to the *Economics in Practice* on p. 69] The growing popularity of coffee in China has had an impact on the market for tea. Draw a supply and demand graph that shows how this increase in demand for coffee has affected the market for tea. Describe what has happened to the equilibrium price and quantity of tea. What could tea producers do to return the price or quantity to the initial equilibrium price or quantity? Briefly explain if it is possible for tea producers to return both the price and quantity to the initial equilibriums without a change in consumer behavior.

14. [Related to the *Economics in Practice* on p. 72] Analyst 1 suggested that the demand curve for newspapers in Baltimore might have shifted to the right because people were becoming more literate. Think of two other plausible stories that would result in this demand curve shifting to the right.

15. Explain whether each of the following statements describes a change in demand or a change in quantity demanded, and specify whether each change represents an increase or a decrease.

   a. Baby Steps Footwear experiences a 40 percent increase in sales of baby shoes during a 3-day, half-price sale.

   b. Tabitha gets a promotion and 15 percent increase in her salary and decides to reward herself by purchasing a new 3-D television.

   c. When the price of peaches unexpectedly rises, many consumers choose to purchase plums instead.

   d. Due to potential problems with its braking system, Asteriod Motors has experienced a decline in sales of its Galactica automobile.

   e. Antonio, an accountant working for the city of Santa Cristina, decides to forego his annual vacation to Hawaii when word leaks out that the city may be cutting all employees' salaries by 10 percent at the end of the year.

16. For each of the five statements (a–e) in the previous question, draw a demand graph representing the appropriate change in quantity demanded or change in demand.

17. Until 2008, General Motors held the title of the world's largest automobile manufacturer for 78 years. The recession of

* Note: Problems marked with an asterisk are more challenging.

2007–2009 and its accompanying financial crisis saw GM declare bankruptcy, receive over $50 billion in government bailout funds, and experience a significant decrease in demand for its products. One area where GM saw huge declines in demand was its highly profitable large truck and SUV sector. In response to the fall in demand, GM drastically reduced the production of large trucks and SUVs, including discontinuing its Hummer brand. Explain what determinants of household demand contributed to the decision by GM to significantly reduce production of its large trucks and SUVs.

18. The market for manicures is made up of five firms, and the data in the following table represents each firm's quantity supplied at various prices. Fill in the column for the quantity supplied in the market, and draw a supply graph showing the market data.

Quantity supplied by:

PRICE	FIRM A	FIRM B	FIRM C	FIRM D	FIRM E	MARKET
$10	3	2	0	2	4	
20	4	4	2	3	5	
30	5	6	3	4	7	
40	6	8	5	5	8	

19. The following table represents the market for disposable digital cameras. Plot this data on a supply and demand graph and identify the equilibrium price and quantity. Explain what would happen if the market price is set at $30, and show this on the graph. Explain what would happen if the market price is set at $15, and show this on the graph.

PRICE	QUANTITY DEMANDED	QUANTITY SUPPLIED
$ 5.00	15	0
10.00	13	3
15.00	11	6
20.00	9	9
25.00	7	12
30.00	5	15
35.00	3	18

Demand and Supply Applications

4

Every society has a system of institutions that determines what is produced, how it is produced, and who gets what is produced. In some societies, these decisions are made centrally, through planning agencies or by government directive. However, in every society, many decisions are made in a *decentralized* way, through the operation of markets.

Markets exist in all societies, and Chapter 3 provided a bare-bones description of how markets operate. In this chapter, we continue our examination of demand, supply, and the price system.

The Price System: Rationing and Allocating Resources

The market system, also called the *price system*, performs two important and closely related functions. First, it provides an automatic mechanism for distributing scarce goods and services. That is, it serves as a **price rationing** device for allocating goods and services to consumers when the quantity demanded exceeds the quantity supplied. Second, the price system ultimately determines both the allocation of resources among producers and the final mix of outputs.

Price Rationing

Consider the simple process by which the price system eliminates a shortage. Figure 4.1 shows hypothetical supply and demand curves for wheat. Wheat is produced around the world, with large supplies coming from Russia and from the United States. Wheat is sold in a world market and used to produce a range of food products, from cereals and breads to processed foods, which line the kitchens of the average consumer. Wheat is thus demanded by large food companies as they produce breads, cereals, and cake for households.

price rationing The process by which the market system allocates goods and services to consumers when quantity demanded exceeds quantity supplied.

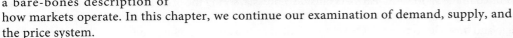

LEARNING OBJECTIVES

Describe the function of price rationing

Discuss the uses and effects of price ceilings, nonprice rationing systems, and price floors

Analyze the economic impact of an oil import tax

Distinguish between consumer surplus and producer surplus and explain the role of each in market efficiency

As Figure 4.1 shows, the equilibrium price of wheat was $160 per millions of metric tons in the spring of 2010. At this price, farmers from around the world were expected to bring 61.7 million metric tons to market. Supply and demand were equal. Market equilibrium existed at a price of $160 per millions of metric tons because at that price, quantity demanded was equal to quantity supplied. (Remember that equilibrium occurs at the point where the supply and demand curves intersect. In Figure 4.1, this occurs at point C.)

In the summer of 2010, Russia experienced its warmest summer on record. Fires swept through Russia, destroying a substantial portion of the Russian wheat crop. With almost a third of the world wheat normally produced in Russia, the effect of this environmental disaster on world wheat supply was substantial. In the figure, the supply curve for wheat, which had been drawn in expectation of harvesting all the wheat planted in Russia along with the rest of the world, now shifted to the left, from $S_{spring\ 2010}$ to $S_{fall\ 2010}$. This shift in the supply curve created a situation of excess demand at the old price of $160. At that price, the quantity demanded is 61.7 million metric tons but the burning of much of the Russia supply left the world with only 35 millions of metric tons expected to be supplied. Quantity demanded exceeded quantity supplied at the original price by 26.7 million metric tons.

The reduced supply caused the price of wheat to rise sharply. As the price rises, the available supply is "rationed." Those who are willing and able to pay the most get it. You can see the market's rationing function clearly in Figure 4.1. As the price rises from $160, the quantity demanded declines along the demand curve, moving from point C (61.7 million tons) toward point B (41.5 million tons). The higher prices mean that prices for products like Pepperidge Farm bread and Shredded Wheat cereal, which use wheat as an essential ingredient, also rise. People bake fewer cakes, and begin to eat more rye bread and switch from Shredded Wheat to Corn Flakes in response to the price changes.

As prices rise, wheat farmers also change their behavior, though supply responsiveness is limited in the short term. Farmers outside of Russia, seeing the price rise, harvest their crops more carefully, getting more precious grains from each stalk. Perhaps some wheat is taken out of storage and brought to market. Quantity supplied increases from 35 million metric tons (point A) to 41.5 million tons (point B). The price increase has encouraged farmers who can to make up for part of the Russia wheat loss.

A new equilibrium is established at a price of $247 per millions of metric tons, with 41.5 million tons transacted. The market has determined who gets the wheat: *The lower total supply is rationed to those who are willing and able to pay the higher price.*

This idea of "willingness to pay" is central to the distribution of available supply, and willingness depends on both desire (preferences) and income/wealth. Willingness to pay does not necessarily mean that only the very rich will continue to buy wheat when the price increases.

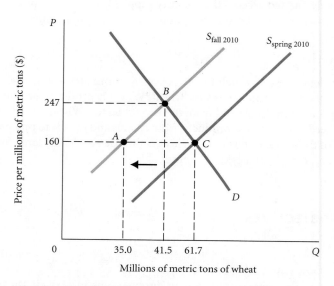

▲ **FIGURE 4.1** **The Market for Wheat**
Fires in Russia in the summer of 2010 caused a shift in the world's supply of wheat to the left, causing the price to increase from $160 per millions of metric tons to $247. The equilibrium moved from C to B.

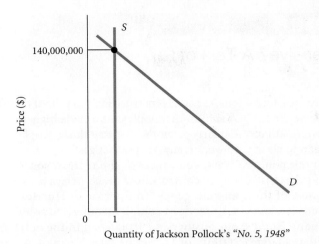

◀ FIGURE 4.2
Market for a Rare Painting
There is some price that will clear any market, even if supply is strictly limited. In an auction for a unique painting, the price (bid) will rise to eliminate excess demand until there is only one bidder willing to purchase the single available painting. Some estimate that the *Mona Lisa* would sell for $600 million if auctioned.

For anyone to continue to buy wheat at a higher price, his or her enjoyment comes at a higher cost in terms of other goods and services.

In sum:

> The adjustment of price is the rationing mechanism in free markets. Price rationing means that whenever there is a need to ration a good—that is, when a shortage exists—in a free market, the price of the good will rise until quantity supplied equals quantity demanded—that is, until the market clears.

There is some price that will clear any market you can think of. Consider the market for a famous painting such as Jackson Pollock's *No. 5, 1948*, illustrated in Figure 4.2. At a low price, there would be an enormous excess demand for such an important painting. The price would be bid up until there was only one remaining demander. Presumably, that price would be very high. In fact, the Pollock painting sold for a record $140 million in 2006. If the product is in strictly scarce supply, as a single painting is, its price is said to be *demand-determined*. That is, its price is determined solely and exclusively by the amount that the highest bidder or highest bidders are willing to pay.

One might interpret the statement that "there is some price that will clear any market" to mean "everything has its price," but that is not exactly what it means. Suppose you own a small silver bracelet that has been in your family for generations. It is quite possible that you would not sell it for *any* amount of money. Does this mean that the market is not working, or that quantity supplied and quantity demanded are not equal? Not at all. It simply means that *you* are the highest bidder. By turning down all bids, you must be willing to forgo what anybody offers for it.

Constraints on the Market and Alternative Rationing Mechanisms

On occasion, both governments and private firms decide to use some mechanism other than the market system to ration an item for which there is excess demand at the current price. Policies designed to stop price rationing are commonly justified in a number of ways.

The rationale most often used is fairness. It is not "fair" to let landlords charge high rents, not fair for oil companies to run up the price of gasoline, not fair for insurance companies to charge enormous premiums, and so on. After all, the argument goes, we have no choice but to pay—housing and insurance are necessary, and one needs gasoline to get to work. The Economics in Practice box on page 82 describes complaints against price increases following Hurricane Sandy in 2012.

Preventing price from rising to equilibrium is justified on several grounds, among them (1) that price-gouging is bad, (2) that income is unfairly distributed, and (3) that some items are

ECONOMICS IN PRACTICE

Why Is My Hotel Room So Expensive? A Tale of Hurricane Sandy

In October 2012 Hurricane Sandy hit the northeastern United States. In New York, New Jersey, and Connecticut flooding in particular caused disruption. In the aftermath of the storm, as individuals and public workers began to clean up, prices for a number of items began to rise. At this point, you should be able to predict which prices likely rose the most.

Before Sandy struck we would expect that most of the markets in these states, as in other areas, were more or less in equilibrium. The only merchants who actually *could* raise prices after the storm are ones who face either a large shift to the right of the demand curve facing them or a shift to the left of the supply curve in their market. Otherwise, if merchants post Sandy raised prices, they would simply end up with surplus goods on the shelf. So if we want to predict which prices rose post Sandy, all we need to do is to look at those businesses facing large shifts in either their demand or supply curves after the storm. With many people forced out of their homes, hotel rooms became scarce. With power out, generators became more valuable. With trees down, tree removal services heard from many more customers. In other words, all of these businesses saw a large shift out of demand curves in their markets and none would find it easy to quickly increase their output levels. One can't really build a Holiday Inn overnight! Higher prices were now possible.

As it turned out, gas prices at the pump also rose. Yet one might well have thought that following Sandy, people would drive less, given the conditions of roads and business closings. Here, the more likely problem was a shift in the supply curve, as delivery trucks found it hard to restock gas stations. A shift in the supply curve made higher prices possible, particularly given the fact that those people who did need to go to work really needed that gas!

As we suggest in the text, in some cases government policy controls how much prices *are allowed* to rise after an emergency. In the case of Hurricane Sandy, all three states lodged complaints of price gouging against numerous businesses, virtually all in the hotel, tree removal, gas station, or generator sales business. In New Jersey, a law against gouging prohibits price increases of more than 10% in an emergency situation. Connecticut and New York are more graphic in their definitions, but less precise. In these states, price gouging involves price increases in emergencies which are "unconscionably excessive." Economics will not be much help in translating that definition into a number. But at this point we hope you can see that economics can very much help us predict what kinds of businesses are likely to be charged with the offense.

THINKING PRACTICALLY

1. Gas prices rose after Sandy as supply shifted to the left, or inward, given transport problems. Transport problems likely also affected the delivery of Cheerios. Do you expect the price of Cheerios to also rise substantially? Why or why not?

necessities and everyone should be able to buy them at a "reasonable" price. Regardless of the rationale, the following examples will make two things clear:

1. Attempts to bypass price rationing in the market and to use alternative rationing devices are more difficult and more costly than they would seem at first glance.
2. Very often such attempts distribute costs and benefits among households in unintended ways.

Oil, Gasoline, and OPEC
One of the most important prices in the world is the price of crude oil. Millions of barrels of oil are traded every day. It is a major input into virtually every product produced. It heats our homes, and it is used to produce the gasoline that runs our cars. Its production has led to massive environmental disasters as well as wars. Its price has fluctuated wildly, leading to major macroeconomic problems. But oil is like other commodities in that its price is determined by the basic forces of supply and demand. Oil provides a good example of how markets work and how markets sometimes fail.

The Organization of the Petroleum Exporting Countries (OPEC) is an organization of twelve countries (Algeria, Angola, Ecuador, Iran, Iraq, Kuwait, Libya, Nigeria, Qatar, Saudi Arabia, the United Arab Emirates, and Venezuela) that together controlled about one-third of the known supply of oil in the year 2010. In 1973 and 1974, OPEC imposed an embargo on shipments of crude oil to the United States. What followed was a drastic reduction in the quantity of gasoline available at local gas pumps.

Had the market system been allowed to operate, refined gasoline prices would have increased dramatically until quantity supplied was equal to quantity demanded. However, the government decided that rationing gasoline only to those who were willing and able to pay the most was unfair, and Congress imposed a **price ceiling**, or maximum price, of $0.57 per gallon of leaded regular gasoline. That price ceiling was intended to keep gasoline "affordable," but it also perpetuated the shortage. At the restricted price, quantity demanded remained greater than quantity supplied, and the available gasoline had to be divided up somehow among all potential demanders.

You can see the effects of the price ceiling by looking carefully at Figure 4.3. If the price had been set by the interaction of supply and demand, it would have increased to approximately $1.50 per gallon. Instead, Congress made it illegal to sell gasoline for more than $0.57 per gallon. At that price, quantity demanded exceeded quantity supplied and a shortage existed. Because the price system was not allowed to function, an alternative rationing system had to be found to distribute the available supply of gasoline.

Several devices were tried. The most common of all nonprice rationing systems is **queuing**, a term that means waiting in line. During 1974, very long lines formed daily at gas stations, starting as early as 5 A.M. Under this system, gasoline went to those people who were willing to pay the most, but the sacrifice was measured in hours and aggravation instead of dollars.[1]

price ceiling A maximum price that sellers may charge for a good, usually set by government.

queuing Waiting in line as a means of distributing goods and services: a nonprice rationing mechanism.

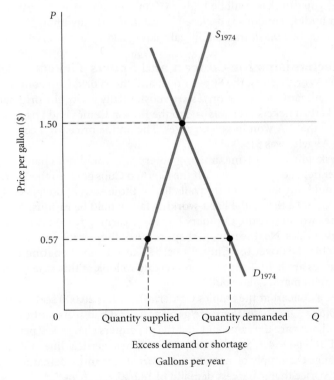

▲ **FIGURE 4.3 Excess Demand (Shortage) Created by a Price Ceiling**
In 1974, a ceiling price of $0.57 cents per gallon of leaded regular gasoline was imposed. If the price had been set by the interaction of supply and demand instead, it would have increased to approximately $1.50 per gallon. At $0.57 per gallon, the quantity demanded exceeded the quantity supplied. Because the price system was not allowed to function, an alternative rationing system had to be found to distribute the available supply of gasoline.

---

[1] You can also show formally that the result is inefficient—that there is a resulting net loss of total value to society. First, there is the cost of waiting in line. Time has a value. With price rationing, no one has to wait in line and the value of that time is saved. Second, there may be additional lost value if the gasoline ends up in the hands of someone who places a lower value on it than someone else who gets no gas. Suppose, for example, that the market price of gasoline if unconstrained would rise to $2 but that the government has it fixed at $1. There will be long lines to get gas. Imagine that to motorist A, 10 gallons of gas is worth $35 but that she fails to get gas because her time is too valuable to wait in line. To motorist B, 10 gallons is worth only $15, but his time is worth much less, so he gets the gas. In the end, A could pay B for the gas and both would be better off. If A pays B $30 for the gas, A is $5 better off and B is $15 better off. In addition, A does not have to wait in line. Thus, the allocation that results from nonprice rationing involves a net loss of value. Such losses are called *deadweight losses*. See p. 92 of this chapter.

favored customers Those who receive special treatment from dealers during situations of excess demand.

A second nonprice rationing device used during the gasoline crisis was that of **favored customers**. Many gas station owners decided not to sell gasoline to the general public, but to reserve their scarce supplies for friends and favored customers. Not surprisingly, many customers tried to become "favored" by offering side payments to gas station owners. Owners also charged high prices for service. By doing so, they increased the actual price of gasoline but hid it in service overcharges to get around the ceiling.

ration coupons Tickets or coupons that entitle individuals to purchase a certain amount of a given product per month.

Yet another method of dividing up available supply is the use of **ration coupons**. It was suggested in both 1974 and 1979 that families be given ration tickets or coupons that would entitle them to purchase a certain number of gallons of gasoline each month. That way, everyone would get the same amount regardless of income. Such a system had been employed in the United States during the 1940s when wartime price ceilings on meat, sugar, butter, tires, nylon stockings, and many other items were imposed.

When ration coupons are used with no prohibition against trading them, however, the result is almost identical to a system of price rationing. Those who are willing and able to pay the most buy up the coupons and use them to purchase gasoline, chocolate, fresh eggs, or anything else that is sold at a restricted price.[2] This means that the price of the restricted good will effectively rise to the market-clearing price. For instance, suppose that you decide not to sell your ration coupon. You are then forgoing what you would have received by selling the coupon. Thus, the "effective" price of the good you purchase will be higher (if only in opportunity cost) than the restricted price. Even when trading coupons is declared illegal, it is virtually impossible to stop black markets from developing. In a **black market**, illegal trading takes place at market-determined prices.

black market A market in which illegal trading takes place at market-determined prices.

Rationing Mechanisms for Concert and Sports Tickets

Tickets for sporting events such as the World Series, the Super Bowl, and the World Cup command huge prices in the open market. In many cases, the prices are substantially above the original issue price. One of the hottest basketball tickets ever was one to the Boston Celtics and Los Angeles Lakers' NBA final series in 2010 that LA won in seven games. The online price for a courtside seat to one of the games in Los Angeles was $19,000.

You might ask why a profit-maximizing enterprise would not charge the highest price it could? The answer depends on the event. If the Chicago Cubs got into the World Series, the people of Chicago would buy all the tickets available for thousands of dollars each. But if the Cubs actually *charged* $2,000 a ticket, the hard-working fans would be furious: "Greedy Cubs Gouge Fans" the headlines would scream. Ordinary loyal fans earning reasonable salaries would not be able to afford those prices. Next season, perhaps some of those irate fans would change loyalties, supporting the White Sox over the Cubs. In part to keep from alienating loyal fans, prices for championship games are held down. It is interesting to look at this case to see how charging a ticket price lower than market plays out.

Let's consider a concert at the Staples Center, which has 20,000 seats. The supply of tickets is thus fixed at 20,000. Of course, there are good seats and bad seats, but to keep things simple, let's assume that all seats are the same and that the promoters charge $50 per ticket for all tickets. This is illustrated in Figure 4.4. Supply is represented by a vertical line at 20,000. Changing the price does not change the supply of seats. In the figure the quantity demanded at the price of $50 is 38,000, so at this price there is excess demand of 18,000.

Who would get to buy the $50 tickets? As in the case of gasoline, a variety of rationing mechanisms might be used. The most common is queuing, waiting in line. The tickets would go on sale at a particular time, and people would show up and wait. Now ticket sellers have virtual waiting rooms online. Tickets for the World Series go on sale at a particular time in September, and the people who log on to team Web sites at the right moment get into an electronic queue and can buy tickets. Often tickets are sold out in a matter of minutes.

There are also, of course, favored customers. Those who get tickets without queuing are local politicians, sponsors, and friends of the artist or friends of the players.

But "once the dust settles," the power of technology and the concept of *opportunity cost* take over. Even if you get the ticket for the (relatively) low price of $50, that is not the true cost.

---

[2] Of course, if you are assigned a number of tickets and you sell them, you are better off than you would be with price rationing. Ration coupons thus serve as a way redistributing income.

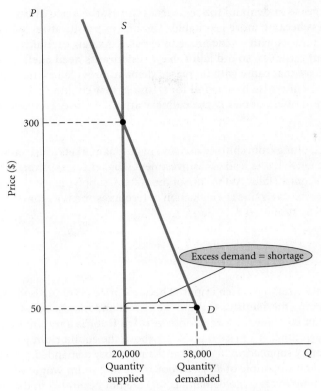

▲ **FIGURE 4.4   Supply of and Demand for a Concert at the Staples Center**
At the face-value price of $50, there is excess demand for seats to the concert. At $50 the quantity demanded is greater than the quantity supplied, which is fixed at 20,000 seats. The diagram shows that the quantity demanded would equal the quantity supplied at a price of $300 per ticket.

The true cost is what you give up to sit in the seat. If people on eBay, StubHub, or Ticketmaster are willing to pay $300 for your ticket, that's what you must pay, or sacrifice, to go to the concert. Many people—even strong fans—will choose to sell that ticket. Once again, it is difficult to stop the market from rationing the tickets to those people who are willing and able to pay the most.

No matter how good the intentions of private organizations and governments, it is very difficult to prevent the price system from operating and to stop people's willingness to pay from asserting itself. Every time an alternative is tried, the price system seems to sneak in the back door. With favored customers and black markets, the final distribution may be even more unfair than what would result from simple price rationing.

Prices and the Allocation of Resources

Thinking of the market system as a mechanism for allocating scarce goods and services among competing demanders is very revealing, but the market determines more than just the distribution of final outputs. It also determines what gets produced and how resources are allocated among competing uses.

Consider a change in consumer preferences that leads to an increase in demand for a specific good or service. During the 1980s, for example, people began going to restaurants more frequently than before. Researchers think that this trend, which continues today, is partially the result of social changes (such as a dramatic rise in the number of two-earner families) and partially the result of rising incomes. The market responded to this change in demand by shifting resources, both capital and labor, into more and better restaurants.

With the increase in demand for restaurant meals, the price of eating out rose and the restaurant business became more profitable. The higher profits attracted new businesses and provided old restaurants with an incentive to expand. As new capital, seeking profits, flowed into the restaurant business, so did labor. New restaurants need chefs. Chefs need training, and the higher wages that came with increased demand provided an incentive for them to get it. In response to the increase in demand for training, new cooking schools opened and existing schools began to offer courses in the culinary arts. This story could go on and on, but the point is clear:

> Price changes resulting from shifts of demand in output markets cause profits to rise or fall. Profits attract capital; losses lead to disinvestment. Higher wages attract labor and encourage workers to acquire skills. At the core of the system, supply, demand, and prices in input and output markets determine the allocation of resources and the ultimate combinations of goods and services produced.

Price Floor

price floor A minimum price below which exchange is not permitted.

minimum wage A price floor set for the price of labor.

As we have seen, price ceilings, often imposed because price rationing is viewed as unfair, result in alternative rationing mechanisms that are inefficient and may be equally unfair. Some of the same arguments can be made for price floors. A **price floor** is a minimum price below which exchange is not permitted. If a price floor is set above the equilibrium price, the result will be excess supply; quantity supplied will be greater than quantity demanded.

The most common example of a price floor is the **minimum wage**, which is a floor set for the price of labor. Employers (who demand labor) are not permitted under federal law to pay a wage less than $7.25 per hour (in 2012) to workers (who supply labor). Critics argue that since the minimum wage is above equilibrium, the result will be wasteful unemployment. At the wage of $7.25, the quantity of labor demanded is less than the quantity of labor supplied. Whenever a price floor is set above equilibrium, there will be an excess supply.

Supply and Demand Analysis: An Oil Import Fee

The basic logic of supply and demand is a powerful tool of analysis. As an extended example of the power of this logic, we will consider a proposal to impose a tax on imported oil. The idea of taxing imported oil is hotly debated, and the tools we have learned thus far will show us the effects of such a tax.

In 2012 the United States imported 45% of its oil. Of the imports, 22% come from the Persian Gulf States. Given the political volatility of that area of the world, many politicians have advocated trying to reduce our dependence on foreign oil. One tool often suggested by both politicians and economists to accomplish this goal has been an import oil tax or tariff.

Supply and demand analysis makes the arguments of the import tax proponents easier to understand. Figure 4.5(a) shows the U.S. market for oil as of late 2012. The world price of oil is at just over $80, and the United States is assumed to be able to buy *all the oil that it wants* at this price. This means that domestic producers cannot charge any more than $80 per barrel. The curve labeled *Supply*$_{US}$ shows the amount that domestic suppliers will produce at each price level. At a price of $80, domestic production is 7 million barrels per day. U.S. producers will produce at point *A* on the supply curve. The total quantity of oil demanded in the United States in 2012 was approximately 13 million barrels per day. At a price of $80, the quantity demanded in the United States is point *B* on the demand curve.

The difference between the total quantity demanded (13 million barrels per day) and domestic production (7 million barrels per day) is total imports (6 million barrels per day).

Now suppose that the government levies a tax of $33\frac{1}{3}$ percent on imported oil. Because the import price is $80, this tax rate translates into a tax of $26.64, which increases the price per barrel paid by U.S. importers to $106.64 ($80 + $26.64). This new, higher price means that U.S. producers can also charge up to $106.64 for a barrel of crude. Note, however, that the tax is paid only on imported oil. Thus, the entire 106.64 paid for domestic crude goes to domestic producers.

Figure 4.5(b) shows the result of the tax. First, because of a higher price, the quantity demanded drops. This is a movement *along* the demand curve from point *B* to point *D*. At the same time, the quantity supplied by domestic producers increases. This is a movement *along* the supply curve from point *A* to point *C*. With an increase in domestic quantity supplied and a decrease in domestic quantity demanded, imports decrease, as we can see clearly as Q_d-Q_c is smaller than the original 6 billions barrels per day.

The tax also generates revenues for the federal government. The total tax revenue collected is equal to the tax per barrel ($26.64) times the number of imported barrels (Q_d-Q_c).

What does all of this mean? In the final analysis, an oil import fee would increase domestic production and reduce overall consumption. To the extent that one believes that Americans are consuming too much oil, the reduced consumption may be a good thing. We also see that the tax increases the price of oil in the United States.

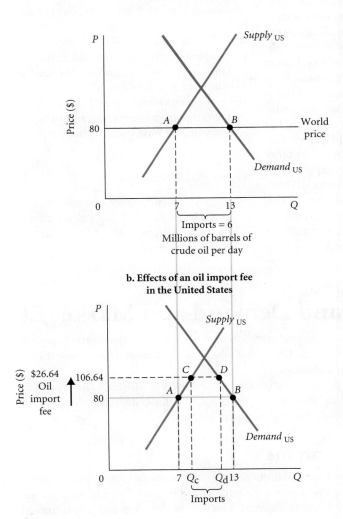

a. U.S. market, 2012

b. Effects of an oil import fee in the United States

◀ **FIGURE 4.5**
The U.S. Market for Crude Oil, 2012

In 2012 the world market price for crude oil was approximately $80 per barrel. Domestic production in the United States that year averaged about 7 million barrels per day, while crude oil demand averaged just under 13 million barrels per day. The difference between production and consumption were made up of net imports of approximately 6 million barrels per day, as we see in panel (a).

If the government imposed a tax in this market of 33.33%, or $26.64, that would increase the world price to $106.64. That higher price causes quantity demanded to fall below its original level of 13 million barrels, while the price increase causes domestic production to rise above the original level. As we see in panel b, the effect is a reduction in import levels.

ECONOMICS IN PRACTICE

The Price Mechanism at Work for Shakespeare

Every summer, New York City puts on free performances of Shakespeare in the Park. Tickets are distributed on a first-come-first-serve basis at the Delacorte Theatre in the park beginning at 1 P.M. on the day of the show. People usually begin lining up at 6 A.M. when the park opens; by 10 A.M. the line has typically reached a length sufficient to give away all available tickets.

When you examine the people standing in line for these tickets, most of them seem to be fairly young. Many carry book bags identifying them as students in one of New York's many colleges. Of course, all college students may be fervent Shakespeare fans, but can you think of another reason for the composition of the line? Further, when you attend one of the plays and look around, the audience appears much older and much sleeker than the people who were standing in line. What is going on?

While the tickets are "free" in terms of financial costs, their true price includes the value of the time spent standing in line. Thus, the tickets are cheaper for people (for example, students) whose time value is lower than they are for high-wage earners, like an investment banker from Goldman Sachs. The true cost of a ticket is $0 plus the opportunity cost of the time spent in line. If the average person spends 4 hours in line, as is done in the Central Park case, for someone with a high wage, the true cost of the ticket might be very high. For example, a lawyer who earns $300 an hour would be giving up $1,200 to wait in line. It should not surprise you to see more people waiting in line for whom the tickets are inexpensive.

What about the people who are at the performance? Think about our discussion of the power of entrepreneurs. In this case, the students who stand in line as consumers of the tickets also can play a role as producers. In fact, the students can produce tickets relatively cheaply by waiting in line. They

can then turn around and sell those tickets to the high-wage Shakespeare lovers. These days eBay is a great source of tickets to free events, sold by individuals with low opportunity costs of their time who queued up. Craigslist even provides listings for people who are willing to wait in line for you.

Of course, now and again we do encounter a busy businessperson in one of the Central Park lines. Recently, one of the authors encountered one and asked him why he was waiting in line rather than using eBay, and he replied that it reminded him of when he was young, waiting in line for rock concerts.

THINKING PRACTICALLY

1. Many museums offer free admission one day a week, on a week day. On that day we observe that museum goers are more likely to be senior citizens than on a typical Saturday. Why?

Supply and Demand and Market Efficiency

Clearly, supply and demand curves help explain the way that markets and market prices work to allocate scarce resources. Recall that when we try to understand "how the system works," we are doing "positive economics."

Supply and demand curves can also be used to illustrate the idea of market efficiency, an important aspect of "normative economics." To understand the ideas, you first must understand the concepts of consumer and producer surplus.

Consumer Surplus

The argument, made several times already, that the market forces us to reveal a great deal about our personal preferences is an extremely important one, and it bears repeating at least once more here. If you are free to choose within the constraints imposed by prices and your income and you decide to buy, for example, a hamburger for $2.50, you have "revealed" that a hamburger is worth at least $2.50 to you.

A simple market demand curve such as the one in Figure 4.6(a) illustrates this point quite clearly. At the current market price of $2.50, consumers will purchase 7 million hamburgers

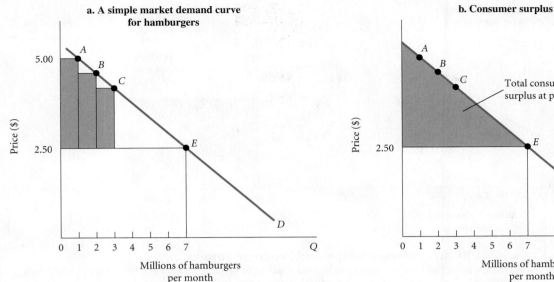

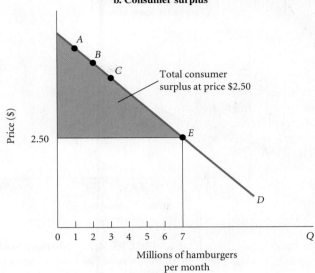

▲ **FIGURE 4.6   Market Demand and Consumer Surplus**
As illustrated in Figure 4.6(a), some consumers (see point *A*) are willing to pay as much as $5.00 each
for hamburgers. Since the market price is just $2.50, they receive a consumer surplus of $2.50 for each
hamburger that they consume. Others (see point *B*) are willing to pay something less than $5.00 and receive
a slightly smaller surplus. Since the market price of hamburgers is just $2.50, the area of the shaded triangle
in Figure 4.6(b) is equal to total consumer surplus.

per month. There is only one price in the market, and the demand curve tells us how many
hamburgers households would buy if they could purchase all they wanted at the posted price of
$2.50. Anyone who values a hamburger at $2.50 or more will buy it. Anyone who does not value
a hamburger that highly will not buy it.

Some people, however, value hamburgers at more than $2.50. As Figure 4.6(a) shows,
even if the price were $5.00, consumers would still buy 1 million hamburgers. If these peo-
ple were able to buy the good at a price of $2.50, they would earn a **consumer surplus.**
Consumer surplus is the difference between the maximum amount a person is willing to pay
for a good and its current market price. The consumer surplus earned by the people willing
to pay $5.00 for a hamburger is approximately equal to the shaded area between point *A* and
the price, $2.50.

The second million hamburgers in Figure 4.6(a) are valued at more than the market price as
well, although the consumer surplus gained is slightly less. Point *B* on the market demand curve
shows the maximum amount that consumers would be willing to pay for the second million hamburgers. The consumer surplus earned by these people is equal to the shaded area between *B* and
the price, $2.50. Similarly, for the third million hamburgers, maximum willingness to pay is given
by point *C*; consumer surplus is a bit lower than it is at points *A* and *B*, but it is still significant.

The total value of the consumer surplus suggested by the data in Figure 4.6(a) is roughly
equal to the area of the shaded triangle in Figure 4.6(b). To understand why this is so, think
about offering hamburgers to consumers at successively lower prices. If the good were actually
sold for $2.50, those near point *A* on the demand curve would get a large surplus; those at
point *B* would get a smaller surplus. Those at point *E* would get no surplus.

consumer surplus   The
difference between the
maximum amount a person is
willing to pay for a good and
its current market price.

Producer Surplus

Similarly, the supply curve in a market shows the amount that firms willingly produce and supply
to the market at various prices. Presumably it is because the price is sufficient to cover the costs
or the opportunity costs of production and give producers enough profit to keep them in business. When speaking of cost of production, we include everything that a producer must give up
in order to produce a good.

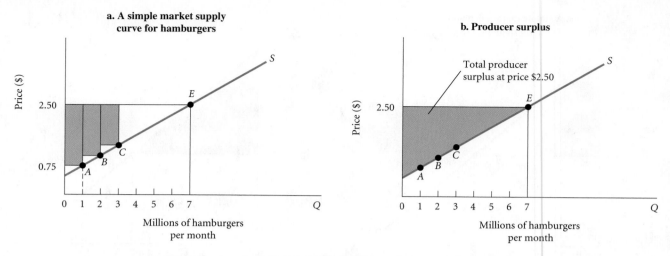

▲ FIGURE 4.7   Market Supply and Producer Surplus
As illustrated in Figure 4.7(a), some producers are willing to produce hamburgers for a price of $0.75 each. Since they are paid $2.50, they earn a producer surplus equal to $1.75. Other producers are willing to supply hamburgers at prices less than $2.50, and they also earn producers surplus. Since the market price of hamburgers is $2.50, the area of the shaded triangle in Figure 4.7(b) is equal to total producer surplus.

A simple market supply curve like the one in Figure 4.7(a) illustrates this point quite clearly. At the current market price of $2.50, producers will produce and sell 7 million hamburgers. There is only one price in the market, and the supply curve tells us the quantity supplied at each price.

Notice, however, that if the price were just $0.75 (75 cents), although production would be much lower—most producers would be out of business at that price—a few producers would actually be supplying burgers. In fact, producers would supply about 1 million burgers to the market. These firms must have lower costs: They are more efficient or they have access to raw beef at a lower price or perhaps they can hire low-wage labor.

If these efficient, low-cost producers are able to charge $2.50 for each hamburger, they are earning what is called a **producer surplus**. Producer surplus is the difference between the current market price and the cost of production for the firm. The first million hamburgers would generate a producer surplus of $2.50 minus $0.75, or $1.75 per hamburger: a total of $1.75 million. The second million hamburgers would also generate a producer surplus because the price of $2.50 exceeds the producers' total cost of producing these hamburgers, which is above $0.75 but much less than $2.50.

The total value of the producer surplus received by producers of hamburgers at a price of $2.50 per burger is roughly equal to the shaded triangle in Figure 4.7(b). Those producers just able to make a profit producing burgers will be near point *E* on the supply curve and will earn very little in the way of surplus.

producer surplus   The difference between the current market price and the cost of production for the firm.

Competitive Markets Maximize the Sum of Producer and Consumer Surplus

In the preceding example, the quantity of hamburgers supplied and the quantity of hamburgers demanded are equal at $2.50. Figure 4.8 shows the total net benefits to consumers and producers resulting from the production of 7 million hamburgers. Consumers receive benefits in excess of the price they pay and equal to the blue shaded area between the demand curve and the price line at $2.50; the area is equal to the amount of consumer surplus being earned. Producers receive compensation in excess of costs and equal to the red-shaded area between the supply curve and the price line at $2.50; the area is equal to the amount of producer surplus being earned.

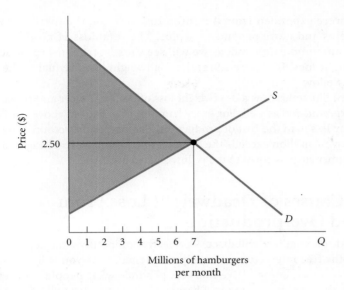

▲ **FIGURE 4.8 Total Producer and Consumer Surplus**
Total producer and consumer surplus is greatest where supply and demand curves intersect at equilibrium.

Now consider the result to consumers and producers if production were to be reduced to 4 million burgers. Look carefully at Figure 4.9(a). At 4 million burgers, consumers are willing to pay $3.75 for hamburgers and there are firms whose costs make it worthwhile to supply at a price as low as $1.50, yet something is stopping production at 4 million. The result is a loss of both consumer and producer surplus. You can see in Figure 4.9(a) that

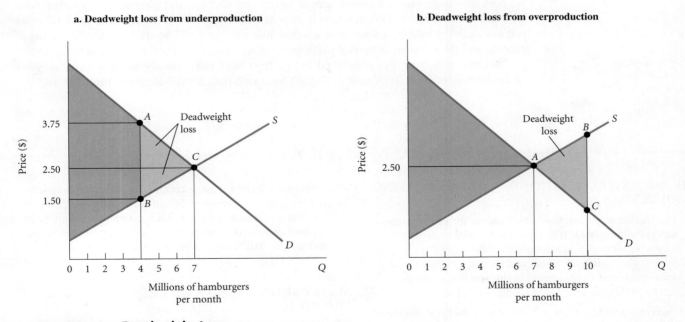

▲ **FIGURE 4.9 Deadweight Loss**
Figure 4.9(a) shows the consequences of producing 4 million hamburgers per month instead of 7 million hamburgers per month. Total producer and consumer surplus is reduced by the area of triangle *ABC* shaded in yellow. This is called the deadweight loss from underproduction. Figure 4.9(b) shows the consequences of producing 10 million hamburgers per month instead of 7 million hamburgers per month. As production increases from 7 million to 10 million hamburgers, the full cost of production rises above consumers' willingness to pay, resulting in a deadweight loss equal to the area of triangle *ABC*.

deadweight loss The total loss of producer and consumer surplus from underproduction or overproduction.

if production were expanded from 4 million to 7 million, the market would yield more consumer surplus and more producer surplus. The total loss of producer and consumer surplus from *underproduction* and, as we will see shortly, from overproduction is referred to as a **deadweight loss**. In Figure 4.9(a) the deadweight loss is equal to the area of triangle *ABC* shaded in yellow.

Figure 4.9(b) illustrates how a deadweight loss of both producer and consumer surplus can result from *overproduction* as well. For every hamburger produced above 7 million, consumers are willing to pay less than the cost of production. The cost of the resources needed to produce hamburgers above 7 million exceeds the benefits to consumers, resulting in a net loss of producer and consumer surplus equal to the yellow shaded area *ABC*.

Potential Causes of Deadweight Loss From Under- and Overproduction

Most of the next few chapters will discuss perfectly competitive markets in which prices are determined by the free interaction of supply and demand. As you will see, when supply and demand interact freely, competitive markets produce what people want at the least cost, that is, they are efficient. Beginning in Chapter 13, however, we will begin to relax assumptions and will discover a number of naturally occurring sources of market failure. Monopoly power gives firms the incentive to underproduce and overprice, taxes and subsidies may distort consumer choices, external costs such as pollution and congestion may lead to over- or underproduction of some goods, and artificial price floors and price ceilings may have the same effects.

Looking Ahead

We have now examined the basic forces of supply and demand and discussed the market/price system. These fundamental concepts will serve as building blocks for what comes next. Whether you are studying microeconomics or macroeconomics, you will be studying the functions of markets and the behavior of market participants in more detail in the following chapters.

Because the concepts presented in the first four chapters are so important to your understanding of what is to come, this might be a good time for you to review this material.

--- **SUMMARY** ---

THE PRICE SYSTEM: RATIONING AND ALLOCATING RESOURCES *p. 79*

1. In a market economy, the market system (or price system) serves two functions. It determines the allocation of resources among producers and the final mix of outputs. It also distributes goods and services on the basis of willingness and ability to pay. In this sense, it serves as a *price rationing* device.

2. Governments as well as private firms sometimes decide not to use the market system to ration an item for which there is excess demand. Examples of nonprice rationing systems include *queuing, favored customers,* and *ration coupons.* The most common rationale for such policies is "fairness."

3. Attempts to bypass the market and use alternative nonprice rationing devices are more difficult and costly than it would seem at first glance. Schemes that open up opportunities for favored customers, black markets, and side payments often end up less "fair" than the free market.

SUPPLY AND DEMAND ANALYSIS: AN OIL IMPORT FEE *p. 86*

4. The basic logic of supply and demand is a powerful tool for analysis. For example, supply and demand analysis shows that an oil import tax will reduce quantity of oil demanded, increase domestic production, and generate revenues for the government.

SUPPLY AND DEMAND AND MARKET
EFFICIENCY *p. 88*

5. Supply and demand curves can also be used to illustrate the
idea of market efficiency, an important aspect of normative
economics.

6. *Consumer surplus* is the difference between the maximum
amount a person is willing to pay for a good and the current
market price.

7. *Producer surplus* is the difference between the current
market price and the cost of production for the firm.

8. At free market equilibrium with competitive markets,
the sum of consumer surplus and producer surplus is
maximized.

9. The total loss of producer and consumer surplus from
underproduction or overproduction is referred to as a
deadweight loss.

REVIEW TERMS AND CONCEPTS

black market, *p. 84*

consumer surplus, *p. 89*

deadweight loss, *p. 92*

favored customers, *p. 84*

minimum wage, *p. 86*

price ceiling, *p. 83*

price floor, *p. 86*

price rationing, *p. 79*

producer surplus, *p. 90*

queuing, *p. 83*

ration coupons, *p. 84*

PROBLEMS

All problems are available on MyEconLab.

1. Illustrate the following with supply and demand curves:
   a. In May 2012, Norwegian artist Edvard Munch's *The Scream*
   was sold in New York for $119.9 million.
   b. In 2013, hogs in the United States were selling for
   97 cents per pound, up from 75 cents per pound a year
   before. This was due primarily to the fact that supply had
   decreased during the period.
   c. Early in 2009, a survey of greenhouses indicated that
   the demand for houseplants was rising sharply. At the
   same time, large numbers of low-cost producers started
   growing plants for sale. The overall result was a drop in
   the average price of houseplants and an increase in the
   number of plants sold.

2. Every demand curve must eventually hit the quantity axis
   because with limited incomes, there is always a price so
   high that there is no demand for the good. Do you agree or
   disagree? Why?

3. When excess demand exists for tickets to a major sporting event
   or a concert, profit opportunities exist for scalpers. Explain
   briefly using supply and demand curves to illustrate. Some
   argue that scalpers work to the advantage of everyone and are
   "efficient." Do you agree or disagree? Explain briefly.

4. In an effort to "support" the price of some agricultural goods,
   the Department of Agriculture pays farmers a subsidy in
   cash for every acre that they leave *unplanted*. The Agriculture

Department argues that the subsidy increases the "cost" of
planting and that it will reduce supply and increase the price of
competitively produced agricultural goods. Critics argue that
because the subsidy is a payment to farmers, it will reduce costs
and lead to lower prices. Which argument is correct? Explain.

5. The rent for apartments in New York City has been rising
   sharply. Demand for apartments in New York City has been
   rising sharply as well. This is hard to explain because the law of
   demand says that higher prices should lead to lower demand.
   Do you agree or disagree? Explain your answer.

6. Illustrate the following with supply and/or demand curves:
   a. The federal government "supports" the price of wheat by
   paying farmers not to plant wheat on some of their land.
   b. An increase in the price of chicken has an impact on the
   price of hamburger.
   c. Incomes rise, shifting the demand for gasoline. Crude
   oil prices rise, shifting the supply of gasoline. At the new
   equilibrium, the quantity of gasoline sold is less than it was
   before. (Crude oil is used to produce gasoline.)

7. Illustrate the following with supply and/or demand curves:
   a. A situation of excess labor supply (unemployment) caused
   by a "minimum wage" law.
   b. The effect of a sharp increase in heating oil prices on the
   demand for insulation material.

---

8. **[Related to the *Economics in Practice* on p. 82]** The feature states that in New Jersey, a law against price gouging prohibits price increases of more than 10 percent in an emergency situation. Assume that prior to Sandy the equilibrium price for portable generators was $100 and the equilibrium quantity was 200 units per month. After Sandy, demand increased to 500 units per month and generator sellers raised prices to the maximum amount allowed by law. Do you think that the new higher price will be high enough to meet the increased demand? Use a supply and demand graph to explain your answer.

9. Suppose that the world price of oil is $90 per barrel and that the United States can buy all the oil it wants at this price. Suppose also that the demand and supply schedules for oil in the United States are as follows:

PRICE ($ PER BARREL)	U.S. QUANTITY DEMANDED	U.S. QUANTITY SUPPLIED
88	16	4
90	15	6
92	14	8
94	13	10
96	12	12

a. On graph paper, draw the supply and demand curves for the United States.

b. With free trade in oil, what price will Americans pay for their oil? What quantity will Americans buy? How much of this will be supplied by American producers? How much will be imported? Illustrate total imports on your graph of the U.S. oil market.

c. Suppose the United States imposes a tax of $4 per barrel on imported oil. What quantity would Americans buy? How much of this would be supplied by American producers? How much would be imported? How much tax would the government collect?

d. Briefly summarize the impact of an oil import tax by explaining who is helped and who is hurt among the following groups: domestic oil consumers, domestic oil producers, foreign oil producers, and the U.S. government.

10. Use the data in the preceding problem to answer the following questions. Now suppose that the United States allows no oil imports.

a. What are the equilibrium price and quantity for oil in the United States?

b. If the United States imposed a price ceiling of $94 per barrel on the oil market and prohibited imports, would there be an excess supply or an excess demand for oil? If so, how much?

c. Under the price ceiling, quantity supplied and quantity demanded differ. Which of the two will determine how much oil is purchased? Briefly explain why.

11. Use the following diagram to calculate total consumer surplus at a price of $8 and production of 6 million meals per day. For the same equilibrium, calculate total producer surplus. Assuming price remained at $8 but production was cut to 3 million meals

per day, calculate producer surplus and consumer surplus. Calculate the deadweight loss from underproduction.

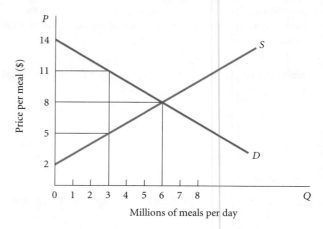

12. In February 2013, the U.S. Energy Information Administration projected that the average retail price for regular-grade gasoline would be $3.57 per gallon for the remainder of the year. Do some research on the price of gasoline. Has this projection been accurate? What is the price of regular-grade gasoline today in your city or town? If it is below $3.57 per gallon, what are the reasons? Similarly, if it is higher than $3.57, what has happened to drive up the price? Illustrate with supply and demand curves.

13. **[Related to the *Economics in Practice* on p. 88]** Many cruise lines offer 5-day trips. A disproportionate number of these trips leave port on Thursday and return late Monday. Why might this be true?

14. **[Related to the *Economics in Practice* on p. 88]** Lines for free tickets to see free Shakespeare in Central Park are often long. A local politician has suggested that it would be a great service if the park provided music to entertain those who are waiting in line. What do you think of this suggestion?

15. Suppose the market demand for burritos is given by $Q_d = 40 - 5P$ and the market supply for burritos is given by $Q_s = 10P - 20$, where P = price (per burrito).

a. Graph the supply and demand schedules for burritos.

b. What is the equilibrium price and equilibrium quantity?

c. Calculate consumer surplus and producer surplus, and identify these on the graph.

16. On April 20, 2010, an oil-drilling platform owned by British Petroleum exploded in the Gulf of Mexico, causing oil to leak into the gulf at estimates of 1.5 to 2.5 million gallons per day for well over 2 months. Due to the oil spill, the government closed over 25 percent of federal waters, which devastated the commercial fishing industry in the area. Explain how the reduction in supply from the reduced fishing waters either increased or decreased consumer surplus and producer surplus, and show these changes graphically.

17. The following graph represents the market for DVDs.

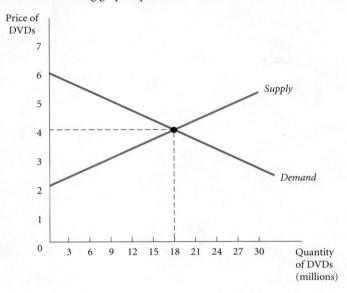

18. The following graph represents the market for wheat. The equilibrium price is $20 per bushel and the equilibrium quantity is 14 million bushels.

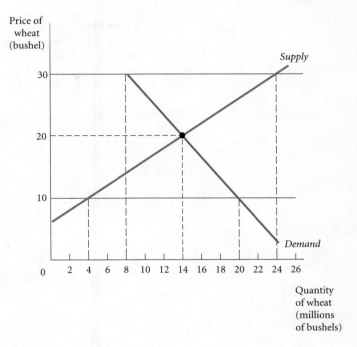

a. Find the values of consumer surplus and producer surplus when the market is in equilibrium, and identify these areas on the graph.

b. If underproduction occurs in this market, and only 9 million DVDs are produced, what happens to the amounts of consumer surplus and producer surplus? What is the value of the deadweight loss? Identify these areas on the graph.

c. If overproduction occurs in this market, and 27 million DVDs are produced, what happens to the amounts of consumer surplus and producer surplus? Is there a deadweight loss with overproduction? If so, what is its value? Identify these areas on the graph.

a. Explain what will happen if the government establishes a price ceiling of $10 per bushel of wheat in this market? What if the price ceiling was set at $30?

b. Explain what will happen if the government establishes a price floor of $30 per bushel of wheat in this market. What if the price floor was set at $10?

 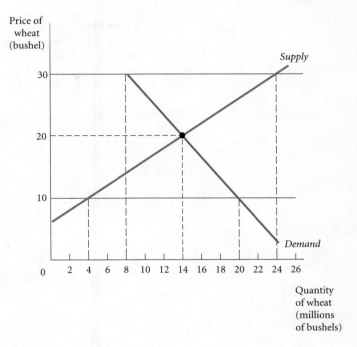

Introduction to Macroeconomics

5

When the macroeconomy is doing well, jobs are easy to find, incomes are generally rising, and profits of corporations are high. On the other hand, if the macroeconomy is in a slump, new jobs are scarce, incomes are not growing well, and profits are low. Students who entered the job market in the boom of the late 1990s in the United States, on average, had an easier time finding a job than did those who entered in the recession of 2008–2009. The sluggish economy that continued into 2013 had negative effects on millions of people. Given the large effect that the macroeconomy can have on our lives, it is important that we understand how it works.

We begin by discussing the differences between microeconomics and macroeconomics that we glimpsed in Chapter 1. **Microeconomics** examines the functioning of individual industries and the behavior of individual decision-making units, typically firms and households. With a few assumptions about how these units behave (firms maximize profits; households maximize utility), we can derive useful conclusions about how markets work and how resources are allocated.

Instead of focusing on the factors that influence the production of particular products and the behavior of individual industries, **macroeconomics** focuses on the determinants of total national output. Macroeconomics studies not household income but *national* income, not individual prices but the *overall* price level. It does not analyze the demand for labor in the automobile industry but instead total employment in the economy.

Both microeconomics and macroeconomics are concerned with the decisions of households and firms. Microeconomics deals with individual decisions; macroeconomics deals with the sum of these individual decisions. *Aggregate* is used in macroeconomics to refer to sums. When we speak of **aggregate behavior**, we mean the behavior of all households as well as the behavior of all firms. We also speak of aggregate consumption and aggregate investment, which refer to total consumption and total investment in the economy, respectively.

Because microeconomists and macroeconomists look at the economy from different perspectives, you might expect that they would reach somewhat different conclusions about the way the economy behaves. This is true to some extent. Microeconomists generally conclude that markets work well. They see prices as flexible, adjusting to maintain equality between quantity supplied and quantity demanded. Macroeconomists, however, observe that important prices in the economy—for example, the wage rate (or price of labor)—often seem "sticky." **Sticky prices**

microeconomics Examines the functioning of individual industries and the behavior of individual decision-making units—firms and households.

macroeconomics Deals with the economy as a whole. Macroeconomics focuses on the determinants of total national income, deals with aggregates such as aggregate consumption and investment, and looks at the overall level of prices instead of individual prices.

aggregate behavior The behavior of all households and firms together.

sticky prices Prices that do not always adjust rapidly to maintain equality between quantity supplied and quantity demanded.

LEARNING OBJECTIVES

Describe the three primary concerns of macroeconomics

Discuss the interaction between the four components of the macroeconomy

Summarize the macroeconomic history of the U.S. between 1929 and 1970

Describe the U.S. economy since 1970

are prices that do not always adjust rapidly to maintain equality between quantity supplied and quantity demanded. Microeconomists do not expect to see the quantity of apples supplied exceeding the quantity of apples demanded because the price of apples is not sticky. On the other hand, macroeconomists—who analyze aggregate behavior—examine periods of high unemployment, where the quantity of labor supplied appears to exceed the quantity of labor demanded. At such times, it appears that wage rates do not fall fast enough to equate the quantity of labor supplied and the quantity of labor demanded.

Macroeconomic Concerns

Three of the major concerns of macroeconomics are

- Output growth
- Unemployment
- Inflation and deflation

Government policy makers would like to have high output growth, low unemployment, and low inflation. We will see that these goals may conflict with one another and that an important point in understanding macroeconomics is understanding these conflicts.

Output Growth

business cycle The cycle of short-term ups and downs in the economy.

aggregate output The total quantity of goods and services produced in an economy in a given period.

Instead of growing at an even rate at all times, economies tend to experience short-term ups and downs in their performance. The technical name for these ups and downs is the **business cycle**. The main measure of how an economy is doing is **aggregate output**, the total quantity of goods and services produced in the economy in a given period. When less is produced (in other words, when aggregate output decreases), there are fewer goods and services to go around and the average standard of living declines. When firms cut back on production, they also lay off workers, increasing the rate of unemployment.

recession A period during which aggregate output declines. Conventionally, a period in which aggregate output declines for two consecutive quarters.

Recessions are periods during which aggregate output declines. It has become conventional to classify an economic downturn as a "recession" when aggregate output declines for two consecutive quarters. A prolonged and deep recession is called a **depression**, although economists do not agree on when a recession becomes a depression. Since the 1930s the United States has experienced one depression (during the 1930s) and eight recessions: 1946, 1954, 1958, 1974–1975, 1980–1982, 1990–1991, 2001, and 2008–2009. Other countries also experienced recessions in the twentieth century, some roughly coinciding with U.S. recessions and some not.

depression A prolonged and deep recession.

expansion *or* **boom** The period in the business cycle from a trough up to a peak during which output and employment grow.

A typical business cycle is illustrated in Figure 5.1. Since most economies, on average, grow over time, the business cycle in Figure 5.1 shows a positive trend—the *peak* (the highest point) of a new business cycle is higher than the peak of the previous cycle. The period from a *trough*, or bottom of the cycle, to a peak is called an **expansion** or a **boom**. During an expansion, output and employment grow. The period from a peak to a trough is called a **contraction, recession**, or **slump**, when output and employment fall.

contraction, recession, *or* **slump** The period in the business cycle from a peak down to a trough during which output and employment fall.

▶ **FIGURE 5.1**
A Typical Business Cycle
In this business cycle, the economy is expanding as it moves through point *A* from the trough to the peak. When the *economy* moves from a peak down to a trough, through point *B*, the economy is in recession.

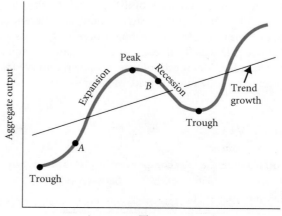

In judging whether an economy is expanding or contracting, note the difference between the level of economic activity and its rate of change. If the economy has just left a trough (point *A* in Figure 5.1), it will be growing (rate of change is positive), but its level of output will still be low. If the economy has just started to decline from a peak (point *B*), it will be contracting (rate of change is negative), but its level of output will still be high. In 2012 the U.S. economy was expanding—it had left the trough of the 2008–2009 recession beginning in 2010—but the level of output was still low and many people were still out of work.

The business cycle in Figure 5.1 is symmetrical, which means that the length of an expansion is the same as the length of a contraction. Most business cycles are not symmetrical, however. It is possible, for example, for the expansion phase to be longer than the contraction phase. When contraction comes, it may be fast and sharp, while expansion may be slow and gradual. Moreover, the economy is not nearly as regular as the business cycle in Figure 5.1 indicates. The ups and downs in the economy tend to be erratic.

Figure 5.2 shows the actual business cycles in the United States between 1900 and 2012. Although many business cycles have occurred in the last 113 years, each is unique. The economy is not so simple that it has regular cycles.

The periods of the Great Depression and World War I and II show the largest fluctuations in Figure 5.2, although other large contractions and expansions have taken place. Note the expansion in the 1960s and the five recessions since 1970. Some of the cycles have been long; some have been very short. Note also that aggregate output actually increased between 1933 and 1937, even though it was still quite low in 1937. The economy did not come out of the Depression until the defense buildup prior to the start of World War II. Note also that business cycles were more extreme before World War II than they have been since then. Finally, note that the recovery from the 2008–2009 recession has been unusually slow.

Unemployment

You cannot listen to the news or read a newspaper without noticing that data on the unemployment rate are released each month. The **unemployment rate**—the percentage of the labor force that is unemployed—is a key indicator of the economy's health. Because the unemployment rate

unemployment rate The percentage of the labor force that is unemployed.

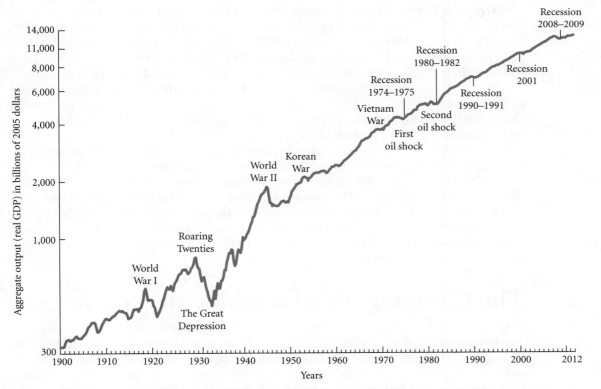

▲ **FIGURE 5.2   U.S. Aggregate Output (Real GDP), 1900–2012**   MyEconLab Real-time data
The periods of the Great Depression and World War I and II show the largest fluctuations in aggregate output.

is usually closely related to the economy's aggregate output, announcements of each month's new figure are followed with great interest by economists, politicians, and policy makers.

Although macroeconomists are interested in learning why the unemployment rate has risen or fallen in a given period, they also try to answer a more basic question: Why is there any unemployment at all? We do not expect to see zero unemployment. At times people decide to quit their jobs and look for something better. Until they find a new job, they will be unemployed. At any time, some firms may go bankrupt due to competition from rivals, bad management, or bad luck. Employees of such firms typically are not able to find new jobs immediately, and while they are looking for work, they will be unemployed. Also, workers entering the labor market for the first time may require a few weeks or months to find a job.

If we base our analysis on supply and demand, we would expect conditions to change in response to the existence of unemployed workers. Specifically, when there is unemployment beyond some minimum amount, there is an excess supply of workers—at the going wage rates, there are people who want to work who cannot find work. In microeconomic theory, the response to excess supply is a decrease in the price of the commodity in question and therefore an increase in the quantity demanded, a reduction in the quantity supplied, and the restoration of equilibrium. With the quantity supplied equal to the quantity demanded, the market clears.

The existence of unemployment seems to imply that the aggregate labor market is not in equilibrium—that something prevents the quantity supplied and the quantity demanded from equating. Why do labor markets not clear when other markets do, or is it that labor markets are clearing and the unemployment data are reflecting something different? This is another main concern of macroeconomists.

Inflation and Deflation

inflation An increase in the overall price level.

Inflation is an increase in the overall price level. Keeping inflation low has long been a goal of government policy. Especially problematic are **hyperinflations**, or periods of very rapid increases in the overall price level.

hyperinflation A period of very rapid increases in the overall price level.

Most Americans are unaware of what life is like under very high inflation. In some countries at some times, people were accustomed to prices rising by the day, by the hour, or even by the minute. During the hyperinflation in Bolivia in 1984 and 1985, the price of one egg rose from 3,000 pesos to 10,000 pesos in 1 week. In 1985, three bottles of aspirin sold for the same price as a luxury car had sold for in 1982. At the same time, the problem of handling money became a burden. Banks stopped counting deposits—a $500 deposit was equivalent to about 32 million pesos, and it just did not make sense to count a huge sack full of bills. Bolivia's currency, printed in West Germany and England, was the country's third biggest import in 1984, surpassed only by wheat and mining equipment.

Skyrocketing prices in Bolivia are a small part of the story. When inflation approaches rates of 2,000 percent per year, the economy and the whole organization of a country begin to break down. Workers may go on strike to demand wage increases in line with the high-inflation rate, and firms may find it hard to secure credit.

Hyperinflations are rare. Nonetheless, economists have devoted much effort to identifying the costs and consequences of even moderate inflation. Does anyone gain from inflation? Who loses? What costs does inflation impose on society? How severe are they? What causes inflation? What is the best way to stop it? These are some of the main concerns of macroeconomists.

deflation A decrease in the overall price level.

A decrease in the overall price level is called **deflation**. In some periods in U.S. history and recently in Japan, deflation has occurred over an extended period of time. The goal of policy makers is to avoid prolonged periods of deflation as well as inflation in order to pursue the macroeconomic goal of stability.

The Components of the Macroeconomy

Understanding how the macroeconomy works can be challenging because a great deal is going on at one time. Everything seems to affect everything else. To see the big picture, it is helpful to divide the participants in the economy into four broad groups: (1) *households*, (2) *firms*, (3) the *government*, and (4) the *rest of the world*. Households and firms make up the private sector, the government is the public sector, and the rest of the world is the foreign sector. These four groups interact in the economy in a variety of ways, many involving either receiving or paying income.

The Circular Flow Diagram

A useful way of seeing the economic interactions among the four groups in the economy is a **circular flow** diagram, which shows the income received and payments made by each group. A simple circular flow diagram is pictured in Figure 5.3.

Let us walk through the circular flow step by step. Households work for firms and the government, and they receive wages for their work. Our diagram shows a flow of wages *into* households as payment for those services. Households also receive interest on corporate and government bonds and dividends from firms. Many households receive other payments from the government, such as Social Security benefits, veterans' benefits, and welfare payments. Economists call these kinds of payments from the government (for which the recipients do not supply goods, services, or labor) **transfer payments**. Together, these receipts make up the total income received by the households.

Households spend by buying goods and services from firms and by paying taxes to the government. These items make up the total amount paid out by the households. The difference between the total receipts and the total payments of the households is the amount that the households save or dissave. If households receive more than they spend, they *save* during the period. If they receive less than they spend, they *dissave*. A household can dissave by using up some of its previous savings or by borrowing. In the circular flow diagram, household spending is shown as a flow *out* of households. Saving by households is sometimes termed a "leakage" from the circular flow because it withdraws income, or current purchasing power, from the system.

Firms sell goods and services to households and the government. These sales earn revenue, which shows up in the circular flow diagram as a flow *into* the firm sector. Firms pay wages, interest, and dividends to households, and firms pay taxes to the government. These payments are shown flowing *out* of firms.

The government collects taxes from households and firms. The government also makes payments. It buys goods and services from firms, pays wages and interest to households, and makes transfer payments to households. If the government's revenue is less than its payments, the government is dissaving.

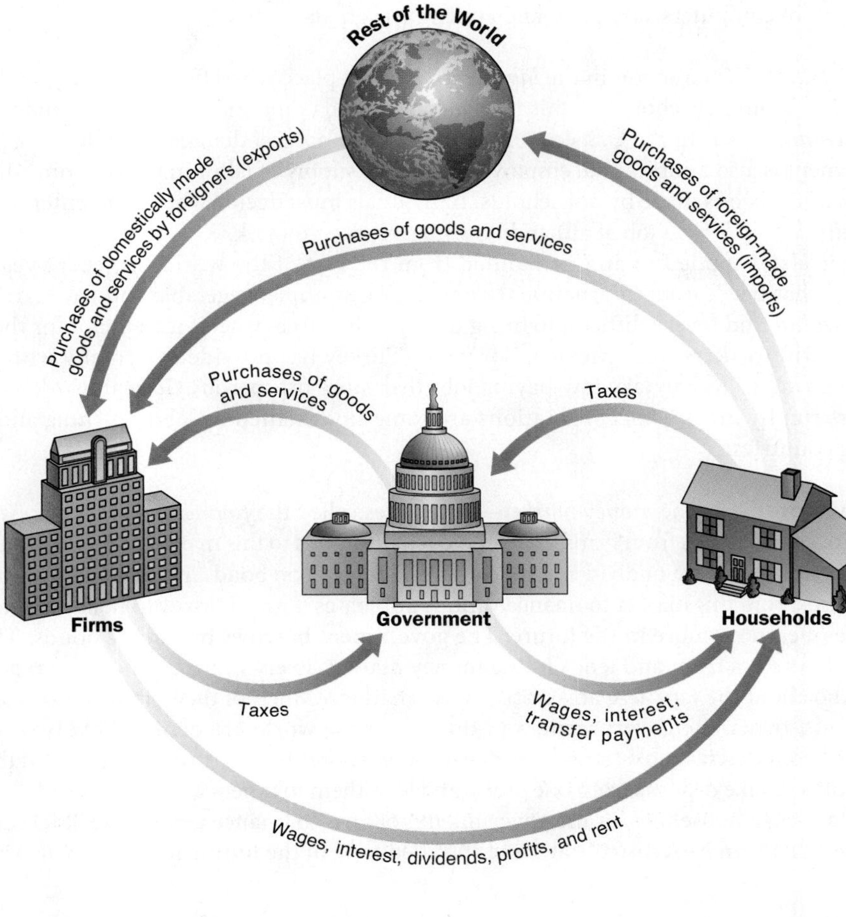

circular flow   A diagram showing the income received and payments made by each sector of the economy.

transfer payments   Cash payments made by the government to people who do not supply goods, services, or labor in exchange for these payments. They include Social Security benefits, veterans' benefits, and welfare payments.

◀ **FIGURE 5.3**
The Circular Flow of Payments

Households receive income from firms and the government, purchase goods and services from firms, and pay taxes to the government. They also purchase foreign-made goods and services (imports). Firms receive payments from households and the government for goods and services; they pay wages, dividends, interest, and rents to households and taxes to the government. The government receives taxes from firms and households, pays firms and households for goods and services—including wages to government workers—and pays interest and transfers to households. Finally, people in other countries purchase goods and services produced domestically (exports).

Note: Although not shown in this diagram, firms and governments also purchase imports.

Finally, households spend some of their income on *imports*—goods and services produced in the rest of the world. Similarly, people in foreign countries purchase *exports*—goods and services produced by domestic firms and sold to other countries.

One lesson of the circular flow diagram is that everyone's expenditure is someone else's receipt. If you buy a personal computer from Dell, you make a payment to Dell, and Dell receives revenue. If Dell pays taxes to the government, it has made a payment and the government has received revenue. Everyone's expenditures go somewhere. It is impossible to sell something without there being a buyer, and it is impossible to make a payment without there being a recipient. Every transaction must have two sides.

The Three Market Arenas

Another way of looking at the ways households, firms, the government, and the rest of the world relate to one another is to consider the markets in which they interact. We divide the markets into three broad arenas: (1) the goods-and-services market, (2) the labor market, and (3) the money (financial) market.

Goods-and-Services Market   Households and the government purchase goods and services from firms in the *goods-and-services market*. In this market, firms also purchase goods and services from each other. For example, Levi Strauss buys denim from other firms to make its blue jeans. In addition, firms buy capital goods from other firms. If General Motors needs new robots on its assembly lines, it may buy them from another firm instead of making them. The *Economics in Practice* in Chapter 1 describes how Apple, in constructing its iPod, buys parts from a number of other firms.

Firms *supply* to the goods-and-services market. Households, the government, and firms *demand* from this market. Finally, the rest of the world buys from and sells to the goods-and-services market. The United States imports hundreds of billions of dollars' worth of automobiles, DVDs, oil, and other goods. In the case of Apple's iPod, inputs come from other firms located in countries all over the world. At the same time, the United States exports hundreds of billions of dollars' worth of computers, airplanes, and agricultural goods.

Labor Market   Interaction in the *labor market* takes place when firms and the government purchase labor from households. In this market, households *supply* labor and firms and the government *demand* labor. In the U.S. economy, firms are the largest demanders of labor, although the government is also a substantial employer. The total supply of labor in the economy depends on the sum of decisions made by households. Individuals must decide whether to enter the labor force (whether to look for a job at all) and how many hours to work.

Labor is also supplied to and demanded from the rest of the world. In recent years, the labor market has become an international market. For example, vegetable and fruit farmers in California would find it very difficult to bring their product to market if it were not for the labor of migrant farm workers from Mexico. For years, Turkey has provided Germany with "guest workers" who are willing to take low-paying jobs that more prosperous German workers avoid. Call centers run by major U.S. corporations are sometimes staffed by labor in India and other developing countries.

Money Market   In the *money market*—sometimes called the *financial market*—households purchase stocks and bonds from firms. Households *supply* funds to this market in the expectation of earning income in the form of dividends on stocks and interest on bonds. Households also *demand* (borrow) funds from this market to finance various purchases. Firms borrow to build new facilities in the hope of earning more in the future. The government borrows by issuing bonds. The rest of the world borrows from and lends to the money market. Every morning there are reports on TV and radio about the Japanese and British stock markets. Much of the borrowing and lending of households, firms, the government, and the rest of the world are coordinated by financial institutions—commercial banks, savings and loan associations, insurance companies, and the like. These institutions take deposits from one group and lend them to others.

When a firm, a household, or the government borrows to finance a purchase, it has an obligation to pay that loan back, usually at some specified time in the future. Most loans also involve payment of interest as a fee for the use of the borrowed funds. When a loan is made, the borrower usually signs a "promise to repay," or *promissory note*, and gives it to the lender. When the federal government borrows, it issues "promises" called **Treasury bonds, notes,** or **bills** in exchange for money. Firms can borrow by issuing **corporate bonds**.

Instead of issuing bonds to raise funds, firms can also issue shares of stock. A **share of stock** is a financial instrument that gives the holder a share in the firm's ownership and therefore the right to share in the firm's profits. If the firm does well, the value of the stock increases and the stockholder receives a *capital gain*[1] on the initial purchase. In addition, the stock may pay **dividends**—that is, the firm may return some of its profits directly to its stockholders instead of retaining the profits to buy capital. If the firm does poorly, so does the stockholder. The capital value of the stock may fall, and dividends may not be paid.

Stocks and bonds are simply contracts, or agreements, between parties. I agree to loan you a certain amount, and you agree to repay me this amount plus something extra at some future date, or I agree to buy part ownership in your firm, and you agree to give me a share of the firm's future profits.

A critical variable in the money market is the *interest rate*. Although we sometimes talk as if there is only one interest rate, there is never just one interest rate at any time. Instead, the interest rate on a given loan reflects the length of the loan and the perceived risk to the lender. A business that is just getting started must pay a higher rate than General Motors pays. A 30-year mortgage has a different interest rate than a 90-day loan. Nevertheless, interest rates tend to move up and down together, and their movement reflects general conditions in the financial market.

Treasury bonds, notes, *and* **bills** Promissory notes issued by the federal government when it borrows money.

corporate bonds Promissory notes issued by firms when they borrow money.

shares of stock Financial instruments that give to the holder a share in the firm's ownership and therefore the right to share in the firm's profits.

dividends The portion of a firm's profits that the firm pays out each period to its shareholders.

The Role of the Government in the Macroeconomy

The government plays a major role in the macroeconomy, so a useful way of learning how the macroeconomy works is to consider how the government uses policy to affect the economy. The two main policies are (1) fiscal policy and (2) monetary policy. Much of the study of macroeconomics is learning how fiscal and monetary policies work.

Fiscal policy refers to the government's decisions about how much to tax and spend. The federal government collects taxes from households and firms and spends those funds on goods and services ranging from missiles to parks to Social Security payments to interstate highways. Taxes take the form of personal income taxes, Social Security taxes, and corporate profits taxes, among others. An *expansionary* fiscal policy is a policy in which taxes are cut and/or government spending increases. A *contractionary* fiscal policy is the reverse.

Monetary policy in the United States is conducted by the Federal Reserve, the nation's central bank. The Fed, as it is usually called, controls the short-term interest rate in the economy. The Fed's decisions have important effects on the economy. In fact, the task of trying to smooth out business cycles in the United States has historically been left to the Fed (that is, to monetary policy). The chair of the Federal Reserve is sometimes said to be the second most powerful person in the United States after the president. As we will see later in the text, the Fed played a more active role in the 2008–2009 recession than it had in previous recessions. Fiscal policy, however, also played a very active role in the 2008–2009 recession and its aftermath.

fiscal policy Government policies concerning taxes and spending.

monetary policy The tools used by the Federal Reserve to control the short-term interest rate.

A Brief History of Macroeconomics

The severe economic contraction and high unemployment of the 1930s, the decade of the **Great Depression**, spurred a great deal of thinking about macroeconomic issues, especially unemployment. Figure 5.2 earlier in the chapter shows that this period had the largest and longest aggregate output contraction in the twentieth century in the United States. The 1920s had been prosperous years for the U.S. economy. Virtually everyone who wanted a job could get one, incomes rose substantially, and prices were stable. Beginning in late 1929, things took a sudden turn for the worse. In 1929, 1.5 million people were unemployed. By 1933, that had increased

Great Depression The period of severe economic contraction and high unemployment that began in 1929 and continued throughout the 1930s.

---

[1] A *capital gain* occurs whenever the value of an asset increases. If you bought a stock for $1,000 and it is now worth $1,500, you have earned a capital gain of $500. A capital gain is "realized" when you sell the asset. Until you sell, the capital gain is *accrued* but not *realized*.

to 13 million out of a labor force of 51 million. In 1933, the United States produced about 27 percent fewer goods and services than it had in 1929. In October 1929, when stock prices collapsed on Wall Street, billions of dollars of personal wealth were lost. Unemployment remained above 14 percent of the labor force until 1940. (See the *Economics in Practice*, p. 105, "Macroeconomics in Literature," for Fitzgerald's and Steinbeck's take on the 1920s and 1930s.)

Before the Great Depression, economists applied microeconomic models, sometimes referred to as "classical" or "market clearing" models, to economy-wide problems. For example, classical supply and demand analysis assumed that an excess supply of labor would drive down wages to a new equilibrium level; as a result, unemployment would not persist.

In other words, classical economists believed that recessions were self-correcting. As output falls and the demand for labor shifts to the left, the argument went, the wage rate will decline, thereby raising the quantity of labor demanded by firms that will want to hire more workers at the new lower wage rate. However, during the Great Depression, unemployment levels remained very high for nearly 10 years. In large measure, the failure of simple classical models to explain the prolonged existence of high unemployment provided the impetus for the development of macroeconomics. It is not surprising that what we now call macroeconomics was born in the 1930s.

One of the most important works in the history of economics, *The General Theory of Employment, Interest and Money*, by John Maynard Keynes, was published in 1936. Building on what was already understood about markets and their behavior, Keynes set out to construct a theory that would explain the confusing economic events of his time.

Much of macroeconomics has roots in Keynes's work. According to Keynes, it is not prices and wages that determine the level of employment, as classical models had suggested; instead, it is the level of aggregate demand for goods and services. Keynes believed that governments could intervene in the economy and affect the level of output and employment. The government's role during periods when private demand is low, Keynes argued, is to stimulate aggregate demand and, by so doing, to lift the economy out of recession. (Keynes was a larger-than-life figure, one of the Bloomsbury group in England that included, among others, Virginia Woolf and Clive Bell.

After World War II and especially in the 1950s, Keynes's views began to gain increasing influence over both professional economists and government policy makers. Governments came to believe that they could intervene in their economies to attain specific employment and output goals. They began to use their powers to tax and spend as well as their ability to affect interest rates and the money supply for the explicit purpose of controlling the economy's ups and downs. This view of government policy became firmly established in the United States with the passage of the Employment Act of 1946. This act established the President's Council of Economic Advisers, a group of economists who advise the president on economic issues. The act also committed the federal government to intervening in the economy to prevent large declines in output and employment.

The notion that the government could and should act to stabilize the macroeconomy reached the height of its popularity in the 1960s. During these years, Walter Heller, the chairman of the Council of Economic Advisers under both President Kennedy and President Johnson, alluded to **fine-tuning** as the government's role in regulating inflation and unemployment. During the 1960s, many economists believed the government could use the tools available to manipulate unemployment and inflation levels fairly precisely.

fine-tuning The phrase used by Walter Heller to refer to the government's role in regulating inflation and unemployment.

The optimism was short-lived. In the 1970s and early 1980s, the U.S. economy had wide fluctuations in employment, output, and inflation. In 1974–1975 and again in 1980–1982, the United States experienced a severe recession. Although not as catastrophic as the Great Depression of the 1930s, these two recessions left millions without jobs and resulted in billions of dollars of lost output and income. In 1974–1975 and again in 1979–1981, the United States also saw very high rates of inflation.

The 1970s was thus a period of stagnation and high inflation, which came to be called stagflation. **Stagflation** is defined as a situation in which there is high inflation at the same time there are slow or negative output growth and high unemployment. Until the 1970s, high inflation had been observed only in periods when the economy was prospering and unemployment was low. The problem of stagflation was vexing both for macroeconomic theorists and policy makers concerned with the health of the economy.

stagflation A situation of both high inflation and high unemployment.

It was clear by 1975 that the macroeconomy was more difficult to control than Heller's words or textbook theory had led economists to believe. The events of the 1970s and early 1980s had an important influence on macroeconomic theory. Much of the faith in the simple

ECONOMICS IN PRACTICE

Macroeconomics in Literature

As you know, the language of economics includes a heavy dose of graphs and equations. But the underlying phenomena that economists study are the stuff of novels as well as graphs and equations. The following two passages, from *The Great Gatsby* by F. Scott Fitzgerald and *The Grapes of Wrath* by John Steinbeck, capture in graphic, although not graphical, form the economic growth and spending of the Roaring Twenties and the human side of the unemployment of the Great Depression.

The Great Gatsby, written in 1925, is set in the 1920s, while *The Grapes of Wrath*, written in 1939, is set in the early 1930s. If you look at Figure 5.2 for these two periods, you will see the translation of Fitzgerald and Steinbeck into macroeconomics.

From *The Great Gatsby*

At least once a fortnight a corps of caterers came down with several hundred feet of canvas and enough colored lights to make a Christmas tree of Gatsby's enormous garden. On buffet tables, garnished with glistening hors d'œuvre, spiced baked hams crowded against salads of harlequin designs and pastry pigs and turkeys bewitched to a dark gold. In the main hall a bar with a real brass rail was set up, and stocked with gins and liquors and with cordials so long forgotten that most of his female guests were too young to know one from another.

By seven o'clock the orchestra has arrived—no thin five piece affair but a whole pit full of oboes and trombones and saxophones and viols and cornets and piccolos and low and high drums. The last swimmers have come in from the beach now and are dressing upstairs; the cars from New York are parked five deep in the drive, and already the halls and salons and verandas are gaudy with primary colors and hair shorn in strange new ways and shawls beyond the dreams of Castile.

From *The Grapes of Wrath*

The moving, questing people were migrants now. Those families who had lived on a little piece of land, who had lived and died on forty acres, had eaten or starved on the produce of forty acres, had now the whole West to rove in. And they scampered about, looking for work; and the highways were streams of people, and the ditch banks were lines of people. Behind them more were coming. The great highways streamed with moving people.

THINKING PRACTICALLY

1. As we indicate in the introduction to this chapter, macroeconomics focuses on three concerns. Which of these concerns is covered in *The Grapes of Wrath* excerpt?

2. What economics textbook is featured in *The Great Gatsby*?
   Hint: Go to fairmodel.econ.yale.edu/rayfair/pdf/2000c.pdf.

Source: From *The Grapes of Wrath* by John Steinbeck, copyright 1939, renewed © 1967 by John Steinbeck. Used by permission of Viking Penguin, a division of Penguin Group (USA) Inc. and Penguin Group (UK) Ltd.

Keynesian model and the "conventional wisdom" of the 1960s was lost. Although we are now 40 years past the 1970s, the discipline of macroeconomics is still in flux and there is no agreed-upon view of how the macroeconomy works. Many important issues have yet to be resolved. This makes macroeconomics hard to teach but exciting to study.

The U.S. Economy Since 1970

In the following chapters, it will be useful to have a picture of how the U.S. economy has performed in recent history. Since 1970, the U.S. economy has experienced five recessions and two periods of high inflation. The period since 1970 is illustrated in Figures 5.4, 5.5, and 5.6. These

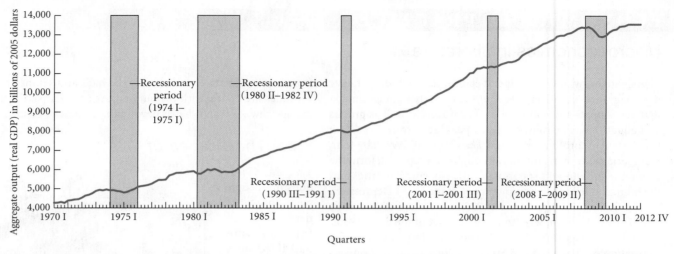

▲ **FIGURE 5.4** **Aggregate Output (Real GDP), 1970 I–2012 IV** MyEconLab Real-time data

Aggregate output in the United States since 1970 has risen overall, but there have been five recessionary periods: 1974 I–1975 I, 1980 II–1982 IV, 1990 III–1991 I, 2001 I–2001 III, and 2008 I–2009 II.

figures are based on quarterly data (that is, data for each quarter of the year). The first quarter consists of January, February, and March; the second quarter consists of April, May, and June; and so on. The Roman numerals I, II, III, and IV denote the four quarters. For example, 1972 III refers to the third quarter of 1972.

Figure 5.4 plots aggregate output for 1970 I–2012 IV. The five recessionary periods are 1974 I–1975 I, 1980 II–1982 IV, 1990 III–1991 I, 2001 I–2001 III, and 2008 I–2009 II.[2] These five periods are shaded in the figure. Figure 5.5 plots the unemployment rate for the same overall period with the same shading for the recessionary periods. Note that unemployment rose in all five recessions. In the 1974–1975 recession, the unemployment rate reached a maximum of 8.8 percent in the second quarter of 1975. During the 1980–1982 recession, it reached a maximum of 10.7 percent in the fourth quarter of 1982. The unemployment rate continued to rise after the 1990–1991 recession and reached a peak of 7.6 percent in the third quarter of 1992. In the 2008-2009 recession it reached a peak of 9.9 percent in the fourth quarter of 2009.

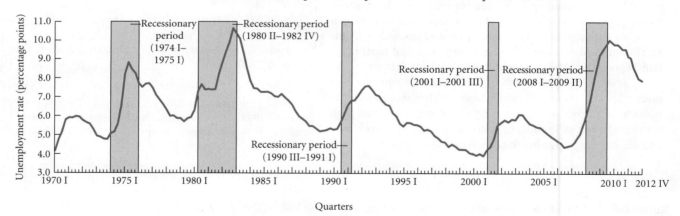

▲ **FIGURE 5.5** **Unemployment Rate, 1970 I–2012 IV** MyEconLab Real-time data

The U.S. unemployment rate since 1970 shows wide variations. The five recessionary reference periods show increases in the unemployment rate.

---

[2] Regarding the 1980 II–1982 IV period, output rose in 1980 IV and 1981 I before falling again in 1981 II. Given this fact, one possibility would be to treat the 1980 II–1982 IV period as if it included two separate recessionary periods: 1980 II–1980 III and 1981 I–1982 IV. Because the expansion was so short-lived, however, we have chosen not to separate the period into two parts. These periods are close to but are not exactly the recessionary periods defined by the National Bureau of Economic Research (NBER). The NBER is considered the "official" decider of recessionary periods. One problem with the NBER definitions is that they are never revised, but the macro data are, sometimes by large amounts. This means that the NBER periods are not always those that would be chosen using the latest revised data. In November 2008 the NBER declared that a recession began in December 2007. In September 2010 it declared that the recession ended in June 2009.

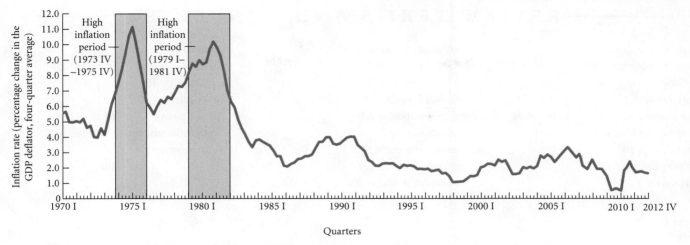

▲ **FIGURE 5.6** **Inflation Rate (Percentage Change in the** MyEconLab Real-time data
GDP Deflator, Four-Quarter Average), 1970 I–2012 IV
Since 1970, inflation has been high in two periods: 1973 IV–1975 IV and 1979 I–1981 IV. Inflation between
1983 and 1992 was moderate. Since 1992, it has been fairly low.

Figure 5.6 plots the inflation rate for 1970 I–2012 IV. The two high inflation periods are
1973 IV–1975 IV and 1979 I–1981 IV, which are shaded. In the first high inflation period, the
inflation rate peaked at 11.1 percent in the first quarter of 1975. In the second high inflation period,
inflation peaked at 10.2 percent in the first quarter of 1981. Since 1983, the inflation rate has been
quite low by the standards of the 1970s. Since 1992, it has been between about 1 and 3 percent.

In the following chapters, we will explain the behavior of and the connections among variables such as output, unemployment, and inflation. When you understand the forces at work
in creating the movements shown in Figures 5.4, 5.5, and 5.6, you will have come a long way in
understanding how the macroeconomy works.

SUMMARY

1. *Microeconomics* examines the functioning of individual
industries and the behavior of individual decision-making
units. *Macroeconomics* is concerned with the sum, or aggregate, of these individual decisions—the consumption of *all*
households in the economy, the amount of labor supplied
and demanded by *all* individuals and firms, and the total
amount of *all* goods and services produced.

MACROECONOMIC CONCERNS p. 98

2. The three topics of primary concern to macroeconomists are
the growth rate of aggregate output; the level of unemployment; and increases in the overall price level, or *inflation*.

THE COMPONENTS OF THE MACROECONOMY p. 100

3. The *circular flow* diagram shows the flow of income received
and payments made by the four groups in the economy—
households, firms, the government, and the rest of the
world. Everybody's expenditure is someone else's receipt—
every transaction must have two sides.

4. Another way of looking at how households, firms, the
government, and the rest of the world relate is to consider
the markets in which they interact: the goods-and-services
market, labor market, and money (financial) market.

5. Among the tools that the government has available for
influencing the macroeconomy are *fiscal policy* (decisions
on taxes and government spending) and *monetary policy*
(control of the short-term interest rate).

A BRIEF HISTORY OF MACROECONOMICS p. 103

6. Macroeconomics was born out of the effort to explain the
Great Depression of the 1930s. Since that time, the discipline
has evolved, concerning itself with new issues as the problems facing the economy have changed. Through the late
1960s, it was believed that the government could "fine-tune"
the economy to keep it running on an even keel at all times.
The poor economic performance of the 1970s, however,
showed that *fine-tuning* does not always work.

THE U.S. ECONOMY SINCE 1970 p. 105

7. Since 1970, the U.S. economy has seen five *recessions* and
two periods of high inflation.

MyEconLab Visit **www.myeconlab.com** to complete these exercises online and get instant
feedback. Exercises that update with real-time data are marked with 🌐.

—— REVIEW TERMS AND CONCEPTS ——

aggregate behavior, *p. 97*

aggregate output, *p. 98*

business cycle, *p. 98*

circular flow, *p. 101*

contraction, recession, *or* slump, *p. 98*

corporate bonds, *p. 103*

deflation, *p. 100*

depression, *p. 98*

dividends, *p. 103*

expansion *or* boom, *p. 98*

fine-tuning, *p. 104*

fiscal policy, *p. 103*

Great Depression, *p. 103*

hyperinflation, *p. 100*

inflation, *p. 100*

macroeconomics, *p. 97*

microeconomics, *p. 97*

monetary policy, *p. 103*

recession, *p. 98*

shares of stock, *p. 103*

stagflation, *p. 104*

sticky prices, *p. 97*

transfer payments, *p. 101*

Treasury bonds, notes, *and* bills, *p. 103*

unemployment rate, *p. 99*

—— PROBLEMS ——

All problems are available on MyEconLab.

1. Define inflation. Assume that you live in a simple economy in which only three goods are produced and traded: fish, fruit, and meat. Suppose that on January 1, 2012, fish sold for $2.50 per pound, meat was $3.00 per pound, and fruit was $1.50 per pound. At the end of the year, you discover that the catch was low and that fish prices had increased to $5.00 per pound, but fruit prices stayed at $1.50 and meat prices had actually fallen to $2.00. Can you say what happened to the overall "price level"? How might you construct a measure of the "change in the price level"? What additional information might you need to construct your measure?

2. Define *unemployment*. Should everyone who does not hold a job be considered "unemployed"? To help with your answer, draw a supply and demand diagram depicting the labor market. What is measured along the demand curve? What factors determine the quantity of labor demanded during a given period? What is measured along the labor supply curve? What factors determine the quantity of labor supplied by households during a given period? What is the opportunity cost of holding a job?

3. [Related to the *Economics in Practice* on *p. 105*] The *Economics in Practice* describes prosperity and recession as they are depicted in literature. In mid-2009, there was a debate about whether the U.S. economy had entered an economic expansion. Look at the data on real GDP growth and unemployment and describe the pattern since 2007. You can find raw data on employment and unemployment at www.bls.gov, and you can find raw data on real GDP growth at www.bea.gov. Summarize what happened in mid-2009. Did the United States enter an economic expansion? Explain.

4. A recession occurred in the U.S. economy during the first three quarters of 2001. National output of goods and services fell during this period. But during the fourth quarter of 2001, output began to increase and it increased at a slow rate through the first quarter of 2003. At the same time, between March 2001 and April 2003, employment declined almost continuously with

a loss of over 2 million jobs. How is it possible that output rises while at the same time employment is falling?

5. Describe the economy of your state. What is the most recently reported unemployment rate? How has the number of payroll jobs changed over the last 3 months and over the last year? How does your state's performance compare to the U.S. economy's performance over the last year? What explanations have been offered in the press? How accurate are they?

6. Explain briefly how macroeconomics is different from microeconomics. How can macroeconomists use microeconomic theory to guide them in their work, and why might they want to do so?

7. During 1993 when the economy was growing very slowly, President Clinton recommended a series of spending cuts and tax increases designed to reduce the deficit. These were passed by Congress in the Omnibus Budget Reconciliation Act of 1993. Some who opposed the bill argued that the United States was pursuing a "contractionary fiscal policy" at precisely the wrong time. Explain their logic.

8. Many of the expansionary periods during the twentieth century occurred during wars. Why do you think this is true?

9. In the 1940s, you could buy a soda for 5 cents, eat dinner at a restaurant for less than $1, and purchase a house for $10,000. From this statement, it follows that consumers today are worse off than consumers in the 1940s. Comment.

10. John Maynard Keynes was the first to show that government policy could be used to change aggregate output and prevent recession by stabilizing the economy. Describe the economy of the world at the time Keynes was writing. Describe the economy of the United States today. What measures were being proposed by the Presidential candidates in the election of 2008 to end the recession which began in early 2008? Were the actions taken appropriate from the standpoint of John Maynard Keynes? Did they have the desired effect?

11. In which of the three market arenas is each of the following goods traded?
    a. U.S. Treasury Bonds
    b. An Amazon Kindle
    c. A Harley-Davidson Softail motorcycle
    d. The business knowledge of Dallas Mavericks' owner Mark Cuban
    e. Shares of Google stock
    f. The crop-harvesting abilities of an orange picker in Florida

12. Assume that the demand for autoworkers declines significantly due to a decrease in demand for new automobiles. Explain what will happen to unemployment using both classical and Keynesian reasoning.

13. Explain why the length and severity of the Great Depression necessitated a fundamental rethinking of the operations of the macroeconomy.

Measuring National Output and National Income

6

We saw in the last chapter that three main concerns of macroeconomics are aggregate output, unemployment, and inflation. In this chapter, we discuss the measurement of aggregate output and inflation. In the next chapter, we discuss the measurement of unemployment. Accurate measures of these variables are critical for understanding the economy. Without good measures, economists would have a hard time analyzing how the economy works and policy makers would have little to guide them on which policies are best for the economy.

Much of the macroeconomic data are from the **national income and product accounts**, which are compiled by the Bureau of Economic Analysis (BEA) of the U.S. Department of Commerce. It is hard to overestimate the importance of these accounts. They are, in fact, one of the great inventions of the twentieth century. (See the *Economics in Practice*, p. 119.) They not only convey data about the performance of the economy but also provide a conceptual framework that macroeconomists use to think about how the pieces of the economy fit together. When economists think about the macroeconomy, the categories and vocabulary they use come from the national income and product accounts.

The national income and product accounts can be compared with the mechanical or wiring diagrams for an automobile engine. The diagrams do not explain how an engine works, but they identify the key parts of an engine and show how they are connected. Trying to understand the macroeconomy without understanding national income accounting is like trying to fix an engine without a mechanical diagram and with no names for the engine parts.

There are literally thousands of variables in the national income and product accounts. In this chapter, we discuss only the most important. This chapter is meant to convey the way the national income and product accounts represent or organize the economy and the *sizes* of the various pieces of the economy.

national income and product accounts Data collected and published by the government describing the various components of national income and output in the economy.

LEARNING OBJECTIVES

Describe GDP fundamentals and differentiate between GDP and GNP

Explain two methods for calculating GDP

Discuss the difference between real GDP and nominal GDP

Discuss the limitations of using GDP to measure well-being

Gross Domestic Product

gross domestic product (GDP) The total market value of all final goods and services produced within a given period by factors of production located within a country.

The key concept in the national income and product accounts is **gross domestic product (GDP)**.

> GDP is the total market value of a country's output. It is the market value of all final goods and services produced within a given period of time by factors of production located within a country.

U.S. GDP for 2012—the value of all output produced by factors of production in the United States in 2012—was $15,676.0 billion.

GDP is a critical concept. Just as an individual firm needs to evaluate the success or failure of its operations each year, so the economy as a whole needs to assess itself. GDP, as a measure of the total production of an economy, provides us with a country's economic report card. Because GDP is so important, we need to take time to explain exactly what its definition means.

Final Goods and Services

final goods and services Goods and services produced for final use.

intermediate goods Goods that are produced by one firm for use in further processing by another firm.

First, note that the definition refers to **final goods and services**. Many goods produced in the economy are not classified as *final* goods, but instead as intermediate goods. **Intermediate goods** are produced by one firm for use in further processing by another firm. For example, tires sold to automobile manufacturers are intermediate goods. The parts that go in Apple's iPod are also intermediate goods. The value of intermediate goods is not counted in GDP.

Why are intermediate goods not counted in GDP? Suppose that in producing a car, General Motors (GM) pays $200 to Goodyear for tires. GM uses these tires (among other components) to assemble a car, which it sells for $24,000. The value of the car (including its tires) is $24,000, not $24,000 + $200. The final price of the car already reflects the value of all its components. To count in GDP both the value of the tires sold to the automobile manufacturers and the value of the automobiles sold to the consumers would result in double counting.

value added The difference between the value of goods as they leave a stage of production and the cost of the goods as they entered that stage.

Double counting can also be avoided by counting only the value added to a product by each firm in its production process. The **value added** during some stage of production is the difference between the value of goods as they leave that stage of production and the cost of the goods as they entered that stage. Value added is illustrated in Table 6.1. The four stages of the production of a gallon of gasoline are: (1) oil drilling, (2) refining, (3) shipping, and (4) retail sale. In the first stage, value added is the value of the crude oil. In the second stage, the refiner purchases the oil from the driller, refines it into gasoline, and sells it to the shipper. The refiner pays the driller $3.00 per gallon and charges the shipper $3.30. The value added by the refiner is thus $0.30 per gallon. The shipper then sells the gasoline to retailers for $3.60. The value added in the third stage of production is $0.30. Finally, the retailer sells the gasoline to consumers for $4.00. The value added at the fourth stage is $0.40; and the total value added in the production process is $4.00, the same as the value of sales at the retail level. Adding the total values of sales at each stage of production ($3.00 + $3.30 + $3.60 + $4.00 = $13.90) would significantly overestimate the value of the gallon of gasoline.

> In calculating GDP, we can sum up the value added at each stage of production or we can take the value of final sales. We do not use the value of total sales in an economy to measure how much output has been produced.

TABLE 6.1 Value Added in the Production of a Gallon of Gasoline (Hypothetical Numbers)

Stage of Production	Value of Sales	Value Added
(1) Oil drilling	$3.00	$3.00
(2) Refining	3.30	0.30
(3) Shipping	3.60	0.30
(4) Retail sale	4.00	0.40
Total value added		$4.00

Exclusion of Used Goods and Paper Transactions

GDP is concerned only with new, or current, production. Old output is not counted in current GDP because it was already counted when it was produced. It would be double counting to count sales of used goods in current GDP. If someone sells a used car to you, the transaction is not counted in GDP because no new production has taken place. Similarly, a house is counted in GDP only at the time it is built, not each time it is resold. In short:

> GDP does not count transactions in which money or goods changes hands but in which no new goods and services are produced.

Sales of stocks and bonds are not counted in GDP. These exchanges are transfers of ownership of assets, either electronically or through paper exchanges, and do not correspond to current production. However, what if you sell the stock or bond for more than you originally paid for it? Profits from the stock or bond market have nothing to do with current production, so they are not counted in GDP. However, if you pay a fee to a broker for selling a stock of yours to someone else, this fee is counted in GDP because the broker is performing a service for you. This service is part of current production. Be careful to distinguish between exchanges of stocks and bonds for money (or for other stocks and bonds), which do not involve current production, and fees for performing such exchanges, which do.

Exclusion of Output Produced Abroad by Domestically Owned Factors of Production

> GDP is the value of output produced by factors of production *located within a country*.

The three basic factors of production are land, labor, and capital. The labor of U.S. citizens counts as a domestically owned factor of production for the United States. The output produced by U.S. citizens abroad—for example, U.S. citizens working for a foreign company—is *not* counted in U.S. GDP because the output is not produced within the United States. Likewise, profits earned abroad by U.S. companies are not counted in U.S. GDP. However, the output produced by foreigners working in the United States is counted in U.S. GDP because the output is produced within the United States. Also, profits earned in the United States by foreign-owned companies are counted in U.S. GDP.

It is sometimes useful to have a measure of the output produced by factors of production owned by a country's citizens regardless of where the output is produced. This measure is called **gross national product (GNP)**. For most countries, including the United States, the difference between GDP and GNP is small. In 2012, GNP for the United States was $15,913.1 billion, which is close to the $15,676.0 billion value for U.S. GDP.

The distinction between GDP and GNP can be tricky. Consider the Honda plant in Marysville, Ohio. The plant is owned by the Honda Corporation, a Japanese firm, but most of the workers employed at the plant are U.S. workers. Although all the output of the plant is included in U.S. GDP, only part of it is included in U.S. GNP. The wages paid to U.S. workers are part of U.S. GNP, while the profits from the plant are not. The profits from the plant are counted in Japanese GNP because this is output produced by Japanese-owned factors of production (Japanese capital in this case). The profits, however, are not counted in Japanese GDP because they were not earned in Japan.

gross national product (GNP) The total market value of all final goods and services produced within a given period by factors of production owned by a country's citizens, regardless of where the output is produced.

Calculating GDP

GDP can be computed two ways. One way is to add up the total amount spent on all final goods and services during a given period. This is the **expenditure approach** to calculating GDP. The other way is to add up the income—wages, rents, interest, and profits—received by all factors

expenditure approach A method of computing GDP that measures the total amount spent on all final goods and services during a given period.

income approach A method of computing GDP that measures the income—wages, rents, interest, and profits—received by all factors of production in producing final goods and services.

of production in producing final goods and services. This is the **income approach** to calculating GDP. These two methods lead to the same value for GDP for the reason we discussed in the previous chapter: *Every payment (expenditure) by a buyer is at the same time a receipt (income) for the seller.* We can measure either income received or expenditures made, and we will end up with the same total output.

Suppose the economy is made up of just one firm and the firm's total output this year sells for $1 million. Because the total amount spent on output this year is $1 million, this year's GDP is $1 million. (Remember: The expenditure approach calculates GDP on the basis of the total amount spent on final goods and services in the economy.) However, *every one* of the million dollars of GDP either is paid to someone or remains with the owners of the firm as profit. Using the income approach, we add up the wages paid to employees of the firm, the interest paid to those who lent money to the firm, and the rents paid to those who leased land, buildings, or equipment to the firm. What is left over is profit, which is, of course, income to the owners of the firm. If we add up the incomes of all the factors of production, including profits to the owners, we get a GDP of $1 million.

The Expenditure Approach

Recall from the previous chapter the four main groups in the economy: households, firms, the government, and the rest of the world. There are also four main categories of expenditure:

- Personal consumption expenditures (C): household spending on consumer goods
- Gross private domestic investment (I): spending by firms and households on new capital, that is, plant, equipment, inventory, and new residential structures
- Government consumption and gross investment (G)
- Net exports (EX − IM): net spending by the rest of the world, or exports (EX) minus imports (IM)

The expenditure approach calculates GDP by adding together these four components of spending. It is shown here in equation form:

$$GDP = C + I + G + (EX - IM)$$

U.S. GDP was $15,676.0 billion in 2012. The four components of the expenditure approach are shown in Table 6.2, along with their various categories.

MyEconLab Real-time data

TABLE 6.2 Components of U.S. GDP, 2012: The Expenditure Approach

	Billions of Dollars		Percentage of GDP	
Personal consumption expenditures (C)	11,119.5		70.9	
Durable goods		1,218.8		7.8
Nondurable goods		2,563.0		16.3
Services		7,337.7		46.8
Gross private domestic investment (I)	2,059.5		13.1	
Nonresidential		1,616.6		10.3
Residential		382.4		2.4
Change in business inventories		60.6		0.4
Government consumption and gross investment (G)	3,063.6		19.5	
Federal		1,214.2		7.7
State and local		1,849.4		11.8
Net exports (EX − IM)	−566.7		−3.6	
Exports (EX)		2,179.7		13.9
Imports (IM)		2,746.3		17.5
Gross domestic product	15,676.0		100.0	

Note: Numbers may not add exactly because of rounding.

Source: U.S. Bureau of Economic Analysis.

ECONOMICS IN PRACTICE

Where Does eBay Get Counted?

eBay runs an online marketplace with over 220 million registered users who buy and sell 2.4 billion items a year, ranging from children's toys to oil paintings. In December 2007, one eBay user auctioned off a 1933 Chicago World's Fair pennant. The winning bid was just over $20.

eBay is traded on the New York Stock Exchange, employs hundreds of people, and has a market value of about $40 billion. With regard to eBay, what do you think gets counted as part of current GDP?

That 1933 pennant, for example, does not get counted. The production of that pennant was counted back in 1933. The many cartons of K'nex bricks sent from one home to another don't count either. Their value was counted when the bricks were first produced. What about a newly minted Scrabble game? One of the interesting features of eBay is that it has changed from being a market in which individuals market their hand-me-downs to a place that small and even large businesses use as a sales site. The value of the new Scrabble game would be counted as part of this year's GDP if it were produced this year.

So do any of eBay's services count as part of GDP? eBay's business is to provide a marketplace for exchange. In doing so, it uses labor and capital and creates value. In return for creating this value, eBay charges fees to the sellers that use its site. The value of these fees do enter into GDP. So while the old knickknacks that people sell on eBay do not contribute to current GDP, the cost of finding an interested buyer for those old goods does indeed get counted.

THINKING PRACTICALLY

1. John has a 2009 Honda Civic. In 2013, he sells it to Mary for $10,000. Is that $10,000 counted in the GDP for 2013?

2. If John is an automobile dealer, does that change your answer to Question 1 at all?

Personal Consumption Expenditures (C)   The largest part of GDP consists of **personal consumption expenditures (C)**. Table 6.2 shows that in 2012, the amount of personal consumption expenditures accounted for 70.9 percent of GDP. These are expenditures by consumers on goods and services.

There are three main categories of consumer expenditures: durable goods, nondurable goods, and services. **Durable goods**, such as automobiles, furniture, and household appliances, last a relatively long time. **Nondurable goods**, such as food, clothing, gasoline, and cigarettes, are used up fairly quickly. Payments for **services**—those things we buy that do not involve the production of physical items—include expenditures for doctors, lawyers, and educational institutions. As Table 6.2 shows, in 2012, durable goods expenditures accounted for 7.8 percent of GDP, nondurables for 16.3 percent, and services for 46.8 percent. Almost half of GDP is now service consumption.

Gross Private Domestic Investment (I)   *Investment*, as we use the term in economics, refers to the purchase of new capital—housing, plants, equipment, and inventory. The economic use of the term is in contrast to its everyday use, where *investment* often refers to purchases of stocks, bonds, or mutual funds.

Total investment in capital by the private sector is called **gross private domestic investment (I)**. Expenditures by firms for machines, tools, plants, and so on make up **nonresidential investment**.[1] Because these are goods that firms buy for their own final use, they are part of "final sales" and counted in GDP. Expenditures for new houses and apartment buildings constitute **residential investment**. The third component of gross private domestic investment, the **change in business inventories**, is the amount by which firms' inventories change during a period. Business inventories can be looked at as the goods that firms produce now but intend to sell later. In 2012, gross private domestic investment accounted for 13.1 percent of GDP. Of that, 10.3 percent was nonresidential investment, 2.4 percent was residential investment, and 0.4 percent was change in business inventories.

personal consumption expenditures (C) Expenditures by consumers on goods and services.

durable goods Goods that last a relatively long time, such as cars and household appliances.

nondurable goods Goods that are used up fairly quickly, such as food and clothing.

services The things we buy that do not involve the production of physical things, such as legal and medical services and education.

gross private domestic investment (I) Total investment in capital—that is, the purchase of new housing, plants, equipment, and inventory by the private (or nongovernment) sector.

nonresidential investment Expenditures by firms for machines, tools, plants, and so on.

residential investment Expenditures by households and firms on new houses and apartment buildings.

---

[1] The distinction between what is considered investment and what is considered consumption is sometimes fairly arbitrary. A firm's purchase of a car or a truck is counted as investment, but a household's purchase of a car or a truck is counted as consumption of durable goods. In general, expenditures by firms for items that last longer than a year are counted as investment expenditures. Expenditures for items that last less than a year are seen as purchases of intermediate goods.

change in business inventories The amount by which firms' inventories change during a period. Inventories are the goods that firms produce now but intend to sell later.

Change in Business Inventories   Why is the change in business inventories considered a component of investment—the purchase of new capital? To run a business most firms hold inventories. Publishing firms print more books than they expect to sell instantly so that they can ship them quickly once they do get orders. Inventories—goods produced for later sale—are counted as capital because they produce value in the future. An increase in inventories is an increase in capital.

Regarding GDP, remember that it is not the market value of total final *sales* during the period, but rather the market value of total final *production*. The relationship between total production and total sales is as follows:

$$\text{GDP} = \text{Final sales} + \text{Change in business inventories}$$

Total production (GDP) equals final sales of domestic goods plus the change in business inventories. In 2012, production in the United States was larger than sales by $60.6 billion. The stock of inventories at the end of 2012 was $60.6 billion *larger* than it was at the end of 2011—the change in business inventories was $60.6 billion.

Gross Investment versus Net Investment   During the process of production, capital (especially machinery and equipment) produced in previous periods gradually wears out. GDP does not give us a true picture of the real production of an economy. GDP includes newly produced capital goods but does not take account of capital goods "consumed" in the production process.

depreciation The amount by which an asset's value falls in a given period.

gross investment The total value of all newly produced capital goods (plant, equipment, housing, and inventory) produced in a given period.

net investment Gross investment minus depreciation.

Capital assets decline in value over time. The amount by which an asset's value falls each period is called its **depreciation**.[2] A personal computer purchased by a business today may be expected to have a useful life of 4 years before becoming worn out or obsolete. Over that period, the computer steadily depreciates.

What is the relationship between gross investment (I) and depreciation? **Gross investment** is the total value of all newly produced capital goods (plant, equipment, housing, and inventory) produced in a given period. It takes no account of the fact that some capital wears out and must be replaced. **Net investment** is equal to gross investment minus depreciation. Net investment is a measure of how much the stock of capital *changes* during a period. Positive net investment means that the amount of new capital produced exceeds the amount that wears out, and negative net investment means that the amount of new capital produced is less than the amount that wears out. Therefore, if net investment is positive, the capital stock has increased, and if net investment is negative, the capital stock has decreased. Put another way, the capital stock at the end of a period is equal to the capital stock that existed at the beginning of the period plus net investment:

$$\text{capital}_{\text{end of period}} = \text{capital}_{\text{beginning of period}} + \text{net investment}$$

government consumption and gross investment (G) Expenditures by federal, state, and local governments for final goods and services.

Government Consumption and Gross Investment (G)   Government

consumption and gross investment (G) include expenditures by federal, state, and local governments for final goods (bombs, pencils, school buildings) and services (military salaries, congressional salaries, school teachers' salaries). Some of these expenditures are counted as government consumption, and some are counted as government gross investment. Government transfer payments (Social Security benefits, veterans' disability stipends, and so on) are not included in G because these transfers are not purchases of anything currently produced. The payments are not made in exchange for any goods or services. Because interest payments on the government debt are also counted as transfers, they are excluded from GDP on the grounds that they are not payments for current goods or services.

As Table 6.2 shows, government consumption and gross investment accounted for $3,063.6 billion, or 19.5 percent of U.S. GDP, in 2012. Federal government consumption and gross investment accounted for 7.7 percent of GDP, and state and local government consumption and gross investment accounted for 11.8 percent.

---

[2] This is the formal definition of economic depreciation. Because depreciation is difficult to measure precisely, accounting rules allow firms to use shortcut methods to approximate the amount of depreciation that they incur each period. To complicate matters even more, the U.S. tax laws allow firms to deduct depreciation for tax purposes under a different set of rules.

TABLE 6.3 National Income, 2012

	Billions of Dollars	Percentage of National Income
National income	13,833.2	100.0
Compensation of employees	8,559.8	61.9
Proprietors' income	1,203.0	8.7
Rental income	463.5	3.4
Corporate profits	1,939.3	14.0
Net interest	504.1	3.6
Indirect taxes minus subsidies	1069.6	7.7
Net business transfer payments	127.9	0.9
Surplus of government enterprises	−34.0	−0.2

Source: See Table 6.2.

Net Exports (EX − IM)

The value of **net exports (EX − IM)** is the difference between *exports* (sales to foreigners of U.S.-produced goods and services) and *imports* (U.S. purchases of goods and services from abroad). This figure can be positive or negative. In 2012, the United States exported less than it imported, so the level of net exports was negative (−$566.7 billion). Before 1976, the United States was generally a net exporter—exports exceeded imports, so the net export figure was positive.

The reason for including net exports in the definition of GDP is simple. Consumption, investment, and government spending (C, I, and G, respectively) include expenditures on goods produced at home and abroad. Therefore, C + I + G overstates domestic production because it contains expenditures on foreign-produced goods—that is, imports (IM), which have to be subtracted from GDP to obtain the correct figure. At the same time, C + I + G understates domestic production because some of what a nation produces is sold abroad and therefore is not included in C, I, or G—exports (EX) have to be added in. If a U.S. firm produces computers and sells them in Germany, the computers are part of U.S. production and should be counted as part of U.S. GDP.

The Income Approach

We now turn to calculating GDP using the income approach, which looks at GDP in terms of who receives it as income rather than as who purchases it.

We begin with the concept of **national income**, which is defined in Table 6.3. National income is the sum of eight income items. **Compensation of employees**, the largest of the eight items by far, includes wages and salaries paid to households by firms and by the government, as well as various supplements to wages and salaries such as contributions that employers make to social insurance and private pension funds. **Proprietors' income** is the income of unincorporated businesses. **Rental income**, a minor item, is the income received by property owners in the form of rent. **Corporate profits**, the second-largest item of the eight, is the income of corporations. **Net interest** is the interest paid by business. (Interest paid by households and the government is not counted in GDP because it is not assumed to flow from the production of goods and services.)

The sixth item, **indirect taxes minus subsidies**, includes taxes such as sales taxes, customs duties, and license fees less subsidies that the government pays for which it receives no goods or services in return. (Subsidies are like negative taxes.) The value of indirect taxes minus subsidies is thus net income received by the government. **Net business transfer payments** are net transfer payments by businesses to others and are thus income of others. The final item is the `surplus of government enterprises`, which is the income of government enterprises. Table 6.3 shows that this item was negative in 2012: government enterprises on net ran at a loss.

National income is the total income of the country, but it is not quite GDP. Table 6.4 shows what is involved in going from national income to GDP. Table 6.4 first shows that in moving from gross domestic product (GDP) to gross national product (GNP), we need to add receipts of factor income from the rest of the world and subtract payments of factor income to the rest of the world. National income is income of the country's citizens, not the income of the residents of the country. So we first need to move from GDP to GNP. This, as discussed earlier, is a minor adjustment.

net exports (EX − IM) The difference between exports (sales to foreigners of U.S.-produced goods and services) and imports (U.S. purchases of goods and services from abroad). The figure can be positive or negative.

national income The total income earned by the factors of production owned by a country's citizens.

compensation of employees Includes wages, salaries, and various supplements—employer contributions to social insurance and pension funds, for example—paid to households by firms and by the government.

proprietors' income The income of unincorporated businesses.

rental income The income received by property owners in the form of rent.

corporate profits The income of corporations.

net interest The interest paid by business.

indirect taxes minus subsidies Taxes such as sales taxes, customs duties, and license fees less subsidies that the government pays for which it receives no goods or services in return.

net business transfer payments Net transfer payments by businesses to others.

surplus of government enterprises Income of government enterprises.

MyEconLab Real-time data

TABLE 6.4 GDP, GNP, NNP, and National Income, 2012

	Dollars (Billions)
GDP	15,676.0
Plus: Receipts of factor income from the rest of the world	+774.1
Less: Payments of factor income to the rest of the world	−537.0
Equals: GNP	15,913.1
Less: Depreciation	−2,011.4
Equals: Net national product (NNP)	13,901.7
Less: Statistical discrepancy	−68.5
Equals: National income	13,833.2

Source: See Table 6.2

net national product (NNP)
Gross national product minus depreciation; a nation's total product minus what is required to maintain the value of its capital stock.

We then need to subtract depreciation from GNP, which is a large adjustment. GNP less depreciation is called **net national product (NNP)**. Why is depreciation subtracted? To see why, go back to the example earlier in this chapter in which the economy is made up of just one firm and total output (GDP) for the year is $1 million. Assume that after the firm pays wages, interest, and rent, it has $100,000 left. Assume also that its capital stock depreciated by $40,000 during the year. National income includes corporate profits (see Table 6.3), and in calculating corporate profits, the $40,000 depreciation is subtracted from the $100,000, leaving profits of $60,000. So national income does not include the $40,000. When we calculate GDP using the expenditure approach, however, depreciation is not subtracted. We simply add consumption, investment, government spending, and net exports. In our simple example, this is just $1 million. We thus must subtract depreciation from GDP (actually GNP when there is a rest-of-the-world sector) to get national income.

statistical discrepancy
Data measurement error.

Table 6.4 shows that net national product and national income are the same except for a **statistical discrepancy**, a data measurement error. If the government were completely accurate in its data collection, the statistical discrepancy would be zero. The data collection, however, is not perfect, and the statistical discrepancy is the measurement error in each period. Table 6.4 shows that in 2012, this error was $68.5 billion, which is small compared to national income of $13,833.2 billion.

personal income The total income of households.

We have so far seen from Table 6.3 the various income items that make up total national income, and we have seen from Table 6.4 how GDP and national income are related. A useful way to think about national income is to consider how much of it goes to households. The total income of households is called **personal income**, and it turns out that almost all of national income is personal income. Table 6.5 shows that of the $13,883.2 billion in national income in 2012, $13,402.4 billion was personal income. The second line in Table 6.5, the amount of national income not going to households, includes the profits of corporations not paid to households in the form of dividends, called the *retained earnings* of corporations. This is income that goes to corporations rather than to households, and so it is part of national income but not personal income.

MyEconLab Real-time data

TABLE 6.5 National Income, Personal Income, Disposable Personal Income, and Personal Saving, 2012

	Dollar (Billions)
National income	13,833.2
Less: Amount of national income not going to households	−430.8
Equals: **Personal income**	13,402.4
Less: Personal income taxes	−1,471.9
Equals: **Disposable personal income**	11,930.6
Less: Personal consumption expenditures	−11,119.5
Personal interest payments	−172.3
Transfer payments made by households	−168.1
Equals: **Personal saving**	470.8
Personal saving as a percentage of disposable personal income:	3.9%

Source: See Table 6.2

ECONOMICS IN PRACTICE

GDP: One of the Great Inventions of the 20th Century

As the 20th century drew to a close, the U.S. Department of Commerce embarked on a review of its achievements. At the conclusion of this review, the Department named the development of the national income and product accounts as "its achievement of the century."

J. Steven Landefeld *Director, Bureau of Economic Analysis*

While the GDP and the rest of the national income accounts may seem to be arcane concepts, they are truly among the great inventions of the twentieth century.

Paul A. Samuelson and William D. Nordhaus

GDP! The right concept of economy-wide output, accurately measured. The U.S. and the world rely on it to tell where we are in the business cycle and to estimate long-run growth. It is the centerpiece of an elaborate and indispensable system of social accounting, the national income and product accounts. This is surely the single most innovative achievement of the Commerce Department in the 20th century. I was fortunate to become an economist in the 1930's when Kuznets, Nathan, Gilbert, and Jaszi were creating this most important set of economic time series. In economic theory, macroeconomics was just beginning at the same time. Complementary, these two innovations deserve much credit for the improved performance of the economy in the second half of the century.

James Tobin

FROM THE *SURVEY OF CURRENT BUSINESS*

Prior to the development of the NIPAs [national income and product accounts], policy makers had to guide the economy using limited and fragmentary information about the state of the economy. The Great Depression underlined the problems of incomplete data and led to the development of the national accounts:

One reads with dismay of Presidents Hoover and then Roosevelt designing policies to combat the Great Depression of the 1930s on the basis of such sketchy data

as stock price indices, freight car loadings, and incomplete indices of industrial production. The fact was that comprehensive measures of national income and output did not exist at the time. The Depression, and with it the growing role of government in the economy, emphasized the need for such measures and led to the development of a comprehensive set of national income accounts.

Richard T. Froyen

In response to this need in the 1930s, the Department of Commerce commissioned Nobel laureate Simon Kuznets of the National Bureau of Economic Research to develop a set of national economic accounts....Professor Kuznets coordinated the work of researchers at the National Bureau of Economic Research in New York and his staff at Commerce. The original set of accounts was presented in a report to Congress in 1937 and in a research report, *National Income, 1929–35....*

The national accounts have become the mainstay of modern macroeconomic analysis, allowing policy makers, economists, and the business community to analyze the impact of different tax and spending plans, the impact of oil and other price shocks, and the impact of monetary policy on the economy as a whole and on specific components of final demand, incomes, industries, and regions....

THINKING PRACTICALLY

1. The articles above emphasize the importance of being able to measure an economy's output to improve government policy. Looking at recent news, can you identify one economic policy debate or action that referenced GDP?

Source: U.S. Department of Commerce, Bureau of Economics, "GDP: One of the Great Inventions of the 20th Century," Survey of Current Business, January 2000, pp. 6–9.

Personal income is the income received by households before they pay personal income taxes. The amount of income that households have to spend or save is called **disposable personal income**, *or* **after-tax income**. It is equal to personal income minus personal income taxes, as shown in Table 6.5.

Because disposable personal income is the amount of income that households can spend or save, it is an important income concept. Table 6.5 shows there are three categories of spending: (1) personal consumption expenditures, (2) personal interest payments, and (3) transfer payments made by households. The amount of disposable personal income left after total personal spending is **personal saving**. If your monthly disposable income is $500 and you spend $450, you have $50 left at the end of the month. Your personal saving is $50 for the month. Your personal saving level can be negative: If you earn $500 and spend $600 during the month, you have *dissaved* $100. To spend $100 more than you earn, you will have to borrow the $100 from someone, take the $100 from your savings account, or sell an asset you own.

disposable personal income *or* **after-tax income** Personal income minus personal income taxes. The amount that households have to spend or save.

personal saving The amount of disposable income that is left after total personal spending in a given period.

personal saving rate The percentage of disposable personal income that is saved. If the personal saving rate is low, households are spending a large amount relative to their incomes; if it is high, households are spending cautiously.

The **personal saving rate** is the percentage of disposable personal income saved, an important indicator of household behavior. A low saving rate means households are spending a large fraction of their income. A high-saving rate means households are cautious in their spending. As Table 6.5 shows, the U.S. personal saving rate in 2012 was 3.9 percent. Saving rates tend to rise during recessionary periods, when consumers become anxious about their future, and fall during boom times, as pent-up spending demand gets released. In 2005 the saving rate got down to 1.3 percent.

Nominal versus Real GDP

current dollars The current prices that we pay for goods and services.

nominal GDP Gross domestic product measured in current dollars.

We have thus far looked at GDP measured in **current dollars**, or the current prices we pay for goods and services. When we measure something in current dollars, we refer to it as a *nominal* value. **Nominal GDP** is GDP measured in current dollars—all components of GDP valued at their current prices.

In most applications in macroeconomics, however, nominal GDP is not what we are after. It is not a good measure of aggregate output over time. Why? Assume that there is only one good—say, pizza, which is the same quality year after year. In each year 1 and 2, one hundred units (slices) of pizza were produced. Production thus remained the same for year 1 and year 2. Suppose the price of pizza increased from $1.00 per slice in year 1 to $1.10 per slice in year 2. Nominal GDP in year 1 is $100 (100 units $\times$ $1.00 per unit), and nominal GDP in year 2 is $110 (100 units $\times$ $1.10 per unit). Nominal GDP has increased by $10 even though no more slices of pizza were produced. If we use nominal GDP to measure growth, we can be misled into thinking production has grown when all that has really happened is a rise in the price level (inflation).

If there were only one good in the economy—for example, pizza—it would be easy to measure production and compare one year's value to another's. We would add up all the pizza slices produced each year. In the example, production is 100 in both years. If the number of slices had increased to 105 in year 2, we would say production increased by 5 slices between year 1 and year 2, which is a 5 percent increase. Alas, however, there is more than one good in the economy.

The following is a discussion of how the BEA adjusts nominal GDP for price changes. As you read the discussion, keep in mind that this adjustment is not easy. Even in an economy of just apples and oranges, it would not be obvious how to add up apples and oranges to get an overall measure of output. The BEA's task is to add up thousands of goods, each of whose price is changing over time.

weight The importance attached to an item within a group of items.

In the following discussion, we will use the concept of a **weight**, either price weights or quantity weights. What is a weight? It is easiest to define the term by an example. Suppose in your economics course there is a final exam and two other tests. If the final exam counts for one-half of the grade and the other two tests for one-fourth each, the "weights" are one-half, one-fourth, and one-fourth. If instead the final exam counts for 80 percent of the grade and the other two tests for 10 percent each, the weights are .8, .1, and .1. The more important an item is in a group, the larger its weight.

Calculating Real GDP

Nominal GDP adjusted for price changes is called *real GDP*. All the main issues involved in computing real GDP can be discussed using a simple three-good economy and 2 years. Table 6.6 presents all the data that we will need. The table presents price and quantity data for 2 years and three goods. The goods are labeled *A*, *B*, and *C*, and the years are labeled 1 and 2. *P* denotes price, and *Q* denotes quantity. Keep in mind that everything in the following discussion, including the discussion of the GDP deflation, is based on the numbers in Table 6.6. Nothing has been brought in from the outside. The table is the entire economy.

The first thing to note from Table 6.6 is that *nominal output*—in current dollars—in year 1 for good *A* is the price of good *A* in year 1 ($0.50) times the number of units of good *A* produced in year 1 (6), which is $3.00. Similarly, nominal output in year 1 is 7 $\times$ $0.30 = $2.10 for good *B* and 10 $\times$ $0.70 = $7.00 for good *C*. The sum of these three amounts, $12.10 in column 5, is nominal GDP in year 1 in this simple economy. Nominal GDP in year 2—calculated by using the year 2 quantities and the year 2 prices—is $19.20 (column 8). Nominal GDP has risen from $12.10 in year 1 to $19.20 in year 2, an increase of 58.7 percent.[3]

---

[3] The percentage change is calculated as $[(19.20 - 12.10)/12.10] \times 100 = .587 \times 100 = 58.7$ percent.

TABLE 6.6 A Three-Good Economy

	(1)	(2)	(3)	(4)	(5)	(6)	(7)	(8)
					GDP in Year 1 in Year 1 Prices	GDP in Year 2 in Year 1 Prices	GDP in Year 1 in Year 2 Prices	GDP in Year 2 in Year 2 Prices
	Production		Price per Unit					
	Year 1 Q_1	Year 2 Q_2	Year 1 P_1	Year 2 P_2	$P_1 \times Q_1$	$P_1 \times Q_2$	$P_2 \times Q_1$	$P_2 \times Q_2$
Good A	6	11	$0.50	$0.40	$ 3.00	$ 5.50	$ 2.40	$ 4.40
Good B	7	4	0.30	1.00	2.10	1.20	7.00	4.00
Good C	10	12	0.70	0.90	7.00	8.40	9.00	10.80
Total					$12.10	$15.10	$18.40	$19.20
					Nominal GDP in year 1			Nominal GDP in year 2

You can see that the price of each good changed between year 1 and year 2—the price of good A fell (from $0.50 to $0.40) and the prices of goods B and C rose (B from $0.30 to $1.00; C from $0.70 to $0.90). Some of the change in nominal GDP between years 1 and 2 is due to price changes and not production changes. How much can we attribute to price changes and how much to production changes? Here things get tricky. The procedure that the BEA used prior to 1996 was to pick a **base year** and to use the prices in that base year as weights to calculate real GDP. This is a **fixed-weight procedure** because the weights used, which are the prices, are the same for all years—namely, the prices that prevailed in the base year.

Let us use the fixed-weight procedure and year 1 as the base year, which means using year 1 prices as the weights. Then in Table 6.6, real GDP in year 1 is $12.10 (column 5) and real GDP in year 2 is $15.10 (column 6). Note that both columns use year 1 prices and that nominal and real GDP are the same in year 1 because year 1 is the base year. Real GDP has increased from $12.10 to $15.10, an increase of 24.8 percent.

Let us now use the fixed-weight procedure and year 2 as the base year, which means using year 2 prices as the weights. In Table 6.6, real GDP in year 1 is $18.40 (column 7) and real GDP in year 2 is $19.20 (column 8). Note that both columns use year 2 prices and that nominal and real GDP are the same in year 2, because year 2 is the base year. Real GDP has increased from $18.40 to $19.20, an increase of 4.3 percent.

This example shows that growth rates can be sensitive to the choice of the base year— 24.8 percent using year 1 prices as weights and 4.3 percent using year 2 prices as weights. The old BEA procedure simply picked one year as the base year and did all the calculations using the prices in that year as weights. The new BEA procedure makes two important changes. The first (using the current example) is to take the average of the two years' price changes, in other words, to "split the difference" between 24.8 percent and 4.3 percent. What does "splitting the difference" mean? One way is to take the average of the two numbers, which is 14.55 percent. What the BEA does is to take the *geometric* average, which for the current example is 14.09 percent.[4] These two averages (14.55 percent and 14.09 percent) are quite close, and the use of either would give similar results. The point here is not that the geometric average is used, but that the first change is to split the difference using some average. Note that this new procedure requires two "base" years because 24.8 percent was computed using year 1 prices as weights and 4.3 percent was computed using year 2 prices as weights.

The second BEA change is to use years 1 and 2 as the base years when computing the percentage change between years 1 and 2, then use years 2 and 3 as the base years when computing the percentage change between years 2 and 3, and so on. The two base years change as the calculations move through time. The series of percentage changes computed this way is taken to be the series of growth rates of real GDP. So in this way, nominal GDP is adjusted for price changes. To make sure you understand this, review the calculations in Table 6.6, which provides all the data you need to see what is going on.

base year The year chosen for the weights in a fixed-weight procedure.

fixed-weight procedure A procedure that uses weights from a given base year.

---

[4] The geometric average is computed as the square root of 124.8 × 104.3, which is 114.09.

Calculating the GDP Deflator

We now switch gears from real GDP, a quantity measure, to the GDP deflator, a price measure. One of economic policy makers' goals is to keep changes in the overall price level small. For this reason, policy makers not only need good measures of how real output is changing but also good measures of how the overall price level is changing. The GDP deflator is one measure of the overall price level. We can use the data in Table 6.6 to show how the BEA computes the GDP deflator.

In Table 6.6, the price of good *A* fell from $0.50 in year 1 to $0.40 in year 2, the price of good *B* rose from $0.30 to $1.00, and the price of good *C* rose from $0.70 to $0.90. If we are interested only in how individual prices change, this is all the information we need. However, if we are interested in how the overall price *level* changes, we need to weight the individual prices in some way. The obvious weights to use are the quantities produced, but which quantities—those of year 1 or year 2? The same issues arise here for the quantity weights as for the price weights in computing real GDP.

Let us first use the fixed-weight procedure and year 1 as the base year, which means using year 1 quantities as the weights. Then in Table 6.6, the "bundle" price in year 1 is $12.10 (column 5) and the bundle price in year 2 is $18.40 (column 7). Both columns use year 1 quantities. The bundle price has increased from $12.10 to $18.40, an increase of 52.1 percent.

Next, use the fixed-weight procedure and year 2 as the base year, which means using year 2 quantities as the weights. Then the bundle price in year 1 is $15.10 (column 6), and the bundle price in year 2 is $19.20 (column 8). Both columns use year 2 quantities. The bundle price has increased from $15.10 to $19.20, an increase of 27.2 percent.

This example shows that overall price increases can be sensitive to the choice of the base year: 52.1 percent using year 1 quantities as weights and 27.2 percent using year 2 quantities as weights. Again, the old BEA procedure simply picked one year as the base year and did all the calculations using the quantities in the base year as weights. First, the new procedure splits the difference between 52.1 percent and 27.2 percent by taking the geometric average, which is 39.1 percent. Second, it uses years 1 and 2 as the base years when computing the percentage change between years 1 and 2, years 2 and 3 as the base years when computing the percentage change between years 2 and 3, and so on. The series of percentage changes computed this way is taken to be the series of percentage changes in the GDP deflator, that is, a series of inflation rates.

The Problems of Fixed Weights

To see why the BEA switched to the new procedure, let us consider a number of problems using fixed-price weights to compute real GDP. First, 1987 price weights, the last price weights the BEA used before it changed procedures, are not likely to be very accurate for, say, the 1950s. Many structural changes took place in the U.S. economy between the 1950s and 1987, and it seems unlikely that 1987 prices are good weights to use for the 1950s. Nor are they likely to be good weights for 2012.

Another problem is that the use of fixed-price weights does not account for the responses in the economy to supply shifts. Perhaps bad weather leads to a lower production of oranges in year 2. In a simple supply-and-demand diagram for oranges, this corresponds to a shift of the supply curve to the left, which leads to an increase in the price of oranges and a decrease in the quantity demanded. As consumers move up the demand curve, they are substituting away from oranges. If technical advances in year 2 result in cheaper ways of producing computers, the result is a shift of the computer supply curve to the right, which leads to a decrease in the price of computers and an increase in the quantity demanded. Consumers are substituting toward computers. (You should be able to draw supply-and-demand diagrams for both cases.) Table 6.6 shows this tendency. The quantity of good *A* rose between years 1 and 2 and the price decreased (the computer case), whereas the quantity of good *B* fell and the price increased (the orange case). The computer supply curve has been shifting to the right over time, due primarily to technical advances. The result has been large decreases in the price of computers and large increases in the quantity demanded.

To see why these responses pose a problem for the use of fixed-price weights, consider the data in Table 6.6. Because the price of good *A* was higher in year 1, the increase in production of good *A* is weighted more if we use year 1 as the base year than if we used year 2 as the base year. Also, because the price of good *B* was lower in year 1, the decrease in production of good *B* is weighted less if we use year 1 as the base year. These effects make the overall change in real GDP larger if we use year 1 price weights than if we use year 2 price weights. Using year 1 price weights ignores the kinds of substitution responses discussed in the previous paragraph and leads to what many believe are too-large estimates of real GDP changes. In the past, the BEA tended to move the base year forward about every 5 years, resulting in the past estimates of real GDP growth being revised downward. It is undesirable to have past growth estimates change simply because of the change to a new base year. The new BEA procedure avoids many of these fixed-weight problems.

Similar problems arise when using fixed-quantity weights to compute price indexes. For example, the fixed-weight procedure ignores the substitution away from goods whose prices are increasing and toward goods whose prices are decreasing or increasing less rapidly. The procedure tends to overestimate the increase in the overall price level. As discussed in the next chapter, there are still a number of price indexes that are computed using fixed weights. The GDP deflator differs because it does not use fixed weights. It is also a price index for all the goods and services produced in the economy. Other price indexes cover fewer domestically produced goods and services but also include some imported (foreign-produced) goods and services.

It should finally be stressed that there is no "right" way of computing real GDP. The economy consists of many goods, each with its own price, and there is no exact way of adding together the production of the different goods. We can say that the BEA's new procedure for computing real GDP avoids the problems associated with the use of fixed weights, and it seems to be an improvement over the old procedure. We will see in the next chapter, however, that the consumer price index (CPI)—a widely used price index—is still computed using fixed weights.

Limitations of the GDP Concept

We generally think of increases in GDP as good. Increasing GDP (or preventing its decrease) is usually considered one of the chief goals of the government's macroeconomic policy. Because some serious problems arise when we try to use GDP as a measure of happiness or well-being, we now point out some of the limitations of the GDP concept as a measure of welfare.

GDP and Social Welfare

If crime levels went down, society would be better off, but a decrease in crime is not an increase in output and is not reflected in GDP. Neither is an increase in leisure time. Yet to the extent that households want extra leisure time (instead of having it forced on them by a lack of jobs in the economy), an increase in leisure is also an increase in social welfare. Furthermore, some increases in social welfare are associated with a *decrease* in GDP. An increase in leisure during a time of full employment, for example, leads to a decrease in GDP because less time is spent on producing output.

Most nonmarket and domestic activities, such as housework and child care, are not counted in GDP even though they amount to real production. However, if I decide to send my children to day care or hire someone to clean my house or drive my car for me, GDP increases. The salaries of day care staff, cleaning people, and chauffeurs are counted in GDP, but the time I spend doing the same things is not counted. A mere change of institutional arrangements, even though no more output is being produced, can show up as a change in GDP.

Furthermore, GDP seldom reflects losses or social ills. GDP accounting rules do not adjust for production that pollutes the environment. The more production there is, the larger the GDP, regardless of how much pollution results in the process.

GDP also has nothing to say about the distribution of output among individuals in a society. It does not distinguish, for example, between the case in which most output goes to a few people and the case in which output is evenly divided among all people. We cannot use GDP to measure the effects of redistributive policies (which take income from some people and give income to others). Such policies have no direct impact on GDP. GDP is also neutral about the kinds of goods an economy produces. Symphony performances, handguns, cigarettes, professional football games, Bibles, soda pop, milk, economics textbooks, and comic books all get counted similarly.

ECONOMICS IN PRACTICE

Green Accounting

The national income and product accounts include all market activities. So purchased child care is included, but child care provided by parents is not. Recently many economists and policy makers have become concerned about the exclusion of one particularly large and important nonmarket activity from the national income accounts: the environment.

Many industries when they produce goods also produce air pollution as a by-product. The market goods these firms produce go into the national income and product accounts, but the environmental costs of air pollution are not subtracted. How much difference does not counting of this by-product make? Recent work by Nick Muller, Robert Mendelsohn, and Bill Nordhaus estimates that for some industries in the United States, like stone mining and

coal-powered electricity generation, including properly valued air pollution in the national income and product accounts as an offset to the value of the marketed goods produced by these industries would make the contribution of these industries to our nation's GDP negative![1]

THINKING PRACTICALLY

1. Why do you think we have not counted pollution in GDP measures in the past?

[1] Nicholas Muller, Robert Mendelsohn and William Nordhaus, "Environmental Accounting for Pollution in the United States Economy," *American Economics Review* August 2011, 1649–1675.

The Informal Economy

Many transactions are missed in the calculation of GDP even though, in principle, they should be counted. Most illegal transactions are missed unless they are "laundered" into legitimate business. Income that is earned but not reported as income for tax purposes is usually missed, although some adjustments are made in the GDP calculations to take misreported income into account. The part of the economy that should be counted in GDP but is not is sometimes called the **informal economy**.

informal economy The part of the economy in which transactions take place and in which income is generated that is unreported and therefore not counted in GDP.

Tax evasion is usually thought to be the major incentive for people to participate in the informal economy. Studies estimate that the size of the U.S. informal economy, ranging from 5 percent to 30 percent of GDP,[5] is comparable to the size of the informal economy in most European countries and probably much smaller than the size of the informal economy in the Eastern European countries. Estimates of Italy's informal economy range from 10 percent to 35 percent of Italian GDP. At the lower end of the scale, estimates for Switzerland range from 3 percent to 5 percent.

Why should we care about the informal economy? To the extent that GDP reflects only a part of economic activity instead of a complete measure of what the economy produces, it is misleading. Unemployment rates, for example, may be lower than officially measured if people work in the informal economy without reporting this fact to the government. Also, if the size of the informal economy varies among countries—as it does—we can be misled when we compare GDP among countries. For example, Italy's GDP would be much higher if we considered its informal sector as part of the economy, while Switzerland's GDP would change very little.

Gross National Income per Capita

gross national income (GNI) GNP converted into dollars using an average of currency exchange rates over several years adjusted for rates of inflation.

Making comparisons across countries is difficult because such comparisons need to be made in a single currency, generally U.S. dollars. Converting GNP numbers for Japan into dollars requires converting from yen into dollars. Since exchange rates can change quite dramatically in short periods of time, such conversions are tricky. Recently, the World Bank adopted a new measuring system for international comparisons. The concept of **gross national income (GNI)** is GNP converted into dollars using an average of currency exchange rates over several years adjusted for rates of inflation. Figure 6.1 lists the gross national income per capita (GNI divided by population) for various countries in 2011. Of the countries in the figure, Norway had the highest per capita GNI, followed by Switzerland, the United States, and the Netherlands. Ethiopia was estimated to have per capita GNI of only $1,110 in 2011. This compares to $61,460 for Norway.

[5] See, for example, Edgar L. Feige, "Defining and Estimating Underground and Informal Economies: The New Industrial Economic Approach," *World Development* 19(7), 1990, and "The Underground Economy in the United States," Occasional Paper No. 2, U.S. Department of Labor, September 1992.

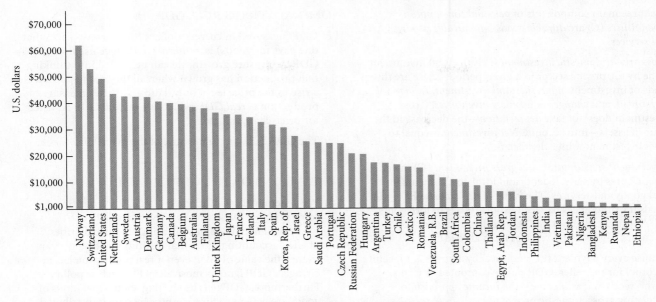

▲ **FIGURE 6.1** **Per-Capita Gross National Income for Selected Countries, 2011** MyEconLab Real-time data

Source: World Bank.

Looking Ahead

This chapter has introduced many key variables in which macroeconomists are interested, including GDP and its components. There is much more to be learned about the data that macroeconomists use. In the next chapter, we will discuss the data on employment, unemployment, and the labor force. In Chapters 10 and 11, we will discuss the data on money and interest rates. Finally, in Chapter 20, we will discuss in more detail the data on the relationship between the United States and the rest of the world.

──────── S U M M A R Y ────────

1. One source of data on the key variables in the macroeconomy is the *national income and product accounts*. These accounts provide a conceptual framework that macroeconomists use to think about how the pieces of the economy fit together.

GROSS DOMESTIC PRODUCT *p. 112*

2. *Gross domestic product* (*GDP*) is the key concept in national income accounting. GDP is the total market value of all final goods and services produced within a given period by factors of production located within a country. GDP excludes *intermediate goods*. To include goods when they are purchased as inputs and when they are sold as final products would be double counting and would result in an overstatement of the value of production.

3. GDP excludes all transactions in which money or goods change hands but in which no new goods and services are produced.

GDP includes the income of foreigners working in the United States and the profits that foreign companies earn in the United States. GDP excludes the income of U.S. citizens working abroad and profits earned by U.S. companies in foreign countries.

4. *Gross national product* (*GNP*) is the market value of all final goods and services produced during a given period by factors of production owned by a country's citizens.

CALCULATING GDP *p. 113*

5. The *expenditure approach* to GDP adds up the amount spent on all final goods and services during a given period. The four main categories of expenditures are *personal consumption expenditures* (*C*), *gross private domestic investment* (*I*), *government consumption and gross investment* (*G*), and *net exports* (*EX* − *IM*). The sum of these categories equals GDP.

6. The three main components of *personal consumption expenditures* (C) are *durable goods, nondurable goods,* and *services.*

7. *Gross private domestic investment* (I) is the total investment made by the private sector in a given period. There are three kinds of investment: *nonresidential investment, residential investment,* and *changes in business inventories.* Gross investment does not take *depreciation*—the decrease in the value of assets—into account. *Net investment* is equal to gross investment minus depreciation.

8. *Government consumption and gross investment* (G) include expenditures by state, federal, and local governments for final goods and services. The value of *net exports* (EX − IM) equals the differences between exports (sales to foreigners of U.S.-produced goods and services) and imports (U.S. purchases of goods and services from abroad).

9. Because every payment (expenditure) by a buyer is a receipt (income) for the seller, GDP can be computed in terms of who receives it as income—the *income approach* to calculating gross domestic product.

10. GNP minus depreciation is *net national product* (NNP). *National income* is the total amount earned by the factors of production in the economy. It is equal to NNP except for a statistical discrepancy. *Personal income* is the total income of households. *Disposable personal income* is what households have to spend or save after paying their taxes. The *personal saving rate* is the percentage of disposable personal income saved instead of spent.

NOMINAL VERSUS REAL GDP *p. 120*

11. GDP measured in current dollars (the current prices that one pays for goods) is *nominal GDP*. If we use nominal GDP to measure growth, we can be misled into thinking that production has grown when all that has happened is a rise in the price level, or inflation. A better measure of production is *real GDP*, which is nominal GDP adjusted for price changes.

12. The GDP deflator is a measure of the overall price level.

LIMITATIONS OF THE GDP CONCEPT *p. 123*

13. We generally think of increases in GDP as good, but some problems arise when we try to use GDP as a measure of happiness or well-being. The peculiarities of GDP accounting mean that institutional changes can change the value of GDP even if real production has not changed. GDP ignores most social ills, such as pollution. Furthermore, GDP tells us nothing about what kinds of goods are being produced or how income is distributed across the population. GDP also ignores many transactions of the *informal economy*.

14. The concept of *gross national income* (GNI) is GNP converted into dollars using an average of currency exchange rates over several years adjusted for rates of inflation.

REVIEW TERMS AND CONCEPTS

base year, *p. 121*

change in business inventories, *p. 116*

compensation of employees, *p. 117*

corporate profits, *p. 117*

current dollars, *p. 120*

depreciation, *p. 116*

disposable personal income, *or* after-tax income, *p. 119*

durable goods, *p. 115*

expenditure approach, *p. 113*

final goods and services, *p. 112*

fixed-weight procedure, *p. 121*

government consumption and gross investment (G), *p. 116*

gross domestic product (GDP), *p. 112*

gross investment, *p. 116*

gross national income (GNI), *p. 124*

gross national product (GNP), *p. 113*

gross private domestic investment (I), *p. 115*

income approach, *p. 114*

indirect taxes minus subsidies, *p. 117*

informal economy, *p. 124*

intermediate goods, *p. 112*

national income, *p. 117*

national income and product accounts, *p. 111*

net business transfer payments, *p. 117*

net exports (EX − IM), *p. 117*

net interest, *p. 117*

net investment, *p. 116*

net national product (NNP), *p. 118*

nominal GDP, *p. 120*

nondurable goods, *p. 115*

nonresidential investment, *p. 115*

personal consumption expenditures (C), *p. 115*

personal income, *p. 118*

personal saving, *p. 119*

personal saving rate, *p. 120*

proprietors' income, *p. 117*

rental income, *p. 117*

residential investment, *p. 115*

services, *p. 115*

statistical discrepancy, *p. 118*

surplus of government enterprises, *p. 117*

value added, *p. 112*

weight, *p. 120*

Equations:

Expenditure approach to GDP: GDP = C + I + G + (EX − IM), *p. 114*

GDP = Final sales + Change in business inventories, *p. 116*

$capital_{end\ of\ period} = capital_{beginning\ of\ period} + net\ investment$, *p. 116*

PROBLEMS

All problems are available on MyEconLab.

1. [Related to the *Economics in Practice* on *p. 115*] In a simple economy, suppose that all income is either compensation of employees or profits. Suppose also that there are no indirect taxes. Calculate gross domestic product from the following set of numbers. Show that the expenditure approach and the income approach add up to the same figure.

Consumption	$5,000
Investment	1,000
Depreciation	600
Profits	900
Exports	500
Compensation of employees	5,300
Government purchases	1,000
Direct taxes	800
Saving	1,100
Imports	700

2. How do we know that calculating GDP by the expenditure approach yields the same answer as calculating GDP by the income approach?

3. As the following table indicates, GNP and real GNP were almost the same in 1972, but there was a $300 billion difference by mid-1975. Explain why. Describe what the numbers here suggest about conditions in the economy at the time. How do the conditions compare with conditions today?

DATE	GNP (BILLIONS OF DOLLARS)	REAL GNP (BILLIONS OF DOLLARS)	REAL GNP (% CHANGE)	GNP DEFLATOR (% CHANGE)
72:2	1,172	1,179	7.62	2.93
72:3	1,196	1,193	5.11	3.24
72:4	1,233	1,214	7.41	5.30
73:1	1,284	1,247	10.93	5.71
73:2	1,307	1,248	.49	7.20
73:3	1,338	1,256	2.44	6.92
73:4	1,377	1,266	3.31	8.58
74:1	1,388	1,253	−4.00	7.50
74:2	1,424	1,255	.45	10.32
74:3	1,452	1,247	−2.47	10.78
74:4	1,473	1,230	−5.51	12.03
75:1	1,480	1,204	−8.27	10.86
75:2	1,517	1,219	5.00	5.07

4. What are some of the problems in using fixed weights to compute real GDP and the GDP deflator? How does the BEA's approach attempt to solve these problems?

5. Explain what double counting is and discuss why GDP is not equal to total sales.

6. The following table gives some figures from forecasts of real GDP (in 2005 dollars) and population done in mid-2012. According to the forecasts, approximately how much real growth will there be between 2015 and 2016? What is the per-capita real GDP projected to be in 2015 and in 2016? Compute the forecast rate of change in real GDP and per-capita real GDP between 2015 and 2016.

Real GDP 2015 (billions)	$15,392
Real GDP 2016 (billions)	$16,084
Population 2015 (millions)	321.4
Population 2016 (millions)	323.8

7. Look at a recent edition of *The Economist*. Go to the section on economic indicators. Go down the list of countries and make a list of the ones with the fastest and slowest GDP growth. Look also at the forecast rates of GDP growth. Go back to the table of contents at the beginning of the journal to see if there are articles about any of these countries. Write a paragraph or two describing the events or the economic conditions in one of the countries. Explain why they are growing or not growing rapidly.

8. During 2002, real GDP in Japan rose about 1.3 percent. During the same period, retail sales in Japan fell 1.8 percent in real terms. What are some possible explanations for retail sales to consumers falling when GDP rises? (*Hint:* Think of the composition of GDP using the expenditure approach.)

9. [Related to the *Economics in Practice* on *p. 119*] Which of the following transactions would not be counted in GDP? Explain your answers.
   a. General Motors issues new shares of stock to finance the construction of a plant.
   b. General Motors builds a new plant.
   c. Company A successfully launches a hostile takeover of company B, in which company A purchases all the assets of company B.
   d. Your grandmother wins $10 million in the lottery.
   e. You buy a new copy of this textbook.
   f. You buy a used copy of this textbook.
   g. The government pays out Social Security benefits.
   h. A public utility installs new antipollution equipment in its smokestacks.
   i. Luigi's Pizza buys 30 pounds of mozzarella cheese, holds it in inventory for one month, and then uses it to make pizza (which it sells).
   j. You spend the weekend cleaning your apartment.
   k. A drug dealer sells $500 worth of illegal drugs.

10. If you buy a new car, the entire purchase is counted as consumption in the year in which you make the transaction. Explain briefly why this is in one sense an "error" in national income accounting. (*Hint:* How is the purchase of a car different from the purchase of a pizza?) How might you correct this error? How is housing treated in the National Income and Product Accounts? Specifically how does owner-occupied housing enter into the accounts? (Hint: Do some Web searching on "imputed rent on owner-occupied housing.")

11. Explain why imports are subtracted in the expenditure approach to calculating GDP.

12. GDP calculations do not directly include the economic costs of environmental damage—for example, global warming and acid rain. Do you think these costs should be included in GDP? Why or why not? How could GDP be amended to include environmental damage costs?

13. Beginning in 2005, the housing market, which had been booming for years, turned. Housing construction dropped sharply in 2006. Go to www.bea.gov. Look at the GDP release and at past releases from 2002–2012. In real dollars, how much private residential fixed investment (houses, apartments, condominiums, and cooperatives) took place in each quarter from 2002–2012? What portion of GDP did housing construction represent? After 2006, residential fixed investment was declining sharply, yet GDP was growing until the end of 2007. What categories of aggregate spending kept things moving between 2006 and the end of 2007?

14. By mid-2009, many economists believed that the recession had ended and the U.S. economy had entered an economic expansion. Define *recession* and *expansion*. Go to www.bea.gov and look at the growth of GDP during 2009. In addition, go to www.bls.gov and look at payroll employment and the unemployment rate. Had the recession ended and had the U.S. economy entered an expansion? What do you see in the data? Can you tell by reading newspapers or watching cable news whether the country had entered an expansion? Explain.

15. Jeannine, a successful real estate agent in San Francisco, occasionally includes one of her home listings in the real estate section on eBay. In December 2012, Jeannine listed a home built in 1934 on eBay for $1.2 million, and she accepted an offer from a buyer in Copenhagen, Denmark, for $1.15 million in January 2013. What part, if any, of this transaction will be included as a part of U.S. GDP in 2013?

16. Larson has started a home wine-making business and he buys all his ingredients from his neighborhood farmers' market and a local bottle manufacturer. Last year he purchased $4,000 worth of ingredients and bottles and produced 2,000 bottles of wine.
He sold all 2,000 bottles of wine to an upscale restaurant for $10 each. The restaurant sold all the wine to customers for $45 each. For the total wine production, calculate the value added of Larson and of the restaurant.

17. [Related to the *Economics in Practice* on p. 124] In 2012, the state of Vermont passed legislation requiring the use of a new measure of economic growth and well-being. The following information is from Vermont bill S.237:
"This bill proposes to…require a genuine progress indicator committee to develop an economic indicator, to be named the "genuine progress indicator," to replace the gross domestic product as a measure of Vermont's economic health.…The genuine progress indicator shall be one that adds in positive factors and subtracts negative factors which are not counted by standard gross domestic product accounting practices."
Go to the following Website to view a copy of this 5-page bill: http://www.leg.state.vt.us/docs/2012/bills/Intro/S-237.pdf
On page 3 of the bill you will find a list of 29 measures to be included in the index (starting on line 12). From this list, choose the 5 items that you think will be the easiest to

quantitatively measure and the 5 items that you think will be the most difficult to quantitatively measure and explain your reasoning.
Source: http://www.leg.state.vt.us/docs/2012/bills/Intro/S-237.pdf

18. Artica is a nation with a simple economy that produces only six goods: oranges, bicycles, magazines, paper, orange juice, and hats. Assume that half of all the oranges are used to produce orange juice and one-third of all the paper is used to produce magazines.
   a. Use the production and price information in the table to calculate nominal GDP for 2011.
   b. Use the production and price information in the table to calculate real GDP for 2009, 2010, and 2011 using 2009 as the base year. What is the growth rate of real GDP from 2009 to 2010 and from 2010 to 2011?
   c. Use the production and price information in the table to calculate real GDP for 2009, 2010, and 2011 using 2010 as the base year. What is the growth rate of real GDP from 2009 to 2010 and from 2010 to 2011?

PRODUCT	2009 QUANTITY	2009 PRICE	2010 QUANTITY	2010 PRICE	2011 QUANTITY	2011 PRICE
Oranges	180	$0.90	200	$1.00	200	$1.25
Bicycles	20	85.00	25	90.00	30	95.00
Magazines	175	3.50	150	3.50	150	3.25
Paper	675	0.60	600	0.50	630	0.50
Orange juice	40	3.50	50	4.00	60	4.50
Hats	70	10.00	80	12.50	100	15.00

19. The following table contains nominal and real GDP data, in billions of dollars, from the U.S. Bureau of Economic Analysis for 2011 and 2012. The data is listed per quarter, and the real GDP data was calculated using 2005 as the base year. Fill in the columns for the GDP deflator and for the percent increase in price level.

QUARTER	NOMINAL GDP	REAL GDP	GDP DEFLATOR	PERCENT INCREASE IN PRICE LEVEL
2011q1	14,867.8	13,227.9		
2011q2	15,012.8	13,271.8		
2011q3	15,176.1	13,331.6		
2011q4	15,294.3	13,422.4		
2012q1	15,478.3	13,506.4		
2012q2	15,585.6	13,548.5		
2012q3	15,811.0	13,652.5		
2012q4	15,864.1	13,665.4		

20. Evaluate the following statement: Even if the prices of a large number of goods and services in the economy increase dramatically, the real GDP for the economy can still fall.

Unemployment, Inflation, and Long-Run Growth

7

Each month the U.S. Bureau of Labor Statistics (BLS) announces the value of the unemployment rate for the previous month. For example, on January 4, 2013, it announced that the unemployment rate for December 2012 was 7.8 percent. The unemployment rate is a key measure of how the economy is doing. This announcement is widely watched, and if the announced unemployment rate is different from what the financial markets expect, there can be large movements in those markets. It is thus important to know how the BLS computes the unemployment rate. The first part of this chapter describes how the unemployment rate is computed and discusses its various components.

Inflation is another key macroeconomic variable. The previous chapter discussed how the GDP deflator, the price deflator for the entire economy, is computed. The percentage change in the GDP deflator is a measure of inflation. There are, however, other measures of inflation, each pertaining to some part of the economy. The most widely followed price index is the consumer price index (CPI), and its measurement is discussed next in this chapter. The CPI is also announced monthly by the BLS, and this announcement is widely followed by the financial markets as well. For example, on January 16, 2013, the BLS announced that the percentage change in the CPI for December 2012 was 0.0. After discussing the measurement of the CPI, this chapter discusses various costs of inflation.

The last topic considered in this chapter is long-run growth. Although much of macroeconomics is concerned with explaining business cycles, long-run growth is also a major concern. The average yearly growth rate of U.S. real GDP depicted in Figure 5.2 in Chapter 5 is 3.2 percent. So while there were many ups and downs during the 113 years depicted in Figure 5.2, on average, the economy was growing at a 3.2 percent rate. In the last part of this chapter, we discuss the sources of this growth.

Keep in mind that this chapter is still descriptive. We begin our analysis of how the economy works in the next chapter.

LEARNING OBJECTIVES

Explain how unemployment is measured
Discuss unemployment trends and costs
Describe the tools used to measure inflation
Discuss the costs and effects of inflation
Discuss the components and implications of long-run growth

Unemployment

We begin our discussion of unemployment with its measurement.

Measuring Unemployment

The unemployment data released each month by the BLS are based on a survey of households. Each month the BLS draws a sample of 60,000 households and completes interviews with all but about 2,500 of them. Each interviewed household answers questions concerning the work activity of household members 16 years of age or older during the calendar week that contains the twelfth of the month. (The survey is conducted in the week that contains the nineteenth of the month.)

If a household member 16 years of age or older worked 1 hour or more as a paid employee, either for someone else or in his or her own business or farm, the person is classified as **employed**. A household member is also considered employed if he or she worked 15 hours or more without pay in a family enterprise. Finally, a household member is counted as employed if the person held a job from which he or she was temporarily absent due to illness, bad weather, vacation, labor-management disputes, or personal reasons, regardless of whether he or she was paid.

Those who are not employed fall into one of two categories: (1) unemployed or (2) not in the labor force. To be considered **unemployed**, a person must be 16 years old or older, available for work, and have made specific efforts to find work during the previous 4 weeks. A person not looking for work because he or she does not want a job or has given up looking is classified as **not in the labor force**. People not in the labor force include full-time students, retirees, individuals in institutions, those staying home to take care of children, and discouraged job seekers.

The total **labor force** in the economy is the number of people employed plus the number of unemployed:

$$\text{labor force} = \text{employed} + \text{unemployed}$$

The total population 16 years of age or older is equal to the number of people in the labor force plus the number not in the labor force:

$$\text{population} = \text{labor force} + \text{not in labor force}$$

With these numbers, several ratios can be calculated. The **unemployment rate** is the ratio of the number of people unemployed to the total number of people in the labor force:

$$\text{unemployment rate} = \frac{\text{unemployed}}{\text{employed} + \text{unemployed}}$$

In December 2012, the labor force contained 155.511 million people, 143.305 million of whom were employed and 12.206 million of whom were unemployed and looking for work. The unemployment rate was 7.8 percent:

$$\frac{12.206}{143.305 + 12.206} = 7.8\%$$

The ratio of the labor force to the population 16 years old or over is called the **labor force participation rate**:

$$\text{labor force participation rate} = \frac{\text{labor force}}{\text{population}}$$

In December 2012, the population of 16 years old or over was 240.584 million. So the labor force participation rate was .65 (=155.511/240.584).

Table 7.1 shows values of these variables for selected years since 1950. Although the unemployment rate has gone up and down over this period, the labor force participation rate grew

---

employed Any person 16 years old or older (1) who works for pay, either for someone else or in his or her own business for 1 or more hours per week, (2) who works without pay for 15 or more hours per week in a family enterprise, or (3) who has a job but has been temporarily absent with or without pay.

unemployed A person 16 years old or older who is not working, is available for work, and has made specific efforts to find work during the previous 4 weeks.

not in the labor force A person who is not looking for work because he or she does not want a job or has given up looking.

labor force The number of people employed plus the number of unemployed.

unemployment rate The ratio of the number of people unemployed to the total number of people in the labor force.

labor force participation rate The ratio of the labor force to the total population 16 years old or older.

TABLE 7.1 Employed, Unemployed, and the Labor Force, 1950–2012

	(1) Population 16 Years Old or Over (Millions)	(2) Labor Force (Millions)	(3) Employed (Millions)	(4) Unemployed (Millions)	(5) Labor Force Participation Rate (Percentage Points)	(6) Unemployment Rate (Percentage Points)
1950	105.0	62.2	58.9	3.3	59.2	5.3
1960	117.2	69.6	65.8	3.9	59.4	5.5
1970	137.1	82.8	78.7	4.1	60.4	4.9
1980	167.7	106.9	99.3	7.6	63.8	7.1
1990	189.2	125.8	118.8	7.0	66.5	5.6
2000	212.6	142.6	136.9	5.7	67.1	4.0
2012	243.3	155.0	142.5	12.5	63.7	8.1

Note: Figures are civilian only (military excluded).
Source: Economic Report of the President, 2012, Table B-35, and U.S. Bureau of Labor Statistics.

steadily between 1950 and 2000. Much of this increase was due to the growth in the participation rate of women between the ages of 25 and 54. Column 3 in Table 7.1 shows how many new workers the U.S. economy has absorbed in recent years. The number of employed workers increased by 40.4 million between 1950 and 1980 and by 43.2 million between 1980 and 2012.

Components of the Unemployment Rate

The unemployment rate by itself conveys some but not all information about the unemployment picture. To get a better picture, it is useful to look at unemployment rates across groups of people, regions, and industries.

Unemployment Rates for Different Demographic Groups   There are large differences in rates of unemployment across demographic groups. Table 7.2 shows the unemployment rate for November 1982—the worst month of the recession in 1982—and for December 2012—also a month with fairly high overall unemployment—broken down by race, sex, and age. In December 2012, when the overall unemployment rate was 7.8 percent, the rate for whites was 6.9 percent while the rate for African Americans was more than twice that—14.0 percent.

TABLE 7.2 Unemployment Rates by Demographic Group, 1982 and 2012

	Years	November 1982	December 2012
Total		10.8	7.8
White		9.6	6.9
Men	20+	9.0	6.2
Women	20+	8.1	6.3
Both sexes	16–19	21.3	21.6
African American		20.2	14.0
Men	20+	19.3	14.0
Women	20+	16.5	12.2
Both sexes	16–19	49.5	40.5

Source: U.S. Bureau of Labor Statistics. Data are seasonally adjusted.

During the recession of 1982, men fared worse than women. For African Americans, 19.3 percent of men 20 years and over and 16.5 percent of women 20 years and over were unemployed. Teenagers between 16 and 19 years of age fared worst. African Americans between 16 and 19 experienced an unemployment rate of 49.5 percent in November 1982. For whites between 16 and 19, the unemployment rate was 21.3 percent. The unemployment rate for teenagers was also quite high in December 2012, and African American men and women continue to have unemployment rates higher than their white counterparts.

Unemployment Rates in States and Regions   Unemployment rates also vary by geographic location. For a variety of reasons, not all states and regions have the same level of unemployment. States and regions have different combinations of industries, which do not all

MyEconLab Real-time data

TABLE 7.3 Regional Differences in Unemployment, 1975, 1982, 1991, 2003, and 2010

	1975	1982	1991	2003	2010
U.S. avg.	8.5	9.7	6.7	6.0	9.6
Cal.	9.9	9.9	7.5	6.7	12.4
Fla.	10.7	8.2	7.3	5.1	11.5
Ill.	7.1	11.3	7.1	6.7	10.3
Mass.	11.2	7.9	9.0	6.7	8.5
Mich.	12.5	15.5	9.2	7.3	12.5
N.J.	10.2	9.0	6.6	5.9	9.5
N.Y.	9.5	8.6	7.2	6.3	8.6
N.C.	8.6	9.0	5.8	6.5	10.6
Ohio	9.1	12.5	6.4	6.1	10.1
Tex.	5.6	6.9	6.6	6.8	8.2

Source: Statistical Abstract of the United States, various editions.

grow and decline at the same time and at the same rate. Also, the labor force is not completely mobile—workers often cannot or do not want to pack up and move to take advantage of job opportunities in other parts of the country.

As Table 7.3 shows, in the last 35 years remarkable changes have occurred in the relative prosperity of regions. In the 1970s Massachusetts was still quite dependent on its industrial base. As textile mills, leather goods plants, and furniture factories closed in the face of competition both from abroad and from lower wage southern states, Massachusetts experienced relatively high unemployment. By the 1980s, the state had moved into more high-technology areas with the birth of firms like Wang Laboratories and Digital Equipment. By 1982 the Massachusetts unemployment rate had moved to being relatively low.

Michigan is another interesting state. As you probably know, Michigan is highly dependent on the automotive industry. Michigan has suffered unemployment rates above the national average for decades as the American automobile industry has lost share to foreign competition, and the state economy has been relatively slow to attract new industries. It should not surprise you that Michigan has one of the highest unemployment rates in 2010, given the state of the U.S. auto industry in the recent period.

Finally, consider Texas. Texas produces about 20 percent of the oil in the United States. (Alaska is another large oil producer.) For most of the last 35 years oil has done well, and for most of this period Texas has had relatively low unemployment rates. In Table 7.3, only in 2003 was Texas' unemployment rate greater than the national average.

Discouraged-Worker Effects Many people believe that the unemployment rate underestimates the fraction of people who are involuntarily out of work. People who stop looking for work are classified as having dropped out of the labor force instead of being unemployed. During recessions, people may become discouraged about finding a job and stop looking. This lowers the unemployment rate as calculated by the BLS because those no longer looking for work are no longer counted as unemployed.

discouraged-worker effect
The decline in the measured unemployment rate that results when people who want to work but cannot find jobs grow discouraged and stop looking, thus dropping out of the ranks of the unemployed and the labor force.

To demonstrate how this **discouraged-worker effect** lowers the unemployment rate, suppose there are 10 million unemployed out of a labor force of 100 million. This means an unemployment rate of 10/100 = .10, or 10 percent. If 1 million of these 10 million unemployed people stopped looking for work and dropped out of the labor force, 9 million would be unemployed out of a labor force of 99 million. The unemployment rate would then drop to 9/99 = .091, or 9.1 percent.

The BLS survey provides some evidence on the size of the discouraged-worker effect. Respondents who indicate that they have stopped searching for work are asked why they stopped. If the respondent cites inability to find employment as the sole reason for not searching, that person might be classified as a discouraged worker.

The number of discouraged workers seems to hover around 1 percent of the size of the labor force in normal times. During the 1980–1982 recession, the number of discouraged workers increased steadily to a peak of 1.5 percent. In December 2012 discouraged workers

ECONOMICS IN PRACTICE

A Quiet Revolution: Women Join the Labor Force

Table 7.1 shows that the labor force participation rate in the United States increased from 59.2 percent in 1950 to 63.7 percent in 2012. Much of this increase was due to the increased participation of women in the labor force. In 1955, the labor force participation rate of women was 36 percent. For married women, the rate was even lower at 29 percent. By the 1990s, these numbers shifted considerably. In 1996, the labor force participation rate was 60 percent for all women and 62 percent for married women. The reasons for these changes are complex. Certainly, in the 1960s, there was a change in society's attitude toward women and paid work. In addition, the baby boom became the baby bust as greater availability of birth control led to fewer births.

By comparison, the participation rate for men declined over this period—from 85 percent in 1955 to 75 percent in 1996. Why the labor force participation rate for men fell is less clear than why the women's rate rose. No doubt, some men dropped out to assume more traditional women's roles, such as child care. Whatever the causes, the economy grew in a way that absorbed virtually all the new entrants during the period in question.

As women began joining the labor force in greater numbers in the 1970s and 1980s, their wages relative to men's wages actually fell. Most economists attribute this decline to the fact that less experienced women were entering the labor force, pointing out the importance of correcting for factors such as experience and education when we analyze labor markets.

At least some of the women entering the labor force at this time hired housecleaners and child care workers to perform tasks they had once done themselves. As we learned in Chapter 6, the salaries of daycare staff and cleaning people are counted in GDP, while the value of these tasks when done by a husband or wife in a household is not part of GDP.

If you are interested in learning more about the economic history of American women, read the book *Understanding the Gender Gap: An Economic History of American Women* by Harvard University economist Claudia Goldin.

THINKING PRACTICALLY

1. When a household decides to hire someone else to clean their house and uses their extra time to watch television, the wages paid to that household worker increase GDP. Is economic output in fact larger?

were estimated to comprise about 0.7 percent of the size of the labor force. Some economists argue that adding the number of discouraged workers to the number who are now classified as unemployed gives a better picture of the unemployment situation.

The Duration of Unemployment The unemployment rate measures unemployment at a given point in time. It tells us nothing about how long the average unemployed worker is out of work. With a labor force of 1,000 people and an annual unemployment rate of 10 percent, we know that at any moment 100 people are unemployed. But a very different picture emerges if it turns out that the same 100 people are unemployed all year, as opposed to a situation in which each of the 1,000 people has a brief spell of unemployment of a few weeks during the year. The duration statistics give us information on this feature of unemployment. Table 7.4 shows that during recessionary periods, the average duration of unemployment rises. Between 1979 and 1983, the average duration of unemployment rose from 10.8 weeks to 20.0 weeks. The slow growth following the 1990–1991 recession resulted in an increase in duration of unemployment to 17.7 weeks in 1992 and to 18.8 weeks in 1994. In 2000, average duration was down to 12.6 weeks, which then rose to 19.6 weeks in 2004. Between 2007 and 2009 average duration rose sharply from 16.8 weeks to 24.4 weeks. Following the recession it rose even more—to 39.4 weeks in 2012. This reflects the slow overall recovery from the recession.

MyEconLab Real-time data

TABLE 7.4 Average Duration of Unemployment, 1970–2012

	Weeks		Weeks		Weeks
1970	8.6	1985	15.6	2000	12.6
1971	11.3	1986	15.0	2001	13.1
1972	12.0	1987	14.5	2002	16.6
1973	10.0	1988	13.5	2003	19.2
1974	9.8	1989	11.9	2004	19.6
1975	14.2	1990	12.0	2005	18.4
1976	15.8	1991	13.7	2006	16.8
1977	14.3	1992	17.7	2007	16.8
1978	11.9	1993	18.0	2008	17.9
1979	10.8	1994	18.8	2009	24.4
1980	11.9	1995	16.6	2010	33.0
1981	13.7	1996	16.7	2011	39.3
1982	15.6	1997	15.8	2012	39.4
1983	20.0	1998	14.5		
1984	18.2	1999	13.4		

Source: U.S. Bureau of Labor Statistics.

The Costs of Unemployment

In the Employment Act of 1946, Congress declared that it was the

> continuing policy and responsibility of the federal government to use all practicable means…to promote maximum employment, production, and purchasing power.

In 1978, Congress passed the Full Employment and Balanced Growth Act, commonly referred to as the *Humphrey-Hawkins Act*, which formally established specific unemployment rate targets. While the Act formally expired in 2000, full employment has remained an important target of federal policy. Why should full employment be a policy objective of the federal government? What costs does unemployment impose on society?

Some Unemployment Is Inevitable Before we discuss the costs of unemployment, we must realize that some unemployment is simply part of the natural workings of the labor market. Remember, to be classified as unemployed, a person must be looking for a job. Every year thousands of people enter the labor force for the first time. Some have dropped out of high school, some are high school or college graduates, and still others are finishing graduate programs. At the same time, new firms are starting up and others are expanding and creating new jobs while other firms are contracting or going out of business.

At any moment, there is a set of job seekers and a set of jobs that must be matched with one another. It is important that the right people end up in the right jobs. The right job for a person will depend on that person's skills, preferences concerning work environment (large firm or small, formal or informal), location of the individual's home, and willingness to commute. At the same time, firms want workers who can meet the requirements of the job and grow with the company.

To make a good match, workers must acquire information on job availability, wage rates, location, and work environment. Firms must acquire information on worker availability and skills. Information gathering consumes time and resources. The search may involve travel, interviews, preparation of a résumé, telephone calls, and hours looking online or through the newspaper. To the extent that these efforts lead to a better match of workers and jobs, they are well spent. As long as the gains to firms and workers exceed the costs of search, the result is efficient.

When we consider the various costs of unemployment, it is useful to categorize unemployment into three types:

- Frictional unemployment
- Structural unemployment
- Cyclical unemployment

ECONOMICS IN PRACTICE

The Consequences of Unemployment Persist

Throughout the recession of 2008–2009 and the slow recovery afterwards many young college graduates found themselves unemployed, many for a number of months. As painful as that experience was, economists had more bad news for them. The negative effect of early unemployment on your career lasts for many years!

Lisa Kahn, a Yale economist, followed graduates of colleges from the period 1979–1989 over the subsequent 17 years.[1] You know from Chapter 5 that within this overall period there was one recession in 1979–1982. Kahn finds that even fifteen years later, wage rates of those with post-college unemployment lagged substantially. Not only did low wages persist, but fewer graduates in recessionary periods were able to enter high prestige jobs, even when the economy recovered.

THINKING PRACTICALLY

1. Describe a mechanism that might help explain the persistence of wage-effects from a recession.

[1]Lisa Kahn, "The Long-Term Labor Consequences of Graduating from College in a Bad Economy," *Labour Economics*, April 2010.

Frictional, Structural, and Cyclical Unemployment   When the BLS does its survey about work activity for the week containing the twelfth of each month, it interviews many people who are involved in the normal search for work. Some are either entering the labor force or switching jobs. This unemployment is both natural and beneficial for the economy. The portion of unemployment due to the normal turnover in the labor market is called **frictional unemployment**. The frictional unemployment rate can never be zero. It may, however, change over time. As jobs become more differentiated and the number of required skills increases, matching skills and jobs becomes more complex and the frictional unemployment rate may rise.

The concept of frictional unemployment is somewhat vague because it is hard to know what "the normal turnover in the labor market" means. The industrial structure of the U.S. economy is continually changing. Manufacturing, for instance, has yielded part of its share of total employment to services and to finance, insurance, and real estate. Within the manufacturing sector, the steel and textile industries have contracted sharply, while high-technology sectors such as electronic components have expanded. Although the unemployment that arises from such structural shifts could be classified as frictional, it is usually called **structural unemployment**. The term *frictional unemployment* is used to denote short-run job/skill-matching problems, problems that last a few weeks. *Structural unemployment* denotes longer-run adjustment problems—those that tend to last for years. Although structural unemployment is expected in a dynamic economy, it is painful to the workers who experience it. In some ways, those who lose their jobs because their skills are obsolete experience the greatest pain. The fact that structural unemployment is natural and inevitable does not mean that it costs society nothing.

Economists sometimes use the term **natural rate of unemployment** to refer to the unemployment rate that occurs in a normal functioning economy. This concept is also vague because it is hard to know what a "normal functioning economy" means. It is probably best to think of the natural rate of unemployment as the sum of the frictional rate and the structural rate. Estimates of the natural rate vary from 4 percent to 6 percent.

There are times when the actual unemployment rate appears to be above the natural rate. Between 2007 and 2009 the actual unemployment rate rose from 4.6 percent to 9.3 percent, and it seems unlikely that all of this rise was simply due to a rise in frictional and structural unemployment. Any unemployment that is above frictional plus structural is called **cyclical unemployment**. It seems likely that much of the unemployment in 2009, during the 2008–2009 recession, was cyclical unemployment.

frictional unemployment
The portion of unemployment that is due to the normal turnover in the labor market; used to denote short-run job/skill-matching problems.

structural unemployment
The portion of unemployment that is due to changes in the structure of the economy that result in a significant loss of jobs in certain industries.

natural rate of unemployment
The unemployment rate that occurs as a normal part of the functioning of the economy. Sometimes taken as the sum of the frictional unemployment rate and the structural unemployment rate.

cyclical unemployment
Unemployment that is above frictional plus structural unemployment.

Social Consequences   The costs of unemployment are neither evenly distributed across the population nor easily quantified. The social consequences of the Depression of the 1930s are perhaps the hardest to comprehend. Few emerged from this period unscathed. At the bottom were the poor and the fully unemployed, about 25 percent of the labor force. Even those who kept their jobs found themselves working part-time. Many people lost all or part of their savings as the stock market crashed and thousands of banks failed.

Congressional committees heard story after story. In Cincinnati, where the labor force totaled about 200,000, about 48,000 were wholly unemployed, 40,000 more were on short time, and relief payments to the needy averaged $7 to $8 per week:

> Relief is given to a family one week and then they are pushed off for a week in the hope that somehow or other the breadwinner may find some kind of work....We are paying no rent at all. That, of course, is a very difficult problem because we are continually having evictions, and social workers...are hard put to find places for people whose furniture has been put out on the street.[1]

From Birmingham, Alabama, in 1932:

> ...we have about 108,000 wage and salary workers in my district. Of that number, it is my belief that not exceeding 8,000 have their normal incomes. At least 25,000 men are altogether without work. Some of them have not had a stroke of work for more than 12 months. Perhaps 60,000 or 70,000 are working from one to five days a week, and practically all have had serious cuts in wages and many of them do not average over $1.50 per day.[2]

Inflation

In a market economy like the U.S. economy, prices of individual goods continually change as supply and demand shift. Indeed, a major concern of microeconomics is understanding the way in which relative prices change—why, for example, have computers become less expensive over time and dental services more expensive? In macroeconomics, we are concerned not with relative price changes, but with changes in the *overall* price level of goods and services. Inflation is defined as an increase in the overall price level, while deflation is a decrease in the overall price level.

The fact that all prices for the multitude of goods and services in our economy do not rise and fall together at the same rate makes measurement of inflation difficult. We have already explored measurement issues in Chapter 6 in defining the GDP deflator, which measures the price level for all goods and services in an economy. We turn now to look at a second, commonly used measure of the price level, the consumer price index.

The Consumer Price Index

consumer price index (CPI) A price index computed each month by the Bureau of Labor Statistics using a bundle that is meant to represent the "market basket" purchased monthly by the typical urban consumer.

The **consumer price index (CPI)** is the most widely followed price index. Unlike the GDP deflator, it is a fixed-weight index. It was first constructed during World War I as a basis for adjusting shipbuilders' wages, which the government controlled during the war. Currently, the CPI is computed by the BLS each month using a bundle of goods meant to represent the "market basket" purchased monthly by the typical urban consumer. The quantities of each good in the bundle that are used for the weights are based on extensive surveys of consumers. In fact, the BLS collects prices each month for about 71,000 goods and services from about 22,000 outlets in 44 geographic areas. For example, the cost of housing is included in the data collection by surveying about 5,000 renters and 1,000 homeowners each month. Figure 7.1 shows the CPI market basket for December 2007.

Table 7.5 shows values of the CPI since 1950. The base period for this index is 1982–1984, which means that the index is constructed to have a value of 100.0 when averaged across these three years. The percentage change for a given year in the table is a measure of inflation in that year. For example, from 1970 to 1971, the CPI increased from 38.8 to 40.5, a percentage change of 4.4 percent. [The percentage change is (40.5 − 38.8)/38.8 times 100.] The table shows the high inflation rates in the 1970s and early 1980s and the fairly low inflation rates since 1992.

Since the CPI is a fixed-weight price index (with the current base period 1982–1984), it suffers from the substitution problem discussed in the last chapter. With fixed weights, it does not account

---

[1] U.S. Senate Hearings before a subcommittee of the Committee of Manufacturers, 72nd Congress, first session (1931), p. 239. Cited in Lester Chandler, *America's Greatest Depression, 1929–1941* (New York: Harper & Row, 1970), p. 43.

[2] Senate Hearings, in Lester Chandler, *America's Greatest Depression, 1929–1941* (New York: Harper & Row, 1970), p. 43.

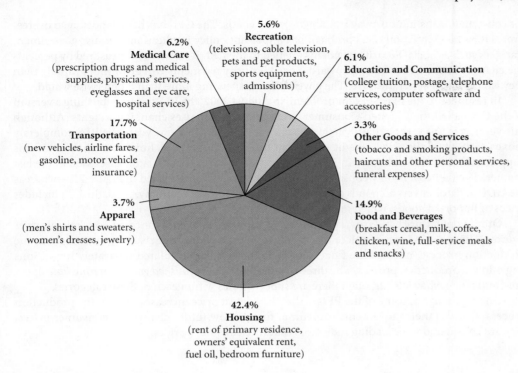

Source: The Bureau of Labor Statistics

◄ FIGURE 7.1
The CPI Market Basket
The CPI market basket shows how a typical consumer divides his or her money among various goods and services. Most of a consumer's money goes toward housing, transportation, and food and beverages.

MyEconLab Real-time data

TABLE 7.5 The CPI, 1950–2012

	Percentage Change in CPI	CPI		Percentage Change in CPI	CPI
1950	1.3	24.1	1982	6.2	96.5
1951	7.9	26.0	1983	3.2	99.6
1952	1.9	26.5	1984	4.3	103.9
1953	0.8	26.7	1985	3.6	107.6
1954	0.7	26.9	1986	1.9	109.6
1955	−0.4	26.8	1987	3.6	113.6
1956	1.5	27.2	1988	4.1	118.3
1957	3.3	28.1	1989	4.8	124.0
1958	2.8	28.9	1990	5.4	130.7
1959	0.7	29.1	1991	4.2	136.2
1960	1.7	29.6	1992	3.0	140.3
1961	1.0	29.9	1993	3.0	144.5
1962	1.0	30.2	1994	2.6	148.2
1963	1.3	30.6	1995	2.8	152.4
1964	1.3	31.0	1996	3.0	156.9
1965	1.6	31.5	1997	2.3	160.5
1966	2.9	32.4	1998	1.6	163.0
1967	3.1	33.4	1999	2.2	166.6
1968	4.2	34.8	2000	3.4	172.2
1969	5.5	36.7	2001	2.8	177.1
1970	5.7	38.8	2002	1.6	179.9
1971	4.4	40.5	2003	2.3	184.0
1972	3.2	41.8	2004	2.7	188.9
1973	6.2	44.4	2005	3.4	195.3
1974	11.0	49.3	2006	3.2	201.6
1975	9.1	53.8	2007	2.8	207.3
1976	5.8	56.9	2008	3.9	215.3
1977	6.5	60.6	2009	−0.4	214.5
1978	7.6	65.2	2010	1.7	218.1
1979	11.3	72.6	2011	3.1	224.9
1980	13.5	82.4	2012	2.1	229.6
1981	10.3	90.9			

Sources: U.S. Bureau of Labor Statistics.

for consumers' substitution away from high-priced goods. The CPI thus has a tendency to overestimate the rate of inflation. This problem has important policy implications because government transfers such as Social Security payments are tied to the CPI. If inflation as measured by percentage changes in the CPI is biased upward, Social Security payments will grow more rapidly than they would with a better measure: The government is spending more than it otherwise would.

In response to the fixed-weight problem, in August 2002, the BLS began publishing a version of the CPI called the Chained Consumer Price Index, which uses changing weights. Although this version is not yet the main version, it may be that within a few years the BLS completely moves away from the fixed-weight version of the CPI. Remember, however, that even if this happens, the CPI will still differ in important ways from the GDP deflator, discussed in the last chapter. The CPI covers only consumer goods and services—those listed in Figure 7.1—whereas the GDP deflator covers all goods and services produced in the economy. Also, the CPI includes prices of imported goods, which the GDP deflator does not.

producer price indexes (PPIs) Measures of prices that producers receive for products at various stages in the production process.

Other popular price indexes are **producer price indexes (PPIs)**, once called *wholesale price indexes*. These are indexes of prices that producers receive for products at various stages in the production process, not just the final stage. The indexes are calculated separately for various stages in the production process. The three main categories are *finished goods, intermediate materials*, and *crude materials*, although there are subcategories within each of these categories.

One advantage of some of the PPIs is that they detect price increases early in the production process. Because their movements sometimes foreshadow future changes in consumer prices, they are considered to be leading indicators of future consumer prices.

The Costs of Inflation

If you asked most people why inflation is bad, they would tell you that it lowers the overall standard of living by making goods and services more expensive. That is, it cuts into people's purchasing power. People are fond of recalling the days when a bottle of Coca-Cola cost a dime and a hamburger cost a quarter. Just think what we could buy today if prices had not changed. What people usually do not think about is what their incomes were in the "good old days." The fact that the cost of a Coke has increased from 10 cents to a dollar does not mean anything in real terms if people who once earned $5,000 now earn $50,000. During inflations, most prices—including input prices like wages—tend to rise together, and input prices determine both the incomes of workers and the incomes of owners of capital and land. So inflation by itself does not *necessarily* reduce one's purchasing power.

Inflation May Change the Distribution of Income Whether you gain or lose during a period of inflation depends on whether your income rises faster or slower than the prices of the things you buy. The group most often mentioned when the impact of inflation is discussed is people living on fixed incomes. If your income is fixed and prices rise, your ability to purchase goods and services falls proportionately.

Although the elderly are often thought of as living on fixed incomes, many pension plans pay benefits that are *indexed* to inflation, as we describe in the *Economics in Practice* on p. 139. The benefits these plans provide automatically increase when the general price level rises. If prices rise 10 percent, benefits also rise 10 percent. The biggest source of income for many elderly people is Social Security. These benefits are fully indexed; when prices rise—that is, when the CPI rises—by 5 percent, Social Security benefits also increase by 5 percent.

Wages are also sometimes indexed to inflation through cost of living adjustments (COLAs) written into labor contracts. These contracts usually stipulate that future wage increases will be larger the larger is the rate of inflation. If wages are fully indexed, workers do not suffer a fall in real income when inflation rises, although wages are not always fully indexed.

One way of thinking about the effects of inflation on the distribution of income is to distinguish between *anticipated* and *unanticipated* inflation. If inflation is anticipated and contracts are made and agreements written with the anticipated value of inflation in mind, there need not be any effects of inflation on income distribution. Consider an individual who is thinking about retiring and has a pension that is not indexed to the CPI. If she knew what inflation was going to be for the next 20 or 30 years of her retirement, there would be no problem. She would just wait to retire until she had enough money to pay for her anticipated growing expenses. The problem occurs if, after she has retired, inflation is higher than she expected. At that point, she

ECONOMICS IN PRACTICE

Chain-Linked Consumer Price Index in the News

The calculations described in Chapter 6 on how to construct a chain-linked price index may seem complicated and a bit arcane to you. But throughout the last months of 2012 and into early 2013, as Republicans and Democrats argued over the federal budget, chain linking became a hot topic.

As we know from the discussion of fixed weights in Chapter 6, chain linking a price index accounts for product substitution that people make in response to relative price changes. Fixed-weight price indices, which do not take into account this substitution, tend to overestimate inflation. There are two versions of the consumer price index (CPI), one using fixed weights and one using chain linking. The fixed-weight version is the one that is used to adjust social security benefits and veteran benefits to price changes. If, say, the CPI increases by 2 percent in a year, benefits are increased by 2 percent. If the chain-linked CPI were used instead, benefits

would tend to increase more slowly because in general the chain-linked CPI increases less than does the fixed-weight CPI (because of product substitution). You may see where this is going. One way to decrease expenditures on social security and veteran benefits in the future would be to use the chain-linked CPI rather than the fixed-weight CPI. The nonpartisan Congressional Budget office estimated that if the chain-linked CPI were adopted, it would save the federal government about $145 billion over a ten year period from the lower benefits.

THINKING PRACTICALLY

1. Tax brackets are also tied to the fixed-weight CPI. How would tax revenue be affected if the chain-linked CPI were used instead?

may face the prospect of having to return to work. Similarly, if I as a landlord expect inflation to be 2 percent per year over the next 3 years and offer my tenants a 3-year lease with a 2 percent rent increase each year, I will be in bad shape if inflation turns out to be 10 percent per year and causes all my costs to rise by 10 percent per year.

For another example, consider debtors versus creditors. It is commonly believed that debtors benefit at the expense of creditors during an inflation because with inflation they pay back less in the future in real terms than they borrowed. But this is not the case if the inflation is anticipated and the loan contract is written with this in mind.

Suppose that you want to borrow $100 from me to be paid back in a year and that we both agree that if there is no inflation the appropriate interest rate is 5 percent. Suppose also that we both anticipate that the inflation rate will be 10 percent. In this case we will agree on a 15 percent interest rate—you will pay me back $115 at the end of the year. By charging you 15 percent I have taken into account the fact that you will be paying me back with dollars worth 10 percent less in real terms than when you borrowed them. I am then not hurt by inflation and you are not helped if the actual inflation rate turns out to equal our anticipated rate. I am earning a 5 percent **real interest rate**—the difference between the interest rate on a loan and the inflation rate.

Unanticipated inflation, on the other hand, is a different story. If the actual inflation rate during the year turns out to be 20 percent, I as a creditor will be hurt. I charged you 15 percent interest, expecting to get a 5 percent real rate of return, when I needed to charge you 25 percent to get the same 5 percent real rate of return. Because inflation was higher than anticipated, I got a negative real return of 5 percent. Inflation that is higher than anticipated benefits debtors; inflation that is lower than anticipated benefits creditors.

To summarize, the effects of anticipated inflation on the distribution of income are likely to be fairly small, since people and institutions will adjust to the anticipated inflation. Unanticipated inflation, on the other hand, may have large effects, depending, among other things, on how much indexing to inflation there is. If many contracts are not indexed and are based on anticipated inflation rates that turn out to be wrong, there can be big winners and losers. In general, there is more uncertainty and risk when inflation is unanticipated. This uncertainty may prevent people from signing long-run contracts that would otherwise be beneficial for both parties.

real interest rate The difference between the interest rate on a loan and the inflation rate.

Administrative Costs and Inefficiencies There may be costs associated even with anticipated inflation. One is the administrative cost associated with simply keeping up. During the rapid inflation in Israel in the early 1980s, a telephone hotline was set up to give the hourly price index. Store owners had to recalculate and repost prices frequently, and this took time that could have been used more efficiently. In Zimbabwe, where the inflation rate in June 2008 was estimated by some to be over 1 million percent at an annual rate, the government was forced to print ever-increasing denominations of money. In 2009 Zimbabwe abandoned its currency and started using the U.S. dollar and the South African Rand to conduct business.

More frequent banking transactions may also be required when anticipated inflation is high. For example, interest rates tend to rise with anticipated inflation. When interest rates are high, the opportunity costs of holding cash outside of banks is high. People therefore hold less cash and need to stop at the bank more often. (We discuss this effect in more detail in the next part of this book.)

Public Enemy Number One? Economists have debated the seriousness of the costs of inflation for decades. Some, among them Alan Blinder, say, "Inflation, like every teenager, is grossly misunderstood, and this gross misunderstanding blows the political importance of inflation out of all proportion to its economic importance."[3] Others such as Phillip Cagan and Robert Lipsey argue, "It was once thought that the economy would in time make all the necessary adjustments [to inflation], but many of them are proving to be very difficult.... For financial institutions and markets, the effects of inflation have been extremely unsettling."[4]

No matter what the real economic cost of inflation, people do not like it. It makes us uneasy and unhappy. In 1974, President Ford verbalized some of this discomfort when he said, "Our inflation, our public enemy number one, will unless whipped destroy our country, our homes, our liberties, our property, and finally our national pride, as surely as any well-armed wartime enemy." [5] In this belief, our elected leaders have vigorously pursued policies designed to stop inflation. In 2013, after many years of low inflation, some observers began to worry about possible future increases in inflation.

Long-Run Growth

output growth The growth rate of the output of the entire economy.

per-capita output growth The growth rate of output per person in the economy.

productivity growth The growth rate of output per worker.

In discussing long-run growth, it will be useful to begin with a few definitions. **Output growth** is the growth rate of the output of the entire economy. **Per-capita output growth** is the growth rate of output per person in the economy. If the population of a country is growing at the same rate as output, then per-capita output is not growing: Output growth is simply keeping up with population growth. Not everyone in a country works, and so output per worker is not the same as output per person. Output per worker is larger than output per person, and it is called productivity. **Productivity growth** is thus the growth rate of *output per worker*.

One measure of the economic welfare of a country is its per-capita output. Per-capita output can increase because productivity increases, as each worker now produces more than he or she did previously, or because there are more workers relative to nonworkers in the population. In the United States, both forces have been at work in increasing per-capita output.

Output and Productivity Growth

We have pointed out that aggregate output in the United States has grown at an annual rate of 3.3 percent since 1900. Some years are better than this and some years worse, but, on average, the growth rate has been 3.3 percent. An area of economics called *growth theory* is concerned with the question of what determines this rate. Why 3.3 percent and not 2 percent or 4 percent? We take up this question in Chapter 17, but a few points are useful to make now.

In a simplified economy, machines (capital) and workers (labor) are needed to produce output. Suppose that an economy consists of six machines and 60 workers, with 10 workers working on each machine, and that the length of the workweek is 40 hours, with this workweek resulting in 50 units of output per month per machine. Total output (GDP) for the month is thus 300 units (6 machines times 50 units per machine) in this simple economy.

How can output increase in this economy? There are a number of ways. One way is to add more workers. If, for example, 12 workers are added, 2 extra per machine, more output can be produced per machine per hour worked because there are more workers helping out on each machine. Another way is to add more machines. For example, if 4 machines are added, the

---

[3] Alan Blinder, *Hard Heads, Soft Hearts: Tough-Minded Economics for a Just Society* (Reading, MA: Addison-Wesley, 1987).
[4] Phillip Cagan and Robert E. Lipsey, "The Financial Effects of Inflation," National Bureau of Economic Research (Cambridge, MA: General Series No. 103, 1978), pp. 67–68.
[5] U.S. President, Weekly Compilation of Presidential Documents, vol. 10, no. 41, p. 1247. Cited in Blinder, *Hard Heads*.

60 workers have a total of 10 machines to work with instead of 6 and more output can be produced per worker per hour worked. A third way is to increase the length of the workweek (for example, from 40 hours to 45 hours). With workers and machines working more hours, more output can be produced. Output can thus increase if labor or capital increases or if the amount of time that labor and capital are working per week increases.

Another way for output to increase in our economy is for the quality of the workers to increase. If, for example, the education of the workers increases, this may add to their skills and thus increase their ability to work on the machines. Output per machine might then rise from 50 units per month to some larger number per month. Also, if workers become more physically fit by exercising more and eating less fat and more whole grains and fresh fruits and vegetables, their greater fitness may increase their output on the machines. People are sometimes said to be adding to their *human capital* when they increase their mental or physical skills.

The quality of the machines used in the workplace may also increase. In particular, new machines that replace old machines may allow more output to be produced per hour with the same number of workers. In our example, it may be that 55 instead of 50 units of output can be produced per month per new machine with 10 workers per machine and a 40-hour workweek. An obvious example is the replacement of an old computer with a new, faster one that allows more to be done per minute of work on the computer.

To summarize, output can increase when there are more workers, more skills per worker, more machines, better machines, or a longer workweek.

Output per worker hour is called *labor productivity* or sometimes just *productivity*. Output per worker hour is plotted in Figure 7.2 for the 1952 I–2012 IV period. Two features are immediately clear from the figure. First, there is an upward trend. Second, there are fairly sizable short-run fluctuations around the trend. We will see in Chapter 16 why there are short-run fluctuations. This has to do with the possibility that the employed workforce is not always fully utilized. For now, however, our main interest is the long-run trend.

To smooth out the short-run fluctuations in Figure 7.2, we have added straight-line segments to the figure, where the segments roughly go through the high values. The slope of each line segment is the growth rate of productivity along the segment. The growth rates are listed in the figure. The different productivity growth rates in the figure tell an interesting story. From the 1950s through the mid-1960s, the growth rate was 3.2 percent. The rate then fell to 2.5 percent in the last half of the 1960s and early 1970s. Between the early 1970s and the early 1990s, the growth rate was much lower at 1.5 percent. Since the early 1990s, it has been 1.9 percent.

Why are the growth rates positive in Figure 7.2? Why has the amount of output that a worker can produce per hour risen in the last half century? Part of the answer is that the amount of capital per worker has increased. In Figure 7.3 capital per worker is plotted for the same 1952 I–2012 IV period. It is clear from the figure that the amount of capital per worker has

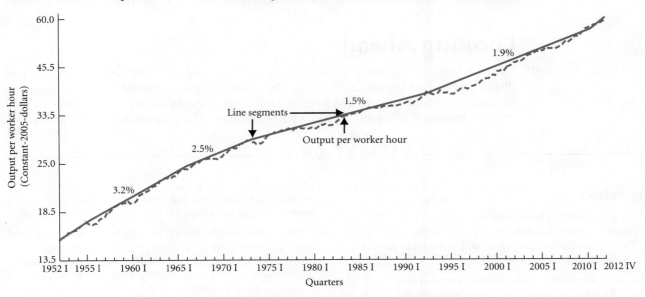

▲ **FIGURE 7.2 Output per Worker Hour (Productivity), 1952 I–2012 IV**
Productivity grew much faster in the 1950s and 1960s than since.

MyEconLab Real-time data

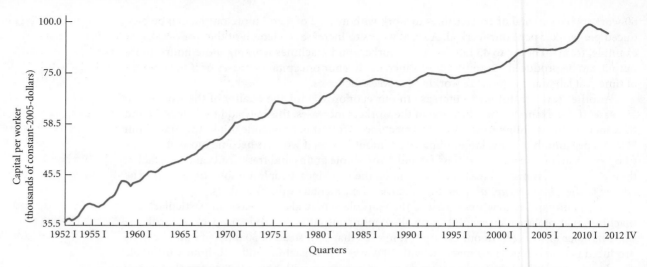

▲ **FIGURE 7.3   Capital per Worker, 1952 I–2012 IV**   MyEconLab Real-time data
Capital per worker grew until about 1980 and then leveled off somewhat.

generally been rising. Therefore, with more capital per worker, more output can be produced per worker. The other part of the answer is that the quality of labor and capital has been increasing. Both the average skill of workers and the average quality of capital have been increasing. This means that more output can be produced per worker for a given quantity of capital because both workers and capital are getting better.

A harder question to answer concerning Figure 7.2 is why the growth rate of productivity was much higher in the 1950s and 1960s than it has been since the early 1970s. Again, part of the answer is that the amount of capital per worker rose more rapidly in the 1950s and 1960s than it has since then. This can be seen in Figure 7.3. The other part of the answer is, of course, that the quality of labor and capital must have increased more in the 1950s and 1960s than later, although this, to some extent, begs the question. The key question is why the quality of labor and capital has grown more slowly since the early 1970s. We take up this question in Chapter 17, where we will see that there seems to be no one obvious answer. An interesting question for the future is whether the continued growth of the Internet will lead to a much larger productivity growth rate, perhaps as large as the growth rate in the 1950s and 1960s. In the present context, you can think about the growth of the Internet as an increase in physical capital (wires, servers, switchers, and so on) and an increase in the quality of capital (an increase in what can be done per minute using the Internet). Time will tell whether the Internet will lead to a "new age" of productivity growth.

Looking Ahead

This ends our introduction to the basic concepts and problems of macroeconomics. The first chapter of this part introduced the field; the second chapter discussed the measurement of national product and national income; and this chapter discussed unemployment, inflation, and long-run growth. We are now ready to begin the analysis of how the macroeconomy works.

——— S U M M A R Y ———

UNEMPLOYMENT *p. 130*

1. The *unemployment rate* is the ratio of the number of *unemployed* people to the number of people in the *labor force*. To be considered unemployed and in the labor force, a person must be looking for work.

2. Big differences in rates of unemployment exist across demographic groups, regions, and industries. African

Americans, for example, experience much higher unemployment rates than whites.

3. A person who decides to stop looking for work is considered to have dropped out of the labor force and is no longer classified as unemployed. People who stop looking because they are discouraged about finding a job are sometimes called *discouraged workers*.

4. Some unemployment is inevitable. Because new workers are continually entering the labor force, because industries and firms are continuously expanding and contracting, and because people switch jobs, there is a constant process of job search as workers and firms try to match the best people to the available jobs. This unemployment is both natural and beneficial for the economy.

5. The unemployment that occurs because of short-run job/skill-matching problems is called *frictional unemployment*. The unemployment that occurs because of longer-run structural changes in the economy is called *structural unemployment*. The *natural rate of unemployment* is the sum of the frictional rate and the structural rate. The increase in unemployment that occurs during recessions and depressions is called *cyclical unemployment*.

INFLATION p. 136

6. The *consumer price index (CPI)* is a fixed-weight price index. It represents the "market basket" purchased by the typical urban consumer.

7. Whether people gain or lose during a period of inflation depends on whether their income rises faster or slower than the prices of the things they buy. The elderly are more insulated from inflation than most people think because Social Security benefits and many pensions are indexed to inflation.

8. Inflation is likely to have a larger effect on the distribution of income when it is unanticipated than when it is anticipated.

LONG-RUN GROWTH p. 140

9. Output growth depends on: (1) the growth rate of the capital stock, (2) the growth rate of output per unit of the capital stock, (3) the growth rate of labor, and (4) the growth rate of output per unit of labor.

10. Output per worker hour (labor productivity) rose faster in the 1950s and 1960s than it rose from the 1970s to 2012. An interesting question is whether labor productivity will rise faster in the future because of the Internet.

REVIEW TERMS AND CONCEPTS

consumer price index (CPI), *p. 136*

cyclical unemployment, *p. 135*

discouraged-worker effect, *p. 132*

employed, *p. 130*

frictional unemployment, *p. 135*

labor force, *p. 130*

labor force participation rate, *p. 130*

natural rate of unemployment, *p. 135*

not in the labor force, *p. 130*

output growth, *p. 140*

per-capita output growth, *p. 140*

producer price indexes (PPIs), *p. 138*

productivity growth, *p. 140*

real interest rate, *p. 139*

structural unemployment, *p. 135*

unemployed, *p. 130*

unemployment rate, *p. 130*

Equations:

labor force = employed + unemployed, *p. 130*

population = labor force + not in labor force, *p. 130*

$$\text{unemployment rate} = \frac{\text{unemployed}}{\text{employed} + \text{unemployed}},$$

p. 130

$$\text{labor force participation rate} = \frac{\text{labor force}}{\text{population}}, p. 130$$

PROBLEMS

All problems are available on MyEconLab.

1. In late 2010 economists were debating whether the U.S. economy was in a recession. GDP seemed to be rising, yet the unemployment rate was stuck at close to 10 percent. In thinking about the economic distress experienced during a recession which is the most important: high unemployment or falling GDP? Defend your answer.

2. When an inefficient firm or a firm producing a product that people no longer want goes out of business, people are unemployed, but that is part of the normal process of economic growth and development. The unemployment is part of the natural rate and need not concern policy makers. Discuss that statement and its relevance to the economy today.

3. What is the unemployment rate in your state today? What was it in 1970, 1975, 1982, and 2008? How has your state done relative to the national average? Do you know or can you determine why?

4. [Related to the *Economics in Practice* on p. 133] For each of the following events, explain what is likely to happen to the labor force participation rate:
   a. The federal minimum wage is raised to $12.50 per hour.
   b. The minimum legal working age is raised from 16 to 18.
   c. The economy is in the midst of a prolonged recession.
   d. The federal government imposes a legal retirement age of 65.
   e. The federal government increases the minimum age requirement for collecting Social Security benefits.

5. Suppose all wages, salaries, welfare benefits, and other sources of income were indexed to inflation. Would inflation still be considered a problem? Why or why not?

6. [Related to the *Economics in Practice* on p. 135] According to the National Bureau of Economic Research (NBER), the United States experienced five recessions from 1980 to 2010. Following

is the NBER's list of the start and end dates for each of these recessions:

January 1980 – July 1980
July 1981 – November 1982
July 1990 – March 1991
March 2001 – November 2001
December 2007 – June 2009

Go to the Bureau of Labor Statistics Web site (www.bls.gov) and look up the monthly unemployment data since 1980. (Find BLS series number LNS14000000 and choose 1980 as the "from" date.) What were the unemployment rates for the starting and ending months for each of the 5 recessions? How long after each recession ended did it take for the unemployment rate to start to decrease, and how long did it take for the unemployment rate to return to the pre-recession level?

7. Go to www.bls.gov and click on the links for state and area employment and unemployment. Look at your home state and describe what changes have taken place in the workforce. Has the labor force participation rate gone up or down? Provide an explanation for the rate change. Are your state's experiences the same as the rest of the country? Provide an explanation of why your state's experiences are the same as or different from the rest of the country.

8. What do the CPI and PPIs measure? Why do we need both of these types of price indexes? (Think about what purpose you would use each one for.)

9. The consumer price index (CPI) is a fixed-weight index. It compares the price of a fixed bundle of goods in one year with the price of the same bundle of goods in some base year. Calculate the price of a bundle containing 100 units of good X, 150 units of good Y, and 25 units of good Z in 2011, 2012, and 2013. Convert the results into an index by dividing each bundle price figure by the bundle price in 2011. Calculate the percentage change in your index between 2011 and 2012 and again between 2012 and 2013. Was there inflation between 2012 and 2013?

GOOD	QUANTITY CONSUMED	2011 PRICES	2012 PRICES	2013 PRICES
X	100	$1.00	$1.50	$1.75
Y	150	1.50	2.00	2.00
Z	25	3.00	3.25	3.00

10. Consider the following statements:
    a. More people are employed in Tappania now than at any time in the past 50 years.
    b. The unemployment rate in Tappania is higher now than it has been in 50 years.
    Can both of those statements be true at the same time? Explain.

11. Policy makers talk about the "capacity" of the economy to grow. What specifically is meant by the "capacity" of the economy? How might capacity be measured? In what ways is capacity limited by labor constraints and by capital constraints? What are the consequences if demand in the economy exceeds capacity? What signs would you look for?

12. [Related to the *Economics in Practice* on *p. 139*] In his 2013 State of the Union speech, President Obama proposed raising the federal minimum wage from $7.25 to $9.00 per hour, and stated that future minimum wage increases should be tied to the

cost of living. Explain how tying the minimum wage to an index like the CPI could impact the economy? Do you suppose the impact would be different if the minimum wage was tied to the chain-linked CPI as opposed to the fixed-weight CPI? Explain.

13. What was the rate of growth in real GDP during the most recent quarter? You can find the answer in publications such as the *Survey of Current Business, The Economist,* and *Business Week*. Has growth been increasing or decreasing? What policies might you suggest for increasing the economy's potential long-run rate of growth?

14. Suppose the stock of capital and the workforce are both increasing at 3 percent annually in the country of Wholand. At the same time, real output is growing at 6 percent. How is that possible in the short run and in the long run?

15. Suppose the number of employed people in an economy is 121,166,640. The unemployment rate in this economy is 10.4 percent, or .104, and the labor force participation rate is 72.5 percent, or .725.
    a. What is the size of the labor force?
    b. How many people are unemployed?
    c. What is the size of the working-age population?

16. On average, nations in Europe pay higher unemployment benefits for longer periods of time than does the United States. How do you suppose this would impact the unemployment rates in these nations? Explain which type of unemployment you think is most directly affected by the size and duration of unemployment benefits.

17. Consider the following four situations. In which situation would a borrower be best off and in which situation would a lender be best off?
    a. The nominal interest rate is 14 percent and the inflation rate is 17 percent.
    b. The nominal interest rate is 7 percent and the inflation rate is 3 percent.
    c. The nominal interest rate is 4 percent and the inflation rate is –2 percent.
    d. The real interest rate is 6 percent and the inflation rate is 2 percent.

18. In each of the following cases, classify the person as cyclically unemployed, structurally unemployed, frictionally unemployed, or not in the labor force. Explain your answers.
    a. Maya just graduated from a top medical school and is currently deciding which hospital emergency room job she will accept.
    b. Hector lost his job as an assembly line worker at Chrysler due to the recession.
    c. Alejandro, an advertising executive in Seattle, quit his job one month ago to look for a more prestigious advertising job in New York City. He is still looking for a job.
    d. Yvonne got laid off from her job as a financial analyst 3 months ago and has not looked for a new job since then.
    e. Taylor lost his job as a welder due to the introduction of robotic welding machines.
    f. Ruby quit her job as a hotel concierge to become a full-time student at a culinary school.

19. The consumer price index is 125 in year 1 and 160 in year 2. All inflation is anticipated. If the Commerce Bank of Beverly Hills charges an interest rate of 35 percent in year 2, what is the bank's real interest rate?

PART III
The Core of Macroeconomic Theory

We now begin our discussion of the theory of how the macroeconomy works. We know how to calculate gross domestic product (GDP), but what factors *determine* it? We know how to define and measure inflation and unemployment, but what circumstances *cause* inflation and unemployment? What, if anything, can government do to reduce unemployment and inflation?

Analyzing the various components of the macroeconomy is a complex undertaking. The level of GDP, the overall price level, and the level of employment—three chief concerns of macroeconomists—are influenced by events in three broadly defined "markets":

- Goods-and-services market
- Financial (money) market
- Labor market

We will explore each market, as well as the links between them, in our discussion of macroeconomic theory. Figure III.1 presents the plan of the next seven chapters, which form the

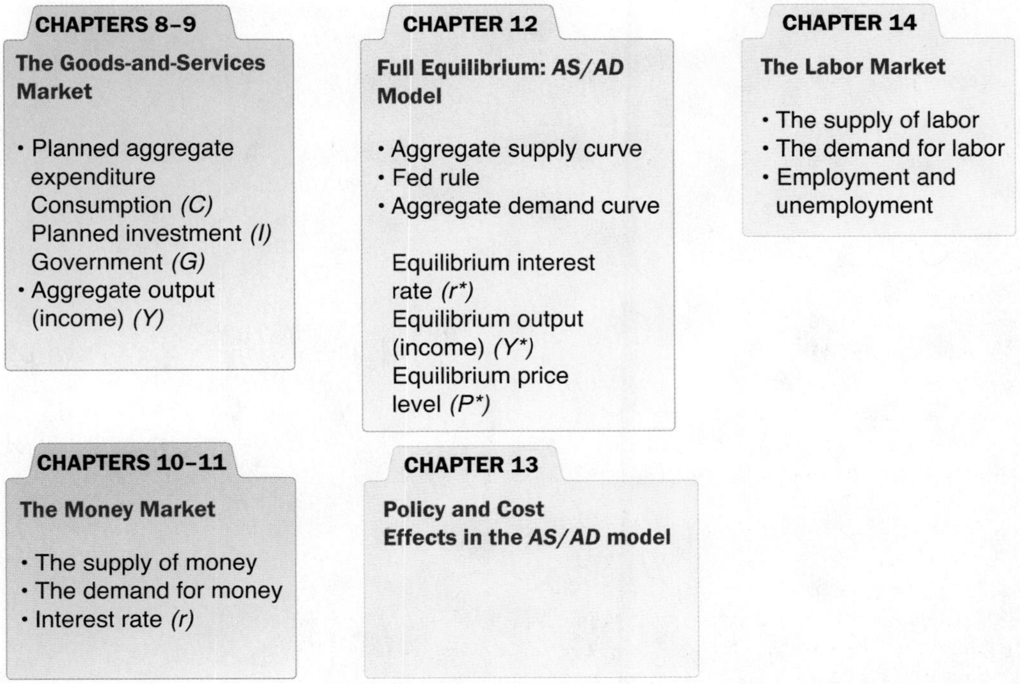

CHAPTERS 8–9

The Goods-and-Services Market

- Planned aggregate expenditure
  Consumption *(C)*
  Planned investment *(I)*
  Government *(G)*
- Aggregate output (income) *(Y)*

CHAPTER 12

Full Equilibrium: *AS/AD* Model

- Aggregate supply curve
- Fed rule
- Aggregate demand curve

  Equilibrium interest rate *(r*)*
  Equilibrium output (income) *(Y*)*
  Equilibrium price level *(P*)*

CHAPTER 14

The Labor Market

- The supply of labor
- The demand for labor
- Employment and unemployment

CHAPTERS 10–11

The Money Market

- The supply of money
- The demand for money
- Interest rate *(r)*

CHAPTER 13

Policy and Cost Effects in the *AS/AD* model

▲ **FIGURE III.1 The Core of Macroeconomic Theory**
We build up the macroeconomy slowly. In Chapters 8 and 9, we examine the market for goods and services. In Chapters 10 and 11, we examine the money market.

core of macroeconomic theory. In Chapters 8 and 9, we describe the market for goods and services, often called the *goods market*. In Chapter 8, we explain several basic concepts and show how the equilibrium level of output is determined in a simple economy with no government and no imports or exports. In Chapter 9, we add the government to the economy.

In Chapters 10 and 11, we focus on the *money market*. Chapter 10 introduces the money market and the banking system and discusses the way the U.S. central bank (the Federal Reserve) controls the money supply. Chapter 11 analyzes the demand for money and the way interest rates are determined.

Chapter 12 introduces the aggregate supply (*AS*) curve. It also discusses the behavior of the Federal Reserve regarding its interest rate decision, which is approximated by a "Fed rule." The Fed rule is then added to the analysis of the goods market to derive the aggregate demand (*AD*) curve. The resulting model, the "*AS/AD*" model, determines the equilibrium values of the interest rate (r), aggregate output (income) (Y), and the price level (P). Chapter 13 uses the *AS/AD* model to analyze policy and cost effects. Finally, Chapter 14 discusses the supply of and demand for labor and the functioning of the labor market in the macroeconomy. This material is essential to understanding how modern, developed economies function.

Aggregate Expenditure and Equilibrium Output

In the last several chapters we described a number of features of the U.S. economy, including real GDP, inflation, and unemployment, and we talked about how they are measured. Now we begin the analytical part of macroeconomics: we begin to explain how it is that the parts of the economy interact to produce the time-profile of the American economy that we described in the last few chapters.

We begin with the simplest case, focusing on households and firms. Once we understand how households and firms interact at the aggregate level, we will introduce government in Chapter 9. Our goal in this chapter is to provide you with a simplified model that will let you see what happens to the economy as a whole when there is an increase in investment. If suddenly all the managers of firms in the economy decided to expand their plants, how would that affect households and aggregate output? Because these are difficult questions, we start with a simple model and then build up chapter by chapter.

As we work through our model of the economy, we will focus, at least initially, on understanding movements in real gross domestic product (GDP), one of the central measures of macroeconomic activity. Because we are interested in tracking real changes in the level of economic activity, we focus on real, rather than nominal, output. So, while we will typically use dollars to measure GDP, you should think about this as dollars corrected for price level changes.

We saw earlier that GDP can be calculated in terms of either income or expenditures. We will use the variable *Y* to refer to both **aggregate output** and **aggregate income.**

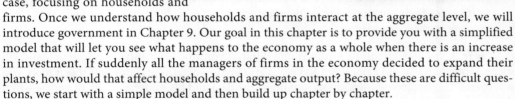

In any given period, there is an exact equality between aggregate output (production) and aggregate income. You should be reminded of this fact whenever you encounter the combined term **aggregate output (income) (*Y*)**.

Aggregate output can also be considered the aggregate quantity supplied because it is the amount that firms are supplying (producing) during a period. In the discussions that follow, we use the term *aggregate output (income)* instead of *aggregate quantity supplied*, but keep in mind that the two are equivalent. Also remember that *aggregate output* means "real GDP." For ease of discussion we will sometimes refer to aggregate output (income) as simply "output" or "income."

aggregate output The total quantity of goods and services produced (or supplied) in an economy in a given period.

aggregate income The total income received by all factors of production in a given period.

aggregate output (income) (*Y*) A combined term used to remind you of the exact equality between aggregate output and aggregate income.

LEARNING OBJECTIVES
Explain the principles of the Keynesian theory of consumption
Explain how equilibrium output is determined
Describe the multiplier process
Use the multiplier equation to calculate changes in equilibrium

From the outset, you must think in "real terms." For example, when we talk about output (Y), we mean real output, not nominal output. Although we discussed in Chapter 6 that the calculation of real GDP is complicated, you can ignore these complications in the following analysis. To help make things easier to read, we will frequently use dollar values for Y. But do not confuse Y with nominal output. The main point is to think of Y as being in real terms—the quantities of goods and services produced, not the dollars circulating in the economy.

Because we are building the model slowly, we are taking as fixed for purposes of this chapter and the next the interest rate (r) and the overall price level (P). The determination of the interest rate is discussed in Chapters 10 and 11, and the determination of the price level is discussed in Chapter 12. The interest rate does, however, play a role in this chapter and the next because, as we will see, it affects planned investment. In fact, a key link between the goods market and the money market is the effect of the interest rate on planned investment. It's just that we take the interest rate as fixed for now.

The Keynesian Theory of Consumption

In 2005, the average American family spent about $1,900 on clothing. For high-income families earning more than $150,000, the amount spent on clothing was substantially higher, at about $5,500. We all recognize that for consumption as a whole, as well as for consumption of most specific categories of goods and services, consumption rises with income. This relationship between consumption and income is central to Keynes's model of the economy. While Keynes recognized that many factors, including wealth and interest rates, play a role in determining consumption levels in the economy, in his classic *The General Theory of Employment, Interest, and Money*, current income played the key role:

> The fundamental psychological law, upon which we are entitled to depend with great confidence both *a priori* from our knowledge of human nature and from the detailed facts of experience, is that men [and women, too] are disposed, as a rule and on average, to increase their consumption as their incomes increase, but not by as much as the increase in their income.[1]

Keynes is telling us two things in this quote. First, if you find your income going up, you will spend more than you did before. But Keynes is also saying something about how much more you will spend: He predicts—based on his looking at the data and his understanding of people—that the rise in consumption will be less than the full rise in income. This simple observation plays a large role in helping us understand the workings of the aggregate economy.

The relationship between consumption and income is called a **consumption function**. Figure 8.1 shows a hypothetical consumption function for an individual household. The curve is labeled $c(y)$, which is read "c is a function of y," or "consumption is a function of income." Note

consumption function
The relationship between consumption and income.

▶ **FIGURE 8.1**
A Consumption Function for a Household
A consumption function for an individual household shows the level of consumption at each level of household income.

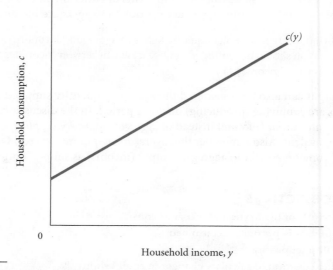

---

[1] John Maynard Keynes, *The General Theory of Employment, Interest, and Money* (1936), First Harbinger Ed. (New York: Harcourt Brace Jovanovich, 1964), p. 96.

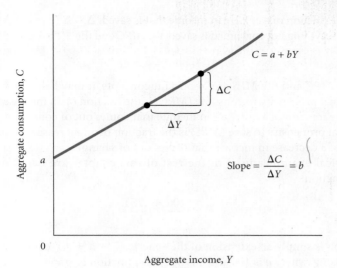

◀ **FIGURE 8.2**
An Aggregate Consumption Function
The aggregate consumption function shows the level of aggregate consumption at each level of aggregate income. The upward slope indicates that higher levels of income lead to higher levels of consumption spending.

that we have drawn the line with an upward slope, reflecting that consumption increases with income. To reflect Keynes's view that consumption increases less than one for one with income, we have drawn the consumption function with a slope of less than 1. The consumption function in Figure 8.1 is a straight line, telling us that an increase in income of $1 leads to the same increase in consumption regardless of the initial value of income. In practice, the consumption function may be curved, with the slope decreasing as income increases. This would tell us that the typical consumer spends less of the incremental income received as his or her income rises.

The consumption function in Figure 8.1 represents an individual household. In macroeconomics, however, we are interested in the behavior of the economy as a whole, the aggregate consumption of all households in the economy in relation to aggregate income. Figure 8.2 shows this aggregate consumption function, again using a straight line, or constant slope, for simplicity. With a straight-line consumption curve, we can use the following equation to describe the curve:

$$C = a + bY$$

Y is aggregate output (income), C is aggregate consumption, and a is the point at which the consumption function intersects the vertical axis—a constant. The letter b is the slope of the line, in this case $\Delta C/\Delta Y$ [because consumption (C) is measured on the vertical axis and income (Y) is measured on the horizontal axis].[2] Every time income increases (say by ΔY), consumption increases by b times ΔY. Thus, $\Delta C = b \times \Delta Y$ and $\Delta C/\Delta Y = b$. Suppose, for example, that the slope of the line in Figure 8.2 is .75 (that is, $b = .75$). An increase in income (ΔY) of $1,000 would then increase consumption by $b\Delta Y = .75 \times \$1,000$, or $750.

The **marginal propensity to consume (MPC)** is the fraction of a change in income that is consumed. In the consumption function here, b is the MPC. An MPC of .75 means consumption changes by .75 of the change in income. The slope of the consumption function is the MPC. An MPC less than 1 tells us that individuals spend less than 100 percent of their income increase, just as Keynes suggested.

marginal propensity to consume (MPC) That fraction of a change in income that is consumed, or spent.

$$\text{marginal propensity to consume} \equiv \text{slope of consumption function} \equiv \frac{\Delta C}{\Delta Y}$$

Aggregate saving (S) in the economy, denoted S, is the difference between aggregate income and aggregate consumption:

$$S \equiv Y - C$$

The triple equal sign means that this equation is an **identity**, or something that is always true by definition. This equation simply says that income that is not consumed must be saved. If $0.75 of a $1.00 increase in income goes to consumption, $0.25 must go to saving. If income decreases by $1.00, consumption will decrease by $0.75 and saving will decrease by $0.25. The **marginal propensity to**

aggregate saving (S) The part of aggregate income that is not consumed.

identity Something that is always true.

marginal propensity to save (MPS) That fraction of a change in income that is saved.

---

[2] The Greek letter Δ (delta) means "change in." For example, ΔY (read "delta Y") means the "change in income." If income (Y) in 2012 is $100 and income in 2013 is $110, then ΔY for this period is $110 − $100 = $10. For a review of the concept of slope, see Appendix, Chapter 1.

save **(MPS)** is the fraction of a change in income that is saved: $\Delta S / \Delta Y$, where ΔS is the change in saving. Because everything not consumed is saved, the MPC and the MPS must add up to 1.

$$MPC + MPS \equiv 1$$

Because the MPC and the MPS are important concepts, it may help to review their definitions. The marginal propensity to consume (MPC) is the fraction of an increase in income that is consumed (or the fraction of a decrease in income that comes out of consumption).

The marginal propensity to save (MPS) is the fraction of an increase in income that is saved (or the fraction of a decrease in income that comes out of saving).

The numerical examples used in the rest of this chapter are based on the following consumption function:

$$C = \underbrace{100}_{a} + \underbrace{.75Y}_{b}$$

This equation is simply an extension of the generic $C = a + bY$ consumption function we have been discussing, where a is 100 and b is .75. This function is graphed in Figure 8.3.

Since saving and consumption by definition add up to income, we can use the consumption curve to tell us about both consumption and saving. We do this in Figure 8.4. In this figure, we have drawn a 45° line from the origin. Everywhere along this line aggregate consumption is equal to aggregate income. Therefore, saving is zero. Where the consumption curve is *above* the 45° line, consumption exceeds income and saving is negative. Where the consumption function *crosses* the 45° line, consumption is equal to income and saving is zero. Where the consumption function is *below* the 45° line, consumption is less than income and saving is positive. Note that the slope of the saving function is $\Delta S / \Delta Y$, which is equal to the marginal propensity to save (MPS). The consumption function and the saving function are mirror images of each other. No information appears in one that does not appear in the other. These functions tell us how

▶ **FIGURE 8.3   The Aggregate Consumption Function Derived from the Equation $C = 100 + .75Y$**

In this simple consumption function, consumption is 100 at an income of zero. As income rises, so does consumption. For every 100 increase in income, consumption rises by 75. The slope of the line is .75.

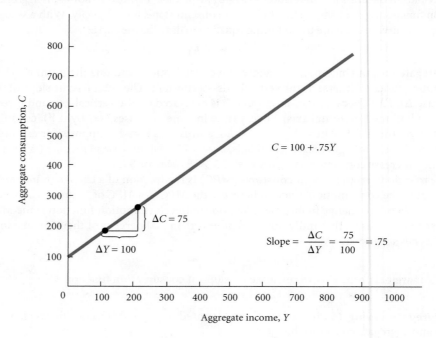

Aggregate Income, Y	Aggregate Consumption, C
0	100
80	160
100	175
200	250
400	400
600	550
800	700
1,000	850

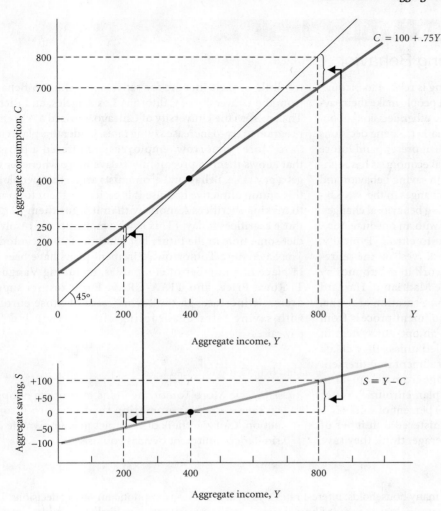

◀ **FIGURE 8.4 Deriving the Saving Function from the Consumption Function in Figure 8.3**
Because $S \equiv Y - C$, it is easy to derive the saving function from the consumption function. A 45° line drawn from the origin can be used as a convenient tool to compare consumption and income graphically. At $Y = 200$, consumption is 250. The 45° line shows us that consumption is larger than income by 50. Thus, $S \equiv Y - C = -50$. At $Y = 800$, consumption is less than income by 100. Thus, $S = 100$ when $Y = 800$.

Y	$-$	C	$=$	S
Aggregate Income		Aggregate Consumption		Aggregate Saving
0		100		−100
80		160		−80
100		175		−75
200		250		−50
400		400		0
600		550		50
800		700		100
1,000		850		150

households in the aggregate will divide income between consumption spending and saving at every possible income level. In other words, they embody aggregate household behavior.

Other Determinants of Consumption

The assumption that consumption depends only on income is obviously a simplification. In practice, the decisions of households on how much to consume in a given period are also affected by their wealth, by the interest rate, and by their expectations of the future. Households with higher wealth are likely to spend more, other things being equal, than households with less wealth.

The boom in the U.S. stock market in the last half of the 1990s and the boom in housing prices between 2003 and 2005, both of which increased household wealth substantially, led households to consume more than they otherwise would have in these periods. In 2009–2010, after a fall in housing prices and the stock market, consumption was less than it otherwise would have been.

ECONOMICS IN PRACTICE

Behavioral Biases in Saving Behavior

This chapter has described how saving is related to income. Economists have generally assumed that people make their saving decisions rationally, just as they make other decisions about choices in consumption and the labor market. Saving decisions involve thinking about trade-offs between present and future consumption. Recent work in behavioral economics has highlighted the role of psychological biases in saving behavior and has demonstrated that seemingly small changes in the way saving programs are designed can result in big behavioral changes.

Many retirement plans are designed with an opt-in feature. That is, you need to take some action to enroll. Typically, when you begin a job, you need to check "yes" on the retirement plan enrollment form. Recent work in economics by James Choi of Yale University, Brigitte Madrian of Harvard and Dennis Shea, head of executive compensation at Aetna, suggests that simply changing the enrollment process from the opt-in structure just described to an opt-out system in which people are automatically enrolled unless they check the "no" box dramatically increases enrollment in retirement pension plans. In one study, the change from an opt-in to an opt-out system increased pension plan enrollment after 3 months of work from 65 percent to 98 percent of workers.

Behavioral economists have administered a number of surveys suggesting that people, on average, think they save too little of their income for retirement. Shlomo Benartzi, from the University of California, Los Angeles, and Richard Thaler, from the University of Chicago, devised a retirement program to try to increase saving rates. Under this plan, called Save More Tomorrow, employees are offered a program that allows them to precommit to save more whenever they get a pay raise. Behavioral economists argue that people find this option attractive because it is easier for them to commit to making sacrifices tomorrow than it is for them to make those sacrifices today. (This is why many people resolve to diet some time in the future but continue to overeat today.) The Save More Tomorrow retirement plans have been put in place in a number of companies, including Vanguard, T. Rowe Price, and TIAA-CREF. Early results suggest dramatic increases in the saving rates of those enrolled, with saving rates quadrupling after 4 years and four pay raises.

THINKING PRACTICALLY

1. The Save More Tomorrow Plans encourage people to save more by committing themselves to future action. Can you think of examples in your own life of similar commitment devices you use?

For many households, interest rates also figure in to consumption and saving decisions. Lower interest rates reduce the cost of borrowing, so lower interest rates are likely to stimulate spending. (Conversely, higher interest rates increase the cost of borrowing and are likely to decrease spending.) Finally, as households think about what fraction of incremental income to consume versus save, their expectations about the future may also play a role. If households are optimistic and expect to do better in the future, they may spend more at present than if they think the future will be bleak.

Household expectations are also important regarding households' responses to changes in their income. If, for example, the government announces a tax cut, which increases after-tax income, households' responses to the tax cut will likely depend on whether the tax cut is expected to be temporary or permanent. If households expect that the tax cut will be in effect for only two years, their responses are likely to be smaller than if they expect the tax cut to be permanent.

We examine these issues in Chapter 16, where we take a closer look at household behavior regarding both consumption and labor supply. But for now, we will focus only on income, given that it is the most important determinant of consumption.

Planned Investment (I) versus Actual Investment

The output of an economy consists not only of goods consumed by households, but investments made by firms. Some firms' investments are in the form of plants and equipment. These are not very different from consumption of households. In a given period, a firm might buy $500,000 of new machinery, which would be part of aggregate output for the period, as would the purchase of automobiles by households. In Chapter 6, you learned that firms' investments also include inventories. Understanding how firms invest in inventories is a little more complicated, but it is important for understanding the way the macroeconomy works.

A firm's inventory is the stock of goods that it has awaiting sale. For many reasons, most firms want to hold some inventory. It is hard to predict exactly when consumers will want to purchase a new refrigerator, and most customers are not patient. Sometimes it is cheaper to produce goods in larger volumes than current demand requires, which leads firms to want to have inventory. From a macroeconomic perspective, however, inventory differs from other capital investments in one very important way: While purchases by firms of machinery and equipment are *always* deliberate, *sometimes* inventories build up (or decline) without any deliberate plan by firms. For this reason, there can be a difference between **planned invest-ment**, which consists of the investments firms *plan* to make, and **actual investment**, which consists of all of firms' investments, including their unplanned changes in inventories.

Why are inventories sometimes different from what was planned? Recall that firms hold planned inventories in anticipation of sales, recognizing that the exact timing of sales may be uncertain. If a firm overestimates how much it will sell in a period, it will end up with more in inventory than it planned to have. On other occasions, inventories may be lower than planned when sales are stronger than expected. We will use I to refer to planned investment, not necessarily actual investment. As we will see shortly, the economy is in equilibrium only when planned investment and actual investment are equal.

planned investment (I) Those additions to capital stock and inventory that are planned by firms.

actual investment The actual amount of investment that takes place; it includes items such as unplanned changes in inventories.

Planned Investment and the Interest Rate (r)

We have seen that there is an important difference between planned investment and actual invest-ment, and this distinction will play a key role in the discussion of equilibrium in this chapter. But another important question is what determines planned investment in the first place? In practice planned investment depends on many factors, as you would expect, but here we focus on just one: the interest rate. Recall that investment refers to a firm's purchase of new capital—new machines and plants. Whether a firm decides to invest in a project depends on whether the expected profits from the project justify its costs. And one cost of an investment project is the interest cost. When a manufacturing firm builds a new plant, the contractor must be paid at the time the plant is built. The money needed to carry out such projects is generally borrowed and paid back over an extended period. The real cost of an investment project thus depends in part on the interest rate—the cost of borrowing. When the interest rate rises, it becomes more expensive to borrow and fewer projects are likely to be undertaken; increasing the interest rate, *ceteris paribus*, is likely to reduce the level of planned investment spending. When the interest rate falls, it becomes less costly to borrow and more investment projects are likely to be undertaken; reducing the interest rate, *ceteris paribus*, is likely to increase the level of planned investment spending.

The relationship between the interest rate and planned investment is illustrated by the downward-sloping demand curve in Figure 8.5. The higher the interest rate, the lower the level of planned investment. At an interest rate of 3 percent, planned investment is I_0. When the inter-est rate rises from 3 to 6 percent, planned investment falls from I_0 to I_1. As the interest rate falls, however, more projects become profitable, so more investment is undertaken. The curve in Figure 8.5 is sometimes called the "marginal efficiency of investment" curve.

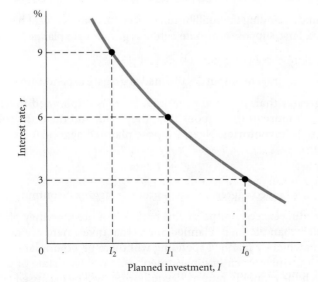

◀ **FIGURE 8.5** **Planned Investment Schedule**
Planned investment spending is a negative function of the interest rate. An increase in the interest rate from 3 percent to 6 percent reduces planned investment from I_0 to I_1.

Other Determinants of Planned Investment

The assumption that planned investment depends only on the interest rate is obviously a simplification, just as is the assumption that consumption depends only on income. In practice, the decision of a firm on how much to invest depends on, among other things, its expectation of future sales. If a firm expects that its sales will increase in the future, it may begin to build up its capital stock—that is, to invest—now so that it will be able to produce more in the future to meet the increased level of sales. The optimism or pessimism of entrepreneurs about the future course of the economy can have an important effect on current planned investment. Keynes used the phrase *animal spirits* to describe the feelings of entrepreneurs, and he argued that these feelings affect investment decisions.

We will come back to this issue in Chapter 16, where we will take a closer look at firm behavior (and household behavior), but until then we will assume that planned investment simply depends on the interest rate.

The Determination of Equilibrium Output (Income)

Thus far, we have described the behavior of firms and households. We now discuss the nature of equilibrium and explain how the economy achieves equilibrium.

equilibrium Occurs when there is no tendency for change. In the macroeconomic goods market, equilibrium occurs when planned aggregate expenditure is equal to aggregate output.

A number of definitions of **equilibrium** are used in economics. They all refer to the idea that at equilibrium, there is no tendency for change. In microeconomics, equilibrium is said to exist in a particular market (for example, the market for bananas) at the price for which the quantity demanded is equal to the quantity supplied. At this point, both suppliers and demanders are satisfied. The equilibrium price of a good is the price at which suppliers want to furnish the amount that demanders want to buy.

planned aggregate expenditure (AE) The total amount the economy plans to spend in a given period. Equal to consumption plus planned investment: $AE \equiv C + I$.

To define equilibrium for the macroeconomy, we start with a new variable, **planned aggregate expenditure (AE)**. Planned aggregate expenditure is, by definition, consumption plus planned investment:

$$AE \equiv C + I$$

Note that I is planned investment spending only. It does not include any unplanned increases or decreases in inventory. Note also that this is a definition. Aggregate expenditure is always equal to $C + I$, and we write it with the triple equal sign.

The economy is defined to be in equilibrium when aggregate output (Y) is equal to planned aggregate expenditure (AE).

$$\text{Equilibrium: } Y = AE$$

Because AE is, by definition, $C + I$, equilibrium can also be written:

$$\text{Equilibrium: } Y = C + I$$

It will help in understanding the equilibrium concept to consider what happens if the economy is out of equilibrium. First, suppose aggregate output is greater than planned aggregate expenditure:

$$Y > C + I$$

aggregate output $>$ planned aggregate expenditure

When output is greater than planned spending, there is unplanned inventory investment. Firms planned to sell more of their goods than they sold, and the difference shows up as an unplanned increase in inventories. Next, suppose planned aggregate expenditure is greater than aggregate output:

$$C + I > Y$$

planned aggregate expenditure $>$ aggregate output

When planned spending exceeds output, firms have sold more than they planned to. Inventory investment is smaller than planned. Planned and actual investment are not equal. Only when output is exactly matched by planned spending will there be no unplanned inventory investment. If there is unplanned inventory investment, this will be a state of disequilibrium. The mechanism by which the economy returns to equilibrium will be discussed later. Equilibrium in

TABLE 8.1 Deriving the Planned Aggregate Expenditure Schedule and Finding Equilibrium. The Figures in Column 2 are Based on the Equation $C = 100 + .75Y$.

(1) Aggregate Output (Income) (Y)	(2) Aggregate Consumption (C)	(3) Planned Investment (I)	(4) Planned Aggregate Expenditure (AE) $C + I$	(5) Unplanned Inventory Change $Y - (C + I)$	(6) Equilibrium? $(Y = AE?)$
100	175	25	200	−100	No
200	250	25	275	−75	No
400	400	25	425	−25	No
500	475	25	500	0	Yes
600	550	25	575	+25	No
800	700	25	725	+75	No
1,000	850	25	875	+125	No

the goods market is achieved only when aggregate output (Y) and planned aggregate expenditure $(C + I)$ are equal, or when actual and planned investment are equal.

Table 8.1 derives a planned aggregate expenditure schedule and shows the point of equilibrium for our numerical example. I is assumed to be fixed and equal to 25 for these calculations. Remember that I depends on the interest rate, but the interest rate is fixed for purposes of this chapter. Remember also that all our calculations are based on $C = 100 + .75Y$. To determine planned aggregate expenditure, we add consumption spending (C) to planned investment spending (I) at every level of income. Glancing down columns 1 and 4, we see one and only one level at which aggregate output and planned aggregate expenditure are equal: $Y = 500$.

Figure 8.6 illustrates the same equilibrium graphically. Figure 8.6a adds planned investment, fixed at 25, to consumption at every level of income. Because planned investment is a constant, the

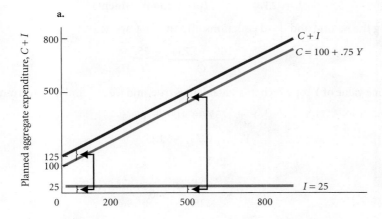

a.

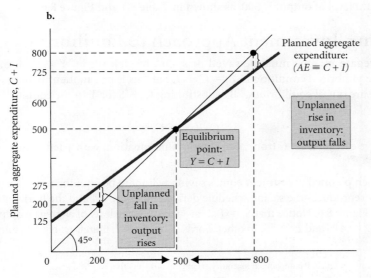

b.

Aggregate output, Y

◀ **FIGURE 8.6**
Equilibrium Aggregate Output
Equilibrium occurs when planned aggregate expenditure and aggregate output are equal. Planned aggregate expenditure is the sum of consumption spending and planned investment spending.

planned aggregate expenditure function is simply the consumption function displaced vertically by that constant amount. Figure 8.6b shows the planned aggregate expenditure function with the 45° line. The 45° line represents all points on the graph where the variables on the horizontal and vertical axes are equal. Any point on the 45° line is a potential equilibrium point. The planned aggregate expenditure function crosses the 45° line at a single point, where $Y = 500$. (The point at which the two lines cross is sometimes called the *Keynesian cross*.) At that point, $Y = C + I$.

Now let us look at some other levels of aggregate output (income). First, consider $Y = 800$. Is this an equilibrium output? Clearly, it is not. At $Y = 800$, planned aggregate expenditure is 725 (see Table 8.1). This amount is less than aggregate output, which is 800. Because output is greater than planned spending, the difference ends up in inventory as unplanned inventory investment. In this case, unplanned inventory investment is 75. In the aggregate, firms have more inventory than desired. As a result, firms have an incentive to change their production plans going forward. In this sense, the economy will not be in equilibrium.

Next, consider $Y = 200$. Is this an equilibrium output? No. At $Y = 200$, planned aggregate expenditure is 275. Planned spending (AE) is greater than output (Y), and there is an unplanned fall in inventory investment of 75. Again, firms in the aggregate will experience a different result from what they expected.

At $Y = 200$ and $Y = 800$, planned investment and actual investment are unequal. There is unplanned investment, and the system is out of balance. Only at $Y = 500$, where planned aggregate expenditure and aggregate output are equal, will planned investment equal actual investment.

Finally, let us find the equilibrium level of output (income) algebraically. Recall that we know the following:

$$Y = C + I \qquad \text{(equilbrium)}$$

$$C = 100 + .75Y \quad \text{(consumption function)}$$

$$I = 25 \qquad \text{(planned investment)}$$

By substituting the second and third equations into the first, we get:

$$Y = \underbrace{100 + .75Y}_{C} + \underbrace{25.}_{I}$$

There is only one value of Y for which this statement is true, and we can find it by rearranging terms:

$$Y - .75Y = 100 + 25$$

$$Y(1 - 0.75) = 125$$

$$.25Y = 125$$

$$Y = \frac{125}{.25} = 500$$

The equilibrium level of output is 500, as shown in Table 8.1 and Figure 8.6.

The Saving/Investment Approach to Equilibrium

Because aggregate income must be saved or spent, by definition, $Y \equiv C + S$, which is an identity. The equilibrium condition is $Y = C + I$, but this is not an identity because it does not hold when we are out of equilibrium.[3] By substituting $C + S$ for Y in the equilibrium condition, we can write:

$$C + S = C + I$$

Because we can subtract C from both sides of this equation, we are left with:

$$S = I$$

Thus, only when planned investment equals saving will there be equilibrium.

Figure 8.7 reproduces the saving schedule derived in Figure 8.4 and the horizontal investment function from Figure 8.6. Notice that $S = I$ at one and only one level of aggregate output, $Y = 500$. At $Y = 500$, $C = 475$ and $I = 25$. In other words, $Y = C + I$; therefore, equilibrium exists.

---

[3] It would be an identity if I included unplanned inventory accumulations—in other words, if I were actual investment instead of planned investment.

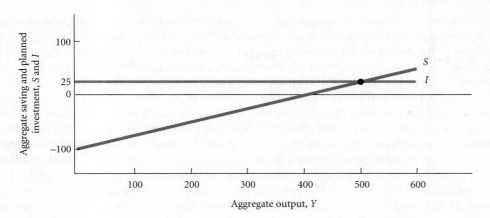

◀ **FIGURE 8.7**
The $S = I$ Approach to Equilibrium
Aggregate output is equal to planned aggregate expenditure only when saving equals planned investment ($S = I$). Saving and planned investment are equal at $Y = 500$.

Adjustment to Equilibrium

We have defined equilibrium and learned how to find it, but we have said nothing about how firms might react to *disequilibrium*. Let us consider the actions firms might take when planned aggregate expenditure exceeds aggregate output (income).

We already know the only way firms can sell more than they produce is by selling some inventory. This means that when planned aggregate expenditure exceeds aggregate output, unplanned inventory reductions have occurred. Firms have sold more than they planned. It seems reasonable to assume that firms will respond to unplanned inventory reductions by increasing output. If firms increase output, income must also increase. (Output and income are two ways of measuring the same thing.) As GM builds more cars, it hires more workers (or pays its existing workforce for working more hours), buys more steel, uses more electricity, and so on. These purchases by GM represent income for the producers of labor, steel, electricity, and so on. When firms try to keep their inventories stable by increasing production, this will generate more income in the economy as a whole. This will lead to more consumption. Remember, when income rises, so does consumption. The adjustment process will continue as long as output (income) is below planned aggregate expenditure. If firms react to unplanned inventory reductions by increasing output, an economy with planned spending greater than output will adjust to equilibrium, with Y higher than before. If planned spending is less than output, there will be unplanned increases in inventories. In this case, firms will respond by reducing output. As output falls, income falls, consumption falls, and so on, until equilibrium is restored, with Y lower than before.

As Figure 8.6 shows, at any level of output above $Y = 500$, such as $Y = 800$, output will fall until it reaches equilibrium at $Y = 500$, and at any level of output below $Y = 500$, such as $Y = 200$, output will rise until it reaches equilibrium at $Y = 500$.[4]

The Multiplier

The model we have developed lets us answer the question we posed at the beginning of this chapter: What happens to the level of real output if all of the managers in the economy suddenly decide to increase planned investment from, say, 25 to 50? It may surprise you to learn that the change in equilibrium output will be *greater* than the initial change in planned investment. In fact, output will change by a multiple of the change in planned investment.

The **multiplier** is defined as the ratio of the change in the equilibrium level of output to a change in some exogenous variable. An **exogenous variable** is a variable that is assumed not to depend on the state of the economy—that is, a variable is exogenous if it does not change in response to changes in the economy. In this chapter, we consider planned investment to be exogenous. This simplifies our analysis and provides a foundation for later discussions.

multiplier The ratio of the change in the equilibrium level of output to a change in some exogenous variable.

exogenous variable A variable that is assumed not to depend on the state of the economy—that is, it does not change when the economy changes.

[4] In discussing simple supply and demand equilibrium in Chapters 3 and 4, we saw that when quantity supplied exceeds quantity demanded, the price falls and the quantity supplied declines. Similarly, when quantity demanded exceeds quantity supplied, the price rises and the quantity supplied increases. In the analysis here, we are ignoring potential changes in prices or in the price level and focusing on changes in the level of real output (income). Later, after we have introduced money and the price level into the analysis, prices will be very important. At this stage, however, only aggregate output (income) (Y) adjusts when aggregate expenditure exceeds aggregate output (with inventory falling) or when aggregate output exceeds aggregate expenditure (with inventory rising).

With planned investment exogenous, we can ask how much the equilibrium level of output changes when planned investment changes. Remember that we are not trying to explain *why* planned investment changes; we are simply asking how much the equilibrium level of output changes when (for whatever reason) planned investment changes. (Beginning in Chapter 12, we will no longer take planned investment as given and will explain how planned investment is determined.)

Consider a sustained increase in planned investment of 25—that is, suppose I increases from 25 to 50 and stays at 50. If equilibrium existed at $I = 25$, an increase in planned investment of 25 will cause a disequilibrium, with planned aggregate expenditure greater than aggregate output by 25. Firms immediately see unplanned reductions in their inventories. As a result, firms begin to increase output.

Let us say the increase in planned investment comes from an anticipated increase in travel that leads airlines to purchase more airplanes, car rental companies to increase purchases of automobiles, and bus companies to purchase more buses (all capital goods). The firms experiencing unplanned inventory declines will be automobile manufacturers, bus producers, and aircraft producers—GM, Ford, Boeing, and so on. In response to declining inventories of planes, buses, and cars, these firms will increase output.

Now suppose these firms raise output by the full 25 increase in planned investment. Does this restore equilibrium? No, it does not because when output goes up, people earn more income and a part of that income will be spent. This increases planned aggregate expenditure even further. In other words, an increase in I also leads indirectly to an increase in C. To produce more airplanes, Boeing has to hire more workers or ask its existing employees to work more hours. It also must buy more engines from General Electric, more tires from Goodyear, and so on. Owners of these firms will earn more profits, produce more, hire more workers, and pay out more in wages and salaries. This added income does not vanish into thin air. It is paid to households that spend some of it and save the rest. The added production leads to added income, which leads to added consumption spending.

If planned investment (I) goes up by 25 initially *and is sustained at this higher level*, an increase of output of 25 will *not* restore equilibrium because it generates even more consumption spending (C). People buy more consumer goods. There are unplanned reductions of inventories of basic consumption items—washing machines, food, clothing, and so on—and this prompts other firms to increase output. The cycle starts all over again.

Output and income can rise significantly more than the initial increase in planned investment, but how much and how large is the multiplier? This is answered graphically in Figure 8.8. Assume that the economy is in equilibrium at point A, where equilibrium output is 500. The increase in

▶ **FIGURE 8.8** **The Multiplier as Seen in the Planned Aggregate Expenditure Diagram**

At point A, the economy is in equilibrium at $Y = 500$. When I increases by 25, planned aggregate expenditure is initially greater than aggregate output. As output rises in response, additional consumption is generated, pushing equilibrium output up by a multiple of the initial increase in I. The new equilibrium is found at point B, where $Y = 600$. Equilibrium output has increased by 100 ($600 - 500$), or *four times* the amount of the increase in planned investment.

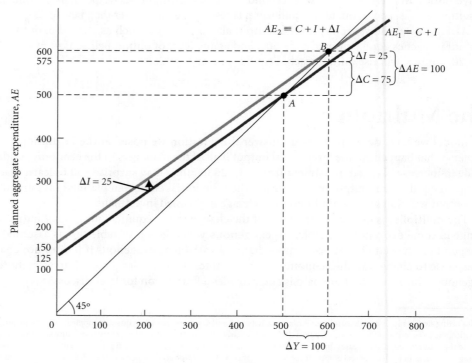

I of 25 shifts the $AE \equiv C + I$ curve up by 25 because I is higher by 25 at every level of income. The new equilibrium occurs at point B, where the equilibrium level of output is 600. Like point A, point B is on the 45° line and is an equilibrium value. Output (Y) has increased by 100 (600–500), or four times the initial increase in planned investment of 25, between point A and point B. The multiplier in this example is 4. At point B, aggregate spending is also higher by 100. If 25 of this additional 100 is investment (I), as we know it is, the remaining 75 is added consumption (C). From point A to point B then, $\Delta Y = 100$, $\Delta I = 25$, and $\Delta C = 75$.

Why doesn't the multiplier process go on forever? The answer is that only a fraction of the increase in income is consumed in each round. Successive increases in income become smaller and smaller in each round of the multiplier process, due to leakage as saving, until equilibrium is restored.

The size of the multiplier depends on the slope of the planned aggregate expenditure line. The steeper the slope of this line, the greater the change in output for a given change in investment. When planned investment is fixed, as in our example, the slope of the $AE \equiv C + I$ line is just the marginal propensity to consume ($\Delta C / \Delta Y$). The greater the MPC, the greater the multiplier. This should not be surprising. A large MPC means that consumption increases a great deal when income increases.

The Multiplier Equation

Is there a way to determine the size of the multiplier without using graphic analysis? Yes, there is.

Assume that the market is in equilibrium at an income level of $Y = 500$. Now suppose planned investment (I)—thus, planned aggregate expenditure (AE)—increases and remains higher by 25. Planned aggregate expenditure is greater than output, there is an unplanned inventory reduction, and firms respond by increasing output (income) (Y). This leads to a second round of increases, and so on.

What will restore equilibrium? Look at Figure 8.7 and recall: Planned aggregate expenditure ($AE \equiv C + I$) is not equal to aggregate output (Y) unless $S = I$; the leakage of saving must exactly match the injection of planned investment spending for the economy to be in equilibrium. Recall also that we assumed that planned investment jumps to a new, higher level and stays there; it is a *sustained* increase of 25 in planned investment spending. As income rises, consumption rises and so does saving. Our $S = I$ approach to equilibrium leads us to conclude that equilibrium will be restored only when saving has increased by exactly the amount of the initial increase in I. Otherwise, I will continue to be greater than S and $C + I$ will continue to be greater than Y. (The $S = I$ approach to equilibrium leads to an interesting paradox in the macroeconomy. See the following *Economics in Practice*, "The Paradox of Thrift.")

It is possible to figure how much Y must increase in response to the additional planned investment before equilibrium will be restored. Y will rise, pulling S up with it until the change in saving is exactly equal to the change in planned investment—that is, until S is again equal to I at its new higher level. Because added saving is a *fraction* of added income (the MPS), the increase in *income* required to restore equilibrium must be a *multiple* of the increase in planned investment.

Recall that the marginal propensity to save (MPS) is the fraction of a change in income that is saved. It is defined as the change in S (ΔS) over the change in income (ΔY):

$$MPS = \frac{\Delta S}{\Delta Y}$$

Because ΔS must be equal to ΔI for equilibrium to be restored, we can substitute ΔI for ΔS and solve:

$$MPS = \frac{\Delta I}{\Delta Y}$$

Therefore,

$$\Delta Y = \Delta I \times \frac{1}{MPS}$$

As you can see, the change in equilibrium income (ΔY) is equal to the initial change in planned investment (ΔI) times $1/MPS$. The multiplier is $1/MPS$:

$$\text{multiplier} \equiv \frac{1}{MPS}$$

ECONOMICS IN PRACTICE

The Paradox of Thrift

An interesting paradox can arise when households attempt to increase their saving. What happens if households become concerned about the future and want to save more today to be prepared for hard times tomorrow? If households increase their planned saving, the saving schedule in the graph below shifts upward from S_0 to S_1. The plan to save more is a plan to consume less, and the resulting drop in spending leads to a drop in income. Income drops by a multiple of the initial shift in the saving schedule. Before the increase in saving, equilibrium exists at point A, where $S_0 = I$ and $Y = 500$. Increased saving shifts the equilibrium to point B, the point at which $S_1 = I$. New equilibrium output is 300—a decrease of 200 (ΔY) from the initial equilibrium.

By consuming less, households have actually *caused* the hard times about which they were apprehensive. Worse, the new equilibrium finds saving at the same level as it was before consumption dropped (25). In their attempt to save more, households have caused a contraction in output, and thus in income. They end up consuming less, but they have not saved any more.

It should be clear why saving at the new equilibrium is equal to saving at the old equilibrium. Equilibrium requires that saving equals planned investment, and because planned investment is unchanged, saving must remain unchanged for equilibrium to exist. This paradox shows that the interactions among sectors in the economy can be of crucial importance.

The paradox of thrift is "paradoxical" because it contradicts the widely held belief that "a penny saved is a penny earned." This may be true for an individual, but when society as a whole saves more, the result is a drop in income but no increased saving.

Does the paradox of thrift always hold? Recall our assumption that the interest rate is fixed. If the extra saving that the households want to do to ward off hard times leads to a fall in the interest rate, this will increase planned investment and thus shift up the I schedule in the figure. The paradox might then be avoided. Planned investment could increase enough so that the new equilibrium occurs at a higher level of income (and saving).

THINKING PRACTICALLY

1. Draw a consumption function corresponding to S_0 and S_1 and describe what is happening.

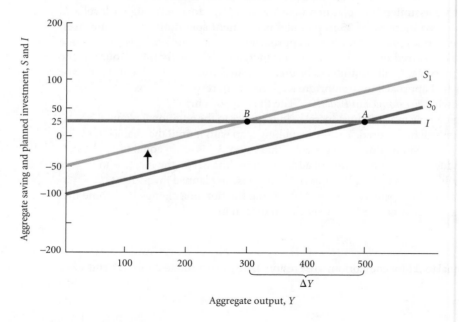

The Paradox of Thrift

An increase in planned saving from S_0 to S_1 causes equilibrium output to decrease from 500 to 300. The decreased consumption that accompanies increased saving leads to a contraction of the economy and to a reduction of income. But at the new equilibrium, saving is the same as it was at the initial equilibrium. Increased efforts to save have caused a drop in income but no overall change in saving.

Because $MPS + MPC \equiv 1$, $MPS \equiv 1 - MPC$. It follows that the multiplier is also equal to

$$\text{multiplier} \equiv \frac{1}{1 - MPC}$$

In our example, the MPC is .75; so the MPS must equal $1 - .75$, or .25. Thus, the multiplier is 1 divided by .25, or 4. The change in the equilibrium level of Y is 4×25, or 100.[5] Also note that the same analysis holds when planned investment falls. If planned investment falls by a certain amount and is sustained at this lower level, output will fall by a multiple of the reduction in I. As the initial shock is felt and firms cut output, they lay people off. The result: Income, and subsequently consumption, falls.

The Size of the Multiplier in the Real World

In considering the size of the multiplier, it is important to realize that the multiplier we derived in this chapter is based on a *very* simplified picture of the economy. First, we have assumed that planned investment is exogenous and does not respond to changes in the economy. Second, we have thus far ignored the role of government, financial markets, and the rest of the world in the macroeconomy. For these reasons, it would be a mistake to move on from this chapter thinking that national income can be increased by $100 billion simply by increasing planned investment spending by $25 billion.

As we relax these assumptions in the following chapters, you will see that most of what we add to make our analysis more realistic has the effect of *reducing* the size of the multiplier. For example:

1. The Appendix to Chapter 9 shows that when tax payments depend on income (as they do in the real world), the size of the multiplier is reduced. As the economy expands, tax payments increase and act as a drag on the economy. The multiplier effect is smaller.
2. We will see in Chapter 12 that adding Fed behavior regarding the interest rate has the effect of reducing the size of the multiplier.
3. We will also see in Chapter 12 that adding the price level to the analysis reduces the size of the multiplier. We will see that part of an expansion of the economy is likely to take the form of an increase in the price level instead of an increase in real output. When this happens, the size of the multiplier is reduced.
4. The multiplier is also reduced when imports are introduced (in Chapter 20), because some domestic spending leaks into foreign markets.

These juicy tidbits give you something to look forward to as you proceed through the rest of this book. For now, however, it is enough to point out that in reality the size of the multiplier is probably about 2. This is much lower than the value of 4 that we used in this chapter.

Looking Ahead

In this chapter, we took the first step toward understanding how the economy works. We assumed that consumption depends on income, that planned investment is fixed, and that there is equilibrium. We discussed how the economy might adjust back to equilibrium when it is out of equilibrium. We also discussed the effects on equilibrium output from a change in planned investment and derived the multiplier. In the next chapter, we retain these assumptions and add the government to the economy.

---

[5] The multiplier can also be derived algebraically, as the Appendix to this chapter demonstrates.

SUMMARY

THE KEYNESIAN THEORY OF CONSUMPTION *p. 148*

1. Aggregate consumption is assumed to be a function of aggregate income.

2. The *marginal propensity to consume (MPC)* is the fraction of a change in income that is consumed, or spent. The *marginal propensity to save (MPS)* is the fraction of a change in income that is saved. Because all income must be saved or spent, $MPS + MPC \equiv 1$.

PLANNED INVESTMENT (*I*) VERSUS ACTUAL INVESTMENT *p. 152*

3. Planned investment may differ from actual investment because of unanticipated changes in inventories.

PLANNED INVESTMENT AND THE INTEREST RATE (*r*) *p. 153*

4. Planned investment depends on the interest rate, which is taken to be fixed for this chapter.

THE DETERMINATION OF EQUILIBRIUM OUTPUT (INCOME) *p. 154*

5. *Planned aggregate expenditure (AE)* equals consumption plus planned investment: $AE \equiv C + I$. *Equilibrium* in the goods market is achieved when planned aggregate expenditure equals aggregate output: $C + I = Y$. This holds if and only if planned investment and actual investment are equal.

6. Because aggregate income must be saved or spent, the equilibrium condition $Y = C + I$ can be rewritten as $C + S = C + I$, or $S = I$. Only when planned investment equals saving will there be equilibrium. This approach to equilibrium is the *saving/ investment approach* to equilibrium.

7. When planned aggregate expenditure exceeds aggregate output (*income*), there is an unplanned fall in inventories. Firms will increase output. This increased output leads to increased income and even more consumption. This process will continue as long as output (income) is below planned aggregate expenditure. If firms react to unplanned inventory reductions by increasing output, an economy with planned spending greater than output will adjust to a new equilibrium, with *Y* higher than before.

THE MULTIPLIER *p. 157*

8. Equilibrium output changes by a multiple of the change in planned investment or any other *exogenous variable*. The *multiplier* is 1/*MPS*.

9. When households increase their planned saving, income decreases and saving does not change. Saving does not increase because in equilibrium, saving must equal planned investment and planned investment is fixed. If planned investment also increased, this *paradox of thrift* could be averted and a new equilibrium could be achieved at a higher level of saving and income. This result depends on the existence of a channel through which additional household saving finances additional investment.

REVIEW TERMS AND CONCEPTS

actual investment, *p. 153*

aggregate income, *p. 147*

aggregate output, *p. 147*

aggregate output (income) (*Y*), *p. 147*

aggregate saving (*S*), *p. 149*

consumption function, *p. 148*

equilibrium, *p. 154*

exogenous variable, *p. 157*

identity, *p. 149*

marginal propensity to consume (*MPC*), *p. 149*

marginal propensity to save (*MPS*), *p. 149*

multiplier, *p. 157*

planned aggregate expenditure (*AE*), *p. 154*

planned investment (*I*), *p. 153*

Equations:

$S \equiv Y - C$, *p. 149*

$MPC \equiv$ slope of consumption

function $\equiv \dfrac{\Delta C}{\Delta Y}$, *p. 149*

$MPC + MPS \equiv 1$, *p. 150*

$AE \equiv C + I$, *p. 154*

Equilibrium condition: $Y = AE$ or $Y = C + I$, *p. 154*

Saving/investment approach to equilibrium: $S = I$, *p. 156*

Multiplier $\equiv \dfrac{1}{MPS} \equiv \dfrac{1}{1 - MPC}$, *p. 161*

PROBLEMS

All problems are available on MyEconLab.

1. Briefly define the following terms and explain the relationship between them:

    MPC..Multiplier

    Actual investment...Planned investment

    Aggregate expenditure..Real GDP

    Aggregate output...Aggregate income

2. Expert econometricians in the Republic of Yuck estimate the following:

    Real GNP (*Y*)...200 billion Yuck dollars

    Planned investment spending...................75 billion Yuck dollars

    Yuck is a simple economy with no government, no taxes, and no imports or exports. Yuckers (citizens of Yuck) are creatures of habit. They have a rule that everyone saves exactly 25 percent of income. Assume that planned investment is fixed and remains at 75 billion Yuck dollars.

You are asked by the business editor of the *Weird Herald*, the local newspaper, to predict the economic events of the next few months. By using the data given, can you make a forecast? What is likely to happen to inventories? What is likely to happen to the level of real GDP? Is the economy at an equilibrium? When will things stop changing?

3. Go to **www.commerce.gov**. Click on "Bureau of Economic Analysis." Click next on "National" and then on the latest GDP release. Look through the report. Which of the components of aggregate expenditure appear to be growing or falling the fastest? What story can you tell about the current economic events from the data?

4. The following questions refer to this table:

AGGREGATE OUTPUT/INCOME	CONSUMPTION	PLANNED INVESTMENT
2.000	2.100	300
2,500	2,500	300
3,000	2,900	300
3,500	3,300	300
4,000	3,700	300
4,500	4,100	300
5,000	4,500	300
5,500	4,900	300

   a. At each level of output, calculate saving. At each level of output, calculate unplanned investment (inventory change). What is likely to happen to aggregate output if the economy produces at each of the levels indicated? What is the equilibrium level of output?

   b. Over each range of income (2,000 to 2,500, 2,500 to 3,000, and so on), calculate the marginal propensity to consume. Calculate the marginal propensity to save. What is the multiplier?

   c. By assuming there is no change in the level of the *MPC* and the *MPS* and planned investment jumps by 200 and is sustained at that higher level, recompute the table. What is the new equilibrium level of *Y*? Is this consistent with what you compute using the multiplier?

5. Explain the multiplier intuitively. Why is it that an increase in planned investment of $100 raises equilibrium output by more than $100? Why is the effect on equilibrium output finite? How do we know that the multiplier is 1/*MPS*?

6. You are given the following data concerning Freedonia, a legendary country:
   (1) Consumption function: $C = 200 + 0.8Y$
   (2) Investment function: $I = 100$
   (3) $AE \equiv C + I$
   (4) $AE = Y$
   a. What is the marginal propensity to consume in Freedonia, and what is the marginal propensity to save?
   b. Graph equations (3) and (4) and solve for equilibrium income.
   c. Suppose equation (2) is changed to (2′) $I = 110$. What is the new equilibrium level of income? By how much does the $10 increase in planned investment change equilibrium income? What is the value of the multiplier?

   d. Calculate the saving function for Freedonia. Plot this saving function on a graph with equation (2). Explain why the equilibrium income in this graph must be the same as in part b.

7. This chapter argues that saving and spending behavior depend in part on wealth (accumulated savings and inheritance), but our simple model does not incorporate this effect. Consider the following model of a very simple economy:

$$C = 10 + .75Y + .04W$$
$$I = 100$$
$$W = 1,000$$
$$Y = C + I$$
$$S = Y - C$$

If you assume that wealth (*W*) and investment (*I*) remain constant (we are ignoring the fact that saving adds to the stock of wealth), what are the equilibrium levels of GDP (*Y*), consumption (*C*), and saving (*S*)? Now suppose that wealth increases by 50 percent to 1,500. Recalculate the equilibrium levels of *Y*, *C*, and *S*. What impact does wealth accumulation have on GDP? Many were concerned with the very large increase in stock values in the late 1990s. Does this present a problem for the economy? Explain.

8. You learned earlier that expenditures and income should always be equal. In this chapter, you learned that *AE* and aggregate output (income) can be different. Is there an inconsistency here? Explain.

9. [Related to the *Economics in Practice* on p. 152] The *Economics in Practice* describes some of the difficulties that households have with regard to decisions involving trade-offs between the present and the future. Explain briefly how the problem of global warming and the problem of adequate household saving are similar. Describe ways in which the concept of opportunity cost can be used to frame these two problems. What barriers might prevent households or societies from achieving satisfactory outcomes?

10. [Related to the *Economics in Practice* on p. 160] If households decide to save more, saving in the aggregate may fall. Explain this in words.

11. Suppose that in the year 2011, Celestial Electronics planned to produce 950,000 units of its portable GPS devices. Of the 950,000 it planned to produce, a total of 25,000 units would be added to the inventory at its new plant in Florida. Also assume that these units have been selling at a price of $100 each and that the price has been constant over time. Suppose further that this year the firm built a new plant for $5 million and acquired $2.5 million worth of equipment. It had no other investment projects, and to avoid complications, assume no depreciation.

   Now suppose that at the end of the year, Celestial had produced 950,000 units but had only sold 900,000 units and that inventories now contained 50,000 units more than they had at the beginning of the year. At $100 each, that means that the firm added $5,000,000 in new inventory.
   a. How much did Celestial actually invest this year?
   b. How much did it plan to invest?
   c. Would Celestial produce more or fewer units next year? Why?

12. Use the graph to answer the questions that follow.
   a. What is the value of the *MPC*?
   b. What is the value of the *MPS*?

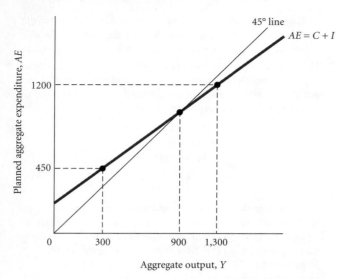

Planned aggregate expenditure, AE

Aggregate output, Y

c. What is the value of the multiplier?

d. What is the amount of unplanned investment at aggregate output of 300, 900, and 1,300?

13. According to the Bureau of Economic Analysis, during the recession of 2007–2009, household saving as a fraction of disposable personal income increased from a low of just over 1 percent in the first quarter of 2008 to 5 percent in the second quarter of 2009. All else equal, what impact would this change in saving have on the *MPC*, *MPS*, and multiplier? How would this change affect equilibrium output when planned investment changes?

14. Assume in a simple economy that the level of saving is –500 when aggregate output equals zero and that the marginal propensity to save is 0.2. Derive the saving function and the consumption function, and draw a graph showing these functions. At what level of aggregate output does the consumption curve cross the 45° line? Explain your answer and show this on the graph.

CHAPTER 8 APPENDIX

Deriving the Multiplier Algebraically

In addition to deriving the multiplier using the simple substitution we used in the chapter, we can also derive the formula for the multiplier by using simple algebra.

Recall that our consumption function is:

$$C = a + bY$$

where b is the marginal propensity to consume. In equilibrium:

$$Y = C + I$$

Now we solve these two equations for Y in terms of I. By substituting the first equation into the second, we get:

$$Y = \underbrace{a + bY}_{C} + I$$

This equation can be rearranged to yield:

$$Y - bY = a + I$$
$$Y(I - b) = a + I$$

We can then solve for Y in terms of I by dividing through by $(I - b)$:

$$Y = (a + I)\left(\frac{1}{1 - b}\right)$$

Now look carefully at this expression and think about increasing I by some amount, ΔI, with a held constant. If I increases by ΔI, income will increase by

$$\Delta Y = \Delta I \times \frac{1}{1 - b}$$

Because $b \equiv MPC$, the expression becomes

$$\Delta Y = \Delta I \times \frac{1}{1 - MPC}$$

The multiplier is

$$\frac{1}{1 - MPC}$$

Finally, because $MPS + MPC \equiv 1$, MPS is equal to $1 - MPC$, making the alternative expression for the multiplier $1/MPS$, just as we saw in this chapter.

The Government and Fiscal Policy

Nothing in macroeconomics or microeconomics arouses as much controversy as the role of government in the economy.

In microeconomics, the active presence of government in regulating competition, providing roads and education, and redistributing income is applauded by those who believe a free market simply does not work well when left to its own devices. Opponents of government intervention say it is the government, not the market, that performs badly. They say bureaucracy and inefficiency could be eliminated or reduced if the government played a smaller role in the economy.

In macroeconomics, the debate over what the government can and should do has a similar flavor. At one end of the spectrum are the Keynesians and their intellectual descendants who believe that the macroeconomy is likely to fluctuate too much if left on its own and that the government should smooth out fluctuations in the business cycle. These ideas can be traced to Keynes's analysis in *The General Theory*, which suggests that governments can use their taxing and spending powers to increase aggregate expenditure (and thereby stimulate aggregate output) in recessions or depressions. At the other end of the spectrum are those who claim that government spending is incapable of stabilizing the economy, or worse, is destabilizing and harmful.

Perhaps the one thing most people can agree on is that, like it or not, governments are important actors in the economies of virtually all countries. For this reason alone, it is worth our while to analyze the way government influences the functioning of the macroeconomy.

The government has a variety of powers—including regulating firms' entry into and exit from an industry, setting standards for product quality, setting minimum wage levels, and regulating the disclosure of information—but in macroeconomics, we study a government with general but limited powers. Specifically, government can affect the macroeconomy through two policy channels: fiscal policy and monetary policy. **Fiscal policy**, the focus of this chapter, refers to the government's spending and taxing behavior—in other words, its budget policy. (The word *fiscal* comes from the root *fisc*, which refers to the "treasury" of a government.) Fiscal policy is generally divided into three categories: (1) policies concerning government purchases of goods and services, (2) policies concerning taxes, and (3) policies concerning transfer payments (such as unemployment compensation, Social Security benefits, welfare payments, and veterans' benefits) to households. **Monetary policy**, which we consider in the next two chapters, refers to the behavior of the nation's central bank, the Federal Reserve, concerning the interest rate.

LEARNING OBJECTIVES

Discuss the influence of fiscal policies on the economy

Describe the effects of three fiscal policy multipliers

Compare and contrast the federal budgets of three U.S. government administrations

Explain the influence of the economy on the federal government budget

fiscal policy The government's spending and taxing policies.

monetary policy The behavior of the Federal Reserve concerning the nation's money supply.

Government in the Economy

Given the scope and power of local, state, and federal governments, there are some economic results over which they exert great control and others that are beyond their control. We need to distinguish between variables that a government controls directly and variables that are a consequence of government decisions *combined with the state of the economy.*

For example, tax rates are controlled by the government. By law, Congress has the authority to decide who and what should be taxed and at what rate. Tax *revenue*, on the other hand, is not subject to complete control by the government. Revenue from the personal income tax system depends on personal tax rates (which Congress sets) *and* on the income of the household sector (which depends on many factors not under direct government control, such as how much households decide to work). Revenue from the corporate profits tax depends on both corporate profits tax rates and the size of corporate profits. The government controls corporate tax rates but not the size of corporate profits.

Some government spending also depends on government decisions and on the state of the economy. For example, in the United States, the unemployment insurance program pays benefits to unemployed people. When the economy goes into a recession, the number of unemployed workers increases and so does the level of government unemployment insurance payments.

Because taxes and spending often go up or down in response to changes in the economy instead of as the result of deliberate decisions by policy makers, we will occasionally use **discretionary fiscal policy** to refer to changes in taxes or spending that are the result of deliberate changes in government policy.

discretionary fiscal policy Changes in taxes or spending that are the result of deliberate changes in government policy.

Government Purchases (G), Net Taxes (T), and Disposable Income (Y_d)

We now add the government to the simple economy in Chapter 8. To keep things simple, we will combine two government activities—the collection of taxes and the payment of transfer payments—into a category we call **net taxes (T)**. Specifically, net taxes are equal to the tax payments made to the government by firms and households minus transfer payments made to households by the government. The other variable we will consider is government purchases of goods and services (G).

Our earlier discussions of household consumption did not take taxes into account. We assumed that all the income generated in the economy was spent or saved by households. When we take into account the role of government, as Figure 9.1 does, we see that as income (Y) flows toward households, the government takes income from households in the form of net taxes (T). The income that ultimately gets to households is called **disposable, or after-tax, income (Y_d):**

net taxes (T) Taxes paid by firms and households to the government minus transfer payments made to households by the government.

disposable, or after-tax, income (Y_d) Total income minus net taxes: $Y - T$.

$$\text{disposable income} \equiv \text{total income} - \text{net taxes}$$

$$Y_d \equiv Y - T$$

Y_d excludes taxes paid by households and includes transfer payments made to households by the government. For now, we are assuming that T does not depend on Y—that is, net taxes do not depend on income. This assumption is relaxed in Appendix B to this chapter. Taxes that do not depend on income are sometimes called *lump-sum taxes.*

As Figure 9.1 shows, the disposable income (Y_d) of households must end up as either consumption (C) or saving (S). Thus,

$$Y_d \equiv C + S$$

This equation is an identity—something that is always true.

Because disposable income is aggregate income (Y) minus net taxes (T), we can write another identity:

$$Y - T \equiv C + S$$

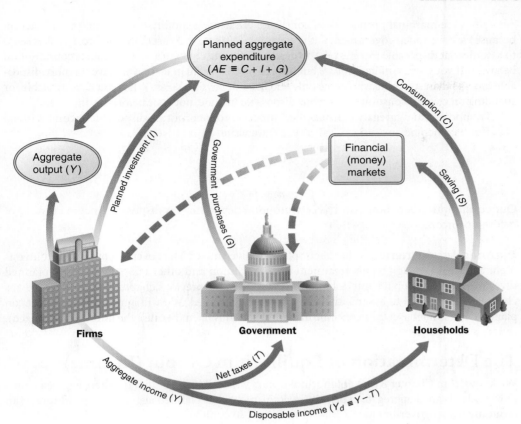

By adding T to both sides:

$$Y \equiv C + S + T$$

This identity says that aggregate income gets cut into three pieces. Government takes a slice (net taxes, T), and then households divide the rest between consumption (C) and saving (S).

Because governments spend money on goods and services, we need to expand our definition of planned aggregate expenditure. Planned aggregate expenditure (AE) is the sum of consumption spending by households (C), planned investment by business firms (I), *and* government purchases of goods and services (G).

$$AE \equiv C + I + G$$

A government's **budget deficit** is the difference between what it spends (G) and what it collects in taxes (T) in a given period:

$$\text{budget deficit} \equiv G - T$$

budget deficit The difference between what a government spends and what it collects in taxes in a given period: $G - T$.

If G exceeds T, the government must borrow from the public to finance the deficit. It does so by selling Treasury bonds and bills (more on this later). In this case, a part of household saving (S) goes to the government. The dashed lines in Figure 9.1 mean that some S goes to firms to finance investment projects and some goes to the government to finance its deficit. If G is less than T, which means that the government is spending less than it is collecting in taxes, the government is running a *surplus*. A budget surplus is simply a negative budget deficit.

Adding Taxes to the Consumption Function In Chapter 8, we assumed that aggregate consumption (C) depends on aggregate income (Y), and for the sake of illustration, we used a specific linear consumption function:

$$C = a + bY$$

where b is the marginal propensity to consume. We need to modify this consumption function because we have added government to the economy. With taxes a part of the picture, it makes sense to assume that disposable income (Y_d), instead of before-tax income (Y), determines consumption behavior. If you earn a million dollars but have to pay $950,000 in taxes, you have no more disposable income than someone who earns only $50,000 but pays no taxes. What you have available for spending on current consumption is your disposable income, not your before-tax income.

To modify our aggregate consumption function to incorporate disposable income instead of before-tax income, instead of $C = a + bY$, we write

$$C = a + bY_d$$

or

$$C = a + b(Y - T)$$

Our consumption function now has consumption depending on disposable income instead of before-tax income.

Planned Investment   What about planned investment? The government can affect investment behavior through its tax treatment of depreciation and other tax policies. Also, planned investment depends on the interest rate, as discussed in the previous chapter. For purposes of this chapter, we continue to assume that the interest rate is fixed. We will ignore any tax effects on planned investment and thus continue to assume that it is fixed (because the interest rate is fixed).

The Determination of Equilibrium Output (Income)

We know from Chapter 8 that equilibrium occurs where $Y = AE$—that is, where aggregate output equals planned aggregate expenditure. Remember that planned aggregate expenditure in an economy with a government is $AE \equiv C + I + G$, so equilibrium is

$$Y = C + I + G$$

The equilibrium analysis in Chapter 8 applies here also. If output (Y) exceeds planned aggregate expenditure ($C + I + G$), there will be an unplanned increase in inventories—actual investment will exceed planned investment. Conversely, if $C + I + G$ exceeds Y, there will be an unplanned decrease in inventories.

An example will illustrate the government's effect on the macroeconomy and the equilibrium condition. First, our consumption function, $C = 100 + .75Y$ before we introduced the government sector, now becomes

$$C = 100 + .75Y_d$$

or

$$C = 100 + .75(Y - T)$$

Second, we assume that G is 100 and T is 100.[1] In other words, the government is running a balanced budget, financing all of its spending with taxes. Third, we assume that planned investment (I) is 100.

Table 9.1 calculates planned aggregate expenditure at several levels of disposable income. For example, at $Y = 500$, disposable income is $Y - T$, or 400. Therefore, $C = 100 + .75(400) = 400$. Assuming that I is fixed at 100 and assuming that G is fixed at 100, planned aggregate expenditure is 600 ($C + I + G = 400 + 100 + 100$). Because output ($Y$) is only 500, planned spending is greater than output by 100. As a result, there is an unplanned inventory decrease of 100, giving firms an incentive to raise output. Thus, output of 500 is below equilibrium.

---

[1] As we pointed out earlier, the government does not have complete control over tax revenues and transfer payments. We ignore this problem here, however, and set T, tax revenues minus transfers, at a fixed amount. Things will become more realistic later in this chapter and in Appendix B.

TABLE 9.1   Finding Equilibrium for $I = 100$, $G = 100$, and $T = 100$

(1) Output (Income) Y	(2) Net Taxes T	(3) Disposable Income $Y_d \equiv Y - T$	(4) Consumption Spending $C = 100 + .75\,Y_d$	(5) Saving S $Y_d - C$	(6) Planned Investment Spending I	(7) Government Purchases G	(8) Planned Aggregate Expenditure $C + I + G$	(9) Unplanned Inventory Change $Y - (C + I + G)$	(10) Adjustment to Disequilibrium
300	100	200	250	−50	100	100	450	−150	Output ↑
500	100	400	400	0	100	100	600	−100	Output ↑
700	100	600	550	50	100	100	750	−50	Output ↑
900	100	800	700	100	100	100	900	0	Equilibrium
1,100	100	1,000	850	150	100	100	1,050	+50	Output ↓
1,300	100	1,200	1,000	200	100	100	1,200	+100	Output ↓
1,500	100	1,400	1,150	250	100	100	1,350	+150	Output ↓

If $Y = 1,300$, then $Y_d = 1,200$, $C = 1,000$, and planned aggregate expenditure is 1,200. Here planned spending is *less* than output, there will be an unplanned inventory increase of 100, and firms have an incentive to cut back output. Thus, output of 1,300 is above equilibrium. Only when output is 900 are output and planned aggregate expenditure equal, and only at $Y = 900$ does equilibrium exist.

In Figure 9.2, we derive the same equilibrium level of output graphically. First, the consumption function is drawn, taking into account net taxes of 100. The old function was $C = 100 + .75Y$. The new function is $C = 100 + .75(Y - T)$ or $C = 100 + .75(Y - 100)$, rewritten as $C = 100 + .75Y - 75$, or $C = 25 + .75Y$. For example, consumption at an income of zero is 25 ($C = 25 + .75Y = 25 + .75(0) = 25$). The marginal propensity to consume has not changed—we assume that it remains .75. Note that the consumption function in Figure 9.2 plots the points in columns 1 and 4 of Table 9.1.

Planned aggregate expenditure, recall, adds planned investment to consumption. Now in addition to 100 in investment, we have government purchases of 100. Because I and G are constant at 100 each at all levels of income, we add $I + G = 200$ to consumption at every level of income. The result is the new AE curve. This curve is just a plot of the points in columns 1 and 8 of Table 9.1. The 45° line helps us find the equilibrium level of real output, which, we already

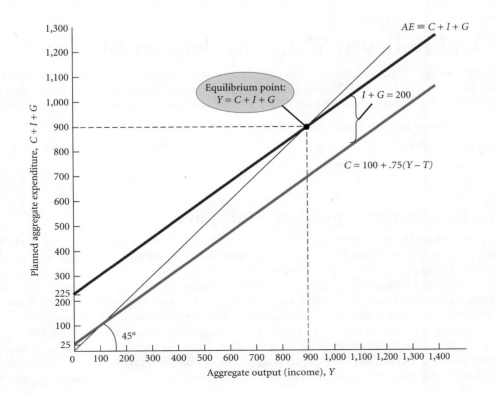

◀ **FIGURE 9.2**
Finding Equilibrium Output/Income Graphically
Because G and I are both fixed at 100, the aggregate expenditure function is the new consumption function displaced upward by $I + G = 200$. Equilibrium occurs at $Y = C + I + G = 900$.

know, is 900. If you examine any level of output above or below 900, you will find disequilibrium. At $Y = 500$, for example, people want to consume 400, which with planned investment of 100 and government purchases of 100, gives planned aggregate expenditure of 600. Output is, however, only 500. Inventories will fall below what was planned, and firms will have an incentive to increase output.

The Saving/Investment Approach to Equilibrium   As in the last chapter, we can also examine equilibrium using the saving/investment approach. Look at the circular flow of income in Figure 9.1. The government takes out net taxes (T) from the flow of income—a leakage—and households save (S) some of their income—also a leakage from the flow of income. The planned spending injections are government purchases (G) and planned investment (I). If leakages ($S + T$) equal planned injections ($I + G$), there is equilibrium:

> saving/investment approach to equilibrium: $S + T = I + G$

To derive this, we know that in equilibrium, aggregate output (income) (Y) equals planned aggregate expenditure (AE). By definition, AE equals $C + I + G$, and by definition, Y equals $C + S + T$. Therefore, at equilibrium

$$C + S + T = C + I + G$$

Subtracting C from both sides leaves:

$$S + T = I + G$$

Note that equilibrium does *not* require that $G = T$ (a balanced government budget) or that $S = I$. It is only necessary that the sum of S and T equals the sum of I and G.

Column 5 of Table 9.1 calculates aggregate saving by subtracting consumption from disposal income at every level of disposable income ($S \equiv Y_d - C$). Because I and G are fixed, $I + G$ equals 200 at every level of income. Using the table to add saving and taxes ($S + T$), we see that $S + T$ equals 200 only at $Y = 900$. Thus, the equilibrium level of output (income) is 900, the same answer we arrived at through numerical and graphic analysis.

Fiscal Policy at Work: Multiplier Effects

You can see from Figure 9.2 that if the government were able to change the levels of either G or T, it would be able to change the equilibrium level of output (income). At this point, we are assuming that the government controls G and T. In this section, we will review three multipliers:

- Government spending multiplier
- Tax multiplier
- Balanced-budget multiplier

The Government Spending Multiplier

Suppose you are the chief economic adviser to the president and the economy is sitting at the equilibrium output pictured in Figure 9.2. Output and income are 900, and the government is currently buying 100 worth of goods and services each year and is financing them with 100 in taxes. The budget is balanced. In addition, firms are investing (producing capital goods) 100. The president calls you into the Oval Office and says, "Unemployment is too high. We need to lower unemployment by increasing output and income." After some research, you determine that an acceptable unemployment rate can be achieved only if aggregate output increases to 1,100.

You now need to determine how the government can use taxing and spending policy—fiscal policy—to increase the equilibrium level of national output. Suppose the president has let it be known that taxes must remain at present levels—Congress just passed a major tax reform package—so adjusting T is out of the question for several years. That leaves you with G. Your only option is to increase government spending while holding taxes constant.

To increase spending without raising taxes (which provides the government with revenue to spend), the government must borrow. When G is bigger than T, the government runs a deficit and the difference between G and T must be borrowed. For the moment, we will ignore the possible effect of the deficit and focus only on the effect of a higher G with T constant.

Meanwhile, the president is awaiting your answer. How much of an increase in spending would be required to generate an increase of 200 in the equilibrium level of output, pushing it from 900 to 1,100 and reducing unemployment to the president's acceptable level? You might be tempted to say that because we need to increase income by 200 (1,100 − 900), we should increase government spending by the same amount. But what will happen if we raise G by 200? The increased government spending will throw the economy out of equilibrium. Because G is a component of aggregate spending, planned aggregate expenditure will increase by 200. Planned spending will be greater than output, inventories will be lower than planned, and firms will have an incentive to increase output. Suppose output rises by the desired 200. You might think, "We increased spending by 200 and output by 200, so equilibrium is restored."

There is more to the story than this. The moment output rises, the economy is generating more income. This was the desired effect: the creation of more employment. The newly employed workers are also consumers, and some of their income gets spent. With higher consumption spending, planned spending will be greater than output, inventories will be lower than planned, and firms will raise output (and thus raise income) again. This time firms are responding to the new consumption spending. Already, total income is over 1,100.

This story should sound familiar. It is the multiplier in action. Although this time it is government spending (G) that is changed rather than planned investment (I), the effect is the same as the multiplier effect we described in Chapter 8. An increase in government spending has the same impact on the equilibrium level of output and income as an increase in planned investment. A dollar of extra spending from either G or I is identical with respect to its impact on equilibrium output. The equation for the government spending multiplier is the same as the equation for the multiplier for a change in planned investment.

$$\text{government spending multiplier} \equiv \frac{1}{MPS} \equiv \frac{1}{1 - MPC}$$

We derive the government spending multiplier algebraically in Appendix A to this chapter.

Formally, the **government spending multiplier** is defined as the ratio of the change in the equilibrium level of output to a change in government spending. This is the same definition we used in the previous chapter, but now the autonomous variable is government spending instead of planned investment.

government spending multiplier
The ratio of the change in the equilibrium level of output to a change in government spending.

Remember that we were thinking of increasing government spending (G) by 200. We can use the multiplier analysis to see what the new equilibrium level of Y would be for an increase in G of 200. The multiplier in our example is 4. (Because b—the MPC—is .75, the MPS must be $1 - .75 = .25$; and $1/.25 = 4$.) Thus, Y will increase by 800 (4 × 200). Because the initial level of Y was 900, the new equilibrium level of Y is $900 + 800 = 1,700$ when G is increased by 200.

The level of 1,700 is much larger than the level of 1,100 that we calculated as being necessary to lower unemployment to the desired level. Let us back up then. If we want Y to increase by 200 and if the multiplier is 4, we need G to increase by only $200/4 = 50$. If G increases by 50, the equilibrium level of Y will change by 200 and the new value of Y will be 1,100 (900 + 200), as desired.

Looking at Table 9.2, we can check our answer to make sure it is an equilibrium. Look first at the old equilibrium of 900. When government purchases (G) were 100, aggregate output (income) was equal to planned aggregate expenditure ($AE \equiv C + I + G$) at $Y = 900$. Now G has increased to 150. At $Y = 900$, ($C + I + G$) is greater than Y, there is an unplanned fall in inventories, and output will rise, but by how much? The multiplier told us that equilibrium income would rise by four times the 50 change in G. Y should rise by 4 × 50 = 200, from 900 to 1,100, before equilibrium is restored. Let us check. If $Y = 1,100$, consumption is $C = 100 + .75Y_d = 100 + .75(1,000) = 850$. Because I equals 100 and G now equals 100 (the original level of G) + 50 (the additional G brought about by the fiscal policy change) = 150, $C + I + G = 850 + 100 + 150 = 1,100$. $Y = AE$, and the economy is in equilibrium.

TABLE 9.2 Finding Equilibrium after a Government Spending Increase of 50 (*G* Has Increased from 100 in Table 9.1 to 150 Here)

(1) Output (Income) Y	(2) Net Taxes T	(3) Disposable Income $Y_d \equiv Y - T$	(4) Consumption Spending $C = 100 + .75 \, Y_d$	(5) Saving S $Y_d - C$	(6) Planned Investment Spending I	(7) Government Purchases G	(8) Planned Aggregate Expenditure $C + I + G$	(9) Unplanned Inventory Change $Y - (C + I + G)$	(10) Adjustment to Disequilibrium
300	100	200	250	−50	100	150	500	−200	Output ↑
500	100	400	400	0	100	150	650	−150	Output ↑
700	100	600	550	50	100	150	800	−100	Output ↑
900	100	800	700	100	100	150	950	−50	Output ↑
1,100	100	1,000	850	150	100	150	1,100	0	Equilibrium
1,300	100	1,200	1,000	200	100	150	1,250	+50	Output ↓

The graphic solution to the president's problem is presented in Figure 9.3. An increase of 50 in *G* shifts the planned aggregate expenditure function up by 50. The new equilibrium income occurs where the new *AE* line (AE_2) crosses the 45° line, at $Y = 1{,}100$.

The Tax Multiplier

Remember that fiscal policy comprises policies concerning government spending *and* policies concerning taxation. To see what effect a change in tax policy has on the economy, imagine the following. You are still chief economic adviser to the president, but now you are instructed to devise a plan to reduce unemployment to an acceptable level *without* increasing the level of government spending. In your plan, instead of increasing government spending (*G*), you decide to cut taxes and maintain the current level of spending. A tax cut increases disposable income, which is likely to lead to added consumption spending. (Remember our general rule that increased income leads to increased consumption.) Would the decrease in taxes affect aggregate output (income) the same as an increase in *G*?

▶ **FIGURE 9.3**
The Government Spending Multiplier
Increasing government spending by 50 shifts the *AE* function up by 50. As *Y* rises in response, additional consumption is generated. Overall, the equilibrium level of *Y* increases by 200, from 900 to 1,100.

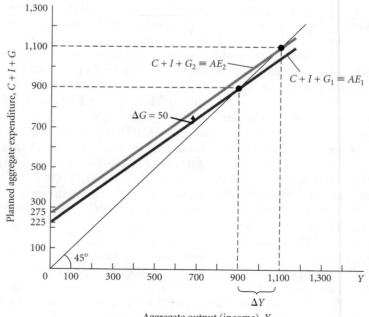

A decrease in taxes would increase income. The government spends no less than it did before the tax cut, and households find that they have a larger after-tax (or disposable) income than they had before. This leads to an increase in consumption. Planned aggregate expenditure will increase, which will lead to inventories being lower than planned, which will lead to a rise in output. When output rises, more workers will be employed and more income will be generated, causing a second-round increase in consumption, and so on. Thus, income will increase by a multiple of the decrease in taxes, but there is a "wrinkle." The multiplier for a change in taxes is *not the same* as the multiplier for a change in government spending. Why does the **tax multiplier**—the ratio of change in the equilibrium level of output to a change in taxes—differ from the spending multiplier? To answer that question, we need to compare the ways in which a tax cut and a spending increase work their way through the economy.

tax multiplier The ratio of change in the equilibrium level of output to a change in taxes.

Look at Figure 9.1. When the government increases spending, there is an immediate and direct impact on the economy's *total* spending. Because G is a component of planned aggregate expenditure, an increase in G leads to a dollar-for-dollar increase in planned aggregate expenditure. When taxes are cut, there is no direct impact on spending. Taxes enter the picture only because they have an effect on the household's disposable income, which influences household's consumption (which is part of total spending). As Figure 9.1 shows, the tax cut flows through households before affecting aggregate expenditure.

Let us assume that the government decides to cut taxes by $1. By how much would spending increase? We already know the answer. The marginal propensity to consume (MPC) tells us how much consumption spending changes when disposable income changes. In the example running through this chapter, the marginal propensity to consume out of disposable income is .75. This means that if households' after-tax incomes rise by $1.00, they will increase their consumption not by the full $1.00, but by only $0.75.[2]

In summary, when government spending increases by $1, planned aggregate expenditure increases initially by the full amount of the rise in G, or $1. When taxes are cut, however, the initial increase in planned aggregate expenditure is only the MPC times the change in taxes. Because the initial increase in planned aggregate expenditure is smaller for a tax cut than for a government spending increase, the final effect on the equilibrium level of income will be smaller.

We figure the size of the tax multiplier in the same way we derived the multiplier for an increase in investment and an increase in government purchases. The final change in the equilibrium level of output (income) (Y) is

$$\Delta Y = \text{(initial increase in aggregate expenditure)} \times \left(\frac{1}{MPS}\right)$$

Because the initial change in aggregate expenditure caused by a tax change of ΔT is $(-\Delta T \times MPC)$, we can solve for the tax multiplier by substitution:

$$\Delta Y = (-\Delta T \times MPC) \times \left(\frac{1}{MPS}\right) = -\Delta T \times \left(\frac{MPC}{MPS}\right)$$

Because a tax cut will cause an *increase* in consumption expenditures and output and a tax increase will cause a *reduction* in consumption expenditures and output, the tax multiplier is a negative multiplier:

$$\text{tax multiplier} \equiv -\left(\frac{MPC}{MPS}\right)$$

We derive the tax multiplier algebraically in Appendix A to this chapter.

---

[2] What happens to the other $0.25? Remember that whatever households do not consume is, by definition, saved. The other $0.25 thus gets allocated to saving.

If the *MPC* is .75, as in our example, the multiplier is −.75/.25 = −3. A tax cut of 100 will increase the equilibrium level of output by −100 × −3 = 300. This is very different from the effect of our government spending multiplier of 4. Under those same conditions, a 100 increase in *G* will increase the equilibrium level of output by 400 (100 × 4). If we wanted to increase output by 400, we would need a tax cut of 400/3 or 133.33.

The Balanced-Budget Multiplier

We have now discussed (1) changing government spending with no change in taxes and (2) changing taxes with no change in government spending. What if government spending and taxes are increased by the same amount? That is, what if the government decides to pay for its extra spending by increasing taxes by the same amount? The government's budget deficit would not change because the increase in expenditures would be matched by an increase in tax income.

You might think in this case that equal increases in government spending and taxes have no effect on equilibrium income. After all, the extra government spending equals the extra amount of tax revenues collected by the government. This is not so. Take, for example, a government spending increase of $40 billion. We know from the preceding analysis that an increase in *G* of 40, with taxes (*T*) held constant, should increase the equilibrium level of income by 40 × the government spending multiplier. The multiplier is 1/*MPS* or 1/.25 = 4. The equilibrium level of income should rise by 160 (40 × 4).

Now suppose that instead of keeping tax revenues constant, we finance the 40 increase in government spending with an equal increase in taxes so as to maintain a balanced budget. What happens to aggregate spending as a result of the rise in *G* and the rise in *T*? There are two initial effects. First, government spending rises by 40. This effect is direct, immediate, and positive. Now the government also collects 40 more in taxes. The tax increase has a *negative* impact on overall spending in the economy, but it does not fully offset the increase in government spending.

The final impact of a tax increase on aggregate expenditure depends on how households respond to it. The only thing we know about household behavior so far is that households spend 75 percent of their added income and save 25 percent. We know that when disposable income falls, both consumption and saving are reduced. A tax *increase* of 40 reduces disposable income by 40, and that means consumption falls by 40 × *MPC*. Because *MPC* = .75, consumption falls by 30 (40 × .75). The net result in the beginning is that government spending rises by 40 and consumption spending falls by 30. Aggregate expenditure increases by 10 right after the simultaneous balanced-budget increases in *G* and *T*.

So a balanced-budget increase in *G* and *T* will raise output, but by how much? How large is this **balanced-budget multiplier?** The answer may surprise you:

balanced-budget multiplier
The ratio of change in the equilibrium level of output to a change in government spending where the change in government spending is balanced by a change in taxes so as not to create any deficit. The balanced-budget multiplier is equal to 1: The change in *Y* resulting from the change in *G* and the equal change in *T* are exactly the same size as the initial change in *G* or *T*.

$$\text{balanced-budget multiplier} \equiv 1$$

Let us combine what we know about the tax multiplier and the government spending multiplier to explain this. To find the final effect of a simultaneous increase in government spending and increase in net taxes, we need to add the multiplier effects of the two. The government spending multiplier is 1/*MPS*. The tax multiplier is −*MPC*/*MPS*. Their sum is (1/*MPS*) + (−*MPC*/*MPS*) ≡ (1 − *MPC*)/*MPS*. Because *MPC* + *MPS* ≡ 1, 1 − *MPC* ≡ *MPS*. This means that (1 − *MPC*)/*MPS* ≡ *MPS*/*MPS* ≡ 1. (We also derive the balanced-budget multiplier in Appendix A to this chapter.)

Returning to our example, recall that by using the government spending multiplier, a 40 increase in *G* would *raise* output at equilibrium by 160 (40 × the government spending multiplier of 4). By using the tax multiplier, we know that a tax hike of 40 will *reduce* the equilibrium level of output by 120 (40 × the tax multiplier, −3). The net effect is 160 minus 120, or 40. It should be clear then that the effect on equilibrium *Y* is equal to the balanced increase in *G* and *T*. In other words, the net increase in the equilibrium level of *Y* resulting from the change in *G* and the change in *T* are exactly the size of the initial change in *G* or *T*.

If the president wanted to raise *Y* by 200 without increasing the deficit, a simultaneous increase in *G* and *T* of 200 would do it. To see why, look at the numbers in Table 9.3. In Table 9.1, we saw an equilibrium level of output at 900. With both *G* and *T* up by 200, the new

TABLE 9.3 Finding Equilibrium after a Balanced-Budget Increase in G and T of 200 Each (Both G and T Have Increased from 100 in Table 9.1 to 300 Here)

(1) Output (Income) Y	(2) Net Taxes T	(3) Disposable Income $Y_d \equiv Y - T$	(4) Consumption Spending $C = 100 + .75Y_d$	(5) Planned Investment Spending I	(6) Government Purchases G	(7) Planned Aggregate Expenditure $C + I + G$	(8) Unplanned Inventory Change $Y - (C + I + G)$	(9) Adjustment to Disequilibrium
500	300	200	250	100	300	650	−150	Output ↑
700	300	400	400	100	300	800	−100	Output ↑
900	300	600	550	100	300	950	−50	Output ↑
1,100	300	800	700	100	300	1,100	0	Equilibrium
1,300	300	1,000	850	100	300	1,250	+50	Output ↓
1,500	300	1,200	1,000	100	300	1,400	+100	Output ↓

TABLE 9.4 Summary of Fiscal Policy Multipliers

	Policy Stimulus	Multiplier	Final Impact on Equilibrium Y
Government spending multiplier	Increase or decrease in the level of government purchases: ΔG	$\dfrac{1}{MPS}$	$\Delta G \times \dfrac{1}{MPS}$
Tax multiplier	Increase or decrease in the level of net taxes: ΔT	$\dfrac{-MPC}{MPS}$	$\Delta T \times \dfrac{-MPC}{MPS}$
Balanced-budget multiplier	Simultaneous balanced-budget increase or decrease in the level of government purchases and net taxes: $\Delta G = \Delta T$	1	ΔG

equilibrium is 1,100—higher by 200. At no other level of Y do we find $(C + I + G) = Y$. An increase in government spending has a direct initial effect on planned aggregate expenditure; a tax increase does not. The initial effect of the tax increase is that households cut consumption by the MPC times the change in taxes. This change in consumption is less than the change in taxes because the MPC is less than 1. The positive stimulus from the government spending increase is thus greater than the negative stimulus from the tax increase. The net effect is that the balanced-budget multiplier is 1.

Table 9.4 summarizes everything we have said about fiscal policy multipliers.

A Warning   Although we have added government, the story told about the multiplier is still incomplete and oversimplified. For example, we have been treating net taxes (T) as a lump-sum, fixed amount, whereas in practice, taxes depend on income. Appendix B to this chapter shows that the size of the multiplier is reduced when we make the more realistic assumption that taxes depend on income. We continue to add more realism and difficulty to our analysis in the chapters that follow.

The Federal Budget

Because fiscal policy is the manipulation of items in the federal budget, that budget is relevant to our study of macroeconomics. The **federal budget** is an enormously complicated document, up to thousands of pages each year. It lists in detail all the things the government plans to spend money on and all the sources of government revenues for the coming year. It is the product of a complex interplay of social, political, and economic forces.

federal budget   The budget of the federal government.

The Budget in 2012

A highly aggregated version of the federal budget is shown in Table 9.5. In 2012, the government had total receipts of $2,674.5 billion, largely from personal income taxes ($1,137.8 billion) and contributions for social insurance ($934.8 billion). (Contributions for social insurance are

MyEconLab Real-time data

TABLE 9.5 Federal Government Receipts and Expenditures, 2012 (Billions of Dollars)

	Amount	Percentage of Total
Current receipts		
Personal income taxes	1,137.8	42.5
Excise taxes and customs duties	116.1	4.3
Corporate income taxes	373.7	14.0
Taxes from the rest of the world	17.3	0.6
Contributions for social insurance	934.8	35.0
Interest receipts and rents and royalties	53.4	2.0
Current transfer receipts from business and persons	59.2	2.2
Current surplus of government enterprises	−17.8	−0.7
Total	2,674.5	100.0
Current expenditures		
Consumption expenditures	1,059.6	28.2
Transfer payments to persons	1,773.2	47.2
Transfer payments to the rest of the world	76.4	2.0
Grants-in-aid to state and local governments	468.0	12.5
Interest payments	318.5	8.5
Subsidies	60.4	1.6
Total	3,756.1	100.0
Net federal government saving–surplus (+) or deficit (−)		
(Total current receipts − Total current expenditures)	−1,081.6	

Source: U.S. Bureau of Economic Analysis.

employer and employee Social Security taxes.) Receipts from corporate income taxes accounted for $373.7 billion, or only 14.0 percent of total receipts. Not everyone is aware of the fact that corporate income taxes as a percentage of government receipts are quite small relative to personal income taxes and Social Security taxes.

The federal government also spent $3,756.1 billion in expenditures in 2012. Of this, $1,773.2 billion represented transfer payments to persons (Social Security benefits, military retirement benefits, and unemployment compensation).[3] Consumption ($1,059.6 billion) was the next-largest component, followed by grants-in-aid given to state and local governments by the federal government ($468.0 billion), and interest payments on the federal debt ($318.5 billion).

federal surplus (+) or deficit (−) Federal government receipts minus expenditures.

The difference between the federal government's receipts and its expenditures is the **federal surplus (+) or deficit (−)**, which is federal government saving. Table 9.5 shows that the federal government spent much more than it took in during 2012, resulting in a deficit of $1,081.6 billion.

Fiscal Policy Since 1993: The Clinton, Bush, and Obama Administrations

Between 1993 and the current edition of this text, the United States has had three different presidents, two Democrats and a Republican. The fiscal policy implemented by each president reflects both the political philosophy of the administration and the differing economic conditions each faced. Figures 9.4, 9.5, and 9.6 trace the fiscal policies of the Clinton (1993–2000), Bush (2001–2008), and first Obama administrations (2009–2012).

Figure 9.4 plots total federal personal income taxes as a percentage of total taxable income. This is a graph of the average personal income tax rate. As the figure shows, the average tax rate increased substantially during the Clinton administrations. Much of this increase was due to a tax bill that was passed in 1993 during the first Clinton administration. The figure then shows the dramatic effects of the tax cuts during the first Bush administration. The large fall in the average tax rate in 2001 III was due to a tax rebate passed after the 9/11 terrorist attacks. Although the average tax rate went back up in 2001 IV, it then fell substantially as the Bush tax cuts began to be felt. The average tax rate remained low during the Obama administration. This was in part due to the large ($787 billion) stimulus bill that was passed in February

---

[3] Remember that there is an important difference between transfer payments and government purchases of goods and services (consumption expenditures). Much of the government budget goes for things that an economist would classify as transfers (payments that are grants or gifts) instead of purchases of goods and services. Only the latter are included in our variable *G*. Transfers are counted as part of net taxes.

2009. The bill consisted of tax cuts and government spending increases, mostly for the 2009–2010 period. In 2011–2012 the average tax rate was somewhat higher than it was in 2009–2010 due to the winding down of the stimulus bill. The overall tax policy of the federal government is thus clear from Figure 9.4. The average tax rate rose sharply under President Clinton, fell sharply under President Bush, and remained low under President Obama.

Table 9.5 shows that the three most important spending variables of the federal government are consumption expenditures, transfer payments to persons, and grants-in-aid to state and local governments. Consumption expenditures, which are government expenditures on goods and services, are part of GDP. Transfer payments and grants-in-aid are not spending on current output (GDP), but just transfers from the federal government to people and state and local governments. Figure 9.5 plots two spending ratios. One is federal government consumption expenditures as a percentage of GDP, and the other is transfer payments to persons plus grants-in-aid to state and local governments as a percentage of GDP. The figure shows that consumption expenditures as a percentage of GDP generally fell during the Clinton administrations, generally rose during the Bush administrations, and remained high during the Obama administration. The increase during the Bush administrations reflects primarily the spending on the Iraq war. The initial increase during the Obama administration reflects the effects of the stimulus bill and increased spending for the Afghanistan war. Expenditures as a fraction of GDP fell slightly in 2011 and 2012, but only slightly.

Figure 9.5 also shows that transfer payments as a percentage of GDP generally rose during the Bush administrations especially near the end, and remained high in the Obama administration. The percent was flat or slightly falling during the Clinton administrations. Some of the fall between 1996 and 2000 was due to President Clinton's welfare reform legislation. Some of the rise from 2001 on is due to increased Medicare payments. The high values in the Obama administration again reflect the effects of the stimulus bill and various extensions.

Figure 9.6 plots the federal government surplus (+) or deficit (−1) as a percentage of GDP. The figure shows that during the Clinton administrations the federal budget moved from substantial deficit to noticeable surplus. This, of course, should not be surprising since the average tax rate generally rose during this period and spending as a percentage of GDP generally fell. Figure 9.6 then shows that the surplus turned into a substantial deficit during the first Bush administration. This also should not be surprising since the average tax rate generally fell during this period and spending as a percentage of GDP generally rose. The deficit rose sharply in the beginning of the Obama administration—to 9.5 percent of GDP by the second quarter of 2009. Again, this is not a surprise. The average tax rate remained low and spending increased substantially. The deficit improved somewhat in 2011 and 2012, but remained large.

To summarize, Figures 9.4, 9.5, and 9.6 show clearly the large differences in the fiscal policies of the three administrations. Tax rates generally rose and spending as a percentage of

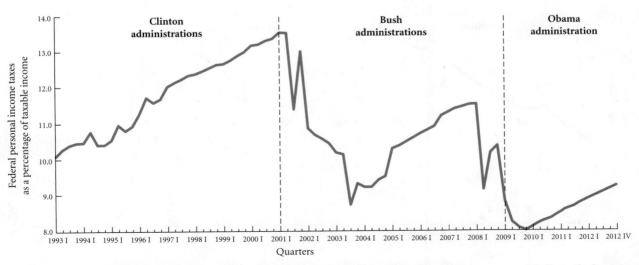

▲ **FIGURE 9.4   Federal Personal Income Taxes as a Percentage of Taxable Income, 1993 I–2012 IV**

MyEconLab Real-time data

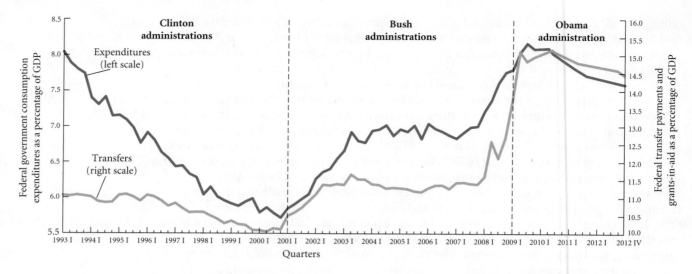

▲ **FIGURE 9.5** **Federal Government Consumption Expenditures as a Percentage of GDP and Federal Transfer Payments and Grants-in-Aid as a Percentage of GDP, 1993 I–2012 IV** MyEconLab Real-time data

GDP generally fell during the Clinton administrations, and the opposite generally happened during the Bush and Obama administrations.

As you look at these differences, you should remember that the decisions that governments make about levels of spending and taxes reflect not only macroeconomic concerns but also microeconomic issues and political philosophy. President Clinton's welfare reform program resulted in a decrease in government transfer payments but was motivated in part by interest in improving market incentives. President Bush's early tax cuts were based less on macroeconomic concerns than on political philosophy, while the increased spending came from international relations. President Obama's fiscal policy, on the other hand, was motivated by macroeconomic concerns. The stimulus bill was designed to mitigate the effects of the recession that began in 2008. Whether tax and spending policies are motivated by macroeconomic concerns or not, they have macroeconomic consequences.

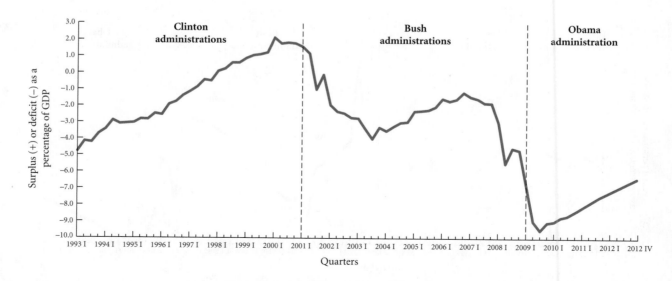

▲ **FIGURE 9.6** **The Federal Government Surplus (+) or Deficit (−) as a Percentage of GDP, 1993 I–2012 IV** MyEconLab Real-time data

ECONOMICS IN PRACTICE

The U.S. Congress Fights about the Budget

In the text we describe the way in which fiscal decisions, about taxes and spending affect the macro economy. In contrast to the decisions about monetary policy, which are made by a small group of people at the Fed, tax and spending decisions are made by Congress.

In the spring of 2013, arguments about the shape of the 2014 budget were raging. The dispute had been several years in the making. Under the Budget Control Act of 2011, Congress committed itself to a series of automatic spending cuts and tax increases if it could not otherwise agree on a less-deficit-producing budget. The automatic—and quite large—nature of these tax increases and spending cuts led observers to refer to the impending "fiscal cliff." On January 2013, the tax increase part of the cliff was diminished as Congress signed the American Tax Relief Act (ATRA), which retained many of the earlier Bush tax cuts, while modifying others. But the specter of automatic spending cuts remained as Congress met to try to agree on a budget.

We can look at the Congressional Record for March 21, 2013 (p. 1800) for a taste of the debate, as members of the House commented on a budget proposal of Paul Ryan, Republican Congressman from Wisconsin. Standing before the House, Representative Eddie Bernice Johnson of Texas, a Democrat, had this to say about Congressman Ryan's bill: "This budget would not only jeopardize seniors, families and the most vulnerable in our society, it would also destroy jobs and put our nation's economic recovery at risk." Several speakers later, the Congress heard a different view from Andy Barr, a new Republican Congressman from Kentucky: "This budget balances our nation's finances in ten years, because it is wrong to keep spending money we do not have. This budget moves us closer to pro-growth tax reform without raising taxes because families and small businesses should be able to keep more of their hard-earned income instead of having it wasted by Washington bureaucrats." Notice the blend of concerns about the state of the economy and ideology. Compromise does not look easy!

THINKING PRACTICALLY

1. How would you describe the views of the two people quoted on the benefits of government spending?

The Federal Government Debt

When the government runs a deficit, it must borrow to finance it. To borrow, the federal government sells government securities to the public. It issues pieces of paper promising to pay a certain amount, with interest, in the future. In return, it receives funds from the buyers of the paper and uses these funds to pay its bills. This borrowing increases the **federal debt**, the total amount owed by the federal government. The federal debt is the total of all accumulated deficits minus surpluses over time. Conversely, if the government runs a surplus, the federal debt falls.

Some of the securities that the government issues end up being held by the federal government at the Federal Reserve or in government trust funds, the largest of which is Social Security. The term **privately held federal debt** refers only to the *privately held* debt of the U.S. government. At the end of September 2011, the federal debt was $14.8 trillion, of which $8.5 trillion was privately held.

The privately held federal government debt as a percentage of GDP is plotted in Figure 9.7 for the 1993 I–2012 IV period. The percentage fell during the second Clinton administration, when the budget was in surplus, and it mostly rose during the Bush administrations, when the budget was in deficit. The rise during the Obama administration has been dramatic. At the beginning of the second Obama administration, many people were concerned about the rising debt/GDP ratio.

federal debt The total amount owed by the federal government.

privately held federal debt The privately held (non-government-owned) debt of the U.S. government.

The Economy's Influence on the Government Budget

We have just seen that an administration's fiscal policy is sometimes affected by the state of the economy. The Obama administration, for example, increased government spending and lowered taxes in response to the recession of 2008–2009. It is also the case, however, that the economy affects the federal government budget even if there are no explicit fiscal policy changes. There are effects that the government has no direct control over. They can be lumped under the general heading of "automatic stabilizers and destabilizers."

Automatic Stabilizers and Destabilizers

Most of the tax revenues of the government result from applying a tax rate decided by the government to a base that reflects the underlying activity of the economy. The corporate profits tax,

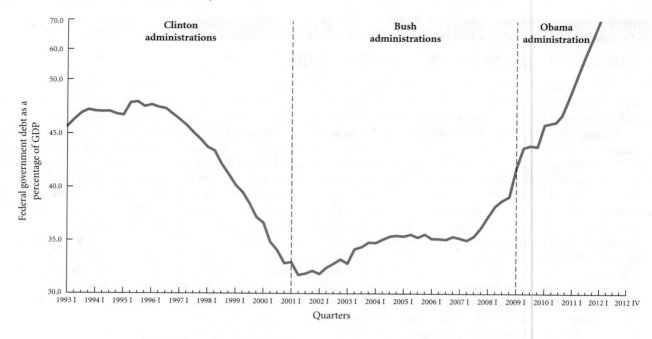

▲ **FIGURE 9.7** **The Federal Government Debt as a Percentage of GDP, 1993 I–2012 IV** MyEconLab Real-time data

for example, comes from applying a rate (say 35 percent) to the profits earned by firms. Income taxes come from applying rates shown in tax tables to income earned by individuals. Tax revenues thus depend on the state of the economy even when the government does not change tax rates. When the economy goes into a recession, tax revenues will fall, even if rates remain constant, and when the economy picks up, so will tax revenues. As a result, deficits fall in expansions and rise in recessions, other things being equal.

Some items on the expenditure side of the government budget also automatically change as the economy changes. If the economy declines, unemployment increases, which leads to an increase in unemployment benefits. Welfare payments, food stamp allotments, and similar transfer payments also increase in recessions and decrease in expansions.

automatic stabilizers
Revenue and expenditure items in the federal budget that automatically change with the state of the economy in such a way as to stabilize GDP.

These automatic changes in government revenues and expenditures are called **automatic stabilizers**. They help stabilize the economy. In recessions, taxes fall and expenditures rise, which creates positive effects on the economy, and in expansions, the opposite happens. The government does not have to change any laws for this to happen.

Another reason that government spending is not completely controllable is that inflation often picks up in an expansion. We saw in Chapter 7 that some government transfer payments are tied to the rate of inflation (changes in the CPI); so these transfer payments increase as inflation increases. Some medical care transfer payments also increase as the prices of medical care rise, and these prices may be affected by the overall rate of inflation. To the extent that inflation is more likely to increase in an expansion than in a recession, inflation can be considered to be an **automatic destabilizer**. Government spending increases as inflation increases, which further fuels the expansion, which is destabilizing. If inflation decreases in a recession, there is an automatic decrease in government spending, which makes the recession worse.

automatic destabilizer
Revenue and expenditure items in the federal budget that automatically change with the state of the economy in such a way as to destabilize GDP.

We will see in later chapters that interest rates tend to rise in expansions and fall in recessions. When interest rates rise, government interest payments to households and firms increase (because households and firms hold much of the government debt), which is interest income to the households and firms. Government spending on interest payments thus tends to rise in expansions and fall in contractions, which, other things being equal, is destabilizing. We will see in later chapters, however, that interest rates also have negative effects on the economy, and these negative effects are generally larger than the positive effects from the increase in government interest payments. The net effect of an increase in interest rates on the economy is thus generally negative. But this is getting ahead of our story.

fiscal drag The negative effect on the economy that occurs when average tax rates increase because taxpayers have moved into higher income brackets during an expansion.

Since 1982 personal income tax brackets have been tied to the overall price level. Prior to this they were not, which led to what was called **fiscal drag**. If tax brackets are not tied to the

ECONOMICS IN PRACTICE

The Debt Clock

Next time you are in New York City, wander by West 44ᵗʰ Street and the Avenue of the Americas. Located on an outside wall is a U.S. Debt Clock, mounted by Seymour Durst, a N.Y. real estate developer. Rather than showing us the passage of time, as would a conventional clock, this clock shows us the mounting of the U.S. debt. Durst was an early worrier about the debt! Needless to say, it sped up during the Obama administration. See Figure 9.7.

> **THINKING PRACTICALLY**
>
> 1. For a few years beginning in 2000, the clock was stopped and covered up. Can you guess why based on the data you have seen in this chapter?

price level, then as the price level rises and thus people's nominal incomes rise, people move into higher brackets; so the average tax rates that they pay increase. This is a "drag" on the economy, hence the name fiscal drag. In 1982, the United States instituted an alternative Minimum Tax (AMT), directed at higher income individuals who had a number of special tax deductions. These individuals were subject to an alternative calculation of their income taxes, which essentially eliminated some deductions and imposed a (lower) flat tax. In contrast to the standard tax tables, the income level at which the AMT would kick in remained constant over the subsequent thirty years until finally indexed to inflation in 2013. For this period, the AMT tax created fiscal drag. It is interesting to note that fiscal drag is actually an automatic stabilizer in that the number of people moving into higher tax brackets increases in expansions and falls in contractions. By indexing the tax brackets to the overall price level, the legislation in 1982 eliminated the fiscal drag caused by inflation from taxes other than the AMT. If incomes rise only because of inflation, there is no change in average tax rates because the brackets are changed each year. The inflation part of the automatic stabilizer has been eliminated.

Full-Employment Budget

Because the condition of the economy affects the budget deficit so strongly, we cannot accurately judge either the intent or the success of fiscal policies just by looking at the surplus or deficit. Instead of looking simply at the size of the surplus or deficit, economists have developed an alternative way to measure how effective fiscal policy actually is. By examining what the budget would be like if the economy were producing at the full-employment level of output—the so-called **full-employment budget**—we can establish a benchmark for evaluating fiscal policy.

The distinction between the actual and full-employment budget is important. Suppose the economy is in a slump and the deficit is $250 billion. Also suppose that if there were full employment, the deficit would fall to $75 billion. The $75 billion deficit that would remain even with full employment would be due to the structure of tax and spending programs instead of the state of the economy. This deficit—the deficit that remains at full employment—is sometimes called the **structural deficit**. The $175 billion ($250 billion − $75 billion) part of the deficit caused by the fact the economy is in a slump is known as the **cyclical deficit**. The existence of the cyclical deficit depends on where the economy is in the business cycle, and it ceases to exist when full employment is reached. By definition, the cyclical deficit of the full-employment budget is zero.

Table 9.5 shows that the federal government deficit in 2012 was approximately $1.1 trillion. How much of this was cyclical and how much was structural? The U.S. economy was still not at full employment in 2012, and so some of the deficit was clearly cyclical.

full-employment budget What the federal budget would be if the economy were producing at the full-employment level of output.

structural deficit The deficit that remains at full employment.

cyclical deficit The deficit that occurs because of a downturn in the business cycle.

Looking Ahead

We have now seen how households, firms, and the government interact in the goods market, how equilibrium output (income) is determined, and how the government uses fiscal policy to influence the economy. In the following two chapters, we analyze the money market and monetary policy—the government's other major tool for influencing the economy.

SUMMARY

1. The government can affect the macroeconomy through two specific policy channels. *Fiscal policy* refers to the government's taxing and spending behavior. *Discretionary fiscal policy* refers to changes in taxes or spending that are the result of deliberate changes in government policy. *Monetary policy* refers to the behavior of the Federal Reserve concerning the nation's money supply.

GOVERNMENT IN THE ECONOMY *p. 166*

2. The government does not have complete control over tax revenues and certain expenditures, which are partially dictated by the state of the economy.

3. As a participant in the economy, the government makes purchases of goods and services (G), collects taxes, and makes transfer payments to households. *Net taxes* (T) is equal to the tax payments made to the government by firms and households minus transfer payments made to households by the government.

4. *Disposable*, or *after-tax, income* (Y_d) is equal to the amount of income received by households after taxes: $Y_d \equiv Y - T$. After-tax income determines households' consumption behavior.

5. The *budget deficit* is equal to the difference between what the government spends and what it collects in taxes: $G - T$. When G exceeds T, the government must borrow from the public to finance its deficit.

6. In an economy in which government is a participant, planned aggregate expenditure equals consumption spending by households (C) plus planned investment spending by firms (I) plus government spending on goods and services (G): $AE \equiv C + I + G$. Because the condition $Y = AE$ is necessary for the economy to be in equilibrium, it follows that $Y = C + I + G$ is the macroeconomic equilibrium condition. The economy is also in equilibrium when leakages out of the system equal injections into the system.

This occurs when saving and net taxes (the leakages) equal planned investment and government purchases (the injections): $S + T = I + G$.

FISCAL POLICY AT WORK: MULTIPLIER EFFECTS *p. 170*

7. Fiscal policy has a multiplier effect on the economy. A change in government spending gives rise to a multiplier equal to $1/MPS$. A change in taxation brings about a multiplier equal to $-MPC/MPS$. A simultaneous equal increase or decrease in government spending and taxes has a multiplier effect of 1.

THE FEDERAL BUDGET *p. 175*

8. During the two Clinton administrations, the federal budget went from being in deficit to being in surplus. This was reversed during the two Bush administrations, driven by tax rate decreases and government spending increases. The deficit has increased further in the Obama administration.

THE ECONOMY'S INFLUENCE ON THE GOVERNMENT BUDGET *p. 179*

9. *Automatic stabilizers* are revenue and expenditure items in the federal budget that automatically change with the state of the economy and that tend to stabilize GDP. For example, during expansions, the government automatically takes in more revenue because people are making more money that is taxed.

10. The *full-employment budget* is an economist's construction of what the federal budget would be if the economy were producing at a full-employment level of output. The *structural deficit* is the federal deficit that remains even at full employment. The *cyclical deficit* is that part of the total deficit caused by the economy operating at less than full employment.

REVIEW TERMS AND CONCEPTS

automatic destabilizer, *p. 180*

automatic stabilizers, *p. 180*

balanced-budget multiplier, *p. 174*

budget deficit, *p. 167*

cyclical deficit, *p. 181*

discretionary fiscal policy, *p. 166*

disposable, *or* after-tax, income (Y_d), *p. 166*

federal budget, *p. 175*

federal debt, *p. 179*

federal surplus (+) *or* deficit (−), *p. 176*

fiscal drag, *p. 180*

fiscal policy, *p. 165*

full-employment budget, *p. 181*

government spending multiplier, *p. 171*

monetary policy, *p. 166*

net taxes (T), *p. 166*

privately held federal debt, *p. 179*

structural deficit, *p. 181*

tax multiplier, *p. 173*

Equations:

Disposable income: $Y_d \equiv Y - T$, *p. 166*

$AE \equiv C + I + G$, *p. 167*

Government budget deficit $\equiv G - T$, *p. 167*

Equilibrium in an economy with a government: $Y = C + I + G$, *p. 168*

Saving/investment approach to equilibrium in an economy with a government: $S + T = I + G$, *p. 170*

Government spending multiplier

$\equiv \dfrac{1}{MPS} \equiv \dfrac{1}{1 - MPC}$, *p. 171*

Tax multiplier $\equiv -\left(\dfrac{MPC}{MPS}\right)$, *p. 173*

Balanced-budget multiplier $\equiv 1$, *p. 174*

PROBLEMS

All problems are available on MyEconLab.

1. You are appointed secretary of the treasury of a recently independent country called Rugaria. The currency of Rugaria is the lav. The new nation began fiscal operations this year, and the budget situation is that the government will spend 10 million lavs and taxes will be 9 million lavs. The 1-million-lav difference will be borrowed from the public by selling 10-year government bonds paying 5 percent interest. The interest on the outstanding bonds must be added to spending each year, and we assume that additional taxes are raised to cover that interest. Assuming that the budget stays the same except for the interest on the debt for 10 years, what will be the accumulated debt? What will the size of the budget be after 10 years?

2. Suppose that the government of Lumpland is enjoying a fat budget surplus with fixed government expenditures of $G = 150$ and fixed taxes of $T = 200$. Assume that consumers of Lumpland behave as described in the following consumption function:

$$C = 150 + 0.75(Y - T)$$

Suppose further that investment spending is fixed at 100. Calculate the equilibrium level of GDP in Lumpland. Solve for equilibrium levels of Y, C, and S. Next, assume that the Republican Congress in Lumpland succeeds in reducing taxes by 20 to a new fixed level of 180. Recalculate the equilibrium level of GDP using the tax multiplier. Solve for equilibrium levels of Y, C, and S after the tax cut and check to ensure that the multiplier worked. What arguments are likely to be used in support of such a tax cut? What arguments might be used to oppose such a tax cut?

3. For each of the following statements, decide whether you agree or disagree and explain your answer:
   a. During periods of budget surplus (when $G < T$), the government debt grows.
   b. A tax cut will increase the equilibrium level of GDP if the budget is in deficit but will decrease the equilibrium level of GDP if the budget is in surplus.
   c. If the $MPS = .90$, the tax multiplier is actually larger than the expenditure multiplier.

4. Define *saving* and *investment*. Data for the simple economy of Newt show that in 2013, saving exceeded investment and the government is running a balanced budget. What is likely to happen? What would happen if the government were running a deficit and saving were equal to investment?

5. Expert economists in the economy of Yuk estimate the following:

	BILLION YUKS
Real output/income	1,000
Government purchases	200
Total net taxes	200
Investment spending (planned)	100

Assume that Yukkers consume 75 percent of their disposable incomes and save 25 percent.

   a. You are asked by the business editor of the *Yuk Gazette* to predict the events of the next few months. By using the data given, make a forecast. (Assume that investment is constant.)
   b. If no changes were made, at what level of GDP (Y) would the economy of Yuk settle?
   c. Some local conservatives blame Yuk's problems on the size of the government sector. They suggest cutting government purchases by 25 billion Yuks. What effect would such cuts have on the economy? (Be specific.)

6. A $1 increase in government spending will raise equilibrium income more than a $1 tax cut will, yet both have the same impact on the budget deficit. So if we care about the budget deficit, the best way to stimulate the economy is through increases in spending, not cuts in taxes. Comment.

7. Assume that in 2013, the following prevails in the Republic of Nurd:

$Y = \$200$	$G = \$0$
$C = \$160$	$T = \$0$
$S = \$40$	
$I \,(\text{planned}) = \$30$	

Assume that households consume 80 percent of their income, they save 20 percent of their income, $MPC = .8$, and $MPS = .2$. That is, $C = .8Y_d$ and $S = .2Y_d$.

   a. Is the economy of Nurd in equilibrium? What is Nurd's equilibrium level of income? What is likely to happen in the coming months if the government takes no action?
   b. If $200 is the "full-employment" level of Y, what fiscal policy might the government follow if its goal is full employment?
   c. If the full-employment level of Y is $250, what fiscal policy might the government follow?
   d. Suppose $Y = \$200$, $C = \$160$, $S = \$40$, and $I = \$40$. Is Nurd's economy in equilibrium?
   e. Starting with the situation in part d, suppose the government starts spending $30 each year with no taxation and continues to spend $30 every period. If I remains constant, what will happen to the equilibrium level of Nurd's domestic product (Y)? What will the new levels of C and S be?
   f. Starting with the situation in part d, suppose the government starts taxing the population $30 each year without spending anything and continues to tax at that rate every period. If I remains constant, what will happen to the equilibrium level of Nurd's domestic product (Y)? What will be the new levels of C and S? How does your answer to part f differ from your answer to part e? Why?

8. Some economists claim World War II ended the Great Depression of the 1930s. The war effort was financed by borrowing massive sums of money from the public. Explain how a war could end a recession. Look at recent and back issues of the *Economic Report of the President* or the *Statistical Abstract of the United States*. How large was the federal government's debt as a percentage of GDP in 1946? How large is it today?

MyEconLab Visit **www.myeconlab.com** to complete these exercises online and get instant feedback. Exercises that update with real-time data are marked with ⬤.

9. Suppose all tax collections are fixed (instead of dependent on income) and all spending and transfer programs are fixed (in the sense that they do not depend on the state of the economy, as, for example, unemployment benefits now do). In this case, would there be any automatic stabilizers in the government budget? Would there be any distinction between the full-employment deficit and the actual budget deficit? Explain.

10. Answer the following:
    a. MPS = .4. What is the government spending multiplier?
    b. MPC = .9. What is the government spending multiplier?
    c. MPS = .5. What is the government spending multiplier?
    d. MPC = .75. What is the tax multiplier?
    e. MPS = .1. What is the tax multiplier?
    f. If the government spending multiplier is 6, what is the tax multiplier?
    g. If the tax multiplier is −2, what is the government spending multiplier?
    h. If government purchases and taxes are increased by $100 billion simultaneously, what will the effect be on equilibrium output (income)?

11. For the data in the following table, the consumption function is C = 200 + 0.8(Y − T). Fill in the columns in the table and identify the equilibrium output.

12. Use your answer to the previous problem to calculate the MPC, MPS, government spending multiplier, and tax multiplier. Draw a graph showing the data for consumption spending, planned aggregate expenditures, and aggregate output. Be sure to identify the equilibrium point on your graph.

13. What is the balanced-budget multiplier? Explain why the balanced-budget multiplier is equal to 1.

14. Evaluate the following statement: For an economy to be in equilibrium, planned investment spending plus government purchases must equal saving plus net taxes.

15. [Related to the *Economics in Practice* on p. 181] In addition to the U.S. Debt Clock in New York City, you can find various versions of the debt clock online. Go to www.usdebtclock.org. On this Website, you will find real-time values for over 50 items, including the national debt, the federal budget deficit, federal spending, and federal tax revenues. Look at the numbers for the above-mentioned four items. Explain the relationships between these items. Which numbers are increasing and which are decreasing? Based on the numbers you see, explain the current fiscal policy actions that appear to be underway in the economy and what actions, if any, would need to be taken in an attempt to reduce the national debt.

OUTPUT	NET TAXES	DISPOSABLE INCOME	CONSUMPTION SPENDING	SAVING	PLANNED INVESTMENT SPENDING	GOVERNMENT PURCHASES	PLANNED AGGREGATE EXPENDITURES	UNPLANNED INVENTORY CHANGE
1,050	50				150	200		
1,550	50				150	200		
2,050	50				150	200		
2,550	50				150	200		
3,050	50				150	200		
3,550	50				150	200		
4,050	50				150	200		

CHAPTER 9 APPENDIX A

Deriving the Fiscal Policy Multipliers

The Government Spending and Tax Multipliers

In the chapter, we noted that the government spending multiplier is 1/MPS. (This is the same as the investment multiplier.) We can also derive the multiplier algebraically using our hypothetical consumption function:

$$C = a + b(Y − T)$$

where b is the marginal propensity to consume. As you know, the equilibrium condition is

$$Y = C + I + G$$

By substituting for C, we get

$$Y = a + b(Y − T) + I + G$$
$$Y = a + bY − bT + I + G$$

This equation can be rearranged to yield

$$Y − bY = a + I + G − bT$$
$$Y(1 − b) = a + I + G − bT$$

Now solve for Y by dividing through by (1 − b):

$$Y = \frac{1}{(1 − b)}(a + I + G − bT)$$

We see from this last equation that if G increases by 1 with the other determinants of Y (a, I, and T) remaining constant, Y increases by 1/(1 − b). The multiplier is, as before, simply 1/(1 − b), where b is the marginal propensity to consume. Of course, 1 − b equals the marginal propensity to save, so the government spending multiplier is 1/MPS.

We can also derive the tax multiplier. The last equation says that when T increases by $1, holding a, I, and G constant, income decreases by b/(1 − b) dollars. The tax multiplier is $-b/(1 - b)$, or $-MPC/(1 - MPC) = -MPC/MPS$. (Remember, the negative sign in the resulting tax multiplier shows that it is a *negative* multiplier.)

The Balanced-Budget Multiplier

It is easy to show formally that the balanced-budget multiplier equals 1. When taxes and government spending are simultaneously increased by the same amount, there are two effects on planned aggregate expenditure: one positive and one negative. The initial impact of a balanced-budget increase in government spending and taxes on aggregate expenditure would be the *increase* in government purchases (ΔG) minus the *decrease* in consumption (ΔC) caused by the tax increase. The decrease in consumption brought about by the tax increase is equal to $\Delta C = \Delta T (MPC)$.

initial increase in spending:	ΔG
− initial decrease in spending:	$\Delta C = \Delta T(MPC)$
= net initial increase in spending	$\Delta G - \Delta T(MPC)$

In a balanced-budget increase, $\Delta G = \Delta T$; so in the above equation for the net initial increase in spending we can substitute ΔG for ΔT.

$$\Delta G - \Delta G(MPC) = \Delta G (1 - MPC)$$

Because $MPS = (1 - MPC)$, the net initial increase in spending is:

$$\Delta G(MPS)$$

We can now apply the expenditure multiplier $\left(\dfrac{1}{MPS}\right)$ to this net initial increase in spending:

$$\Delta Y = \Delta G(MPS)\left(\frac{1}{MPS}\right) = \Delta G$$

Thus, the final total increase in the equilibrium level of Y is just equal to the initial balanced increase in G and T. That means the balanced-budget multiplier equals 1, so the final increase in real output is of the same magnitude as the initial change in spending.

CHAPTER 9 APPENDIX B

The Case in Which Tax Revenues Depend on Income

In this chapter, we used the simplifying assumption that the government collects taxes in a lump sum. This made our discussion of the multiplier effects somewhat easier to follow. Now suppose that the government collects taxes not solely as a lump sum that is paid regardless of income but also partly in the form of a proportional levy against income. This is a more realistic assumption. Typically, tax collections either are based on income (as with the personal income tax) or follow the ups and downs in the economy (as with sales taxes). Instead of setting taxes equal to some fixed amount, let us say that tax revenues depend on income. If we call the amount of net taxes collected T, we can write $T = T_0 + tY$.

This equation contains two parts. First, we note that net taxes (T) will be equal to an amount T_0 if income (Y) is zero. Second, the tax rate (t) indicates how much net taxes change as income changes. Suppose T_0 is equal to −200 and t is 1/3. The resulting tax function is $T = -200 + 1/3Y$, which is graphed in Figure 9B.1. Note that when income is zero, the government collects "negative net taxes," which simply means that it makes transfer payments of 200. As income rises, tax collections increase because every extra dollar of income generates $0.33 in extra revenues for the government.

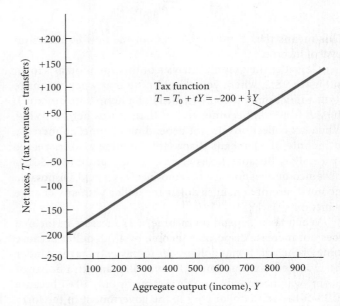

▲ FIGURE 9B.1   **The Tax Function**
This graph shows net taxes (taxes minus transfer payments) as a function of aggregate income.

How do we incorporate this new tax function into our discussion? All we do is replace the old value of T (in the example in the chapter, T was set equal to 100) with the new value, $-200 + 1/3Y$. Look first at the consumption equation. Consumption (C) still depends on disposable income, as it did before. Also, disposable income is still $Y - T$, or income minus taxes. Instead of disposable income equaling $Y - 100$, however, the new equation for disposable income is

$$Y_d \equiv Y - T$$
$$Y_d \equiv Y - (-200 + 1/3Y)$$
$$Y_d \equiv Y + 200 - 1/3Y$$

Because consumption still depends on after-tax income, exactly as it did before, we have

$$C = 100 + .75Y_d$$
$$C = 100 + .75(Y + 200 - 1/3Y)$$

Nothing else needs to be changed. We solve for equilibrium income exactly as before, by setting planned aggregate expenditure equal to aggregate output. Recall that planned aggregate expenditure is $C + I + G$ and aggregate output is Y. If we assume, as before, that $I = 100$ and $G = 100$, the equilibrium is

$$Y = C + I + G$$
$$Y = \underbrace{100 + .75(Y + 200 - 1/3Y)}_{C} + \underbrace{100}_{I} + \underbrace{100}_{G}$$

This equation may look difficult to solve, but it is not. It simplifies to

$$Y = 100 + .75Y + 150 - 25Y + 100 + 100$$
$$Y = 450 + .5Y$$
$$.5Y = 450$$

This means that $Y = 450/.5 = 900$, the new equilibrium level of income.

Consider the graphic analysis of this equation as shown in Figure 9B.2, where you should note that when we make taxes a function of income (instead of a lump-sum amount), the AE function becomes *flatter* than it was before. Why? When tax collections do not depend on income, an increase in income of $1 means disposable income also increases by a dollar. Because taxes are a constant amount, adding more income does not raise the amount of taxes paid. Disposable income therefore changes dollar for dollar with any change in income.

When taxes depend on income, a $1 increase in income does not increase disposable income by a full dollar because some of the additional dollar goes to pay extra taxes. Under the modified tax function of Figure 9B.2, an extra dollar of income will increase disposable income by only $0.67 because $0.33 of the extra dollar goes to the government in the form of taxes.

No matter how taxes are calculated, the marginal propensity to consume out of disposable (or after-tax) income is the same—each extra dollar of disposable income will increase consumption spending by $0.75. However, a $1 change in before-tax income does not have the same effect on disposable income in each case. Suppose we were to increase

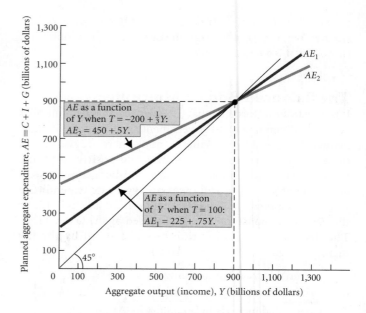

▲ **FIGURE 9B.2 Different Tax Systems**
When taxes are strictly lump-sum ($T = 100$) and do not depend on income, the aggregate expenditure function is steeper than when taxes depend on income.

income by $1. With the lump-sum tax function, disposable income would rise by $1.00, and consumption would increase by the MPC times the change in Y_d, or $0.75. When taxes depend on income, disposable income would rise by only $0.67 from the $1.00 increase in income and consumption would rise by only the MPC times the change in disposable income, or $0.75 \times .67 = 0.50.

If a $1.00 increase in income raises expenditure by $0.75 in one case and by only $0.50 in the other, the second aggregate expenditure function must be flatter than the first.

The Government Spending and Tax Multipliers Algebraically

All this means that if taxes are a function of income, the three multipliers (investment, government spending, and tax) are less than they would be if taxes were a lump-sum amount. By using the same linear consumption function we used in Chapters 7 and 8, we can derive the multiplier:

$$C = a + b(Y - T)$$
$$C = a + b(Y - T_0 - tY)$$
$$C = a + bY - bT_0 - btY$$

We know that $Y = C + I + G$. Through substitution we get

$$Y = \underbrace{a + bY - bT_0 - btY}_{C} + I + G$$

Solving for Y:

$$Y = \frac{1}{1 - b + bt}(a + I + G - bT_0)$$

This means that a $1 increase in G or I (holding a and T_0 constant) will increase the equilibrium level of Y by

$$\frac{1}{1 - b + bt}$$

If $b = MPC = .75$ and $t = .20$, the spending multiplier is 2.5. (Compare this to 4, which would be the value of the spending multiplier if taxes were a lump sum, that is, if $t = 0$.)

Holding a, I, and G constant, a fixed or lump-sum tax cut (a cut in T_0) will increase the equilibrium level of income by

$$\frac{b}{1 - b + bt}$$

Thus, if $b = MPC = .75$ and $t = .20$, the tax multiplier is -1.875. (Compare this to -3, which would be the value of the tax multiplier if taxes were a lump sum.)

—————————— APPENDIX SUMMARY ——————————

1. When taxes depend on income, a $1 increase in income does not increase disposable income by a full dollar because some of the additional dollar must go to pay extra taxes. This means that if taxes are a function of income,

the three multipliers (investment, government spending, and tax) are less than they would be if taxes were a lump-sum amount.

—————————— APPENDIX PROBLEMS ——————————

1. Assume the following for the economy of a country:
   a. Consumption function: $C = 85 + 0.5Y_d$
   b. Investment: $I = 85$
   c. Government spending: $G = 60$
   d. Net taxes: $T = -40 + 0.25Y$
   e. Disposable income: $Y_d \equiv Y - T$
   f. Equilibrium: $Y = C + I + G$

Solve for equilibrium income. (*Hint*: Be very careful in doing the calculations. They are not difficult, but it is easy to make careless mistakes that produce wrong results.) How much does the government collect in net taxes when the economy is in equilibrium? What is the government's budget deficit or surplus?

The Money Supply and the Federal Reserve System

10

In the last two chapters, we explored how consumers, firms, and the government interact in the goods market. In this chapter and the next, we show how money markets work in the macroeconomy. We begin with what money is and what role it plays in the U.S. economy. We then discuss the forces that determine the supply of money and show how banks create money. Finally, we discuss the workings of the nation's central bank, the Federal Reserve (the Fed), and the tools at its disposal to control the money supply.

Microeconomics has little to say about money. Microeconomic theories and models are concerned primarily with *real* quantities (apples, oranges, hours of labor) and *relative* prices (the price of apples relative to the price of oranges or the price of labor relative to the prices of other goods). Most of the key ideas in microeconomics do not require that we know anything about money. As we shall see, this is not the case in macroeconomics.

An Overview of Money

You often hear people say things like, "He makes a lot of money" (in other words, "He has a high income") or "She's worth a lot of money" (meaning "She is very wealthy"). It is true that your employer uses money to pay you your income, and your wealth may be accumulated in the form of money. However, *money is not income, and money is not wealth.*

To see that money and income are not the same, think of a $20 bill. That bill may pass through a thousand hands in a year, yet never be used to pay anyone a salary. Suppose you get a $20 bill from an automatic teller machine, and you spend it on dinner. The restaurant puts that $20 bill in a bank in the next day's deposit. The bank gives it to a woman cashing a check the following day; she spends it at a baseball game that night. The bill has been through many hands but not as part of anyone's income.

LEARNING OBJECTIVES

Define money and discuss its functions

Explain how banks create money

Describe the functions and structure of the Federal Reserve System

Discuss the three policy tools the Federal Reserve uses to manage the money supply

What Is Money?

Most people take the ability to obtain and use money for granted. When the whole monetary system works well, as it generally does in the United States, the basic mechanics of the system are virtually invisible. People take for granted that they can walk into any store, restaurant, boutique, or gas station and buy whatever they want as long as they have enough green pieces of paper.

The idea that you can buy things with money is so natural and obvious that it seems absurd to mention it, but stop and ask yourself: "How is it that a store owner is willing to part with a steak and a loaf of bread that I can eat in exchange for some pieces of paper that are intrinsically worthless?" Why, on the other hand, are there times and places where it takes a shopping cart full of money to purchase a dozen eggs? The answers to these questions lie in what money is—a means of payment, a store of value, and a unit of account.

barter The direct exchange of goods and services for other goods and services.

A Means of Payment, or Medium of Exchange Money is vital to the working of a market economy. Imagine what life would be like without it. The alternative to a monetary economy is **barter**, people exchanging goods and services for other goods and services directly instead of exchanging via the medium of money.

How does a barter system work? Suppose you want bacon, eggs, and orange juice for breakfast. Instead of going to the store and buying these things with money, you would have to find someone who has the items and is willing to trade them. You would also have to have something the bacon seller, the orange juice purveyor, and the egg vendor want. Having pencils to trade will do you no good if the bacon, orange juice, and egg sellers do not want pencils.

A barter system requires a *double coincidence of wants* for trade to take place. That is, to effect a trade, you have to find someone who has what you want and that person must also want what you have. Where the range of goods traded is small, as it is in relatively unsophisticated economies, it is not difficult to find someone to trade with and barter is often used. In a complex society with many goods, barter exchanges involve an intolerable amount of effort. Imagine trying to find people who offer for sale all the things you buy in a typical trip to the supermarket and who are willing to accept goods that you have to offer in exchange for their goods.

medium of exchange, *or* means of payment What sellers generally accept and buyers generally use to pay for goods and services.

Some agreed-to **medium of exchange** (*or* **means of payment**) neatly eliminates the double-coincidence-of-wants problem. Under a monetary system, money is exchanged for goods or services when people buy things; goods or services are exchanged for money when people sell things. No one ever has to trade goods for other goods directly. Money is a lubricant in the functioning of a market economy.

store of value An asset that can be used to transport purchasing power from one time period to another.

A Store of Value Economists have identified other roles for money aside from its primary function as a medium of exchange. Money also serves as a **store of value**—an asset that can be used to transport purchasing power from one time period to another. If you raise chickens and at the end of the month sell them for more than you want to spend and consume immediately, you may keep some of your earnings in the form of money until the time you want to spend it.

There are many other stores of value besides money. You could have decided to hold your "surplus" earnings by buying such things as antique paintings, baseball cards, or diamonds, which you could sell later when you want to spend your earnings. Money has several advantages over these other stores of value. First, it comes in convenient denominations and is easily portable. You do not have to worry about making change for a Renoir painting to buy a gallon of gasoline. Second, because money is also a means of payment, it is easily exchanged for goods at all times. (A Renoir is not easily exchanged for other goods.) These two factors compose the **liquidity property of money**. Money is easily spent, flowing out of your hands like liquid. Renoirs and ancient Aztec statues are neither convenient nor portable and are not readily accepted as a means of payment.

liquidity property of money The property of money that makes it a good medium of exchange as well as a store of value: It is portable and readily accepted and thus easily exchanged for goods.

The main disadvantage of money as a store of value is that the value of money falls when the prices of goods and services rise. If the price of potato chips rises from $1 per bag to $2 per bag, the value of a dollar bill in terms of potato chips falls from one bag to half a bag. When this happens, it may be better to use potato chips (or antiques or real estate) as a store of value.

unit of account A standard unit that provides a consistent way of quoting prices.

A Unit of Account Money also serves as a **unit of account**—a consistent way of quoting prices. All prices are quoted in monetary units. A textbook is quoted as costing $90, not 150 bananas or 5 pizzas, and a banana is quoted as costing 60 cents, not 1.4 apples or 6 pages of a textbook. Obviously, a standard unit of account is extremely useful when quoting prices. This function of money may have escaped your notice—what else would people quote prices in except money?

ECONOMICS IN PRACTICE

Don't Kill the Birds!

In most countries commodity monies were abandoned many years ago. At one point, sea shells and other artifacts from nature were commonly used. One of the more interesting examples of a commodity money is described by David Houston, an ethno-ornithologist.[1]

In the nineteenth century, elaborate rolls of red feathers harvested from the Scarlet Honeyeater bird were used as currency between the island of Santa Cruz and nearby Pacific Islands. Feathers were made into rolls of more than 10 meters in length and were never worn, displayed, or used. Their sole role was to serve as currency in a complex valuation system. Houston tells us that more than 20,000 of these birds were killed each year to create this "money," adding considerably to bird mortality. Running the printing presses is much easier.

Today, one of the few remaining uses of commodity monies is the use of dolphin teeth in the Solomon Islands. Apparently there is even a problem with counterfeiting as people try to pass off fruit bat teeth as dolphin teeth![2]

THINKING PRACTICALLY

1. Why do red feather rolls and dolphin teeth make good commodity monies, whereas coconut shells would not?

[1]David Houston, "The Impact of the Red Feather Currency on the Population of the Scarlet Honeyeater on Santa Cruz," in Sonia Tidemann and Andrew Gosler, eds., *Ethno-Ornithology: Birds, Indigenous Peoples, Culture and Society* (London, Earthscan Publishers, 2010), pp. 55–66.
[2] *The Wall Street Journal*, excerpted from "Shrinking Dollar Meets Its Match in Dolphin Teeth" by Yaroslav Trofimov. Copyright 2008 by *Dow Jones & Company, Inc.* Reproduced with permission of *Dow Jones & Company, Inc.* via Copyright Clearance Center.

Commodity and Fiat Monies

Introductory economics textbooks are full of stories about the various items that have been used as money by various cultures—candy bars, cigarettes (in World War II prisoner-of-war camps), huge wheels of carved stone (on the island of Yap in the South Pacific), cowrie shells (in West Africa), beads (among North American Indians), cattle (in southern Africa), and small green scraps of paper (in contemporary North America). The list goes on. The Economics in Practice box above describes the use of bird feathers as money. These various kinds of money are generally divided into two groups, commodity monies and fiat money.

Commodity monies are those items used as money that also have an intrinsic value in some other use. For example, prisoners of war made purchases with cigarettes, quoted prices in terms of cigarettes, and held their wealth in the form of accumulated cigarettes. Of course, cigarettes could also be smoked—they had an alternative use apart from serving as money. Gold represents another form of commodity money. For hundreds of years gold could be used directly to buy things, but it also had other uses, ranging from jewelry to dental fillings.

commodity monies Items used as money that also have intrinsic value in some other use.

By contrast, money in the United States today is mostly fiat money. **Fiat money**, sometimes called **token money**, is money that is intrinsically worthless. The actual value of a 1-, 10-, or 50-dollar bill is basically zero; what other uses are there for a small piece of paper with some green ink on it?

fiat, or token, money Items designated as money that are intrinsically worthless.

Why would anyone accept worthless scraps of paper as money instead of something that has some value, such as gold, cigarettes, or cattle? If your answer is "because the paper money is backed by gold or silver," you are wrong. There was a time when dollar bills were convertible directly into gold. The government backed each dollar bill in circulation by holding a certain amount of gold in its vaults. If the price of gold were $35 per ounce, for example, the government agreed to sell 1 ounce of gold for 35 dollar bills. However, dollar bills are no longer backed by any commodity—gold, silver, or anything else. They are exchangeable only for dimes, nickels, pennies, other dollars, and so on.

The public accepts paper money as a means of payment and a store of value because the government has taken steps to ensure that its money is accepted. The government declares its paper money to be **legal tender**. That is, the government declares that its money must be accepted in settlement of debts. It does this by fiat (hence *fiat money*). It passes laws defining

legal tender Money that a government has required to be accepted in settlement of debts.

certain pieces of paper printed in certain inks on certain plates to be legal tender, and that is that. Printed on every Federal Reserve note in the United States is "This note is legal tender for all debts, public and private." Often the government can get a start on gaining acceptance for its paper money by requiring that it be used to pay taxes. (Note that you cannot use chickens, baseball cards, or Renoir paintings to pay your taxes.)

Aside from declaring its currency legal tender, the government usually does one other thing to ensure that paper money will be accepted: It promises the public that it will not print paper money so fast that it loses its value. Expanding the supply of currency so rapidly that it loses much of its value has been a problem throughout history and is known as **currency debasement**. Debasement of the currency has been a special problem of governments that lack the strength to take the politically unpopular step of raising taxes. Printing money to be used on government expenditures of goods and services can serve as a substitute for tax increases, and weak governments have often relied on the printing press to finance their expenditures. An interesting example is Zimbabwe. In 2007, faced with a need to improve the public water system, Zimbabwe's president, Robert Mugabe, said, "Where money for projects cannot be found, we will print it" (reported in the *Washington Post*, July 29, 2007). In later chapters we will see the way in which this strategy for funding public projects can lead to serious inflation.

currency debasement
The decrease in the value of money that occurs when its supply is increased rapidly.

Measuring the Supply of Money in the United States

We now turn to the various kinds of money in the United States. Recall that money is used to buy things (a means of payment), to hold wealth (a store of value), and to quote prices (a unit of account). Unfortunately, these characteristics apply to a broad range of assets in the U.S. economy in addition to dollar bills. As we will see, it is not at all clear where we should draw the line and say, "Up to this is money, beyond this is something else."

To solve the problem of multiple monies, economists have given different names to different measures of money. The two most common measures of money are transactions money, also called M1, and broad money, also called M2.

M1: Transactions Money What should be counted as money? Coins and dollar bills, as well as higher denominations of currency, must be counted as money—they fit all the requirements. What about checking accounts? Checks, too, can be used to buy things and can serve as a store of value. Debit cards provide even easier access to funds in checking accounts. In fact, bankers call checking accounts *demand deposits* because depositors have the right to cash in (demand) their entire checking account balance at any time. That makes your checking account balance virtually equivalent to bills in your wallet, and it should be included as part of the amount of money you hold.

If we take the value of all currency (including coins) held outside of bank vaults and add to it the value of all demand deposits, traveler's checks, and other checkable deposits, we have defined **M1, or transactions money**. As its name suggests, this is the money that can be directly used for transactions—to buy things.

M1, *or* transactions money
Money that can be directly used for transactions.

> M1 ≡ currency held outside banks + demand deposits + traveler's checks + other checkable deposits

M1 at the end of December 2012 was $2,440.1 billion. M1 is a stock measure—it is measured at a point in time. It is the total amount of coins and currency outside of banks and the total dollar amount in checking accounts *on a specific day*. Until now, we have considered supply as a flow—a variable with a time dimension: the quantity of wheat supplied *per year*, the quantity of automobiles supplied to the market *per year*, and so on. However, M1 is a stock variable.

M2: Broad Money Although M1 is the most widely used measure of the money supply, there are others. Should savings accounts be considered money? Many of these accounts cannot be used for transactions directly, but it is easy to convert them into cash or to transfer funds from a savings account into a checking account. What about money market accounts (which allow only a few checks per month but pay market-determined interest rates) and money market mutual funds (which sell shares and use the proceeds to purchase short-term securities)? These can be used to write checks and make purchases, although only over a certain amount.

If we add **near monies**, close substitutes for transactions money, to M1, we get **M2**, called **broad money** because it includes not-quite-money monies such as savings accounts, money market accounts, and other near monies.

$$M2 \equiv M1 + \text{Savings accounts} + \text{Money market accounts} + \text{Other near monies}$$

M2 at the end of December 2012 was $10,402.4 billion, considerably larger than the total M1 of $2,440.1 billion. The main advantage of looking at M2 instead of M1 is that M2 is sometimes more stable. For instance, when banks introduced new forms of interest-bearing checking accounts in the early 1980s, M1 shot up as people switched their funds from savings accounts to checking accounts. However, M2 remained fairly constant because the fall in savings account deposits and the rise in checking account balances were both part of M2, canceling each other out.

Beyond M2 Because a wide variety of financial instruments bear some resemblance to money, some economists have advocated including almost all of them as part of the money supply. In recent years, for example, credit cards have come to be used extensively in exchange. Everyone who has a credit card has a credit limit—you can charge only a certain amount on your card before you have to pay it off. Usually we pay our credit card bills with a check. One of the very broad definitions of money includes the amount of available credit on credit cards (your charge limit minus what you have charged but not paid) as part of the money supply.

There are no rules for deciding what is and is not money. This poses problems for economists and those in charge of economic policy. However, *for our purposes, "money" will always refer to transactions money, or M1*. For simplicity, we will say that M1 is the sum of two *general* categories: currency in circulation and deposits. Keep in mind, however, that M1 has *four* specific components: currency held outside banks, demand deposits, traveler's checks, and other checkable deposits.

The Private Banking System

Most of the money in the United States today is "bank money" of one sort or another. M1 is made up largely of checking account balances instead of currency, and currency makes up an even smaller part of M2 and other broader definitions of money. Any understanding of money requires some knowledge of the structure of the private banking system.

Banks and banklike institutions borrow from individuals or firms with excess funds and lend to those who need funds. For example, commercial banks receive funds in various forms, including deposits in checking and savings accounts. They take these funds and loan them out in the form of car loans, mortgages, commercial loans, and so on. Banks and banklike institutions are called **financial intermediaries** because they "mediate," or act as a link between people who have funds to lend and those who need to borrow.

The main types of financial intermediaries are commercial banks, followed by savings and loan associations, life insurance companies, and pension funds. Since about 1970, the legal distinctions among the different types of financial intermediaries have narrowed considerably. It used to be, for example, that checking accounts could be held only in commercial banks and that commercial banks could not pay interest on checking accounts. Savings and loan associations were prohibited from offering certain kinds of deposits and were restricted primarily to making loans for mortgages.

The Depository Institutions Deregulation and Monetary Control Act, enacted by Congress in 1980, eliminated many of the previous restrictions on the behavior of financial institutions. Many types of institutions now offer checking accounts, and interest is paid on many types of checking accounts. Savings and loan associations now make loans for many things besides home mortgages.

How Banks Create Money

So far we have described the general way that money works and the way the supply of money is measured in the United States, but how much money is available at a given time? Who supplies it, and how does it get supplied? We are now ready to analyze these questions in detail. In particular, we want to explore a process that many find mysterious: the way banks *create money*.

---

near monies Close substitutes for transactions money, such as savings accounts and money market accounts.

M2, *or* broad money M1 plus savings accounts, money market accounts, and other near monies.

financial intermediaries Banks and other institutions that act as a link between those who have money to lend and those who want to borrow money.

A Historical Perspective: Goldsmiths

To begin to see how banks create money, consider the origins of the modern banking system. In the fifteenth and sixteenth centuries, citizens of many lands used gold as money, particularly for large transactions. Because gold is both inconvenient to carry around and susceptible to theft, people began to place their gold with goldsmiths for safekeeping. On receiving the gold, a goldsmith would issue a receipt to the depositor, charging him a small fee for looking after his gold. After a time, these receipts themselves, rather than the gold that they represented, began to be traded for goods. The receipts became a form of paper money, making it unnecessary to go to the goldsmith to withdraw gold for a transaction. The receipts of the de Medici's, who were both art patrons and goldsmith-bankers in Italy in the Renaissance period, were reputedly accepted in wide areas of Europe as currency.

At this point, all the receipts issued by goldsmiths were backed 100 percent by gold. If a goldsmith had 100 ounces of gold in his safe, he would issue receipts for 100 ounces of gold, and no more. Goldsmiths functioned as warehouses where people stored gold for safekeeping. The goldsmiths found, however, that people did not come often to withdraw gold. Why should they, when paper receipts that could easily be converted to gold were "as good as gold"? (In fact, receipts were better than gold—more portable, safer from theft, and so on.) As a result, goldsmiths had a large stock of gold continuously on hand.

Because they had what amounted to "extra" gold sitting around, goldsmiths gradually realized that they could lend out some of this gold without any fear of running out of gold. Why would they do this? Because instead of just keeping their gold idly in their vaults, they could earn interest on loans. Something subtle, but dramatic, happened at this point. The goldsmiths changed from mere depositories for gold into banklike institutions that had the power to create money. This transformation occurred as soon as goldsmiths began making loans. Without adding any more real gold to the system, the goldsmiths increased the amount of money in circulation by creating additional claims to gold—that is, receipts that entitled the bearer to receive a certain number of ounces of gold on demand.[1] Thus, there were more claims than there were ounces of gold.

A detailed example may help to clarify this. Suppose you go to a goldsmith who is functioning only as a depository, or warehouse, and ask for a loan to buy a plot of land that costs 20 ounces of gold. Also suppose that the goldsmith has 100 ounces of gold on deposit in his safe and receipts for exactly 100 ounces of gold out to the various people who deposited the gold. If the goldsmith decides he is tired of being a mere goldsmith and wants to become a real bank, he will loan you some gold. You don't want the gold itself, of course; rather, you want a slip of paper that represents 20 ounces of gold. The goldsmith in essence "creates" money for you by giving you a receipt for 20 ounces of gold (even though his entire supply of gold already belongs to various other people).[2] When he does, there will be receipts for 120 ounces of gold in circulation instead of the 100 ounces worth of receipts before your loan and the supply of money will have increased.

People think the creation of money is mysterious. Far from it! The creation of money is simply an accounting procedure, among the most mundane of human endeavors. You may suspect the whole process is fundamentally unsound or somehow dubious. After all, the banking system began when someone issued claims for gold that already belonged to someone else. Here you may be on slightly firmer ground.

Goldsmiths-turned-bankers did face certain problems. Once they started making loans, their receipts outstanding (claims on gold) were greater than the amount of gold they had in their vaults at any given moment. If the owners of the 120 ounces worth of gold receipts all presented their receipts and demanded their gold at the same time, the goldsmith would be in trouble. With only 100 ounces of gold on hand, people could not get their gold at once.

In normal times, people would be happy to hold receipts instead of real gold, and this problem would never arise. If, however, people began to worry about the goldsmith's financial safety, they might begin to have doubts about whether their receipts really were as good as gold. Knowing there were more receipts outstanding than there were ounces of gold in the goldsmith's vault, they might start to demand gold for receipts.

---

[1] Remember, these receipts circulated as money, and people used them to make transactions without feeling the need to cash them in—that is, to exchange them for gold itself.
[2] In return for lending you the receipt for 20 ounces of gold, the goldsmith expects to get an IOU promising to repay the amount (in gold itself or with a receipt from another goldsmith) with interest after a certain period of time.

This situation leads to a paradox. It makes perfect sense for people to hold paper receipts (instead of gold) if they know they can always get gold for their paper. In normal times, goldsmiths could feel perfectly safe in loaning out more gold than they actually had in their possession. But once people start to doubt the safety of the goldsmith, they are foolish not to demand their gold back from the vault.

A run on a goldsmith (or in our day, a **run on a bank**) occurs when many people present their claims at the same time. These runs tend to feed on themselves. If I see you going to the goldsmith to withdraw your gold, I may become nervous and decide to withdraw my gold as well. It is the *fear* of a run that usually causes the run. Runs on a bank can be triggered by a variety of causes: rumors that an institution may have made loans to borrowers who cannot repay, wars, failures of other institutions that have borrowed money from the bank, and so on. As you will see later in this chapter, today's bankers differ from goldsmiths—today's banks are subject to a "required reserve ratio." Goldsmiths had no legal reserve requirements, although the amount they loaned out was subject to the restriction imposed on them by their fear of running out of gold.

run on a bank Occurs when many of those who have claims on a bank (deposits) present them at the same time.

The Modern Banking System

To understand how the modern banking system works, you need to be familiar with some basic principles of accounting. Once you are comfortable with the way banks keep their books, the whole process of money creation will seem logical.

A Brief Review of Accounting   Central to accounting practices is the statement that "the books always balance." In practice, this means that if we take a snapshot of a firm—any firm, including a bank—at a particular moment in time, then by definition:

$$\text{Assets} - \text{Liabilities} \equiv \text{Net Worth}$$
$$\text{or}$$
$$\text{Assets} \equiv \text{Liabilities} + \text{Net Worth}$$

Assets are things a firm owns that are worth something. For a bank, these assets include the bank building, its furniture, its holdings of government securities, cash in its vaults, bonds, stocks, and so on. Most important among a bank's assets, for our purposes at least, are the loans it has made. A borrower gives the bank an *IOU*, a promise to repay a certain sum of money on or by a certain date. This promise is an asset of the bank because it is worth something. The bank could (and sometimes does) sell the IOU to another bank for cash.

Other bank assets include cash on hand (sometimes called *vault cash*) and deposits with the U.S. central bank—the **Federal Reserve Bank (the Fed)**. As we will see later in this chapter, federal banking regulations require that banks keep a certain portion of their deposits on hand as vault cash or on deposit with the Fed.

Federal Reserve Bank (the Fed)   The central bank of the United States.

A firm's *liabilities* are its debts—what it owes. A bank's liabilities are the promises to pay, or IOUs, that it has issued. A bank's most important liabilities are its deposits. *Deposits* are debts owed to the depositors because when you deposit money in your account, you are in essence making a loan to the bank.

The basic rule of accounting says that if we add up a firm's assets and then subtract the total amount it owes to all those who have lent it funds, the difference is the firm's net worth. *Net worth* represents the value of the firm to its stockholders or owners. How much would you pay for a firm that owns $200,000 worth of diamonds and had borrowed $150,000 from a bank to pay for them? The firm is worth $50,000—the difference between what it owns and what it owes. If the price of diamonds were to fall, bringing their value down to only $150,000, the firm would be worth nothing.

We can keep track of a bank's financial position using a simplified balance sheet called a T-account. By convention, the bank's assets are listed on the left side of the T-account and its liabilities and net worth are on the right side. By definition, the balance sheet always balances, so that the sum of the items on the left side of the T-account is equal to the sum of the items on the right side.

The T-account in Figure 10.1 shows a bank having $110 million in *assets*, of which $20 million are **reserves**, the deposits the bank has made at the Fed, and its cash on hand (coins and currency). Reserves are an asset to the bank because it can go to the Fed and get cash for them,

reserves   The deposits that a bank has at the Federal Reserve bank plus its cash on hand.

▶ **FIGURE 10.1**
T-Account for a Typical Bank (millions of dollars)
The balance sheet of a bank must always balance, so that the sum of assets (reserves and loans) equals the sum of liabilities (deposits and net worth).

	Assets		Liabilities	
Reserves	20	100		Deposits
Loans	90	10		Net worth
Total	110	110		Total

the same way you can go to the bank and get cash for the amount in your savings account. Our bank's other asset is its loans, worth $90 million.

Why do banks hold reserves/deposits at the Fed? There are many reasons, but perhaps the most important is the legal requirement that they hold a certain percentage of their deposit liabilities as reserves. The percentage of its deposits that a bank must keep as reserves is known as the **required reserve ratio**. If the reserve ratio is 20 percent, a bank with deposits of $100 million must hold $20 million as reserves, either as cash or as deposits at the Fed. To simplify, we will assume that banks hold all of their reserves in the form of deposits at the Fed.

On the liabilities side of the T-account, the bank has deposits of $100 million, which it owes to its depositors. This means that the bank has a net worth of $10 million to its owners ($110 million in assets − $100 million in liabilities = $10 million net worth). The net worth of the bank is what "balances" the balance sheet. Remember that when some item on a bank's balance sheet changes, there must be at least one other change somewhere else to maintain balance. If a bank's reserves increase by $1, one of the following must also be true: (1) Its other assets (for example, loans) decrease by $1, (2) its liabilities (deposits) increase by $1, or (3) its net worth increases by $1. Various fractional combinations of these are also possible.

required reserve ratio The percentage of its total deposits that a bank must keep as reserves at the Federal Reserve.

The Creation of Money

Like the goldsmiths, today's bankers seek to earn income by lending money out at a higher interest rate than they pay depositors for use of their money.

In modern times, the chances of a run on a bank are fairly small, and even if there is a run, the central bank protects the private banks in various ways. Therefore, banks usually make loans up to the point where they can no longer do so because of the reserve requirement restriction. A bank's required amount of reserves is equal to the required reserve ratio times the total deposits in the bank. If a bank has deposits of $100 and the required ratio is 20 percent, the required amount of reserves is $20. The difference between a bank's actual reserves and its required reserves is its **excess reserves**:

excess reserves The difference between a bank's actual reserves and its required reserves.

$$\text{excess reserves} \equiv \text{actual reserves} - \text{required reserves}$$

If banks make loans up to the point where they can no longer do so because of the reserve requirement restriction, this means that banks make loans up to the point where their excess reserves are zero.

To see why, note that when a bank has excess reserves, it has credit available and it can make loans. Actually, a bank can make loans *only* if it has excess reserves. When a bank makes a loan, it creates a demand deposit for the borrower. This creation of a demand deposit causes the bank's excess reserves to fall because the extra deposits created by the loan use up some of the excess reserves the bank has on hand. An example will help demonstrate this.

Assume that there is only one private bank in the country, the required reserve ratio is 20 percent, and the bank starts off with nothing, as shown in panel 1 of Figure 10.2. Now suppose dollar bills are in circulation and someone deposits 100 of them in the bank. The bank deposits the $100 with the central bank, so it now has $100 in reserves, as shown in panel 2. The bank now has assets (reserves) of $100 and liabilities (deposits) of $100. If the required reserve ratio is 20 percent, the bank has excess reserves of $80.

Panel 1		Panel 2		Panel 3	
Assets	Liabilities	Assets	Liabilities	Assets	Liabilities
Reserves 0	0 Deposits	Reserves 100	100 Deposits	Reserves 100 Loans 400	500 Deposits

▲ **FIGURE 10.2 Balance Sheets of a Bank in a Single-Bank Economy**
In panel 2, there is an initial deposit of $100. In panel 3, the bank has made loans of $400.

How much can the bank lend and still meet the reserve requirement? For the moment, let us assume that anyone who gets a loan keeps the entire proceeds in the bank or pays them to someone else who does. Nothing is withdrawn as cash. In this case, the bank can lend $400 and still meet the reserve requirement. Panel 3 shows the balance sheet of the bank after completing the maximum amount of loans it is allowed with a 20 percent reserve ratio. With $80 of excess reserves, the bank can have up to $400 of additional deposits. The $100 in reserves plus $400 in loans (which are made as deposits) equals $500 in deposits. With $500 in deposits and a required reserve ratio of 20 percent, the bank must have reserves of $100 (20 percent of $500)—and it does. The bank can lend no more than $400 because that is all its $100 of reserves will support, given its initial deposit. When a bank has no excess reserves and thus can make no more loans, it is said to be *loaned up*.

Remember, the money supply (M1) equals cash in circulation plus deposits. Before the initial deposit, the money supply was $100 ($100 cash and no deposits). After the deposit and the loans, the money supply is $500 (no cash outside bank vaults and $500 in deposits). It is clear then that when loans are converted into deposits, the supply of money will increase.

The bank whose T-accounts are presented in Figure 10.2 is allowed to make loans of $400 based on the assumption that loans that are made *stay in the bank* in the form of deposits. Now suppose you borrow from the bank to buy a personal computer and you write a check to the computer store. If the store also deposits its money in the bank, your check merely results in a reduction in your account balance and an increase to the store's account balance within the bank. No cash has left the bank. As long as the system is closed in this way—remember that so far we have assumed that there is only one bank—the bank knows that it will never be called on to release any of its $100 in reserves. It can expand its loans up to the point where its total deposits are $500.

Of course, there are many banks in the country, a situation that is depicted in Figure 10.3. As long as the banking system as a whole is closed, it is still possible for an initial deposit of $100 to result in an expansion of the money supply to $500, but more steps are involved when there is more than one bank.

To see why, assume that Mary makes an initial deposit of $100 in bank 1 and the bank deposits the entire $100 with the Fed (panel 1 of Figure 10.3). All loans that a bank makes are withdrawn from the bank as the individual borrowers write checks to pay for merchandise. After Mary's deposit, bank 1 can make a loan of up to $80 to Bill because it needs to keep only $20 of its $100 deposit as reserves. (We are assuming a 20 percent required reserve ratio.) In other words, bank 1 has $80 in excess reserves.

Bank 1's balance sheet at the moment of the loan to Bill appears in panel 2 of Figure 10.3. Bank 1 now has loans of $80. It has credited Bill's account with the $80, so its total deposits are $180 ($80 in loans plus $100 in reserves). Bill then writes a check for $80 for a set of shock absorbers for his car. Bill wrote his check to Sam's Car Shop, and Sam deposits Bill's check in bank 2. When the check clears, bank 1 transfers $80 in reserves to bank 2. Bank 1's balance sheet now looks like the top of panel 3. Its assets include reserves of $20 and loans of $80; its liabilities are $100 in deposits. Both sides of the T-account balance: The bank's reserves are 20 percent of its deposits, as required by law, and it is fully loaned up.

Now look at bank 2. Because bank 1 has transferred $80 in reserves to bank 2, bank 2 now has $80 in deposits and $80 in reserves (panel 1, bank 2). Its reserve requirement is also 20 percent, so it has excess reserves of $64 on which it can make loans.

Now assume that bank 2 loans the $64 to Kate to pay for a textbook and Kate writes a check for $64 payable to the Manhattan College Bookstore. The final position of bank 2, after it honors Kate's $64 check by transferring $64 in reserves to the bookstore's bank, is reserves of $16, loans of $64, and deposits of $80 (panel 3, bank 2).

	Panel 1		Panel 2		Panel 3	
	Assets	Liabilities	Assets	Liabilities	Assets	Liabilities
Bank 1	Reserves 100	100 Deposits	Reserves 100 Loans 80	180 Deposits	Reserves 20 Loans 80	100 Deposits
Bank 2	Reserves 80	80 Deposits	Reserves 80 Loans 64	144 Deposits	Reserves 16 Loans 64	80 Deposits
Bank 3	Reserves 64	64 Deposits	Reserves 64 Loans 51.20	115.20 Deposits	Reserves 12.80 Loans 51.20	64 Deposits

Summary:	Loans	Deposits
Bank 1	80	100
Bank 2	64	80
Bank 3	51.20	64
Bank 4	40.96	51.20
⋮	⋮	⋮
Total	400.00	500.00

▲ **FIGURE 10.3** **The Creation of Money When There Are Many Banks**
In panel 1, there is an initial deposit of $100 in bank 1. In panel 2, bank 1 makes a loan of $80 by creating a deposit of $80. A check for $80 by the borrower is then written on bank 1 (panel 3) and deposited in bank 2 (panel 1). The process continues with bank 2 making loans and so on. In the end, loans of $400 have been made and the total level of deposits is $500.

The Manhattan College Bookstore deposits Kate's check in its account with bank 3. Bank 3 now has excess reserves because it has added $64 to its reserves. With a reserve ratio of 20 percent, bank 3 can loan out $51.20 (80 percent of $64, leaving 20 percent in required reserves to back the $64 deposit).

As the process is repeated over and over, the total amount of deposits created is $500, the sum of the deposits in each of the banks. Because the banking system can be looked on as one big bank, the outcome here for many banks is the same as the outcome in Figure 10.2 for one bank.[3]

The Money Multiplier

In practice, the banking system is not completely closed—there is some leakage out of the system, as people send money abroad or even hide it under their mattresses! Still, the point here is that an increase in bank reserves leads to a greater than one-for-one increase in the money supply. Economists call the relationship between the final change in deposits and the change in reserves that caused this change the money multiplier. Stated somewhat differently, the **money multiplier** is the multiple by which deposits can increase for every dollar increase in reserves. Do not confuse the money multiplier with the spending multipliers we discussed in the last two chapters. They are not the same thing.

In the example we just examined, reserves increased by $100 when the $100 in cash was deposited in a bank and the amount of deposits increased by $500 ($100 from the initial deposit, $400 from the loans made by the various banks from their excess reserves). The money multiplier in this case is $500/$100 = 5. Mathematically, the money multiplier can be defined as follows:[4]

money multiplier The multiple by which deposits can increase for every dollar increase in reserves; equal to 1 divided by the required reserve ratio.

$$\text{money multiplier} \equiv \frac{1}{\text{required reserve ratio}}$$

---

[3] If banks create money when they make loans, does repaying a loan "destroy" money? The answer is yes.
[4] To show this mathematically, let rr denote the reserve requirement ratio, like 0.20. Say someone deposits 100 in bank 1 in Figure 10.3. Bank 1 can create $100(1 - rr)$ in loans, which are then deposits in bank 2. Bank 2 can create $100(1 - rr)(1 - rr)$ in loans, which are then deposits in bank 3, and so on. The sum of the deposits is thus $100[1 + (1 - rr) + (1 - rr)^2 + (1 - rr)^3 + \ldots]$. The sum of the infinite series in brackets is $1/rr$, which is the money multiplier.

In the United States, the required reserve ratio varies depending on the size of the bank and the type of deposit. For large banks and for checking deposits, the ratio is currently 10 percent, which makes the potential money multiplier $1/.10 = 10$. This means that an increase in reserves of $1 could cause an increase in deposits of $10 if there were no leakage out of the system.

It is important to remember that the money multiplier is derived under the assumption that banks hold no excess reserves. For example, when Bank 1 gets the deposit of $100, it loans out the maximum that it can, namely $100 times 1 minus the reserve requirement ratio. If instead Bank 1 held the $100 as excess reserves, the increase in the money supply would just be the initial $100 in deposits (brought in, say, from outside the banking system).

The Federal Reserve System

We have seen how the private banking system creates money by making loans. However, private banks are not free to create money at will. Their ability to create money is controlled by the volume of reserves in the system, which is controlled by the Fed. The Fed therefore has the ultimate control over the money supply. We will now examine the structure and function of the Fed.

Founded in 1913 by an act of Congress (to which major reforms were added in the 1930s), the Fed is the central bank of the United States. The Fed is a complicated institution with many responsibilities, including the regulation and supervision of about 6,000 commercial banks. The organization of the Federal Reserve System is presented in Figure 10.4.

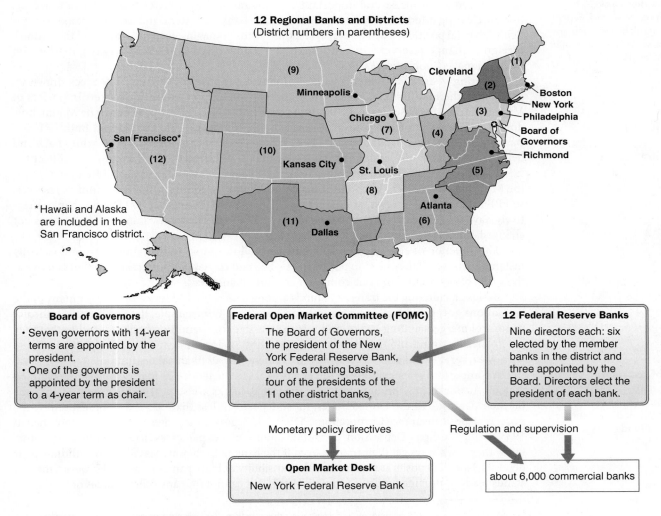

▲ FIGURE 10.4 **The Structure of the Federal Reserve System**

The *Board of Governors* is the most important group within the Federal Reserve System. The board consists of seven members, each appointed for 14 years by the president of the United States. The *chair* of the Fed, who is appointed by the president and whose term runs for 4 years, usually dominates the entire Federal Reserve System and is sometimes said to be the second most powerful person in the United States. The Fed is an independent agency in that it does not take orders from the president or from Congress.

The United States is divided into 12 Federal Reserve districts, each with its own Federal Reserve bank. These districts are indicated on the map in Figure 10.4. The district banks are like branch offices of the Fed in that they carry out the rules, regulations, and functions of the central system in their districts and report to the Board of Governors on local economic conditions.

Federal Open Market Committee (FOMC) A group composed of the seven members of the Fed's Board of Governors, the president of the New York Federal Reserve Bank, and four of the other 11 district bank presidents on a rotating basis; it sets goals concerning the money supply and interest rates and directs the operation of the Open Market Desk in New York.

U.S. monetary policy is formally set by the **Federal Open Market Committee (FOMC)**. The FOMC consists of the seven members of the Fed's Board of Governors; the president of the New York Federal Reserve Bank; and on a rotating basis, four of the presidents of the 11 other district banks. The FOMC sets goals concerning interest rates, and it directs the **Open Market Desk** in the New York Federal Reserve Bank to buy and/or sell government securities. (We discuss the specifics of open market operations later in this chapter.)

Functions of the Federal Reserve

The Fed is the central bank of the United States. Central banks are sometimes known as "bankers' banks" because only banks (and occasionally foreign governments) can have accounts in them. As a private citizen, you cannot go to the nearest branch of the Fed and open a checking account or apply to borrow money.

Open Market Desk The office in the New York Federal Reserve Bank from which government securities are bought and sold by the Fed.

The Fed performs several important administrative functions for banks. These functions include clearing interbank payments, regulating the banking system, and assisting banks in a difficult financial position. The Fed is also responsible for managing exchange rates and the nation's foreign exchange reserves.[5] In addition, it is often involved in intercountry negotiations on international economic issues.

Clearing interbank payments works as follows. Suppose you write a $100 check drawn on your bank, the First Bank of Fresno (FBF), to pay for tulip bulbs from Crockett Importers of Miami, Florida. Because Crockett Importers does not bank at FBF, but at Banco de Miami, how does your money get from your bank to the bank in Florida? The Fed does it. Both FBF and Banco de Miami have accounts at the Fed. When Crockett Importers receives your check and deposits it at Banco de Miami, the bank submits the check to the Fed, asking it to collect the funds from FBF. The Fed presents the check to FBF and is instructed to debit FBF's account for the $100 and to credit the account of Banco de Miami. Accounts at the Fed count as reserves, so FBF loses $100 in reserves, and Banco de Miami gains $100 in reserves. The two banks effectively have traded ownerships of their deposits at the Fed. The *total* volume of reserves has not changed, nor has the money supply.

This function of clearing interbank payments allows banks to shift money around virtually instantaneously. All they need to do is wire the Fed and request a transfer, and the funds move at the speed of electricity from one computer account to another.

Besides facilitating the transfer of funds among banks, the Fed is responsible for many of the regulations governing banking practices and standards. For example, the Fed has the authority to control mergers among banks, and it is responsible for examining banks to ensure that they are financially sound and that they conform to a host of government accounting regulations. As we saw earlier, the Fed also sets reserve requirements for all financial institutions.

lender of last resort One of the functions of the Fed: It provides funds to troubled banks that cannot find any other sources of funds.

An important responsibility of the Fed is to act as the **lender of last resort** for the banking system. As our discussion of goldsmiths suggested, banks are subject to the possibility of runs on their deposits. In the United States, most deposits of less than $250,000 are insured by the Federal Deposit Insurance Corporation (FDIC), a U.S. government agency that was established in 1933 during the Great Depression. Deposit insurance makes panics less likely. Because depositors know they can always get their money, even if the bank fails, they are less likely to withdraw their deposits. Not all deposits are insured, so the possibility of bank panics remains. However, the Fed stands ready to provide funds to a troubled bank that cannot find any other sources of funds.

---

[5] *Foreign exchange reserves* are holdings of the currencies of other countries—for example, Japanese yen—by the U.S. government. We discuss exchange rates and foreign exchange markets at length in Chapter 20.

The Fed is the ideal lender of last resort for two reasons. First, providing funds to a bank that is in dire straits is risky and not likely to be very profitable, and it is hard to find private banks or other private institutions willing to do this. The Fed is a nonprofit institution whose function is to serve the overall welfare of the public. Thus, the Fed would certainly be interested in preventing catastrophic banking panics such as those that occurred in the late 1920s and the 1930s.

Second, the Fed has an essentially unlimited supply of funds with which to help banks facing the possibility of runs. The reason, as we shall see, is that the Fed can create reserves at will. A promise by the Fed that it will support a bank is very convincing. Unlike any other lender, the Fed can never run out of dollars. Therefore, the explicit or implicit support of the Fed should be enough to assure depositors that they are in no danger of losing their funds.

Expanded Fed Activities Beginning in 2008

In March 2008, faced with many large financial institutions simultaneously in serious financial trouble, the Fed began to broaden its role in the banking system. No longer would it be simply a lender of last resort to banks, but would become an active participant in the private banking system. How did this change come about?

Beginning in about 2003, the U.S. economy experienced rapidly rising housing prices, in what some called a "housing bubble." Financial institutions began issuing mortgages with less oversight, in some cases to households with poor credit ratings (so-called sub prime borrowers). Some households bought homes they could not afford based on their incomes, expecting to eventually "cash in" on the rising housing prices. Regulation, by the Fed or other federal or state agencies, was lax, and many financial firms took very large risks. When housing prices began to fall in late 2005, the stage was set for a financial crisis. Financial institutions, even very large ones, began to experience very large losses, as home owners began defaulting on their loans, setting off a chain reaction that many people thought threatened the economic system.

The Fed responded to these events in a number of ways. In March 2008 it participated in a bailout of Bear Stearns, a large financial institution, by guaranteeing $30 billion of Bear Stearns' liabilities to JPMorgan. On September 7, 2008, it participated in a government takeover of the Federal National Mortgage Association (Fannie Mae) and the Federal Home Loan Mortgage Corporation (Freddie Mac), which at that time owned or guaranteed about half of the $12 trillion mortgage market in the United States. On September 17, 2008, the Fed loaned $85 billion to the American International Group (AIG) insurance company to help it avoid bankruptcy. In mid September the Fed urged Congress to pass a $700 billion bailout bill, which was signed into law on October 3.

In the process of bailing out Fannie Mae and Freddie Mac, in September 2008, the Fed began buying securities of these two associations, called "federal agency debt securities." We will see in the next section that by the end of January 2013 the Fed held $75 billion of these securities. More remarkable, however, is that in January 2009 the Fed began buying mortgage-backed securities, securities that the private sector was reluctant to hold because of their perceived riskiness. We will see in the next section that by the end of January 2013 the Fed held $966 billion of these securities. In September 2012 the Fed opted to buy mortgage-backed securities and long-term government bonds to the tune of $85 billion per month. Most of these purchases show up as an increase in excess reserves of commercial banks.

As is not surprising, there has been much political discussion of whether the Fed should have regulated financial institutions more in 2003–2005 and whether its subsequent active role in the system was warranted. Whatever one's views, it is certainly the case that the Fed has taken a much more active role in financial markets since 2008.

The Federal Reserve Balance Sheet

Although the Fed is a special bank, it is similar to an ordinary commercial bank in that it has a balance sheet that records its asset and liability position at any moment of time. Among other things, this balance sheet is useful for seeing the Fed's current involvement in private financial markets. The balance sheet for January 30, 2013, is presented in Table 10.1.

On January 30, 2013, the Fed had $3,052 billion in assets, of which $11 billion was gold, $1,710 billion was U.S. Treasury securities, $75 billion was federal agency debt securities, $966 billion was mortgage-backed securities, and $290 billion was other.

MyEconLab Real-time data

TABLE 10.1 Assets and Liabilities of the Federal Reserve System, January 30, 2013 (Billions of Dollars)

Assets			Liabilities
Gold	$ 11	$1,156	Currency in circulation
U.S. Treasury securities	1,710	1,645	Reserve balances (about 110 required)
Federal agency debt securities	75	71	U.S. Treasury deposits
Mortgage-backed securities	966	180	All other liabilities and net worth
All other assets	290	$3,052	Total
Total	$3,052		

Source: Board of Governors of the Federal Reserve System.

Gold is trivial. *Do not think that this gold has anything to do with money in circulation.* Most of the gold was acquired during the 1930s, when it was purchased from the U.S. Treasury Department. Since 1934, the dollar has not been backed by (is not convertible into) gold. You cannot take a dollar bill to the Fed to receive gold for it; all you can get for your old dollar bill is a new dollar bill.[6] Although it is unrelated to the money supply, the Fed's gold counts as an asset on its balance sheet because it is something of value the Fed owns.

U.S. Treasury securities are the traditional assets held by the Fed. These are obligations of the federal government that the Fed has purchased over the years. The Fed controls the money supply by buying and selling these securities, as we will see in the next section. Before the change in Fed behavior in 2008, almost all of its assets were in the form of U.S. Treasury securities. For example, in the ninth edition of this text, the balance sheet presented was for October 24, 2007, where total Fed assets were $885 billion, of which $780 billion were U.S. Treasury securities.

The new assets of the Fed (since 2008) are federal agency debt securities and mortgage-backed securities. (These were both zero in the October 24, 2007 balance sheet.) They now total $1,041 billion. The Fed's intervention discussed at the end of the previous section has been huge.

Of the Fed's liabilities, $1,156 billion is currency in circulation, $1,645 billion is reserve balances, $71 billion is U.S. Treasury deposits, and $180 billion is other. Regarding U.S. Treasury deposits, the Fed acts as a bank for the U.S. government and these deposits are held by the U.S. government at the Fed. When the government needs to pay for something like a new aircraft carrier, it may write a check to the supplier of the ship drawn on its "checking account" at the Fed. Similarly, when the government receives revenues from tax collections, fines, or sales of government assets, it may deposit these funds at the Fed.

Currency in circulation accounts for about 38 percent of the Fed's liabilities. The dollar bill that you use to buy a pack of gum is clearly an asset from your point of view—it is something you own that has value. Because every financial asset is by definition a liability of some other agent in the economy, whose liability is the dollar bill? The dollar bill is a liability—an IOU—of the Fed. It is, of course, a strange IOU because it can only be redeemed for another IOU of the same type. It is nonetheless classified as a liability of the Fed.

Reserve balances account for about 54 percent of the Fed's liabilities. These are the reserves that commercial banks hold at the Fed. Remember that commercial banks are required to keep a certain fraction of their deposits at the Fed. These deposits are assets of the commercial banks and liabilities of the Fed. What is remarkable about the $1,645 billion in reserve balances at the Fed is that only about $110 billion are required reserves. The rest—over $1,500 billion—are excess reserves, reserves that the commercial banks could lend to the private sector if they wanted to. One of the reasons the Fed said it was buying mortgage-backed securities was to provide funds to the commercial banks for loans to consumers and businesses. Think of a commercial bank that owns $10 million in mortgage-backed securities. The Fed buys these securities by taking the securities and crediting the commercial bank's account at the Fed with $10 million in reserves. The bank is now in a position to lend this money out. Instead, what the banks have mostly done is keep the reserves as deposits at the Fed. Banks earn a small interest rate from the Fed on their excess reserves. So as a first approximation, one can think of the Fed's purchase of

---

[6] The fact that the Fed is not obliged to provide gold for currency means it can never go bankrupt. When the currency was backed by gold, it would have been possible for the Fed to run out of gold if too many of its depositors came to it at the same time and asked to exchange their deposits for gold. If depositors come to the Fed to withdraw their deposits today, all they can get is dollar bills. The dollar was convertible into gold internationally until August 15, 1971.

mortgage-backed securities as putting mortgage-backed securities on the asset side of its balance sheet and excess reserves on the liability side. This also means that there is no money multiplier, which is derived under the assumption that banks hold no excess reserves. The money supply increases only as the excess reserves are loaned out. Banks' holding excess reserves limits the ability of the Fed to control the money supply, as is discussed in the next section.

How the Federal Reserve Controls the Money Supply

To see how, in usual times when banks are not holding excess reserves, the Fed controls the supply of money in the U.S. economy, we need to understand the role of reserves. As we have said, the required reserve ratio establishes a link between the reserves of the commercial banks and the deposits (money) that commercial banks are allowed to create. The reserve requirement effectively determines how much a bank has available to lend. If the required reserve ratio is 20 percent, each $1 of reserves can support $5 in deposits. A bank that has reserves of $100,000 cannot have more than $500,000 in deposits. If it did, it would fail to meet the required reserve ratio.

If you recall that the *money supply* is equal to the sum of deposits inside banks and the currency in circulation outside banks, you can see that reserves provide the leverage that the Fed needs to control the money supply. If the Fed wants to increase the supply of money, it creates more reserves, thereby freeing banks to create additional deposits by making more loans. If it wants to decrease the money supply, it reduces reserves.

Three tools are available to the Fed for changing the money supply: (1) changing the required reserve ratio, (2) changing the discount rate, and (3) engaging in open market operations. Although (3) is almost exclusively used to change the money supply, an understanding of how (1) and (2) work is useful in understanding how (3) works. We thus begin our discussion with the first two tools. The following discussion assumes that banks hold no excess reserves. On p. 208 we consider the case in which banks hold excess reserves.

The Required Reserve Ratio

One way for the Fed to alter the supply of money is to change the required reserve ratio. This process is shown in Table 10.2. Let us assume the initial required reserve ratio is 20 percent.

In panel 1, a simplified version of the Fed's balance sheet (in billions of dollars) shows that reserves are $100 billion and currency outstanding is $100 billion. The total value of the Fed's

---

TABLE 10.2 A Decrease in the Required Reserve Ratio from 20 Percent to 12.5 Percent Increases the Supply of Money (All Figures in Billions of Dollars)

Panel 1: Required Reserve Ratio = 20%

| Federal Reserve | | | | Commercial Banks | | | |
Assets		Liabilities		Assets		Liabilities	
Government securities	$200	$100	Reserves	Reserves	$100	$500	Deposits
		$100	Currency	Loans	$400		

Note: Money supply (M1) = currency + deposits = $600.

Panel 2: Required Reserve Ratio = 12.5%

| Federal Reserve | | | | Commercial Banks | | | |
Assets		Liabilities		Assets		Liabilities	
Government securities	$200	$100	Reserves	Reserves	$100	$800 (+$300)	Deposits
		$100	Currency	Loans (+$300)	$700		

Note: Money supply (M1) = currency + deposits = $900.

assets is $200 billion, which we assume to be all in government securities. Assuming there are no excess reserves—banks stay fully loaned up—the $100 billion in reserves supports $500 billion in deposits at the commercial banks. (Remember, the money multiplier equals 1/required reserve ratio = 1/.20 = 5. Thus, $100 billion in reserves can support $500 billion [$100 billion × 5] in deposits when the required reserve ratio is 20 percent.) The supply of money (M1, or transactions money) is therefore $600 billion: $100 billion in currency and $500 billion in (checking account) deposits at the commercial banks.

Now suppose the Fed wants to increase the supply of money to $900 billion. If it lowers the required reserve ratio from 20 percent to 12.5 percent (as in panel 2 of Table 10.2), the same $100 billion of reserves could support $800 billion in deposits instead of only $500 billion. In this case, the money multiplier is 1/.125, or 8. At a required reserve ratio of 12.5 percent, $100 billion in reserves can support $800 billion in deposits. The total money supply would be $800 billion in deposits plus the $100 billion in currency, for a total of $900 billion.[7]

Put another way, with the new lower reserve ratio, banks have excess reserves of $37.5 billion. At a required reserve ratio of 20 percent, they needed $100 billion in reserves to back their $500 billion in deposits. At the lower required reserve ratio of 12.5 percent, they need only $62.5 billion of reserves to back their $500 billion of deposits; so the remaining $37.5 billion of the existing $100 billion in reserves is "extra." With that $37.5 billion of excess reserves, banks can lend out more money. If we assume the system loans money and creates deposits to the *maximum* extent possible, the $37.5 billion of reserves will support an additional $300 billion of deposits ($37.5 billion × the money multiplier of 8 = $300 billion). The change in the required reserve ratio has injected an additional $300 billion into the banking system, at which point the banks will be fully loaned up and unable to increase their deposits further. Decreases in the required reserve ratio allow banks to have more deposits with the existing volume of reserves. As banks create more deposits by making loans, the supply of money (currency + deposits) increases. The reverse is also true: If the Fed wants to restrict the supply of money, it can raise the required reserve ratio, in which case banks will find that they have insufficient reserves and must therefore reduce their deposits by "calling in" some of their loans.[8] The result is a decrease in the money supply.

For many reasons, the Fed has tended not to use changes in the reserve requirement to control the money supply. In part, this reluctance stems from the era when only some banks were members of the Fed and therefore subject to reserve requirements. The Fed reasoned that if it raised the reserve requirement to contract the money supply, banks might choose to stop being members. This argument no longer applies. Since the passage of the Depository Institutions Deregulation and Monetary Control Act in 1980, all depository institutions are subject to Fed requirements.

It is also true that changing the reserve requirement ratio is a crude tool. Because of lags in banks' reporting to the Fed on their reserve and deposit positions, a change in the requirement today does not affect banks for about 2 weeks. (However, the fact that changing the reserve requirement expands or reduces credit in every bank in the country makes it a very powerful tool when the Fed does use it—assuming no excess reserves held.)

The Discount Rate

discount rate The interest rate that banks pay to the Fed to borrow from it.

Banks may borrow from the Fed. The interest rate they pay the Fed is the **discount rate**. When banks increase their borrowing, the money supply increases. To see why this is true, assume that there is only one bank in the country and that the required reserve ratio is 20 percent. The initial position of the bank and the Fed appear in panel 1 of Table 10.3, where the money supply (currency + deposits) is $480 billion. In panel 2, the bank has borrowed $20 billion from the Fed. By using this $20 billion as a reserve, the bank can increase its loans by $100 billion, from

---

[7] To find the maximum volume of deposits (D) that can be supported by an amount of reserves (R), divide R by the required reserve ratio. If the required reserve ratio is g, because $R = gD$, then $D = R/g$.

[8] To reduce the money supply, banks never really have to "call in" loans before they are due. First, the Fed is almost always expanding the money supply slowly because the real economy grows steadily and, as we shall see, growth brings with it the need for more circulating money. So when we speak of "contractionary monetary policy," we mean the Fed is slowing down the rate of money growth, not reducing the money supply. Second, even if the Fed were to cut reserves (instead of curb their expansion), banks would no doubt be able to comply by reducing the volume of new loans they make while old ones are coming due.

TABLE 10.3 The Effect on the Money Supply of Commercial Bank Borrowing from the Fed (All Figures in Billions of Dollars)

Panel 1: No Commercial Bank Borrowing from the Fed

Federal Reserve				Commercial Banks			
Assets		Liabilities		Assets		Liabilities	
Securities	$160	$80	Reserves	Reserves	$80	$400	Deposits
		$80	Currency	Loans	$320		

Note: Money supply (M1) = currency + deposits = $480.

Panel 2: Commercial Bank Borrowing $20 from the Fed

Federal Reserve				Commercial Banks			
Assets		Liabilities		Assets		Liabilities	
Securities	$160	$100	Reserves (+$20)	Reserves (+$20)	$100	$500	Deposits (+$100)
Loans (+$20)	$20	$80	Currency	Loans (+$100)	$420	$20	Amount owed to Fed (+$20)

Note: Money supply (M1) = currency + deposits = $580.

$320 billion to $420 billion. (Remember, a required reserve ratio of 20 percent gives a money multiplier of 5; having excess reserves of $20 billion allows the bank to create an additional $20 billion × 5, or $100 billion, in deposits.) The money supply has thus increased from $480 billion to $580 billion. Bank borrowing from the Fed thus leads to an increase in the money supply if the banks loan out their excess reserves.

The Fed can influence bank borrowing, and thus the money supply, through the discount rate. The higher the discount rate, the higher the cost of borrowing and the less borrowing banks will want to do. If the Fed wants to curtail the growth of the money supply, for example, it will raise the discount rate and discourages banks from borrowing from it, restricting the growth of reserves (and ultimately deposits).

Historically, the Fed has not used the discount rate to control the money supply. Prior to 2003 it usually set the discount rate lower than the rate that banks had to pay to borrow money in the private market. Although this provided an incentive for banks to borrow from the Fed, the Fed discouraged borrowing by putting pressure in various ways on the banks not to borrow. This pressure was sometimes called **moral suasion**. On January 9, 2003, the Fed announced a new procedure. Henceforth, the discount rate would be set above the rate that banks pay to borrow money in the private market and moral suasion would no longer be used. Although banks could then borrow from the Fed if they wanted to, they were unlikely to do so except in unusual circumstances because borrowing was cheaper in the private market. In 2008, for the first time since the Great Depression, the Fed opened its discount window not only to depository banks but also to primary dealer credit institutions such as Credit Suisse, which does not take bank deposits. This practice was ended in February 2010, and economists expect the Fed to return to its historical policy of not using the discount window as a regular tool to try to change the money supply.

moral suasion   The pressure that in the past the Fed exerted on member banks to discourage them from borrowing heavily from the Fed.

Open Market Operations

By far the most significant of the Fed's tools for controlling the supply of money is **open market operations**. Congress has authorized the Fed to buy and sell U.S. government securities in the open market. When the Fed purchases a security, it pays for it by writing a check that, when cleared, *expands* the quantity of reserves in the system, increasing the money supply. When the Fed sells a bond, private citizens or institutions pay for it with their bank deposits, which *reduces* the quantity of reserves in the system.

To see how open market operations and reserve controls work, we need to review several key ideas.

open market operations The purchase and sale by the Fed of government securities in the open market; a tool used to expand or contract the amount of reserves in the system and thus the money supply.

Two Branches of Government Deal in Government Securities   The fact that the Fed is able to buy and sell government securities—bills and bonds—may be confusing. In fact, *two* branches of government deal in financial markets for different reasons, and you must keep the two separate in your mind.

First, keep in mind that the Treasury Department is responsible for collecting taxes and paying the federal government's bills. Salary checks paid to government workers, payments to General Dynamics for a new Navy ship, Social Security checks to retirees, and so on, are all written on accounts maintained by the Treasury. Tax receipts collected by the Internal Revenue Service, a Treasury branch, are deposited to these accounts.

If total government spending exceeds tax receipts, the law requires the Treasury to borrow the difference. Recall that the government deficit is $(G - T)$, or government purchases minus net taxes. To finance the deficit, $(G - T)$ is the amount the Treasury must borrow each year. This means that the Treasury *cannot* print money to finance the deficit. The Treasury borrows by issuing bills, bonds, and notes that pay interest. These government securities, or IOUs, are sold to individuals and institutions. Often foreign countries as well as U.S. citizens buy them. As discussed in Chapter 9, the total amount of privately held government securities is the *privately held federal debt*.

The Fed is not the Treasury. Instead, it is a quasi-independent agency authorized by Congress to buy and sell *outstanding* (preexisting) U.S. government securities on the open market. The bonds and bills initially sold by the Treasury to finance the deficit are continuously resold and traded among ordinary citizens, firms, banks, pension funds, and so on. The Fed's participation in that trading affects the quantity of reserves in the system, as we will see.

Because the Fed owns some government securities, some of what the government owes it owes to itself. Recall that the Federal Reserve System's largest single asset is government securities. These securities are nothing more than bills and bonds initially issued by the Treasury to finance the deficit. They were acquired by the Fed over time through direct open market purchases that the Fed made to expand the money supply as the economy expanded.

The Mechanics of Open Market Operations

How do open market operations affect the money supply? Look again at Table 10.1. As you can see, more than half of the Fed's assets consist of the government securities we have been talking about (U.S. Treasury securities).

Suppose the Fed wants to decrease the supply of money. If it can reduce the volume of bank reserves on the liabilities side of its balance sheet, it will force banks, in turn, to reduce their own deposits (to meet the required reserve ratio). Since these deposits are part of the supply of money, the supply of money will contract. (We are continuing to assume that banks hold no excess reserves.)

What will happen if the Fed sells some of its holdings of government securities to the general public? The Fed's holdings of government securities must decrease because the securities it sold will now be owned by someone else. How do the purchasers of securities pay for what they have bought? They pay by writing checks drawn on their banks and payable to the Fed.

Let us look more carefully at how this works, with the help of Table 10.4. In panel 1, the Fed initially has $100 billion of government securities. Its liabilities consist of $20 billion of deposits (which are the reserves of commercial banks) and $80 billion of currency. With the required reserve ratio at 20 percent, the $20 billion of reserves can support $100 billion of deposits in the commercial banks. The commercial banking system is fully loaned up. Panel 1 also shows the financial position of a private citizen, Jane Q. Public. Jane has assets of $5 billion (a large checking account deposit in the bank) and no debts, so her net worth is $5 billion.

Now imagine that the Fed sells $5 billion in government securities to Jane. Jane pays for the securities by writing a check to the Fed, drawn on her bank. The Fed then reduces the reserve account of her bank by $5 billion. The balance sheets of all the participants after this transaction are shown in panel 2. Note that the supply of money (currency plus deposits) has fallen from $180 billion to $175 billion.

This is not the end of the story. As a result of the Fed's sale of securities, the amount of reserves has fallen from $20 billion to $15 billion, while deposits have fallen from $100 billion to $95 billion. With a required reserve ratio of 20 percent, banks must have $.20 \times \$95$ billion, or $19 billion, in reserves. Banks are under their required reserve ratio by $4 billion [$19 billion (the amount they should have) minus $15 billion (the amount they do have)]. What can banks do to get back into reserve requirement balance? Look back on the bank balance sheet. Banks had made

TABLE 10.4 Open Market Operations (The Numbers in Parentheses in Panels 2 and 3 Show the Differences Between Those Panels and Panel 1. All Figures in Billions of Dollars)

Panel 1

Federal Reserve				Commercial Banks				Jane Q. Public			
Assets		Liabilities		Assets		Liabilities		Assets		Liabilities	
Securities	$100	$20	Reserves	Reserves	$20	$100	Deposits	Deposits	$5	$0	Debts
		$80	Currency	Loans	$80					$5	Net Worth

Note: Money supply (M1) = currency + deposits = $180.

Panel 2

Federal Reserve				Commercial Banks				Jane Q. Public			
Assets		Liabilities		Assets		Liabilities		Assets		Liabilities	
Securities (−$5)	$95	$15 (−$5)	Reserves	Reserves (−$5)	$15	$95	Deposits (−$5)	Deposits (−$5)	$0	$0	Debts
		$80	Currency	Loans	$80			Securities (+$5)	$5	$5	Net Worth

Note: Money supply (M1) = currency + deposits = $175.

Panel 3

Federal Reserve				Commercial Banks				Jane Q. Public			
Assets		Liabilities		Assets		Liabilities		Assets		Liabilities	
Securities (−$5)	$95	$15 (−$5)	Reserves	Reserves (−$5)	$15	$75	Deposits (−$25)	Deposits (−$5)	$0	$0	Debts
		$80	Currency	Loans (−$20)	$60			Securities (+$5)	$5	$5	Net Worth

Note: Money supply (M1) = currency + deposits = $155.

loans of $80 billion, supported by the $100 billion deposit. With the smaller deposit, the bank can no longer support $80 billion in loans. The bank will either "call" some of the loans (that is, ask for repayment) or more likely reduce the number of new loans made. As loans shrink, so do deposits in the overall banking system.

The final equilibrium position is shown in panel 3, where commercial banks have reduced their loans by $20 billion. Notice that the change in deposits from panel 1 to panel 3 is $25 billion, which is five times the size of the change in reserves that the Fed brought about through its $5 billion open market sale of securities. This corresponds exactly to our earlier analysis of the money multiplier. The change in money (−$25 billion) is equal to the money multiplier (5) times the change in reserves (−$5 billion).

Now consider what happens when the Fed *purchases* a government security. Suppose you hold $100 in Treasury bills, which the Fed buys from you. The Fed writes you a check for $100, and you turn in your Treasury bills. You then take the $100 check and deposit it in your local bank. This increases the reserves of your bank by $100 and begins a new episode in the money expansion story. With a reserve requirement of 20 percent, your bank can now lend out $80. If that $80 is spent and ends up back in a bank, that bank can lend $64, and so on. (Review Figure 10.3.) The Fed can expand the money supply by buying government securities from people who own them, just the way it reduces the money supply by selling these securities.

Each business day the Open Market Desk in the New York Federal Reserve Bank buys or sells millions of dollars' worth of securities, usually to large security dealers who act as intermediaries between the Fed and the private markets. We can sum up the effect of these open market operations this way:

■ An open market *purchase* of securities by the Fed results in an *increase* in reserves and an *increase* in the supply of money by an amount equal to the money multiplier times the change in reserves.

■ An open market *sale* of securities by the Fed results in a *decrease* in reserves and a *decrease* in the supply of money by an amount equal to the money multiplier times the change in reserves.

Open market operations are the Fed's preferred means of controlling the money supply for several reasons. First, open market operations can be used with some precision. If the Fed needs to change the money supply by just a small amount, it can buy or sell a small volume of government securities. If it wants a larger change in the money supply, it can buy or sell a larger amount. Second, open market operations are extremely flexible. If the Fed decides to reverse course, it can easily switch from buying securities to selling them. Finally, open market operations have a fairly predictable effect on the supply of money. Because banks are obliged to meet their reserve requirements, an open market sale of $100 in government securities will reduce reserves by $100, which will reduce the supply of money by $100 times the money multiplier.

Where does the Fed get the money to buy government securities when it wants to expand the money supply? The Fed simply creates it! In effect, it tells the bank from which it has bought a $100 security that its reserve account (deposit) at the Fed now contains $100 more than it did previously. This is where the power of the Fed, or any central bank, lies. The Fed has the ability to create money at will. In the United States, the Fed exercises this power when it creates money to buy government securities.

Excess Reserves and the Supply Curve for Money

In September 2008 commercial banks began holding huge quantities of excess reserves. This has continued through the time of this writing (March 2013). This is evident from the Fed's balance sheet for January 30, 2013, in Table 10.1, where all but about $110 billion of the $1,645 billion in reserve balances are excess reserves. The holding of excess reserves by commercial banks obviously affects the ability of the Fed to control the money supply. The previous discussion of the three tools assumes that when banks get reserves, they loan them out to the limit they are allowed. Conversely, if they lose reserves, they must cut back loans to get back in compliance with their reserve requirements. The three tools work through the Fed changing the amount of reserves in the banking system, which then affects loans and the money supply. If banks simply hold increased reserves as excess reserves and adjust to a decrease in reserves by decreasing their excess reserves, the tools do not work.

How long this holding of excess reserves will continue is unclear. Banks earn more on their loans than they do on their excess reserves, and as the effects of the 2008–2009 recession ease, banks are likely to go back to making more loans. This excess reserve holding may thus be temporary. In the following chapters we will assume that the Fed can control the money supply, but you should keep in mind that there are times when this assumption may not be realistic. We will in fact relax this assumption in Chapter 12. For now, however, we assume that the supply curve for money is vertical, as depicted in Figure 10.5. It is assumed that the Fed can achieve any particular value of the money supply through one of its three tools.

▶ **FIGURE 10.5**
The Supply of Money
The money supply curve is assumed to be vertical. It is assumed that the Fed can achieve any particular value of the money supply through one of its three tools.

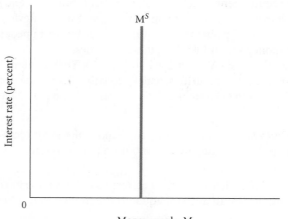

Looking Ahead

This chapter has discussed only the supply side of the money market. In the next chapter, we turn to the demand side of the money market. We will examine the demand for money and see how the supply of and demand for money determine the equilibrium interest rate.

SUMMARY

AN OVERVIEW OF MONEY *p. 189*

1. Money has three distinguishing characteristics: (1) a *means of payment*, or *medium of exchange*; (2) *a store of value*; and (3) *a unit of account*. The alternative to using money is *barter*, in which goods are exchanged directly for other goods. Barter is costly and inefficient in an economy with many different kinds of goods.

2. *Commodity monies* are items that are used as money and that have an intrinsic value in some other use—for example, gold and cigarettes. *Fiat monies* are intrinsically worthless apart from their use as money. To ensure the acceptance of fiat monies, governments use their power to declare money *legal tender* and promise the public they will not debase the currency by expanding its supply rapidly.

3. There are various definitions of money. Currency plus demand deposits plus traveler's checks plus other checkable deposits compose M1, or *transactions money*—money that can be used directly to buy things. The addition of savings accounts and money market accounts (*near monies*) to M1 gives M2, or *broad money*.

HOW BANKS CREATE MONEY *p. 193*

4. The *required reserve ratio* is the percentage of a bank's deposits that must be kept as *reserves* at the nation's central bank, the *Federal Reserve*.

5. Banks create money by making loans. When a bank makes a loan to a customer, it creates a deposit in that customer's account. This deposit becomes part of the money supply. Banks can create money only when they have *excess reserves*—reserves in excess of the amount set by the required reserve ratio.

6. The *money multiplier* is the multiple by which the total supply of money can increase for every dollar increase in reserves. The money multiplier is equal to 1/required reserve ratio.

THE FEDERAL RESERVE SYSTEM *p. 199*

7. The Fed's most important function is controlling the nation's money supply. The Fed also performs several other functions: It clears interbank payments, is responsible for many of the regulations governing banking practices and standards, and acts as a *lender of last resort* for troubled banks that cannot find any other sources of funds. The Fed also acts as the bank for the U.S. government. Beginning in 2008 the Fed greatly expanded its lending activities to the private sector.

HOW THE FEDERAL RESERVE CONTROLS THE MONEY SUPPLY *p. 203*

8. The key to understanding how the Fed controls the money supply is the role of reserves. If the Fed wants to increase the supply of money, it creates more reserves, freeing banks to create additional deposits. If it wants to decrease the money supply, it reduces reserves.

9. The Fed has three tools to control the money supply: (1) changing the required reserve ratio, (2) changing the *discount rate* (the interest rate member banks pay when they borrow from the Fed), and (3) engaging in *open market operations* (the buying and selling of already-existing government securities). To increase the money supply, the Fed can create additional reserves by lowering the discount rate or by buying government securities, or the Fed can increase the number of deposits that can be created from a given quantity of reserves by lowering the required reserve ratio. To decrease the money supply, the Fed can reduce reserves by raising the discount rate or by selling government securities or it can raise the required reserve ratio. If commercial banks hold large quantities of excess reserves, the ability of the Fed to control the money supply is severely limited.

10. For now the money supply curve is assumed to be vertical. It is assumed that the Fed can achieve any particular value of the money supply through one of its three tools.

REVIEW TERMS AND CONCEPTS

barter, *p. 190*

commodity monies, *p. 191*

currency debasement, *p. 192*

discount rate, *p. 204*

excess reserves, *p. 196*

Federal Open Market Committee (FOMC), *p. 200*

Federal Reserve Bank (the Fed), *p. 195*

fiat, *or token, money, p. 191*

financial intermediaries, *p. 193*

legal tender, *p. 191*

lender of last resort, *p. 200*

liquidity property of money, *p. 190*

M1, *or transactions money, p. 192*

M2, *or broad money, p. 193*

MyEconLab Visit **www.myeconlab.com** to complete these exercises online and get instant feedback. Exercises that update with real-time data are marked with 🌐.

medium of exchange, *or* means of payment, *p. 190*

money multiplier, *p. 198*

moral suasion, *p. 205*

near monies, *p. 193*

Open Market Desk, *p. 200*

open market operations, *p. 205*

required reserve ratio, *p. 196*

reserves, *p. 195*

run on a bank, *p. 195*

store of value, *p. 190*

unit of account, *p. 190*

Equations:

M1 ≡ currency held outside banks + demand deposits + traveler's checks + other checkable deposits, *p. 192*

M2 ≡ M1 + savings accounts + money market accounts + other near monies, *p. 193*

Assets ≡ Liabilities + Net Worth, *p. 195*

Excess reserves ≡ actual reserves − required reserves, *p. 196*

$$\text{Money multiplier} \equiv \frac{1}{\text{required reserve ratio}}, \text{ p. 198}$$

PROBLEMS

All problems are available on MyEconLab.

1. In the Republic of Ragu, the currency is the rag. During 2012, the Treasury of Ragu sold bonds to finance the Ragu budget deficit. In all, the Treasury sold 50,000 10-year bonds with a face value of 100 rags each. The total deficit was 5 million rags. Further, assume that the Ragu Central Bank reserve requirement was 20 percent and that in the same year, the bank bought 500,000 rags' worth of outstanding bonds on the open market. Finally, assume that all of the Ragu debt is held by either the private sector (the public) or the central bank.
   a. What is the combined effect of the Treasury sale and the central bank purchase on the total Ragu debt outstanding? On the debt held by the private sector?
   b. What is the effect of the Treasury sale on the money supply in Ragu?
   c. Assuming no leakage of reserves out of the banking system, what is the effect of the central bank purchase of bonds on the money supply?

2. In 2000, the federal debt was being paid down because the federal budget was in surplus. Recall that surplus means that tax collections (*T*) exceed government spending (*G*). The surplus (*T* − *G*) was used to buy back government bonds from the public, reducing the federal debt. As we discussed in this chapter, the main method by which the Fed increases the money supply is to buy government bonds by using open market operations. What is the impact on the money supply of using the fiscal surplus to buy back bonds? In terms of their impacts on the money supply, what is the difference between Fed open market purchases of bonds and Treasury purchases of bonds using tax revenues?

3. For each of the following, determine whether it is an asset or a liability on the accounting books of a bank. Explain why in each case.
   Cash in the vault
   Demand deposits
   Savings deposits
   Reserves
   Loans
   Deposits at the Federal Reserve

4. [Related to the *Economics in Practice* on p. 191] It is well known that cigarettes served as money for prisoners of war in World War II. Do an internet search using the key word cigarettes and write a description of how this came to be and how it worked.

5. If the head of the Central Bank of Japan wanted to expand the supply of money in Japan in 2009, which of the following would do it? Explain your answer.
   Increase the required reserve ratio
   Decrease the required reserve ratio
   Increase the discount rate
   Decrease the discount rate
   Buy government securities in the open market
   Sell government securities in the open market

6. Suppose in the Republic of Madison that the regulation of banking rested with the Madison Congress, including the determination of the reserve ratio. The Central Bank of Madison is charged with regulating the money supply by using open market operations. In April 2013, the money supply was estimated to be 52 million hurls. At the same time, bank reserves were 6.24 million hurls and the reserve requirement was 12 percent. The banking industry, being "loaned up," lobbied the Congress to cut the reserve ratio. The Congress yielded and cut required reserves to 10 percent. What is the potential impact on the money supply? Suppose the central bank decided that the money supply should not be increased. What countermeasures could it take to prevent the Congress from expanding the money supply?

7. The U.S. money supply (M1) at the beginning of 2000 was $1,148 billion broken down as follows: $523 billion in currency, $8 billion in traveler's checks, and $616 billion in checking deposits. Suppose the Fed decided to reduce the money supply by increasing the reserve requirement from 10 percent to 11 percent. Assuming all banks were initially loaned up (had no excess reserves) and currency held outside of banks did not change, how large a change in the money supply would have resulted from the change in the reserve requirement?

8. As king of Medivalia, you are constantly strapped for funds to pay your army. Your chief economic wizard suggests the following plan: "When you collect your tax payments from your subjects, insist on being paid in gold coins. Take those gold coins, melt them down, and remint them with an extra 10 percent of brass thrown in. You will then have 10 percent more money than you started with." What do you think of the plan? Will it work?

9. Why is M2 sometimes a more stable measure of money than M1? Explain in your own words using the definitions of M1 and M2.

10. Do you agree or disagree with each of the following statements? Explain your answers.
    a. When the Treasury of the United States issues bonds and sells them to the public to finance the deficit, the money supply remains unchanged because every dollar of money taken in by the Treasury goes right back into circulation through government spending. This is not true when the Fed sells bonds to the public.
    b. The money multiplier depends on the marginal propensity to save.

*11. When the Fed adds new reserves to the system, some of these new reserves find their way out of the country into foreign banks or foreign investment funds. In addition, some portion of the new reserves ends up in people's pockets and under their mattresses instead of in bank vaults. These "leakages" reduce the money multiplier and sometimes make it very difficult for the Fed to control the money supply precisely. Explain why this is true.

12. You are given this account for a bank:

ASSETS		LIABILITIES	
Reserves	$ 500	$3,500	Deposits
Loans	3,000		

The required reserve ratio is 10 percent.
    a. How much is the bank required to hold as reserves given its deposits of $3,500?
    b. How much are its excess reserves?
    c. By how much can the bank increase its loans?
    d. Suppose a depositor comes to the bank and withdraws $200 in cash. Show the bank's new balance sheet, assuming the bank obtains the cash by drawing down its reserves. Does the bank now hold excess reserves? Is it meeting the required reserve ratio? If not, what can it do?

13. After suffering two years of staggering hyperinflation, the African nation of Zimbabwe officially abandoned its currency, the Zimbabwean dollar, in April 2009 and made the U.S. dollar its official currency. Why would anyone in Zimbabwe be willing to accept U.S. dollars in exchange for goods and services?

14. The following is from an article in *USA TODAY*.

    A small but growing number of cash-strapped communities are printing their own money. Borrowing from a Depression-era idea, they are aiming to help consumers make ends meet and support struggling local businesses. The systems generally work like this: Businesses and individuals form a network to print currency. Shoppers buy it at a discount—say, 95 cents for $1 value—and spend the full value at stores that accept the currency. . . .

    Source: From *USA TODAY*, a division of Gannett Co., Inc. Reprinted with Permission.

    These local currencies are being issued in communities as diverse as small towns in North Carolina and Massachusetts to cities as large as Detroit, Michigan. Do these local currencies qualify as money based on the description of what money is in the chapter?

15. Suppose on your 21st birthday, your eccentric grandmother invites you to her house, takes you into her library, removes a black velvet painting of Elvis Presley from the wall, opens a hidden safe where she removes 50 crisp $100 bills, and hands them to you as a present, claiming you are her favorite grandchild. After thanking your grandmother profusely (and helping her rehang the picture of Elvis), you proceed to your bank and deposit half of your gift in your checking account and half in your savings account. How will these transactions affect M1 and M2? How will these transactions change M1 and M2 in the short run? What about the long run?"

16. Suppose Fred deposits $8,000 in cash into his checking account at the Bank of Bonzo. The Bank of Bonzo has no excess reserves and is subject to a 5 percent required reserve ratio.
    a. Show this transaction in a T-account for the Bank of Bonzo.
    b. Assume the Bank of Bonzo makes the maximum loan possible from Fred's deposit to Clarice and show this transaction in a new T-account.
    c. Clarice decides to use the money she borrowed to take a trip to Tahiti. She writes a check for the entire loan amount to the Tropical Paradise Travel Agency, which deposits the check in its bank, the Iceberg Bank of Barrow, Alaska. When the check clears, the Bonzo Bank transfers the funds to the Iceberg Bank. Show these transactions in a new T-account for the Bonzo Bank and in a T-account for the Iceberg Bank.
    d. What is the maximum amount of deposits that can be created from Fred's initial deposit?
    e. What is the maximum amount of loans that can be created from Fred's initial deposit?

17. What are the three tools the Fed can use to change the money supply? Briefly describe how the Fed can use each of these tools to either increase or decrease the money supply.

* Note: Problems marked with an asterisk are more challenging.

Money Demand and the Equilibrium Interest Rate

11

Having discussed the supply of money in the last chapter, we now turn to the *demand* for money. One goal of this and the previous chapter is to provide a theory of how the interest rate is determined in the macroeconomy. Once we have seen how the interest rate is determined, we can turn to how the Federal Reserve (Fed) affects the interest rate.

Interest Rates and Bond Prices

Interest is the fee that borrowers pay to lenders for the use of their funds. Firms and governments borrow funds by issuing bonds, and they pay interest to the lenders that purchase the bonds. Households also borrow, either directly from banks and finance companies or by taking out mortgages.

Some loans are very simple. You might borrow $1,000 from a bank to be paid back a year from the date you borrowed the funds. If the bank charged you, say, $100 for doing this, the interest rate on the loan would be 10 percent. You would receive $1,000 now and pay back $1,100 at the end of the year—the original $1,000 plus the interest of $100. In this simple case the interest rate is just the interest payment divided by the amount of the loan, namely 10 percent.

Bonds are more complicated loans. Bonds have several properties. First, they are issued with a face value, typically in denominations of $1,000. Second, they come with a maturity date, which is the date the borrower agrees to pay the lender the face value of the bond. Third, there is a fixed payment of a specified amount that is paid to the bondholder each year. This payment is known as a coupon.

Say that company XYZ on January 2, 2014, issued a 15-year bond that had a face value of $1,000 and paid a coupon of $100 per year. On this date the company sold the bond in the bond market. The price at which the bond sold would be whatever price the market determined it to be. Say that the market-determined price was in fact $1,000. (Firms when issuing bonds try to choose the coupon to be such that the price that the bond initially sells for is roughly equal to its face value.) The lender would give XYZ a check for $1,000 and every January for the next 14 years XYZ would send the lender a check for $100. Then on January 2, 2029, XYZ

interest The fee that borrowers pay to lenders for the use of their funds.

LEARNING OBJECTIVES
Define interest and discuss the relationship between interest rates and bond prices

Describe the determinants of money demand

Explain how the equilibrium interest rate is determined

ECONOMICS IN PRACTICE

Professor Serebryakov Makes an Economic Error

In Chekhov's play *Uncle Vanya*, Alexander Vladimirovitch Serebryakov, a retired professor, but apparently not of economics, calls his household together to make an announcement. He has retired to his country estate, but he does not like living there. Unfortunately, the estate does not derive enough income to allow him to live in town. To his gathered household, he thus proposes the following:

> Omitting details, I will put it before you in rough outline. Our estate yields on an average not more than two per cent, on its capital value. I propose to sell it. If we invest the money in suitable securities, we should get from four to five per cent, and I think we might even have a few thousand roubles to spare for buying a small villa in Finland.

This idea was not well received by the household, especially by Uncle Vanya, who lost it for a while and tried to kill Professor Serebryakov, but no one pointed out that this was bad economics. As the beginning of this chapter discusses, if you buy a bond and interest rates rise, the price of your bond falls. What Professor Serebryakov does not realize is that what he is calling the capital value of the estate, on which he is earning 2 percent, is not the value for which he could sell the estate if the interest rate on "suitable" securities is 5 percent. If an investor in Russia can earn 5 percent on these securities, why would he or she buy an estate earning only 2 percent? The price of the estate would have to fall until the return to the investor was 5 percent. To make matters worse, it may have been that the estate was a riskier investment

than the securities, and if this were so, a return higher than 5 percent would have been required on the estate purchase to compensate the investor for the extra risk. This would, of course, lower the price of the estate even more. In short, this is not a scheme by which the professor could earn more money than what the estate is currently yielding. Perhaps had Uncle Vanya taken an introductory economics course and known this, he would have been less agitated.

THINKING PRACTICALLY

1. What would happen to the value of the estate if the interest rate on the securities that Professor Serebryakov is talking about fell?

would send the lender a check for the face value of the bond—$1,000—plus the last coupon payment—$100—and that would square all accounts. In this example the interest rate that the lender receives each year on his or her $1,000 investment is 10 percent. If, on the other hand, the market-determined price of the XYZ bond at the time of issue were only $900, then the interest rate that the lender receives would be larger than 10 percent. The lender pays $900 and receives $100 each year. This is an interest rate of roughly 11.1 percent.

A key relationship that we will use in this chapter is that market-determined prices of existing bonds and interest rates are inversely related. The fact that the coupon on a bond is unchanged over time does not mean that a bond's price is insulated from interest rate movements. Say that after XYZ issued its bond, interest rates went up so that a company similar to XYZ when issuing a 15-year bond had to choose a coupon of $200 to have its bond initially sell for $1,000. At $1,000 this bond is clearly a better deal than the XYZ bond at $1,000 because the coupon is larger. If the owner of the XYZ bond wanted to sell it, what price could he or she get? It should be obvious that he or she could not get $1,000 since people could buy the other bond for $1,000 and earn more. The price of the XYZ bond would have to fall to have investors be indifferent between buying it and buying the other bond. In other words, when interest rates rise, the prices of existing bonds fall.

It is important to realize that the bond market directly determines prices of bonds, not interest rates. Given a bond's market-determined price, its face value, its maturity, and its coupon, the interest rate, or yield, on that bond can be calculated. Interest rates are thus *indirectly* determined by the bond market. Although each bond generally has at least a slightly different interest rate, we will assume for simplicity in this and the following chapters that there is only one interest rate. (Appendix A to this chapter provides some detail on various types of interest rates.) In fact, we will assume in the following analysis that there is only one type of bond. The (one) interest rate is the market-determined interest rate on this bond.

The Demand for Money

The factors and forces determining the demand for money are central issues in macroeconomics. As we shall see, the interest rate and nominal income influence how much money households and firms choose to hold.

Before we proceed, we must emphasize one point that may be troublesome. When we speak of the demand for money, we are not asking these questions: How much cash would you like to have? How much income would you like to earn? How much wealth would you like? (The answer to these questions is presumably "as much as possible.") Instead, we are concerned with how much of your financial assets you want to hold *in the form of money*, which does not earn interest, versus how much you want to hold in interest-bearing securities such as bonds. We take as given the *total* amount of financial assets. Our concern here is with how these assets are divided between money and interest-bearing securities.

The Transaction Motive

How much money to hold involves a trade-off between the liquidity of money and the interest income offered by other kinds of assets. The main reason for holding money instead of interest-bearing assets is that money is useful for buying things. Economists call this the **transaction motive**. This rationale for holding money is at the heart of the discussion that follows.[1]

To keep our analysis of the demand for money clear, we need a few simplifying assumptions. First, we assume that there are only two kinds of assets available to households: bonds and money. By "bonds" we mean interest-bearing securities of all kinds. As previously noted, we are assuming that there is only one type of bond and only one market-determined interest rate. By "money" we mean currency in circulation and deposits in checking accounts that do not pay interest.[2]

Second, we assume that income for the typical household is "bunched up." It arrives once a month at the beginning of the month. Spending, by contrast, is spread out over time; we assume that spending occurs at a completely uniform rate throughout the month—that is, that the same amount is spent each day (Figure 11.1). The mismatch between the timing of money inflow and the timing of money outflow is sometimes called the **nonsynchronization of income and spending**.

Finally, we assume that spending for the month is equal to income for the month. Because we are focusing on the transactions demand for money and not on its use as a store of value, this assumption is perfectly reasonable.

transaction motive   The main reason that people hold money—to buy things.

nonsynchronization of income and spending   The mismatch between the timing of money inflow to the household and the timing of money outflow for household expenses.

◀ **FIGURE 11.1**
The Nonsynchronization of Income and Spending
Income arrives only once a month, but spending takes place continuously.

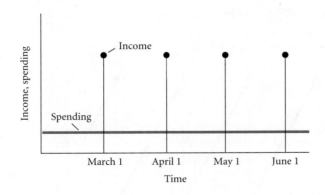

---

[1] The model that we discuss here is known in the economics profession as the Baumol/Tobin model, after the two economists who independently derived it, William Baumol and James Tobin.

[2] Although we are assuming that checking accounts do not pay interest, many do. Fortunately, all that we really need to assume here is that the interest rate on checking accounts is less than the interest rate on "bonds." Suppose bonds pay 10 percent interest and checking accounts pay 5 percent. (Checking accounts must pay less than bonds. Otherwise, everyone would hold all their wealth in checking accounts and none in bonds because checking accounts are more convenient.) When it comes to choosing whether to hold bonds or money, the difference in the interest rates on the two matters. People are concerned about how much extra interest they will earn from holding bonds instead of money. For simplicity, we are assuming in the following discussion that the interest rate on checking accounts is zero.

Given these assumptions, how would a rational person (household) decide how much of monthly income to hold as money and how much to hold as interest-bearing bonds? Suppose Jim decides to deposit his entire paycheck in his checking account. Let us say that Jim earns $1,200 per month. The pattern of Jim's bank account balance is illustrated in Figure 11.2. At the beginning of the month, Jim's balance is $1,200. As the month rolls by, Jim draws down his balance, writing checks or withdrawing cash to pay for the things he buys. At the end of the month, Jim's bank account balance is down to zero. Just in time, he receives his next month's paycheck, deposits it, and the process begins again.

One useful statistic we need to calculate is the *average balance* in Jim's account. Jim spends his money at a constant $40 per day ($40 per day times 30 days per month = $1,200). His average balance is just his starting balance ($1,200) plus his ending balance (0) divided by 2, or ($1,200 + 0)/2 = $600. For the first half of the month, Jim has more than his average of $600 on deposit, and for the second half of the month, he has less than his average.

Is anything wrong with Jim's strategy? Yes. If he follows the plan described, Jim is giving up interest on his funds, interest he could be earning if he held some of his funds in interest-bearing bonds instead of in his checking account. How could he manage his funds to give himself more interest?

Instead of depositing his entire paycheck in his checking account at the beginning of the month, Jim could put half his paycheck into his checking account and buy a bond with the other half. By doing this, he would run out of money in his checking account halfway through the month. At a spending rate of $40 per day, his initial deposit of $600 would last only 15 days. Jim would have to sell his bond halfway through the month and deposit the $600 from the sale of the bond in his checking account to pay his bills during the second half of the month.

Jim's money holdings (checking account balances) if he follows this strategy are shown in Figure 11.3. When he follows the buy-a-$600-bond strategy, Jim reduces the average amount of money in his checking account. Comparing the dashed green lines (old strategy) with the solid green lines (buy-$600-bond strategy), his average bank balance is exactly half of what it was with the first strategy.[3]

The buy-a-$600-bond strategy seems sensible. The object of this strategy was to keep some funds in bonds, where they could earn interest, instead of being "idle" money. Why should he stop there? Another possibility would be for Jim to put only $400 into his checking account on the first of the month and buy two $400 bonds. The $400 in his account will last only 10 days if he spends $40 per day, so after 10 days he must sell one of the bonds and deposit the $400 from the sale in his checking account. This will last through the 20th of the month, at which point he must sell the second bond and deposit the other $400. This strategy lowers Jim's average money holding (checking account balance) even further, reducing his money holdings to an average of only $200 per month, with correspondingly higher average holdings of interest-earning bonds.

▶ **FIGURE 11.2**
Jim's Monthly Checking Account Balances: Strategy 1
Jim could decide to deposit his entire paycheck ($1,200) into his checking account at the start of the month and run his balance down to zero by the end of the month. In this case, his average balance would be $600.

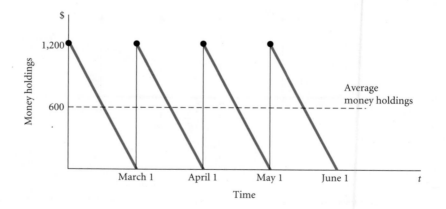

---

[3] Jim's average balance for the first half of the month is (starting balance + ending balance)/2, or ($600 + 0)/2 = $300. His average for the second half of the month is also $300. His average for the month as a whole is $300. For simplicity, we are ignoring in this discussion the interest income that Jim earns on his bond strategy. His total income is in fact higher than $1,200 per month when he holds some bonds during the month because of the interest income he is earning.

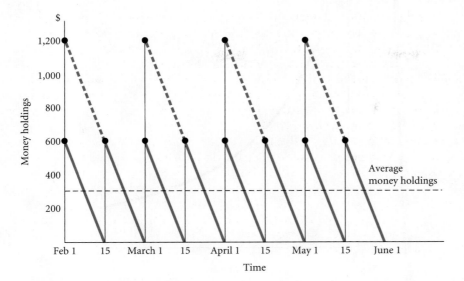

◀ **FIGURE 11.3**
Jim's Monthly Checking Account Balances: Strategy 2
Jim could also choose to put half of his paycheck into his checking account and buy a bond with the other half of his income. At midmonth, Jim would sell the bond and deposit the $600 into his checking account to pay the second half of the month's bills. Following this strategy, Jim's average money holdings would be $300.

You can imagine Jim going even further. Why not hold all wealth in the form of bonds (where it earns interest) and make transfers from bonds to money every time he makes a purchase? If selling bonds, transferring funds to checking accounts, and making trips to the bank were without cost, Jim would never hold money for more than an instant. Each time he needed to pay cash for something or to write a check, he would go to the bank or call the bank, transfer the exact amount of the transaction to his checking account, and withdraw the cash or write the check to complete the transaction. If he did this constantly, he would squeeze the most interest possible out of his funds because he would never hold assets that did not earn interest.

In practice, money management of this kind is costly. There are brokerage fees and other costs to buy or sell bonds, and time must be spent waiting in line at the bank or at an ATM. At the same time, it is costly to hold assets in non-interest-bearing form because they lose potential interest revenue.

We have a trade-off problem of the type that pervades economics. Switching more often from bonds to money raises the interest revenue Jim earns (because the more times he switches, the less, on average, he has to hold in his checking account and the more he can keep in bonds), but this increases his money management costs. Less switching means more interest revenue lost (because average money holdings are higher) but lower money management costs (fewer purchases and sales of bonds, less time spent waiting in bank lines, fewer trips to the bank, and so on). Given this trade-off, there is a level of average money balances that earns Jim the most profit, taking into account both the interest earned on bonds and the costs paid for switching from bonds to money. This level is his *optimal balance.*

How does the interest rate affect the number of switches that Jim makes and thus the average money balance he chooses to hold? It is easy to see why an increase in the interest rate lowers the optimal money balance. If the interest rate were only 2 percent, it would not be worthwhile to give up much liquidity by holding bonds instead of cash or checking balances. However, if the interest rate were 30 percent, the opportunity cost of holding money instead of bonds would be quite high and we would expect people to keep most of their funds in bonds and to spend considerable time managing their money balances. The interest rate represents the opportunity cost of holding money (and therefore not holding bonds, which pay interest). The higher the interest rate, the higher the opportunity cost of holding money and the less money people will want to hold. When interest rates are high, people want to take advantage of the high return on bonds, so they choose to hold very little money. Appendix B to this chapter provides a detailed example of this principle.

A demand curve for money, with the interest rate representing the "price" of money, would look like the curve labeled M^d in Figure 11.4. At higher interest rates, bonds are more attractive than money, so people hold less money because they must make a larger sacrifice in interest for each dollar of money they hold. The curve in Figure 11.4 slopes downward, just like an ordinary

▶ **FIGURE 11.4**

The Demand Curve for Money Balances

The quantity of money demanded (the amount of money households and firms want to hold) is a function of the interest rate. Because the interest rate is the opportunity cost of holding money balances, increases in the interest rate reduce the quantity of money that firms and households want to hold and decreases in the interest rate increase the quantity of money that firms and households want to hold.

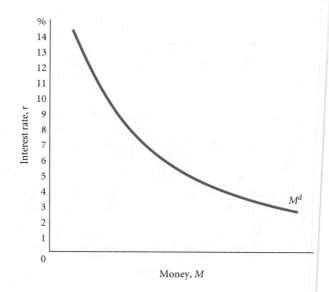

demand curve for oranges or shoes. There is an inverse relationship between the interest rate and the quantity of money demanded.[4]

The Speculation Motive

A number of other theories have been offered to explain why the quantity of money households want to hold may rise when interest rates fall and fall when interest rates rise. One theory involves household expectations and the fact, as discussed at the beginning of this chapter, that interest rates and bond prices are inversely related.

Consider your desire to hold money balances instead of bonds. If market interest rates are higher than normal, you may expect them to come down in the future. If and when interest rates fall, the bonds that you bought when interest rates were high will increase in price. When interest rates are high, the opportunity cost of holding cash balances is high and there is a **speculation motive** for holding bonds in lieu of cash. You are "speculating" that interest rates will fall in the future and thus that bond prices will rise.

speculation motive One reason for holding bonds instead of money: Because the market price of interest-bearing bonds is inversely related to the interest rate, investors may want to hold bonds when interest rates are high with the hope of selling them when interest rates fall.

Similarly, when market interest rates are lower than normal, you may expect them to rise in the future. Rising interest rates will bring about a decline in the price of existing bonds. Thus, when interest rates are low, it is a good time to be holding money and not bonds. When interest rates are low, not only is the opportunity cost of holding cash balances low, but also there is a speculative motive for holding a larger amount of money. Why should you put money into bonds now when you expect interest rates to rise in the future and thus bond prices to fall?

The Total Demand for Money

So far we have talked only about household demand for checking account balances. However, the total quantity of money demanded in the economy is the sum of the demand for checking account balances *and cash* by both households *and firms*.

The trade-off for firms is the same as it was for Jim. Like households, firms must manage their money. They have payrolls to meet and purchases to make, they receive cash and checks from sales, and many firms that deal with the public must make change—they need cash in the cash register. Thus, just like Jim, firms need money to engage in ordinary transactions.

---

[4] The theory of money demand presented here assumes that people know the exact timing of their income and spending. In practice, both have some uncertainty attached to them. For example, some income payments may be unexpectedly delayed a few days or weeks, and some expenditures may arise unexpectedly (such as the cost of repairing a plumbing problem). Because people know that this uncertainty exists, as a precaution against unanticipated delays in income receipts or unanticipated expenses, they may choose to hold more money than the strict transactions motive would suggest. This reason for holding money is sometimes called the *precautionary motive*.

ECONOMICS IN PRACTICE

ATMs and the Demand for Money

Years ago the typical college student spent many a Friday afternoon visiting a bank to make sure he or she had enough cash for weekend activities. Today the typical student, whether in the United States or abroad, doesn't need to plan ahead. As a result of automated teller machines (ATMs), access to your bank account is available 24-7. What difference has the spread of ATMs made on the demand for money?

Italy makes a great case study of the effects of the spread of ATMs on the demand for money. In Italy, virtually all checking accounts pay interest. What doesn't pay interest is cash. So from the point of view of the model in this chapter, we can think of Italian checking accounts as (interest-earning) "bonds" and cash as (non-interest-earning) "money." In other words, in Italy there is an interest cost to carrying cash instead of depositing the cash in a checking account. A recent paper by three economists—Orazio Attanasio from University College London, Luigi Guiso from the Einaudi Institute for Economics and Finance (EIEF), and Tullio Jappelli from the University of Naples Federico II, Italy—took advantage of this institutional fact to see how the availability of ATMs influence the demand for cash (non-interest-earning money).[1]

Why do we think there might be an effect? Think back to the college student of 20 years ago. On Friday, he or she might have withdrawn cash in excess of expected weekly needs just in case. With ATMs everywhere, cash can be withdrawn as needed. This means that the amount of cash needed to support a given level of consumption should fall as ATMs proliferate. This is exactly what Attansio, Guiso, and Jappelli found in Italy in the first six years of ATM adoption. In 1989, ATM adoption in Italy was relatively low, about 15 percent of the population. By 1995, ATM use had risen to about 40 percent. What happened to cash holdings in this period? The amount of cash divided by total consumption fell from 3.8 percent to 2.8 percent. The study also found, as we would expect from our discussion in the text, that the demand for cash responds to changes in the interest rate paid on checking accounts. The higher the interest rate, the less cash held. In other words, when the interest rate on checking accounts rises, people go to ATM machines more often and take out less in cash each time, thereby keeping, on average, more in checking accounts earning the higher interest rate.

THINKING PRACTICALLY

1. Suppose most or all ATM machines increased the fee they charged *per transaction*. What would this do to the transaction demand for money?

[1] Orazio Attanasio, Luigi Guiso, and Tullio Jappelli, *"The Demand for Money, Financial Innovation and the Welfare Costs of Inflation: An Analysis with Household Data,"* Journal of Political Economy, *April 2002.*

However, firms as well as households can hold their assets in interest-earning form. Firms manage their assets the same way households do, keeping some in cash, some in their checking accounts, and some in bonds. A higher interest rate raises the opportunity cost of money for firms as well as for households and thus reduces the demand for money.

The same trade-off holds for cash. We all walk around with some money in our pockets, but not thousands of dollars, for routine transactions. We carry, on average, about what we think we will need, not more, because there are costs—risks of being robbed and forgone interest. At any given moment, there is a demand for money—for cash and checking account balances. Although households and firms need to hold balances for everyday transactions, their demand has a limit. For both households and firms, the quantity of money demanded at any moment depends on the opportunity cost of holding money, a cost determined by the interest rate.

The Effect of Nominal Income on the Demand for Money

In the model we began constructing in Chapter 8, we let Y denote aggregate output and income. We noted at the beginning of Chapter 8 that you should think of Y as being in real terms rather than in nominal terms. This has in fact made no difference so far because we have not yet introduced the aggregate price level. We now need to do this, and we will let P denote the aggregate price level. Y is real output and income and $P \cdot Y$ is nominal output and income.

We need to introduce nominal income at this stage because in the above theory of the demand for money, everything is nominal. Jim's income of $1,200 per month is nominal, and his money holdings are nominal. In the demand for money curve in Figure 11.4, the quantity of money, M, is nominal. Figure 11.4 says that the nominal demand for money depends on the interest rate.

▶ **FIGURE 11.5** **An Increase in Nominal Aggregate Output (Income) ($P \cdot Y$) Shifts the Money Demand Curve to the Right**

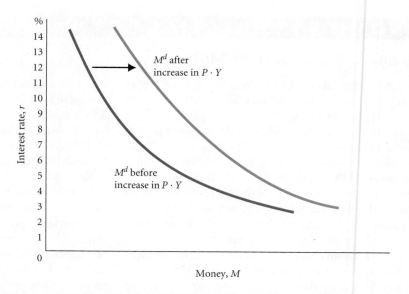

TABLE 11.1 Determinants of Money Demand

1. The interest rate: r (The quantity of money demanded is a negative function of the interest rate.)
2. Aggregate nominal output (income) $P \cdot Y$
   a. Real aggregate output (income): Y (An increase in Y shifts the money demand curve to the right.)
   b. The aggregate price level: P (An increase in P shifts the money demand curve to the right.)

What happens to Jim's strategy if his income is $2,400 per month rather than $1,200 per month? If we continue to assume that he spends all of his income during the month, then everything is just double from what it was before. If, for example, his optimal strategy was to go to the bank once during the middle of the month (as in Figure 11.3), then his average money holdings will now be $600, double the $300 when his income was $1,200 per month. The demand for (nominal) money thus increases as nominal income increases. This means that the demand for money curve in Figure 11.4 shifts out when nominal income increases. This is drawn in Figure 11.5. An increase in $P \cdot Y$ shifts the curve out.

It is important to realize that $P \cdot Y$ can increase because P increases or because Y increases (or both). Thus an increase in P, the aggregate price level, increases the demand for money, as does an increase in Y, real aggregate income.

Table 11.1 summarizes everything we have said about the demand for money. The demand for money depends negatively on the interest rate, r, and positively on real income, Y, and the price level, P.

The Equilibrium Interest Rate

We are now in a position to consider one of the key questions in macroeconomics: How is the interest rate determined in the economy?

Financial markets (what we call the money market) work very well in the United States. Almost all financial markets clear—that is, almost all reach an equilibrium where quantity demanded equals quantity supplied. In the money market, the point at which the quantity of money demanded equals the quantity of money supplied determines the equilibrium interest rate in the economy. This explanation sounds simple, but it requires elaboration.

Supply and Demand in the Money Market

We saw in Chapter 10 that the Fed can control the money supply through its manipulation of the amount of reserves in the economy by using one of the three tools (the reserve requirement ratio, the discount rate, and open market operations). For now we are assuming that the money supply curve is vertical. (Review Figure 10.5 on p. 208.)

Figure 11.6 superimposes the vertical money supply curve from Figure 10.5 on the downward-sloping money demand curve. Only at interest rate r^* is the quantity of money in circulation (the money supply) equal to the quantity of money demanded. To understand why r^* is an equilibrium, we need to ask what forces drive the interest rate to r^*. Keep in mind in the following discussion that when the Fed fixes the money supply it also fixes the supply of bonds. The decision of households and firms is to decide what fraction of their funds to hold in non-interest-bearing money versus interest-bearing bonds. At the equilibrium interest rate r^* in Figure 11.6 the demand for bonds by households and firms is equal to the supply.

Consider r_0 in Figure 11.6, an interest rate higher than the equilibrium rate. At this interest rate households and firms would want to hold more bonds than the Fed is supplying (and less money than the Fed is supplying). They would bid the price of bonds up and thus the interest rate down. The bond market would clear when the price of bonds rose enough to correspond to an interest rate of r^*. At interest rate r_1 in Figure 11.6, which is lower than the equilibrium rate, households and firms would want to hold fewer bonds than the fed is supplying (and more money than the Fed is supplying). They would bid the price of bonds down and thus the interest rate up. The bond market would clear when the price of bonds fell enough to correspond to an interest rate of r^*.

Changing the Money Supply to Affect the Interest Rate

With an understanding of equilibrium in the money market, we now see how the Fed can affect the interest rate. Suppose the current interest rate is 7 percent and the Fed wants to reduce the interest rate. To do so, it would expand the money supply. Figure 11.7 shows how such an expansion would work. To expand M^s, the Fed can reduce the reserve requirement, cut the discount rate, or buy U.S. government securities on the open market. All these practices expand the quantity of reserves in the system. Banks can make more loans, and the money supply expands even more. (Review Chapter 10 if you are unsure why.) In Figure 11.7, the initial money supply curve, M_0^s, shifts to the right, to M_1^s. At M_1^s the supply of bonds is smaller than it was at M_0^s.

As the money supply expands from M_0^s to M_1^s, the supply of bonds is decreasing, which drives up the price of bonds. At M_1^s the equilibrium price of bonds corresponds to an interest rate of 4 percent. So the new equilibrium interest rate is 4 percent.

If the Fed wanted to increase the interest rate, it would contract the money supply. It could do so by increasing the reserve requirement, by raising the discount rate, or by selling U.S. government securities in the open market. Whichever tool the Fed chooses, the result would be lower reserves and a lower supply of money. The supply of money curve in Figure 11.7 would shift to the left, and the equilibrium interest rate would rise. (As an exercise, draw a graph of this situation and explain why the interest rate would rise.)

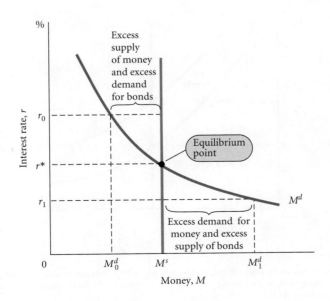

◀ **FIGURE 11.6**
Adjustments in the Money Market
Equilibrium exists in the money market when the supply of money is equal to the demand for money and thus when the supply of bonds is equal to the demand for bonds. *At* r_0 the price of bonds would be bid up (and thus the interest rate down), and at r_1 the price of bonds would be bid down (and thus the interest rate up).

▶ **FIGURE 11.7**
The Effect of an Increase in the Supply of Money on the Interest Rate
An increase in the supply of money from M_0^s to M_1^s lowers the rate of interest from 7 percent to 4 percent.

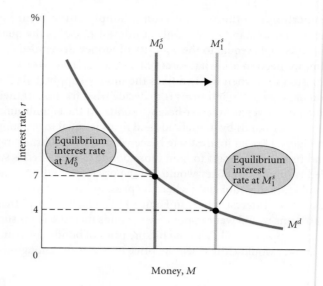

Increases in $P \cdot Y$ and Shifts in the Money Demand Curve

Changes in the supply of money are not the only factors that influence the equilibrium interest rate. Shifts in money demand can do the same thing.

Recall that the demand for money depends on both the interest rate, r, and nominal income $(P \cdot Y)$. An increase in $P \cdot Y$ shifts the money demand curve to the right. This is illustrated in Figure 11.8. If the increase in $P \cdot Y$ is such as to shift the money demand curve from M_0^d to M_1^d, the result is an increase in the equilibrium level of the interest rate from 4 percent to 7 percent. A decrease in $P \cdot Y$ would shift M^d to the left, and the equilibrium interest rate would fall. Remember that $P \cdot Y$ can change because the price level P changes or because real income Y changes (or both).

Zero Interest Rate Bound

By the middle of 2008 the Fed had driven the short-term interest rate close to zero, and it has remained at essentially zero through the time of this writing (March 2013). The Fed does this, of course, by increasing the money supply until the intersection of the money supply at the demand for money curve is at an interest rate of roughly zero. At a zero interest rate people are indifferent whether they hold non-interest-bearing money or zero interest-bearing bonds. The Fed cannot drive the interest rate lower than zero.[5]

▶ **FIGURE 11.8**
The Effect of an Increase in Nominal Income ($P \cdot Y$) on the Interest Rate
An increase in nominal income ($P \cdot Y$) shifts the money demand curve from M_0^d to M_1^d, which raises the equilibrium interest rate from 4 percent to 7 percent.

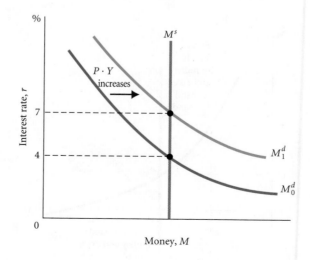

---

[5] In fact there are times when an interest rate can be negative. Financial institutions may at times be willing to hold bonds with a negative interest rate over cash (with a zero interest rate) for security purposes. The financial institutions in effect pay a small fee to hold the bonds—the fee being the negative interest rate.

Looking Ahead

One of the main aims of this chapter and the last one has been to explain how the Fed can change the interest rate and the money supply through open market operations. Purchases of government securities lowers the interest rate and expands the money supply, and sales of government securities raises the interest rate and contracts the money supply. We have not yet discussed, however, why the Fed might want to change the interest rate. We have also not considered the determination of the aggregate price level. We discuss both of these issues in the next chapter. It is the key chapter regarding the core of macro theory.

SUMMARY

INTEREST RATES AND BOND PRICES *p. 213*

1. *Interest* is the fee that borrowers pay to lenders for the use of their funds. Interest rates and bond prices are inversely related. Although there are many different interest rates in the United States, we assume for simplicity that there is only one interest rate in the economy.

THE DEMAND FOR MONEY *p. 215*

2. The demand for money depends negatively on the interest rate. The higher the interest rate, the higher the opportunity cost (more interest forgone) from holding money and the less money people will want to hold. An increase in the interest rate reduces the quantity demanded for money, and the money demand curve slopes downward.

3. The demand for money depends positively on nominal income. Aggregate nominal income is $P \cdot Y$, where P is the aggregate price level and Y is the aggregate real income.

An increase in either P or Y increases the demand for money.

THE EQUILIBRIUM INTEREST RATE *p. 220*

4. The point at which the quantity of money supplied equals the quantity of money demanded determines the equilibrium interest rate in the economy. An excess supply of money will cause households and firms to buy more bonds, driving the interest rate down. An excess demand for money will cause households and firms to move out of bonds, driving the interest rate up.

5. The Fed can affect the equilibrium interest rate by changing the supply of money using one of its three tools—the required reserve ratio, the discount rate, or open market operations.

6. An increase in either P or Y, which shifts the money demand curve to the right, increases the equilibrium interest rate. A decrease in either P or Y decreases the equilibrium interest rate.

REVIEW TERMS AND CONCEPTS

interest, *p. 213*

nonsynchronization of income and spending, *p. 215*

speculation motive, *p. 218*

transaction motive, *p. 215*

PROBLEMS

All problems are available on MyEconLab.

1. State whether you agree or disagree with the following statements and explain why.
   a. When the real economy expands (Y rises), the demand for money expands. As a result, households hold more cash and the supply of money expands.
   b. Inflation, a rise in the price level, causes the demand for money to decline. Because inflation causes money to be worth less, households want to hold less of it.
   c. If the Fed buys bonds in the open market and at the same time we experience a recession, interest rates will no doubt rise.

2. During 2003, we began to stop worrying that inflation was a problem. Instead, we began to worry about deflation, a decline in the price level. Assume that the Fed decided to hold the money supply constant. What impact would deflation have on interest rates?

3. [Related to the *Economics in Practice* on *p. 219*] How many times a week do you use an ATM? If ATMs were not available, would you carry more cash? Would you keep more money in your checking account? How many times a day do you use cash?

4. What if, at a low level of interest rates, the money demand curve became nearly horizontal, as in the following graph. That is, with interest rates so low, the public would not find it attractive to hold bonds; thus, money demand would be very high. Many argue that this was the position of the U.S. economy in 2003. If the Fed decided to expand the money supply in the graph, what would be the impact on interest rates?

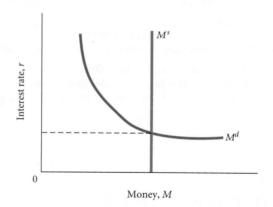

5. [Related to the *Economics in Practice* on *p. 214*] The *Economics in Practice* states that the capital value of Professor Serebryakov's estate is not the value for which he could sell the estate if the interest rate on "suitable" securities is higher than the average yield from the estate. What would happen to:
   a. the value of the estate if the interest rate on "suitable" securities rose?
   b. the value of the estate if investment in the estate was suddenly viewed as being less risky than investment in the securities?
   c. the yield on the securities if the securities were suddenly viewed as being more risky than was previously thought?

6. During the fourth quarter of 1993, real GDP in the United States grew at an annual rate of over 7 percent. During 1994, the economy continued to expand with modest inflation.

(Y rose at a rate of 4 percent and P increased about 3 percent.) At the beginning of 1994, the prime interest rate (the interest rate that banks offer their best, least risky customers) stood at 6 percent, where it remained for over a year. By the beginning of 1995, the prime rate had increased to over 8.5 percent.
   a. By using money supply and money demand curves, show the effects of the increase in Y and P on interest rates, assuming *no change* in the money supply.
   b. On a separate graph, show that the interest rate can rise even if the Federal Reserve expands the money supply as long as it does so more slowly than money demand is increasing.

7. Illustrate the following situations using supply and demand curves for money:
   a. The Fed buys bonds in the open market during a recession.
   b. During a period of rapid inflation, the Fed increases the reserve requirement.
   c. The Fed acts to hold interest rates constant during a period of high inflation.
   d. During a period of no growth in GDP and zero inflation, the Fed lowers the discount rate.
   e. During a period of rapid real growth of GDP, the Fed acts to increase the reserve requirement.

8. During a recession, interest rates may fall even if the Fed takes no action to expand the money supply. Why? Use a graph to explain.

9. During the summer of 1997, Congress and the president agreed on a budget package to balance the federal budget. The "deal," signed into law by President Clinton in August as the Taxpayer Relief Act of 1997, contained substantial tax cuts and expenditure reductions. The tax reductions were scheduled to take effect immediately, however, while the expenditure cuts would come mostly in 1999 to 2002. Thus, in 1998, the package was seen by economists to be mildly expansionary. If the result is an increase in the growth of real output/income, what would you expect to happen to interest rates if the Fed holds the money supply (or the rate of growth of the money supply) constant? What would the Fed do if it wanted to raise interest rates? What if it wanted to lower interest rates? Illustrate with graphs.

10. The demand for money in a country is given by

$$M^d = 10,000 - 10,000r + P \cdot Y$$

where M^d is money demand in dollars, r is the interest rate (a 10 percent interest rate means $r = 0.1$), and $P \cdot Y$ is national income. Assume that $P \cdot Y$ is initially 5,000.
   a. Graph the amount of money demanded (on the horizontal axis) against the interest rate (on the vertical axis).
   b. Suppose the money supply (M^s) is set by the central bank at $10,000. On the same graph you drew for part a., add the money supply curve. What is the equilibrium rate of interest? Explain how you arrived at your answer.
   c. Suppose income rises from $P \cdot Y = 5,000$ to $P \cdot Y = 7,500$. What happens to the money demand curve you drew in part a.? Draw the new curve if there is one. What happens to the equilibrium interest rate if the central bank does not change the supply of money?
   d. If the central bank wants to keep the equilibrium interest rate at the same value as it was in part b., by how much

should it increase or decrease the supply of money given the new level of national income?

e. Suppose the shift in part c. has occurred and the money supply remains at $10,000 but there is no observed change in the interest rate. What might have happened that could explain this?

11. The United States entered a deep recession at the end of 2007. The Fed under Ben Bernanke used aggressive monetary policy to prevent the recession from becoming another Great Depression. The Fed Funds target rate was 5.25 percent in the fall of 2007; by mid-2008, it stood at 2 percent; and in January 2009, it went to a range of 0-0.25 percent, where it still stood through mid-2013. Lower interest rates reduce the cost of borrowing and encourage firms to borrow and invest. They also have an effect on the value of the bonds (private and government) outstanding in the economy. Explain briefly but clearly why the value of bonds changes when interest rates change. Go to federalreserve.gov, click on "Economic Research & Data," and click on "Flow of Funds." Look at the most recent release and find balance sheet table B.100. How big is the value of Credit Market Instruments held by households?

12. Normally, people in the United States and from around the world think of highly-rated corporate or government bonds as a safe place to put their savings relative to common stocks. Because the stock market had performed so poorly during the recession and because many foreigners turned to the United States as a safe place to invest, bond sales boomed.

If you were a holder of high-grade fixed-rate bonds that you purchased a few years earlier when rates were much higher, you found yourself with big capital gains. That is, as rates went lower, the value of previously issued bonds increased. Many investment advisers in late 2010 were telling their clients to avoid bonds because inflation was going to come back.

a. Suppose you bought a $10,000 ten-year fixed-rate bond issued by the U.S. Treasury in July 2007 that paid 5% interest. In July 2010, new seven-year fixed-rate bonds were being sold by the Treasury that paid 2.43%. Explain clearly what was likely to have happened to the value of your bond which still has 7 years to run paying 5%.

b. Why would bond prices rise if people feared a recession was coming?

c. Why would fear of inflation lead to losses for bondholders?

d. Look back and see what happened in late 2010 into 2011. Did the Fed keep rates low? Did the recession end? Did we see the start of inflation? Explain.

13. Explain what will happen to holdings of bonds and money if there is an excess supply of money in the economy. What will happen if there is an excess demand for money in the economy? What will happen to interest rates in each of these cases?

14. The island nation of Macadamia recently experienced an 800 percent jump in tourism, increasing income throughout the island. Suppose the Macadamia money market was in equilibrium prior to the rise in tourism. What impact will the increase in income have on the equilibrium interest rate in Macadamia, assuming no change in the supply of money? What will the Macadamia Central Bank have to do to keep the increase in income from impacting the interest rate?

15. All else equal, what effect will an expansionary fiscal policy have on the money market, and how will this change impact the effectiveness of the fiscal policy? Draw a graph to illustrate your answer.

16. Explain the differences between the transaction motive for holding money and the speculation motive for holding money.

CHAPTER 11 APPENDIX A

The Various Interest Rates in the U.S. Economy

Although there are many different interest rates in the economy, they tend to move up or down with one another. Here we discuss some of their differences. We first look at the relationship between interest rates on securities with different *maturities*, or terms. We then briefly discuss some of the main interest rates in the U.S. economy.

The Term Structure of Interest Rates

The *term structure of interest rates* is the relationship among the interest rates offered on securities of different maturities. The key here is understanding issues such as these: How are these different rates related? Does a 2-year security (an IOU that promises to repay principal, plus interest, after 2 years) pay a lower annual rate than a 1-year security (an IOU to be repaid, with interest, after 1 year)? What happens to the rate of interest offered on 1-year securities if the rate of interest on 2-year securities increases?

Assume that you want to invest some money for 2 years and at the end of the 2 years you want it back. Assume that you want to buy government securities. For this analysis, we restrict your choices to two: (1) You can buy a 2-year security today and hold it for 2 years, at which time you cash it in (we will assume that the interest rate on the 2-year security is 9 percent per year), or (2) you can buy a 1-year security today. At the end of 1 year, you must cash this security in; you can then buy another 1-year security. At the end of the second year, you will cash in the second security. Assume that the interest rate on the first 1-year security is 8 percent.

Which would you prefer? Currently, you do not have enough data to answer this question. To consider choice (2) sensibly, you need to know the interest rate on the 1-year security that you intend to buy in the second year. This rate will not be known until the second year. All you know now is the rate on the 2-year security and the rate on the current 1-year security. To decide what to do, you must form an *expectation* of the rate on the 1-year security a year from now. If you expect the 1-year rate (8 percent) to remain the same in the second year, you should buy the 2-year security. You would earn 9 percent per year on the 2-year security but only 8 percent per year on the two 1-year securities. If you expect the 1-year rate to rise to 12 percent a year from now, you should make the second choice. You would earn 8 percent in the first year, and you expect to earn 12 percent in the second year. The expected rate of return over the 2 years is about 10 percent, which is better than the 9 percent you can get on the 2-year security. If you expect the 1-year rate a year from now to be 10 percent, it does not matter very much which of the two choices you make. The rate of return over the 2-year period will be roughly 9 percent for both choices.

We now alter the focus of our discussion to get to the topic we are really interested in—how the 2-year rate is determined. Assume that the 1-year rate has been set by the Fed and it is 8 percent. Also assume that people expect the 1-year rate a year from now to be 10 percent. What is the 2-year rate? According to a theory called the *expectations theory of the term structure of interest rates*, the 2-year rate is equal to the average of the current 1-year rate and the 1-year rate expected a year from now. In this example, the 2-year rate would be 9 percent (the average of 8 percent and 10 percent).

If the 2-year rate were lower than the average of the two 1-year rates, people would not be indifferent as to which security they held. They would want to hold only the short-term 1-year securities. To find a buyer for a 2-year security, the seller would be forced to increase the interest rate it offers on the 2-year security until it is equal to the average of the current 1-year rate and the expected 1-year rate for next year. The interest rate on the 2-year security will continue to rise until people are once again indifferent between one 2-year security and two 1-year securities.[1]

Let us now return to Fed behavior. We know that the Fed can affect the short-term interest rate by changing the money supply, but does it also affect long-term interest rates? The answer is "somewhat." Because the 2-year rate is an average of the current 1-year rate and the expected 1-year rate a year from now, the Fed influences the 2-year rate to the extent that it influences the current 1-year rate. The same holds for 3-year rates and beyond. The current short-term rate is a means by which the Fed can influence longer-term rates.

In addition, Fed behavior may directly affect people's expectations of the future short-term rates, which will then affect long-term rates. If the chair of the Fed testifies before Congress that raising short-term interest rates is under consideration, people's expectations of higher future short-term interest rates are likely to increase. These expectations will then be reflected in current long-term interest rates.

Types of Interest Rates

The following are some widely followed interest rates in the United States.

Three-Month Treasury Bill Rate Government securities that mature in less than a year are called *Treasury bills*, or sometimes *T-bills*. The interest rate on 3-month Treasury bills is probably the most widely followed short-term interest rate.

Government Bond Rate Government securities with terms of 1 year or more are called *government bonds*. There are 1-year bonds, 2-year bonds, and so on, up to 30-year bonds. Bonds of different terms have different interest rates. The relationship among the interest rates on the various maturities is the term structure of interest rates that we discussed in the first part of this Appendix.

Federal Funds Rate Banks borrow not only from the Fed but also from each other. If one bank has excess reserves, it can lend some of those reserves to other banks through the federal funds market. The interest rate in this market is called the *federal funds rate*—the rate banks are charged to borrow reserves from other banks.

The federal funds market is really a desk in New York City. From all over the country, banks with excess reserves to lend and banks in need of reserves call the desk and negotiate a rate of interest. Account balances with the Fed are changed for the period of the loan without any physical movement of money.

This borrowing and lending, which takes place near the close of each working day, is generally for 1 day ("overnight"), so the federal funds rate is a 1-day rate. It is the rate on which the Fed has the most effect through its open market operations.

Commercial Paper Rate Firms have several alternatives for raising funds. They can sell stocks, issue bonds, or borrow from a bank. Large firms can also borrow directly from the public by issuing "commercial paper," which is essentially short-term corporate IOUs that offer a designated rate of interest. The interest rate offered on commercial paper depends on the financial condition of the firm and the maturity date of the IOU.

Prime Rate Banks charge different interest rates to different customers depending on how risky the banks perceive the customers to be. You would expect to pay a higher interest rate

---

[1] For longer terms, additional future rates must be averaged in. For a 3-year security, for example, the expected 1-year rate a year from now and the expected 1-year rate 2 years from now are added to the current 1-year rate and averaged.

for a car loan than General Motors would pay for a $1 million loan to finance investment. Also, you would pay more interest for an unsecured loan, a "personal" loan, than for one that was secured by some asset, such as a house or car, to be used as collateral.

The *prime rate* is a benchmark that banks often use in quoting interest rates to their customers. A very low-risk corporation might be able to borrow at (or even below) the prime rate. A less well-known firm might be quoted a rate of "prime plus three-fourths," which means that if the prime rate is, say, 10 percent, the firm would have to pay interest of 10.75 percent. The prime rate depends on the cost of funds to the bank; it moves up and down with changes in the economy.

AAA Corporate Bond Rate Corporations finance much of their investment by selling bonds to the public. Corporate bonds are classified by various bond dealers according to their risk. Bonds issued by General Motors are in less risk of default than bonds issued by a new risky biotech research firm. Bonds differ from commercial paper in one important way: Bonds have a longer maturity.

Bonds are graded in much the same way students are. The highest grade is AAA, the next highest AA, and so on. The interest rate on bonds rated AAA is the *triple A corporate bond rate*, the rate that the least risky firms pay on the bonds that they issue.

APPENDIX A PROBLEMS

1. The following table gives three key U.S. interest rates in 1980 and again in 1993:

	1980 (%)	1993 (%)
Three-month U.S. government bills	11.39	3.00
Long-term U.S. government bonds	11.27	6.59
Prime rate	15.26	6.00

Provide an explanation for the extreme differences that you see. Specifically, comment on (1) the fact that rates in 1980 were much higher than in 1993 and (2) the fact that the long-term rate was higher than the short-term rate in 1993 but lower in 1980.

CHAPTER 11 APPENDIX B

The Demand For Money: A Numerical Example

This Appendix presents a numerical example showing how optimal money management behavior can be derived.

We have seen that the interest rate represents the opportunity cost of holding funds in non-interest-bearing checking accounts (as opposed to bonds, which yield interest). We have also seen that costs are involved in switching from bonds to money. Given these costs, our objective is to determine the optimum amount of money for an individual to hold. The optimal average level of money holdings is the amount that maximizes the profits from money management. Interest is earned on average bond holdings, but the cost per switch multiplied by the number of switches must be subtracted from interest revenue to obtain the net profit from money management.

Suppose the interest rate is .05 (5 percent), it costs $2 each time a bond is sold,[1] and the proceeds from the sale

are deposited in one's checking account. Suppose also that the individual's income is $1,200 and that this income is spent evenly throughout the period. This situation is depicted in the top half of Table 11B.1. The optimum value for average money holdings is the value that achieves the largest possible profit in column 6 of the table. When the interest rate is 5 percent, the optimum average money holdings are $150 (which means that the individual makes three switches from bonds to money).

In the bottom half of Table 11B.1, the same calculations are performed for an interest rate of 3 percent instead of 5 percent. In this case, the optimum average money holdings is $200 (which means the person/household makes two instead of three switches from bonds to money). The lower interest rate has led to an increase in the optimum average money holdings. Under the assumption that people behave optimally, the demand for money is a negative function of the interest rate: The lower the rate, the more money on average is held, and the higher the rate, the less money on average is held.

---

[1] In this example, we will assume that the $2 cost does not apply to the original purchase of bonds.

TABLE 11B.1 Optimum Money Holdings

1 Number of Switches[a]	2 Average Money Holdings[b]	3 Average Bond Holdings[c]	4 Interest Earned[d]	5 Cost of Switching[e]	6 Net Profit[f]
			$r = 5$ percent		
0	$600.00	$ 0.00	$ 0.00	$0.00	$ 0.00
1	300.00	300.00	15.00	2.00	13.00
2	200.00	400.00	20.00	4.00	16.00
3	150.00*	450.00	22.50	6.00	16.50
4	120.00	480.00	24.00	8.00	16.00

Assumptions: Interest rate $r = 0.05$. Cost of switching from bonds to money equals $2 per transaction.

			$r = 3$ percent		
0	$600.00	$ 0.00	$ 0.00	$0.00	$0.00
1	300.00	300.00	9.00	2.00	7.00
2	200.00*	400.00	12.00	4.00	8.00
3	150.00	450.00	13.50	6.00	7.50
4	120.00	480.00	14.40	8.00	6.40

Assumptions: Interest rate $r = 0.03$. Cost of switching from bonds to money equals $2 per transaction.

*Optimum money holdings. [a]That is, the number of times you sell a bond. [b]Calculated as 600/(col. 1 + 1). [c]Calculated as 600 − col. 2. [d]Calculated as r × col. 3, where r is the interest rate. [e]Calculated as t × col. 1, where t is the cost per switch ($2). [f]Calculated as col. 4 − col. 5.

APPENDIX B PROBLEMS

1. Sherman Peabody earns a monthly salary of $1,500, which he receives at the beginning of each month. He spends the entire amount each month at the rate of $50 per day. (Assume 30 days in a month.) The interest rate paid on bonds is 10 percent per month. It costs $4 every time Peabody sells a bond.

   a. Describe briefly how Mr. Peabody should decide how much money to hold.

   b. Calculate Peabody's optimal money holdings. (*Hint*: It may help to formulate a table such as Table 11B.1 in this Appendix. You can round to the nearest $0.50, and you

   need to consider only average money holdings of more than $100.)

   c. Suppose the interest rate rises to 15 percent. Find Peabody's optimal money holdings at this new interest rate. What will happen if the interest rate increases to 20 percent?

   d. Graph your answers to b. and c. with the interest rate on the vertical axis and the amount of money demanded on the horizontal axis. Explain why your graph slopes downward.

The Determination of Aggregate Output, the Price Level, and the Interest Rate

12

In the last four chapters we have been exploring the key elements of the macroeconomy one element at a time. In Chapters 8 and 9 we looked at how the output level in the economy is determined, keeping the interest rate and the price level fixed. In Chapters 10 and 11 we turned our attention to the interest rate, holding output and the price level fixed. We are now ready to bring these key pieces of the economy—output, the price level, and the interest rate—together at the same time.

This chapter and the next one will give you the ability to think about the key issues policy makers face in trying to manage the economy. We will see how the output level is determined. We will see what forces push the overall price level up, creating inflation, in an economy. By the time you finish these two chapters, we hope you will be much better able to understand what lies behind many of the current policy debates in the United States.

As we complete the story in this chapter, we will focus on the behavior of two key players in the macroeconomy: firms, who make price and output decisions, and the Federal Reserve (the Fed), which controls the interest rate. We begin with the price and output decisions of firms, which will be summarized in an Aggregate Supply curve.

The Aggregate Supply (*AS*) Curve

Aggregate supply is the total supply of goods and services in an economy. The **aggregate supply (*AS*) curve** shows the relationship between the aggregate quantity of output supplied by all the firms in an economy and the overall price level. To understand the aggregate supply curve, we need to understand something about the behavior of the individual firms that make up the economy.

aggregate supply The total supply of all goods and services in an economy.

aggregate supply (*AS*) curve A graph that shows the relationship between the aggregate quantity of output supplied by all firms in an economy and the overall price level.

LEARNING OBJECTIVES

Define the aggregate supply curve and discuss shifts in the short-run *AS* curve

Discuss the *IS* curve and the Fed rule and identify factors that cause *IS* curve and Fed rule shifts

Derive the aggregate demand curve and explain why the *AD* curve is downward sloping

Discuss the shape of the long-run aggregate supply curve and explain long-run market adjustment to potential GDP

In developing the *AS* curve, macroeconomists think about a firm as simultaneously making decisions about its level of output and its price. In contrast to perfectly competitive firms, who simply take the market price as given and only make an output decision, imperfectly competitive firms, which macroeconomics emphasizes, choose both quantity and price. Imperfectly competitive firms do not have individual supply curves because these firms are choosing both output and price at the same time. To derive an individual supply curve, we need to imagine calling out a price to a firm and having the firm tell us how much output it will supply at that price. We cannot do this if firms are also setting prices. What this means is that you should not think of the *AS* curve as being the sum of individual supply curves. If individual supply curves do not exist, we certainly can't add them together!

So if the *AS* curve is *not* the sum of individual supply curves, what is it? The *AS* curve shows what happens to the price level and output as aggregate demand rises and falls. It reflects the behavior of firms as they face changing overall demand. When an imperfectively competitive firm faces an outward shift in its demand curve with its marginal cost curve unchanged, it responds by raising its output and price. If all firms are facing outward shifts, all outputs and prices will be rising, which means that aggregate output and the aggregate price level will be rising. The *AS* curve traces out aggregate output and aggregate price level points corresponding to different levels of demand. Although it is called an aggregate *supply* curve, it is really misnamed. It is better thought of as a "price/output response" curve—a curve that traces out the price decisions and output decisions of all firms in the economy under different levels of aggregate demand.

What might such a curve look like?

Aggregate Supply in the Short Run

The *AS* curve (or price-output response curve) shows how changes in aggregate demand affect the price level and output in an economy. When aggregate demand in an economy increases, how much, if at all, does the price level increase? How much does output increase? Most economists believe that, at least for a period of time, an increase in aggregate demand will result in an increase in *both* the price level and output. Many economists also believe that how much a demand increase affects the price level versus output depends on the strength of the economy at the time the demand increase occurred. Figure 12.1 shows a curve reflecting these ideas. At very low levels of aggregate output—for example, when the economy is in a recession—the aggregate

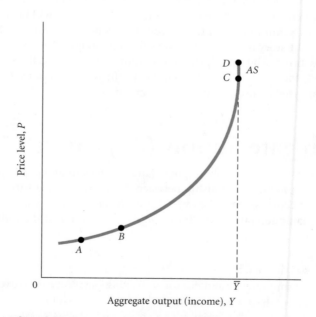

▲ **FIGURE 12.1 The Short-Run Aggregate Supply Curve**
In the short run, the aggregate supply curve (the price/output response curve) has a positive slope. At low levels of aggregate output, the curve is fairly flat. As the economy approaches capacity, the curve becomes nearly vertical. At capacity, $\overline{Y}$, the curve is vertical.

supply curve is fairly flat and that at high levels of output—for example, when the economy is experiencing a boom—it is vertical or nearly vertical.

Why an Upward Slope?   Why might a higher price level be associated with more output, giving the *AS* curve a positive slope? Suppose that when aggregate demand increases, all prices, including wages, increase at the same time. After all, when we talk about aggregate price level, we are talking about not only output prices but also prices of inputs, including the price of labor, or wages. If wages and prices are both rising, firms get more for their products and pay proportionately more for workers. The *AS* curve in this case would be vertical. Product prices would increase, but firms would not increase output because it would not be profitable to do so. Suppose, on the other hand, that wages and prices do not move at the same time. If wages respond more slowly to a demand change than do product prices, firms will increase output as product prices rise. Here the *AS* curve will have an upward slope, rather than being vertical.

So a key question in whether the *AS* curve slopes up or is vertical is whether wages are "sticky," moving more slowly than other prices. With sticky wages, demand increases occur without proportional wage increases and so firms' marginal cost curves do not shift proportionally. In practice, wages do tend to lag behind prices. We discuss in Chapter 14 various reasons that have been advanced for why wages might be sticky in the short run.

We should add a word of caution at this point. It may be that some of a firm's input costs are rising even in the short run after the aggregate demand increase has taken place because some of a firm's inputs may be purchased from other firms who are raising prices. For example, one input to a Dell computer is a chip produced by Intel or AMD. The fact that some of a firm's input costs rise along with a shift in the demand for its product complicates the picture because it means that at the same time there is an outward shift in a firm's demand curve, there is some upward shift in its marginal cost curve. In deriving an upward-sloping *AS* curve, we are in effect assuming that these kinds of input costs are small relative to wage costs. So the story is that wages are a large fraction of total costs and that wage changes lag behind price changes. This gives us an upward-sloping short-run *AS* curve.

Why the Particular Shape?   Notice the *AS* curve in Figure 12.1 begins with a flat section and ends with a more-or-less vertical section. Why might the *AS* curve have this shape? Consider the vertical portion first. At some level the overall economy is using all its capital and all the labor that wants to work at the market wage. At this level ($\overline{Y}$), increased demand for output can be met only by increased prices and similarly for increased demand for labor. Neither wages nor prices are likely to be sticky at this level of economic activity.

What about the flat portion of the curve? Here we are at levels of output that are low relative to historical levels. Many firms are likely to have excess capacity in terms of their plant and equipment and their workforce. With excess capacity, firms may be able to increase output from *A* to *B* without a proportionate cost increase. Small price increases may thus be associated with relatively large output responses. We may also observe relatively sticky wages upward at this point on the *AS* curve if firms have held any excess workers in the downturn as a way to preserve worker morale.

Shifts of the Short-Run Aggregate Supply Curve

The *AS* curve shows how the overall price level and output move with a change in aggregate demand, and we have seen that the answer to whether the price level or output is more affected depends on how the economy is doing at the time of the change. Now we can think about how other features of the economy might affect, or *shift*, the position of the *AS* curve.

What does a rightward shift of the *AS* curve mean? A rightward shift says that society can get a larger aggregate output at a given price level. What might cause such a shift? Clearly, if a society had an increase in labor or capital, the *AS* curve would shift to the right, since the capacity of the economy would increase. Also, technical changes that increased productivity would shift the *AS* curve to the right by lowering marginal costs of production in the economy. Recall that the vertical part of the short-run *AS* curve represents the economy's maximum (capacity) output. This maximum output is determined by the economy's existing resources,

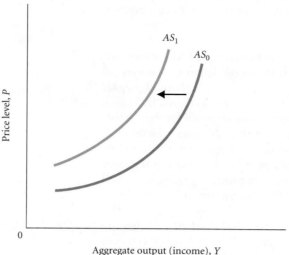

a. A decrease in aggregate supply

A leftward shift of the AS curve from AS_0 to AS_1
could be caused by an increase in costs—for example,
an increase in wage rates or energy prices.

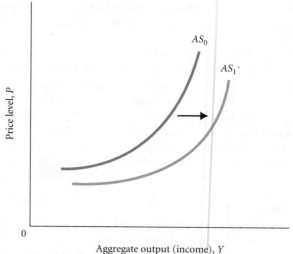

b. An increase in aggregate supply

A rightward shift of the AS curve from AS_0 to AS_1
could be caused by a decrease in costs—for example,
a decrease in wage rates or energy prices or technical change.

▲ **FIGURE 12.2** **Shifts of the Short-Run Aggregate Supply Curve**

like the size of its labor force, capital stock, and the current state of technology. The labor force grows naturally with an increase in the working-age population, but it can also increase for other reasons. Since the 1960s, for example, the percentage of women in the labor force has grown sharply. This increase in the supply of women workers has shifted the AS curve to the right. Immigration can also shift the AS curve. During the 1970s, Germany, faced with a serious labor shortage, opened its borders to large numbers of "guest workers," largely from Turkey. The United States has experienced significant immigration, legal and illegal, from Mexico, from Central and South American countries, and from Asia. (We discuss economic growth in more detail in Chapter 17.)

We have focused on labor and capital as factors of production, but for a modern economy, energy is also an important input. New discoveries of oil or problems in the production of energy can also shift the AS curve through effects on the marginal cost of production in many parts of the economy.

Figures 12.2(a) and (b) show the effects of shifts in the short-run AS curve coming from changes in wage rates or energy prices. This type of shift is sometimes called a **cost shock** *or* **supply shock**. Oil has historically had quite volatile prices and has often been thought to contribute to shifts in the AS curve that, as we will shortly see, contribute to economy-wide fluctuations.

cost shock, *or* **supply shock** A change in costs that shifts the short-run aggregate supply (AS) curve.

The Aggregate Demand (AD) Curve

The AS curve in Figure 12.1 shows us all possible combinations of aggregate output and the price level consistent with firms' output and price decisions. But where on the curve will an economy be? To answer this question we need to consider the demand side of the economy. In this section we will derive an aggregate demand (AD) curve. This curve is derived from the model of the goods market in Chapters 8 and 9 and from the behavior of the Fed. We begin with the goods market.

Planned Aggregate Expenditure and the Interest Rate

We can use the fact that planned investment depends on the interest rate to consider how planned aggregate expenditure (AE) depends on the interest rate. Recall that planned aggregate expenditure is the sum of consumption, planned investment, and government purchases. That is,

$$AE \equiv C + I + G$$

We know that there are many possible levels of I, each corresponding to a different interest rate. When the interest rate rises, planned investment falls. Therefore, a rise in the interest rate (r) will lead to a fall in total planned spending ($C + I + G$) as well.[1]

Figure 12.3 shows what happens to planned aggregate expenditure and output when the interest rate rises from 3 percent to 6 percent. At the higher interest rate, planned investment is lower; planned aggregate expenditure thus shifts *downward*. Recall from Chapters 8 and 9 that a fall in any component of aggregate spending has an even larger (or "multiplier") effect on output. When the interest rate rises, planned investment (and thus planned aggregate expenditure) falls and equilibrium output (income) falls by even more than the fall in planned investment. In Figure 12.3, equilibrium output falls from Y_0 to Y_1 when the interest rate rises from 3 percent to 6 percent.

We can summarize the effects of a change in the interest rate on the equilibrium level of output in the goods market. The effects of a change in the interest rate include:

- A high interest rate (r) discourages planned investment (I).

- Planned investment is a part of planned aggregate expenditure (AE).

- Thus, when the interest rate rises, planned aggregate expenditure (AE) at every level of income falls.

- Finally, a decrease in planned aggregate expenditure lowers equilibrium output (income) (Y) by a multiple of the initial decrease in planned investment.

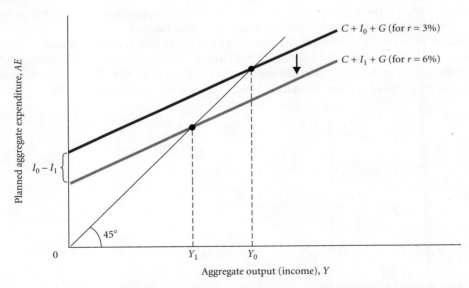

▲ **FIGURE 12.3   The Effect of an Interest Rate Increase on Planned Aggregate Expenditure and Equilibrium Output**
An increase in the interest rate from 3 percent to 6 percent lowers planned aggregate expenditure and thus reduces equilibrium output from Y_0 to Y_1.

---

[1] When we look in detail in Chapter 16 at the behavior of households in the macroeconomy, we will see that consumption spending (C) is also stimulated by lower interest rates and discouraged by higher interest rates.

Using a convenient shorthand:

$$r{\uparrow} \rightarrow I{\downarrow} \rightarrow AE{\downarrow} \rightarrow Y{\downarrow}$$

$$r{\downarrow} \rightarrow I{\uparrow} \rightarrow AE{\uparrow} \rightarrow Y{\uparrow}$$

IS curve Relationship between aggregate output and the interest rate in the goods market.

This relationship between output and the interest rate is summarized in Figure 12.4. This curve is called the **IS curve**. Any point on the IS curve is an equilibrium in the goods market for the particular interest rate. Equilibrium means that planned investment equals saving, hence the IS notation. It is noted in the box in the figure that an increase in government spending (G) shifts the IS curve to the right. *With the interest rate fixed*, an increase in G increases AE and thus Y in equilibrium. Just to be clear, this shift is shown in Figure 12.5. If for a given interest rate, an increase in G increases output from Y_1 to Y_2, this is a shift of the IS curve from IS_1 to IS_2.

The Behavior of the Fed

The IS curve shows the relationship between the interest rate and output. When the interest rate is high, planned investment is low, so output is low. When the interest rate is low, planned investment is high, so output is high. But where on the curve is the actual economy? To answer this question we need to know the value of the interest rate. We know from Chapters 10 and 11 how the Fed controls the interest rate—through the reserve requirement ratio, the discount rate, and open market operations, but almost always open market operations. Review this material if necessary. All we need for present purposes is the fact that the Fed can control the interest rate, but you should know how it does this.

We will now consider *why* the Fed might want to change the interest rate. Every six weeks, the Federal Open Market Committee (FOMC) meets. This committee is headed by the chair of the Fed, currently Ben Bernanke, who usually dominates the meeting. The FOMC decides on the value of the interest rate (the exact rate it sets is called the "federal funds" rate). After the meeting, it instructs the Open Market Desk at the New York Federal Reserve Bank to buy or sell government securities until the desired interest rate value is reached.

The FOMC usually announces the interest rate value at 2:15 P.M. eastern time on the day it meets. This is a key time for financial markets around the world. At 2:14 P.M., thousands of people are staring at their computer screens waiting from word on high. If the announcement is a surprise, it can have large and immediate effects on bond and stock markets.

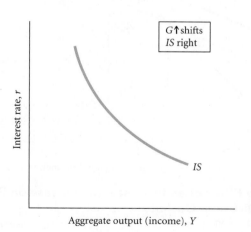

▲ **FIGURE 12.4 The IS Curve**

In the goods market, there is a negative relationship between output and the interest rate because planned investment depends negatively on the interest rate. Any point on the IS curve is an equilibrium in the goods market for the given interest rate.

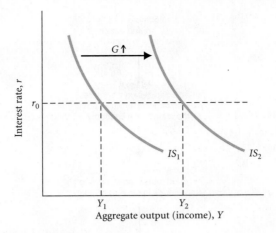

▲ **FIGURE 12.5 Shift of the *IS* Curve**
An increase in government spending (*G*) with the interest rate fixed increases output (*Y*), which is a shift of the *IS* curve to the right.

How does the Fed decide on what interest rate value to choose? The Fed's main goals are high levels of output and employment and a low rate of inflation. From the Fed's point of view, the best situation is a fully employed economy with a low inflation rate. The worst situation is stagflation—high unemployment and high inflation. In fact, the Humphrey-Hawkins Full Employment Act of 1978 mandated the Fed to aim for full employment and price stability, and when the bill was sunsetted in 2000, the expectation was that the Fed would continue to aim for full employment and price stability.

Figure 12.6 summarizes the decision-making process of the Fed in terms of its interest rate setting. The Fed examines data on the current state of the economy, particularly output and inflation, and also considers the likely future course of the economy. In this setting, the Fed faces some hard choices. It knows—as we do from the *IS* curve in Figure 12.4—that increasing the interest rate will result in lower output, while reducing the interest rate will result in higher output. So one factor the Fed uses to choose the interest rate value is whether it believes output to be too low, too high, or about right. But we know that the Fed also cares about inflation. If the Fed finds inflation higher than it wishes, it will raise the interest rate, other things being equal, and vice versa if it finds inflation lower than it wishes.

The discussion so far has focused on output and inflation as the two main inputs into the Fed's interest rate decision. But the Fed is not just a mechanical calculator. The Fed chair brings to the FOMC meeting his or her own considerable expertise about the working of the economy. Ben Bernanke, as you likely know, was a distinguished researcher and Princeton professor prior to his appointment. Most of the other members of the FOMC have long experience in business and economics. As the Fed thinks about its interest rate setting, it considers factors other than current output and inflation. Levels of consumer confidence, possible fragility of the domestic banking sector, and possible financial problems abroad, say a potential euro crisis, may play a role in its interest rate decision. For our purposes we will label all these factors (all factors except output and inflation) as "Z" factors. These factors lie outside our model, and they are likely to vary from period to period in ways that are hard to predict.

If we put all of this together, we can describe the interest rate behavior of the Fed by using a simple linear equation, which we will call the **Fed rule**:

$$r = \alpha Y + \beta P + \gamma Z$$

Fed rule Equation that shows how the Fed's interest rate decision depends on the state of the economy.

▶ **FIGURE 12.6**
Fed Behavior

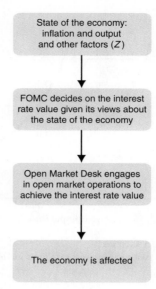

Describing the Fed rule via an equation will allow us to incorporate Fed behavior formally into the *AS/AD* model we are building.[2] It is, of course, only an approximation as to how the Fed actually behaves.

What does this equation tell us? We will assume that the three coefficients, α, β, and γ, are positive. When output is high, all else equal, the Fed favors a higher interest rate then it would in a low-output economy. Likewise, when the price level is high, all else equal, the Fed favors a higher interest rate then it would when price stability is not a problem. High interest rates will thus be associated with high output and price levels. Positive coefficients tell us that the Fed "leans against the wind." That is, when output and/or the price level are high, the Fed sets a high interest rate to try to rein the economy in. Note that we are using the price level, P, as the variable in the rule. In practice, the Fed cares about inflation, which is the change in P, rather than the level of P, and we are approximating this by using just the level of P.

Z in the rule stands for all the factors that affect the Fed's interest rate decision except for Y and P. Since we have taken γ to be positive, the factors in Z are defined to be such that a high value of a factor makes the Fed inclined to have a high interest-rate value, other things being equal.

We are now ready to add the Fed rule to our model. Figure 12.7 adds the Fed rule to the *IS* curve from Figure 12.4. The line depicting the Fed rule in the graph shows the relationship between the Fed's choice of the interest rate and aggregate output, holding the price level and the Z factors constant. The slope is positive because the coefficient α in the Fed rule is positive: When output is high, the interest rate that the Fed sets is high, other things being equal. The intersection of the *IS* curve and the Fed rule determines the equilibrium values of output and the interest rate. At this point there is equilibrium in the goods market *and* the value of the interest rate is what the Fed rule calls for.

---

[2] The Fed rule used here differs somewhat from that advocated for teaching purposes by David Romer, "Keynesian Macroeconomics without the LM Curve," *Journal of Economic Perspectives,* 14, Spring 2000, 149–169. First, the left-hand side variable is the nominal interest rate *(r)* rather than the real interest rate advocated by Romer. The Fed does in fact set the nominal rate at each FOMC meeting, so the use of the nominal rate is more realistic and easier to understand for students. Second, the price level, not the rate of inflation, is used in the rule. The *AS/AD* model is a static model. Introducing inflation brings in dynamics, which complicates the analysis. P is used here instead of the change in P. The insights still hold, and the story is much simpler. Third, the nominal interest rate is used in the (real) goods market in the determination of planned investment. Again, this is an approximation to avoid dynamics, and the insights still hold.

The research of one of the authors (Fair) actually supports the use of the nominal rate in the goods market. The results suggest that people (both consumers and investors) respond more to nominal rates than to real rates. Also, the left-hand side variable in Fair's price equation in his U.S. macroeconometric model is the (log) price level rather than the rate of inflation. This equation is consistent with the discussion behind the *AS* curve, where the two decision variables of a firm are taken to be the firm's price level and level of output, not the change in the price level and level of output.

ECONOMICS IN PRACTICE

What Does Ben Bernanke Really Care About?

We describe in this chapter a "Fed rule," using an equation. Underneath this equation are the goals and ideas of the men and women who make the decisions at the Fed. As we suggested, the most important of these decision makers is the chair of the Fed, Ben Bernanke.

As the economy sputtered along in late 2012 and early 2013, a number of newspaper articles began to appear focusing on what Ben Bernanke really cared about. One article was titled "Does Ben Bernanke Care Too Much About Jobs?"[1] while another journalist opined "Ben Bernanke Doesn't Care about the Price of Your Hamburger."[2] At this point you should see that these colorful headlines are just asking what are the variables in the Fed rule!

THINKING PRACTICALLY

1. In his research work while a professor at Princeton, Bernanke emphasized the dangers of inflation. As Fed Chair, he has spent more time worrying about output. Why is this? (Hint: go back and look at the data graphs.).

[1] Bohan and Hollinder, *National Journal*, March 2, 2013.
[2] Mark O'Brian, *The Atlantic*, July 26, 2012.

Figure 12.7 shows the equilibrium values of output and the interest rate for given values of government spending (*G*), the price level (*P*), and all factors in *Z*. Suppose the government decides to increase its spending. How do the equilibrium values of the interest rate and output change? Remember that an increase in government spending shifts the *IS* curve to the right. This will in Figure 12.7 increase the equilibrium values of both the interest rate and output. Now what happens if instead of a change in government spending, we have an increase in the price level? Remember that the price level is in the Fed rule–the Fed cares about price stability. The Fed would thus respond to an increase in the price level by raising the interest rate. This means that in Figure 12.7 an increase in the price level shifts the Fed rule to the left—for a given value of output, the interest rate is higher for a higher value of the price level. Finally, if any of the "Z" factors we described increase, like an increase in consumer confidence, this leads the Fed to increase the interest rate, which also shifts the Fed rule to the left in Figure 12.7.

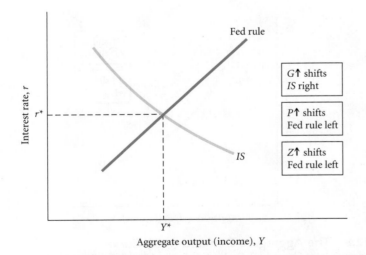

▲ **FIGURE 12.7   Equilibrium Values of the Interest Rate and Output**
In the Fed rule, the Fed raises the interest rate as output increases, other things being equal. Along the *IS* curve, output falls as the interest rate increases because planned investment depends negatively on the interest rate. The intersection of the two curves gives the equilibrium values of output and the interest rate for given values of government spending (*G*), the price level (*P*), and the factors in *Z*.

Deriving the *AD* Curve

We can now derive the *AD* curve. The *AD* curve (and the *AS* curve) is a relationship between the overall price level *(P)* and aggregate output (income) *(Y)*. We know from Figure 12.7 that an increase in *P* shifts the Fed rule to the left (and has no effect on the *IS* curve). When the Fed rule shifts to the left along an unchanged *IS* curve, the new equilibrium is at a higher interest rate and a lower level of output. Be sure you understand why output is lower when *P* is higher. When *P* increases, the Fed, according to the rule, responds by raising the interest rate, other things being equal. The higher interest rate has a negative effect on planned investment and thus on *AE* and thus on *Y*. This is the relationship reflected in the *IS* curve. Conversely, a decrease in *P* shifts the Fed rule to the right, resulting in a new equilibrium with a lower interest rate and higher level of output. There is thus a negative relationship between *P* and *Y* in the goods market with the Fed rule, and this is the *AD* curve. The *AD* curve is presented in Figure 12.8.

It is noted in Figure 12.8 that an increase in government spending *(G)* shifts the *AD* curve to the right. We can see this from Figure 12.7. When *G* increases, the *IS* curve shifts to the right since *AE* and thus *Y* are larger for a given value of the interest rate. (Remember that *AE = C + I + G*.) The new equilibrium for the *G* increase has a higher interest rate and a higher level of output. The higher level of output means that the *AD* curve shifts to the right when *G* increases.

It is also noted in Figure 12.8 that an increase in *Z* shifts the *AD* curve to the left. Remember that an increase in *Z* means that the Fed is raising the interest rate, other things being equal: The coefficient *γ* is positive. We can see why the *AD* curve shifts to the left when *Z* increases from Figure 12.7. When *Z* increases, the Fed rule shifts to the left in Figure 12.7, which results in a higher interest rate and a lower level of output. The lower level of output means that the *AD* curve shifts to the left when *Z* increases.

It is important to realize that the *AD* curve is *not* a market demand curve, and it is *not* the sum of all market demand curves in the economy. To understand why, recall the logic behind a simple downward-sloping household demand curve. A demand curve shows the quantity of output demanded (by an individual household or in a single market) at every possible price, *ceteris paribus*. In drawing a simple demand curve, we are assuming that *other prices* and *income* are fixed. From these assumptions, it follows that one reason the quantity demanded of a particular good falls when its price rises is that other prices do *not* rise. The good in question therefore becomes more expensive relative to other goods, and households respond by

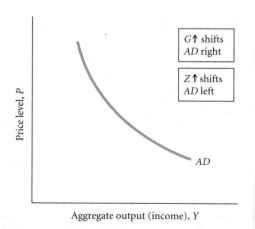

▲ **FIGURE 12.8** **The Aggregate Demand (*AD*) Curve**
The *AD* curve is derived from Figure 12.7. Each point on the *AD* curve is an equilibrium point in Figure 12.7 for a given value of *P*. When *P* increases, the Fed raises the interest rate (the Fed rule in Figure 12.7 shifts to the left), which has a negative effect on planned investment and thus on *Y*. The *AD* curve reflects this negative relationship between *P* and *Y*.

substituting other goods for the good whose price increased. In addition, if income does not rise when the price of a good does, real income falls. This may also lead to a lower quantity demanded of the good whose price has risen.

Things are different when the *overall price level* rises. When the overall price level rises, many prices rise together. For this reason, we cannot use the *ceteris paribus* assumption to draw the *AD* curve. The logic that explains why a simple demand curve slopes downward fails to explain why the *AD* curve also has a negative slope. Aggregate demand falls when the price level increases because the higher price level leads the Fed to raise the interest rate, which decreases planned investment and thus aggregate output. *It is the higher interest rate that causes aggregate output to fall.*

The Final Equilibrium

Figure 12.9 combines the *AS* curve from Figure 12.1 and the *AD* curve from Figure 12.8. Consider for a moment what these two curves have embedded in them. Every point on the *AS* curve is one in which firms make output and price decisions to maximize their profits. Every point on the *AD* curve reflects equilibrium in the goods market with the Fed behaving according to the Fed rule. The intersection of these two curves is the final equilibrium. The equilibrium values of aggregate output (Y) and the price level (P) are determined. Behind the scenes, equilibrium values of the interest rate (r), consumption (C), and planned investment (I) are determined. Also determined behind the scenes are equilibrium values of the demand for and supply of money. The demand for money is determined from the demand for money equation in Chapter 10, and the supply of money is determined as a result of the open market operations of the Fed that it uses to achieve the interest rate value called for by the Fed rule. The supply of money is whatever is needed to achieve the desired value of the interest rate, given the demand for money equation. In equilibrium, the supply of money equals the demand for money.

The variables that are exogenous to the *AS/AD* model (i.e., not explained by the model) are government spending (G), the factors in Z, and exogenous costs, like oil prices, that shift the *AS* curve. Net taxes (T), which have not been discussed in this chapter but are discussed in Chapter 9, are also exogenous. (Net taxes are part of the expanded model of the goods market in Chapter 9.) It is noted in Figure 12.9 that an increase in G shifts the *AD* curve to the right and that an increase in Z shifts the *AD* curve to the left. These shifts have already been discussed. The figure also notes that an increase in costs shifts the *AS* curve to the left. These costs are best thought of as costs like oil prices.

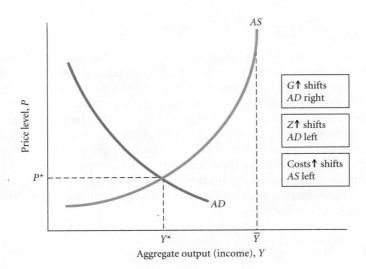

◀ **FIGURE 12.9**
Equilibrium Output and the Price Level

The rest of this chapter discusses the *AD* and *AS* curves in a little more detail, and then Chapter 13 uses the *AS/AD* framework to analyze monetary and fiscal policy effects and other macroeconomic issues. Chapter 13 shows the power of the *AS/AD* model to analyze many interesting and important questions in macroeconomics.

Other Reasons for a Downward-Sloping *AD* Curve

The *AD* curve slopes down in the above analysis because the Fed raises the interest rate when *P* increases and because planned investment depends negatively on the interest rate. It is also the case in practice that consumption depends negatively on the interest rate, so planned investment depending on the interest rate is not the only link between the interest rate and planned aggregate expenditure. We noted briefly in Chapter 8 that consumption depends on the interest rate, and we will discuss this in more detail in Chapter 16. The main point here is that planned investment does not bear the full burden of linking changes in the interest rate to changes in planned aggregate expenditure and thus the downward-sloping *AD* curve.

There is also a real wealth effect on consumption that contributes to a downward-sloping *AD* curve. We noted in Chapter 8 and will discuss in detail in Chapter 16 that consumption depends on wealth. Other things being equal, the more wealth households have, the more they consume. Wealth includes holdings of money, shares of stock, bonds, and housing, among other things. If household wealth decreases, the result will be less consumption now and in the future. The price level has an effect on some kinds of wealth. Suppose you are holding $1,000 in a checking account or in a money market fund and the price level rises by 10 percent. Your holding is now worth 10 percent less because the prices of the goods that you could buy with your $1,000 have all increased by 10 percent. The purchasing power (or "real value") of your holding has decreased by 10 percent. An increase in the price level may also lower the real value of stocks and housing, although whether it does depends on what happens to stock prices and housing prices when the overall price level rises. If stock prices and housing prices rise by the same percentage as the overall price level, the real value of stocks and housing will remain unchanged. If an increase in the price level does lower the real value of wealth, this is another reason for the downward slope of the *AD* curve. If real wealth falls, this leads to a decrease in consumption, which leads to a decrease in planned aggregate expenditure. So if real wealth falls when there is an increase in the price level, there is a negative relationship between the price level and output through this **real wealth effect**.

real wealth effect The change in consumption brought about by a change in real wealth that results from a change in the price level.

The Long-Run *AS* Curve

We derived the short-run *AS* curve under the assumption that wages were sticky. This does not mean, however, that stickiness persists forever. Over time, wages adjust to higher prices. When workers negotiate with firms over their wages, they take into account what prices have been doing in the recent past. If wages fully adjust to prices in the long run, then the long-run *AS* curve will be vertical. We can see why in Figure 12.10. Initially, the economy is in equilibrium at a price level of P_0 and aggregate output of Y_0 (the point *A* at which AD_0 and AS_0 intersect). Now imagine a shift of the *AD* curve from AD_0 to AD_1. In response to this shift, both the price level and aggregate output rise in the short run, to P_1 and Y_1, respectively (the point *B* at which AD_1 and AS_0 intersect). The movement along the upward-sloping AS_0 curve as *Y* increases from Y_0 to Y_1 assumes that wages lag prices. At point *B* real wages (nominal wages divided by prices) are lower then they are at point *A*.

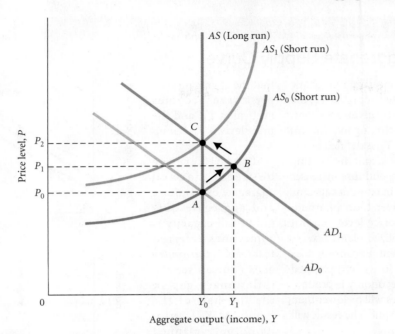

▲ **FIGURE 12.10   The Long-Run Aggregate Supply Curve**
When the *AD* curve shifts from AD_0 to AD_1, the equilibrium price level initially rises from P_0 to P_1 and output rises from Y_0 to Y_1. Wages respond in the longer run, shifting the *AS* curve from AS_0 to AS_1. If wages fully adjust, output will be back to Y_0. Y_0 is sometimes called *potential GDP*.

Now, as wages increase, the short-run *AS* curve shifts to the left. If wages fully adjust, the *AS* curve will over time have shifted from AS_0 to AS_1 in Figure 12.10, and output will be back to Y_0 (the point *C* at which AD_1 and AS_1 intersect). So when wages fully adjust to prices, the long-run *AS* curve is vertical. At point *C* real wages are back to where they were at point *A*. The price level is, of course, higher.

By looking at Figure 12.10, you can begin to see why arguments about the shape of the *AS* curve are so important in policy debates. If the long-run *AS* curve is vertical as we have drawn it, factors that shift the *AD* curve to the right—such as increasing government spending—simply end up increasing the price level. If the short-run *AS* curve also is quite steep, even in the short run most of the effect of any shift in the *AD* curve will be felt in an increase in the price level rather than an increase in aggregate output. If the *AS* curve, on the other hand, is flat, *AD* shifts can have a large effect on aggregate output, at least in the short run. We discuss these effects of policy in more detail in the next chapter.

Potential GDP

Recall that even the short-run *AS* curve becomes vertical at some particular level of output. The vertical portion of the short-run *AS* curve exists because there are physical limits to the amount that an economy can produce in any given time period. At the physical limit, all plants are operating around the clock, many workers are on overtime, and there is no cyclical unemployment.

Note that the vertical portions of the short-run *AS* curves in Figure 12.10 are to the right of Y_0. If the vertical portions of the short-run *AS* curves represent "capacity," what is the nature of Y_0, the level of output corresponding to the long-run *AS* curve? Y_0 represents the level of aggregate output that can be *sustained* in the long run without inflation. It is

ECONOMICS IN PRACTICE

The Simple "Keynesian" Aggregate Supply Curve

There is a great deal of disagreement concerning the shape of the *AS* curve. One view of the aggregate supply curve, the simple "Keynesian" view, holds that at any given moment, the economy has a clearly defined capacity, or maximum, output. This maximum output, denoted by Y_F, is defined by the existing labor force, the current capital stock, and the existing state of technology. If planned aggregate expenditure increases when the economy is producing *below* this maximum capacity, this view holds, inventories will be lower than planned, and firms will increase output, but the price level will not change. Firms are operating with underutilized plants (excess capacity), and there is cyclical unemployment. Expansion does not exert any upward pressure on prices. However, if planned aggregate expenditure increases when the economy is producing near or at its maximum (Y_F), inventories will be lower than planned, but firms cannot increase their output. The result will be an increase in the price level, or inflation.

This view is illustrated in the figure. In the top half of the diagram, aggregate output (income) (Y) and planned aggregate expenditure ($C + I + G \equiv AE$) are initially in equilibrium at AE_1, Y_1, and price level P_1. Now suppose an increase in government spending increases planned aggregate expenditure. If such an increase shifts the *AE* curve from AE_1 to AE_2 and the corresponding aggregate demand curve from AD_1 to AD_2, the equilibrium level of output will rise from Y_1 to Y_F. (Remember, an expansionary policy shifts the *AD* curve to the right.) Because we were initially producing below capacity output (Y_1 is lower than Y_F), the price level will be unaffected, remaining at P_1.

Now consider what would happen if *AE* increased even further. Suppose planned aggregate expenditure shifted from AE_2 to AE_3, with a corresponding shift of AD_2 to AD_3. If the economy were producing below capacity output, the equilibrium level of output would rise to Y_3. However, the output of the economy cannot exceed the maximum output of Y_F. As inventories fall below what was planned, firms encounter a fully employed labor market and fully utilized plants. Therefore, they cannot increase their output. The result is

that the aggregate supply curve becomes vertical at Y_F, and the price level is driven up to P_3.

The difference between planned aggregate expenditure and aggregate output at full capacity is sometimes referred to as an *inflationary gap*. You can see the inflationary gap in the top half of the figure. At Y_F (capacity output), planned aggregate expenditure (shown by AE_3) is greater than Y_F. The price level rises to P_3 until the aggregate quantity supplied and the aggregate quantity demanded are equal.

Despite the fact that the kinked aggregate supply curve provides some insights, most economists find it unrealistic. It does not seem likely that the whole economy suddenly runs into a capacity "wall" at a specific level of output. As output expands, some firms and industries will hit capacity before others.

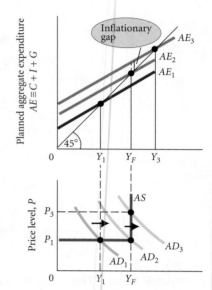

With planned aggregate expenditure of AE_1 and aggregate demand of AD_1, equilibrium output is Y_1. A shift of planned aggregate expenditure to AE_2, corresponding to a shift of the *AD* curve to AD_2, causes output to rise but the price level to remain at P_1. If planned aggregate expenditure and aggregate demand exceed Y_F, however, there is an inflationary gap and the price level rises to P_3.

THINKING PRACTICALLY

1. Why is the distance between AE_3 and AE_2 called an inflationary gap?

---

potential output, *or* **potential GDP** The level of aggregate output that can be sustained in the long run without inflation.

sometimes called **potential output** *or* **potential GDP**. Output can be pushed above Y_0 under a variety of circumstances, but when it is, there is upward pressure on wages. (Remember that real wages are lower at point *B* than at point *A* in Figure 12.10.) As the economy approaches short-run capacity, wage rates tend to rise as firms try to attract more people into the labor force and to induce more workers to work overtime. Rising wages shift the short-run *AS* curve to the left (in Figure 12.10 from AS_0 to AS_1) and drive output back to Y_0.

Short-Run Equilibrium Below Potential Output   Thus far, we have argued that if the short-run aggregate supply and aggregate demand curves intersect to the right of Y_0 in Figure 12.10, wages will rise, causing the short-run AS curve to shift to the left and pushing aggregate output back down to Y_0. Although different economists have different opinions on how to determine whether an economy is operating at or above potential output, there is general agreement that there is a maximum level of output (below the vertical portion of the short-run aggregate supply curve) that can be sustained without inflation.

What about short-run equilibria that occur to the *left* of Y_0? If the short-run aggregate supply and aggregate demand curves intersect at a level of output below potential output, what will happen? Here again economists disagree. Those who believe the aggregate supply curve is vertical in the long run believe that when short-run equilibria exist below Y_0, output will tend to rise—just as output tends to fall when short-run equilibria exist above Y_0. The argument is that when the economy is operating below full employment with excess capacity and high unemployment, wages are likely to *fall*. A decline in wages shifts the aggregate supply curve to the *right*, causing the price level to fall and the level of aggregate output to rise back to Y_0. This automatic adjustment works only if wages fall quickly when excess capacity and unemployment exist. We will discuss wage adjustment during periods of unemployment in detail in Chapter 14.

SUMMARY

THE AGGREGATE SUPPLY (*AS*) CURVE p. 229

1. *Aggregate supply* is the total supply of goods and services in an economy. The *aggregate supply (AS) curve* shows the relationship between the aggregate quantity of output supplied by all the firms in the economy and the overall price level. The *AS* curve is *not* a market supply curve, and it is *not* the simple sum of individual supply curves. For this reason, it is helpful to think of the *AS* curve as a "price/output response" curve—that is, a curve that traces out the price and output decisions of all firms in the economy under a given set of circumstances.

2. The shape of the short-run *AS* curve is a source of much controversy in macroeconomics. Many economists believe that at low levels of aggregate output, the *AS* curve is fairly flat and that at high levels of aggregate output, the *AS* curve is vertical or nearly vertical.

3. Anything that affects an individual firm's marginal cost curve can shift the *AS* curve. The two main factors are wage rates and energy prices.

THE AGGREGATE DEMAND (*AD*) CURVE p. 232

4. The *IS* curve summarizes the relationship between the interest rate and equilibrium output in the goods market. Government spending (*G*) shifts the *IS* curve.

5. Fed behavior is described by an interest rate rule, the *Fed rule*. The Fed's choice of the interest rate value depends on the state of the economy, approximated in the rule by output (*Y*), the

price level (*P*), and other factors (*Z*). The Fed uses open market operations to achieve the interest rate value that it wants.

6. Each point on the *AD* curve is, for a given value of *P*, an equilibrium in the goods market with the Fed rule. Increases in *G* shift the *AD* curve to the right, and increases in *Z* shift the *AD* curve to the left.

THE FINAL EQUILIBRIUM p. 239

7. The final equilibrium is the point of intersection of the *AS* and *AD* curves. Determined at this point are equilibrium values of output, the price level, the interest rate, consumption, planned investment, the demand for money, and the supply of money. Exogenous variables (variables not explained by the model) are government spending, the factors in *Z*, net taxes (used in the next chapter), and cost shocks.

OTHER REASONS FOR A DOWNWARD-SLOPING *AD* CURVE p. 240

8. Consumption as well as planned investment depends on the interest rate, and this is another reason for a downward-sloping *AD* curve. Another reason is that consumption also depends on real wealth.

THE LONG-RUN *AS* CURVE p. 240

9. The long-run *AS* curve is vertical if wages adjust completely to prices in the long run.

─── **REVIEW TERMS AND CONCEPTS** ───

aggregate supply, *p. 229*

aggregate supply (*AS*) curve, *p. 229*

cost shock, or supply shock, *p. 232*

Fed rule, *p. 235*

IS curve, *p. 234*

potential output, or potential GDP, *p. 242*

real wealth effect, *p. 240*

Equations:

$AE \equiv C + I + G$, *p. 233*

$r = \alpha Y + \beta P + \gamma Z$, *p. 235*

─── **PROBLEMS** ───

All problems are available on MyEconLab.

1. On June 5, 2003, the European Central Bank acted to decrease the short-term interest rate in Europe by half a percentage point, to 2 percent. The bank's president at the time, Willem Duisenberg, suggested that, in the future, the bank could reduce rates further. The rate cut was made because European countries were growing very slowly or were in recession. What effect did the bank hope the action would have on the economy? Be specific. What was the hoped-for result on C, I, and Y?

2. Some economists argue that the "animal spirits" of investors are so important in determining the level of investment in the economy that interest rates do not matter at all. Suppose that this were true – that investment in no way depends on interest rates.
   a. How would Figure 12.4 be different?
   b. What would happen to the level of planned aggregate expenditures if the interest rate changed?

3. Describe the Fed's tendency to "lean against the wind." Do the Fed's policies tend to stabilize or destabilize the economy?

4. The economy of Mayberry is currently in equilibrium at point A on the graph. Prince Barney of Mayberry has decided that he wants the economy to grow and has ordered the Royal Central Bank of Mayberry to print more currency so banks can

expand their loans to stimulate growth. Explain what will most likely happen to the economy of Mayberry as a result of Prince Barney's actions and show the result on the graph.

5. Illustrate each of the following situations with a graph showing the *IS* curve and the Fed rule, and explain what happens to the equilibrium values of the interest rate and output:
   a. An increase in G with the money supply held constant by the Fed
   b. An increase in G with the Fed changing M^s by enough to keep interest rates constant
   c. An increase in P with no change in government spending
   d. A decrease in Z with no change in government spending
   e. A decrease in P and an increase in G

6. Two separate capacity constraints are discussed in this chapter: (1) the actual physical capacity of existing plants and equipment, shown as the vertical portion of the short-run *AS* curve, and (2) potential GDP, leading to a vertical long-run *AS* curve. Explain the difference between the two. Which is greater, full-capacity GDP or potential GDP? Why?

7. During 1999 and 2000, a debate raged over whether the United States was at or above potential GDP. Some economists feared the economy was operating at a level of output above potential GDP and inflationary pressures were building. They urged the Fed to tighten monetary policy and increase interest rates to slow the economy. Others argued that a worldwide glut of cheap products was causing input prices to be lower, keeping prices from rising.

   By using aggregate supply and demand curves and other useful graphs, illustrate the following:
   a. Those pushing the Fed to act were right, and prices start to rise more rapidly in 2000. The Fed acts belatedly to slow money growth (contract the money supply), driving up interest rates and pushing the economy back to potential GDP.
   b. The worldwide glut gets worse, and the result is a falling price level (deflation) in the United States despite expanding aggregate demand.

8. Illustrate each of the following situations with a graph showing aggregate supply and aggregate demand curves, and explain what happens to the equilibrium values of the price level and aggregate output:
   a. An increase in G with the money supply held constant by the Fed
   b. An increase in the price of oil with no change in government spending

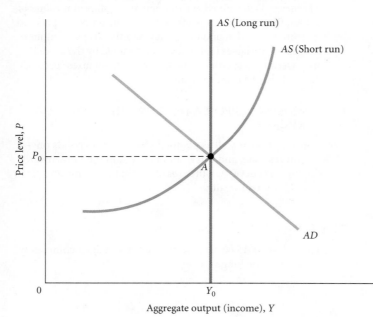

c. A decrease in Z with no change in government spending

d. A decrease in the price of oil and an increase in G

9. The aggregate demand curve slopes downward because when the price level is lower, people can afford to buy more and aggregate demand rises. When prices rise, people can afford to buy less and aggregate demand falls. Is this a good explanation of the shape of the AD curve? Why or why not?

10. In the first few chapters of this book, we introduced the notion of supply and demand. One of the first things we did was to derive the relationship between the price of a product and the quantity demanded per time period by an individual household. Now we have derived what is called the *aggregate* demand curve. The two look the same and both seem to have a negative slope, but the logic is completely different. Tell one story that explains the negative slope of a simple demand curve and another story that explains the more complex aggregate demand curve (AD).

11. Using aggregate supply and aggregate demand curves to illustrate, describe the effects of the following events on the price level and on equilibrium GDP in the *long run* assuming that input prices fully adjust to output prices after some lag:

a. An increase occurs in the money supply above potential GDP

b. GDP is above potential GDP, and a decrease in government spending and in the money supply occurs

c. Starting with the economy at potential GDP, a war in the Middle East pushes up energy prices temporarily. The Fed expands the money supply to accommodate the inflation.

12. [Related to the *Economics in Practice* on p. 242] The *Economics in Practice* describes the simple Keynesian aggregate supply curve as one in which there is a maximum level of output given the constraints of a fixed capital stock and a fixed supply of labor. The presumption is that increases in demand when firms are operating below capacity will result in output increases and no input price or output price changes but that at levels of output above full capacity, firms have no choice but to raise prices if demand increases. In reality, however, the short-run aggregate supply curve isn't flat and then vertical. Rather, it becomes steeper as we move from left to right on the diagram. Explain why. What circumstances might lead to an equilibrium at a very flat portion of the AS curve? At a very steep portion?

Policy Effects and Costs Shocks in the *AS/AD* Model

13

In the budget crisis in the fall of 2012, Republicans and Democrats argued vehemently about the overall government budget. What should be done to raise or lower taxes? What about government spending? Much of this debate was ideological, as U.S. political leaders differed in questions like how big the government should be. Although perhaps ideologically motivated, decisions made in the political process about taxes and spending have important macroeconomic consequences. The *AS/AD* model developed in the last chapter is a key tool in allowing us to explore these consequences.

Fiscal Policy Effects

In Chapter 12, we used government spending on goods and services (*G*) as our fiscal policy variable. We know from Chapter 9, however, that the government also collects taxes and spends money on transfer payments. We used *T* to denote net taxes, that is, taxes minus transfer payments. We will continue this notation in this chapter. The level of net taxes is obviously an important fiscal policy variable along with government spending. In fact, much of the political debate in the United States in 2012 regarding the government budget was about taxes and transfers, not about government purchases of goods and services. We know from Chapter 9 that the tax multiplier is smaller in absolute value than is the government spending multiplier. (You might want to review this material.) Although the sizes of the multipliers differ, the main point for this chapter is that both a decrease in net taxes and an increase in government spending increase output (*Y*). We know from Figure 12.8 in Chapter 12 that an increase in *G* shifts the *AD* curve to the right. We can also add that a decrease in net taxes shifts the *AD* curve to the right (just not as much because of the smaller multiplier). We will use this feature in this chapter.

LEARNING OBJECTIVES

Use the *AS/AD* model to analyze the short-run and long-run effects of fiscal policy

Use the *AS/AD* model to analyze the short-run and long-run effects of monetary policy

Describe the effects of monetary policy under a binding situation

Explain how economic shocks affect the *AS/AD* model

Discuss monetary policy since 1970

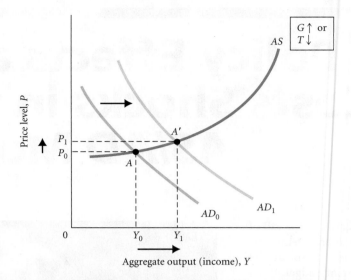

▲ **FIGURE 13.1** **A Shift of the *AD* Curve When the Economy is on the Nearly Flat Part of the *AS* Curve**

We now want to consider what happens to the economy when government spending or net taxes change, say, an increase in government spending or a decrease in net taxes. We first must be careful to note where along the *AS* curve the economy is at the time of the change. In Figure 13.1, the economy is assumed to be on the nearly flat portion of the *AS* curve (point *A*). Here the economy is not producing close to capacity. An expansionary fiscal policy—increase in *G* or decrease in *T*—shifts the *AD* curve to the right. In the figure, this results in a small price increase relative to the output increase. The increase in equilibrium *Y* (from Y_0 to Y_1) is much greater than the increase in equilibrium *P* (from P_0 to P_1). This is the case in which an expansionary fiscal policy works well. There is an increase in output with little increase in the price level. When the economy is producing on the nearly flat portion of the *AS* curve, firms are producing well below capacity, and they will respond to an increase in demand by increasing output much more than they increase prices.

Figure 13.2 shows what happens when the economy is operating on the steep part of the *AS* curve (point *B*), where the economy is already operating at a high level relative to its resources. In this case, an expansionary fiscal policy results in a small change in equilibrium output (from Y_0 to Y_1) and a large change in the equilibrium price level (from P_0 to P_1). Here, an expansionary fiscal policy does not work well. The output multiplier is close to zero. Output is initially close to capacity, and attempts to increase it further mostly lead to a higher price level.

Make sure you understand what is happening behind the scenes in Figure 13.2. For example, in the case of a government spending increase, why does output not increase much on the steep part of the *AS* curve? When there is an increase in *G*, the demand for firms' goods increases. Because firms are near capacity, they respond by mostly raising their prices instead of increasing their outputs. The rise in prices raises the overall price level (*P*). Now the Fed enters. The price level is in the Fed rule, and when *P* rises, the Fed increases the interest rate (*r*). The higher interest rate lowers planned investment. If total output cannot be increased very much because the economy is near capacity, the interest rate must rise enough to decrease planned investment enough to offset the increase in government spending in the new equilibrium. In this case there is almost complete crowding out of planned investment.

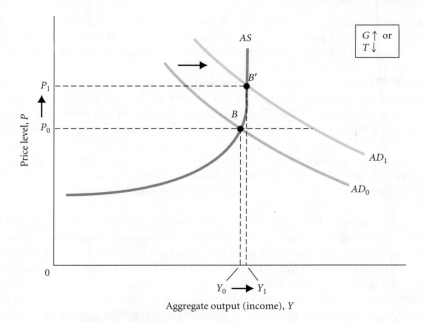

▲ **FIGURE 13.2** **A Shift of the *AD* Curve When the Economy is Operating at or Near Capacity**

What is behind the scenes if there is a decrease in net taxes (T) in Figure 13.2 on the steep part of the *AS* curve? In this case, consumption demand increases (because after tax income has increased), which is also a demand increase for firms' goods. Firms again mostly raise their prices, so P increases, and so the Fed raises the interest rate, which lowers planned investment. If total output is little changed, the interest rate must rise such that the decrease in planned investment is roughly equal to the increase in consumption in the new equilibrium. In this case, consumption rather than government spending crowds out planned investment. Consumption is higher even though output is little changed because after tax income is higher due to the decrease in T (disposable income, $Y-T$, is higher).

Note that in Figure 13.1, where the economy is on the flat part of the *AS* curve, there is very little crowding out of planned investment. Output expands to meet the increased demand. Because the price level increases very little, the Fed does not raise the interest rate much, and so there is little change in planned investment.

Fiscal Policy Effects in the Long Run

We can now turn to look at the long-run effects of fiscal policy. Most economists believe that in the long run wages adjust to some extent to match rising prices. Eventually, as prices rise, we would expect workers to demand and get higher wages. If wages adjust fully, then the long-run *AS* curve is vertical. In this case it is easy to see that fiscal policy will have no effect on output. If the government increases G or decreases T, thus shifting up the *AD* curve, the full effect is felt on the price level. Here, the long-run response to fiscal policy looks very much like that on the steep part of the short-run *AS* curve.

So we see that the key question, much debated in macroeconomics, is how fast wages adjust to changes in prices. If wages adjust to prices in a matter of a few months, the *AS* curve quickly becomes vertical and fiscal policy will be short-lived. If wages are slower to adjust, the *AS* curve might retain some upward slope for a long period and one would be more confident about the usefulness of fiscal policy. While most economists believe that wages are slow to adjust in the short run and therefore that fiscal policy has potential effects in the short run, there is less consensus about the shape of the long-run *AS* curve. In an interesting way, economists' views about how effective fiscal policy can be—whether the government can *ever* spend itself out of a low output state—is summarized in whether they believe the long-run *AS* curve is vertical or upward sloping.

Another source of disagreement among macroeconomists centers on whether equilibria below potential output, $\overline{Y}$ in Figure 12.9 in Chapter 12, are self-correcting (that is, without government intervention). Recall that those who believe in a vertical long-run *AS* curve believe that slack in the economy will put downward pressure on wages, causing the short-run *AS* curve to shift to the right and pushing aggregate ouput back toward potential output. However, some argue that wages do *not* fall much during slack periods and that the economy can get "stuck" at an equilibrium below potential output. In this case, monetary and fiscal policy would be necessary to restore full employment. We will return to this debate in Chapter 14.

The "new classical" economics, which we will discuss in Chapter 18, assumes that prices and wages are fully flexible and adjust very quickly to changing conditions. New classical economists believe, for example, that wage rate changes do not lag behind price changes. The new classical view is consistent with the existence of a vertical *AS* curve, even in the short run. At the other end of the spectrum is what is sometimes called the simple "Keynesian" view of aggregate supply. Those who hold this view believe there is a kink in the *AS* curve at capacity output, as we discussed in the *Economics in Practice*, "The Simple 'Keynesian' Aggregate Supply Curve," in Chapter 12. As we have seen, these differences in perceptions of the way the markets act have large effects on the advice economists give to the government.

Monetary Policy Effects

Monetary policy is controlled by the Fed, which we are assuming behaves according to the Fed rule described in Chapter 12. The interest rate value that the Fed chooses *(r)* depends on output *(Y)*, the price level *(P)*, and other factors *(Z)*. The Fed achieves the interest rate value that it wants though open market operations. But how effective is the Fed in moving the economy as it follows its rule? There are several features of the *AS/AD* model that we need to consider regarding the effectiveness of the Fed, which we turn to now.

The Fed's Response to the Z Factors

We noted in Chapter 12 that the Fed is not just a mechanical calculator, responding in a mechanical way to *Y* and *P*. The Fed is affected by things outside of our model. Looking at reports of consumer sentiment, the Fed may decide that the economy is more fragile than one might have thought looking at only output and the price level. Or perhaps the Fed is worried about something unfavorable in the international arena. If one of these "Z" factors, as we have called them, changes, the Fed may decide to set the interest rate above or below what the values of *Y* and *P* alone call for in the rule.

Since *Z* is outside of the *AS/AD* model (that is, exogenous to the model), we can ask what changes in *Z* do to the model. We have in fact already seen the answer to this question in Figure 12.8 in Chapter 12. An increase in *Z*, like an increase in consumer confidence, shifts the *AD* curve to the left. Remember that an increase in *Z* is a tightening of monetary policy in that the interest rate is set higher than what *Y* and *P* alone would call for. Similarly, a decrease in *Z* shifts the *AD* curve to the right. This is an easing of monetary policy.

In the previous section, we used that fact that *G* and *T* shift the *AD* curve to analyze the effectiveness of fiscal policy in different situations (flat, normal, or steep part of the *AS* curve). This same analysis pertains to *Z*. Monetary policy in the form of changes in *Z* has the same issues as does fiscal policy in the form of changes in *G* and *T*. (You should review in Chapter 12 why changes in *Z* shift the *AD* curve if this is not clear.)

ECONOMICS IN PRACTICE

Alternative Tools for the Federal Reserve

Twice a year, Ben Bernanke, as chair of the Federal Reserve, testifies before Congress and is grilled by Republicans and Democrats alike on Fed policy. In December 2012, Bernanke talked about Fed reactions to the on-going "almost Zero" interest rates.

As we noted in the text, with negative interest rates not possible, a zero interest rate poses challenges for a Fed that wants to further stimulate the economy. In his December 2012 remarks, Bernanke mentioned two alternative policies the Fed was pursuing to stimulate the economy. First, the Fed was purchasing long-term government securities with the aim of driving down long-term interest rates (which, unlike short-term interest rates, were not zero).

Second, the Fed was engaging in what Bernanke called "forward guidance." Not only does the Fed now say at regular intervals what its current interest-rate policy is, but it gives guidance as to what it will do in the future. In its December 2012 meeting, for example, the Fed indicated that interest rates would stay close to zero as long as the unemployment rate was over 6.5 percent and inflation was less than 2.5 percent. Clearly, the Fed believes that one key to stimulating a currently sluggish economy is reassuring households and firms that it will continue to stimulate!

THINKING PRACTICALLY

1. Does the Fed's choice of 6.5 percent for the unemployment rate in its statement suggest that it thinks that the full employment unemployment rate is 6.5 percent?

Shape of the *AD* Curve When the Fed Cares More About the Price Level than Output

In the equation representing the Fed rule, we used a weight of α for output and a weight of β for the price level. The relative size of these two coefficients can be thought of as a measure of how much the Fed cares about output versus the price level.[1] If α is small relative to β, this means that the Fed has a strong preference for stable prices relative to output. In this case, when the Fed sees a price increase, it responds with a large increase in the interest rate, thus driving down planned investment and thus output. In this case, the *AD* curve is relatively flat, as depicted in Figure 13.3. The Fed is willing to accept large changes in *Y* to keep *P* stable. We will return to Figure 13.3 when we discuss cost shocks.

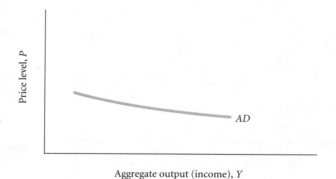

▲ **FIGURE 13.3   The Shape of the *AD* Curve When the Fed Has a Strong Preference for Price Stability Relative to Output**

---

[1] Remember that the Fed actually cares about inflation, the change in *P*, rather than the level of *P* itself. We are using *P* as an approximation.

The issue of how much weight the Fed puts on the price level relative to output is related to the issue of inflation targeting, which is discussed at the end of this chapter. If a monetary authority is engaged in inflation targeting, then it behaves as if inflation is the only variable in its interest rate rule. This is not, however, the way the Fed operates—it does care about output. In fact, in late 2012, the Fed explicitly set 6.5 percent as a target for the unemployment rate before it would begin to raise the interest rate. See the Economics in Practice on page 563.

What Happens When There is a Zero Interest Rate Bound?

Since 2008 short-term interest rates in the United States have been close to zero. For all practical purposes, an interest rate cannot be negative. We don't charge people when they save money or pay them to borrow money. The fact that the interest rate is bounded by zero has implications for the shape of the AD curve, which we will now explain.

zero interest rate bound
The interest rate cannot go below zero.

Let us begin with the Fed rule. Suppose the conditions of the economy in terms of output, the price level, and the Z factors are such that the Fed wants a *negative* interest rate. In this case, the best that the Fed can do is to choose zero for the value of r, which again it has mostly done since 2008 (at the time of this writing). (This is called a **zero interest rate bound**.) If Y or P or Z begin to increase, there is some point at which the rule will call for a positive value of r, at which time the Fed will move from zero to the positive value. The fact that the interest rate has remained at roughly zero for many years in the United States suggests that Y, P, and Z can be calling for a negative interest rate for many years. This is the situation we are concerned with in this section—the case in which the values of Y, P, and Z are far below what they would have to be to call for a positive interest rate in the Fed rule. We will call this situation a **binding situation**.

binding situation State of the economy in which the Fed rule calls for a negative interest rate.

What does Figure 12.7 in Chapter 12 look like in a binding situation? This is shown in Figure 13.4. In this situation the interest rate is always zero, and so equilibrium is just where the IS curve crosses zero. In this binding situation, changes in P and Z do not shift anything (as they did in Figure 12.7) because the interest rate is always zero. In a binding situation the AD curve is vertical, as shown in Figure 13.5. It is easy to see why. In the normal case, an increase in P leads the Fed through the rule to increase the interest rate, which lowers planned investment and thus output. A decrease in P leads to the opposite. In the binding case, the interest rate does not change when P changes (it is always zero), and so planned investment

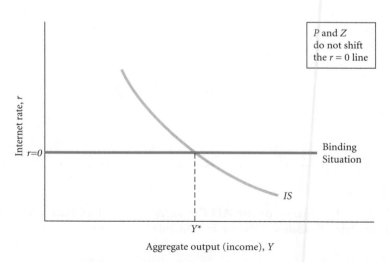

▲ **FIGURE 13.4 Equilibrium In the Goods Market When the Interest Rate is Zero.** In a binding situation changes in P and Z do not shift the $r = 0$ line.

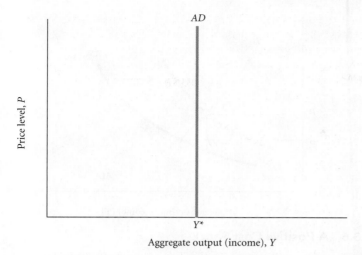

▲ **FIGURE 13.5   The *AD* Curve in a Binding Situation.** In a binding situation the interest rate is always zero.

and thus output do not change. In order for the *AD* curve to have a slope, the interest rate must change when the price level changes, which does not happen in the binding situation. Note also that changes in *Z* do not shift the *AD* curve in a binding situation (unlike the case in Figure 12.8 in Chapter 12). Again, the interest rate is always zero—it does not change when *Z* changes in a binding situation.

You should note that changes in government spending (*G*) and net taxes (*T*) still shift the *AD* curve even if it is vertical. In fact, since there is no crowding out of planned investment or consumption when *G* increases or *T* decreases because the interest rate does not increase, the shift is even greater. With a vertical *AD* curve, fiscal policy can be used to increase output, but monetary policy cannot. You might ask, what if the economy is on the nearly vertical part of the *AS* curve and a vertical *AD* curve is shifted to the right of the vertical part? Alas, there would be no intersection any more. Here the model would break down, but fortunately this is not a realistic case. If the economy is on the nearly vertical part of the *AS* curve, it is highly unlikely that a binding situation will exist and thus highly unlikely that the *AD* curve will be vertical. If the economy is on the nearly vertical part of the *AS* curve, output and possibly the price level would be high, and it is unlikely the Fed would want a negative interest rate in this case.

Shocks to the System

Cost Shocks

Suppose we have a sudden and severe cold spell that kills off a large fraction of the feeder-fish stock in the world. Or suppose that war breaks out in the Middle East and oil supplies from the region are cut off. How do events like these affect aggregate output and the price level in an economy? When things like this happen, what is the Fed likely to do? The *AS/AD* model can help guide us through to answers to these questions.

These examples are cost shocks, which were introduced in Chapter 12. We chose the examples carefully. In both cases the shock occurred in products that are used as inputs into a wide variety of other products. So a disaster in the fish or oil markets is likely to increase all at once the costs of many firms. The *AS* curve shifts to the left as firms who experience these new costs raise their prices to cover their new higher costs.

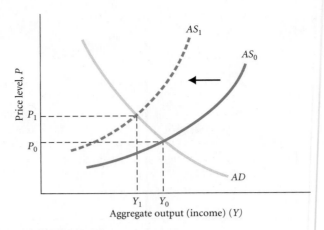

▲ **FIGURE 13.6** **A Positive Cost Shock**

Figure 13.6 shows what happens to the economy when the *AS* curve shifts to the left. This leads to stagflation. Equilibrium output falls from Y_0 to Y_1, and the equilibrium price level rises from P_0 to P_1. The reason output falls is that the increase in *P* leads the Fed to raise the interest rate, which lowers planned investment and thus output. Remember that the Fed rule is a "leaning against the wind" rule, and when the price level rises the Fed leans against the wind by raising the interest rate.

We have seen in the previous two sections that when analyzing the effects of changing *G*, *T*, and *Z*, the shape of the *AS* curve matters. When analyzing the effects of cost shocks, on the other hand, it is the shape of the *AD* curve that matters. Consider, for example, the case where the *AD* curve is fairly flat, as in Figure 13.3. This is the case where the Fed puts a large weight on price stability relative to output. In this case, a leftward shift of the *AS* curve results in a large decrease in output relative to the increase in the price level. Behind the scenes the Fed is raising the interest rate a lot, thus lowering planned investment and thus output a lot, to offset much of the price effect of the cost shock. The price level rises less and output falls more than it would if the *AD* curve were shaped more like the one in Figure 13.6.

An interesting case is when the *AD* curve is vertical, as in Figure 13.5. Remember that this is the case of a binding situation with a zero interest rate. When the *AD* curve is vertical and the *AS* curve shifts to the left, there is no change in output. The only change is a higher price level. In a binding situation the increase in *P* does not change *r* (*r* is still zero), so planned investment is unaffected, and thus output is unaffected. Remember that this story holds only as long as the situation remains binding. At some point if there are large leftward shifts in the *AS* curve, *P* will be high enough that the binding situation no longer holds. When this happens, Figure 13.5 is not relevant, and we are back to Figure 13.6.

When the price level rises because the *AS* curve shifts to the left, this is called **cost-push,** *or* **supply-side, inflation**. As we have seen, this is accompanied by lower output. There is thus higher inflation and lower output, or **stagflation**.

Demand-Side Shocks

We know from the previous two sections that an expansionary fiscal policy (an increase in *G* or a decrease in *T*) and an expansionary monetary policy (a decrease in *Z*) shifts the *AD* curve to the right and results in a higher price level. This is an increase in the price level caused by an increase in demand and is called **demand-pull inflation**. Contrary to cost-push inflation, demand-pull inflation corresponds to higher output rather than lower.

There are other sources of demand shifts, exogenous to the model, that are interesting to consider. These we can put under the general heading of demand-side shocks. As mentioned

cost-push, *or* **supply-side, inflation** Inflation caused by an increase in costs.

stagflation Occurs when output is falling at the same time that prices are rising.

demand-pull inflation Inflation that is initiated by an increase in aggregate demand.

ECONOMICS IN PRACTICE

A Bad Monsoon Season Fuels Indian Inflation

In 2012, the Indian monsoons came with less rain than normal. For the rice crop, this was a large and adverse shock. Rice is grown in water-laden paddies, and domestic production fell dramatically with the weather shock. The result for India, which is a large consumer of rice, was a substantial increase in the price of rice. Nearby countries also growing rice, like Thailand, were not able to make up for India's production deficiencies, and rice prices rose throughout much of Southeast Asia.

For a country like the United States, a rise in rice prices would likely have little effect on overall prices. There are many substitutes for rice in the United States and rice plays a small role in the average household budget. The same is not true for India, which is both poorer (meaning that food in general is a larger part of the budget) and much more dependent on rice. For India, the weather shock on rice threatened to increase the overall inflation rate, which at 10 percent was already high by U.S. standards, and the Indian government struggled to try to manage this (supply) shock.

THINKING PRACTICALLY

1. What two features of the Indian economy meant that an increase in rice prices was likely to spread through the economy and influence the overall inflation rate?

in Chapter 5, in the 1930's when macroeconomics was just beginning, John Maynard Keynes introduced the idea of "animal spirits" of investors. Keynes' animal spirits were his way of describing a kind of optimism about the economy that helped propel it forward. Animal spirits, while maybe important to the economy, are not explained by our model. Within the present context, an improvement in animal spirits—for example, a rise in consumer confidence—can be thought of as a "demand-side shock."

What happens when, say, there is a positive demand-side shock? The *AD* curve shifts to the right. This will lead to some increase in output and some increase in the price level, how much of each depends on where the economy is on the *AS* curve. There is nothing new to our story about aggregate demand increases except that instead of being triggered by a fiscal or monetary policy change, the demand increase is triggered by something outside of the model. Any price increase that results from a demand-side shock is also considered demand-pull inflation.

Expectations

Animal spirits can be considered expectations of the future. Expectations in general likely have important effects on the economy, but they are hard to predict or to quantify. However formed, firms' expectations of future prices may affect their current price decisions. If a firm expects that its competitors will raise their prices, it may raise its own price in anticipation of this. An increase in future price expectations may thus shift the *AS* curve to the left and thus act like a cost shock. How might this work?

Consider a firm that manufactures toasters in an imperfectly competitive market. The toaster maker must decide what price to charge retail stores for its toaster. If it overestimates price and charges much more than other toaster manufacturers are charging, it will lose many customers. If it underestimates price and charges much less than other toaster makers are charging, it will gain customers but at a considerable loss in revenue per sale. The firm's *optimum price*—the price that maximizes the firm's profits—is presumably not too far from the average of its competitors' prices. If it does not know its competitors' projected prices before it sets its own price, as is often the case, it must base its price on what it expects its competitors' prices to be.

Suppose inflation has been running at about 10 percent per year. Our firm probably expects its competitors will raise their prices about 10 percent this year, so it is likely to raise the price of its own toaster by about 10 percent. This response is how expectations can get "built into the system." If every firm expects every other firm to raise prices by 10 percent, every firm will raise prices by about 10 percent. Every firm ends up with the price increase it expected.

The fact that expectations can affect the price level is vexing. Expectations can lead to an inertia that makes it difficult to stop an inflationary spiral. If prices have been rising and if people's expectations are *adaptive*—that is, if they form their expectations on the basis of past pricing behavior—firms may continue raising prices even if demand is slowing or contracting. In terms of the *AS/AD* diagram, an increase in inflationary expectations that causes firms to increase their prices shifts the *AS* curve to the left. Remember that the *AS* curve represents the price/output responses of firms. If firms increase their prices because of a change in inflationary expectations, the result is a leftward shift of the *AS* curve.

Given the importance of expectations in inflation, the central banks of many countries survey consumers about their expectations. In Great Britain, for example, a February 2013 survey by the Bank of England found that consumers expected inflation of 3.2 percent for the period 2013–2014. A similar survey by the Bank of India found consumer expectations of inflation in this period to be in the 10 percent range. One of the aims of central banks is to try to keep these expectations low.

Monetary Policy since 1970

At the end of Chapter 9, we compared the fiscal policies of the Clinton, Bush, and Obama administrations. In this section, we will review what monetary policy has been like since 1970. Remember by monetary policy we mean the interest rate behavior of the Fed. How has the Fed changed the interest rate in response to economic conditions?

Figure 13.7 plots three variables that can be used to discuss Fed behavior since 1970. The interest rate is the 3-month Treasury bill rate, which moves closely with the interest rate that the Fed actually controls, which is the federal funds rate. For simplicity, we will take the 3-month Treasury bill rate to be the rate that the Fed controls and we will just call it "the interest rate." Inflation is the percentage change in the GDP deflator over the previous 4 quarters. This variable is also plotted in Figure 5.6 on p. 107. Output is the percentage deviation of real GDP from its trend. (Real GDP itself is plotted in Figure 5.4 on p. 106.) It is easier to see fluctuations in real GDP by looking at percentage deviations from its trend.

Recall from Chapter 5 that we have called five periods since 1970 "recessionary periods" and two periods "high inflation periods." These periods are highlighted in Figure 13.7. The recessionary and high inflation periods have considerable overlap in the last half of the 1970s and early 1980s. After 1981, there are no more high inflation periods and three more recessionary periods. There is thus some stagflation in the early part of the period since 1970 but not in the later part.

We know from earlier in this chapter that stagflation is bad news for policy makers. No matter what the Fed does, it will result in a worsening of either output or inflation. Should the Fed raise the interest rate to lessen inflation at a cost of making the output situation worse, or should it lower the interest rate to help output growth at a cost of making inflation worse? What did the Fed actually do? You can see from Figure 13.7 that the Fed generally raised the interest rate when inflation was high—even when output was low. So, the Fed seems to have worried more in this period about inflation. The interest rate was very high in the 1979–1983 period even though output was low. Had the Fed not had such high interest rates in this period, the recession would likely have been less severe, but inflation would have been even worse. Paul Volcker, Fed chair at that time, was both hailed as an inflation-fighting hero and pilloried for what was labeled the "Volcker recession."

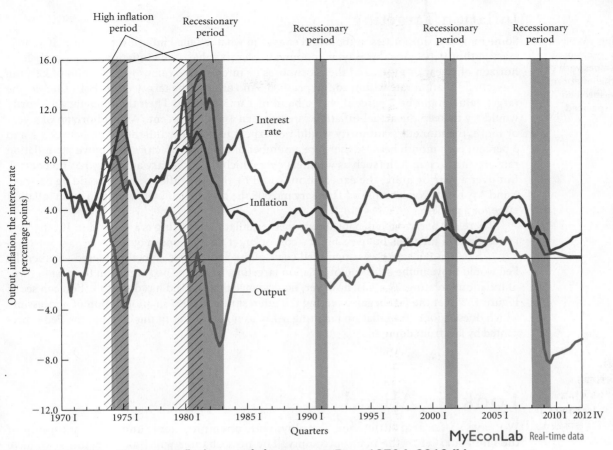

▲ FIGURE 13.7   Output, Inflation, and the Interest Rate 1970 I–2012 IV
The Fed generally had high interest rates in the two inflationary periods and low interest rates from the
mid-1980s on. It aggressively lowered interest rates in the 1990 III–1991 I, 2001 I–2001 III, and 2008 I–2009
II recessions. Output is the percentage deviation of real GDP from its trend. Inflation is the 4-quarter average
of the percentage change in the GDP deflator. The interest rate is the 3-month Treasury bill rate.

After inflation got back down to about 4 percent in 1983, the Fed began lowering the
interest rate, which helped to increase output. The Fed increased the interest rate in 1988
as inflation began to pick up a little and output was strong. The Fed acted aggressively in
lowering the interest rate during the 1990–1991 recession and again in the 2001 recession.
The Treasury bill rate got below 1 percent in 2003. The Fed then reversed course, and the
interest rate rose to nearly 5 percent in 2006. The Fed then reversed course again near the
end of 2007 and began lowering the interest rate in an effort to fight a recession that it
expected was coming. The recession did come, and the Fed lowered the interest rate to near
zero beginning in 2008 IV. The interest rate has remained at essentially zero since then. This
is the zero interest rate bound discussed earlier in this chapter. The period 2008 IV–2012 IV
is a "binding situation" period.

Fed behavior in the period since 1970 is thus fairly easy to summarize. The Fed generally
had high interest rates in the 1970s and early 1980s as it fought inflation. Since 1983, inflation
has been low by historical standards, and the Fed focused between 1983 and 2008 on trying
to smooth fluctuations in output. Since the end of 2008, there has been a zero interest rate
bound.

Inflation Targeting

inflation targeting When a monetary authority chooses its interest rate values with the aim of keeping the inflation rate within some specified band over some specified horizon.

Some monetary authorities in the world engage in what is called **inflation targeting**. If a monetary authority behaves this way, it announces a *target* value of the inflation rate, usually for a horizon of a year or more, and then it chooses its interest rate values with the aim of keeping the actual inflation rate within some specified band around the target value. For example, the target value might be 2 percent with a band of 1 to 3 percent. Then the monetary authority would try to keep the actual inflation rate between 1 and 3 percent. With a horizon of a year or more, the monetary authority would not expect to keep the inflation rate between 1 and 3 percent each month because there are a number of temporary factors that move the inflation rate around each month (such as weather) over which the monetary authority has no control. But over a year or more, the expectation would be that the inflation rate would be between 1 and 3 percent. For example, in Hungary in 2008 the central bank set a medium-term inflation target of 3 percent.

There has been much debate about whether inflation targeting is a good idea. It can lower fluctuations in inflation, but possibly at a cost of larger fluctuations in output.

When Ben Bernanke was appointed chair of the Fed in 2006, some wondered whether the Fed would move in the direction of inflation targeting. Bernanke had argued in the past in favor of inflation targeting. There is, however, no evidence that the Fed has done this. You can see in Figure 13.7 that the Fed began lowering the interest rate in 2007 in anticipation of a recession, which doesn't look like inflation targeting. Also, as noted earlier in this chapter, the Fed is prevented by law from doing so.

Looking Ahead

We have so far said little about employment, unemployment, and the functioning of the labor market in the macroeconomy. The next chapter will link everything we have done so far to this third major market arena—the labor market—and to the problem of unemployment.

SUMMARY

FISCAL POLICY EFFECTS *p. 247*

1. Increases in government spending (*G*) and decreases in net taxes (*T*) shift the *AD* curve to the right and increase output and the price level. How much each increases depends on where the economy is on the *AS* curve before the change.

2. If the *AS* curve is vertical in the long run, then changes in *G* and *T* have no effect on output in the long run.

MONETARY POLICY EFFECTS *p. 249*

3. Monetary policy is determined by the Fed rule, which includes output, the price level, and the factors in *Z*. Changes in *Z* shift the *AD* curve.

4. The *AD* curve is flatter the more the Fed weights price stability relative to output.

5. A binding situation is a state of the economy in which the Fed rule calls for a negative interest rate. In this case the best the Fed can do is have a zero interest rate.

6. The *AD* curve is vertical in a binding situation.

SHOCKS TO THE SYSTEM *p. 252*

7. Positive cost shocks shift the *AS* curve to the left, creating *cost-push inflation*.

8. Positive demand-side shocks shift the *AD* curve to the right, creating *demand-pull inflation*.

MONETARY POLICY SINCE 1970 *p. 255*

9. The Fed generally had high interest rates in the 1970s and early 1980s as it fought inflation. Since 1983, inflation has been low by historical standards, and the Fed focused between 1983 and 2008 on trying to smooth fluctuations in output. Since the end of 2008, there has been a zero interest rate bound.

10. Inflation targeting is the case where the monetary authority weights only inflation. It chooses its interest rate value with the aim of keeping the inflation rate within some specified band over some specified horizon.

REVIEW TERMS AND CONCEPTS

binding situation, *p. 251*

cost-push, *or* supply-side inflation, *p. 253*

demand-pull inflation, *p. 253*

inflation targeting, *p. 257*

stagflation, *p. 253*

zero interest rate bound, *p. 251*

PROBLEMS

All problems are available on MyEconLab.

1. During the third quarter of 1997, Japanese GDP was falling at a rate of over 11 percent. Many blamed the big increase in Japan's taxes in the spring of 1997, which was designed to balance the budget. Explain how an increase in taxes with the economy growing slowly could precipitate a recession. Do not skip steps in your answer. If you were head of the Japanese central bank, how would you respond? What impact would your policy have on the level of investment?

2. For each of the following scenarios, tell a story and predict the effects on the equilibrium level of aggregate output (*Y*) and the interest rate (*r*):

   a. During 2005, the Federal Reserve was tightening monetary policy in an attempt to slow the economy. Congress passed a substantial cut in the individual income tax at the same time.

   b. During the summer of 2003, Congress passed and President George W. Bush signed the third tax cut in 3 years. Many of the tax cuts took effect in 2005. Assume that the Fed holds M^s fixed.

   c. In 1993, the government raised taxes. At the same time, the Fed was pursuing an expansionary monetary policy.

   d. In 2005, conditions in Iraq led to a sharp drop in consumer confidence and a drop in consumption. Assume that the Fed holds the money supply constant.

   e. The Fed attempts to increase the money supply to stimulate the economy, but plants are operating at 65 percent of their capacities and businesses are pessimistic about the future.

3. Paranoia, the largest country in central Antarctica, receives word of an imminent penguin attack. The news causes

expectations about the future to be shaken. As a consequence, there is a sharp decline in investment spending plans.

a. Explain in detail the effects of such an event on the economy of Paranoia, assuming no response on the part of the central bank or the Treasury (M^s, T, and G all remain constant.) Make sure you discuss the adjustments in the goods market and the money market.

b. To counter the fall in investment, the King of Paranoia calls for a proposal to increase government spending. To finance the program, the Chancellor of the Exchequer has proposed three alternative options:

(1) Finance the expenditures with an equal increase in taxes

(2) Keep tax revenues constant and borrow the money from the public by issuing new government bonds

(3) Keep taxes constant and finance expenditures by printing new money

Consider the three financing options and rank them from most expansionary to least expansionary. Explain your ranking.

4. By late summer 2010, the target federal funds rate was between zero and 0.25 percent. At the same time, "animal spirits" were dormant and there was excess capacity in most industries. That is, businesses were in no mood to build new plant and equipment if they were not using their already existing capital. Interest rates were at or near zero, and yet investment demand remained quite low. The unemployment rate was 9.6 percent in August 2010. These conditions suggest that monetary policy is likely to be a more effective tool to promote expansion than fiscal policy. Do you agree or disagree? Explain your answer.

5. Describe the policy mix that would result in each of the following situations.

a. The interest rate decreases, investment increases, and the change in aggregate output is indeterminate.

b. Aggregate output increases, and the interest rate change is indeterminate.

c. The interest rate increases, investment decreases, and the change in aggregate output is indeterminate.

d. Aggregate output decreases, and the interest rate change is indeterminate.

6. Expansionary policies are designed to stimulate the economy by increasing aggregate output. Explain why expansionary fiscal policy and expansionary monetary policy have opposite effects on the interest rate despite having the same goal of increasing aggregate output. Illustrate your answer with graphs of the money market.

7. Explain the effect, if any, that each of the following occurrences should have on the aggregate demand curve.

a. The Fed lowers the discount rate.

b. The price level decreases.

c. The federal government increases federal income tax rates in an effort to reduce the federal deficit.

d. Pessimistic firms decrease investment spending.

e. The inflation rate falls by 3 percent.

f. The federal government increases purchases to stimulate the economy.

8. In Japan during the first half of 2000, the Bank of Japan kept interest rates at a near zero level in an attempt to stimulate demand. In addition, the government passed a substantial increase in government expenditure and cut taxes. Slowly, Japanese GDP began to grow with absolutely no sign of an increase in the price level. Illustrate the position of the Japanese economy with aggregate supply and aggregate demand curves. Where on the short-run *AS* curve was Japan in 2000?

9. In 2008, the price of oil rose sharply on world markets. What impact would you expect there to be on the aggregate price level and on real GDP? Illustrate your answer with aggregate demand and aggregate supply curves. What would you expect to be the effect on interest rates if the Fed held the money supply constant? Tell a complete story.

10. By using aggregate supply and aggregate demand curves to illustrate your points, discuss the impacts of the following events on the price level and on equilibrium GDP (*Y*) in the *short run*:

a. A tax cut holding government purchases constant with the economy operating at near full capacity

b. An increase in the money supply during a period of high unemployment and excess industrial capacity

c. An increase in the price of oil caused by a war in the Middle East, assuming that the Fed attempts to keep interest rates constant by accommodating inflation

d. An increase in taxes and a cut in government spending supported by a cooperative Fed acting to keep output from falling

11. In country A, all wage contracts are indexed to inflation. That is, each month wages are adjusted to reflect increases in the cost of living as reflected in changes in the price level. In country B, there are no cost-of-living adjustments to wages, but the workforce is completely unionized. Unions negotiate 3-year contracts. In which country is an expansionary monetary policy likely to have a larger effect on aggregate output? Explain your answer using aggregate supply and aggregate demand curves.

12. During 2001, the U.S. economy slipped into a recession. For the next several years, the Fed and Congress used monetary and fiscal policies in an attempt to stimulate the economy. Obtain data on interest rates (such as the prime rate or the federal funds rate). Do you see evidence of the Fed's action? When did the Fed begin its expansionary policy? Obtain data on total federal expenditures, tax receipts, and the deficit. (Try www.commerce.gov). When did fiscal policy become "expansionary"? Which policy seems to have suffered more from policy lags?

13. From the following graph, identify the initial equilibrium, the short-run equilibrium, and the long-run equilibrium based on the scenarios below. Explain your answers and identify what happened to the price level and aggregate output.

Scenario 1. The economy is initially in long-run equilibrium at point *A*, and a cost shock causes cost-push inflation. The government reacts by implementing an expansionary fiscal policy.

Scenario 2. The economy is initially in long-run equilibrium at point *A*, and an increase in government purchases causes

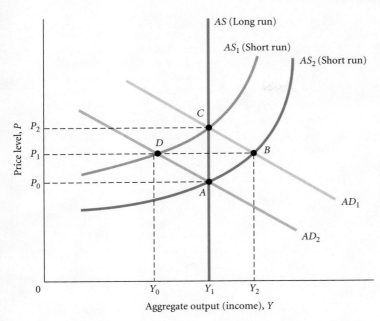

demand-pull inflation. In the long run, wages respond to the inflation.

Scenario 3. The economy is initially in long-run equilibrium at point *C*, and the federal government implements an increase in corporate taxes and personal income taxes. In the long run, firms and workers adjust to the new price level and costs adjust accordingly.

Scenario 4. The economy is initially in long-run equilibrium at point *C*, and energy prices decrease significantly. The government reacts by implementing a contractionary fiscal policy.

14. Evaluate the following statement: In the short run, if an economy experiences inflation of 10 percent, the cause of the inflation is unimportant. Whatever the cause, the only important issue the government needs to be concerned with is the 10 percent increase in the price level.

The Labor Market In the Macroeconomy

14

In Chapter 7 we described some features of the U.S. labor market and explained how the unemployment rate is measured. In Chapter 12 we considered the labor market briefly in our discussion of the aggregate supply curve. Because labor is an input, what goes on in the labor market affects the shape of the aggregate supply (*AS*) curve. Sticky wages cause the *AS* curve to be upward sloping; if wages are completely flexible and rise every time the price level rises by the same percentage, the *AS* curve will be vertical.

In this chapter, we look further at the labor market's role in the macroeconomy. First, we consider the classical view, which holds that wages always adjust to clear the labor market, that is, to equate the supply of and demand for labor. We then consider why the labor market may not always clear and why unemployment may exist. Finally, we discuss the relationship between inflation and unemployment. As we go through the analysis, it is important to recall why unemployment is one of the three primary concerns of macroeconomics. Go back and reread "The Costs of Unemployment" in Chapter 7 (pp. 134–135). It is clear that unemployment imposes heavy costs on the unemployed and on society. In December 2012 there were 12.2 million people unemployed.

The Labor Market: Basic Concepts

On the first Friday of every month, the Labor Department releases the results of a household survey that provides an estimate of the number of people with a job, the employed (*E*), as well as the number of people who are looking for work but cannot find a job, the unemployed (*U*). The labor force (*LF*) is the number of employed plus unemployed:

$$LF = E + U$$

The **unemployment rate** is the number of people unemployed as a percentage of the labor force:

$$\text{unemployment rate} = \frac{U}{LF}$$

To repeat, to be unemployed, a person must be out of a job and actively looking for work. When a person stops looking for work, he or she is considered *out of the labor force* and is no longer counted as unemployed.

LEARNING OBJECTIVES

Define fundamental concepts of the labor market

Explain the classical view of the labor market

Discuss four reasons for the existence of unemployment

Analyze the short-run relationship between unemployment and inflation

Discuss the long-run relationship between unemployment and output

unemployment rate The number of people unemployed as a percentage of the labor force.

It is important to realize that even if the economy is running at or near full capacity, the unemployment rate will never be zero. The economy is dynamic. Students graduate from schools and training programs; some businesses make profits and grow, while others suffer losses and go out of business; people move in and out of the labor force and change careers. It takes time for people to find the right job and for employers to match the right worker with the jobs they have. This **frictional** and **structural unemployment** is inevitable and in many ways desirable. (Review Chapter 7 if these terms are hazy to you.)

In this chapter, we are concerned with **cyclical unemployment**, the increase in unemployment that occurs during recessions and depressions. When the economy contracts, the number of people unemployed and the unemployment rate rise. The United States has experienced several periods of high unemployment. During the Great Depression, the unemployment rate remained high for nearly a decade. In December 1982, more than 12 million people were unemployed, putting the unemployment rate at 10.8 percent. In the recession of 2008–2009, the unemployment rate rose to over 10 percent.

In one sense, the reason employment falls when the economy experiences a downturn is obvious. When firms cut back on production, they need fewer workers, so people get laid off. Employment tends to fall when aggregate output falls and to rise when aggregate output rises. *Nevertheless, a decline in the demand for labor does not necessarily mean that unemployment will rise.* If markets work as we described in Chapters 3 and 4, a decline in the demand for labor will initially create an excess supply of labor. As a result, the wage rate should fall until the quantity of labor supplied again equals the quantity of labor demanded, restoring equilibrium in the labor market. At the new lower wage rate, everyone who wants a job will have one.

If the quantity of labor demanded and the quantity of labor supplied are brought into equilibrium by rising and falling wage rates, there should be no persistent unemployment above the frictional and structural amount. Labor markets should behave just like output markets described by supply and demand curves. This was the view held by the classical economists who preceded Keynes, and it is still the view of a number of economists. Other economists believe that the labor market is different from other markets and that wage rates adjust only slowly to decreases in the demand for labor. If true, economies can suffer bouts of involuntary unemployment.

The Classical View of the Labor Market

The classical view of the labor market is illustrated in Figure 14.1. Classical economists assumed that the wage rate adjusts to equate the quantity demanded with the quantity supplied, thereby implying that unemployment does not exist. If we see people out of work, it just means that they are not interested in working at the going market wage for someone with their skills. To see how wage adjustment might take place, we can use the supply and demand curves in Figure 14.1. Curve D_0 is the **labor demand curve**. Each point on D_0 represents the amount of labor firms want to employ at each given wage rate. Each firm's decision about how much labor to demand is part of its overall profit-maximizing decision. A firm makes a profit by selling output to households. It will hire workers if the value of its output is sufficient to justify the wage that is being paid. Thus, the amount of labor that a firm hires depends on the value of output that workers produce.

Figure 14.1 also shows a **labor supply curve**, labeled S. Each point on the labor supply curve represents the amount of labor households want to supply at each given wage rate. Each household's decision concerning how much labor to supply is part of the overall consumer choice problem of a household. Each household member looks at the market wage rate, the prices of outputs, and the value of leisure time (including the value of staying at home and working in the yard or raising children) and chooses the amount of labor to supply (if any). A household member not in the labor force has decided that his or her time is more valuable in nonmarket activities.

In Figure 14.1 the labor market is initially in equilibrium at W_0 and L_0. Now consider what classical economists think would happen if there is a decrease in the demand for labor. The demand for labor curve shifts in from D_0 to D_1. The new demand curve intersects the labor supply curve at L_1 and W_1. There is a new equilibrium at a lower wage rate, in which fewer people are employed. Note that the fall in the demand for labor has not caused any unemployment. There are fewer people working, but all people interested in working at the wage W_1 are in fact employed.

The classical economists saw the workings of the labor market—the behavior of labor supply and labor demand—as optimal from the standpoint of both individual households and

frictional unemployment The portion of unemployment that is due to the normal working of the labor market; used to denote short-run job/skill matching problems.

structural unemployment The portion of unemployment that is due to changes in the structure of the economy that result in a significant loss of jobs in certain industries.

cyclical unemployment The increase in unemployment that occurs during recessions and depressions.

labor demand curve A graph that illustrates the amount of labor that firms want to employ at each given wage rate.

labor supply curve A graph that illustrates the amount of labor that households want to supply at each given wage rate.

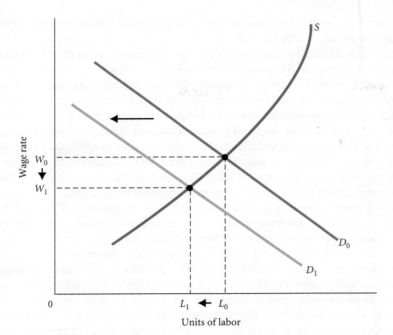

The Classical Labor Market
Classical economists believe that the labor market always clears. If the demand for labor shifts from D_0 to D_1, the equilibrium wage will fall from W_0 to W_1. Anyone who wants a job at W_1 will have one.

firms and from the standpoint of society. If households want more output than is currently being produced, output demand will increase, output prices will rise, the demand for labor will increase, the wage rate will rise, and more workers will be drawn into the labor force. (Some of those who preferred not to be a part of the labor force at the lower wage rate will be lured into the labor force at the higher wage rate.) At equilibrium, prices and wages reflect a trade-off between the value households place on outputs and the value of time spent in leisure and nonmarket work. At equilibrium, the people who are not working have *chosen* not to work at that market wage. There is always *full employment* in this sense. The classical economists believed that the market would achieve the optimal result if left to its own devices, and there is nothing the government can do to make things better.

The Classical Labor Market and the Aggregate Supply Curve

How does the classical view of the labor market relate to the theory of the vertical *AS* curve we covered in Chapter 12? The classical idea that wages adjust to clear the labor market is consistent with the view that wages respond quickly to price changes. In the absence of sticky wages, the *AS* curve will be vertical. In this case, monetary and fiscal policy will have no effect on real output. Indeed, in this view, there is no unemployment problem to be solved!

The Unemployment Rate and the Classical View

If, as the classical economists assumed, the labor market works well, how can we account for the fact that the unemployment rate at times seems high? There seem to be times when millions of people who want jobs at prevailing wage rates cannot find them. How can we reconcile this situation with the classical assumption about the labor market?

Some economists answer by arguing that the unemployment rate is not a good measure of whether the labor market is working well. We know the economy is dynamic and at any given time some industries are expanding and some are contracting. Consider, for example, a carpenter who is laid off because of a contraction in the construction industry. He had probably developed specific skills related to the construction industry—skills not necessarily useful for jobs in other industries. If he were earning $40,000 per year as a carpenter, he may be able to earn only $30,000 per year in another industry. He may eventually work his way back up to a salary of $40,000 in the new industry as he develops new skills, but this process will take time. Will this carpenter take a job at $30,000? There are at least two reasons he may not. First, he may believe that the slump in the construction industry is temporary and that he will soon get his job back.

Second, he may mistakenly believe that he can earn more than $30,000 in another industry and will continue to look for a better job.

If our carpenter decides to continue looking for a job paying more than $30,000 per year, he will be considered unemployed because he is actively looking for work. This does not necessarily mean that the labor market is not working properly. The carpenter has *chosen* not to work for a wage of $30,000 per year, but if his value to any firm outside the construction industry is no more than $30,000 per year, we would not expect him to find a job paying more than $30,000. In this case, a positive unemployment rate as measured by the government does not necessarily indicate that the labor market is working poorly. It just tells us that people are slow to adjust their expectations.

If the degree to which industries are changing in the economy fluctuates over time, there will be more people like our carpenter at some times than at others. This variation will cause the measured unemployment rate to fluctuate. Some economists argue that the measured unemployment rate may sometimes *seem* high even though the labor market is working well. The quantity of labor supplied at the current wage is equal to the quantity demanded at the current wage. The fact that there are people willing to work at a wage higher than the current wage does not mean that the labor market is not working. Whenever there is an upward-sloping supply curve in a market (as is usually the case in the labor market), the quantity supplied at a price higher than the equilibrium price is always greater than the quantity supplied at the equilibrium price.

Economists who view unemployment this way do not see it as a major problem. Yet the haunting images of the bread lines in the 1930s are still with us, and many find it difficult to believe everything was optimal when over 12 million people were counted as unemployed in 2012. There are other views of unemployment, as we will now see.

Explaining the Existence of Unemployment

If unemployment is a major macroeconomic problem—and many economists believe that it is—then we need to explore some of the reasons that have been suggested for its existence. Among these are sticky wages, efficiency wages, imperfect information, and minimum wage laws.

Each of these explanations for unemployment focuses on a particular reason that wage rates do not completely adjust when the demand for labor falls. Because wage rates do not fall as far or as fast as needed, there will be more people who wish to work at the current wage rates than there are jobs for those people. This is what one means by unemployment.

Sticky Wages

sticky wages The downward rigidity of wages as an explanation for the existence of unemployment.

One explanation for unemployment (above and beyond normal frictional and structural unemployment) is that wages are **sticky** on the downward side. We described this briefly in our building of the AS curve. This situation is illustrated in Figure 14.2, where the equilibrium wage gets stuck at W_0 (the original wage) and does not fall to W^* when demand decreases from D_0 to D_1. The result is unemployment of the amount $L_0 - L_1$, where L_0 is the quantity of labor that households want to supply at wage rate W_0 and L_1 is the amount of labor that firms want to hire at wage rate W_0. $L_0 - L_1$ is the number of workers who would like to work at W_0 but cannot find jobs.

The sticky wage explanation of unemployment, however, begs the question. *Why* are wages sticky, if they are, and *why* do wages not fall to clear the labor market during periods of high unemployment? Many answers have been proposed, but as yet no one answer has been agreed on. This lack of consensus is one reason macroeconomics has been in a state of flux for so long. The existence of unemployment continues to be a puzzle. Although we will discuss the major theories that economists have proposed to explain why wages may not clear the labor market, we can offer no conclusions. The question is still open.

social, *or* implicit, contracts Unspoken agreements between workers and firms that firms will not cut wages.

Social, or Implicit, Contracts   One explanation for downwardly sticky wages is that firms enter into **social, *or* implicit, contracts** with workers not to cut wages. It seems that extreme events—deep recession, deregulation, or threat of bankruptcy—are necessary for firms to cut wages. Wage cuts did occur in the Great Depression, in the airline industry following deregulation of the industry in the 1980s, and recently when some U.S. manufacturing firms found themselves in danger of bankruptcy from stiff foreign competition. Even then, wage cuts were typically imposed only on new workers, not existing workers, as in the auto industry in 2008–2009. Broad-based wage cuts are exceptions to the general rule. For reasons that may be more sociological than economic, cutting wages

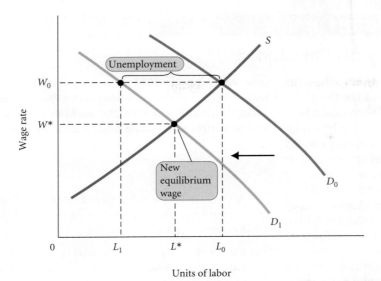

◀ FIGURE 14.2
Sticky Wages
If wages "stick" at W_0 instead
of falling to the new equilibrium
wage of W^* following a shift
of demand from D_0 to D_1, the
result will be unemployment
equal to $L_0 - L_1$.

seems close to being a taboo. In one study, Truman Bewley of Yale University surveyed hundreds of managers about why they did not reduce wage rates in downturns. The most common response was that wage cuts hurt worker morale and thus negatively affect worker productivity. Breaking the taboo and cutting wages may be costly in this sense. Firms seem to prefer laying off existing workers to lowering their wages.

A related argument, the **relative-wage explanation of unemployment**, holds that workers are concerned about their wages *relative* to the wages of other workers in other firms and industries and may be unwilling to accept wage cuts unless they know that other workers are receiving similar cuts. Because it is difficult to reassure any one group of workers that all other workers are in the same situation, workers may resist any cut in their wages. There may be an implicit understanding between firms and workers that firms will not do anything that would make their workers worse off relative to workers in other firms.

Explicit Contracts Many workers—in particular unionized workers—sign 1- to 3-year employment contracts with firms. These contracts stipulate the workers' wages for each year of the contract. Wages set in this way do not fluctuate with economic conditions, either upward or downward. If the economy slows down and firms demand fewer workers, the wage will not fall. Instead, some workers will be laid off.

Although **explicit contracts** can explain why some wages are sticky, a deeper question must also be considered. Workers and firms surely know at the time a contract is signed that unforeseen events may cause the wages set by the contract to be too high or too low. Why do firms and workers bind themselves in this way? One explanation is that negotiating wages is costly. Negotiations between unions and firms can take a considerable amount of time—time that could be spent producing output—and it would be very costly to negotiate wages weekly or monthly. Contracts are a way of bearing these costs at no more than 1-, 2-, or 3-year intervals. There is a trade-off between the costs of locking workers and firms into contracts for long periods of time and the costs of wage negotiations. The length of contracts that minimizes negotiation costs seems to be (from what we observe in practice) between 1 and 3 years.

Some multiyear contracts adjust for unforeseen events by **cost-of-living adjustments (COLAs)** written into the contract. COLAs tie wages to changes in the cost of living: The greater the rate of inflation, the more wages are raised. COLAs thus protect workers from unexpected inflation, although many COLAs adjust wages by a smaller percentage than the percentage increase in prices.

Efficiency Wage Theory

Another explanation for unemployment centers on the **efficiency wage theory**, which holds that the productivity of workers increases with the wage rate. If this is true, firms may have an incentive to pay wages *above* the wage at which the quantity of labor supplied is equal to the quantity of labor demanded.

relative-wage explanation of unemployment An explanation for sticky wages (and therefore unemployment): If workers are concerned about their wages relative to the wages of other workers in other firms and industries, they may be unwilling to accept a wage cut unless they know that all other workers are receiving similar cuts.

explicit contracts Employment contracts that stipulate workers' wages, usually for a period of 1 to 3 years.

cost-of-living adjustments (COLAs) Contract provisions that tie wages to changes in the cost of living. The greater the inflation rate, the more wages are raised.

efficiency wage theory An explanation for unemployment that holds that the productivity of workers increases with the wage rate. If this is so, firms may have an incentive to pay wages above the market-clearing rate.

ECONOMICS IN PRACTICE

Congress Extends Unemployment Insurance

In the United States unemployment insurance benefits are paid out to workers who qualify to cushion the losses associated with spells of unemployment. The standard benefits are managed by states and typically last for 26 weeks. In the recent recession the federal government has provided extended benefits to the unemployed, offering as much as an additional 47 weeks to workers who remain unemployed. Part of the debate surrounding the so-called fiscal cliff in Congress involved whether these benefits should be continued, absent a plan to raise taxes to cover the $30 billion per-year cost of this insurance. In the end, the benefits were continued until December 2013.

How much does extending these benefits matter? The data in Table 7.4 in Chapter 7 show that the recent recession is characterized by unemployment of longer duration than in other recessions. In 2012 the average duration of unemployment was 39.4 weeks. Following the 1980–1982 recession, the average duration peaked at 20.0 weeks in 1983, and following the 1990–1991 recession, it peaked at 18.8 weeks in 1994.

THINKING PRACTICALLY

1. Can you think of any reasons that long-term unemployment is higher in this recession than it has been in the past?

2. Some policy makers worry that extending unemployment benefits will actually increase unemployment. Can you think of any reason this might be true?

The key argument of the efficiency wage theory is that by offering workers a wage in excess of the market wage, the productivity of those workers is increased. Some economists have likened the payment of this higher wage to a gift-exchange: Firms pay a wage in excess of the market wage, and in return, workers work harder or more productively than they otherwise would. Under these circumstances, there will be people who want to work at the wage paid by firms and cannot find employment. Indeed, for the efficiency wage theory to operate, it must be the case that the wage offered by firms is above the market wage. It is the gap between the two that motivates workers who do have jobs to outdo themselves.

Empirical studies of labor markets have identified several potential benefits that firms receive from paying workers more than the market-clearing wage. Among them are lower turnover, improved morale, and reduced "shirking" of work. Even though the efficiency wage theory predicts some unemployment, the behavior it is describing is unlikely to account for much of the observed large cyclical fluctuations in unemployment over time.

Imperfect Information

Thus far we have been assuming that firms know exactly what wage rates they need to set to clear the labor market. They may not choose to set their wages at this level, but at least they know what the market-clearing wage is. In practice, however, firms may not have enough information at their disposal to know what the market-clearing wage is. In this case, firms are said to have *imperfect information*. If firms have imperfect or incomplete information, they may simply set wages wrong—wages that do not clear the labor market.

If a firm sets its wages too high, more workers will want to work for that firm than the firm wants to employ, resulting in some potential workers being turned away. The result is, of course, unemployment. One objection to this explanation is that it accounts for the existence of unemployment only in the very short run. As soon as a firm sees that it has made a mistake, why would it not immediately correct its mistake and adjust its wages to the correct market-clearing level? Why would unemployment *persist*?

If the economy were simple, it should take no more than a few months for firms to correct their mistakes, but the economy is complex. Although firms may be aware of their past mistakes and may try to correct them, new events are happening all the time. Because constant change—including a constantly changing equilibrium wage level—is characteristic of the economy, firms may find it hard to adjust wages to the market-clearing level. The labor market is not like the

ECONOMICS IN PRACTICE

The Longer You are Unemployed, the Harder it is to Get a Job

Almost everyone has been or will be unemployed for a period of time during his or her work career. After graduation, it may take you a while to find a new job. If your firm closes, you may not find something right away. But in some cases, for some people, unemployment lasts a long time. What are the consequences of long-term unemployment?

Simply comparing job market results for people who are unemployed for a long time versus those with no or short spells of unemployment clearly does not tell us the answer. In most cases, people with long spells of unemployment do not look exactly like those with only short spells, and at least some of the differences across those groups may be hard to observe. The authors of a recent paper conducted an interesting experiment to try to figure out what long-term unemployment does to one's eventual job prospects.

Kory Kroft, Fabian Lange, and Matthew Notowidigdo sent out fictitious job resumes to real job postings in 100 U.S. cities.[1] Over 12,000 resumes were sent in response to 3,000 job postings. Fictitious job applicants were randomly assigned unemployment durations of 1 to 36 months. The researchers then tracked "call backs" to these resumes. The result? Call backs decreased dramatically as a response to unemployment duration. This effect was especially strong in cities that had strong job markets. The researchers suggested that employers were likely inferring low worker quality based on long duration of unemployment.

THINKING PRACTICALLY

1. What does this result tell us about how easy it is for firms to see worker quality?

[1] Kory Kroft, Fabian Lange, Matthew Notowidigdo, "Duration Dependence and Labor Market Conditions: Theory and Evidence From a Field Experiment." NBER Working Paper, September 2012.

stock market or the market for wheat, where prices are determined in organized exchanges every day. Instead, thousands of firms are setting wages and millions of workers are responding to these wages. It may take considerable time for the market-clearing wages to be determined after they have been disturbed from an equilibrium position.

Minimum Wage Laws

Minimum wage laws explain at least a small fraction of unemployment. These laws set a floor for wage rates—a minimum hourly rate for any kind of labor. In 2013, the federal minimum wage was $7.25 per hour. If the market-clearing wage for some groups of workers is below this amount, this group will be unemployed. In Figure 14.2, if the minimum wage is W_0 and the market-clearing wage is W^*, the number of unemployed will be $L_0 - L_1$.

minimum wage laws Laws that set a floor for wage rates—that is, a minimum hourly rate for any kind of labor.

Out-of-school teenagers, who have relatively little job experience, are most likely to be hurt by minimum wage laws. If some teenagers can produce only $6.90 worth of output per hour, no firm would be willing to hire them at a wage of $7.25. To do so would incur a loss of $0.35 per hour. In an unregulated market, these teenagers would be able to find work at the market-clearing wage of $6.90 per hour. If the minimum wage laws prevent the wage from falling below $7.25, these workers will not be able to find jobs and they will be unemployed. Others who may be hurt include people with very low skills and some recent immigrants.

Some economists and political observers believe that one of the causes of unemployment is government programs, like unemployment insurance, that reduce the costs of being jobless. The *Economics in Practice* on p. 268 describes a recent extension of unemployment insurance.

An Open Question

As we have seen, there are many explanations for why the labor market may not clear. The theories we have just set forth are not necessarily mutually exclusive, and there may be elements of truth in all of them. The aggregate labor market is very complicated, and there are no simple answers to why there is unemployment. Much current work in macroeconomics is concerned directly or indirectly with this question, and it is an exciting area of study. Which argument or arguments will win out in the end is an open question.

The Short-Run Relationship Between the Unemployment Rate and Inflation

We know from chapter 12 that the Fed cares about both output and the price level. In practice, the Fed typically describes its interests as being unemployment on the one hand and inflation on the other. For example, Ben Bernanke, the Fed chair, gave a speech in June 2008 in which he referred to the "upside risk to inflation" and the "unwelcome rise in the unemployment rate." We are now in a position to connect the Fed interest in output with the unemployment rate and to explore the connection between unemployment and prices.

We begin by looking at the relation between aggregate output (income) (Y) and the unemployment rate (U). For an economy to increase aggregate output, firms must hire more labor to produce that output. Thus, more output implies greater employment. An increase in employment means more people working (fewer people unemployed) and a lower unemployment rate. An increase in Y corresponds to a *decrease* in U. Thus, U and Y are *negatively* related: When Y rises, the unemployment rate falls, and when Y falls, the unemployment rate rises.

What about the relationship between aggregate output and the overall price level? The AS curve, reproduced in Figure 14.3, shows the relationship between Y and the overall price level (P). The relationship is a positive one: When P increases, Y increases, and when P decreases, Y decreases.

As you will recall from the last chapter, the shape of the AS curve is determined by the behavior of firms and how they react to an increase in demand. If aggregate demand shifts to the right and the economy is operating on the nearly flat part of the AS curve—far from capacity—output will increase, but the price level will not change much. However, if the economy is operating on the steep part of the AS curve—close to capacity—an increase in demand will drive up the price level, but output will be constrained by capacity and will not increase much.

Now let us put the two pieces together and think about what will happen following an event that leads to an increase in aggregate demand. First, firms experience an unanticipated decline in inventories. They respond by increasing output (Y) and hiring workers—the unemployment rate falls. If the economy is not close to capacity, there will be little increase in the price level. If, however, aggregate demand continues to grow, the ability of the economy to increase output will eventually reach its limit. As aggregate demand shifts farther and farther to the right along the AS curve, the price level increases more and more and output begins to reach its limit. At the point at which the AS curve becomes vertical, output cannot rise any farther. If output cannot grow, the unemployment rate cannot be pushed any lower. There is a negative relationship between the unemployment rate and the price level. As the unemployment rate declines in response to the economy's moving closer and closer to capacity output, the overall price level rises more and more, as shown in Figure 14.4.

The AS curve in Figure 14.3 shows the relationship between the price level and aggregate output and thus implicitly between the price level and the unemployment rate, which is depicted in Figure 14.4. In policy formulation and discussions, however, economists have focused less on the relationship between the price level and the unemployment rate than on the relationship

▶ **FIGURE 14.3**
The Aggregate Supply Curve
The AS curve shows a positive relationship between the price level (P) and aggregate output (income) (Y).

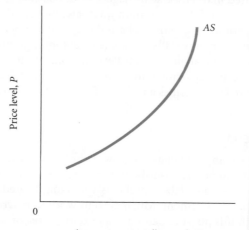

Aggregate output (income), Y

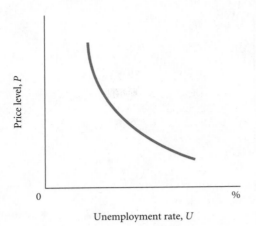

◀ **FIGURE 14.4**
The Relationship Between the Price Level and the Unemployment Rate
This curve shows a negative relationship between the price level (*P*) and the unemployment rate (*U*). As the unemployment rate declines in response to the economy's moving closer and closer to capacity output, the price level rises more and more.

between the **inflation rate**—the percentage change in the price level—and the unemployment rate. Note that the price level and the percentage change in the price level are not the same. The curve describing the relationship between the inflation rate and the unemployment rate, which is shown in Figure 14.5, is called the **Phillips Curve**, after British economist A. W. Phillips, who first examined it using data for the United Kingdom. Fortunately, the analysis behind the *AS* curve (and thus the analysis behind the curve in Figure 14.4) will enable us to see both why the Phillips Curve initially looked so appealing as an explanation of the relationship between inflation and the unemployment rate and how more recent history has changed our views of the interpretation of the Phillips Curve.

inflation rate   The percentage change in the price level.

Phillips Curve   A curve showing the relationship between the inflation rate and the unemployment rate.

The Phillips Curve: A Historical Perspective

In the 1950s and 1960s, there was a remarkably smooth relationship between the unemployment rate and the rate of inflation, as Figure 14.6 shows for the 1960s. As you can see, the data points fit fairly closely around a downward-sloping curve; in general, the higher the unemployment rate is, the lower the rate of inflation. The Phillips Curve in Figure 14.6 shows a trade-off between inflation and unemployment. The curve says that to lower the inflation rate, we must accept a higher unemployment rate, and to lower the unemployment rate, we must accept a higher rate of inflation.

Textbooks written in the 1960s and early 1970s relied on the Phillips Curve as the main explanation of inflation. Things seemed simple—inflation appeared to respond in a fairly predictable way to changes in the unemployment rate. Policy discussions in the 1960s often revolved around the Phillips Curve. The role of the policy maker, it was thought, was to choose a point on the curve. Conservatives usually argued for choosing a point with a low rate of inflation and were willing to accept a higher unemployment rate in exchange for this. Liberals usually argued for accepting more inflation to keep unemployment at a low level.

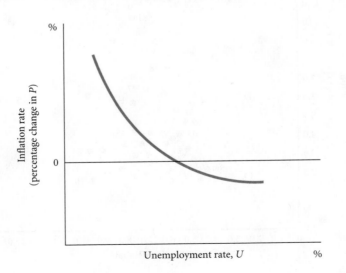

◀ **FIGURE 14.5**
The Phillips Curve
The Phillips Curve shows the relationship between the inflation rate and the unemployment rate.

▶ **FIGURE 14.6**
**Unemployment and
Inflation, 1960–1969**
During the 1960s, there
seemed to be an obvious
trade-off between inflation and
unemployment. Policy debates
during the period revolved
around this apparent trade-off.
Source: See Table 7.5

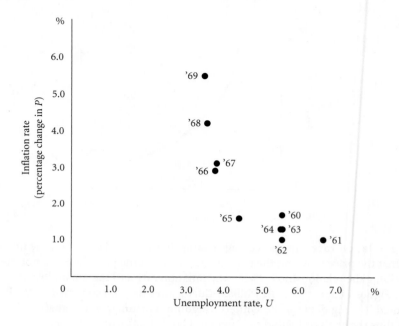

Life did not turn out to be quite so simple. The Phillips Curve broke down in the 1970s
and 1980s. This change can be seen in Figure 14.7, which graphs the unemployment rate and
inflation rate for the period from 1970 to 2012. The points in Figure 14.7 show no particular
relationship between inflation and the unemployment rate.

Aggregate Supply and Aggregate Demand Analysis and the Phillips Curve

How can we explain the stability of the Phillips Curve in the 1950s and 1960s and the lack of
stability after that? To answer, we need to return to *AS/AD* analysis.

If the *AD* curve shifts from year to year but the *AS* curve does not, the values of *P* and *Y* each
year will lie along the *AS* curve [Figure 14.8(a)]. The plot of the relationship between *P* and *Y*
will be upward sloping. Correspondingly, the plot of the relationship between the unemployment rate (which decreases with increased output) and the rate of inflation will be a curve that

▶ **FIGURE 14.7**
**Unemployment and
Inflation, 1970–2012**
From the 1970s on, it became
clear that the relationship between
unemployment and inflation was
anything but simple.
Source: See Table 7.5

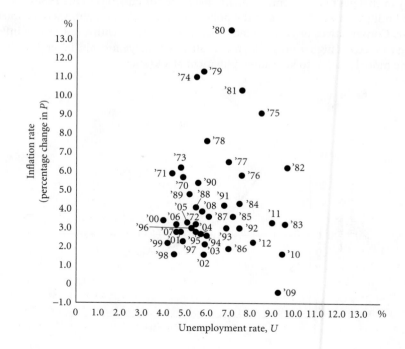

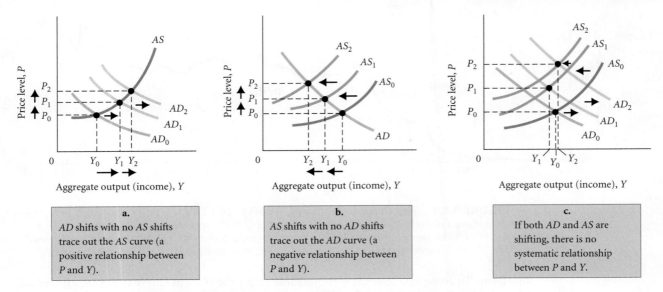

a.	**b.**	**c.**
AS shifts with no *AS* shifts trace out the *AS* curve (a positive relationship between *P* and *Y*).	*AS* shifts with no *AD* shifts trace out the *AD* curve (a negative relationship between *P* and *Y*).	If both *AD* and *AS* are shifting, there is no systematic relationship between *P* and *Y*.

▲ FIGURE 14.8   **Changes in the Price Level and Aggregate Output Depend on Shifts in Both Aggregate Demand and Aggregate Supply**

slopes downward. In other words, we would expect to see a negative relationship between the unemployment rate and the inflation rate, just as we see in Figure 14.6 for the 1960's.

However, the relationship between the unemployment rate and the inflation rate will look different if the *AS* curve shifts from year to year, perhaps from a change in oil prices, but the *AD* curve does not move. A leftward shift of the *AS* curve will cause an *increase* in the price level (*P*) and a *decrease* in aggregate output (*Y*) [Figure 14.8(b)]. When the *AS* curve shifts to the left, the economy experiences both inflation *and* an increase in the unemployment rate (because decreased output means increased unemployment). In other words, if the *AS* curve is shifting from year to year, we would expect to see a positive relationship between the unemployment rate and the inflation rate.

If both the *AS* and the *AD* curves are shifting simultaneously, however, there is no systematic relationship between *P* and *Y* [Figure 14.8(c)] and thus no systematic relationship between the unemployment rate and the inflation rate. One explanation for the change in the Phillips Curve between the 1960s and later periods is that both the *AS* and the *AD* curves appear to be shifting in the later periods—both shifts from the supply side and shifts from the demand side. This can be seen by examining a key cost variable: the price of imports.

The Role of Import Prices   We discussed in the previous chapter that one of the main factors that causes the *AS* curve to shift are energy prices, particularly the price of oil. Since the United States imports much of its oil, the price index of U.S. imports is highly correlated with the (world) price of oil. We can thus consider that a change in the U.S. import price index, which we will call "the price of imports," shifts the *AS* curve. The price of imports is plotted in Figure 14.9 for the 1960 I–2012 IV period. As you can see, the price of imports changed very little between 1960 and 1970. There were no large shifts in the *AS* curve in the 1960s due to changes in the price of imports. There were also no other large changes in input prices in the 1960s, so overall the *AS* curve shifted very little during the decade. The main variation in the 1960s was in aggregate demand, so the shifting *AD* curve traced out points along the *AS* curve.

Figure 14.9 also shows that the price of imports increased considerably in the 1970s. This rise led to large shifts in the *AS* curve during the decade, but the *AD* curve was also shifting throughout the 1970s. With both curves shifting, the data points for *P* and *Y* were scattered all over the graph and the observed relationship between *P* and *Y* was not at all systematic.

This story about import prices and the *AS* and *AD* curves in the 1960s and 1970s carries over to the Phillips Curve. The Phillips Curve was stable in the 1960s because the primary source of variation in the economy was demand, not costs. In the 1970s, both demand *and* costs were varying so no obvious relationship between the unemployment rate and the inflation rate was

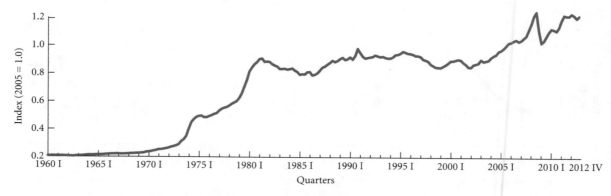

▲ **FIGURE 14.9** **The Price of Imports, 1960 I–2012 IV**   MyEconLab Real-time data

The price of imports changed very little in the 1960s and early 1970s. It increased substantially in 1974 and again in 1979–1980. Between 1981 and 2002, the price of imports changed very little. It generally rose between 2003 and 2008, fell somewhat in late 2008 and early 2009, rose slightly to 2011 and than remained flat.

apparent. To some extent, what is remarkable about the Phillips Curve is not that it was not smooth after the 1960s, but that it ever was smooth.

Expectations and the Phillips Curve

Another reason the Phillips Curve is not stable concerns expectations. We saw in Chapter 13 that if a firm expects other firms to raise their prices, the firm may raise the price of its own product. If all firms are behaving this way, prices will rise because they are expected to rise. In this sense, expectations are self-fulfilling. Similarly, if inflation is expected to be high in the future, negotiated wages are likely to be higher than if inflation is expected to be low. Wage inflation is thus affected by expectations of future price inflation. Because wages are input costs, prices rise as firms respond to the higher wage costs. Price expectations that affect wage contracts eventually affect prices themselves.

If the rate of inflation depends on expectations, the Phillips Curve will shift as expectations change. For example, if inflationary expectations increase, the result will be an increase in the rate of inflation even though the unemployment rate may not have changed. In this case, the Phillips Curve will shift to the right. If inflationary expectations decrease, the Phillips Curve will shift to the left—there will be less inflation at any given level of the unemployment rate.

It so happened that inflationary expectations were quite stable in the 1950s and 1960s. The inflation rate was moderate during most of this period, and people expected it to remain moderate. With inflationary expectations not changing very much, there were no major shifts of the Phillips Curve, a situation that helps explain its stability during the period.

Near the end of the 1960s, inflationary expectations began to increase, primarily in response to the actual increase in inflation that was occurring because of the tight economy caused by the Vietnam War. Inflationary expectations increased even further in the 1970s as a result of large oil price increases. These changing expectations led to shifts of the Phillips Curve and are another reason the curve was not stable during the 1970s.

Inflation and Aggregate Demand

It is important to realize that the fact that the Phillips Curve broke down during the 1970s does not mean that aggregate demand has no effect on inflation. It simply means that inflation is affected by more than just aggregate demand. If, say, inflation is also affected by cost variables like the price of imports, there will be no stable relationship between just inflation and aggregate demand unless the cost variables are not changing. Similarly, if the unemployment rate is taken to be a measure of aggregate demand, where inflation depends on both the unemployment rate and cost variables, there will be no stable Phillips Curve unless the cost variables are not changing. Therefore, the unemployment rate can have an important effect on inflation even though this will not be evident from a plot of inflation against the unemployment rate—that is, from the Phillips Curve.

The Long-Run Aggregate Supply Curve, Potential Output, and the Natural Rate of Unemployment

Thus far we have been discussing the relationship between inflation and unemployment, looking at the short-run AS and AD curves. We turn now to look at the long run, focusing on the connection between output and unemployment.

Recall from Chapter 13 that many economists believe that in the long run, the AS curve is vertical. We have illustrated this case in Figure 14.10. Assume that the initial equilibrium is at the intersection of AD_0 and the long-run aggregate supply curve. Now consider a shift of the aggregate demand curve from AD_0 to AD_1. If wages are sticky and lag prices, in the short run, aggregate output will rise from Y_0 to Y_1. (This is a movement along the short-run AS curve AS_0.) In the longer run, wages catch up. For example, next year's labor contracts may make up for the fact that wage increases did not keep up with the cost of living this year. If wages catch up in the longer run, the AS curve will shift from AS_0 to AS_1 and drive aggregate output back to Y_0. If wages ultimately rise by exactly the same percentage as output prices, firms will produce the same level of output as they did before the increase in aggregate demand.

In Chapter 13, we said that Y_0 is sometimes called *potential output*. Aggregate output can be pushed above Y_0 in the short run. When aggregate output exceeds Y_0, however, there is upward pressure on input prices and costs. The unemployment rate is already quite low, firms are beginning to encounter the limits of their plant capacities, and so on. At levels of aggregate output above Y_0, costs will rise, the AS curve will shift to the left, and the price level will rise. Thus, potential output is the level of aggregate output that can be sustained in the long run without inflation.

This story is directly related to the Phillips Curve. Those who believe that the AS curve is vertical in the long run at potential output also believe that the Phillips Curve is vertical in the long run at some natural rate of unemployment. Changes in aggregate demand—including increases in government spending—increase prices, but do not change employment. Recall from Chapter 7 that the **natural rate of unemployment** refers to unemployment that occurs as a normal part of the functioning of the economy. It is sometimes taken as the sum of frictional unemployment and structural unemployment. The logic behind the vertical Phillips Curve is that whenever the

natural rate of unemployment
The unemployment that occurs as a normal part of the functioning of the economy. Sometimes taken as the sum of frictional unemployment and structural unemployment.

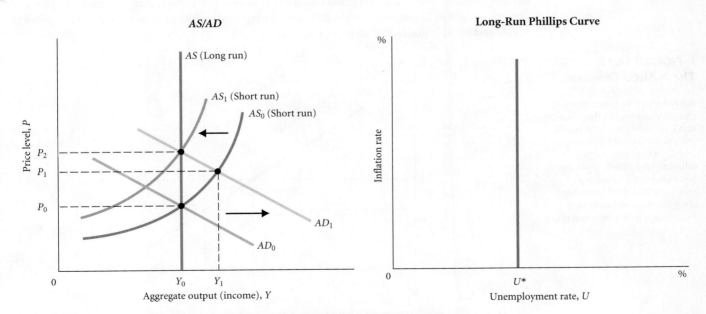

▲ **FIGURE 14.10   The Long-Run Phillips Curve: The Natural Rate of Unemployment**
If the AS curve is vertical in the long run, so is the Phillips Curve. In the long run, the Phillips Curve corresponds to the natural rate of unemployment—that is, the unemployment rate that is consistent with the notion of a fixed long-run output at potential output. U^* is the natural rate of unemployment.

unemployment rate is pushed below the natural rate, wages begin to rise, thus pushing up costs. This leads to a *lower* level of output, which pushes the unemployment rate back up to the natural rate. At the natural rate, the economy can be considered to be at full employment.

The Nonaccelerating Inflation Rate of Unemployment (NAIRU)

In Figure 14.10, the long-run vertical Phillips Curve is a graph with the inflation rate on the vertical axis and the unemployment rate on the horizontal axis. The natural rate of unemployment is U^*. In the long run, with a long-run vertical Phillips Curve, the actual unemployment rate moves to U^* because of the natural workings of the economy.

Another graph of interest is Figure 14.11, which plots the *change in* the inflation rate on the vertical axis and the unemployment rate on the horizontal axis. Many economists believe that the relationship between the change in the inflation rate and the unemployment rate is as depicted by the *PP* curve in the figure. The value of the unemployment rate where the *PP* curve crosses zero is called the *nonaccelerating inflation rate of unemployment* (**NAIRU**). If the actual unemployment rate is to the left of the NAIRU, the change in the inflation rate will be positive. As depicted in the figure, at U_1, the change in the inflation rate is 1. Conversely, if the actual unemployment rate is to the right of the NAIRU, the change in the inflation rate is negative: At U_2, the change is -1.

Consider what happens if the unemployment rate decreases from the NAIRU to U_1 and stays at U_1 for many periods. Assume also that the inflation rate at the NAIRU is 2 percent. Then in the first period the inflation rate will increase from 2 percent to 3 percent. The inflation rate does not, however, just stay at the higher 3 percent value. In the next period, the inflation rate will increase from 3 percent to 4 percent and so on. The price level will be accelerating—that is, the change in the inflation rate will be positive—when the actual unemployment rate is below the NAIRU. Conversely, the price level will be decelerating—that is, the change in the inflation rate will be negative—when the actual unemployment rate is above the NAIRU.[1]

The *PP* curve in Figure 14.11 is like the *AS* curve in Figure 14.3—the same factors that shift the *AS* curve, such as cost shocks, can also shift the *PP* curve. Figure 12.2 on p. 232 summarizes the various factors that can cause the *AS* curve to shift, and these are also relevant for the *PP* curve. A favorable shift for the *PP* curve is to the left because the *PP* curve crosses zero at a lower unemployment rate, indicating that the NAIRU is lower. Some have argued that one possible recent source of favorable shifts is increased foreign competition, which may have kept wage costs and other input costs down.

NAIRU The nonaccelerating inflation rate of unemployment.

▶ **FIGURE 14.11**
The NAIRU Diagram
To the left of the NAIRU, the price level is accelerating (positive changes in the inflation rate); to the right of the NAIRU, the price level is decelerating (negative changes in the inflation rate). Only when the unemployment rate is equal to the NAIRU is the price level changing at a constant rate (no change in the inflation rate).

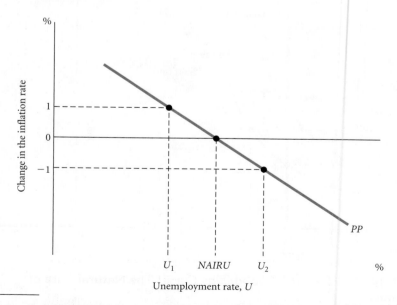

Unemployment rate, U

---

[1] The NAIRU is actually misnamed. It is the *price level* that is accelerating or decelerating, not the inflation rate, when the actual unemployment rate differs from the NAIRU. The inflation rate is not accelerating or decelerating, but simply changing by the same amount each period. The namers of the NAIRU forgot their physics.

Before about 1995, proponents of the NAIRU theory argued that the value of the NAIRU in the United States was around 6 percent. By the end of 1995, the unemployment rate declined to 5.6 percent, and by 2000, the unemployment rate was down to 3.8 percent. If the NAIRU had been 6 percent, one should have seen a continuing increase in the inflation rate beginning about 1995. In fact, the 1995 to 2000 period saw slightly declining inflation. Not only did inflation not continually increase, it did not even increase once to a new, higher value and then stay there. As the unemployment rate declined during this period, proponents of the NAIRU lowered their estimates of it, more or less in line with the actual fall in the unemployment rate. This recalibration can be justified by arguing that there have been continuing favorable shifts of the *PP* curve, such as possible increased foreign competition. Critics, however, have argued that this procedure is close to making the NAIRU theory vacuous. Can the theory really be tested if the estimate of the NAIRU is changed whenever it is not consistent with the data? How trustworthy is the appeal to favorable shifts?

Macroeconomists are currently debating whether equations estimated under the NAIRU theory are good approximations. More time is needed before any definitive answers can be given.

Looking Ahead

This chapter concludes our basic analysis of how the macroeconomy works. In the preceding seven chapters, we have examined how households and firms behave in the three market arenas—the goods market, the money market, and the labor market. We have seen how aggregate output (income), the interest rate, and the price level are determined in the economy, and we have examined the relationship between two of the most important macroeconomic variables, the inflation rate and the unemployment rate. In Chapter 15, we use everything we have learned up to this point to examine a number of important policy issues.

— SUMMARY —

THE LABOR MARKET: BASIC CONCEPTS *p. 263*

1. Because the economy is dynamic, *frictional* and *structural unemployment* are inevitable and in some ways desirable. Times of *cyclical unemployment* are of concern to macroeconomic policy makers.

2. In general, employment tends to fall when aggregate output falls and rise when aggregate output rises.

THE CLASSICAL VIEW OF THE LABOR MARKET *p. 264*

3. Classical economists believe that the interaction of supply and demand in the labor market brings about equilibrium and that unemployment (beyond the frictional and structural amounts) does not exist.

4. The classical view of the labor market is consistent with the theory of a vertical aggregate supply curve.

EXPLAINING THE EXISTENCE OF UNEMPLOYMENT *p. 266*

5. Some economists argue that the unemployment rate is not an accurate indicator of whether the labor market is working properly. Unemployed people who are considered part of the labor force may be offered jobs but may be unwilling to take those jobs at the offered salaries. Some of the

unemployed may have chosen not to work, but this result does not mean that the labor market has malfunctioned.

6. Those who do not subscribe to the classical view of the labor market suggest several reasons why unemployment exists. Downwardly *sticky wages* may be brought about by *social (implicit)* or *explicit contracts* not to cut wages. If the equilibrium wage rate falls but wages are prevented from falling also, the result will be unemployment.

7. *Efficiency wage theory* holds that the productivity of workers increases with the wage rate. If this is true, firms may have an incentive to pay wages above the wage at which the quantity of labor supplied is equal to the quantity of labor demanded. At all wages above the equilibrium, there will be an excess supply of labor and therefore unemployment.

8. If firms are operating with incomplete or imperfect information, they may not know what the market-clearing wage is. As a result, they may set their wages incorrectly and bring about unemployment. Because the economy is so complex, it may take considerable time for firms to correct these mistakes.

9. *Minimum wage laws*, which set a floor for wage rates, are one factor contributing to unemployment of teenagers and very low-skilled workers. If the market-clearing wage for some groups of workers is below the minimum wage, some members of this group will be unemployed.

THE SHORT-RUN RELATIONSHIP BETWEEN THE UNEMPLOYMENT RATE AND INFLATION p. 270

10. There is a negative relationship between the unemployment rate (U) and aggregate output (income) (Y): When Y rises, U falls. When Y falls, U rises.

11. The relationship between the unemployment rate and the price level is negative: As the unemployment rate declines and the economy moves closer to capacity, the price level rises more and more.

12. The *Phillips Curve* represents the relationship between the *inflation rate* and the *unemployment rate*. During the 1950s and 1960s, this relationship was stable and there seemed to be a predictable trade-off between inflation and unemployment. As a result of import price increases (which led to shifts in aggregate supply), the relationship between the inflation rate and the unemployment rate was

erratic in the 1970s. Inflation depends on more than just the unemployment rate.

THE LONG-RUN AGGREGATE SUPPLY CURVE, POTENTIAL OUTPUT, AND THE NATURAL RATE OF UNEMPLOYMENT p. 275

13. Those who believe that the *AS* curve is vertical in the long run also believe that the Phillips Curve is vertical in the long run at the *natural rate of unemployment*. The natural rate is generally the sum of the frictional and structural rates. If the Phillips Curve is vertical in the long run, then there is a limit to how low government policy can push the unemployment rate without setting off inflation.

14. The *NAIRU* theory says that the price level will accelerate when the unemployment rate is below the NAIRU and decelerate when the unemployment rate is above the NAIRU.

REVIEW TERMS AND CONCEPTS

cost-of-living adjustments (COLAs), *p. 267*

cyclical unemployment, *p. 264*

efficiency wage theory, *p. 267*

explicit contracts, *p. 267*

frictional unemployment, *p. 264*

inflation rate, *p. 271*

labor demand curve, *p. 264*

labor supply curve, *p. 264*

minimum wage laws, *p. 269*

NAIRU, *p. 276*

natural rate of unemployment, *p. 275*

Phillips Curve, *p. 271*

relative-wage explanation of unemployment, *p. 267*

social, *or implicit*, contracts, *p. 266*

sticky wages, *p. 266*

structural unemployment, *p. 264*

unemployment rate, *p. 263*

PROBLEMS

All problems are available on MyEconLab.

1. In April 2000, the U.S. unemployment rate dropped below 4 percent for the first time in 30 years. At the same time, inflation remained at a very low level by historical standards. Can you offer an explanation for what seems to be an improved trade-off between inflation and unemployment? What factors might improve the trade-off? What factors might make it worse?

2. [Related to the *Economics in Practice* on p. 268] Economists and politicians have long debated the extent to which unemployment benefits affect the duration of unemployment. The table below represents unemployment and unemployment benefit data for five high-income countries. The unemployment rate and the duration of unemployment benefits for each of these countries are shown for 2007, prior to the recession of 2008–2009,

and for July 2010. As the data shows, three of these countries extended the duration of unemployment benefits as a result of the recession. The data for both 2007 and 2010 show a positive relationship between the duration of unemployment benefits and the unemployment rate. Discuss whether you believe the length of time in which a person can receive unemployment benefits directly affects the unemployment rate, and whether your answer applies to both 2007 and 2010. Look up the unemployment rates in each of the five countries. Discuss whether a positive relationship still exists between the duration of unemployment benefits and the unemployment rate, and whether you believe the extension of unemployment benefits in three of those countries played a role in their current unemployment rates.

COUNTRY	2007 UNEMPLOYMENT RATE	AVERAGE UNEMPLOYMENT BENEFITS DURATION, 2007	JULY 2010 UNEMPLOYMENT RATE	AVERAGE UNEMPLOYMENT BENEFITS DURATION, 2010
Canada	6.4 %	50 weeks	8.0 %	50 weeks
France	8.7 %	52 weeks	10.0 %	104 weeks
Great Britain	5.3 %	26 weeks	7.8 %	26 weeks
Japan	3.9 %	13 weeks	5.3 %	21 weeks
United States	4.6 %	26 weeks	9.5 %	99 weeks

3. Obtain monthly data on the unemployment rate and the inflation rate for the last 2 years. (This data can be found at www.bls.gov or in a recent issue of the *Survey of Current Business* or in the *Monthly Labor Review* or *Employment and Earnings*, all published by the government and available in many college libraries.)

   a. What trends do you observe? Can you explain what you see using aggregate supply and aggregate demand curves?

   b. Plot the 24 monthly rates on a graph with the unemployment rate measured on the x-axis and the inflation rate on the y-axis. Is there evidence of a trade-off between these two variables? Provide an explanation.

4. [Related to the *Economics in Practice* on p. 269] The *Economics in Practice* states that job applicants who have been unemployed for a long period of time have a more difficult time getting job interviews than do those applicants who have been unemployed for a shorter time period. Go to www.bls.gov and do a search for "Table A-12: Unemployed persons by duration of unemployment". Look at the seasonally-adjusted data for the current month and for the same month in the previous year. What happened to the "number of unemployed" and the "percent distribution" over that year for those who were unemployed 15 to 26 weeks and for those who were unemployed 27 weeks and over? Does this data seem to support the findings in the *Economics in Practice*? Explain.

5. In 2012, the country of Ruba was suffering from a period of high unemployment. The new president, Clang, appointed Laurel Tiedye as his chief economist. Ms. Tiedye and her staff estimated these supply and demand curves for labor from data obtained from the secretary of labor, Robert Small:

$$Q_D = 100 - 5W$$
$$Q_S = 10W - 20$$

   where Q is the quantity of labor supplied/demanded in millions of workers and W is the wage rate in slugs, the currency of Ruba.

   a. Currently, the law in Ruba says that no worker shall be paid less than 9 slugs per hour. Estimate the quantity of labor supplied, the number of unemployed, and the unemployment rate.

   b. President Clang, over the objection of Secretary Small, has recommended to Congress that the law be changed to allow the wage rate to be determined in the market. If such a law was passed and the market adjusted quickly, what would happen to total employment, the size of the labor force, and the unemployment rate? Show the results graphically.

   c. Will the Rubanese labor market adjust quickly to such a change in the law? Why or why not?

6. The following policies have at times been advocated for coping with unemployment. Briefly explain how each might work and explain which type or types of unemployment (frictional, structural, or cyclical) each policy is designed to alter.

   a. A computer list of job openings and a service that matches employees with job vacancies (sometimes called an "economic dating service")

   b. Lower minimum wage for teenagers

   c. Retraining programs for workers who need to learn new skills to find employment

   d. Public employment for people without jobs

   e. Improved information about available jobs and current wage rates

   f. The president's going on nationwide TV and attempting to convince firms and workers that the inflation rate next year will be low

7. Your boss offers you a wage increase of 10 percent. Is it possible that you are worse off with the wage increase than you were before? Explain your answer.

8. How will the following affect labor force participation rates, labor supply, and unemployment?

   a. Because the retired elderly are a larger and larger fraction of the U.S. population, Congress and the president decide to raise the Social Security tax on individuals to continue paying benefits to the elderly.

   b. A national child care program is enacted, requiring employers to provide free child care services.

   c. The U.S. government reduces restrictions on immigration into the United States.

   d. The welfare system is eliminated.

   e. The government subsidizes the purchase of new capital by firms (an investment tax credit).

9. Draw a graph to illustrate the following:

   a. A Phillips Curve based on the assumption of a vertical long-run aggregate supply curve

   b. The effect of a change in inflationary expectations on a recently stable Phillips Curve

   c. Unemployment caused by a recently enacted minimum wage law

10. Obtain data on "average hourly earnings of production workers" and the unemployment rate for your state or area over a recent 2-year period. Has unemployment increased or decreased? What has happened to wages? Does the pattern of unemployment help explain the movement of wages? Provide an explanation.

11. Suppose the inflation–unemployment relationship depicted by the Phillips Curve was stable. Do you think the U.S. trade-off and the Japanese trade-off would be identical? If not, what kinds of factors might make the trade-offs dissimilar?

12. The unemployment rate stood at 9.6 percent late in 2010. Despite the fact that the economy had been growing out of the recession for over a year (real GDP was up 3 percent by Q2 2010), there was only modest job growth during 2010. While a fiscal stimulus package provided some help, labor was "stuck in the mud." Which of the following factors contributed to the problem and which ones were important?

   a. Employment and unemployment are always lagging indicators since it is difficult to hire and fire in a downturn.

   b. Productivity has grown considerably this decade; people are working hard and being paid less—in short, firms are "mean and lean."

   c. Construction employment, which is a traditional engine of growth in recoveries, has gone nowhere largely because of the fact that we dramatically overbuilt.

   d. We have minimum wage laws in the United States.

   e. Wages are sticky on the downward side, preventing the labor market from clearing.

   f. The Census Bureau hired and then fired thousands of workers, throwing all the numbers off.
   Choose two of these statements and write a short essay. Use data to support your claims.

13. How might social, or implicit, contracts result in sticky wages? Use a labor market graph to show the effect of social contracts on wages and on unemployment if the economy enters a recession.

Financial Crises, Stabilization, and Deficits

15

We have seen that fiscal policy can affect the economy through tax and spending changes and that monetary policy can affect the economy through interest rate changes. Given that this has been known for many decades, you might ask why fluctuations in the economy are still so large? From Figure 5.5 on p. 106, you can see that there have been large fluctuations in the unemployment rate since 1990. Why can't policy makers do better? This chapter covers a number of topics, but they are all concerned at least indi-

rectly with trying to help answer this question. We will be considering the various constraints that policy makers face in trying to stabilize the economy.

The structure of the chapter is as follows. In the next section we will consider the stock market and the housing market. We will see that both of these markets have important effects on the economy through a household wealth effect. When, say, stock prices or housing prices rise, household wealth rises, and households respond to this by consuming more. Stock prices and housing prices are asset prices, and changes in these prices are, for the most part, unpredictable. Neither policy makers nor anyone else in the economy have the ability to predict how the stock and housing markets will behave in the future. This is then the first problem that policy makers face. If stock and housing prices have important effects on the economy and if changes in these prices are unpredictable, there is an important source of variation that policy makers can do nothing about. At best, policy makers can try to react quickly to these changes once they occur. We also discuss in this section what is meant by "financial crises" and what policy makers can and cannot do about them.

A second problem with trying to stabilize the economy is getting the timing right. This is the subject matter of the second section. We will see that there is a danger of overreacting to changes in the economy—making the fluctuations in the economy even worse than they otherwise would be.

The third section considers government deficit issues. We discussed at the end of Chapter 9 that it is important to distinguish between cyclical deficits and structural deficits. One expects that the government will run a deficit in a recession since tax revenue is down

LEARNING OBJECTIVES

Describe the fundamentals of the stock market

Discuss the causes and effects of historical fluctuations in the stock and housing markets

Explain the purpose of stabilization policies and differentiate between three types of time lags

Discuss the effects of government deficits and deficit targeting

because of the sluggish economy and spending may be up as the government tries to stimulate the economy. If at full employment the government is *still* running a deficit, this part of the deficit is described as a structural deficit.

In 2012 many countries, including the United States, faced serious structural deficit problems. We discuss various problems that may arise if a government runs large deficits year after year. We will see, returning to the subject matter of the first section, that one possible reaction is a financial crisis. The U.S. government also ran large structural deficits in the 1980s, and we conclude with a discussion of this period. There was an attempt in the late 1980s to legislate a requirement that the budget be balanced, and we examine how stabilization policy is affected by such a requirement.

The Stock Market, the Housing Market, and Financial Crises

Introductory macroeconomic textbooks written before 1990 could largely ignore the stock and housing markets. The effects of these markets on the macroeconomy were small enough to be put aside in introductory discussions. This changed in the 1990s for the stock market and after 2000 for the housing market. The stock market contributed to the boom in the last half of the 1990s and to the recession that followed. The housing market contributed to the expansion in 2002–2007 and to the recession that followed. For this reason, even introductory macroeconomics courses must spend some time looking at these two markets. We first turn to some background material on the stock market.

Stocks and Bonds

It will be useful to begin by briefly discussing the three main ways in which firms borrow or raise money to finance their investments. How do firms use financial markets in practice?

When a firm wants to make a large purchase to build a new factory or buy machines, it often cannot pay for the purchase out of its own funds. In this case, it must "finance" the investment. One way to do this is to borrow from a bank. The bank loans the money to the firm, the firm uses the money to buy the factory or machine, and the firm pays back the loan (with interest) to the bank over time.

Another possible way for a firm to borrow money is for the firm to issue a bond. If you buy a bond from a firm, you are making a loan to the firm. Bonds were discussed at the beginning of Chapter 11.

stock A certificate that certifies ownership of a certain portion of a firm.

A third way for a firm to finance an investment is for it to issue additional shares of **stock**. When a firm issues new shares of stock, it does not add to its debt. Instead, it brings in additional owners of the firm, owners who agree to supply it with funds. Such owners are treated differently than bondholders, who are owed the amount they have loaned.

A share of common stock is a certificate that represents the ownership of a share of a business, almost always a corporation. For example, Lincoln Electric is a Cleveland-based company that makes welding and cutting equipment. The company has 41 million shares of common stock that are owned by tens of thousands of shareholders, some of whom are simply private individuals, some of whom are institutions such as Carleton College, and some of whom may be employees of the firm. Shareholders are entitled to a share of the company's profit. When profits are paid directly to shareholders, the payment is called a *dividend*. In a recent year, Lincoln Electric made a profit of $54 million, which was $1.31 per share, of which $0.43 was paid out to shareholders as dividends and the rest was retained for investment.

capital gain An increase in the value of an asset.

realized capital gain The gain that occurs when the owner of an asset actually sells it for more than he or she paid for it.

Stockholders who own stocks that increase in value earn what are called **capital gains**. **Realized capital gains** (or losses) are increases (or decreases) in the value of assets, including stocks, that households receive when they actually sell those assets. The government considers realized capital gains net of losses to be income, although their treatment under the tax code has been very complex and subject to change every few years. The total return that an owner of a share of stock receives is the sum of the dividends received and the capital gain or loss.

Determining the Price of a Stock

What determines the price of a stock? If a share of stock is selling for $25, why is someone willing to pay that much for it? As we have noted, when you buy a share of stock, you own part of the firm. If a firm is making profits, it may be paying dividends to its shareholders. If it is not paying dividends but is making profits, people may expect that it will pay dividends in the future. Microsoft, for example, only began paying dividends in 2003 as it entered a more mature phase of its business. Apple began paying dividends in 2012. Dividends are important in thinking about stocks because dividends are the form in which shareholders receive income from the firm. So one thing that is likely to affect the price of a stock is what people expect its future dividends will be. The larger the expected future dividends, the larger the current stock price, other things being equal.

Another important consideration in thinking about the price of a stock is the time the dividends are expected to be paid. A $2-per-share dividend that is expected to be paid 4 years from now is worth less than a $2-per-share dividend that is expected to be paid next year. In other words, the farther into the future the dividend is expected to be paid, the more it will be "discounted." The amount by which expected future dividends are discounted depends on the interest rate. The higher the interest rate, the more expected future dividends will be discounted. If the interest rate is 10 percent, I can invest $100 today and receive $110 a year from now. I am thus willing to pay $100 today to someone who will pay me $110 in a year. If instead, the interest rate were only 5 percent, I would be willing to pay $104.76 today to receive $110 a year from now because the alternative of $104.76 today at a 5 percent interest rate also yields $110.00 at the end of the year. I am thus willing to pay more for the promise of $110 a year from now when the interest rate is lower. In other words, I "discount" the $110 less when the interest rate is lower.

Another discount factor aside from the interest rate must be taken into account; it is the discount for risk. People prefer certain outcomes to uncertain ones for the same expected values. For example, I prefer a certain $50 over a bet in which there is a 50 percent chance I will get $100 and a 50 percent chance I will get nothing. The expected value of the bet is $50, but I prefer the certain $50 over the bet, where there is a 50 percent chance that I will end up with nothing. The same reasoning holds for future dividends. If, say, I expect dividends for both firms A and B to be $2 per share next year but firm B has a much wider range of possibilities (is riskier), I will prefer firm A. Put another way, I will "discount" firm B's expected future dividends more than firm A's because the outcome for firm B is more uncertain.

We can thus say that the price of a stock should equal the discounted value of its expected future dividends, where the discount factors depend on the interest rate and risk. If for some reason (say, a positive surprise news announcement from the firm) expected future dividends increase, this development should lead to an increase in the price of the stock. If the interest rate falls, this decrease should also lead to a stock price increase. Finally, if the perceived risk of a firm falls, this perception should increase the firm's stock price.

Some stock analysts talk about the possibility of stock market "bubbles." Given the preceding discussion, what might a bubble be? Assume that given your expectations about the future dividends of a firm and given the discount rate, you value the firm's stock at $20 per share. Is there any case in which you would pay more than $20 for a share? You can, of course, buy the stock and sell it later; you don't need to hold the stock forever. If the stock is currently selling for $25, which is above your value of $20, but you think that the stock will rise to $30 in the next few months, you might buy it now in anticipation of selling it later for a higher price. If others have similar views, the price of the stock may be driven up.

In this case, what counts is not the discounted value of expected future dividends, but rather your view of what others will pay for the stock in the future. If everyone expects that everyone else expects that the price will be driven up, the price may be driven up. One might call this outcome a bubble because the stock price depends on what people expect that other people expect and so on.

When a firm's stock price has risen rapidly, it is difficult to know whether the reason is that people have increased their expectations of the firm's future dividends or that there is a bubble. Because people's expectations of future dividends are not directly observed, it is hard to test alternative theories.

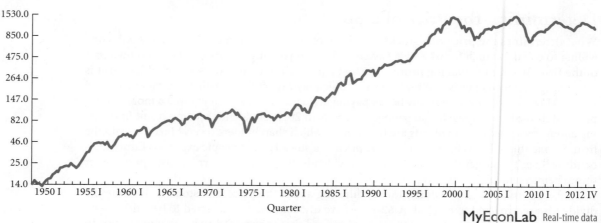

▲ **FIGURE 15.1** **The S&P 500 Stock Price Index, 1948 I–2012 IV**

The Stock Market Since 1948

Dow Jones Industrial Average An index based on the stock prices of 30 actively traded large companies. The oldest and most widely followed index of stock market performance.

NASDAQ Composite An index based on the stock prices of over 5,000 companies traded on the NASDAQ Stock Market. The NASDAQ market takes its name from the National Association of Securities Dealers Automated Quotation System.

Standard and Poor's 500 (S&P 500) An index based on the stock prices of 500 of the largest firms by market value.

If you follow the stock market at all, you know that much attention is paid to two stock price indices: the **Dow Jones Industrial Average** and the **NASDAQ Composite**. From a macroeconomic perspective, however, these two indices cover too small a sample of firms. One would like an index that includes firms whose total market value is close to the market value of all firms in the economy. For this purpose a much better measure is the **Standard and Poor's 500 stock price index**, called the **S&P 500**. This index includes most of the larger companies in the economy by market value.

The S&P 500 index is plotted in Figure 15.1 for 1948 I–2012 IV. What perhaps stands out most in this plot is the huge increase in the index between 1995 and 2000. Between December 31, 1994, and March 31, 2000, the S&P 500 index rose 226 percent, an annual rate of increase of 25 percent. This is by far the largest stock market boom in U.S. history, completely dominating the boom of the 1920s. Remember that we are talking about the S&P 500 index, which includes most of the firms in the U.S. economy by market value. We are not talking about just a few dot-com companies. The entire stock market went up 25 percent per year for 5 years! This boom added roughly $14 trillion to household wealth, about $2.5 trillion per year.

What caused this boom? You can see from Figure 13.7 in Chapter 13 that interest rates did not change much in the last half of the 1990s, so the boom cannot be explained by any large fall in interest rates. Perhaps profits rose substantially during this period, and this growth led to a large increase in expected future dividends? We know from the preceding discussion that if expected future dividends increase, stock prices should increase. Figure 15.2 plots for 1948 I–2012 IV the ratio of after-tax profits to GDP. It is clear from the figure that nothing unusual happened in the last half of the 1990s. The share of after-tax profits in GDP rose from the middle of 1995 to the middle of 1997, but then generally fell after that through 2000. Thus, there does not appear to be any surge of profits that would have led people to expect much higher future dividends.

It could be that the perceived riskiness of stocks fell in the last half of the 1990s. This change would have led to smaller discount rates for stocks and thus, other things being equal, to higher stock prices. Although this possibility cannot be completely ruled out, there is no strong independent evidence that perceived riskiness fell.

The stock market boom is thus a puzzle, and many people speculate that it was simply a bubble. For some reason, stock prices started rising rapidly in 1995 and people expected that other people expected that prices would continue to rise. This led stock prices to rise further, thus fulfilling the expectations, which led to expectations of further increases, and so on. Bubble believers note that once stock prices started falling in 2000, they fell a great deal. It is not the case that stock prices just leveled out in 2000; they fell rapidly. People of the bubble view argue that this is simply the bubble bursting.

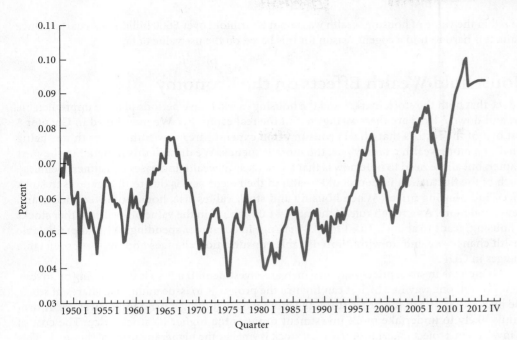

MyEconLab Real-time data

◀ **FIGURE 15.2**
Ratio of After-Tax Profits to GDP, 1948 I–2012 IV

The first problem then for the stability of the macroeconomy is the large and seemingly unpredictable swings in the stock market. As we will see, these swings induce behavior changes by households and firms that affect the real economy. Before we explore this link, however, we turn to a second volatile series: housing prices.

Housing Prices Since 1952

Figure 15.3 plots the relative price of housing for 1952 I–2012 IV. The plotted figure is the ratio of an index of housing prices to the GDP deflator. When this ratio is rising, it means that housing prices are rising faster than the overall price level, and vice versa when the ratio is falling.

The plot in Figure 15.3 is remarkable. Housing prices grew roughly in line with the over-all price level until about 2000. The increase between 2000 and 2006 was then huge, followed by a huge fall between 2006 and 2009. Between 2000 I and 2006 I the value of housing wealth increased by about $13 trillion, roughly $500 billion per quarter. Between 2006 II and 2009 I

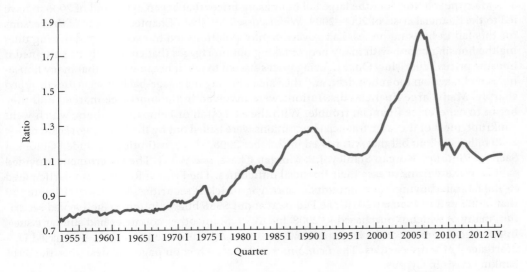

MyEconLab Real-time data

◀ **FIGURE 15.3**
Ratio of a Housing Price Index to the GDP Deflator, 1952 I–2012 IV

the fall in the value of housing wealth was about $7 trillion, over $600 billion per quarter. Once again, it is hard to find a cogent reason for this based on the use value of housing.

Household Wealth Effects on the Economy

We see that both the stock market and the housing market have periods of large unpredictable ups and downs. How are these swings felt in the real economy? We mentioned in Chapter 8 that one of the factors that affects consumption expenditures is wealth. Other things being equal, the more wealth a family has, the more it spends. We discuss this in detail in the next chapter, but all we need to note now is that an increase in wealth increases consumer spending. Much of the fluctuation in household wealth in the recent past is due to fluctuations in stock prices and housing prices. When housing and stock values rise, households feel richer and they spend more. As a rough rule of thumb, a $1.00 change in the value of wealth (either stocks or housing) leads to about a $0.03 to $0.04 change in consumer spending. With unpredictable wealth change, we end up with unpredictable consumption changes and thus unpredictable changes in GDP.

An increase in stock prices may also increase investment. If a firm is considering an investment project, one way in which it can finance the project is to issue additional shares of stock. The higher the price of the firm's stock, the more money it can get per additional share. A firm is thus likely to undertake more investment projects the higher its stock price. The cost of an investment project in terms of shares of stock is smaller the higher the price of the stock. This is the way a stock market boom may increase investment and a stock market contraction may decrease investment. Stock price changes affect a firm's cost of capital.

Financial Crises and the 2008 Bailout

It is clear that the stock market boom in the last half of the 1990s contributed to the strong economy in that period and that the contraction in the stock market after that contributed to the 2000–2001 recession. It is also clear that the boom in housing prices in the 2000–2005 period contributed to the expansion that followed the 2000–2001 recession and that the collapse of housing prices between 2006 and 2009 contributed to the 2008–2009 recession. This is just the household wealth effect at work combined in the case of stock prices with an effect on the investment spending of firms.

The recession of 2008–2009 was also characterized by some observers as a period of financial crisis. While there is no precise definition of a financial crisis, most financial writers identify financial crises as periods in which the financial institutions that facilitate the movement of capital across households and firms cease to work smoothly. In a financial crisis, macroeconomic problems caused by the wealth effect of a falling stock market or housing market are accentuated.

Many people consider the large fall in housing prices that began at the end of 2006 to have led to the financial crisis of 2008–2009. We discussed briefly in Chapter 10 some of the reasons for this fall in housing prices. Lax government regulations led to excessive risk taking during the housing boom, with many people taking out mortgages that could only be sustained if housing prices kept rising. Once housing prices started to fall, it became clear that many households had taken on too much debt, and the value of many mortgage-backed securities dropped sharply. Many large financial institutions were involved in the mortgage market, and they began to experience financial trouble. With the exception of Lehman Brothers, which went bankrupt, most of the large financial institutions were bailed out by the federal government—a $700 billion bailout bill that was passed in October 2008. These institutions included Goldman Sachs, Citigroup, Morgan Stanley, J.P. Morgan Chase, and A.I.G. The government provided capital to these firms to ease their financial difficulties. The Federal Reserve also participated in the bailout, buying huge amounts of mortgage-backed securities. We saw in Chapter 10 that at the end of January 2013, the Fed held about $966 billion in mortgage-backed securities, many of which it purchased in 2008 and 2009. Many other countries had similar issues, in part because many of the large financial institutions in other countries had purchased U.S. mortgage-backed securities. The *Economics in Practice* box on page 288 describes the 2013 banking crisis in Cyprus.

What would have happened had the U.S. government not bailed out the large financial institutions? This is a matter of debate among economists and politicians. But some effects are clear. Absent intervention, the negative wealth effect would have been larger. Some of the financial institutions would have gone bankrupt, which would have wiped out their bond-holders. Many of these bonds are held by the household sector, so household wealth would have fallen from the loss in value of the bonds. The fall in overall stock prices would also likely have been larger, thus contributing to the negative wealth effect. The government bailout thus reduced the fall in wealth that took place during this period. Some people also argue that lending to businesses would have been lower had there been no bailout. This would have forced businesses to cut investment, thereby contributing to the contraction in aggregate demand. It is not clear how important this effect is since, as seen in Chapter 10, much of the Fed's purchase of mortgage-backed securities ended up as excess reserves in banks, not as increased loans.

It is important to distinguish between the stimulus measures the government took to fight the 2008–2009 recession, which were tax cuts and spending increases, and the bailout activity, which was direct help to financial institutions to keep them from failing. Putting aside the stimulus measures, was the bailout a good idea? On the positive side, it lessened the negative wealth effect and possibly led to more loans to businesses. Also, much of the lending to the financial institutions has or will be repaid; so the final total cost will be less than $700 billion. On the negative side, there were political and social costs. Most of the people who benefited from the bailout were wealthy—certainly wealthier than average. The wealth that didn't fall because of the bailout was mostly wealth of high-income people—people holding the bonds of the financial institutions. Also, the jobs in the financial institutions that were saved were mostly jobs of high-income earners. People who will pay for the bailout in the long run are the U.S. taxpayers, who are on average less wealthy than those who benefited from the bailout. The bailout thus likely had, or at least was perceived by many to have had, bad income distribution consequences, which put a strain on the body politic. Even though much of the money will be repaid, not all of it will, and the perception lingers that the rich were bailed out. We come back to this in the third section of this chapter, but the bailout will probably make it harder to increase tax rates on middle-income people in the future.

Asset Markets and Policy Makers

It should be clear by now that stock prices and housing prices have played a large role in the economy since the 1990s. The problem for policy makers trying to stabilize the economy is that it is hard to predict changes in stock and housing prices. Who could have predicted ahead of time the boom in the stock market that began in 1995, or the boom in housing prices that began in 2000, or the collapse of housing prices that began in 2006? Changes in asset prices like these are essentially unpredictable, so policy makers can only react after the fact to such changes. Their ability to stabilize the economy is thus considerably restricted by the fact that changes in asset prices affect the economy and are not predictable. One exception, however, that is often cited is that perhaps the U.S. government (including the Fed) should have seen in the 2002–2005 period the excessive risk that was being taken and instituted added government regulation. In 2010 a financial regulation bill, known as the Dodd-Frank bill, was passed to try to tighten up financial regulations in the hope of preventing a recurrence of the 2008–2009 financial crisis.

Time Lags Regarding Monetary and Fiscal Policy

We have so far seen that asset-price changes are difficult for policy makers to deal with because they can't be predicted ahead of time. At best, policy makers deal with these changes only after they occur. Even once problems are recognized, however, responding to these problems takes time. Consider the two possible time paths for aggregate output (income) (Y) shown in Figure 15.4. In path B (the light blue line), the fluctuations in GDP

ECONOMICS IN PRACTICE

Depositors in Cyprus End Up as Shareholders!

As many of you may know, Cyprus is a small sun-baked island-country off the coast of Greece. In the early part of 2013, newspaper readers around the world were also reminded that Cyprus is part of the Euro Zone, as we watched it struggle with a banking crisis that looked a lot like the ones we saw earlier in the United States and Iceland in 2008.

Cyprus's two largest banks, the Bank of Cyprus and Cyprus Popular (also known as Laiki), have the lion's share of the banking business in Cyprus. While a number of their depositors were Cypriots, Russian business people also used Cyprus as a place to park large deposits in what many described as an attempt to reduce or evade taxes. As you know from the text, when people deposit money in banks, bankers hold some in reserve, but lend out the rest, earning interest in excess of what they have to pay those depositors. In the case of the Cypriot banks, many of the loans went to businesses in neighboring Greece. But in the period 2012 and 2013, Greece business faltered badly as the Greek government struggled to reduce its very large debt to conform to requirements of the European Union (EU), of which it also was a member. The result? Many Greek businesses failed and took with them the Cypriot bank investments. Cyprus's banks had also invested in Greek sovereign debt, losing much of these investments when the EU forced Greece to restructure that debt.

By early 2013, both the Bank of Cyprus and Laiki were near failure, and the government of Cyprus, worried about the effect of a bank failure on the rest of the already-fragile economy, had to figure out a way to bail them out. Their solution? Laiki, the second largest bank, was closed, and deposits still left were transferred to the Bank of Cyprus. That bank too had little money left and needed recapitalization. Where did it get the new money? In the United States, funds to support failing banks came from the Fed. Cyprus, on the Euro, did not have this option. Some cash came (with strings) from the European Union. But, much help also came (forcibly) from bank depositors, most from outside Cyprus, with accounts in excess of 100,000 Euros. The government of Cyprus decided to wipe out a fraction—on the order of 40 percent or more for large depositors—of the deposits on the books of the banks, essentially wiping out part of the bank's liabilities (remember, deposits are liabilities to a bank). In return for these deposits, the large depositors received shares of stock in the bank. Much of the help needed to restore the Cyprus banks in effect came, not willingly, from Russian oligarchs as funds they considered cash, accessible by ATM, were now turned into shares of hard-to-trade and perhaps worthless shares of stock.

THINKING PRACTICALLY

1. When the Central Bank "took" part of large depositors' accounts, what happened to the reserves needed for the bank?

---

stabilization policy Describes both monetary and fiscal policy, the goals of which are to smooth out fluctuations in output and employment and to keep prices as stable as possible.

are smaller than those in path A (the dark blue line). One aim of **stabilization policy** is to smooth out fluctuations in output to try to move the economy along a path like B instead of A. Stabilization policy is also concerned with the stability of prices. Here the goal is not to prevent the overall price level from rising at all, but instead to achieve an inflation rate that is as close as possible to a target rate of about 2 percent given the government's other goals of high and stable levels of output and employment.

▶ **FIGURE 15.4**
Two Possible Time Paths for GDP
Path A is less stable—it varies more over time—than path B. Other things being equal, society prefers path B to path A.

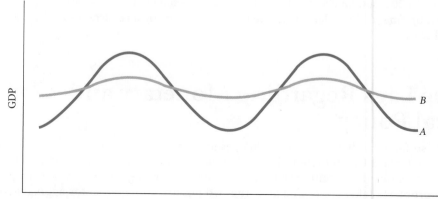

Stabilization goals are not easy to achieve. The existence of various kinds of **time lags**, or delays in the response of the economy to stabilization policies, can make the economy difficult to control. Economists generally recognize three kinds of time lags: recognition lags, implementation lags, and response lags.

time lags Delays in the economy's response to stabilization policies.

Stabilization

Figure 15.5 shows timing problems a government may face when trying to stabilize the economy. Suppose the economy reaches a peak and begins to slide into recession at point A (at time t_0). Given the need to collect and process economic data, policy makers do not observe the decline in GDP until it has sunk to point B (at time t_1). By the time they have begun to stimulate the economy (point C, time t_2), the recession is well advanced and the economy has almost bottomed out. When the policies finally begin to take effect (point D, time t_3), the economy is already on its road to recovery. The policies push the economy to point E'—a much greater fluctuation than point E, which is where the economy would have been without the stabilization policy. Sometime after point D, policy makers may begin to realize that the economy is expanding too quickly. By the time they have implemented contractionary policies and the policies have made their effects felt, the economy is starting to weaken. The contractionary policies therefore end up pushing GDP to point F' instead of point F.

Because of the various time lags, the expansionary policies that should have been instituted at time t_0 do not begin to have an effect until time t_3, when they are no longer needed. The light blue line in Figure 15.5 shows how the economy behaves as a result of the "stabilization" policies. The dark blue line shows the time path of GDP if the economy had been allowed to run its course and no stabilization policies had been attempted. In this case, stabilization policy makes income more erratic, not less—the policy results in a peak income of E' as opposed to E and a trough income of F' instead of F.

Critics of stabilization policy argue that the situation in Figure 15.5 is typical of the interaction between the government and the rest of the economy. This claim is not necessarily true. We need to know more about the nature of the various kinds of lags before deciding whether stabilization policy is good or bad.

Recognition Lags

It takes time for policy makers to recognize a boom or a slump. Many important data—those from the national income and product accounts, for example—are available only quarterly. It usually takes several weeks to compile and prepare even the preliminary estimates for these

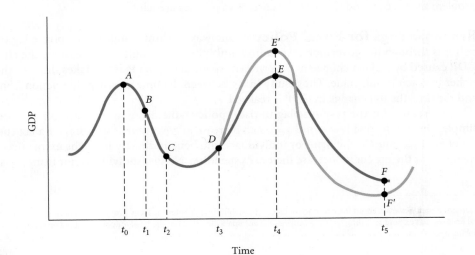

◀ **FIGURE 15.5**
Possible Stabilization Timing Problems
Attempts to stabilize the economy can prove destabilizing because of time lags. An expansionary policy that should have begun to take effect at point A does not actually begin to have an impact until point D, when the economy is already on an upswing. Hence, the policy pushes the economy to points E' and F' (instead of points E and F). Income varies more widely than it would have if no policy had been implemented.

figures. If the economy goes into a slump on January 1, the recession may not be detected until the data for the first quarter are available at the end of April.

Moreover, the early national income and product accounts data are only preliminary, based on an incomplete compilation of the various data sources. These estimates can, and often do, change as better data become available. (For example, when the Bureau of Economic Analysis first announced the results for the fourth quarter of 2012, it indicated that the economy had negative growth, −0.1%. This announcement was at the end of January 2013. At the end of February the growth rate was revised to plus 0.1%. Then at the end of March it was further revised to plus 0.4%.) This situation makes the interpretation of the initial estimates difficult, and **recognition lags** result.

recognition lag The time it takes for policy makers to recognize the existence of a boom or a slump.

Implementation Lags

The problems that lags pose for stabilization policy do not end once economists and policy makers recognize that the economy is in a boom or a slump. Even if everyone knows that the economy needs to be stimulated or reined in, it takes time to put the desired policy into effect, especially for actions that involve fiscal policy. **Implementation lags** result.

Each year Congress decides on the federal government's budget for the coming year. The tax laws and spending programs embodied in this budget are hard to change once they are in place. If it becomes clear that the economy is entering a recession and is in need of a fiscal stimulus during the middle of the year, there is a limited amount that can be done. Until Congress authorizes more spending or a cut in taxes, changes in fiscal policy are not possible.[1]

implementation lag The time it takes to put the desired policy into effect once economists and policy makers recognize that the economy is in a boom or a slump.

Monetary policy is less subject to the kinds of restrictions that slow down changes in fiscal policy. As we saw in Chapter 10, the Fed's main tool for controlling the supply of money or the interest rate is open market operations—buying and selling government securities. Transactions in these securities take place in a highly developed market, and if the Fed chooses, it can buy or sell a large volume of securities in a very short period of time. The implementation lag for monetary policy is generally much shorter than for fiscal policy. When the Fed wants to change the interest rate, it goes into the open market and purchases government securities. As the interest rate falls the economy is stimulated to expand.

Response Lags

Even after a macroeconomic problem has been recognized and the appropriate corrective policies have been implemented, there are **response lags**—lags that occur because of the operation of the economy itself. Even after the government has formulated a policy and put it into place, the economy takes time to adjust to the new conditions. Although monetary policy can be adjusted and implemented more quickly than fiscal policy, it takes longer to make its effect felt on the economy because of response lags. What is most important is the total lag between the time a problem first occurs and the time the corrective policies are felt.

response lag The time that it takes for the economy to adjust to the new conditions after a new policy is implemented; the lag that occurs because of the operation of the economy itself.

Response Lags for Fiscal Policy One way to think about the response lag in fiscal policy is through the government spending multiplier. This multiplier measures the change in GDP caused by a given change in government spending or net taxes. It takes time for the multiplier to reach its full value. The result is a lag between the time a fiscal policy action is initiated and the time the full change in GDP is realized.

The reason for the response lag in fiscal policy—the delay in the multiplier process—is simple. During the first few months after an increase in government spending or a tax cut, there is not enough time for the firms or individuals who benefit directly from the extra government spending or the tax cut to increase their own spending. Neither individuals nor firms revise their

---

[1] Do not forget, however, about the existence of automatic stabilizers (Chapter 9). Many programs contain built-in countercyclical features that expand spending or cut tax collections automatically (without the need for congressional or executive action) during a recession.

spending plans instantaneously. Until they can make those revisions, extra government spending does not stimulate extra private spending.

Changes in government purchases are a component of aggregate expenditure. When G rises, aggregate expenditure increases directly; when G falls, aggregate expenditure decreases directly. When personal taxes are changed, however, an additional step intervenes, giving rise to another lag. Suppose a tax cut has lowered personal income taxes across the board. Each household must decide what portion of its tax cut to spend and what portion to save. This decision is the extra step. Before the tax cut gets translated into extra spending, households must take the step of increasing their spending, which usually takes some time.

With a business tax cut, there is a further complication. Firms must decide what to do with their added after-tax profits. If they pay out their added profits to households as dividends, the result is the same as with a personal tax cut. Households must decide whether to spend or to save the extra funds. Firms may also retain their added profits and use them for investment, but investment is a component of aggregate expenditure that requires planning and time.

In practice, it takes about a year for a change in taxes or in government spending to have its full effect on the economy. This response lag means that if we increase spending to counteract a recession today, the full effects will not be felt for 12 months. By that time, the state of the economy might be very different.

Response Lags for Monetary Policy Monetary policy works by changing interest rates, which then change planned investment. Interest rates can also affect consumption spending, as we discuss further in Chapter 16. For now, it is enough to know that lower interest rates usually stimulate consumption spending and that higher interest rates decrease consumption spending.

The response of consumption and investment to interest rate changes takes time. Even if interest rates were to drop by 5 percent overnight, firms would not immediately increase their investment purchases. Firms generally make their investment plans several years in advance. If General Motors (GM) wants to respond to a decrease in interest rates by investing more, it will take time—perhaps up to a year—for the firm to come up with plans for a new factory or assembly line. While drawing up such plans, GM may spend little on new investments. The effect of the decrease in interest rates may not make itself felt for quite some time.

The response lags for monetary policy are even longer than response lags for fiscal policy. When government spending changes, there is a direct change in the sales of firms, which sell more as a result of the increased government purchases. When interest rates change, however, the sales of firms do not change until households change their consumption spending and/or firms change their investment spending. It takes time for households and firms to respond to interest rate changes. In this sense, interest rate changes are like tax-rate changes. The resulting change in firms' sales must wait for households and firms to change their purchases of goods.

Summary

Stabilization is thus not easily achieved even if there are no surprise asset-price changes. It takes time for policy makers to recognize the existence of a problem, more time for them to implement a solution, and yet more time for firms and households to respond to the stabilization policies taken. Monetary policy can be adjusted more quickly and easily than taxes or government spending, making it a useful instrument in stabilizing the economy. However, because the economy's response to monetary changes is probably slower than its response to changes in fiscal policy, tax and spending changes may also play a useful role in macroeconomic management.

Government Deficit Issues

If a government is trying to stimulate the economy through tax cuts or spending increases, this, other things being equal, will increase the government deficit. One thus expects deficits in recessions—cyclical deficits. These deficits are temporary and do not impose any long-run problems, especially if modest surpluses are run when there is full employment. If, however, at

ECONOMICS IN PRACTICE

Social Security Changes: Long, Long Implementation Lags!

Just over 20 percent of the U.S. budget is spent each year on Social Security payments to the elderly and disabled. It is one of the largest "entitlement" programs in the country. An entitlement program is one in which the benefits are conferred by rights and legislation. Medicare is another such program. In the case of both Medicare and Social Security, the eventual recipients of these benefits will typically have paid into the funds, though under the U.S. system there is no one-to-one matching of payments in and benefits out. Higher-earning individuals will typically have paid in more than they eventually recoup in benefits, while lower-income earners will typically get more than the paid-in earning, assuming an average life span. With large and growing deficits, more policy makers are looking at these entitlement programs as possible places spending could be cut as a way to control the budget. Despite the term "entitlement," beneficiaries are by no means guaranteed a set of specific Social Security benefits.

Reducing spending from Social Security, however, is a complicated matter. For a number of the elderly, these benefits form a substantial part of their retirement income. Making a big change in benefits for those about-to-retire or already retired strikes many citizens as bad policy. Few 80-year-olds want to return to work if their retirement income gets cut in half by Congress! As a result, most changes in Social Security benefits kick in only many years in the future.

In 1983, Congress enacted just such a change. As life spans increased, many began to question the existing retirement age provisions of the Social Security Act. Longer lives mean that if people retire at a given age they collect Social Security over

a longer time span than they would have done when Social Security was first instituted. Long life spans is one reason Social Security expenditures are so high. So in 1983, Congress decided to control Social Security spending by raising the age at which one could retire and receive full benefits. When did the age change kick in? Only for those people who were born after 1938; this group was 45 years old in 1983 and was thought to have enough time to adjust to the policy change. In fact, the retirement age change was slowly adjusted, two months at a time, until it reached the age of 67 for those born after 1960.

A more recent proposal to trim Social Security expenditures involves changing the way inflation is adjusted for in the benefits (see *Economics in Practice* in Chapter 7, page 139). Here too if the proposal is passed the phase-in will be very slow and substantial spending reductions a long time in the future.

You should now be able to see some of the issues involved with using spending changes in Social Security as a fiscal tool! Any substantial changes will likely be put in place only very slowly, over many years. In the text we talked about implementation lags and response time lags. For programs affecting the elderly like Social Security and to some extent Medicare, rapid spending level changes are very hard to do.

THINKING PRACTICALLY

1. Defense spending is another large fraction of the U.S. budget. How easy is it to reduce this spending?

full employment the deficit—the structural deficit—is still large, this can have negative long-run consequences.

We saw in Table 9.5, in Chapter 9, that the U.S. government deficit in 2012 was $1.1 trillion. It was clear by at least 2010 that the United States was facing a huge structural deficit problem. Figure 9.5, in Chapter 9, shows how this problem developed. At the beginning of 2001, the government was running a surplus, and by the end of the year, it was in deficit. Most of this was a cyclical deficit because the economy was in a recession. Deficits persisted after the recession, however, and in the roughly full employment years of 2005–2007, the deficit was between about 1.5 and 2.0 percent of GDP. These deficits were all full employment deficits since the economy was at full employment. The recession hit in 2008 and the deficits soared. The deficit as a percent of GDP reached 9.5 percent in 2009. In 2012, the percent was still about 7 percent. Although some of the deficit was still cyclical, much was structural.

The large deficits beginning in 2008 on led to a large rise in the ratio of the federal government debt to GDP. By 2012 IV the ratio had risen to 61 percent, up from about 36 percent at the end of 2007. In 2010 and 2011 political leaders in the United States were reluctant to do much about the structural deficit problem because the economy was recovering only slowly from the 2008–2009 recession. In addition, the Republicans and Democrats were at odds on whether the deficit problem should be tackled with spending cuts or tax increases. A modest change was made at the end of 2012. The Bush tax cuts, which had been in effect for 12 years, were not extended for high-income tax payers. In addition, the payroll tax cut, which had been in effect for two years, was not extended. The increased revenue from these changes is not nearly enough to prevent the debt/GDP ratio from continuing to rise. In the beginning of 2013 the second Obama administration and the Congress were trying to come up with more significant measures. Again, a serious problem was the different views that Republicans and Democrats had over tax increases versus spending cuts. At the time of this writing (March 2013) no deal was in sight. Without significant new measures, the debt/GDP ratio is projected to continue to rise.

What happens if a country like the United States continues to run large structural deficits year after year? Deficits require that the government borrow money to finance them. In the case of the United States, the U.S. Treasury must sell bills and bonds. If the Fed buys them, this increases the money supply, which means that the government is simply financing the deficit by printing money. This is not a viable long-run strategy. It will eventually lead to excess aggregate demand and hyperinflation. If the Treasury is forced to sell the bonds to the U.S. public and foreigners, this may drive down the price of bonds and thus drive up the interest rate on the bonds. High interest rates, other things being equal, increase the government deficit because of higher government interest payments. The government has to hope that the public and foreigners are willing to buy the bonds with only modest decreases in their prices. This can continue for a long time. In 2012 the U.S. Treasury was able to sell large quantities of government bonds with negligible effects on bond prices. The public and foreigners were gobbling them up. Some economists are concerned that this demand may dry up.

One long-run concern from continuing deficits is that interest rates are driven up, thus exacerbating the deficit problem. Another concern is the possibility of a negative reaction from the stock market. If the market perceives that at some point interest rates will rise and that because of this the government will be forced to raise taxes or cut spending, this decreases expected future dividends, which drives down stock prices. So there could be a negative wealth effect even before bond rates begin to rise if the stock market expects this to happen. In short, possible negative asset-market reactions may discipline the long-run deficit strategy of the government. The asset markets may force the government to get its budget in control. This is another constraint on the ability of policy makers to stabilize the economy. If there is a structural deficit problem, policy makers may not have the freedom to lower taxes or raise spending to mitigate a downturn.

Deficit Targeting

The year 2010 was not the first time in which deficit issues played a major role in policy discussions. In the 1980s the U.S. government was spending much more than it was receiving in taxes. In response to the large deficits, in 1986 the U.S. Congress passed and President Reagan signed the **Gramm-Rudman-Hollings Act** (named for its three congressional sponsors), referred to as GRH. It is interesting to look back on this in the context of the current deficit problem. GRH set a target for reducing the federal deficit by a set amount each year. As Figure 15.6 shows, the

Gramm-Rudman-Hollings Act Passed by the U.S. Congress and signed by President Reagan in 1986, this law set out to reduce the federal deficit by $36 billion per year, with a deficit of zero slated for 1991.

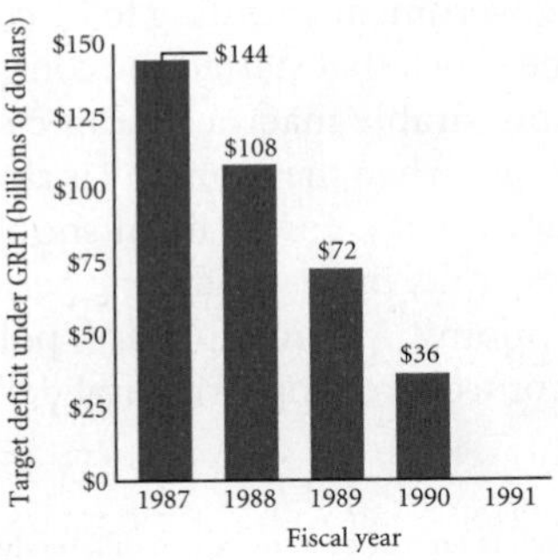

◀ FIGURE 15.6
Deficit Reduction Targets under Gramm-Rudman-Hollings
The GRH legislation, passed in 1986, set out to lower the federal deficit by $36 billion per year. If the plan had worked, a zero deficit would have been achieved by 1991.

deficit was to decline by $36 billion per year between 1987 and 1991, with a deficit of zero slated for fiscal year 1991. What was interesting about the GRH legislation was that the targets were not merely guidelines. If Congress, through its decisions about taxes and spending programs, produced a budget with a deficit larger than the targeted amount, GRH called for automatic spending cuts. The cuts were divided proportionately among most federal spending programs so that a program that made up 5 percent of total spending was to endure a cut equal to 5 percent of the total spending cut.[2]

In 1986, the U.S. Supreme Court declared part of the GRH bill unconstitutional. In effect, the Court said that Congress would have to approve the "automatic" spending cuts before they could take place. The law was changed in 1986 to meet the Supreme Court ruling and again in 1987, when new targets were established. The new targets had the deficit reaching zero in 1993 instead of 1991. The targets were revised again in 1991, when the year to achieve a zero deficit was changed from 1993 to 1996. In practice, these targets never came close to being achieved. As time wore on, even the revised targets became completely unrealistic, and by the end of the 1980s, the GRH legislation was not taken seriously.

Although the GRH legislation is history, it is useful to consider the stabilization consequences of deficit targeting. What if deficit targeting is taken seriously? Is this good policy? The answer is probably not. We will now show how deficit targeting can make the economy more unstable.

In a world with no deficit targeting, the Congress and the president make decisions each year about how much to spend and how much to tax. The federal government deficit is a result of these decisions and the state of the economy. However, with deficit targeting, the size of the deficit is set in advance. Taxes and government spending must be adjusted to produce the required deficit. In this situation, the deficit is no longer a consequence of the tax and spending decisions. Instead, taxes and spending become a consequence of the deficit decision.

What difference does it make whether Congress chooses a target deficit and adjusts government spending and taxes to achieve that target or decides how much to spend and tax and lets the deficit adjust itself? The difference may be substantial. Consider a leftward shift of the *AD* curve caused by some negative demand shock. A negative demand shock is something that causes a negative shift in consumption or investment schedules or that leads to a decrease in U.S. exports.

We know that a leftward shift of the *AD* curve lowers aggregate output (income), which causes the government deficit to increase. In a world without deficit targeting, the increase in the deficit during contractions provides an **automatic stabilizer** for the economy. (Review Chapter 9 if this point is hazy.) The contraction-induced decrease in tax revenues and increase in transfer payments tend to reduce the fall in after-tax income and consumer spending due to the negative demand shock. Thus, the decrease in aggregate output (income) caused by the negative demand shock is lessened somewhat by the growth of the deficit [Figure 15.7(a)].

In a world with deficit targeting, the deficit is not allowed to rise. Some combination of tax increases and government spending cuts would be needed to offset what would have otherwise been an increase in the deficit. We know that increases in taxes or cuts in spending are contractionary in themselves. The contraction in the economy will therefore be larger than it would have been without deficit targeting because the initial effect of the negative demand shock is worsened by the rise in taxes or the cut in government spending required to keep the deficit from rising. As Figure 15.7(b) shows, deficit targeting acts as an **automatic destabilizer**. It requires taxes to be raised and government spending to be cut during a contraction. This reinforces, rather than counteracts, the shock that started the contraction.

Deficit targeting thus has undesirable macroeconomic consequences. It requires cuts in spending or increases in taxes at times when the economy is already experiencing problems. This drawback does not mean, of course, that a government should ignore structural deficit problems. But locking in spending cuts or tax increases during periods of negative demand shocks is not a good way to manage the economy. Moving forward, policy makers around the globe will have to devise other methods to control growing structural deficits.

automatic stabilizers
Revenue and expenditure items in the federal budget that automatically change with the economy in such a way as to stabilize GDP.

automatic destabilizers
Revenue and expenditure items in the federal budget that automatically change with the economy in such a way as to destabilize GDP.

---

[2] Programs such as Social Security were exempt from cuts or were treated differently. Interest payments on the federal debt were also immune from cuts.

a. Without Deficit Targeting

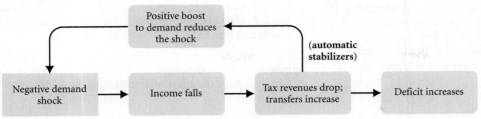

◀ **FIGURE 15.7**
Deficit Targeting as an Automatic Destabilizer
Deficit targeting changes the way the economy responds to negative demand shocks because it does not allow the deficit to increase. The result is a smaller deficit but a larger decline in income than would have otherwise occurred.

b. With Deficit Targeting

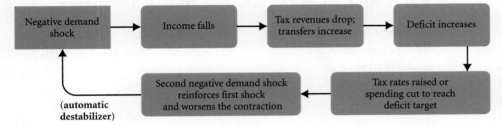

SUMMARY

THE STOCK MARKET, THE HOUSING MARKET, AND FINANCIAL CRISES *p. 282*

1. A firm can finance an investment project by borrowing from banks, by issuing *bonds*, or by issuing new shares of its stock. People who own shares of *stock* own a fraction of the firm.

2. The price of a stock should equal the discounted value of its expected future dividends, where the discount factors depend on the interest rate and risk.

3. A bubble exists when the price of a stock exceeds the discounted value of its expected future dividends. In this case what matters is what people expect that other people expect about how much the stock can be sold for in the future.

4. The largest stock market boom in U.S. history occurred between 1995 and 2000, when the S&P 500 index rose by 25 percent per year. The boom added $14 trillion to household wealth.

5. Why there was a stock market boom in 1995–2000 appears to be a puzzle. There was nothing unusual about earnings that would predict such a boom. Many people believe that the boom was merely a bubble.

6. Housing prices rose rapidly between 2000 and 2006 and fell rapidly between 2006 and 2009. Many consider that the fall in housing prices beginning in 2006 led to the recession and financial crisis of 2008–2009.

7. Changes in stock prices and housing prices change household wealth, which affects consumption and thus the real economy. Changes in stock and housing prices are largely unpredictable, which makes many fluctuations in the economy unpredictable.

TIME LAGS REGARDING MONETARY AND FISCAL POLICY *p. 287*

8. *Stabilization policy* describes both fiscal and monetary policy, the goals of which are to smooth out fluctuations in output and employment and to keep prices as stable as possible. Stabilization goals are not necessarily easy to achieve because of the existence of certain *time lags*, or delays in the response of the economy to macroeconomic policies.

9. A *recognition lag* is the time it takes for policy makers to recognize the existence of a boom or a slump. An *implementation lag* is the time it takes to put the desired policy into effect once economists and policy makers recognize that the economy is in a boom or a slump. A *response lag* is the time it takes for the economy to adjust to the new conditions after a new policy is implemented—in other words, a lag that occurs because of the operation of the economy itself. In general, monetary policy can be implemented more rapidly than fiscal policy but fiscal policy generally has a shorter response lag than monetary policy.

GOVERNMENT DEFICIT ISSUES *p. 291*

10. The U.S. government has been running a large structural deficit at least since 2010. There is currently much debate about what to do, but no agreed-upon long-run plan. Large deficits year after year may lead to negative asset-market reactions, such as large decreases in bond and stock prices.

11. In 1986 Congress passed and President Reagan signed the *Gramm-Rudman-Hollings Act* (*GRH*), which set deficit targets for each year. The aim was to reduce the large structural deficit that existed.

12. Deficit-targeting measures that call for automatic spending cuts to eliminate or reduce the deficit, like the GRH legislation, may have the effect of destabilizing the economy.

———— REVIEW TERMS AND CONCEPTS ————

automatic destabilizers, *p. 294*

automatic stabilizers, *p. 294*

capital gain, *p. 282*

Dow Jones Industrial Average, *p. 284*

Gramm-Rudman-Hollings Act, *p. 293*

implementation lag, *p. 290*

NASDAQ Composite, *p. 284*

realized capital gain, *p. 282*

recognition lag, *p. 290*

response lag, *p. 290*

stabilization policy, *p. 288*

Standard and Poor's 500 (S&P 500), *p. 284*

stock, *p. 282*

time lags, *p. 289*

———— PROBLEMS ————

All problems are available on **MyEconLab**.

1. In July 2003, the S&P 500 index was at 1,000.
   a. What is the S&P 500 index?
   b. Where is the S&P today?
   c. If you had invested $10,000 in July 2003 and your investments had increased in value by the same percentage as the S&P 500 index had increased, how much would you have today?
   d. Assume that the total stock market holdings of the household sector were about $12 trillion and that the entire stock market went up/down by the same percentage as the S&P. Evidence suggests that the "wealth effect" of stock market holdings on consumer spending is about 4 percent of wealth annually. How much additional or reduced spending would you expect to see as a result of the stock market moves since July 2003? Assuming a multiplier of 2 and a GDP of $10,000 billion, how much additional/less GDP would you predict for next year if all of this was true?

2. During 1997, stock markets in Asia collapsed. Hong Kong's was down nearly 30 percent, Thailand's was down 62 percent, and Malaysia's was down 60 percent. Japan and Korea experienced big drops as well. What impacts would these events have on the economies of the countries themselves? Explain your answer. In what ways would you have expected these events to influence the U.S. economy? How might the spending of Asians on American goods be affected? What about Americans who have invested in these countries?

3. Explain why the government deficit rises as the economy contracts.

4. You are given the following information about the economy in 2012 (all in billions of dollars):

Consumption function:	$C = 100 + (.8 \times Y_d)$
Taxes:	$T = -150 + (.25 \times Y)$
Investment function:	$I = 60$
Disposable income:	$Y_d = Y - T$
Government spending:	$G = 80$
Equilibrium:	$Y = C + I + G$

Hint: Deficit is $D = G - T = G - [-150 + (.25 \times Y)]$.

   a. Find equilibrium income. Show that the government budget deficit (the difference between government spending and tax revenues) is $5 billion.
   b. Congress passes the Foghorn-Leghorn (F-L) amendment, which requires that the deficit be zero this year. If the budget adopted by Congress has a deficit that is larger than zero, the deficit target must be met by cutting spending. Suppose spending is cut by $5 billion (to $75 billion). What is the new value for equilibrium GDP? What is the new deficit? Explain carefully why the deficit is not zero.
   c. Suppose the F-L amendment was not in effect and planned investment falls to $I = 55$. What is the new value of GDP? What is the new government budget deficit? What happens to GDP if the F-L amendment is in effect and spending is cut to reach the deficit target? (*Hint:* Spending must be cut by $21.666 billion to balance the budget.)

5. Some states are required to balance their budgets. Is this measure stabilizing or destabilizing? Suppose all states were

committed to a balanced-budget philosophy and the economy moved into a recession. What effects would this philosophy have on the size of the federal deficit?

6. Explain why stabilization policy may be difficult to carry out. How is it possible that stabilization policies can actually be destabilizing?

7. Since the year 2000, several countries have defaulted on their sovereign bonds. Do some research to find information on three countries that have defaulted since 2000. For each of the three countries you have researched, explain when the default occurred, how much debt was involved in the default, what interest rates each government had to pay on its bonds immediately following the default, and what interest rates the government is now paying on its bonds. How do these interest rates compare to the interest rates being paid on current U.S. government bonds? ·

8. Suppose the government decides to decrease spending and increase taxes in an attempt to decrease its deficit. Is it possible for the Fed to ease the macroeconomic effects of the spending and tax changes? Explain.

9. If the government implements a spending and tax policy in which it promises to neither increase nor decrease spending and taxes, is it still possible for the budget deficit to increase or decrease? Explain.

10. Explain why the implementation lag is generally longer and the response lag is generally shorter for fiscal policy than they are for monetary policy.

11. In February 2013, the Congressional Budget Office (CBO) issued a report estimating that the federal budget deficit for 2013 was expected to fall to $845 billion, or 5.3 percent of GDP. Working under the assumption that current laws affecting the budget will not change (i.e., no revisions in planned tax changes or fiscal stimulus spending), the CBO also estimated that the deficit as a percentage of GDP would fall to 2.4 percent by 2015. Go to www.cbo.gov and look up the current and estimated deficit-to-GDP ratios. Were the CBO's estimates accurate, and have its projections changed? Explain whether any policy changes enacted since February 2013 might have been responsible for changes in the CBO's projections.

Household and Firm Behavior in the Macroeconomy: A Further Look*

16

In Chapters 8 through 14, we considered the interactions of households, firms, and the government in the goods, money, and labor markets. The macroeconomy is complicated, and there is much to learn about these interactions. To keep our discussions as uncomplicated as possible, we assumed simple behavior of households and firms—the two basic decision-making units in the economy. We assumed that household consumption (C)

depends only on income and that firms' planned investment (I) depends only on the interest rate. We did not consider that households make consumption and labor supply decisions simultaneously and that firms make investment and employment decisions simultaneously.

Now that we understand the basic interactions in the economy, we present a more realistic picture of the influences on households' consumption and labor supply decisions and on firms' investment and employment decisions. We then use what we have learned to analyze more macroeconomic issues.

Households: Consumption and Labor Supply Decisions

For most of our analysis so far, we have been assuming that consumption depends simply on income. While this is a useful starting point, and income is in fact the most important determinant of consumption, it is not the only thing that determines household consumption decisions. We need to consider other theories of consumption to build a more realistic description of household behavior.

* This chapter is somewhat more advanced, but it contains a lot of interesting information!

LEARNING OBJECTIVES

Describe factors that affect household consumption and labor supply decisions

Summarize the behavior of aggregate household variables since 1970

Describe factors that affect the investment and employment decisions of firms

Analyze aggregate investment and employment variables since 1970

Describe the short-run relationship between output and unemployment

Identify factors that affect multiplier size

The Life-Cycle Theory of Consumption

Most people make consumption decisions based not only on current income but also on what they expect to earn later in life. Many of you, as young college students, are consuming more than you currently earn as you anticipate future earnings, while a number of your instructors are consuming less than they currently earn as they save for retirement without labor earnings. The model of consumption that is based on the idea that people track lifetime income when they make consumption decisions is called the **life-cycle theory of consumption**.

The lifetime income and consumption pattern of a representative individual is shown in Figure 16.1. As you can see, this person has a low income during the first part of her life, high income in the middle, and low income again in retirement. Her income in retirement is not zero because she has income from sources other than her own labor—Social Security payments, interest and dividends, and so on.

The consumption path as drawn in Figure 16.1 is constant over the person's life. This is an extreme assumption, but it illustrates the point that the path of consumption over a lifetime is likely to be more stable than the path of income. We consume an amount greater than our incomes during our early working careers. We do so by borrowing against future income by taking out a car loan, a mortgage to buy a house, or a loan to pay for college. This debt is repaid when our incomes have risen and we can afford to use some of our income to pay off past borrowing without substantially lowering our consumption. The reverse is true for our retirement years. Here, too, our incomes are low. Because we consume less than we earn during our prime working years, we can save up a "nest egg" that allows us to maintain an acceptable standard of living during retirement.

Fluctuations in wealth are also an important component of the life-cycle story. Many young households borrow in anticipation of higher income in the future. Some households actually have *negative wealth*—the value of their assets is less than the debts they owe. A household in its prime working years saves to pay off debts and to build up assets for its later years, when income typically goes down. Households whose assets are greater than the debts they owe have *positive wealth*. With its wage earners retired, a household consumes its accumulated wealth. Generally speaking, wealth starts out negative, turns positive, and then approaches zero near the end of life. Wealth, therefore, is intimately linked to the cumulative saving and dissaving behavior of households.

The key difference between the Keynesian theory of consumption and the life-cycle theory is that the life-cycle theory suggests that consumption and saving decisions are likely to be based not only on current income but also on expectations of future income. The consumption behavior of households immediately following World War II clearly supports the life-cycle story. Just after the war ended, income fell as wage earners moved out of war-related work. However, consumption spending did not fall commensurately, as Keynesian theory would predict. People expected to find jobs in other sectors eventually, and they did not adjust their consumption spending to the temporarily lower incomes they were earning in the meantime.

life-cycle theory of consumption A theory of household consumption: Households make lifetime consumption decisions based on their expectations of lifetime income.

▶ **FIGURE 16.1**
Life-Cycle Theory of Consumption
In their early working years, people consume more than they earn. This is also true in the retirement years. In between, people save (consume less than they earn) to pay off debts from borrowing and to accumulate savings for retirement.

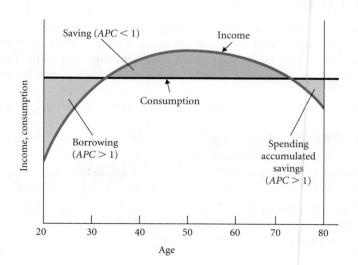

The term **permanent income** is sometimes used to refer to the average level of a person's expected future income stream. If you expect your income will be high in the future (even though it may not be high now), your permanent income is said to be high. With this concept, we can sum up the life-cycle theory by saying that current consumption decisions are likely to be based on permanent income instead of current income.[1] This means that policy changes such as tax-rate changes are likely to have more of an effect on household behavior if they are expected to be permanent instead of temporary.

One-time tax rebates such as we saw in the United States in 2001 and 2008 provide an interesting test of the permanent income hypothesis. In both cases, the tax rebate was a one-time stimulus. In 2008, for example, the tax rebate was $300 to $600 for individual tax payers eligible for the rebate. How much would we expect this rebate to influence consumption? The simple Keynesian model that we introduced earlier in this text would just apply the marginal propensity to consume to the $600. If the marginal propensity to consume is .8, we would expect the $600 to generate $480 in incremental spending per rebate. The permanent income hypothesis instead looks at the $600 in the context of an individual's permanent income. As a fraction of one's lifetime income, $600 is a modest number, and we would thus expect individuals to increase their spending only modestly in response to the rebate. Research on the 2001 tax rebate by Matthew Shapiro and Joel Slemrod, based on surveys of consumers, suggested that most people planned to use their rebates to lower debt, rather than increase spending. This is consistent with the life cycle model.

Although the life-cycle model enriches our understanding of the consumption behavior of households, the analysis is still missing something. What is missing is the other main decision of households: the labor supply decision.

permanent income The average level of a person's expected future income stream.

The Labor Supply Decision

The size of the labor force in an economy is of obvious importance. A growing labor force is one of the ways in which national income/output can be expanded, and the larger the percentage of people who work, the higher the potential output per capita.

So far we have said little about what determines the size of the labor force. Of course, demographics are a key element; the number of children born in 2010 will go a long way toward determining the potential number of 20-year-old workers in 2030. In addition, immigration, both legal and illegal, plays a role.

Behavior also plays a role. Households make decisions about whether to work and how much to work. These decisions are closely tied to consumption decisions because for most households, the bulk of their spending is financed out of wages and salaries. Households make consumption and labor supply decisions simultaneously. Consumption cannot be considered separately from labor supply because it is precisely by selling your labor that you earn income to pay for your consumption.

As we discussed in Chapter 3, the alternative to supplying your labor in exchange for a wage or a salary is leisure or other nonmarket activities. Nonmarket activities include raising a child, going to school, keeping a house, or—in a developing economy—working as a subsistence farmer. What determines the quantity of labor supplied by a household? Among the list of factors are the wage rate, prices, wealth, and nonlabor income.

The Wage Rate A changing wage rate can affect labor supply, but whether the effect is positive or negative is ambiguous. An increase in the wage rate affects a household in two ways. First, work becomes more attractive relative to leisure and other nonmarket activities. Because every hour spent in leisure now requires giving up a higher wage, the opportunity cost of leisure is higher. As a result, you would expect that a higher wage would lead to a larger quantity of labor supplied—a larger workforce. This is called the *substitution effect of a wage rate increase.*

On the other hand, household members who work are clearly better off after a wage rate increase. By working the same number of hours as they did before, they will earn more income.

---

[1] The pioneering work on this topic was done by Milton Friedman, *A Theory of the Consumption Function* (Princeton, NJ: Princeton University Press, 1957). In the mid-1960s, Franco Modigliani did closely related work that included the formulation of the life-cycle theory.

If we assume that leisure is a normal good, people with higher income will spend some of it on leisure by working less. This is the *income effect of a wage rate increase.*

When wage rates rise, the substitution effect suggests that people will work more, while the income effect suggests that they will work less. The ultimate effect depends on which separate effect is more powerful. The data suggest that the substitution effect seems to win in most cases. That is, higher wage rates usually lead to a larger labor supply and lower wage rates usually lead to a lower labor supply.

Prices   Prices also play a major role in the consumption/labor supply decision. In our discussions of the possible effects of an increase in the wage rate, we have been assuming that the prices of goods and services do not rise at the same time. If the wage rate and all other prices rise simultaneously, the story is different. To make things clear, we need to distinguish between the nominal wage rate and the real wage rate.

nominal wage rate   The wage rate in current dollars.

real wage rate   The amount the nominal wage rate can buy in terms of goods and services.

The **nominal wage rate** is the wage rate in current dollars. When we adjust the nominal wage rate for changes in the price level, we obtain the **real wage rate**. The real wage rate measures the amount that wages can buy in terms of goods and services. Workers do not care about their nominal wage—they care about the purchasing power of this wage—the real wage.

Suppose skilled workers in Indianapolis were paid a wage rate of $20 per hour in 2010. Now suppose their wage rate rose to $22 in 2011, a 10 percent increase. If the prices of goods and services were the same in 2011 as they were in 2010, the real wage rate would have increased by 10 percent. An hour of work in 2011 ($22) buys 10 percent more than an hour of work in 2010 ($20). What if the prices of all goods and services also increased by 10 percent between 2010 and 2011? The purchasing power of an hour's wages has not changed. The real wage rate has not increased at all. In 2011, $22 bought the same quantity of goods and services that $20 bought in 2010.

To measure the real wage rate, we adjust the nominal wage rate with a price index. As we saw in Chapter 7, there are several such indexes that we might use, including the consumer price index and the GDP price index.[2]

We can now apply what we have learned from the life-cycle theory to our wage/price story. Recall that the life-cycle theory says that people look ahead in making their decisions. Translated to real wage rates, this idea says that households look at expected future real wage rates as well as the current real wage rate in making their current consumption and labor supply decisions. Consider, for example, medical students who expect that their real wage rate will be higher in the future. This expectation obviously has an effect on current decisions about things like how much to buy and whether to take a part-time job.

Wealth and Nonlabor Income   Life-cycle theory implies that wealth fluctuates over the life cycle. Households accumulate wealth during their working years to pay off debts accumulated when they were young and to support themselves in retirement. This role of wealth is clear, but the existence of wealth poses another question. Consider two households that are at the same stage in their life cycle and have similar expectations about future wage rates, prices, and so on. They expect to live the same length of time, and both plan to leave the same amount to their children. They differ only in their wealth. Because of a past inheritance, household 1 has more wealth than household 2. Which household is likely to have a higher consumption path for the rest of its life? Household 1 is because it has more wealth to spread out over the rest of its life. Holding everything else constant (including the stage in the life cycle), the more wealth a household has, the more it will consume both now and in the future.

Now consider a household that has a sudden unexpected increase in wealth, perhaps an inheritance from a distant relative. How will the household's consumption pattern be affected? Few spend the entire inheritance all at once. Most households will increase consumption both now and in the future, spending the inheritance over the course of the rest of their lives.

nonlabor, *or* **nonwage, income**   Any income received from sources other than working—inheritances, interest, dividends, transfer payments, and so on.

An increase in wealth can also be looked on as an increase in nonlabor income. **Nonlabor,** *or* **nonwage, income** is income received from sources other than working—inheritances, interest, dividends, and transfer payments, such as welfare payments and Social Security payments.

---

[2] To calculate the real wage rate, we divide the nominal wage rate by the price index. Suppose the wage rate rose from $10 per hour in 1998 to $18 per hour in 2010 and the price level rose 50 percent during the same period. Using 1998 as the base year, the price index would be 1.00 in 1998 and 1.50 in 2010. The real wage rate is W/P, where W is the nominal wage rate and P is the price level. Using 1998 as the base year, the real wage rate is $10 in 1998 ($10.00/1.00) and $12 in 2010 ($18.00/1.50).

As with wealth, an unexpected increase in nonlabor income will have a positive effect on a household's consumption.

What about the effect of an increase in wealth or nonlabor income on labor supply? We already know that an increase in income results in an increase in the consumption of normal goods, including leisure. Therefore, an unexpected increase in wealth or nonlabor income results in an increase in consumption and an increase in leisure. With leisure increasing, labor supply must fall. So an unexpected increase in wealth or nonlabor income leads to a *decrease* in labor supply. This point should be obvious. If you suddenly win a million dollars in the state lottery or make a killing in the stock market, you will probably work less in the future than you otherwise would have.

Interest Rate Effects on Consumption

Recall from the last few chapters that the interest rate affects a firm's investment decision. A higher interest rate leads to a lower level of planned investment and vice versa. This was a key link between the money market and the goods market, and it was the channel through which monetary policy had an impact on planned aggregate expenditure.

We can now expand on this link: The interest rate also affects household behavior. Consider the effect of a fall in the interest rate on consumption. A fall in the interest rate lowers the reward to saving. If the interest rate falls from 10 percent to 5 percent, you earn 5¢ instead of 10¢ per year on every dollar saved. This means that the opportunity cost of spending a dollar today (instead of saving it and consuming it plus the interest income a year from now) has fallen. You will substitute toward current consumption and away from future consumption when the interest rate falls: You consume more today and save less. A rise in the interest rate leads you to consume less today and save more. This effect is called the *substitution effect*.

There is also an *income effect* of an interest rate change on consumption. If a household has positive wealth and is earning interest on that wealth, a fall in the interest rate leads to a fall in interest income. This is a decrease in its nonlabor income, which, as we just saw, has a negative effect on consumption. For households with positive wealth, the income effect works in the opposite direction from the substitution effect. On the other hand, if a household is a debtor and is paying interest on its debt, a fall in the interest rate will lead to a fall in interest payments. The household is better off in this case and will consume more. In this case, the income and substitution effects work in the same direction. The total household sector in the United States has positive wealth, and so in the aggregate, the income and substitution effects work in the opposite direction.

On balance, the data suggest that the substitution effect dominates the income effect so that the interest rate has a negative net effect on consumption: Interest rate increases cause consumption to fall. There is also some evidence, however, that the income effect is getting larger over time. U.S. households own most of the U.S. government debt, and the size of this debt has increased dramatically in the last 25 years. This means that the change in government interest payments (and so the change in household interest income) is now larger for a given change in interest rates than before, which leads to a larger income effect than before for a given change in interest rates. On net, this tells us that interest rate increases will cause consumption to fall less as the income effect grows.

Government Effects on Consumption and Labor Supply: Taxes and Transfers

The government influences household behavior mainly through income tax rates and transfer payments. When the government raises income tax rates, after-tax real wages decrease, lowering consumption. When the government lowers income tax rates, after-tax real wages increase, raising consumption. A change in income tax rates also affects labor supply. If the substitution effect dominates, as we are generally assuming, an increase in income tax rates, which lowers after-tax wages, will lower labor supply. A decrease in income tax rates will increase labor supply.

Transfer payments are payments such as Social Security benefits, veterans' benefits, and welfare benefits. An increase in transfer payments is an increase in nonlabor income, which we have seen has a positive effect on consumption and a negative effect on labor supply. Increases in transfer payments thus increase consumption and decrease labor supply, while decreases in transfer payments decrease consumption and increase labor supply. Table 16.1 summarizes these results.

TABLE 16.1 The Effects of Government on Household Consumption and Labor Supply

	Income Tax Rates		Transfer Payments	
	Increase	Decrease	Increase	Decrease
Effect on consumption	Negative	Positive	Positive	Negative
Effect on labor supply	Negative*	Positive*	Negative	Positive

* If the substitution effect dominates.

Note: The effects are larger if they are expected to be permanent instead of temporary.

A Possible Employment Constraint on Households

Our discussion of the labor supply decision has so far proceeded as if households were free to choose how much to work each period. If a member of a household decides to work an additional 5 hours a week at the current wage rate, we have assumed that the person *can* work 5 hours more—that work is available. If someone who has not been working decides to work at the current wage rate, we have assumed that the person *can find a job*.

There are times when these assumptions do not hold. The Great Depression, when unemployment rates reached 25 percent of the labor force, led to the birth of macroeconomics in the 1930s. Since the mid-1970s, the United States has experienced five recessions, with high unemployment rates. When there is unemployment, some households feel an additional constraint on their behavior. Some people may want to work 40 hours per week at the current wage rates but may find only part-time work. Others may not find any work at all.

How does a household respond when it is constrained from working as much as it would like? It consumes less. If your current wage rate is $10 per hour and you normally work 40 hours a week, your normal income from wages is $400 per week. If your average tax rate is 20 percent, your after-tax wage income is $320 per week. You are likely to spend much of this income during the week. If you are prevented from working, this income will not be available to you and you will have less to spend. You will spend something, of course. You may receive some form of nonlabor income, and you may have assets such as savings deposits or stocks and bonds that can be withdrawn or sold. You also may be able to borrow during your period of unemployment. Even though you will spend something during the week, you almost certainly will spend less than you would have if you had your usual income of $320 in after-tax wages.

A household constrained from working as much as it would like at the current wage rate faces a different decision from the decision facing a household that can work as much as it wants. The work decision of the former household is, in effect, forced on it. The household works as much as it can—a certain number of hours per week or perhaps none at all—but this amount is less than the household would choose to work at the current wage rate if it could find more work. The amount that a household would like to work at the current wage rate if it could find the work is called its **unconstrained supply of labor**. The amount that the household actually works in a given period at current wage rates is called its **constrained supply of labor**.

A household's constrained supply of labor is not a variable over which it has any control. The amount of labor the household supplies is imposed on it from the outside by the workings of the economy. However, the household's consumption *is* under its control. We have just seen that the less a household works—that is, the smaller the household's constrained supply of labor is—the lower its consumption. Constraints on the supply of labor are an important determinant of consumption when there is unemployment.

unconstrained supply of labor The amount a household would like to work within a given period at the current wage rate if it could find the work.

constrained supply of labor The amount a household actually works in a given period at the current wage rate.

Keynesian Theory Revisited   Recall the Keynesian theory that current income determines current consumption. We now know the consumption decision is made jointly with the labor supply decision and the two depend on the real wage rate. It is incorrect to think that consumption depends only on income, at least when there is full employment. However, if there is unemployment, Keynes is closer to being correct because the level of income (at least workers' income) depends exclusively on the employment decisions made by firms and not on household decisions. In this case, it is income that affects consumption, not the wage rate. For this reason Keynesian theory is considered to pertain to periods of unemployment. It was, of course, precisely during such a period that the theory was developed.

A Summary of Household Behavior

This completes our discussion of household behavior in the macroeconomy. Household consumption depends on more than current income. Households determine consumption and labor supply simultaneously, and they look ahead in making their decisions.

The following factors affect household consumption and labor supply decisions:

■ Current and expected future real wage rates

■ Initial value of wealth

■ Current and expected future nonlabor income

■ Interest rates

■ Current and expected future tax rates and transfer payments

If households are constrained in their labor supply decisions, income is directly determined by firms' hiring decisions. In this case, we can say (in the traditional, Keynesian way) that "income" affects consumption.

The Household Sector Since 1970

To better understand household behavior, let us examine how some of the aggregate household variables have changed over time. We will discuss the period 1970 I–2012 IV. (Remember, Roman numerals refer to quarters, that is, 1970 I means the first quarter of 1970.) Within this span, there have been five recessionary periods: 1974 I–1975 I, 1980 II–1982 IV, 1990 III–1991 I, 2001 I–2001 III, and 2008 I–2009 II. How did the household variables behave during each period?

Consumption Data on the total consumption of the household sector are in the national income accounts. As we saw in Table 6.2 in Chapter 6, personal consumption expenditures accounted for 70.9 percent of GDP in 2012. The three basic categories of consumption expenditures are services, nondurable goods, and durable goods.

Figure 16.2 plots the data for consumption expenditures on services and nondurable goods combined and for consumption expenditures on durable goods. The variables are in real terms. You can see that expenditures on services and nondurable goods are "smoother" over time than expenditures on durable goods. For example, the decrease in expenditures on services and nondurable goods was much smaller during the five recessionary periods than the decrease in expenditures on durable goods.

Why do expenditures on durables fluctuate more than expenditures on services and nondurables? When times are bad, people can postpone the purchase of durable goods, which they do. It follows that expenditures on these goods change the most. When times are tough, you do not *have* to have a new car or a new smartphone; you can make do with your old Chevy

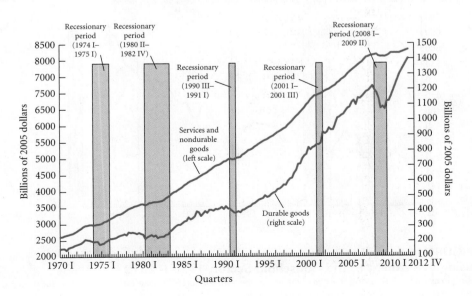

MyEconLab Real-time data

◀ **FIGURE 16.2**
Consumption Expenditures, 1970 I–2012 IV
Over time, expenditures on services and nondurable goods are "smoother" than expenditures on durable goods.

ECONOMICS IN PRACTICE

Measuring Housing Price Changes

We have suggested in the text that the rapid rise in housing prices in the period from 2000 to 2006 and the subsequent rapid fall of those prices after 2006 may have played a role in the 2008–2009 recession. There has been a good deal of work in economics tracing the links between what has been called the housing bubble and that recession, particularly on the bursting of the bubble on bank stability.

But how do we measure housing price changes? After all, houses are all different. Measuring price changes in houses is much harder than measuring price changes in oil, or even price changes in milk or cans of tuna fish. One possibility is to look at changes in the *average* price of a house in a city over time. However, if in year 1 mostly modest split-levels change hands, while in year 2 most of the houses sold are McMansions, then changes in the average price will not do a very good job of capturing housing price inflation. An alternative is to try to standardize the house type, say looking at the change in the average price of a four-bedroom house in an area over time. This is better, but still leaves one with a lot of heterogeneity. In fact, one of the authors of this text, Karl Case, working with Robert Shiller,

a behavioral finance economist, developed an index (aptly named the Case-Shiller index) that neatly solves the problem that houses are all different. The Case-Shiller index looks only at houses that have sold multiple times and asks the question: How much does an identical house sell for now versus that same house in the past? The index, developed first in Boston, is now computed for a number of large housing areas. In fact, the index itself is commonly reported on the financial pages and shows housing price changes for 10 city and 20 city bundles.

So what does the Case-Shiller index tell us about the present? From 1996 to 2006, the Case-Shiller index increased by 125 percent, only to fall by 38 percent from 2006 to 2011. But 2012 and early 2013 looked much better, with an annual increase of 7.3 percent in the 10-city index and 8.1 percent for the 20-city index as of April 2013.

THINKING PRACTICALLY

1. Who, other than macroeconomists, might be interested in trading the Case-Schiller index?

---

or iPhone until things get better. When your income falls, it is not as easy to postpone the service costs of day care or health care. Nondurables fall into an intermediate category, with some items (such as new clothes) easier to postpone than others (such as food).

Housing Investment Another important expenditure of the household sector is housing investment (purchases of new housing), plotted in Figure 16.3. Housing investment is the most easily postponable of all household expenditures, and it has large fluctuations. The fluctuations are remarkable between 2003 and 2010. Housing investment rose rapidly between 2003 and 2005 and then came crashing down. As discussed in Chapter 15, much of this was driven by a huge increase and then decrease in housing prices.

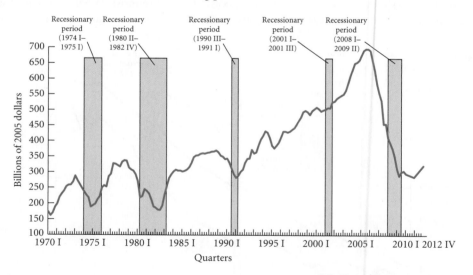

▲ **FIGURE 16.3**　　　　　　　　　　　　　　　　　　MyEconLab Real-time data

Housing Investment of the Household Sector, 1970 I–2012 IV

Housing investment fell during the five recessionary periods since 1970. Like expenditures for durable goods, expenditures for housing investment are postponable.

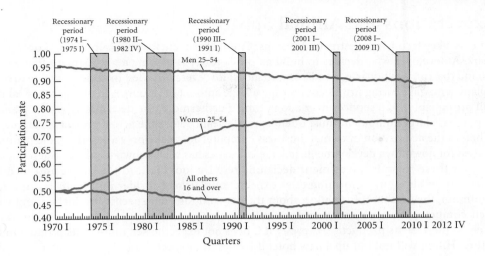

MyEconLab Real-time data

◀ **FIGURE 16.4 Labor Force Participation Rates for Men 25 to 54, Women 25 to 54, and All Others 16 and Over, 1970 I–2012 IV**

Since 1970, the labor force participation rate for prime-age men has been decreasing slightly. The rate for prime-age women has been increasing dramatically. The rate for all others 16 and over has been declining since 1979 and shows a tendency to fall during recessions (the discouraged-worker effect).

Labor Supply   As we noted in Chapters 7 and 14, a person is considered a part of the labor force when he or she is working or has been actively looking for work in the past few weeks. The ratio of the labor force to the total working-age population—those 16 and over—is the *labor force participation rate.*

It is informative to divide the labor force into three categories: males 25 to 54, females 25 to 54, and all others 16 and over. Ages 25 to 54 are sometimes called "prime" ages, presuming that a person is in the prime of working life during these ages. The participation rates for these three groups are plotted in Figure 16.4.

As the figure shows, most men of prime age are in the labor force, although the participation rate has fallen since 1970—from .961 in 1970 I to .886 in 2012 IV. (A rate of .886 means that 88.6 percent of prime-age men were in the labor force.) The participation rate for prime-age women, on the other hand, rose dramatically between 1970 and 1990—from .501 in 1970 I to .741 in 1990 I. Although economic factors account for some of this increase, a change in social attitudes and preferences probably explains much of the increase. Since 1990, the participation rate for prime-age women has changed very little. In 2012 IV, it was .745, still considerably below the .886 rate for prime-age men.

Figure 16.4 also shows the participation rate for all individuals 16 and over except prime-age men and women. This rate has some cyclical features—it tends to fall in recessions and to rise or fall less during expansions. These features reveal the operation of the *discouraged-worker effect,* discussed in Chapter 7. During recessions, some people get discouraged about ever finding a job. They stop looking and are then not considered a part of the labor force. During expansions, people become encouraged again. Once they begin looking for jobs, they are again considered a part of the labor force. Because prime-age women and men are likely to be fairly attached to the labor force, the discouraged-worker effect for them is quite small.

Firms: Investment and Employment Decisions

Having taken a closer look at the behavior of households in the macroeconomy, we now look more closely at the behavior of firms—the other major decision-making unit in the economy. In discussing firm behavior earlier, we assumed that planned investment depends only on the interest rate. However, there are several other determinants of planned investment. We now discuss them and the factors that affect firms' employment decisions. Once again, microeconomic theory can help us gain some insight into the working of the macroeconomy.

In a market economy, firms determine which goods and services are available to consumers today and which will be available in the future, how many workers are needed for what kinds of jobs, and how much investment will be undertaken. Stated in macroeconomic terms, the decisions of firms, taken together, determine output, labor demand, and investment.

Expectations and Animal Spirits

Time is a key factor in investment decisions. Capital has a life that typically extends over many years. A developer who decides to build an office tower is making an investment that will be around (barring earthquakes, floods, or tornadoes) for several decades. In deciding where to build a plant, a manufacturing firm is committing a large amount of resources to purchase capital that will presumably yield services over a long time. Furthermore, the decision to build a plant or to purchase large equipment must often be made years before the actual project is completed. Whereas the acquisition of a small business computer may take only a few days, the planning process for downtown developments in large U.S. cities has been known to take decades.

For these reasons, investment decisions require looking into the future and forming expectations about it. In forming their expectations, firms consider numerous factors. At a minimum, they gather information about the demand for their specific products, about what their competitors are planning, and about the macroeconomy's overall health. A firm is not likely to increase its production capacity if it does not expect to sell more of its product in the future. Hilton will not put up a new hotel if it does not expect to fill the rooms at a profitable rate. Ford will not build a new plant if it expects the economy to enter a long recession.

Forecasting the future is fraught with dangers. Many events cannot be foreseen. Investments are therefore always made with imperfect knowledge. Keynes pointed this out in 1936:

> The outstanding fact is the extreme precariousness of the basis of knowledge on which our estimates of prospective yield have to be made. Our knowledge of the factors which will govern the yield of an investment some years hence is usually very slight and often negligible. If we speak frankly, we have to admit that our basis of knowledge for estimating the yield ten years hence of a railway, a copper mine, a textile factory, the goodwill of a patent medicine, an Atlantic liner, a building in the City of London amounts to little and sometimes nothing.

animal spirits of entrepreneurs
A term coined by Keynes to describe investors' feelings.

Keynes concludes from this line of thought that much investment activity depends on psychology and on what he calls the **animal spirits of entrepreneurs**:

> Our decisions . . . can only be taken as a result of animal spirits. In estimating the prospects of investment, we must have regard, therefore, to nerves and hysteria and even the digestions and reactions to the weather of those upon whose spontaneous activity it largely depends.[3]

Because expectations about the future are, as Keynes points out, subject to great uncertainty, they may change often. Thus, animal spirits help to make investment a volatile component of GDP.

The Accelerator Effect Expectations, at least in part, are thus likely to determine the level of planned investment spending. At any interest rate, the level of investment is likely to be higher if businesses are optimistic and lower if they are pessimistic. A key question is then what determines expectations? One possibility is that expectations are optimistic when aggregate output (Y) is rising and pessimistic when aggregate output is falling. At any given level of the interest rate, expectations may be more optimistic and planned investment higher when output is growing rapidly than when it is growing slowly or falling. It is easy to see why this might be so. When firms expect future prospects to be good, they may plan now to add productive capacity, and one indicator of future prospects is the current growth rate.

accelerator effect
The tendency for investment to increase when aggregate output increases and to decrease when aggregate output decreases, accelerating the growth or decline of output.

If this is the case, the result will be what is called an **accelerator effect**. If aggregate output (income) (Y) is rising, investment will increase even though the level of Y may be low. Higher investment spending leads to an added increase in output, further "accelerating" the growth of aggregate output. If Y is falling, expectations are dampened and investment spending will be cut even though the level of Y may be high, accelerating the decline.

---

[3] John Maynard Keynes, *The General Theory of Employment, Interest, and Money (1936)*, First Harbinger Ed. (New York: Harcourt Brace Jovanovich, 1964), pp. 149, 152.

Excess Labor and Excess Capital Effects

In practice, firms appear at times to hold what we will call **excess labor** and/or **excess capital**. A firm holds excess labor (or capital) if it can reduce the amount of labor it employs (or capital it holds) and still produce the same amount of output. Why would a firm want to employ more workers or have more capital on hand than it needs? Both labor and capital are costly—a firm has to pay wages to its workers, and it forgoes interest on funds tied up in machinery or buildings. Why would a firm want to incur costs that do not yield revenue?

To see why, suppose a firm suffers a sudden and large decrease in sales, but it expects the lower sales level to last only a few months, after which it believes sales will pick up again. In this case, the firm is likely to lower production in response to the sales change to avoid too large an increase in its stock of inventories. This decrease in production means that the firm could get rid of some workers and some machines because it needs less labor and less capital to produce the now-lower level of output.

However, things are not that simple. Decreasing its workforce and capital stock quickly can be costly for a firm. Abrupt cuts in the workforce hurt worker morale and may increase personnel administration costs, and abrupt reductions in capital stock may be disadvantageous because of the difficulty of selling used machines. These types of costs are sometimes called **adjustment costs** because they are the costs of adjusting to the new level of output. There are also adjustment costs to increasing output. For example, it is usually costly to recruit and train new workers.

Adjustment costs may be large enough that a firm chooses not to decrease its workforce and capital stock when production falls. The firm may at times choose to have more labor and capital on hand than it needs to produce its current amount of output simply because getting rid of them is more costly than keeping them. In practice, excess labor takes the form of workers not working at their normal level of activity (more coffee breaks and more idle time, for instance). Some of this excess labor may receive new training so that productivity will be higher when production picks up again.

The existence of excess labor and capital at any given moment is likely to affect future employment and investment decisions. Suppose a firm already has excess labor and capital due to a fall in its sales and production. When production picks up again, the firm will not need to hire as many new workers or acquire as much new capital as it would otherwise. The more excess capital a firm already has, the less likely it is to invest in new capital in the future. The more excess labor it has, the less likely it is to hire new workers in the future.

> **excess labor, excess capital** Labor and capital that are not needed to produce the firm's current level of output.

> **adjustment costs** The costs that a firm incurs when it changes its production level—for example, the administration costs of laying off employees or the training costs of hiring new workers.

Inventory Investment

We now turn to a brief discussion of the inventory investment decision. **Inventory investment** is the change in the stock of inventories. Although inventory investment is another way in which a firm adds to its capital stock, the inventory investment decision is quite different from the plant-and-equipment investment decision.

> **inventory investment** The change in the stock of inventories.

The Role of Inventories Recall the distinction between a firm's sales and its output. If a firm can hold goods in inventory, which is usually the case unless the good is perishable or unless the firm produces services, then within a given period, it can sell a quantity of goods that differs from the quantity of goods it produces during that period. When a firm sells more than it produces, its stock of inventories decreases; when it sells less than it produces, its stock of inventories increases.

> Stock of inventories (end of period) = Stock of inventories (beginning of period)
> + Production − Sales

If a firm starts a period with 100 umbrellas in inventory, produces 15 umbrellas during the period, and sells 10 umbrellas in this same interval, it will have 105 umbrellas (100 + 15 − 10) in inventory at the end of the period. A change in the stock of inventories is actually investment because inventories are counted as part of a firm's capital stock. In our example, inventory investment during the period is a positive number, 5 umbrellas (105 − 100). When the number of goods produced is less than the number of goods sold, such as 5 produced and 10 sold, inventory investment is negative.

The Optimal Inventory Policy

We can now consider firms' inventory decisions. Firms are concerned with what they are going to sell and produce in the future as well as what they are selling and producing currently. At each point in time, a firm has some idea of how much it is going to sell in the current period and in future periods. Given these expectations and its knowledge of how much of its good it already has in stock, a firm must decide how much to produce in the current period. Inventories are costly to a firm because they take up space and they tie up funds that could be earning interest. However, if a firm's stock of inventories gets too low, the firm may have difficulty meeting the demand for its product, especially if demand increases unexpectedly. The firm may lose sales. The point between too low and too high a stock of inventory is called the **desired, *or* optimal, level of inventories**. This is the level at which the extra cost (in lost sales) from decreasing inventories by a small amount is just equal to the extra gain (in interest revenue and decreased storage costs).

A firm that had no costs other than inventory costs would always aim to produce in a period exactly the volume of goods necessary to make its stock of inventories at the end of the period equal to the desired stock. If the stock of inventory fell lower than desired, the firm would produce more than it expected to sell to bring the stock up. If the stock of inventory grew above the desired level, the firm would produce less than it expected to sell to reduce the stock.

There are other costs to running a firm besides inventory costs. In particular, large and abrupt changes in production can be very costly because it is often disruptive to change a production process geared to a certain rate of output. If production is to be increased, there may be adjustment costs for hiring more labor and increasing the capital stock. If production is to be decreased, there may be adjustment costs in laying off workers and decreasing the capital stock.

Because holding inventories and changing production levels are both costly, firms face a trade-off between them. Because of adjustment costs, a firm is likely to smooth its production path relative to its sales path. This means that a firm is likely to have its production fluctuate less than its sales, with changes in inventories to absorb the difference each period. However, because there are incentives not to stray too far from the optimal level of inventories, fluctuations in production are not eliminated completely. Production is still likely to fluctuate, just not as much as sales fluctuate.

Two other points need to be made here. First, if a firm's stock of inventories is unusually or unexpectedly high, the firm is likely to produce less in the future than it otherwise would have in order to decrease its high stock of inventories. In other words, although the stock of inventories fluctuates over time because production is smoothed relative to sales, at any point in time, inventories may be unexpectedly high or low because sales have been unexpectedly low or high. An unexpectedly high stock will have a negative effect on production in the future, and an unexpectedly low stock will have a positive effect on production in the future. An unexpected increase in inventories has a negative effect on future production, and an unexpected decrease in inventories has a positive effect on future production.

Second, firms do not know their future sales exactly. They have expectations of future sales, and these expectations may not turn out to be exactly right. This has important consequences. If sales turn out to be less than expected, inventories will be higher than expected and there will be less production in the future. Furthermore, *future* sales expectations are likely to have an important effect on *current* production. If a firm expects its sales to be high in the future, it will adjust its planned production path accordingly. Even though a firm smooths production relative to sales, over a long time, it must produce as much as it sells. If it does not, it will eventually run out of inventories. The level of a firm's planned production path depends on the level of its expected future sales path. If a firm's expectations of the level of its future sales path decrease, the firm is likely to decrease the level of its planned production path, including its actual production in the current period. Current production depends on expected future sales.

Because production is likely to depend on expectations of the future, animal spirits may play a role. If firms become more optimistic about the future, they are likely to produce more now. Keynes's view that animal spirits affect investment is also likely to pertain to output.

desired, *or* optimal, level of inventories The level of inventory at which the extra cost (in lost sales) from lowering inventories by a small amount is just equal to the extra gain (in interest revenue and decreased storage costs).

A Summary of Firm Behavior

The following factors affect firms' investment and employment decisions:

- Firms' expectations of future output
- Wage rate and cost of capital (The interest rate is an important component of the cost of capital.)
- Amount of excess labor and excess capital on hand

The most important points to remember about the relationship among production, sales, and inventory investment are

- Inventory investment—that is, the change in the stock of inventories—equals production minus sales.
- An unexpected increase in the stock of inventories has a negative effect on future production.
- Current production depends on expected future sales.

The Firm Sector Since 1970

To close our discussion of firm behavior, we now examine some aggregate investment and employment variables for the period 1970 I–2012 IV.

Plant-and-Equipment Investment   Plant-and-equipment investment by the firm sector is plotted in Figure 16.5. Investment fared poorly in the five recessionary periods after 1970. This observation is consistent with the observation that investment depends in part on output. An examination of the plot of real GDP in Figure 5.4 in Chapter 5 and the plot of investment in Figure 16.5 shows that investment generally does poorly when GDP does poorly and that investment generally does well when GDP does well.

Figure 16.5 also shows that investment fluctuates greatly. This is not surprising. The animal spirits of entrepreneurs are likely to be volatile, and if animal spirits affect investment, it follows that investment too will be volatile.

Despite the volatility of plant-and-equipment investment, however, it is still true that housing investment fluctuates more than plant-and-equipment investment (as you can see by comparing Figures 16.3 and 16.5). Plant-and-equipment investment is not the most volatile component of GDP.

Employment   Employment in the firm sector is plotted in Figure 16.6, which shows that employment fell in all five recessionary periods. This is consistent with the theory that employment depends in part on output. Otherwise, employment has grown over time in

MyEconLab Real-time data
◀ **FIGURE 16.5**
Plant-and-Equipment Investment of the Firm Sector, 1970 I–2012 IV
Overall, plant-and-equipment investment declined in the five recessionary periods since 1970.

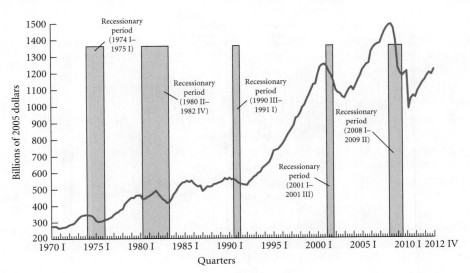

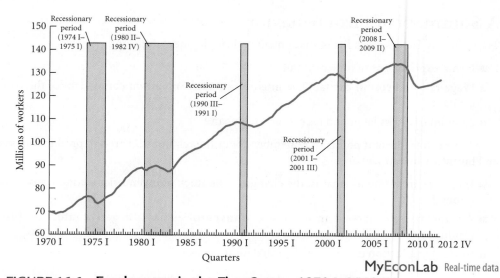

▲ FIGURE 16.6   Employment in the Firm Sector, 1970 I–2012 IV
Growth in employment was generally negative in the five recessions the U.S. economy has experienced since 1970.

response to the growing economy. Employment in the firm sector rose from 59.4 million in 1970 I to 131.9 million in 2007 IV (before the recession of 2008–2009). During the 2008–2009 recession, employment fell by 9.5 million—from 131.9 million in 2007 IV to 122.4 million in 2009 IV. You can see that it only recovered modestly in 2010–2012.

Inventory Investment   Recall that *inventory investment* is the difference between the level of output and the level of sales. Recall also that some inventory investment is usually unplanned. This occurs when the actual level of sales is different from the expected level of sales.

Inventory investment of the firm sector is plotted in Figure 16.7. Also plotted in this figure is the ratio of the stock of inventories to the level of sales—the *inventory/sales ratio*. The figure shows that inventory investment is very volatile—more volatile than housing investment and plant-and-equipment investment. Some of this volatility is undoubtedly due to the unplanned component of inventory investment, which is likely to fluctuate greatly from one period to the next.

When the inventory/sales ratio is high, the actual stock of inventories is likely to be larger than the desired stock. In such a case, firms have overestimated demand and produced too much relative to sales and they are likely to want to produce less in the future to draw down their stock. You can find several examples of this trend in Figure 16.7—the clearest occurred

MyEconLab Real-time data

▶ **FIGURE 16.7**

Inventory Investment of the Firm Sector and the Inventory/Sales Ratio, 1970 I–2012 IV

The inventory/sales ratio is the ratio of the firm sector's stock of inventories to the level of sales. Inventory investment is very volatile.

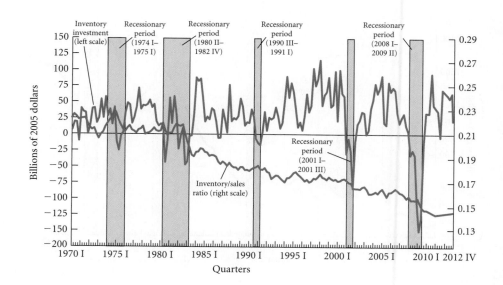

during the 1974–1975 period. At the end of 1974, the stock of inventories was very high relative to sales, an indication that firms probably had undesired inventories at the end of 1974. In 1975, firms worked off these undesired inventories by producing less than they sold. Thus, inventory investment was very low in 1975. The year 1975 is clearly a year in which output would have been higher had the stock of inventories at the beginning of the year not been so high. There were large declines in inventory investment in the recessions of 2001 and 2008–2009.

On average, the inventory/sales ratio has been declining over time, evidence that firms are becoming more efficient in their management of inventory stocks. Firms are becoming more efficient in the sense of being able (other things equal) to hold smaller and smaller stocks of inventories relative to sales.

Productivity and the Business Cycle

We can now use what we have just learned about firm behavior to analyze movements in productivity. **Productivity**, sometimes called **labor productivity**, is defined as output per worker hour. If output is Y and the number of hours worked in the economy is H, productivity is Y/H. Simply stated, productivity measures how much output an average worker produces per hour.

productivity, *or* labor productivity Output per worker hour.

Productivity fluctuates over the business cycle, tending to rise during expansions and fall during contractions. See Figure 7.2 in Chapter 7 for a plot of productivity for 1952 I–2012 IV. You can see from this figure that productivity fluctuates up and down around a positive trend. The fact that firms at times hold excess labor explains why productivity fluctuates in the same direction as output.

Figure 16.8 shows the pattern of employment and output over time for a hypothetical economy. Employment does not fluctuate as much as output over the business cycle. It is precisely this pattern that leads to higher productivity during periods of high output and lower productivity during periods of low output. During expansions in the economy, output rises by a larger percentage than employment and the ratio of output to workers rises. During downswings, output falls faster than employment and the ratio of output to workers falls.

The existence of excess labor when the economy is in a slump means that productivity as measured by the ratio Y/H tends to fall at such times. Does this trend mean that labor is in some sense "less productive" during recessions than before? Not really: It means only that firms choose to employ more labor than would be profit-maximizing. For this reason, some workers are in effect idle some of the time even though they are considered employed. They are not less productive in the sense of having less potential to produce output; they are merely not working part of the time that they are *counted* as working.

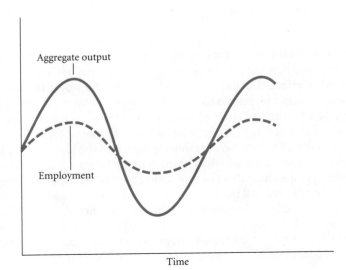

◀ **FIGURE 16.8**
Employment and Output over the Business Cycle
In general, employment does not fluctuate as much as output over the business cycle. As a result, measured productivity (the output-to-labor ratio) tends to rise during expansionary periods and decline during contractionary periods.

The Short-Run Relationship Between Output and Unemployment

We can also use what we have learned about household and firm behavior to analyze the relationship between output and unemployment. When we discussed the connections between the *AS/AD* diagram and the Phillips Curve in Chapter 14, we mentioned that output (*Y*) and the unemployment rate (*U*) are inversely related. When output rises, the unemployment rate falls, and when output falls, the unemployment rate rises. At one time, it was believed that the short-run relationship between the two variables was fairly stable. **Okun's Law** (after U.S. economist Arthur Okun, who first studied the relationship) stated that in the short run the unemployment rate decreased about 1 percentage point for every 3 percent increase in real GDP. As with the Phillips Curve, Okun's Law has not turned out to be a "law." The economy is far too complex for there to be such a simple and stable relationship between two macroeconomic variables.

Although the short-run relationship between output and the unemployment rate is not the simple relationship Okun believed, it is true that a 1 percent increase in output tends to correspond to a less than 1 percentage point decrease in the unemployment rate in the short run. In other words, there are a number of "slippages" between changes in output and changes in the unemployment rate.

The first slippage is between the change in output and the change in the number of jobs in the economy. When output increases by 1 percent, the number of jobs does not tend to rise by 1 percent in the short run. There are two reasons for this. First, a firm is likely to meet some of the increase in output by increasing the number of hours worked per job. Instead of having the labor force work 40 hours per week, the firm may pay overtime and have the labor force work 42 hours per week. Second, if a firm is holding excess labor at the time of the output increase, at least part of the increase in output can come from putting the excess labor back to work. For both reasons, the number of jobs is likely to rise by a smaller percentage than the increase in output.

The second slippage is between the change in the number of *jobs* and the change in the *number of people employed*. If you have two jobs, you are counted twice in the job data but only once in the persons-employed data. Because some people have two jobs, there are more jobs than there are people employed. When the number of jobs increases, some of the new jobs are filled by people who already have one job (instead of by people who are unemployed). This means that the increase in the number of people employed is less than the increase in the number of jobs. This is a slippage between output and the unemployment rate because the unemployment rate is calculated from data on the number of people employed, not the number of jobs.

The third slippage concerns the response of the labor force to an increase in output. Let *E* denote the number of people employed, let *L* denote the number of people in the labor force, and let *u* denote the unemployment rate. In these terms, the unemployment rate is

$$u = 1 - E/L$$

The unemployment rate is 1 minus the employment rate, *E/L*.

When we discussed how the unemployment rate is measured in Chapter 7, we introduced the **discouraged-worker effect**. A discouraged worker is one who would like a job but has stopped looking because the prospects seem so bleak. When output increases, job prospects begin to look better and some people who had stopped looking for work begin looking again. When they do, they are once again counted as part of the labor force. The labor force increases when output increases because discouraged workers are moving back into the labor force. This is another reason the unemployment rate does not fall as much as might be expected when output increases.

These three slippages show that the link from changes in output to changes in the unemployment rate is complicated. All three combine to make the change in the unemployment rate less than the percentage change in output in the short run. They also show that the relationship between changes in output and changes in the unemployment rate is not likely to be stable. The size of the first slippage, for example, depends on how much excess labor is being held at the time of the output increase, and the size of the third slippage depends on what else is

Okun's Law The theory, put forth by Arthur Okun, that in the short run the unemployment rate decreases about 1 percentage point for every 3 percent increase in real GDP. Later research and data have shown that the relationship between output and unemployment is not as stable as Okun's "Law" predicts.

discouraged-worker effect The decline in the measured unemployment rate that results when people who want to work but cannot find work grow discouraged and stop looking, dropping out of the ranks of the unemployed and the labor force.

affecting the labor force (such as changes in real wage rates) at the time of the output increase. The relationship between output and unemployment depends on the state of the economy at the time of the output change.

The Size of the Multiplier

We can finally bring together the material in this chapter and in previous chapters to consider the size of the multiplier. We mentioned in Chapter 8 that much of the analysis we would do after deriving the simple multiplier would have the effect of decreasing the size of the multiplier. We can now summarize why.

1. There are *automatic stabilizers*. We saw in the Appendix to Chapter 9 that if taxes are not a fixed amount but instead depend on income (which is surely the case in practice), the size of the multiplier is decreased. When the economy expands and income increases, the amount of taxes collected increases. The rise in taxes acts to offset some of the expansion (thus, a smaller multiplier). When the economy contracts and income decreases, the amount of taxes collected decreases. This decrease in taxes helps to lessen the contraction. Some transfer payments also respond to the state of the economy and act as automatic stabilizers, lowering the value of the multiplier. Unemployment benefits are the best example of transfer payments that increase during contractions and decrease during expansions.

2. There is the *interest rate*. We saw in Chapter 12 that in normal times the Fed increases the interest rate as output increases, which decreases planned investment. The increase in output from a government spending increase is thus smaller than if the interest rate did not rise because of the crowding out of planned investment. As we saw earlier in this chapter, increases in the interest rate also have a negative effect on consumption. Consumption is also crowded out in the same way that planned investment is, and this effect lowers the value of the multiplier even further.

3. There is the response of the *price level*. We also saw in Chapter 12 that some of the effect of an expansionary policy is to increase the price level. The multiplier is smaller because of this price response. The multiplier is particularly small when the economy is on the steep part of the *AS* curve, where most of the effect of an expansionary policy is to increase prices.

4. There are *excess capital* and *excess labor*. When firms are holding excess labor and capital, part of any output increase can come from putting the excess labor and capital back to work instead of increasing employment and investment. This lowers the value of the multiplier because (1) investment increases less than it would have if there were no excess capital and (2) consumption increases less than it would have if employment (and thus household income) had increased more.

5. There are *inventories*. Part of any initial increase in sales can come from drawing down inventories instead of increasing output. To the extent that firms draw down their inventories in the short run, the value of the multiplier is lower because output does not respond as quickly to demand changes.

6. There are people's *expectations* about the future. People look ahead, and they respond less to temporary changes than to permanent changes. The multiplier effects for policy changes perceived to be temporary are smaller than those for policy changes perceived to be permanent.

The Size of the Multiplier in Practice   In practice, the multiplier probably has a value of around 2.0. Its size also depends on how long ago the spending increase began. For example, in the first quarter of an increase in government spending, the multiplier is only about 1.1. If government spending rises by $1 billion, GDP will increase by about $1.1 billion during the first quarter. In the second quarter, the multiplier will rise to about 1.6. The multiplier then will rise to its peak of about 2.0 in the fourth quarter.

One of the main points to remember here is that if the government is contemplating a monetary or fiscal policy change, the response of the economy to the change is not likely to be large and quick. It takes time for the full effects to be felt, and in the final analysis, the effects are much smaller than the simple multiplier we discussed in Chapter 8 would lead one to believe.

A good way to review much of the material since Chapter 8 is to make sure you clearly understand how the value of the multiplier is affected by each of the additions to the simple model in Chapter 8. We have come a long way since then, and this review may help you to put all the pieces together.

SUMMARY

HOUSEHOLDS: CONSUMPTION AND LABOR SUPPLY DECISIONS *p. 299*

1. The *life-cycle theory of consumption* says that households make lifetime consumption decisions based on their expectations of lifetime income. Generally, households consume an amount less than their incomes during their prime working years and an amount greater than their incomes during their early working years and after they have retired.

2. Households make consumption and labor supply decisions simultaneously. Consumption cannot be considered separately from labor supply because it is precisely by selling your labor that you earn the income that makes consumption possible.

3. There is a trade-off between the goods and services that wage income will buy and leisure or other nonmarket activities. The wage rate is the key variable that determines how a household responds to this trade-off.

4. Changes in the wage rate have both an income effect and a substitution effect. The evidence suggests that the substitution effect seems to dominate for most people, which means that the aggregate labor supply responds positively to an increase in the wage rate.

5. Consumption increases when the wage rate increases.

6. The *nominal wage rate* is the wage rate in current dollars. The *real wage rate* is the amount the nominal wage can buy in terms of goods and services. Households look at expected future real wage rates as well as the current real wage rate in making their consumption and labor supply decisions.

7. Holding all else constant (including the stage in the life cycle), the more wealth a household has, the more it will consume both now and in the future.

8. An unexpected increase in *nonlabor income* (any income received from sources other than working, such as inheritances, interest, and dividends) will have a positive effect on a household's consumption and will lead to a decrease in labor supply.

9. The interest rate also affects consumption, although the direction of the total effect depends on the relative sizes of the income and substitution effects. There is some evidence that the income effect is larger now than it used to be, making monetary policy less effective than it used to be.

10. The government influences household behavior mainly through income tax rates and transfer payments. If the substitution effect dominates, an increase in tax rates lowers after-tax income, decreases consumption, and decreases the labor supply; a decrease in tax rates raises after-tax income, increases consumption, and increases labor supply. Increases in transfer payments increase consumption and decrease labor supply; decreases in transfer payments decrease consumption and increase labor supply.

11. During times of unemployment, households' labor supply may be constrained. Households may want to work a certain number of hours at current wage rates but may not be allowed to do so by firms. In this case, the level of income (at least workers' income) depends exclusively on the employment decisions made by firms. Households consume less if they are constrained from working.

FIRMS: INVESTMENT AND EMPLOYMENT DECISIONS *p. 307*

12. Expectations affect investment and employment decisions. Keynes used the term *animal spirits of entrepreneurs* to refer to investors' feelings.

13. At any level of the interest rate, expectations are likely to be more optimistic and planned investment is likely to be higher when output is growing rapidly than when it is growing slowly or falling. The result is an *accelerator effect* that can cause the economy to expand more rapidly during an expansion and contract more quickly during a recession.

14. *Excess labor and capital* are labor and capital not needed to produce a firm's current level of output. Holding excess labor and capital may be more efficient than laying off workers or selling used equipment. The more excess capital a firm has, the less likely it is to invest in new capital in the future. The more excess labor it has, the less likely it is to hire new workers in the future.

15. Holding inventories is costly to a firm because they take up space and they tie up funds that could be earning interest. Not holding inventories can cause a firm to lose sales if demand increases. The *desired*, or *optimal*, *level of inventories* is the level at which the extra cost (in lost sales) from lowering inventories by a small amount is equal to the extra gain (in interest revenue and decreased storage costs).

16. An unexpected increase in inventories has a negative effect on future production, and an unexpected decrease in inventories has a positive effect on future production.

17. The level of a firm's planned production path depends on the level of its expected future sales path. If a firm's expectations of its future sales path decrease, the firm is likely to decrease the level of its planned production path, including its actual production in the current period.

PRODUCTIVITY AND THE BUSINESS CYCLE *p. 313*

18. *Productivity*, or *labor productivity*, is output per worker hour—the amount of output produced by an average worker in 1 hour. Productivity fluctuates over the business cycle, tending to rise during expansions and fall during contractions. That workers are less productive during contractions does not mean that they have less potential to produce output; it means that excess labor exists and that workers are not working at their capacity.

THE SHORT-RUN RELATIONSHIP BETWEEN OUTPUT AND UNEMPLOYMENT *p. 314*

19. There is a negative relationship between output and unemployment: When output (Y) rises, the unemployment rate (U) falls, and when output falls, the unemployment rate rises. *Okun's Law* states that in the short run the unemployment rate decreases about 1 percentage point for every 3 percent increase in GDP. Okun's Law is not a "law"—the economy is too complex for there to be a stable relationship between two macroeconomic variables. In general, the relationship between output and unemployment depends on the state of the economy at the time of the output change.

THE SIZE OF THE MULTIPLIER *p. 315*

20. There are several reasons why the actual value of the multiplier is smaller than the size that would be expected from the simple multiplier model: (1) Automatic stabilizers help to offset contractions or limit expansions. (2) When government spending increases, the increased interest rate crowds out planned investment and consumption spending. (3) Expansionary policies increase the price level. (4) Firms sometimes hold excess capital and excess labor. (5) Firms may meet increased demand by drawing down inventories instead of increasing output. (6) Households and firms change their behavior less when they expect changes to be temporary instead of permanent.

21. In practice, the size of the multiplier at its peak is about 2.

REVIEW TERMS AND CONCEPTS

accelerator effect, *p. 308*

adjustment costs, *p. 309*

animal spirits of entrepreneurs, *p. 308*

constrained supply of labor, *p. 304*

desired, *or* optimal, level of inventories, *p. 310*

discouraged-worker effect, *p. 314*

excess labor, excess capital, *p. 309*

inventory investment, *p. 309*

life-cycle theory of consumption, *p. 300*

nominal wage rate, *p. 302*

nonlabor, *or* nonwage, income, *p. 302*

Okun's Law, *p. 314*

permanent income, *p. 301*

productivity, *or* labor productivity, *p. 313*

real wage rate, *p. 302*

unconstrained supply of labor, *p. 304*

PROBLEMS

All problems are available on MyEconLab.

1. Between October 2004 and October 2005, real GDP in the United States increased by 3.6 percent, while nonfarm payroll jobs increased by only 1.4 percent. How is it possible for output to increase without a proportional increase in the number of workers?

2. During 2005, the Federal Reserve Bank raised interest rates in an effort to prevent an increase in the rate of inflation.
   a. What direct effects do higher interest rates have on household and firm behavior?
   b. One of the consequences of higher interest rates was that the value of existing bonds (both corporate bonds and government bonds) fell substantially. Explain why higher interest rates would decrease the value of existing fixed-rate bonds held by the public.
   c. Some economists argue that the wealth effect of higher interest rates on consumption is as important as the direct effect of higher interest rates on investment. Explain what economists mean by "wealth effects on consumption" and illustrate with AS/AD curves.

3. In 2005, President Bush's tax reform commission proposed and Congress enacted a decrease in taxes. One of the cuts was in the income tax rate for higher-income wage earners. Republicans claimed that raising the rewards for working (the net after-tax wage rate) would lead to more work effort and a higher labor supply. Critics of the tax cuts replied that this claim was baseless because it "ignored the income effect of the tax cut (net wage increase)." Explain what these critics meant.

4. Graph the following two consumption functions:

$$(1)\ C = 300 + .5Y$$
$$(2)\ C = .5Y$$

   a. For each function, calculate and graph the average propensity to consume (APC) when income is $100, $400, and $800.
   b. For each function, what happens to the APC as income rises?
   c. For each function, what is the relationship between the APC and the marginal propensity to consume?
   d. Under the first consumption function, a family with income of $50,000 consumes a smaller proportion of its income than a family with income of $20,000; yet if we take a dollar of income away from the rich family and give it to the poor family, total consumption by the two families does not change. Explain how this is possible.

5. From 2001 to 2005, the price of houses increased steadily around the country.
   a. What impact would you expect increases and decreases in home value to have on the consumption behavior of home owners? Explain.
   b. In what ways might events in the housing market have influenced the rest of the economy through their effects on consumption spending? Be specific.

*6. Adam Smith is 45 years old. He has assets (wealth) of $20,000 and has no debts or liabilities. He knows that he will work for

20 more years and will live 5 years after that, when he will earn nothing. His salary each year for the rest of his working career is $14,000. (There are no taxes.) He wants to distribute his consumption over the rest of his life in such a way that he consumes the same amount each year. He cannot consume in total more than his current wealth plus the sum of his income for the next 20 years. Assume that the rate of interest is zero and that Smith decides not to leave any inheritance to his children.
   a. How much will Adam consume this year and next year? How did you arrive at your answer?
   b. Plot on a graph Adam's income, consumption, and wealth from the time he is 45 until he is 70 years old. What is the relationship between the annual increase in his wealth and his annual saving (income minus consumption)? In what year does Adam's wealth start to decline? Why? How much wealth does he have when he dies?
   c. Suppose Adam receives a tax rebate of $100 per year, so his income is $14,100 per year for the rest of his working career. By how much does his consumption increase this year and next year?
   d. Now suppose Adam receives a 1-year-only tax refund of $100—his income this year is $14,100; but in all succeeding years, his income is $14,000. What happens to his consumption this year? in succeeding years?

7. Explain why a household's consumption and labor supply decisions are interdependent. What impact does this interdependence have on the way in which consumption and income are related?

8. Why do expectations play such an important role in investment demand? How, if at all, does this explain why investment is so volatile?

9. How can a firm maintain a smooth production schedule even when sales are fluctuating? What are the benefits of a smooth production schedule? What are the costs?

10. Explain the effect that each of the following situations will have on the size of the multiplier.
   a. Firms have excess inventories as the economy begins to recover from a recession.
   b. Expansionary policy causes the price level to increase.
   c. People expect a $500 tax rebate to be a one-time occurrence.
   d. The government decreases spending, and the Fed does not change the money supply.
   e. The economy expands, and income taxes are progressive.
   f. The government extends unemployment benefits as a response to a lingering recession.

11. The Bureau of Labor Statistics reported that in June 2010, the unemployment rate in the United States was 9.5 percent. In November 2007, prior to the beginning of the recession of 2007–2009, the BLS reported an unemployment rate of 4.7 percent.
   a. According to Okun's Law, by how much would GDP need to increase for the unemployment rate to decrease from the June 2010 rate back to the pre-recession rate of November 2007?
   b. In June 2010, the annual GDP growth rate in the United States was 2.4 percent. At this rate of growth, how long does

*Note: Problems marked with an asterisk are more challenging.

Okun's Law predict it would take for the economy to return to the unemployment rate of November 2007?

12. In the short run, the percentage increase in output tends to correspond to a smaller percentage decrease in the unemployment rate due to "slippages." Explain the three slippages between changes in output and changes in the unemployment rate.

13. George Jetson has recently been promoted to inventory control manager at Spacely Sprockets, and he must decide on the optimal level of sprockets to keep in inventory. How should Jetson decide on the optimal level of inventory? How would a change in interest rates affect the optimal level of inventory? What costs and benefits will Spacely Sprockets experience by holding inventory?

14. Futurama Medical is a high-tech medical equipment manufacturer that uses custom-designed machinery and a highly skilled, well-trained labor force in its production factory. Gonzo Garments is a mid-level clothing manufacturer that uses mass-produced machinery and readily available labor in its production factory. Which of these two firms would you expect to have more significant adjustment costs? Which firm would be more likely to hold excess labor? excess capital? Explain your answers.

Long-Run Growth 17

Think about how many hours your great-grandparents had to work to pay for basic necessities like food and clothing. Now think about how many hours you will have to work for the same thing. You will likely spend many fewer hours. People on average will earn in real terms more per hour than did people of earlier generations. This is true in almost all economies, but certainly in all developed economies. Another way of saying this is that in almost all economies the amount of output produced per worker has risen over time. Why? Why are we able to produce more per hour than prior generations did? This is the subject matter of this chapter. We explore the long-run growth process.

We briefly introduced long-run growth in Chapter 7. We distinguished between **output growth**, which is the growth rate of output of the entire economy, and **per-capita output growth**, which is the growth rate of output per person in the economy. Another important concept, as mentioned in the previous paragraph, is the growth rate of output per worker, called **labor productivity growth**. Output per capita is a measure of the standard of living in a country. It is not the same as output per worker because not everyone in the population works. Output per capita can fall even when output per worker is increasing if the fraction of the population that is working is falling (as it might be in a country with an increasing number of children per working-age adult). Output per capita is a useful measure because it tells us how much output each person would receive if total output were evenly divided across the entire population. Output per worker is a useful measure because it tells us how much output each worker on average is producing.

We begin this chapter with a brief history of economic growth since the Industrial Revolution. We then discuss the sources of growth—answering the question why output per worker has risen over time. We then turn to look more narrowly at the U.S. growth picture. We conclude with a discussion of growth and the environment, returning to the world perspective.

output growth The growth rate of the output of the entire economy.

per-capita output growth The growth rate of output per person in the economy.

labor productivity growth The growth rate of output per worker.

LEARNING OBJECTIVES

Summarize the history and process of economic growth

Describe the sources of economic growth

Discuss environmental issues associated with economic growth

The Growth Process: From Agriculture to Industry

The easiest way to understand the growth process and to identify its causes is to think about a simple economy. Recall from Chapter 2, Colleen and Bill washed up on a deserted island. At first, they had only a few simple tools and whatever human capital they brought with them to the island. They gathered nuts and berries and built a small cabin. Their "GDP" consisted of basic food and shelter.

Over time, things improved. The first year they cleared some land and began to cultivate a few vegetables they found growing on the island. They made some tools and dug a small reservoir to store rainwater. As their agricultural efforts became more efficient, they shifted their resources—their time—into building a larger, more comfortable home.

Colleen and Bill were accumulating capital in two forms. First, they built *physical capital*, material things used in the production of goods and services—a better house, tools, a water system, perhaps a boat to let them fish farther off shore. Second, they acquired more *human capital*—knowledge, skills, and talents. Through trial and error, they learned about the island and its soil and its climate and learned what did and did not work. Both kinds of capital made them more efficient and increased their productivity. Because it took less time to produce the food they needed to survive, they could devote more energy to producing other things or to leisure.

At any given time, Colleen and Bill faced limits on what they could produce. These limits were imposed by the existing state of their technical knowledge and the resources at their disposal. Over time, they expanded their possibilities, developed new technologies, accumulated capital, and made their labor more productive. In Chapter 2, we defined a society's *production possibility frontier (ppf)*, which shows all possible combinations of output that can be produced given present technology and whether all available resources are fully and efficiently employed. Economic growth expands those limits and shifts society's production possibilities frontier out to the right, as Figure 17.1 shows.

Before the Industrial Revolution in Great Britain, every society in the world was agrarian. Towns and cities existed here and there, but almost everyone lived in rural areas. People spent most of their time producing food and other basic subsistence goods. Then beginning in England around 1750, technical change and capital accumulation increased productivity significantly in two important industries: agriculture and textiles. New and more efficient methods of farming were developed. New inventions and new machinery in spinning and weaving meant that more could be produced with fewer resources. Just as new technology, capital equipment, and resulting higher productivity made it possible for Colleen and Bill to spend time working on other projects and new "products," the British turned from agricultural production to industrial production. In both cases, growth meant new products, more output, and wider choice.

Those changes meant that peasants and workers in eighteenth-century England who in the past would have continued in subsistence farming could make a better living as urban workers. A rural agrarian society was very quickly transformed into an urban industrial society.

▶ **FIGURE 17.1**
Economic Growth Shifts Society's Production Possibility Frontier Up and to the Right

The production possibility frontier shows all the combinations of output that can be produced if all society's scarce resources are fully and efficiently employed. Economic growth expands society's production possibilities, shifting the *ppf* up and to the right.

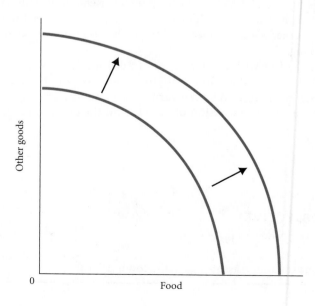

The transition from agriculture to industry has been more recent in developing countries in Asia. One of the hallmarks of current growth in China and Vietnam, for example, has been the focus on manufacturing exports as a growth strategy. A visitor to Vietnam cannot help but be struck by the pace of industrialization.

Economic growth continues today in the developed world. And while the underlying process is still the same, the face is different. Just as Colleen and Bill devoted time to building a boat and designing tools, the developed economies are still creating capital to increase productivity. Just as a shovel makes it possible to dig a bigger hole, new microwave towers bring cell phone service to places that had been out of range. Scientists work on finding a cure for Alzheimer's disease using tools they couldn't have dreamed of a decade ago. Tools available on the Web make it possible for a single law clerk in a busy law office to check hundreds of documents for the opinions of potential expert witnesses in a court case in an hour, a task that took a dozen law clerks weeks to perform just a few years ago. In each case, we have become more proficient at producing what we want and need and we have freed up resources to produce new things that we want and need. For Colleen and Bill, it was a better diet; with a boat, they could catch more fish in less time. Today it may be better cell phone service, a fast, inexpensive color printer, or a better medical procedure.

The basic building blocks are the same. Growth comes from a bigger workforce and more productive workers. Higher productivity comes from tools (capital), a better-educated and more highly skilled workforce (human capital), and increasingly from innovation and technical change (new techniques of production) and newly developed products and services.

Table 17.1 provides estimates of the growth of GDP for a number of developed and developing countries for the 20 years 1993–2012. One fact that should strike you as you look at these numbers is the high rates of growth of China and India relative to those of the developed countries. Some economists argue that when poorer, less developed countries begin to develop, they typically have higher growth rates as they **catch-up** with the more developed countries. This idea is called *convergence theory* since it suggests that gaps in national incomes tend to close over time. Indeed, more than 50 years ago, the economic historian Alexander Gerschenkron coined the term *the advantages of backwardness* as a description of the phenomenon by which less developed countries could leap ahead by borrowing technology from more developed countries. This idea seems to fit the current experiences of China and India, as shown in the table. On the other hand, growth rates in sub-Saharan Africa are more modest, although still higher than those for the developed countries. We turn now to look at the sources of economic growth.

catch-up The theory stating that the growth rates of less developed countries will exceed the growth rates of developed countries, allowing the less developed countries to catch up.

MyEconLab Real-time data

TABLE 17.1 Growth of Real GDP: 1993–2012	
Country	Average Growth Rates per Year, Percentage Points, 1993–2012
United States	2.5
Japan	0.8
Germany	1.2
France	1.5
United Kingdom	2.1
China	10.1
India	6.9
Sub-Saharan Africa	4.6

Source: *Economic Report of the President, 2012*, Table B-112

Sources of Economic Growth

It will be useful to begin with a simple case where the quality of labor, L, and the quality of capital, K, do not change over time. A worker is a worker is a worker, and a machine is a machine is a machine. Output, Y, is produced in a production process using L and K. In most situations it seems reasonable to assume that as labor and capital increase, so will output. The exact relationship between these inputs and output can be described with an **aggregate production function**, which is a mathematical relationship stating that total GDP (output) (Y) depends on the total amount of labor used (L) and the total amount of capital (K) used. (Land is another possible input in the production

aggregate production function A mathematical relationship stating that total GDP (output) depends on the total amount of labor used and the total amount of capital used.

ECONOMICS IN PRACTICE

Government Strategy for Growth

Figure 17.1 shows how a country's production possibility frontier shifts out with technology. Another characteristic of a country that you might want to think about is how far an individual country is from the technological frontier of the rest of the world and how distance from that frontier might influence growth strategies pursued by a country.

One of the puzzles in the growth area has been the fact that government strategies for growth seem to succeed in one place and then fail dismally in another. Work by Acemoglu, Aghion, and Zilibotti suggests that one key to successful government policies is how far a country is from the world frontier.[1]

Suppose a country is behind relative to the world at large. A government's job here is helping its industries to catch up. What policies work for this? Acemoglu et al suggest that industrial policy like that used by Japan and South Korea may be helpful for this case. Here the government knows what the right technology is and just has to help its firms find the world frontier. As firms develop, however, and approach the world technological frontier, things change. Now growth comes through innovation, by finding out new ways to do things that are the best in the world. How does the government help in this task? Here, markets with sharp incentives and some encouragement of risk taking likely will be more useful. For this, policies to support entrepreneurship and improve the workings of venture capital will likely work better. Acemoglu and his colleagues argue that governments often shift too late from policies supporting adoption of other countries' ideas to support of their own innovative efforts.

THINKING PRACTICALLY

1. In recent years China has begun to strengthen its laws on patents. How does this fit in with the research described here?

[1] Daron Acemoglu, Philippe Aghion, and Fabrizio Zilibotti, "Distance to Frontier, Selection, and Economic Growth," *Journal of the European Economic Association*, March 2006, 37–74.

process, but we are assuming that land is fixed.) The numbers that are used in Tables 17.2 and 17.4, which follow, are based on the simple production function $Y = 3 \times K^{1/3} L^{2/3}$. Both capital and labor are needed for production (if either is equal to zero, so is output) and increases in either result in more output. Using this construct we can now explore exactly how an economy achieves higher output levels over time as it experiences changes in labor and capital.

Increase in Labor Supply

In our example of Colleen and Bill on an island, it is clear that adding another individual exactly like Colleen and Bill to the workforce would increase output. A key question is how large would the increase be? In fact, both economic theory and practice tell us that in the absence of increases in the capital stock, as labor increases, less and less output will be added by each new worker. This effect is called *diminishing returns*. It has been discussed for well over a hundred years, beginning with early economists like Thomas Malthus and David Ricardo who began thinking about the effects of population growth.

Malthus and Ricardo focused on agricultural output for which the central form of capital was land. With land in limited supply, the economists reckoned that new farm laborers would be forced to work the land more intensively or to bring less productive land into the agricultural sector. In either case, as labor supply grew, output would increase, but at a declining rate. Increases in the labor supply would reduce labor productivity, or output per worker.

TABLE 17.2 Economic Growth from an Increase in Labor—More Output but Diminishing Returns and Lower Labor Productivity

Period	Quantity of Labor L	Quantity of Capital K	Total Output Y	Labor Productivity Y/L	Marginal Return to Labor $\Delta Y/\Delta L$
1	100	100	300	3.0	—
2	110	100	320	2.9	2.0
3	120	100	339	2.8	1.9
4	130	100	357	2.7	1.8

TABLE 17.3 Employment, Labor Force, and Population Growth, 1960–2011

	Civilian Noninstitutional Population 16 and Over (Millions)	Civilian Labor Force		Employment (Millions)
		Number (Millions)	Percentage of Population	
1960	117.3	69.6	59.3	65.8
1970	137.1	82.8	60.4	78.7
1980	167.7	106.9	63.7	99.3
1990	189.2	125.8	66.5	118.8
2000	212.6	142.6	67.1	136.9
2011	239.6	153.6	64.1	139.9
Total percentage change, 1960–2011	+104.3%	+120.7%		+112.6%
Percentage change at an annual rate	+1.4%	+1.6%		+1.6 %

Source: Economic Report of the President, 2012, Table B-35.

In developed economies, labor works not so much with land as with other forms of capital—machines, computers, and the like. But diminishing returns occur in this setting as well. Table 17.2 provides an arithmetic example of diminishing returns using the aggregate production function discussed previously. Notice in the table the relationship between the level of output and the level of labor. With capital fixed at 100, as labor increases from 100 to eventually 130, total output increases, but at a diminishing rate. In the last column, we see that labor productivity falls. Simply increasing the amount of labor with no other changes in the economy decreases labor productivity because of diminishing returns.

The U.S. population and labor force have grown over time. Table 17.3. shows the growth of the population, labor force, and employment between 1960 and 2011. In this period, the population 16 and over grew at an annual rate of 1.4 percent, the labor force grew at an annual rate of 1.6 percent, and employment grew at an annual rate of 1.6 percent. We will come back to this table later in the chapter. We would expect that this increase in labor would, by itself, end up increasing overall output levels in the United States.

Increase in Physical Capital

It is easy to see how physical capital contributes to output. Bill and Colleen digging a garden with one shovel will be able to do more if a second shovel is added. How much more? We saw that there are diminishing returns to labor as more and more labor is added to a fixed amount of capital. There are likewise diminishing returns to capital as more and more capital is added to a fixed supply of labor. The extra output from the garden that Bill and Colleen can produce when a second shovel is added is likely to be smaller than the extra output that was produced when the first shovel was added. If a third shovel were added, even less extra output would likely be produced (if any).

Table 17.4 shows how an increase in capital without a corresponding increase in labor increases output. It uses the same aggregate production function employed in Table 17.2. Observe two things about these numbers. First, additional capital increases labor productivity—it rises from 3.0 to 3.3 as capital is added. Second, there are diminishing returns to capital. Increasing capital by 10 first increases output by 10—from 300 to 310. However, the second increase of 10 yields only an output increase of 9, and the third increase of 10 yields only an output increase of 8 or 0.8 per unit of capital. The last column in the table shows the decline in output per capital as capital is increased.

TABLE 17.4 Economic Growth from an Increase in Capital—More Output, Diminishing Returns to Added Capital, Higher Labor Productivity

Period	Quantity of Labor L	Quantity of Capital K	Total Output Y	Labor Productivity Y/L	Output per Capital Y/K	Marginal Return to Capital $\Delta Y/\Delta K$
1	100	100	300	3.0	3.0	—
2	100	110	310	3.1	2.8	1.0
3	100	120	319	3.2	2.7	0.9
4	100	130	327	3.3	2.5	0.8

TABLE 17.5 Fixed Private Nonresidential Net Capital Stock, 1960–2011 (Billions of 2005 Dollars)

	Equipment	Structures
1960	670.9	3,001.4
1970	1,154.0	4,149.2
1980	1,931.6	5,480.4
1990	2,620.0	7,257.7
2000	4,230.8	8,570.7
2011	5,509.6	9,878.6
Total percentage change, 1960–2011	+721.2%	+229.1%
Percentage change at an annual rate	+4.2%	+2.4%

Source: U.S. Department of Commerce, Bureau of Economic Analysis.

The U.S. capital stock has grown over time, also contributing to output growth. Table 17.5 shows the growth of capital equipment and capital structures between 1960 and 2011. (The increase in the capital stock is the difference between gross investment and depreciation. Remember that some capital becomes obsolete and some wears out each year.) Between 1960 and 2011 the stock of equipment grew at an annual rate of 4.2 percent and the stock of structures grew at an annual rate of 2.4 percent.

Notice the growth rates of capital in Table 17.5 (4.2 percent and 2.4 percent) are larger than the growth rate of labor in Table 17.3 (1.5 percent). Capital has grown relative to labor in the United States. As a result, each U.S. worker has more capital to work with now than he or she had a hundred years ago. We see in Table 17.4 that adding more capital relative to labor increases labor productivity. We thus have one answer so far as to why labor productivity has grown over time in the United States—the amount of capital per worker has grown. You are able to produce more output per hour than your grandparents did because you have more capital to work with. In almost all economies, capital has been growing faster than labor, which is an important source of labor productivity growth in these economies.

The importance of capital in a country's economic growth naturally leads one to ask the question of what determines a country's stock of capital. In the modern open economy, new capital can come from the saving of a country's residents and/or from the investments of foreigners. **Foreign direct investment** is any investment in enterprises made in a country by residents outside that country. Foreign direct investment has been quite influential in providing needed capital for growth in much of Southeast Asia. In Vietnam, for example, rapid growth has been led by foreign direct investment. Very recently, we have seen signs of Chinese foreign direct investment in parts of Africa and in other parts of Asia.

foreign direct investment (FDI) Investment in enterprises made in a country by residents outside that country.

Recent work in economics has focused on the role that institutions play in creating a capital-friendly environment that encourages home savings and foreign investment. In a series of papers, LaPorta, Lopez de Silanes, Shleifer, and Vishny argue that countries with English common-law origins (as opposed to French) provide the strongest protection for shareholders, less corrupt governments, and better court systems. In turn, these financial and legal institutions promote growth by encouraging capital investment. Countries with poor institutions, corruption, and inadequate protection for lenders and investors struggle to attract capital. The World Bank calls countries with weak institutions *fragile countries*.

Many of the World Bank's fragile countries are in sub-Saharan Africa. Many observers believe that the relative stagnation of some of the sub-Saharan African nations comes in part from their relatively weak institutions. High costs of doing business, including corruption and investment risks associated with conflict, have made countries such as Zimbabwe less attractive to domestic and foreign capital. Ethnic and linguistic fractionalization have also played a role. In the United States case, growth has been facilitated by the use of foreign capital, much of which was attracted by strong institutions in the United States.

Increase in the Quality of the Labor Supply (Human Capital)

So far we have looked at what happens when an economy gets more units of identical workers. But as we well know, in most societies, populations have grown more educated and healthier over time. The quality of labor has changed, as well as its quantity, and this too leads to long-run growth.

TABLE 17.6 Years of School Completed by People Over 25 Years Old, 1940–2010

	Percentage with Less than 5 Years of School	Percentage with 4 Years of High School or More	Percentage with 4 Years of College or More
1940	13.7	24.5	4.6
1950	11.1	34.3	6.2
1960	8.3	41.1	7.7
1970	5.5	52.3	10.7
1980	3.6	66.5	16.2
1990	NA	77.6	21.3
2000	NA	84.1	25.6
2010	NA	87.1	29.9

NA = not available.

Source: Statistical Abstract of the United States, 1990, Table 215, and 2012, Table 229.

When the quality of labor increases, this is referred to as an increase in human capital. If a worker's human capital has increased, he or she can produce more output working with the same amount of physical capital. Labor input in efficiency terms has increased.

Human capital can be produced in many ways. Individuals can invest in themselves by going to college or by completing vocational training programs. Firms can invest in human capital through on-the-job training. The government invests in human capital with programs that improve health and that provide schooling and job training. In many developing economies, we have seen very high returns from educating women who had previously been largely unschooled.

In the developing countries of sub-Saharan Africa, health is a major issue due to the high incidence of HIV and other diseases. Programs to improve the health of the population increase, among other things, the quality of the labor force, which increases output. Workers who are ill are obviously less productive than those who are not.

In the United States, considerable resources have been put into education over the decades. Table 17.6 shows that the level of educational attainment in the United States has risen significantly since 1940. The percentage of the population with at least 4 years of college rose from 4.6 percent in 1940 to 29.9 percent in 2010. In 1940 less than one person in four had completed high school; in 2010 87.1 percent had. This is a substantial increase in human capital. We thus have our second answer as to why labor productivity has increased in the United States—the quality of labor has increased through more education. Policy makers in many developed economies are concerned about their ability to continue to generate growth through human capital improvements.

Increase in the Quality of Capital (Embodied Technical Change)

Just as workers have changed in the last one hundred years, so have machines. A present-day word processor is quite different from the manual typewriter of the mid-20th century. An increase in the quality of a machine will increase output in the production process for the same amount of labor used. How does an increase in the quality of capital come about? It comes about in what we will call **embodied technical change**. Some technical innovation takes place, such as a faster computer chip, which is then incorporated into machines. Usually the technical innovations are incorporated into new machines, with older machines simply discarded when they become obsolete. In this case the quality of the total capital stock increases over time as more efficient new machines replace less efficient old ones. In some cases, however, innovations are incorporated into old machines. Commercial airplanes last for many decades, and many innovations that affect airplanes are incorporated into existing ones. But in general, one thinks of embodied technical change as showing up in new machines rather than existing ones.

embodied technical change
Technical change that results in an improvement in the quality of capital.

An increase in the quality of capital increases labor productivity (more output for the same amount of labor). We thus have our third answer as to why labor productivity has increased over time—the quality of capital has increased because of embodied technical change.

We will come back to embodied technical change, but to finish the train of thought we turn next to disembodied technical change.

ECONOMICS IN PRACTICE

German Jewish Émigrés Contribute to U.S. Growth

Sometimes terrible events in history can be used by social scientists to test theories in ways not as easily done in normal times. The emigration of Jewish scientists from Germany in the late 1930s and early 1940s is an example.

By the time World War II began, over 133,000 Jewish émigrés found their way to the United States. Among them were several thousand academics, including many scientists. Petra Moser, Alessandra Voena, and Fabian Waldinger in a recent paper decided to see if they could find any effect of this move on the well-being of the United States.[1]

Among the émigrés were a number of chemists. Moser et al, using a series of directories, identified all of the chemists who relocated to the United States in this period along with their fields within chemistry. The chemists brought with them their considerable human capital. From the point of view of this chapter, the United States experienced an unexpected shift in the human capital of its population. Moser and her colleagues then compared the rate of patenting in the United States in the period before the emigration with the one right after, looking specifically at the fields within chemistry in which the new émigrés worked. Their results? The work indicates that these new U.S. citizens may have increased patent rates in their fields by more than 30%!

THINKING PRACTICALLY

1. Show on a production possibility frontier the effects of the new German emigration.

[1] Petra Moser, Alessandra Voena, and Fabian Waldinger, "German-Jewish émigrés and U.S. Invention," Stanford Working paper, March 21, 2011.

Disembodied Technical Change

In some situations we can achieve higher levels of output over time even if the quantity and quality of labor and capital don't change. How might we do this? Perhaps we learn how to better organize the plant floor or manage the labor force. In recent years operational improvements like lean manufacturing and vendor inventory management systems have increased the ability of many manufacturing firms to get more output from a fixed amount and quality of labor and capital. Even improvements in information and accounting systems or incentive systems can lead to improved output levels. A type of technical change that is not specifically embedded in either labor or capital but works instead to allow us to get more out of both is called **disembodied technical change**.

disembodied technical change Technical change that results in a change in the production process.

Recent experiences in the Chinese economy provide an interesting example of what might be considered disembodied technical change broadly defined. Working at the IMF, Zuliu Hu and Mohsin Khan have pointed to the large role of productivity gains in the 20 years following the market reforms in China. In the period after the reforms, productivity growth rates tripled, averaging almost 4 percent a year. Hu and Khan argue that the productivity gains came principally from the unleashing of profit incentives that came with opening business to the private sector. Better incentives produced better use of labor and capital.

Disembodied technical change can be negative, though this is unusual. An example is environmental regulations that require the whole production process to pollute less and thus, say, be more costly from a private perspective. Another example is health and safety regulations that require the production process to run slower to reduce injuries to workers. There is an important caveat here, however. In these examples, private output is smaller, but the analysis does not include the improved quality of air, water, health, and safety that results from the regulations. So you can think about disembodied technical change in these cases as being negative using the private measure of output, but not necessarily a broader measure of welfare.

To the extent that disembodied technical changes are mostly positive, this is our fourth answer as to why labor productivity has increased. People have figured out how to run production processes and how to manage firms more efficiently.

More on Technical Change

We have seen that both embodied and disembodied technical change increase labor productivity. It is not always easy to decide whether a particular technical innovation is embodied or disembodied, and in many discussions this distinction is not made. In the rest of this section we will not make the distinction, but just talk in general about technical innovations.

The main point to keep in mind is that technical change, regardless of how it is categorized, increases labor productivity.

The Industrial Revolution was in part sparked by new technological developments. New techniques of spinning and weaving—the invention of the machines known as the mule and the spinning jenny, for example—were critical. The high-tech boom that swept the United States in the early 1980s was driven by the rapid development and dissemination of semiconductor technology. The high-tech boom in the 1990s was driven by the rise of the Internet and the technology associated with it. In India in the 1960s, new high-yielding seeds helped to create a "green revolution" in agriculture.

Technical change generally takes place in two stages. First, there is an advance in knowledge, or an **invention**. However, knowledge by itself does nothing unless it is used. When new knowledge is used to produce a new product or to produce an existing product more efficiently, there is **innovation**.

Given the centrality of innovation to growth, it is interesting to look at what has been happening to research in the United States over time. A commonly used measure of inputs into research is the fraction of GDP spent. In 2011, the United States spent 2.7 percent of it GDP on R&D, down slightly from a high of 2.9 percent in the early 1960s. Over time the balance of research funding has shifted away from government toward industry. Since industry research tends to be more applied, some observers are concerned that the United States will lose some of its edge in technology unless more funding is provided. In 2007, the National Academies of Science argued as follows:

> Although many people assume that the United States will always be a world leader in science and technology, this may not continue to be the case inasmuch as great minds and ideas exist throughout the world. We fear the abruptness with which a lead in science and technology can be lost—and the difficulty of recovering a lead once lost, if indeed it can be recovered at all.[1]

As we suggested earlier, the theory of convergence suggests that newly developing countries can leap forward by exploiting the technology of the developed countries. Indeed, all countries benefit when a better way of doing things is discovered. Innovation and the diffusion of that innovation push the production possibility frontier outward. But there is at least some evidence that a country that leads in a discovery retains some advantage in exploiting it, at least for some time.

What evidence do we have that the United States might be losing its edge? Looking at R&D as a share of GDP, the United States ranked seventh among OECD countries in 2006. If we look at patenting data, the evidence is more encouraging: For patents simultaneously sought in the United States, Japan, and the European Union (EU), known as triadic patents, U.S. inventors are the leading source, having taken the lead from the EU in 1989. On the output side, then, the United States appears still to be quite strong in the area of research.

invention An advance in knowledge.

innovation The use of new knowledge to produce a new product or to produce an existing product more efficiently.

U.S. Labor Productivity: 1952 I–2012 IV

Now that we have considered the various answers as to why U.S. labor productivity has increased over time, we can return to the data and see what the actual growth has been. In Figure 7.2 in Chapter 7, we presented a plot of U.S. labor productivity for the 1952 I–2012 IV period. This figure is repeated in Figure 17.2. Remember that the line segments are drawn to smooth out the short-run fluctuations in productivity. We saw in the last chapter that given how productivity is measured, it moves with the business cycle because firms tend to hold excess labor in recessions. We are not interested in business cycles in this chapter, and the line segments are a way of ignoring business cycle effects.

There was much talk in the late 1970s and early 1980s about the U.S. "productivity problem." Some economics textbooks published in the early 1980s had entire chapters discussing the decline in productivity that seemed to be taking place during the late 1970s. In January 1981, the Congressional Budget Office published a report, *The Productivity Problem: Alternatives for Action*.

It is clear from Figure 17.2 that there was a slowdown in productivity growth in the 1970s. The growth rate went from 3.2 percent in the 1950s and first half of the 1960s to 2.5 percent in the last half of the 1960s and early 1970s and then to 1.5 percent from the early 1970s to the

---

[1] National Academies, "Rising Above the Gathering Storm: Energizing the Employing America for a Brighter Future," National Academies Press, 2007.

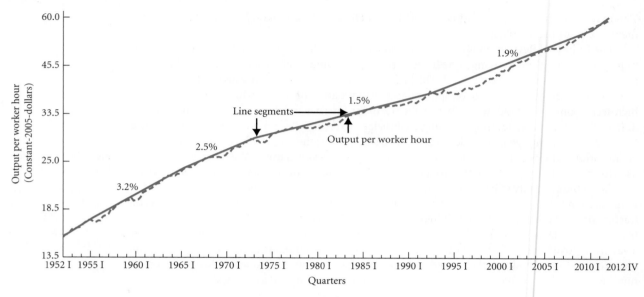

▲ FIGURE 17.2 **Output per Worker Hour (Productivity),** MyEconLab Real-time data
1952 I–2012 IV

1990s. Many explanations were offered at the time for the productivity slowdown of the late 1970s and early 1980s. Some economists pointed to the low rate of saving in the United States compared with other parts of the world. Others blamed increased environmental and government regulation of U.S. business. Still others argued that the country was not spending as much on R&D as it should have been. Finally, some suggested that high energy costs in the 1970s led to investment designed to save energy instead of to enhance labor productivity.

Many of these factors turned around in the 1980s and 1990s and yet, as you can see from Figure 17.2, productivity growth rose to 1.9 percent in the 1990s and through 2012. This early discussion is now quite dated. The interesting question as we move into the second decade of the twenty-first century is whether the continued growth of the Internet and wireless devices will return productivity growth to the values observed in the 1950s and 1960s or whether the period of the 1950s and 1960s was simply an unusually good period for productivity growth and the United States will continue to have productivity growth of around 2 percent.

Growth and the Environment and Issues of Sustainability

In 2000, the United Nations unanimously adopted the Millennium Development Goals, a set of quantifiable, time-based targets for developing countries to meet. Included in these targets, as you might expect, were measures of education, mortality, and income growth. But the UN resolution also included a set of environmental criteria. Specific criteria have been developed around clean air, clean water, and conservation management. Table 17.7 provides the 2005 ranking of a series of developing countries on the UN index.

The inclusion of environmental considerations in the development goals speaks to the importance of environmental infrastructure in the long-run growth prospects of a country. Environmental considerations also address some concerns that in the process of growth, environmental degradation will occur. Evidence on global warming has increased some of the international concerns about growth and the environment. The connections between the environment and growth are complex and remain debated among economists.

The classic work on growth and the environment was done in the mid-1990s by Gene Grossman and Alan Krueger.[2] It is well known that as countries develop, they typically generate air

---

[2] Gene Grossman and Alan Krueger, "Economic Growth and the Environment," *Quarterly Journal of Economics*, May 1995.

TABLE 17.7 Environmental Scores in the World Bank Country Policy and Institutional Assessment 2005 Scores (min = 1, max = 6)	
Albania	3
Angola	2.5
Bhutan	4.5
Cambodia	2.5
Cameroon	4
Gambia	3
Haiti	2.5
Madagascar	4
Mozambique	3
Papua New Guinea	1.5
Sierra Leone	2.5
Sudan	2.5
Tajikistan	2.5
Uganda	4
Vietnam	3.5
Zimbabwe	2.5

Source: International Bank for Reconstruction and Development / The World Bank: World Development Indicators Database 2005.

and water pollutants. China's recent rapid growth provides a strong example of this fact. Grossman and Krueger found, however, that as growth progresses and countries become richer, pollution tends to fall. The relationship between growth, as measured in per-capita income, and pollution is an inverted *U*. Figure 17.3 shows Grossman and Krueger's evidence on one measure of air pollution.

How do we explain the inverted *U*? Clean water and clean air are what economists call *normal goods*. That is, as people get richer, they want to consume more of these goods. You have already seen in the Keynesian model that aggregate consumption increases with income. As it happens, microeconomics finds that this relationship is true for most individual types of goods as well. Demand for clean water and clean air turns out to increase with income levels. As countries develop, their populace increasingly demands improvements on these fronts. We have seen an increasing number of public projects about the environment in China, for example. So while increased industrialization with growth initially degrades the environment, in the long run environmental quality typically improves.

Grossman and Krueger found this inverted *U* in a number of countries. Economic historians remind us that in the heyday of industrialization, northern England suffered from very serious air pollution. Some of you may recall the description of air pollution in nineteenth-century English novels such as Elizabeth Gaskell's *North and South*.

If environmental pollution eventually declines as growth brings rising per-capita incomes, why should we be worried? First, as Grossman and Krueger point out, the inverted *U* represents historical experience, but it is not inevitable. In particular, if public opinion moves governments

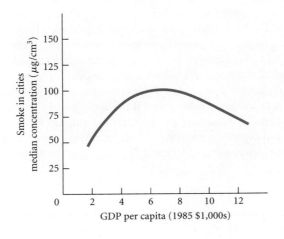

◀ FIGURE 17.3 **The Relationship Between Per-Capita GDP and Urban Air Pollution**

One measure of air pollution is smoke in cities. The relationship between smoke concentration and per-capita GDP is an inverted *U*: As countries grow wealthier, smoke increases and then declines.

Source: Gene Grossman and Alan Krueger, *QJE*, May 1995.

and the economy at large toward technologies that reduce pollution, this requires an empowered populace and a responsive government. Here too we see the importance of institutions in growth. A second issue arises in cases in which high levels of current emissions produce irreversible outcomes. Some would argue that by the time nations such as China and Vietnam develop enough to reduce their emissions, it will be too late. Many believe that global warming is such an example.

Another important problem that has made itself known recently comes from pollution sources that move across country boundaries. Carbon emissions associated with global warming are one such by-product of increased industrialization. Other air pollution problems move across national borders as well. In the heyday of industrialization by the Soviet Union, prevailing winds blew much of the Soviet-produced pollution to Finland. Choices that countries make about levels of growth and levels of environmental control affect the well-being of other countries' populations. Nor is it easy for countries at very different levels of GDP per capita to agree on common standards of environmental control. As we suggested earlier, demand for clean air increases with income, when needs for food and shelter are better met. It should surprise no one who has studied economics that there are debates between developing countries and developed countries about optimal levels of environmental control. These debates are further complicated when we recognize the gains that consumers in developed economies reap from economic activity in the developing world. Much of the increased carbon emitted by Chinese businesses, for example, is associated with goods that are transported and traded to Europe and the United States. These consumers thus share the benefits of this air pollution through the cheaper goods they consume.

Much of Southeast Asia has fueled its growth through export-led manufacturing. For countries that have based their growth on resource extraction, there is another set of potential sustainability issues. Many of the African nations are in this category. Nigeria relies heavily on oil; South Africa and the Congo are large producers of diamonds and other gems. Extraction methods, of course, may carry environmental problems. Many people also question whether growth based on extraction is economically sustainable: What happens when the oil or minerals run out? The answer is quite complicated and depends in some measure on how the profits from the extraction process are used. Because extraction can be accomplished without a well-educated labor force, while other forms of development are more dependent on a skilled-labor base, public investment in infrastructure is especially important. To the extent that countries use the revenues from extraction to invest in infrastructure such as roads and schools and to increase the education and health of their populace, the basis for growth can be shifted over time. With weak institutions, these proceeds may be expropriated by corrupt governments or invested outside the country, and long-run sustainable growth will not result.

The question of whether the natural resource base imposes strong natural limits on growth has been debated since the time of Malthus. Earlier in this chapter we described the concerns of Thomas Malthus that population growth in England would outstrip the ability of the land to provide. In that case, technology stepped in.

In 1972, the Club of Rome, a group of "concerned citizens," contracted with a group at MIT to do a study entitled *The Limits to Growth*.[3] The book-length final report presented the results of computer simulations that assumed present growth rates of population, food, industrial output, and resource exhaustion. According to these data, sometime after the year 2000 the limits will be reached and the entire world economy will come crashing down:

Collapse occurs because of nonrenewable resource depletion. The industrial capital stock grows to a level that requires an enormous input of resources. In the very process of that growth, it depletes a large fraction of the resource reserves available. As resource prices rise and mines are depleted, more and more capital must be used for obtaining resources, leaving less to be invested for future growth. Finally, investment cannot keep up with depreciation and the industrial base collapses, taking with it the service and agricultural systems, which have become dependent on industrial inputs (such as fertilizers, pesticides, hospital laboratories, computers, and especially energy for mechanization)....Population finally decreases when the death rate is driven upward by the lack of food and health services.[4]

[3] Donella H. Meadows et al., *The Limits to Growth* (Washington, D.C.: Potomac Associates, 1972).
[4] Meadows et al., pp. 131–132.

This argument is similar to one offered almost 200 years ago by Thomas Malthus, mentioned earlier in this chapter.

In the early 1970s, many thought that the Club of Rome's predictions had come true. It seemed the world was starting to run up against the limits of world energy supplies. In the years since, new reserves have been found and new sources of energy, including large reserves of gas and oil produced by fracking, have been discovered and developed. At present, issues of global warming and biodiversity are causing many people to question the process of growth. How should one trade off the obvious gains from growth in terms of the lives of those in the poorer nations against environmental goals? Recognizing the existence of these trade-offs and trying to design policies to deal with them is one of the key tasks of policy makers.

——— SUMMARY ———

1. In almost all countries output per worker, *labor productivity*, has been growing over time.

THE GROWTH PROCESS: FROM AGRICULTURE TO INDUSTRY *p. 322*

2. All societies face limits imposed by the resources and technologies available to them. Economic growth expands these limits and shifts society's production possibilities frontier up and to the right.

3. There is considerable variation across the globe in growth rates. Some countries—particularly in Southeast Asia—appear to be catching up.

4. The process by which some less developed, poorer countries experience high growth and begin to catch up to more developed areas is known as convergence.

SOURCES OF ECONOMIC GROWTH *p. 323*

5. An *aggregate production function* embodies the relationship between inputs—the labor force and the stock of capital—and total national output.

6. A number of factors contribute to economic growth: (1) an increase in the labor supply, (2) an increase in physical capital—plant and equipment, (3) an increase in the quality of the labor supply—human capital, (4) an increase in the quality of physical capital—embodied technical change, and (5) disembodied technical change—for example, an increase in managerial skills.

7. The growth rate of labor productivity in the United States has decreased from about 3.2 percent in the 1950s and 1960s to about 1.9 percent in the 1990s and 2000s. It was only about 1.5 percent in the 1970s.

GROWTH AND THE ENVIRONMENT AND ISSUES OF SUSTAINABILITY *p. 330*

8. As countries begin to develop and industrialize, environmental problems are common. As development progresses further, however, most countries experience improvements in their environmental quality.

9. The limits placed on a country's growth by its natural resources have been debated for several hundred years. Growth strategies based on extraction of resources may pose special challenges to a country's growth.

——— REVIEW TERMS AND CONCEPTS ———

aggregate production function, *p. 323*
catch-up, *p. 323*
disembodied technical change, *p. 328*
embodied technical change, *p. 327*

foreign direct investment (FDI), *p. 326*
innovation, *p. 329*
invention, *p. 329*

labor productivity growth, *p. 321*
output growth, *p. 321*
per-capita output growth, *p. 321*

——— PROBLEMS ———

All problems are available on MyEconLab.

1. One way that less developed countries catch up with the growth of the more developed countries is by adopting the technology of the developed countries. On average, however, developed countries are capital-rich and labor-short relative to the developing nations. Think of the kinds of technology that a typical developing country with a short supply of capital and a large marginally employed labor force would find when "shopping" for technology in a more developed country. As a hint, the Japanese have developed the field of robotics such as assembly line machines. Such machines are designed to replace expensive workers with capital (robots) in order to lower the overall cost of production. In what ways does it help a developing country to transfer and use a new technology in its country? What are the costs?

2. Tables 1, 2, and 3 present some data on three hypothetical economies. Complete the tables by figuring the measured productivity of labor and the rate of output growth. What do the data tell you about the causes of economic growth? (*Hint:* How fast are *L* and *K* growing?)

TABLE 1

PERIOD	L	K	Y	Y/L	GROWTH RATE OF OUTPUT
1	1,052	3,065	4,506		
2	1,105	3,095	4,674		
3	1,160	3,126	4,842		
4	1,218	3,157	5,019		

TABLE 2

PERIOD	L	K	Y	Y/L	GROWTH RATE OF OUTPUT
1	1,052	3,065	4,506		
2	1,062	3,371	4,683		
3	1,073	3,709	4,866		
4	1,084	4,079	5,055		

TABLE 3

PERIOD	L	K	Y	Y/L	GROWTH RATE OF OUTPUT
1	1,052	3,065	4,506		
2	1,062	3,095	4,731		
3	1,073	3,126	4,967		
4	1,084	4,157	5,216		

3. Go to a recent issue of *The Economist* magazine. In the back of each issue is a section called "economic indicators." That section lists the most recent growth data for a substantial number of countries. Which countries around the world are growing most rapidly according to the most recent data? Which countries around the world are growing more slowly? Flip through the stories in *The Economist* to see if there is any explanation for the pattern that you observe. Write a brief essay on current general economic conditions around the world.

4. In the fall of 2005, the president's tax reform commission issued a final report. The commission called for a general cut in marginal tax rates; lower tax rates on dividends, capital gains, and interest income; and, more importantly, the expensing of investment in capital equipment. These provisions were argued to be "pro-growth." In what ways would you expect each of these proposals to be favorable to economic growth?

5. [Related to the *Economics in Practice* on p. 324] In a March 2013 press release, the World Bank announced its support to assist Indonesia in accelerating its economic growth through the Research and Innovation in Science and Technology Project (RISET). This project is designed to boost research and innovation in Indonesia and assist the country in evolving into a knowledge-based economy. According to Stefan G. Koeberle, World Bank Country Director for Indonesia, "Improving human resources and national capabilities in science and technology is a key pillar in Indonesia's masterplan to accelerate and expand its economy. Shifting from a resource-based economy to a knowledge-based economy will bring Indonesia up the value chain in a wide range of sectors, with the help of homegrown innovation and a vast pool of human resources." The press release states that a large part of the RISET program will involve assistance in raising the academic credentials of Indonesian researchers involved with science and

engineering, and it is hoped that the program will eventually lead to increased investment in R&D, where as a percentage of GDP, Indonesia's R&D investment falls significantly below many of its Asian neighbors. Using the information presented in this chapter, explain how increasing research and innovation and raising the academic credentials of researchers can assist in increasing long-run economic growth in Indonesia.

Source: "World Bank Supports Move to Accelerate Indonesia's Economic Growth through Science, Technology, and Innovation," www.worldbank.org, March 29, 2013.

6. Education is an area in which it has been hard to create productivity gains that reduce costs. Collect data on the tuition rates of your own college in the last twenty years and compare that increase to the overall rate of inflation using the CPI. What do you observe? Can you suggest some productivity-enhancing measures?

7. Economists generally agree that high budget deficits today will reduce the growth rate of the economy in the future. Why? Do the reasons for the high budget deficit matter? In other words, does it matter whether the deficit is caused by lower taxes, increased defense spending, more job-training programs, and so on?

8. Why can growth lead to a more unequal distribution of income? By assuming this is true, how is it possible for the poor to benefit from economic growth?

9. According to the Bureau of Labor Statistics, productivity in the United States grew at an annual rate of 3.7 percent from 2008 to 2009. During this same time, real GDP in the United States declined by 2.5 percent. Explain how productivity can increase when real GDP is declining.

10. The data in the following table represents real GDP from 2009–2012 for five countries.
    a. Calculate the growth rate in real GDP for all five countries from 2009–2010. Which country experienced the highest rate of economic growth from 2009–2010?
    b. Calculate the growth rate in real GDP for all five countries from 2010–2011. Which country experienced the highest rate of economic growth from 2010–2011?
    c. Calculate the growth rate in real GDP for all five countries from 2011–2012. Which country experienced the highest rate of economic growth from 2011–2012?
    d. Calculate the average annual growth rate in real GDP for all five countries from 2009–2012. Which country experienced the highest average annual rate of economic growth from 2009–2012?

COUNTRY	2009	2010	2011	2012
United States	12758.00	13063.00	13299.10	13583.85
El Salvador	18.39	18.57	18.84	19.20
Republic of South Africa	280.47	288.44	297.45	305.27
Cambodia	8.02	8.55	9.09	9.71
Russia	870.12	905.22	944.47	980.07

All values are in 2005 U.S. dollars.
Source: United States Department of Agriculture.

11. The data in the following table represents real GDP per capita in 1972 and 2012 for five countries. Fill in the table by calculating the annual growth rate in real GDP per capita from 1972 to 2012. Is the data in the completed table consistent with convergence theory? Explain.

COUNTRY	REAL GDP PER CAPITA IN 1972	REAL GDP PER CAPITA IN 2012	ANNUAL GROWTH IN REAL GDP PER CAPITA 1972–2012
United States	22,189	43,219	
El Salvador	2,352	3,152	
Repubilc of South Africa	4,677	6,254	
Cambodia	113	649	
Russia	4,084	6,877	

All values are in 2005 U.S. dollars.
Source: United States Department of Agriculture.

12. How do each of the following relate to the rates of productivity and growth in an economy?
    a. Spending on research and development
    b. Government regulation
    c. Changes in human capital
    d. Output per worker hour
    e. Embodied technical change
    f. Disembodied technical change

13. Use the data in the following table to explain what happened with respect to economic growth and the standard of living in each of the three countries.

COUNTRY	REAL GDP 2012	REAL GDP 2011	POPULATION 2012	POPULATION 2011
Astoria	10,600	9,750	1,500	1,325
Tiberius	3,500	3,150	650	585
Zorba	47,750	49,100	12,500	13,440

14. [Related to the *Economics in Practice* on *p. 328*] One source of long-run economic growth is an increase in the quality of labor, or human capital, of which education plays a major role. Go to www.bls.gov and look up the current unemployment rate. Compare this to the current unemployment rates for those without a high school diploma, those with only a high school diploma, and those with a bachelor's degree or higher. What does this data suggest about education requirements for jobs in the United States? Then go to www.census.gov and look at the current population survey historical table A-2. Find the percentage of the total population 25 years and older who have completed four years of high school or more and the percentage who have completed four years of college or more. Compare this data with the unemployment data. What does this information suggest about future productivity and growth for the U.S. economy?

Alternative Views in Macroeconomics

18

Throughout this book, we have noted that there are many disagreements and questions in macroeconomics. For example, economists disagree on whether the aggregate supply curve is vertical, either in the short run or in the long run. Some economists even doubt that the aggregate supply curve is a useful macroeconomic concept. There are different views on whether cyclical employment exists and, if it does, what causes it. Economists disagree about whether monetary and fiscal policies are effective at stabilizing the economy, and they support different views on the primary determinants of consumption and investment spending.

We discussed some of these disagreements in previous chapters, but only briefly. In this chapter, we discuss in more detail a number of alternative views of how the macroeconomy works.

Keynesian Economics

John Maynard Keynes's *General Theory of Employment, Interest, and Money*, published in 1936, remains one of the most important works in economics. While a great deal of the material in the previous 10 chapters is drawn from modern research that postdates Keynes, much of the material is built around a framework constructed by Keynes.

What exactly is *Keynesian economics*? In one sense, it is the foundation of all of macroeconomics. Keynes was the first to emphasize aggregate demand and links between the money market and the goods market. Keynes also emphasized the possible problem of sticky wages. In recent years, the term *Keynesian* has been used more narrowly. Keynes believed in an activist federal government. He believed that the government had a role to play in fighting inflation and unemployment, and he believed that monetary and fiscal policies should be used to manage the macroeconomy. This is why *Keynesian* is sometimes used to refer to economists who advocate active government intervention in the macroeconomy.

During the 1970s and 1980s, it became clear that managing the macroeconomy was more easily accomplished on paper than in practice. The inflation problems of the 1970s and early 1980s and the seriousness of the recessions of 1974–1975 and 1980–1982 led many economists to challenge the idea of active government intervention in the economy. Some of the challenges were simple

LEARNING OBJECTIVES

Summarize Keynesian economics and explain the principles of monetarism

Explain the fundamentals of supply-side economics

Discuss the principles and implications of the rational-expectations hypothesis and the Lucas supply function

Discuss the real business cycle theory and new Keynesian economics

attacks on the bureaucracy's ability to act in a timely manner. Others were theoretical assaults that claimed to show that monetary and fiscal policies had no or little effect on the economy.

We begin with an old debate—that between Keynesians and monetarists.

Monetarism

The Velocity of Money

velocity of money
The number of times a dollar bill changes hands, on average, during a year; the ratio of nominal *GDP* to the stock of money.

A key variable in monetarism is the **velocity of money**. Think of velocity as the number of times a dollar bill changes hands, on average, during a year. Suppose on January 1 you buy a new ballpoint pen with a $5 bill. The owner of the stationery store does not spend your $5 right away. She may hold it until, say, May 1, when she uses it to buy a dozen doughnuts. The doughnut store owner does not spend the $5 he receives until July 1, when he uses it (along with other cash) to buy 100 gallons of oil. The oil distributor uses the bill to buy an engagement ring for his fiancée on September 1, but the $5 bill is not used again in the remaining 3 months of the year. Because this $5 bill has changed hands four times during the year, its velocity of circulation is 4. A velocity of 4 means that the $5 bill stays with each owner for an average of 3 months, or one quarter of a year.

In practice, we use gross domestic product (GDP), instead of the total value of all transactions in the economy, to measure velocity[1] because GDP data are more readily available. The income velocity of money (V) is the ratio of nominal GDP to the stock of money (M):

$$V \equiv \frac{GDP}{M}$$

If $12 trillion worth of final goods and services is produced in a year and if the money stock is $1 trillion, then the velocity of money is $12 trillion ÷ $1 trillion, or 12.0.

We can expand this definition slightly by noting that nominal income (GDP) is equal to real output (income) (Y) times the overall price level (P):

$$GDP \equiv P \times Y$$

Through substitution:

$$V \equiv \frac{P \times Y}{M}$$

or

$$M \times V \equiv P \times Y$$

At this point, it is worth pausing to ask whether our definition has provided us with any insights into the workings of the economy. The answer is no. Because we defined V as the ratio of GDP to the money supply, the statement $M \times V \equiv P \times Y$ is an identity—it is true by definition. It contains no more useful information than the statement "A bachelor is an unmarried man." The definition does not, for example, say anything about what will happen to $P \times Y$ when M changes. The final value of $P \times Y$ depends on what happens to V. If V falls when M increases, the product $M \times V$ could stay the same, in which case the change in M would have had no effect on nominal income. To give monetarism some economic content, a simple version of monetarism known as the **quantity theory of money** is used.

quantity theory of money
The theory based on the identity $M \times V \equiv P \times Y$ and the assumption that the velocity of money (V) is constant (or virtually constant).

The Quantity Theory of Money

The key assumption of the quantity theory of money is that the velocity of money is constant (or virtually constant) over time. If we let V denote the constant value of V, the equation for the quantity theory can be written as follows:

$$M \times \overline{V} = P \times Y$$

[1] Recall that GDP does not include transactions in intermediate goods (for example, flour sold to a baker to be made into bread) or in existing assets (for example, the sale of a used car). If these transactions are made using money, however, they do influence the number of times money changes hands during the course of a year. GDP is an imperfect measure of transactions to use in calculating the velocity of money.

Note that the double equal sign has replaced the triple equal sign because the equation is no longer an identity. The equation is true if velocity is constant (and equal to V) but not otherwise. If the equation is true, it provides an easy way to explain nominal GDP. Given M, which can be considered a policy variable set by the Federal Reserve (Fed), nominal GDP is just $M \times \overline{V}$. In this case, the effects of monetary policy are clear. Changes in M cause equal percentage changes in nominal GDP. For example, if the money supply doubles, nominal GDP also doubles. If the money supply remains unchanged, nominal GDP remains unchanged.

The key is whether the velocity of money is really constant. Early economists believed that the velocity of money was determined largely by institutional considerations, such as how often people are paid and how the banking system clears transactions between banks. Because these factors change gradually, early economists believed velocity was essentially constant.

When there is equilibrium in the money market, then the quantity of money supplied is equal to the quantity of money demanded. That could mean that M in the quantity-theory equation equals both the quantity of money supplied and the quantity of money demanded. If the quantity-theory equation is looked on as a demand-for-money equation, it says that the demand for money depends on nominal income (GDP, or $P \times Y$), but *not* on the interest rate. If the interest rate changes and nominal income does not, the equation says that the quantity of money demanded will not change. This is contrary to the theory of the demand for money in Chapter 11, which had the demand for money depending on both income and the interest rate.

Testing the Quantity Theory of Money   One way to test the validity of the quantity theory of money is to look at the demand for money using recent data on the U.S. economy. The key is this: Does money demand depend on the interest rate? Most empirical work says yes. When demand-for-money equations are estimated (or "fit to the data"), the interest rate usually turns out to be a significant factor. The demand for money does not appear to depend only on nominal income.

Another way of testing the quantity theory is to plot velocity over time and see how it behaves. Figure 18.1 plots the velocity of money for the 1960 I–2012 IV period. The data show that velocity is far from constant. There was a positive trend until 2007, but also large fluctuations around this trend. For example, velocity rose from 6.1 in 1980 III to 6.7 in 1981 III, fell to 6.3 in 1983 I, rose to 6.7 in 1984 III, and fell to 5.7 in 1986 IV. Changes of a few tenths of a point may seem small, but they are actually large. For example, the money supply in 1986 IV was $800 billion. If velocity changes by 0.3 with a money supply of this amount and if the money supply is unchanged, we have a change in nominal GDP ($P \times Y$) of $240 billion (0.3 × $800 billion), which is about 5 percent of the level of GDP in 1986. The change in velocity in since 2008 has been remarkable. Velocity fell from 9.5 in 2008 I to 5.9 in 2012 IV!

The debate over monetarist theories is more subtle than our discussion so far indicates. First, there are many definitions of the money supply. M1 is the money supply variable used for the graph in Figure 18.1, but there may be some other measure of the money supply that

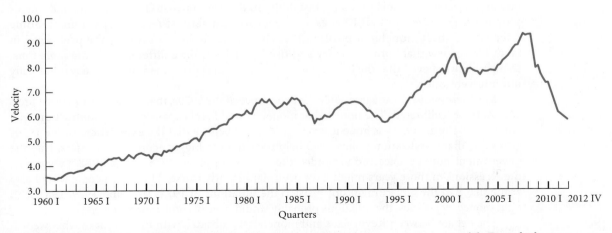

▲ **FIGURE 18.1   The Velocity of Money, 1960 I–2012 IV**   MyEconLab Real-time data
Velocity has not been constant over the period from 1960 to 2012. This was a long-term positive trend, which has now reversed.

would lead to a smoother plot. For example, many people shifted their funds from checking account deposits to money market accounts when the latter became available in the late 1970s. Because GDP did not change as a result of this shift while M1 decreased, velocity—the ratio of GDP to M1—must have gone up. Suppose instead we measured the supply of money by M2 (which includes both checking accounts and money market accounts). In this case, the decrease in checking deposits would be exactly offset by the rise in money market account deposits and M2 would not change. With no change in GDP and no change in M2, the velocity of money would not change. Whether or not velocity is constant may depend partly on how we measure the money supply.

Second, there may be a time lag between a change in the money supply and its effects on nominal GDP. Suppose we experience a 10 percent increase in the money supply today, but it takes 1 year for nominal GDP to increase by 10 percent. If we measured the ratio of today's money supply to today's GDP, it would seem that velocity had fallen by 10 percent. However, if we measured today's money supply against GDP 1 year from now, when the increase in the supply of money had its full effect on income, velocity would have been constant.

The debate over the quantity theory of money is primarily empirical. It is a debate that can be resolved by looking at facts about the real world and seeing whether they are in accord with the predictions of theory. Is there a measure of the money supply and a choice of the time lag between a change in the money supply and its effects on nominal GDP such that V is in effect constant? If so, the monetarist theory is a useful approach to understanding how the macroeconomy works and how changes in the money supply will cause a proportionate increase in nominal GDP. If not, some other theory is likely to be more appropriate. (We discuss the testing of alternative theories at the end of this chapter.)

The Keynesian/Monetarist Debate

The debate between Keynesians and monetarists was perhaps the central controversy in macroeconomics in the 1960s. The leading spokesman for monetarism was Milton Friedman from the University of Chicago. Most monetarists, including Friedman, blamed much of the instability in the economy on the Federal Reserve, arguing that the high inflation that the United States encountered from time to time could have been avoided if only the Fed had not expanded the money supply so rapidly. Monetarists were skeptical of the Fed's ability to "manage" the economy—to expand the money supply during bad times and contract it during good times. A common argument against such management is the one discussed in Chapter 15: Time lags may make attempts to stimulate and contract the economy counterproductive.

Friedman advocated instead a policy of steady and slow money growth—specifically, that the money supply should grow at a rate equal to the average growth of real output (income) (Y). That is, the Fed should pursue a constant policy that accommodates real growth but not inflation.

Many Keynesians, on the other hand, advocated the application of coordinated monetary and fiscal policy tools to reduce instability in the economy—to fight inflation and unemployment. However, not all Keynesians advocated an activist federal government. Some rejected the strict monetarist position that changes in money affect only the price level in favor of the view that both monetary and fiscal policies make a difference. *At the same time*, though, they believed that the best possible policy for the government to pursue was basically noninterventionist.

Most economists now agree, after the experience of the 1970s, that monetary and fiscal tools are not finely calibrated. The notion that monetary and fiscal expansions and contractions can "fine-tune" the economy is gone forever. Still, many believe that the experiences of the 1970s also show that stabilization policies can help prevent even bigger economic disasters. Had the government not cut taxes and expanded the money supply in 1975 and in 1982, they argue, the recessions of those years might have been significantly worse. The same people would also argue that had the government not resisted the inflations of 1974–1975 and 1979–1981 with tight monetary policies, the inflations probably would have become much worse.

The debate between Keynesians and monetarists subsided with the advent of what we will call "new classical macroeconomics." Before turning to this, however, it will be useful to consider a minor but interesting footnote in macroeconomic history: supply-side economics.

Supply-Side Economics

From our discussion of equilibrium in the goods market, beginning with the simple multiplier in Chapter 8 and continuing through Chapter 13, we have focused primarily on *demand*. Supply increases and decreases in response to changes in aggregate expenditure (which is closely linked to aggregate demand). Fiscal policy works by influencing aggregate expenditure through tax policy and government spending. Monetary policy works by influencing investment and consumption spending through increases and decreases in the interest rate. The theories we have been discussing are "demand-oriented." *Supply-side economics,* as the name suggests, focuses on the supply side.

The argument of the supply-siders about the economy in the late 1970s and early 1980s was simple. The real problem, they said, was not demand, but high rates of taxation and heavy regulation that reduced the incentive to work, to save, and to invest. What was needed was not a demand stimulus, but better incentives to stimulate *supply*.

If we cut taxes so people take home more of their paychecks, the argument continued, they will work harder and save more. If businesses get to keep more of their profits and can get away from government regulations, they will invest more. This added labor supply and investment, or capital supply, will lead to an expansion of the supply of goods and services, which will reduce inflation and unemployment at the same time.

At their most extreme, supply-siders argued that the incentive effects of supply-side policies were likely to be so great that a major cut in tax rates would actually *increase* tax revenues. Even though *tax rates* would be lower, more people would be working and earning income and firms would earn more profits, so that the increases in the *tax bases* (profits, sales, and income) would then outweigh the decreases in rates, resulting in increased government revenues.

The Laffer Curve

Figure 18.2 presents a key diagram of supply-side economics. The tax rate is measured on the vertical axis, and tax revenue is measured on the horizontal axis. The assumption behind this curve is that there is some tax rate beyond which the supply response is large enough to lead to a decrease in tax revenue for further increases in the tax rate. There is obviously some tax rate between zero and 100 percent at which tax revenue is at a maximum. At a tax rate of zero, work effort is high but there is no tax revenue. At a tax rate of 100, the labor supply is presumably zero because people are not allowed to keep any of their income. Somewhere between zero and 100 is the maximum-revenue rate.

The big debate in the 1980s was whether tax rates in the United States put the country on the upper or lower part of the curve in Figure 18.2. The supply-side school claimed that the United States was around *A* and that taxes should be cut. Others argued that the United States was nearer *B* and that tax cuts would lead to lower tax revenue.

The diagram in Figure 18.2 is the **Laffer curve**, named after economist Arthur Laffer, who, legend has it, first drew it on the back of a napkin at a cocktail party. The Laffer curve had some influence on the passage of the Economic Recovery Tax Act of 1981, the tax package put forward by the Reagan administration that brought with it substantial cuts in both personal and business taxes.

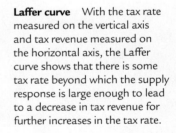

Laffer curve With the tax rate measured on the vertical axis and tax revenue measured on the horizontal axis, the Laffer curve shows that there is some tax rate beyond which the supply response is large enough to lead to a decrease in tax revenue for further increases in the tax rate.

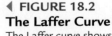

◀ **FIGURE 18.2**
The Laffer Curve
The Laffer curve shows that the amount of revenue the government collects is a function of the tax rate. It shows that when tax rates are very high, an increase in the tax rate could cause tax revenues to fall. Similarly, under the same circumstances, a cut in the tax rate could generate enough additional economic activity to cause revenues to rise.

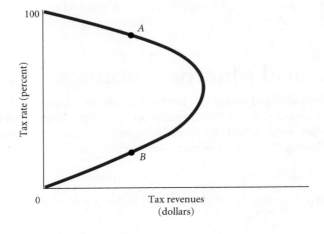

Individual income tax rates were cut by as much as 25 percent over 3 years. Corporate taxes were cut sharply in a way designed to stimulate capital investment. The new law allowed firms to depreciate their capital at a rapid rate for tax purposes, and the bigger deductions led to taxes that were significantly lower than before.

Evaluating Supply-Side Economics

Supporters of supply-side economics claim that Reagan's tax policies were successful in stimulating the economy. They point to the fact that almost immediately after the tax cuts of 1981 were put into place, the economy expanded and the recession of 1980–1982 came to an end. In addition, inflation rates fell sharply from the high rates of 1980 and 1981. Except for 1 year, federal receipts continued to rise throughout the 1980s despite the cut in tax rates.

Critics of supply-side policies do not dispute these facts, but offer an alternative explanation of how the economy recovered. The Reagan tax cuts were enacted just as the U.S. economy was in the middle of its deepest recession since the Great Depression. The unemployment rate stood at 10.7 percent in the fourth quarter of 1982. It was the recession, critics argue, that was responsible for the reduction in inflation—not the supply-side policies. Also among the criticisms of supply-side economics is that it is unlikely a tax cut would substantially increase the supply of labor. In addition, in theory, a tax cut could even lead to a *reduction* in labor supply. Recall our discussion of income and substitution effects in Chapter 16. Although it is true that a higher after-tax wage rate provides a higher reward for each hour of work and thus more incentive to work, a tax cut also means that households receive a higher income for a given number of hours of work. Because they can earn the same amount of money working fewer hours, households might choose to work *less*. They might spend some of their added income on leisure. Research done during the 1980s suggests that tax cuts seem to increase the supply of labor somewhat but that the increases are very modest.

What about the recovery from the recession? Why did real output begin to grow rapidly in late 1982, precisely when the supply-side tax cuts were taking effect? Two reasons have been suggested. First, the supply-side tax cuts had large *demand*-side effects that stimulated the economy. Second, the Fed pumped up the money supply and drove interest rates down at the same time the tax cuts were being put into effect. The money supply expanded about 20 percent between 1981 and 1983, and interest rates fell. In the third quarter of 1981, the average 3-month U.S. Treasury bill paid 15 percent interest. By the first quarter of 1983, the rate had dropped to 8.1 percent.

Certainly, traditional theory suggests that a huge tax cut will lead to an increase in disposable income and, in turn, an increase in consumption spending (a component of aggregate expenditure). In addition, although an increase in planned investment (brought about by a lower interest rate) leads to added productive capacity and added supply in the long run, it also increases expenditures on capital goods (new plant and equipment investment) in the short run.

Whether the recovery from the 1981–1982 recession was the result of supply-side expansion or supply-side policies that had demand-side effects, one thing is clear: The extreme promises of the supply-siders did not materialize. President Reagan argued that because of the effect depicted in the Laffer curve, the government could maintain expenditures (and even increase defense expenditures sharply), cut tax rates, *and* balance the budget. This was not the case. Government revenues fell sharply from levels that would have been realized without the tax cuts. After 1982, the federal government ran huge deficits, with about $2 trillion added to the national debt between 1983 and 1992.

New Classical Macroeconomics

The challenge to Keynesian and related theories has come from a school sometimes referred to as the new classical macroeconomics.[2] Like monetarism and Keynesianism, this term is vague. No two new classical macroeconomists think exactly alike, and no single model completely represents this school. The following discussion, however, conveys the flavor of the new classical views.

---

[2] The term *new classical* is used because many of the assumptions and conclusions of this group of economists resemble those of the classical economists—that is, those who wrote before Keynes.

The Development of New Classical Macroeconomics

A key complaint of new classical macroeconomics is the way traditional models treat expectations. Keynes himself recognized that expectations (in the form of "animal spirits") play a big part in economic behavior. The problem is that traditional models assume that expectations are formed in naive ways. A common assumption, for example, is that people form their expectations of future inflation by assuming present inflation will continue. If they turn out to be wrong, they adjust their expectations by some fraction of the difference between their original forecast and the actual inflation rate. Suppose you expect 10 percent inflation next year. When next year comes, the inflation rate turns out to be only 5 percent, so you have made an error of 5 percentage points. You might then predict an inflation rate for the following year of 7.5 percent, halfway between your earlier expectation (10 percent) and actual inflation last year (5 percent).

The problem with this treatment of expectations is that it is not consistent with the assumptions of microeconomics. It implies that people systematically overlook information that would allow them to make better forecasts, even though there are costs to being wrong. If, as microeconomic theory assumes, people are out to maximize their satisfaction and firms are out to maximize their profits, they should form their expectations in a smarter way. Instead of naively assuming the future will be like the past or the present, they should actively seek to forecast the future. Any other behavior is not in keeping with the microeconomic view of the forward-looking, rational people who compose households and firms.

Rational Expectations

In previous chapters we emphasized households' and firms' expectations about the future. A firm's decision to build a new plant depends on its expectations of future sales. The amount of saving a household undertakes today depends on its expectations about future interest rates, wages, and prices.

How are expectations formed? Do people assume that things will continue as they are at present (such as predicting rain tomorrow because it is raining today)? What information do people use to make their guesses about the future? Questions such as these have become central to current macroeconomic thinking and research. One theory, the **rational-expectations hypothesis**, offers a powerful way of thinking about expectations.

Suppose we want to forecast inflation. What does it mean to say that my expectations of inflation are "rational"? The rational-expectations hypothesis assumes that people know the "true model" that generates inflation—they know how inflation is determined in the economy—and they use this model to forecast future inflation rates. If there were no random, unpredictable events in the economy and if people knew the true model generating inflation, their forecasts of future inflation rates would be perfect. Because it is true, the model would not permit mistakes and thus the people using it would not make mistakes.

However, many events that affect the inflation rate are not predictable—they are random. By "true" model, we mean a model that is, *on average*, correct in forecasting inflation. Sometimes the random events have a positive effect on inflation, which means that the model underestimates the inflation rate, and sometimes they have a negative effect, which means that the model overestimates the inflation rate. On average, the model is correct. Therefore, rational expectations are correct on average even though their predictions are not exactly right all the time.

To see why, suppose you have to forecast how many times a fair coin will come up heads out of 100 tosses. The true model in this case is that the coin has a 50/50 chance of coming up heads on any one toss. Because the outcome of the 100 tosses is random, you cannot be sure of guessing correctly. If you know the true model—that the coin is fair—your rational expectation of the outcome of 100 tosses is 50 heads. You are not likely to be exactly right—the actual number of heads is likely to be slightly higher or slightly lower than 50—but *on average*, you will be correct.

Sometimes people are said to have rational expectations if they use "all available information" in forming their expectations. This definition is vague because it is not always clear what "all available information" means. The definition is precise if by "all available information" we mean that people know and use the true model. We cannot have more or better information than the true model!

If information can be obtained at no cost, people are not behaving rationally when they fail to use all available information. Because there are usually costs to making a wrong

rational-expectations hypothesis The hypothesis that people know the "true model" of the economy and that they use this model to form their expectations of the future.

ECONOMICS IN PRACTICE

How Are Expectations Formed?

A current debate among macroeconomists and policy makers is how people form expectations about the future state of the economy. Of particular interest is the formation of inflationary expectations. One possible way that inflation can be transmitted in an economy is if individuals expect there to be inflation and then, because of these expectations, demand higher wages, leading in turn to increases in inflation. In 2010, a number of economists began to worry about the possibility of inflationary expectations heating up in the United States in the next few years because of the large federal government deficit.

How, in fact, are expectations formed? Are expectations rational, as some macroeconomists believe, reflecting an accurate understanding of how the economy works? Or are they formed in simpler, more mechanical ways? A recent research paper by Ronnie Driver and Richard Windram from the Bank of England sheds some light on this issue. Since 1999, the Bank of England has done a survey four times a year of 2,000 British consumers about their views of future inflation and future interest rates. The surveys suggest that consumers tend to expect future inflation to be what they perceive past inflation to have been. Also, there are some differences between what consumers perceive past inflation to have been and the actual estimates of past inflation made by the government. In other words, consumers are more influenced by their own experiences than by actual government numbers and their expectations of the future are based on

their past experiences. Consumers mostly expect the future to look the way they perceive the past to have looked. Two factors that appear to be important in influencing consumer perceptions of inflation are gas prices and the attention the media pays to price increases. All this suggests that, at least for the British consumers surveyed, the formation of inflationary expectations is a less sophisticated process than some economic theorists suggest. This research also suggests that to the extent that gas prices increase and media attention to inflation increases, inflationary expectations will increase.

THINKING PRACTICALLY

1. Why do you think that consumers are so sensitive to gas prices in forming their expectations?

forecast, it is not rational to overlook information that could help improve the accuracy of a forecast as long as the costs of acquiring that information do not outweigh the benefits of improving its accuracy.

Rational Expectations and Market Clearing If firms have rational expectations and if they set prices and wages on this basis, on average, prices and wages will be set at levels that ensure equilibrium in the goods and labor markets. When a firm has rational expectations, it knows the demand curve for its output and the supply curve of labor that it faces, except when random shocks disrupt those curves. Therefore, on average, the firm will set the market-clearing prices and wages. The firm knows the true model, and it will not set wages different from those it expects will attract the number of workers it wants. If all firms behave this way, wages will be set in such a way that the total amount of labor supplied will, on average, be equal to the total amount of labor that firms demand. In other words, on average, there will be full employment.

In Chapter 14, we argued that there might be disequilibrium in the labor market (in the form of either unemployment or excess demand for workers) because firms may make mistakes in their wage-setting behavior due to expectation errors. If, on average, firms do not make errors, on average, there will be equilibrium. When expectations are rational, disequilibrium exists only temporarily as a result of random, unpredictable shocks—obviously an important conclusion. If true, it means that disequilibrium in any market is only temporary because firms, on average, set market-clearing wages and prices.

The assumption that expectations are rational radically changes the way we can view the economy. We go from a world in which unemployment can exist for substantial periods and the multiplier can operate to a world in which (on average) all markets clear and there is full employment. In this world, there is no need for government stabilization policies. Unemployment is not a problem that governments need to worry about; if it exists at all, it is because of unpredictable shocks that, on average, amount to zero. There is no more reason for the government to try to change the outcome in the labor market than there is for it to change the outcome in the banana market. On average, prices and wages are set at market-clearing levels.

The Lucas Supply Function   The **Lucas supply function**, named after Robert E. Lucas of the University of Chicago, is an important part of a number of new classical macroeconomic theories. It yields, as we shall see, a surprising policy conclusion. The function is deceptively simple. It says that real output (Y) depends on (is a function of) the difference between the actual price level (P) and the expected price level (P^e):

$$Y = f(P - P^e)$$

The actual price level minus the expected price level ($P - P^e$) is the **price surprise**. Before considering the policy implications of this function, we should look at the theory behind it.

Lucas begins by assuming that people and firms are specialists in production but generalists in consumption. If someone you know is a manual laborer, the chances are that she sells only one thing—labor. If she is a lawyer, she sells only legal services. In contrast, people buy a large bundle of goods—ranging from gasoline to ice cream and pretzels—on a regular basis. The same is true for firms. Most companies tend to concentrate on producing a small range of products, but they typically buy a larger range of inputs—raw materials, labor, energy, and capital. According to Lucas, this divergence between buying and selling creates an asymmetry. People know more about the prices of the things they sell than they do about the prices of the things they buy.

At the beginning of each period, a firm has some expectation of the average price level for that period. If the actual price level turns out to be different, there is a price surprise. Suppose the average price level is higher than expected. Because the firm learns about the actual price level slowly, some time goes by before it realizes that all prices have gone up. The firm *does* learn *quickly* that the price of its *output* has gone up. The firm perceives—incorrectly, it turns out—that its price has risen relative to other prices, and this perception leads it to produce more output.

A similar argument holds for workers. When there is a positive price surprise, workers at first believe that their "price"—their wage rate—has increased relative to other prices. Workers believe that their real wage rate has risen. We know from theory that an increase in the real wage is likely to encourage workers to work more hours.[3] The real wage has not actually risen, but it takes workers a while to figure this out. In the meantime, they supply more hours of work than they would have. This increase means that the economy produces more output when prices are unexpectedly higher than when prices are at their expected level.

This is the rationale for the Lucas supply function. Unexpected increases in the price level can fool workers and firms into thinking that relative prices have changed, causing them to alter the amount of labor or goods they choose to supply.

Policy Implications of the Lucas Supply Function   The Lucas supply function in combination with the assumption that expectations are rational implies that anticipated policy changes have no effect on real output. Consider a change in monetary policy. In general, the change will have some effect on the average price level. If the policy change is announced to the public, people will know the effect on the price level because they have rational expectations (and know the way changes in monetary policy affect the price level). This means that the change in monetary policy affects the actual price level and the expected price level in the same way. The new price level minus the new expected price level is zero—no price surprise. In such a case, there will be no change in real output because the Lucas supply function states that real output can change from its fixed level only if there is a price surprise.

The general conclusion is that *any* announced policy change—in fiscal policy or any other policy—has no effect on real output because the policy change affects both actual and expected price levels in the same way. If people have rational expectations, known policy changes can

Lucas supply function The supply function embodies the idea that output (Y) depends on the difference between the actual price level and the expected price level.

price surprise Actual price level minus expected price level.

---

[3] This is true if we assume that the substitution effect dominates the income effect (see Chapter 17).

produce no price surprises—and no increases in real output. The only way any change in government policy can affect real output is if it is kept in the dark so it is not generally known. Government policy can affect real output only if it surprises people; otherwise, it cannot. Rational-expectations theory combined with the Lucas supply function proposes a very small role for government policy in the economy.

Real Business Cycle Theory and New Keynesian Economics

real business cycle theory
An attempt to explain business cycle fluctuations under the assumptions of complete price and wage flexibility and rational expectations. It emphasizes shocks to technology and other shocks.

Research that followed Lucas's work was concerned with whether the existence of business cycles can be explained under the assumptions of complete price and wage flexibility (market clearing) and rational expectations. This work is called **real business cycle theory**. As we discussed in Chapter 12, if prices and wages are completely flexible, then the *AS* curve is vertical, even in the short run. If the *AS* curve is vertical, then events or phenomena that shift the *AD* curve (such as changes in government spending, and taxes) have no effect on real output. Real output does fluctuate over time, so the puzzle is how the fluctuations can be explained if they are not due to policy changes or other shocks that shift the *AD* curve. Solving this puzzle is one of the main missions of real business cycle theory.

It is clear that if shifts of the *AD* curve cannot account for real output fluctuations (because the *AS* curve is vertical), then shifts of the *AS* curve must be responsible. However, the task is to come up with convincing explanations as to what causes these shifts and why they persist over a number of periods. The problem is particularly difficult when it comes to the labor market. If prices and wages are completely flexible, then there is never any unemployment aside from frictional unemployment. For example, because the measured U.S. unemployment rate was 4.0 percent in 2000 and 9.3 percent in 2009, the puzzle is to explain why so many more people chose not to work in 2009 than in 2000.

Early real business cycle theorists emphasized shocks to the production technology. Suppose there is a negative shock in a given year that causes the marginal product of labor to decline. This leads to a fall in the real wage, which leads to a decrease in the quantity of labor supplied. People work less because the negative technology shock has led to a lower return from working. The opposite happens when there is a positive shock: The marginal product of labor rises, the real wage rises, and people choose to work more. This research was not as successful as some had hoped because it required what seemed to be unrealistically large shocks to explain the observed movements in labor supply over time.

new Keynesian economics
A field in which models are developed under the assumptions of rational expectations and sticky prices and wages.

What has come to be called **new Keynesian economics** retains the assumption of rational expectations, but drops the assumption of completely flexible prices and wages. Prices and wages are assumed to be sticky. The existence of menu costs is often cited as a justification of the assumption of sticky prices. It may be costly for firms to change prices, which prevents firms from having completely flexible prices. Sticky wages are discussed in Chapter 14, and some of the arguments given there as to why wages might be sticky may be relevant to new Keynesian models. A main issue regarding these models is that any justification has to be consistent with all agents in the model having rational expectations.

Current research in new Keynesian economics broadly defined is vast. There are many models, often called dynamic stochastic general equilibrium (DSGE) models. The properties of these models vary, but most have the feature—because of the assumption of sticky prices and wages—that monetary policy can affect real output. The government generally has some role to play in these models.

Evaluating the Rational Expectations Assumption

Almost all models in new classical macroeconomics—Lucas's model, real business cycle models, new Keynesian models—assume rational expectations. A key question concerning how realistic these models are is thus how realistic the assumption of rational expectations is. If this assumption approximates the way expectations are actually formed, then it calls into question any theory that relies at least in part on expectation errors for the existence of disequilibrium. The arguments in favor of the rational expectations assumption sound persuasive from the perspective of microeconomic theory. When expectations are not rational, there are likely to be unexploited profit opportunities, and most economists believe such opportunities are rare and short-lived.

The argument *against* rational expectations is that it requires households and firms to know too much. This argument says that it is unrealistic to think that these basic decision-making units know as much as they need to know to form rational expectations. People must know the true model (or at least a good approximation of the true model) to form rational expectations, and this knowledge is a lot to expect. Even if firms and households are capable of learning the true model, it may be costly to take the time and gather the relevant information to learn it. The gain from learning the true model (or a good approximation of it) may not be worth the cost. In this sense, there may not be unexploited profit opportunities around. Gathering information and learning economic models may be too costly to bother with, given the expected gain from improving forecasts.

Although the assumption that expectations are rational seems consistent with the satisfaction-maximizing and profit-maximizing postulates of microeconomics, the rational expectations assumption is more extreme and demanding because it requires more information on the part of households and firms. Consider a firm engaged in maximizing profits. In some way or other, it forms expectations of the relevant future variables, and given these expectations, it figures out the best thing to do from the point of view of maximizing profits. Given a set of expectations, the problem of maximizing profits may not be too hard. What may be hard is forming accurate expectations in the first place. This requires firms to know much more about the overall economy than they are likely to, so the assumption that their expectations are rational is not necessarily realistic. Firms, like the rest of us—so the argument goes—grope around in a world that is difficult to understand, trying to do their best but not always understanding enough to avoid mistakes.

In the final analysis, the issue is empirical. Does the assumption of rational expectations stand up well against empirical tests? This question is difficult to answer. Much work is currently being done to answer it. There are no conclusive results yet, although the results discussed in the *Economics in Practice* on p. 344 are not supportive of the rational expectations assumption.

Testing Alternative Macroeconomic Models

You may wonder why there is so much disagreement in macroeconomics. Why can't macroeconomists test their models against one another and see which performs best?

One problem is that macroeconomic models differ in ways that are hard to standardize. If one model takes the price level to be given, or not explained within the model, and another one does not, the model with the given price level may do better in, for instance, predicting output—not because it is a better model but simply because the errors in predicting prices have not been allowed to affect the predictions of output. The model that takes prices as given has a head start, so to speak.

Another problem arises in the testing of the rational expectations assumption. Remember, if people have rational expectations, they are using the true model to form their expectations. Therefore, to test this assumption, we need the true model. There is no way to be sure that whatever model is taken to be the true model is in fact the true one. Any test of the rational expectations hypothesis is therefore a *joint* test: (1) that expectations are formed rationally and (2) that the model being used is the true one. If the test rejects the hypothesis, it may be that the model is wrong rather than that the expectations are not rational.

Another problem for macroeconomists is the small amount of data available. Most empirical work uses data beginning about 1950, which in 2012 was about 63 years' (252 quarters) worth of data. Although this may seem like a lot of data, it is not. Macroeconomic data are fairly "smooth," which means that a typical variable does not vary much from quarter to quarter or from year to year. For example, the number of business cycles within this 61-year period is small, about eight. Testing various macroeconomic hypotheses on the basis of eight business cycle observations is not easy, and any conclusions must be interpreted with caution.

To give an example of the problem of a small number of observations, consider trying to test the hypothesis that import prices affect domestic prices. Import prices changed very little in the 1950s and 1960s. Therefore, it would have been very difficult at the end of the 1960s to estimate the effect of import prices on domestic prices. The variation in import prices was not great enough to show any effects. We cannot demonstrate that changes in import prices help explain changes in domestic prices if import prices do not change. The situation was different by the end of the 1970s because by then, import prices had varied considerably. By the end of the 1970s, there were good estimates of the import price effect, but not before. This kind of problem is encountered again and again in empirical macroeconomics. In many cases, there are not enough observations for much to be said and hence there is considerable room for disagreement.

We said in Chapter 1 that it is difficult in economics to perform controlled experiments. Economists, are for the most part, at the mercy of the historical data. If we were able to perform experiments, we could probably learn more about the economy in a shorter time. Alas, we must wait. In time, the current range of disagreements in macroeconomics should be considerably narrowed.

SUMMARY

KEYNESIAN ECONOMICS *p. 337*

1. In a broad sense, Keynesian economics is the foundation of modern macroeconomics. In a narrower sense, *Keynesian* refers to economists who advocate active government intervention in the economy.

MONETARISM *p. 338*

2. The monetarist analysis of the economy places a great deal of emphasis on the *velocity of money*, which is defined as the number of times a dollar bill changes hands, on average, during the course of a year. The velocity of money is the ratio of nominal GDP to the stock of money, or $V \equiv GDP/M \equiv (P \times Y)/M$. Alternately, $M \times V \equiv P \times Y$.

3. The *quantity theory of money* assumes that velocity is constant (or virtually constant). This implies that changes in the supply of money will lead to equal percentage changes in nominal GDP. The quantity theory of money equation is $M \times \overline{V} = P \times Y$. The equation says that demand for money does not depend on the interest rate.

4. Most monetarists blame most of the instability in the economy on the federal government and are skeptical of the government's ability to manage the macroeconomy. They argue that the money supply should grow at a rate equal to the average growth of real output (income) (Y)—the Fed should expand the money supply to accommodate real growth but not inflation.

SUPPLY-SIDE ECONOMICS *p. 341*

5. *Supply-side economics* focuses on incentives to stimulate supply. Supply-side economists believe that if we lower taxes, workers will work harder and save more and firms will invest more and produce more. At their most extreme, supply-siders argue that incentive effects are likely to be so great that a major cut in taxes will actually increase tax revenues.

6. The *Laffer curve* shows the relationship between tax rates and tax revenues. Supply-side economists use it to argue

that it is possible to generate higher revenues by cutting tax rates. This does not appear to have been the case during the Reagan administration, however, where lower tax rates decreased tax revenues significantly and contributed to the large increase in the federal debt during the 1980s.

NEW CLASSICAL MACROECONOMICS *p. 342*

7. *New classical macroeconomics* uses the assumption of rational expectations. The *rational expectations hypothesis* assumes that people know the "true model" that generates economic variables. For example, rational expectations assumes that people know how inflation is determined in the economy and use this model to forecast future inflation rates.

8. The *Lucas supply function* assumes that real output (Y) depends on the actual price level minus the expected price level, or the *price surprise*. This function combined with the assumption that expectations are rational implies that anticipated policy changes have no effect on real output.

9. *Real business cycle theory* is an attempt to explain business cycle fluctuations under the assumptions of complete price and wage flexibility and rational expectations. It emphasizes shocks to technology and other shocks.

10. *New Keynesian economics* relaxes the assumption of complete price and wage flexibility. There is usually a role for government policy in these models.

TESTING ALTERNATIVE MACROECONOMIC MODELS *p. 347*

11. Economists disagree about which macroeconomic model is best for several reasons: (1) Macroeconomic models differ in ways that are hard to standardize; (2) when testing the rational-expectations assumption, we are never sure that whatever model is taken to be the true model is the true one; and (3) the amount of data available is fairly small.

REVIEW TERMS AND CONCEPTS

Laffer curve, *p. 341*
Lucas supply function, *p. 345*
new Keynesian economics, *p. 346*
price surprise, *p. 345*

quantity theory of money, *p. 338*
rational expectations hypothesis, *p. 343*
real business cycle theory, *p. 346*
velocity of money, *p. 338*

Equations:
$$V \equiv \frac{GDP}{M}, p.\ 338$$
$$M \times V \equiv P \times Y, p.\ 338$$
$$M \times \overline{V} = P \times Y, p.\ 338$$

PROBLEMS

All problems are available on MyEconLab.

1. The table gives estimates of the rate of money supply growth and the rate of real GDP growth for five countries in 2000:

	RATE OF GROWTH IN MONEY SUPPLY (M1)	RATE OF GROWTH OF REAL GDP
Australia	+9.3	+4.4
Britain	+7.6	+4.4
Canada	+18.7	+4.9
Japan	+9.0	+0.7
United States	+0.2	+5.1

   a. If you were a monetarist, what would you predict about the rate of inflation across the five countries?

   b. If you were a Keynesian and assuming activist central banks, how might you interpret the same data?

2. The three diagrams in Figure 1 represent in a simplified way the predictions of the three theories presented in this chapter about the likely effects of a major tax cut.

   a. Match each of the following theories with a graph: (1) Keynesian economics, (2) supply-side economics, (3) rational expectations/monetarism. Explain the logic behind the three graphs.

   b. Which theory do you find most convincing? Explain.

3. [Related to the *Economics in Practice* on p. 344] Suppose you are thinking about where to live after you finish your degree. You discover that an apartment building near your new job has identical units—one is for rent and the other for sale as a condominium. Given your salary, both are affordable and you like them. Would you buy or rent? How would you go about deciding? Would your expectations play a role? Be specific. Where do you think those expectations come from? In what ways could expectations change things in the housing market as a whole?

4. In 2000, a well-known economist was heard to say, "The problem with supply-side economics is that when you cut taxes, they have both supply and demand side effects and you cannot separate the effects." Explain this comment. Be specific and use the 1997 tax cuts or the Reagan tax cuts of 1981 as an example.

5. A cornerstone of new classical economics is the notion that expectations are "rational." What do you think will happen to the prices of single-family homes in your community over the next several years? On what do you base your expectations? Is your thinking consistent with the notion of rational expectations? Explain.

6. You are a monetarist given the following information: The money supply is $1,000. The velocity of money is 5. What is nominal income? real income? What happens to nominal income if the money supply is doubled? What happens to real income?

7. When Bill Clinton took office in January 1993, he faced two major economic problems: a large federal budget deficit and high unemployment resulting from a very slow recovery from the recession of 1990 to 1991. In his first State of the Union message, the president called for spending cuts and substantial tax increases to reduce the deficit. Most of these proposed spending cuts were in the defense budget. The following day Alan Greenspan, chair of the Federal Reserve Board of Governors, signaled his support for the president's plan. Many elements of the president's original plan were later incorporated into the deficit reduction bill passed in 1993.

   a. Some said at the time that without the Fed's support, the Clinton plan would be a disaster. Explain this argument.

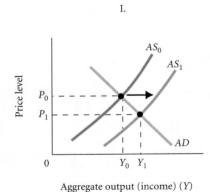
I.

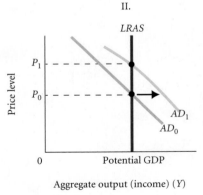
II.

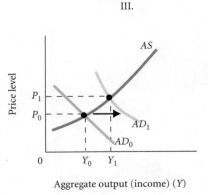
III.

▲ **FIGURE 1**

b. Supply-side economists and monetarists were very worried about the plan and the support it received from the Fed. What specific problems might a monetarist and a supply-side economist worry about?

c. Suppose you were hired by the Federal Reserve Bank of St. Louis to report on the events of 1995 and 1996. What specific evidence would you look for to see whether the Clinton plan was effective or whether the critics were right to be skeptical?

8. In an economy with reasonably flexible prices and wages, full employment is almost always maintained. Explain why that statement is true.

9. During the 1980 presidential campaign, Ronald Reagan promised to cut taxes, increase expenditures on national defense, and balance the budget. During the New Hampshire primary of 1980, George Bush called this policy "voodoo economics." The two men were arguing about the relative merits of supply-side economics. Explain their disagreement.

10. In a hypothetical economy, there is a simple proportional tax on wages imposed at a rate t. There are plenty of jobs around, so if people enter the labor force, they can find work. We define total government receipts from the tax as

$$T = t \times W \times L$$

where t = the tax rate, W = the gross wage rate, and L = the total supply of labor. The net wage rate is

$$W_n = (1 - t) W$$

The elasticity of labor supply is defined as

$$\frac{\text{Percentage of change in } L}{\text{Percentage of change in } W_n} = \frac{\Delta L / \Delta L}{\Delta W_n / W_n}$$

Suppose t was cut from .25 to .20. For such a cut to *increase* total government receipts from the tax, how elastic must the supply of labor be? (Assume a constant gross wage.) What does your answer imply about the supply-side assertion that a cut in taxes can increase tax revenues?

11. The following is data from 2012 for the tiny island nation of Papaya: money supply = 600 million; price level = 2.5; velocity of money = 4. Use the quantity theory of money to answer the following questions.

a. What is the value of real output (income) in 2012?

b. What is the value of nominal GDP in 2012?

c. If real output doubled, by how much would the money supply need to change?

d. If velocity is constant and Papaya was experiencing a recession in 2012, what impact would an easy money policy have on nominal GDP?

e. If the annual GDP growth rate is 8 percent in Papaya, by how much will the money supply need to change in 2013?

12. In the nation of Lower Vicuna, the velocity of money is fairly constant, and in the nation of Upper Vicuna, the velocity of money fluctuates greatly. For which nation would the quantity theory of money better explain changes in nominal GDP? Explain.

13. The economy of Carmona is represented by the following Lucas supply function: $Y = 600 + 40(P - P^e)$. The current price level in Carmona is 1.8, and the expected price level is 1.95.

a. What will be the new level of real output if inflation expectations are correct?

b. What will be the new level of real output if inflation expectations are wrong and the actual price level rises to 2.0?

c. What will be the new level of real output if the actual price level does not change?

d. What is the value of the "price surprise" in parts a, b, and c?

14. If households and firms have rational expectations, is it possible for the unemployment rate to exceed the natural rate of unemployment? Explain.

15. Assume people and firms have rational expectations. Explain how each of the following events will affect aggregate output and the price level.

a. The Fed unexpectedly decreases the required reserve ratio.

b. Congress passes a tax reduction bill which will go into effect in one year and last for ten years.

c. The Fed announces it will decrease the supply of money.

d. Without notice, OPEC cuts oil production by 50 percent.

e. The government passes a previously unannounced emergency defense spending bill, authorizing an immediate $500 billion increase in funding.

*Note: Problems marked with an asterisk are more challenging.

International Trade, Comparative Advantage, and Protectionism

19

Over the last 42 years, international transactions have become increasingly important to the U.S. economy. In 1970, imports represented only about 5.4 percent of U.S. gross domestic product (GDP). The share in 2012 was 17.7 percent. In 2010, the United States imported about $220 billion worth of goods and services each month. The increased trade we observe in the United States is mirrored throughout the world. From 1980 to 2012, world trade in real terms grew more than six-fold. This trend has been especially rapid in the newly industrialized Asian economies, but many developing countries such as Malaysia and Vietnam have been increasing their openness to trade.

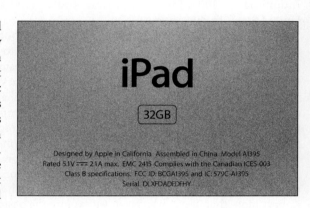

The "internationalization" or "globalization" of the U.S. economy has occurred in the private and public sectors, in input and output markets, and in firms and households. Once uncommon, foreign products are now everywhere, from the utensils we eat with to the cars we drive. Chinese textiles and Indian software are commonplace. It might surprise you to learn that many of the cut flowers sold in the United States are grown in Africa and South America. In fact, most products today are made in a number of countries. Back in Chapter 1, we presented an *Economics in Practice* that described the production of Apple's iPod. An iPod contains 451 parts made in countries scattered around the world including Korea, Japan, China, and the United States. The bottom of the iPod has the following information: "Designed by Apple in California, Assembled in China." Suzuki makes cars in Hungary and employs workers from Romania and Slovakia. Honda started producing Japanese motorcycles in Ohio in 1977 with 64 employees in Marysville. The company now employs almost 12,000 workers who assemble Honda automobiles in four different locations in Ohio.

LEARNING OBJECTIVES

Differentiate between comparative advantage and absolute advantage in international trade

Discuss how terms of trade and exchange rates affect international trade

Describe the sources of comparative advantage

Analyze the economic effects of trade barriers

Evaluate the arguments over free trade and protectionism

TABLE 19.1
U.S. Balance of Trade (Exports Minus Imports), 1929–2012 (Billions of Current Dollars)

	Exports Minus Imports
1929	+0.4
1933	+0.1
1945	−0.8
1955	+0.5
1960	+4.2
1965	+5.6
1970	+4.0
1975	+16.0
1976	−1.6
1977	−23.1
1978	−25.4
1979	−22.5
1980	−13.1
1981	−12.5
1982	−20.0
1983	−51.7
1984	−102.7
1985	−115.2
1986	−132.5
1987	−145.0
1988	−110.1
1989	−87.9
1990	−77.6
1991	−27.0
1992	−32.8
1993	−64.4
1994	−92.7
1995	−90.7
1996	−96.3
1997	−101.4
1998	−161.8
1999	−262.1
2000	−382.1
2001	−371.0
2002	−427.2
2003	−504.1
2004	−618.7
2005	−722.7
2006	−769.3
2007	−713.1
2008	−709.7
2009	−388.7
2010	−511.6
2011	−568.1
2012	−566.7

Source: U.S. Bureau of Economic Analysis.

trade surplus The situation when a country exports more than it imports.

trade deficit The situation when a country imports more than it exports.

At the same time, the United States exports billions of dollars' worth of agricultural goods, aircraft, and industrial machinery. Korea imports substantial amounts of U.S. beef. In addition, the United States exports and imports large quantities of services. When a Pakistani student enrolls in an American college or university, or a sick woman from Chile seeks medical attention in a U.S. hospital, or a Kenyan hires a lawyer in Miami to help him with a real estate deal, or a tourist from Indonesia eats at a restaurant in New York City, the United States is exporting a service. Similarly, when a student from the United States takes her junior year abroad in Scotland, or a tourist stays in a hotel in Singapore or gets a massage at a spa in Jamaica, the United States is importing a service.

Nor are the patterns of trade that we observe in one period set in stone. Consider the case of textiles and apparel. As recently as 2000, Mexico was the major supplier to the United States of textiles and apparel with almost 15 percent of total U.S. imports in this category. By 2006, China had overtaken Mexico's lead with 29 percent of the share of U.S. textile and apparel imports. The Dominican Republic and Honduras, which had been the fourth and fifth largest sources of U.S. imports, respectively, had been replaced by Bangladesh and Indonesia. In 2004, for the first time, India became one of the top five exporters to the United States in this category.

In addition to the fact that goods and services (outputs) flow easily across borders, so too do inputs: capital and labor. Certainly, it is very easy to buy financial assets abroad. Millions of Americans own shares in foreign stocks or have invested in bonds issued by foreign countries. At the same time, millions of foreigners have put money into the U.S. stock and bond markets.

Outsourcing is also changing the nature of the global labor market. It is now simple and very common for a customer service call to a software company from a user of its product in Bend, Oregon, to be routed to Bangalore, India, where a young, ambitious Indian man or woman provides assistance to a customer over the Internet. The Internet has in essence made it possible for some types of labor to flow smoothly across international borders.

To get you more acquainted with the international economy, this chapter discusses the economics of international trade. First, we describe the recent tendency of the United States to import more than it exports. Next, we explore the basic logic of trade. Why should the United States or any other country engage in international trade? Finally, we address the controversial issue of protectionism. Should a country provide certain industries with protection in the form of import quotas or tariffs, which are taxes imposed on imports? Should a country help a domestic industry compete in international markets by providing subsidies?

Trade Surpluses and Deficits

Until the 1970s, the United States generally exported more than it imported. When a country exports more than it imports, it runs a **trade surplus**. When a country imports more than it exports, it runs a **trade deficit**. Table 19.1 shows that before 1976 the United States generally ran a trade surplus. This changed in 1976, and since 1976 the United States has run a trade deficit. The deficit reached a local peak of $145.0 billion in 1987, fell to $27.0 billion in 1991, and then rose dramatically to over $700 billion by 2005. In 2012 it was $566.7 billion.

The large trade deficits in the middle and late 1980s sparked political controversy that continues today. Foreign competition hit U.S. markets hard. Less expensive foreign goods— among them steel, textiles, and automobiles—began driving U.S. manufacturers out of business, and thousands of jobs were lost in important industries. Cities such as Pittsburgh, Youngstown, and Detroit had major unemployment problems. In more recent times, the outsourcing of software development to India has caused complaints from white-collar workers.

The natural reaction to trade-related job dislocation is to call for protection of U.S. industries. Many people want the president and Congress to impose taxes and import restrictions that would make foreign goods less available and more expensive, protecting U.S. jobs. This argument is not new. For hundreds of years, industries have petitioned governments for protection and societies have debated the pros and cons of free and open trade. For the last century and a half, the principal argument against protection has been the theory of comparative advantage, first discussed in Chapter 2.

The Economic Basis for Trade: Comparative Advantage

Perhaps the best-known debate on the issue of free trade took place in the British Parliament during the early years of the nineteenth century. At that time, the landed gentry—the landowners—controlled Parliament. For a number of years, imports and exports of grain had been subject to a set of tariffs, subsidies, and restrictions collectively called the **Corn Laws**. Designed to discourage imports of grain and to encourage exports, the Corn Laws' purpose was to keep the price of food high. The landlords' incomes, of course, depended on the prices they got for what their land produced. The Corn Laws clearly worked to the advantage of those in power.

With the Industrial Revolution, a class of wealthy industrial capitalists emerged. The industrial sector had to pay workers at least enough to live on, and a living wage depended greatly on the price of food. Tariffs on grain imports and export subsidies that kept grain and food prices high increased the wages that capitalists had to pay, cutting into their profits. The political battle raged for years. However, as time went by, the power of the landowners in the House of Lords was significantly reduced. When the conflict ended in 1848, the Corn Laws were repealed.

On the side of repeal was David Ricardo, a businessman, economist, member of Parliament, and one of the fathers of modern economics. Ricardo's principal work, *Principles of Political Economy and Taxation*, was published in 1817, two years before he entered Parliament. Ricardo's **theory of comparative advantage**, which he used to argue against the Corn Laws, claimed that trade enables countries to specialize in producing the products they produce best. According to the theory specialization and free trade will benefit all trading partners (real wages will rise), even those that may be absolutely less efficient producers. This basic argument remains at the heart of free-trade debates even today, as policy makers argue about the effects of tariffs on agricultural development in sub-Saharan Africa and the gains and losses from outsourcing software development to India.

The easiest way to understand the theory of comparative advantage is to examine a simple two-person society. Suppose Bill and Colleen, stranded on a deserted island in Chapter 2, have only two tasks to accomplish each week: gathering food to eat and cutting logs to construct a house. If Colleen could cut more logs than Bill in a day and Bill could gather more berries and fruits, specialization would clearly benefit both of them.

But suppose Bill is slow and clumsy and Colleen is better at cutting logs *and* gathering food. Ricardo's point is that it still pays for them to specialize. They can produce more in total by specializing than they can by sharing the work equally. We now turn to look at the application of the powerful idea of comparative advantage to international trade.

Corn Laws The tariffs, subsidies, and restrictions enacted by the British Parliament in the early nineteenth century to discourage imports and encourage exports of grain.

theory of comparative advantage Ricardo's theory that specialization and free trade will benefit all trading partners (real wages will rise), even those that may be absolutely less efficient producers.

Absolute Advantage versus Comparative Advantage

A country enjoys an **absolute advantage** over another country in the production of a good if it uses fewer resources to produce that good than the other country does. Suppose country A and country B produce wheat, but A's climate is more suited to wheat and its labor is more productive. Country A will produce more wheat per acre than country B and use less labor in growing it and bringing it to market. Country A enjoys an absolute advantage over country B in the production of wheat.

A country enjoys a **comparative advantage** in the production of a good if that good can be produced at lower cost *in terms of other goods*. Suppose countries C and D both produce wheat and corn and C enjoys an absolute advantage in the production of both—that is, C's climate is better than D's and fewer of C's resources are needed to produce a given quantity of both wheat and corn. Now C and D must each choose between planting land with either wheat or corn. To produce more wheat, either country must transfer land from corn production; to produce more corn, either country must transfer land from wheat production. The cost of wheat in each country can be measured in bushels of corn, and the cost of corn can be measured in bushels of wheat.

Suppose that in country C, a bushel of wheat has an opportunity cost of 2 bushels of corn. That is, to produce an additional bushel of wheat, C must give up 2 bushels of corn. At the same time, producing a bushel of wheat in country D requires the sacrifice of only 1 bushel of corn. Even though C has an *absolute* advantage in the production of both products, D enjoys a *comparative* advantage in the production of wheat because the *opportunity cost* of producing wheat is lower in D. Under these circumstances, Ricardo claims, D can benefit from trade if it specializes in the production of wheat.

absolute advantage The advantage in the production of a good enjoyed by one country over another when it uses fewer resources to produce that good than the other country does.

comparative advantage The advantage in the production of a good enjoyed by one country over another when that good can be produced at lower cost in terms of other goods than it could be in the other country.

Gains from Mutual Absolute Advantage   To illustrate Ricardo's logic in more detail, suppose Australia and New Zealand each have a fixed amount of land and do not trade with the rest of the world. There are only two goods—wheat to produce bread and cotton to produce clothing. This kind of two-country/two-good world does not exist, but its operations can be generalized to many countries and many goods.

To proceed, we have to make some assumptions about the preferences of the people living in New Zealand and the people living in Australia. If the citizens of both countries walk around naked, there is no need to produce cotton, so all the land can be used to produce wheat. However, assume that people in both countries have similar preferences with respect to food and clothing: The populations of both countries use both cotton and wheat, and preferences for food and clothing are such that both countries consume equal amounts of wheat and cotton.

Finally, we assume that each country has only 100 acres of land for planting and that land yields are as given in Table 19.2. New Zealand can produce 3 times the wheat that Australia can on 1 acre of land, and Australia can produce 3 times the cotton that New Zealand can in the same space. New Zealand has an absolute advantage in the production of wheat, and Australia has an absolute advantage in the production of cotton. In cases like this, we say the two countries have *mutual absolute advantage*.

If there is no trade and each country divides its land to obtain equal units of cotton and wheat production, each country produces 150 bushels of wheat and 150 bales of cotton. New Zealand puts 75 acres into cotton but only 25 acres into wheat, while Australia does the reverse (Table 19.3).

We can organize the same information in graphic form as production possibility frontiers for each country. In Figure 19.1, which presents the positions of the two countries before trade, each country is constrained by its own resources and productivity. If Australia put all its land into cotton, it would produce 600 bales of cotton (100 acres $\times$ 6 bales/acre) and no wheat; if it put all its land into wheat, it would produce 200 bushels of wheat (100 acres $\times$ 2 bushels/acre) and no cotton. The opposite is true for New Zealand. Recall from Chapter 2 that a country's production possibility frontier represents all combinations of goods that can be produced, given the country's resources and state of technology. Each country must pick a point along its own production possibility curve.

When both countries have an absolute advantage in the production of one product, it is easy to see that specialization and trade will benefit both. Australia should produce cotton, and New Zealand should produce wheat. Transferring all land to wheat production in New Zealand yields 600 bushels, while transferring all land to cotton production in Australia yields 600 bales. An agreement to trade 300 bushels of wheat for 300 bales of cotton would double both wheat and cotton consumption in both countries. (Remember, before trade, both countries produced 150 bushels of wheat and 150 bales of cotton. After trade, each country will have 300 bushels of wheat and 300 bales of cotton to consume. Final production and trade figures are provided in Table 19.4 and Figure 19.2.) Trade enables both countries to move beyond their previous resource and productivity constraints.

The advantages of specialization and trade seem obvious when one country is technologically superior at producing one product and another country is technologically superior at producing another product. However, let us turn to the case in which one country has an absolute advantage in the production of *both* goods.

TABLE 19.2 Yield per Acre of Wheat and Cotton

	New Zealand	Australia
Wheat	6 bushels	2 bushels
Cotton	2 bales	6 bales

TABLE 19.3 Total Production of Wheat and Cotton Assuming No Trade, Mutual Absolute Advantage, and 100 Available Acres

	New Zealand	Australia
Wheat	25 acres $\times$ 6 bushels/acre = 150 bushels	75 acres $\times$ 2 bushels/acre = 150 bushels
Cotton	75 acres $\times$ 2 bales/acre = 150 bales	25 acres $\times$ 6 bales/acre = 150 bales

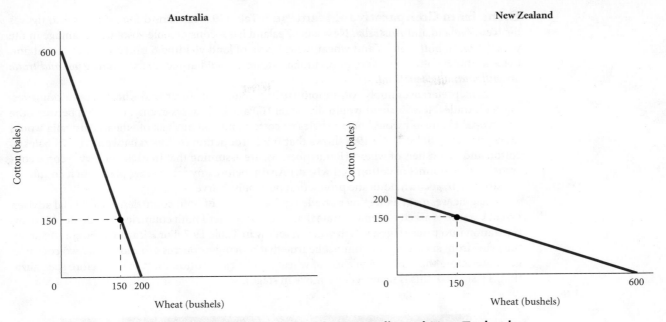

▲ FIGURE 19.1   **Production Possibility Frontiers for Australia and New Zealand Before Trade**

Without trade, countries are constrained by their own resources and productivity.

TABLE 19.4 Production and Consumption of Wheat and Cotton After Specialization

	Production		Consumption	
	New Zealand	Australia		New Zealand	Australia
Wheat	100 acres ✕ 6 bushels/acre 600 bushels	0 acres 0	Wheat	300 bushels	300 bushels
Cotton	0 acres 0	100 acres ✕ 6 bales/acre 600 bales	Cotton	300 bales	300 bales

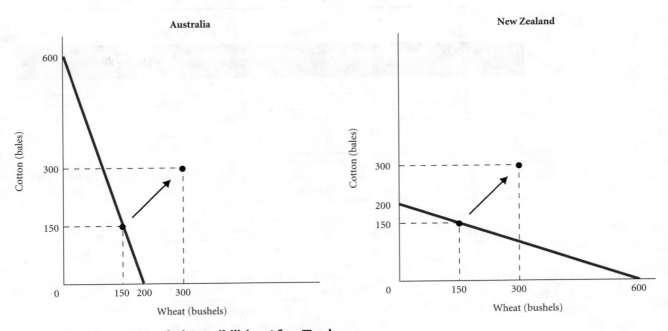

▲ FIGURE 19.2   **Expanded Possibilities After Trade**

Trade enables both countries to move beyond their own resource constraints—beyond their individual production possibility frontiers.

Gains from Comparative Advantage   Table 19.5 contains different land yield figures for New Zealand and Australia. Now New Zealand has a considerable absolute advantage in the production of both cotton and wheat, with 1 acre of land yielding 6 times as much wheat and twice as much cotton as 1 acre in Australia. Ricardo would argue that *specialization and trade are still mutually beneficial.*

Again, preferences imply consumption of equal units of cotton and wheat in both countries. With no trade, New Zealand would divide its 100 available acres evenly, or 50/50, between the two crops. The result would be 300 bales of cotton and 300 bushels of wheat. Australia would divide its land 75/25. Table 19.6 shows that final production in Australia would be 75 bales of cotton and 75 bushels of wheat. (Remember, we are assuming that in each country, people consume equal amounts of cotton and wheat.) Again, before any trade takes place, each country is constrained by its own domestic production possibility curve.

Imagine we are at a meeting of trade representatives of both countries. As a special adviser, David Ricardo is asked to demonstrate that trade can benefit both countries. He divides his demonstration into three stages, which you can follow in Table 19.7. For Ricardo to be correct about the gains from specialization, it must be true that moving resources around in the two countries generates more than the 375 bushels of wheat and bales of cotton that we had before specialization. To see how this is managed, we move in stages.

TABLE 19.5 Yield per Acre of Wheat and Cotton

	New Zealand	Australia
Wheat	6 bushels	1 bushel
Cotton	6 bales	3 bales

TABLE 19.6 Total Production of Wheat and Cotton Assuming No Trade and 100 Available Acres

	New Zealand	Australia
Wheat	50 acres × 6 bushels/acre 300 bushels	75 acres × 1 bushel/acre 75 bushels
Cotton	50 acres × 6 bales/acre 300 bales	25 acres × 3 bales/acre 75 bales

TABLE 19.7 Realizing a Gain from Trade When One Country Has a Double Absolute Advantage

	STAGE 1			STAGE 2	
	New Zealand	Australia		New Zealand	Australia
Wheat	50 acres × 6 bushels/acre 300 bushels	0 acres 0	Wheat	75 acres × 6 bushels/acre 450 bushels	0 acres 0
Cotton	50 acres × 6 bales/acre 300 bales	100 acres × 3 bales/acre 300 bales	Cotton	25 acres × 6 bales/acre 150 bales	100 acres × 3 bales/acre 300 bales

STAGE 3		
	New Zealand	Australia
Wheat	100 bushels (trade) → 350 bushels (after trade)	100 bushels
Cotton	200 bales (trade) ← 350 bales (after trade)	100 bales

In Stage 1, let Australia move all its land into cotton production, where it is least disadvantaged. Australia would then produce 300 bales of cotton, as we see in Stage 1 of Table 19.7. Now the question is whether Ricardo can help us use New Zealand's land to add at least 75 bales of cotton to the total while producing more than the original 375 bushels of wheat. In Stage 2, Ricardo tells New Zealand to use 25 acres to produce cotton and 75 acres for wheat production. With that allocation of land, New Zealand produces 450 bushels of wheat (far more than the total produced in the nonspecialization case by both countries) and 150 bales of cotton, leaving us with 450 bales of cotton as well. Specialization has increased the world production of both wheat and cotton by 75 units! With trade, which we show in Stage 3 for the case in which both countries prefer equal consumption of the two goods, both countries can be better off than they were earlier.

Why Does Ricardo's Plan Work?   To understand why Ricardo's scheme works, let us return to the definition of comparative advantage.

The real cost of producing cotton is the wheat that must be sacrificed to produce it. *When we think of cost this way, it is less costly to produce cotton in Australia than to produce it in New Zealand, even though an acre of land produces more cotton in New Zealand.* Consider the "cost" of 3 bales of cotton in the two countries. In terms of opportunity cost, 3 bales of cotton in New Zealand cost 3 bushels of wheat; in Australia, 3 bales of cotton cost only 1 bushel of wheat. Because 3 bales are produced by 1 acre of Australian land, to get 3 bales, an Australian must transfer 1 acre of land from wheat to cotton production. Because an acre of land produces a bushel of wheat, losing 1 acre to cotton implies the loss of 1 bushel of wheat. *Australia has a comparative advantage in cotton production* because its opportunity cost, in terms of wheat, is lower than New Zealand's. This is illustrated in Figure 19.3.

Conversely, New Zealand has a comparative advantage in wheat production. A unit of wheat in New Zealand costs 1 unit of cotton, while a unit of wheat in Australia costs 3 units of cotton. When countries specialize in producing goods in which they have a comparative advantage, they maximize their combined output and allocate their resources more efficiently.

Terms of Trade

Ricardo might suggest a number of options for exchanging wheat and cotton to the trading partners. The one we just examined benefited both partners; in percentage terms, Australia made out slightly better. Other deals might have been more advantageous to New Zealand.

The ratio at which a country can trade domestic products for imported products is the **terms of trade**. The terms of trade determine how the gains from trade are distributed among trading partners. In the case just considered, the agreed-to terms of trade were 1 bushel of wheat for 2 bales of cotton. Such terms of trade benefit New Zealand, which can get 2 bales of cotton for each bushel of wheat. If it were to transfer its own land from wheat to cotton, it would get only 1 bale of cotton. The same terms of trade benefit Australia, which can get 1 bushel of wheat for 2 bales of cotton. A direct transfer of its own land would force it to give up 3 bales of cotton for 1 bushel of wheat.

terms of trade The ratio at which a country can trade domestic products for imported products.

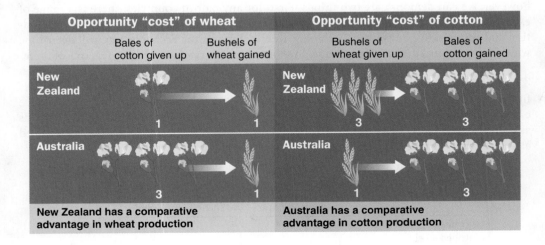

Opportunity "cost" of wheat		Opportunity "cost" of cotton	
Bales of cotton given up	Bushels of wheat gained	Bushels of wheat given up	Bales of cotton gained
New Zealand 1	1	**New Zealand** 3	3
Australia 3	1	**Australia** 1	3
New Zealand has a comparative advantage in wheat production		**Australia has a comparative advantage in cotton production**	

◀ FIGURE 19.3
Comparative Advantage Means Lower Opportunity Cost
The real cost of cotton is the wheat sacrificed to obtain it. The cost of 3 bales of cotton in New Zealand is 3 bushels of wheat (a half acre of land must be transferred from wheat to cotton—refer to Table 19.5). However, the cost of 3 bales of cotton in Australia is only 1 bushel of wheat. Australia has a comparative advantage over New Zealand in cotton production, and New Zealand has a comparative advantage over Australia in wheat production.

If the terms of trade changed to 3 bales of cotton for every bushel of wheat, only New Zealand would benefit. At those terms of trade, *all* the gains from trade would flow to New Zealand. Such terms do not benefit Australia at all because the opportunity cost of producing wheat domestically is *exactly the same* as the trade cost: A bushel of wheat costs 3 bales of cotton. If the terms of trade went the other way—1 bale of cotton for each bushel of wheat—only Australia would benefit. New Zealand gains nothing because it can already substitute cotton for wheat at that ratio. To get a bushel of wheat domestically, however, Australia must give up 3 bales of cotton, and one-for-one terms of trade would make wheat much less costly for Australia.

Both parties must have something to gain for trade to take place. In this case, you can see that both Australia and New Zealand will gain when the terms of trade are set between 1:1 and 3:1, cotton to wheat.

Exchange Rates

The examples used thus far have shown that trade can result in gains to both parties. When trade is free—unimpeded by government-instituted barriers—patterns of trade and trade flows result from the independent decisions of thousands of importers and exporters and millions of private households and firms.

Private households decide whether to buy Toyotas or Chevrolets, and private firms decide whether to buy machine tools made in the United States or machine tools made in Taiwan, raw steel produced in Germany or raw steel produced in Pittsburgh.

But how does this trade actually come about? Before a citizen of one country can buy a product made in another country or sold by someone in another country, a currency swap must take place. Consider Shane, who buys a Toyota built in Japan from a dealer in Boston. He pays in dollars, but the Japanese workers who made the car receive their salaries in yen. Somewhere between the buyer of the car and the producer, a currency exchange must be made. The regional distributor probably takes payment in dollars and converts them into yen before remitting the proceeds to Japan.

To buy a foreign-produced good, a consumer, or an intermediary, has to buy foreign currency. The price of Shane's Toyota in dollars depends on the price of the car stated in yen and the dollar price of yen. You probably know the ins and outs of currency exchange very well if you have ever traveled in another country.

In February 2013, the British pound was worth $1.57. Now suppose you are in London having dinner. On the menu is a nice bottle of wine for 15 pounds. How can you figure out whether you want to buy it? You know what dollars will buy in the United States, so you have to convert the price into dollars. Each pound will cost you $1.57, so 15 pounds will cost you $1.57 \times 15 = $23.55.

exchange rate The ratio at which two currencies are traded. The price of one currency in terms of another.

The attractiveness of foreign goods to U.S. buyers and of U.S. goods to foreign buyers depends in part on the **exchange rate**, the ratio at which two currencies are traded. In May 2008, the British pound was worth $1.97, and that same bottle of wine would have cost $29.55.

To understand the patterns of trade that result from the actions of hundreds of thousands of independent buyers and sellers—households and firms—we must know something about the factors that determine exchange rates. Exchange rate determination is very complicated. Here, however, we can demonstrate two things. First, for any pair of countries, there is a range of exchange rates that can lead automatically to both countries' realizing the gains from specialization and comparative advantage. Second, within that range, the exchange rate will determine which country gains the most from trade. In short, exchange rates determine the terms of trade.

Trade and Exchange Rates in a Two-Country/Two-Good World   Consider first a simple two-country/two-good model. Suppose both the United States and Brazil produce only two goods—raw timber and rolled steel. Table 19.8 gives the current prices of both goods as domestic buyers see them. In Brazil, timber is priced at 3 reals (R) per foot and steel is priced at 4 R per meter. In the United States, timber costs $1 per foot and steel costs $2 per meter.

TABLE 19.8 Domestic Prices of Timber (per Foot) and Rolled Steel (per Meter) in the United States and Brazil		
	United States	Brazil
Timber	$1	3 Reals
Rolled steel	$2	4 Reals

Suppose U.S. and Brazilian buyers have the option of buying at home or importing to meet their needs. The options they choose will depend on the exchange rate. For the time being, we will ignore transportation costs between countries and assume that Brazilian and U.S. products are of equal quality.

Let us start with the assumption that the exchange rate is $1 = 1 R. From the standpoint of U.S. buyers, neither Brazilian steel nor Brazilian timber is competitive at this exchange rate. A dollar buys a foot of timber in the United States, but if converted into a real, it will buy only one-third of a foot. The price of Brazilian timber to an American is $3 because it will take $3 to buy the necessary 3 R. Similarly, $2 buys a meter of rolled steel in the United States, but the same $2 buys only half a meter of Brazilian steel. The price of Brazilian steel to an American is $4, twice the price of domestically produced steel.

At this exchange rate, however, Brazilians find that U.S.-produced steel and timber are less expensive than steel and timber produced in Brazil. Timber at home—Brazil—costs 3 R, but 3 R buys $3, which buys 3 times as much timber in the United States. Similarly, steel costs 4 R at home, but 4 R buys $4, which buys twice as much U.S.-made steel. At an exchange rate of $1 = 1 R, Brazil will import steel and timber and the United States will import nothing.

However, now suppose the exchange rate is 1 R = $0.25. This means that 1 dollar buys 4 R. At this exchange rate, the Brazilians buy timber and steel at home and the Americans import both goods. At this exchange rate, Americans must pay a dollar for a foot of U.S. timber, but the same amount of timber can be had in Brazil for the equivalent of $0.75. (Because 1 R costs $0.25, 3 R can be purchased for $0.75.) Similarly, steel that costs $2 per meter in the United States costs an American half as much in Brazil because $2 buys 8 R, which buys 2 meters of Brazilian steel. At the same time, Brazilians are not interested in importing because both goods are cheaper when purchased from a Brazilian producer. In this case, the United States imports both goods and Brazil imports nothing.

So far we can see that at exchange rates of $1 = 1 R and $1 = 4 R, we get trade flowing in only one direction. Let us now try an exchange rate of $1 = 2 R, or 1 R = $0.50. First, Brazilians will buy timber in the United States. Brazilian timber costs 3 R per foot, but 3 R buys $1.50, which is enough to buy 1.5 feet of U.S. timber. Buyers in the United States will find Brazilian timber too expensive, but Brazil will import timber from the United States. At this same exchange rate, however, both Brazilian and U.S. buyers will be indifferent between Brazilian and U.S. steel. To U.S. buyers, domestically produced steel costs $2. Because $2 buys 4 R, a meter of imported Brazilian steel also costs $2. Brazilian buyers also find that steel costs 4 R, whether domestically produced or imported. Thus, there is likely to be no trade in steel.

What happens if the exchange rate changes so that $1 buys 2.1 R? While U.S. timber is still cheaper to both Brazilians and Americans, Brazilian steel begins to look good to U.S. buyers. Steel produced in the United States costs $2 per meter, but $2 buys 4.2 R, which buys more than a meter of steel in Brazil. When $1 buys more than 2 R, trade begins to flow in both directions: Brazil will import timber, and the United States will import steel.

If you examine Table 19.9 carefully, you will see that trade flows in both directions as long as the exchange rate settles between $1 = 2 R and $1 = 3 R. Stated the other way around, trade will flow in both directions if the price of a real is between $0.33 and $0.50.

Exchange Rates and Comparative Advantage If the foreign exchange market drives the exchange rate to anywhere between 2 and 3 R per dollar, the countries will automatically adjust and comparative advantage will be realized. At these exchange rates, U.S. buyers begin buying all their steel in Brazil. The U.S. steel industry finds itself in trouble. Plants close,

TABLE 19.9 Trade Flows Determined by Exchange Rates		
Exchange Rate	Price of Real	Result
$1 = 1 R	$ 1.00	Brazil imports timber and steel.
$1 = 2 R	.50	Brazil imports timber.
$1 = 2.1 R	.48	Brazil imports timber; United States imports steel.
$1 = 2.9 R	.34	Brazil imports timber; United States imports steel.
$1 = 3 R	.33	United States imports steel.
$1 = 4 R	.25	United States imports timber and steel.

and U.S. workers begin to lobby for tariff protection against Brazilian steel. At the same time, the U.S. timber industry does well, fueled by strong export demand from Brazil. The timber-producing sector expands. Resources, including capital and labor, are attracted into timber production.

The opposite occurs in Brazil. The Brazilian timber industry suffers losses as export demand dries up and Brazilians turn to cheaper U.S. imports. In Brazil, lumber companies turn to the government and ask for protection from cheap U.S. timber. However, steel producers in Brazil are happy. They are not only supplying 100 percent of the domestically demanded steel but also selling to U.S. buyers. The steel industry expands, and the timber industry contracts. Resources, including labor, flow into steel.

With this expansion-and-contraction scenario in mind, let us look again at our original definition of comparative advantage. If we assume that prices reflect resource use and resources can be transferred from sector to sector, we can calculate the opportunity cost of steel/timber in both countries. In the United States, the production of a meter of rolled steel consumes twice the resources that the production of a foot of timber consumes. Assuming that resources can be transferred, the opportunity cost of a meter of steel is 2 feet of timber (Table 19.8). In Brazil, a meter of steel uses resources costing 4 R, while a unit of timber costs 3 R. To produce a meter of steel means the sacrifice of only four-thirds (or one and one-third) feet of timber. Because the opportunity cost of a meter of steel (in terms of timber) is lower in Brazil, we say that Brazil has a comparative advantage in steel production.

Conversely, consider the opportunity cost of timber in the two countries. Increasing timber production in the United States requires the sacrifice of half a meter of steel for every foot of timber—producing a meter of steel uses $2 worth of resources, while producing a foot of timber requires only $1 worth of resources. Nevertheless, each foot of timber production in Brazil requires the sacrifice of three-fourths of a meter of steel. Because the opportunity cost of timber is lower in the United States, the United States has a comparative advantage in the production of timber. If exchange rates end up in the right ranges, the free market will drive each country to shift resources into those sectors in which it enjoys a comparative advantage. Only in a country with a comparative advantage will those products be competitive in world markets.

The Sources of Comparative Advantage

Specialization and trade can benefit all trading partners, even those that may be inefficient producers in an absolute sense. If markets are competitive and if foreign exchange markets are linked to goods-and-services exchange, countries will specialize in producing products in which they have a comparative advantage.

So far, we have said nothing about the sources of comparative advantage. What determines whether a country has a comparative advantage in heavy manufacturing or in agriculture? What explains the actual trade flows observed around the world? Various theories and empirical work on international trade have provided some answers. Most economists look to **factor endowments**—the quantity and quality of labor, land, and natural resources of a country—as the principal sources of comparative advantage. Factor endowments seem to explain a significant portion of actual world trade patterns.

The Heckscher-Ohlin Theorem

Eli Heckscher and Bertil Ohlin, two Swedish economists who wrote in the first half of the twentieth century, expanded and elaborated on Ricardo's theory of comparative advantage. The **Heckscher-Ohlin theorem** ties the theory of comparative advantage to factor endowments. It assumes that products can be produced using differing proportions of inputs and that inputs are mobile between sectors in each economy, but that factors are not mobile *between* economies. According to this theorem, a country has a comparative advantage in the production of a product if that country is relatively well endowed with inputs used intensively in the production of that product.

This idea is simple. A country with a great deal of good fertile land is likely to have a comparative advantage in agriculture. A country with a large amount of accumulated capital is likely to have a comparative advantage in heavy manufacturing. A country well-endowed with human capital is likely to have a comparative advantage in highly technical goods.

factor endowments The quantity and quality of labor, land, and natural resources of a country.

Heckscher-Ohlin theorem A theory that explains the existence of a country's comparative advantage by its factor endowments: A country has a comparative advantage in the production of a product if that country is relatively well endowed with inputs used intensively in the production of that product.

Other Explanations for Observed Trade Flows

Comparative advantage is not the only reason countries trade. It does not explain why many countries import and export the same kinds of goods. The United States, for example, exports Velveeta cheese and imports blue cheese.

Just as industries within a country differentiate their products to capture a domestic market, they also differentiate their products to please the wide variety of tastes that exists worldwide. The Japanese automobile industry, for example, began producing small, fuel-efficient cars long before U.S. automobile makers did. In doing so, the Japanese auto industry developed expertise in creating products that attracted a devoted following and considerable brand loyalty. BMWs, made mostly in Germany, and Lexus, made mostly in Japan, also have their champions in many countries. Just as product differentiation is a natural response to diverse preferences within an economy, it is also a natural response to diverse preferences across economies. Paul Krugman did some of the earliest work in this area, sometimes called New Trade Theory.

New trade theory also relies on the idea of comparative advantage. If the Japanese developed skills and knowledge that gave them an edge in the production of fuel-efficient cars, that knowledge can be thought of as a very specific kind of capital that is not currently available to other producers. Toyota in producing the Lexus, invested in a form of intangible capital called *goodwill*. That goodwill, which may come from establishing a reputation for performance and quality over the years, is one source of the comparative advantage that keeps Lexus selling on the international market. Some economists distinguish between gains from *acquired comparative advantages* and gains from *natural comparative advantages*.

Trade Barriers: Tariffs, Export Subsidies, and Quotas

Trade barriers—also called *obstacles to trade*—take many forms. The three most common are tariffs, export subsidies, and quotas. All are forms of **protection** shielding some sector of the economy from foreign competition.

A **tariff** is a tax on imports. The average tariff on imports into the United States is less than 5 percent. Certain protected items have much higher tariffs. For example, in 2009 President Obama imposed a tariff of 35 percent on tire imports from China.

Export subsidies—government payments made to domestic firms to encourage exports— can also act as a barrier to trade. One of the provisions of the Corn Laws that stimulated Ricardo's musings was an export subsidy automatically paid to farmers by the British government when the price of grain fell below a specified level. The subsidy served to keep domestic prices high, but it flooded the world market with cheap subsidized grain. Foreign farmers who were not subsidized were driven out of the international marketplace by the artificially low prices.

Farm subsidies remain a part of the international trade landscape today. Many countries continue to appease their farmers by heavily subsidizing exports of agricultural products. The political power of the farm lobby in many countries has had an important effect on recent international trade negotiations aimed at reducing trade barriers. The prevalence of farm subsidies in the developed world has become a major rallying point for less developed countries as they strive to compete in the global marketplace. Many African nations, in particular, have a comparative advantage in agricultural land. In producing agricultural goods for export to the world marketplace, however, they must compete with food produced on heavily subsidized farms in Europe and the United States. Countries such as France have particularly high farm subsidies, which, it argues, helps preserve the rural heritage of France. One side effect of these subsidies, however, is to make it more difficult for some of the poorer nations in the world to compete. Some have argued that if developed nations eliminated their farm subsidies, this would have a much larger effect on the economies of some African nations than is currently achieved by charitable aid programs.

Closely related to subsidies is **dumping**. Dumping occurs when a firm or industry sells its products on the world market at prices lower than its cost of production. Charges of dumping are often brought by a domestic producer that believes itself to be subject to unfair competition.

protection The practice of shielding a sector of the economy from foreign competition.

tariff A tax on imports.

export subsidies Government payments made to domestic firms to encourage exports.

dumping A firm's or an industry's sale of products on the world market at prices below its own cost of production.

ECONOMICS IN PRACTICE

Globalization Improves Firm Productivity

In the text we described the way in which free trade allows countries to make the most of what they do well. Recent work in the trade area has also described the way in which free trade improves the productivity of firms within a country.[1]

Within a country we typically see firms of varying productivity. If firms were in fact all producing exactly the same product, we would expect higher-cost firms to be driven out of business. In fact, firms are often producing products that are close substitutes, but not identical. Matchbox cars are like Hot Wheels cars, but not identical. Under these conditions, industries will have firms with a range of productivity levels since some people will pay a little more for the particular product a firm supplies.

What happens when trade opens up? Now competition grows. Firms with good products and low costs can expand to serve markets elsewhere. They grow and often improve their cost through scale economies while doing so. Less productive firms find themselves facing tough competition from both

foreign producers and from their domestic counterparts who now look even more productive than before. Melitz and other economists have found that when we look at the distribution of firm productivity after big trade changes (like the free trade agreement between the United States and Canada in 1989) we see a big drop-off in the less productive firms.

Trade not only exploits comparative advantage of countries, but it improves the efficiency of firms more generally.

THINKING PRACTICALLY

1. What do you expect to see happen to average prices after trade opens up?

[1] Marc Melitz at Harvard did much of the early work in this area. For a review see Marc Melitz and Daniel Trefler, "Gains from Trade when Firms Matter," *Journal of Economic Perspectives*, Spring 2012, 90–117. See also Andrew B. Bernard, Jonathan Eaton, J. Bradford Jensen and Samuel Kortum, "Plants and Productivity in International Trade," *American Economic Review*, Winter 2003, 1268–90.

In the United States, claims of dumping are brought before the International Trade Commission. In 2007, for example, a small manufacturer of thermal paper charged China and Germany with dumping. In 2006, the European Union charged China with dumping shoes. In 2009, China brought a dumping charge against U.S. chicken producers. Determining whether dumping has actually occurred can be difficult. Domestic producers argue that foreign firms will dump their product in the United States, drive out American competitors, and then raise prices, thus harming consumers. Foreign exporters, on the other hand, claim that their prices are low simply because their costs are low and that no dumping has occurred. Figuring out the costs for German thermal paper or Chinese shoes is not easy. In the case of the Chinese shoe claim, for example, the Chinese government pointed out that shoes are a very labor-intensive product and that given China's low wages, it should not be a surprise that it is able to produce shoes very cheaply. In other words, the Chinese claim that shoes are an example of the theory of comparative advantage at work rather than predatory dumping.

quota A limit on the quantity of imports.

A **quota** is a limit on the quantity of imports. Quotas can be mandatory or "voluntary," and they may be legislated or negotiated with foreign governments. The best-known voluntary quota, or "voluntary restraint," was negotiated with the Japanese government in 1981. Japan agreed to reduce its automobile exports to the United States by 7.7 percent, from the 1980 level of 1.82 million units to 1.68 million units. Many quotas limit trade around the world today. Perhaps the best-known recent case is the textile quota imposed in August 2005 by the European Union on imports of textiles from China. Because China had exceeded quotas that had been agreed to earlier in the year, the EU blocked the entry of Chinese-produced textiles into Europe; as a result, more than 100 million garments piled up in European ports. In the *Economics in Practice* box on page 363 we look at the effects of lifting quotas.

Smoot-Hawley tariff The U.S. tariff law of the 1930s, which set the highest tariffs in U.S. history (60 percent). It set off an international trade war and caused the decline in trade that is often considered one of the causes of the worldwide depression of the 1930s.

U.S. Trade Policies, GATT, and the WTO

The United States has been a high-tariff nation, with average tariffs of over 50 percent, for much of its history. The highest were in effect during the Great Depression following the **Smoot-Hawley tariff**, which pushed the average tariff rate to 60 percent in 1930. The Smoot-Hawley tariff set off an international trade war when U.S. trading partners retaliated with tariffs of their own.

ECONOMICS IN PRACTICE

What Happens When We Lift a Quota?

Prior to 2005, textiles and clothing from China and much of the emerging world, heading for the United States, Canada, and the European Union, were subject to quotas. In an interesting new paper, Peter Schott from Yale and Amit Khandelwal and Shang-Jin Wei from Columbia University, investigated what happened once the quota was lifted.[1]

It should come as no surprise that lifting the quota increased the textiles and clothing exported to all three areas. A more interesting question is what happened to the composition of the firms doing the exporting after quotas were lifted. Did the same firms just send more goods, for example?

When an exporting country faces a quota on its products, someone has to decide which firms get the privilege of sending their goods abroad. Typically, governments make this decision. In some cases, governments auction off the rights to export, seeking to maximize public revenue; here we might expect that more efficient firms would be the most likely exporters since they could bid the most due to their cost advantage in selling the goods. In other cases, governments may give export rights to friends and family.

In this case, Schott et al. did not know how China had allocated the export rights or what objective it had in mind. But the results they found were very instructive. After quotas were lifted in 2005, exports did increase dramatically. Moreover, most of the exports were produced not by the older firms which had dominated the quota-laden era, but by new entrants! Without quotas, firms need to be efficient to export and most of the older firms now subject to the new competition rapidly lost market share. The evidence of this paper tells us that however China was allocating its licenses, it was not to the most efficient firms.

THINKING PRACTICALLY

1. If in fact the Chinese government were allocating the rights to export under a quota to the most productive firms, what would you expect to see happen once the quota is lifted?

[1] Amit Khandelwal, Peter Schott, Shang-Jin Wei, "Trade Liberalization and Embedded Institutional Reform: Evidence from Chinese Exporters," *American Economic Review*, forthcoming, 2013.

Many economists say the decline in trade that followed was one of the causes of the worldwide depression of the 1930s.[1]

In 1947, the United States, with 22 other nations, agreed to reduce barriers to trade. It also established an organization to promote liberalization of foreign trade. The **General Agreement on Tariffs and Trade (GATT)** proved to be very successful in helping reduce tariff levels and encourage trade. In 1986, GATT sponsored a round of world trade talks known as the Uruguay Round that were focused on reducing trade barriers further. After much debate, the Uruguay Round was signed by the U.S. Congress in 1993 and became a model for multilateral trade agreements.

In 1995, the **World Trade Organization (WTO)** was established as a negotiating forum to deal with the rules of trade established under GATT and other agreements. It remains the key institution focused on facilitating freer trade across nations and negotiating trade disputes. The WTO consists of 153 member nations and serves as a negotiating forum for countries as they work through complexities of trade under the Uruguay Round and other agreements. At this time, the WTO is the central institution for promoting and facilitating free trade.

While the WTO was founded to promote free trade, its member countries clearly have different incentives as they confront trade cases. In recent years, differences between developed and developing countries have come to the fore. In 2001, at a WTO meeting in Doha, Qatar, the WTO launched a new initiative, the **Doha Development Agenda**, to deal with some of the issues that intersect the areas of trade and development. In 2007, the Doha Development Agenda continued to struggle over the issue of agriculture and farm subsidies that were described earlier in this chapter. The less developed countries, with sub-Saharan Africa taking the lead, seek to eliminate all farm subsidies currently paid by the United States and the European Union.

General Agreement on Tariffs and Trade (GATT) An international agreement signed by the United States and 22 other countries in 1947 to promote the liberalization of foreign trade.

World Trade Organization (WTO) A negotiating forum dealing with rules of trade across nations.

Doha Development Agenda An initiative of the World Trade Organization focused on issues of trade and development.

[1] See especially Charles Kindleberger, *The World in Depression 1929–1939* (London: Allen Lane, 1973).

The EU has, for its part, tried to push the less developed countries toward better environmental policies as part of a broader free trade package. As of 2013, the Doha declaration remained stalled and its future uncertain.

The movement in the United States has been away from tariffs and quotas and toward freer trade. The Reciprocal Trade Agreements Act of 1934 authorized the president to negotiate trade agreements on behalf of the United States. As part of trade negotiations, the president can confer *most-favored-nation status* on individual trading partners. Imports from countries with most-favored-nation status are taxed at the lowest negotiated tariff rates. In addition, in recent years, several successful rounds of tariff-reduction negotiations have reduced trade barriers to their lowest levels ever.

Despite this general trend toward freer trade, most American presidents in the last 50 years have made exceptions to protect one economic sector or another. Eisenhower and Kennedy restricted imports of Japanese textiles; Johnson restricted meat imports to protect Texas beef producers; Nixon restricted steel imports; Reagan restricted automobiles from Japan. In early 2002, President George W. Bush imposed a 30 percent tariff on steel imported from the EU. In 2003, the WTO ruled that these tariffs were unfair and allowed the EU to slap retaliatory tariffs on U.S. products. Shortly thereafter, the steel tariffs were rolled back, at least on EU steel. At present, the United States has high tariffs on sugar-based ethanol, an energy source competitive with corn-based ethanol, and on tires imported from China.

Economic Integration

economic integration Occurs when two or more nations join to form a free-trade zone.

European Union (EU) The European trading bloc composed of 27 countries (of the 27 countries in the EU, 17 have the same currency—the euro).

U.S.-Canadian Free Trade Agreement An agreement in which the United States and Canada agreed to eliminate all barriers to trade between the two countries by 1998.

North American Free Trade Agreement (NAFTA) An agreement signed by the United States, Mexico, and Canada in which the three countries agreed to establish all North America as a free-trade zone.

Economic integration occurs when two or more nations join to form a free-trade zone. In 1991, the European Community (EC, or the Common Market) began forming the largest free-trade zone in the world. The economic integration process began that December, when the 12 original members (the United Kingdom, Belgium, France, Germany, Italy, the Netherlands, Luxembourg, Denmark, Greece, Ireland, Spain, and Portugal) signed the Maastricht Treaty. The treaty called for the end of border controls, a common currency, an end to all tariffs, and the coordination of monetary and political affairs. The **European Union (EU)**, as the EC is now called, has 27 members (for a list, see the Summary, p. 371). On January 1, 1993, all tariffs and trade barriers were dropped among the member countries. Border checkpoints were closed in early 1995. Citizens can now travel among member countries without passports.

The United States is not a part of the EU. However, in 1988, the United States (under President Reagan) and Canada (under Prime Minister Mulroney) signed the **U.S.-Canadian Free Trade Agreement**, which removed all barriers to trade, including tariffs and quotas, between the two countries by 1998.

During the last days of the George H. W. Bush administration in 1992, the United States, Mexico, and Canada signed the **North American Free Trade Agreement (NAFTA)**, with the three countries agreeing to establish all of North America as a free-trade zone. The agreement eliminated all tariffs over a 10- to 15-year period and removed restrictions on most investments. During the presidential campaign of 1992, NAFTA was hotly debated. Both Bill Clinton and George Bush supported the agreement. Industrial labor unions that might be affected by increased imports from Mexico (such as those in the automobile industry) opposed the agreement, while industries whose exports to Mexico might increase as a result of the agreement—for example, the machine tool industry—supported it. Another concern was that Mexican companies were not subject to the same environmental regulations as U.S. firms, so U.S. firms might move to Mexico for this reason.

NAFTA was ratified by the U.S. Congress in late 1993 and went into effect on the first day of 1994. The U.S. Department of Commerce estimated that as a result of NAFTA, trade between the United States and Mexico increased by nearly $16 billion in 1994. In addition, exports from the United States to Mexico outpaced imports from Mexico during 1994. In 1995, however, the agreement fell under the shadow of a dramatic collapse of the value of the peso. U.S. exports to Mexico dropped sharply, and the United States shifted from a trade surplus to a large trade deficit with Mexico. Aside from a handful of tariffs, however, all of NAFTA's commitments were fully implemented by 2003, and an 8-year report signed by all three countries declared the pact a success. The report concludes, "Eight years of expanded trade, increased employment and investment, and enhanced opportunity for the citizens of all three countries have demonstrated that NAFTA works and will continue to work." From 1993–2011 trade among NAFTA countries more than tripled from $288 billion to $1 trillion.

Free Trade or Protection?

One of the great economic debates of all time revolves around the free-trade-versus-protection controversy. We briefly summarize the arguments in favor of each.

The Case for Free Trade

In one sense, the theory of comparative advantage *is* the case for free trade. Trade has potential benefits for all nations. A good is not imported unless its net price to buyers is below the net price of the domestically produced alternative. When the Brazilians in our earlier example found U.S. timber less expensive than their own, they bought it, yet they continued to pay the same price for homemade steel. Americans bought less expensive Brazilian steel, but they continued to buy domestic timber at the same lower price. Under these conditions, *both Americans and Brazilians ended up paying less and consuming more.*

At the same time, resources (including labor) move out of steel production and into timber production in the United States. In Brazil, resources (including labor) move out of timber production and into steel production. The resources in both countries are used more efficiently. Tariffs, export subsidies, and quotas, which interfere with the free movement of goods and services around the world, reduce or eliminate the gains of comparative advantage.

We can use supply and demand curves to illustrate this. Suppose Figure 19.4 shows domestic supply and demand for textiles. In the absence of trade, the market clears at a price of $4.20. At equilibrium, 450 million yards of textiles are produced and consumed.

Assume now that textiles are available at a world price of $2. This is the price in dollars that Americans must pay for textiles from foreign sources. If we assume that an unlimited quantity of textiles is available at $2 and there is no difference in quality between domestic and foreign textiles, no domestic producer will be able to charge more than $2. In the absence of trade barriers, the world price sets the price in the United States. As the price in the United States falls from $4.20 to $2.00, the quantity demanded by consumers increases from 450 million yards to 700 million yards, but the quantity supplied by domestic producers drops from 450 million yards to 200 million yards. The difference, 500 million yards, is the quantity of textiles imported.

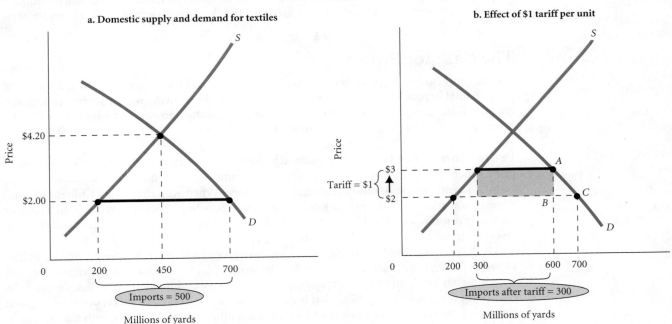

▲ **FIGURE 19.4   The Gains from Trade and Losses from the Imposition of a Tariff**
A tariff of $1 increases the market price facing consumers from $2 per yard to $3 per yard. The government collects revenues equal to the gray shaded area in **b**. The loss of efficiency has two components. First, consumers must pay a higher price for goods that could be produced at lower cost. Second, marginal producers are drawn into textiles and away from other goods, resulting in inefficient domestic production. The triangle labeled ABC in **b** is the deadweight loss or excess burden resulting from the tariff.

The argument for free trade is that each country should specialize in producing the goods and services in which it enjoys a comparative advantage. If foreign producers can produce textiles at a much lower price than domestic producers, they have a comparative advantage. As the world price of textiles falls to $2, domestic (U.S.) quantity supplied drops and resources are transferred to other sectors. These other sectors, which may be export industries or domestic industries, are not shown in Figure 19.4a. It is clear that the allocation of resources is more efficient at a price of $2. Why should the United States use domestic resources to produce what foreign producers can produce at a lower cost? U.S. resources should move into the production of the things it produces best.

Now consider what happens to the domestic price of textiles when a trade barrier is imposed. Figure 19.4b shows the effect of a set tariff of $1 per yard imposed on imported textiles. The tariff raises the domestic price of textiles to $2 + $1 = $3. The result is that some of the gains from trade are lost. First, consumers are forced to pay a higher price for the same good. The quantity of textiles demanded drops from 700 million yards under free trade to 600 million yards because some consumers are not willing to pay the higher price. Notice in Figure 19.4b the triangle labeled ABC. This is the deadweight loss or excess burden resulting from the tariff. Absent the tariff, these 100 added units of textiles would have generated benefits in excess of the $2 that each one cost.

At the same time, the higher price of textiles draws some marginal domestic producers who could not make a profit at $2 into textile production. (Recall that domestic producers do not pay a tariff.) As the price rises to $3, the quantity supplied by domestic producers rises from 200 million yards to 300 million yards. The result is a decrease in imports from 500 million yards to 300 million yards.

Finally, the imposition of the tariff means that the government collects revenue equal to the shaded area in Figure 19.4b. This shaded area is equal to the tariff rate per unit ($1) times the number of units imported after the tariff is in place (300 million yards). Thus, receipts from the tariff are $300 million.

What is the final result of the tariff? Domestic producers receiving revenues of only $2 per unit before the tariff was imposed now receive a higher price and earn higher profits. However, these higher profits are achieved at a loss of efficiency. Trade barriers prevent a nation from reaping the benefits of specialization, push it to adopt relatively inefficient production techniques, and force consumers to pay higher prices for protected products than they would otherwise pay.

The Case for Protection

A case can also be made in favor of tariffs and quotas. Over the course of U.S. history, protectionist arguments have been made so many times by so many industries before so many congressional committees that it seems all pleas for protection share the same themes. We describe the most frequently heard pleas next.

Protection Saves Jobs   The main argument for protection is that foreign competition costs Americans their jobs. When Americans buy imported Toyotas, U.S.-produced cars go unsold. Layoffs in the domestic auto industry follow. When Americans buy Chinese textiles, American workers may lose their jobs. When Americans buy shoes or textiles from Korea or Taiwan, the millworkers in Maine and Massachusetts, as well as in South Carolina and Georgia, lose their jobs.

It is true that when we buy goods from foreign producers, domestic producers suffer. However, there is no reason to believe that the workers laid off in the contracting sectors will not ultimately be reemployed in expanding sectors. Foreign competition in textiles, for example, has meant the loss of U.S. jobs in that industry. Thousands of textile workers in New England lost their jobs as the textile mills closed over the last 40 years. Nevertheless, with the expansion of high-tech industries, the unemployment rate in Massachusetts fell to one of the lowest in the country in the mid-1980s, and New Hampshire, Vermont, and Maine also boomed.

The adjustment is far from costless. The knowledge that some other industry, perhaps in some other part of the country, may be expanding is of little comfort to the person whose skills become obsolete or whose pension benefits are lost when his or her company abruptly closes a plant or goes bankrupt.

ECONOMICS IN PRACTICE

A Petition

While most economists argue in favor of free trade, it is important to recognize that some groups are likely to lose from freer trade. Arguments by the losing groups against trade have been around for hundreds of years. In the following article, you will find an essay by a French satirist of the nineteenth century, Frederic Bastiat, complaining about the unfair competition that the sun provides to candle makers. You see that the author proposes a quota, as opposed to a tariff, on the sun.

From the Manufacturers of Candles, Tapers, Lanterns, Sticks, Street Lamps, Snuffers, and Extinguishers, and from Producers of Tallow, Oil, Resin, Alcohol, and Generally of Everything Connected with Lighting.

To the Honourable Members of the Chamber of Deputies.

Gentlemen:

You are on the right track. You reject abstract theories and [have] little regard for abundance and low prices. You concern yourselves mainly with the fate of the producer. You wish to free him from foreign competition, that is, to reserve the *domestic market* for *domestic industry*.

We come to offer you a wonderful opportunity for your—what shall we call it? Your theory? No, nothing is more deceptive than theory. Your doctrine? Your system? Your principle? But you dislike doctrines, you have a horror of systems, as for principles, you deny that there are any in political economy; therefore we shall call it your practice —your practice without theory and without principle.

We are suffering from the ruinous competition of a rival who apparently works under conditions so far superior to our own for the production of light that he is *flooding* the *domestic market* with it at an incredibly low price; for the moment he appears, our sales cease, all the consumers turn to him, and a branch of French industry whose ramifications are innumerable is all at once reduced to complete stagnation. This rival, which is none other than the sun, is waging war on us so mercilessly we suspect he is being stirred up against us by perfidious Albion (excellent diplomacy nowadays!), particularly because he has for that

haughty island a respect that he does not show for us. [A reference to Britain's reputation as a foggy island.]

We ask you to be so good as to pass a law requiring the closing of all windows, dormers, skylights, inside and outside shutters, curtains, casements, bull's-eyes, deadlights, and blinds—in short, all openings, holes, chinks, and fissures through which the light of the sun is wont to enter houses, to the detriment of the fair industries with which, we are proud to say, we have endowed the country, a country that cannot, without betraying ingratitude, abandon us today to so unequal a combat.

Screening out the sun would increase the demand for candles. Should candlemakers be protected from unfair competition?

THINKING PRACTICALLY

1. Using supply and demand curves, show the effect of screening out the sun on the price of candles.

Source: An Open Letter to the French Parliament by Frederic Bastiat (1801–1850), originally published in 1845.

These problems can be addressed in two ways. We can ban imports and give up the gains from free trade, acknowledging that we are willing to pay premium prices to save domestic jobs in industries that can produce more efficiently abroad, or we can aid the victims of free trade in a constructive way, helping to retrain them for jobs with a future. In some instances, programs to relocate people in expanding regions may be in order. Some programs deal directly with the transition without forgoing the gains from trade.

Some Countries Engage in Unfair Trade Practices   Attempts by U.S. firms to monopolize an industry are illegal under the Sherman and Clayton acts. If a strong company decides to drive the competition out of the market by setting prices below cost, it would be aggressively prosecuted by the Antitrust Division of the Justice Department. However, the argument goes, if we will not allow a U.S. firm to engage in predatory pricing or monopolize an industry or a market, can we stand by and let a German firm or a Japanese firm do so in the name of free trade? This is a legitimate argument and one that has gained significant favor in recent years. How should we respond when a large international company or a country behaves strategically against a domestic firm or industry? Free trade may be the best solution when everybody plays by the rules, but sometimes we have to fight back. The WTO is the vehicle currently used to negotiate disputes of this sort.

Cheap Foreign Labor Makes Competition Unfair   Let us say that a particular country gained its "comparative advantage" in textiles by paying its workers low wages. How can U.S. textile companies compete with companies that pay wages that are less than a quarter of what U.S. companies pay? Questions like this are often asked by those concerned with competition from China and India.

First, remember that wages in a competitive economy reflect productivity: a high ratio of output to units of labor. Workers in the United States earn higher wages because they are more productive. The United States has more capital per worker; that is, the average worker works with better machinery and equipment and its workers are better trained. Second, trade flows not according to *absolute* advantage, but according to *comparative* advantage: All countries benefit, even if one country is more efficient at producing everything.

Protection Safeguards National Security   Beyond saving jobs, certain sectors of the economy may appeal for protection for other reasons. The steel industry has argued for years with some success that it is vital to national defense. In the event of a war, the United States would not want to depend on foreign countries for a product as vital as steel. Even if we acknowledge another country's comparative advantage, we may want to protect our own resources.

Virtually no industry has ever asked for protection without invoking the national defense argument. Testimony that was once given on behalf of the scissors and shears industry argued that "in the event of a national emergency and imports cutoff, the United States would be without a source of scissors and shears, basic tools for many industries and trades essential to our national defense." The question lies not in the merit of the argument, but in just how seriously it can be taken if *every* industry uses it.

Protection Discourages Dependency   Closely related to the national defense argument is the claim that countries, particularly small or developing countries, may come to rely too heavily on one or more trading partners for many items. If a small country comes to rely on a major power for food or energy or some important raw material in which the large nation has a comparative advantage, it may be difficult for the smaller nation to remain politically neutral. Some critics of free trade argue that larger countries, such as the United States, Russia, and China have consciously engaged in trade with smaller countries to create these kinds of dependencies.

Therefore, should small, independent countries consciously avoid trading relationships that might lead to political dependence? This objective may involve developing domestic industries in areas where a country has a comparative disadvantage. To do so would mean protecting that industry from international competition.

Environmental Concerns   In recent years, concern about the environment has led some people to question advantages of free trade. Some environmental groups, for example, argue that the WTO's free trade policies may harm the environment. The central argument is that poor countries will become havens for polluting industries that will operate their steel and auto factories with few environmental controls.

These issues are quite complex, and there is much dispute among economists about the interaction between free trade and the environment. One relatively recent study of sulphur dioxide, for example, found that in the long run, free trade reduces pollution, largely by increasing the income of countries; richer countries typically choose policies to improve the environment.[2] Thus, while free trade and increased development initially may cause pollution levels to rise, in the long run, prosperity is a benefit to the environment. Many also argue that there are complex trade-offs to be made between pollution control and problems such as malnutrition and health for poor countries. The United States and Europe both traded off faster economic growth and

---

[2] Werner Antweiler, Brian Copeland, and M. Scott Taylor, "Is Free Trade Good for the Environment?" *American Economic Review*, September, 2001.

income against cleaner air and water at earlier times in their development. Some argue that it is unfair for the developed countries to impose their preferences on other countries facing more difficult trade-offs.

Nevertheless, the concern with global climate change has stimulated new thinking in this area. A recent study by the Tyndall Centre for Climate Change Research in Britain found that in 2004, 23 percent of the greenhouse gas emissions produced by China were created in the production of exports. In other words, these emissions come not as a result of goods that China's population is enjoying as its income rises, but as a consequence of the consumption of the United States and Europe, where most of these goods are going. In a world in which the effects of carbon emissions are global and all countries are not willing to sign binding global agreements to control emissions, trade with China may be a way for developed nations to avoid their commitments to pollution reduction. Some have argued that penalties could be imposed on high-polluting products produced in countries that have not signed international climate control treaties as a way to ensure that the prices of goods imported this way reflect the harm that those products cause the environment.[3] Implementing these policies is, however, likely to be very complex, and some have argued that it is a mistake to bundle trade and environmental issues. As with other areas covered in this book, there is still disagreement among economists as to the right answer.

Protection Safeguards Infant Industries   Young industries in a given country may have a difficult time competing with established industries in other countries. In a dynamic world, a protected **infant industry** might mature into a strong industry worldwide because of an acquired, but real, comparative advantage. If such an industry is undercut and driven out of world markets at the beginning of its life, that comparative advantage might never develop.

Yet efforts to protect infant industries can backfire. In July 1991, the U.S. government imposed a 62.67 percent tariff on imports of active-matrix liquid crystal display screens (also referred to as "flat-panel displays" used primarily for laptop computers) from Japan. The Commerce Department and the International Trade Commission agreed that Japanese producers were selling their screens in the U.S. market at a price below cost and that this dumping threatened the survival of domestic laptop screen producers. The tariff was meant to protect the infant U.S. industry until it could compete head-on with the Japanese.

Unfortunately for U.S. producers of laptop computers and for consumers who purchase them, the tariff had an unintended (although predictable) effect on the industry. Because U.S. laptop screens were generally recognized to be of lower quality than their Japanese counterparts, imposition of the tariff left U.S. computer manufacturers with three options: (1) They could use the screens available from U.S. producers and watch sales of their final product decline in the face of *higher-quality* competition from abroad, (2) they could pay the tariff for the higher-quality screens and watch sales of their final product decline in the face of *lower-priced* competition from abroad, or (3) they could do what was most profitable for them to do—move

infant industry   A young industry that may need temporary protection from competition from the established industries of other countries to develop an acquired comparative advantage.

Changes in Openness to Trade Over Time across the World

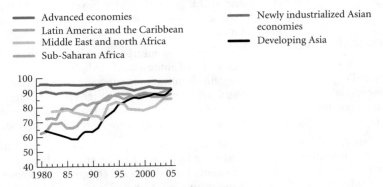

— Advanced economies
— Latin America and the Caribbean
— Middle East and north Africa
— Sub-Saharan Africa
— Newly industrialized Asian economies
— Developing Asia

Source: International Monetary Fund, *2007 World Economic Outlook.*
Trade openness is measured as 100 minus the average effective tariff rate in the region.

◀ FIGURE 19.5 **Trade Openness Across the World (Index is 100 minus the average effective tariff rate in the region.)**

---

[3] Judith Chevalier, "A Carbon Cap That Starts in Washington," *New York Times*, December 16, 2007.

their production facilities abroad to avoid the tariff completely. The last option is what Apple and IBM did. In the end, not only were the laptop industry and its consumers hurt by the imposition of the tariff (due to higher costs of production and to higher laptop computer prices), but the U.S. screen industry was hurt as well (due to its loss of buyers for its product) by a policy specifically designed to help it.

The case for free trade has been made across the world as increasing numbers of countries have joined the world marketplace. Figure 19.5 on page 369 traces the path of tariffs across the world from 1980–2005. The lines show an index of trade openness, calculated as 100 minus the tariff rate. (So higher numbers mean lower tariffs.) We see rapid reductions in the last 25 years across the world, most notably in countries in the emerging and developing markets.

An Economic Consensus

You now know something about how international trade fits into the structure of the economy.

Critical to our study of international economics is the debate between free traders and protectionists. On one side is the theory of comparative advantage, formalized by David Ricardo in the early part of the nineteenth century. According to this view, all countries benefit from specialization and trade. The gains from trade are real, and they can be large; free international trade raises real incomes and improves the standard of living.

On the other side are the protectionists, who point to the loss of jobs and argue for the protection of workers from foreign competition. Although foreign competition can cause job loss in specific sectors, it is unlikely to cause net job loss in an economy and workers will, over time, be absorbed into expanding sectors. Foreign trade and full employment can be pursued simultaneously. Although economists disagree about many things, the vast majority of them favor free trade.

SUMMARY

1. All economies, regardless of their size, depend to some extent on other economies and are affected by events outside their borders.

TRADE SURPLUSES AND DEFICITS *p. 352*

2. Until the 1970s, the United States generally exported more than it imported—it ran a *trade surplus*. In the mid-1970s, the United States began to import more merchandise than it exported—a *trade deficit*.

THE ECONOMIC BASIS FOR TRADE: COMPARATIVE ADVANTAGE *p. 353*

3. The *theory of comparative advantage*, dating to David Ricardo in the nineteenth century, holds that specialization and free trade will benefit all trading partners, even those that may be absolutely less efficient producers.

4. A country enjoys an *absolute advantage* over another country in the production of a product if it uses fewer resources to produce that product than the other country does. A country has a *comparative advantage* in the production of a product if that product can be produced at a lower cost in terms of other goods.

5. Trade enables countries to move beyond their previous resource and productivity constraints. When countries specialize in producing those goods in which they have a comparative advantage, they maximize their combined output and allocate their resources more efficiently.

6. When trade is free, patterns of trade and trade flows result from the independent decisions of thousands of importers and exporters and millions of private households and firms.

7. The relative attractiveness of foreign goods to U.S. buyers and of U.S. goods to foreign buyers depends in part on *exchange rates*, the ratios at which two currencies are traded for each other.

8. For any pair of countries, there is a range of exchange rates that will lead automatically to both countries realizing the gains from specialization and comparative advantage. Within that range, the exchange rate will determine which country gains the most from trade. This leads us to conclude that exchange rates determine the terms of trade.

9. If exchange rates end up in the right range (that is, in a range that facilitates the flow of goods between nations), the free market will drive each country to shift resources into those sectors in which it enjoys a comparative advantage. Only those products in which a country has a comparative advantage will be competitive in world markets.

THE SOURCES OF COMPARATIVE ADVANTAGE *p. 360*

10. The *Heckscher-Ohlin theorem* looks to relative *factor endowments* to explain comparative advantage and trade flows. According to the theorem, a country has a comparative advantage in the production of a product if that country is relatively well endowed with the inputs that are used intensively in the production of that product.

11. A relatively short list of inputs—natural resources, knowledge capital, physical capital, land, and skilled and unskilled labor—explains a surprisingly large portion of world trade patterns. However, the simple version of the theory of comparative advantage cannot explain why many countries import and export the same goods.

12. Some theories argue that comparative advantage can be acquired. Just as industries within a country differentiate their products to capture a domestic market, they also differentiate their products to please the wide variety of tastes that exists worldwide. This theory is consistent with the theory of comparative advantage.

TRADE BARRIERS: TARIFFS, EXPORT SUBSIDIES, AND QUOTAS *p. 361*

13. Trade barriers take many forms. The three most common are *tariffs, export subsidies*, and *quotas*. All are forms of *protection* through which some sector of the economy is shielded from foreign competition.

14. Although the United States has historically been a high-tariff nation, the general movement is now away from tariffs and quotas. The *General Agreement on Tariffs and Trade (GATT)*, signed by the United States and 22 other countries in 1947, continues in effect today; its purpose is to reduce barriers to world trade and keep them down. Also important are the *U.S.-Canadian Free Trade Agreement*, signed in 1988, and the *North American Free Trade Agreement*, signed by the United States, Mexico, and Canada in the last days of the George H. W. Bush administration in 1992, taking effect in 1994.

15. The World Trade Organization (WTO) was set up by GATT to act as a negotiating forum for trade disputes across countries.

16. The *European Union (EU)* is a free-trade bloc composed of 27 nations: Austria, Belgium, Bulgaria, Cyprus, the Czech Republic, Denmark, Estonia, Finland, France, Germany, Greece, Hungary, Ireland, Italy, Latvia, Lithuania, Luxembourg, Malta, the Netherlands, Poland, Portugal, Romania, Slovakia, Slovenia, Spain, Sweden, and the United Kingdom. Many economists believe that the advantages of free trade within the bloc, a reunited Germany, and the ability to work well as a bloc will make the EU the most powerful player in the international marketplace in the coming decades.

FREE TRADE OR PROTECTION? *p. 365*

17. In one sense, the theory of comparative advantage is the case for free trade. Trade barriers prevent a nation from reaping the benefits of specialization, push it to adopt relatively inefficient production techniques, and force consumers to pay higher prices for protected products than they would otherwise pay.

18. The case for protection rests on a number of propositions, one of which is that foreign competition results in a loss of domestic jobs, but there is no reason to believe that the workers laid off in the contracting sectors will not be ultimately reemployed in other expanding sectors. This adjustment process is far from costless, however.

19. Other arguments for protection hold that cheap foreign labor makes competition unfair; that some countries engage in unfair trade practices; that free trade might harm the environment; and that protection safeguards the national security, discourages dependency, and shields *infant industries*. Despite these arguments, most economists favor free trade.

<hr>

REVIEW TERMS AND CONCEPTS

PROBLEMS

All problems are available on MyEconLab.

1. Suppose Germany and France each produce only two goods, guns and butter. Both are produced using labor alone. Assuming both countries are at full employment, you are given the following information:

Germany: 10 units of labor required to produce 1 gun
5 units of labor required to produce 1 pound of butter
Total labor force: 1,000,000 units

France: 15 units of labor required to produce 1 gun
10 units of labor required to produce 1 pound of butter
Total labor force: 750,000 units

a. Draw the production possibility frontiers for each country in the absence of trade.
b. If transportation costs are ignored and trade is allowed, will France and Germany engage in trade? Explain.
c. If a trade agreement is negotiated, at what rate (number of guns per unit of butter) would they agree to exchange?

2. The United States and Russia each produce only bearskin caps and wheat. Domestic prices are given in the following table:

	RUSSIA	UNITED STATES	
Bearskin caps	10 Ru	$ 7	Per hat
Wheat	15 Ru	$10	Per bushel

On April 1, the Zurich exchange listed an exchange rate of $1 = 1 Ru.

a. Which country has an absolute advantage in the production of bearskin caps? wheat?
b. Which country has a comparative advantage in the production of bearskin caps? wheat?
c. If the United States and Russia were the only two countries engaging in trade, what adjustments would you predict assuming exchange rates are freely determined by the laws of supply and demand?

3. The following table shows imports and exports of goods during 2009 for the United States:

	EXPORTS	IMPORTS
Total	1,068.0	1,575.0
Civilian aircraft	35.0	10.0
Apparel, household goods—textile	5.0	74.0
Crude oil	1.0	189.0
Vehicles, parts, and engines	82.0	158.0
Foods, feeds, and beverages	94.0	81.0

All figures are rounded to the nearest billion dollars.
Source: www.census.gov.

What, if anything, can you conclude about the comparative advantage that the United States has relative to its trading partners in the production of goods? What stories can you tell about the wide disparities in apparel and aircraft?

4. The following table gives recent figures for yield per acre in Illinois and Kansas:

	WHEAT	SOYBEANS
Illinois	48	39
Kansas	40	24

Source: U.S. Department of Agriculture, Crop Production.

a. If we assume that farmers in Illinois and Kansas use the same amount of labor, capital, and fertilizer, which state has an absolute advantage in wheat production? soybean production?
b. If we transfer land out of wheat into soybeans, how many bushels of wheat do we give up in Illinois per additional bushel of soybeans produced? in Kansas?
c. Which state has a comparative advantage in wheat production? in soybean production?
d. The following table gives the distribution of land planted for each state in millions of acres in the same year.

	TOTAL ACRES UNDER TILL	WHEAT	SOYBEANS
Illinois	22.9	1.9 (8.3%)	9.1 (39.7%)
Kansas	20.7	11.8 (57.0%)	1.9 (9.2%)

Are these data consistent with your answer to part c? Explain.

5. You can think of the United States as a set of 50 separate economies with no trade barriers. In such an open environment, each state specializes in the products that it produces best.
a. What product or products does your state specialize in?
b. Can you identify the source of the comparative advantage that lies behind the production of one or more of these products (for example, a natural resource, plentiful cheap labor, or a skilled labor force)?
c. Do you think that the theory of comparative advantage and the Heckscher-Ohlin theorem help to explain why your state specializes the way that it does? Explain your answer.

6. Australia and the United States produce white and red wines. Current domestic prices for each wine are given in the following table:

	AUSTRALIA	UNITED STATES
White wine	5 AU$	10 US$
Red wine	10 AU$	15 US$

Suppose the exchange rate is 1 AU$ = 1 US$.
a. If the price ratios within each country reflect resource use, which country has a comparative advantage in the production of red wine? white wine?
b. Assume that there are no other trading partners and that the only motive for holding foreign currency is to buy foreign goods. Will the current exchange rate lead to trade flows in both directions between the two countries? Explain.

c. What adjustments might you expect in the exchange rate? Be specific.

d. What would you predict about trade flows between Australia and the United States after the exchange rate has adjusted?

7. Some empirical trade economists have noted that for many products, countries are both importers and exporters. For example, the United States both imports and exports shirts. How do you explain this?

8. [Related to the *Economics in Practice* on p. 362] As is stated in the text, NAFTA was ratified by the U.S. Congress in 1993 and went into effect on January 1, 1994, and aside from a few tariffs, all of NAFTA's commitments were fully implemented by 2003. Go to http://www.usa.gov" and do a search for "NAFTA: A Decade of Success" to find a document from the Office of the United States Trade Representative which details the benefits of this free-trade agreement between the United States, Canada, and Mexico. Describe what happened to the following in the NAFTA countries by 2003, when NAFTA's commitments were fully implemented: economic growth, exports, total trade volume, and productivity. Now conduct a Web search to find any disadvantages of NAFTA and see how they relate to the arguments for protectionism in the text. Explain whether you believe any of these disadvantages outweigh the benefits you described regarding economic growth, exports, trade volume, and productivity.

9. [Related to the *Economics in Practice* on p. 367] When a president presents a trade agreement for ratification to Congress, many domestic industries fight the ratification. In 2005, the United States was negotiating the Central America-Dominican Republic Free Trade Agreement (CAFTA-DR). Write a brief essay on the U.S. political opposition to CAFTA-DR in 2004 and 2005. What industries in the United States opposed the trade agreement? Is it fair to compare the arguments of these industries to the arguments posed by the candle makers?

10. The following graph represents the domestic supply and demand for coffee a number of years ago.

a. In the absence of trade, what is the equilibrium price and equilibrium quantity?

b. The government opens the market to free trade, and Colombia enters the market, pricing coffee at $1 per pound. What will happen to the domestic price of coffee? What will be the new domestic quantity supplied and domestic quantity demanded? How much coffee will be imported from Colombia?

c. After numerous complaints from domestic coffee producers, the government imposes a $0.50 per pound tariff on all imported coffee. What will happen to the domestic price of

coffee? What will be the new domestic quantity supplied and domestic quantity demanded? How much coffee will now be imported from Colombia?

d. How much revenue will the government receive from the $0.50 per pound tariff?

e. Who ultimately ends up paying the $0.50 per pound tariff? Why?

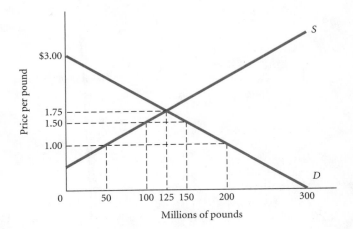

11. Refer to the previous problem. Assume the market is opened to trade and Colombia still enters the market by pricing coffee at $1.00 per pound. But as a response to complaints from domestic coffee producers, instead of imposing a $0.50 per pound tariff, the government imposes an import quota of 50 million pounds on Colombian coffee. How will the results of the quota differ from the results of the tariff?

12. The nation of Pixley has an absolute advantage in everything it produces compared to the nation of Hooterville. Could these two nations still benefit by trading with each other? Explain.

13. Evaluate the following statement: If lower exchange rates increase a nation's exports, the government should do everything in its power to ensure that the exchange rate for its currency is as low as possible.

14. [Related to the *Economics in Practice* on p. 363] Since the 1960s, the United States has had an embargo in place on Cuba, virtually eliminating all trade between the two countries. Suppose the United States decided to lift the embargo on exports to Cuba while maintaining the embargo on Cuban imports. Explain whether this one-sided change would benefit neither country, just one country, or both countries?

Open-Economy Macroeconomics: The Balance of Payments and Exchange Rates

20

The economies of the world have become increasingly interdependent over the last four decades. No economy operates in a vacuum, and economic events in one country can have significant repercussions on the economies of other countries.

International trade is a major part of today's world economy. U.S. imports now account for about 17 percent

of U.S. gross domestic product (GDP), and billions of dollars flow through the international capital market each day. In Chapter 19, we explored the main reasons why there is international exchange. Countries trade with one another to obtain goods and services they cannot produce themselves or to take advantage of the fact that other countries can produce goods and services at a lower cost than they can. You can see the various connections between the domestic economy and the rest of the world in the circular flow diagram in Figure 20.3 in Chapter 5. Foreign countries supply goods and services to the United States, and the United States supplies goods and services to the rest of the world.

From a macroeconomic point of view, the main difference between an international transaction and a domestic transaction concerns currency exchange. When people in countries with different currencies buy from and sell to each other, an exchange of currencies must also take place. Brazilian coffee exporters cannot spend U.S. dollars in Brazil—they need Brazilian reals. A U.S. wheat exporter cannot use Brazilian reals to buy a tractor from a U.S. company or to pay the rent on warehouse facilities. Somehow international exchange must be managed in a way that allows both partners in the transaction to wind up with their own currency.

LEARNING OBJECTIVES

Explain how the balance of payments is calculated

Discuss how equilibrium output is determined in an open economy

Describe the trade feedback effect and the price feedback effect

Discuss factors that affect exchange rates in an open economy with a floating system

Summarize the implications of floating exchange rates

Discuss the effectiveness of monetary and fiscal policies in economies with fixed and flexible exchange rate systems

exchange rate The price of one country's currency in terms of another country's currency; the ratio at which two currencies are traded for each other.

As you know from Chapter 19, the direction of trade between two countries depends on **exchange rates**—the price of one country's currency in terms of the other country's currency. If the Japanese yen were very expensive (making the dollar cheap), both Japanese and Americans would buy from U.S. producers. If the yen were very cheap (making the U.S. dollar expensive), both Japanese and Americans would buy from Japanese producers. Within a certain range of exchange rates, trade flows in both directions, each country specializes in producing the goods in which it enjoys a comparative advantage, and trade is mutually beneficial.

Because exchange rates are a factor in determining the flow of international trade, the way they are determined is very important. Since 1900, the world monetary system has been changed several times by international agreements and events. In the early part of the twentieth century, nearly all currencies were backed by gold. Their values were fixed in terms of a specific number of ounces of gold, which determined their values in international trading—exchange rates.

In 1944, with the international monetary system in chaos as the end of World War II drew near, a large group of experts unofficially representing 44 countries met in Bretton Woods, New Hampshire, and drew up a number of agreements. One of those agreements established a system of essentially fixed exchange rates under which each country agreed to intervene by buying and selling currencies in the foreign exchange market when necessary to maintain the agreed-to value of its currency.

In 1971, most countries, including the United States, gave up trying to fix exchange rates formally and began allowing them to be determined essentially by supply and demand. For example, without government intervention in the marketplace, the price of British pounds in dollars is determined by the interaction of those who want to exchange dollars for pounds (those who "demand" pounds) and those who want to exchange pounds for dollars (those who "supply" pounds). If the quantity of pounds demanded exceeds the quantity of pounds supplied, the price of pounds will rise, just as the price of peanuts or paper clips would rise under similar circumstances. A more detailed discussion of the various monetary systems that have been in place since 1900 is provided in the Appendix to this chapter.

In this chapter, we explore in more detail what has come to be called *open-economy macroeconomics*. First, we discuss the *balance of payments*—the record of a nation's transactions with the rest of the world. We then go on to consider how the analysis changes when we allow for the international exchange of goods, services, and capital.

The Balance of Payments

foreign exchange All currencies other than the domestic currency of a given country.

We sometimes lump all foreign currencies—euros, Swiss francs, Japanese yen, Brazilian reals, and so forth—together as "foreign exchange." **Foreign exchange** is simply all currencies other than the domestic currency of a given country (in the case of the United States, the U.S. dollar). U.S. demand for foreign exchange arises because its citizens want to buy things whose prices are quoted in other currencies, such as Australian jewelry, vacations in Mexico, and bonds or stocks issued by Sony Corporation of Japan. Whenever U.S. citizens make these purchases, they first buy the foreign currencies and then make the purchases.

Where does the *supply* of foreign exchange come from? The answer is simple: The United States (actually U.S. citizens or firms) earns foreign exchange when it sells products, services, or assets to another country. Just as Mexico earns foreign exchange when U.S. tourists visit Cancún, the United States earns foreign exchange (in this case, Mexican pesos) when Mexican tourists come to the United States to visit Disney World. Similarly, Saudi Arabian purchases of stock in General Motors and Colombian purchases of real estate in Miami increase the U.S. supply of foreign exchange.

balance of payments The record of a country's transactions in goods, services, and assets with the rest of the world; also the record of a country's sources (supply) and uses (demand) of foreign exchange.

The record of a country's transactions in goods, services, and assets with the rest of the world is its **balance of payments**. The balance of payments is also the record of a country's sources (supply) and uses (demand) of foreign exchange.[1]

---

[1] Bear in mind the distinction between the balance of payments and a balance sheet. A *balance sheet* for a firm or a country measures that entity's stock of assets and liabilities at a moment in time. The *balance of payments*, by contrast, measures *flows*, usually over a period of a month, a quarter, or a year. Despite its name, the balance of payments is *not* a balance sheet.

The Current Account

The balance of payments is divided into two major accounts, the *current account* and the *capital account*. These are shown in Table 20.1, which provides data on the U.S. balance of payments for 2011. We begin with the current account.

The first item in the current account is U.S. trade in goods. This category includes exports of computer chips, and potato chips, and imports of Scotch whiskey, Chinese toys, and Mexican oil. U.S. exports *earn* foreign exchange for the United States and are a credit (+) item on the current account. U.S. imports *use up* foreign exchange and are a debit (−) item. In 2011, the United States imported $738.4 billion more in goods than it exported.

Next in the current account is services. Like most other countries, the United States buys services from and sells services to other countries. For example, a U.S. firm shipping wheat to England might purchase insurance from a British insurance company. A Dutch flower grower may fly flowers to the United States aboard an American airliner. In the first case, the United States is importing services and therefore using up foreign exchange; in the second case, it is selling services to foreigners and earning foreign exchange. In 2011 the United States exported $178.6 billion more in services than it imported.

The difference between a country's exports of goods and services and its imports of goods and services is its **balance of trade**. When exports of goods and services are less than imports of goods and services, a country has a **trade deficit**. The U.S. trade deficit in 2011 was large: $559.8 billion (that is, $738.4 billion less $178.6 billion).

The third item in the current account concerns investment income. U.S. citizens hold foreign assets (stocks, bonds, and real assets such as buildings and factories). Dividends, interest, rent, and profits paid to U.S. asset holders are a source of foreign exchange. Conversely, when foreigners earn dividends, interest, and profits on assets held in the United States, foreign exchange is used up. In 2011, investment income received from foreigners exceeded investment income paid to foreigners by $227.0 billion.

The fourth item in Table 20.1 is net transfer payments. Transfer payments from the United States to foreigners are another use of foreign exchange. Some of these transfer payments are

balance of trade A country's exports of goods and services minus its imports of goods and services.

trade deficit Occurs when a country's exports of goods and services are less than its imports of goods and services.

TABLE 20.1 United States Balance of Payments, 2011

All transactions that bring foreign exchange into the United States are credited (+) to the current account; all transactions that cause the United States to lose foreign exchange are debited (−) to the current account

Current Account	Billions of dollars
Goods exports	1,497.4
Goods imports	−2,235.8
(1) Net export of goods	−738.4
Exports of services	606.0
Imports of services	−427.4
(2) Net export of services	178.6
Income received on investments	744.6
Income payments on investments	−517.6
(3) Net investment income	227.0
(4) Net transfer payments	−133.1
(5) Balance on current account (1 + 2 + 3 + 4)	−465.9
Capital Account	
(6) Change in private U.S. assets abroad (increase is −)	−364.1
(7) Change in foreign private assets in the United States	789.2
(8) Change in U.S. government assets abroad (increase is −)	−119.5
(9) Change in foreign government assets in the United States	211.8
(10) Balance on capital account (6 + 7 + 8 + 9)	517.4
(11) Net capital account transactions and financial derivatives	37.7
(12) Statistical discrepancy	−89.2
(13) Balance of payments (5 + 10 + 11 + 12)	0

Source: U.S. Bureau of Economic Analysis.

from private U.S. citizens, and some are from the U.S. government. You may send a check to a relief agency in Africa. Many immigrants in the United States send remittances to their countries of origin to help support extended families. Conversely, some foreigners make transfer payments to the United States. *Net* refers to the difference between payments from the United States to foreigners and payments from foreigners to the United States.

balance on current account
Net exports of goods plus net exports of services plus net investment income plus net transfer payments.

If we add net exports of goods, net export of services, net investment income, and net transfer payments, we get the **balance on current account**. The balance on current account shows how much a nation has spent on foreign goods, services, investment income payments, and transfers relative to how much it has earned from other countries. When the balance is negative, which it was for the United States in 2011, a nation has spent more on foreign goods and services (plus investment income and transfers paid) than it has earned through the sales of its goods and services to the rest of the world (plus investment income and transfers received). If a nation has spent more on foreign goods, services, investment income payments, and transfers than it has earned, its net wealth position vis-à-vis the rest of the world must decrease. By *net*, we mean a nation's assets abroad minus its liabilities to the rest of the world. The capital account of the balance of payments records the changes in these assets and liabilities. We now turn to the capital account.

The Capital Account

For each transaction recorded in the current account, there is an offsetting transaction recorded in the capital account. Consider the purchase of a Japanese car by a U.S. citizen. Say that the yen/dollar exchange rate is 100 yen to a dollar and that the yen price of the car is 2.0 million yen, which is $20,000. The U.S. citizen (probably an automobile dealer) takes $20,000, buys 2.0 million yen, and then buys the car. In this case, U.S. imports are increased by $20,000 in the current account and foreign assets in the United States (in this case, Japanese holdings of dollars) are increased by $20,000 in the capital account. The net wealth position of the United States vis-à-vis the rest of the world has decreased by $20,000. The key point to realize is that an increase in U.S. imports results in an increase in foreign assets in the United States. The United States must "pay" for the imports, and whatever it pays with (in this example, U.S. dollars) is an increase in foreign assets in the United States. Conversely, an increase in U.S. exports results in an increase in U.S. assets abroad because foreigners must pay for the U.S. exports.

balance on capital account
In the United States, the sum of the following (measured in a given period): the change in private U.S. assets abroad, the change in foreign private assets in the United States, the change in U.S. government assets abroad, and the change in foreign government assets in the United States.

Table 20.1 shows that U.S. assets abroad are divided into private holdings (line 6) and U.S. government holdings (line 8). Similarly, foreign assets in the United States are divided into foreign private (line 7) and foreign government (line 9). The sum of lines 6, 7, 8, and 9 is the **balance on capital account** (line 10). The next item is called net capital account transactions and financial derivatives, (line 11). It includes things such as U.S. government debt forgiveness. These kinds of transactions affect the capital account but not the current account. Ignoring this item, if there were no errors of measurement in the data collection, the balance on capital account would equal the negative of the balance on current account because, as mentioned previously, for each transaction in the current account, there is an offsetting transaction in the capital account. Another way of looking at the balance on capital account is that it is the change in the net wealth position of the country vis-à-vis the rest of the world. When the balance on capital account is positive, this means that the change in foreign assets in the country is greater than the change in the country's assets abroad, which is a decrease in the net wealth position of the country.

Table 20.1 shows that in 2011, the U.S. balance on current account was −$465.9 billion, which means that the United States spent considerably more than it made vis-à-vis the rest of the world. If the balance on current account is measured correctly, the net wealth position of the United States vis-à-vis the rest of the world should have decreased by $465.9 billion in 2011 minus the $37.7 billion in line 11, or $428.2 billion. The balance on capital account (line 10) is in fact $517.4 billion; so the error of measurement, called the statistical discrepancy, is −$89.2 billion (line 12) in 2011. The balance of payments (line 13) is the sum of the

ECONOMICS IN PRACTICE

The Composition of Trade Gaps

Trade gaps, or deficits, occur when a country's imports of goods and services outweigh its exports. These trade gaps can change because an entrepreneur from one country invents and produces something that generates big sales abroad or because imports from one country have a big price change. Denmark, for example, runs a trade surplus with Japan largely because of its sales of Legos. Norway's exports are dominated by fish and crude oil, and its trade balance as a result is relatively volatile following oil price movements.

For France, energy prices are key to its trade deficit, as it imports most of its oil. You might be surprised to know that one of the United States' largest exports is agricultural products.

THINKING PRACTICALLY

1. Although one of the largest exports in the United States is agricultural products, the United States has very few farm workers. How do you explain this?

balance on current account, the balance on capital account, net capital account transactions and financial derivatives, and the statistical discrepancy. By construction, it is always zero.

It is important to note from Table 20.1 that even though the net wealth position of the United States decreased in 2011, the change in U.S. assets abroad increased ($364.1 billion private plus $119.5 billion government). How can this be? Because there was an even larger increase in foreign assets in the United States ($789.2 billion private plus $211.8 billion government). It is the *net* change (that is, the change in foreign assets in the United States minus the change in U.S. assets abroad) that is equal to the negative of the balance on current account (aside from the statistical discrepancy), not the change in just U.S. assets abroad. Much of the increase of $211.8 billion in foreign government assets was the accumulation of dollars and U.S. Treasury securities by China.

Many transactions get recorded in the capital account that do not pertain to the current account. Consider a purchase of a U.K. security by a U.S. resident. This is done by the U.S. resident's selling dollars for pounds and using the pounds to buy the U.K. security. After this transaction, U.S. assets abroad have increased (the United States now holds more U.K. securities) and foreign assets in the United States have increased (foreigners now hold more dollars). The purchase of the U.K. security is recorded as a minus item in line 6 in Table 20.1, and the increase in foreign holdings of dollars is recorded as a plus item in line 7. These two balance out. This happens whenever there is a switch of one kind of asset for another vis-à-vis the rest of the world. In recent years, a number of business people from the oil-rich Middle East and Russia purchased apartments in U.S. cities like New York and San Francisco. These real estate investments increased foreign assets in the United States (real estate) and increased U.S. assets abroad (foreign currency from the Middle East).

The United States as a Debtor Nation

If a country has a positive net wealth position vis-à-vis the rest of the world, it can be said to be a creditor nation. Conversely, if it has a negative net wealth position, it can be said to be a debtor nation. Remember that a country's net wealth position increases if it has a positive current account balance and decreases if it has a negative current account balance. It is important to realize that the *only* way a country's net wealth position can change is if its current account balance is nonzero. Simply switching one form of asset for another, such as trading real estate for foreign currency, is not a change in a country's net wealth position. Another way of putting this is that a country's net wealth position is the sum of all its past current account balances.

Prior to the mid-1970s, the United States had generally run current account surpluses, and thus its net wealth position was positive. It was a creditor nation. This began to turn around in the mid-1970s, and by the mid-1980s, the United States was running large current account deficits. Sometime during this period, the United States changed from having a positive net wealth position vis-à-vis the rest of the world to having a negative position. In other words, the United States changed from a creditor nation to a debtor nation. The current account deficits persisted into the 1990s, and the United States is now the largest debtor nation in the world. In 2011 foreign assets in the United States totaled $25.2 trillion and U.S. assets abroad totaled $21.1 trillion.[2] The U.S. net wealth position was thus −$4.1 trillion. This large negative position reflects the fact that the United States spent much more in the 1980s, 1990s, and 2000s on foreign goods and services (plus investment income and transfers paid) than it earned through the sales of its goods and services to the rest of the world (plus investment income and transfers received).

Equilibrium Output (Income) in an Open Economy

Everything we have said so far has been descriptive. Now we turn to analysis. How are all these trade and capital flows determined? What impacts do they have on the economies of the countries involved? To simplify our discussion, we will assume that exchange rates are fixed. We will relax this assumption later.

The International Sector and Planned Aggregate Expenditure

Our earlier descriptions of the multiplier took into account the consumption behavior of households (C), the planned investment behavior of firms (I), and the spending of the government (G). We defined the sum of those three components as planned aggregate expenditure (AE).

To analyze the international sector, we must include the goods and services a country exports to the rest of the world as well as what it imports. If we call our exports of goods and services EX, it should be clear that EX is a component of total output and income. A U.S. razor sold to a buyer in Mexico is as much a part of U.S. production as a similar razor sold in Pittsburgh. Exports simply represent demand for domestic products not by domestic households and firms and the government, but by the rest of the world.

What about imports (IM)? Remember, imports are *not a part of domestic output* (Y). By definition, imports are not produced by the country that is importing them. Remember also, when we look at households' total consumption spending, firms' total investment spending, and total government spending, imports are included. Therefore, to calculate domestic output correctly, we must subtract the parts of consumption, investment, and government spending that constitute imports. The definition of planned aggregate expenditure becomes:

Planned aggregate expenditure in an open economy:

$$AE \equiv C + I + G + EX - IM$$

net exports of goods and services ($EX - IM$) The difference between a country's total exports and total imports.

The last two terms ($EX - IM$) together are the country's **net exports of goods and services**.

Determining the Level of Imports What determines the level of imports and exports in a country? For now, we assume that the level of imports is a function of income (Y). The rationale is simple: When U.S. income increases, U.S. citizens buy more of everything, including U.S. cars and peanut butter, Japanese TV sets, and Korean steel and smartphones. When income rises, imports tend to go up. Algebraically,

$$IM = mY$$

where Y is income and m is some positive number. (m is assumed to be less than 1; otherwise, a $1 increase in income generates an increase in imports of more than $1, which is unrealistic.)

---

[2] U.S. Bureau of Economic Analysis.

Recall from Chapter 8 that the marginal propensity to consume (*MPC*) measures the change in consumption that results from a $1 change in income. Similarly, the **marginal propensity to import**, abbreviated as *MPM* or *m*, is the change in imports caused by a $1 change in income. If *m* = .2, or 20 percent, and income is $1,000, then imports, *IM*, are equal to .2 × $1,000 = $200. If income rises by $100 to $1,100, the change in imports will equal *m* × (the change in income) = .2 × $100 = $20.

For now we will assume that exports (*EX*) are given (that is, they are not affected, even indirectly, by the state of the domestic economy.) This assumption is relaxed later in this chapter.

marginal propensity to import (*MPM*) The change in imports caused by a $1 change in income.

Solving for Equilibrium Given the assumption about how imports are determined, we can solve for equilibrium income. This procedure is illustrated in Figure 20.1. Starting from the consumption function (blue line) in Figure 20.1(a), we gradually build up the components of planned aggregate expenditure (red line). Assuming for simplicity that planned investment, government purchases, and exports are all constant and do not depend on income, we move easily from the blue line to the red line by adding the fixed amounts of *I*, *G*, and *EX* to consumption at every level of income. In this example, we take *I* + *G* + *EX* to equal 80.

C + *I* + *G* + *EX*, however, includes spending on imports, which are not part of domestic production. To get spending on domestically produced goods, we must subtract the amount that is imported at each level of income. In Figure 20.1(b), we assume *m* = .25, which is the assumption that 25 percent of total income is spent on goods and services produced in foreign countries. Imports under this assumption are a constant fraction of total income; therefore, at higher levels of income, a larger amount is spent on foreign goods and services. For example, at *Y* = 200, *IM* = .25 *Y*, or 50. Similarly, at *Y* = 400, *IM* = .25 *Y*, or 100. Figure 20.1(b) shows the planned *domestic* aggregate expenditure curve.

Equilibrium is reached when planned domestic aggregate expenditure equals domestic aggregate output (income). This is true at only one level of aggregate output, *Y** = 200, in Figure 20.1(b). If *Y* were below *Y**, planned expenditure would exceed output, inventories would be lower than planned, and output would rise. At levels above *Y**, output would exceed planned expenditure, inventories would be larger than planned, and output would fall.

The Open-Economy Multiplier All of this has implications for the size of the multiplier. Recall the multiplier, introduced in Chapter 8, and consider a sustained rise in government purchases (*G*). Initially, the increase in *G* will cause planned aggregate expenditure to

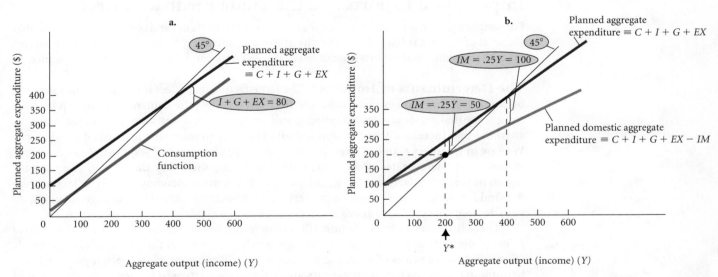

▲ **FIGURE 20.1 Determining Equilibrium Output in an Open Economy**
In **a.**, planned investment spending (*I*), government spending (*G*), and total exports (*EX*) are added to consumption (*C*) to arrive at planned aggregate expenditure. However, *C* + *I* + *G* + *EX* includes spending on imports. In **b.**, the amount imported at every level of income is subtracted from planned aggregate expenditure. Equilibrium output occurs at *Y** = 200, the point at which planned domestic aggregate expenditure crosses the 45-degree line.

MyEconLab Real-time data

be greater than aggregate output. Domestic firms will find their inventories to be lower than planned and thus will increase their output, but added output means more income. More workers are hired, and profits are higher. Some of the added income is saved, and some is spent. The added consumption spending leads to a second round of inventories being lower than planned and raising output. Equilibrium output rises by a multiple of the initial increase in government purchases. This is the multiplier.

In Chapters 8 and 9, we showed that the simple multiplier equals $1/(1 - MPC)$, or $(1/MPS)$. That is, a sustained increase in government purchases equal to ΔG will lead to an increase in aggregate output (income) of $\Delta G [1/(1 - MPC)]$. If the MPC were .75 and government purchases rose by \$10 billion, equilibrium income would rise by $4 \times \$10$ billion, or \$40 billion. The multiplier is $[1/(1 - .75)] = [1/.25] = 4.0$.

In an open economy, some of the increase in income brought about by the increase in G is spent on imports instead of domestically produced goods and services. The part of income spent on imports does not increase domestic income (Y) because imports are produced by foreigners. To compute the multiplier, we need to know how much of the increased income is used to increase domestic consumption. (We are assuming all imports are consumption goods. In practice, some imports are investment goods and some are goods purchased by the government.) In other words, we need to know the marginal propensity to consume *domestic* goods. Domestic consumption is $C - IM$. So the marginal propensity to consume domestic goods is the marginal propensity to consume all goods (the MPC) minus the marginal propensity to import (the MPM). The marginal propensity to consume domestic goods is $(MPC - MPM)$. Consequently,

$$\text{open-economy multiplier} = \frac{1}{1 - (MPC - MPM)}$$

If the MPC is .75 and the MPM is .25, then the multiplier is $1/.5$, or 2.0. This multiplier is smaller than the multiplier in which imports are not taken into account, which is $1/.25$, or 4.0. The effect of a sustained increase in government spending (or investment) on income—that is, the multiplier—is smaller in an open economy than in a closed economy. The reason: When government spending (or investment) increases and income and consumption rise, some of the extra consumption spending that results is on foreign products and not on domestically produced goods and services.

Imports and Exports and the Trade Feedback Effect

For simplicity, we have so far assumed that the level of imports depends only on income and that the level of exports is fixed. In reality, the amount of spending on imports depends on factors other than income and exports are not fixed. We will now consider the more realistic picture.

The Determinants of Imports   The same factors that affect households' consumption behavior and firms' investment behavior are likely to affect the demand for imports because some imported goods are consumption goods and some are investment goods. For example, anything that increases consumption spending is likely to increase the demand for imports. We saw in Chapters 8 and 11 that factors such as the after-tax real wage, after-tax nonlabor income, and interest rates affect consumption spending; thus, they should also affect spending on imports. Similarly, anything that increases investment spending is likely to increase the demand for imports. A decrease in interest rates, for example, should encourage spending on both domestically produced goods and foreign-produced goods.

There is one additional consideration in determining spending on imports: the *relative prices* of domestically produced and foreign-produced goods. If the prices of foreign goods fall relative to the prices of domestic goods, people will consume more foreign goods relative to domestic goods. When Japanese cars are inexpensive relative to U.S. cars, consumption of Japanese cars should be high and vice versa.

The Determinants of Exports   We now relax our assumption that exports are fixed. The foreign demand for U.S. exports is identical to the foreign countries' imports from the United States. Germany imports goods, some of which are U.S.-produced. France, Spain,

ECONOMICS IN PRACTICE

The Recession Takes Its Toll on Trade

During recessions, people in many countries become more protectionist and seek to protect jobs in their own home industries by limiting imports. Chapter 19 described some of the economic costs of this protectionism. What fewer people recognize is the effect of recessions on the overall level of trade in the world. As the text describes, there is a trade-feedback effect in which growth in one country leads to growth in other countries, further enhancing growth in the first country. In the recession of 2008–2009, this feedback effect was quite apparent (in the negative direction).

The Paris-based Organization for Economic Cooperation and Development (OECD) collects data on trade levels for a number of countries. The figure below shows the rise in trade levels in the world over the period 2005 to the middle of 2008 followed by large declines in the 2008–2009 recession. By 2011 (not shown on the chart) trade levels had returned to their 2008 peak.

THINKING PRACTICALLY

1. Why do you think trade rose in the 2005–2008 period?

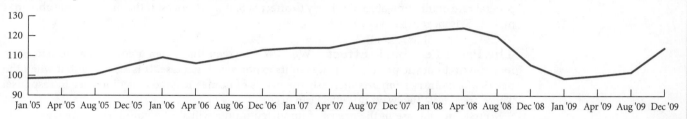

and so on do the same. Total expenditure on imports in Germany is a function of the factors we just discussed except that the variables are German variables instead of U.S. variables. This is true for all other countries as well. The demand for U.S. exports depends on economic activity in the rest of the world—rest-of-the-world real wages, wealth, nonlabor income, interest rates, and so forth—as well as on the prices of U.S. goods relative to the price of rest-of-the-world goods. When foreign output increases, U.S. exports tend to increase. U.S. exports also tend to increase when U.S. prices fall relative to those in the rest of the world.

The Trade Feedback Effect We can now combine what we know about the demand for imports and the demand for exports to discuss the **trade feedback effect**. Suppose the United States finds its exports increasing, perhaps because the world suddenly decides it prefers U.S. computers to other computers. Rising exports will lead to an increase in U.S. output (income), which leads to an increase in U.S. imports. Here is where the trade feedback begins. Because U.S. imports are somebody else's exports, the extra import demand from the United States raises the exports of the rest of the world. When other countries' exports to the United States go up, their output and incomes also rise, in turn leading to an increase in the demand for imports from the rest of the world. Some of the extra imports demanded by the rest of the world come from the United States, so U.S. exports increase. The increase in U.S. exports stimulates U.S. economic activity even more, triggering a further increase in the U.S. demand for imports and so on. An increase in U.S. imports increases other countries' exports, which stimulates those countries' economies and increases their imports, which increases U.S. exports, which stimulates the U.S. economy and increases its imports, and so on. This is the trade feedback effect. In other words, an increase in U.S. economic activity leads to a worldwide increase in economic activity, which then "feeds back" to the United States.

trade feedback effect
The tendency for an increase in the economic activity of one country to lead to a worldwide increase in economic activity, which then feeds back to that country.

Import and Export Prices and the Price Feedback Effect

We have talked about the price of imports, but we have not yet discussed the factors that influence import prices. The consideration of import prices is complicated because more than one currency is involved. When we talk about "the price of imports," do we mean the price in dollars, in yen, in U.K. pounds, in Mexican pesos, and so on? Because the exports of one country are the imports of another, the same question holds for the price of exports.

When Mexico exports auto parts to the United States, Mexican manufacturers are interested in the price of auto parts in terms of pesos because pesos are what they use for transactions in Mexico. U.S. consumers are interested in the price of auto parts in dollars because dollars are what they use for transactions in the United States. The link between the two prices is the dollar/peso exchange rate.

Suppose Mexico is experiencing inflation and the price of radiators in pesos rises from 1,000 pesos to 1,200 pesos per radiator. If the dollar/peso exchange rate remains unchanged at, say, $0.10 per peso, Mexico's export price for radiators in terms of dollars will also rise, from $100 to $120 per radiator. Because Mexico's exports to the United States are, by definition, U.S. imports from Mexico, an increase in the dollar prices of Mexican exports to the United States means an increase in the prices of U.S. imports from Mexico. Therefore, when Mexico's export prices rise with no change in the dollar/peso exchange rate, U.S. import prices rise. Export prices of other countries affect U.S. import prices.

A country's export prices tend to move fairly closely with the general price level in that country. If Mexico is experiencing a general increase in prices, this change likely will be reflected in price increases of all domestically produced goods, both exportable and nonexportable. The general rate of inflation abroad is likely to affect U.S. import prices. If the inflation rate abroad is high, U.S. import prices are likely to rise.

The Price Feedback Effect We have just seen that when a country experiences an increase in domestic prices, the prices of its exports will increase. It is also true that when the prices of a country's *imports* increase, the prices of domestic goods may increase in response. There are at least two ways this effect can occur.

First, an increase in the prices of imported inputs will shift a country's aggregate supply curve to the left. In Chapter 13, we discussed the macroeconomy's response to a cost shock. Recall that a leftward shift in the aggregate supply curve due to a cost increase causes aggregate output to fall and prices to rise (stagflation).

Second, if import prices rise relative to domestic prices, households will tend to substitute domestically produced goods and services for imports. This is equivalent to a rightward shift of the aggregate demand curve. If the domestic economy is operating on the upward-sloping part of the aggregate supply curve, the overall domestic price level will rise in response to an increase in aggregate demand. Perfectly competitive firms will see market-determined prices rise, and imperfectly competitive firms will experience an increase in the demand for their products. Studies have shown, for example, that the price of automobiles produced in the United States moves closely with the price of imported cars.

Still, this is not the end of the story. Suppose a country—say, Mexico—experiences an increase in its domestic price level. This will increase the price of its exports to Canada (and to all other countries). The increase in the price of Canadian imports from Mexico will lead to an increase in domestic prices in Canada. Canada also exports to Mexico. The increase in Canadian prices causes an increase in the price of Canadian exports to Mexico, which then further increases the Mexican price level.

This is called the **price feedback effect**, in the sense that inflation is "exportable." An increase in the price level in one country can drive up prices in other countries, which in turn further increases the price level in the first country. Through export and import prices, a domestic price increase can "feed back" on itself.

It is important to realize that the discussion so far has been based on the assumption of fixed exchange rates. Life is more complicated under flexible exchange rates, to which we now turn.

price feedback effect The process by which a domestic price increase in one country can "feed back" on itself through export and import prices. An increase in the price level in one country can drive up prices in other countries. This in turn further increases the price level in the first country.

The Open Economy with Flexible Exchange Rates

floating, *or* **market-determined, exchange rates** Exchange rates that are determined by the unregulated forces of supply and demand.

To a large extent, the fixed exchange rates set by the Bretton Woods agreements served as international monetary arrangements until 1971. Then in 1971, the United States and most other countries decided to abandon the fixed exchange rate system in favor of **floating,** *or* **market-determined, exchange rates**. Although governments still intervene to ensure that exchange rate movements are "orderly," exchange rates today are largely determined by the unregulated forces of supply and demand.

Understanding how an economy interacts with the rest of the world when exchange rates are not fixed is not as simple as when we assume fixed exchange rates. Exchange rates determine the price of imported goods relative to domestic goods and can have significant effects on the level of imports and exports. Consider a 20 percent drop in the value of the dollar against the British pound. Dollars buy fewer pounds, and pounds buy more dollars. Both British residents, who now get more dollars for pounds, and U.S. residents, who get fewer pounds for dollars, find that U.S. goods and services are more attractive. Exchange rate movements have important impacts on imports, exports, and the movement of capital between countries.

The Market for Foreign Exchange

What determines exchange rates under a floating rate system? To explore this question, we assume that there are just two countries, the United States and Great Britain. It is easier to understand a world with only two countries, and most of the points we will make can be generalized to a world with many trading partners.

The Supply of and Demand for Pounds Governments, private citizens, banks, and corporations exchange pounds for dollars and dollars for pounds every day. In our two-country case, those who *demand* pounds are holders of dollars seeking to exchange them for pounds. Those who *supply* pounds are holders of pounds seeking to exchange them for dollars. It is important not to confuse the supply of dollars (or pounds) on the foreign exchange market with the U.S. (or British) money supply. The latter is the sum of all the money currently in circulation. The supply of dollars on the foreign exchange market is the number of dollars that holders seek to exchange for pounds in a given time period. The demand for and supply of dollars on foreign exchange markets determine *exchange* rates; the demand for money balances, and the total domestic money supply determine the *interest* rate.

The common reason for exchanging dollars for pounds is to buy something produced in Great Britain. U.S. importers who purchase Jaguar automobiles or Scotch whiskey must pay with pounds. U.S. citizens traveling in Great Britain who want to ride the train, stay in a hotel, or eat at a restaurant must acquire pounds for dollars to do so. If a U.S. corporation builds a plant in Great Britain, it must pay for that plant in pounds.

At the same time, some people may want to buy British stocks or bonds. Implicitly, when U.S. citizens buy a bond issued by the British government or by a British corporation, they are making a loan, but the transaction requires a currency exchange. The British bond seller must ultimately be paid in pounds.

On the supply side of the market, the situation is reversed. Here we find people—usually British citizens—holding pounds they want to use to buy dollars. Again, the common reason is to buy things produced in the United States. If a British importer decides to import golf carts made in Georgia, the producer must be paid in dollars. British tourists visiting New York may ride in cabs, eat in restaurants, and tour Ellis Island. Doing those things requires dollars. When a British firm builds an office complex in Los Angeles, it must pay the contractor in dollars.

In addition to buyers and sellers who exchange money to engage in transactions, some people and institutions hold currency balances for speculative reasons. If you think that the U.S. dollar is going to decline in value relative to the pound, you may want to hold some of your wealth in the form of pounds. Table 20.2 summarizes some of the major categories of private foreign exchange demanders and suppliers in the two-country case of the United States and Great Britain.

Figure 20.2 shows the demand curve for pounds in the foreign exchange market. When the price of pounds (the exchange rate) is lower, it takes fewer dollars to buy British goods and services, to build a plant in Liverpool, to travel to London, and so on. Lower net prices (in dollars) should increase the demand for British-made products and encourage investment and travel in Great Britain. If prices (in pounds) in Britain do not change, an increase in the quantity of British goods and services demanded by foreigners will increase the quantity of pounds demanded. The demand-for-pounds curve in the foreign exchange market has a negative slope.

TABLE 20.2 Some Buyers and Sellers in International Exchange Markets: United States and Great Britain

The Demand for Pounds (Supply of Dollars)

1. Firms, households, or governments that import British goods into the United States or want to buy British-made goods and services
2. U.S. citizens traveling in Great Britain
3. Holders of dollars who want to buy British stocks, bonds, or other financial instruments
4. U.S. companies that want to invest in Great Britain
5. Speculators who anticipate a decline in the value of the dollar relative to the pound

The Supply of Pounds (Demand for Dollars)

1. Firms, households, or governments that import U.S. goods into Great Britain or want to buy U.S.-made goods and services
2. British citizens traveling in the United States
3. Holders of pounds who want to buy stocks, bonds, or other financial instruments in the United States
4. British companies that want to invest in the United States
5. Speculators who anticipate a rise in the value of the dollar relative to the pound

▶ **FIGURE 20.2**
The Demand for Pounds in the Foreign Exchange Market
When the price of pounds falls, British-made goods and services appear less expensive to U.S. buyers. If British prices are constant, U.S. buyers will buy more British goods and services and the quantity of pounds demanded will rise.

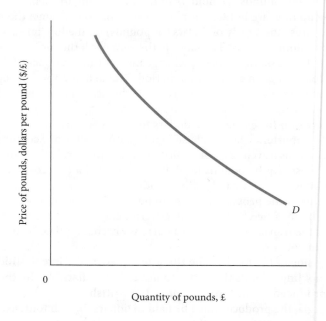

Figure 20.3 shows a supply curve for pounds in the foreign exchange market. At a higher exchange rate, each pound buys more dollars, making the price of U.S.-produced goods and services lower to the British. The British are more apt to buy U.S.-made goods when the price of pounds is high (the value of the dollar is low). An increase in British demand for U.S. goods and services is likely to increase the quantity of pounds supplied. The curve representing the supply of pounds in the foreign exchange market has a positive slope.

The Equilibrium Exchange Rate   When exchange rates are allowed to float, they are determined the same way other prices are determined: The equilibrium exchange rate occurs at the point at which the quantity demanded of a foreign currency equals the quantity of that currency supplied. This is illustrated in Figure 20.4. An excess demand for pounds

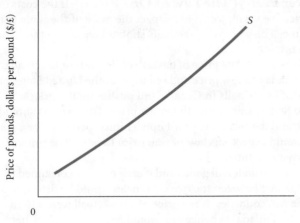

◀ **FIGURE 20.3**
The Supply of Pounds in the Foreign Exchange Market
When the price of pounds rises, the British can obtain more dollars for each pound. This means that U.S.-made goods and services appear less expensive to British buyers. Thus, the quantity of pounds supplied is likely to rise with the exchange rate.

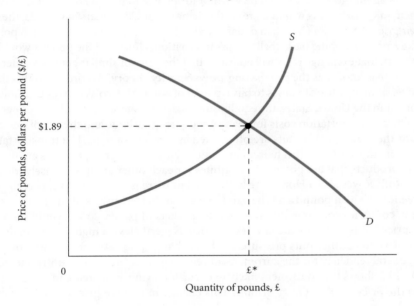

◀ **FIGURE 20.4**
The Equilibrium Exchange Rate
When exchange rates are allowed to float, they are determined by the forces of supply and demand. An excess demand for pounds will cause the pound to appreciate against the dollar. An excess supply of pounds will lead to a depreciating pound.

(quantity demanded in excess of quantity supplied) will cause the price of pounds to rise—the pound will **appreciate** relative to the dollar. An excess supply of pounds will cause the price of pounds to fall—the pound will **depreciate** relative to the dollar.[3]

Factors That Affect Exchange Rates

We now know enough to discuss the factors likely to influence exchange rates. Anything that changes the behavior of the people in Table 20.2 can cause demand and supply curves to shift and the exchange rate to adjust accordingly.

appreciation of a currency
The rise in value of one currency relative to another.

depreciation of a currency
The fall in value of one currency relative to another.

---

[3] Although Figure 20.3 shows the supply-of-pounds curve in the foreign exchange market with a positive slope, under certain circumstances the curve may bend back. Suppose the price of a pound rises from $1.50 to $2.00. Consider a British importer who buys 10 Chevrolets each month at $15,000 each, including transportation costs. When a pound exchanges for $1.50, he will supply 100,000 pounds per month to the foreign exchange market—100,000 pounds brings $150,000, enough to buy 10 cars. Now suppose the cheaper dollar causes him to buy 12 cars. Twelve cars will cost a total of $180,000; but at $2 = 1 pound, he will spend only 90,000 pounds per month. The supply of pounds on the market falls when the price of pounds rises. The reason for this seeming paradox is simple. The number of pounds a British importer needs to buy U.S. goods depends on both the quantity of goods he buys and the price of those goods in pounds. If demand for imports is inelastic so that the percentage decrease in price resulting from the depreciated currency is greater than the percentage increase in the quantity of imports demanded, importers will spend fewer pounds and the quantity of pounds supplied in the foreign exchange market will fall. The supply of pounds will slope upward as long as the demand for U.S. imports is elastic.

Purchasing Power Parity: The Law of One Price

If the costs of transporting goods between two countries are small, we would expect the price of the same good in both countries to be roughly the same. The price of basketballs should be roughly the same in Canada and the United States, for example.

It is not hard to see why. If the price of basketballs is cheaper in Canada, it will benefit someone to buy balls in Canada at a low price and sell them in the United States at a higher price. This decreases the supply of basketballs in Canada and pushes up the price and increases the supply of balls in the United States, and pushes down the price. This process should continue as long as the price differential, and therefore the profit opportunity, persists. For a good with trivial transportation costs, we would expect this **law of one price** to hold. The price of a good should be the same regardless of where we buy it.

If the law of one price held for all goods and if each country consumed the same market basket of goods, the exchange rate between the two currencies would be determined simply by the relative price levels in the two countries. If the price of a basketball were $10 in the United States and $12 in Canada, the U.S.–Canada exchange rate would have to be $1 U.S. per $1.20 Canadian. If the rate were instead one-to-one, it would be worth it for people to buy the balls in the United States and sell them in Canada. This would increase the demand for U.S. dollars in Canada, thereby driving up their price in terms of Canadian dollars to $1 U.S. per $1.2 Canadian, at which point no one could make a profit shipping basketballs across international lines and the process would cease.[4]

The theory that exchange rates will adjust so that the price of similar goods in different countries is the same is known as the **purchasing-power-parity theory**. According to this theory, if it takes 10 times as many Mexican pesos to buy a pound of salt in Mexico as it takes U.S. dollars to buy a pound of salt in the United States, the equilibrium exchange rate should be 10 pesos per dollar.

In practice, transportation costs for many goods are quite large and the law of one price does not hold for these goods. (Haircuts are often cited as a good example. The transportation costs for a U.S. resident to get a British haircut are indeed large unless that person is an airline pilot.) Also, many products that are potential substitutes for each other are not precisely identical. For instance, a Rolls Royce and a Honda are both cars, but there is no reason to expect the exchange rate between the British pound and the yen to be set so that the prices of the two are equalized. In addition, countries consume different market baskets of goods, so we would not expect the aggregate price levels to follow the law of one price. Nevertheless, a high rate of inflation in one country relative to another puts pressure on the exchange rate between the two countries, and there is a general tendency for the currencies of relatively high-inflation countries to depreciate.

Figure 20.5 shows the adjustment likely to occur following an increase in the U.S. price level relative to the price level in Great Britain. This change in relative prices will affect citizens of

law of one price If the costs of transportation are small, the price of the same good in different countries should be roughly the same.

purchasing-power-parity theory A theory of international exchange holding that exchange rates are set so that the price of similar goods in different countries is the same.

▶ **FIGURE 20.5**
Exchange Rates Respond to Changes in Relative Prices
The higher price level in the United States makes imports relatively less expensive. U.S. citizens are likely to increase their spending on imports from Britain, shifting the demand for pounds to the right, from D_0 to D_1. At the same time, the British see U.S. goods getting more expensive and reduce their demand for exports from the United States. The supply of pounds shifts to the left, from S_0 to S_1. The result is an increase in the price of pounds. The pound appreciates, and the dollar is worth less.

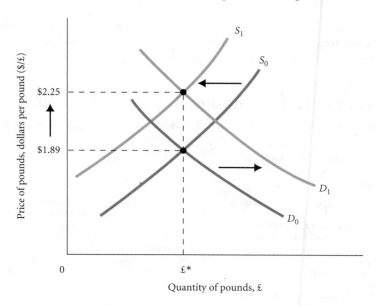

[4] Of course, if the rate were $1 U.S. to $2 Canadian, it would benefit people to buy basketballs in Canada (at $12 Canadian, which is $6 U.S.) and sell them in the United States. This would weaken demand for the U.S. dollar, and its price would fall from $2 Canadian until it reached $1.20 Canadian.

both countries. Higher prices in the United States make imports relatively less expensive. U.S. citizens are likely to increase their spending on imports from Britain, shifting the demand for pounds to the right, from D_0 to D_1. At the same time, the British see U.S. goods getting more expensive and reduce their demand for exports from the United States. Consequently, the supply of pounds shifts to the left, from S_0 to S_1. The result is an increase in the price of pounds. Before the change in relative prices, 1 pound sold for $1.89; after the change, 1 pound costs $2.25. The pound appreciates, and the dollar depreciates.

Relative Interest Rates   Another factor that influences a country's exchange rate is the level of its interest rate relative to other countries' interest rates. If the interest rate is 6 percent in the United States and 8 percent in Great Britain, people with money to lend have an incentive to buy British securities instead of U.S. securities. Although it is sometimes difficult for individuals in one country to buy securities in another country, it is easy for international banks and investment companies to do so. If the interest rate is lower in the United States than in Britain, there will be a movement of funds out of U.S. securities into British securities as banks and firms move their funds to the higher-yielding securities.

How does a U.S. bank buy British securities? It takes its dollars, buys British pounds, and uses the pounds to buy the British securities. The bank's purchase of pounds drives up the price of pounds in the foreign exchange market. The increased demand for pounds increases the price of the pound (and decreases the price of the dollar). A high interest rate in Britain relative to the interest rate in the United States tends to depreciate the dollar.

Figure 20.6 shows the effect of rising interest rates in the United States on the dollar–pound exchange rate. Higher interest rates in the United States attract British investors. To buy U.S. securities, the British need dollars. The supply of pounds (the demand for dollars) shifts to the right, from S_0 to S_1. The same relative interest rates affect the portfolio choices of U.S. banks, firms, and households. With higher interest rates at home, there is less incentive for U.S. residents to buy British securities. The demand for pounds drops at the same time the supply increases and the demand curve shifts to the left, from D_0 to D_1. The net result is a depreciating pound and an appreciating dollar. The price of pounds falls from $1.89 to $1.25.

The Effects of Exchange Rates on the Economy

We are now ready to discuss some of the implications of floating exchange rates. Recall, when exchange rates are fixed, households spend some of their incomes on imports and the multiplier is smaller than it would be otherwise. Imports are a "leakage" from the circular flow, much like

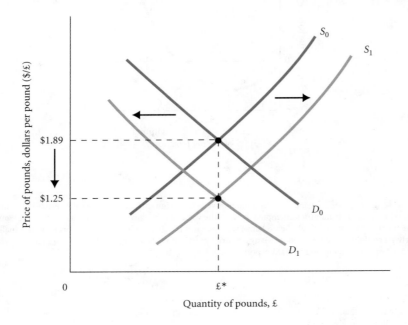

◀ **FIGURE 20.6**
Exchange Rates Respond to Changes in Relative Interest Rates
If U.S. interest rates rise relative to British interest rates, British citizens holding pounds may be attracted into the U.S. securities market. To buy bonds in the United States, British buyers must exchange pounds for dollars. The supply of pounds shifts to the right, from S_0 to S_1. However, U.S. citizens are less likely to be interested in British securities because interest rates are higher at home. The demand for pounds shifts to the left, from D_0 to D_1. The result is a depreciated pound and a stronger dollar.

taxes and saving. Exports, in contrast, are an "injection" into the circular flow; they represent spending on U.S.-produced goods and services from abroad and can stimulate output.

The world is far more complicated when exchange rates are allowed to float. First, the level of imports and exports depends on exchange rates as well as on income and other factors. When events cause exchange rates to adjust, the levels of imports and exports will change. Changes in exports and imports can, in turn, affect the level of real GDP and the price level. Further, exchange rates themselves also adjust to changes in the economy. Suppose the government decides to stimulate the economy with an expansionary monetary policy. This will affect interest rates, which may affect exchange rates.

Exchange Rate Effects on Imports, Exports, and Real GDP   As we already know, when a country's currency depreciates (falls in value), its import prices rise and its export prices (in foreign currencies) fall. When the U.S. dollar is cheap, U.S. products are more competitive with products produced in the rest of the world and foreign-made goods look expensive to U.S. citizens.

A depreciation of a country's currency can serve as a stimulus to the economy. Suppose the U.S. dollar falls in value, as it did sharply between 1985 and 1988 and again, more moderately from 2002–2008 and 2012–2013. If foreign buyers increase their spending on U.S. goods, and domestic buyers substitute U.S.-made goods for imports, aggregate expenditure on domestic output will rise, inventories will fall, and real GDP (Y) will increase. A depreciation of a country's currency is likely to increase its GDP.[5]

Exchange Rates and the Balance of Trade: The J Curve   Because a depreciating currency tends to increase exports and decrease imports, you might think that it also will reduce a country's trade deficit. In fact, the effect of a depreciation on the balance of trade is ambiguous.

Many economists believe that when a currency starts to depreciate, the balance of trade is likely to worsen for the first few quarters (perhaps three to six). After that, the balance of trade may improve. This effect is graphed in Figure 20.7. The curve in this figure resembles the letter J, and the movement in the balance of trade that it describes is sometimes called the **J-curve effect**. The point of the J shape is that the balance of trade gets worse before it gets better following a currency depreciation.

J-curve effect   Following a currency depreciation, a country's balance of trade may get worse before it gets better. The graph showing this effect is shaped like the letter J, hence the name J-curve effect.

▶ **FIGURE 20.7**   **The Effect of a Depreciation on the Balance of Trade (the J Curve)**
Initially, a depreciation of a country's currency may worsen its balance of trade. The negative effect on the price of imports may initially dominate the positive effects of an increase in exports and a decrease in imports.

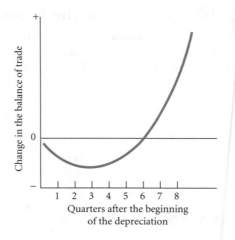

Quarters after the beginning of the depreciation

---

[5] For this reason, some countries are tempted at times to intervene in foreign exchange markets, depreciate their currencies, and stimulate their economies. If all countries attempted to lower the value of their currencies simultaneously, there would be no gain in income for any of them. Although the exchange rate system at the time was different, such a situation actually occurred during the early years of the Great Depression. Many countries practiced so-called *beggar-thy-neighbor* policies of competitive devaluations in a desperate attempt to maintain export sales and employment.

ECONOMICS IN PRACTICE

China's Increased Flexibility

As we indicate in the text, most economies in the world operate with flexible exchange rates so that the value of a dollar relative to the euro, for example, is set in the market and reflects the underlying markets for goods and services. One exception among the major trading countries has been China, whose government has acted to keep the value of its currency, the yuan, stable and relatively low. An undervalued yuan, of course, increases demand for Chinese goods from abroad, but it also hurts the Chinese population by making foreign goods more expensive. In the late spring of 2010, after much pressure from its trading partners, the Chinese government announced that it would make the yuan more flexible. From 2005–2011, the yuan appreciated 28%.

THINKING PRACTICALLY

1. What mechanisms could the Chinese government use to keep the value of the yuan low?

How does the J curve come about? Recall that the balance of trade is equal to export revenue minus import costs, including exports and imports of services:

> balance of trade = dollar price of exports × quantity of exports
> − dollar price of imports × quantity of imports

A currency depreciation affects the items on the right side of this equation as follows: First, the quantity of exports increases and the quantity of imports decreases; both have a *positive* effect on the balance of trade (lowering the trade deficit or raising the trade surplus). Second, the dollar price of exports is not likely to change very much, at least not initially. The dollar price of exports changes when the U.S. price level changes, but the initial effect of a depreciation on the domestic price level is not likely to be large. Third, the dollar price of imports increases. Imports into the United States are more expensive because $1 U.S. buys fewer yen, euros, and so on, than before. An increase in the dollar price of imports has a *negative* effect on the balance of trade.

An example to clarify this last point follows: The dollar price of a Japanese car that costs 1,200,000 yen rises from $10,000 to $12,000 when the exchange rate moves from 120 yen per dollar to 100 yen per dollar. After the currency depreciation, the United States ends up spending more (in dollars) for the Japanese car than it did before. Of course, the United States will end up buying fewer Japanese cars than it did before. Does the number of cars drop enough so that the quantity effect is bigger than the price effect or vice versa? Does the value of imports increase or decrease?

The net effect of a depreciation on the balance of trade could go either way. The depreciation stimulates exports and cuts back imports, but it also increases the dollar price of imports. It seems that the negative effect dominates initially. The impact of a depreciation on the price of imports is generally felt quickly, while it takes time for export and import quantities to respond to price changes. In the short run, the value of imports increases more than the value of exports, so the balance of trade worsens. The initial effect is likely to be negative, but after exports and imports have had time to respond, the net effect turns positive.

The more elastic the demand for exports and imports, the larger the eventual improvement in the balance of trade.

Exchange Rates and Prices

The depreciation of a country's currency tends to increase its price level. There are two reasons for this effect. First, when a country's currency is less expensive, its products are more competitive on world markets, so exports rise. In addition, domestic buyers tend to substitute domestic products for the now-more-expensive imports. This means that planned aggregate expenditure on domestically produced goods and services rises and that the aggregate demand curve shifts to the right. The result is a higher price level, a higher output, or both. (You may want to draw an *AS/AD* diagram to verify this outcome.) If the economy is close to capacity, the result is likely to be higher prices. Second, a depreciation makes imported inputs more expensive. If costs increase, the aggregate supply curve shifts to the left. If aggregate demand remains unchanged, the result is an increase in the price level.

Monetary Policy with Flexible Exchange Rates

Let us now put everything in this chapter together and consider what happens when monetary policy is used first to stimulate the economy and then to contract the economy.

Suppose the economy is below full employment and the Federal Reserve (Fed) lowers the interest rate. The lower interest rate stimulates planned investment spending and consumption spending. Output thus increases. But there are additional effects: (1) The lower interest rate has an impact in the foreign exchange market. A lower interest rate means a lower demand for U.S. securities by foreigners, so the demand for dollars drops. (2) U.S. investment managers will be more likely to buy foreign securities (which are now paying relatively higher interest rates), so the supply of dollars rises. Both events push down the value of the dollar. A cheaper dollar is a good thing if the goal of the Fed is to stimulate the domestic economy because a cheaper dollar means more U.S. exports and fewer imports. If consumers substitute U.S.-made goods for imports, both the added exports and the decrease in imports mean more spending on domestic products, so the multiplier actually increases. Flexible exchange rates thus help the Fed in its goal to stimulate the economy.

Now suppose inflation is a problem and the Fed raises the interest rate. Here again, floating exchange rates help. The higher interest rate lowers planned investment and consumption spending, reducing output and lowering the price level. The higher interest rate also attracts foreign buyers into U.S. financial markets, driving up the value of the dollar, which reduces the price of imports. The reduction in the price of imports causes a shift of the aggregate supply curve to the right, which helps fight inflation, which is what the Fed wants to do. Flexible exchange rates thus help the Fed in its goal to fight inflation.

Fiscal Policy with Flexible Exchange Rates

While we have just seen that flexible exchange rates help the Fed achieve its goals, the opposite is the case for the fiscal authorities in normal times when there is no zero lower interest rate bound and the Fed is following the Fed rule. Say that the administration and Congress want to stimulate the economy, and they increase government spending to do this. This increases output in the usual way (shift of the *AD* curve to the right). This usual way means that the interest rate is also higher (from the Fed rule because output and the price level are higher). The higher interest rate leads, as discussed above, to an appreciation of the dollar. An appreciation, other things being equal, increases imports and decreases exports, which has a negative effect on output. The increase in output is thus less than it would have been had there been no appreciation. The appreciation also leads to a decrease in import prices, which shifts the *AS* curve to the right, thus decreasing the price level, other things being equal. Although the price level is lower than otherwise, the main worry was output, and output is lower, other things being equal. Flexible exchange rates thus hurt the fiscal authorities in their goal to stimulate the economy.

ECONOMICS IN PRACTICE

Losing Monetary Policy Control

In 1999 the European Central Bank (ECB) was created and a common currency for much of Europe, the euro, was introduced. Countries across Europe, from Germany and France to Italy, Spain, and Portugal, dismantled their own monetary authorities, turning their central banks into research institutions, and ceded control over monetary policy to the ECB.

In a recent speech, Martin Feldstein, Harvard professor and former advisor to President Reagan, argued the following:

"When interest and principal on the British government debt come due, the British Government can always create additional pounds to meet those obligations. By contrast, the French government and the French central bank cannot create euros.... If France cannot borrow to finance that deficit, France will be forced to default."[1]

THINKING PRACTICALLY

1. With the creation of the ECB some have argued that overspending by the French and Italian governments becomes Germany's problem. Why?

[1] Quoted in *The Telegraph*, Feb 2, 2013.

Flexible exchange rates also hurt the fiscal authorities if they want to contract the economy to fight inflation. Say there is a decrease in government spending. This shifts the *AD* curve to the left, which decreases output and the price level. The interest rate is also lower (from the Fed rule because output and the price level are lower), which leads to a depreciation of the dollar. The depreciation, other things being equal, decreases imports and increases exports, which has a positive effect on output. However, the depreciation also leads to an increase in import prices, which shifts the *AS* curve to the left, thus increasing the price level, other things being equal. Although output is higher than otherwise, the main worry was inflation, and the price level is higher, other things being equal. So flexible exchange rates also hurt the fiscal authorities in their goal to fight inflation.

Note that the appreciation or depreciation occurs because of the Fed rule. If the Fed does not change the interest rate in response to the fiscal policy change, either because there is a zero lower bound or because it just doesn't want to, there is no appreciation or depreciation and thus no offset to what the fiscal authorities are trying to do from the existence of flexible exchange rates.

Monetary Policy with Fixed Exchange Rates   Although most major countries in the world today have a flexible exchange rate (counting for this purpose the euro zone countries as one country), it is interesting to ask what role monetary policy can play when a country has a fixed exchange rate. The answer is, no role. For a country to keep its exchange rate fixed to, say, the U.S. dollar, its interest rate cannot change relative to the U.S. interest rate. If the monetary authority of the country lowered the interest rate because it wanted to stimulate the economy, the country's currency would depreciate (assuming the U.S. interest rate did not change). People would want to sell the country's currency and buy dollars and invest in U.S. securities because the country's interest rate would have fallen relative to the U.S. interest rate. In other words, the monetary authority cannot change its interest rate relative to the U.S. interest rate without having its exchange rate change. The monetary authority is at the mercy of the United States, and it has no independent way of changing its interest rate if it wants to keep its exchange rate fixed to the dollar.

When the various European countries moved in 1999 to a common currency, the euro, each country gave up its monetary policy. Monetary policy is decided for all of the euro zone countries by the European Central Bank (ECB). The Bank of Italy, for example, no longer has any influence over Italian interest rates. Interest rates are influenced by the ECB. This is the price Italy paid for giving up the lira. See the *Economics in Practice*, "Losing Monetary Policy Control," on p. 393 for problems that may arise when there is a common currency.

The one case in which a country can change its interest rate and keep its exchange rate fixed is if it imposes capital controls. Imposing capital controls means that the country limits or prevents people from buying or selling its currency in the foreign exchange markets. A citizen of the country may be prevented, for example, from using the country's currency to buy dollars. The problem with capital controls is that they are hard to enforce, especially for large countries and for long periods of time.

An Interdependent World Economy

The increasing interdependence of countries in the world economy has made the problems facing policy makers more difficult. We used to be able to think of the United States as a relatively self-sufficient region. Forty years ago economic events outside U.S. borders had relatively little effect on its economy. This situation is no longer true. The events of the past four decades have taught us that the performance of the U.S. economy is heavily dependent on events outside U.S. borders.

This chapter and the previous chapter have provided only the bare bones of open-economy macroeconomics. If you continue your study of economics, more will be added to the basic story we have presented. The next chapter concludes with a discussion of the problems of developing countries.

--- SUMMARY ---

1. The main difference between an international transaction and a domestic transaction concerns currency exchange: When people in different countries buy from and sell to each other, an exchange of currencies must also take place.

2. The *exchange rate* is the price of one country's currency in terms of another country's currency.

THE BALANCE OF PAYMENTS *p. 376*

3. *Foreign exchange* is all currencies other than the domestic currency of a given country. The record of a nation's transactions in goods, services, and assets with the rest of the world is its *balance of payments*. The balance of payments is also the record of a country's sources (supply) and uses (demand) of foreign exchange.

EQUILIBRIUM OUTPUT (INCOME) IN AN OPEN ECONOMY *p. 380*

4. In an open economy, some income is spent on foreign produced goods instead of domestically produced goods. To measure planned domestic aggregate expenditure in an open economy, we add total exports but subtract total imports: $C + I + G + EX - IM$. The open economy is in equilibrium when domestic aggregate output (income) (Y) equals planned domestic aggregate expenditure.

5. In an open economy, the multiplier equals

$$1/[1 - (MPC - MPM)],$$

where MPC is the marginal propensity to consume and MPM is the marginal propensity to import. The *marginal propensity to import* is the change in imports caused by a $1 change in income.

6. In addition to income, other factors that affect the level of imports are the after-tax real wage rate, after-tax nonlabor income, interest rates, and relative prices of domestically produced and foreign-produced goods. The demand for exports is determined by economic activity in the rest of the world and by relative prices.

7. An increase in U.S. economic activity leads to a worldwide increase in economic activity, which then "feeds back" to the United States. An increase in U.S. imports increases other countries' exports, which stimulates economies and increases their imports, which increases U.S. exports, which stimulates the U.S. economy and increases its imports, and so on. This is the *trade feedback effect*.

8. Export prices of other countries affect U.S. import prices. The general rate of inflation abroad is likely to affect U.S. import prices. If the inflation rate abroad is high, U.S. import prices are likely to rise.

9. Because one country's exports are another country's imports, an increase in export prices increases other countries' import prices. An increase in other countries' import prices leads to an increase in their domestic prices—and their export prices. In short, export prices affect import prices and vice versa. This *price feedback effect* shows that inflation is "exportable"; an increase in the price level in one country can drive up prices in other countries, making inflation in the first country worse.

THE OPEN ECONOMY WITH FLEXIBLE EXCHANGE RATES *p. 384*

10. The equilibrium exchange rate occurs when the quantity demanded of a foreign currency in the foreign exchange market equals the quantity of that currency supplied in the foreign exchange market.

11. *Depreciation of a currency* occurs when a nation's currency falls in value relative to another country's currency. *Appreciation of a currency* occurs when a nation's currency rises in value relative to another country's currency.

12. According to the *law of one price*, if the costs of transportation are small, the price of the same good in different countries should be roughly the same. The theory that exchange rates are set so that the price of similar goods in different countries is the same is known as the *purchasing-power-parity* theory. In practice, transportation costs are significant for many goods, and the law of one price does not hold for these goods.

13. A high rate of inflation in one country relative to another country puts pressure on the exchange rate between the two countries. There is a general tendency for the currencies of relatively high-inflation countries to depreciate.

14. A depreciation of the dollar tends to increase U.S. GDP by making U.S. exports cheaper (hence, more competitive

abroad) and by making U.S. imports more expensive (encouraging consumers to switch to domestically produced goods and services).

15. The effect of a depreciation of a nation's currency on its balance of trade is unclear. In the short run, a currency depreciation may increase the balance-of-trade deficit because it raises the price of imports. Although this price increase causes a decrease in the quantity of imports demanded, the impact of a depreciation on the price of imports is generally felt quickly, but it takes time for export and import quantities to respond to price changes. The initial effect is likely to be negative, but after exports and imports have had time to respond, the net effect turns positive. The tendency for the balance-of-trade deficit to widen and then to decrease as the result of a currency depreciation is known as the *J-curve effect*.

16. The depreciation of a country's currency tends to raise its price level for two reasons. First, a currency depreciation increases planned aggregate expenditure, an effect that shifts the aggregate demand curve to the right. If the economy is close to capacity, the result is likely to be higher prices. Second, a depreciation makes imported inputs more expensive. If costs increase, the aggregate supply curve shifts to the left. If aggregate demand remains unchanged, the result is an increase in the price level.

17. When exchange rates are flexible, a U.S. expansionary monetary policy decreases the interest rate and stimulates planned investment and consumption spending. The lower interest rate leads to a lower demand for U.S. securities by foreigners and a higher demand for foreign securities by U.S. investment-fund managers. As a result, the dollar depreciates. A U.S. contractionary monetary policy appreciates the dollar.

18. Flexible exchange rates do not always work to the advantage of policy makers. An expansionary fiscal policy can appreciate the dollar and work to reduce the multiplier.

———— R E V I E W   T E R M S   A N D   C O N C E P T S ————

appreciation of a currency, *p. 387*

balance of payments, *p. 376*

balance of trade, *p. 377*

balance on capital account, *p. 378*

balance on current account, *p. 378*

depreciation of a currency, *p. 387*

exchange rate, *p. 376*

floating, *or* market-determined, exchange rates, *p. 384*

foreign exchange, *p. 376*

J-curve effect, *p. 390*

law of one price, *p. 388*

marginal propensity to import (*MPM*), *p. 381*

net exports of goods and services (*EX* − *IM*), *p. 380*

price feedback effect, *p. 384*

purchasing-power-parity theory, *p. 388*

trade deficit, *p. 377*

trade feedback effect, *p. 383*

Equations:

Planned aggregate expenditure in an open economy:

$AE \equiv C + I + G + EX - IM$, *p. 380*

Open-economy multiplier =

$\dfrac{1}{1 - (MPC - MPM)}$, *p. 382*

PROBLEMS

All problems are available on MyEconLab.

1. In April 2013, the euro was trading at $1.31. Check the Internet or any daily newspaper to see what the "price" of a euro is today. What explanations can you give for the change? Make sure you check what has happened to interest rates and economic growth.

2. Suppose the following graph shows what prevailed on the foreign exchange market in 2012 with floating exchange rates.
   a. Name three phenomena that might shift the demand curve to the right.
   b. Which, if any, of these three phenomena might cause a simultaneous shift of the supply curve to the left?
   c. What effects might each of the three phenomena have on the balance of trade if the exchange rate floats?

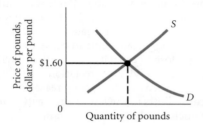

3. Obtain a recent issue of *The Economist*. Turn to the section entitled "Financial Indicators." Look at the table entitled "Trade, exchange rates and budgets." Which country had the largest trade deficit over the last year and during the last month? Which country had the largest trade surplus over the last year and during the last month? How does the current account deficit/surplus compare to the overall trade balance? How can you explain the difference?

4. The exchange rate between the U.S. dollar and the Japanese yen is floating freely—both governments do not intervene in the market for each currency. Suppose a large trade deficit with Japan prompts the United States to impose quotas on certain Japanese products imported into the United States and, as a result, the quantity of these imports falls.
   a. The decrease in spending on Japanese products increases spending on U.S.-made goods. Why? What effect will this have on U.S. output and employment and on Japanese output and employment?
   b. What happens to U.S. imports from Japan when U.S. output (or income) rises? If the quotas initially reduce imports from Japan by $25 billion, why is the final reduction in imports likely to be less than $25 billion?
   c. Suppose the quotas do succeed in reducing imports from Japan by $15 billion. What will happen to the demand for yen? Why?
   d. What will happen to the dollar–yen exchange rate? Why? (*Hint:* There is an excess supply of yen, or an excess demand for dollars.) What effects will the change in the value of each currency have on employment and output in the United States? What about the balance of trade? (Ignore complications such as the J curve.)
   e. Considering the macroeconomic effects of a quota on Japanese imports, could a quota reduce employment and output in the United States? have no effect at all? Explain.

5. What effect will each of the following events have on the current account balance and the exchange rate if the exchange rate is fixed? if the exchange rate is floating?
   a. The U.S. government cuts taxes and income rises.
   b. The U.S. inflation rate increases, and prices in the United States rise faster than those in countries with which the United States trades.
   c. The United States adopts an expansionary monetary policy. Interest rates fall (and are now lower than those in other countries) and income rises.
   d. The textile companies' "Buy American" campaign is successful, and U.S. consumers switch from purchasing imported products to buying products made in the United States.

6. You are given the following model that describes the economy of Hypothetica.
   (1) Consumption function: $C = 100 + .8Y_d$
   (2) Planned investment: $I = 38$
   (3) Government spending: $G = 75$
   (4) Exports: $EX = 25$
   (5) Imports: $IM = .05 Y_d$
   (6) Disposable income: $Y_d \equiv Y - T$
   (7) Taxes: $T = 40$
   (8) Planned aggregate expenditure:

   $$AE \equiv C + I + G + EX - IM$$

   (9) Definition of equilibrium income: $Y = AE$
   a. What is equilibrium income in Hypothetica? What is the government deficit? What is the current account balance?
   b. If government spending is increased to $G = 80$, what happens to equilibrium income? Explain using the government spending multiplier. What happens to imports?
   c. Now suppose the amount of imports is limited to $IM = 40$ by a quota on imports. If government spending is again increased from 75 to 80, what happens to equilibrium income? Explain why the same increase in G has a bigger effect on income in the second case. What is it about the presence of imports that changes the value of the multiplier?
   d. If exports are fixed at $EX = 25$, what must income be to ensure a current account balance of zero? (*Hint:* Imports depend on income, so what must income be for imports to be equal to exports?) By how much must we cut government spending to balance the current account? (*Hint:* Use your answer to the first part of this question to determine how much of a decrease in income is needed. Then use the multiplier to calculate the decrease in G needed to reduce income by that amount.)

7. [Related to the *Economics in Practice* on p. 391] Do a Web search and find a Website where you can look up historical exchange rates. Find the exchange rates between the U.S. dollar and the euro, the Canadian dollar, the Japanese yen, and the Chinese yuan at the beginning of 2008 and at the end of 2008. Did the U.S. dollar appreciate or depreciate against these currencies during 2008? Go to www.census.gov and find the value of U.S. exports, imports, and the U.S. trade balance at

the beginning of 2008 and at the end of 2008. Did these values increase or decrease during 2008? Explain how the changes in the exchange rates may have had an impact on the changes in U.S exports, imports, and the trade balance.

8. Suppose the exchange rate between the Mexican peso and the U.S. dollar is 12 MXN = $1 and the exchange rate between the Hungarian forint and the U.S. dollar is 215 HUF = $1.
   a. Express both of these exchange rates in terms of dollars per unit of the foreign currency.
   b. What should the exchange rate be between the Mexican peso and the Hungarian forint? Express the exchange rate in terms of 1 peso and in terms of 1 forint.
   c. Suppose the exchange rate between the peso and the dollar changes to 9 MXN = $1 and the exchange rate between the forint and the dollar changes to 240 HUF = $1. For each of the three currencies, explain whether the currency has appreciated or depreciated against the other two currencies.

9. Suppose the exchange rate between the British pound and the U.S. dollar is £1 = $1.50.
   a. Draw a graph showing the demand and supply of pounds for dollars.
   b. If the Bank of England implements a contractionary monetary policy, explain what will happen to the exchange rate between the pound and the dollar and show this on a graph. Has the dollar appreciated or depreciated relative to the pound? Explain.
   c. If the U.S. government implements an expansionary fiscal policy, explain what will happen to the exchange rate between the pound and the dollar and show this on a graph. Has the dollar appreciated or depreciated relative to the pound? Explain.

10. Canada is the largest trading partner for the United States. In 2009, U.S. exports to Canada were more than $171 billion and imports from Canada totaled more than $224 billion. On January 1, 2009, the exchange rate between the Canadian dollar and the U.S. dollar was 1.224 Canadian dollars = 1 U.S. dollar. On January 1, 2010, the exchange rate was 1.05 Canadian dollars = 1 U.S. dollar. Explain how this change in exchange rates could impact U.S. consumers and firms?

11. [Related to the *Economics in Practice* on p. 379] The United States is the largest oil importer in the world, importing an average of 10.6 million barrels of crude oil per day in 2012. According to the *Economics in Practice*, energy prices are key to France's trade deficit, and in the first half of 2012, France's trade deficit fell as a result of lower oil prices. Go to www.inflationdata.com to look up crude oil prices for the past 10 years; then go to www.census.gov to look up the U.S. trade balance for the past 10 years. Does there appear to be a relationship between the price of crude oil and the U.S. trade balance? Briefly explain the results of your findings.

12. [Related to the *Economics in Practice* on p. 383] The *Economics in Practice* states that trade levels declined during the 2008-2009 recession, reaching a low point toward the beginning of 2009. Search the Internet for export and import data since 2008 for developed nations. By how much have the values of these exports and imports increased or decreased since 2009? Explain if the changes in the values reflect the trade feedback effect.

13. [Related to the *Economics in Practice* on p. 393] Explain why the European Central Bank cannot selectively change interest rates in any of the 17 EU countries that have adopted the euro—for example, lowering the interest rate to stimulate the economies of Greece, Ireland, or Spain, while maintaining the interest rate in other countries.

CHAPTER 20 APPENDIX

World Monetary Systems Since 1900

Since the beginning of the twentieth century, the world has operated under a number of different monetary systems. This Appendix provides a brief history of each and a description of how they worked.

The Gold Standard

The gold standard was the major system of exchange rate determination before 1914. All currencies were priced in terms of gold—an ounce of gold was worth so much in each currency. When all currencies exchanged at fixed ratios to gold, exchange rates could be determined easily. For instance, 1 ounce of gold was worth $20 U.S.; that same ounce of gold exchanged for £4 (British pounds). Because $20 and £4 were each worth 1 ounce of gold, the exchange rate between dollars and pounds was $20/£4, or $5 to £1.

For the gold standard to be effective, it had to be backed up by the country's willingness to buy and sell gold at the determined price. As long as countries maintain their currencies at a fixed value in terms of gold *and* as long as each country is willing to buy and sell gold, exchange rates are fixed. If at the given exchange rate the number of U.S. citizens who want to buy things produced in Great Britain is equal to the number of British citizens who want to buy things produced in the United States, the currencies of the two countries will simply be exchanged. What if U.S. citizens suddenly decide they want to drink imported Scotch instead of domestic bourbon? If the British do not have an increased desire for U.S. goods, they will still accept U.S. dollars because those dollars can be redeemed in gold. This gold can then be immediately turned into pounds.

As long as a country's overall balance of payments remained in balance, no gold would enter or leave the country and the economy would be in equilibrium. If U.S. citizens bought more from the British than the British bought from the United States, however, the U.S. balance of payments would be in deficit and the U.S. stock of gold would begin to fall. Conversely, Britain would start to accumulate gold because it would be exporting more than it spent on imports.

Under the gold standard, gold was a big determinant of the money supply.[1] An inflow of gold into a country caused that country's money supply to expand, and an outflow of gold caused that country's money supply to contract. If gold were flowing from the United States to Great Britain, the British money supply would expand and the U.S. money supply would contract.

Now recall from earlier chapters the impacts of a change in the money supply. An expanded money supply in Britain will lower British interest rates and stimulate aggregate demand. As a result, aggregate output (income) and the price level in Britain will increase. Higher British prices will discourage U.S. citizens from buying British goods. At the same time, British citizens will have more income and will face relatively lower import prices, causing them to import more from the States.

On the other side of the Atlantic, U.S. citizens will face a contracting domestic money supply. This will cause higher interest rates, declining aggregate demand, lower prices, and falling output (income). The effect will be lower demand in the United States for British goods. Thus, changes in relative prices and incomes that resulted from the inflow and outflow of gold would automatically bring trade back into balance.

Problems with the Gold Standard

Two major problems were associated with the gold standard. First, the gold standard implied that a country had little control over its money supply. The reason, as we have just seen, is that the money stock increased when the overall balance of payments was in surplus (gold inflow) and decreased when the overall balance was in deficit (gold outflow). A country that was experiencing a balance-of-payments deficit could correct the problem only by the painful process of allowing its money supply to contract. This contraction brought on a slump in economic activity, a slump that would eventually restore balance-of-payments equilibrium, but only after reductions in income and employment. Countries could (and often did) act to protect their gold reserves, and this precautionary step prevented the adjustment mechanism from correcting the deficit.

Making the money supply depend on the amount of gold available had another disadvantage. When major new gold fields were discovered (as in California in 1849 and South Africa in 1886), the world's supply of gold (and therefore of money) increased. The price level rose and income increased. When no new gold was discovered, the supply of money remained unchanged and prices and income tended to fall.

When President Reagan took office in 1981, he established a commission to consider returning the nation to the gold standard. The final commission report recommended against such a move. An important part of the reasoning behind this recommendation was that the gold standard puts enormous economic power in the hands of gold-producing nations.

Fixed Exchange Rates and the Bretton Woods System

As World War II drew to a close, a group of economists from the United States and Europe met to formulate a new set of rules for exchange rate determination that they hoped would avoid the difficulties of the gold standard. The rules they designed became known as the *Bretton Woods system*, after the town in New Hampshire where the delegates met. The Bretton Woods system was based on two (not necessarily compatible) premises. First, countries were to maintain fixed exchange rates with one another. Instead of pegging their currencies directly to gold, however, currencies were fixed in terms of the U.S. dollar, which was fixed in value at $35 per ounce of gold. The British pound, for instance, was fixed at roughly $2.40, so that an ounce of gold was worth approximately £14.6. As we shall see, the pure system of fixed exchange rates would work in a manner very similar to the pre-1914 gold standard.

The second aspect of the Bretton Woods system added a new wrinkle to the operation of the international economy. Countries experiencing a "fundamental disequilibrium" in their balance of payments were allowed to change their exchange rates. (The term *fundamental disequilibrium* was necessarily vague, but it came to be interpreted as a large and persistent current account deficit.) Exchange rates were not really fixed under the Bretton Woods system; they were, as someone remarked, only "fixed until further notice."

The point of allowing countries with serious current account problems to alter the value of their currency was to avoid the harsh recessions that the operation of the gold standard would have produced under these circumstances. However, the experience of the European economies in the years between World War I and World War II suggested that it might not be a good idea to give countries complete freedom to change their exchange rates whenever they wanted.

During the Great Depression, many countries undertook so-called competitive devaluations to protect domestic output and employment. That is, countries would try to encourage exports—a source of output growth and employment—by attempting to set as low an exchange rate as possible, thereby making their exports competitive with foreign-produced goods. Unfortunately, such policies had a built-in flaw. A devaluation of the pound against the French franc might help encourage British exports to France, but if those additional British exports cut into French output and employment, France would likely respond by devaluing the franc against the pound, a move that, of course, would undo the effects of the pound's initial devaluation.

To solve this exchange rate rivalry, the Bretton Woods agreement created the International Monetary Fund (IMF). Its job was to assist countries experiencing temporary current

---

[1] In the days when currencies were tied to gold, changes in the amount of gold influenced the supply of money in two ways. A change in the quantity of gold coins in circulation had a direct effect on the supply of money; indirectly, gold served as a backing for paper currency. A decrease in the central bank's gold holdings meant a decline in the amount of paper money that could be supported.

account problems.[2] It was also supposed to certify that a "fundamental disequilibrium" existed before a country was allowed to change its exchange rate. The IMF was like an international economic traffic cop whose job was to ensure that all countries were playing the game according to the agreed-to rules and to provide emergency assistance where needed.

"Pure" Fixed Exchange Rates

Under a pure fixed exchange rate system, governments set a particular *fixed* rate at which their currencies will exchange for one another and then commit themselves to maintaining that rate. A true fixed exchange rate system is like the gold standard in that exchange rates are supposed to stay the same forever. Because currencies are no longer backed by gold, they have no fixed, or standard, value relative to one another. There is, therefore, no automatic mechanism to keep exchange rates aligned with each other, as with the gold standard.

The result is that under a pure fixed exchange rate system, governments must at times intervene in the foreign exchange market to keep currencies aligned at their established values. Economists define government intervention in the foreign exchange market as the buying or selling of foreign exchange for the purpose of manipulating the exchange rate. What kind of intervention is likely to occur under a fixed exchange rate system, and how does it work?

We can see how intervention works by looking at Figure 20A.1. Initially, the market for Australian dollars is in equilibrium. At the fixed exchange rate of 0.96, the supply of dollars is exactly equal to the demand for dollars. No government intervention is necessary to maintain the exchange rate at this level. Now suppose Australian wines are found to be contaminated with antifreeze and U.S. citizens switch to California wines. This substitution away from the Australian product shifts the U.S. demand curve for Australian dollars to the left: The United States demands fewer Australian dollars at every exchange rate (cost of an Australian dollar) because it is purchasing less from Australia than it did before.

If the price of Australian dollars were set in a completely unfettered market, the shift in the demand curve would lead to a fall in the price of Australian dollars, just the way the price of wheat would fall if there was an excess supply of wheat. Remember, the Australian and U.S. governments have committed themselves to maintaining the rate at 0.96. To do so, either the U.S. government or the Australian government (or both) must buy up the excess supply of Australian dollars to keep its price from falling. In essence, the fixed exchange rate policy commits governments to making up any difference between the supply of a currency and the demand so as to keep the price of

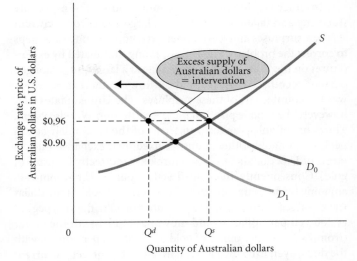

▲ **FIGURE 20A.1   Government Intervention in the Foreign Exchange Market**
If the price of Australian dollars were set in a completely unfettered market, one Australian dollar would cost 0.96 U.S. dollars when demand is D_0 and 0.90 when demand is D_1. If the government has committed to keeping the value at 0.96, it must buy up the excess supply of Australian dollars ($Q^s - Q^d$).

the currency (exchange rate) at the desired level. The government promises to act as the supplier (or demander) of last resort, who will ensure that the amount of foreign exchange demanded by the private sector will equal the supply at the fixed price.

Problems with the Bretton Woods System

As it developed after the end of World War II, the system of more-or-less fixed exchange rates had some flaws that led to its abandonment in 1971.

First, there was a basic asymmetry built into the rules of international finance. Countries experiencing large and persistent current account deficits—what the Bretton Woods agreements termed "fundamental disequilibria"—were obliged to devalue their currencies and/or take measures to cut their deficits by contracting their economies. Both of these alternatives were unpleasant because devaluation meant rising prices and contraction meant rising unemployment. However, a country with a current account deficit had no choice because it was losing stock of foreign exchange reserves. When its stock of foreign currencies became exhausted, it had to change its exchange rate because further intervention (selling off some of its foreign exchange reserves) became impossible.

Countries experiencing current account surpluses were in a different position because they were gaining foreign exchange reserves. Although these countries were supposed to stimulate their economies and/or revalue their currencies to restore balance to their current account, they were not obliged to do so. They could easily maintain their fixed exchange rate by buying up any excess supply of foreign exchange with their own currency, of which they had plentiful supply.

---

[2] The idea was that the IMF would make short-term loans to a country with a current account deficit. The loans would enable the country to correct the current account problem gradually, without bringing on a deep recession, running out of foreign exchange reserves, or devaluing the currency.

In practice, this meant that some countries—especially Germany and Japan—tended to run large and chronic current account surpluses and were under no compulsion to take steps to correct the problem. The U.S. economy, stimulated by expenditures on the Vietnam War, experienced a large and prolonged current account deficit (capital outflow) in the 1960s, which was the counterpart of these surpluses. The United States was, however, in a unique position under the Bretton Woods system. The value of gold was fixed in terms of the U.S. dollar at $35 per ounce of gold. Other countries fixed their exchange rates in terms of U.S. dollars (and therefore only indirectly in terms of gold). Consequently, the United States could never accomplish anything by devaluing its currency in terms of gold. If the dollar was devalued from $35 to $40 per ounce of gold, the yen, pegged at 200 yen per dollar, would move in parallel with the dollar (from 7,000 yen per ounce of gold to 8,000 yen per ounce), with the dollar–yen exchange rate unaffected. To correct its current account deficits vis-à-vis Japan and Germany, it would be necessary for those two countries to adjust their currencies' exchange rates with the dollar. These countries were reluctant to do so for a variety of reasons. As a result, the U.S. current account was chronically in deficit throughout the late 1960s.

A second flaw in the Bretton Woods system was that it permitted devaluations only when a country had a "chronic" current account deficit and was in danger of running out of foreign exchange reserves. This meant that devaluations could often be predicted quite far in advance, and they usually had to be rather large if they were to correct any serious current account problem. The situation made it tempting for speculators to "attack" the currencies of countries with current account deficits.

Problems such as these eventually led the United States to abandon the Bretton Woods rules in 1971. The U.S. government refused to continue pegging the value of the dollar in terms of gold. Thus, the prices of all currencies were free to find their own levels.

The alternative to fixed exchange rates is a system that allows exchange rates to move freely or flexibly in response to market forces. Two types of flexible exchange rate systems are usually distinguished. In a *freely floating system*, governments do not intervene at all in the foreign exchange market.[3] They do not buy or sell currencies with the aim of manipulating the rates. In a *managed floating system*, governments intervene if markets are becoming "disorderly"—fluctuating more than a government believes is desirable. Governments may also intervene if they think a currency is increasing or decreasing too much in value even though the day-to-day fluctuations may be small.

Since the demise of the Bretton Woods system in 1971, the world's exchange rate system can be described as "managed floating." One of the important features of this system has been times of large fluctuations in exchange rates. For example, the yen–dollar rate went from 347 in 1971 to 210 in 1978, to 125 in 1988, and to 80 in 1995. Those are very large changes, changes that have important effects on the international economy, some of which we have covered in this text.

---

[3] However, governments may from time to time buy or sell foreign exchange for their own needs (instead of influencing the exchange rate). For example, the U.S. government might need British pounds to buy land for a U.S. embassy building in London. For our purposes, we ignore this behavior because it is not "intervention" in the strict sense of the word.

APPENDIX SUMMARY

1. The gold standard was the major system of exchange rate determination before 1914. All currencies were priced in terms of gold. Difficulties with the gold standard led to the Bretton Woods agreement following World War II. Under this system, countries maintained fixed exchange rates with one another and fixed the value of their currencies in terms of the U.S. dollar. Countries experiencing a "fundamental disequilibrium" in their current accounts were permitted to change their exchange rates.

2. The Bretton Woods system was abandoned in 1971. Since then, the world's exchange rate system has been one of managed floating rates. Under this system, governments intervene if foreign exchange markets are fluctuating more than the government thinks desirable.

APPENDIX PROBLEMS

1. The currency of Atlantis is the wimp. In 2012, Atlantis developed a balance-of-payments deficit with the United States as a result of an unanticipated decrease in exports; U.S. citizens cut back on the purchase of Atlantean goods. Assume Atlantis is operating under a system of fixed exchange rates.
   a. How does the drop in exports affect the market for wimps? Identify the deficit graphically.
   b. How must the government of Atlantis act (in the short run) to maintain the value of the wimp?

   c. If Atlantis had originally been operating at full employment (potential GDP), what impact would those events have had on its economy? Explain your answer.
   d. The chief economist of Atlantis suggests an expansionary monetary policy to restore full employment; the Secretary of Commerce suggests a tax cut (expansionary fiscal policy). Given the fixed exchange rate system, describe the effects of these two policy options on Atlantis's current account.
   e. How would your answers to a, b, and c change if the two countries operated under a floating rate system?

Economic Growth in Developing and Transitional Economies

21

Our primary focus in this text has been on countries with modern industrialized economies that rely heavily on markets to allocate resources, but what about the economic problems facing countries such as Somalia and Haiti? Can we apply the same economic principles that we have been studying to these less-developed nations?

Yes. All economic analysis deals with the problem of making choices under conditions of scarcity, and the problem of satisfying people's wants and needs is as real for Somalia and Haiti as it is for the United States, Germany, and Japan. The universality of scarcity is what makes economic analysis relevant to all nations, regardless of their level of material well-being or ruling political ideology.

The basic tools of supply and demand, theories about consumers and firms, and theories about the structure of markets all contribute to an understanding of the economic problems confronting the world's developing nations. However, these nations often face economic problems quite different from those that richer, more developed countries face. In developing nations, an economist may have to worry about chronic food shortages, explosive population growth, and hyperinflations that reach triple, and even quadruple, digits.

The instruments of economic management also vary from nation to nation. The United States has well-developed financial market institutions and a strong central bank (the Federal Reserve) through which the government can control the macroeconomy to some extent. Even limited intervention is impossible in some of the developing countries. In the United States, tax laws can be changed to stimulate saving, to encourage particular kinds of investments, or to redistribute income. In many developing countries, there are neither meaningful personal income taxes nor effective tax policies.

LEARNING OBJECTIVES

Discuss the characteristics of developing nations

Describe the sources of economic development

Summarize the strategies for economic development

Discuss the intervention methods used by development economists

Summarize the six basic requirements for the successful transition to a market economy

Even though economic problems and the policy instruments available to tackle them vary across nations, economic thinking about these problems can be transferred easily from one setting to another. In this chapter, we discuss several of the economic problems specific to developing nations in an attempt to capture some of the insights that economic analysis can offer.

Life in the Developing Nations: Population and Poverty

In 2012, the population of the world reached over 7 billion people. Most of the world's more than 200 nations belong to the developing world, in which about three-fourths of the world's population lives.

In the early 1960s, the nations of the world could be assigned rather easily to categories: The *developed countries* included most of Europe, North America, Japan, Australia, and New Zealand; the *developing countries* included the rest of the world. The developing nations were often referred to as the *Third World* to distinguish them from the Western industrialized nations (the *First World*) and the former Socialist bloc of Eastern European nations (the *Second World*).

In 2012, the world did not divide easily into three neat parts. Rapid economic progress brought some developing nations closer to developed economies. Countries such as Argentina and Chile, still considered to be "developing," are often referred to as middle-income or newly industrialized countries. Russia and many countries in the former Soviet bloc had also climbed to middle-income status. Other countries, such as those in much of sub-Saharan Africa and some in South Asia, have stagnated and fallen so far behind the economic advances of the rest of the world that the term *Fourth World* has been used to describe them. China and India, while usually labeled developing countries, are fast becoming economic superpowers.

Although the countries of the developing world exhibit considerable diversity in both their standards of living and their particular experiences of growth, marked differences continue to separate them from the developed nations. The developed countries have a higher average level of material well-being (the amount of food, clothing, shelter, and other commodities consumed by the average person). Comparisons of gross national income (GNI) are often used as a crude index of the level of material well-being across nations. GNI is a measure of a nation's income, computed using a more accurate way of converting purchasing power into dollars. See Table 21.1, where GNI per-capita in the industrial market economies significantly exceeds GNI of both the low- and middle-income developing economies.

Other characteristics of economic development include improvements in basic health and education. The degree of political and economic freedom enjoyed by individual citizens might also be part of what it means to be a developed nation. Some of these criteria are easy to quantify. Table 21.1 presents data for different types of economies according to some of the more easily measured indexes of development. As you can see, the industrial market economies enjoy higher standards of living according to whatever indicator of development is chosen.

Behind these statistics lies the reality of the very difficult life facing the people of the developing world. The great majority of the population lives in rural areas where agricultural work is hard and extremely time-consuming. Productivity (output produced per worker) is low because

TABLE 21.1 Indicators of Economic Development

Country Group	Population, 2011 (billions)	Gross National Income per Capita, 2011 (dollars)	Literacy Rate, 2010 (percent over 15 years of age)	Infant Mortality, 2011 (deaths before age 5 per 1,000 births)	Internet Users per 1,000 people, 2011
Low-income	0.8	569	62.9	62.8	59
Lower middle-income	2.5	1,764	71.0	46.0	160
Upper middle-income	2.5	6,563	93.6	15.9	383
High-income	1.1	39,861	98.3	5.0	767

Source: Data from International Bank for Reconstruction and Development/The World Bank: World Bank Development Report 2002.

household plots are small and only the crudest of farm implements are available. Low productivity means farm output per person is barely sufficient to feed a farmer's own family. School-age children may receive some formal education, but illiteracy remains chronic for young and old. Infant mortality runs 10 times higher than in the United States. Although parasitic infections are common and debilitating, there is only one physician per 5,000 people. In addition, many developing nations are engaged in civil and external warfare.

Life in the developing nations is a continual struggle against the circumstances of poverty, and prospects for dramatic improvements in living standards for most people are dim. As with all generalizations, there are exceptions. In any given nation an elite group often lives in considerable luxury. India is on the World Bank's list of low-income countries, yet Mumbai, a state capital, is one of the top 10 centers of commerce in the world, home to Bollywood, the world's largest film industry.

Poverty—not affluence—dominates the developing world. Recent studies suggest that 40 percent of the population of the developing nations has an annual income insufficient to provide for adequate nutrition. While the developed nations account for only about one-quarter of the world's population, they are estimated to consume three-quarters of the world's output. This leaves the developing countries with about three-fourths of the world's people but only one-fourth of the world's income.

Inequality in the world distribution of income is also substantial. When we look at the world population, the poorest one-fifth of the families earns about 0.5 percent and the richest one-fifth earns 79 percent of total world income.

Economic Development: Sources and Strategies

Economists have been trying to understand economic growth and development since Adam Smith and David Ricardo in the eighteenth and nineteenth centuries, but the study of development economics as it applies to the developing nations has a much shorter history. The geopolitical struggles that followed World War II brought increased attention to the developing nations and their economic problems. During this period, the new field of development economics asked simply: Why are some nations poor and others rich? If economists could understand the barriers to economic growth that prevent nations from developing and the prerequisites that would help them to develop, economists could prescribe strategies for achieving economic advancement.

The Sources of Economic Development

Although a general theory of economic development applicable to all nations has not emerged, some basic factors that limit a poor nation's economic growth have been suggested. These include insufficient capital formation, a shortage of human resources and entrepreneurial ability, and a lack of social overhead capital.

Capital Formation   One explanation for low levels of output in developing nations is insufficient quantities of necessary inputs. Developing nations have diverse resource endowments—Congo, for instance, is abundant in natural resources, while Bangladesh is resource-poor. Almost all developing nations have a scarcity of capital relative to other resources, especially labor. The small stock of physical capital (factories, machinery, farm equipment, and other productive capital) constrains labor's productivity and holds back national output.

Nevertheless, citing capital shortages as the cause of low productivity does not explain much. We need to know why capital is in such short supply in developing countries. There are many explanations. One, the **vicious-circle-of-poverty hypothesis**, suggests that a poor nation must consume most of its income just to maintain its already low standard of living. Consuming most of national income implies limited saving, and this implies low levels of investment. Without investment, the capital stock does not grow, the income remains low, and the vicious circle is complete. Poverty becomes self-perpetuating.

vicious-circle-of-poverty hypothesis Suggests that poverty is self-perpetuating because poor nations are unable to save and invest enough to accumulate the capital stock that would help them grow.

The difficulty with the vicious-circle argument is that if it were true, no nation would ever develop. Japanese GDP per capita in 1900 was well below that of many of today's developing nations, yet today it is among the affluent, developed nations. Among the many nations with low levels of capital per capita, some—like China—have managed to grow and develop in the last 20 years, while others remain behind. In even the poorest countries, there remains some capital surplus that could be harnessed if conditions were right. Many current observers believe that scarcity of capital in some developing countries may have more to do with a lack of incentives for citizens to save and invest productively than with any absolute scarcity of income available for capital accumulation. Many of the rich in developing countries invest their savings in Europe or in the United States instead of in their own country, which may have a riskier political climate. Savings transferred to the United States do not lead to physical capital growth in the developing countries. The term **capital flight** refers to the fact that both human capital and financial capital (domestic savings) leave developing countries in search of higher expected rates of return elsewhere or returns with less risk. Government policies in the developing nations—including price ceilings, import controls, and even outright appropriation of private property—tend to discourage investment. There has been increased attention to the role that financial institutions, including accounting systems and property right rules, play in encouraging domestic capital formation.

capital flight The tendency for both human capital and financial capital to leave developing countries in search of higher expected rates of return elsewhere with less risk.

Whatever the causes of capital shortages, it is clear that the absence of productive capital prevents income from rising in any economy. The availability of capital is a necessary, but not a *sufficient*, condition for economic growth. The landscape of the developing countries is littered with idle factories and abandoned machinery. Other ingredients are required to achieve economic progress.

Human Resources and Entrepreneurial Ability

Capital is not the only factor of production required to produce output. Labor is equally important. First of all, to be productive, the workforce must be healthy. Disease today is the leading threat to development in much of the world. In 2011, almost a million people died of malaria, almost all of them in Africa. The Gates Foundation has targeted malaria eradication as one of its key goals in the next decade. HIV/AIDS was still responsible for almost 2 million deaths in 2011, again mostly in Africa, and has left Africa with more than 14 million AIDS orphans. Iron deficiency and parasites sap the strength of many workers in the developing world.

Health is not the only issue. Look back at Table 21.1. You will notice that low-income countries lag behind high-income countries not only in health but also in literacy rates. To be productive, the workforce must be educated and trained. Basic literacy as well as specialized training in farm management, for example, can yield high returns to both the individual worker and the economy. Education has grown to become the largest category of government expenditure in many developing nations, in part because of the belief that human resources are the ultimate determinant of economic advance. Nevertheless, in many developing countries, many children, especially girls, receive only a few years of formal education.

Just as financial capital seeks the highest and safest return, so does human capital. Thousands of students from developing countries, many of whom were supported by their governments, graduate every year from U.S. colleges and universities. After graduation, these people face a difficult choice: to remain in the United States and earn a high salary or to return home and accept a job at a much lower salary. Many remain in the United States. This **brain drain** siphons off many of the most talented minds from developing countries.

brain drain The tendency for talented people from developing countries to become educated in a developed country and remain there after graduation.

It is interesting to look at what happens to the flow of educated workers as countries develop. Increasingly, students who have come from China and India to study are returning to their home countries eager to use their skills in their newly growing economies. The return flow of this human capital stimulates growth and is a signal that growth is occurring. Indeed, development economists have found evidence that in India, schooling choices made by parents for their children respond quite strongly to changes in employment opportunities.[1] The connection between growth and human capital is in fact a two-way street.

---

[1] The classic work in this area was done by Kaivan Munshi and Mark Rosenzweig, "Traditional Institutions Meet the Modern World: Caste, Gender, and Schooling Choice in a Globalizing Economy," *American Economic Review*, September 2006, 1225–1252. More recent work includes Emily Oster and Bryce Millett, "Do Call Centers Promote School Enrollment? Evidence from India," Chicago Booth Working Paper, June 2010.

ECONOMICS IN PRACTICE

Corruption

Many people have argued that one barrier to economic development in a number of countries is the level of corruption and inefficiency in the government. Measuring levels of corruption and inefficiency can be difficult. Some researchers have tried surveys and experiments. Ray Fisman[1] had a more unusual way to measure the way in which political connections interfere with the workings of the market in Indonesia.

From 1967 to 1998, Indonesia was ruled by President Suharto. While Suharto ruled, his children and longtime allies were affiliated with a number of Indonesian companies. Fisman had the clever idea of looking at what happened to the stock market prices of those firms connected to the Suharto clan relative to unaffiliated firms when Suharto unexpectedly fell ill. Fisman found a large and significant reduction in the value of those affiliated firms on rumors of illness. What does this tell us? A firm's stock price reflects investors' views of what earnings the firm can expect to have. In the case of firms

connected to Suharto, the decline in their stock prices tells us that a large part of the reason investors think that those firms are doing well is because of the family connection rather than the firm's inherent efficiency. One reason corruption is bad for an economy is that it often leads to the wrong firms, the less efficient firms, producing the goods and services in the society.

The following chart shows the World Bank's rating of corruption levels in a number of countries around the world. The countries are ranked from those with the strongest controls on corruption—Germany and France—to those with the lowest controls—Pakistan and Nigeria. Indonesia, as you can see, is near the bottom of the list.

THINKING PRACTICALLY

1. As corruption falls in a country, cost of production often falls. Why?

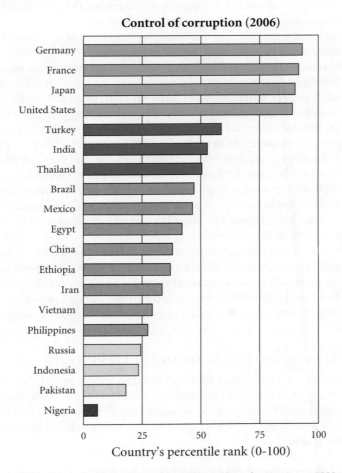

Control of corruption (2006)

Country's percentile rank (0-100)

Source: International Bank for Reconstruction and Development / The World Bank: *World Development Report* 2002.
Note: The governance indicators presented here aggregate the views on the quality of governance provided by a large number of enterprise, citizen, and expert survey respondents in industrial and developing countries. These data are gathered from a number of survey institutes, think tanks, nongovernmental organizations, and international organizations. The aggregate indicators do not reflect the official views of the World Bank, its executive directors, or the countries they represent.

[1] Raymond Fisman, "Estimating the Value of Political Connections," *The American Economic Review,* September 2001, 1095–1102.

Even when educated workers leave for the developed world, they may contribute to the growth of their home country. Recently, economists have begun studying *remittances*, compensation sent back from recent immigrants to their families in less developed countries. While measurement is difficult, estimates of these remittances are approximately $100 billion per year. Remittances fund housing and education for families left behind, but they also can provide investment capital for small businesses. In 2007, it appeared that remittances from illegal immigrants in the United States to Mexico, which had been growing by 20 percent per year, were beginning to fall with tightening of enforcement of immigration rules. Remittances fell further in 2008–2009 with the recession.

In recent years, we have become increasingly aware of the role of entrepreneurship in economic development. Many of the iconic firms in the nineteenth century that contributed so strongly to the early industrial growth of the United States—Standard Oil, U.S. Steel, Carnegie Steel—were begun by entrepreneurs starting with little capital. In China, one of the top search engines is Baidu, a firm started in 2000 by two Chinese nationals, Eric Xu and Robin Li, and now traded on NASDAQ. Providing opportunities and incentives for creative risk takers seems to be an increasing part of what needs to be done to promote development.

Social Overhead Capital Anyone who has spent time in a developing nation knows how difficult it can be to carry on everyday life. Problems with water supplies, poor roads, frequent electrical power outages—in the few areas where electricity is available—and often ineffective mosquito and pest control make life and commerce difficult.

social overhead capital Basic infrastructure projects such as roads, power generation, and irrigation systems.

In any economy, developing or otherwise, the government plays an investment role. In a developing economy, the government must create a basic infrastructure—roads, power generation, and irrigation systems. Such projects, referred to as **social overhead capital**, often cannot successfully be undertaken by the private sector. Many of these projects operate with economies of scale, which means they can be efficient only if they are very large, perhaps too large for any private company or group of companies to carry out. In other cases, the benefits from a development project, while extraordinarily valuable, cannot be easily bought and sold. The availability of clean air and potable water are two examples. Here government must play its role before the private sector can proceed. For example, some observers have recently argued that India's growth prospects are being limited by its poor rail transport system. Goods from Singapore to India move easily over water in less than a day, but they can take weeks to move from port cities to supply factories in the interior. China, by contrast, spent the bulk of its stimulus money in the 2008–2009 period trying to build new transportation networks in part because the government understood how key this social overhead capital was to economic growth. The *Economics in Practice* box on page 407 describes one of the unexpected results of government infrastructure provision in Bangladesh.

To build infrastructure requires public funding. Many less developed countries struggle with raising tax revenues to support these projects. In the last few years, Greece has struggled to repay its debt partly because of widespread tax evasion by its wealthiest citizens. In many less-developed countries, corruption limits the public funds available for productive government investments, as the *Economics in Practice* box on page 405 suggests.

Strategies for Economic Development

Just as no single theory appears to explain lack of economic advancement, no one development strategy will likely succeed in all nations. How active a role should government play in directing economic development? What sectors should be emphasized? Should one focus on new business as a growth engine? These questions are being debated by economists and governments across the globe.

International Monetary Fund (IMF) An international agency whose primary goals are to stabilize international exchange rates and to lend money to countries that have problems financing their international transactions.

Governments or Markets? Soviet-style development was accomplished with detailed central planning, state ownership, and control of prices and output. Today in developing economies, the market plays a much stronger role. In most parts of the world, including nondemocratic countries like China, state ownership has declined and prices are mostly set in markets. International agencies like the **International Monetary Fund (IMF)**, whose primary goals are to stabilize international exchange rates and to lend money to countries with problems financing

ECONOMICS IN PRACTICE

Who You Marry May Depend on the Rain

In Bangladesh, as in many other low-lying countries, river flooding often leaves large swaths of land under water for substantial portions of the year. By building embankments on the side of the river, governments can extend the growing season, allowing several seasons of crops. The result is a wealth increase for people living in affected rural areas. In a recent paper, several economists traced through some unusual consequences of increasing the wealth of rural populations by creating embankments.[1]

In Bangladesh marriages require dowries, paid by the bride's family to the groom. For poor families, raising these dowries can be difficult. Nor is it easy to marry now and promise a dowry-by-installment later on. Making people live up to their promises and pay debts is no easier in Bangladesh than it is elsewhere in the world! The result? In hard times and among the poorer families, people in Bangladesh often marry cousins; promises within an extended family are more easily enforced and wealth sharing inside families also more common.

Now let us think about what happens when the government builds a flood embankment, allowing farmers on one side of the embankment to till the land over most of the year, while those on the other side are faced with six-month flooding. Farmers on the flooded side of the river continue to use marriage within the extended family as a strategy to essentially provide dowries on credit. For those farmers on the more stable side of the river, cousin marriages fell quite substantially.

Since marriage of cousins can have health risks, investments in rural infrastructure can have unforeseen positive effects in an area.

THINKING PRACTICALLY

1. What do you think happens to the overall marriage rate as a result of the embankment?

[1] Ahmed Mushfiq Mobarak, Randall Kuhn, Christina Peters, "Consanguinity and Other Marriage Market Effects of a Wealth Shock in Bangladesh," *Demography*, forthcoming 2013.

---

international transactions, and the **World Bank**, which lends money to countries for development projects, have pushed hard for market-oriented reforms.

Market-oriented reforms, however, have not eliminated the role of government. As indicated earlier, governments play a vital role in creating institutions that allow markets to work effectively—physical institutions like roads and schools, and business and legal institutions such as accounting systems and enforcement of property rights. Many governments also use their taxing and expenditure policies to favor specific sectors over others as they try to grow. **Industrial policy**, in which governments actively pick industries to support as a base for economic development, is still carried on at some level in most developing nations. The greater central control of the economy in China was very evident during the recent recession in the speed with which China could direct its government expenditures as it sought to stimulate its economy.

World Bank An international agency that lends money to individual countries for projects that promote economic development.

industrial policy A policy in which governments actively pick industries to support as a base for economic development.

Agriculture or Industry?   Consider the data in Table 21.2. The richest countries listed—the United States, Japan, and Korea—generate much of their GDP in services, with little value contributed by agricultural production. The poorest countries, on the other hand, have

TABLE 21.2 The Structure of Production in Selected Developed and Developing Economies, 2008

Country	Per-Capita Gross National Income (GNI)	Percentage of Gross Domestic Product		
		Agriculture	Industry	Services
Tanzania	$ 460	30	23	47
Bangladesh	570	19	29	52
China	3,040	11	47	40
Thailand	3,640	12	44	44
Colombia	4,640	8	35	57
Brazil	7,490	6	28	66
Korea (Rep.)	21,430	3	36	61
Japan	37,840	1	27	71
United States	47,890	1	21	78

Source: The World Bank.

substantial agricultural sectors, although as you can see, the service sector is also large in a number of these economies. A casual look at the data might well lead one to conclude that moving out of agriculture was the path to development. And, indeed, industrialization was the path that Eastern Europe and other economies pursued in the post-World War II period.

In many countries, however, industrialization has been unsuccessful. Some have argued that a move out of agriculture may be a result of development, rather than a cause. Others have suggested that industrialization worked for the Western economies but may not work as well for economies with other distributions of human and physical capital. Indeed, in the last several decades the agricultural sector has received more attention as a source of economic development. Many agricultural projects with large productivity enhancement potential have relatively low capital requirements and thus may better match the capital-poor developing world. Agricultural development also improves the lot of the rural population, where more of the poor typically live. Finally, improving agriculture may slow the move of the poor to cities, where infrastructure is inadequate for the growing population.

Experience over the last three decades suggests that some balance between industrialization and agricultural reform leads to the best outcome—that is, it is important and effective to pay attention to both industry and agriculture. The Chinese have referred to this dual approach to development as "walking on two legs."

Exports or Import Substitution?   As developing nations expand their industrial activities, they must decide what type of trade strategy to pursue. Development economists discuss two alternatives: import substitution or export promotion.

import substitution An industrial trade strategy that favors developing local industries that can manufacture goods to replace imports.

Import substitution is a strategy used to develop local industries that can manufacture goods to replace imports. If fertilizer is imported, import substitution calls for a domestic fertilizer industry to produce replacements for fertilizer imports. This strategy gained prominence throughout South America in the 1950s. At that time, most developing nations exported agricultural and mineral products, goods that faced uncertain and often unstable international markets. Under these conditions, the call for import substitution policies was understandable. Special government actions, including tariff and quota protection and subsidized imports of machinery, were set up to encourage new domestic industries. Multinational corporations were also invited into many countries to begin domestic operations.

Most economists believe that import substitution strategies have failed almost everywhere they have been tried. With domestic industries sheltered from international competition by high tariffs (often as high as 200 percent), major economic inefficiencies were created. For example, Peru has a population of approximately 29 million, only a tiny fraction of whom can afford to buy an automobile. Yet at one time, the country had five or six different automobile manufacturers, each of which produced only a few thousand cars per year. Because there are substantial economies of scale in automobile production, the cost per car was much higher than it needed to be, and valuable resources that could have been devoted to another, more productive, activity were squandered producing cars.

Furthermore, policies designed to promote import substitution often encouraged capital-intensive production methods, which limited the creation of jobs and hurt export activities. A country such as Peru could not export automobiles because it could produce them only at a cost far greater than their price on the world market. Worse still, import substitution policies encouraged the use of expensive domestic products, such as tractors and fertilizer, instead of lower-cost imports. These policies taxed the sectors that might have successfully competed in world markets.

export promotion A trade policy designed to encourage exports.

As an alternative to import substitution, some nations have pursued strategies of export promotion. **Export promotion** is the policy of encouraging exports. As an industrial market economy, Japan was a striking example to the developing world of the economic success that exports can provide. Japan had an average annual per-capita real GDP growth rate of roughly 6 percent per year from 1960–1990. This achievement was, in part, based on industrial production oriented toward foreign consumers.

Several countries in the developing world have attempted to emulate Japan's early success. Starting around 1970, Hong Kong, Singapore, Korea, and Taiwan (the "four little dragons" between the two "big dragons," China and Japan) began to pursue export promotion of manufactured goods. Today their growth rates have surpassed Japan's. Other nations, including Brazil, Colombia, and Turkey, have also had some success at pursuing an outward-looking trade policy. China's growth has been mostly export-driven as well.

Government support of export promotion has often taken the form of maintaining an exchange rate favorable enough to permit exports to compete with products manufactured in developed economies. For example, many people believe China has kept the value of the yuan artificially low. Because a "cheap" yuan means inexpensive Chinese goods in the United States, sales of these goods increased dramatically.

A big issue for countries growing or trying to grow by selling exports on world markets is free trade. African nations in particular have pushed for reductions in tariffs imposed on their agricultural goods by Europe and the United States, arguing that these tariffs substantially reduce Africa's ability to compete in the world marketplace.

Microfinance　In the mid 1970s, Muhammad Yunus, a young Bangladeshi economist created the Grameen Bank in Bangladesh. Yunus, who trained at Vanderbilt University and was a former professor at Middle Tennessee State University, used this bank as a vehicle to introduce microfinance to the developing world. In 2006, Yunus received a Nobel Peace Prize for his work. Microfinance is the practice of lending very small amounts of money, with no collateral, and accepting very small savings deposits.[2] It is aimed at introducing entrepreneurs in the poorest parts of the developing world to the capital market. By 2002, more than 2,500 institutions were making these small loans, serving over 60 million people. Two-thirds of borrowers were living below the poverty line in their own countries, the poorest of the poor.

Yunus, while teaching economics in Bangladesh, began lending his own money to poor households with entrepreneurial ambitions. He found that with even very small amounts of money, villagers could start simple businesses: bamboo weaving or hair dressing. Traditional banks found these borrowers unprofitable: The amounts were too small, and it was too expensive to figure out which of the potential borrowers was a good risk. With a borrower having no collateral, information about his or her character was key but was hard for a big bank to discover. Local villagers, however, typically knew a great deal about one another's characters. This insight formed the basis for Yunus's microfinance enterprise. Within a village, people who are interested in borrowing money to start businesses are asked to join lending groups of five people. Loans are then made to two of the potential borrowers, later to a second two, and finally to the last. As long as everyone is repaying their loans, the next group receives theirs. But if the first borrowers fail to pay, all members of the group are denied subsequent loans. What does this do? It makes community pressure a substitute for collateral. Moreover, once the peer lending mechanism is understood, villagers have incentives to join only with other reliable borrowers. The mechanism of peer lending is a way to avoid the problems of imperfect information described in an earlier chapter.

The Grameen model grew rapidly. By 2002, Grameen was lending to two million members. Thirty countries and thirty U.S. states have microfinance lending copied from the Grameen model. Relative to traditional bank loans, microfinance loans are much smaller, repayment begins very quickly, and the vast majority of the loans are made to women (who, in many cases, have been underserved by mainstream banks). A growing set of evidence shows that providing opportunities for poor women has stronger spillovers in terms of

---

[2] An excellent discussion of microfinance is contained in Beatriz Armendariz de Aghion and Jonathan Morduch, *The Economics of Microfinance*, (MIT Press, 2005.)

ECONOMICS IN PRACTICE

Cell Phones Increase Profits for Fishermen in India

Kerala is a poor state in a region of India. The fishing industry is a major part of the local economy, employing more than one million people and serving as the main source of protein for the population. Every day fishing boats go out; and when they return, the captain of the ship needs to decide where to take the fish to sell. There is much uncertainty in this decision: How much fish will they catch; what other boats will come to a particular location; how many buyers will there be at a location? Moreover, fuel costs are high and timing is difficult, so that once a boat comes ashore, it does not pay for the fishermen to search for a better marketplace. In a recent study of this area, Robert Jensen[1] found on a Tuesday morning in November 1997, 11 fishermen in Badagara were dumping their load of fish because they faced no buyers at the dock. However, unbeknownst to them, 15 kilometers away, 27 buyers were leaving their marketplace empty-handed, with unsatisfied demand for fish.

Beginning in 1997 and continuing for the next several years, mobile phone service was introduced to this region of India. By 2001, the majority of the fishing fleet had mobile phones, which they use to call various vendors ashore to confirm where the buyers are. What was the result? Once the phones were introduced, waste, which had averaged 5 to 8 percent of the total catch, was virtually eliminated. Moreover, just as we would have predicted from the simple laws of supply and demand, the prices of fish across the various villages along the fishing market route were closer to each other than they were before. Jensen found that with less waste fishermen's profits rose on average by 8 percent, while the average price of fish fell by 4 percent.

In fact, cell phones are improving the way markets in less-developed countries work by providing price and quantity information so that both producers and consumers can make better economic decisions.

THINKING PRACTICALLY

1. Use a supply and demand graph to show the impact of cell phones in India on prices in the fishing market.

[1] Robert Jensen, "The Digital Provide: Information Technology, Market Performance, and Welfare in the South Indian Fisheries Sector," *The Quarterly Journal of Economics*, August 2007.

improving the welfare of children than does providing comparable opportunities for men. While the field of microfinance has changed considerably since Yunus's introduction and some people question how big a role it will ultimately play in spurring major development and economic growth, it has changed many people's views about the possibilities of entrepreneurship for the poor of the world.

Two Examples of Development: China and India

China and India provide two interesting examples of rapidly developing economies. While low per-capita incomes still mean that both countries are typically labeled developing as opposed to developed countries, many expect that to change in the near future. In the 25-year period from 1978 to 2003, China grew, on average, 9 percent per year, a rate faster than any other country in the world. Even during the 2008–2009 U.S. recession, China continued to grow, and it has continued to do so. While India's surge has been more recent, in the last 8 years, it too has seen annual growth rates in the 6 to 8 percent range. Many commentators expect India and China to dominate the world economy in the twenty-first century.

How did these two rather different countries engineer their development? Consider institutions: India is a democratic country, has a history of the rule of law, and has an English-speaking heritage—all factors typically thought to provide a development advantage. China is still an authoritarian country politically, and property rights are still not well established—both characteristics that were once thought to hinder growth. Both China and India have embraced free market economics, with China taking the lead as India has worked to remove some of its historical regulatory apparatus.

What about social capital? Both India and China remain densely populated. While China is the most populous country in the world, India, with a smaller land mass, is the more densely populated. Nevertheless, as is true in most developing nations, birth rates in both countries have fallen. Literacy rates and life expectancy in China are quite high, in part a legacy from an earlier period. India, on the other hand, has a literacy rate that is less than that of China's and a lower life expectancy. In terms of human capital, China appears to have the edge, at least for now.

What about the growth strategies used by the two countries? China has adopted a pragmatic, gradual approach to market development, sharply in contrast to that adopted some years ago in Poland. China's approach has been called *moshi guohe*, or "Crossing the river by feeling for stepping stones." In terms of sector, most of China's growth has been fueled by manufacturing. The focus on manufacturing is one reason that China's energy consumption and environmental issues have increased so rapidly in the last decade. In India, services have led growth, particularly in the software industry. In sum, it is clear from comparing India and China that there is no single recipe for development.

Development Interventions

To this point we have used the terms *growth* and *development* interchangeably, assuming that as an economy grows in its level of income, it will develop to provide benefits to most of its population. Since the 1970s at least, however, economists and policy makers have questioned the relationship between growth and development. A 1974 World Bank study concluded that "More than a decade of rapid growth in underdeveloped countries has been of little or no benefit to perhaps a third of their population." In the last 20 years, development economists have increasingly turned to much narrower, more microeconomically oriented programs to see if they can figure out which interventions do help the condition of the bottom of the income distribution in developing countries and how to replicate those successful programs.

Random and Natural Experiments: Some New Techniques in Economic Development

Suppose we were trying to decide whether it was worthwhile in terms of student achievement to hire another teacher to reduce the student-faculty ratio. One traditional way we might try to answer that question is to find two classrooms with different enrollments in otherwise similar school systems and look at the educational performance of the students. We see comparisons of this sort everyday in newspaper discussions of policies, and many research projects take a variant of this approach. But the approach is subject to serious criticism. It is possible that differences in the two classrooms beyond the enrollment numbers also matter to performance—differences we have failed to correct in the comparisons we make. Crowded classrooms may be in poorer areas (indeed, this may account for the crowding); they may have less effective teachers; they may lack other resources. In the social sciences, it is very difficult to ensure that we have comparisons that differ only in the one element in which we are interested. The fact that our interventions involve people makes it even harder. In the case of the classrooms with small enrollment, it may well be that the most attentive parents have pushed to have their children in these classrooms, believing them to be better. Perhaps the best teachers apply to lead these classrooms, and their higher quality makes it more likely that they get their first choice of classrooms. If either of these things happens, the two classrooms will differ in systematic ways that bias the results in favor of finding better performance in the smaller classrooms. More attentive parents may provide home support that results in better test outcomes for their children even if the classrooms are crowded. Better teachers improve performance no matter how crowded the classrooms are. Problems of this sort, sometimes called selection bias, plague social science research.

In recent years, a group of development economists began using a technique borrowed from the natural sciences, the **random experiment**, to try to get around the selection problem in evaluating interventions. Instead of looking at results from classrooms that have made different choices about class size or textbooks, for example, the experimenters randomly assign otherwise identical-looking classes to either follow or not follow an intervention. Students

random experiment
(Sometimes referred to as a randomized experiment.) A technique in which outcomes of specific interventions are determined by using the intervention in a randomly selected subset of a sample and then comparing outcomes from the exposed and control group.

and teachers are not allowed to shift around. By comparing the outcomes of large numbers of randomly selected subjects with control groups, social scientists hope to identify effects of interventions in much the same way natural scientists evaluate the efficacy of various drugs.

The leading development group engaged in random experiments in the education and health areas is the Poverty Research Lab at MIT, run by Esther Duflo and Abhijit Banerjee. By working with a range of NGOs and government agencies in Africa, Latin America, and Asia, these economists have looked at a wide range of possible investments to help improve outcomes for the poorest of the poor.

Of course, not all policies can be evaluated this way. Experimenters do not always have the luxury of random assignment. An alternative technique is to rely on what have been called **natural experiments** to mimic the controlled experiment. Suppose I am interested in the effect of an increase in wealth on the likelihood that a poor family will enroll its daughters in school. Comparing school behavior of rich and poor families is obviously problematic because they are likely to differ in too many ways to control adequately. Nor does it seem feasible to substantially increase the wealth of a large number of randomly selected parents. But in an agrarian community we may observe random, annual weather occurrences that naturally lead to occasional years of plenty, and by observing behavior in those years versus other years, we may learn a good deal. The weather in this case has created a natural experiment.

Empirical development economics thus has added experimental methods to its tool kit as a way to answer some of the very difficult and important questions about what does and does not work to improve the lot of the poor in developing nations. We turn now to look at some of the recent work in the fields of education and health, focusing on this experimental work, to provide some sense of the exciting work going on in this field.

natural experiment Selection of a control versus experimental group in testing the outcome of an intervention is made as a result of an exogenous event outside the experiment itself and unrelated to it.

Education Ideas

As we suggested earlier, human capital is an important ingredient in the economic growth of a nation. As economies grow, returns to education also typically grow. As we move from traditional agrarian economies to more diversified and complex economies, the advantages to an individual from education rises. So if we want a nation's poor to benefit from growth, improving their educational outcomes is key. This leads us to one of the central preoccupations of development economists in the last decade or so: Of the many investments one could make in education, which have the highest payoffs? Is it better to invest in more books or more teachers? How much does the quality of teachers matter? Are investments most important in the first years of education or later? In a world with limited resources in which educational outcomes are very important, getting the right answers to these questions is vital.

For most middle-class American students, it may come as a surprise that in the developing world, teacher absenteeism is a serious problem. A recent study led by researchers from the World Bank found, for example, that on an average day, 27 percent of Ugandan and 25 percent of Indian teachers are not at work. Across six poor countries, teacher absences averaged 19 percent. The Poverty Research Lab has conducted a number of experiments in a range of developing countries to see how one might reduce these absences. The most successful intervention was introduced in Rajasthan, India, by an NGO called Seva Mandir. Each day when he or she arrived, the teachers in half of Seva Mandir's 160-single teacher schools were asked to have their picture taken with the children. Cameras were date-stamped. This evidence of attendance fed into the compensation of the teacher. Teacher absentee rates were cut in half relative to the seemingly identical classrooms in which no cameras were introduced.

Student absenteeism is also a problem throughout the developing world, reducing educational outcomes even when schools are well staffed with qualified teachers. Several countries, including Mexico, have introduced cash payments to parents for sending their children to school regularly. Since the Mexican government introduced these payments over time, in ways not likely to be related to educational outcomes, researchers could compare student absenteeism across seemingly identical areas with and without the cash incentives as a form of natural experiment. There is some evidence that cash payments do increase school attendance. Natural experiments have also been used to look at the effect of industrialization that improves educational returns as a way to induce better school attendance; the results have been positive.

Work using experiments, both natural and random, is still at an early stage in development economics. While many reform ideas have proven helpful in improving educational outcomes in different developing countries, it has proven hard up to now to find simple answers that work across the globe. Nevertheless, these new techniques appear to offer considerable promise as a way of tackling issues of improving education for the poor of the developing world.

Health Improvements

Poor health is a second major contributor to individual poverty. In the developing world, estimates are that one-quarter of the population is infected with intestinal worms that sap the energy of children and adults alike. Malaria remains a major challenge in Africa, as does HIV/AIDS.

In the case of many interventions to improve health, human behavior plays an important role, and here is where development economics has focused. For many diseases, we have workable vaccines. But we need to figure out how to encourage people to walk to health clinics or schools to get those vaccines. We want to know if charging for a vaccine will substantially reduce uptake. For many waterborne diseases, treatment of drinking water with bleach is effective, but the taste is bad and bleach is not free. How do we induce usage? Treated bed nets can reduce malaria, but only if they are properly used. In each of these cases, there are benefits to the individual from seeking treatment or preventive care, but also costs. In the last several years, a number of development economists have explored the way in which individuals in developing economies have responded to policies that try to change these costs and benefits.

Intestinal worms, quite common in areas of Africa with inadequate sanitation, are treatable with periodic drugs at a relatively low cost. Michael Kremer and Ted Miguel, working with the World Bank, used random experiments in Kenya to examine the effect of health education and user fees on families' take-up of treatment of their children. Kremer and Miguel found a number of interesting results, results very much in keeping with economic principles. First, a program of charging user fees—even relatively low ones—dramatically reduced treatment rates. The World Bank's attempts to make programs more financially self-sustaining, if used in this area, were likely to have large, adverse public health effects. Elasticities were well above one. Kremer and Miguel also found that as the proportion of vaccinated people in a village grew, and thus the risk of contagion fell, fewer people wanted treatment, indicating some sensitivity to costs and benefit calculations by the villagers. Disappointingly, health education did not seem to make much difference.

As with the area of education, much remains for development economists to understand in the area of health and human behavior. Development economics continues to be one of the most exciting areas in economics.

Population Issues

The population growth of many developing countries has been and remains very high. For poor countries, rapid population growth can strain infrastructure and may impede development. For this reason, population control has at times been part of the development strategy of a number of countries.

Figure 21.1 provides the long historical record of population growth in the world. More than 200 years ago, the Reverend Thomas Malthus, England's first professor of political economy, expressed his fears about this record of population growth. Malthus believed that populations inexorably grew geometrically at a constant growth rate, while the diminishing productivity of land caused food supplies to grow more slowly. Looking at the two phenomena together led Malthus to predict the increasing impoverishment of the world's people unless population could be slowed.

Malthus's fears for Europe and America proved unfounded. Technological changes revolutionized agriculture so that food supplies grew despite the scarcity of land. At the same time, population growth fell dramatically in Europe and America. Nor did Malthus fully see the causal connection between technical change, economic growth, and population. As early as the mid 1960s, economist T. W. Schultz argued that technical progress increased the returns to education by making it harder for children to simply move into the jobs of their parents. Faced with this recognition, more parents in the developing world reduced their family sizes to better consolidate resources for education. Economists have referred to this reduction in family size and increase in child education levels as trading quantity of children for quality. In some countries, market forces pushing populations toward reduced family size have been helped along by government policies aimed at reducing populations.

Of course, there are parts of the developing world in which population growth continues at high levels. Uganda, with a GDP of $300 per capita, had a population growth rate in 2012 of 3.1 percent, one of the highest in the world. As an agrarian economy with high infant mortality rates, Uganda, as well as a number of other countries, still values large families. In agrarian societies, children are sources of farm labor and they may make significant contributions to household income. In societies without public old-age-support or social security programs, children may also provide a source of income for parents who are too old to support

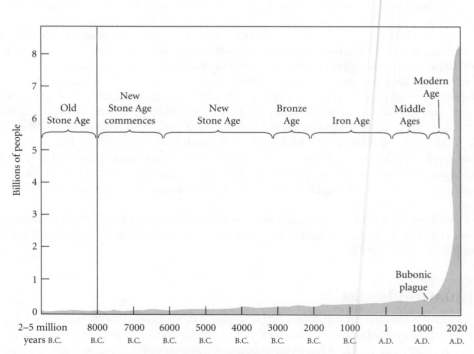

▲ **FIGURE 21.1**   **The Growth of World Population, Projected to A.D. 2020**
For thousands of years, population grew slowly. From A.D. 1 until the mid 1600s, population grew at about .04 percent per year. Since the Industrial Revolution, population growth has occurred at an unprecedented rate.

themselves. With the high value of children coupled with high rates of infant mortality, it is no wonder that families try to have many children to ensure that a sufficient number will survive into adulthood.

Economic theories of population growth suggest that fertility decisions made by poor families should not be viewed as uninformed and uncontrolled. An individual family may find that having many children is a rational strategy for economic survival given the conditions in which it finds itself. Only when the relationship between the costs and benefits of having children changes, in places like Uganda, will fertility rates decline. This does not mean, however, that having many children is in general a net benefit to society as a whole. When a family decides to have a large number of children, it imposes costs on the rest of society; the children must be educated, their health provided for, and so on. In other words, what makes sense for an individual household may create negative effects for the nation as a whole.

The Transition to a Market Economy

In the last several decades, a number of countries have made the transition from a planned economy to a market economy. Russia and the formerly Communist countries of Eastern Europe led the way in this transition beginning in the late-1980s. For a number of these countries, the early transition period was difficult, and there has been considerable debate about the optimal speed of transitions and ways to manage the social upheaval that often comes with economic reform.

For example, between 1992 and 2002, while per-capita income grew by 57 percent in Poland, it shrank by 38 percent in the Ukraine. Countries of the former USSR seem to have had a particularly difficult transition to market economies. Economists have attributed differences in ease of transition to reform strategies (slow versus fast), resource endowments of the country, and differences in institutions.

In more recent years, China and Vietnam have joined the collection of transition economies, coming to rely less on central planning for economic decisions and more on the market. India too is sometimes thought to be a transition economy, as it has in the last decade dismantled much of its government ownership and elaborate rules governing market transactions.

Six Basic Requirements for Successful Transition

Economists generally agree on six basic requirements for a successful transition to a market-based system: (1) macroeconomic stabilization, (2) deregulation of prices and liberalization of trade, (3) privatization of state-owned enterprises and development of new private industry, (4) establishment of market-supporting institutions such as property and contract laws and accounting systems, (5) a social safety net to deal with unemployment and poverty, and (6) external assistance. We now discuss each component.

Macroeconomic Stabilization   Many countries in transition have had a problem with inflation, but few have been worse than Russia. As economic conditions worsened, the government found itself with serious budget problems. As tax revenue flows slowed and expenditure commitments increased, large government budget deficits resulted. At the same time, each of the new republics established its own central bank. Each central bank began issuing "ruble credits" to keep important enterprises afloat and to pay the government's bills. The issuance of these credits, which were generally accepted as a means of payment throughout the country, led to a dramatic expansion of the money supply.

Almost from the beginning, the expanded money supply meant too much money was chasing too few goods. This was made worse by government-controlled prices set substantially below market-clearing levels. The combination of monetary expansion and price control was deadly. Government-run shops that sold goods at controlled prices were empty. People waited in line for days and often became violent when their efforts to buy goods at low official prices were thwarted. At the same time, suppliers found that they could charge much higher prices for their products on the black market—which grew bigger by the day, further exacerbating the shortage of goods at government shops. Over time, the ruble became worth less and less as black market prices continued to rise more rapidly. Russia found itself with near hyperinflation in 1992. To achieve a properly functioning market system, prices must be stabilized. To do so, the government must find a way to move toward a balanced budget and to bring the supply of money under control. China and India, in contrast to Russia and Eastern European states, initially suffered only modest inflation as they decontrolled their prices, though more recently inflation appears to be increasing in China.

Deregulation of Prices and Liberalization of Trade

To move successfully from central planning to a market system, individual prices must be deregulated. A system of freely moving prices forms the backbone of a market system. When people want more of a good than is currently being produced, its price will rise. This higher price increases producers' profits and provides an incentive for existing firms to expand production and for new firms to enter the industry. Conversely, if an industry is producing a good for which there is no market or a good that people no longer want in the same quantity, the result will be excess supply and the price of that good will fall. This outcome reduces profits or creates losses, providing an incentive for some existing firms to cut back on production and for others to go out of business. In short, an unregulated price mechanism ensures an efficient allocation of resources across industries. Until prices are deregulated, this mechanism cannot function. In practice, transition economies have moved at varying speeds in decontrolling prices. Vietnam, for example, decontrolled prices very quickly in moving to a market economy, as did Poland. China, on the other hand, took a slower path in freeing prices from state control.

Trade barriers must also be removed. Reform-minded countries must be able to import capital, technology, and ideas. In addition, it makes no sense to continue to subsidize industries that cannot be competitive on world markets. If it is cheaper to buy steel from an efficient West German steel mill than to produce it in a subsidized antiquated Russian mill, the Russian mill should be modernized or shut down. Ultimately, as the theory of comparative advantage suggests, liberalized trade will push each country to produce the products it produces best.

Deregulating prices and eliminating subsidies can bring serious political problems. Many products in Russia and the rest of the socialist world were priced below market-clearing levels for equity reasons. Housing, food, and clothing were considered by many to be entitlements. Making them more expensive, at least relative to their prices in previous times, is not likely to be popular. In 2008, rising rice prices in Southeast Asia caused considerable unrest in Vietnam, Thailand, and Cambodia. In addition, forcing inefficient firms to operate without subsidies will lead many of them to go out of business, and jobs will be lost. So while price deregulation and trade liberalization are necessary, they are very difficult politically.

Privatization

One problem with a system of central ownership is a lack of accountability. Under a system of private ownership, owners reap the rewards of their successes and suffer the consequences of their failures. Private ownership provides a strong incentive for efficient operation, innovation, and hard work that is lacking when ownership is centralized and profits are distributed to the people.

tragedy of commons The idea that collective ownership may not provide the proper private incentives for efficiency because individuals do not bear the full costs of their own decisions but do enjoy the full benefits.

The classic story to illustrate this point is called the **tragedy of commons**, which is the idea that collective ownership may not provide the proper private incentives for efficiency because individuals do not bear the full costs of their own decisions but do enjoy the full benefits. Suppose an agricultural community has 10,000 acres of grazing land. If the land was held in common so that all farmers had unlimited rights to graze their animals, each farmer would have an incentive to overgraze. He or she would reap the full benefits from grazing additional calves while the costs of grazing the calves would be borne collectively. The system provides no incentive to manage the land efficiently. Similarly, if the efficiency and benefits of your hard work and managerial skills accrue to others or to the state, what incentive do you have to work hard or to be efficient?

One solution to the tragedy of commons attempted in eighteenth-century Britain was to divide up the land into private holdings. Today, many economists argue, the solution to the incentive problem encountered in state-owned enterprises is to privatize them and let the owners compete.

In addition to increasing accountability, privatization means creating a climate in which new enterprises can flourish. If there is market demand for a product not currently being produced, individual entrepreneurs should be free to set up a business and make a profit. During the last months of the Soviet Union's existence, private enterprises such as taxi services, car repair services, restaurants, and even hotels began to spring up all over the country.

Like deregulation of prices, privatization is difficult politically. Privatization means that many protected enterprises will go out of business because they cannot compete at world prices, resulting in a loss of jobs, at least temporarily.

Market-Supporting Institutions   Between 1991 and 1997, U.S. firms entered Eastern Europe in search of markets and investment opportunities and immediately became aware of a major obstacle. The institutions that make the market function relatively smoothly in the United States did not exist in Eastern Europe. For example, the capital market, which channels private saving into productive capital investment in developed capitalist economies, is made up of hundreds of different institutions. The banking system, venture capital funds, the stock market, the bond market, commodity exchanges, brokerage houses, investment banks, and so on, have developed in the United States over hundreds of years, and they could not be replicated overnight in the formerly Communist world.

Similar problems exist today in the Chinese economy. While the Chinese equity market has grown rapidly in the last decade, that growth has been accompanied by problems with weak governance and lack of transparency. These issues discourage investments by western firms.

Many market-supporting institutions are so basic that Americans take them for granted. The institution of private property, for example, is a set of rights that must be protected by laws that the government must be willing to enforce. Suppose the French hotel chain Novotel decides to build a new hotel in Moscow or Beijing. Novotel must first acquire land. Then it will construct a building based on the expectation of renting rooms to customers. These investments are made with the expectation that the owner has a right to use them and a right to the profits that they produce. For such investments to be undertaken, these rights must be guaranteed by a set of property laws. This is equally true for large business firms and for local entrepreneurs who want to start their own enterprises. China's ambiguous property rights laws may also be problematic. While farmers can own their own homes, for example, all rural land is collectively owned by villages. Farmers have the right to manage farmland, but not own it. As a result, transfer of land is difficult.

Similarly, the law must provide for the enforcement of contracts. In the United States, a huge body of law determines what happens if you break a formal promise made in good faith. Businesses exist on promises to produce and promises to pay. Without recourse to the law when a contract is breached, contracts will not be entered into, goods will not be manufactured, and services will not be provided.

Protection of intellectual property rights is also an important feature of developed market economies. When an artist puts out a record, the artist and his or her studio are entitled to reap revenues from it. When Apple developed the iPod, it too earned the right to collect revenue for its patent ownership. Many less developed countries lack laws and enforcement mechanisms to protect intellectual property of foreign investments and their own current and future investors. The lack of protection discourages trade and home-grown invention. For example, in late 2007, China, in recognition of some of these issues, began drafting a new set of laws for intellectual property protection.

Another seemingly simple matter that turns out to be quite complex is the establishment of a set of accounting principles. In the United States, the rules of the accounting game are embodied in a set of generally accepted accounting principles (GAAP) that carry the force of law. Companies are required to keep track of their receipts, expenditures, assets, and liabilities so that their performance can be observed and evaluated by shareholders, taxing authorities, and others who have an interest in the company. If you have taken a course in accounting, you know how detailed these rules have become. Imagine trying to do business in a country operating under hundreds of different sets of rules. That is what happened in Russia during its transition.

Another institution is insurance. Whenever a venture undertakes a high-risk activity, it buys insurance to protect itself. Some years ago Amnesty International (a nonprofit organization that works to protect civil liberties around the world) sponsored a worldwide concert tour with a number of well-known rock bands and performers. The most difficult part of organizing the tour was obtaining insurance for the artists and their equipment when they played in the then-Communist countries of Eastern Europe.

Social Safety Net   In a centrally-planned socialist economy, the labor market does not function freely. Everyone who wants a job is guaranteed one somewhere. The number of jobs is determined by a central plan to match the number of workers. There is essentially no unemployment. This, it has been argued, is one of the great advantages of a planned system. In addition, a central planning system provides basic housing, food, and clothing at very affordable levels for all. With no unemployment and necessities available at very low prices, there is no need for unemployment insurance, welfare, or other social programs.

Transition to a free labor market and liberalization of prices means that some workers will end up unemployed and that everyone will pay higher prices for necessities. Indeed, during the early phases of the transition process, unemployment will be high. Inefficient state-owned enterprises will go out of business; some sectors will contract while others expand. As more and more people experience unemployment, popular support for reform is likely to drop unless some sort of social safety net is erected to ease the transition. This social safety net might include unemployment insurance, aid for the poor, and food and housing assistance. The experiences of the developed world have shown that such programs are expensive.

External Assistance   Very few believe that the transition to a market system can be achieved without outside support and some outside financing. Knowledge of and experience with capitalist institutions that exist in the United States, Western Europe, and Japan are of vital interest to the Eastern European nations. The basic skills of accounting, management, and enterprise development can be taught to developing nations; many say it is in everyone's best interest to do so.

There is little agreement about the extent of *financial* support that should be given, however. In the case of Russia, the United States pushed for a worldwide effort to provide billions of dollars in aid, to stabilize its macroeconomy, and to buy desperately needed goods from abroad. For China, no such aid was thought to be necessary.

Shock Therapy or Gradualism?   Although economists generally agreed on what the former socialist economies needed to do, they debated the sequence and timing of specific reforms.

The popular press described the debate as one between those who believe in "shock therapy" (sometimes called the Big Bang approach) and those who prefer a more gradual approach. Advocates of **shock therapy** believe that the economies in transition should proceed immediately on all fronts. They should stop printing money, deregulate prices and liberalize trade, privatize, develop market institutions, build a social safety net, and acquire external aid—all as quickly as possible. The pain will be severe, the argument goes, but in the end, it will be forgotten as the transition raises living standards. Advocates of a *gradualist* approach believe the best course is to build up market institutions first, gradually decontrol prices, and privatize only the most efficient government enterprises first.

shock therapy The approach to transition from socialism to market capitalism that advocates rapid deregulation of prices, liberalization of trade, and privatization.

Those who favor moving quickly point to the apparent success of Poland, which moved rapidly through the first phases of reform. Russia's experience during the first years of its transition demonstrated that, at least in that country, change must, to some extent, be gradual. In theory, stabilization and price liberalization can be achieved instantaneously. To enjoy the benefits of liberalization, a good deal of privatization must have taken place—and that takes time. One analyst has said that privatization means "selling assets with no value to people with no money." Some estimates suggest that half of Russian state-owned enterprises were incapable of making a profit at world prices. Simply cutting them loose would create chaos. In a sense, Russia had no choice but to move slowly.

SUMMARY

1. The economic problems facing the developing countries are often quite different from those confronting industrialized nations. The policy options available to governments may also differ. Nonetheless, the tools of economic analysis are as useful in understanding the economies of less developed countries as in understanding the U.S. economy.

LIFE IN THE DEVELOPING NATIONS: POPULATION AND POVERTY *p. 402*

2. The central reality of life in the developing countries is poverty. Although there is considerable diversity across the developing nations, most of the people in most developing countries are extremely poor by U.S. standards.

ECONOMIC DEVELOPMENT: SOURCES AND STRATEGIES *p. 403*

3. Almost all developing nations have a scarcity of physical capital relative to other resources, especially labor. The *vicious-circle-of-poverty hypothesis* says that poor countries cannot escape from poverty because they cannot afford to postpone consumption—that is, to save—to make investments. In its crude form, the hypothesis is wrong inasmuch as some prosperous countries were at one time poorer than many developing countries are today. However, it is often difficult to mobilize saving efficiently in many developing nations.

4. Human capital—the stock of education and skills embodied in the workforce—plays a vital role in economic development.

5. Developing countries are often burdened by inadequate *social overhead capital*, ranging from poor public health and sanitation facilities to inadequate roads, telephones, and court systems. Such social overhead capital is often expensive to provide, and many governments are not in a position to undertake many useful projects because they are too costly.

6. Inefficient and corrupt bureaucracies also play a role in retarding economic development in places.

7. Among the many questions governments in developing nations must answer as they seek a road to growth and development is how much to rely on free working markets versus central planning. In recent decades, the pendulum has shifted toward market-based strategies, with governments playing more of a role in creating institutions supportive of markets.

8. Because developed economies are characterized by a large share of output and employment in the industrial sector, many developing countries seem to believe that development and industrialization are synonymous. In many cases, developing countries have pursued industry at the expense of agriculture, with mixed results. Recent evidence suggests that some balance between industry and agriculture leads to the best outcome.

9. *Import-substitution* policies, a trade strategy that favors developing local industries that can manufacture goods to replace imports, were once very common in developing nations. In general, such policies have not succeeded as well as those promoting open, export-oriented economies.

10. The failure of many central planning efforts has brought increasing calls for less government intervention and more market orientation in developing economies.

11. Microfinance—lending small amounts to poor borrowers using peer lending groups—has become an important new tool in encouraging entrepreneurship in developing countries.

12. China and India have followed quite different paths in recent development.

DEVELOPMENT INTERVENTIONS *p. 411*

13. Development economists have begun to use randomized experiments as a way to test the usefulness of various interventions. In these experiments, modeled after the natural sciences, individuals or even villages are randomly assigned to receive various interventions and the outcomes they experience are compared with those of control groups. In the areas of education and health, random experiments have been most prevalent.

14. Development economists also rely on natural experiments to learn about the efficacy of various interventions. In a natural experiment, we compare areas with differing conditions that emerge as a consequence of an unrelated outside force.

15. Many of the newer economic studies focus on understanding how to motivate individuals to take actions that support policy interventions: to use health equipment properly, to attend schools, to receive vaccinations.

16. Rapid population growth is characteristic of many developing countries. Large families can be economically rational because parents need support in their old age or because children offer an important source of labor. However, having many children does not mean a net benefit to society as a whole. Rapid population growth can put a strain on already overburdened public services such as education and health.

THE TRANSITION TO A MARKET ECONOMY *p. 415*

17. Economists generally agree on six requirements for a successful transition from socialism to a market-based system: (1) macroeconomic stabilization, (2) deregulation of prices and liberalization of trade, (3) privatization, (4) establishment of market-supporting institutions, (5) a social safety net, and (6) external assistance.

18. Much debate exists about the sequence and timing of specific reforms. The idea of *shock therapy* is to proceed immediately on all six fronts, including rapid deregulation of prices and privatization. The *gradualist* approach is to build up market institutions first, gradually decontrol prices, and privatize only the most efficient government enterprises first.

REVIEW TERMS AND CONCEPTS

brain drain, *p. 404*

capital flight, *p. 404*

export promotion, *p. 408*

import substitution, *p. 408*

industrial policy, *p. 407*

International Monetary Fund (IMF), *p. 406*

natural experiment, *p. 412*

random experiment, *p. 411*

shock therapy, *p. 418*

social overhead capital, *p. 406*

tragedy of commons, *p. 416*

vicious-circle-of-poverty hypothesis, *p. 403*

World Bank, *p. 407*

PROBLEMS

All problems are available on MyEconLab.

1. For a developing country to grow, it needs capital. The major source of capital in most countries is domestic saving, but the goal of stimulating domestic saving usually is in conflict with government policies aimed at reducing inequality in the distribution of income. Comment on this trade-off between equity and growth. How would you go about resolving the issue if you were the president of a small, poor country?

2. The GDP of any country can be divided into two kinds of goods: capital goods and consumption goods. The proportion of national output devoted to capital goods determines, to some extent, the nation's growth rate.
   a. Explain how capital accumulation leads to economic growth.
   b. Briefly describe how a market economy determines how much investment will be undertaken each period.
   c. Consumption versus investment is a more painful conflict to resolve for developing countries. Comment on that statement.
   d. If you were the benevolent dictator of a developing country, what plans would you implement to increase per-capita GDP?

3. The World Bank and the International Monetary Fund were scheduled to formally cancel the debts of 18 very poor countries in 2006, and the African Development Bank was committed to taking the same action during its 2006 annual meeting. Go online and find out whether these debts were indeed canceled. How much debt was forgiven during that year in each of the countries involved? What are the expected benefits to those countries?

4. Poor countries are trapped in a vicious circle of poverty. For output to grow, they must accumulate capital. To accumulate capital, they must save (consume less than they produce). Because they are poor, they have little or no extra output available for savings—it must all go to feed and clothe the present generation. Thus they are doomed to stay poor forever. Comment on each step in that argument.

5. Famines are acts of God resulting from bad weather or other natural disasters. There is nothing we can do about them except to send food relief after they occur. Explain why that position is inaccurate. Concentrate on agricultural pricing policies and distributional issues.

6. In China, rural property is owned collectively by the village while being managed under long-term contracts by individual farmers. Why might this be a problem in terms of optimal land managment, use, and allocation?

7. How does peer lending used in microfinance help to solve the problem of adverse selection?

8. [Related to the *Economics in Practice* on p. 410] Find another example of the use of cell phones as a way to improve market functioning in a developing economy.

9. [Related to the *Economics in Practice* on p. 405] Corruption in a government is often accompanied by inefficiency in the economy. Why should this be true?

10. The distribution of income in a capitalist economy is likely to be more unequal than it is in a socialist economy. Why is this so? Is there a tension between the goal of limiting inequality and the goal of motivating risk taking and hard work? Explain your answer in detail.

11. The following quote is from the *Encyclopedia of the Developing World*: "[Some scholars] suggest that poor people are not poor because they have large families, but rather they have large families because they are poor." Explain the logic behind this quote.

Source: Thomas M. Leonard, editor, *Encyclopedia of the Developing World*, Vol. 3, p. 1297, 2006.

12. [Related to the *Economics in the Practice* on p. 407] In addition to fewer marriages within extended families, explain what other positive effects are likely to occur in the rural, flood-prone areas of Bangladesh due to increased government spending on infrastructure projects like the building of river embankments and the resulting increase in wealth of the affected rural population.

13. Explain how each of the following can limit the economic growth of developing nations.
    a. Insufficient capital formation
    b. A shortage of human resources
    c. A lack of social overhead capital

14. Of the roughly 7 billion people in the world, more than 75 percent live in developing countries, and one issue of economic concern in many of these countries is that of population growth. In the summary report of the Population Reference Bureau's *2008 World Population Data Sheet*, PRB president Bill Butz made the following comment: "Nearly all of world population growth is now concentrated in the world's poorer countries. Even the small amount of overall growth in the wealthier nations will largely result from immigration." Explain how rapid population growth can limit a nation's productivity. Are there any ways in which population growth can have a positive economic effect? Explain.

Source: "2008 World Population Data Sheet," Population Reference Bureau, August 19, 2008.

15. You have been hired as an economic consultant for the nation of Ishtar. Ishtar is a developing nation that has recently emerged from a 10-year civil war; as a result, it has experienced appreciable political instability. Ishtar has a serious lack of capital formation, and capital flight has been a problem since before the civil war began. As an economic consultant, what policy recommendations would you make for the economic development of Ishtar?

Glossary

absolute advantage A producer has an absolute advantage over another in the production of a good or service if he or she can produce that product using fewer resources (a lower absolute cost per unit); the advantage in the production of a good enjoyed by one country over another when it uses fewer resources to produce that good than the other country does. *p. 29 p. 353*

accelerator effect The tendency for investment to increase when aggregate output increases and to decrease when aggregate output decreases, accelerating the growth or decline of output. *p. 308*

actual investment The actual amount of investment that takes place; it includes items such as unplanned changes in inventories. *p. 153*

adjustment costs The costs that a firm incurs when it changes its production level—for example, the administration costs of laying off employees or the training costs of hiring new workers. *p. 309*

aggregate behavior The behavior of all households and firms together. *p. 97*

aggregate income The total income received by all factors of production in a given period. *p. 147*

aggregate output The total quantity of goods and services produced (or supplied) in an economy in a given period. *p. 98 p. 147*

aggregate output (income) (Y) A combined term used to remind you of the exact equality between aggregate output and aggregate income. *p. 147*

aggregate production function A mathematical relationship stating that total GDP (output) depends on the total amount of labor used and the total amount of capital used. *p. 323*

aggregate saving (S) The part of aggregate income that is not consumed. *p. 149*

aggregate supply The total supply of all goods and services in an economy. *p. 229*

aggregate supply (AS) curve A graph that shows the relationship between the aggregate quantity of output supplied by all firms in an economy and the overall price level. *p. 229*

animal spirits of entrepreneurs A term coined by Keynes to describe investors' feelings. *p. 308*

appreciation of a currency The rise in value of one currency relative to another. *p. 387*

automatic destabilizer Revenue and expenditure items in the federal budget that automatically change with the state of the economy in such a way as to destabilize GDP. *p. 180 p. 294*

automatic stabilizers Revenue and expenditure items in the federal budget that automatically change with the state of the economy in such a way as to stabilize GDP. *p. 180 p. 294*

balance of payments The record of a country's transactions in goods, services, and assets with the rest of the world; also the record of a country's sources (supply) and uses (demand) of foreign exchange. *p. 376*

balance of trade A country's exports of goods and services minus its imports of goods and services. *p. 377*

balance on capital account In the United States, the sum of the following (measured in a given period): the change in private U.S. assets abroad, the change in foreign private assets in the United States, the change in U.S. government assets abroad, and the change in foreign government assets in the United States. *p. 378*

balance on current account Net exports of goods plus net exports of services plus net investment income plus net transfer payments. *p. 378*

balanced-budget multiplier The ratio of change in the equilibrium level of output to a change in government spending where the change in government spending is balanced by a change in taxes so as not to create any deficit. The balanced-budget multiplier is equal to 1: The change in Y resulting from the change in G and the equal change in T are exactly the same size as the initial change in G or T. *p. 174*

barter The direct exchange of goods and services for other goods and services. *p. 190*

base year The year chosen for the weights in a fixed-weight procedure. *p. 121*

binding situation State of the economy in which the Fed rule calls for a negative interest rate *p. 252*

black market A market in which illegal trading takes place at market-determined prices. *p. 84*

brain drain The tendency for talented people from developing countries to become educated in a developed country and remain there after graduation. *p. 404*

budget deficit The difference between what a government spends and what it collects in taxes in a given period: G − T. *p. 167*

business cycle The cycle of short-term ups and downs in the economy. *p. 98*

capital Things that are produced and then used in the production of other goods and services. *p. 26*

capital flight The tendency for both human capital and financial capital to leave developing countries in search of higher expected rates of return elsewhere with less risk. *p. 404*

capital gain An increase in the value of an asset. *p. 282*

capital market The input/factor market in which households supply their savings, for interest or for claims to future profits, to firms that demand funds to buy capital goods. *p. 49*

catch-up The theory stating that the growth rates of less developed countries will exceed the growth rates of developed countries, allowing the less developed countries to catch up. *p. 323*

ceteris paribus, *or* **all else equal** A device used to analyze the relationship between two variables while the values of other variables are held unchanged. *p. 9*

change in business inventories The amount by which firms' inventories change during a period. Inventories are the goods that firms produce now but intend to sell later. *p. 116*

circular flow A diagram showing the income received and payments made by each sector of the economy. *p. 101*

command economy An economy in which a central government either directly or indirectly sets output targets, incomes, and prices. *p. 39*

commodity monies Items used as money that also have intrinsic value in some other use. *p. 191*

comparative advantage A producer has a comparative advantage over another in the production of a good or service if he or she can produce that product at a lower *opportunity cost*; the advantage in the production of a good enjoyed by one country over another when that good can be produced at lower cost in terms of other goods than it could be in the other country. *p. 29 p. 353*

compensation of employees Includes wages, salaries, and various supplements—employer contributions to social insurance and pension funds, for example—paid to households by firms and by the government. *p. 117*

complements, complementary goods Goods that "go together"; a decrease in the price of one results in an increase in demand for the other and vice versa. *p. 55*

constrained supply of labor The amount a household actually works in a given period at the current wage rate. *p. 304*

consumer goods Goods produced for present consumption. *p. 31*

consumer price index (CPI) A price index computed each month by the Bureau of Labor Statistics using a bundle that is meant to represent the "market basket" purchased monthly by the typical urban consumer. *p. 136*

consumer sovereignty The idea that consumers ultimately dictate what will be produced (or not produced) by choosing what to purchase (and what not to purchase). *p. 40*

consumer surplus The difference between the maximum amount a person is willing to pay for a good and its current market price. *p. 89*

consumption function The relationship between consumption and income. *p. 148*

contraction, recession, *or* **slump** The period in the business cycle from a peak down to a trough during which output and employment fall. *p. 98*

Corn Laws The tariffs, subsidies, and restrictions enacted by the British Parliament in the early nineteenth century to discourage imports and encourage exports of grain. *p. 353*

corporate bonds Promissory notes issued by firms when they borrow money. *p. 103*

corporate profits The income of corporations. *p. 117*

cost shock, *or* **supply shock** A change in costs that shifts the short-run aggregate supply (*AS*) curve. *p. 232*

cost-of-living adjustments (COLAs) Contract provisions that tie wages to changes in the cost of living. The greater the inflation rate, the more wages are raised. *p. 267*

cost-push, *or* **supply-side, inflation** Inflation caused by an increase in costs. *p. 254*

currency debasement The decrease in the value of money that occurs when its supply is increased rapidly. *p. 192*

current dollars The current prices that we pay for goods and services. *p. 120*

cyclical deficit The deficit that occurs because of a downturn in the business cycle. *p. 181*

cyclical unemployment Unemployment that is above frictional plus structural unemployment; the increase in unemployment that occurs during recessions and depressions. *p. 135 p. 264*

deadweight loss The total loss of producer and consumer surplus from underproduction or overproduction. *p. 92*

deflation A decrease in the overall price level. *p. 100*

demand curve A graph illustrating how much of a given product a household would be willing to buy at different prices. *p. 51*

demand schedule Shows how much of a given product a household would be willing to buy at different prices for a given time period. *p. 51*

demand-pull inflation Inflation that is initiated by an increase in aggregate demand. *p. 254*

depreciation The decline in an asset's economic value over time; the amount by which an asset's value falls in a given period; *p. 116*

depreciation of a currency The fall in value of one currency relative to another. *p. 387*

depression A prolonged and deep recession. *p. 98*

desired, *or* **optimal, level of inventories** The level of inventory at which the extra cost (in lost sales) from lowering inventories by a small amount is just equal to the extra gain (in interest revenue and decreased storage costs). *p. 310*

discount rate The interest rate that banks pay to the Fed to borrow from it. *p. 204*

discouraged-worker effect The decline in the measured unemployment rate that results when people who want to work but cannot find jobs grow discouraged and stop looking, thus dropping out of the ranks of the unemployed and the labor force. *p. 132 p. 314*

discretionary fiscal policy Changes in taxes or spending that are the result of deliberate changes in government policy. *p. 166*

disembodied technical change Technical change that results in a change in the production process. *p. 328*

disposable personal income *or* **after-tax income** Personal income minus personal income taxes. The amount that households have to spend or save. *p. 119*

disposable, *or* **after-tax, income (Y_d)** Total income minus net taxes: $Y - T$. *p. 166*

dividend(s) Payment made to shareholders of a corporation; the portion of a firm's profits that the firm pays out each period to its shareholders. *p. 103*

Doha Development Agenda An initiative of the World Trade Organization focused on issues of trade and development. *p. 363*

Dow Jones Industrial Average An index based on the stock prices of 30 actively traded large companies. The oldest and most widely followed index of stock market performance. *p. 284*

dumping A firm's or an industry's sale of products on the world market at prices below its own cost of production. *p. 361*

durable goods Goods that last a relatively long time, such as cars and household appliances. *p. 115*

economic growth An increase in the total output of an economy. Growth occurs when a society acquires new resources or when it learns to produce more using existing resources. *p. 12 p. 36*

economic integration Occurs when two or more nations join to form a free-trade zone. *p. 364*

economics The study of how individuals and societies choose to use the scarce resources that nature and previous generations have provided. *p. 2*

efficiency In economics, *allocative efficiency*. An efficient economy is one that produces what people want at the least possible cost; the condition in which the economy is producing what people want at least possible cost. *p. 11*

efficiency wage theory An explanation for unemployment that holds that the productivity of workers increases with the wage rate. If this is so, firms may have an incentive to pay wages above the market-clearing rate. *p. 267*

efficient market A market in which profit opportunities are eliminated almost instantaneously. *p. 3*

embodied technical change Technical change that results in an improvement in the quality of capital. *p. 327*

empirical economics The collection and use of data to test economic theories. *p. 10*

employed Any person 16 years old or older (1) who works for pay, either for someone else or in his or her own business for 1 or more hours per week, (2) who works without pay for 15 or more hours per week in a family enterprise, or (3) who has a job but has been temporarily absent with or without pay. *p. 130*

entrepreneur A person who organizes, manages, and assumes the risks of a firm, taking a new idea or a new product and turning it into a successful business. *p. 48*

equilibrium The condition that exists when quantity supplied and quantity demanded are equal. At equilibrium, there is no tendency for price to change; occurs when there is≈no tendency for change. In the macroeconomic goods market, equilibrium occurs when planned aggregate expenditure is equal to aggregate output. *p. 65 p. 154*

European Union (EU) The European trading bloc composed of 27 countries (of the 27 countries in the EU, 17 have the same currency—the euro). *p. 364*

excess demand *or* **shortage** The condition that exists when quantity demanded exceeds quantity supplied at the current price. *p. 66*

excess labor, excess capital Labor and capital that are not needed to produce the firm's current level of output. *p. 309*

excess reserves The difference between a bank's actual reserves and its required reserves. *p. 196*

excess supply *or* **surplus** The condition that exists when quantity supplied exceeds quantity demanded at the current price. *p. 67*

exchange rate The ratio at which two currencies are traded for each other; the price of one country's currency in terms of another country's currency. *p. 358 p. 376*

exogenous variable A variable that is assumed not to depend on the state of the economy—that is, it does not change when the economy changes. *p. 157*

expansion *or* **boom** The period in the business cycle from a trough up to a peak during which output and employment grow. *p. 98*

expenditure approach A method of computing GDP that measures the total amount spent on all final goods and services during a given period. *p. 113*

explicit contracts Employment contracts that stipulate workers' wages, usually for a period of 1 to 3 years. *p. 267*

export promotion A trade policy designed to encourage exports. *p. 408*

export subsidies Government payments made to domestic firms to encourage exports. *p. 361*

factor endowments The quantity and quality of labor, land, and natural resources of a country. *p. 360*

factors of production The inputs into the production process. Land, labor, and capital are the three key factors of production. *p. 49*

factors of production (*or* **factors**) The inputs into the process of production. Another term for resources. *p. 26*

fallacy of composition The erroneous belief that what is true for a part is necessarily true for the whole. *p. 10*

favored customers Those who receive special treatment from dealers during situations of excess demand. *p. 84*

Fed rule Equation that shows how the Fed's interest rate decision depends on the state of the economy. *p. 235*

federal budget The budget of the federal government. *p. 175*

federal debt The total amount owed by the federal government. *p. 179*

Federal Open Market Committee (FOMC) A group composed of the seven members of the Fed's Board of Governors, the president of the New York Federal Reserve Bank, and four of the other 11 district bank presidents on a rotating basis; it sets goals concerning the money supply and interest rates and directs the operation of the Open Market Desk in New York. *p. 200*

Federal Reserve Bank (the Fed) The central bank of the United States. *p. 195*

federal surplus (+) *or* **deficit** (−) Federal government receipts minus expenditures. *p. 176*

fiat, *or* **token, money** Items designated as money that are intrinsically worthless. *p. 191*

final goods and services Goods and services produced for final use. *p. 112*

financial intermediaries Banks and other institutions that act as a link between those who have money to lend and those who want to borrow money. *p. 193*

fine-tuning The phrase used by Walter Heller to refer to the government's role in regulating inflation and unemployment. *p. 104*

firm An organization that transforms resources (inputs) into products (outputs). Firms are the primary producing units in a market economy. *p. 48*

fiscal drag The negative effect on the economy that occurs when average tax rates increase because taxpayers have moved into higher income brackets during an expansion. *p. 180*

fiscal policy Government policies concerning taxes and spending. *p. 103 p. 165*

fixed-weight procedure A procedure that uses weights from a given base year. *p. 121*

floating, *or* **market-determined, exchange rates** Exchange rates that are determined by the unregulated forces of supply and demand. *p. 384*

foreign direct investment (FDI) Investment in enterprises made in a country by residents outside that country. *p. 326*

foreign exchange All currencies other than the domestic currency of a given country. *p. 376*

free enterprise The freedom of individuals to start and operate private businesses in search of profits. *p. 40*

frictional unemployment The portion of unemployment that is due to the normal turnover in the labor market; used to denote short-run job/skill-matching problems. *p. 135 p. 264*

full-employment budget What the federal budget would be if the economy were producing at the full-employment level of output. *p. 181*

General Agreement on Tariffs and Trade (GATT) An international agreement signed by the United States and 22 other countries in 1947 to promote the liberalization of foreign trade. *p. 363*

government consumption and gross investment (G) Expenditures by federal, state, and local governments for final goods and services. *p. 116*

government spending multiplier The ratio of the change in the equilibrium level of output to a change in government spending. *p. 171*

Gramm-Rudman-Hollings Act Passed by the U.S. Congress and signed by President Reagan in 1986, this law set out to reduce the federal deficit by $36 billion per year, with a deficit of zero slated for 1991. *p. 293*

Great Depression   The period of severe economic contraction and high unemployment that began in 1929 and continued throughout the 1930s. *p. 103*

gross domestic product (GDP)   The total market value of all final goods and services produced within a given period by factors of production located within a country. *p. 112*

gross investment   The total value of all newly produced capital goods (plant, equipment, housing, and inventory) produced in a given period. *p. 116*

gross national income (GNI)   GNP converted into dollars using an average of currency exchange rates over several years adjusted for rates of inflation. *p. 124*

gross national product (GNP)   The total market value of all final goods and services produced within a given period by factors of production owned by a country's citizens, regardless of where the output is produced. *p. 113*

gross private domestic investment (*I*)   Total investment in capital—that is, the purchase of new housing, plants, equipment, and inventory by the private (or nongovernment) sector. *p. 115*

Heckscher-Ohlin theorem   A theory that explains the existence of a country's comparative advantage by its factor endowments: A country has a comparative advantage in the production of a product if that country is relatively well endowed with inputs used intensively in the production of that product. *p. 360*

households   The consuming units in an economy. *p. 48*

hyperinflation   A period of very rapid increases in the overall price level. *p. 100*

identity   Something that is always true. *p. 149*

implementation lag   The time it takes to put the desired policy into effect once economists and policy makers recognize that the economy is in a boom or a slump. *p. 289*

import substitution   An industrial trade strategy that favors developing local industries that can manufacture goods to replace imports. *p. 408*

income   The sum of all a household's wages, salaries, profits, interest payments, rents, and other forms of earnings in a given period of time. It is a flow measure. *p. 54*

income approach   A method of computing GDP that measures the income—wages, rents, interest, and profits—received by all factors of production in producing final goods and services. *p. 114*

indirect taxes minus subsidies   Taxes such as sales taxes, customs duties, and license fees less subsidies that the government pays for which it receives no goods or services in return. *p. 117*

industrial policy   A policy in which governments actively pick industries to support as a base for economic development. *p. 407*

Industrial Revolution   The period in England during the late eighteenth and early nineteenth centuries in which new manufacturing technologies and improved transportation gave rise to the modern factory system and a massive movement of the population from the countryside to the cities. *p. 3*

infant industry   A young industry that may need temporary protection from competition from the established industries of other countries to develop an acquired comparative advantage. *p. 369*

inferior goods   Goods for which demand tends to fall when income rises. *p. 54*

inflation   An increase in the overall price level. *p. 100*

inflation rate   The percentage change in the price level. *p. 271*

inflation targeting   When a monetary authority chooses its interest rate values with the aim of keeping the inflation rate within some specified band over some specified horizon. *p. 258*

informal economy   The part of the economy in which transactions take place and in which income is generated that is unreported and therefore not counted in GDP. *p. 124*

innovation   The use of new knowledge to produce a new product or to produce an existing product more efficiently. *p. 329*

input *or* factor markets   The markets in which the resources used to produce goods and services are exchanged. *p. 48*

inputs *or* resources   Anything provided by nature or previous generations that can be used directly or indirectly to satisfy human wants. *p. 26*

interest   The payments made for the use of money; the fee that borrowers pay to lenders for the use of their funds. *p. 213*

intermediate goods   Goods that are produced by one firm for use in further processing by another firm. *p. 112*

International Monetary Fund (IMF)   An international agency whose primary goals are to stabilize international exchange rates and to lend money to countries that have problems financing their international transactions. *p. 406*

invention   An advance in knowledge. *p. 329*

inventory investment   The change in the stock of inventories. *p. 309*

investment   The process of using resources to produce new capital *p. 32*

IS curve   Relationship between aggregate output and the interest rate in the goods market *p. 234*

J-curve effect   Following a currency depreciation, a country's balance of trade may get worse before it gets better. The graph showing this effect is shaped like the letter *J*, hence the name J-curve effect. *p. 390*

labor demand curve A graph that illustrates the amount of labor that firms want to employ at each given wage rate. *p. 264*

labor force The number of people employed plus the number of unemployed. *p. 130*

labor force participation rate The ratio of the labor force to the total population 16 years old or older. *p. 130*

labor market The input/factor market in which households supply work for wages to firms that demand labor. *p. 49*

labor productivity growth The growth rate of output per worker. *p. 321*

labor supply curve A graph that illustrates the amount of labor that households want to supply at each given wage rate. *p. 264*

Laffer curve With the tax rate measured on the vertical axis and tax revenue measured on the horizontal axis, the Laffer curve shows that there is some tax rate beyond which the supply response is large enough to lead to a decrease in tax revenue for further increases in the tax rate. *p. 341*

laissez-faire economy Literally from the French: "allow [them] to do." An economy in which individual people and firms pursue their own self-interest without any central direction or regulation. *p. 40*

land market The input/factor market in which households supply land or other real property in exchange for rent. *p. 49*

law of demand The negative relationship between price and quantity demanded: *Ceteris paribus,* as price rises, quantity demanded decreases; as price falls, quantity demanded increases. *p. 52*

law of one price If the costs of transportation are small, the price of the same good in different countries should be roughly the same. *p. 388*

law of supply The positive relationship between price and quantity of a good supplied: An increase in market price will lead to an increase in quantity supplied, and a decrease in market price will lead to a decrease in quantity supplied. *p. 61*

legal tender Money that a government has required to be accepted in settlement of debts. *p. 191*

lender of last resort One of the functions of the Fed: It provides funds to troubled banks that cannot find any other sources of funds. *p. 200*

life-cycle theory of consumption A theory of household consumption: Households make lifetime consumption decisions based on their expectations of lifetime income. *p. 300*

liquidity property of money The property of money that makes it a good medium of exchange as well as a store of value: It is portable and readily accepted and thus easily exchanged for goods. *p. 190*

Lucas supply function The supply function embodies the idea that output (Y) depends on the difference between the actual price level and the expected price level. *p. 345*

M1, *or* **transactions money** Money that can be directly used for transactions. *p. 192*

M2, *or* **broad money** M1 plus savings accounts, money market accounts, and other near monies. *p. 193*

macroeconomics The branch of economics that examines the economic behavior of aggregates—income, employment, output, and so on—on a national scale; deals with the economy as a whole. Macroeconomics focuses on the determinants of total national income, deals with aggregates such as aggregate consumption and investment, and looks at the overall level of prices instead of individual prices. *p. 5 p. 97*

marginal propensity to consume *(MPC)* That fraction of a change in income that is consumed, or spent. *p. 149*

marginal propensity to import *(MPM)* The change in imports caused by a $1 change in income. *p. 381*

marginal propensity to save *(MPS)* That fraction of a change in income that is saved. *p. 149*

marginal rate of transformation (MRT) The slope of the production possibility frontier (ppf). *p. 33*

marginalism The process of analyzing the additional or incremental costs or benefits arising from a choice or decision. *p. 2*

market The institution through which buyers and sellers interact and engage in exchange. *p. 40*

market demand The sum of all the quantities of a good or service demanded per period by all the households buying in the market for that good or service. *p. 59*

market supply The sum of all that is supplied each period by all producers of a single product. *p. 64*

medium of exchange, *or* **means of payment** What sellers generally accept and buyers generally use to pay for goods and services. *p. 190*

microeconomics The branch of economics that examines the functioning of individual industries and the behavior of individual decision-making units—that is, firms and households. *p. 4 p. 97*

minimum wage A price floor set for the price of labor; the lowest wage that firms are permitted to pay workers. *p. 86*

minimum wage laws Laws that set a floor for wage rates—that is, a minimum hourly rate for any kind of labor. *p. 269*

model A formal statement of a theory, usually a mathematical statement of a presumed relationship between two or more variables. *p. 8*

monetary policy The tools used by the Federal Reserve to control the short-term interest rate; the behavior of the Federal Reserve concerning the nation's money supply. *p. 103 p. 166*

money multiplier The multiple by which deposits can increase for every dollar increase in reserves; equal to 1 divided by the required reserve ratio. *p. 198*

moral suasion The pressure that in the past the Fed exerted on member banks to discourage them from borrowing heavily from the Fed. *p. 205*

movement along a demand curve The change in quantity demanded brought about by a change in price. *p. 57*

movement along a supply curve The change in quantity supplied brought about by a change in price. *p. 63*

multiplier The ratio of the change in the equilibrium level of output to a change in some exogenous variable. *p. 157*

NAIRU The nonaccelerating inflation rate of unemployment. *p. 276*

NASDAQ Composite An index based on the stock prices of over 5,000 companies traded on the NASDAQ Stock Market. The NASDAQ market takes its name from the National Association of Securities Dealers Automated Quotation System. *p. 284*

national income The total income earned by the factors of production owned by a country's citizens. *p. 117*

national income and product accounts Data collected and published by the government describing the various components of national income and output in the economy. *p. 111*

natural experiment Selection of a control versus experimental group in testing the outcome of an intervention is made as a result of an exogenous event outside the experiment itself and unrelated to it. *p. 412*

natural rate of unemployment The unemployment rate that occurs as a normal part of the functioning of the economy. Sometimes taken as the sum of frictional unemployment rate and structural unemployment rate. *p. 135 p. 275*

near monies Close substitutes for transactions money, such as savings accounts and money market accounts. *p. 193*

net business transfer payments Net transfer payments by businesses to others. *p. 117*

net exports (EX – IM) The difference between exports (sales to foreigners of U.S.- produced goods and services) and imports (U.S. purchases of goods and services from abroad). The figure can be positive or negative. *p. 117*

net exports of goods and services (EX – IM) The difference between a country's total exports and total imports. *p. 380*

net interest The interest paid by business. *p. 117*

net investment Gross investment minus depreciation. *p. 116*

net national product (NNP) Gross national product minus depreciation; a nation's total product minus what is required to maintain the value of its capital stock. *p. 118*

net taxes (T) Taxes paid by firms and households to the government minus transfer payments made to households by the government. *p. 166*

new Keynesian economics A field in which models are developed under the assumptions of rational expectations and sticky prices and wages. *p. 346*

nominal GDP Gross domestic product measured in current dollars. *p. 120*

nominal wage rate The wage rate in current dollars. *p. 302*

nondurable goods Goods that are used up fairly quickly, such as food and clothing. *p. 115*

nonlabor, or nonwage, income Any income received from sources other than working—inheritances, interest, dividends, transfer payments, and so on. *p. 302*

nonresidential investment Expenditures by firms for machines, tools, plants, and so on. *p. 115*

nonsynchronization of income and spending The mismatch between the timing of money inflow to the household and the timing of money outflow for household expenses. *p. 215*

normal goods Goods for which demand goes up when income is higher and for which demand goes down when income is lower. *p. 54*

normative economics An approach to economics that analyzes outcomes of economic behavior, evaluates them as good or bad, and may prescribe courses of action. Also called *policy economics*. *p. 8*

North American Free Trade Agreement (NAFTA) An agreement signed by the United States, Mexico, and Canada in which the three countries agreed to establish all North America as a free-trade zone. *p. 364*

not in the labor force A person who is not looking for work because he or she does not want a job or has given up looking. *p. 130*

Ockham's razor The principle that irrelevant detail should be cut away. *p. 8*

Okun's Law The theory, put forth by Arthur Okun, that in the short run the unemployment rate decreases about 1 percentage point for every 3 percent increase in real GDP. Later research and data have shown that the relationship between output and unemployment is not as stable as Okun's "Law" predicts. *p. 314*

Open Market Desk The office in the New York Federal Reserve Bank from which government securities are bought and sold by the Fed. *p. 200*

open market operations The purchase and sale by the Fed of government securities in the open market; a tool used to expand or contract the amount of reserves in the system and thus the money supply. *p. 205*

opportunity cost The best alternative that we forgo, or give up, when we make a choice or a decision. *p. 2 p. 27*

output growth The growth rate of the output of the entire economy. *p. 140 p. 321*

outputs Goods and services of value to households. *p. 26*

per-capita output growth The growth rate of output per person in the economy. *p. 140 p. 321*

perfect substitutes Identical products. *p. 55*

permanent income The average level of a person's expected future income stream. *p. 301*

personal consumption expenditures (C) Expenditures by consumers on goods and services. *p. 115*

personal income The total income of households. *p. 118*

personal saving The amount of disposable income that is left after total personal spending in a given period. *p. 119*

personal saving rate The percentage of disposable personal income that is saved. If the personal saving rate is low, households are spending a large amount relative to their incomes; if it is high, households are spending cautiously. *p. 120*

Phillips Curve A curve showing the relationship between the inflation rate and the unemployment rate. *p. 271*

planned aggregate expenditure (AE) The total amount the economy plans to spend in a given period. Equal to consumption plus planned investment: $AE + C + I$. *p. 154*

planned investment (I) Those additions to capital stock and inventory that are planned by firms. *p. 153*

positive economics An approach to economics that seeks to understand behavior and the operation of systems without making judgments. It describes what exists and how it works. *p. 8*

post hoc, ergo propter hoc Literally, "after this (in time), therefore because of this." A common error made in thinking about causation: If Event A happens before Event B, it is not necessarily true that A caused B. *p. 10*

potential output, or potential GDP The level of aggregate output that can be sustained in the long run without inflation. *p. 242*

price ceiling A maximum price that sellers may charge for a good, usually set by government. *p. 83*

price feedback effect The process by which a domestic price increase in one country can "feed back" on itself through export and import prices. An increase in the price level in one country can drive up prices in other countries. This in turn further increases the price level in the first country. *p. 384*

price floor A minimum price below which exchange is not-permitted. *p. 86*

price rationing The process by which the market system allocates goods and services to consumers when quantity demanded exceeds quantity supplied. *p. 79*

price surprise Actual price level minus expected price level. *p. 345*

privately held federal debt The privately held (non-government-owned) debt of the U.S. government. *p. 179*

producer price indexes (PPIs) Measures of prices that producers receive for products at various stages in the production process. *p. 138*

producer surplus The difference between the current market price and the cost of production for the firm. *p. 90*

product or output markets The markets in which goods and services are exchanged. *p. 48*

production The process that transforms scarce resources into useful goods and services. *p. 26*

production possibility frontier (ppf) A graph that shows all the combinations of goods and services that can be produced if all of society's resources are used efficiently. *p. 32*

productivity growth The growth rate of output per worker. *p. 140*

productivity, or labor productivity Output per worker hour. *p. 313*

profit The difference between revenues and costs. *p. 60*

proprietors' income The income of unincorporated businesses. *p. 117*

protection The practice of shielding a sector of the economy from foreign competition. *p. 361*

purchasing-power-parity theory A theory of international exchange holding that exchange rates are set so that the price of similar goods in different countries is the same. *p. 388*

quantity demanded The amount (number of units) of a product that a household would buy in a given period if it could buy all it wanted at the current market price. *p. 50*

quantity supplied The amount of a particular product that a firm would be willing and able to offer for sale at a particular price during a given time period. *p. 61*

quantity theory of money The theory based on the identity $M \times V \equiv P \times Y$ and the assumption that the velocity of money (V) is constant (or virtually constant). *p. 338*

queuing Waiting in line as a means of distributing goods and services: a nonprice rationing mechanism. *p. 83*

quota A limit on the quantity of imports. *p. 362*

random experiment (Sometimes referred to as a randomized experiment.) A technique in which outcomes of specific interventions are determined by using the intervention in a randomly selected subset of a sample and then comparing outcomes from the exposed and control group. *p. 411*

ration coupons Tickets or coupons that entitle individuals to purchase a certain amount of a given product per month. *p. 84*

rational-expectations hypothesis The hypothesis that people know the "true model" of the economy and that they use this model to form their expectations of the future. *p. 343*

real business cycle theory An attempt to explain business cycle fluctuations under the assumptions of complete price and wage flexibility and rational expectations. It emphasizes shocks to technology and other shocks. *p. 346*

real interest rate The difference between the interest rate on a loan and the inflation rate. *p. 139*

real wage rate The amount the nominal wage rate can buy in terms of goods and services. *p. 302*

real wealth effect The change in consumption brought about by a change in real wealth that results from a change in the price level. *p. 240*

realized capital gain The gain that occurs when the owner of an asset actually sells it for more than he or she paid for it. *p. 282*

recession A period during which aggregate output declines. Conventionally, a period in which aggregate output declines for two consecutive quarters. *p. 98*

recognition lag The time it takes for policy makers to recognize the existence of a boom or a slump. *p. 289*

relative-wage explanation of unemployment An explanation for sticky wages (and therefore unemployment): If workers are concerned about their wages relative to other workers in other firms and industries, they may be unwilling to accept a wage cut unless they know that all other workers are receiving similar cuts. *p. 267*

rental income The income received by property owners in the form of rent. *p. 117*

required reserve ratio The percentage of its total deposits that a bank must keep as reserves at the Federal Reserve. *p. 196*

reserves The deposits that a bank has at the Federal Reserve bank plus its cash on hand. *p. 195*

residential investment Expenditures by households and firms on new houses and apartment buildings. *p. 115*

response lag The time that it takes for the economy to adjust to the new conditions after a new policy is implemented; the lag that occurs because of the operation of the economy itself. *p. 290*

run on a bank Occurs when many of those who have claims on a bank (deposits) present them at the same time. *p. 195*

scarce Limited. *p. 2*

services The things we buy that do not involve the production of physical things, such as legal and medical services and education. *p. 115*

shares of stock Financial instruments that give to the holder a share in the firm's ownership and therefore the right to share in the firm's profits. *p. 103*

shift of a demand curve The change that takes place in a demand curve corresponding to a new relationship between quantity demanded of a good and price of that good. The shift is brought about by a change in the original conditions. *p. 57*

shift of a supply curve The change that takes place in a supply curve corresponding to a new relationship between quantity supplied of a good and the price of that good. The shift is brought about by a change in the original conditions. *p. 63*

shock therapy The approach to transition from socialism to market capitalism that advocates rapid deregulation of prices, liberalization of trade, and privatization. *p. 418*

Smoot-Hawley tariff The U.S. tariff law of the 1930s, which set the highest tariffs in U.S. history (60 percent). It set off an international trade war and caused the decline in trade that is often considered one of the causes of the worldwide depression of the 1930s. *p. 362*

social overhead capital Basic infrastructure projects such as roads, power generation, and irrigation systems. *p. 406*

social, *or* implicit, contracts Unspoken agreements between workers and firms that firms will not cut wages. *p. 266*

speculation motive One reason for holding bonds instead of money: Because the market price of interest-bearing bonds is inversely related to the interest rate, investors may want to hold bonds when interest rates are high with the hope of selling them when interest rates fall. *p. 218*

stability A condition in which national output is growing steadily, with low inflation and full employment of resources. *p. 12*

stabilization policy Describes both monetary and fiscal policy, the goals of which are to smooth out fluctuations in output and employment and to keep prices as stable as possible. *p. 287*

stagflation A situation of both high inflation and high unemployment; occurs when output is falling at the same time that prices are rising. *p. 104 p. 254*

Standard and Poor's 500 (S&P 500) An index based on the stock prices of 500 of the largest firms by market value. *p. 284*

statistical discrepancy Data measurement error. *p. 118*

sticky prices Prices that do not always adjust rapidly to maintain equality between quantity supplied and quantity demanded. *p. 97*

sticky wages The downward rigidity of wages as an explanation for the existence of unemployment. *p. 266*

stock A certificate that certifies ownership of a certain portion of a firm. *p. 282*

store of value An asset that can be used to transport purchasing power from one time period to another. *p. 190*

structural deficit The deficit that remains at full employment. *p. 181*

structural unemployment The portion of unemployment that is due to changes in the structure of the economy that result in a significant loss of jobs in certain industries. *p. 135 p. 264*

substitutes Goods that can serve as replacements for one another; when the price of one increases, demand for the other increases. *p. 55*

supply curve A graph illustrating how much of a product a firm will sell at different prices. *p. 61*

supply schedule Shows how much of a product firms will sell at alternative prices. *p. 61*

surplus of government enterprises Income of government enterprises. *p. 117*

tariff A tax on imports. *p. 361*

tax multiplier The ratio of change in the equilibrium level of output to a change in taxes. *p. 173*

terms of trade The ratio at which a country can trade domestic products for imported products. *p. 357*

theory of comparative advantage Ricardo's theory that specialization and free trade will benefit all trading partners (real wages will rise), even those that may be absolutely less efficient producers. *p. 28 p. 353*

time lags Delays in the economy's response to stabilization policies. *p. 287*

trade deficit Occurs when a country's exports of goods and services are less than its imports of goods and services. *p. 352 p. 377*

trade feedback effect The tendency for an increase in the economic activity of one country to lead to a worldwide increase in economic activity, which then feeds back to that country. *p. 383*

trade surplus The situation when a country exports more than it imports. *p. 352*

tragedy of commons The idea that collective ownership may not provide the proper private incentives for efficiency because individuals do not bear the full costs of their own decisions but do enjoy the full benefits. *p. 416*

transaction motive The main reason that people hold money—to buy things. *p. 215*

transfer payments Cash payments made by the government to people who do not supply goods, services, or labor in exchange for these payments. They include Social Security benefits, veterans' benefits, and welfare payments. *p. 101*

Treasury bonds, notes, *and* bills Promissory notes issued by the federal government when it borrows money. *p. 103*

U.S.-Canadian Free Trade Agreement An agreement in which the United States and Canada agreed to eliminate all barriers to trade between the two countries by 1998. *p. 364*

unconstrained supply of labor The amount a household would like to work within a given period at the current wage rate if it could find the work. *p. 304*

unemployed A person 16 years old or older who is not working, is available for work, and has made specific efforts to find work during the previous 4 weeks. *p. 130*

unemployment rate The percentage of the labor force that is unemployed; the ratio of the number of people unemployed to the total number of people in the labor force. *p. 99 p. 130 p. 263*

unit of account A standard unit that provides a consistent way of quoting prices. *p. 190*

value added The difference between the value of goods as they leave a stage of production and the cost of the goods as they entered that stage. *p. 112*

variable A measure that can change from time to time or from observation to observation. *p. 8*

velocity of money The number of times a dollar bill changes hands, on average, during a year; the ratio of nominal GDP to the stock of money. *p. 338*

vicious-circle-of-poverty hypothesis   Suggests that poverty is self-perpetuating because poor nations are unable to save and invest enough to accumulate the capital stock that would help them grow. *p. 403*

wealth *or* **net worth**   The total value of what a household owns minus what it owes. It is a stock measure. *p. 54*

weight   The importance attached to an item within a group of items. *p. 120*

World Bank   An international agency that lends money to individual countries for projects that promote economic development. *p. 407*

World Trade Organization (WTO)   A negotiating forum dealing with rules of trade across nations. *p. 363*

zero interest rate bound   The interest rate cannot go below zero *p. 252*

Index

Notes: Key terms and the page on which they are defined appear in **boldface**. Page numbers followed by *n* refer to information in footnotes.

Photo Credits

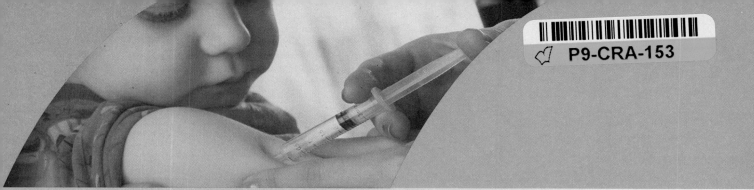

Public Health 101
Healthy People–Healthy Populations

Richard Riegelman, MD, MPH, PhD

Professor and Founding Dean
The George Washington University
School of Public Health and Health Services
Washington, DC

JONES & BARTLETT
LEARNING

World Headquarters

Jones & Bartlett Learning
40 Tall Pine Drive
Sudbury, MA 01776
978-443-5000
info@jblearning.com
www.jblearning.com

Jones & Bartlett Learning Canada
6339 Ormindale Way
Mississauga, Ontario L5V 1J2
Canada

Jones & Bartlett Learning International
Barb House, Barb Mews
London W6 7PA
United Kingdom

Jones & Bartlett Learning books and products are available through most bookstores and online booksellers. To contact Jones & Bartlett Learning directly, call 800-832-0034, fax 978-443-8000, or visit our website, www.jblearning.com.

Substantial discounts on bulk quantities of Jones & Bartlett Learning publications are available to corporations, professional associations, and other qualified organizations. For details and specific discount information, contact the special sales department at Jones & Bartlett Learning via the above contact information or send an email to specialsales@jblearning.com.

This publication is designed to provide accurate and authoritative information in regard to the Subject Matter covered. It is sold with the understanding that the publisher is not engaged in rendering legal, accounting, or other professional service. If legal advice or other expert assistance is required, the service of a competent professional person should be sought.

To order this product, use ISBN: 978-1-4496-0149-2

Production Credits
Publisher: Michael Brown
Editorial Assistant: Catie Heverling
Editorial Assistant: Teresa Reilly
Senior Production Editor: Tracey Chapman
Senior Marketing Manager: Sophie Fleck
Manufacturing and Inventory Control Supervisor: Amy Bacus
Composition: Auburn Associates, Inc.
Cover Design: Kristin E. Parker
Cover Image: (left to right, top to bottom) © Temelko Temelkov/ShutterStock, Inc.; © sergel telegin/ShutterStock, Inc.;
    © Muriel Lasure/ShutterStock, Inc.; © Bill Jonscher/Dreamstime.com
Printing and Binding: Courier Stoughton
Cover Printing: John Pow Company

Library of Congress Cataloging-in-Publication Data
Riegelman, Richard K.
    Public health 101 : healthy people - healthy populations / Richard Riegelman.
        p.   ; cm.
    Includes bibliographical references and index.
    ISBN-13: 978-0-7637-6044-1 (pbk.)
    ISBN-10: 0-7637-6044-7 (pbk.)
    1. Public health—Textbooks.   I. Title.
    [DNLM: 1. Public Health. WA 100 R554p 2009]
    RA425.R36 2009
    362.1—dc22

                                                2009004511

6048
Printed in the United States of America
14   13   12   11   10   10 9 8 7 6 5 4

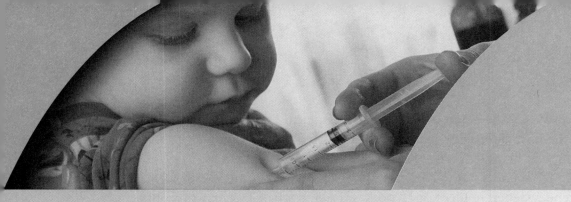

Contents

Section II Tools of Population Health   39

Chapter 3   Health Informatics and Health Communications   41

Chapter 4   Social and Behavioral Sciences and Public Health   55

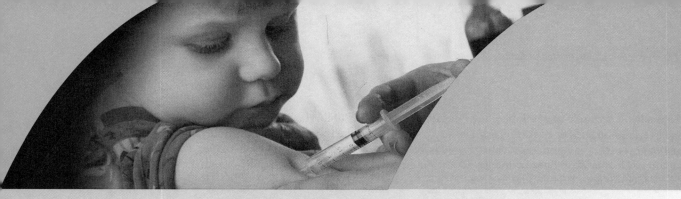

The Essential Public Health Series

*Log on to **www.essentialpublichealth.com** for the most current information on availability.*

CURRENT AND FORTHCOMING TITLES IN THE *ESSENTIAL PUBLIC HEALTH SERIES*:

ABOUT THE EDITOR:

Richard K. Riegelman, MD, MPH, PhD, is Professor of Epidemiology-Biostatistics, Medicine, and Health Policy, and founding dean of The George Washington University School of Public Health and Health Services in Washington,

DC. He has taken a lead role in developing the Educated Citizen and Public Health initiative which has brought together arts and sciences and public health education associations to implement the Institute of Medicine of the National Academies' recommendation that ". . .all undergraduates should have access to education in public health." Dr. Riegelman also led the development of George Washington's undergraduate public health major and minor and currently teaches "Public Health 101" and "Epidemiology 101" to undergraduates.

Dedication

To Nancy Alfred Persily, whose enthusiasm for teaching public health to undergraduates inspired *Public Health 101: Healthy People–Healthy Populations.*

Acknowledgments

Public Health 101: Healthy People–Healthy Populations is the culmination of a decade of effort aimed at introducing public health to undergraduates. The effort began with the teaching of an introductory course in public health in 1998 at the then newly created George Washington University School of Public Health and Health Services. The new course organized by Nancy Alfred Persily inspired my own efforts to teach and to learn from a new generation. The approach was designed as part of a liberal arts education stimulating the movement which came to be called The Educated Citizen and Public Health.

Efforts to think through the content of an introductory course in public health has involved a large number of people throughout the United States. Public health, arts and sciences, and clinical educators all participated in the 2006 Consensus Conference on Public Health Education which put forward the framework for "Public Health 101" upon which this book is based. Among those who led and continue to lead this effort is Susan Albertine whose insights into the relationship between public health and liberal education has formed the basis for much of The Educated Citizen and Public Health movement.

I have taught "Public Health 101" since 2002, providing an opportunity to teach and to learn from over 300 undergraduate students at The George Washington University. Their feedback and input has been central to writing and rewriting this book. Madison Hardee and Katie Harter deserve special recognition for their extensive feedback on many chapters of the book. Laura Olsen provided extremely valuable editing assistance. Paul Marantz from Albert Einstein School of Medicine utilized a draft of the book in teaching an introductory undergraduate course. His students also provided helpful feedback. I'd also like to thank Alan Greenberg and Dante Verme, the chair and vice chair of the Department of Epidemiology and Biostatistics at The George Washington University School of Public Health and Health Services, for their support of my efforts to expand the audience for undergraduate public health.

The draft of the text went through extensive review and feedback. I am grateful to all those who read chapters and provided constructive input. These include Doug Anderson, Constance Battle, Amanda Castel, James Cawley, Ellen Dawson, Diane Dewar, Mark Edberg, Leonard Friedman, Jaime Gofin, Michael Gough, Marc Hiller, Rebecca Katz, Ruth Long, Manya Magnus, David Michaels, Marjorie Rubenson, Richard Skolnik, Joel Teitelbaum, and Sara Wilensky.

Mike Brown, Publisher of public health books for Jones and Bartlett, has made an extraordinary contribution to this book and the series as a whole. His vision has helped craft the series and his publishing expertise made it happen. Catie Heverling, Tracey Chapman, Sophie Fleck, and Jessica Cormier of the editorial, production, and marketing staff of Jones and Bartlett deserve special recognition. Their commitment to this book and the entire *Essential Public Health* series has gone well beyond the expectations of their job. They have watched over this project to ensure that it meets the highest publishing standards and finds its role in the education of an entire generation of students new to public health. Sarah Hajduk's copyediting helped improve the clarity and consistency of this text.

Last, but by no means least, is my wife, Linda Riegelman, who encouraged this book and the *Essential Public Health* series from the beginning. She saw the need to reach out to students and make real the roles that public health plays in their everyday lives. Linda went the extra mile by reading and rereading every word I wrote. She deserves the credit for what works but the blame for what fails is all mine.

Confronting the challenge of putting together *Public Health 101* has been one of the great joys of my professional life. I hope that it will bring both joy and a challenge to you as enter into the important and engaging world of public health.

Richard Riegelman, MD, MPH, PhD
April 2009
Washington, DC

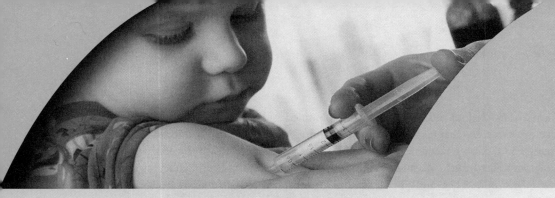

Preface: What Is *Public Health 101 All About?*

Health care is vital to all of us some of the time, but public health is vital to all of us all of the time.
—C. Everett Koop[1]

Public health is about what makes us sick, what keeps us healthy, and what we can do TOGETHER about it. When we think about health, what often comes to mind first is individual health and wellness. In public health, what should come to mind first is the health of communities and society as a whole. Thus, in public health the focus shifts from the individual to the population, from me to us. Whether the issue is influenza, AIDS, climate change, or the cost of health care, we need to look at the impact on individuals and groups at risk as well as the population as a whole.

Public Health 101: Healthy People–Healthy Populations will introduce you to the population health approach to public health. Population health asks basic questions about what determines health and disease. It puts on the table the full range of options for intervention to promote health and prevent disease. These options can range from individualized medical care, to community-wide efforts to protect health and detect disease, to society-wide interventions ranging from laws to taxes.

Public Health 101 is divided into five sections:

- Section I—Principles of Population Health
- Section II—Tools of Population Health
- Section III—Preventing Disease, Disability, and Death
- Section IV—Health Professionals, Healthcare Institutions, and Healthcare Systems
- Section V—Public Health Institutions and Systems

Section I provides an overview of the principles of population health. We outline what determines disease and disability. We see how we can use evidence to come up with strategies for protecting health and reducing disease, disability, and death. In Chapter 1, we see how public health affects our daily life in ways that we often take for granted. We see how public health focuses on the needs of society as a whole, as well as the needs of populations with special vulnerabilities to disease and disability. We also explore the full range of potential interventions for protecting health and preventing disease, disability, and death. Chapter 2 demonstrates how population health places special emphasis on using evidence to define health problems; to understand the etiology or cause of disease; to develop recommendations for addressing health problems; and to implement and evaluate the benefits and harms of these interventions.

Section II examines the tools of population health designed to reach large numbers of people. These tools include: health information and communications; social and behavioral sciences; and health policy, law, and ethics. In Chapter 3, called Health

Informatics and Health Communications, we look at how health data is obtained and compiled and how it can be conveyed or communicated and used to make decisions. In Chapter 4, we look at the contributions of social sciences to our understanding of the sources of health and disease and the tools available to reduce disease, disability, and death. To do this, we examine how social, economic, and cultural factors affect health. We also examine how individual and group behavior can be changed to improve health. In Chapter 5, we take a look at how health policies and laws can be used to improve health. We also examine the legal, policy, and ethical limitations on their use.

Section III looks at the types of conditions that produce disability and death which include: non-communicable disease, communicable diseases, and environmental disease and injury. We explore the types of interventions that are available to protect health, and prevent disease, disability, and death for each of these types of conditions. Chapter 6 looks at a wide range of non-communicable diseases, including most cancers and diseases of the heart and blood vessels, as well as diseases that affect our mental health, from depression to Alzheimer's. We look at a range of options for intervention including: screening for risk factors and for early detection; genetic modification; and use of cost-effective treatments. Chapter 7 examines communicable diseases or diseases that can be transmitted from person-to-person or from other species to humans. It reviews the options for eliminating or controlling the impacts of these conditions. Options for intervention include: barriers to prevent spread of disease ranging from hand washing to quarantine; immunizations designed to protect individuals, as well as populations; and screening, case finding, and preventive treatment designed to cure and control disease. Chapter 8 explores the impact of the physical environment. We look at the health impacts of the unaltered or natural environment; the human-impacted or altered environment; and the impact of the physical environment built for human use including issues of injuries or safety. We explore the multiple ways that we interact with the physical environment and the resulting potential for disease and injury. We also explore approaches to reducing risk.

In Section IV, we step back and take a look from the population health perspective at health care and healthcare systems focused on the care of individuals one at a time. The healthcare system is such a large enterprise that it has consequences far beyond the individuals it directly serves. In Chapter 9, we examine the range of health professionals, including physicians, nurses, and public health professionals. We ask what we mean by a health professional and look at the roles that education and training play in that process. We also look at how society regulates and compensates health professionals. Chapter 10 examines the types of healthcare institutions in the United States, from hospitals to hospice. It examines how these organizations fit together to address issues of coordination and quality of health care. It asks what we can do to connect the components to ensure coordination and quality of care. In Chapter 11, we build upon what we have learned about healthcare professionals and healthcare institutions and examine the healthcare system as a whole. To do this, we need a basic understanding of how the healthcare system is financed and we look at the issue of access to care and the cost of health care. We examine choices you may need to make when selecting health insurance, as well as choices society as a whole needs to make to provide health care to everyone.

Finally, in Section V we look at the public health system, including the governmental structures that make public health *public*. We also ask basic questions about where we go from here as we explore the future of public health. Chapter 12 examines public health agencies at the local, state, federal, and global levels, and explores the roles that public health agencies are expected to play. It recognizes that even with close collaboration among agencies, the job of population health requires involvement of many other groups. We examine approaches to cooperation with other governmental agencies, nongovernmental organizations, and healthcare professionals. Chapter 13 concludes the book by asking you to think about the future of public health. We examine the emerging emphasis on protection of health through disaster preparation and response. We also see how we can plan for the future by learning lessons from the past and understanding current trends that are likely to continue.

How will we go about accomplishing all this? *Public Health 101: Healthy People–Healthy Populations* will not try to overload your mind with facts. It is about providing you with frameworks for thinking, and applying these frameworks to real situations and thought-provoking scenarios.

Each chapter begins and ends with scenarios designed to show you the types of situations you may confront. After each section, there are cases that relate to one or more chapters in the section. They provide realistic case studies and open-ended questions to help you think through the application of the key concepts presented in each section.

Public Health 101: Healthy People–Healthy Populations has been designed to fulfill the recommendations for "Public Health 101" developed as part of the faculty development program sponsored by the Association for Prevention Teaching and Research (APTR) and the Association of American Colleges and Universities (AAC&U) and funded by the Centers for Disease Control and Prevention (CDC).[2] These recommendations include learning outcomes, as well as enduring understandings, designed to identify key concepts and frameworks that students should take away from "Public Health 101" and integrate into their thinking, their work, and their lifelong learning.

Public Health 101 is designed as a gateway to the world of public health. You should take advantage of the Public Health 101 Web site at www.publichealth101.org.

Hopefully, you will come away from reading *Public Health 101* with an appreciation of how the health of the public is influenced by and can be improved by efforts directed at the population, as well as at the individual level. Let us begin in Chapter 1 by exploring the ways that public health affects everyone's daily life.

REFERENCES

1. C. Everett Koop. What is Public Health? Available at: http://sphcm.washington.edu/about/whatis.asp. Accessed April 2, 2009.
2. Association for Prevention Teaching and Research and Association of American Colleges and Universities. Recommendations for Undergraduate Public Health Education. Available at: http://www.aptrweb.org/resources/pdfs/Recommendations.pdf. Accessed April 2, 2009.

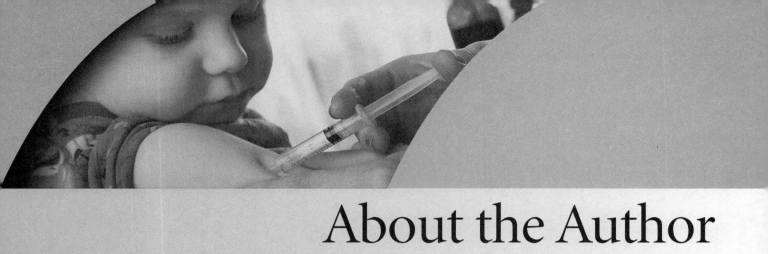

About the Author

Richard Riegelman, MD, MPH, PhD, is Professor of Epidemiology–Biostatistics, Medicine, and Health Policy, and founding dean of The George Washington University School of Public Health and Health Services. His education includes an MD from the University of Wisconsin, plus a MPH and PhD in Epidemiology from The Johns Hopkins University. Dr. Riegelman practiced primary care internal medicine for over 20 years.

Dr. Riegelman has over 70 publications, including six books for students and practitioners of medicine and public health. He is currently editor of the Jones and Bartlett book series *Essential Public Health*. The series provides books and ancillary materials for the full spectrum of curricula for undergraduate public health education, as well as the core and crosscutting competencies covered by the Certification in Public Health examination of the National Board of Public Health Examiners.

Dr. Riegelman has spearheaded efforts to fulfill the Institute of Medicine's recommendation that "…all undergraduates should have access to education in public health." His work with national public health and arts and sciences organizations has developed into The Educated Citizen and Public Health Movement. This movement now includes efforts by the Association of Schools of Public Health (ASPH), the Association for Prevention Teaching and Research (APTR), the Association of American Colleges and Universities (AAC&U), and the American Public Health Association (APHA), to implement undergraduate public health education. Richard Riegelman teaches medical school, graduate, and undergraduate public health courses, which include "Public Health 101" and "Epidemiology 101."

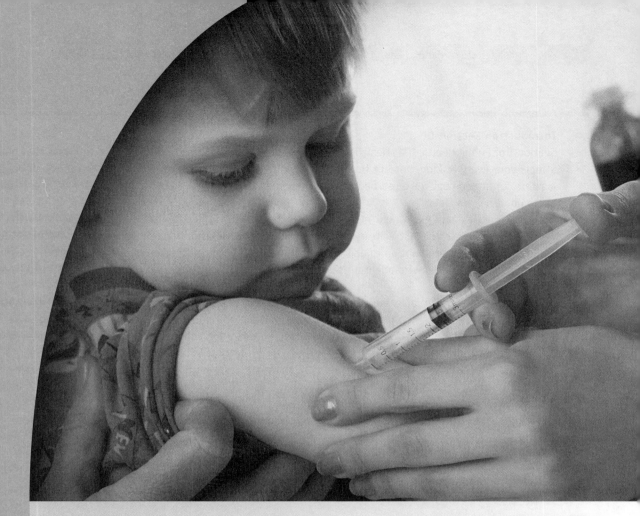

SECTION I

Principles of Population Health

Introduction Section I

Section I of Public Health 101: Healthy People—Healthy Populations introduces you to the ways that public health affects your every waking moment from the food you eat, to the water you drink, to the car you drive. Even sleep matters. In public health we use bed nets to prevent malaria as well as beds that prevent back pain and encourage a good night's sleep.

In Section I we will examine a range of approaches to public health that have been used over the centuries. Then we will focus on a 21st century approach known as population health. Population health includes the full range of options for intervention to address health problems from healthcare systems to community control of communicable disease and environmental health to public policies such as taxation and laws designed to reduce cigarette smoking.

In this section we will also examine an evidence-based approach to population health that focuses on defining the problem, establishing the etiology, making evidence-based recommendations, and evaluating the impacts of interventions. The population health and evidence-based approaches introduced in section I provide an underpinning for all that follows.

At the end of Section I, as with each section, there are cases with discussion questions that draw on chapters from the section. Each case is designed as a realistic description of the types of problems we face as we seek to achieve healthy people and healthy populations.

So with no further ado, let's take a look at how public health can and does affect your daily lives.

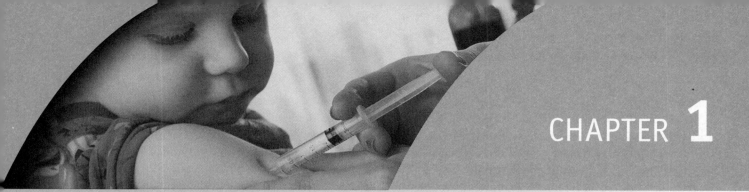

CHAPTER 1

Public Health: The Population Health Approach

LEARNING OBJECTIVES:

By the end of this chapter the student will be able to:

- identify multiple ways that public health affects daily life.
- define eras of public health from ancient times to the early 21st century.
- define the meaning of population health.
- illustrate the uses of health care, traditional public health, and social interventions in population health.
- identify a range of determinants of disease.

I woke up this morning, got out of bed, and went to the bathroom where I used the toilet, washed my hands, brushed and flossed my teeth, drank a glass of water, and took my blood pressure medicine, cholesterol medication, and an aspirin. Then, I did my exercises and took a shower.

On the way to the kitchen, I didn't even notice the smoke detector I passed or the old ashtrays in the closet. I took a low fat yogurt out of the refrigerator and prepared hot cereal in the microwave oven for my breakfast.

Then, I walked out my door into the crisp clean air and got in my car. I put on my seat belt, saw the light go on for the air bag, and safely drove to work. I got to my office where I paid little attention to the new defibrillator at the entrance, the "no smoking" signs, or the absence of asbestos. I arrived safely in my well-ventilated office and got ready to teach Public Health 101.

It wasn't a very eventful morning, but then it's all in a morning's work when it comes to public health.

This rather mundane morning is made possible by a long list of achievements that reflect the often-ignored history of

public health.[1] We take for granted the fact that water chlorination, hand washing, and indoor plumbing largely eliminated the transmission of common bacterial disease, which so often killed the young and not-so-young for centuries. Don't overlook the impact of prevention on our teeth and gums. Teeth brushing, flossing, and fluoridation of water have made a dramatic impact on dental health of children and adults.

The more recent advances in the prevention of heart disease have been a major public health achievement. Preventive successes include: the reduction of blood pressure and cholesterol, cigarette cessation efforts, use of low-dose aspirin, an understanding of the role of exercise, and the widespread availability of defibrillators. These can be credited with at least half the dramatic reductions in heart disease that have reduced the death rate from coronary artery disease by approximately 50 percent in the United States and most other developed countries in the last half century.

The refrigerator was one of the most important advances in food safety which illustrates the impact of social change and innovation not necessarily intended to improve health. Food and product safety are public health achievements that require continued attention. It was public pressure for food safety that in large part brought about the creation of the U.S. Food and Drug Administration. The work of this public health agency continues to affect all of our lives from the safety of the foods we eat to the drugs and cosmetics we use.

Radiation safety, like radiation itself, usually goes unnoticed from the regulation of microwave ovens to the reduction of radon in buildings. We rarely notice when disease does not occur.

Highway safety illustrates the wide scope of activities required to protect the public's health. From seat belts, child restraints, and air bags to safer cars, highways, designated driver programs and enforcement of drunk driving laws, public health efforts require collaboration with professionals not usually thought of as having a health focus.

The physical environment too has been made safer by the efforts of public health. Improvement in the quality of the air we breathe both outdoors and indoors has been an ongoing accomplishment of what we will call "population health." Our lives are safer today because of interventions ranging from installation of smoke detectors to removal of asbestos from buildings. However, the challenges continue. Globalization increases the potential for the spread of existing and emerging diseases and raises concerns about the safety of the products we use. Climate change and ongoing environmental deterioration continue to produce new territory for "old" diseases, such as malaria. Overuse of technologies, such as antibiotics, have encouraged the emergence of resistant bacteria.

The 20th century saw an increase in life expectancy of almost 30 years in most developed countries, much of it due to the successes of public health initiatives.[2] We cannot assume that these trends will continue indefinitely. The epidemic of obesity already threatens to slow down or reverse the progress we have been making. The challenges of 21st century public health include protection of health and continued improvement in its quality, not just its quantity.

To understand the role of public health in these achievements and ongoing challenges, let us start at the beginning and ask: what do we mean by public health?

WHAT DO WE MEAN BY PUBLIC HEALTH?

Ask your parents what public health means and they might say "health care for the poor." Well, they are right that public health has always been about providing services for those with special vulnerabilities either directly or through the healthcare system. But that is only one of the ways that public health serves the most needy and vulnerable in our population. Public health efforts often focus on the most vulnerable populations from reducing exposure to lead paint in deteriorating buildings to food supplementation to prevent birth defects and goiters. Addressing the needs of vulnerable populations has always been a cornerstone of public health. As we will see, however, the definition of vulnerable populations continues to change as do the challenges of addressing their needs.

Ask your grandparents what public health means and they might say "washing your hands." Well, they are right too—public health has always been about determining risks to health and providing successful interventions that are applicable to everyone. But hand washing is only the tip of the iceberg. The types of interventions that apply to everyone and benefit everyone span an enormous range: from food and drug safety to controlling air pollution; from measures to prevent the spread of tuberculosis to vaccinating against childhood diseases; from prevention and response to disasters to detection of contaminants in our water.

The concerns of society as a whole are always in the forefront of public health. These concerns keep changing and the methods for addressing them keep expanding. New technologies and global, local, and national interventions are becoming a necessary part of public health. To understand what public health has been and what it is becoming, let us look at some definitions of public health. The following are two definitions of public health—one from the early 20th century and one from more recent years.

Public health is ". . . the science and art of preventing disease, prolonging life and promoting health . . . through organized community effort. . . ."[3]

The substance of public health is the "organized community efforts aimed at the prevention of disease and the promotion of health."[4]

These definitions show how little the concept of public health changed in the 20th century, however the concept of public health in the 21st century is beginning to undergo important changes in a number of ways including:

- The goal of prolonging life is being complemented by an emphasis on the quality of life.
- Protection of health when it already exists is becoming a focus along with promoting health when it is at risk.
- Use of new technologies, such as the Internet, are redefining "community," as well as offering us new ways to communicate.
- The enormous expansion in the options for intervention, as well as the increasing awareness of potential harms and costs of intervention programs, require a new science of "evidence-based" public health.
- Public health and clinical care, as well as public and private partnerships, are coming together in new ways to produce collaborative efforts rarely seen in the 20th century.

Thus, a new 21st century definition of public health is needed. One such definition might read as follows:

The totality of all evidence-based public and private efforts that preserve and promote health and prevent disease, disability, and death.

This broad definition recognizes public health as the umbrella for a range of approaches which need to be viewed as a part of a big picture or population perspective. Specifically, this definition enlarges the traditional scope of public health to include:

- An examination of the full range of environmental, social, and economic determinants of health—not just those traditionally addressed by the public health and clinical health care
- An examination of the full range of interventions to address health issues, including the structure and function of healthcare delivery systems, plus the role of public policies that affect health even when health is not their intended effect

If you are asked by your children what is public health, you might respond: *"It is about the big picture issues that affect our own health and the health of our community every day of our lives. It is about protecting health in the face of disasters; preventing disease from addictions such as cigarettes; controlling infections such as the human immunodeficiency virus (HIV); and developing systems to ensure the safety of the food we eat and the water we drink."*

A variety of terms have been used to describe this big picture perspective that takes into account the full range of factors that affect health and considers their interactions.[5] A variation of this approach has been called the social-ecological model, systems thinking, or the **population health approach**. We will use the latter term. Before exploring what we mean by the population health approach, let us examine how the approaches to public health have changed over time.[a]

HOW HAS THE APPROACH OF PUBLIC HEALTH CHANGED OVER TIME?

Organized community efforts to promote health and prevent disease go back to ancient times.[6, 7] The earliest human civilizations integrated concepts of prevention into their culture, their religion, and their laws. Prohibitions against specific foods—including pork, beef, and seafood—plus customs for food preparation, including officially-designated methods of killing cattle and methods of cooking, were part of the earliest practices of ancient societies. Prohibitions against alcohol or its limited use for religious ceremony have long been part of societies' efforts to control behavior, as well as prevent disease. Prohibition of cannibalism, the most

universal of food taboos, has strong grounding in the protection of health.[b]

Sexual practices have been viewed as having health consequences from the earliest civilizations. Male circumcision, premarital abstinence, and marital fidelity have all been shown to have impacts on health.

Quarantine or isolation of individuals with disease or exposed to disease has likewise been practiced for thousands of years. The intuitive notion that isolating individuals with disease could protect individuals and societies led to some of the earliest organized efforts to prevent the spread of disease. At times they were successful, but without a solid scientific basis. Efforts to separate individuals and communities from epidemics sometimes led to misguided efforts, such as the unsuccessful attempts to control the black plague by barring outsiders from walled towns and not recognizing that it was the rats and fleas that transmitted the disease.

During the 18th and first half of the 19th century individuals occasionally produced important insights into the prevention of disease. In the 1740s, British naval commander James Lind demonstrated that lemons and other citrus fruit could prevent and treat scurvy, a then-common disease of sailors whose daily nourishment was devoid of citrus fruit, the best source of vitamin C.

In the last years of the 18th century, English physician Edward Jenner recognized that cowpox, a common mild ailment of those who milked cows, protected those who developed it against life-threatening smallpox. He developed what came to be called a vaccine—derived from the Latin "*vacs*," meaning cows. He placed fluid from cowpox sores under the skin of recipients, including his son, and exposed them to smallpox. Despite the success of these smallpox prevention efforts, widespread use of vaccinations was slow to develop partially because at that time there was not an adequate scientific basis to explain the reason for its success.

All of these approaches to disease prevention were known before organized public health existed. Public health awareness began to emerge in Europe and America in the mid-19th century. The American public health movement had its origins in Europe where concepts of disease as the consequence of social conditions took root in the 1830s and 1840s. This movement, which put forth the idea that disease emerges from social conditions of inequality, produced the concept of

---

[a] Turnock[2] has described several meanings of public health. These include the system and social enterprise, the profession, the methods, the government services, and the health of the public. The population health approach used in this book may be thought of as subsuming all of these different perspectives on public health.

[b] In recent years, this prohibition has been indirectly violated by feeding beef products containing bones and brain matter to other cattle. The development of "mad cow" disease and its transmission to humans has been traced to this practice, which can be viewed as analogous to human cannibalism.

social justice. Many attribute public health's focus on vulnerable populations to this tradition.

While early organized public health efforts paid special attention to vulnerable members of society, they also focused on the hazards that affected everyone: contamination of the environment. This focus on sanitation and public health was often called the hygiene movement, which began even before the development of the germ theory of disease. Despite the absence of an adequate scientific foundation, the hygiene movement made major strides in controlling infectious diseases, such as tuberculosis, cholera, and waterborne diseases largely through alteration of the physical environment.

The fundamental concepts of epidemiology also developed during this era. In the 1850s, John Snow, often called the father of epidemiology, helped establish the importance of careful data collection and documentation of rates of disease before and after an intervention to evaluate effectiveness. He is known for his efforts to close down the Broad Street pump, which supplied water contaminated by cholera to a district of London. His actions quickly terminated that epidemic of cholera. John Snow's approach has become a symbol of the earliest epidemiological thinking.

Semmelweis, an Austrian physician, used much the same approach in the mid-19th century to control puerperal fever—or fever of childbirth—then a major cause of maternal mortality. Noting that physicians frequently went from autopsy room to delivery room without washing their hands, he instituted a hand washing procedure and was able to document a dramatic reduction in the frequency of puerperal fever. Unfortunately, he was unable to convince many of his contemporaries to accept this intervention without a clear mechanism of action. Until the acceptance of the germ theory of disease, puerperal fever continued to be the major cause of maternal deaths in Europe and North America.

The mid-19th century in England also saw the development of birth and death records, or vital statistics, which formed the basis of population-wide assessment of health status. From the beginning, there was controversy over how to define the cause of death. Two key figures in the early history of organized public health took opposing positions that reflect this continuing controversy. Edwin Chadwick argued that specific pathological conditions or diseases should be the basis for the cause of death. William Farr argued that underlying factors, including what we would today call risk factors and social conditions, should be seen as the actual causes of death.

Thus, the methods of public health were already being established before the development of the germ theory of disease by Louis Pasteur and his European colleagues in the mid-1800s. The revolutions in biology that they ignited ushered in a new era in public health. American physicians and public health leaders often went to Europe to study new techniques and approaches and brought them back to America to use at home.

After the Civil War, American public health began to produce its own advances and organizations. In 1872, the American Public Health Association (APHA) was formed. According to its own historical account, "the APHA's founders recognized that two of the association's most important functions were advocacy for adoption by the government of the most current scientific advances relevant to public health, and public education on how to improve community health."[8]

The biological revolution of the late 19th and early 20th centuries that resulted from the germ theory of disease laid the groundwork for the modern era of public health. An understanding of the contributions of bacteria and other organisms to disease produced novel diagnostic testing capabilities. For example, scientists could now identify tuberculosis cases through skin testing, bacterial culture, and the newly discovered chest X-ray. Concepts of vaccination advanced with the development of new vaccines against toxins produced by tetanus- and diphtheria-causing bacteria. Without antibiotics or other effective cures, much of public health in this era relied on prevention, isolation of those with disease, and case-finding methods to prevent further exposure.

In the early years of the 20th century, epidemiology methods continued to contribute to the understanding of disease. The investigations of pellagra by Goldberger and the United States Public Health Service overthrew the assumption of the day that pellagra was an infectious disease and established that it was a nutritional deficiency that could be prevented or easily cured with vitamin B-6 (niacin) or a balanced diet. Understanding of the role of nutrition was central to public health's emerging focus on prenatal care and childhood growth and development. Incorporating key scientific advances, these efforts matured in the 1920s and 1930s and introduced a growing alphabet of vitamins and nutrients to the American vocabulary.

A new public health era of effective intervention against active disease began in force after World War II. The discovery of penicillin and its often miraculous early successes convinced scientists, public health practitioners, and the general public that a new era in medicine and public health had arrived.

During this era, public health's focus was on filling the holes in the healthcare system. In this period, the role of public health was often seen as assisting clinicians to effectively deliver clinical services to those without the benefits of private medical care and helping to integrate preventive efforts into the practice of medicine. Thus, the great public health success of organized campaigns for the eradication of polio was mistakenly seen solely as a victory for medicine. Likewise, the successful passage of Medicaid and Medicare, outgrowths of public health's commitment to social justice, was simply viewed as efforts to expand the private practice of medicine.

This period, however, did lay the foundations for the emergence of a new era in public health. Epidemiological methods designed for the study of noncommunicable diseases demonstrated the major role that cigarette smoking plays in lung cancer and a variety of other diseases. The emergence of the randomized clinical trial and the regulation of drugs, vaccines, and other interventions by the Food and Drug Administration developed the foundations for what we now call evidence-based public health and evidence-based medicine.

The 1980s and much of the 1990s were characterized by a focus on individual responsibility for health and interventions at the individual level. Often referred to as health promotion and disease prevention, these interventions targeted individuals to effect behavioral change and combat the risk factors for diseases. As an example, to help prevent coronary artery disease, efforts were made to help individuals address high blood pressure and cholesterol, cigarette smoking, and obesity. Behavioral change strategies were also used to help prevent the spread of the newly emerging HIV/AIDS epidemic. Efforts aimed at individual prevention and early detection as part of medical practice began to bear some fruit with the widespread introduction of mammography for detection of breast cancer and the worldwide use of Pap smears for the detection of cervical cancer. Newborn screening for genetic disease became a widespread and often legally-mandated program, combining individual and community components.

Major public health advances during this era resulted from the environmental movement, which brought public awareness to the health dangers of lead in gasoline and paint. The environmental movement also focused on reducing cancer by controlling radiation exposure from a range of sources including sunlight and radon, both naturally-occurring radiation sources. In a triumph of global cooperation, governments worked together to address the newly-discovered hole in the ozone layer. In the United States, reductions in air pollution levels and smoking rates during this era had an impact on the frequency of chronic lung disease, asthma, and most likely coronary artery disease.

The heavy reliance on individual interventions that characterized much of the last half of the 20th century changed rapidly in the beginning of the 21st century. A new era in public health that is often called "population health" has begun to transform professional and public thought about health. From the potential for bioterrorism to the high costs of health care to the control of pandemic influenza and AIDS, the need for

community-wide or population-wide, public health efforts have become increasingly evident. This new era is characterized by a global perspective and the need to address international health issues. It includes a focus on the potential impacts of climate change, emerging and reemerging infectious diseases, and the consequences of trade in potentially contaminated or dangerous products, ranging from food to toys.

Table 1-1 outlines these eras of public health, identifies their key defining elements, and highlights important events that symbolize each era.[9]

Thus, today we have entered an era in which a focus on the individual is increasingly coupled with a focus on what needs to be done at the community and population level. This era of public health can be viewed as "the era of population health."

WHAT IS MEANT BY POPULATION HEALTH?

The concept of population health has emerged in recent years as a broader concept of public health that includes all the ways that society as a whole or communities within society are affected by health issues and how they respond to these issues. Population health provides an intellectual umbrella for thinking about the wide spectrum of factors that can and do affect the health of individuals and the population as a whole. Figure 1-1 provides an overview of what falls under the umbrella of population health.

Population health also provides strategies for considering the broad range of potential **interventions** to address these issues. By intervention we mean the full range of strategies designed to protect health, and prevent disease, disability, and death. Interventions include: preventive efforts, such as nutrition and vaccination; curative efforts, such as antibiotics and cancer surgery; and efforts to prevent complications and restore function—from chemotherapy to physical therapy. Thus, population health is about *healthy people and healthy populations*.

The concept of population health can be seen as a comprehensive way of thinking about the modern scope of public health. It utilizes an evidence-based approach to analyze the determinants of health and disease and the options for intervention to preserve and improve health. Population health requires us to define what we mean by **health issues** and what we mean by **population(s)**. It also requires us to define what we mean by **society's shared health concerns**, as well as **society's vulnerable groups**.

To understand population health, we therefore need to define what we mean by each of these four components:

- Health issues
- Population(s)
- Society's shared health concerns
- Society's vulnerable groups

TABLE 1-1 Eras of Public Health

Eras of public health	Focus of attention/ Paradigm	Action framework	Notable events and movements in public health and epidemiology
Health protection (Antiquity–1830s)	Authority-based control of individual and community behaviors	Religious and cultural practices and prohibited behaviors	Quarantine for epidemics; sexual prohibitions to reduce disease transmission; dietary restrictions to reduce food-borne disease
Hygiene movement (1840–1870s)	Sanitary conditions as basis for improved health	Environmental action on a community-wide basis distinct from health care	Snow on Cholera; Semmelweis and puerperal fever; collection of vital statistics as empirical foundation for public health and epidemiology
Contagion control (1880–1940s)	Germ theory: demonstration of infectious origins of disease	Communicable disease control through environmental control, vaccination, sanatoriums, and outbreak investigation in general population	Linkage of epidemiology, bacteriology, and immunology to form TB sanatoriums; outbreak investigation, e.g., Goldberger and pellagra
Filling holes in the medical care system (1950s–mid-1980s)	Integration of control of communicable diseases; modification of risk factors; and care of high-risk population as part of medical care	Public system for care of and control of specific infectious diseases and vulnerable populations distinct from general health care system; Integrated health maintenance organizations with integration of preventive services into general health care system	Antibiotics; randomized clinical trials; concept of risk factors; Surgeon General reports on cigarette smoking; Framingham study on cardiovascular risks; health maintenance organizations and community health centers with integration of preventive services into general healthcare system
Health promotion/ Disease prevention (Mid-1980–2000)	Focus on individual behavior and disease detection in vulnerable and general populations	Clinical and population-oriented prevention with focus on individual control of decision making and multiple interventions	AIDS epidemic and need for multiple interventions to reduce risk; reductions in coronary heart disease through multiple interventions
Population health (21st century)	Coordination of public health and health care delivery based upon shared evidence-based systems thinking	Evidence-based recommendations and information management; focus on harms and costs as well as benefits of interventions; globalization	Evidence-based medicine and public health; information technology; medical errors; antibiotic resistance; global collaboration, e.g., SARS, tobacco control, climate change

Source: Awofeso N. What's new about the "New Public Health"? *American Journal of Public Health.* 2004;94(5):705–709.

FIGURE 1-1 The full spectrum of population health

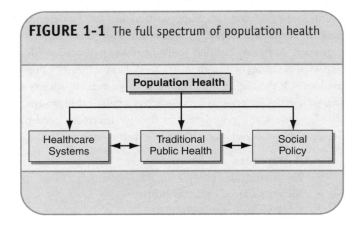

What Are the Implications of Each of the Four Components of Population Health?

All four of the key components of public health have changed in recent years. Let us take a look at the historical, current, and emerging scopes of each component and consider their implications.

For most of the history of public health, the term "health" focused solely on physical health. Mental health has now been recognized as an important part of the definition; conditions such as depression and substance abuse make enormous contributions to disability in populations throughout the world. The boundaries of what we mean by health continue to expand and the limits of health are not clear. Many novel medical interventions, including modification of genes and treatments to increase height, improve cosmetic appearance, and improve sexual performance, confront us with the question: are these health issues?

The definition of a population, likewise, is undergoing fundamental change. For most of recorded history, a population was defined geographically. Geographic communities, such as cities, states, and countries, defined the structure and functions of public health. The current definition of population has expanded to include the idea of a global community, recognizing the increasingly interconnected issues of global health. The definition of population is also focusing more on nongeographic communities. Universities now include the distance-learning community; health care is delivered to members of a health plan; and the Internet is creating new social communities. All of these new definitions of a population are affecting the thinking and approaches needed to address public health issues.

What about the meaning of society-wide concerns—have they changed as well? Historically, public health and communicable disease were nearly synonymous, as symbolized by the field of epidemiology which actually derives its name from the study of communicable disease epidemics. In recent decades, the focus of society-wide concerns has greatly expanded to include toxic exposures from the physical environment, transportation safety, and the costs of health care. However, communicable disease never went away as a focus of public health and the 21st century is seeing a resurgence in concern over emerging infectious diseases, including HIV/AIDS, pandemic flu, and newly drug-resistant diseases, such as staph infections and tuberculosis. Additional concerns, ranging from the impact of climate change to the harms and benefits of new technologies, are altering the meaning of society-wide concerns.

Finally, the meaning of vulnerable populations continues to transform. For most of the 20th century, public health focused on maternal and child health and high risk occupations as the operational definition of vulnerable populations. While these groups remain important to public health, additional groups now receive more attention, including the disabled, the frail elderly, and those without health insurance. Attention is also beginning to focus on the immune-suppressed among those living with HIV/AIDS, who are at higher risk of infection and illness, and those whose genetic code documents their special vulnerability to disease.

Public health has always been about our shared health concerns as a society and our concerns about vulnerable populations. These concerns have changed over time, and new concerns continue to emerge. Table 1-2 outlines historical, current, and emerging components of the population health approach to public health. As is illustrated by communicable diseases, past concerns cannot be relegated to history.

SHOULD WE FOCUS ON EVERYONE OR ON VULNERABLE GROUPS?

Public health is often confronted with the potential conflict of focusing on everyone and addressing society-wide concerns

---

TABLE 1-2 Components of Population Health

	Health	Population	Examples of society-wide concerns	Examples of vulnerable groups
Historical	Physical	Geographically limited	Communicable disease	High risk maternal and child, high risk occupations
Current	Physical and mental	Local, state, national, global, governmentally-defined	Toxic substances, product and transportation safety, communicable diseases, costs of health care	Disabled, frail elderly, uninsured
Emerging	Cosmetic, genetic, social functioning	Defined by local, national, and global communications	Disasters, climate change, technology hazards, emerging infectious diseases	Immune-suppressed, genetic vulnerability

versus focusing on the needs of vulnerable populations.[10] This conflict is reflected in the two different approaches to addressing public health problems. We will call them the **high-risk approach** and the **improving-the-average approach**.

The high-risk approach focuses on those with the highest probability of developing the disease and aims to bring their risk close to the levels experienced by the rest of the population. Figure 1-2A illustrates the high risk approach.

The success of the high-risk approach, as shown in Figure 1-2B, assumes that those with a high probability of developing disease are heavily concentrated among those with exposure to what we call **risk factors**. Risk factors include a wide range of exposures from cigarette smoke and other toxic substances to high risk sexual behaviors.

The improving-the-average approach focuses on the entire population and aims to reduce the risk for everyone. Figure 1-3 illustrates this approach.

The improving-the-average approach assumes that everyone is at some degree of risk and the risk increases with the extent of exposure. In this situation, most of the disease occurs

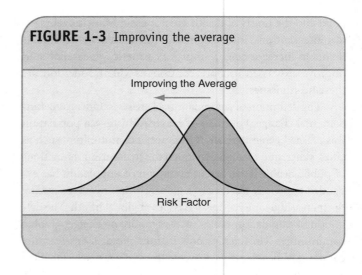

FIGURE 1-3 Improving the average

among the large number of people who have only modestly increased exposure. The successful reduction in average cholesterol levels through changes in the American diet and the anticipated reduction in diabetes via a focus on weight reduction among children illustrate this approach.

One approach may work better than the other in specific circumstances, but in general both approaches are needed if we are going to successfully address today's and tomorrow's health issues. These two approaches parallel public health's longstanding focus on both the health of vulnerable populations and society-wide health concerns.[c]

Now that we understand what is meant by population health, let us take a look at the range of approaches that may be used to promote and protect health.

WHAT ARE THE APPROACHES AVAILABLE TO PROTECT AND PROMOTE HEALTH?

The wide range of strategies that have been, are being, and will be used to address health issues can be divided into three general categories: health care, traditional public health, and social interventions.

Health care includes the delivery of services to individuals on a one-on-one basis. It includes services for those who are sick or disabled with illness or diseases, as well as for those who are asymptomatic. Services delivered as part of clinical prevention have been categorized as vaccinations, behav-

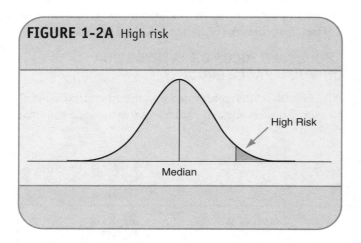

FIGURE 1-2A High risk

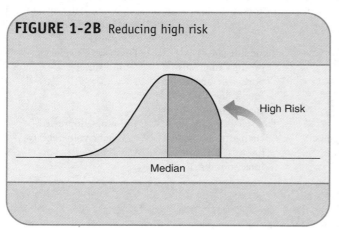

FIGURE 1-2B Reducing high risk

---

[c] An additional approach includes reducing disparities by narrowing the curve. For instance, this might be accomplished by transferring financial and/or health services from the low risk to the high risk category through taxation or other methods. Depending on the distribution of the factors affecting health, this approach may or may not reduce the overall frequency of disease more than the other approaches. The distribution of risk in Figures 1-1 and 1-2 assumes a bell-shaped or normal distribution. The actual distribution of factors affecting health may not follow this distribution.

ioral counseling, screening for disease, and preventive medications.[11]

Traditional public health efforts have a population-based preventive perspective utilizing interventions targeting communities or populations, as well as defined high risk or vulnerable groups. Communicable disease control, reduction of environmental hazards, food and drug safety, and nutritional and behavioral risk factors have been key areas of focus of traditional public health approaches.

Both health care and traditional public health approaches share a goal to directly affect the health of those they reach. In contrast, social interventions are primarily aimed at achieving other nonhealth goals, such as increasing convenience, pleasure, economic growth, and social justice. Social interventions range from improving housing, improving education and services for the poor, to increased global trade. These interventions may have dramatic and sometimes unanticipated positive or negative health consequences. Social interventions, like increased availability of food, may improve health, while the availability of high-fat or high-calorie foods may pose a risk to health.

Table 1-3 describes the characteristics of health care, traditional public health, and social approaches to population health and provides examples of each approach.

None of these approaches is new. However, they have traditionally been separated or put into silos in our thinking process with the connections between them often ignored. As we will see in subsequent chapters, connecting the pieces is an important part of the 21st century challenge of defining public health.

Now that we have explained what we mean by public health and seen the scope and methods that we call population health, let us continue our big-picture approach by taking a look at what we mean by the determinants of health and disease.

WHAT FACTORS DETERMINE THE OCCURRENCE OF DISEASE, DISABILITY, AND DEATH?

To complete our look at the big picture issues in public health, we need to gain an understanding of the forces that determine disease and the outcome of disease including what in public health has been called morbidity (disability) and mortality (death).[d]

As we will see in Chapter 2, we need to establish what are called contributory causes based on evidence. **Contributory causes** can be thought of as causes of disease. For instance, the HIV virus and cigarette smoking are two well-established contributory causes of disease, disability, and death. They produce disease, as well as disability and death. However, knowing these contributory causes of disease is often not enough. We need to ask: what determines whether people will smoke or come in contact with the HIV virus? What determines their course once exposed to cigarettes or HIV? In public health we use the term **determinants** to identify these underlying factors that ultimately bring about disease.

Determinants look beyond the known contributory causes of disease to factors that are at work often years before a dis-

---

[d] We will use the term "disease" as shorthand for the broad range of outcomes that includes injuries and exposures that result in death and disability.

TABLE 1-3 Approaches to Population Health

	Characteristics	Examples
Health care	Systems for delivering one-on-one individual health services including those aimed at prevention, cure, palliation, and rehabilitation	Clinical preventive services including: vaccinations, behavioral counseling, screening for disease, and preventive medications
Traditional public health	Group- and community-based interventions directed at health promotion and disease prevention	Communicable disease control, control of environmental hazards, food and drug safety, reduction in risk factors for disease
Social	Interventions with another nonhealth-related purpose, which have secondary impacts on health	Interventions that improve the built environment, increase education, alter nutrition, or address socioeconomic disparities through changes in tax laws; globalization and mobility of goods and populations

ease develops.[12,13] These underlying factors may be thought of as "upstream" forces. Like great storms, we know the water will flow downstream, often producing flooding and destruction along the way. We just don't know exactly when and where the destruction will occur.

There is no official list or agreed-upon definition of what is included in determinants of disease.[e] Nonetheless, there is wide agreement that the following factors are among those that can be described as determinants in that they increase or at times decrease the chances of developing conditions that threaten the quantity and/or quality of life.

Behavior
Infections
Genetics

Geography
Environment
Medical care
Socio-economic-cultural

BIG GEMS provides a convenient device for remembering these determinants of disease. Let's see what we mean by each of the determinants.

Behavior—Behavior implies actions that increase exposure to the factors that produce disease or protect individuals from disease. Actions such as cigarette smoking, exercise, diet, alcohol consumption, unprotected intercourse, and seat belt use are all examples of the ways that behaviors help determine the development of disease.

Infection—Infections are often the direct cause of disease. In addition, we are increasingly recognizing that early or long-standing exposures to infections may contribute to the development of disease or even protection against disease. Diseases as diverse as gastric and duodenal ulcers, gallstones, and hepatoma or cancer originating in the liver, are increasingly suspected to have infection as an important determinant of the disease. Early exposure to infections may actually reduce diseases ranging from polio to asthma.

Genetics—The revolution in genetics has focused our attention on roles that genetic factors play in the development and outcome of disease. Even when contributory causes, such as cigarettes, have been clearly established as producing lung cancer, genetic factors also play a role in the development and progression of the disease. While genetic factors play a role in many diseases, they are only occasionally the most important determinant of disease.

Geography—Geographic location influences the frequency and even the presence of disease. Infectious diseases such as malaria, Chagas disease, schistosomiasis, and Lyme disease occur only in defined geographic areas. Geography may also imply local geological conditions, such as those that produce high levels of radon—a naturally-occurring radiation that contributes to the development of lung cancer.

Environment—Environmental factors determine disease and the course of disease in a number of ways. The unaltered or "natural" physical world around us may produce disability and death from sudden natural disasters, such as earthquakes and volcanic eruptions, to iodine deficiencies due to low iodine content in the food-producing soil. The altered physical environment produced by human intervention includes exposures to toxic substances in occupational or nonoccupational settings. The physical environment built for use by humans—the **built environment**—produces determinants ranging from indoor air pollution, to "infant-proofed" homes, to hazards on the highway.

Medical care—Access to and the quality of medical care can be a determinant of disease. When a high percentage of individuals are protected by vaccination, nonvaccinated individuals in the population may be protected as well. Cigarette smoking cessation efforts may help smokers to quit, and treatment of infectious disease may reduce the spread to others. Medical care, however, often has its major impact on the course of disease by attempting to prevent or minimize the disability and death once disease develops.

Social-economic-cultural—In the United States, socioeconomic factors have been defined as education, income, and occupational status. These measures have all been shown to be determinants of diseases as varied as breast cancer, tuberculosis, and occupational injuries. Cultural and religious factors are increasingly being recognized as determinants of diseases because beliefs sometimes influence decisions about treatments, in turn affecting the outcome of the disease. While most diseases are more frequent in lower socioeconomic groups, others such as breast cancer are often more common in higher socioeconomic groups.

We will return to determinants again and again as we explore the work of population health. Historically, understanding determinants has often allowed us to prevent diseases and their consequences even when we did not fully understand the

---

[e] Health Canada[12] has identified 12 determinants of health that are: 1) income and social status; 2) employment; 3) education; 4) social environments; 5) physical environments; 6) healthy child development; 7) personal health practices and coping skills; 8) health services; 9) social support networks; 10) biology and genetic endowment; 11) gender; and 12) culture. Many of these are subsumed under socio-economic-cultural determinants in the BIG GEMS framework. The World Health Organization's Commission on Social Determinants of Health has also produced a list of determinants that is consistent with the BIG GEMS framework.[13]

mechanism by which the determinants produced their impact. For instance:

- Scurvy was controlled by citrus fruits well before vitamin C was identified.
- Malaria was partially controlled by clearing swamps before the relationship to mosquito transmission was appreciated.
- Hepatitis B and HIV infections were partially controlled even before the organisms were identified through reduction in use of contaminated needles and blood transfusions.
- Tuberculosis death rates were greatly reduced through less crowded housing, the use of TB sanitariums, and better nutrition.

Using asthma as an example, Box 1-1 illustrates the many ways that determinants can affect the development and course of a disease.

Thus, population health focuses on the big picture issues and the determinants of disease. Increasingly, public health also emphasizes a focus on the research evidence as a basis for understanding the cause or etiology of disease and the intervention that can improve the outcome. Let us now turn our attention to Chapter 2 which explores what we mean by evidence-based public health.

BOX 1-1 Asthma and the Determinants of Disease.

Jennifer, a teenager living in an urban rundown apartment in a city with high levels of air pollution, develops severe asthma. Her mother also has severe asthma, yet both of them smoke cigarettes. Her clinician prescribed medications to prevent asthma attacks, but she takes them only when she experiences severe symptoms. Jennifer is hospitalized twice with pneumonia due to common bacterial infections. She then develops an antibiotic-resistant infection. During this hospitalization, she requires intensive care on a respirator. After several weeks of intensive care and every known treatment to save her life, she dies suddenly.

Asthma is an inflammatory disease of the lung coupled with an increased reactivity of the airways, which together produce a narrowing of the airways of the lungs. When the airways become swollen and inflamed, they become narrower, allowing less air through to the lung tissue and causing symptoms such as wheezing, coughing, chest tightness, breathing difficulty, and predisposition to infection. Once considered a minor ailment, asthma is now the most common chronic disorder of childhood. It affects over six million children under the age of 18 in the United States alone.

Jennifer's tragic history illustrates how a wide range of determinants of disease may affect the occurrence, severity, and development of complications of a disease. Let's walk through the BIG GEMS framework and see how each determinant impacts in Jennifer's story.

Behavior—Behavioral factors play an important role in the development of asthma attacks and in their complications. Cigarette smoking makes asthma attacks more frequent and more severe. It also predisposes individuals to developing infections such as pneumonia. Treatment for severe asthma requires regular treatments along with more intensive treatment when an attack occurs. It is difficult for many people, especially teenagers, to take medication regularly, yet failure to adhere to treatment greatly complicates the disease.

Infection—Infection is a frequent precipitant of asthma and asthma increases the frequency and severity of infections. Infectious diseases, especially pneumonia, can be life-threatening in asthmatics requiring prompt and high quality medical care. The increasing development of antibiotic-resistant infections pose special risks to those with asthma.

Genetics—Genetic factors predispose people to childhood asthma. However, many children and adults without a family history develop asthma.

Geography—Asthma is more common in geographic areas with high levels of naturally occurring allergens due to flowering plants. However, today even populations in desert climates in the United States are often affected by asthma, as irrigation results in the planting of allergen-producing trees and other plants.

Environment—The physical environment, including that built for use by humans, has increasingly been recognized as a major factor affecting the development of asthma and asthma attacks. Indoor air pollution is the most common form of air pollution in many developing countries. Along with cigarette smoke, air pollution inflames the lungs acutely and chronically. Cockroaches often found in rundown buildings have been found to be highly allergenic and predisposing to asthma. Other factors in the built environment, including mold and exposure to pet dander, can also trigger wheezing in susceptible individuals.

(continues)

BOX 1-1 continued.

Medical care—The course of asthma can be greatly affected by medical care. Management of the acute and chronic effects of asthma can be positively affected by efforts to understand an individual's exposures, reducing the chronic inflammation with medications, managing the acute symptoms, and avoiding life-threatening complications.

Socio-economic-cultural—Disease and disease progression are often influenced by an individual's socioeconomic status. Air pollution is often greater in lower socioeconomic neighborhoods of urban areas. Mold and cockroach infestations may be greater in poor neighborhoods. Access to and quality of medical care may be affected by social, economic, and cultural factors.

Thus, asthma is a condition which demonstrates the contributions made by the full range of determinants included in the BIG GEMS framework. No one determinant alone explains the bulk of the disease. The large number of determinants and their interactions provide opportunities for a range of health care, traditional public health, and social interventions.

Key Words

- Population health approach
- Social justice
- Interventions
- Health issues
- Population(s)
- Society's shared health concerns
- Society's vulnerable groups
- High-risk approach
- Improving-the-average approach
- Risk factor
- Contributory causes
- Determinants
- Built environment
- Behavior
- Infections
- Genetics
- Geography
- Environment
- Medical care
- Socio-economic-cultural

Discussion Question

1. Think about a typical day in your life and identify ways that public health affects it.

REFERENCES

1. Pfizer Global Pharmaceuticals. *Milestones in Public Health: Accomplishments in Public Health over the Last 100 Years.* New York: Pfizer Global Pharmaceuticals; 2006.

2. Turnock BJ. *Public Health: What It Is and How It Works,* 4th ed. Sudbury, MA: Jones and Bartlett Publishers; 2009.

3. Winslow CEA. The untilled field of public health. *Mod. Med.* 1920; 920;2:183–191.

4. Institute of Medicine. *The Future of Public Health.* Washington, DC: National Academy Press; 1988:41.

5. Young TK. *Population Health: Concepts and Methods.* New York: Oxford University Press; 1998.

6. Rosen G. *A History of Public Health.* Baltimore: Johns Hopkins University Press; 1993.

7. Porter D. *Health, Civilization, and the State: A History of Public Health from Ancient to Modern Times.* Oxford: Rutledge; 1999.

8. American Public Health Association. APHA History and Timeline. Available at: http://www.apha.org/about/news/presskit/aphahistory.htm? NRMODE=Published&NRNODEGUID=%7b8AF0A3FE-8B29-4952-87EF-2757B9B2668F%7d&NRORIGINALURL=%2fabout%2fnews%2fpresskit% 2faphahistory.htm&NRCACHEHINT=NoModifyGuest&PF=true. Accessed March 12, 2009.

9. Awofeso N. What's new about the "New Public Health"? *American Journal of Public Health.* 2004;94(5):705–709.

10. Rose G, Khaw KT, Marmot M. *Rose's Strategy of Preventive Medicine.* New York: Oxford University Press; 2008.

11. Agency for Healthcare Research and Quality. Preventive Services. Available at: http://www.ahrq.gov/. Accessed March 12, 2009.

12. Public Health Agency of Canada. Population Health Approach—What Determines Health? Available at: http://www.phac-aspc.gc.ca/ph-sp/ determinants/index-eng.php. Accessed March 12, 2009.

13. Commission on Social Determinants of Health. *Closing the gap in a generation: health equity through action on the social determinants of health. Final Report of the Commission on Social Determinants of Health.* Geneva: World Health Organization; 2008.

Evidence-based Public Health

LEARNING OBJECTIVES

By the end of this chapter the student will be able to:

- explain the steps in the evidence-based public health process.
- describe a public health problem in terms of morbidity and mortality.
- describe the approach used in public health to identify a contributory cause of a disease or other condition and establish the efficacy of an intervention.
- describe the process of grading evidence-based recommendations.
- use an approach to identify options for intervention based on "when, who, and how."
- explain the role that evaluation plays in establishing effectiveness as part of evidence-based public health.

Tobacco was introduced to Europe as a new world crop in the early 1600s. Despite the availability of pipe tobacco and later, cigars, the mass production and consumption of tobacco through cigarette smoking did not begin until the development of the cigarette rolling machine by James Duke in the 1880s. This invention allowed mass production and distribution of cigarettes for the first time. Men were the first mass consumers of cigarettes. During World War I, cigarettes were widely distributed free of charge to American soldiers.

Cigarette smoking first became popular among women in the 1920s—an era noted for changes in the role and attitudes of women—and at this time advertising of cigarettes began to focus on women. The mass consumption of cigarettes by women, however, trailed that of men by at least two decades. By the 1950s, over 50 percent of adult males and approximately 25 percent of adult females were regular cigarette smokers.

The health problems of cigarette smoking were not fully recognized until decades after the habit became widespread. As late as the 1940s, R.J. Reynolds advertised that "more doctors smoke Camels than any other cigarette."

Epidemiologists observed that lung cancer deaths were increasing in frequency in the 1930s and 1940s. The increase in cases did not appear to be due to changes in efforts to recognize the disease, ability to recognize the disease, or the definition of the disease. Even after the increasing average life span and aging of the population was taken into account, it was evident that the rate of death from lung cancer was increasing—and more rapidly for men than women. In addition, it was noted that residents of states with higher rates of smoking had higher rates of lung cancer. In the 1950s, the number of lung cancer deaths in females also began to increase and by the 1960s, the disease had become the most common cause of cancer-related deaths in males and was still rising among women.[1, 2]

This type of information was the basis for describing the problems of cigarette smoking and lung cancer and developing ideas or hypotheses about its etiology, or cause. Let us take a look at how the evidence-based public health approach has been used to address the problem of cigarette smoking. There are four basic questions that we need to ask that together make up what we will call the evidence-based public health approach.[3]

1. **P**roblem: What is the health problem?
2. **E**tiology: What is/are the contributory cause(s)?
3. **R**ecommendations: What works to reduce the health impacts?
4. **I**mplementation: How can we get the job done?

These four questions provide a framework for defining, analyzing, and addressing a wide range of public health issues and can be applied to cigarette smoking for the purposes of this chapter.[4] We will call this framework the **P.E.R.I. process**. This process is really circular as illustrated in Figure 2-1. If the evaluation suggests that more needs to be done, the cycle can and should be repeated. Thus, it is an ongoing process.

Using cigarette smoking as an example, we will illustrate the steps needed to apply the evidence-based public health approach.

HOW CAN WE DESCRIBE A HEALTH PROBLEM?

The first step in addressing a health problem is to describe its impact. That is, we need to begin by understanding the occurrence of disability and death due to a disease, which we call the **burden of disease**. In public heath, disability is often called **morbidity** and death is called **mortality**. We also need to determine whether there has been a recent change in the impact of the disease. Thus, the first question we ask in describing a health problem is: what is the burden of disease in terms of morbidity and mortality and has it changed over time?

The second question we need to ask is: are there differences in the distribution of disease and can these differences generate ideas or hypotheses about the disease's etiology (cause)? That is, we need to examine how the disease is spread out or distributed in a population. We call this the **distribution of disease**. Public health professionals called **epidemiologists** investigate factors known as "person" and "place" to see if they can find patterns or associations in the frequency of a disease. We call these **group associations**. Group associations may suggest ideas or hypotheses about the cause, or etiology of a disease.

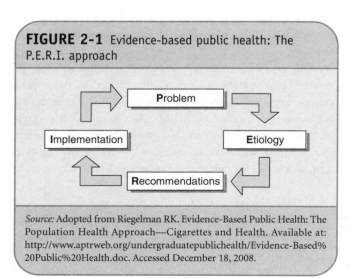

FIGURE 2-1 Evidence-based public health: The P.E.R.I. approach

Source: Adopted from Riegelman RK. Evidence-Based Public Health: The Population Health Approach—Cigarettes and Health. Available at: http://www.aptrweb.org/undergraduatepublichealth/Evidence-Based%20Public%20Health.doc. Accessed December 18, 2008.

"Person" includes demographic characteristics which describe people, such as age, gender, race, and socioeconomic factors. It also includes behaviors or exposures, such as cigarette smoking, exercise, radiation exposure, and use of medications. "Place" implies geographic location, such as a city or state, but it also includes connections between people, such as a university community or a shared Internet site. When these types of factors occur more frequently among groups with the disease than among groups without the disease we call them **risk indicators** or **risk markers**.[a]

Finally, epidemiologists take a scientific approach to addressing public health problems. They are often skeptical of initial answers to a question and ask: could there be another explanation for the differences or changes in the distribution of disease? They often ask: are the differences or changes real or are they artifactual? **Artifactual** implies that the apparent association is actually the result of the data collection process.

When trying to determine whether an association is artifactual or real, epidemiologists ask whether, the observed changes or differences may be due to comparing apples to oranges—for example comparing groups of subjects of different average ages. Age is especially important to epidemiologists because it is very strongly related to the occurrence of disease. Thus, the third question that we need to ask in describing a problem is: are the differences or changes used to suggest group associations artifactual or real?

Before we can answer these three questions we need to understand more about the measurements that epidemiologists use to describe a health problem. We need to look carefully at how we measure the changes or differences in disease, disability, and death. In public health, we use **rates** to summarize our measurement. Let us begin by looking at what we mean by rates and then we will return to the three questions that need to be addressed when describing a health problem.

WHAT DO WE NEED TO KNOW ABOUT RATES IN ORDER TO DESCRIBE A HEALTH PROBLEM?

The term "rate" will be used to describe the types of measurements that have a numerator and a denominator where the numerator is a subset of the denominator—that is, the numerator includes only individuals who are also included in the denominator. In a rate, the numerator measures the number of times an event, such as the diagnosis of lung cancer, occurs. The denominator measures the number of times the event

---

[a] The term risk indicator or risk marker needs to be distinguished from the term risk factor. A risk factor is a candidate for being a contributory cause and implies that at least an association at the individual level has been established as we will discuss later in this chapter. We will also add "time" to "person" and "place" as a basic characteristic for generating hypotheses.

could occur. We often use the entire population in the denominator, but at times we may only use the **at-risk population**. For instance, when measuring the rate of cervical cancer we would only use the population of women in the denominator and when measuring rates of prostate cancer we would only use the population of men in the denominator.[b]

There are two basic types of rates that are key to describing a disease.[5, 6] These are called **incidence** rates and **prevalence**. Incidence rates measure the chances of developing a disease over a period of time—usually one year. That is, incidence rates are the number of new cases of a disease that develop during a year divided by the number of people in the at-risk population, as in the following equation:

$$Incidence \ rate = \frac{\# \ of \ new \ cases \ of \ a \ disease \ in \ a \ year}{\# \ of \ people \ in \ the \ at\text{-}risk \ population}$$

We often express incidence rates as the number of events per 100,000 population in the denominator. For instance, the incidence rate of lung cancer might be 100 per 100,000 per year. In evidence-based public health, comparing incidence rates is often a useful starting point when trying to establish the cause of a problem.

Mortality rates are a special type of incidence rate that measure the incidence of death due to a disease during a particular year. When most people who develop a disease die from the disease, as is the situation with lung cancer, the mortality rate and the incidence rates are very similar. Thus, if the incidence rate of lung cancer is 100 per 100,000 per year, the mortality rate might be 95 per 100,000 per year. When mortality rates and incidence rates are similar and mortality rates are more easily or more reliably obtained, epidemiologists may substitute mortality rates for incidence rates.[c]

The relationship between the incidence rate and the mortality rate is important since it estimates the chances of dying from the disease once it is diagnosed. We call this the **case-fatality**. In our example, the chances of dying from lung cancer—the morality rate divided by the incidence rate—is 95 percent, which indicates that lung cancer results in a very poor prognosis once it is diagnosed.

Prevalence is the number of individuals who have a disease at a particular time divided by the number of individuals who could potentially have the disease. It can be represented by the following equation:

$$Prevalence = \frac{\# \ living \ with \ a \ particular \ disease}{\# \ in \ the \ at\text{-}risk \ population}$$

Thus, prevalence tells us the proportion or percentage of individuals who have the disease.[5, 6]

Despite the fact that lung cancer has become the most common cancer, the prevalence will be low—perhaps one-tenth of one percent or less—because those who develop lung cancer do not generally live for a long period of time. Therefore, you will rarely see people with lung cancer. The prevalence of chronic diseases of prolonged duration, such as asthma or chronic obstructive pulmonary disease (COPD), is often relatively high, hence you will often see people with these diseases.[d]

Prevalence is often useful when trying to assess the total impact or burden of a health problem in a population and can help identify the need for services. For example, knowledge that there is a high prevalence of lung cancer in a certain region may indicate that there is a need for healthcare services in that area. Prevalence is also very useful in clinical medicine as the starting point for screening and diagnosis, as we will discuss in Chapter 6. Now that we have addressed rates, we can return to the three questions for describing a health problem.

WHAT IS THE BURDEN OF DISEASE IN TERMS OF MORBIDITY AND MORTALITY AND HAS IT CHANGED OVER TIME?

As we have seen, lung cancer is a disease with a very poor prognosis; therefore, the burden of disease is high as measured by its high mortality rate. This was the situation in the past and to a large extent continues to be the situation.

Mortality rates have been obtained from death certificates for many years. The cause of death on death certificates is classified using a standardized coding system known as the International Classification of Diseases (ICD). No equally complete or accurate system has been available for collecting data on the incidence rate of lung cancer. However, as we learned in

---

[b] When talking about the term "rate," many epidemiologists also include a unit of time, such as a day or a year, over which the number of events in the numerator is measured. This may also be called a **true rate**. The term "rate," as used in this book includes true rates, as well as proportions. A **proportion** is a fraction in which the numerator is a subset of the denominator. A time period is not required for a proportion, however, it often reflects the situation at one point in time.

[c] This is an example of the pragmatic approach that is often taken by epidemiologists when they are limited by the available data. The question facing epidemiologists is frequently: is the data good enough to address the question? Thus, epidemiology can be thought of as an approximation science.

[d] The relationship between incidence and prevalence rates is approximately: the incidence rate × average duration of the disease = the prevalence rate. Both the incidence rate and the average duration affect the prevalence of the disease. Together, the incidence, prevalence, and case-fatality rates provide a population-based summary of the course of a disease. Incidence reflects the chance of developing the disease, prevalence indicates the chances of having the disease, and case-fatality indicates the prognosis or chance of dying from the disease.

our discussion of rates, the incidence rates and mortality rates for lung cancer are very similar. Therefore, we can use mortality data as a substitute for incidence data when evaluating the overall burden of lung cancer in a population.

By the 1930s, epidemiologists had concluded from the study of death certificates that lung cancer deaths were rapidly increasing. This increase continued through the 1950s—with cancer occurring two decades or more after the growth in consumption of cigarettes. Therefore, it was not immediately obvious that the two were related. In order to hypothesize that cigarettes were a cause of lung cancer, one needed to conclude that there was a long delay and/or a need for long-term exposure to cigarettes before lung cancer developed. There was a need for more evidence linking cigarettes and lung cancer. Let us turn our attention to the second question to see where this evidence came from.

ARE THERE DIFFERENCES IN THE DISTRIBUTION OF DISEASE AND CAN THESE DIFFERENCES GENERATE IDEAS OR HYPOTHESES ABOUT THEIR ETIOLOGY OR CAUSE?

In looking at the distribution of disease and the potential risk factors, epidemiologists found some important relationships.

In terms of "person," the increases in lung cancer mortality observed in the 1930s through 1950s were far more dramatic among men than among women, though by the 1950s the mortality rate among women had begun to increase as well. It was noted that cigarette use had increased first in men and later among women. There appeared to be a delay of several decades between the increase in cigarette smoking and the increase in lung cancer mortality among both men and women. This illustrates that "time" along with "person" and "place" is important in generating hypotheses.

In terms of "place," it was found that the relationship between cigarette smoking and lung cancer mortality was present throughout the United States, but was strongest in those states where cigarette smoking was most common. Therefore, changes over time and the distribution of disease using "person" and "place" led epidemiologists to the conclusion that there was an association between groups of people who smoked more frequently and the group's mortality rates due to lung cancer. These relationships generated the idea that cigarettes might be a cause of lung cancer. Box 2-1 illustrates some other examples of how distributions of disease by "person", "place," and "time" can generate hypotheses about their cause.

BOX 2-1   Generating Hypotheses from Distributions of Person and Place.

An increased frequency of disease based upon occupation has often provided the initial evidence of a group association based upon a combination of "person" and "place." The first recognized occupational disease was found among chimney sweeps often exposed for long periods of time to large quantities of coal dust who were found to have a high incidence of testicular cancer.

The Mad Hatter described in *Alice's Adventures in Wonderland* by Lewis Carroll made infamous the 19th century recognition that exposure to mercury fumes was associated with mental changes. Mercury fumes were created when making the felt used for hats, hence the term "mad as a hatter."

The high frequency of asbestosis among those who worked in shipyards suggested a relationship decades before the dangers of asbestos were fully recognized and addressed. A lung disease known as silicosis among those who worked in the mining industry likewise suggested a relationship that led to in-depth investigation and greater control of the risks.

More recently, a rare tumor called angiosarcoma was found to occur among those exposed over long periods to polyvinyl chloride (PVC), a plastic widely used in construction. The initial report of four cases of this unusual cancer among workers in one PVC plant was enough to strongly suggest a cause-and-effect relationship based upon "place" alone.

An important example of the impact that "place" can have on generating ideas or hypotheses about causation is the history of fluoride and cavities. In the early years of the 20th century, children in the town of Colorado Springs, Colorado, were found to have a very high incidence of brown discoloration of the teeth. It was soon recognized that this condition was limited to those who obtained their water from a common source. Ironically, those with brown teeth were also protected from cavities. This clear relationship to "place" was followed by over two decades of research that led to the understanding that fluoride in the water reduces the risk of cavities, while very high levels of the compound also lead to brown teeth. Examination of the levels of fluoride in other water systems eventually led to the establishment of levels of fluoride that could protect against cavities without producing brown teeth.

Such strong and clear-cut relationships are important, but relatively unusual. Often, examinations of the characteristics of "person," "place," and "time" in populations suggests hypotheses that can be followed-up among individuals to establish cause and effect relationships.[5, 6]

It is important to realize that these mortality rates are group rates. This data did not include any information about whether those who died from lung cancer were smokers. It merely indicated that groups who smoked more, such as males, also had higher mortality rates from lung cancer. The most that we can hope to achieve from this data is to generate hypotheses based on associations between groups or group associations. When we try to establish causation or etiology, we will need to go beyond group association and focus on associations at the individual level. However, before addressing etiology, we need to ask our third question:

ARE THE DIFFERENCES OR CHANGES USED TO SUGGEST GROUP ASSOCIATIONS ARTIFACTUAL OR REAL?

As we have seen from the 1930s through the 1950s, a large number of studies established that lung cancer deaths were increasing among men, but not among women. That is, there was a change over time and a difference between groups. When epidemiologists observe these types of changes and differences in rates, they ask: are the changes or differences in rates real or could they be artificial or artifactual? There are three basic reasons that changes in rates may be artifactual rather than real:

- Changes in the interest in identifying the disease
- Changes in the ability to identify the disease
- Changes in the definition of the disease

For some conditions, such as HIV/AIDS, these changes have all occurred. New and effective treatments have increased the interest in detecting the infection. Improved technology has increased the ability to detect HIV infections at an earlier point in time. In addition, there have been a number of modifications of the definition of AIDS based on new opportunistic infections and newly recognized complications. Therefore, with HIV/AIDS we need to be especially attentive to the possibility that artifactual changes have occurred.

With lung cancer, on the other hand, the diagnosis at the time of death has been of great interest for many years. The ability to diagnose the disease has not changed substantially. In addition, the use of ICD codes on death certificates has helped standardize the definition of the disease. Epidemiologists concluded that it was unlikely that changes in interest, ability, or definition explained the changes in the rates of lung cancer observed in males, thus they concluded that the changes were not artifactual, but real.[e]

However, it was still possible that the increased mortality rates from lung cancer were due to the increasing life span that

was occurring between 1930 and 1960, along with the subsequent aging of the population. Perhaps older people are more likely to develop lung cancer and the aging of the population itself explains the real increase in the rates. To address this issue, epidemiologists use what is called **age adjustment**. To conduct age adjustment, epidemiologists look at the rates of the disease in each age group and also the **age distribution** or the number of people in each age group in the population. Then, they combine the rates for each age group taking into account or adjusting for the age distribution of a population.[f]

Taking into account the age distribution of the population in 1930 and 1960 did have a modest impact on the changes in the mortality rates from lung cancer, but large differences remained. As a result, epidemiologists concluded that lung cancer mortality rates changed over this period especially among men; the changes in rates were real; and the changes could not be explained simply by the aging of the population. Thus, epidemiologists had established the existence of a group association between groups that smoked more cigarettes and groups that developed lung cancer.

WHAT IS THE IMPLICATION OF A GROUP ASSOCIATION?

Group associations are established by investigations that use information on groups or a population without having information on the specific individuals within the group. These studies have been called **population comparisons** or **ecological studies**. Having established the existence of a group association, we still don't know if the individuals who smoke cigarettes are the same ones who develop lung cancer. We can think of a group association as a hypothesis that requires investigation at the individual level. The group association between cigarettes and lung cancer was the beginning of a long road to establish that cigarettes are a cause of lung cancer.

Not all group associations are also individual associations. Imagine the following situation: the mortality rates from drowning are higher in southern states than northern states. The per capita consumption of ice cream is also higher in southern states than northern states. Thus, a group association was established between ice cream consumption and drowning. In thinking about this relationship, you will soon realize that there is another difference between southern and northern states. The average temperature is higher in southern states and higher temperatures are most likely associated with

[e] There are actually several types of lung cancer defined by the ICD codes. Most, but not all, types of lung cancer are strongly associated with cigarette smoking.

[f] Adjustment for age is often performed by combining the rates in each age group using the age distribution of what is called a standard population. The age distribution of the U.S. population in 2000 is currently used as the standard population. Adjustment is not limited to age and may at times be conducted using other characteristics that may differ among the groups, such as gender or race, which may affect the probability of developing a disease.

more swimming and also more ice cream consumption. Ice cream consumption is therefore related both to swimming and to drowning. We call this type of factor a **confounding variable**. In this situation, there is no evidence that those who drown actually consumed ice cream. That is, there is no evidence of an association at the individual level. Thus group associations can be misleading if they suggest relationships that do not exist at the individual level.

Epidemiology research studies that look at associations at the individual level are key to establishing etiology, or cause. Etiology is the second component of the P.E.R.I. approach. Let us turn our attention to how to establish etiology.

ETIOLOGY: HOW DO WE ESTABLISH CONTRIBUTORY CAUSE?

Understanding the reasons for disease is fundamental to the prevention of disability and death. We call these reasons etiology or causation. In evidence-based public health, we use a very specific definition of causation—**contributory cause**. The evidence-based public health approach relies on epidemiological research studies to establish a contributory cause. This requires that we go beyond group association and establish three definitive requirements.[7]

1. The "cause" is associated with the "effect" at the individual level. That is, the potential "cause" and the potential "effect" occur more frequently in the same individual than would be expected by chance. Therefore, we need to establish that individuals with lung cancer are more frequently smokers than individuals without lung cancer.

2. The "cause" precedes the "effect" in time. That is, the potential "cause" is present at an earlier time than the potential "effect." Therefore, we need to establish that cigarette smoking comes before the development of lung cancer.

3. Altering the "cause" alters the "effect." That is, when the potential "cause" is reduced or eliminated, the potential "effect" is also reduced or eliminated. Therefore, we need to establish that reducing cigarette smoking reduces lung cancer rates.

Box 2-2 illustrates the logic behind using these three criteria to establish a cause-and-effect relationship, as well as what the implications of a contributory cause are.

These three definitive requirements are ideally established using three different types of studies, all of which relate potential "causes" to potential "effects" at the individual level. That is, they investigate whether individuals who smoke cigarettes are the same individuals that develop lung cancer.[6] The three basic types of investigations are called **case-control** or **retrospective studies**, **cohort studies** or **prospective studies**, and **randomized clinical trials** or **experimental studies**.

Case-control studies are most useful for establishing requirement #1 previously, i.e., the "cause" is associated with the "effect" at the individual level. Case-control studies can demonstrate that cigarettes and lung cancer occur together more

---

BOX 2-2   Lightning, Thunder, and Contributory Cause.

The requirements for establishing the type of cause-and-effect relationship known as contributory cause used in evidence-based public health can be illustrated by the cause-and-effect relationship between lightning and thunder that human beings have recognized from the earliest times of civilization.

First, lightning is generally associated with thunder, that is, the two occur together far more often than one would expect if there were no relationship. Second, with careful observation it can be concluded that the lightning is seen a short time before the thunder is heard. That is, the potential "cause" (the lightning) precedes in time the "effect" (the thunder). Finally, when the lightning stops, so does the thunder—thus, altering the "cause" alters the "effect."

Notice that lightning is not always associated with thunder. "Heat lightning" may not produce audible thunder or the lightning may be too far away for the thunder to be heard. Lightning is not sufficient in and of itself to guarantee that our ears will subsequently always hear thunder. Conversely, in recent years it has been found that the sound of thunder does not always require lightning. Other reasons for rapidly expansion of air, such as an explosion, can also create a sound similar or identical to thunder.

The recognition of lightning as a cause of thunder came many centuries before human beings had any understanding of electricity or today's appreciation for the science of light and sounds. Similarly, cause-and-effect relationships established by epidemiological investigations do not always depend on understanding the science behind the relationships.

frequently than would be expected by chance alone. To accomplish this, cases with the disease (lung cancer) are compared to controls without the disease to determine whether the cases and the controls previously were exposed to the potential "cause" (cigarette smoking).

When a factor such as cigarettes has been demonstrated to be associated on an individual basis with an outcome such as lung cancer, we often refer to that factor as a **risk factor**.[g]

During the 1940s and early 1950s, a number of case-control studies established that individuals who developed lung cancer were far more likely to be regular smokers compared to similar individuals who did not smoke cigarettes. These case-control studies established requirement #1—the "cause" is associated with the "effect" at the individual level. They established that cigarettes are a risk factor for lung cancer.

Cohort studies are most useful for establishing requirement #2 previously—the "cause" precedes the "effect." Those with the potential "cause" or risk factor (cigarette smoking) and those without the potential "cause" are followed over time to determine who develops the "effect" (lung cancer).[h]

Several large scale cohort studies were conducted in the late 1950s and early 1960s. One conducted by the American Cancer Society followed nearly 200,000 individuals over three or more years to determine the chances that smokers and nonsmokers would develop lung cancer. Those who smoked regularly at the beginning of the study had a greatly increased chance of developing lung cancer over the course of the study, thus establishing requirement #2, the "cause" precedes the "effect" in time.

Randomized clinical trials are most useful for establishing requirement #3—altering the "cause" alters the "effect." Using a chance process known as **randomization**, individuals are assigned to be exposed or not exposed to the potential "cause" (cigarette smoking). Individuals with and without the potential "cause" are then followed over time to determine who develops the "effect." Conducting a randomized clinical trial of cigarettes and lung cancer would require investigators to randomize individuals to smoke cigarettes or not smoke cigarettes

and follow them over many years. This illustrates the obstacles that can occur in seeking to definitively establish contributory cause. Once there was a strong suspicion that cigarettes might cause lung cancer, randomized clinical trials were not practical or ethical as a method for establishing cigarette smoking as a contributory cause of lung cancer. Therefore, we need to look at additional criteria that we can use to help us establish the existence of contributory cause.[i]

Figure 2-2 illustrates the requirements for definitively establishing contributory cause and the types of studies that may be used to satisfy each of the requirements. Notice that the requirements for establishing contributory cause are the same as the requirements for establishing **efficacy**. Efficacy implies that an intervention works, that is, it increases positive outcomes or benefits in the population being investigated.

WHAT CAN WE DO IF WE CANNOT DEMONSTRATE ALL THREE REQUIREMENTS TO DEFINITIVELY ESTABLISH CONTRIBUTORY CAUSE?

When we cannot definitively establish a contributory cause, we often need to look for additional supportive evidence.[7] In evidence-based public health, we often utilize what have been called **supportive** or **ancillary criteria** to make scientific judgments about cause and effect. A large number of these criteria have been used and debated. However, four of them are widely used and pose little controversy. They are:

- Strength of the relationship
- Dose-response relationship
- Consistency of the relationship
- Biological plausibility

Let us examine what we mean by each of these criteria. The **strength of the relationship** implies that we are interested in knowing how closely related the risk factor (cigarette smoking) is to the disease (lung cancer). In other words, we want to know the probability of lung cancer among those who smoke cigarettes compared to the probability of lung cancer among those who do not smoke cigarettes. To measure the strength of the relationship we calculate what we call the **relative risk**. The

---

[g] A risk factor, as we just discussed, usually implies that the factor is associated with the disease at the individual level. At times it may be used to imply that the factor not only is associated with the disease at the individual level, but that it precedes the disease in time. Despite the multiple uses of the term, a risk factor does not in and of itself imply that a cause-and-effect relationship is present, though it may be considered a possible cause.

[h] It may seem obvious that cigarette smoking precedes the development of lung cancer. However, the sequence of events is not always so clear. For instance, those who have recently quit smoking cigarettes have an increased chance of being diagnosed with lung cancer. This may lead to the erroneous conclusion that stopping cigarette smoking is a cause of lung cancer. It is more likely that early symptoms of lung cancer lead individuals to quit smoking. The conclusion that stopping cigarette smoking causes lung cancer is called **reverse causality**. Thus, it was important that cohort studies followed smokers and nonsmokers for several years to establish that the cigarette smoking came first.

[i] At times, a special form of a cohort study called a **natural experiment** can help establish that altering the cause alters the effect. A natural experiment implies that an investigator studies the results of a change in one group, but not in another similar group that was produced by forces outside the investigator's control. For instance, after the Surgeon General's *1964 Report on Smoking and Health* was released, approximately 100,000 physicians stopped smoking. This did not happen among other professionals. Over the next decade, the rates of lung cancer among physicians dropped dramatically, but not among other professionals. Despite the fact that natural experiments can be very useful, they are not considered as reliable as randomized clinical trials. Randomization, especially in large studies, eliminates differences between groups or potential confounding differences, even when these differences in characteristics are not recognized by the investigators.

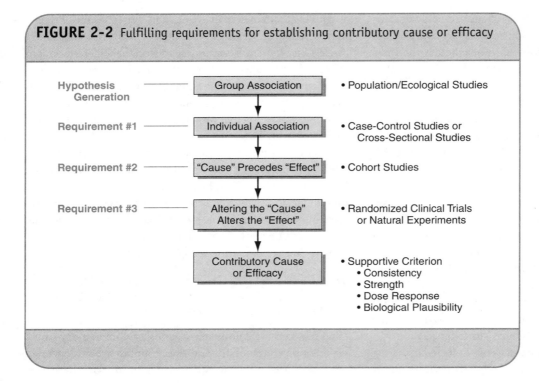

FIGURE 2-2 Fulfilling requirements for establishing contributory cause or efficacy

ask whether smoking more cigarettes is associated with a greater chance of developing lung cancer. If it is, then we say there is a **dose-response relationship**. For instance, smoking one pack of cigarettes per day over many years increases the chances of developing lung cancer compared to smoking half a pack per day. Similarly, smoking two packs per day increases the chances of developing the disease compared to smoking one pack per day. These examples show that a dose-response relationship is present.[k]

Consistency implies that studies in different geographic areas and among a wide range of groups produce similar results. A very large number of studies of cigarettes and lung cancer in many countries and among those of nearly every race and socioeconomic group have consistently demonstrated a strong individual association between cigarette smoking and lung cancer.

The final support criterion is **biological plausibility**. This term implies that we can explain the occurrence of disease based upon known and accepted biological mechanisms. We can explain the occurrence of lung cancer by the fact that cigarette smoke contains a wide range of potentially toxic chemicals which reach the locations in the body where lung cancer occurs.

Thus, the ancillary criteria add support to the argument that cigarette smoking is a contributory cause of lung cancer. Table 2-1 summarizes the use of ancillary or support criteria in making scientific judgments about contributory cause and illustrates these principles using the cigarette smoking and lung cancer scenario. It also cautions to use these criteria carefully because a cause-and-effect relationship may be present even when some or all of these criteria are not fulfilled.[7]

We have now summarized the approach used in evidence-based public health to establish a contributory cause. We

relative risk is the probability of developing the disease if the risk factor is present compared to the probability of the disease if the risk factor is not present. Therefore, the relative risk for cigarette smoking is calculated as:

$$Relative\ risk = \frac{probability\ of\ lung\ cancer\ for\ cigarette\ smokers}{probability\ of\ lung\ cancer\ for\ nonsmokers}$$

The relative risk for cigarette smoking and lung cancer is approximately ten. A relative risk of ten is very large. It tells us that the chances or probability of developing lung cancer are ten times as great for the average smoker compared to the average nonsmoker.[j]

In addition to looking at the strength of the overall relationship between smoking cigarettes and lung cancer, we can

---

[j] A relative risk of ten does not tell us the **absolute risk**. The absolute risk is the actual chance or probability of developing the disease (lung cancer) in the presence of the risk factor (cigarette smoking), expressed numerically—for example, as 0.03 or 3%. A relative risk of ten might imply an increase from 1 in 1000 individuals to 1 in 100 individuals. Alternatively it might imply an increase from 1 in 100 individuals to 1 in 10 individuals. A relative risk can be calculated whenever we have follow-up data on groups of individuals; therefore, it does not in and of itself imply that a contributory cause is present. We need to be careful not to imply that the risk factor will increase the chances of developing the disease or that reducing or eliminating the risk factor will reduce or eliminate the disease unless we have evidence of contributory cause. For case-control studies, a measure known as the **odds ratio** can be calculated and is often used as an approximation of relative risk.

---

[k] A dose-response relationship may also imply that greater exposure to a factor is associated with reduced probability of developing the disease, such as with exercise and coronary artery disease. In this case, the factor may be called a **protective factor** rather than a risk factor.

TABLE 2-1 Ancillary or Supportive Criteria—Cigarettes and Lung Cancer

Criteria	Meaning of the criteria	Evidence for cigarettes and lung cancer	Cautions in using criteria
Strength of the relationship	The relative risk for those with the risk factor is greatly increased compared to those without the risk factor	The relative risk is large or substantial. The relative risk is greater than 10 for the average smoker implying that the average smoker has more than 10 times the probability of developing lung cancer compared to nonsmokers	Even relatively modest relative risks may make important contributions to disease when the risk factor is frequently present. A relative risk of 2 for instance implies a doubling of the probability of developing a disease.
Dose-response relationship	Higher levels of exposure and/or longer duration of exposure to the "cause" is associated with increased probability of the "effect"	Studies of cigarette and lung cancer establish that smoking half a pack a day over an extended period of time increases the risk compared to no smoking. Smoking one pack per day and two packs per day further increases the risk	No dose-response relationship may be evident between no smoking and smoking one cigarette a day or between smoking three and four packs per day
Consistency of the relationship	Studies at the individual level produce similar results in multiple locations among populations of varying socioeconomic and cultural backgrounds	Hundreds of studies in multiple locations and populations consistently establish an individual association between cigarettes and lung cancer	Consistency requires the availability of numerous studies that may not have been conducted
Biological plausibility	Known biological mechanisms can convincingly explain a cause-and-effect relationship	Cigarette smoke directly reaches the areas where lung cancer appears	Exactly which component(s) of cigarette smoking produce lung cancer are just beginning to be understood

started with the development of group associations that generate hypotheses and moved on to look at the definitive requirements for establishing contributory cause. We also looked at the ancillary or supportive criteria that are often needed to make scientific judgments about contributory cause. Table 2-2 summarizes this process and applies it to cigarette smoking and lung cancer.

WHAT DOES CONTRIBUTORY CAUSE IMPLY?

Establishing a contributory cause on the basis of evidence is a complicated, and often a time, consuming job. In practice, our minds often too quickly jump to the conclusion that a cause-and-effect relationship exists. Our language has a large number of words which may subtly imply a cause-and-effect relationship, even in the absence of evidence. Box 2-3 illustrates how we often rapidly draw conclusions about cause and effect.

It is important to understand what the existence of a contributory cause implies and what it does not imply. Despite the convincing evidence that cigarette smoking is a contributory cause of lung cancer, some individuals never smoke and still develop lung cancer. Therefore, cigarettes are not what we call a **necessary cause** of lung cancer. Others smoke cigarettes all their lives and do not develop lung cancer. Thus, cigarettes are not what we call a **sufficient cause** of lung cancer.

TABLE 2-2 Cigarettes and Lung Cancer—Establishing Cause and Effect

Requirements for contributory cause	Meaning of the requirements	Types of studies that can establish the requirement	Evidence for cigarette smoking and lung cancer
Associated at a population level (Group association)	A group relationship between a "cause" and an "effect."	Ecological study or population comparison study: a comparison of population rates between an exposure and a disease.	Men began mass consumption of cigarettes decades before women and their rates of lung cancer increased decades before those of women.
Individual association: "Requirement #1"	Individuals with a disease ("effect") also have an increased chance of having a potential risk factor ("cause").	Case-control studies: cases with the disease are compared to similar controls without the disease to see who had the exposure.	Lung cancer patients were found to have 10 times or greater chance of smoking cigarettes regularly compared to those without lung cancer.
Prior association: "Requirement #2"	The potential risk factor precedes—in time—the outcome.	Cohort studies: exposed and similar nonexposed individuals are followed over time to determine who develops the disease.	Large cohort studies found that those who smoke cigarettes regularly have a 10 times or greater chance of subsequently developing lung cancer.
Altering the "cause" alters the "effect": "Requirement #3"	Active intervention to expose one group to the risk factor results in a greater chance of the outcome.	Randomized clinical trials allocating individuals by chance to be exposed or not exposed are needed to definitively establish contributory cause. Note: these studies are not always ethical or practical.	Alternatives to randomized clinical trials, such as "natural experiments" established that those who quit smoking have greatly reduced chances of developing lung cancer. In addition, the four supportive criteria also suggest contributory cause.

The fact that not every smoker develops lung cancer implies that there must be factors that protect some individuals from lung cancer. The fact that some nonsmokers develop lung cancer implies that there must be additional contributory causes of lung cancer. Thus, the existence of a contributory cause implies that the "cause" increases the chances that the "effect" will develop. Its presence does not guarantee that the disease will develop. In addition the absence of cigarette smoking does not guarantee that the disease will not develop.

Despite the fact that cigarettes have been established as a contributory cause of lung cancer, they are not a necessary or a sufficient cause of lung cancer. In fact, the use of the concepts of necessary and sufficient cause is not considered useful in the evidence-based public health approach because so few, if any, diseases fulfill the definitions of necessary and sufficient

cause. These criteria are too demanding to be used as standards of proof in public health or medicine.

By 1964, the evidence that cigarette smoking was a contributory cause of lung cancer was persuasive enough for the Surgeon General of the United States to produce the first Surgeon General's *Report on Smoking and Health*. The report concluded that cigarettes are an important cause of lung cancer. Over the following decades, the Surgeon General's reports documented the evidence that cigarette smoking not only caused lung cancer, but other cancers—including cancer of the throat and larynx. Cigarette smoking is also a contributory cause of chronic obstructive pulmonary disease (COPD) and coronary artery disease. Smoking during pregnancy poses risks to the unborn child and passive or second-hand smoke creates increased risks to those exposed—especially children.[8] Based on the Surgeon

BOX 2-3 Words that Imply Causation.

Often when reading the newspaper or other media you will find that conclusions about cause and effect are made based upon far less rigorous examination of the data than we have indicated are needed to definitively establish cause and effect. In fact, we often draw conclusions about cause and effect without even consciously recognizing we have done so. Our language has a large number of words that imply a cause-and-effect relationship, some of which we use rather casually.

Let's take a look at the many ways that a hypothetical newspaper article might imply the existence of a cause-and-effect relationship or a contributory cause even when the evidence is based only upon a group association or upon speculation about the possible relationships.

*Over several decades the mortality rates from breast cancer in the United States were observed to increase each year. This trend was **due to** and can be **blamed on** a variety of factors including the increased use of estrogens and exposure to estrogens in food. The recent reduction in breast cancer **resulted from** and can be **attributed to** the declining use of estrogens for menopausal and postmenopausal women. The declining mortality rate was also **produced by** the increased use of screening tests for breast cancer that were **responsible for** early detection and treatment. These trends **demonstrate that** reduced use of estrogens and increased use of screening tests have **contributed to** and **explain** the reduction in breast cancer.*

While these conclusions sound reasonable and may well be cause-and-effect relationships, note that they rely heavily on assertions for which there is no direct evidence provided. For instance, the following words are often used to imply a cause-and-effect relationship when evidence is not or cannot be presented to support the relationship:

- due to
- blamed on
- result from
- attributable to
- produced by
- responsible for
- contributed to
- explained by

It is important to be aware of conscious or unconscious efforts to imply cause-and-effect relationships when the data suggest only group associations and do not meet our more stringent criteria establishing cause and effect.

General's findings, there is clearly overwhelming evidence that cigarette smoking is a contributory cause of lung cancer and a growing list of other diseases. Thus, let us turn our attention to the third component of the P.E.R.I. process: recommendations.

RECOMMENDATIONS: WHAT WORKS TO REDUCE THE HEALTH IMPACT?

The evidence for cigarette smoking as a cause of lung cancer, as well as other diseases, was so strong that it cried out for action. In evidence-based public health, however, action should be grounded in **recommendations** that incorporate evidence. That is, evidence serves not only to establish contributory cause, but is central to determining whether or not specific interventions work.[9, 10] Recommendations are built upon the evidence from studies of interventions. Thus, recommendations are summaries of the evidence of which interventions

work to reduce the health impacts and they indicate whether actions should be taken. These studies utilize the same types of investigations we discussed for contributory cause. In fact, the requirements of contributory cause are the same as those for establishing that an intervention works or has efficacy on the particular population that was studied.

In the decades since the Surgeon General's initial report, a long list of interventions have been implemented and evaluated. As we have discussed, the term intervention is a very broad term in public health. Interventions range from individual counseling and prescription of pharmaceutical drugs which aid smoking cessation; to group efforts, such as peer support groups; to social interventions, such as cigarette taxes and legal restriction on smoking in restaurants.

Recommendations for action have been part of public health and medicine for many years. Evidence-based recommendations, however, are relatively new. They have been contrasted with the traditional *eminence-based* recommendation, which uses the opinion of a respected authority as its foundation. Evidence-based recommendations ask about the research evidence supporting the benefits and harms of potential interventions. In evidence-based recommendations the opinions of experts are most important when research evidence does not or cannot provide answers.

Before looking at the evidence-based recommendations on cigarette smoking made by the Centers for Disease Control and Prevention (CDC), let us look at how they are often made and can be graded. Evidence-based recommendations are based upon two types of criteria—the quality of the evidence and the magnitude of the impact. Each of these criteria is given what is called a **score**.[9, 10] The quality of the evidence is scored based in large part upon the types of investigations and how well the investigation was conducted. Well-conducted randomized clinical trials that fully address the health problem are considered the highest quality evidence. Often, however, cohort and case control studies are needed and are used as part of the recommendation.

Expert opinion, though lowest on the hierarchy of evidence, is often essential to fill in the holes in the research evidence.[9, 10] The quality of the evidence also determines whether the data collected during an intervention is relevant to its use in a particular population or setting. Data from young adults may not be relevant to children or the elderly. Data from severely ill patients may not be relevant to mildly ill patients. Thus, high quality evidence needs to be based not only on the research which can establish efficacy in one particular population, but on the **effectiveness** of the intervention in the specific population in which it will be used.

In evidence-based public health the quality of the evidence is often scored as good, fair, or poor. Good quality implies that the evidence fulfills all the criteria for quality. Poor quality evidence implies that there are fatal flaws in the evidence and recommendations cannot be made. Fair quality lies in between having no fatal flaws.[l]

In addition to looking at the quality of the evidence, it is also important to look at the magnitude of the impact of the intervention. The magnitude of the impact asks the question: how much of the disability and/or death due to the disease can be potentially removed by the intervention? In measuring the magnitude of the impact, evidence-based recommendations take into account the potential benefits of an intervention, as well as the

potential harms. Therefore, we can regard the magnitude of the impact as the benefits minus the harms, or the "net benefits."[m]

The magnitude of the impact, like the quality of the evidence, is scored based upon a limited number of potential categories. In one commonly-used system, the magnitude of the impact is scored as substantial, moderate, small, and zero/negative.[9] A substantial impact may imply that the intervention works extremely well for a small number of people, such as a drug treatment for cigarette cessation. These are the types of interventions that are often the focus of individual clinical care. A substantial impact may also imply that the intervention has a modest net benefit for any one individual, but can be applied to large numbers of people, such as in the form of media advertising or taxes on cigarettes. These are the types of interventions that are most often the focus of traditional public health and social policy.

Evidence-based recommendations combine the score for the quality of the evidence with the score for the impact of the intervention.[9] Table 2-3 summarizes how these aspects can be combined to produce a classification of the strength of the recommendation—graded as A, B, C, D, and I.

It may be useful to think of these grades as indicating the following:

A = Must—A strong recommendation
B = Should—In general, the intervention should be used unless there are good reasons or contraindications for not doing so.
C = May—The use of judgment is often needed on an individual-by-individual basis. Individual recommendations depend on the specifics of an individual's situation, risk-taking attitudes, and values.
D = Don't—There is enough evidence to recommend against using the intervention.
I = Indeterminant, insufficient or I don't know—The evidence is inadequate to make a recommendation for or against the use of the intervention at the present time.

Notice that evidence-based public health and medicine rely primarily on considerations of benefits and harms.

---

[l] To fulfill the criteria for good quality data, evidence is also needed to show that the outcome being measured is a clinically important outcome. Short-term outcomes called **surrogate outcomes**, such as changes in laboratory tests, may not reliably indicate longer term or clinically important outcomes.

[m] The magnitude of the impact can be measured using the relative risk calculation. When dealing with interventions, the people who receive the intervention are often placed in the numerator. Thus, an intervention that reduces the bad outcomes by half would have a relative risk of 0.5. The smaller the relative risk is, the greater the measured impact of the intervention. If the relative risk is 0.20, then those with the intervention have only 20 percent of the risk remaining. Their risk of a bad outcome has been reduced by 80 percent. The reduction in bad outcome is called the **attributable risk percentage** or the **percent efficacy**. The intervention can only be expected to accomplish this potential reduction in risk when a contributory cause is present and the impact of the "cause" can be immediately and completely eliminated.

TABLE 2-3 Classification of Recommendations

	Magnitude of the impact			
	Net benefit: substantial	Net benefit: moderate	Net benefit: small	Net benefit: zero/negative
Quality of the evidence				
Good	A	B	C	D
Fair	B	B	C	D
Poor (insufficient evidence)	I	I	I	I

Source: Agency for Healthcare Research and Quality, U.S. Preventive Services Task Force Guide to Clinical Preventive Services Vol 1, AHRQ Pub. No.02-500.

portant to appreciate the source of the recommendations, as well as the methods used to develop them.[7]

Let us take a look at some examples of how interventions to prevent smoking, detect lung cancer early, or cure lung cancer have been graded. The CDC publishes *The Guide to Community Prevention Services*.[10] This guide indicates that the following interventions are recommended, implying a grade of A or B:

However, recently issues of financial cost have begun to be integrated into evidence-based recommendations. At this point, however, cost considerations are generally only taken into account for "close calls." Close calls are often situations where the net benefits are small to moderate and the costs are large.

The evidence-based public health approach increasingly relies on the use of evidence-based recommendations that are graded based on the quality of the evidence and the expected impact of the intervention. The recommendations are made by a wide array of organizations as discussed in Box 2-4. It is im-

- Clean indoor air legislation prohibiting tobacco use in indoor public and private workplaces
- Federal, state, and local efforts to increase taxes on tobacco products as an effective public health intervention to promote tobacco use cessation and to reduce the initiation of tobacco use among youths
- The funding and implementation of long-term, high-intensity mass media campaigns using paid broadcast times and media messages developed through formative research

BOX 2-4   Who Develops Evidence-Based Recommendations?

Evidence-based recommendations may be developed by a range of groups including government, practitioner-oriented organizations, consumer-oriented organizations, organized health care systems, and even for-profit organizations. Organizations developing evidence-based recommendations, however, are expected to acknowledge their authorship and identify the individuals who participated in the process, as well as their potential conflicts of interest. In addition, regardless of the organization, the evidence-based recommendations should include a description of the process used to collect the data and make the recommendations.

For-profit organizations may make evidence-based recommendations. However, their obvious conflicts of interest often lead them to fund other groups to make recommendations. Thus, the funding source(s) supporting the development of evidence-based recommendations should also be acknowledged as part of the report.

One well-regarded model for development of evidence-based recommendations is the task force model used by the United States Preventive Services Task Force of the Agency for Healthcare Research and Quality (AHRQ), as well as by the Task Force on Community Preventive Services of the Centers for Disease Control and Prevention (CDC).[9, 10] The task force model aims to balance potential conflicts of interest and ensures a range of expertise by selecting a variety of experts, as well as community participants based upon a public nomination process. Once the task force members are appointed, their recommendations are made by a vote of the task force and do not require approval by the government agency.

Thus, as a reader of evidence-based recommendations, it is important that you begin by looking at which group developed the recommendations, whether they have disclosed their membership including potential conflicts of interest, and the groups' procedures for developing the recommendations.

- Proactive telephone cessation support services (quit lines)
- Reduced or eliminated copayments for effective cessation therapies
- Reminder systems for healthcare providers (encouraging them to reinforce the importance of cigarette cessation)
- Efforts to mobilize communities to identify and reduce the commercial availability of tobacco products to youths

Additional recommendations encourage clinicians to specifically counsel patients against smoking, prescribe medications for adults, encourage support groups for smoking cessation, and treat lung cancer with the best available treatments when detected.

Of interest is the grade of D for recommending against screening for early detection of lung cancer using traditional chest X-rays. The evidence strongly suggests that screening using this method may detect cancer at a slightly earlier stage, but not early enough to alter the course of the disease. Therefore early detection does not alter the outcome of the diseases. Research continues to find better screening methods to detect lung cancer in time to make a difference.

Recommendations are not the end of the process. There may be a large number of recommendations among which we may need to choose. In addition, we need to decide the best way(s) to put the recommendations into practice. Thus, implementation is not an automatic process. Issue of ethics, culture, politics, and risk-taking attitudes can and should have major impacts on implementation. A fourth step in the evidence-base public health approach requires us to look at the options for implementation and to develop a strategy for getting the job done.

IMPLEMENTATION: HOW DO WE GET THE JOB DONE?

Strong recommendations based upon the evidence are ideally the basis of implementation. At times, however, it may not be practical or ethical to obtain the evidence needed to establish contributory cause and develop evidence-based recommendations. Naturally-occurring implementation itself may be part of the process of establishing causation, as it was for cigarette smoking in the 1960s when 100,000 physicians stopped smoking and their rates of lung cancer declined rapidly, as compared to other similar professionals who did not stop smoking.

Today, there are often a large number of interventions with adequate data to consider implementation. Many of the interventions have potential harms, as well as potential bene-

fits. The large and growing array of possible interventions means that health decisions require a systematic method for deciding which interventions to use and how to combine them in the most effective and efficient ways. One method for examining the options for implementation uses a structure we will call the "When-Who-How" approach.

"When" asks about the timing in the course of disease in which an intervention occurs. This timing allows us to categorize interventions as **primary**, **secondary**, and **tertiary**. Primary interventions take place before the onset of the disease. They aim to prevent the disease from occurring. Secondary interventions occur after the development of a disease or risk factor, but before symptoms appear. They are aimed at early detection of disease or reducing risk factors while the patient is asymptomatic. Tertiary interventions occur after the initial occurrence of symptoms, but before irreversible disability. They aim to prevent irreversible consequences of the disease. In the cigarette smoking and lung cancer scenario, primary interventions aim to prevent cigarette smoking. Secondary interventions aim to reverse the course of disease by smoking cessation efforts or screening to detect early disease. Tertiary interventions diagnose and treat diseases caused by smoking in order to prevent permanent disability and death.

"Who" asks: at whom should we direct the intervention? Should it be directed at individuals one at a time as part of clinical care? Alternatively, should it be directed at groups of people, such as vulnerable populations, or should it be directed at everyone in a community or population?[n]

Finally, we need to ask: how should we implement interventions? There are three basic types of interventions when addressing the need for behavioral change. These interventions can be classified as: information (education), motivation (incentives), and obligation (requirements).[o]

---

[n] The CDC defines four levels of intervention: the individual, the relationship (e.g., the family), the community, and society or the population as a whole. This framework has the advantage of separating immediate family interventions from community interventions. The group or at-risk group relationship used here may at times refer to the family unit or geographic communities. It may also refer to institutions or at-risk vulnerable groups within the community. The use of group or at-risk group relationship provides greater flexibility allowing application to a wider range of situations. In addition, the three levels used here correlate with the measurements of relative risk, attributable risk percentage, and population attributable percentage, which are the fundamental epidemiological measurements applied to the magnitude of the impact of an intervention.[7]

[o] An additional option is innovation. Innovation implies a technical or engineering solution. The development of a safer cigarette might be an innovation. A distinct advantage of technical or engineering solutions is that they often require far less behavior change. Changing human behavior is frequently difficult. Nonetheless, it is an essential component of most, if not all, successful public health interventions. Certainly, that is the case with cigarette smoking.

TABLE 2-4 Framework of Options for Implementation

	When	Who	How
Levels	1) Primary—Prior to disease or condition 2) Secondary—Prior to symptoms 3) Tertiary—Prior to irreversible complications	1) Individual 2) At-risk group 3) General population/community	1) Information (education) 2) Motivation (incentives) 3) Obligation (requirement)
Meaning of levels	1) Primary—Remove underlying cause, increase resistance, or reduce exposure 2) Secondary—Post-exposure intervention, identify and treat risk factors or screen for asymptomatic disease 3) Tertiary—Reverse the course of disease (cure), prevent complications, restore function	1) Individual often equals patient care 2) At-risk implies groups with common risk factors 3) General population includes defined populations with and without the risk factor	1) Information—Efforts to communicate information and change behavior on basis of information 2) Motivation—Rewards to encourage or discourage without legal requirement 3) Obligation—Required by law or institutional sanction
Cigarette smoking example	1) Primary—Prevention of smoking, reduction in second-hand exposure 2) Secondary—Assistance in quitting, screening for cancer if recommended 3) Tertiary—Health care to minimize disease impact	1) Individual smoker 2) At-risk—Groups at risk of smoking or disease caused by smoking, e.g., adolescents as well as current and ex-smokers 3) Population—Entire population including those who never have or never will smoke	1) Information—Stop smoking campaigns, advertising, warning on package, clinician advice 2) Motivation—Taxes on cigarettes, increased cost of insurance 3) Obligation—Prohibition on sales to minors, exclusion from athletic eligibility, legal restrictions on indoor public smoking

An information or education strategy aims to change behavior through individual encounters, group interactions, or the mass media. Motivation implies use of incentives for changing or maintaining behavior. It implies more than strong or enthusiastic encouragement, it implies tangible reward. Obligation relies on law and regulations requiring specific behaviors. Table 2-4 illustrates how options for intervention for cigarettes might be organized using the "When-Who-How" approach. To better understand the "who" and "how" of the options for intervention when behavior change is needed, refer to Table 2-5, which outlines nine different options.

Deciding when, who, and how to intervene depends in large part upon the available options and the evidence that they work. They also depend in part on our attitudes toward different types of interventions. In American society, we prefer to rely on information or educational strategies. These approaches preserve freedom of choice which we value in public, as well as private, decisions. Use of mass media informational strategies may be quite economically efficient relative to the large number of individuals they reach though messages often need to be tailored to different audiences. However, information is often ineffective in accomplishing behavioral change—at least on its own.

Strategies based upon motivation, such as taxation and other incentives, may at times be more effective than information alone, though educational strategies are still critical to justify and rein-

TABLE 2-5 Examples of "Who" and "How" Related to Cigarette Smoking

	Information	Motivation	Obligation
Individual	Clinician provides patient with information explaining reasons for changing behavior	Clinician encourages patient to change behavior in order to qualify for a service or gain a benefit, e.g., status or financial	Clinician denies patient a service unless patient changes behavior
	Example: Clinician distributes educational packet to a smoker and discusses his or her own smoking habit	*Example: Clinician suggests that the financial savings from not buying cigarettes be used to buy a luxury item*	*Example: Clinician implements recommendation to refuse birth control pills to women over 35 who smoke cigarettes*
High-risk group	Information is made available to all those who engage in a behavior	Those who engage in a behavior are required to pay a higher price	Those who engage in a behavior are barred from an activity or job
	Example: Warning labels on cigarette packages	*Examples: Taxes on cigarettes*	*Example: Smokers banned from jobs that will expose them to fumes that may damage their lungs*
Population	Information is made available to the entire population, including those who do not engage in the behavior	Incentives are provided for those not at risk to discourage the behavior in those at risk	An activity is required or prohibited for those at risk and also for those not at risk of the condition
	Example: Media information on the dangers of smoking	*Example: Lower health care costs for everyone results from reduced percentage of smokers*	*Example: Cigarettes sales banned for those under 18*

force motivational interventions. Motivational interventions should be carefully constructed and judiciously used or they may result in what has been called **victim blaming**. For example, victim blaming in the case of cigarette smoking implies that we regard the consequences of smoking as the smokers' own fault.

The use of obligation or legally-required action can be quite effective if clear-cut behavior and relatively simple enforcement, such as restrictions on indoor public smoking, are used. These types of efforts may be regarded by some as a last resort, but others may see them as a key to effective use of other strategies. Obligation inevitably removes freedom of choice and if not effectively implemented with regard for individual rights, the strategy may undermine respect for the law. Enforcement may become invasive and expensive, thus obligation requires careful consideration before use as a strategy.

Understanding the advantages and disadvantages of each type of approach is key to deciphering many of the controversies we face in deciding how to implement programs to address public health problems; however, implementation is not the end of the evidence-based public health process.

WHAT HAPPENS AFTER IMPLEMENTATION?

Public health problems are rarely completely eliminated with one intervention—there are few magic bullets in this field. Therefore, it is important to evaluate whether an intervention or combination of interventions has been successful in reducing the problem. It is also critical to measure how much of the problem has been eliminated by the intervention(s).

For instance, studies of cigarette smoking between the mid-1960s and the late 1990s demonstrated that there was nearly a 50 percent reduction in cigarette smoking in the United States and that the rates of lung cancer were beginning to fall—at least among males. However, much of the problem still existed because the rates among adolescent males and females remained high and smoking among adults was preceded by smoking as adolescents nearly 90 percent of the time. Thus, an evaluation of the success of cigarette smoking interventions led to a new cycle of the P.E.R.I. process. It focused on how to address the issue of adolescent smoking and nicotine addiction among adults. Many of the interventions being used today grew out of this effort to cycle once again through the evidence-based public health process and look for a new understanding of the problem, its etiology, evidence-based recommendations, and options for implementation as illustrated in Figure 2-3.

Deciding the best combination of approaches to address a public health problem remains an important part of the judgment needed for the practice of public health. In general, multiple approaches are often needed to effectively address a complex problem like cigarette smoking. Population and high risk group approaches, often used by public health professionals, and individual approaches, often used in as part of health care, should be seen as complementary. Often using both types of interventions is more effective than either approach alone. Social interventions, such as cigarette taxes and restrictions on public smoking are also important interventions to consider when asking how to intervene.

The scope of public health problems and the options for intervention are expanding rapidly and now include global, as well as local and national efforts. In China, for instance, 75 percent of adult males are reported to be smokers making China—with its large population—number one in terms of the number of smokers, as well as the number of deaths caused by smoking. An important example of a social intervention is global collaboration to address smoking and health. World Health Organization's (WHO) efforts have led to what the WHO calls the Framework Convention on Tobacco Control (WHO FCTC).[11]

Today, an enormous body of evidence exists on the relationship between tobacco and health. Understanding the nature of the problems, the etiology or cause-and-effect relationships, the evidence-based recommendations, and the approaches for implementing and evaluating the options for interventions, remain key to the public health approach to smoking and health.[4] Figure 2-3 diagrams the full P.E.R.I approach. Table 2-6 summarizes the questions to ask in the evidence-based public health approach.

The P.E.R.I. process summarizes as a mneumonic the steps in evidence-based public health. It emphasizes the need to understand the nature of the problem and its underlying causes. It also helps structure the use of evidence to make recommendations and decide on which options to put into practice. Finally the circular nature of the P.E.R.I. process reminds us that the job of improving health goes on often requiring multiple efforts to understand and address the problem.[12]

Now that we have an understanding of the basic approach of evidence-based public health let us turn our attention in Section II to the fundamental tools at our disposal for addressing public health problems.

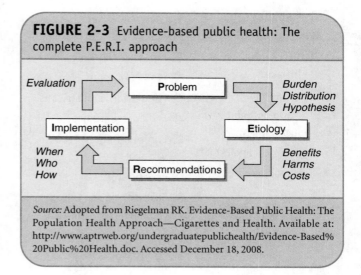

FIGURE 2-3 Evidence-based public health: The complete P.E.R.I. approach

Source: Adopted from Riegelman RK. Evidence-Based Public Health: The Population Health Approach—Cigarettes and Health. Available at: http://www.aptrweb.org/undergraduatepublichealth/Evidence-Based%20Public%20Health.doc. Accessed December 18, 2008.

TABLE 2-6 Questions to Ask—Evidence-Based Public Health Approach

1. **Problem**—What is the health problem?
   - What is the burden of disease and has it changed over time?
   - Are there differences in the distribution of disease and can these differences generate ideas or hypotheses about their etiology?
   - Are the differences or changes used to suggest group associations artifactual or real?
2. **Etiology**—What are the contributory cause(s)?
   - Has an association been established at the individual level?
   - Does the "cause" precede the "effect"?
   - Has altering the "cause" been shown to alter the "effect" (if not use ancillary criteria)?
3. **Recommendations**—What works to reduce the health impacts?
   - What is the quality of the evidence for the intervention?
   - What is the impact of the intervention in terms of benefits and harms?
   - What grade should be given indicating the strength of the recommendation?
4. **Implementations**—How can we get the job done?
   - When should the implementation occur?
   - At whom should the implementation be directed?
   - How should the intervention(s) be implemented?

Source: Adapted from Riegelman RK. Evidence-Based Public Health: The Population Health Approach—Cigarettes and Health. Available at: http://www.aptrweb.org/undergraduatepublichealth/Evidence-Based%20Public%20Health.doc. Accessed December 18, 2008.

Key Words

- P.E.R.I. process
- Burden of disease
- Morbidity
- Mortality
- Distribution of disease
- Epidemiologists
- Group associations
- Risk indicators (or risk markers)
- Artifactual
- Rate
- At-risk population
- True rate

- Incidence rate
- Prevalence rate
- Case-fatality
- Age adjustment
- Age distribution
- Standard population
- Population comparisons
- Ecological studies
- Confounding variable
- Contributory cause
- Case-control or retrospective studies
- Cohort or prospective studies

- Randomized clinical trials or experimental studies
- Risk factor
- Reverse causality
- Randomization
- Natural experiment
- Efficacy
- Supportive criteria
- Ancillary criteria
- Relative risk
- Absolute risk
- Odds ratio
- Dose-response relationship
- Protective factor

- Biological plausibility
- Necessary cause
- Sufficient cause
- Effectiveness
- Surrogate outcomes
- Attributable risk percentage (or the percent efficacy)
- Primary, secondary, and tertiary interventions
- Victim blaming
- Proportion
- Consistency
- Recommendation
- Evidence

Discussion Questions

1. Use the P.E.R.I. framework and the list of questions to outline how each step in the P.E.R.I. process was accomplished for cigarette smoking.

2. How would you use the P.E.R.I. process to address the remaining issues of cigarette smoking?

REFERENCES

1. Cable News Network. Focus: Tobacco Under Attack. Available at: http://www.cnn.com/US/9705/tobacco/history/#cigars.htm. Accessed December 20, 2008.

2. Johnson, Dr. G. A Long Trail of Evidence Links Cigarette Smoking to Lung Cancer. ON SCIENCE column. Available at: http://www.txtwriter.com/Onscience/Articles/smokingcancer2.html. Accessed March 12, 2009.

3. Centers for Disease Control and Prevention. The Public Health Approach to Violence Prevention. Available at: http://www.cdc.gov/ncipc/dvp/PublicHealthApproachTo_ViolencePrevention.htm. Accessed March 12, 2009.

4. Riegelman RK. The Population Health Approach—Cigarettes and Health. Available at: http://www.teachprevention.org/. Accessed March 12, 2009.

5. Gordis L. *Epidemiology,* 4th ed. Philadelphia: Elsevier Saunders; 2009.

6. Friis RH, Sellers TA. *Epidemiology for Public Health Practice,* 4th ed. Sudbury, MA: Jones and Bartlett Publishers; 2009.

7. Riegelman RK. *Studying a Study and Testing a Test: How to Read the Medical Evidence,* 5th ed. Philadelphia: Lippincott, Williams & Wilkins; 2005.

8. United States Department of Health and Human Services. Surgeon General's Reports on Smoking and Tobacco Use. Available at: http://www.cdc.gov/tobacco/data_statistics/sgr/index.htm. Accessed March 12, 2009.

9. Agency for Healthcare Research and Quality, *U.S. Preventive Services Task Force Guide to Clinical Preventive Services.* 2002; Vols. 1 and 2, AHRQ Pub. No. 02-500.

10. Centers for Disease Control and Prevention. The Community Guide. Available at: http://www.thecommunityguide.org/. Accessed March 12, 2009.

11. World Health Organization. Global tobacco treaty enters into force with 57 countries already committed. Available at: http://www.who.int/mediacentre/news/releases/2005/pr09/en/index.html. Accessed March 12, 2009.

12. Centers for Disease Control and Prevention. The Social-Ecological Model: A Framework for Prevention. Available at: http://www.cdc.gov/ncipc/dvp/social-ecological-model_dvp.htm. Accessed March 12, 2009.

Section I:
Cases and Discussion Questions

❋ HIV/AIDS Determinants and Control of the Epidemic

A report appeared in the CDC's Morbidity and Mortality Weekly Report (MMWR) on June 5, 1981 describing a previously unknown deadly disease in five young homosexual males all in Los Angeles. The disease was characterized by dramatically reduced immunity allowing otherwise innocuous organisms to become "opportunistic infections," rapidly producing fatal infections or cancer. Thus, acquired immune deficiency syndrome (AIDS) first became known to the public health and medical communities. It was soon traced to rectal intercourse, blood transfusions, and reuse of injection needles as methods of transmission. Reuse of needles was a common practice in poor nations. It was also widespread among intravenous drug abusers. Within several years the disease was traced to a previously unknown retrovirus which came to be called the human immunodeficiency virus (HIV).

A test was developed to detect the disease and was first used in testing blood for transfusion. Within a short period of time, the blood supply was protected by testing all donated blood and transmission of HIV by blood transfusion became a rare event. Diagnostic tests for HIV/AIDS soon became available for testing individuals. For many years, these were used by clinicians only for high risk individuals. More recently, the CDC has moved toward recommending universal testing as part of routine health care.

In subsequent years, much has been learned about HIV/AIDS. Today it is primarily a heterosexually-transmitted disease with greater risk of transmission from male to females than females to males. In the United States, African-Americans are at the greatest risk. Condoms have been demonstrated to reduce the risk of transmission. Abstinence and monogamous sexual relationship likewise eliminate or greatly reduce the

risk. Even serial monogamy reduces the risk compared to multiple simultaneous partners. Male circumcision has been shown to reduce the potential to acquire HIV infection by approximately 50 percent.

In major U.S. cities, the frequency of HIV is often greater than 1 percent of the population fulfilling the CDC definition of high risk. In these geographic areas the risk of unprotected intercourse is substantially greater than in most suburban or rural areas. Nearly everyone is susceptible to HIV infection despite the fact that a small number of people have well documented protection on a genetic basis.

Maternal-to-child transmission is quite frequent and has been shown to be largely preventable by treatments during pregnancy and at the time of delivery. CDC recommendations for universal testing of pregnant women and intervention for all HIV-positive patients has been widely implemented by clinicians and hospitals and have resulted in greatly reduced frequency of maternal-to-child transmissions in the developed countries and in developing countries as well in recent years.

Medication is now available that greatly reduces the load of HIV present in the blood. These medications delay the progression of HIV, and also reduce the ease of spread of the disease. These treatments were rapidly applied to HIV/AIDS patients in developed countries, but it required about a decade before they were widely used in most developing countries. Inadequate funding from developed countries and controversies over patent protection for HIV/AIDS drugs delayed widespread use of these treatments in developing countries.

New and emerging approaches to HIV prevention include use of antiviral medications during breast feeding, postcoital treatments, and rapid diagnosis and follow-up to detect and treat those recently exposed.

Discussion Questions

❋ 1. Use the BIG GEMS framework to examine the factors in addition to infection that have affected the spread of HIV and control or failure to control the HIV/AIDS epidemic.

2. What roles has health care played in controlling or failing to control the HIV/AIDS epidemic?

3. What roles has traditional public health played in controlling or failing to control the HIV/AIDS epidemic?

4. What roles have social factors (beyond the sphere of health care or public health) played in controlling or failing to control the HIV/AIDS epidemic?

Smoking and Adolescents— The Continuing Problem

The rate of smoking in the United States has been reduced by approximately one-half since the 1960s. However, the rate of smoking among teenagers increased in the 1980s and 1990s, especially among teenage females. This raised concerns that young women would continue smoking during pregnancy. In addition, it was found that nearly 90 percent of those who smoked started before the age of 18, and in many cases at a considerably younger age.

In the 1980s and most of the 1990s, smoking was advertised to teenagers and even preteens or "tweens," through campaigns such as Joe Camel. In recent years, a series of interventions directed at teenagers and tweens were put into effect. These included elimination of cigarette vending machines, penalties for those who sell cigarettes to those under 18, and elimination of most cigarette advertising aimed at those under 18. In addition, the Truth® campaign aimed to convince adolescents that not smoking was a sign of independence from the tobacco companies who sought to control their behavior, rather than seeing smoking as a sign of independence from their parents. Evaluation studies concluded that these interventions have worked to reduce adolescent smoking by about one-third.

Despite the successes of the early years of the 21st century in lowering the rates of cigarette smoking among adolescents, the rates have now stabilized at over 20 percent. Evidence indicates that adolescents who smoke generally do not participate in athletics, more often live in rural areas, and more often white and less often African-American. Males and females smoke about the same amount overall, but white females smoke more and Asian females smoke less than their male counterparts.

New drugs have recently been shown to increase the rates of success in smoking cessation among adults with few side effects. Evidence that the benefits are greater than the harms in adolescents is insufficient to recommend them for widespread use because of increased potential for adverse effects including suicide. A series of interventions has been suggested for addressing the continuing problem of adolescent smoking. These include:

- Expulsion from school for cigarette smoking
- Focus on adolescents in tobacco warning labels
- Selective use of prescriptions for cigarette cessation drugs
- No smoking rules for sporting events, music concerts, and other adolescent-oriented events
- Fines for adolescents who falsify their age and purchase cigarettes
- Higher taxes on tobacco products
- Rewards to students in schools with the lowest smoking rates in a geographic area
- Higher auto insurance premiums for adolescents who smoke
- Application of technology to reduce the quantity of nicotine allowed in tobacco products to reduce the potential for addiction
- Testing of athletes for nicotine and exclusion from competition if they test positive
- Research to develop safer types of cigarettes
- Provision of tobacco counseling as part of medical care covered through insurance

As a recent high school graduate, you are asked to participate in a focus group to determine which of these interventions is likely to be most successful.

Discussion Questions

1. How does this case illustrate the P.E.R.I. process?
2. Which of these interventions do you think would be most successful? Explain.
3. How would you classify each of these potential interventions as education (information), motivation (incentives), obligation (required), or innovation (technological change)?
4. What other interventions can you suggest to reduce adolescent smoking?

Reye's Syndrome: A Public Health Success Story

Reye's Syndrome is a potentially fatal disease of childhood which typically occurs in the winter months at the end of an episode of influenza, chicken pox, or other acute viral infection. It is characterized by progressive stages of nausea and vomiting, liver dysfunction, and mental impairment that progress over hours to days and result in a range of symptoms from irritability to confusion to deepening stages of loss of consciousness. Reye's Syndrome is diagnosed by putting together a pattern of signs and symptoms. There is no definitive diagnostic test for the disease.

Reye's Syndrome was first defined as a distinct condition in the early 1960s. By the 1980s, over 500 cases per year were being diagnosed in the United States. When Reye's Syndrome was diagnosed there was over a 30 percent case-fatality rate. Early diagnosis and aggressive efforts to prevent brain damage were shown to reduce the deaths and limit the mental complications, but there is no cure for Reye's Syndrome.

In the late 1970s and early 1980s, a series of case-control studies compared Reye's Syndrome children with similar children who also had an acute viral infection, but did not develop the syndrome. These studies suggested that use of aspirin, then called "baby aspirin," was strongly associated with Reye's Syndrome with over 90 percent of those children afflicted with the syndrome having recently used aspirin.

Cohort studies were not practical because they would require observing very large numbers of children who might be given or not given aspirin by their caretakers. Randomized clinical trials were neither feasible nor ethical. Fortunately, it was considered safe and acceptable to reduce or eliminate aspirin use in children because there was a widely-used alternative—acetaminophen (often used as the brand name Tylenol)—that was not implicated in the studies of Reye's Syndrome.

As early as 1980, the CDC cautioned physicians and parents about the potential dangers of aspirin. In 1982, the U.S. Surgeon General issued an advisory on the danger of aspirin for use in children. By 1986, the U.S. Food and Drug Administration required a Reye's Syndrome warning be placed on all aspirin-containing medications. These efforts were coupled with public service announcements, informational brochures, and patient education by pediatricians and other health professionals who cared of children. The use of the term "baby aspirin" was strongly discouraged.

In the early 1980s, there were over 500 cases of Reye's Syndrome per year in the United States. In recent years, there have often been less than 5 per year. The success of the efforts to reduce or eliminate the use of "baby aspirin" and the subsequent dramatic reduction in the frequency of Reye's Syndrome provided convincing evidence that aspirin was a contributory cause of the condition and its removal from use was an effective intervention.

Discussion Questions

1. How does the Reye's Syndrome history illustrate the use of each of the steps in the P.E.R.I process?
2. What unique aspects of Reye's Syndrome made it necessary and feasible to rely on case-control studies to provide the evidence to help reduce the frequency of the syndrome?
3. What types of methods for implementation were utilized as part of the implementation process? Can you classify them in terms of when, who, and how?
4. How does the Reye's Syndrome history illustrate the use of evaluation to demonstrate whether the implementation process was successful?

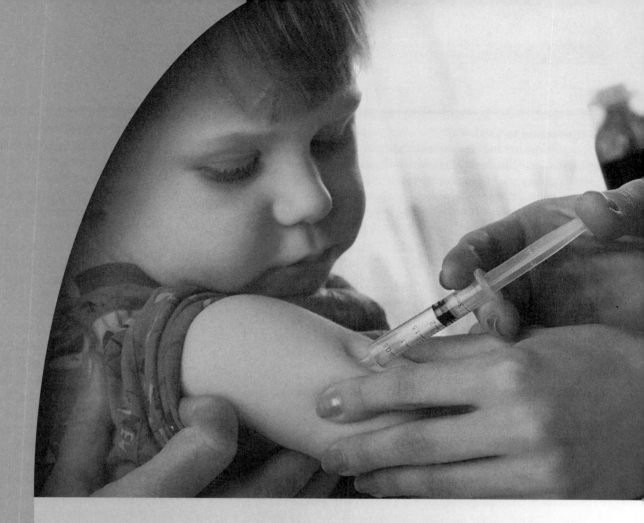

SECTION II

Tools of Population Health

Introduction to Section II

In order to protect and promote health and prevent disease, disability, and death, public health uses an array of tools. In this section, we will examine three of the basic tools of public health: health informatics and health communications; social and behavioral sciences; and health policy, laws, and ethics. Figure 2-A provides a framework for thinking about the tools used in the population health approach and indicates where they are addressed in the book.

In Chapter 3, we will explore how health information is collected, compiled, and presented, as well as how it is perceived, combined, and used to make decisions in the arena of health informatics and health communications. Chapter 4 will examine the contributions of the social and behavioral sciences in helping us to understand the sources of health and disease and strategies available to reduce disease, disability, and death. To do this we will explore how social and economic factors affect health. We will also examine how individual and group behavior can be changed to improve health. Finally, in Chapter 5, we will learn how health policies and laws can be used to improve health, as well as how ethical and philosophical issues limit their use.

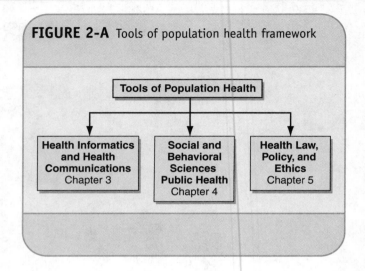

FIGURE 2-A Tools of population health framework

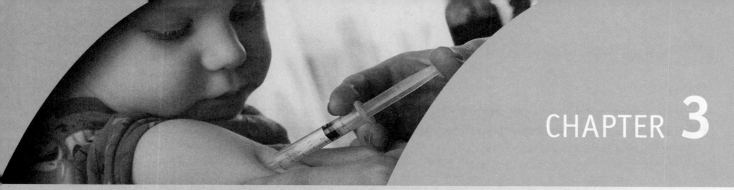

Health Informatics and Health Communications

By the end of this chapter the student will be able to:

- identify six basic types of public health data.
- explain the meaning, use, and limitations of the infant mortality rate and life expectancy measurements.
- explain the meanings and uses of HALEs and DALYs.
- identify criteria for evaluating the quality of information presented on a Web site.
- explain ways that perceptions affect how people interpret information.
- explain the roles of probabilities, utilities, and the timing of events in combining public health data.
- explain how attitudes, such as risk-taking attitudes, may affect decision making.
- identify three different approaches to clinical decision making and their advantages and disadvantages.

You read that the rate of use of cocaine among teenagers has fallen by 50 percent in the last decade. You wonder where that information might come from?

You hear that life expectancy in the United States is now approximately 80 years. You wonder what that implies about how long you will live and what that means for your grandmother who is 82 and in good health?

You hear on the news the gruesome description of a shark attack on a young boy from another state and decide to keep your son away from the beach. While playing at a friend's house your son nearly drowns after falling into the backyard pool. You ask why so many people think that drowning in a backyard pool is unusual when it is far more common than shark attacks?

Balancing the harms and benefits is essential to making decisions, your clinician says. The treatment you are considering

has an 80 percent chance of working but there is also a 20 percent chance of side effects. What do you need to consider when balancing the harms and the benefits, you ask?

You are faced with a decision to have a medical procedure, One physician tells you there's no other choice and you must undergo the procedure, another tells you about the harms and benefits and advises you to go ahead, and the third lays out the options and tells you it's your decision. Why are there such different approaches to making decisions these days?

These are the types of issues and questions that we will address as we look at health informatics and health communications.

WHAT ARE HEALTH INFORMATICS AND HEALTH COMMUNICATIONS?

The term "**health informatics**" deals with the methods for collecting, compiling, and presenting health information, while the term "**health communications**" deals with how we perceive information, combine information, and use information to make decisions. Thus, together these concepts are about information from its collection to its use. Figure 3-1 displays how these parts of the process fit into a continuous flow of information.

The fields of health informatics and health communications has been growing at the speed of the Internet. These fields have implications for most, if not all, aspects of public health, as well as health care. Therefore, we will focus on key issues in each of the above-mentioned components of this burgeoning field. We will look at the following aspects of health informat-

FIGURE 3-1 Health informatics and health communications and the flow of information

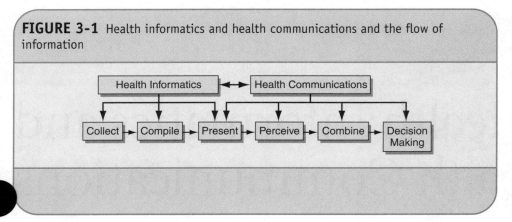

that can be rapidly and flexibly accessed by computers to address a wide range of questions. These systems have great potential to provide useful information to contribute to evidence-based public health. This information can help describe problems, examine etiology, assist with evidence-based recommendations, and examine the options for implementation, as well as help evaluate the outcomes. Despite their great potential, integrated databases also create the potential for abuse of the most intimate health information. Thus, protecting the privacy of data is now of great concern as part of the development of integrated databases.

Data can be used for a wide range of purposes in public health and health care. One particularly important use is the compilation of data to generate summary measurements of the health of a group or population. Let us take a look at how we compile this data.

HOW IS PUBLIC HEALTH INFORMATION COMPILED TO MEASURE THE HEALTH OF A POPULATION?

Measurements that summarize the health of populations are called **population health status measures**. For over a century, public health professionals have focused on how to summarize the health status of large populations, such as countries and large groups within countries—for example, males and females or large racial groups of a particular nation. In the 20th century, two measurements became standard for summarizing the health status of populations—the **infant mortality rate** and **life expectancy**. These measurements rely on death and birth certificate data, as well as census data. Toward the latter part of the 20th century, these sources of data became widely available and quite accurate in most parts of the world.

The infant mortality rate estimates the rate of death in the first year of life. For many years, it has been used as the primary measurement of child health. Life expectancy has been used to measure the overall health of the population using the probability of dying at each year of life.[1, 2] These measures were the mainstay of 20th century population health measurements. Let us look at each of these measures and see why additional health status measurements are needed for the 21st century.

At the turn of the 20th century, infant mortality rates were high even in today's developed countries. It was not usual for

ics and health communications and ask the following questions:

- *Collecting data:* Where does public health data come from?
- *Compiling information:* How is public health information compiled or put together to measure the health of a population?
- *Presenting information:* How can we evaluate the quality of the presentation of public health information?
- *Perceiving information:* What factors affect how we perceive public health information?
- *Combing information:* What types of information need to be combined to make health decisions?
- *Decision making:* How do we utilize information to make health decisions?

We can only highlight key issues in this complex field of health informatics and health communications. To do this, we will use the above questions and provide frameworks and approaches to explore possible answers.

WHERE DOES PUBLIC HEALTH DATA COME FROM?

Public health **data** is collected in a wide variety of ways.[a]

These methods are often referred to as **public health surveillance**. Data of this type comes from a growing variety of sources. It is helpful, however, to classify these sources according to the way they are collected. Table 3-1 outlines the most common types of public health data, provides examples of each type, and indicates important uses, as well as the advantages and disadvantages of each type of data.

Data from different sources are increasingly being combined to create integrated health data systems or **databases**

---

[a] Data is usually defined as facts or representation of facts while **information** implies that the data is compiled and/or presented in a way designed for a range of uses. Thus the term data is used here only in the context of collection.

TABLE 3-1 The 6 Ss of Sources of Public Health Data

Type	Examples	Uses	Advantages/Disadvantages
Single case or small series	Case reports of one or a small number of cases, such as SARS, anthrax, mad cow disease and new diseases (e.g., first report of AIDS)	Alert to new disease or resistant disease; alert to potential spread beyond initial area	Useful for dramatic, unusual, and new conditions; requires alert clinicians and rapid ability to disseminate information
Statistics ("Vital Statistics") and reportable diseases	Vital statistics: birth, death, marriage, divorce; reporting of key communicable and specially-selected noncommunicable diseases (e.g., elevated lead levels, child and spouse abuse, etc.)	Required by law—sometimes penalties imposed for noncompliance; births and deaths key to defining leading causes of disease; reportable disease may be helpful in identifying changes over time	Vital statistics very complete because of social and financial consequences; reportable disease often relies on institutional reporting rather than individual clinicians; frequent delays in reporting data
Surveys—sampling	National Health and Nutrition Examination Survey (NHANES); Behavioral Risk Factor Surveillance System (BRFSS)	Drawing conclusions about overall population and subgroups from representative samples	Well conducted surveys allow inference to be drawn about larger populations; frequent delays in reporting data
Self-reporting	Adverse effect monitoring of drugs and vaccines as reported by those affected	May help identify unrecognized or unusual events	Useful when unusual events closely follow initial use of drug or vaccine; tends to be incomplete; difficult to evaluate meaning because of selective process of reporting
Sentinel monitoring	Influenza monitoring to identify start of outbreak and changes in virus type	Early warnings or warning of previously unrecognized events	Can be used for "real-time" monitoring; requires considerable knowledge of patterns of disease and use of services to develop
Syndromic surveillance	Use of symptom patterns (e.g., headaches, cough/fever or gastrointestinal symptoms, plus increased sales of over-the-counter drugs) to raise alert of possible new or increased disease	May be able to detect unexpected and subtle changes, such as bioterrorism or new epidemic producing commonly occurring symptoms	May be used for early warning even when no disease is diagnosed; does not provide a diagnosis and may have false positives

over 100 of every 1000 newborns to die in the first year of life. In many parts of the world during this time, infant mortality far exceeded the death rate in any later years of childhood. For this reason, the infant mortality rate was often used as a surrogate or substitute measure for overall rates of childhood death. In the first half of the 20th century, however, great improvements in infant mortality occurred in what are today's developed countries. During the second half of the century, many developing countries also saw greatly reduced infant mortal-

ity rates. Today, many countries have achieved infant mortality rates below 10 per 1000 and a growing number of nations have achieved rates below 5 per 1000.[b]

---

[b] The infant mortality rate is measured using the number of deaths among those ages 0–1 in a particular year divided by the total number of live births in the same year. If the number of live births is stable from year to year, then the infant mortality rate is a measure of the rate of deaths. Health status measurements of child health have not sought to incorporate disability on the less-than-completely-accurate assumption that disability is not a major factor among children.

The degree of success in reducing mortality among children aged two to five has not been as great.[3] Malnutrition and old and new infectious diseases continue to kill young children. In addition, improvements in the care of severely ill newborns have extended the lives of many children—only to have them die after the first year of life. Children with HIV/AIDS often die not in the first year of life, but in the second, third or fourth year. Once a child survives to age five, they have a very high probability of surviving into adulthood in most countries. Thus, a new measurement known as **under-5 mortality** has now become the standard health status measure used by the World Health Organization (WHO) to summarize the health of children.

Let us take a look at the second traditional measure of population health status—life expectancy. Life expectancy is a snapshot of a population incorporating the probability of dying at each age of life in a particular year. Life expectancy tells us how well a country is doing in terms of deaths in a particular year. As an example, life expectancy at birth in a developed country might be 80 years. Perhaps in 1900, life expectancy at birth in that same country was only 50 years. In 2020, life expectancy might be 85 years. Thus, this metric allows us to make comparisons between countries and within a single country over time.

Despite its name, life expectancy cannot be used to accurately predict the future—that would require assuming that nothing will change. That is, it assumes that the death rates at all ages will remain the same in future years. We have seen increases in life expectancy in most countries over the last century, but declines occurred in Sub-Saharan Africa and countries of the former Soviet Union in the late 20th century.[c]

Life expectancy tells us only part of what we want to know. It reflects the impact of dying, but not the impact of disabilities. When considering the health status of a population in the 21st century, we need to consider disability, as well as death.

Today the World Health Organization (WHO) uses a measurement known as the **health-adjusted life expectancy (HALE)** to summarize the health of populations.[4] The HALE measurement starts with life expectancy and then incorporates measurements of the quality of health. The WHO utilizes survey data to obtain a country's overall measurement of quality of health. This measurement incorporates key components including:[d]

- Mobility—the ability to walk without assistance
- Cognition—mental function including memory
- Self-care—activities of daily living including dressing, eating, bathing, and use of the toilet
- Pain—regular pain that limits function
- Mood—alteration in mood that limits function
- Sensory organ function—impairment in vision or hearing that impairs function

From these measurements, an overall quality of health score is obtained. In most countries, these range from 85 to 90 percent. We might consider a score of less than 85 percent as poor and greater than 90 percent as very good. A quality of health measurement of 90 percent indicates that the average person in the country loses 10 percent of their full health over their lifetime to one or more disabilities.

The quality of health measurement is multiplied by the life expectancy to obtain the HALE. Thus, a country which has achieved a life expectancy of 80 years and an overall quality of health score of 90 percent can claim a HALE of $80.00 \times 0.90 = 72.00$. Table 3-2 displays WHO data on life expectancy and HALEs at birth for a variety of large countries.[e]

Thus, today the under-5 mortality and HALEs are used by the WHO as the standard measures reflecting child health and the overall health of a population. An additional measure, known as the **disability-adjusted life year (DALY)**, has been developed and used by the WHO to allow for comparisons and changes based on categories of diseases and conditions.[5] Box 3-1 describes DALYs and some of the data and conclusions that have come from using this measurement.

Table 3-3 displays DALYs according to these categories of diseases and conditions for the same large countries for which HALEs are displayed in Table 3-2.

---

[c] Life expectancy is greater than you might expect at older ages. For instance, in a country with a life expectancy of 80 years, a 60-year-old may still have a life expectancy of 25 years, not 20 years, because they escaped the risks of death during the early years of life. At age 80, the chances of death are very dependent on an individual's state of health because life expectancy combines the probability of death of those in good health and those in poor health. Healthy 80-year-olds have a very high probability of living to 90 and beyond.

[d] It can be argued that use of these measurements associate disability primarily with the elderly. Note that these qualities of health do not specifically include measures of the ability to work, engage in social interactions, or have satisfying sexual relationships, all of which may be especially important to younger populations.

[e] Not all countries accept the HALE as the method for expressing disabilities. A measurement known as the **health-related quality of life (HRQOL)** has been developed and used in the United States. The HRQOL incorporates a measure of unhealthy days. Unhealthy days are measured by asking a representative sample of individuals the number of days in the last 30 during which the status of either their mental or physical health kept them from their usual activities. It then calculates a measure of the quality of health by adding together the number of unhealthy days due to mental plus physical health. The quality of health is then obtained by dividing the number of healthy days by 30. This measurement is relatively easy to collect and calculate, but unlike the HALE, it does not reflect objective measures of disability and cannot be directly combined with life expectancy to produce an overall measure of health. That is, it does not include the impact of mortality.

TABLE 3-2 Life Expectancy and Health Adjusted Life Expectancy for a Range of Large Countries

Country	Life expectancy	Health-adjusted life expectancy (HALE)
Nigeria	48.8	41.5
India	62.8	53.5
Russian Federation	66.4	58.4
Brazil	71.7	59.8
China	73.4	64.1
United States	78.0	69.3
United Kingdom	79.2	70.6
Canada	80.6	72.0
Japan	82.6	75.0

Source: Data from World Health Organization. World Health Report 2004 Statistical Appendix 4; Geneva: World Health Organization; 2004.

The Global Burden of Disease (GBD) project has produced a number of important conclusions using DALYs including:

- Depression is a major contributor to most nation's DALY and may become the number one contributor in the next few decades in developing, as well as developed countries.
- Chronic disabling diseases, including hookworm, malaria, and HIV, affect the young and working-age population and are the greatest contributors to the burden of disease in many developing countries.
- Cancers—such as breast cancer, hepatomas (primary liver cancer), and colon cancer—which affect the working-age population and are common in many developing countries—have an important impact on the burden of disease as expressed in DALYs.
- Motor vehicle, occupational, and other forms of unintentional injuries have a disproportionate impact on the burden of disease compared to merely measuring deaths

BOX 3-1 DALYs.

Disability-adjusted life years (DALYs) are designed to examine the impacts that specific diseases and risk factors have on populations, as well as provide an overall measure of population health status. They allow comparisons between countries or within countries over time, based not only on overall summary numbers, such as life expectancy and HALEs, but based on specific diseases and risk factors. The DALY compares a country's performance to the country with the longest life expectancy, which is currently Japan. Japan has a life expectancy that is approximately 83 years. In a country with zero DALYs, the average person would live approximately 83 years without any disability and would then die suddenly. Of course, this does not occur even in Japan, so all countries have DALYs of greater than zero. The measurement is usually presented as DALYs per 1000 population in a particular country.[f]

Calculations of DALYs require much more data on specific diseases and disability than other measurements, such as life expectancy or HALEs. However, the WHO's Global Burden of Disease (GBD) project has made considerable progress in obtaining worldwide data collected using a consistent approach.[5] Data is often not available on the disability produced by a disease. The WHO then uses expert opinion to estimate the impact.

The GBD project presents data on DALYs divided into the following categories. Data is also available on specific diseases and risk factors.

- Communicable disease, maternal, neonatal and nutritional conditions
- Noncommunicable diseases
- Injuries

[f] The DALY is a complex and technical measurement. If, in a country with zero DALYs, 1000 newborns suddenly died, there would be a loss of as much as 83,000 DALYs from the death of these 1000 newborns. Thus, the total DALYs a country can lose in a particular year can range from zero to approximately 83,000 per 1000 persons. This somewhat overstates the possible loss due to the discounting and weighing that occurs in the calculation of DALYs. Nonetheless when interpreting a country's total DALYs, it may be useful to compare the number of DALYs to this maximum possible loss. It is also important to recognize that DALYs require a number of policy decisions that are hidden in the numbers. For instance, it was decided to emphasize the importance of death and disability among those of working age by giving them greater weight or importance in the calculation of this measurement. Working age was defined as age 16–60, which reflects a concept of working age more often used in developing countries. Death and disability at ages greater than the approximately 83 years of life expectancies of Japan do not add to the DALYs. In calculating DALYs, separate maximum life expectancies are used for males (~80 years) and females (>85 years), implying that loss of life among females is given slightly greater importance. These issues illustrate that in order to understand quantitative measures such as DALYs, you need to recognize that policy decisions are often subtly integrated into quantitative measurements. We need to appreciate the policy and sometimes the ethical decisions that are part of what appears to be objective measurements.

TABLE 3-3 DALYs Lost by Disease Categories and Total of All Categories Per 1,000 Population

Country	DALYs lost due to communicable diseases; maternal, neonatal, and nutritional conditions	DALYs lost due to noncommunicable diseases	DALYs lost due to injuries (unintentional + intentional)	Total DALYs lost
Nigeria	41,251	10,279	4,815	56,345
India	12,958	11,824	3,793	28,575
Russian Federation	2,189	18,752	6,411	27,352
Brazil	4,361	13,113	3,247	20,721
China	2,847	10,217	2,314	15,378
United States	941	11,939	1,387	14,267
United Kingdom	855	11,192	744	12,791
Canada	585	10,256	967	11,808
Japan	588	8,791	1,051	10,430

Source: Reprinted from World Health Organization. Global Burden of Disease Project 2004. Geneva: World Health Organization; 2004.

because these injuries produce long-term disabilities, as well as death at young ages.

- Obesity is rapidly overtaking malnutrition as a burden of disease in developing countries as early onset diabetes, heart disease, and strokes become major causes of death and disabilities among younger populations.

We have now looked at important sources of public health data and examined one key way that data is compiled to generate population health status measurements. Now, let us look at a third issue—the presentation of public health information.

HOW CAN WE EVALUATE THE QUALITY OF THE PRESENTATION OF HEALTH INFORMATION?

Having information is not enough. A key role and essential tool of public health is to effectively present the information in ways that serve as a basis for understanding and decision making. Issues of information presentation are increasingly important and increasingly complex. They require the study of a range of disciplines from mass media, to computer graphics, to statistics.[g] Public health information is often presented as graphics. Graphics create a picture in our mind of what is going on and a picture is truly worth a thousand words. Graphical presentations can accurately inform, but they can also mislead us in a

wide variety of ways. The accurate presentation of visual information has become an art, as well as a science that deserves attention from all those who use information.[6]

Issues of quality are key to the presentation of information. The Internet is increasingly the primary source of public health information for the user. Thus, when we address issues of quality, we need to have a set of criteria for judging the quality of information presented on the Internet. Before relying on a Web site for health information, you should ask yourself key questions.[7] These questions are summarized in Table 3-4. Try these out the next time that you view a health information Web site.

The presentation of data may be viewed as the end of health informatics, but also the beginning of health communications. Even the most accurate data presentation does not tell us how the data will be perceived by the user. Let us take a look at the rapidly-growing component of health communications that deals with how we perceive information.

WHAT FACTORS AFFECT HOW WE PERCEIVE PUBLIC HEALTH INFORMATION?

Regardless of how accurately information is presented, communication also needs to consider how the information is perceived by the recipient. Therefore, we also need to look at factors known to affect the perception of information or the subjective interpretation of what the information means for an individual.

At least three types of effects can greatly influence our perceptions of potential harms and benefits.[8] We will call them

---

[g] The use of statistics is one approach to data presentation. It asks questions, such as: what are the strengths of the relationships between risk factors and diseases?. This is known as **estimation**. Statistical analysis also draws conclusions from data on small groups (**samples**) about larger groups or populations—this is called **inference** or **statistical significance testing**.

TABLE 3-4 Quality Standards for Health Information on the Internet

Criteria	Questions to Ask
Overall site quality	• Is the purpose of the site clear? • Is the site easy to navigate? • Are the site's sponsors clearly identified? • Are advertising and sales separated from health information?
Authors	• Are the authors of the information clearly identified? • Do the authors have health credentials? • Is contact information provided?
Information	• Does the site get its information from reliable sources? • Is the information useful and easy to understand? • Is it easy to tell the difference between fact and opinion?
Relevance	• Are there answers to your specific questions?
Timeliness	• Can you tell when the information was written? • Is it current?
Links	• Do the internal links work? • Are there links to related sites for more information?
Privacy	• Is your privacy protected? • Can you search for information without providing information about yourself?

Source: Data from American Public Health Association. Criteria for Assessing the Quality of Health Information on the Internet. Available at: http://www.apha.org/NR/rdonlyres/36630D3D-D50E-4215-8835-4B80298B0685/0/November152000.pdf. Accessed November 13, 2008.

the **dread effect**, the **unfamiliarity effect**, and the **uncontrollability effect**. The dread effect is present with hazards that easily produce very visualizable and feared consequences. It explains why we often fear shark attacks more than drowning in a swimming pool. The dread effect may also be elicited by the potential for catastrophic events, ranging from nuclear meltdowns to a poisoning of the water supply. Our degree of familiarity with a potential harm or a potential benefit can greatly influence how we perceive data and translate it for our own situation. Knowing a friend or relative who died of lung cancer may influence how we perceive the information on the hazards of smoking or the presence of radon. It also may explain why we often see the danger of sun exposure as low and food irradiation as high, despite the fact that the data indicates that the degree of harm is the other way around.

Finally, the uncontrollability effect may have a major impact on our perceptions and actions. We often consider hazards that we perceive as in our control as less threatening than ones that we perceive as out of our control. Automobile collisions, for instance, are often seen as less hazardous than airplane crashes, despite the fact that statistics show that commercial air travel is far safer than travel by automobile.

Perception of bad outcomes (or harms) and good outcomes (or benefits) needs to be considered along with the numbers if

we are going to understand the ways information is used to make decisions. Not everyone perceives harms and benefits the same way. The selection of accurate and effective methods for conveying data is key to health communications.[h]

One approach to addressing differing perceptions of information is the use of a method known as **decision analysis**. Decision analysis relies on the vast information-processing ability of computers to formally combine information on benefits and harms to reach quantitative decisions. It provides us with insight into the types of information that need to be combined. Let us look at how we combine information—the next question in our flow of health information.

WHAT TYPE OF INFORMATION NEEDS TO BE COMBINED TO MAKE HEALTH DECISIONS?

Decision analysis focuses on three key types of information that need to be combined as the basis for making decisions. We can better understand these types of information by asking the following questions:

• *How likely?*—what is the probability or chance that the particular outcome will occur?
• *How important?*—what is the value or importance we place on a good or a bad outcome?
• *How soon?*—when, on average, will the particular outcome happen if it is going to happen?

When expressing the chances that an outcome will occur, we often express the results as a percentage from 0 to 100.

---

[h] For instance, we generally have difficulty distinguishing between small and very small numbers. The difference between 1 in 10,000 and 1 in 100,000 is difficult for most of us to grasp and incorporate into our decisions. When comparing these types of probabilities it is tempting to compare the outcomes to ones that are better known, such as those with similar emotional impacts. We might compare the chances of dying from a motorcycle accident with that of a truck or automobile accident. Comparison of different types of outcomes, such as between being struck by lightning compared to dying from a chronic exposure to chemicals or radiation, is far less informative.

Probabilities, on the other hand, range from 0 to 1. Percentages and probabilities are often used interchangeably—the probability of 0.10 can be converted to 10 percent and vice versa. When faced with a percentage or probability we need to ask: what period of time is being considered? For instance, if you hear that the chances of developing a blood clot while taking high-dose estrogen birth control pills is 5 percent, what does that mean? Does it mean 5 percent per cycle, 5 percent per year, or 5 percent over the time period that the average user is on the pill?

Outcomes vary from death to disabilities. Some outcomes greatly affect our function and limit our future, while we can learn to live with some outcomes despite the limitations they impose. When dealing with a quantitative approach, we are forced to place numbers on the value or importance of specific outcomes. A scale known as a **utility scale** is one method to measure and compare the value or importance that different people place on different outcomes.[9] This scale is intended to parallel the scale of probabilities, that is, it extends from 0 to 1 or from 0 to 100 percent. It defines 1 or 100 percent as the state of health in which there are no health-related limitations. Zero is defined as immediate death. On the utility scale there is nothing worse than immediate death. Figure 3-2 displays the utility scale.[i] Box 3-2 illustrates how we can use the utility scale to assign numbers to specific outcomes.

Utilities are important especially when we need to combine potential harms with potential benefits. Probabilities alone often do not give us the answers we need when addressing issues of hazards ranging from environmental toxins to unhealthy behaviors. Utilities are also critical when looking at particular interventions, such as prevention or treatment options that include positive benefits, but also involve side effects or harms. Thus, whenever we need to combine or balance benefits and harms, we need to consider the utility of the outcomes along with the chances or probabilities of the outcomes.

The expected timing of the occurrence of good and bad outcomes can also affect how we view the outcome. Most people view the occurrence of a bad outcome as worse if it occurs in the immediate future compared to its occurrence years from now. Conversely, we usually view a good outcome as more valuable if it occurs in the immediate future. Thus, whenever we consider harms and benefits and try to combine them, we need to ask: when are the outcomes expected to occur?[9] When both the good and the bad outcomes occur in the immediate future, the timing is not an issue. In public health and medi-

FIGURE 3-2 Scale used to measure utilities

100%   0%
|————————————————————————————————————|
Full Health   Immediate Death

cine, however, this is rarely the case. When dealing with many treatments the benefits come first while the harms may occur at a later time. When dealing with vaccines and surgery, the pain and side effects often precedes the potential gain. The timing of the benefits is rarely the same as the timing of the harms. Thus, we need to take this into account. This process is known as **discounting**. Discounting is a quantitative process in which we give greater emphasis or weight to events which are expected to occur in the immediate future compared to events which are expected to occur in the distant future.[k]

We have seen that probabilities, utilities, and timing are key components of health communications that need to be combined when making public health and healthcare decisions.[l] However, there are other factors that are characteristic not of the data itself, but of the **decision maker**. A decision maker may be an individual, a health professional, or it may be an organization like a nonprofit, a corporation, or a government agency. Let

---

[i] Many people consider prolonged incapacity or vegetative states as worse than death. The utility scale does not generally take this into account. This is a specific example of the more general limitation of quantitative decision making—that it focuses on the outcome and not on the process of getting there.

---

[k] The exact amount of discounting that should occur is controversial, but there is agreement that we should place less importance on outcomes that occur in the distant future than those which occur in the immediate future. There is also agreement that the rate of discounting for harms and for benefits should be the same. The concept of discounting comes from economics and can be most easily understood with a financial example. Let us imagine that we want to discount at 5 percent per year. A discount rate of 5 percent implies that I am willing to give you $95 today if you are willing to give me $100 one year from now.[9] Discounting is above and beyond inflation, so the actual return might be $100 plus the rate of inflation. Note that economists try to set the rate based on the average real return on money invested over a large number of years. In the past, this has been about 3 percent in most developed countries. When making decisions on a subjective basis, we often discount the future at a much higher rate. This is especially true of those who are very sick and are often focused heavily on the immediate future.

[l] Decision analysis is not the usual method used to combine information. Because the task of combining information is so complex and the ability of our minds to handle large quantities of information is so limited, we often use rules of thumb known as **heuristics**.[8] Heuristics allow us to make decisions more rapidly and often with less information. For instance, we often prefer to structure decisions to allow only one of two choices, rather than choosing from a large number of options presented to us at the same time. Thus, we often narrow the field of candidates in primary elections to allow side-by-side comparisons in the general elections. The one-on-one comparisons allow manipulation of the results by getting rid of candidates in the primaries who might have fared better in the general election.

BOX 3-2 Obtaining a Utility Score.

Let us see how we can use the utility scale to put numbers on a specific outcome—complete and permanent blindness. Using the scale in Figure 3–2, place a number on the importance or value that you give to complete and permanent blindness.

In large groups of individuals, the average utility placed on blindness is quite predictable—about 50 percent. However, the range of values among a group is generally quite wide ranging from 20 to 80 percent and sometimes even wider. Predicting an individual's utility is quite difficult since gender, socioeconomic group, and other predictors have little impact.[j]

Individuals who place a high utility on complete and permanent blindness usually indicate that they can learn to live with blindness and it will not greatly affect their enjoyment of life. Those who place a low utility on blindness generally say just the opposite. Thus, we need to understand that a utility of 50 percent is an average including some with a much higher and some with a much lower utility. Therefore the best way to know the value or utility that an individual places on a particular outcome such as blindness is to ask them.

[j] There are at least two predictors that are of some value. Those who have experienced an outcome usually find that they can adapt to it to a certain extent and usually rate its utility as somewhat higher than those who have not experienced the outcome. Second, age does have an impact on the scoring of utility. Younger people generally rate the utility of an outcome as somewhat worse or lower than older people, perhaps due to the longer-term impact the disability has on their future options. The average utility placed on blindness by college students, for instance, is often closer to 40 percent. Neither of these impacts is large on average, nor can they be used to successfully predict the utility of any one individual.

us turn our attention to decision makers and ask about how we can go about making decisions. To do this we need to address issues beyond probability, utility, and timing.

HOW DO WE UTILIZE INFORMATION TO MAKE HEALTH DECISIONS?

There are two key questions that we can ask to gain an understanding of how we use information to make health decisions:

- How do our risk-taking attitudes affect the way we make decisions?
- How do we incorporate information into our decisions?

There are a large number of attitudes that can affect the way we make decisions. One of the most important is known as our **risk-taking attitudes**.[m]

Let us examine what we mean by this term and see what type of risk-taking attitude you use in making decisions. Attitudes toward risk greatly influence the choices that we all make in the prevention and treatment of disease.[9] Box 3-3 illustrates how you can understand your own attitudes toward risk taking by making some choices. We will assume that you understand what we mean by utilities and that you have thought through what a wide range of utilities means to you personally.

[m] In addition to a risk-taking attitude, there are other attitudes that affect our decision making. For instance, decision making may depend on whether we regard an error of omission as equal to an error of commission. Decision analysis and most ethicists regard them as equal, but many people see errors of omission as more acceptable than errors of commission. That is, most people consider a bad outcome resulting from inaction as more tolerable than a bad outcome resulting from their own actions.

Understanding attitudes toward risk is important for analyzing how individuals make decisions about their own lives. It is also key when trying to understand how group decisions are made that require society to balance harms and benefits. Perhaps the most common health decisions that you will make are the decisions related to your health care and that of your family. Therefore, let us complete our examination of health communications by looking at three different approaches that can be used to make clinical healthcare decisions.

There are three basic approaches to clinical decision making. We will call these approaches **inform of decision**, **informed consent**, and **shared decision making**. Preferences for these types of approaches have changed over time, yet all three are currently part of clinical practice.

The inform of decision approach implies that the clinician has all the essential information and can make decisions that are in the patient's best interest. The role of the clinician is then merely to inform the patient of what needs to be done, to prescribe the treatment, or write the orders. At one point in time, this type of decision-making approach was standard for practicing clinicians. In the not-too-distant past, clinicians rarely told patients that they had cancer—justifying their silence by arguments that the knowledge might make the patient depressed, which could interfere with their response to the disease and to the treatment. The decision to have many tests and receive a range of medications is still often done using the inform of decision approach.

A second type of decision-making approach is called informed consent. It rests on the principle that ultimately patients need to give their permission or consent before major

BOX 3-3   Risk-Taking Attitudes.

Review the following situations and write down your decisions.

Situation A

Imagine that you have coronary artery disease and have a reduced quality of life with a utility of 0.80 compared to your previous state of full health with a utility of 1.00. You are offered the pair of options below. You can select only one option. Which of the following two options do you prefer?

OPTION #1: A treatment with the following possible outcomes:
  50% chance of raising the quality of your health (your utility) from 0.80 to 1.00
  50% chance of reducing the quality of your health (your utility) from 0.80 to 0.60
OPTION #2: Refuse the above treatment and accept a quality of your health (your utility) of 0.80

Situation B

Imagine that you have coronary artery disease and have a reduced quality of life that has a utility of 0.20 compared to your previous state of full health that had a utility of 1.00. You are offered the pair of options below. You can select only one option. Which of the following two options do you prefer?

OPTION #1: A treatment with the following possible outcomes:
  10% chance of raising the quality of your health (your utility) from 0.20 to 1.00
  90% chance of reducing the quality of your health (your utility) from 0.20 to 0.11
OPTION #2: Refuse the above treatment and accept a quality of your health (your utility) of 0.20

What was your answer in Situation A? Situation B? To understand the meaning of your answers you need to appreciate that in terms of the probabilities and utilities presented in each situation, these options are a "toss-up." That is, taking into account the probabilities and the utilities, there is no difference between these options.[n]

Thus, the information does not determine your choice; it must be your attitude toward taking chances, which is your attitude toward risk taking.

Did you choose Option #2 in Situation A and Option #1 in Situation B? Most, but not all, people make these choices. In Situation A, we begin with a utility of 0.80. For many people, this is a tolerable situation and they do not want to take any chances of being reduced to a lower, perhaps intolerable utility. Thus, they want to guarantee a tolerable level of health. We can call this the certainty effect. In Situation B, we begin with a utility of 0.20. For many people, this is an intolerable situation. Thus people are usually willing to take their chances of getting even worse in the hopes of a major improvement in their health. When the quality of life is bad enough, most, if not all, people are willing to take their chances or "go for it." This risk-taking behavior can be called the long-shot effect. Thus, risk-taking and risk-avoiding choices are both common, defensible, and reasonably predictable. Most of us are risk takers when conditions are intolerable and risk avoiders when conditions are tolerable.

A few people will choose Option #1 in both Situation A and B. These individuals are willing to take their chances in a range of situations in order to improve their outcome. We call them risk takers. Are you one of them? The only way to know is to ask yourself. Similarly, a few people will choose Option #2 in both situations. These individuals seek to avoid taking chances in a range of situations in order to preserve their current state of health. We call them risk avoiders. Are you one of them? Only you can answer that question.[o]

---

[n] Notice that the outcomes occur in the immediate future so there is no issue of timing or need to discount the benefits or the harms.

[o] There is a fourth option, which is to choose Option #2 in Situation A and Option #1 in Situation B. The small number of individuals who make this choice usually have a very different perception of what utilities mean to them. For instance, they might perceive little difference between a 0.80 and a 0.20 utility.

interventions, such as surgery, radiation, or chemotherapy, can be undertaken. Informed consent may be written, spoken, or implied. Clinically, informed consent implies that individuals have the right to know what will be done, why it will be done, and what the known benefits and harms are. Patients have the right to ask questions, including inquiring about the availability of other options. Informed consent does not mean that all possible options are presented to the patient, but it does imply that a clinician has made a recommendation for a specific intervention.

The third type of decision-making is called shared decision making. In this approach, the clinician's job is to provide information to the patient with which he or she can make a decision. This might include directly giving information to the patient, providing consultations, or referring patients to sources of information often on the Internet. Shared decision making places a far greater burden on the patient to seek out, understand, and use information. Using this approach, clinicians are not required to provide recommendations on specific interventions, though patients are free to ask for a clinician's opinion.

All three types of decision-making approaches are currently in use today. Table 3-5 outlines the process and roles implied by each of these approaches, as well as some of the potential advantages and disadvantages of each approach.

Health informatics and health communications are key tools for population health. We have taken a look at important issues related to each of them. We have asked questions about how public health data and information is collected, compiled, presented, perceived, combined, and used in decision making. Data and information are key public health tools for guiding our decision making. We will find ourselves coming back again and again to these principles as we study the population health approach. Now, let us turn our attention to Chapter 4, which discusses a second key tool—utilization of the social and behavioral sciences.

TABLE 3-5 Types of Individual Decision Making

Type of decision making	Process/Roles	Advantages	Disadvantages
Inform of decision	Clinician has all the essential information to make a decision that is in the patient's best interest Clinician aims to convey their decision as a clear and unambiguous action or order Patients accept the clinician's recommendation without necessarily understanding or agreeing with the underlying reasoning	May be efficient and effective when patients seek clear direction provided by an authoritative and trusted source Patient may favor if they do not seek out or feel they cannot handle independent decision-making responsibilities	Patient may not gain information and understanding of the nature of the problem or the nature of the treatment Patient may not be prepared to participate in the implementation of the decision Patient may not accept responsibility for the outcome of the treatment
Informed consent	Clinician has the responsibility to convey a recommendation to the patient Harms and benefits of treatment are weighed by the clinician in making a recommendation Clinician has a responsibility to provide information on the aim of the recommendation, the potential benefits, the known harms, and the process that will occur. The patient has the right to ask additional questions about the treatment and the availability of other alternatives	Patient gains information and understanding of the nature of the problem or the nature of the treatment Patient may be prepared to participate in the implementation of the decision Patient may accept responsibility for the outcome of the treatment	Time consuming compared to informing of the decision May require elaborate paperwork to implement formal informed consent process May increase emphasis on legal documents and malpractice law
Shared decision making	Clinicians serve as a source of information for patients including providing it directly or identifying means of obtaining information	May increase the control of the patients over their own lives May increase the types of information considered in decision making	May be time consuming for patients and clinicians May increase the costs of health care

continues

TABLE 3-5 Types of Individual Decision Making (continued)

Type of decision making	Process/Roles	Advantages	Disadvantages
	Patients can expect to be informed of the existence of a range of accepted options and be assisted in their efforts to obtain information	May reduce the adversarial nature of the relationship between clinicians and patients	May increase the stress/anxiety for patients
	Patients may seek information on experimental or alternative approaches and can discuss the advantages and disadvantages of these approaches with a clinician	May improve the outcome of care by increasing the patient's understanding and commitment to the chosen course of care	May shift the responsibility for bad outcomes from the clinician to the patient, i.e., takes the clinician off the hook/ clinician does not need to do the hard work of thinking through the decision and making a recommendation
	Considerations besides benefits and harms are part of the decision-making process, including such considerations as cost, risk-taking attitudes, and the distress/discomforts associated with the treatment		
	Patients are often directly involved in the implementation of care		

Key Words

- Health informatics
- Health communications
- Data
- Public health surveillance
- Databases
- Population health status measures
- Infant mortality rate
- Life expectancy
- Under-5 mortality
- Health-adjusted life expectancy (HALE)
- Disability-adjusted live year (DALY)
- Decision analysis
- Utility scale
- Discounting
- Decision maker
- Risk-taking attitude
- Dread effect
- Unfamiliarity effect
- Uncontrollability effect
- Inform of decision
- Informed consent
- Shared decision making
- Certainty effect
- Long-shot effect
- Risk takers
- Risk avoiders

Discussion Questions

Take a look at the questions posed in the following scenarios which were presented at the beginning of this chapter. See whether you can now answer these questions.

1. You read that the rate of use of cocaine among teenagers has fallen by 50 percent in the last decade. You wonder where that information might come from?

2. You hear that life expectancy in the United States is now approximately 80 years. You wonder what that implies about how long you will live and what that means for your grandmother who is 82 and in good health?

3. You hear on the news the gruesome description of a shark attack on a young boy from another state and decide to keep your son away from the beach. While playing at a friend's house your son nearly drowns after falling into the backyard pool. You ask why so many people think that drowning in a backyard pool is unusual when it is far more common than shark attacks?

4. Balancing the harms and benefits is essential to making decisions, your clinician says. The treatment you are considering has an 80 percent chance of working but there is also a 20 percent chance of side effects. What do you need to consider when balancing the harms and the benefits, you ask?

5. You are faced with a decision to have a medical procedure. One physician tells you there's no other choice and you must undergo the procedure, another tells you about the harms and benefits and advises you to go ahead, and the third lays out the options and tells you it's your decision. Why are there such different approaches to making decisions these days?

REFERENCES

1. Gordis L. *Epidemiology*, 4th ed. Philadelphia: Elsevier Saunders; 2009.
2. Friis RH Sellers TA. *Epidemiology for Public Health Practice*, 4th ed. Sudbury, MA; Jones and Bartlett Publishers; 2009.
3. Skolnik R. *Essentials of Global Health*. Sudbury, MA: Jones and Bartlett Publishers; 2008.
4. World Health Organization. Healthy life expectancy (HALE) at birth (years). Available at: http://www.who.int/whosis/indicators/compendium/2008/1hat/en/index.html. Accessed March 12, 2009.
5. World Health Organization. Global Burden of Disease. Available at: http://www.who.int/healthinfo/global_burden_disease/en/. Accessed March 12, 2009.
6. Tufte ER. *The Visual Display of Quantitative Information*, 2nd ed. Cheshire, CT: Graphics Press; 2001.
7. American Public Health Association. Criteria for Assessing the Quality of Health Information on the Internet. Available at: http://www.apha.org/NR/rdonlyres/36630D3D-D50E-4215–8835–4B80298B0685/0/November152000.pdf. Accessed March 12, 2009.
8. Dawes RM, Hastie R. *Rational Choice in an Uncertain World*. Thousand Oaks, CA: Sage Publications; 2001.
9. Riegelman RK. *Measures of Medicine: Benefits, Harms and Costs*. Cambridge, MA: Blackwell Science; 1995.

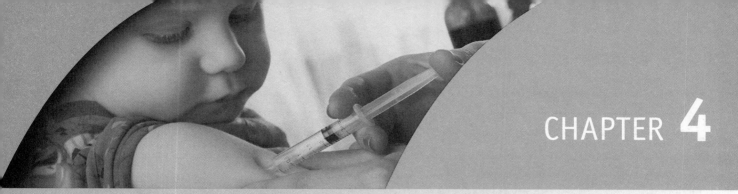

CHAPTER **4**

Social and Behavioral Sciences and Public Health

LEARNING OBJECTIVES

By the end of this chapter the student will be able to:

- explain relationships between the social and behavioral sciences and public health.
- illustrate how socioeconomic status affects health.
- illustrate how culture and religion affects health.
- identify and illustrate the stages in behavioral change that constitute the Stages of Change model.
- identify ways that interventions at the individual level and at the social level can reinforce each other to influence behavioral change.
- explain the principles of social marketing.

You travel to a country in Asia and find that their culture affects most parts of life. From the food they eat and their method of cooking, to their attitudes toward medical care, to their beliefs about the cause of disease and the ability to alter it through public health and medical interventions, this country is profoundly different from the United States. You ask: how does culture affect health?

You are working in a country with strict Islamic practices and find that religion, like culture, can have major impacts on health. Religious practices differ widely—from beliefs about food and alcohol; to sexual practices, such as male circumcision and female sexual behavior; to acceptance or rejection of interventions aimed at women's health. You ask: how does religion affect health?

You're trying to help your spouse quit smoking cigarettes and your kids from starting. You know that gentle encouragement and support on a one-on-one basis are essential, but often are not enough because cigarettes are an addiction that produces withdrawal and long-term cravings. Like most addictions, it requires a combination of individual motivation, support from

family and friends, and sometimes the use of medications; but you wonder: do warning labels on cigarettes, taxes on cigarettes, and "no smoking" zones in public places make any difference?

Your efforts to convince your friends to avoid smoking (or at least stop smoking) focus on giving them the facts about how cigarettes cause lung cancer, throat cancer, and serious heart disease. You are frustrated by how little impact you have on your friends. You wonder, whether you would be more successful by focusing on the immediate negative impacts, such as stained teeth and bad breath, as well as the loss of control that goes along with addiction to nicotine?

As a new parent, you hear from your pediatrician, nurses in the hospital, and even from the makers of your brand of diapers, that babies should sleep on their backs. They call it "back-to-sleep." You're surprised to find that it's part of the class on babysitting given by the local community center and a required part of the training for those who work in registered day care centers. You find out that it's all part of a social marketing campaign that has reduced in half the number of deaths from sudden infant death syndrome. You ask: why has the "back-to-sleep" campaign been so successful?

Each of these cases illustrates ways that an understanding of social and behavioral sciences can contribute to an understanding of public health. Let us explore these connections.

HOW IS PUBLIC HEALTH RELATED TO THE SOCIAL AND BEHAVIORAL SCIENCES?

The development of social and behavioral sciences in the 19th and 20th centuries is closely connected with the

TABLE 4-1 Examples of Contributions of Social and Behavioral Sciences to Public Health

Social science discipline[a]	Examples of disciplinary contributions to public health
Psychology	Theories of the origins of behavior and risk taking tendencies and methods for altering individual and social behaviors
Sociology	Theories of social development, organizational behavior, and systems thinking. Social impacts on individual and group behaviors
Anthropology	Social and cultural influences on individual and population decision making for health with a global perspective
Political science/Public policy	Approaches to government and policy making related to public health. Structures for policy analysis and the impact of government on public health decision making
Economics	Understanding the micro- and macroeconomic impact on public health and health care systems
Communications	Theory and practice of mass and personalized communication and the role of media in communicating health information and health risks
Demography	Understanding demographic changes in populations globally due to aging, migration, and differences in birth rates, plus their impact on health and society
Geography	Understanding of the impacts of geography on disease and determinants of disease, as well as methods for displaying and tracking the location of disease occurrence

[a] A similar list of contributions of the humanities could be developed including the contributions of literature, the arts, history and philosophy, and ethics. These contributions of the social sciences are in addition to contributions of the sciences, mathematics, and humanities. Biology, chemistry, and statistics underpin much of epidemiology and environmental health. Languages and culture, history, and the arts provide key contributions to health communications and health policy. Thus, a broad arts and sciences education is often considered a key part of preparation for public health.

development of public health. These subject areas share a fundamental belief that understanding the organization and motivation behind social forces, along with a better understanding of the behavior of individuals, can be used to improve the lives of individuals, as well as those of society as a whole.[1]

The 19th century development of social and behavioral sciences, as well as public health, grew out of the Industrial Revolution in Europe, and later in America. It was grounded in efforts to address the social and economic inequalities that developed during this period and provided an intellectual and institutional structure for what was and is now called social justice. Social justice implies a society that provides fair treatment and a fair share of the rewards of society to individuals and groups of individuals. Early public health reformers advocated for social justice and saw public health as an integral aspect of it.

The intellectual link between social and behavioral sciences and public health is so basic and so deep that it is often taken for granted. As students with opportunities to learn about both social sciences and public health, it is important to understand the key contributions that social sciences make to public health. It is not an exaggeration to view public health as an application of the social sciences, i.e., as an applied social science. Table 4–1 summarizes many of the contributions that the social sciences make to public health.

Let us start with a key question that needs to be addressed to understand the relationship between social forces and health.

How Does Socioeconomic Status Affect Health?

Beginning in the 19th century, social scientists developed the concept of **socioeconomic status**. They also developed elaborate systems to operationalize the definition of socioeconomic status and classify individuals. In the United States, the definition has generally included measures that are primarily economic including:[b]

- family income
- educational level or parents' educational level
- professional status or parents' professional status

Let us examine how socioeconomic status has been shown to affect health. Then, we will examine additional social factors that affect health and the response to disease.

[b] A more formal social hierarchy has traditionally existed in Europe. European social scientists utilized the concept of social class when categorizing individuals by socioeconomic status. In Europe, economics alone was not thought to be adequate to explain socioeconomic status or categorize individuals.

Health status, at least as measured by life expectancy, is strongly associated with socioeconomic status.[2, 3] Greater longevity is associated with higher social status with a gradient of increasing longevity from lowest to highest on the socioeconomic scale.

It is also important to recognize that socioeconomic impact are not solely related to a person's income Above an annual threshold income level of about $10,000 per person, the association of longevity with income is best explained by the disparities in income, rather than the absolute level. Thus, developed countries with smaller disparities of income, such as Japan, Sweden, and Canada, have greater average longevity and smaller disparities in longevity between their richest and poorest citizens than compared to a country like the United States. In the United States, greater disparities in income and longevity exist between the richest and poorest citizens. However, the enormous diversity of the population of the United States in terms culture and religion as well as socioeconomic level may also help explain the disparities in longevity.[c]

We understand many, but not all, of the ways that socioeconomic factors affect health. Greater economic wealth usually implies access to healthier living conditions. Improved sanitation, less crowding, greater access to health care, and safer methods for cooking and eating are all strongly associated with higher economic status in developed, as well as developing countries.

Education is also strongly associated with better health. It may change health outcomes and increase longevity by encouraging behaviors that provide protection against disease and likewise reduce exposure to behaviors that put individuals at risk of disease. Higher education levels, coupled with the increased resources that greater wealth can provide, may increase access to better medical care and provide greater ability to protect against health hazards.

Individuals of lower socioeconomic status are more likely to be exposed to health hazards at work and in the physical environment through toxic exposure in the air they breathe, in the water they drink, and in the food they eat. Table 4–2 outlines a number of mechanisms by which socioeconomic status can directly and indirectly influence health.

These factors, while important, explain only about half of the observed differences in life expectancy among individuals of different socioeconomic status. For instance, the rates of coronary heart disease are considerably higher among those of lower socioeconomic status—even after taking into account cigarette smoking, high blood pressure, cholesterol levels, and blood sugar counts.[3]

Considerable research is now being directed to better understand these and other effects of socioeconomic status. One theory suggests that social control and social participation may help explain these substantial differences in health. It contends that control over individual and group decision making is much greater among individuals of higher socioeconomic status. The theory holds that the ability to control one's life may be associated with biological changes that affect health and disease.[3] Additional research is needed to confirm or reject this theory and/or provide an adequate explanation for these important, yet unexplained, differences in health based upon socioeconomic status.

What Other Social Factors Explain Differences in Health and Response to Disease?

Culture and religion have effects on health above and beyond socioeconomic status as measured by income, education, and professional status. They can be viewed as behaviors, values, and beliefs that are learned from others and shared with others.

Culture

Culture, in a broad sense, helps people make judgments about the world and decisions about behavior. Culture defines what is good or bad, and what is healthy and unhealthy. This may relate to lifestyle patterns, beliefs about risk, and beliefs about body type—for example, a large body type in some cultures symbolizes health and well-being, not overweight or other negative conditions.

Culture directly affects the daily habits of life. Food choice and methods of food preparation and preservation are all affected by culture, as well as socioeconomic status. The Mediterranean diet, which includes olive oil, seafood, vegetables, nuts, and fruits, has been shown to have benefits for the heart even when used in countries far removed from the Mediterranean.

There are often clear-cut negative and/or positive impacts on disability related to cultural traditions as diverse as feet

---

[c] The association between socioeconomic status and longevity is most strongly associated with an individual's socioeconomic status as an adult. The socioeconomic status of an individual's parents has a much weaker association. This suggests that genetic factors have little to do with the association between socioeconomic status and life expectancy. Education has a stronger association with health status than income or professional status. Lower socioeconomic status leads to poor health rather than poor health leading to lower socioeconomic status. Socioeconomic factors are associated with an increase in relative risk of death of 1.5 to 2.0 when comparing the lowest and highest socioeconomic groups. This means that those in the lowest group have more than a 50 percent increase in the death rate compared to the highest group. This relative risk steadily increases as the socioeconomic level decreases. The relationship has a dose-response relationship, that is, there is an increase in longevity with every increase in socioeconomic status. Thus, the impact is not limited to those with the lowest status. The largest contributors to the differences in the death rate are: cardiovascular disease, violence, and increasingly AIDS; however the death rate is impacted in general by a wide range of diseases—most being malignancies and infectious diseases.[3]

TABLE 4-2 Examples of Ways that Socioeconomic Status May Affect Health

Type	Examples
Living conditions	Increases in sanitation, reductions in crowding, methods of heating and cooking
Overall educational opportunities	Education is the strongest association with health behaviors and health outcomes.
	May be due to better appreciation of factors associated with disease and greater ability to control these factors
Educational opportunities for women	Education for women has an impact on the health of children and families
Occupational exposures	Lower socioeconomic jobs are traditionally associated with increased exposures to health risks
Access to goods and services	Ability to access goods, such as protective devices and high quality foods and services, including medical and social services to protect and promote health
Family size	Large family size affects health and is traditionally associated with lower socioeconomic status and with lower health status
Exposures to high risk behaviors	Social alienation related to poverty may be associated with violence, drugs, other high risk behaviors
Environmental	Lower socioeconomic status associated with greater exposure to environmental pollution, "natural" disasters, and dangers of the "built environment"

binding in China and female genital mutilation in some parts of Africa. Some societies reject strenuous physical activity for those who have the status and wealth to be served by others.

Culture is also related to an individual's response to symptoms and acceptance of interventions. In many cultures, medical care is exclusively for those with symptoms and is not part of prevention. Many traditional cultures have developed sophisticated systems of self-care and self-medication supported by family and traditional healers. These traditions greatly affect how an individual responds to symptoms, how they communicate the symptoms, and the types of medical and public health interventions that they will accept.

Many cultures allow and even encourage the use of traditional approaches alongside Western medical and public health approaches. In some cultures, traditional healers are considered appropriate for health problems whose causes are not thought to be biological, but related to spiritual and other phenomena. Recent studies of alternative, or complementary, medicine have provided evidence that specific traditional interventions, such as acupuncture and specific osteopathic and chiropractic manipulation, have measurable benefits. Thus, cultural differences should not be viewed as problems to be addressed, but rather as practices to be understood. Table 4-3 summarizes a number of the ways that culture can affect health.

Religion

Social factors affecting health include religion along with culture. Religion can have a major impact on health particularly for specific practices that are encouraged or condemned by a particular religious group. For instance, we now know that male circumcision reduces susceptibility to HIV/AIDS. Religious attitudes that condone or condemn the use of condoms, alcohol, and tobacco have direct and indirect impacts on health as well.

Some religions prohibit specific healing practices, such as blood transfusions or abortion, or totally reject medical interventions altogether, as is practiced by Christian Scientists. Religious individuals may see medical and public health interventions as complementary to religious practice or may substitute prayer for medical interventions in response to symptoms of disease. Table 4-4 outlines some of the ways that religion may affect health.

We have examined a number of ways that socioeconomic, cultural, and religious factors may affect health and the response to disease. Many, but not all, of these factors ultimately influence the health-related behavior of individuals. Thus, we need to look at the relationship between behavior and health and the ways that we can use knowledge from the social sciences to improve health.

TABLE 4-3 Examples of Ways that Culture Can Affect Health

Ways that culture may affect health	Examples
Culture is related to behavior—social practices may put individuals and groups at increased or reduced risk	Food preferences—vegetarian, Mediterranean diet Cooking methods History of binding of feet in China Female genital mutilation Role of exercise
Culture is related to response to symptoms, such as the level of urgency to recognize symptoms, seek care, and communicate symptoms	Cultural differences in seeking care and self-medication Social, family, and work structures provide varying degree of social support—low degree of social support may be associated with reduced health-related quality of life
Culture is related to the types of interventions that are acceptable	Variations in degree of acceptance of traditional Western medicine including reliance on self-help and traditional healers
Culture is related to the response to disease and to interventions	Cultural differences in follow-up, adherence to treatment, and acceptance of adverse outcome

TABLE 4-4 Examples of Ways that Religion May Affect Health

Ways that religion affects health	Examples
Religion may affect social practices that put individuals at increased or reduced risk	Sexual: circumcision, use of contraceptive Food: avoidance of seafood, pork, beef Alcohol use: part of religion versus prohibited Tobacco use: actively discouraged by Mormons and Seventh-Day Adventists as part of their religion
Religion may affect response to symptoms	Christian Scientists reject medical care as a response to symptoms
Religion may affect the types of interventions that are acceptable	Prohibition against blood transfusions Attitudes toward stem cell research Attitudes toward abortion End-of-life treatments
Religion may affect the response to disease and to interventions	Role of prayer as an intervention to alter outcome.

Can Health Behavior Be Changed?

Much of the preventable disease and disability today in the United States and other developed countries is related to the behavior of individuals. From cigarette smoking to obesity, from intentional to unintentional injuries, from sexual behavior to drug abuse, health issues can be traced to the behavior of individuals. At times, we hear discouraging messages that behavior cannot be changed. However, if we take a relatively long-term view, we find that there are many examples of behavioral change that have occurred for the better. For instance:

- Cigarette smoking in the United States among males has been reduced from approximately 50 percent in the 1960s to less than 25 percent today.
- Infants today generally are placed on their backs for sleeping and napping and not on their stomachs, as was the usual practice in the 1980s and earlier. "Back-to-sleep" campaigns are believed to have reduced Sudden Infant Death Syndrome (SIDS) by nearly 50 percent in the United States.
- Seat belt use in the United States has increased from less than 25 percent in the 1970s to over 80 percent currently.
- Drunk driving in the United States has been dramatically reduced with a resulting decline in automobile-related fatalities.
- Mammography use increased by approximately 50 percent during the 1990s and has been credited with beginning to reduce the previously-rising mortality rates from breast cancer.

The potential to change behavior can make health worse as well. The following changes for the worse have also occurred in the United States in recent years:

- Over the last three decades, Americans have increased their caloric intake and reduced their average amount of exercise, resulting in a doubling of the obesity rate to approximately one-third of all adults.
- Between the 1960s and the 1990s, teenage girls and young adult women increased their cigarette smoking, subjecting their unborn children to additional hazards of low birthweight.

Thus, behaviorial change is possible for the better and for the worse. Some behaviors, however, are easier to change than others. Let's take a look at why this is.

Why Are Some Individual Health Behaviors Easier to Change Than Others?

Some behaviors are relatively easy to change, while others are extremely difficult. Being able to recognize the difference is an important place to start when trying to alter behavior. It is relatively easy when one behavior can be substituted for a similar one and results in a potentially large payoff. In these situations, knowledge often goes a long way. For instance, the substitution of acetaminophen (Tylenol) for aspirin to prevent Reye's Syndrome was relatively easy. Similarly, the "back-to-sleep" campaign was quite successful in reducing the rate of death from SIDS. In both of these cases, an acceptable and convenient substitute was available making the needed behavioral change much easier to accomplish.

Along with knowledge, incentives—such as reduced cost, increased availability, or improvements in ease-of-use—can encourage rapid acceptance and motivate behavioral change. For instance, easier-to-install child restraint systems have increased their use. Greater insurance coverage and widespread availability of modern mammography equipment has led to an increase in the number of mammograms performed.

The most difficult behaviors to change are those that have a physiological component, such as obesity, or an addictive element, such as cigarette smoking. Individual interventions aimed at smoking cessation or long-term weight control generally succeed less than 30 percent of the time—even among motivated individuals. Even intensive interventions with highly-motivated individuals cannot be expected to be successful more than 50 percent of the time, as was illustrated by the Multiple Risk Factor Intervention Trial (MRFIT), which attempted intensive interventions to reduce risk factors for cardiovascular disease.

In addition, physical, social and economic barriers can stand in the way of behavior change, even if individuals themselves are motivated. If health care is not accessible, or if survival needs require individuals to engage in risks they might not take otherwise, change in behavior may be impeded.

Successful behavioral change requires that we understand as much as we can about how behavior can be changed and what we can do to help.

How Can Individual Behavior Be Changed?

The behavior of individuals is often the final common pathway through which disease, disability, and death can be prevented. The fact that individual behavior has a clearly observable connection with these factors does not necessarily imply that the best or only way to address the behavior of individuals is to focus exclusively on individuals. The forces at work to mold individual behaviors are sometimes referred to as **downstream factors**, **mainstream factors**, and **upstream factors**. Downstream factors are those that directly involve an individual and can potentially be altered by individual interventions, such as an addiction to nicotine. Mainstream factors are those that result from the relationship of an individual with a larger group or population, such as peer pressure to smoke or the level of taxation on cigarettes. These factors require attention at the group or population level. Finally, upstream factors are often grounded in social structures and policies, such as government-sponsored programs that encourage tobacco production. These require us to look beyond traditional health care and public health interventions to the broader social and economic forces that affect health.

Thus, changes in behavior often require more than individual motivation and determination to change. They require encouragement and support from groups ranging from friends and families to work and peer groups. Behavioral change may also require social policies and expectations that reinforce individual efforts. It also requires us to examine the stages that individuals experience as they struggle to change behaviors, especially those habits with physiological challenges.

What Stages Do Individuals Go Through in Making Behavioral Changes?

The process of individual behavioral changes can be described using what has been called the **Stages of Change model**.[4-6] This model provides a useful longitudinal description of five steps that individuals go through in changing behavior. It also suggests steps that can be taken to help individuals make changes.[d]

The first stage, called **precontemplation**, implies that an individual has not yet considered changing their behavior. At this stage, efforts to encourage change are not likely to be successful. However, efforts to educate and offer help in the future may lay the groundwork for later success.

The second phase, known as **contemplation**, implies that an individual is actively thinking about the benefits and barriers to change. At this stage, information focused on short- and immediate-term gains, as well as long-term benefits, can be especially useful. In addition, the contemplation stage lends itself to developing a baseline—that is, establishing the current severity or extent of the problem in order to measure future progress.

The third phase is called **preparation**. During this phase the individual is developing a plan of action. At this point, the individual may be especially receptive to setting goals, considering a range of strategies, and developing a timetable. Help in recognizing and preparing for unanticipated barriers can be especially useful to the individual during this phase.

The fourth phase is the **action** phase when the change in behavior takes place. This is the time to bring together all possible outside support to reinforce and reward the new behavior and help with problems or setbacks that occur.

The fifth—and hopefully final phase—is the **maintenance** phase in which the new behavior becomes a permanent part of an individual's lifestyle. The maintenance phase requires education on how to anticipate the long-term nature of behavioral change, especially how to resist the inevitable temptations to resume the old behavior. Using the cigarette smoking as illustration again, Table 4–5 summarizes the stages of behavioral change and the specific actions that can be helpful at each of the stages.

Notice that individual behavioral change is made easier when group and social efforts are also brought to bear. Higher taxes on cigarettes, peer attitudes and support, and enforcement of laws restricting the permissible locations for smoking, all can be effective social interventions that increase the chances of entering the precontemplation phase, reinforce individual efforts to change behavior, and assist with the maintenance phase. Thus, when looking at how to change individual behavior, we also need to consider how group behaviors can be changed.

How Can Group Behaviors Be Changed?

In recent years, public health has begun to apply marketing approaches to try to better understand and change the health behaviors of groups of people—especially those like cigarette smokers who are at high risk of health impacts of their behavior. **Social marketing**, a use and extension of traditional product marketing, has become a key component of a public health approach to behavioral change.[7] Social marketing campaigns were first successfully used in the developing world for promoting a range of products and behaviors, including family planning and pediatric rehydration therapy. In recent years, social marketing efforts have been widely and successfully used in developed countries, including such efforts as:

- The truth® campaign—Developed by the American Legacy Foundation, it aims to redirect smoking from being seen as a teenage rebellion to not smoking being a rebellion against the alleged behavior-controlling tobacco industry.
- The National Youth Anti-Drug campaign—It uses social marketing efforts directed at young people, including the "Parents. The anti-drug." campaign.
- The VERB™ campaign—It focused on 9 to 13 year olds, or "tweens," with a goal of making exercise fun and "cool" for everyone, not just competitive athletes.

[d]Designing interventions based upon the Stages of Change model has not been uniformly successful. One potential reason for this may be that individuals are often in different stages of change for different types of interventions. With complex interventions, such as those required to address obesity, an individual may be in one stage of change for exercise, another for adding fruits and vegetables to his/her diet, and in a different stage in terms of calorie reduction.

TABLE 4-5 Stages of Behavioral Change

Stages of change	Actions	Example—Cigarette Smoking
Precontemplation	**Prognosticate**	
Individuals not considering change	Assessing readiness for change—timing is key	Determine individual's readiness to quit. If not ready, indicate receptivity to help in the future
		Look for receptive timing such as during acute respiratory symptoms
		Social factors, such as workplace and indoor restriction on smoking and taxation, increase likelihood of entering precontemplation phase
Contemplation	**Motivate change**	
Individual thinks actively about the health risk and action required to reduce that risk	Provide information focused on short and intermediate gains from behavioral change, as well as long-term benefits	Reinforce increase in exercise level, reduction in cough, financial savings, serving as example to children, protection of fetus, etc.
Issue of change is on the individual's agenda but no action planned	Doubtful, dire, and distant impacts are less effective	Also continue to inform of longer term effects on health
	Establish baseline to assess severity of the problem; focus attention on the problem and provide basis for comparison	Develop log of timing, frequency, and quantity of smoking, as well as associated events
Preparation	**Plan change**	
Prepare for action including developing a plan and setting a timetable	Set specific measurable and obtainable goals with deadlines	Quit date or possible tapering if heavy smoker
	Two or more well chosen simultaneous interventions may maximize effectiveness	Family support, peer support, individual planning, medication, etc.—may reinforce and multiply impacts
	Recognize habitual nature of existing behavior and remove associated activities	Remove cigarettes, ashtrays, and other associated smoking equipment
		Remove personal and environmental impacts of past smoking, such as teeth cleaning and cleaning of drapery
		Anticipate temptations, such as associations with food, drink, and social occasions
Action	**Reinforce change**	
Observable changes in behavior with potential for relapse	Provide/suggest tangible rewards	Provide rewards, such as alternative use of money—focus on personal hygiene or personal environment
	Positive feedback encouragement of new behavior	Focus on measurable progress toward new behavior
		Provide receptive environment, but avoid focus on excuses
	Anticipate adverse effects and frustrations	Take short term one-day-at-a-time approach
		Recognize cravings and have plan including use of medications
		Recognize potential for symptoms to worsen at first before improvement occurs
		Anticipate potential for weight gain and encourage exercise and other behaviors to reduce potential for weight gain
	Utilize group/peer support	Family and peer reinforcement critical during action phase

continues

TABLE 4-5 Stages of Behavioral Change (continued)

Maintenance	Maintain change	
New behavior needs to be consolidated as part of permanent lifestyle change	Practice/reinforce methods for maintaining new behavior	Avoid old associations and prepare/practice response when encountering old circumstances
	Recognize long term nature of behavioral change and need for supportive peers and social reinforcement	Negative social attitudes toward smoking among peers and society along with social restrictions, such as limiting public indoor smoking and social actions, such as taxation, help prevent smoking and reinforce maintenance of cessation

Source: Data from Prochaska JO, DiClemente CC. Stages and processes of self-change of smoking: toward an integrative model of change. *J Consult Clin Psychol.* 1983;51:390–395.

Social marketing incorporates the "4 Ps," which are widely used to structure traditional marketing efforts. These are:

- **Product**: Identifying the behavior or innovation that is being marketed
- **Price**: Identifying the benefits, the barriers, as well as the financial costs
- **Place**: Identifying the target audiences and how to reach them
- **Promotion**: Organizing a campaign or program to reach the target audience(s)

Social marketing has incorporated concepts from the **diffusion of innovation theory**. This theory, like the stages of behavioral change, contends that adoption of new behaviors requires a series of phases or steps. These move from knowledge of the innovation, to persuasion of its benefits, to the decision to adapt, to implementation, and confirmation.[1] The diffusion of innovation theory has contributed the concept of different types of adopters including: **early adopters**—those who seek to experiment with innovative ideas; **early majority adopters**—often opinion leaders whose social status frequently influences others to adopt the behavior; and **late adopters** (or laggards)—those who need support and encouragement to make adoption as easy as possible.

A different approach is often needed to engage each of these groups. For instance, marketing efforts may initially target early adopters with an approach encouraging innovation and creativity. This may be followed by an approach to opinion leaders who can help the innovation or behavior change become mainstream. A different approach emphasizing ease-of-use and widespread acceptance may be most helpful for encouraging late adopters.

Social marketing, like product marketing, often relies on what marketers call **branding**. Branding includes words and symbols that help the target audience identify with the service; however, it goes deeper than just words and symbols. It can be seen as a method of implementing the fourth "P," or promotion. It also builds upon the first three "Ps":

- Branding requires a clear understanding of the product or the behavior to be changed (product).
- Successful branding puts forth strategies for reducing the financial and psychological costs (price).
- Branding identifies the audience and segments of the audience and asks how each segment can be reached (place).

Thus, branding is the public face of social marketing, but it also needs to be integrated into the core of the marketing plan.[e]

Social marketing efforts in developing and developed countries have demonstrated that it is possible to change key

---

[e] Social marketing has not only incorporated traditional product marketing approaches, it has extended them to address the special circumstances of not-for-profit and government organizations. The use of social marketing in public health has required modifications and enhancements that have been described using four more "Ps": publics, partnerships, policies, and purse strings. "Publics" refers to the need to reach not only a target audience whose behavior we seek to change, but also those people who influence the target audience—be they parents, employers, or opinion leaders. For example, a campaign to address obesity, cigarettes, or high-risk sexual behavior in schools, requires support from parents. "Partnerships" refers to the need for collaborations to achieve most public health goals. The VERB™ campaign, for instance, partnered with television stations appealing to "tweens" and schools to help get its message out. Successful efforts to reduce adolescent smoking, increase exercise, and reduce drug use, also require changing institutional policies, which means reaching adult decision makers. Finally, the "purse string" aspect is money—few public health social marketing campaigns have adequate resources to do the job. Funding issues may require public health marketing teams to incorporate a long-term approach and look for nontraditional sources of funding.

BOX 4-1 VERB™ Campaign.

The VERB™ social marketing campaign was funded through the Centers for Disease Control and Prevention (CDC), which worked with advertising agencies to reach "tweens" to make exercise "cool." After a series of focus groups and other efforts to define and understand the market, they concluded that the message should not be one of improving health, but rather of having fun with friends, exploring new activities with a sense of adventure, and being free to experiment without being judged on performance.

Marketing efforts also identified barriers including time constraints and the attraction of other activities from social occasions to television to computers. Barriers included lack of access to facilities, as well as negative images of competition, embarrassment, and the inability to become an elite athlete.

The VERB™ campaign implied action and used the tagline "*It's what you do.*" Initial messages used animated figures of children covered with verbs being physically active. Later, messages turned these animated verb-covered kids into real kids actively playing. Widely-used logos were developed and promoted as part of the branding effort. The VERB™ campaign partnered with television channels that successfully reach "tweens," sponsored outreach events, and distributed promotional materials.

During the four years of the VERB™ campaign, "tweens" developed widespread recognition of the program and rated it highly in terms of "saying something important to me" and "makes me want to get more active" with maximum levels of recognition of 64 percent and 68 percent, respectively. Despite the documented success of VERB™, it was discontinued because of cuts in the federal budget.

health behaviors of well-defined groups of people, including adolescents, which are often regarded as the hardest to reach. An example of the use of social marketing to reach young people, the VERB™ campaign, is examined in Box 4-1.[8]

To be most successful, behavior-changing efforts need to include individual, group, and social aspects. Let us look at some approaches to combining these efforts.

How Can We Combine Individual, Group, and Social Efforts to Implement Behavioral Change?

As we have seen, behavioral change is most successful when it combines efforts aimed at the individuals, the at-risk group, and the population, or society as a whole. It can be useful to look again at the Stages of Change model to see how interventions can be successfully combined at each stage in the behavior change process. Let us return to cigarette smoking as an example.

In the precontemplation and contemplation stages, individual interventions are focused on education, assessing readiness to change, and offering help. Interventions targeting at-risk groups and populations, such as taxation on cigarettes and restriction on public and workplace smoking, can be very useful in smoking cessation preparation and preventing individuals from starting smoking in the first place.

The preparation stage requires individual action, but it can be encouraged and reinforced by family and friends, as well as via national efforts, such as the American Cancer Society's annual Great American Smokeout®, which encourages smokers to quit for a lifetime by starting with just one day. The action phase may appear to be exclusively based on individual action; however, it can be supported and encouraged by family and peers and reinforced by social efforts, such as health insurance polices that provide payment for support groups and medications.

The maintenance phase also relies on individual, group, and population/social interventions. Individual interventions often focus on education about the long-term nature of behavioral change and the efforts necessary to resist the temptation to resume smoking. Group support and reinforcement continue to be important in encouraging maintenance of the new behavior. The same types of social interventions that encourage individuals to stop cigarette smoking, such as taxation and restrictions on public and workplace smoking, also help encourage them to continue their smoke-free behavior. Table 4-6 summarizes the roles that individual, group, and population intervention can play in changing cigarette smoking behavior.

We have now looked at how health informatics and health communications, as well as social and behavioral interventions, can be used in population health. In Chapter 5, we will turn our attention to another set of key tools of population health: law, policy, and ethics.

TABLE 4-6 Stages of Change—Individual, Group and Population/Social Interventions to Change Cigarette Smoking Behavior

Stage of change	Individual	At-risk group	Population/society
Precontemplation	Assess readiness for change and offer future help	Social marketing aimed at specific groups Restriction on smoking at work	Cost affected by taxes, restrictions on smoking in public places, warning labels on packages
Contemplation	Information on hazards of smoking and gains from quitting	More receptive to social marketing aimed at specific groups Restriction on smoking at work	More receptive to costs of cigarettes, restrictions on smoking in public places, and warning labels
Preparation	Set individual goals and develop strategy Medication may be helpful	Support group/friends and family reinforce individual preparation; telephone "quit lines"	National efforts, e.g., American Cancer Society National Quit Day
Action	Remove connections between cigarettes and pleasurable activities Use of medications if needed	Public commitment to action—announce to family, friends, and work colleagues	Pay for medication and other assistance with cessation as part of insurance
Maintenance	Education regarding long term physical addiction and potential for relapse	Continued reinforcement at work and by peer and social groups	Continued reinforcement by social marketing, taxes, and restriction on public smoking

Key Words

- Stages of Change model
- Social marketing
- Diffusion of innovation theory
- Branding
- Downstream factors
- Mainstream factors
- Upstream factors
- Precontemplation
- Contemplation
- Preparation
- Action
- Maintenance
- Product
- Price
- Place
- Promotion
- Early adopters
- Early majority adopters
- Late adopters

Discussion Questions

Take a look at the questions posed in the following scenarios, which were presented at the beginning of this chapter. See now whether you can answer these questions.

1. You travel to a country in Asia and find that their culture affects most parts of life. From the food they eat and their method of cooking to their attitudes toward medical care to their beliefs about the cause of disease and the ability to alter it through public health and medical interventions, this country is profoundly different from the United States. You ask: how does culture affect health?

2. You are working in a country with strict Islamic practices and find that religion like culture can have major impacts on health. Religious practices differ widely—from beliefs about food and alcohol; to sexual practices, such as male circumcision and female sexual behavior; to acceptance or rejection of interventions aimed at women's health. You ask: how does religion affect health?

3. You're trying to help your spouse quit smoking cigarettes and your kids from starting. You know that gentle encouragement and support on a one-on-one basis are essential, but often are not enough because cigarettes are an addiction that produces withdrawal and long-term cravings. Like most addictions, it requires a combination of individual motivation, support from family and friends, and sometimes the use of medications; but you wonder: do warning labels on cigarettes, taxes on cigarettes, and "no smoking" zones in public places make any difference?

4. Your efforts to convince your friends to avoid smoking (or at least stop smoking) focus on giving them the facts about how cigarettes cause lung cancer, throat cancer, and serious heart disease. You are frustrated by how little impact you have on your friends. You wonder, whether you would be more successful by focusing on the immediate negative impacts, such as stained teeth and bad breath, as well as the loss of control that goes along with addiction to nicotine?

5. As a new parent, you hear from your pediatrician, nurse in the hospital, and even from the makers of your brand of diapers, that babies should sleep on their backs. They call it "back-to-sleep." You're surprised to find that it's part of the class on babysitting given by the local community center and a required part of the training for those who work in registered day care centers. You find out that it's a part of a social marketing campaign that has reduced in half the number of deaths from sudden infant death syndrome. You ask: why has the "back-to-sleep" campaign been so successful?

REFERENCES

1. Edberg M. *Essentials of Health Behavior: Social and Behavioral Theory in Public Health.* Sudbury, MA: Jones and Bartlett Publishers; 2007

2. Commission on Social Determinants of Health. *Closing the Gap in a Generation: Health Equity through Action on the Social Determinants of Health. Final Report of the Commission on Social Determinants of Health.* Geneva, Switzerland: World Health Organization; 2008.

3. Marmot M. *The Status Syndrome: How Social Standing Affects Our Health and Longevity.* New York: Henry Holt and Company; 2004.

4. DiClemente CC, Prochaska JO. Self-change and therapy change of smoking behavior: a comparison of processes of change in cessation and maintenance. *Addict Behav.* 1982;7:133–142.

5. Prochaska JO, DiClemente CC. Stages and processes of self-change of smoking: toward an integrative model of change. *J Consult Clin Psychol.* 1983;51:390–395.

6. Jenkins CD. *Building Better Health: A Handbook of Behavioral Change* (Technical Publication No. 590). Washington, DC: Pan American Health Organization; 2003.

7. Weinreich NK. What is social marketing? Available at: http://www.social-marketing.com/Whatis.html. Accessed March 12, 2009.

8. Wong F, Huhman M, Asbury L, Mueller RB, McCarthy S, Londe P, et al. VERB™—A social marketing campaign to increase physical activity among youth. *Prev Chronic Disease.* 2004;3(1):1–7.

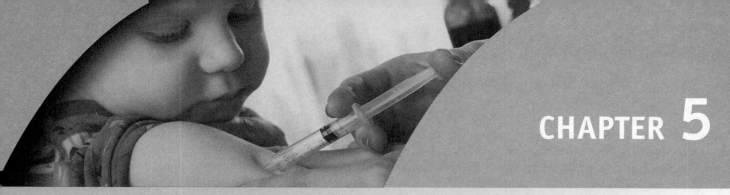

Health Law, Policy, and Ethics

LEARNING OBJECTIVES

By the end of this chapter the student will be able to:

- explain the scope of health law, policy, and ethics.
- identify key legal principles that form the basis for public health law.
- identify four types of law.
- explain the differences between market and social justice.
- illustrate the potential tensions between individual rights and the needs of society using public health examples.
- discuss key principles that underlie the ethics of human research.

A new statute and subsequent administrative regulations give only a temporary license to newly-licensed drivers, prohibiting late night driving, the use of cell phones and limiting the number of passengers. You ask: should elderly drivers be subject to these same types of regulations, such as being required to take a driver's test?

You decide not to enroll in the health plan offered by your employer because it seems so expensive and you are young and healthy. Shortly thereafter, your car is struck by a hit-and-run driver and you find yourself on the way to the nearest hospital. After stabilizing you as required by law, they transfer you to the public hospital, which is the only one in town that will take care of you without insurance. You ask: do you have a right to health care?

You hear that a new drug has shown extremely promising results, but will not be available for a least a couple of years. You wonder: why do you have to wait so long to take the newest prescription medicine while your e-mail fills up with promotions for

the untested ways to enhance your energy, beauty, and sexual performance?

You hear that a neighbor has TB and refuses treatment. You wonder: what if he has the type of TB that can't be cured with drugs? You ask: can't they make him take his medicine or at least get him out of your neighborhood?

You hear an advertisement about participating in a new research study. It sounds like you're eligible, so you check into it. You're surprised to find that even if you participate you may not receive the new drug and won't even be told which treatment you are receiving. Despite your willingness to take your chances, you're told that you are not eligible for the study due to conditions that put you at increased risk of developing side effects. You ask: why can't I participate if I'm willing to take the risks?

These are the types of issues that are part of health law, policy, and ethics. Let us begin by examining the scope of these issues.

WHAT IS THE SCOPE OF HEALTH LAW, POLICY, AND ETHICS?

Health law, policy, and ethics reflect a wide range of tools that society uses to encourage and discourage behaviors by individuals and groups. These tools apply to health care, as well as to traditional public health. In addition, in recent years a field called **bioethics** has been defined, which includes elements of both health care and public health and focuses on applying morals or values to areas of potential conflict.[1]

Health law, policy, and ethics affect the full range of issues that confront us in population health. They address such things as the access to and the quality and cost of health care. They also address the organizational and professional structures designed to deliver health care. Health law, policy, and ethics are also key tools for accomplishing the goals of traditional public health ranging from occupational safety to drug and highway safety and from control of communicable diseases to non-communicable and environmental diseases. Bioethics lies at the intersection of health law and policy and attempts to apply individual and group values and morals to controversial issues, such as abortion, stem cell research, and end-of-life care. Table 5-1 outlines a range of issues that are addressed by health law, policy, and ethics.

The scope of health law, policy, and ethics is so vast that we will focus on first defining key principles and philosophies that underlie our society's approach to these issues. Then, we will focus on three examples that illustrate key issues confronted in the healthcare, public health, and bioethics arenas. These are:

1. Is there a right to health care?
2. How does public health balance the rights of individuals and the needs of society?
3. How can bioethical principles be applied to protecting individuals who participate in research?[1]

Let us start by taking a look at key legal principles that underlie the approach to public health and health care in the United States.

What Legal Principles Underlie Public Health and Health Care?

In order to better appreciate the issue of health policy and law, it is important to understand some key legal principles that

underlie both public health and healthcare law in the United States.[1] First, the U.S. Constitution is a fundamental document that governs the issues of public health and healthcare law. However, the U.S. Constitution does not mention health. As a result, public health and health care are among those issues that are left primarily to the authority of the states unless delegated by the state-to-local jurisdictions, such as cities or counties. The use of this authority, known as **police power**, allows states to pass legislation and take actions to protect the common good. The authority to protect the common good may justify a wide range of state actions including: the regulation of healthcare professionals and facilities; the establishment of health and safety standards in retail, as well as other occupational settings; and the control of hazards ranging from requiring use of car restraint systems to vaccinations to restricting the sale of tobacco products.[1, 2]

The use of state police power is limited by the protections afforded to individuals. These protections are known as **rights** and are created either through the U.S. Constitution, through a state's constitution, or through laws passed at the federal or state levels. The U.S. Constitution allows, but does not require, governments to act to protect public health or to provide healthcare services. This has been referred to as the **negative constitution**. Thus, while governments often have the authority to act, they are not required to do so. For instance, the Supreme Court has not found an obligation on the part of states to act to prevent child or spousal abuse even when the state is fully aware of specific circumstances or a court has issued a restraining order.[1]

Second, the Interstate Commerce Clause of the U.S. Constitution is the major source of federal authority in public health and health care. It provides the federal government

TABLE 5-1 Components of Health Law, Policy, and Ethics

Component	Scope	Examples of issues
Health care	Access, quality, and cost of health care Organizational and professional structures for the delivery of care	Rules governing Medicare and Medicaid, as well as laws governing private insurance Hospital governance and professional licensure
Public health	Population health and safety, including governmental efforts to provide services to entire populations, as well as vulnerable groups	Food and drug laws and procedures, environmental laws and procedures, regulations for control of communicable diseases
Bioethics	Application of individual and group values and morals to controversial areas	End-of-life care, stem cell research, abortion, protection of research subjects

with authority to tax, spend, and regulate interstate commerce.[2] This authority has been used to justify a wide range of federal involvement in health care and public health. Federal authority is often exerted through incentives to the states. For instance, states may be offered federal funding or matching funding if they enact specific types of legislation, such as the rules governing Medicaid or definitions of blood-alcohol levels for driving under the influence.[3] The U.S. Constitution's supremacy clause declares that legitimate federal laws are the supreme laws of the land and they preempt or overrule state laws that conflict with them.[a] This provision has been used by federal public health agencies, such as the Food and Drug Administration and the Environmental Protection Agency, to justify national standards that overrule and limit state rules and regulations ranging from quality controls on drugs to levels of permissible exposures to toxic substances.[1,2]

Third, the U.S. Constitution grants individual rights. Some of them, such as freedom of speech, religion, assembly, and the right to bear arms, are explicit in the document. Others have been inferred by the U.S. Supreme Court, such as the right to procreation, privacy, bodily integrity, and travel. These inferred rights are often the basis for individual protections in public health and health care, including the right to utilize contraception, have an abortion, and limit the state and federal authority to use quarantine and other travel restrictions.[1,2] Unless the U.S. Constitution explicitly includes a right or one has been "found" by the Supreme Court of the United States, no right exists. However, federal and state legislatures may create rights through legislation ranging from access to education to access to medical care. The existence of a right implies that state and/or federal courts are expected to uphold and enforce the right.[b]

---

[a] Another implication of constitutional law is the supremacy of the U.S. Constitution even over international law. Human rights and standards incorporated into international documents are not directly enforceable in the United States. These rights and standards are only enforceable in the United States through enactment of federal or state laws.[1]

[b] Enforcement is required by law to occur based on due process. Due process includes **substantive due process**, which refers to the grounds for depriving an individual of a right, as well as **procedural due process**, which refers to the processes that must be undertaken to deprive an individual of a right. The former implies that state and federal governments must justify depriving an individual of life, liberty, and property. When fundamental rights are involved or laws are based on suspect classifications, such as gender or race, the court applies strict criteria that place difficult burdens of proof on the government to justify these types of actions. Procedural due process implies that when a right exists, governments may not deny individuals the right in an arbitrary or unfair way. This process requires that acceptable legal processes be followed before an individual can be deprived of a right. The Supreme Court has considered a fundamental right as one that is explicit in the U.S. Constitution, that has been "found" in the U.S. Constitution by the Supreme Court, or that is rooted in the nation's history and traditions.[1,2]

Health law is based upon these rules governing the authority of federal and state governments and also the rights of individuals. It is derived from four sources that are summarized in Box 5-1.[1]

Thus, health law refers to a vast array of legal issues that influence much of what goes on in public health and health care. However, the influence of health policy often extends beyond that of the formal legal system. Let us take a look at what we mean by health policy.

What Do We Mean by Health Policy?

Within the constraints set by law, there is considerable latitude for governments, as well as private groups, to develop policies that affect the ways that public health and health care are conducted. Health policy is a subset of the larger arena of public policy. According to Teitelbaum and Wilensky, "when deciding on whether something is a public policy decision, the focus is not only on who is making the decision, but also on what kind of decision is being made."[4] They define individuals or groups that make public policy based on the ability of the individual or group to make an **authoritative decision**. An authoritative decision is a decision made by an individual or group that has the power to implement the decision. A range of governmental and private groups make public policy decisions in areas such as cigarette smoking. In government, authoritative sions might be made by an executive branch official, such as the president or a governor, or administrative officials, such as federal, state, or local health officers. These may range from policies that discourage the growing of tobacco to policies that encourage the sale of tobacco products abroad to policies that restrict smoking in public places or tax tobacco sales. These polices may or may not be incorporated into laws or statutes.

At times, health policy may be made by private groups, including professional societies, such as the American Public Health Association, or commercial trade associations representing hospitals, the drug industry, the insurance industry, etc. Policies that affect large numbers of people, such as those that restrict smoking in hospitals, encourage clinicians to incorporate smoking prevention and cessation programs, compensate clinicians' efforts through insurance, and encourage the development of new drugs to assist with smoking cessation, are all examples of health polices that may be set by groups outside of government. Thus, the "public" in public policies does not necessarily imply that the policies were developed or implemented by government.

According to Teitelbaum and Wilensky, in addition to being authoritative, a public policy decision must be one that "goes beyond the individual sphere and affects the greater community."[4] Decisions to seek vaccination or screenings, to smoke

BOX 5-1   Types of Law.

To appreciate the complex relationship between the law and public health and health care, it is important to appreciate that there are four sources of law. These may be classified as **constitutional law, legislative statutes, administrative regulations**, and **judicial law** (also called case law or common law).

Constitutional law includes not only the United States Constitution, but the constitutions of the 50 states. The provisions of state constitutions are important because the responsibilities for health lie with the states unless the federal constitution grants authority to the federal government. As we have seen, the commerce clause and the due process clauses of the constitution have been the basis for extensions of federal authority into areas of health. State constitutions are often easier to amend than the federal constitutions, and thus can and do change more frequently. Constitutions often limit the role of government and define its processes. Constitutional law, however, does not usually directly mandate roles for government in the area of health.

Legislative law, or statutes, is/are written by legislative bodies at local, state, and federal levels. Federal statutes preempt, that is they over-rule, conflicting state statutes, as long as they are consistent with the limitation placed on the federal government by the U.S. Constitution. Statutes often directly address health issues. Legislative law may place requirements or prohibition on future activities. Statutes may authorize governmental regulation, such as professional or institutional licensure; require specific activities, such as a restaurant inspections; prohibit other activities, such as smoking in public places; or provide funding to pay for governmental services or reimburse those who provide the services, such as health care.

Administrative law is produced by executive agencies of the federal, state, and local governments in order to implement legislative statutes, which are often written in quite general language. Executive agencies must follow legally-defined processes and stay within what is called the legislative intent of the statute. Administrative law can be seen as operationalizing statutes passed by legislative bodies. These types of laws may define who is eligible for services, how these services may be provided, the levels of reimbursement received, and a large number of other important details that affect the day-to-day operations of government services and programs. Administrative law affects public health in many ways from the regulation of septic tanks to requirements for immunization to enroll in public education. Executive agencies often set up quasi-judicial processes to review contested cases. These judicial processes usually provide for limited access to the court system to contest their decisions.

Judicial, case, or common law, is law made by courts when applying constitutional, statutory, or administrative law to specific cases. In addition, common law may fill in the holes when statutory law does not provide guidance. For instance case law may be the basis for addressing environmental health issues which the law defines as "nuisances" ranging from excess noise to disposal of garbage. Judges' primary responsibility is to apply previous rulings or precedence to new cases that come before them; however, they may take into account existing traditions and customs of society when applying the law to specific cases. Higher courts including appellate courts, and ultimately the U.S. Supreme Court, and in some instances, state Supreme Courts may decide that a statute violates the relevant constitutions. That is, they can rule a statute unconstitutional.

---

cigarettes at home, or to purchase a particular type of health insurance are individual decisions. Public policy issues revolve around incentives or requirements to encourage or discourage these actions by groups of individuals or the society as a whole. Health policy often rests upon the attitude or philosophy that a group takes toward the role that different types of institutions should play in public health and health care. Specifically, the appropriate role of government is often a controversial subject.

How Do Philosophies Toward the Role of Government Affect Health Policies?

One of the most fundamental differences within our society is the attitude or philosophy about the roles that government

and the economic market should play in advancing health. To appreciate this issue, it is useful to look at two contrasting philosophies regarding the government's role in health care and public health. These philosophies are called **social justice** and **market justice**.

Understanding these quite different approaches is helpful because our current system of health care and public health borrows from both of these basic approaches to varying degrees. Table 5-2 outlines the contrasting characteristics of market justice and social justice. Table 5-3 examines many of the implications of the two different philosophies.[5]

Market and social justice approaches are useful for understanding the structure of healthcare systems, as we will see

TABLE 5-2 Characteristics of Market and Social Justice

Market Justice	Social Justice
Views health care as an economic good	Views health care as a social resource
Assumes free market conditions for health services delivery	Requires active government involvement in health services delivery
Assumes that markets are more efficient in allocating resources equitably	Assumes that the government is more efficient in allocating health resources equitably
Production and distribution of health care determined by market-based demand	Medical resource allocation determined by central planning
Medical care distribution based on people's ability to pay	Ability to pay inconsequential for receiving medical care
Access to medical care viewed as an economic reward for personal effort and achievement	Equal access to medical services viewed as a basic right

Source: Shi L, Singh D. *Delivering Health Care in America.* 3rd ed. Sudbury, MA: Jones and Bartlett Publishers; 2004: 59.

TABLE 5-3 Implications of Market and Social Justice

Market Justice	Social Justice
Individual responsibility for health	Collective responsibility for health
Benefits based on individual purchasing power	Everyone is entitled to a basic package of services
Limited obligation to the collective good	Strong obligation to the collective good
Emphasis on individual well-being	Community well-being supersedes that of the individual
Private solutions to social problems	Public solutions to social problems
Rationing based on ability to pay	Planned rationing of health care

Source: Shi L, Singh D. *Delivering Health Care in America.* 3rd ed. Sudbury, MA: Jones and Bartlett Publishers; 2004: 59.

in Chapter 11. They are also useful in understanding the evolution of public health approaches and institutions, such as those of the United States Food and Drug Administration[6] illustrated in Box 5-2.

We have now looked at key principles and approaches of health law and health policy that underlie our approach to health care and public health. To see how these principles operate in practice, let us review the three questions introduced earlier:

1. Is there a right to health care?
2. How does public health balance the rights of individuals and the needs of society?
3. How can bioethical principles be applied to protecting individuals who participate in research?

Is There a Right to Health Care?

In 1948, a right to health care was incorporated into the Universal Declaration of Human Rights and the Constitution of the World Health Organization. The former states that "(e)veryone has the right to a standard of living adequate for the health and well-being of himself and his family, including…medical care…and the right to security in the event of…sickness…."[7] Most developed countries have incorporated a right to health

BOX 5-2 The United States Food and Drug Administration and Market Justice versus Social Justice.

The arguments over the use of the market mechanism and the governmental regulatory mechanism in public health are well illustrated by the history of the U.S. Food and Drug Administration. These opposing philosophies are highlighted as we as a nation have attempted to balance market approaches versus regulatory or social justice approaches.

Until the early years of the 20th century, the market controlled the availability of drugs. Narcotics and other addictive substances were widely sold in the marketplace totally within the law. Drugs were falsely advertised to produce miraculous cures. There were few limitations on what could be advertised or what substances the miracle cures of the day could contain.

The "muckrakers," aggressive journalists of the early 20th century, brought to public attention many abuses, from the sale of drugs laced with narcotics, cocaine, and alcohol, to the abuses in the meatpacking industry so vividly portrayed in Upton Sinclair famous novel, *The Jungle*. In 1906, these efforts finally resulted in the passage of federal legislation establishing the Food and Drug Administration (FDA). The FDA act is often considered a key accomplishment of what has been called the Progressive Era of American politics.

Though this legislation creating the FDA provided the foundation for modern food and drug regulation, the original law only required that products be accurately labeled indicating their ingredients. The burden was on the FDA to demonstrate safety problems before a drug could be removed from the market. It was not until the late 1930s that the authority of the FDA was expanded. This expansion was justified by use of the interstate commerce clause since most drugs are part of commerce between two or more states.

In 1937, a Tennessee drug company producing a pediatric liquid form of sulfa, the first antibiotic precipitated the changes in FDA law. The solvent in this untested product was a highly toxic chemical related to antifreeze. Over 100 people died, mostly children. The public outcry brought Congress to action with the passage of the 1938 FDA amendments. These amendments required safety testing prior to making a new drug available to the market. The process of safety regulation soon resulted in an additional requirement that certain drugs be prescribed only by a physician, while others were available over-the-counter.

Over the years, the FDA's authority has been repeatedly increased in the wake of highly-publicized tragedies. The production and distribution of a batch of polio vaccine that itself caused polio led to the regulation of vaccines in the 1950s. The Dalkon Shield, an intrauterine device (IUD) that produced thousands of cases of infection and subsequent infertility, brought about regulations of medical devices in the mid-1970s. Perhaps the most famous U.S. disaster was the one that did not happen. In the early 1960s, FDA safety regulations resulted in a delay in approving a new, very effective sleeping pill called thalidomide. In Europe, the drug produced thousands of grossly-deformed newborns, an event which did not occur in the United States. Ironically, the thalidomide case resulted in the Kefauver-Harris Drug Amendments, which focused on efficacy, not safety, and mandated efficacy testing before a drug could be approved and marketed. This landmark legislation laid the groundwork for today's process of drug approval and for the evolution of evidence-based medicine and public health.

The authority of the FDA, however, has not continued to expand. The 1980s and 1990s produced a social movement that sought smaller government and less authority over the lives of individuals. In 1994, Congress created a new category of substances—carved from the definition of drugs—dietary supplements. These included not only vitamins and minerals, but also herbal remedies. Dietary supplements, as opposed to drugs, were subject to far less regulation. As long as they did not claim therapeutic value for specific diseases, dietary supplements could be advertised and sold without demonstrating either safety or efficacy. In parallel with the 1906 legislation, only accurate labeling was required and the burden was on the FDA to prove problems with safety.

The move back to market control also resulted from an early 1990s Supreme Court decision that allowed advertising of prescription drugs. The enormous expansion of prescription drug promotion produced a flood of direct advertisement to consumers and a rapid expansion of the quantity of prescription drugs marketed and prescribed. During this period of rapid expansion, the FDA focused on premarket regulation of the safety and efficacy of drugs. However, once approved, the FDA did not have the authority to further evaluate the drug's safety. Rare, but often serious, side effects of drugs were evident only after the drugs were prescribed to large numbers of patients in clinical practice. The short period of premarket observation also hid side effects that only appeared after longer term use. In addition, individuals included in premarket trials often had one disease and were not taking other medications. Patients with multiple diseases on multiple medications often experienced far more side effects.

Most recently, a widely-publicized tragedy has led to new legislation and approaches to regulation. Vioxx®, one of a new class of medications for pain relief and reduction in inflammation, was widely advertised and used by tens of millions of people before it was recognized that it increased the incidence of heart disease. The drug was estimated to have caused tens of thousands of deaths from heart disease. The FDA amendments of 2007 aimed to address safety issues by giving the FDA authority for the first time to require pharma-

(continues)

BOX 5-2 continued.

ceutical companies to perform postmarket data collection; by authorizing programs to utilize large national prescription databases to search for adverse drug effects; and by encouraging FDA review of direct-to-consumer drug advertising before it is seen by consumers.

The history of the FDA reflects the tension in American society between governmental efforts to regulate and efforts to allow market regulation through the choices made by individuals. This tension has been a part of the regulation of drugs, vaccines, and medical devices for over 100 years and is likely to continue to be important in coming years.

care in their constitution or have created rights to health care as part of the legislative process, usually as part of a healthcare system that provides universal coverage. This internationally recognized right to health care cannot be enforced in the United States unless it is found to be recognized by the U.S. Constitution or a state constitution or has been incorporated into federal, state, or local statutes. Therefore, we need to examine what has happened within the legal system of the United States.

As we have discussed, the U.S. Constitution does not mention the word health. Rights, however, can be "found" or created by the Supreme Court through their interpretation of the Constitution. Rights to travel and privacy, for example, have been "found" by the Supreme Court, while a right to health care has not been. State courts, such as the Supreme Court of Indiana, have addressed the meaning of a license to practice medicine in *Hurley v. Eddingfield*. In the case, a licensed physician refused services to a pregnant woman despite being offered prepayment and despite the fact that the physician knew that no other qualified physician was available. As a result, the woman did not receive medical care and both she and her unborn child died.[1] The court established what has been called the **no-duty principle**. This principle holds that healthcare providers (whether they are individuals or institutions) do not have an obligation to provide health services. A right to health care can be created within a state via its constitution. It can also be created in the United States or within a state by legislative action.[1]

Limited rights to health care have been established by legislative action. For instance, federal law includes the 1986 Treatment for Emergency Medical Conditions and Women in Labor Act, which provides a right to emergency medical care usually provided through hospital emergency departments.[c] This act establishes a right to health care by those seeking emergency services and establishes a duty on the part of hospital emergency department to provide these services.

This right and the corresponding duty, however, are quite limited. Patients have the right to receive care and the hospital has a duty to provide an "appropriate" examination. The institution also has the duty to stabilize an emergency situation by providing as much treatment as possible within its capacity. When a hospital does not have the capacity to treat the emergency condition, it is required to transfer the patient to another facility in a medically-appropriate fashion. These rights and duties are limited to emergency conditions in hospital emergency departments and do not provide more general rights to health care.[d]

Thus, a right to health care in the United States has not been generally established. As with health law and policies in general, this issue has not been definitively settled. As the state and federal governments struggle with the problems of providing health care for everyone, the right to health care is again emerging as an issue for debate and consideration. Let us now take a look at another fundamental issue that is at the core of public health law and policy—the balance between the rights of the individual and the needs of society.

How Does Public Health Balance the Rights of Individuals and the Needs of Society?

Public health interventions often create a level of tension between the concerns of individuals and the needs of society. This is the situation even when individual rights are not involved. For instance, the courts have been clear that a driver's license is a privilege and not a right. Thus, it can be regulated by states without having to justify that individuals who are denied a driver's license are being denied a right. The regulation of driver's licenses is a state responsibility and as such there is

_____

[c] This act is often referred to as EMTALA which is an acronym for the law's original name—the Emergency Medical Treatment and Active Labor Act.

[d] Another example of legislation that has established rights to health care is the Medicaid program. Medicaid establishes defined criteria for eligibility to enroll that are partially governed by federal law and partially by state law, as we will discuss in Chapter 11. During the time that an individual is qualified for Medicaid, they have certain rights to health care that can be enforced by individuals in the courts.

enormous variation in factors such as age requirement, the length and requirement for learning permits, the type of examination required, the rules for suspension of a driver's license, and requirements for renewal of a driver's license.

Motor vehicle injuries remain a major cause of death and disability. It is widely accepted that there are two age groups at highest risk of death and disability from motor vehicles. The first are adolescents during their initial years of driving and the second are elderly individuals. Until recently, most states imposed minimum or no barriers to either group once an initial driver's license had been issued. In many states, these limitations have now been imposed for one or both age groups. Possible public health interventions include raising the driving age, requiring stricter standards for licensure, and placing initial limitations on new drivers including restricting night time driving, the number of passengers, and the use of cell phones. Common restrictions on older drivers include vision and hearing tests and reexamination including road testing.

The tension level between the individual and society is even greater when fundamental rights are denied as is the case with the use of quarantine. Box 5-3 examines the historical and current uses of quarantine.[8]

The dynamic between individual and societal needs is also key to understanding most bioethical issues. The modern field of bioethics grew out of the efforts to protect participants in research, while ensuring that society can benefit from the results of ethical human research. Let us look at how these standards developed and how research subjects are protected today.

How Can Bioethical Principles Be Applied to Protecting Individuals Who Participate in Research?

Ethical issues pervade nearly every aspect of public health and medical practice. However, ethical considerations have had an especially strong impact on the conduct of research. The mod-

---

BOX 5-3   Quarantine as a Public Health Authority.

Quarantine, the compulsory physical separation of those with a disease—or at high risk of developing a disease—from the rest of the population goes back to ancient times when it was used to restrict entry of ships into ports where epidemic diseases threatened. Attempts to control epidemics of yellow fever, smallpox, and other infectious disease by quarantine were very much a part of the early history of the United States.

In the 19th century, tuberculosis (TB) sanatoriums often isolated those afflicted on a voluntary basis. Laws existed and were occasionally used that allowed quarantine of patients who felt well though were thought to be carriers of TB and other contagious diseases, such as typhoid. The infamous "Typhoid Mary" was quarantined on an island in New York after she refused to voluntarily refrain from working as a food handler.

Quarantine was only occasionally used to control disease in the 20th century. However, in the early 21st century it again became a public health issue precipitated by the recognition of SARS and the fear of rapid global spread of SARS and other communicable diseases. The spread of resistant and extremely resistant tuberculosis has again made use of quarantine for TB an ongoing important public health issue.

Quarantine laws are in the process of revision. The issues of quarantine reflect many of the tensions between the right of the individual and the rights of society. For instance, a recent *New England Journal of Medicine* article on use of quarantine for control of extremely resistant TB states:

> In recent decades, courts have clarified the legal rights of patients with tuberculosis who are subject to compulsory isolation. Drawing an analogy between isolation orders and civil commitment for mental illness, courts have affirmed that patients who are isolated by law have many procedural due-process rights, including the right to counsel and a hearing before an independent decision maker. States must also provide "clear and convincing" evidence that isolation is necessary to prevent a significant risk of harm to others. Most important, some courts have held that isolation must be the least restrictive alternative for preventing such a risk. If the government can protect public health without relying on involuntary detention, it must and should do so."[8]

The use of quarantine is thus likely to be restricted and used very infrequently in the future. Increasingly, the emphasis on the rights of the individual outweighs any value that quarantine might have in protecting the public's health.

ern field of bioethics in general and research ethics in particular grew out of the Nuremberg trials of German physicians who performed experiments on prisoners in Nazi concentration camps. These crimes included exposure to extremes of temperature, mutilating surgery, and deliberate infection with a variety of lethal germs. The report of the Nuremberg trials established internationally-accepted principles known as the Nuremberg Code shown in Box 5-4.[9]

Abuse of individuals participating in research has not been limited to victims of Nazi concentration camps. In the United States from the late 1930s through the early 1970s, the Tuskegee Syphilis Study used disadvantaged, rural black men to study the untreated course of syphilis. These men were recruited to a study of "bad blood," and were misled into believing that they were receiving effective treatment; in addition, they were provided deceptive information in order to retain them in the study. These subjects were deprived of penicillin treatment in order not to interrupt the research, long after such treatment became generally available for syphilis. The Tuskegee Study was a major reason for the creation of The National Commission for the Protection of Human Subjects of Biomedical and Behavioral Research, which produced what has come to be called the **Belmont Report.** The Belmont Report focused on the key issues of defining informed consent and selection of participants and led to the development of **Institutional Review Boards** (**IRBs**), which now must approve most human research. The report remains a vital part of the framework for defining the rights of research subjects.[10] The followed excerpts outline three basic ethical principles:

1. **Respect for Persons**—Respect for persons incorporates at least two ethical convictions: first, individuals should be treated as autonomous agents, and second, that persons with diminished autonomy are entitled to protection. The principle of respect for persons thus divides into two separate moral requirements: the requirement to acknowledge autonomy and the requirement to protect those with diminished autonomy.
2. **Beneficence**—Persons are treated in an ethical manner not only by respecting their decisions and protecting them from harm, but also by making efforts to secure their well-being. Such treatment falls under the

---

BOX 5-4 **The Ten Principles Contained in the Nuremberg Code.**

1. The voluntary consent of the human subject is absolutely essential....
2. The experiment should be such as to yield fruitful results for the good of society, unprocurable by other methods or means of study, and not random and unnecessary in nature.
3. The experiment should be so designed and based on the results of animal experimentation and knowledge of the natural history of the disease or other problem under study that the anticipated results will justify the performance of the experiment.
4. The experiment should be so conducted as to avoid all unnecessary physical and mental suffering and injury.
5. No experiment should be conducted where there is an a priori reason to believe that death or disabling injury will occur; except, perhaps, in those experiments where the experimental physicians also serve as subjects.
6. The degree of risk to be taken should never exceed that determined by the humanitarian importance of the problem to be solved by the experiment.
7. Proper preparations should be made and adequate facilities provided to protect the experimental subject against even remote possibilities of injury, disability, or death.
8. The experiment should be conducted only by scientifically qualified persons. The highest degree of skill and care should be required through all stages of the experiment of those who conduct or engage in the experiment.
9. During the course of the experiment the human subject should be at liberty to bring the experiment to an end if he has reached the physical or mental state where continuation of the experiment seems to him to be impossible.
10. During the course of the experiment the scientist in charge must be prepared to terminate the experiment at any stage, if he has probable cause to believe, in the exercise of the good faith, superior skill and careful judgment required of him that a continuation of the experiment is likely to result in injury, disability, or death to the experimental subject.

Source: United States Government. Trials of War Criminals before the Nuremberg Military Tribunals under Control Council Law No. 10, Vol. 2. Washington, DC: U.S. Government Printing Office; 1949: 181–182.

principle of beneficence. . . . Two general rules have been formulated as complementary expressions of beneficent actions in this sense: (1) do no harm and (2) maximize possible benefits and minimize possible harms.

3. **Justice**—Who ought to receive the benefits of research and bear its burdens? This is a question of justice, in the sense of fairness in distribution or what is deserved. An injustice occurs when some benefit to which a person is entitled is denied without good reason or when some burden is imposed unduly. Another way of conceiving the principle of justice is that equals ought to be treated equally.

Institutional Review Boards were created to ensure the ethical conduct of research. The code of federal regulations outlines the following key roles that the Institutional Review Board is expected to play. In order to approve research, the IRB shall determine that all of the following requirements are satisfied:[11]

1. Risks to subjects are minimized.
2. Risks to subjects are reasonable in relation to anticipated benefits.
3. Selection of subjects is equitable.
4. Informed consent will be sought from each prospective subject or the subject's legally-authorized representative.
5. The research plan makes adequate provision for monitoring the data collected to ensure the safety of subjects.
6. When appropriate, there are adequate provisions to protect the privacy of subjects and to maintain the confidentiality of data.
7. When some or all of the subjects are likely to be vulnerable to coercion or undue influence, such as children, prisoners, pregnant women, mentally disabled persons, or economically or educationally disadvantaged persons, additional safeguards have been included in the study to protect the rights and welfare of these subjects.

We have come a long way from the days when human research was conducted without informed consent on individuals who could be coerced to participate. The standards of research, however, continue to evolve and will most likely continue to change through identification of ethical limitations of current studies.[e]

We have now examined key principles of health law, policy, and ethics and their applications to issues in health care, public health, and bioethics. These principles are key tools, along with health informatics, health communications, as well as the social and behavioral sciences, and can be considered options for implementation when striving to achieve the goals of public health. They are especially powerful tools because they often carry with them the compulsory authority of government. The police powers of public health are increasingly being used cautiously and with careful consideration of the rights of individuals. In many ways, the use of laws is seen as a last resort when provision of information and incentives for change has not been successful. Now that we have examined key tools of population health, let us turn our attention in Section III to efforts to prevent disease, disability, and death for non-communicable diseases, communicable disease, and environmental health and safety.

---

[e] Recent changes in research ethics include limitations on the use of placebos and requirements to register randomized clinical trials before they begin. Placebos are now considered ethical only when no effective active intervention is accepted as the standard of care. The requirement to register randomized clinical trials before they begin was put into effect after randomized clinical trials came to public attention that were never submitted for publication because the results were in conflict with the interests of the trial's sponsor.

Key Words

- Bioethics
- Police power
- Rights
- Negative constitution
- Substantive due process
- Procedural due process
- Authoritative decision
- Social justice
- Market justice
- No-duty principle
- The Belmont Report
- Institutional Review Boards (IRBs)
- Respect for Persons
- Beneficence
- Justice

Discussion Questions

Take a look at the questions posed in the following scenarios which were presented at the beginning of this chapter. See now whether you can answer them.

1. *A new statute and subsequent administrative regulations give only a temporary license to newly-licensed drivers, prohibiting late night driving and the use of cell phones and limiting the number of passengers. You ask: should elderly drivers be subject to these same types of regulations, such as being required to take a driver's test?*

2. *You decide not to enroll in the health plan offered by your employer because it seems so expensive and you are young and healthy. Shortly thereafter, your car is struck by a hit-and-run driver and you find yourself on the way to the nearest hospital. After stabilizing you as required by law, they transfer you to the public hospital, which is the only one in town that will take care of you without insurance. You ask: do you have a right to health care?*

3. *You hear that a new drug has shown extremely promising results, but will not be available for a least a couple of years. You wonder: why do you have to wait so long to take the newest prescription medicine while your e-mail fills up with promotions for the untested ways to enhance your energy, beauty, and sexual performance?*

4. *You hear that a neighbor has TB and refuses treatment. You wonder: what if he has the type of TB that can't be cured with drugs? You ask: can't they make him take his medicine or at least get him out of your neighborhood?*

5. *You hear an advertisement about participating in a new research study. It sounds like you're eligible, so you check into it. You're surprised to find that even if you participate you may not receive the new drug and won't even be told which treatment you are receiving. Despite your willingness to take your chances, you're told that you are* not eligible for the study due to conditions that put you at increased risk of developing side effects. You ask: why can't I participate if I'm willing to take the risks?

REFERENCES

1. Teitelbaum JB, Wilensky SE. *Essentials of Health Policy and Law.* Sudbury, MA: Jones and Bartlett Publishers; 2007.

2. Gostin LA. *Public Health Law: Power, Duty, Restraint.* Berkeley and New York: University of California Press and Milbank Memorial Fund; 2000.

3. Turnock BJ. *Public Health: What It Is and How It Works.* 4th ed. Sudbury, MA: Jones and Bartlett Publishers; 2009.

4. Teitelbaum JB, Wilensky SE. *Essentials of Health Policy and Law.* Sudbury, MA: Jones and Bartlett Publishers; 2007: 12.

5. Shi L, Singh D. *Delivering Health Care in America.* 3rd ed. Sudbury, MA: Jones and Bartlett Publishers; 2004.

6. United States Food and Drug Administration. FDA History. Available at: http://www.fda.gov/oc/history/default.htm. Accessed March 18, 2009.

7. United Nations General Assembly. The Universal Declaration of Human Rights. Available at: http://www.un.org/Overview/rights.html. Accessed March 18, 2009.

8. Parmet WE. Legal power and legal rights—isolation and quarantine in the case of drug-resistant tuberculosis. *New England Journal Medicine* 2007; 357: 434.

9. United States Government. Trials of War Criminals before the Nuremberg Military Tribunals under Control Council Law No. 10, Vol. 2. Washington, DC: U.S. Government Printing Office; 1949: 181–182.

10. The National Commission for the Protection of Human Subjects of Biomedical and Behavioral Research. The Belmont Report: Ethical Principles and Guidelines for the Protection of Human Subjects of Research. Available at: http://ohsr.od.nih.gov/guidelines/belmont.html. Accessed March, 2009.

11. United States Department of Health and Human Services. Title 45 Public Welfare Department of Health and Human Services, Part 46 Protection of Human Subjects. Available at: http://www.hhs.gov/ohrp/humansubjects/guidance/45cfr46.htm. Accessed March 18, 2009.

Section II:
Cases and Discussion Questions

Don's Diabetes

Don had been a diabetic for over a decade and took his insulin pretty much as the doctor ordered. Every morning, after checking his blood sugar levels, he would adjust his insulin dose according to the written instructions. From the beginning, Don's doctor worried about the effect of the diabetes—he ordered tests, adjusted dosages and prescriptions, and sent his patient to the ophthalmologist for assessment and laser treatment to prevent blindness.

It was the amputation of his right foot that really got Don's attention. Don wasn't exactly athletic, but he did play a round of golf once in a while. He first noticed a little scratch on his foot after a day on the golf course. It wasn't until a week later that he noticed the swelling and the redness in his foot and an ulceration that was forming. He was surprised that his foot didn't hurt, but the doctor informed him that diabetic foot ulcers often don't cause pain. That's part of the problem with diabetes—you lose your sensation in your feet.

After six months of receiving treatment on a weekly basis, a decision had to be made. "There isn't any choice," his doctor said, "the foot infection is spreading and if we don't amputate the foot, we might have to amputate to the knee or even higher." So after describing the potential benefits and harms of the surgery and asking whether there were any questions, the doctor asked Don to sign a form. The next morning, Don's leg was amputated above the ankle leaving him with a stump in place of a foot.

The surgeon came to Don's room the day after surgery to take a look at his amputation. "Beautiful work," he said with a big smile on his face. Maybe it was a beautiful stump, Don thought to himself, but it doesn't work like my old foot. At first, he felt sorry for himself—thinking of what lay ahead to literally get back on his feet.

The physical therapist who visited Don in the hospital told him, "You got off lucky—now, are you going to take control or let diabetes control you?" But, diabetes was already controlling him, Don thought to himself—daily insulin, blood sugar testing, weekly trips to the doctor, and now despite it all—an amputated foot. "Diabetes is a bad disease," his doctor told him. "We're doing everything we can do and you're still experiencing complications."

Maybe the doctors were doing everything they could, but Don wondered what else was possible. He enrolled in a self-help group for diabetics. They shared stories of medical care, new advances in diabetes management, and their own frustrations with the disease and with their medical care. Don realized he had received good medical care, but he also acknowledged that good care by good doctors is not enough. There needs to be a system that makes the pieces work together, but there also needs to be a patient who takes charge of his care.

So take charge, he did. He worked closely with the practice's physician assistant and nurse practitioner, who were experts in diabetic management. He learned how to interpret his blood tests and how they were useful for day-to-day monitoring of his disease. He also learned about hemoglobin A1c blood tests, which measure how well his diabetes is doing over periods of months. After several months, his clinicians taught him how to adjust his dose of insulin to accommodate for changes in his routine or during minor illnesses. They always let him know that care was available and that he did not need to make decisions all by himself. Don also learned to examine his feet and how to prevent minor injuries from turning into major problems. His sporadic eye doctor appointments turned into regular question-and-answer sessions comparing the most recent photographs of his retina to those from the past.

Don found himself keeping his own records to be sure that he had them all in one place—fearing that one doctor would not talk to another and that the records in one office or one hospital would never make their way to the next. Don's fears were well-founded when his kidney function began to deteriorate and his primary care doctor sent him to a kidney specialist, who sent him to a transplant surgeon, and then to a vascular surgeon to prepare him for dialysis. Sure enough, the only records the dialysis doctors could rely upon were the ones that Don had kept on his own.

Soon the dialysis doctor told Don that he had a tough decision to make. Did he want to come into the dialysis center for half a day twice a week where they take care of everything or did he want to learn home dialysis and take care of this treatment on his own? Don had lots of questions. He needed to understand what each dialysis scenario entailed and the advantages and disadvantages of both options, including the costs and discomforts. He also wanted to know about any other potential treatments. Don asked questions of his doctors, learned as much as he could about dialysis on the Internet, and outlined the pros and cons of home dialysis. After that, is was an easy decision for Don. "Sure, I'll learn how to do it myself. I want to be in charge of my own care. I want to stand on my own two feet," he told the doctor without a moment's hesitation.

Discussion Questions

1. What type of decision-making process was going on during the early stages of Don's diabetes? Explain.
2. What type of decision-making process was used to reach the decision to have an amputation? Explain.
3. What type of decision-making process occurred in the decision about dialysis? Explain.
4. In Don's case, what are the advantages and disadvantages of each of these approaches to decision making from both the patient and the clinician's perspective? Explain.

José and Jorge—Identical Twins without Identical Lives

José and Jorge were identical twins separated at birth. José grew up in a large family in an impoverished slum in the middle of a crime-ridden and polluted district of a major city. Jorge grew up in an upper-middle-class professional family with one other brother in a suburban community in the same city. Despite the fact the José and Jorge were identical twins, their lives and health could not have been more different.

José had few opportunities for medical care or public health services as a child. His nutrition was always marginal and he developed several severe cases of diarrhea before he was one year of age. He received a polio vaccine as part of a community vaccination program, but never received vaccinations for measles, mumps, rubella, or other childhood illnesses. At age four, he developed measles and was so sick his mother was sure he would not make it.

As a child, José developed asthma which seemed to worsen when he played outdoors on hot smoggy days. Dropping out of school at age 14, José went to work in a factory, but quit when he found himself panting for breath at the end of the day.

As a teenager José was repeatedly exposed to crime and drugs. Once, he was caught in the crossfire of gangs fighting for control of drugs in his community. Experimenting with drugs with his teenage friends, José contracted HIV from use of contaminated needles. José did not know he had HIV until he was nearly 30 years old and developed tuberculosis (TB). He did receive treatment for the TB free-of-charge from the health department, but once he felt better he didn't follow-up with treatment.

By the time the TB returned, José had lost 30 pounds and could barely make it into the emergency room of the public hospital because of his shortness of breath. He was hospitalized for the last two months of his life, mostly to prevent others from being exposed to what was now drug-resistant tuberculosis. No one ever knew how many people José exposed to HIV or TB.

Jorge's life as a child was far less eventful. He received "well child" care from an early age. His family hardly noticed that he rarely developed diarrhea and had few sick days from "diseases of childhood." He did well in school, but like José, he developed asthma. With good treatment, Jorge was able to play on sports teams at least until he began to smoke cigarettes at age 14.

Jorge soon began to gain weight and by the time he graduated from college was rapidly becoming obese. In his twenties, he developed high blood pressure, and in his 30s he had early signs of diabetes. Jorge had a heart attack in his mid 40s and underwent bypass surgery a few years later. The treatments for diabetes, hypertension, and high cholesterol worked well and Jorge was able to lead a productive professional life into his 40s.

By the time that Jorge turned 50, his diabetes began to worsen and he developed progressive kidney disease. Jorge soon needed twice-a-week dialysis, which kept him alive as he awaited a kidney transplant.

Discussion Questions

1. How do social and economic factors contribute to the different disease patterns of José and Jorge?
2. How do factors in the physical environmental explain differences in the health of José and Jorge?
3. What role does medical care play in the differences between the health outcomes of José and Jorge?
4. What roles do public health services play in the health outcomes of José and Jorge?

Changing Behavior—Cigarette Smoking

It wasn't going to be easy for Steve to stop smoking. He had been at it for 30 years—ever since he took it up on a dare at age 16 and found that it was a good way to socialize. In his 20s, it seemed to make dealing with the work pressure easier and in those days you could smoke in your office and didn't even need to shut the door—much less deal with those dirty looks he was getting now.

Steve always was confident that he could take them or leave them. He'd quit when he was good and ready and a few cigarettes couldn't hurt. But, then he talked to some friends who had quit for a decade or more and said they'd go back in a minute if they thought cigarettes were safe. Maybe for some people those cravings just never go away, he worried to himself. However, there was that bout of walking pneumonia and then the cough that just didn't seem to go away. The cough was so bad that he had trouble smoking more than a few cigarettes a day. The physician assistant let him know that these symptoms were early warning signs of things to come, however Steve just wasn't ready to stop. So, the physician assistant gave him a fact sheet and let Steve know there was help available when he was ready.

It might have been his fears about his 10-year-old son that finally tipped the scales. "Daddy, those cigarettes are bad for you," or maybe it was when he found cigarette butts in the backyard after his 16-year-old daughter's birthday party. Steve knew enough to believe that a father who smokes has a child who smokes. So this time he would do it right.

Steve's physician assistant recognized that Steve was finally ready to quit. He let him know in no uncertain terms that it was important to quit totally, completely, and forever. He also informed Steve that he could rely on help—that he was not alone. With the encouragement of his physician assistant, Steve joined a support group and set a quit date and announced it to his friends and family. The new medication he was prescribed seemed to relieve the worst cravings and the feeling he called "crawling the walls."

His wife Dorothy was supportive. She cleared the cigarette butts and ashtrays out of the house and dealt with the smell by having all the drapes cleaned. She also helped by getting him up after dinner and taking a walk, which kept him from his old habit of having a cigarette with dessert and coffee. It also helped keep him from gaining too much weight, which she confided was her greatest fear. Dorothy's quiet encouragement and subtle reinforcement without nagging worked wonders when Steve needed them the most.

Saving a couple of dollars a day didn't hurt. Steve collected those dollars and put them in a special hiding place. On his first year anniversary of quitting, he wrapped up the dollar bills in a box and gave them to Dorothy as a present. The note inside said: "A trip for us for as long as the money lasts." Dorothy was delighted, but feared the worst when Steve began to open up his present to himself. As he unwrapped a box of cigars, he smiled a big smile and said, "I'm congratulating myself on quitting smoking."

Discussion Questions

1. How are each of the phases of the stages of behavioral change model illustrated in Steve's case?
2. Which techniques for successful cigarette cessation are illustrated in Steve's case?
3. Which effective public health (or population) approaches does this case illustrate?
4. What is the impact of combining individual clinical approaches and public health (or population) approaches?

The Elderly Driver

It was late in the afternoon on a sunny April day. Maybe it was the sun in her eyes, but 82-year-old Janet found herself in her car in a ditch at the side of the road, unsure of how she got there. Once at the hospital, her son and daughter joined her and heard the good news that Janet had escaped with just a broken arm. The police report strongly suggested that she had swerved off the road, but it was not clear why.

This was not Janet's first driving "episode"; in fact, her driving had been a constant worry to her daughter for over two years. Her daughter often offered to take her Mom shopping and insisted that she do the driving when they were together. "Don't you trust me?" was the only thanks the daughter received. When alone, Janet continued to drive herself, staying off the freeway and increasingly driving only during the day. She knew it wasn't as easy as it used to be, but it was her lifeline to independence.

Then, a few months after the April accident, the form for Janet's license renewal arrived. A vision test and a physical exam were required, along with a doctor's certification that Janet was in good health and capable of driving; however, no road test was required. So Janet made a doctor's appointment and at the end of it she left the forms with a note for the doctor saying, "To the best doctor I've ever had. Thanks for filling this out. You know how much driving means to me."

On Janet's way home from the doctor's office, it happened. She was driving down the road when suddenly she was crossing that yellow line and heading toward an oncoming car. The teenage driver might have been going a little fast, but Janet was in the wrong lane and the head-on collision killed the 16-year-old passenger in the front seat who was not wearing a seatbelt. The 18-year-old driver walked way from the accident unharmed, thanks to an inflated airbag.

Janet was never the same emotionally. And despite escaping the accident with just a few bruises, the loss of her driver's license symbolized the end for her. Those lost weekly shopping trips and the strangers in the Assisted Living Center were not the same as living in her own home. The young man in the accident screaming for help woke her up almost every night. It was only a year after the accident when Janet died, and it was just like she had said: "Take my license away and it will kill me."

Discussion Questions

1. How does this case reflect the important issue of balancing the legal rights of the individual and the rights of society as a whole?
2. What role do you believe healthcare providers should play in implementing driving laws and regulations?
3. Identify any changes you would make to prevent the types of outcomes that occurred in this case study.
4. How would you communicate the lessons learned in this case to new and inexperienced drivers?

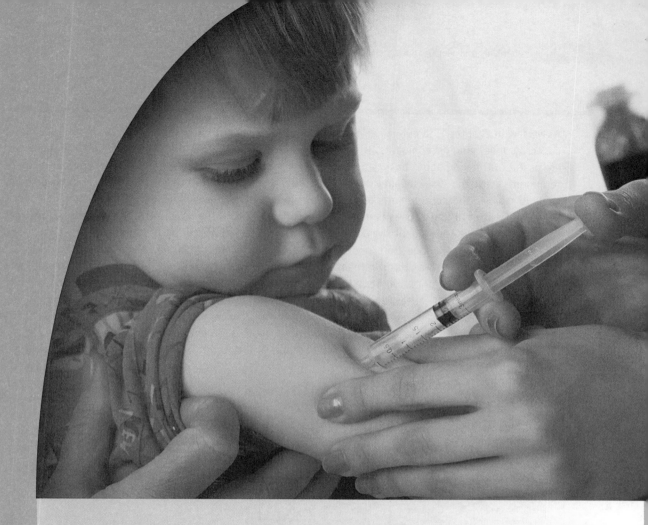

SECTION III

Preventing Disease, Disability, and Death

As we saw in Chapter 1, in public health we are increasingly identifying disease, disability, and death as being produced by underlying determinants, which we organized using the BIG GEMS mnemonic. While these determinants are useful in thinking about basic reasons for disease and disability, it is often difficult to link the underlying determinants with the diseases and disabilities that result. As we discussed in chapter 1 with asthma, at times many or most of the determinants of disease play a role in the development of a disease.

The concept of **actual causes** is more closely connected with the development of disease. It provides a way of organizing what we know about the prevention of disease and disability into categories that we can measure. Thus, it allows us to ask a key question: how much disease and disability can be prevented?[1] Actual causes of disease can then be linked to three basic categories: non-communicable diseases, communicable diseases, and environmental diseases and injuries. Figure 3-A illustrates the framework we will use in this section to connect determinants of disease, actual causes, and categories of disease and injury.

The concept of actual causes of disease is a relatively new concept which has been successfully applied to the causes of death, though not to disability. Table 3-A provides the most recent data on the actual causes of death. It indicates that nearly half of all deaths in the United States are related to nine potentially preventable actual causes.[a]

The concept of actual causes of disease provides us with a framework for thinking about the underlying problems that lead to death. As indicated in the table, nearly half of all deaths can be ascribed to one of these actual causes. Actual causes can help guide us in placing priorities on where we should put our attention and spend our money to prevent disease.

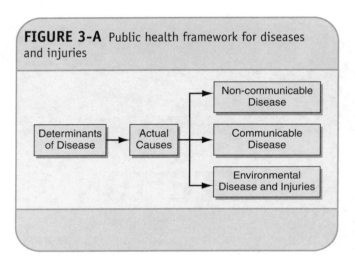

FIGURE 3-A Public health framework for diseases and injuries

---

[a] Causes of death on death certificates have traditionally been defined in terms of specific diseases that have been formally incorporated with thousands of listings in the International Code of Diseases (ICD codes). This coding system includes a wide range of specific diseases, as well as injuries and other conditions. These items are then categorized based upon organ system or another biological framework.

TABLE 3-A Actual Causes of Death in the United States

Actual Cause	Number of Deaths
Tobacco	435,000
Diet and Physical Inactivity	400,000
Alcohol consumption	85,000
Microbial agents (infections)	75,000
Toxic agents	55,000
Motor vehicles	43,000
Firearms	29,000
Sexual behavior	20,000
Illicit drug use	17,000
Total	**1,159,000 (total deaths = 2,403,351)**

Source: Data from: Mokdad AM, Marks JS, Stroup DF, Gerberding JL. Actual causes of death in the United States 2000. *JAMA.* 2004; 291: 1238–1245.

A substantial portion of the actual causes of death are related to the development of non-communicable disease including tobacco, diet and physical inactivity, alcohol and illicit drug use. Communicable disease remains an important category related not only to microbial agents, but also to sexual behavior. Finally, a broad range of environmental diseases and injuries are related to toxic agents, motor vehicle- and firearm-related injuries. In Chapters 6, 7, and 8, we will address non-communicable and communicable diseases, and environmental health and injury and examine the public health strategies that have been used to address them. We will aim to better understand the burden of disease and strategies for addressing it. Let us begin with the largest category of disease in the United States today—non-communicable diseases.

Key Words

- Actual causes

REFERENCES

1. Mokdad AM, Marks JS, Stroup DF, Gerberding JL. Actual causes of death in the United States 2000. *JAMA*. 2004; 291: 1238–1245.

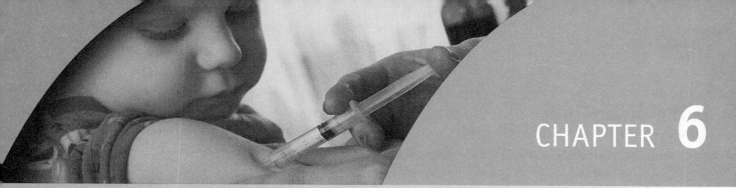

CHAPTER 6

Non-Communicable Diseases

LEARNING OBJECTIVES

By the end of this chapter the student will be able to:

- describe the burden of non-communicable diseases on mortality and morbidity in the United States.
- describe the epidemiological transition and the current distribution of disease in developed and developing countries.
- describe the ideal criteria for a screening program.
- explain the multiple risk factor intervention approach to control of a non-communicable disease.
- describe the meaning of cost-effectiveness.
- describe several ways that genetic interventions can affect the burden of non-communicable diseases.
- describe ways that population interventions can be combined with individual interventions to more effectively reduce the burden of non-communicable diseases.

Sasha didn't want to think about the possibility of breast cancer, but as she turned 50 she agreed to have a mammography which, as she feared, was positive or "suspicious," as her doctor put it. Waiting for the results of the follow-up biopsy was the worst part, but the relief she felt when the results were negative brought tears of joy to her and her family. Then she wondered: is it common to have a positive mammography when no cancer is present?

The first sign of Michael's coronary heart disease was his heart attack. Looking back, he had been at high risk for many years since he smoked, had high blood pressure, and high cholesterol. His lack of exercise and obesity only made the situation worse. Michael asked: what are the risk factors for coronary heart disease and what can be done to identify and address these factors for himself and his family?

John's knee injury from skiing continued to produce swelling and pain, greatly limiting his activities. His physician informed him

that the standard procedure today is to look inside with a flexible scope and do any surgery that is needed through the scope. It's simpler, cheaper, and does not even require hospitalization. "We call it 'cost-effective,'" his doctor said. John wondered: what does cost effective really mean?

Jennifer and her husband George were tested for the cystic fibrosis gene and both were found to have it. Cystic fibrosis causes chronic lung infections and greatly shortens the length of life. They now ask: what does this mean for our chances of having a child with cystic fibrosis? Can we find out whether our child has cystic fibrosis early in pregnancy?

Fred's condition deteriorated slowly, but persistently. He just couldn't remember anything and repeated himself endlessly. The medications helped for a short time, but before long he didn't recognize his family and couldn't take care of himself. The diagnosis was Alzheimer's and he was not alone. Almost everyone in the nursing home seemed to be affected. No one seems to understand the cause of Alzheimer's disease. The family asked: what else can be done, not only for Fred, but for those who come after Fred?

Alcohol use is widespread on your campus. You don't see it as a problem as long as you walk home or have a designated driver. Your mind changes one day after you hear about a classmate who nearly died from alcohol poisoning as a result of binge drinking. You ask yourself: what should be done on my campus to address binge drinking?

Each of these scenarios represents one of the approaches to non-communicable diseases that we will examine in this chapter.

WHAT IS THE BURDEN OF NON-COMMUNICABLE DISEASE?

Non-communicable disease represents a wide range of diseases from cardiovascular disease, to cancers, to depression, Alzheimer's, and chronic arthritis. Together, they represent the majority of causes of death and disability in most developed countries. Today, cardiovascular diseases and cancer alone each represent nearly 25 percent of the causes of death as reflected on death certificates in the United States.

The impact of non-communicable diseases on death only reflects part of the impact. Chronic disabilities, largely due to non-communicable diseases, are now the most rapidly growing component of morbidity in most developing as well as developed countries. As populations age, non-communicable diseases increase in frequency. The presence of two or more chronic diseases makes progressive disability particularly likely. The consequences of the rapidly growing pattern of disability due to non-communicable diseases has enormous economic implications. The great increase in direct costs for health care is in part due to the increased burden of non-communicable diseases. The impact extends beyond healthcare costs as it affects the quality of life and may limit the ability of those who wish to work to continue to do so.

Non-communicable diseases have not always dominated the types of diseases which impact a society. Box 6-1 discusses the **epidemiological transition**[1] and provides a perspective on where we stand today.

There are a wide range of preventive, curative, and rehabilitative approaches to non-communicable diseases. However, there are a limited number of basic strategies being used that are part of the population health approach including:

- screening for early detection and treatment of disease
- multiple risk factor interventions
- identification of cost effective treatments
- genetics counseling and intervention
- research

We will take a look at each of these approaches. Finally, we will see how many of these approaches can be combined using the population health approach. Let us begin with what we call **screening** for disease.

BOX 6-1　The Epidemiological Transition and Non-Communicable Diseases.

Disease patterns have not always been the same and will continue to evolve. To gain a big picture understanding of this process of change, it is useful to understand the concept known as the epidemiological or public health transition.

The epidemiological transition describes the changing pattern of disease that has been seen in many countries as they have experienced social and economic development. Its central message is that prior to social and economic development, communicable diseases—or microbial agents using the term from actual causes—represent the dominant cause of disease and disability. In countries in early stages of development, infections are a key cause of mortality either directly or indirectly. For instance, in undeveloped countries maternal and perinatal conditions, as well as nutritional disorders, are often identified as the causes of death. Microbial agents play a key role in maternal and perinatal deaths, as well as deaths ascribed to nutrition. Most maternal deaths are due to infection not necessarily transmitted from others, but related to exposure to microbial agents at the time of birth and in the early postpartum period.

Similarly, most deaths among young children in undeveloped countries are related directly or indirectly to infection. Inadequate nutrition predisposes children to infection and interferes with their ability to fight off infection when it does occur. Many of the deaths among children with malnutrition are related to acute infections, especially acute infectious diarrhea and acute respiratory infections.

As social and economic development progresses, non-communicable diseases including cardiovascular diseases, diabetes, cancers, chronic respiratory ailments, and neuropsychiatric diseases, such as depression and Alzheimer's, predominate as the causes of disability and death. Depression is rapidly becoming one of the major causes of disability and the World Health Organization (WHO) estimates that it will produce more disability than any other single condition in coming years. In addition, illicit drug use has become a major cause of death among the young and includes not only illegal use of drugs, but also abuse of prescription drugs.

In much of the developing world, the same basic patterns are occurring in the developing regions within these countries. Often, earlier distributions of disease dominated by communicable diseases coexist with patterns of non-communicable disease typical of developed countries. Thus, is it not unusual to find that malnutrition and obesity are often present side-by-side in the same developing country.

The epidemiologic transition does not imply that once countries reach the stage where non-communicable diseases dominate that this pattern will persist indefinitely. Newly-emerging diseases, such as HIV/AIDS, pandemic flu, and drug-resistant bacterial infections, raise the possibility that communicable diseases will once again dominate the pattern of disease and death in developed countries.

HOW CAN SCREENING FOR DISEASE ADDRESS THE BURDEN OF NON-COMMUNICABLE DISEASES?

Screening for disease implies the use of tests on individuals who do not have symptoms of a specific disease. These individuals are **asymptomatic**. This implies that he or she does not have symptoms related to the disease being investigated. He or she may have symptoms of other diseases. Screening for disease can result in detection of disease at an early stage under the assumption that early detection will allow for treatment that will improve outcome. Screening has been successful for a range of non-communicable diseases including breast cancer and colon cancer, as well as childhood conditions, including vision and hearing impairments. In all of these conditions, screening has resulted in reduced disability and/or deaths. Not all non-communicable diseases, however, are good candidates for screening and in some cases screening programs have yet to be devised and studied for some non-communicable diseases for which early detection could be useful.

Four criteria need to be fulfilled for an ideal screening program.[2] While few, if any, health conditions completely fulfill all four requirements, these criteria provide a standard against which to judge the potential of a screening program. These criteria are:

1. The disease produces substantial death and/or disability.
2. Early detection is possible and improves outcome.
3. There is a feasible testing strategy for screening.
4. Screening is acceptable in terms of harms, costs, and patient acceptance.

The first criterion is perhaps the easiest to evaluate. Conditions, such as breast and colon cancer, result in substantial death and disability rates. Breast cancer is the second-most common cancer in terms of causes of death and is the most common cancer-related cause of death among women in their 50s. Colon cancer is among the most common causes of cancer death in both men and women. Childhood conditions, such as hearing loss and visual impairment, are not always obvious, however they cause considerable disability.

Determining whether early detection is possible and will improve outcomes is not as easy as it might appear. Screening may result in early detection, but if effective treatment is not available it may merely alert the clinician and the patient to the disease at an earlier point in time without offering hope of an improved outcome. Screening cigarette smokers for lung cancer using X-rays would seem reasonable because lung cancer is the number one cancer killer of both men and women. However, X-ray screening of smokers has been beneficial only in terms of early detection. By the time lung cancer can be seen via chest X-ray, it is already too late to cure. This early detection without improved outcome is called **lead-time bias**.[a]

As indicated in the third criteria, in order to implement a successful screening program, there must be a feasible testing strategy.[b] This usually requires identification of a high-risk population. It also requires a strategy for using two or more tests to distinguish what are called **false positives** and **false negatives** from those who truly have and do not have the disease. False positives are individuals who have positive results on a screening test but do not turn out to have the disease. Similarly, false negatives are those who have negative results on the screening test but turn out to have the disease.

How can we develop feasible testing strategies?[3] To understand the need for and use of feasible testing strategies, it is important to recognize that screening for diseases is usually conducted on groups that are at an increased risk for the condition. For instance, screening men and women for colon cancer and women for breast cancer is often conducted on people aged 50 years and older. This type of group is considered high-risk usually with a chance or risk of having the disease being 1 percent or more. Use of high-risk groups like these allows tests that are less than perfect to serve as initial screening tests.

For instance, mammography has a substantial number of false positives and false negatives. A 50-year-old woman with a positive mammography has only about a 10 to 15 percent chance of having breast cancer. That is, most of the initial positive results will turn out to be false positives.[c]

Therefore, screening for diseases such as breast cancer almost always requires two or more tests. These tests need to be combined using a testing strategy. The most commonly used testing strategy is called **sequential testing** or **two-stage testing**. This approach implies that an initial screening test is followed by one or more definitive or diagnostic test. Sequen-

---

[a] The concept of lead time implies that screening produces an earlier diagnosis that may be effectively used to intervene prior to diagnosis without screening.

[b] A prerequisite to use of tests in screening and other situations is establishing the cut-off line that differentiates a positive test and a negative test. Often this is done by using what is called a **reference interval**. This range is often established by utilize populations that are believed to be free of a disease. The central 95 percent of the range of values (or the mean plus or minus two standard deviations) for this population is then used as the reference interval or range of normal. This approach has a number of limitations including equating existing levels on a test with desirable levels. When data is available on the desirable levels, it is preferable to utilize these levels to establish a reference interval and to define a positive and negative test result. Establishing the desirable level for a test result requires long term follow-up. For such measurements as blood pressure, cholesterol, and fasting blood sugar, desirable levels are now available.

[c] This assumes a 1 percent pretest probability and a **sensitivity** and **specificity** of 90 percent. A moderately accurate test, such as a mammography, may have a sensitivity of about 90 percent and a similar specificity. Sensitivity implies that the test is about 90 percent accurate in the presence of disease (i.e., present in disease) while specificity tells us the mammography is about 90 percent accurate in the absence of disease (i.e., negative in health).

tial testing is used in breast cancer, hearing and vision testing, and most other forms of screening for non-communicable diseases. It is generally the most cost-effective form of screening because only one negative test is needed to rule out the disease.

Sequential testing by definition misses those who have false negative results because a negative test occurs and the testing process is over at least for the immediate future. Thus, a testing strategy needs to consider how to detect those missed by screening. We need to ask: is there a need for repeat screening and if so, when should it occur?[d]

Finally, an ideal screening test should be acceptable in terms of harms, costs and patient acceptance. Harms must be judged by looking at the entire testing strategy—not just the initial test. Physical examination, blood tests, and urine tests often are used as initial screening tests. These tests are virtually harmless. The real question is: what needs to be done if the initial test is positive? If invasive tests such as catheterization or surgery are required, the overall testing strategy may present substantial potential harms.

Screenings and diagnostic tests themselves can be quite costly. In addition, costs are related to the length of time between testing. Testing every year will be far more costly than testing every five or ten years. The frequency of testing depends on the speed at which the disease develops and progresses, as well as the number of people who can be expected to be missed on the initial test. Mammographic screening is traditionally conducted every year because breast cancer can develop and spread rapidly. In the case of colon cancer, however, longer periods between testing are acceptable because the disease is much slower to develop. Thus, cost considerations may be taken into account when choosing between technologies and when setting the interval between screenings.[e]

Finally, patient acceptance is key to successful screening. Many screening strategies present little problem with patient acceptance. However, colon cancer screening has had its challenges with patience acceptance because many consider it an invasive and uncomfortable procedure. Far less then half the people who qualify for screening based upon current recommendations currently pursue and receive colon cancer screening. This contrasts dramatically with mammography where a substantial majority now receives the recommended screening.

The screening tests that completely fulfill these ideal criteria are few and many more are successfully used despite not fulfilling all these criteria. Screening may still be useful as long as we are aware of its limitations and prepared to accept its inherent problems. Table 6-1 illustrates how commonly-used screening tests for risk factors for cardiovascular disease and common cancers perform based upon the four criteria we have outlined.

These criteria do help identify types of screening that should not be done. In general, we do not screen for disease when early detection does not improve outcome. We do not screen for rare diseases, such as many types of cancer, especially when the available tests are only moderately accurate. Finally, we do not screen for diseases when the testing strategy produces substantial harms. Screening for disease is not the only population health approach that can be used to address the burden of non-communicable disease. Multiple risk factor reduction is a second strategy that we will examine.

HOW CAN IDENTIFICATION AND TREATMENT OF MULTIPLE RISK FACTORS BE USED TO ADDRESS THE BURDEN OF NON-COMMUNICABLE DISEASE?

As we have seen, the concept of risk factors is fundamental to the work of public health. Risk factors ranging from high levels of blood pressure and LDL cholesterol to multiple sexual partners and anal intercourse help us identify groups that are most likely to develop a disease. Evidence-based recommendations often focus on addressing risk factors and implementation efforts often address the best way(s) to target high-risk groups. Thus, identifying and reducing risk factors is an inherent part of the population health approach to non-communicable diseases.

A special form of intervention aimed at risk factors is called **multiple risk factor reduction**. As the name implies, this strategy intervenes simultaneously in a series of risk factors all of which contribute to a particular outcome, such as cardiovascular disease or lung cancer. Multiple risk factor reduction is most effective when there are constellations or groups of risk factors that cluster together in definable groups of people. It may also be useful when the presence of two or more risk factor increases the risk more than would be expected by adding together the impact of each risk factor.

The success of the last half century in addressing coronary artery disease exemplifies multiple risk factor reduction. Box 6-2 discusses the impact of the strategy on coronary

---

[d] A sequential testing strategy also requires a decision on the order of administering the tests. Issues of cost and safety are often the overriding consideration in determining which test to use first and which to use to confirm an initial positive test. At times, a testing strategy known as **simultaneous testing** or **parallel testing** is used. In this scenario, two tests are used initially if one test can be expected to detect one type of disease and the other test can be expected to detect a different type of disease. Traditionally, flexible sigmoidoscopy, which examines the lower approximately 35 cm of the colon, has been used along with tests for occult blood in the stool. Tests for occult blood attempt to screen for cancer in the large section of colon proximal to the sigmoid region. Using both of these tests has been shown to be more accurate for screening than use of either test alone because each attempts to find cancer in different anatomical sites.

[e] Today, there is a wide range of methods for screening for colon cancer including colonoscopy, which examines the entire colon, and virtual colonoscopy, which does not require an internal examination. These newer tests are much more costly than sigmoidoscopy and occult stool testing. Which is the most accurate and cost-effective test remains controversial. However, the need for and benefits of screening for colon cancer are widely accepted.

TABLE 6-1 Examples of Screening Tests for Heart Disease and Cancer and Ideal Criteria

	Substantial mortality and/or morbidity	Early detection possible and alters outcome	Screening is feasible (can identify a high-risk population and a testing strategy)	Screening acceptable in terms of harms, costs, and patient acceptance
Hypertension	Contributory cause of strokes, myocardial infarctions, kidney disease	High blood pressure precedes bad outcomes often by decades and effective treatment is available	Test everyone—desirable range has been established	Screening itself is free of harms, low cost, and acceptable to patients Treatments, however, may be complicated and have harms, costs, and side effects
LDL cholesterol	Contributory cause of strokes, myocardial infarctions, and other vascular diseases	Precedes the development of disease by decades and treatment is effective in altering outcome	Test everyone—desirable range has been established	Screening itself is free of harm, low cost, and acceptable to patients Treatment has rare side effects, which can be detected by symptoms and low-cost blood tests
Breast cancer	2nd most common fatal cancer among women and most common for women under 70	Early detection improves outcome	For those 50 and over, combination of mammography and follow-up biopsy shown to be feasible	Harm may occur due to false positives, low risk of harm from radiation, patient acceptance good, but test can be somewhat painful Screening younger women increases costs and false positives
Cervical cancer	If undetected and untreated—may be fatal	Early treatment dramatically reduces the risk of death	Pap smear and follow-up testing have been extremely successful	Pap results in substantial number of false positives New DNA testing may be used to separate true and false positives
Colon cancer	2nd most common fatal cancer in men and third in women	Early detection of polyps reduces development of cancer and early detection of cancer improves chances of survival	Men and women 50 and older, plus those with high risk types of colon disease Options for screening include: fecal occult blood testing, plus flexible sigmoidoscopy, colonoscopy, and virtual colonoscopy	Patient acceptance has been major barrier, small probability of harm from procedure, substantial cost for colonoscopy and virtual colonoscopy

BOX 6-2 Coronary Artery Disease and Multiple Risk Factor Reduction.

An epidemic of coronary artery disease and subsequent heart attacks spread widely through mid-20th century America. Sudden death, especially among men in their 50s and even younger, became commonplace in nearly every neighborhood in suburban America. To better understand this epidemic, which caused nearly half of all deaths in Americans in the 1940s and 1950s, the National Institutes of Health began the Framingham Heart Study in the late 1940s.[4]

In those days, there were only suggestions that cholesterol and hypertension contributed to heart disease and little, if any, recognition that cigarettes played a role. The Framingham Heart Study enrolled a cohort of over 7000 individuals in Framingham, Massachusetts: questioning, examining, and taking blood samples from them every other year to explore a large number of conceivable connections with coronary artery disease—the cause of heart attacks. Now well into its second half-century after thousands of publications and hundreds of thousands of examinations, the Framingham Heart Study continues to follow the children and grandchildren of the original Framingham cohort.

The study has provided us with extensive long-term data on a cohort of individuals. These form the basis for many of the numbers we use to estimate the strength of risk factors for coronary artery disease. It has helped demonstrate not only the risk factors for the disease, but also the protective or resilience factors. The use of aspirin, regular exercise, and modest alcohol consumption have been suggested as protective factors despite the fact that no one ever thought of them in the 1940s.[f]

The Framingham Heart Study demonstrated that high blood pressure preceded strokes and heart attacks by years and often decades. It took the Veterans Administration's randomized clinical trials of the early 1970s to convince the medical and public health communities that high blood pressure needed and benefited from aggressive detection and treatment. Through a truly joint effort by public health and medicine, high blood pressure detection and treatment came to public and professional recognition as a major priority in the 1970s.

The impact of elevated levels of low-density lipoprotein (LDL), the bad cholesterol, were likewise suggested by the Framingham Heart Study, but it was not until the development of a new class of medications called statins in the mid-1980s that treatment of high levels of LDL cholesterol took off. These drugs have been able to achieve remarkable reductions in LDL and equally remarkable reductions in coronary artery disease with only rare side effects. These drugs have been so successful that some countries have made them available over-the-counter. Clinicians are using them more and more aggressively to achieve levels of LDL cholesterol that are less than half those sought a generation ago.[g]

Although diabetes has been treated with insulin since the 1920s and oral treatments beginning after World War II, the treatment of diabetes to prevent its consequences—including coronary artery disease—was not definitely established as effective until the 1990s. Our current understanding of diabetes has come from a series of randomized clinical trials and long-term follow-ups that demonstrate the key role that diabetes can play in diseases of the heart and blood vessels and the impressive role that aggressive treatment can play in reducing the risks of these diseases.

Efforts aimed at early detection and treatment of heart attacks and prevention of second heart attacks through the use of medications have become routine parts of medical practice. Medical procedures, including angioplasty and surgical bypass of diseased coronary arteries, have also been widely used. Widespread availability of defibrillators in public areas is one of the most recent effort to prevent the fatal consequences of coronary artery disease.

Between the 1950s and the early years of the 21st century, the death rate from coronary artery disease has declined by over 50 percent. The impact is even greater among those in their 50s and 60s. Sudden death from coronary artery disease among men in their 50s is now a relatively rare event.

For years medicine and public health professionals debated whether public health and clinical preventive interventions or medical and surgical interventions deserved the lion's share of the credit for these achievements. The evidence suggests that both prevention and treatment have had important impacts.[6] When medicine and public health work together, the public's health is the winner.

---

[f] The data developed for the Surgeon General's Reports on Smoking and Health in the 1960s and beyond, strongly pointed to substantial effects of cigarettes not only on lung disease, but on coronary artery disease as well. In fact, given the large number of deaths from coronary artery disease compared to lung disease, it became evident that in terms of number of deaths the biggest impact of cigarette smoking is on heart disease, not lung disease.

[g] Recent data even suggests that for individuals with levels of LDL cholesterol within the currently accepted range of normal, statins may be beneficial in the presence of evidence of inflammation as measured by a test called C-reactive protein.[5]

artery disease. Multiple risk factor reduction strategies are being attempted for a range of diseases from asthma to diabetes.

Multiple risk factor reduction is most successful when a number of risk factors are at work in the same individual. As we have seen with asthma, factors like indoor and outdoor air pollution, cockroaches and other allergens, and a lack of adherence to medications, tend to occur together and may be most effectively addressed together. Similarly, obesity and lack of exercise tend to reinforce each other often requiring a comprehensive multiple risk factor reduction approach.[h]

Screening for disease and multiple risk factor reduction are key approaches to using testing as part of secondary intervention.[i] The enormous burden of non-communicable disease cannot be totally prevented even by maximizing the use of these strategies. It is important to couple them with cost-effective treatment. Thus, a third population health strategy for addressing the burden of non-communicable disease is to develop cost-effective interventions to treat common diseases.

HOW CAN COST-EFFECTIVE INTERVENTIONS HELP US ADDRESS THE BURDEN OF NON-COMMUNICABLE DISEASES?

Clinicians today have a wide range of interventions to treat disease. Many of these interventions have some impact on the course of a disease. The proliferation of interventions means that it is especially important to identify which provide the greatest benefits at the lowest cost. In order to understand how cost-effective interventions can help address the burden of non-communicable disease, we need to understand what we mean by cost-effective.

Cost-effectiveness is a concept that combines issues of benefits and harms with issues of financial costs. It starts by considering the benefits and harms of an intervention to determine

its **net-effectiveness**. Net-effectiveness implies that the benefits are substantially greater than the harms even after the value (or utility), as well as the timing of the harms and benefits, are taken into account. Only after establishing net-effectiveness do we take into account the financial costs.

Cost-effectiveness compares a new intervention to the current or standard intervention. It usually asks: is the additional net-effectiveness of an intervention worth the additional cost? At times it may also require us to ask: is a small loss of net-effectiveness worth the considerable savings in cost? Figure 6-1 is a tool for categorizing interventions in order to analyze their costs and net-effectiveness.

Box 6-3 provides more details on the use of cost-effectiveness analysis.[7]

Preventive interventions often undergo cost-effectiveness analysis. Many interventions, ranging from mammography to most childhood vaccinations to cigarette cessation programs, get high or at least passing grades on cost-effectiveness. However, many widely-used treatment interventions do not or would not meet the current standards of cost-effectiveness. The application of cost-effectiveness criteria to common clinical interventions is considered a population health intervention aimed at getting maximum value for the dollars spent.

The results of cost-effectiveness analysis have already had an impact on a number of common clinical procedures. For instance, cost-effective treatments include: the use of minimally-invasive orthopedic surgery, such as knee surgery; the reduced length of intensive care and hospitalization for coronary artery disease; and the use of home health care for intravenous administration of antibiotics and other medications. These efforts to

---

[h] In some situations the existence of multiple risk factors does more than add together to produce disease. At times, the existence of two or more factors multiply the risk. In these situations addressing even one of the factors can have a major impact on disease. For instance, it is now well established that asbestos exposure and cigarette smoking multiply the risks of lung cancer. Thus, if the relative risk for cigarettes is 10 and the relative risk for asbestos exposure is 5, then the relative risk if both factors are present is approximately 50. If an individual who has previously been exposed to both risk factors stops smoking cigarettes and the effects of cigarette smoking are immediately and completely reversible, we can expect the relative risk of lung cancer to decline from approximately a fifty-fold increase to a five-fold increase. We will take up this issue again in Chapter 8 because this type of interaction is increasingly central to addressing complex public health issues.

[i] The principles of testing discussed here are not limited to screening for disease and identification of risk factors. They are also useful as part of a cost-effective approach to diagnosis of symptomatic diseases. In addition, testing is often used for a range of applications in medicine and public health, including monitoring response to treatment, identifying side effects, identifying genetic predictors of disease, and establishing baseline levels for future testing. Public health applications include the use of environmental testing and testing for disease prevalence.

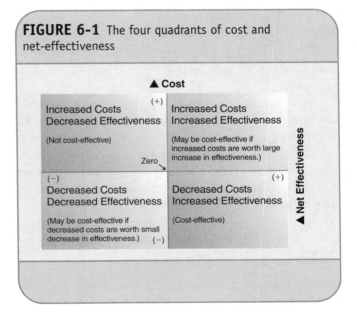

FIGURE 6-1 The four quadrants of cost and net-effectiveness

▲ Cost

(+)

Increased Costs
Decreased Effectiveness

(Not cost-effective)

Increased Costs
Increased Effectiveness

(May be cost-effective if increased costs are worth large increase in effectiveness.)

Zero

(−)

Decreased Costs
Decreased Effectiveness

(May be cost-effective if decreased costs are worth small decrease in effectiveness.) (−)

(+)

Decreased Costs
Increased Effectiveness

(Cost-effective)

▲ Net Effectiveness

BOX 6-3   Cost-Effectiveness and Its Calculations.

Cost-effectiveness is often judged by comparing the costs of a new intervention to the cost of the current, standard, or state-of-the-art intervention. A measure known as the **incremental cost-effectiveness ratio** is then obtained. This ratio represents the additional cost relative to the additional net-effectiveness.

Net-effectiveness may measure a diagnosis made, a death prevented, or a disability prevented, etc. To operationize the concept of net-effectiveness requires us to define, measure, and combine the probabilities and utilities of benefits with the probabilities and utilities of harm and take into account the timing of the benefits and the harms. Thus, the process of calculating net-effectiveness can be quite complex.

Similarly, calculating costs can be challenging. Most economists argue that the costs are not limited to the costs of providing the intervention and the current and future medical care, but should also include the cost of transportation, loss of income, and other expenses associate with obtaining health care and being disabled. Thus, calculating a cost-effectiveness ratio has become a complex undertaking.

The criteria for establishing cost effectiveness have changed over time. Most experts in cost-effectiveness prefer the use of a measurement called **quality-adjusted life years** or **QALYs**. QALYs ask about the number of life-years saved by an intervention, rather than the number of lives. Thus, one QALY may be thought of as one year of life at full health compared to immediate death.

In cost-effectiveness analysis, a financial value is usually placed on a QALY reflecting what a society can afford to pay for the average QALY as measured by its per capita gross domestic product (GDP). In the United States, where the GPD is approaching $50,000 there is a general consensus that a QALY currently should be valued at $50,000. Thus, when you hear that a formal cost-effectiveness analysis has shown that an intervention is cost-effective, it generally implies that the addition cost is less than $50,000 per QALY.[j]

The ideal intervention is one in which the cost goes down and the effectiveness goes up. Cost-saving, quality-increasing interventions have a negative incremental cost-effectiveness ratio. That is, QALYs go up while the costs go down. These cost-reducing, QALY-increasing interventions, while highly desirable, are very rare. Usually we need to spend more to get additional QALYs. One example of an intervention that reduces costs and at the same time produces additional QALYs is treatment of hypertension in high risk individuals, such as those with diabetes.[k]

---

[j] An increase of one QALY may be the result of obtaining small improvements in utility from a large number of people. For instance, if ten people increase their utility from 0.1 to 0.2, the result is an increase of one QALY. The value of a QALY is often set slightly above the average gross domestic product (GDP) or sum of all goods and services produced per person. In the United States, the GDP now exceeds $40,000 per person per year. Thus, setting the value of a QALY at $50,000 reflects how much we can afford to pay rather than strictly reflecting how much we think a QALY is worth.

[k] Another example is the use of influenza vaccine among the elderly and those with chronic disease predisposing them to the complications of influenza. It is important to distinguish these types of interventions from those that reduce the costs, but also reduce the QALYs, because at times both are referred to as cost-saving measures.

---

increase the cost-effectiveness of routine healthcare procedures are becoming key to maximizing the benefits obtained from the vast amount of money spent on health care as we will discuss in Chapter 11.

Applying cost-effectiveness analysis to routine clinical interventions is often coupled with efforts to better predict the outcome of disease and treatment. Improving the ability to predict the outcome of diseases and interventions can help us know when, how, and if to intervene. Improved prediction holds out the hope of increased effectiveness, as well as reduced costs by tailoring the treatment to the individual patient.[l]

In addition to screening, multiple risk factor reduction, and cost-effective intervention using prediction rules, the revolution in genetics has opened up another possible strategy for addressing the burden of non-communicable diseases.

HOW CAN GENETIC COUNSELING AND INTERVENTION BE USED TO ADDRESS THE BURDEN OF CHRONIC DISEASES?

Interventions based upon genetics have been part of medical and public health practice since at least the 1960s, when it was recognized that abnormalities of single genes for such condi-

---

[l] Research designed to develop **prediction rules** has become a major focus of clinical, as well as public health research. This challenging type of research may be able to improve evidence-based recommendations by providing different recommendations for groups with different prognoses and/or different responses

to treatment. Efforts to improve the effectiveness of breast cancer treatments, for instance, are now focused on testing patients to determine the best type of chemotherapy to use to treat their particular cancer. This approach shows promise of producing greater benefit and less harm at reduced cost.

tions as Tay-Sachs disease (found among Ashkenazi Jews) and sickle cell anemia (found among African-Americans) could be detected by testing potential parents who could then be counseled on the risks associated with childbearing.

It was also recognized that chromosomal abnormalities that produce Down Syndrome, the most commonly-recognized cause of mental retardation, could be detected at an early stage in pregnancy. In addition, certain genetic defects such as phenylketonuria (PKU) can be recognized at birth and relatively simple dietary interventions can prevent the severe retardation of mental development that would otherwise occur.

In light of all this valuable knowledge, today genetic testing and counseling are often offered to prospective parents. Testing for Down Syndrome is a standard part of prenatal care; and testing for a wide range of rare, but serious disorders is a population health intervention. In fact, in most states these tests are legally required soon after birth. The triumph of the human genome project in the early years of the 21st century has sparked interest in expanding the applicability of genetic interventions in medicine and public health. For instance, the gene for cystic fibrosis, the most common genetic disorder among whites in the United States, has been identified and screening of large numbers of couples is now possible. Even among whites without a history of cystic fibrosis, the chance of carrying the gene is about three percent. If both the mother and the father carry the gene, the chances of having a child with cystic fibrosis is 25 percent with each pregnancy. The fetus can be tested for the disease early in pregnancy.

There are a wide range of current and developing applications of genetics including:[8]

- **Genetic prevention**—This approach incorporates efforts to prevent the occurrence of single genes or multiple gene combinations that are likely to produce disease. This includes: expanded use of genetic counseling, prenatal testing, and early abortion or fetal therapies. Knowledge of the human genome holds promise for expanding this approach beyond diseases caused by single-gene defects to diseases that depend on multiple genes. It is important to recognize that diseases that are dependent on multiple genes will be more difficult to predict than resulting from a single-gene.

- **Genetic detection prior to disease**—This approach includes efforts aimed at detection of genetic defects and implementation of early intervention to prevent what is called the **phenotypic expression of genes**. Building on the success of treatment of PKU and other inborn errors of metabolism, risk factors for common diseases, such as high cholesterol, high blood sugar, or obesity

might be detected early and aggressively managed during childhood.

- **Gene-environmental protection**—Genetic testing holds out the possibility of defining combinations of genes that identify individuals who are especially likely to develop disease when they experience specific environmental exposures, such as those interactions that occur in occupational settings where workers are exposed to specific chemicals often at low doses. Identification of gene-environment interactions may lead to identification of those who are at high risk if they work in certain occupational settings.

- **Genotypic-based screening for early disease**—Combinations of genes may identify groups that are at high risk of common diseases and that can be targeted for screening. For instance, studies suggest that for certain common cancers, such as those of the breast, prostate, and colon, genetic factors are associated with 30–40 percent of these diseases. Finding predisposing genetic patterns early in life may be useful for identifying those who need earlier or more intensive screening for early detection.

Each of these potential uses of genetics in public health present ethical as well as technological issues. Questions to consider include: Should we identify diseases when little can be done to prevent or treat them? How can we identify genetic risk factors without stigmatizing or putting those with the genes at a disadvantage? Will screening programs be improved by identifying groups at genetic risk of disease or will high risk groups without genetic risk factors unfairly be passed over for screenings?

These and other approaches based on the rapidly accumulating knowledge of genetics are likely to become routine medical and public health strategies for primary, secondary, and tertiary interventions for non-communicable disease in the coming years. Their successful adoption, however, will require careful attention by those in the fields of public health and medicine to ensure that benefits are gained and harms minimized. Despite the enormous advances that have occurred in public health and medicine in recent decades, there is still much to be learned. A final strategy for non-communicable diseases addresses the question: what can we do when highly-effective interventions don't exist?

WHAT CAN WE DO WHEN HIGHLY-EFFECTIVE INTERVENTIONS DON'T EXIST?

Alzheimer's disease reflects the challenge of what to do when the cause of a disease is not known and the treatment is not highly effective.[9] Alzheimer's is among the most rapidly increasing condition among those that we classify as non-communicable diseases. The aging of the population has been and is expected to be associated with many more cases of Alzheimer's, which primarily affects the quality of life with its progressive damage to memory—especially short-term memory.[m]

Today we have limited treatment options for those afflicted with Alzheimer's. Several drugs are available that have modest positive impacts on memory. Efforts to stimulate mental activity through keeping active mentally and physically have also been shown to have positive, yet modest impacts. Public health efforts have encouraged the use of these existing interventions especially when there is evidence that they allow individuals to function on their own or with limited assistance for longer periods of time.

The population health approach to Alzheimer's disease, however, also stresses the need for additional research. Epidemiological research has helped produce the modest advances in preventing progression and treating the symptoms of the disease. A population health approach, however, needs to acknowledge the need for a basic biological understanding of what causes Alzheimer's. As we learned in Chapter 2, the P.E.R.I. process asks us to address the etiology as the basis for evidence-based recommendations and intervention. Thus, the population health approach to Alzheimer's, as with other diseases of unknown etiology, requires us to ask basic questions about the biology of the disease and to learn more about its cause(s). Fortunately, an increasingly sophisticated and well-financed effort is being directed at understanding the etiology of Alzheimer's. We can now have hope and increasing confidence that the epidemic being faced by many of your grandparents will be brought under control in the not-too-distant future.

We have now explored the major population health strategies for addressing non-communicable diseases. These include screening, multiple risk factor reduction, cost-effective treatments, genetic counseling, and more research. A complex problem often requires us to combine many of these approaches.

HOW CAN WE COMBINE STRATEGIES TO ADDRESS COMPLEX PROBLEMS OF NON-COMMUNICABLE DISEASES?

Multiple interventions combining health care, traditional public health approaches, and social interventions are often needed to address the complex problems presented by non-communicable diseases. The combined and integrated use of

---

[m] Not all cases of memory loss or dementia are due to Alzheimer's. Additional causes include: strokes and cerebral vascular disease, chronic alcoholism, thyroid disease, specific infectious diseases (such as syphilis and AIDS), as well as the effects of drugs and a long list of rare diseases. Today, however, Alzheimer's is the most common and the most important cause of memory loss and dementia. We tend to classify a disease as non-communicable unless there is convincing evidence that it can be transmitted or that it is due in large part to environmental exposures or injuries. Despite the fact that we do not yet know the etiology of Alzheimer's disease, it is generally classified as non-communicable.

BOX 6-4   Alcohol Abuse and the Population Health Approach.

Alcohol has been a central feature of American society and American medicine and public health since the early days of the country. It was among the earliest painkillers and was used routinely to allow surgeons to perform amputations during the Civil War and earlier conflicts. The social experiment of alcohol prohibition during the 1920s and early 1930s ended in failure as perceived by a great majority of Americans.

Efforts to control the consequences of alcohol took a new direction after World War II. Americans began to focus on the consequences of the disease, including liver disease, fetal alcohol syndrome, automobile accidents, and intentional and unintentional violence.

Population health interventions became the focus of alcohol control efforts. For instance, taxation of alcohol based upon 1950s legislation raised the price of alcohol enough to substantially reduce consumption. Restrictions on advertising and higher taxes on hard liquor with its greater alcohol content eventually contributed to greater use of beer and wine. Despite the continued growth in alcohol consumption, the number of cases of liver disease and other alcohol-related health problems have declined. In recent years, efforts to alert pregnant women to the health effects of drinking through product labeling and other health communications efforts have had an impact.

The highway safety impacts of alcohol use have led to population health efforts in cooperation with transportation and police departments. Greatly increased police efforts to catch drunk drivers and stripping of the licenses of repeat offenders have become routine and have been attributed to impressive reductions in automotive accidents related to alcohol. Efforts such as the designated driver movement originated by Mothers Against Drunk Drivers (MADD) have demonstrated the often-critical role that private citizens can play in implementing population health interventions.

(continues)

BOX 6-4 continued.

Focusing on high-risk groups, as well as using what we have called "improving-the-average" strategies, has had an important impact. Alcoholics Anonymous (AA) and other peer support groups have focused on encouraging individuals to acknowledge their alcohol problems. These groups often provide important encouragement and support for long-term abstinence.

Medical efforts to control alcohol consumption have been aimed primarily at those with clear evidence of alcohol abuse—often those in need of alcohol withdrawal or "drying out." Drugs are available that provide modest help in controlling an individual's alcohol consumption. Screening for alcohol abuse has become a widespread part of health care. These interventions have been aimed at those with the highest levels of risk. The combination of individual, group, and population interventions has reduced the overall impact of alcohol use without requiring its prohibition. In fact, modest levels of consumption, up to one drink per day for women and two for men, may help protect against coronary artery disease.

The issue of alcohol and public health has not gone away. The focus today has returned to identifying high-risk groups and intervening to prevent bad outcomes. A key risk factor today is binge drinking with its risk of acute alcohol poisoning, as well as unintentional and intentional violence. College students are among the highest risk group. One episode of binge drinking dramatically increases the probability of additional episodes suggesting that intervention strategies are needed to reduce the risk. We've made a great deal of progress controlling the impacts of alcohol, but we clearly have more to do.

multiple interventions is central to the population health approach. Box 6-4 looks at what we can learn about the population health approach to non-communicable diseases from the long history of alcohol use and abuse, as well as the substantial recent success in addressing disease due to alcohol.[10]

We have now taken a look at strategies to control non-communicable diseases that are currently the most common reason for disability and death in most developed countries. Now, let us look at a second category—communicable disease—which has been central to the history of public health and threatens to become central to its future.

Key Words

- Epidemiological transition
- Screening
- Asymptomatic
- Lead-time bias
- Watchful waiting
- False positives
- False negatives
- Reference interval
- Sensitivity
- Specificity
- Sequential testing (or two-stage testing)
- Simultaneous testing (or parallel testing)
- Multiple risk factor reduction
- Cost-effectiveness
- Net-effectiveness
- Prediction rules
- Phenotypic expression of genes

Discussion Questions

Take a look at the questions poised in the following scenarios which were presented at the beginning of this chapter. See now whether you can answer them.

1. *Sasha didn't want to think about the possibility of breast cancer, but as she turned 50 she agreed to have a mammography which, as she feared, was positive or "suspicious," as her doctor put it. Waiting for the results of the follow-up biopsy was the worst part, but the relief she felt when the results were negative brought tears of joy to her and her family. Then she wondered: is it common to have a positive mammography when no cancer is present?*

2. *The first sign of Michael's coronary heart disease was his heart attack. Looking back, he had been at high risk for many years since he smoked, had high blood pressure, and high cholesterol. His lack of exercise and obesity only made the situation worse. Michael asked: what are the risk factors for coronary heart disease and what can be done to identify and address these factors for himself and his family?*

3. *John's knee injury from skiing continued to produce swelling and pain, greatly limiting his activities. His physician informed him that the standard procedure today is to look inside with a flexible scope and do any surgery that is needed through the scope. It's simpler, cheaper, and does not even require hospitalization. "We call it 'cost-effective,'" his doctor said. John wondered: what does cost effective really mean?*

4. *Jennifer and her husband George were tested for the cystic fibrosis gene and both were found to have it. Cystic fibrosis causes chronic lung infections and greatly shortens the length of life. They now ask: what does this mean for our chances of having a child with cystic fibrosis? Can we find out whether our child has cystic fibrosis early in pregnancy?*

5. *Fred's condition deteriorated slowly, but persistently. He ju couldn't remember anything and repeated himself endless The medications helped for a short time, but before long I didn't recognize his family and couldn't take care of himse The diagnosis was Alzheimer's and he was not alone. Almo everyone in the nursing home seemed to be affected. No on seems to understand the cause of Alzheimer's disease. T family asked: what else can be done, not only for Fred, but f those who come after Fred?*

6. *Alcohol use is widespread on your campus. You don't see it a problem as long as you walk home or have a designate driver. Your mind changes one day after you hear about classmate who nearly died from alcohol poisoning as a rest of binge drinking. You ask yourself: what should be done on n campus to address binge drinking?*

REFERENCES

1. Omran AR. The epidemiologic transition: a theory of the epidemic ogy of population change. *The Milbank Memorial Fund Quarterly*. 1971; 49(4 509–538.

2. Riegelman RK. *Studying a Study and Testing a Test: How to Read t Medical Evidence*. Philadelphia: Lippincott, Williams & Wilkins; 2005.

3. Gordis L. *Epidemiology*. 4th ed. Philadelphia: Elsevier Saunders; 200

4. Framingham Heart Study. History of the Framingham Heart Stud Available at: http://www.framinghamheartstudy.org/about/history.htm Accessed March 18, 2009.

5. Ridker PM, Danielson E, Foneseca FAH, Genest J, et al. Rosuvastat to prevent vascular events in men and women with elevated C-reactive pr tein. *N Engl J Med*. 2008; 259(21): 2195–2207.

6. Critchley J, Capwell S, Unal B. Life-years gained from coronary hea disease mortality reduction in Scotland—prevention or treatment? *J Clin E* 2003; 56(6): 583–590.

7. Gold MR, Siegel JE, Russell LB, Weinstein MC. *Cost-Effectiveness Health and Medicine*. New York: Oxford University Press; 1996.

8. Khoury MJ, Burke W, Thomson EJ. *Genetics and Public Health in t 21st Century: Using Genetic Information to Improve Health and Prevent Diseas* New York: Oxford University Press; 2000.

9. National Institute on Aging. Alzheimer's Disease Fact Sheet. Availab at: http://www.nia.nih.gov/Alzheimers/Publications/adfact.htm. Accesse March 18, 2009.

10. Room R, Babor T, Rehm J. Alcohol and public health. *Lancet*. 200 365(9458): 519–530.

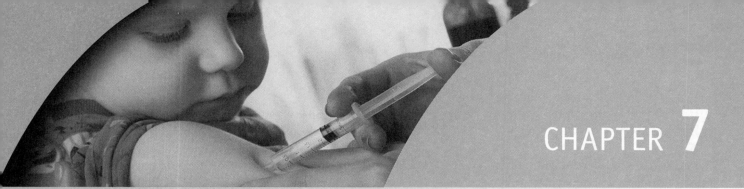

CHAPTER 7

Communicable Diseases

LEARNING OBJECTIVES

By the end of this chapter, the student will be able to:

- describe the burden of disease caused by communicable diseases.
- identify the roles that barrier protections play in preventing communicable diseases.
- identify the roles that vaccinations can play in preventing communicable diseases.
- identify the roles that screening, case finding, and contact treatment can play in preventing communicable diseases.
- identify the conditions that make eradication of a disease feasible.
- describe a range of options for controlling the HIV/AIDS epidemic.

Your college roommate went to bed not feeling well one night and early the next morning you had trouble arousing her. She was rushed to the hospital just in time to be effectively diagnosed and treated for meningococcal meningitis. The health department recommends immediate antibiotic treatment for everyone that was in close contact with your roommate. They set up a process to watch for additional cases to be sure an outbreak is not in progress. Fortunately, no more cases occur. You ask yourself: should your college require that all freshmen have the meningococcal vaccine before they can register for classes?

As a health advisor to a worldwide HIV/AIDS foundation, you are asked to advise on ways to address the HIV and developing tuberculosis (TB) epidemics. You are asked to do some long-range thinking and to come up with a list of potential approaches to control the epidemics, or at least ways reduce the development of TB. The first recommendation you make is to forget about eradicating HIV/AIDS. How did you come to that conclusion?

Your hometown of 100,000 is faced with a crisis as an airplane lands containing a passenger thought to have a new form of severe influenza that has recently gained the ability to spread from person to person through airborne spread. As the mayor of the city, what do you decide to do?

You are a principal at a local high school. One of your top athletes is in the hospital with a spreading bacterial infection due to a staphylococcus bacteria resistant to all known antibiotics. The infection occurred after what appeared to be a minor injury during practice. As the principal, what do you decide to do?

Diseases due to infection form a large part of the history of public health and are again a central part of its present and its future. Infections of public health importance may be caused by a wide variety of organisms ranging from bacteria, to viruses, to a spectrum of parasites including malaria and hookworm. Let us examine the burden of disease due to infections.[a]

---

[a] The term **infectious disease** is intended to include both communicable disease and disease caused by organisms that are not communicable. The central feature that distinguishes **communicable disease** from other diseases caused by organisms is its ability to be transmitted from person to person or from animals or the physical environment to humans by a variety of routes: from air and water, from contaminated articles (fomites), or from insect and animal bites. Other **infections** of public health interest are caused by organisms, such as pneumococcus (streptococcus pneumoniae), which usually coexist with healthy individuals, but are capable of causing disease when relocated to areas of the body with increased susceptibility or when they are provided opportunities to multiply or invade new areas because of an individual's decreased resistance. It is important to note that the distinction between infectious diseases and communicable diseases is not always made and at times they are considered synonyms.

WHAT IS THE BURDEN OF DISEASE CAUSED BY COMMUNICABLE DISEASES?

For many centuries, communicable diseases were the leading cause of death and disability among all ages, but especially among the young and the old. Communicable diseases were not only the causes of great epidemics, but they were the causes of routine deaths. These included a key role in maternal deaths associated with childbirth, infant and early childhood deaths, as well as deaths of malnourished infants and children.

The last half of the 20th century saw a brief respite from deaths and disabilities caused by communicable diseases and other infections. This was due in large part to medical efforts to treat infections with drugs and public health efforts to prevent infections (often with vaccines) and to eradicate or control other infections. Even as these great accomplishments were underway, warning signs of bacteria resistant to antibiotics began to appear. Staphylococcus organisms resistant to current antibi-otics began to plague hospitals in the 1950s until new antibiotics were developed. Resistance of gonorrhea and pneumococcus to a range of antibiotics became widespread. World Health Organization (WHO)—and U.S. government-sponsored pro-grams, such as those to promote the eradication of malaria and TB, were not able to have sustained impacts and the goals were trimmed back to control rather than eradication.

The early 21st century has seen the return of infections that were previously under control, as well as an emergence of new diseases. Tuberculosis, the great epidemic of the 18th and 19th centuries, has returned in force partially as a result of HIV/AIDS. Box 7-1 looks at the history of TB and the histor-ical and current burden of disease caused by it.[1,2]

Over a dozen previously-unknown infections have emerged in recent decades—the majority of which are believed to have originated in animal species. In the United States, the presence of Lyme Disease and West Nile virus were unknown until the late 20th century, but have now spread to extensive

---

BOX 7-1   The Burden of TB.

"If the importance of a disease for mankind is measured by the number of fatalities it causes, then tuberculosis must be considered much more important than those most feared infectious diseases, plague, cholera and the like. One in seven of all human beings die from tuberculosis. If one only considers the productive middle-age groups, tuberculosis carries away one-third, and often more."[1]

Robert Koch, March 24, 1882

The history of tuberculosis (TB) goes back to ancient times, but beginning in the 18th century it took center stage in much of Europe and America. It has been estimated that in the two centuries from 1700 to 1900, tuberculosis was responsible for the deaths of ap-proximately one billion human beings. The annual death rate from TB when Koch made his discovery was approximately seven million people.[1] Today that would be the equivalent of over 30 million people considering today's population.

Robert Koch's discovery of the association between the tuberculosis bacilli, its culture and isolation, and its transmission to a vari-ety of animal species provided a clear demonstration that the bacilli are a contributory cause of the disease. While the tuberculosis bacilli are clearly a contributory cause of the disease tuberculosis, they are not sufficient alone to produce disease. A large percentage of the world's population harbors tuberculosis. Other factors are needed to produce active disease. These factors include reduced im-munity and nutrition, as well as genetic factors.[b]

The discovery of the tuberculosis bacilli actually followed the development of what was called the sanitarium movement, which began in Europe and America. Sanitariums isolated tuberculosis victims, while providing good nutrition and clean air. The sanitarium move-ment was coupled in the early 20th century with the use of the Bacillus Calmette-Guérin (BCG) vaccine, purified protein derivative (PPD) skin tests, and the recently-invented chest X-ray. These three early and rather crude technologies are still in use today and were de-signed to prevent and diagnose TB. In addition, the understanding of the epidemiology of the tuberculosis bacteria led to a clear vic-tory for public health with the near elimination of TB from the milk supply early in the 20th century.

Thus, even before the ability to actively treat tuberculosis, public health interventions were able to dramatically reduce the frequency of the disease at least in Europe and America. A second round of efforts to control TB began in the 1940s with the discovery of strep-tomycin, the first anti-TB drug, followed over the next decade by para-aminosalicylic acid (PAS) and isoniazid (INH). Combination drug treatments proved highly effective. In addition, INH was found to be effective on its own to prevent skin-test-positive TB from pro-gressing to active disease. Public health and medical efforts to conduct screening for positive skin tests and selectively treating with INH became widespread.

continues

BOX 7-1 continued.

Thus, by the late 1950s and 1960s, TB was brought under control by the combination of medical and public health advances. The success of this effort resulted in the closing of TB sanitariums, gradual cutbacks in screening and treatment programs, and a general loss of interest in TB. From the mid-1960s on, there was little interest or research on TB. Tuberculosis became a treatable disease usually handled as part of routine medical care. Most medical and public health practitioners regarded it as a disease ready for eradication.

Unfortunately, TB was prematurely pronounced dead. It had never come under control in many parts of the world and approximately one-third of those living in developing countries today are estimated to harbor the TB bacillus. That is, they carry TB organisms which may multiply and spread in the future.

Soon after the beginning of the AIDS epidemic that began in the 1980s, active TB came back with a vengeance. AIDS patients with latent TB often developed active TB quite early in their battle with AIDS. They then became contagious to others. Tuberculosis may be more difficult to diagnose and may progress faster in AIDS patients.

Coupled with the return of TB as a public health problem, resistance to TB drugs began to emerge. The problem was successfully combated in the 1990s by the simple public health intervention known as directly-observed therapy or DOT. DOT helped ensure that patients received all the prescribed treatment, thus greatly increasing adherence to effective treatment.

Nonetheless, in recent years resistance to TB drugs and extreme resistance to drug treatments have increased all over the world. Today, we are faced with a triple threat of limited recent research leaving us without modern diagnostic aids or new drugs; a rapidly emerging threat from multiple-drug-resistant tuberculosis, and a spreading epidemic of HIV/AIDS predisposing patients to active tuberculosis. In the past, TB has been exceptionally responsive to a wide range of public health and medical efforts to control its spread. There is hope that with increased awareness and increased further research this will happen again.[2]

---

[b] Establishing that an organism is a contributory cause of the disease traditionally relied on **Koch's postulates.** Koch's postulates hold that in order to definitely establish a cause-and-effect relationship, the following four conditions must be met: 1) the organism must be shown to be present in every case of the disease by isolation of the organism; 2) the organism must not be found in cases of other disease; 3) once isolated, the organism must be capable of replicating the disease in an experimental animal; and 4) the organism must be recoverable from the animal. Ironically, TB cannot be shown to fulfill Koch's postulates. However, a very useful set of **Modern Koch's posulates** has been developed by the National Institute of Allergy and Infectious Disease. It requires evidence of an epidemiological association, isolation, and transmissions to establish that an organism is a contributory cause of the disease.[3]

---

areas of the country. Long-established diseases, such as malaria, are extending their geographic range and further extension is expected with global warming. Influenza is anticipated to return again in pandemic form, as has occurred repeatedly in prior centuries. A pandemic is most likely to occur when ongoing mutations produce new strains capable of person-to-person transmission. Whether you live in a dorm, are a public health professional, a politician, a high school principal, or in almost any profession, the types of questions illustrated in these cases are part of your present and your future.

History suggests that public health and medical interventions have and will continue to have major impacts on the burden of communicable diseases. Let us look at the tools available to address this burden.

WHAT PUBLIC HEALTH TOOLS ARE AVAILABLE TO ADDRESS THE BURDEN OF COMMUNICABLE DISEASES?

A range of public health tools are available to address the burden of communicable diseases. Some of these are useful in addressing non-communicable diseases as well, but they have special applications when directed toward infections. These include:

- Barrier protections, including isolation and quarantine
- Immunizations designed to protect individuals, as well as populations
- Screening and case finding
- Treatment and contact treatment
- Efforts to maximize effectiveness of treatments and prevent resistance

Let us look at each of these tools.

How Can Barriers Against Disease Be Used to Address the Burden of Communicable Diseases?

Examples of barriers to the spread of infections are as old as hand washing and as new as insecticide-impregnated bed nets that have had a major impact on the rate of malaria. Barrier protection, such as condoms, is believed by many to be the most successful intervention to prevent sexually-transmitted diseases. The use of masks may be effective in reducing the spread of disease in healthcare institutions, such as hospitals. The same measures may be preventative in the community at large and are a routine part of winter weather habits in much of Asia.

A special form of barrier protection consists of separating individuals with disease from the healthy population to prevent exposure. As we discussed previously, sanitariums had a major impact in reducing outbreaks of TB in the 19th and first half of the 20th century. Today, once again, we are faced with issues of isolation and occasionally have to legally enforce quarantine as we saw in our discussion of health law and policy in Chapter 5.

A second traditional public health approach to infections is the use of immunizations. Let us take a look at a range of ways that immunizations can be used to address the burden of infections.

How Can Immunizations Be Used to Address the Burden of Communicable Disease?

Immunization refers to the strengthening of the immune system to prevent or control disease. Injections of antibodies may be administered to achieve **passive immunity**, which may provide effective short-term protection. **Inactivated (dead)** and **live vaccines (attenuated live)** can often stimulate the body's own antibody production. Live vaccines utilize living organisms that also stimulate cell-mediated immunity and produce long-term protection that more closely resemble the body's own response to infection.

Vaccines are now available for a wide range of bacterial and viral diseases and are being developed and increasingly used to prevent infections as varied as malaria and hookworm.[4] Unfortunately, if has been difficult to produce effective vaccines for some diseases, such as HIV/AIDS. Vaccines, like medications, are rarely 100 percent effective and may produce side effects including allergic reactions that can be life threatening. Live vaccines have the potential to cause injury to a fetus and can themselves produce disease particularly in those with reduced immunity. Some vaccines are not effective for the very young and the elderly. Therefore, the use of vaccines requires extensive investigations to define its effectiveness and safety as well as to identify high risk groups for whom it should be recommended.

For instance college students and military recruits who tend to live in close quarters represent two high-risk groups for meningococcal disease. This bacterial infection can be rapidly life-threatening and when present it requires testing and antibiotic treatment of close contacts. Effective vaccination is now a key tool for controlling this disease. Ideally, vaccination occurs before exposure, however when an outbreak occurs, vaccination of large numbers of potentially exposed individuals living in the surrounding area may be key to effective control. Thus public health uses of vaccines need to consider who should receive the vaccine, when it should be administered, and how it should be administered.

Vaccines administration has traditionally been limited to injections as shots or ingestion as pills. New methods of administration including nasal sprays are now being developed. In addition, it is often possible to combine vaccines increasing the ease of administration. Inactivated vaccines may not produce long term immunity and may require follow-up vaccines or boosters. Thus the use of vaccinations requires the development of a population health strategy which gives careful attention to who, when, and how.

Some infections, especially those viruses that are highly contagious, can be controlled by vaccinating a substantial proportion of the population often in the range of 70 to 90 percent. In this situation, those who are susceptible rarely, if ever, encounter an individual with the disease. This is known as **herd immunity**. When a population has been vaccinated at these types of levels for infections—such as chicken pox, measles, and polio—those who have not been vaccinated are often protected. For some vaccines, such as live polio vaccine, herd immunity is facilitated by the fact that the virus in the vaccine can itself be spread from person to person providing protection for the unvaccinated. Thus, public health authorities are interested in the levels of protection in the community, that is the level of protection of the unvaccinated as well as the vaccinated.

In addition to tools for preventing disease in individuals and populations, public health efforts are often directed at screening for disease and conducting what is called case-finding.

How Can Screening and Case Finding Be Used to Address the Burden of Communicable Disease?

Ideally, screening for infections fulfills the same criteria for non-communicable diseases, which we discussed in Chapter 6, and has played a role in controlling the spread of a number of infections. For example, screening for tuberculosis and syphilis was an effective part of the control of these infections well before they could be cured with antibiotics. Today, screening for sexually-transmitted diseases, including gonorrhea and chlamydia, are a routine part of clinical care. HIV screening has long been recommended for high-risk individuals and for populations with an estimated prevalence above one percent. Today, universal screening is increasingly being adopted as a basic strategy for control of HIV/AIDS.

Screening for communicable diseases has often been linked with the public health practice known as **case finding**. Case finding implies confidential interviewing of those diagnosed with a disease and asking for their recent close physical or sexual contacts. Case finding techniques have been key to the control of syphilis and to a large extent TB both before and after the availability of effective treatment. The advent of effective treatment meant that case finding was of benefit both to those diagnosed with the disease and those located through case finding.

Successful case finding aims to maintain confidentiality. However, when following-up sexual contacts confidentiality is difficult to maintain. The potential for public recognition and the attendant social sigma has inhibited the use of case finding in HIV/AIDS in many parts of the world. The reluctance to utilize case finding may change in coming years as early diagnosis and perhaps early treatment become more effective in controlling the epidemic.

In addition to the use of barrier protections, vaccination of individuals and populations, as well as the use of screening and case finding, public health tools also encompass treatment of those with disease and their contacts.

How Can Treatment of Those Diagnosed and Their Contacts Help to Address the Burden of Communicable Disease?

Treatment of symptomatic disease may in and of itself reduce the risk of transmission. Successful treatment of HIV has been shown to reduce the viral load and thereby reduce the ease of transmission. Similarly, treatment of active TB reduces its infectivity. In addition to direct treatment, a public health tool known as **epidemiological treatment** or treatment of contacts has been effective in controlling a number of communicable diseases. Sexual partners of those with gonorrhea and chlamydia are routinely treated even when their infections cannot be detected. This approach presumably works because early and low-level infections caused by these organisms may be difficult to detect. As we saw in the meningococcal scenario, epidemiological treatment may be the most effective way to halt the rapid spread of a disease.

Contact treatment of HIV/AIDS may become a routine part of controlling the disease. It is already recommended and widely used for treatment of needlestick injuries in healthcare settings. Let us look at one additional public health tool being increasingly used to maximize effectiveness of treatment and prevent resistance.

How Can Public Health Efforts Maximize Effectiveness of Treatment and Prevent Resistance?

In recent years, the impact of antibiotic resistance has become painfully obvious—resistant pneumococcus, gonococcus, and tuberculosis have become widespread. In fact, extremely drug-resistant strains of TB exist in many areas of the world today. Efforts to control resistance have been modest compared to the forces encouraging resistance. Forces encouraging drug resistance include: overuse of prescribed antibiotics, over-the-counter sales of antibiotics in many countries, and widespread use of antibiotics to stimulate modest growth in agricultural animals.

As we have seen, one successful effort known as directly observer therapy (DOT) has led to a more effective treatment of TB. As the name implies, DOT aims to ensure complete adherence to TB treatment by observing individuals taking their daily or at less frequent intervals of treatment. This effort has been credited with success even in areas of drug resistance perhaps on the basis that the body can handle resistant TB if most of the organisms are effectively treated. Efforts are now underway to reduce or eliminate the use of antibiotics for animal growth and to place increased restrictions on the prescribing of highly useful new antibiotics.

The recent emergence of methicillin-resistant staphylococcus aureus (MRSA) outside hospitals has drawn long-overdue attention. It is spreading to communities and beginning to affect otherwise healthy individuals, including athletes and others simply in close physical contact. An effective program to control MRSA will require the use of a range of interventions. This is the situation for many of today's increasingly complex communicable diseases.

Let us now turn our attention to strategies that combine many of the specific public health tools designed to address the problems of infection. We will look at two basic strategies for combating complex infections: elimination and control.

HOW CAN PUBLIC HEALTH STRATEGIES BE USED TO ELIMINATE SPECIFIC COMMUNICABLE DISEASES?

Smallpox was the first human disease to be eradicated. An international effort is hopefully nearing completion to eradicate polio. These two viral diseases are the only ones that have been successfully targeted for eradication. As we have discussed, programs to eradicate TB and malaria have never come close to meeting their goals. Talk of the end of HIV/AIDS is even more unrealistic. Let us see what it takes to successfully eradicate a disease and why so few diseases are on the short list for potential eradication.

The history of smallpox has a unique place in public health. The disease goes back thousands of years and it played a prominent role in colonial America where epidemics often killed a quarter or more of its victims, especially children, and left most others, including George Washington, with severe facial scars for life. As we discussed in Chapter 1, the concept of vaccination and the first successful vaccination was developed for smallpox. During the 19th and early 20th centuries, smallpox was largely eliminated from most developed and developing countries through modest improvement on Jenner's basic approach to vaccination, despite the many side effects of this quite crude treatment.[c]

Despite the control of smallpox in most developed countries, there were still over 10 million cases annually of the disease in over 30 countries during the early 1960s. In 1967, the WHO began a campaign to eliminate smallpox. The success of the campaign over the next decade depended on extraordinary organizational management and cooperation, but the prerequisite for success were the unique epidemiological characteristics of smallpox that made it possible. Let us outline the characteristics of smallpox that made eradication possible:[5]

- **No animal reservoir**—Smallpox is an exclusively human disease. That is, there is no reservoir of the disease in animals. It does not affect other species that can then infect additional humans. This also means that if the disease is eliminated from humans, it has nowhere to hide and later reappear in human populations.
- **Short persistence in environment**—The smallpox virus requires human contact and cannot persist for more than a brief time in the environment without a human host. Thus, droplets from sneezing or coughing need to find an immediate victim and are not easily transmitted except by human-to-human contact.
- **Absence of a long-term carrier state**—Once an individual recovers from smallpox, they no longer carry the virus and cannot transmit it to others. Some diseases, like HIV/AIDS and hepatitis B, can maintain long-term carrier states and be infectious to others for years or decades.
- **The disease produces long-term immunity**—Once having recovered from smallpox, very effective immunity is established preventing a second infection.
- **Vaccination also establishes long-term immunity**—As with the disease itself, the live smallpox vaccine pro-

duces very successful long-term immunity. Smallpox has not mutated to become more infectious despite the extensive use of vaccination.
- **Herd immunity protects those who are susceptible**—Long-term immunity from the disease or the vaccine makes it possible to protect large populations. At least 80 percent of the population needs to be vaccinated to interrupt the spread of the infection to the remaining susceptible people.
- **Easily-identified disease**—The classic presentation of smallpox is relatively easy to identify by clinicians with experience observing the disease, as well as by the average person. This makes it possible to quickly diagnose the disease and protect others from being exposed.
- **Effective postexposure vaccination**—The smallpox vaccine is effective even after exposure to smallpox. This enables effective use of what is called **ring vaccination**. Ring vaccination involves identification of a case of smallpox, vaccination of household and close contacts, followed by vaccination of all those within a mile radius of the smallpox case. In the past, households within ten miles were typically searched for additional cases of smallpox. These surveillance and containment efforts were successful even in areas without high levels of vaccination.

The presence of these characteristics makes a disease ideal for eradication. While fulfilling all of them may not be necessary for eradication, the absence of a large number of them makes efforts at eradication less likely to succeed. Table 7-1 outlines these characteristics of smallpox and compares them to polio—the current viral candidate for eradication—as well as to measles. Based upon the content of the table, you should not be surprised to learn that the polio campaign has been much more difficult and has taken much longer than that of smallpox. The potential for a successful measles eradication campaign is still being debated.[d]

Finally, take a look at Table 7-2, which applies these characteristics to HIV infection. It demonstrates why the eradication of HIV/AIDS is not on the horizon.

Unfortunately, eradication of most diseases is not a viable strategy. Thus, public health measures are usually focused on control of infections. In order to understand the range of strategies that are available and useful for controlling communicable diseases, we will take a look at three important and quite different diseases—HIV, influenza A, and rabies.

---

[c] While the vaccine against smallpox is very effective, it has many side effects. The live virus contained in the vaccine can itself cause disease in those vaccinated especially if they have widespread skin disease or have compromised immune system. Today, these side effects might have prevented the widespread use of the smallpox vaccine because it could threaten the lives of the large number of HIV positive individuals many of whom are unaware of their HIV infection. Allergic reactions to the vaccine are also quite common. Allergic reactions to the smallpox vaccine, including inflammation of the lining of the heart, prompted discontinuation of a campaign to vaccinate first responders and healthcare professionals soon after the 9/11 attack.

---

[d] Efforts are underway for the eradication of Guinea Worm, which exhibits a number of favorable characteristics for eradication.

TABLE 7-1 Eradication of Human Diseases—What Makes It Possible?

	Smallpox	Polio	Measles
Disease is limited to humans, i.e., no animal reservoir?	Yes	Yes	Yes
Limited persistence in the environment?	Yes	Yes	Yes
Absence of long-term carrier state?	Yes	Yes—Absent, but may occur in immune-compromised individuals	Yes—Absent, but may occur in immune-compromised individuals
Long-term immunity results from infection?	Yes	Yes—But may not be sustained in immune-compromised individuals	Yes—But may not be sustained in immune-compromised individuals
Vaccination confers long-term immunity?	Yes	Yes—But may not be sustained in immune-compromised individuals Virus used for production of the live vaccine can produce polio-like illness and has potential to revert back to "wild type infection"	Yes—But may not be sustained in immune-compromised individuals
Herd immunity prevents perpetuation of an epidemic?	Yes	Yes	Yes
Easily-diagnosed disease?	Yes—Disease easily identified	Yes/No Disease relatively easy to identify, but large number of asymptomatic infections	No Disease may be confused with other diseases by those unfamiliar with measles
Vaccination effective postexposure?	Yes Postexposure vaccination effective	No Postexposure vaccination not effective	No Postexposure vaccination not effective

WHAT OPTIONS ARE AVAILABLE FOR THE CONTROL OF HIV/AIDS?

HIV/AIDS has been a uniquely difficult epidemic to control. An understanding of the biology of the HIV virus helps us understand many of the reasons for this. The HIV virus attacks the very cells designed to control it. The virus can avoid exposure to treatments by residing inside cells without replicating. Many treatments work by interrupting the process of replication and thus are not effective when replication stops. The virus establishes a chronic carrier state enabling long-term infectivity. High mutation rates reduce the effectiveness of drugs, as well as the effectiveness of the body's own immune system to fight the disease.

Despite these monumental challenges, considerable progress has been made by reducing the load of virus through drug treatment and preventing the transmission of the disease through a variety of public health interventions. To appreciate the efforts to control transmission of HIV/AIDS, it is important to understand the large number of ways that it can be transmitted.

TABLE 7-2 Potential for Eradication of HIV/AIDS

	HIV/AIDS
Disease is limited to humans, i.e., no animal reservoir?	No—Animal reservoirs exist
Limited persistence in the environment?	No—May persist on contaminated needles long enough for transmission
Absence of long-term carrier state?	No—Carrier state is routine
Long-term immunity results from infection?	No—Effective long-term immunity does not usually occur
Vaccination confers long-term immunity?	No—None currently available and will be difficult to achieve
Herd immunity prevents perpetuation of an epidemic?	No—Large number of previously-infected individuals increases the risk to the uninfected
Easily-diagnosed disease?	No—Requires testing
Vaccination effective postexposure?	No—None currently available

HIV is most infectious when transmitted directly by blood. Blood transfusions were an early source of the spread of the virus. The introduction of HIV virus testing in the mid 1980s led to dramatic improvement in the safety of the blood supply. Nonetheless, the safest blood transfusions are those that come from an individual's own blood. Thus, donation of one's own blood for later transfusion when needed has become a routine part of surgery preparation in many parts of the world. The most dangerous forms of transfusions are those that come from blood or blood products pooled from large numbers of individuals. Hemophiliacs in many developed countries used pooled blood products to control their bleeding in the 1980s. They suffered perhaps the world's highest rate of HIV infection before this hazard was recognized and addressed. A more recent pooling of blood products occurred in China and contributed to a surge of the disease.

Unprotected anal intercourse is a highly infectious way to transmit HIV. This may help to explain the early spread of the disease among male homosexuals. Today, however, heterosex-

ual transmission is the most common route of infection; additionally, there is a higher risk of transmission from male to female than from female to male. A series of public health interventions have now been shown to be effective: properly used latex condoms, male circumcision, and abstinence are being promoted in efforts to control the disease throughout the world. Aggressive treatment of AIDS at an early stage reduces the viral load and the ease of transmission to others.[e]

Maternal-to-child transmission of HIV was a common, but not universal event before the advent of effective drug treatment. The use of treatment during pregnancy and at the time of delivery has dramatically reduced the maternal-to-child transmission of the infection. Today, this route of transmission is close to being eliminated, which is an important public health achievement. Breastfeeding represents an ongoing and more controversial route of transmission. Up to 25 percent of HIV-positive breastfeeding women may transmit HIV to their children. In countries where breastfeeding provides an essential defense against a wide range of infections, the issue of whether or not to breastfeed has been very controversial. Drug treatment of HIV infections during breastfeeding has been shown to reduce, but not eliminate transmission.

Finally, HIV can be transmitted through contaminated needles. Thus, the risk of HIV transmission needs to be addressed in two very different populations—healthcare workers and those who abuse intravenous drugs. New needle technologies and better disposal methods have reduced the likelihood of needlestick injuries in healthcare settings. Postexposure treatment with drugs has been quite successful in reducing health care-related HIV infections. Reductions in HIV transmission through intravenous drug use have also occurred in areas where public health efforts have focused attention on this method of transmission. Needle exchange programs have met resistance and remain controversial, but most likely contribute to transmission reductions when the programs are carefully designed and administered.

Thus, a range of existing interventions linked to the method of transmission of HIV have been moderately successful in controlling the disease. New methods of control are needed and are being investigated and increasingly applied. Unfortunately, vaccination is not one of them. In fact, randomized clinical trials so far have demonstrated no substantial degree of protection from vaccinations and have raised the concern that vaccination may actually increase the probability of acquiring HIV.

---

[e] It has been suggested that serial monogamy reduces the risk of HIV transmission in populations compared to having two or more concurrent partners. Serial monogamy contributes to only one chain of transmission at a time and thus may slow, if not halt, the speed or spread of the epidemic in a population.

The recognition that effective vaccinations are not likely in the foreseeable future has brought forth a wide array of ideas on how to control the spread of infection. Antiviral creams, postcoital treatments, and early testing and case finding may become effective interventions. Antiviral creams may become both an adjunct to condom use, as well as a substitute in those situations where condom use is not acceptable. The success of postneedlestick interventions in the healthcare setting has raised the possibility that postexposure treatment may also be effective after high risk sexual contact. Finally, new diagnostic tests for HIV that allow for detection of the disease in the most contagious early weeks of the infection are being investigated for widespread use. To be effective, testing for early disease would need to be coupled with rapid case finding to identify and ideally treat contacts.

It is encouraging to know that existing and emerging interventions for HIV hold out possibility of effective control. Public health and medical intervention complement each other and are both needed if we are to effectively address the most widespread epidemic of the 21st century. Table 7-3 summarizes the routes of transmission and the estimated transmission rates per exposure.[6] Finally, it outlines the potential interventions that we have discussed.

WHAT OPTIONS ARE AVAILABLE FOR THE CONTROL OF INFLUENZA?

Pandemic influenza is not a new problem. The influenza epidemic of 1918 is estimated to have killed an estimated 50 million people in a world populated with 2 billion people. Today, that would translate to over 150 million deaths. The history of the 1918 influenza pandemic is briefly summarized in Box 7.2.[7] The 1958 pandemic of Asian flu caused a similar, if less deadly pandemic. Thus, we should not be surprised if pandemic flu returns in the coming years.

Influenza A is a viral infection that has long been capable of pandemic or worldwide spread.[f] Its ability to be rapidly

[f] Influenza B can also cause epidemics of influenza, however it is not thought to pose the same hazard of pandemic disease that is possible with Influenza A.

TABLE 7-3 Mode and Chances of Transmission of HIV and Existing Interventions

Route of transmission	Estimated transmission rate per exposure	Potential interventions
Blood transfusion Blood and blood products, such as pooled blood products previously used in U.S. by hemophiliacs	Contaminated blood over 90% chance of transmission; pooling of blood dramatically increases infection	Screening of blood to detect HIV early Use of individual's own blood for surgery
Sexual contact—Anal higher than vaginal, which is much higher than oral	Range from 0.1% to 10% with unprotected receptive anal intercourse posing highest risk Vaginal male to female greater than female to male Circumcision reduces risk by half Other sexually-transmitted diseases may increase risk	Latex condom Circumcision Abstinence Serial monogamy reduces spread compared to two or more concurrent partners
Mother-to-child transmission	15% to 40% higher in developing countries Highest rate of transmission at time of vaginal delivery	Cesarean delivery Drug treatment during pregnancy and at time of delivery for mother and child
Breast-feeding	Very low per exposure, but up to 25% over year or more of breast-feeding	Continuation of drug treatment reduces, but does not eliminate transmission
Needlestick exposures Healthcare occupational risk	Less than 0.5% of HIV positive needlesticks result in transmission	Postexposure treatment with drugs established as effective prevention
Injection drug use	Less than 1% per episode of needle sharing	Needle exchange programs

Source: Data from Population Reference Bureau. Facing the HIV/AIDS Pandemic. *Population Bulletin* 2002: 57(3).

BOX 7-2   The Influenza Pandemic of 1918.

The history of the influenza pandemic of 1918 is summarized by the United States National Archives and Records Administration as follows:[7]

World War I claimed an estimated 16 million lives. The influenza epidemic that swept the world in 1918 killed an estimated 50 million people. One fifth of the world's population was attacked by this deadly virus. Within months, it had killed more people than any other illness in recorded history.

The plague emerged in two phases. In late spring of 1918, the first phase, known as the "three-day fever," appeared without warning. Few deaths were reported. Victims recovered after a few days. When the disease surfaced again that fall, it was far more severe. Scientists, doctors, and health officials could not identify this disease which was striking so fast and so viciously, eluding treatment and defying control. Some victims died within hours of their first symptoms. Others succumbed after a few days; their lungs filled with fluid and they suffocated to death.

The plague did not discriminate. It was rampant in urban and rural areas, from the densely populated East coast to the remotest parts of Alaska. Young adults, usually unaffected by these types of infectious diseases, were among the hardest hit groups along with the elderly and young children. The flu afflicted over 25 percent of the U.S. population. In one year, the average life expectancy in the United States dropped by 12 years.

---

transmitted through the air from person to person and its short incubation period have made it an ongoing public health problem. It often kills the very young, the very old, and those with chronic illnesses, particularly those with respiratory diseases and suppressed immune systems. In addition, the disease continues to mutate creating new types against which previous infections and previous vaccinations have little or no impact. Thus, new vaccines are required every flu season. Seasonal influenza kills over 30,000 people in the United States alone in the average year despite the increasingly widespread use of vaccinations.

A variety of public health and medical interventions have been and continue to be used to address the current and potential threat posed by influenza. They may well all be needed to address future threats. Let us take a look at these interventions.

Inactivated or dead vaccines have been the mainstay of immunization against influenza. Unfortunately, current technology requires approximately six months lead time to produce large quantities of the vaccine. Thus, influenza experts need to make educated guesses about next year's dominant strains of influenza. In some years, they have been wrong and the deaths and disability from seasonal influenza have increased. New technologies for vaccine production are greatly needed and are being extensively researched.

In recent years, live vaccines administered through nasal spray have been developed and increasingly used. These vaccines are more acceptable than shots to most patients and are now considered safe for a wide range of age groups. They raise the hope of greater acceptance and wider use of influenza vaccinations in coming years.

Medications to treat influenza and modestly shorten the course of the disease have also been developed. Influenza experts view these drugs as most useful to temporarily slow the spread of new strains providing additional time for the development of vaccines to specifically target the new strain. Widespread use of influenza drugs has already resulted in resistance raising concerns that these drugs will not be effective when we need them the most. Efforts are underway to develop new drugs and reserve their use solely for potential pandemic conditions.

Despite our best efforts, influenza is expected to continue its annual seasonal epidemic and to pose a risk of pandemic spread. The use of barrier protection such as masks, isolation methods, and even quarantine has been considered part of a comprehensive effort to control influenza. It is clear that we have a variety of public health methods to help control the impact of the disease. It is likely that we will need all of these efforts and new ones if we are going to control the potential deaths and disabilities due to influenza in coming years.[8] Now, let us look at our last example of the development of public health strategies to control communicable diseases—that of rabies.

WHAT OPTIONS ARE AVAILABLE FOR THE CONTROL OF RABIES?

Rabies is an ancient disease that has plagued human beings for over 4000 years. It is caused by a ribonucleic acid (RNA) virus that is transmitted through saliva of infected animals and slowly replicates. It spreads to nerve cells and gradually invades the central nervous system over a 20- to 60-day incubation period. Once the central nervous system is involved, the disease progresses almost inevitably to death within one to two weeks. Any warm-blooded animal can be infected with rabies, but some species are particularly susceptible—most commonly raccoons, skunks, and bats. Cats and dogs can also be infected and transmit the virus.

A multicomponent vaccination strategy has been very successful in preventing the development of rabies in humans. In most recent years, there have been between one and five fatal cases of rabies per year in the United States despite the persistence and periodic increase in rabies among wildlife populations. Let us take a look at how this quite remarkable control effort has occurred.

The ability to successfully vaccinate humans against rabies after the occurrence of a rabies-prone bite has long been a component of the success of rabies reduction among humans. The use of postexposure vaccination was first demonstrated by Louis Pasteur in 1887 and was used to dramatically save the life of a young victim. Early live vaccines had frequent and severe side effects. They were sequentially replaced by inactivated vaccines grown in animal nerve tissue. These replacement vaccines still led to occasional acute neurological complications and gave the treatment a reputation of being dangerous. The development of a vaccine grown in human cell cultures in the 1970s led to safety records comparable to those of other commonly-used vaccines. Today, over 30,000 rabies vaccination series are administered annually in the United States.

The success of rabies control is a result of a series of coordinated efforts to utilize vaccinations in different settings: Vaccines are administered to individuals who are bitten by suspicious species of wild animals including raccoons, bats, skunks, foxes, and coyotes. Victims of suspected rabies bites by dogs and cats may await the results of quarantine of the animal and observation over a 10-day period. When substantial doubt still exists after this time frame, vaccination is recommended. Laws requiring rabies vaccination of dogs and cats have been enforced in the United States for decades and have greatly reduced the number of reported infections in these animals. Today only ten percent or fewer of suspect rabies-prone bites come from dogs and cats.

Wildlife remains the greatest source of rabies—wildlife epidemics occur with regularity. Rabies-prone bites still occur especially from raccoons, which regularly feed from garbage cans in rural, suburban, and occasionally urban America. Recent development of effective oral vaccinations that can be administered to wildlife through baits have been credited with reducing the number of infected animals, especially those residing in close proximity to humans.

Rabies illustrates the variety of ways that a key intervention—vaccination—can be used to address a disease. As with many complex diseases of public health importance, a carefully designed and coordinated strategy is required to maximize the benefit of available technology. In addition, ongoing research is needed to continue to develop new and improved approaches to the control of communicable diseases.[9]

HIV/AIDS, influenza A, and rabies represent three very different communicable diseases. However, they all require the use of multiple interventions, close collaboration between the public health and healthcare systems, and continuing efforts to find new and more effective methods for their control.

Efforts to control infectious diseases have increased in recent years along with the increase in emerging and reemerging infectious diseases. Technological advances have provided encouragement for the future but at times have raised concerns about the safety of our interventions.[g] New technology, new strategies for applying technology, and new ways to effectively organize our efforts are needed to ensure the effectiveness and safety of our efforts to prevent, eradicate and control communicable diseases.

Now let us turn our attention to our third category of disease in chapter 8 that of environmental diseases and injuries.

---

[g] In recent decades the number of vaccinations used in children has increased dramatically. The potential for new side effect from multiple vaccinations has been of recent concern especially the previous use of a mercury containing compound designed to help preserve vaccines. Concerns have been raised that multiple vaccines have increased the risk of autism. Despite investigations which do not support an association, these concerns have persisted.

Key Words

- Infectious disease
- Communicable disease
- Infections
- Immunization
- Passive immunity
- Inactived (dead) vaccine
- Live vaccines
- Herd immunity
- Case finding
- Epidemiological treatment
- Ring vaccination

Discussion Questions

Take a look at the questions posed in the following scenarios which were presented at the beginning of this chapter. See now whether you can answer them.

1. *Your college roommate went to bed not feeling well one night and early the next morning you had trouble arousing her. She was rushed to the hospital just in time to be effectively diagnosed and treated for meningococcal meningitis. The health department recommends immediate antibiotic treatment for everyone that was in close contact with your roommate. They set up a process to watch for additional cases to be sure an outbreak is not in progress. Fortunately, no more cases occur. You ask yourself: should your college require that all freshmen have the meningococcal vaccine before they can register for classes?*

2. *As a health advisor to a worldwide HIV/AIDS foundation, you are asked to advise on ways to address the HIV and developing tuberculosis (TB) epidemics. You are asked to do some long-range thinking and to come up with a list of potential approaches to control the epidemics, or at least ways reduce the development of TB. The first recommendation you make is to forget about eradicating HIV/AIDS. How did you come to that conclusion?*

3. *Your hometown of 100,000 is faced with a crisis as an airplane lands containing a passenger thought to have a new form of severe influenza that has recently gained the ability to spread from person to person through airborne spread. As the mayor of the city, what do you decide to do?*

4. *You are a principal at a local high school. One of your top athletes is in the hospital with a spreading bacterial infection due to a staphylococcus bacteria resistant to all known antibiotics. The infection occurred after what*

appeared to be a minor injury during practice. As the principal, what do you decide to do?

REFERENCES

1. Nobelprize.org. Robert Koch and Tuberculosis. Available at: http://nobelprize.org/educational_games/medicine/tuberculosis/readmore.htm. Accessed March 18, 2009.

2. New Jersey Medical School Global Tuberculosis Institute. History of TB. Available at: http://www.umdnj.edu/ntbcweb/tbhistory.htm. Accessed March 18, 2009.

3. National Institute of Allergy and Infectious Diseases. The Evidence that HIV causes AIDS. Available at: http://www3.niaid.nih.gov/topics/HIVAIDS/Understanding/HIVcausesAIDS.htm. Accessed March 18, 2009.

4. Centers for Disease Control and Prevention. Vaccines. Available at: http://www.cdc.gov/vaccines/. Accessed March 18, 2009.

5. Sompayrac L. *How Pathogenic Viruses Work.* Sudbury, MA: Jones and Bartlett Publishers; 2002.

6. Lamptey P, Wigley M, Carr D, Collymore Y. Facing the HIV/AIDS pandemic. *Population Bulletin.* 2002; 57(3): 1–3.

7. National Archives and Records Administration. The Deadly Vines: The Influenza Epidemic of 1918. Available at: http://www.archives.gov/exhibits/influenza-epidemic/. Accessed May 12, 2009.

8. World Health Organization. Global Agenda for Influenza Surveillance and Control. Available at: http://www.who.int/csr/disease/influenza/globalagenda/en/index.html. Accessed March 18, 2009.

9. Centers for Disease Control and Prevention. Rabies Home. Available at: http://www.cdc.gov/rabies/. Accessed March 18, 2009.

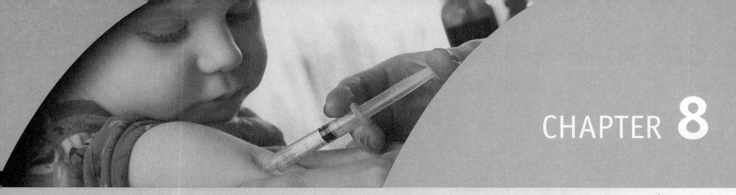

CHAPTER 8

Environmental Health and Safety

LEARNING OBJECTIVES

By the end of this chapter the student will be able to:

- define the scope of morbidity and mortality caused by the physical environment.
- identify the range of interactions that occur between human beings and the physical environment.
- identify the components of environmental risk assessment and apply them to an environmental hazard, such as lead.
- distinguish between a risk assessment, a public health assessment, and an ecological assessment.
- discuss the meaning of interactions and how they may impact the size of risks.
- illustrate how safety issues, such as motor vehicle injuries, have been addressed using a systems thinking approach.

Joe grew up in an industrial district of town. His family lived in an old apartment building and he played in a playground near a major intersection. By the age of 6, Joe was found to have high lead levels in his blood and was not doing well in school. Where could all that lead come from, his mother wondered?

Jill is pregnant and loves fish, which she has eaten almost daily for years as part of her effort to stay healthy. She hears that fish should not be eaten regularly during pregnancy. Why, she wonders, should I cut down on eating something as healthy as fish?

Ralph and Sonya, a prosperous professional couple, and their two children live in an older suburban home. They feel secure that their environment is safe. They were surprised to find when they wanted to put their house up for sale that it did not pass the safety tests for radon. Where did the radon come from, they wondered, and what can be done about it?

Sandra worked for an international agency that had successfully addressed the danger of radiation due to the hole in the ozone

layer. She was shocked when she was told that she had a life-threatening skin cancer called melanoma. She asked, what could cause melanoma? Could years of sun exposure have played a role?

With your seat belt on, children buckled in, and airbags activated, you head out of the driveway to face the world. You didn't see that truck coming when it hit you from the side. The ambulance responded within minutes and took your family to the nearest emergency room. You all made it through with only minor injuries. You ask yourself, was it just luck or did the system work?

All of these situations are part of what we mean by the burden of environmental disease and injury. In order to understand the impact of the environment on disease, we need to define what we mean by it and appreciate the many ways that we interact with it.

WHAT IS MEANT BY "ENVIRONMENT"?

Environment is an ambiguous term. It is sometimes used to imply all influences other than genetic influences including social, economic, and cultural influences. We will define the environment as the physical environment. The physical environment can be thought of in three categories: unaltered ("natural"), altered, and the built environment.[a] Figure 8-1 diagrams the scope of environmental diseases and injuries.

---

[a] The term "natural" is used in quotations because it can be a misleading term. We often think that the term "natural disasters" implies that human actions had nothing to do with the events. Increasingly, human actions precipitate, worsen, and even cause "natural disasters." Construction on vulnerable lands increases the damage from storms, fires, earthquakes, and even volcanoes. Global warming caused by human activities is also beginning to have its impacts. Our planet has been altered in so many ways that the unaltered environment is becoming difficult to find.

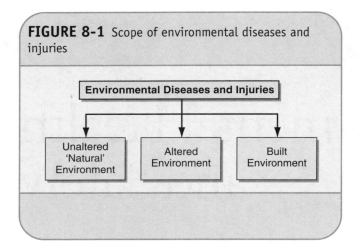

FIGURE 8-1 Scope of environmental diseases and injuries

The health of human beings was affected by the physical environment long before we had the capacity to substantially alter it. Floods, earthquakes, and volcanoes have always been a part of the physical environment. In addition to these intermittent and often isolated impacts, daily exposure to infectious diseases in water and food have always been a part of the unaltered environment.

In recent years, we have recognized more subtle impacts of the **unaltered environment**. Radon, a common naturally-occurring breakdown product of uranium, increases the risk of lung cancer. Exposure to naturally-occurring sunlight increases the chances of skin cancer including melanoma—a potentially lethal skin cancer—especially among light-skinned individuals.

Human activity has altered nearly every aspect of our physical environment. Some alterations to our environment may improve human health—from water treatment, to waste management, to mosquito and flood control. Nonetheless, we need to consider the overall impacts that these changes have on the physical environment. The sheer growth in the number of human beings—we are rapidly approaching a planet population of 7 billion—is likely to magnify our impact on all aspects of our physical environment in the future.

We often think of the **altered environment** as reflecting the impact of chemicals, radiation, and biological products that we introduce into the environment. The list of intentional or unintentional introductions is in fact very long. It ranges from industrial chemicals, such as pesticides, benzene, and chlorofluorocarbons (CFCs), to elements mined from the earth, such as mercury and lead. It also includes radiation from nuclear energy and medical wastes. Biological impacts encompass the introduction of invasive species and the management of biological wastes.

The concept of the **built environment** is a relatively new term that includes all the impacts of the physical environment

as a result of human construction. The impacts of it include injuries and exposures in the home, the transportation system, and where we work and play. It also includes factors ranging from the way we build and heat our buildings and cook our food, to the way we travel from place to place. The built environment influences our safety through its impact on injuries and hazardous exposures. It also influences our activity levels and our social interactions that impact our health.[1]

The impact of the built environment is wide-ranging throughout the world, but differs greatly by geography and stage of social and economic development. Indoor air pollution from cooking is the most prominent source of air pollution in much of the developing world. Motor vehicle injuries are the most deadly consequences of the built environment in most developed countries. The built environment has subtle impacts as well. The way we build our cities affects the amount of exercise we get and the quantity of noise pollution we experience. Construction methods affect air systems in buildings and can increase our exposure to "sick buildings." Let us take a look at the burden of disease that results from the physical environment.

WHAT IS THE BURDEN OF DISEASE DUE TO THE PHYSICAL ENVIRONMENT?

Measuring the impact of the physical environment on health is difficult because of the many types of impacts and the often subtle effects that occur. The impacts we experience today may pale in comparison to what we can expect in the future. Nonetheless, it is useful to appreciate the current estimates of the magnitude of the direct and indirect burden.

As we saw in the introduction to this section, motor vehicle injuries and exposure to toxic substances are two important actual causes of death that represent the largest known impact of the physical environment. Together, these incidents are estimated to cause nearly 100,000 deaths, representing about 20 percent of preventable deaths in the United States and approximately 10 percent of all deaths in the United States according to the Centers for Disease Control and Prevention's (CDC's) calculations.[2] Motor vehicle injuries and other unintentional injuries have especially heavy impacts on the young; in fact, they are the number one cause of death in the United States among those 1 to 24 years of age.[3] As a cause of disability, injuries also rank high especially considering their disproportionate impact on the young.[b]

---

[b] The role of environmental factors in asthma is difficult to separate from the impact of cigarettes, genetics, and other determinants of health and disease, etc. Subtle, but important impacts are increasingly being recognized. Air pollution, especially very small particle air pollution, is being linked increasingly to coronary artery disease. Attributing a portion of the many deaths from coronary artery disease to air pollution substantially increases the estimates of the environmental burden of disease.

Approximately 5000 deaths due to injuries occur in the occupational setting per year. Certain occupations are particularly vulnerable to injuries including mining, construction, and agriculture. Occupational injuries have been declining in recent years, but remain an important cause of death and disability.[4]

The impact of toxic substances on death and disability is difficult to measure due to the length of time the substances may take to affect the body. It may be years after an exposure before an individual experiences negative health effects on their kidneys, liver, nerves, and other organs. Many toxic exposures occur in occupational settings. Occupational exposures that result in morbidity and mortality include lung diseases caused by exposures to hazardous dusts, hearing loss from loud noises, and back pain from excessive lifting, as well as a wide range of other mechanical problems, including carpal tunnel syndrome often caused by repetitive motion of the hand and wrist.[4]

Cancer caused by occupational exposures has been of particular concern. As much as five percent of cancer deaths in males have been estimated to be due to occupational exposures.[5] Cancers of the lung, bladder, and white blood cells (leukemia), are particularly likely to result from chronic exposures to chemicals, such as formaldehyde, benzene, and organic dyes. Reductions in occupational exposures in the last 25 years have resulted in a declining burden of disease from these exposures in the United States. The opposite is being seen in many newly industrializing countries where current exposures are increasing and may result in more cases of cancer and other diseases in the not-too-distant future.

Finally, we cannot evaluate the impact of toxic exposures solely by tracing them to human deaths and disabilities. The altered environment has impacts on entire ecosystems of plants and animals. The ecological impact of environmental factors can have long-term and largely irreversible consequences. Once chemicals, radiation, and biological products are released into the environment, the process cannot generally be easily reversed. Thus, we need to take a broad and long-term perspective when we address environmental health. To understand how the physical environment—be it the unaltered, altered, or built environment—affects health, we need to explore the myriad ways that we interact with it. Box 8-1 illustrates this concept.

Because of the complexity of the interactions between human beings and the physical environment, a range of approaches has been developed for addressing these issues. We will categorize and examine these approaches as follows:

- **Risk assessment**
- **Public health assessment**
- **Ecological assessment**
- **Interaction analysis**
- **Systems analysis**

We can think of these strategies as a progression of approaches of increasing complexity. We will organize our approach to environmental diseases and injuries starting with risk assessment and proceeding in order to examine each of these strategies.

HOW DOES RISK ASSESSMENT ADDRESS THE IMPACTS OF THE PHYSICAL ENVIRONMENT?

Risk assessment is a formal process that aims to measure the potential impact of known **hazards**. A hazard indicates the inherent danger of an exposure, while a risk assessment aims to take into account not only the inherent danger, but the quantity, route, and timing of the exposure.[6] The risk assessment approach to environmental hazards represents the mainstay of our current approach. The underlying principles have a long history in public health often resulting from the investigation of specific occupational exposures.

One of the earliest occupational investigations occurred among chimney sweeps in 18th-century England. Their high-dose exposure to carbon residues in smokestacks led to early and frequent testicular cancer. Nineteenth century industrializing countries also provided ample opportunities to study the impacts of work-related exposures. For instance, the dangers of radiation came to light after high levels of cancer were detected in workers who painted watches with radiation-containing paint for the purposes of nighttime illumination. The dangers of asbestos became evident after high-dose exposures among ship workers during World War II resulted in cases of lung cancer many years later. The dangers of exposure to polyvinyl chloride (PVC), a common industrial compound, was recognized after five workers from the same manufacturing plant came down with a rare liver tumor in the 1970s.

Risk assessment today has become a complex technical effort requiring quantitative measures of the magnitude of the risk. The history of risk assessment in the United States is closely tied to the investigations and regulations surrounding benzene. Box 8-2 provides an overview of the history of the study and regulation of this chemical hazard.[7, 8]

The formal process of risk assessment represents the current approach to environmental hazards in the United States.[9, 10] Figure 8-2 illustrates the four step risk assessment process as used by the U.S. EPA.

Risk assessment attempts to evaluate the impact of environmental exposures one at a time and to measure the types and magnitudes of the impacts. If a substantial risk is found

BOX 8-1   How We Interact with Our Environment.

We are exposed to the physical environment every minute of our lives through multiple routes. For each of these routes of exposure, the body has mechanisms for protection. We are primarily exposed to the environment via the skin; the respiratory tract (from the nose to the lungs); the alimentary tract or digestive tract (from the mouth to the anus); and the genital-urinary tract.

Each bodily surface that is directly exposed to the physical environment has developed a form of barrier protection. The skin provides direct protection against radiation, organisms, and physical contact, as well as providing some protections against heat and cold. The respiratory tract is guarded by mucous production and by small hair-like structures called cilia, whose motion in conjunction with coughing removes materials that we breathe into our lungs. Cells called phagocytes literally consume organisms and large particles. Antibodies, along with cell-mediated immunity, also protect against access of harmful particles and organisms through the lungs. The alimentary or digestive tract is protected by saliva, mucous membranes, and antibodies, as well as strong acidity in the stomach. The genital-urinary tract is protected by mucous membrane barriers, antibody and cell-mediated immunity, and at times by an acid environment.[c]

Therefore, we need to recognize that the impacts of the environment on health are very complex.[5] We should expect to find that the following issues affect the risk:

- *Route of exposure*—The consequences of exposures to heavy metals including mercury, lead, and cadmium, for instance, depend on whether the exposure is via the skin or the respiratory or gastrointestinal tracts.
- *Timing of exposure*—Short-term high-dose impacts often will not be the same as long-term low-dose impacts even if the total exposure and the routes of exposure are the same. For instance, a small number of severe episodes of sunburn during childhood have been found to greatly increase the risk of skin cancers far more than multiple milder adult sunburns. Chronic low-dose exposures may produce different and more subtle impacts.
- *Stage of life*—The impact on the very young and the very old are likely to be different than the impact for people at other stages of life. We need to be especially concerned about exposures during pregnancy, early childhood, and the later years of life.
- *Other diseases*—The presence of other diseases will affect how the body is impacted by an environmental exposure. We need to be especially concerned about environmental exposures for those with chronic lung diseases and those with suppressed immune systems, such as those living with AIDS.
- *Special sensitivities*—A few individuals will be hypersensitive to specific environmental exposures that have no measurable impact on the vast majority of individuals. We need to be concerned about how to identify and protect these individuals without depriving them of rights or opportunities.

---

[c]The effectiveness of our bodily defenses depends on a number of factors, for instance, genetic factors. Skin pigmentation reduces the penetration of radiation and reduces the risk of skin cancers, including melanoma, the most serious of skin cancers. Other diseases affect how well our defenses operate—for instance chronic obstructive lung disease and cystic fibrosis can alter the ability of the cilia in the lung to operate effectively. Age can affect the ability of our skin to serve as an effective barrier as well as the ability of the immune system to respond. The elderly are especially prone to the effects of heat and cold. They are also more susceptible to a range of infections and cancers. Our defense mechanisms can overreact to environmental stimuli and themselves produce ailments, including allergies and autoimmune disease. The impacts of environmental exposures may be limited to a small number of susceptible individuals whose immune systems react especially strongly to specific environmental exposures. For instance, allergies to peanuts or household or industrial chemicals can produce unusual, but severe reactions in a small number of susceptible individuals.

to exist, the process then reviews options to protect, detect, and react to the risk to minimize the burden of disease on humans.

The risk assessment process builds in a margin of error designed to provide extra protection for especially vulnerable individuals or populations. Thus those exposed to levels above the recommended maximum levels of exposure will not necessarily experience adverse effects. Table 8-1 outlines the four steps in the risk assessment process and uses a simplified example of how airborne exposure to benzene in occupational settings might be presented in this framework.

Now let us take a look at what is meant by public health assessment.

WHAT IS A PUBLIC HEALTH ASSESSMENT?

Risk assessment is distinguished from what is called a public health assessment. A public health assessment goes beyond a risk assessment by including data on actual exposure in a community.

Public health assessments have the potential for major impacts on large numbers of people because they address the risks not just in a specific location, such as in an occupational

BOX 8-2 Benzene and Risk Assessment.

Benzene is an organic chemical that is used as a solvent in the chemical and pharmaceutical industries. Because it readily becomes a gas at room temperature, airborne exposure is an important concern. Benzene is one of the most widely-used organic chemicals. It is estimated that over 250,000 American workers are exposed to benzene, particularly in the chemical, printing, paint, and petroleum industries.[d]

A range of toxic effects have been documented from benzene over the last 150 years. These include neurological effects of acute and chronic exposure, as well as life-threatening suppression of the production of red blood cells called aplastic anemia.

In the 1960s and 1970s, it was increasingly recognized that benzene caused cancer, particularly leukemia. Early studies of benzene and leukemia were conducted by Muzaffer Aksoy, a Turkish physician, who observed leukemia among many shoemakers in Turkey where benzene was being used as a solvent in the manufacturing of leather products. His large cohort study helped establish the chemical as a presumed cause of leukemia.

Based on a series of studies that documented the risk of leukemia, in 1978 the federal government established a standard for exposure to benzene in the air of 1 part per million (1 ppm), as opposed to the former approach of limiting the exposure to 10 parts per million (10 ppm). One part per million is approximately the equivalent of one drop in 40 gallons of liquid. In 1980, the United States Supreme Court overturned the new standard based upon the argument that the Environmental Protection Agency (EPA) had not documented the impact of the new 1 ppm standard in terms of number of lives saved or compared it to the 10 ppm level. The Supreme Court concluded that "safe" did not mean risk-free, giving the analogies of driving a car and breathing city air. The Supreme Court insisted that standards be set based upon the preponderance of evidence from a formal risk assessment. As a result of this Supreme Court decision, the EPA developed a risk-assessment approach that grew into the current risk-assessment process. The 1 part per million standard was supported by quantitative measures of the impact: the federal government estimated that there would be 14 to 17 excess deaths per 1000 workers exposed to 10 ppm of benzene for a working lifetime, compared to being exposed to the new 1 ppm standard.

Thus, risk assessment today is a highly technical and quantitative activity designed to establish a maximum level of allowed exposure to one particular hazard. The levels set are designed to conform to the Supreme Court's definition of "significant risk," which is characterized by one that is "not acceptable to society" in "ordinary life".[7]

---

[d] Benzene is also a component of gasoline therefore, the entire population has some exposure to benzene. This discussion focuses on the hazard assessment of benzene in the occupational setting.

---

setting, but risks to large numbers of individuals and often to the population as a whole. These types of risk assessments have been very controversial and have taken years—often decades—to complete. An expert panel for the National Academy of Sciences has recommended a major overhaul of public health assessments.[11] A classic example of the importance and potential impacts of the public health assessment process and its ongoing challenges is discussed in Box 8-3, which looks at the health risks due to lead.[12, 13]

Risk assessments and public health assessments both focus exclusively on the health impacts on human beings. Let us take a look at an additional type of assessment conducted by the EPA that looks at the impact of an exposure on plants and animals.

WHAT IS AN ECOLOGICAL RISK ASSESSMENT?

Environmental health cannot be viewed solely on the basis of current impacts on human health. The impacts of environmental contamination or pollution on plants and animals and

FIGURE 8-2 The 4-step risk assessment process

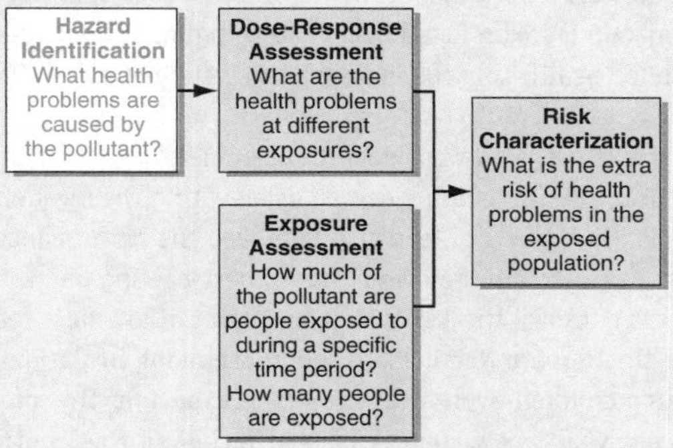

Source: Reprinted from U.S. Environmental Protection Agency. Risk Assessment Portal Available at http://www.epa.gov/risk/hazardousidentification.htm Accessed December 14, 2008.

TABLE 8-1 Four-Step Risk Assessment and Simplified Example—Benzene

Components	Simplified example—benzene
Hazard Identification What health effects are caused by the pollutant?	Benzene causes leukemia Strong evidence from cohort studies and supportive animal data exist
Dose-response Relationship What are the health problems at different exposures?	Strong dose-response relationship among occupational workers with level of 1 ppm over a working lifetime. The impact of exposure at 1 ppm is indistinguishable from unexposed with rapid increase in rates of leukemia above that level
Exposure Assessment How much of the pollutant are people exposed to during a specific time period? How many people are exposed?	Industrial exposures above 1 ppm common in a range of industries at the time the standard was set Over 250,000 workers exposed to benzene
Risk Characterization What is the extra risk of health problems in the exposed population?	14–17 excess cases of leukemia per 1000 workers exposed to 10 ppm throughout a working lifetime

Source: Awofeso N. What's new about the "New Public Health"? *American Journal of Public Health.* 2004; 94(5): 705–709.

the ecosystems in which they exist often has important long-term consequences.

The modern environmental movement in the United States was ignited in large part by Rachel Carson's book, *Silent Spring*, which described how the widespread use of DDT had threatened the American Eagle and other birds as it became deposited in and weakened their eggs.[14] Broader concern about the impacts of contaminants on ecological systems ranging from chemicals, to radiation, to genetically-altered crops has made clear the importance of ecological risk assessments. Human health consequences remain an important, but not necessarily a direct consequence of the impacts of environmental contamination or pollution as described in Box 8-4, which explores the impacts of mercury.[15]

Up to this point, we have addressed the impact of environmental exposures one at a time. Increasingly, we find that the

BOX 8-3   Health Risks Due to Lead.

Knowledge of the potential for lead poisoning goes back to ancient civilizations, where the metal was widely used—for example, it was a component of water pipes and part of the process of making wine. In Rome, lead was used as a method of abortion and high-dose exposures led to a range of mental effects. It is said the Roman emperors were affected by the high levels of lead in Roman wine.

Benjamin Franklin listed every known profession for which lead posed a health hazard and predicted that many years would pass before the public health consequences of lead were addressed. Of course, Benjamin Franklin was right. Things were to get worse before they got better.

In the 1920s, lead was added to gasoline to make for smoother driving. It was highly effective in getting the "knocks" out of early versions of the piston engine, as well as elevating the level of lead in the air. Even today, the lead from gasoline lies in the soil of many playgrounds. High levels of lead also improved the performance of paints. Houses built before the 1970s, and especially before the 1950s, still pose a threat to children who often ingest peeling paint.

It was not until the 1970s that the effect of low-dose lead exposure on the development of intellectual function became clear. The studies of Dr. Herbert Needleman and subsequent investigators documented clear-cut negative effects on the intellectual development of young children even at low levels of exposure. This prompted efforts to remove lead from gasoline, paints, and many other products. In recent years, new sources of lead including toys, pottery, and water have been given increased attention. In short, lead is a well-recognized hazard that is still with us.

continues

BOX 8-3 continued.

Efforts to protect the environment have been coupled with efforts to detect and react to elevated lead levels. It is now standard practice in pediatrics and public health to monitor blood levels in high-risk children, investigate their home environments, and treat persistently-elevated levels. Lead standards for playgrounds, lead abatement programs for homes, and lead monitoring of consumer products, all aim to reduce or eliminate the hazards of lead. The system is by no means foolproof and in recent years elevated levels of the metal have been found from such divergent sources as toys manufactured in China and water in Washington, D.C. Table 8-2 summarizes the potential exposures to lead, including their sources, and offers potential means of reducing or eliminating the hazard.[13]

TABLE 8-2 Where Does Lead in our Bodies Come From and What Can Be Done About It?

How lead enters our bodies	Where it comes from	Ways to reduce exposure
Inhalation	Workers in many lead-exposure industries: including mining, smelting, metal repair, or foundry work Demolition and renovation activities that generate fumes and dust, including home renovations and hobby activities Addition of lead to gasoline Once inhaled deep into the lungs may remain for long periods and be absorbed into blood over time	Occupational controls Phase-out of lead in gasoline in U.S. from 1976 to 1996
Ingestion	Children—normal ingestion of dirt and dust by infants and young children with up to 5% of children who ingest large quantities—a condition called "pica." Children absorb greater percentage of ingested lead than adults Children's toys and objects that are placed in the mouth are especially important sources Soil near old high traffic areas often contaminated from previous lead in gas Glazed pottery often includes lead that can leach into food	Removal of lead paint from older homes—lead levels in paint in the 1950s and earlier were as much as 50% lead Enforce elimination of lead paint from children's toys Monitoring and control of lead levels in soil in young children's play areas Very high blood levels may require "chelation"—treatment to reduce lead levels in blood
Water	Pipes especially in older water supplies and homes built before the mid-1980s often contain lead Lead used in pipes outside and within the home can leach into water—especially warm water—over time	Regulation of levels of lead in public water supply Run home water before use—especially after away for extended period. Use cold water for cooking
In-utero	Pregnant women absorb higher percentage of ingested lead compared to children and can cross placenta Mother's previous lead exposure stored in her bones can be resorbed into her blood during pregnancy	Special effort to reduce exposure by pregnant women including special care with home renovations during pregnancy especially homes built before 1970

Source: Data from Agency for Toxic Substance and Disease Registry. Case Studies in Environmental Medicine—Lead. Available at: http://www.epa.gov/radon/healthrisks.html. Accessed November 8, 2008.

BOX 8-4   Health Risks of Mercury in the Environment.

The impact of high-dose mercury on mental function has been recognized since the 19th century. More recently, it was established that much lower levels of mercury pose risks to the fetus. Neurological damage, including learning disabilities and hearing loss, have been documented at low levels of exposure. The human risks of mercury exposure need to be understood as part of the impact of mercury on an entire ecological system.

For much of the late 19th and 20th centuries, mercury was a common product of industry that heavily contaminated the Great Lakes of the United States. The impacts were not appreciated despite the high levels of contamination and the impacts on animal species. Mercury in bodies of water is filtered by fish species and can concentrate in their fat. Thus, certain fish species can and do accumulate high concentrations of mercury. These species may be eaten by fish-eating birds and pose a risk to a number of endangered avian species. There is no technologically-feasible method for removing mercury from the Great Lakes or other bodies of water. Your children's children will most likely be living with mercury contamination.

Recommendations for limiting the consumption of fish, especially by pregnant women, have been the mainstay of efforts to address this problem. These efforts are complicated by the fact that the consumption of fish also carries health benefits. Today, the challenge is how to minimize the amount of mercury consumed by women without losing the benefits of fish consumption. Because some fish have much higher mercury levels than others, the March of Dimes recommends that pregnant women avoid shark, swordfish, king mackerel, and tilefish. They indicate that "it's ok" to eat a limited amount of fish that contain small amounts of mercury, including salmon, pollock, catfish, and canned light tuna.[16] The details of how much fish is safe for pregnant women to eat remains controversial. For today and many years to come, we will be living with the impacts of past environmental contamination on entire ecosystems.

---

interactions between exposures produce unexpectedly large impacts. We will take a look at two types of strategies that are being developed to address more than one problem at a time. We will begin by looking at a strategy called an interaction analysis. Finally, we will build upon this approach to see how systems analysis is becoming an important approach for addressing issues of environmental health and safety.

WHAT IS AN INTERACTION ANALYSIS APPROACH TO ENVIRONMENTAL DISEASES?

The term interaction analysis implies that to understand and control the impacts of environmental exposures, it is necessary to take into account the effect of two or more exposures. Risk assessment approaches make the assumption that each exposure stands on its own. Thus, if there is more than one type of exposure, we need to make the assumption that the total impact is the sum of the two impacts. For example, if one exposure has a relative risk of 4 and a second has a relative risk of 6, we assume that exposure to both results in a relative risk of 10. Many times adding together the relative risks does provide an approximation of the risk of two or more exposures. However, in an increasing number of situations we are recognizing that there are interactions between exposures themselves so that the presence of both exposures results in

an overall impact much greater than expected. For instance, we might find that having both exposures results in a relative risk of a bad outcome of 4 times 6 or 24 instead of 10. This type of interaction is called **multiplicative interaction**. Box 8-5 examines the multiplicative interaction between radon and cigarette smoking.[17]

WHAT IS A SYSTEMS ANALYSIS APPROACH TO ENVIRONMENTAL HEALTH AND SAFETY?

As we have seen, the traditional risk assessment approach to environmental hazards assumes that each factor acts on its own without explicitly recognizing the interactions that occur. In addition, traditional risk assessment assumes that more is worse and that a very low exposure has little if any impact. That is, it assumes the existence of a dose-response relationship to estimate the magnitude of the potential harm. Not all environmental hazards conform to these major assumptions. As we have seen, both radon and asbestos exposure interact with cigarette smoking and multiply the risk of disease.

Not all risks for environmental disease require high-level or long-term exposure. In addition to causing lung cancer, asbestos has also been shown to cause a form of cancer called mesothelioma, which originates in the lining of the lung or pleura. Even small and short-term exposures to asbestos may

BOX 8-5   Interaction Between Radon and Cigarettes.

Radon is a naturally-occurring radioactive gas. It is colorless and odorless. Radon is produced by the decay of uranium in soil, rock, and groundwater. It emits ionizing radiation during its radioactive decay. Radon is found all over the country though there are areas of the country with substantially higher levels than other areas. Radon gets into the indoor air primarily by entering via the soil under homes and other buildings at the basement or lowest level.

Today, it is recognized that radon is the second most important cause of lung cancer after cigarettes and the most common cause of cancer among nonsmokers. The EPA estimates that radon accounts for over 20,000 cases of lung cancer, as compared with the over 100,000 cases attributed to cigarettes. The average indoor level in the United States is about 1.3pCi/L. The EPA has set a level of 2pCi/L as an attainable level and a level of 4pCi/L as the maximum recommended level. Approximately 15 percent of homes in the United States have basement radon levels above 4pCi/L.

Cigarette smoking and radon exposure are multiplicative; that is, when both are present, the hazard is multiplied. For instance, using the EPA's figures, the relative risk of lung cancer for the average smoker is approximately nine times the risk compared to a nonsmoker. The relative risk from radon when the level is 10pCi/L compared to 2pCi/L is over 4.5. When both cigarette smoking and a level of radon exposure of 10pCi/L are present, the relative risk of lung cancer increases almost 40 times.

The recognition that radon and also asbestos multiply the impacts of cigarette smoking has had a key impact on the approaches used to address these potential hazards. For smokers with exposure to these hazards the risk can be greatly reduced by reductions in radon and asbestos, as well as by stopping smoking. Because both radon and asbestos are potentially controllable environmental exposures, there has been a great deal of attention and money given to control of these hazards. Thus, the recognition of interactions which multiply or greatly increase the risk have become an important tool for setting priorities and developing approaches to risk reduction.

---

cause mesothelioma as evidenced by well-documented cases among household members who washed the clothing of those exposed. Low-dose environmental exposures to estrogen-like substances may pose threats to the reproductive health of animal species and could even affect the human rate of breast cancer. New technologies, such as nanotechnology, are raising concerns that the risks of low-level exposure need to be investigated as much as those of high level exposure.

Addressing these types of issues requires us to focus on the interactions between multiple factors which together form a system. Environmental problems often come from multiple sources. A now-classic success story of environmental understanding and collaboration in addressing multiple factors at once is the history of the hole in the ozone layer,[18] which is discussed in Box 8-6.

Systems analysis approaches are an increasingly important strategy for addressing environmental health and safety. A systems analysis approach has been used successfully to address the problem of death and disabilities due to transportation injuries. Vast improvements in motor vehicle safety have occurred in recent decades—from bikes to boats to airplanes. Today, for instance, the commercial airline safety system has become a model. It includes a range of connected interventions from aircraft construction to routine maintenance, from efforts to reduce human error to investigation of near misses and actual crashes. The success of these efforts is evidenced by the fact that the goal of zero deaths per year from commercial airlines is nearing reality in the United States. We have also made great progress in land transportation.[19] Much of this progress has resulted from using a systems analysis approach as discussed in Box 8-7.

We have now taken a look at a series of progressively complex approaches being used to address the issues of environmental disease and injuries. The problems of environmental health and safety require increasingly sophisticated solutions. As we will see in future sections, the lessons learned from these efforts have potential applications to other aspects of public health and health care.

We have now looked at the non-communicable diseases, communicable diseases, and environmental health and safety as the way of organizing the major causes of disability and death. Now, let us turn our attention to the organized systems that have been developed for addressing these problems. First, we will look at the healthcare system in general in Section IV. Section V will explore the traditional public health system.

BOX 8-6 Addressing the Problem of the Hole in the Ozone Layer.

It was first recognized in 1985 that the layer of ozone above Antarctica was being depleted at an alarming rate. Ozone in the upper atmosphere is known to protect against damaging radiation from the sun. Fears were raised that the hole in the ozone would expand progressively and encompass populated areas in the southern hemisphere and involve the northern hemisphere as well.

It was quickly recognized that the problem was linked to multiple interacting human and naturally-occurring systems. The use of chloro-fluorocarbons (CFCs) in such products as refrigerators and air conditioning equipment was quickly identified as a major contributor. In addition, commonly-used aerosol sprays from deodorants to hair sprays contained CFCs. More concerning was the use of CFC in devices to deliver medications.

The timely accumulation of data, the rapid understanding of the multiple contributors to the problem, and a worldwide media campaign soon brought together a remarkably effective response to the problem. By 1987, an international agreement, known as the Montreal Protocol, was developed and quickly implemented by most nations. The agreement and subsequent revisions resulted in the rapid phase-out of most uses of CFC with more graduate elimination of CFCs in medical devices.

The hole in the ozone layer continues to expand due to the extremely long half-life of CFCs. The projections, however, are for a turn-around in the near future and a resolution of the problem by 2050. The coordinated scientific, public health, health communications, and political responses have encouraged future efforts to recognize and jointly address multifactor environmental health problems.

BOX 8-7 A Systems Analysis Approach to Motor Vehicle Injuries.

The approach used to address the complex problem of motor vehicle collisions has been a systems analysis approach. It has incorporated elements of health care, traditional public health, as well as social interventions. Motor vehicle injuries in the United States have been the leading cause of death for children and young adults for at least the last half century. Today, they remain a critical problem, however, the death rates from motor vehicle injuries in the United States over the last half-century have fallen so dramatically that the CDC classified highway safety as one of the ten great public health achievements of the 20th century. This progress has not been due to any one intervention—it is the combination of coordinated interventions that have made the difference. Highway safety can be thought of as a systems analysis success story not only because of the progress that has been made, but because of the potential for continued progress in the future. Interventions have often relied upon engineering solutions or technical innovations. Improvements in automobile design, airbags, and in highway construction have been essential elements in preventing and surviving motor vehicle crashes.

Education has played a role as well. Educational efforts have included instructing parents in the use of child restraints, teaching all drivers and passengers to wear seat belts, and encouraging the widespread use of the designated driver concept. Motivational efforts have included lower insurance rates for safe drivers and progressive stages of licensing for young drivers. Mandatory or obligatory efforts have included enforcement of drunk driver laws and seat belt laws.

Connecting the pieces with an emergency medical system has been key to a successful systems analysis approach. The first hour after a serious injury is often called the golden hour—a period of time when emergency interventions can save many lives. A coordinated emergency response, emergency department preparedness, and increased use of modern communications equipment have all helped to create a system out of what was formally a series of disconnected interventions.

The challenge of making transportation safe is by no means over. New innovations and new strategies are needed. The success of the systems analysis approach so far gives us encouragement that more progress is on the way.

Key Words

- Unaltered environment
- Altered environment
- Built environment
- Hazards
- Multiplicative interaction

Discussion Questions

Take a look at the questions posed in the following scenarios which were presented at the beginning of this chapter. See now whether you can answer them.

1. *Joe grew up in an industrial district of town. His family lived in an old apartment building and he played in a playground near a major intersection. By the age of 6, Joe was found to have high lead levels in his blood and was not doing well in school. Where could all that lead come from, his mother wondered?*

2. *Jill is pregnant and loves fish, which she has eaten almost daily for years as part of her effort to stay healthy. She hears that fish should not be eaten regularly during pregnancy. Why, she wonders, should I cut down on eating something as healthy as fish?*

3. *Ralph and Sonya, a prosperous professional couple, and their two children live in an older suburban home. They feel secure that their environment is safe. They were surprised to find when they wanted to put their house up for sale that it did not pass the safety tests for radon. Where did the radon come from, they wondered, and what can be done about it?*

4. *Sandra worked for an international agency that had successfully addressed the danger of radiation due to the hole in the ozone layer. She was shocked when she was told that she had a life-threatening skin cancer called melanoma. She asked, what could cause melanoma? Could years of sun exposure have played a role?*

5. *With your seat belt on, children buckled in, and airbags activated, you head out of the driveway to face the world. You didn't see that truck coming when it hit you from the side. The ambulance responded within minutes and took your family to the nearest emergency room. You all made it through with only minor injuries. You ask yourself, was it just luck or did the system work?*

REFERENCES

1. Prevention Institute. The Built Environment and Health. Available at: http://www.preventioninstitute.org/builtenv.html. Accessed March 19, 2009.

2. Mokdad AM, Marks JS, Stroup DF, Gerberding JL. Actual causes of death in the United States 2000. *JAMA*. 2004; 291: 1238–1245.

3. Centers for Disease Control and Prevention National Center for Health Statistics. Deaths—Leading Causes. Available at: http://www.cdc.gov/nchs/FASTATS/lcod.htm. Accessed March 19, 2009.

4. Friis RH. *Essentials of Environmental Health*. Sudbury, MA: Jones and Bartlett Publishers; 2007.

5. Oncology Encyclopedia. Occupational Exposures and Cancer. Available at: http://www.answers.com/topic/occupational-exposures-and-cancer. Accessed March 19, 2009.

6. Centers for Disease Control and Prevention. Environmental Hazards and Health Effects. Available at: http://www.cdc.gov/vaccines/. Accessed March 19, 2009.

7. Greenberg MR. *Environmental Policy Analysis and Practice*. Piscataway, NJ: Rutgers University Press; 2008.

8. Rom WN, Markowitz SB. *Environmental and Occupational Medicine*. Philadelphia: Lippincott, Williams & Wilkins; 2006.

9. U.S. Environmental Protection Agency. Risk Assessment Portal. Available at: http://www.epa.gov/risk/hazardous-identification.htm. Accessed December 14, 2008.

10. Agency for Toxic Substances and Disease Registry. A Citizen's Guide to Risk Assessments and Public Health Assessments. Available at: http://www.atsdr.cdc.gov/publications/citizensGuidetoRiskAssessments.html. Accessed November 21, 2008.

11. Environmental Health News. EPA must overhaul risk assessments to protect public health, panel says. Available at: http://www.environmental healthnews.org/ehs/news/panel-advises-epa-to-overhaul-risk-assessments. Accessed December 13, 2008.

12. Agency for Toxic Substance and Disease Registry. ToxFAQs™ for Lead. Available at: http://www.atsdr.cdc.gov/tfacts13.html. Accessed November 9, 2008.

13. Agency for Toxic Substance and Disease Registry. Case Studies in Environmental Medicine—Lead. Available at: http://www.epa.gov/radon/healthrisks.html. Accessed March 19, 2009.

14. National Defense Resource Council. The Story of Silent Spring. Available at: http://www.nrdc.org/health/pesticides/hcarson.asp. Accessed March 19, 2009.

15. U.S. Environmental Protection Agency. Mercury Study Report to Congress, Volume I, Executive Summary. Available at: http://www.epa.gov/ttn/oarpg/t3/reports/volume1.pdf. Accessed March 19, 2009.

16. March of Dimes. Pregnancy and Newborn Health Education Center. Available at: http://www.marchofdimes.com/pnhec/159_823.asp. Accessed March 19, 2009.

17. United States Environmental Protection Agency. Radon. Available at: http://www.epa.gov/radon/. Accessed March 19, 2009.

18. National Aeronautics and Space Administration. Ozone Hole Watch. Available at: http://ozonewatch.gsfc.nasa.gov/facts/hole.html#nav_bypass. Accessed March 19, 2009.

19. Pfizer Global Pharmaceuticals. *Milestones in Public Health: Accomplishments in Public Health over the Last 100 Years*. New York: Pfizer Global Pharmaceuticals; 2006.

Section III:
Cases and Discussion Questions

High Blood Pressure: A Public Health and Healthcare Success

Elevated levels of blood pressure, or hypertension, have been observed since the development of blood pressure measurements in the 19th century. It was soon recognized that populations with a high frequency of elevated blood pressure were also populations with a high frequency of strokes, yet the dangers of high blood pressure often went unappreciated until recent years.

High blood pressure is a condition that historically has affected both the privileged and the underprivileged in our society. Presidents Woodrow Wilson and Franklin Delano Roosevelt both had high blood pressure and suffered strokes and heart disease. Today, the condition is disproportionately present among African Americans—15 to 20 percent have some degree of elevated blood pressure.

For many years, high blood pressure was considered a consequence of disease rather than its cause. Clinicians seeing a patient with a stroke, for instance, often attributed their elevation in blood pressure to the stroke rather than the other way around. Long-term studies, such as the Framingham Heart Study that followed a large number of individuals for many years, established that the high blood pressure actually preceded strokes and not the other way around. High blood pressure as a contributory cause of strokes, as well as heart and kidney disease, was fully confirmed only after randomized clinical trials in the late 1960s and early 1970s established that lower blood pressure leads to reduced frequency of these afflictions. Screening for high blood pressure became widespread in the same period in large part as a result of these investigations. Elevated levels were initially defined as 140/100 or greater, based upon a range of normal obtained by measuring the blood pressure on large numbers of adult Americans. What were once considered acceptable levels of blood pressure have been redefined as elevated levels in recent years. Today, the desirable level is considered 120/80 or lower. These changing levels are justified by follow-up data from a large number of individuals that demonstrate that even levels of blood pressure only slightly above 120/80 are associated with increased risk of stroke and heart disease.

The fluctuating levels of blood pressure often make it difficult to establish an individual's average level. Electronic monitoring of blood pressure over a 24-hour period has become a feasible and acceptable gold standard for establishing an individual's average level. Early detection and successful treatments have been shown to effectively reduce the consequences of high blood pressure. Weight loss and salt restriction are often prescribed initially with subsequent introduction of one or more drugs. Most, if not all individuals with elevated blood pressure, respond to drug treatment with tolerable or no side effects, but need to continue treatment for many years—usually for the rest of their lives.

A national public health campaign began in the 1970s to encourage individuals to know their blood pressure and to urge clinicians to treat detected elevated levels. In recent decades, national surveys have indicated that a gradually increasing percentage of patients with elevated blood pressures are being successfully treated and that there has been a substantial reduction in strokes and deaths from strokes. Recent evidence showing that reducing the high salt levels in the American diet can reduce the average level of blood pressure has prompted renewed public health efforts to change eating habits and the contents of commercial foods.

Today, treatment of high blood pressure is recognized as one of the most cost-effective interventions. Its cost per quality-adjusted life year saved is only a few thousand dollars a year for the average person. For high-risk groups, such as those with diabetes, it actually saves money to monitor and treat high blood pressure rather than allow it to cause or exacerbate other health problems requiring more expensive treatments.

1. How does this history of high blood pressure demonstrate the problem description and etiology components of the P.E.R.I. process? What different types of studies were used to establish etiology or contributory cause?

2. How does this history of high blood pressure illustrate the evidence-based recommendations and implementation/evaluation components of the P.E.R.I. process?

3. Explain the justification for updating the definition of what is considered a "healthy" blood pressure level.

4. How does this history of high blood pressure demonstrate the application of the four criteria for a successful screening program?

5. Using the four quadrants of cost and effectiveness, how would you classify treatment of hypertension for the average person? For those with diabetes?

Testing and Screening

Ken had just turned 40 and with a little encouragement from his wife, he decided that it was time to have a physical—it would be his first real visit to a doctor since he broke his arm as a kid. Seeing a doctor hadn't made sense to him before. He was in great shape, felt fine, and didn't smoke. Maybe it was his 65-year-old father's sudden death from a heart attack just a few weeks after his retirement that finally convinced Ken to find himself a doctor. He knew that his father had had high cholesterol, but he was told his own cholesterol level and electrocardiogram results were okay when he entered the military at age 18. Besides, Ken wasn't big on desserts and only ate a Big Mac when he took the kids out after their soccer games.

The examination was quite uneventful and Ken was reassured when the doctor couldn't find anything of concern. A few recommendations on nutrition and better ways to exercise were about all that came out of the visit. Then he got the call from the doctor's office—could he make a follow-up appointment to discuss his cholesterol?

His low-density lipoprotein (LDL, or "bad" cholesterol) was 165 and his high-density lipoprotein (HDL, or "good" cholesterol) was 40. "We used to think these levels were okay since they are so common," his doctor began." However, now we consider your LDL cholesterol too high because it increases your chances of developing heart and other blood vessel diseases. There's no evidence of heart disease at this point, but your cholesterol needs attention."

"What do you mean by attention?" Ken replied. "I exercise, don't smoke, and generally keep my fats down." Ken soon learned a lot more about cholesterol. He first tried his best at changing his diet—it helped a little, but just didn't do the trick. Ken's doctor told him: "For some people there is a strong genetic component to high cholesterol levels and while diet is still important, it just can't always reduce LDL cholesterol enough by itself. Exercise helps, especially by increasing the good cholesterol, but it doesn't do much for the bad cholesterol. Medication may be needed and there is now evidence that if taken regularly, it reduces the chances of having a heart attack or at least delays its occurrence."

Taking medication every day was not so easy for Ken, but he stuck with the plan. His doctor asked him to have his cholesterol levels checked every few months for the first year. Ken was amazed at how well the medicine worked. His LDL fell from 165 to less than 100 on only a modest dose. In addition to routine cholesterol checks, Ken had his blood tested for potential side effects from the medication, such as impacts to his liver, and he was required to report any long-lasting muscle aches and pains. The good news was that he couldn't tell he was taking the medication—he felt just fine.

Now that the cholesterol levels had dropped, he thought maybe he could go off the medication if he just watched his diet closely. His doctor let him try that for a month, but after the 30 days were up his LDL level was back up to 160. "Looks like you're hooked on medication for life," his doctor said with a wry smile, adding, "at least the extra cost is worth the extra benefit." Ken and his wife were told the high cholesterol levels were a genetic condition. Not only did Ken need to take the medication on a permanent basis, but the pediatricians began testing his kids. The doctors said, "we are beginning to understand the genetics behind this condition and would like to do some genetic testing on the children, including that new baby of yours." Ken wondered if the information on his children's cholesterol levels would be part of their medical records for the rest of their lives. "You're not planning to put that on the Internet, are you?" Ken joked nervously as they drew blood from his newborn son.

1. How are the range of normal- and desirable-range approaches to establishing a reference interval and defining a positive and negative test illustrated in this case? Explain.

2. What arguments are presented in this case that fulfill the criteria for screening for high cholesterol? Explain.

3. What definition of cost-effectiveness is being used to justify screening and treatment of elevated LDL cholesterol?

4. What ethical issues need to be considered in screening for conditions such as elevated LDL cholesterol? Explain.

What to Do about Lyme Disease?

You have just moved into a new subdivision—your first home with your young family. The first week you are there, a neighbor tells you that her son has developed Lyme disease and now has chronic arthritis that requires extensive treatment.

Lyme disease is an increasingly common disease that can cause acute and chronic arthritis if not treated early and correctly. In rare instances, it can cause life-threatening heart disease and temporary paralysis often to one side of the face due to nerve damage. The disease is caused by an organism known as a spirochete, which is spread from deer ticks to humans via tick bites. Lyme disease is especially common in communities with large deer populations.

Ticks must remain in place on the human skin at least 12 to 24 hours in order to extract human blood and inject the spirochete organism at the site of the bite. Complete removal of the small, but visible tick within 24 hours usually prevents the disease. Deer ticks are most abundant in the late spring and tend to live on tall grasses from which they can easily move to the bare legs of children and adults. The disease frequently first appears as a circular red rash around the site of the bite. At this stage, early diagnosis and treatment with antibiotics is usually successful. Several weeks or months later, the onset of arthritis may occur and can be difficult to diagnose. A missed diagnosis may result in severe arthritis that is difficult to treat. A vaccine has been developed and briefly marketed to prevent the disease, but it was quite expensive and only partially successful.

In your new hometown, the local health department is charged with developing a plan for control or elimination of Lyme disease. As an informed and concerned citizen, you are invited to give input on the plan identifying possible interventions.

1. What primary interventions would you consider?
2. What secondary interventions would you consider?
3. What tertiary interventions would you consider?
4. What educational interventions do you recommend?
5. Can Lyme disease be eradicated? Can it be controlled?

Sharma's Village

Sharma lives in a small farming village in south Asia, but she could just as well be living in Haiti, Ethiopia, Ghana, or several dozen other countries classified by the World Bank as low-income economies. Her home is a small hut and she works daily with her mother to gather firewood for their small indoor fireplace that acts as the kitchen stove. The smoke often makes her eyes water because there is no chimney or other ventilation. At night, she sleeps with her extended family in a room where mosquitoes bite her regularly. Despite the fact that Sharma lives in a rural community, the villagers live in crowded quarters. The water the family drinks is carried by the women from a well several hundred yards from their home. The water sometimes tastes bad, but it is all they have to drink.

The family farms a small plot of land on the hillside, which had become eroded from years of cutting trees. The last big

monsoon to hit the area created a landslide, which left the village underwater for several weeks creating mold in nearly every home. Most of the adults have goiters from the lack of iodine in the soil. The addition of iodine to salt has prevented goiters in the children. Pesticides are used widely to control mosquitoes and agricultural pests, but the farmers receive little education on their safe use. Recently, a new road was built connecting her village with the neighboring towns. Despite the advantages of having the new road, cars and trucks now speed through her village, rarely stopping to let people cross the road.

In Sharma's village, the life expectancy is 49 years. Babies often die of diarrheal diseases in the first year of life and mothers occasionally die in childbirth. Malaria is widespread and hookworm disease is present among those who farm the fields and in children, whose ability to learn is often affected. Malnutrition is also widespread despite the fact that farming is the major occupation in the village. Chronic lung disease among adults and asthma among the young is surprisingly common even though cigarette smoking is rare. Tuberculosis is widespread and a major cause of death, however there are few cases of HIV/AIDS in the area. Unexplained neurological diseases among farm workers occur regularly. The most common cause of death among teenagers is motor vehicle injuries along the new road even though there is only one truck in the village.

1. What environmental risk factors contributing to disease and other health conditions are illustrated in this case? Classify each as an unaltered, altered, or built environment factor.
2. Discuss at least two examples of how disease or other conditions found in the village can be explained by the environmental risk factors?
3. Identify at least two interventions that would make a large difference in the health of this village.
4. What changes do you expect to occur in this village as social and economic development take place?

Asthma—It's in the Air

Joe had asthma for as long as he could remember. Struggling to keep up with his friends on the playground was among one of his earliest memories. In those days no one worried about it—"you'll outgrow it"—they'd tell him. He grew up not too far from an oil refinery and lots of kids had asthma. He can still remember the debate in town about whether it was worth the costs to reduce the pollution. Asthma kept him out of sports, but turned his attention to schoolwork. He always said the asthma was the key to his academic success. It even kept him from smoking—the wheezing just got too bad whenever he inhaled deeply.

When he left home for college, his asthma seemed to improve. He could now take long walks without discomfort. However, it was more than a little embarrassing for him when he had to stop near the top of a small hill to catch his breath while taking a short hike with his girlfriend. With her encouragement, he finally agreed to go to the clinic to see what could be done. The doctor prescribed an inhaler and told him to work with the physician assistant to see if they "could get down to the bottom of this." The inhaler worked so well and so quickly that Joe decided just to use it whenever he exercised. He even found that he could use it before a cigarette and could now smoke just to be sociable.

Joe didn't return to the clinic again until the prescription ran out. This time, the physician assistant insisted that he learn more about asthma. Joe learned the danger of cigarettes, the need to stay on treatment even when he was doing well, and the importance of rapidly treating worsening symptoms. He also began to understand the importance of getting an annual influenza vaccine and taking that pneumococcal vaccine that he'd originally rejected.

Things went well for a couple of years until despite his best efforts at prevention, he suffered a full-blown asthma attack. The antibiotics he was prescribed didn't do the trick and he ended up in the hospital requiring a ventilator for a couple of days. He couldn't understand what had happened to him—he had tried to do everything right. "It's not your fault," his doctor and physician assistant told him. "Those antibiotics have been used so much that they don't touch some of the bugs anymore. We had to give you some new and expensive drugs that aren't even available as pills."

Joe seemed to understand—there were things he could and should do, but it wasn't all in his control. He now realized that with asthma there were bigger issues—it's in the air, as well as in the lungs, and it can also be in the genes. These words really hit home when his son experienced his first asthma attack before his first birthday. Joe now knew that you don't always outgrow asthma.

1. What does this case illustrate about the relationship of genetics and environmental causes of disease?
2. What preventive efforts are illustrated in this case?
3. What do you think are the advantages and disadvantages of emphasizing better treatment of asthma versus control of air pollution?
4. What do you think is the proper role of cost considerations in addressing environmental issues such as asthma?

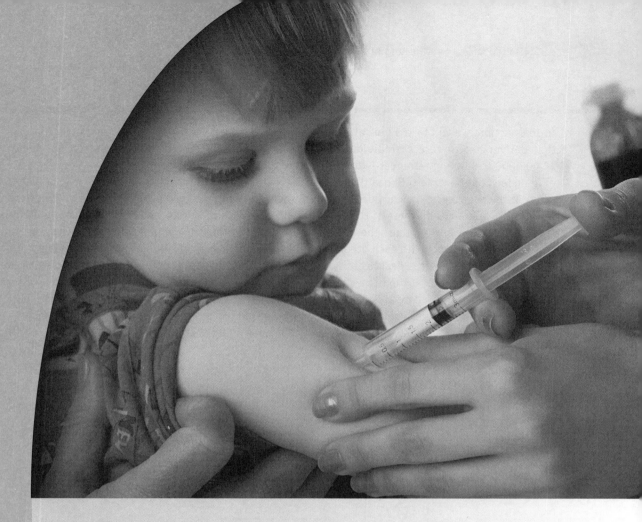

Health Professionals, Healthcare Institutions, and Healthcare Systems

In this section, we will take a look at healthcare systems, the people, institutions, and organizational structures that deliver health care to individuals. In the United States, the healthcare system consumes well over $2,000,000,000,000 in resources—that's two TRILLION dollars.

To understand how the U.S. healthcare system functions and is organized, we will start in Chapter 9 by taking a look at the people who provide health services. There are over 15 million people involved in the delivery of health services. We will focus on three of the largest groups: physicians, nurses, and the public health professionals.

In Chapter 10, we will discuss the institutions involved in the delivery of healthcare services and how they interact or do not interact with each other. We will also examine methods for maximizing the quality of health care. Finally, we will examine the healthcare system as a whole in Chapter 11. We will aim to understand how the system is financed and look at the issue of access to care and the costs of that care. These particular issues have become the center of the debate about what needs to be addressed to improve the U.S. healthcare system. To provide perspective, we will also examine the characteristics of some other healthcare systems in developed countries.

Figure 4-A displays the components of a healthcare system that will guide our discussion of this complex subject.

Let us begin in Chapter 9 by turning our attention to the types of clinical and public health professionals that are part of the health workforce.

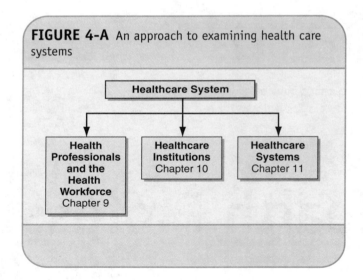

FIGURE 4-A An approach to examining health care systems

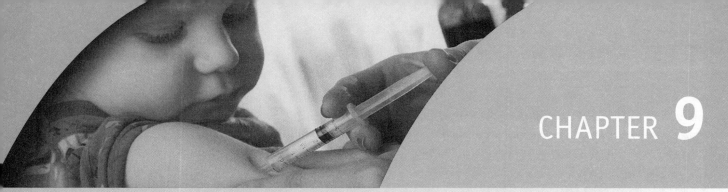

CHAPTER 9

Health Professionals and the Health Workforce

Upon arrival at the hospital, the nurse specialist examines you and consults with the radiologists, the gastroenterologist, and the general surgeon. Your medication is reviewed by the PharmD, and your meals by the clinical nutritionist. Throughout the hospitalization you are followed by a hospitalist. Once you get back home, the home care team comes to see you regularly for the first two weeks and the physician assistant and registered nurse see you in the office. You realize that health care is no longer just about doctors and nurses. You ask yourself: what roles do all of these health professionals play in the healthcare system?

Jenna decides that after college she wants to become a doctor and practice medicine. "I thought there was only one kind of doctor who could diagnose disease and prescribe medicine," she mentions at a career counseling meeting. "Not so, anymore," says her advisor. "There are allopathic and osteopathic physicians. In

addition, there are nurse practitioners who are authorized to diagnose and prescribe medications, and there are physician assistants who do the same under a physician's supervision. The universe of "doctors" now includes doctors of nursing practice, as well as other doctoral degree professionals, such as pharmacists and physical therapists." Understanding careers in health care can be as difficult for students as it is for patients, Jenna thinks to herself. Now she understands why her advisor asked: "what do you mean by 'practice'? What do you mean by 'doctor'?"

Sarah was about to begin medical school and was expecting two years of "preclinical" classroom lectures focusing on the basic sciences, followed by the study of clinical diseases. Then, as she'd heard from her physician father, she expected two years of clinical hospital "rotations" and electives investigating specialties. She is surprised to find that medical school has changed. There are small group problem-based learning sessions where she needs to be able to locate and read the research literature. There is contact with patients and their problems right from the beginning. There is increasingly a four-year approach instead of a preclinical and clinical approach to medical education. She wonders: are these changes for the better? What else needs to be done to improve medical education?

You are interested in clinical care, as well as public health. "I need to make a choice," you think to yourself. "Not necessarily," your advisor says. "There are many ways to combine clinical care with public health." After a little investigation, you find out that undergraduate public health education is increasingly seen as preparation for clinical education and clinical prevention and population health are increasingly becoming part of clinical care. In addition, many careers from health administration, to health policy, to clinical research, combine the individual orientation of clinical care with the population perspective of public health. So what's the best pathway to a public health career for you?

WHAT DO WE MEAN BY A HEALTH PROFESSIONAL?

Until the early years of the 20th century, education and practice for the health professions was an informal process often without standardized admissions requirements, curricula, or even formal recognition of a profession. Throughout the 20th century and into the 21st, there has been an ongoing movement to formalize the education process for health professionals. These formal requirements have come to define what we mean by a health professional and include admission prerequisites, coursework requirements, examinations of competency, official recognition of educational achievements, and granting of permission to practice. Today, the list of formal health professions is very long. Clinical health professions may be classified as physicians, nurses, dentists, pharmacists, optometrists, psychologists, podiatrists, and chiropractors. They also include nurse practitioners, physician assistants, health services administrators, and allied health practitioners.[1] "Allied health practitioner" is a broad category in its own right, ranging from graduate degree trained professionals, such as physical therapists, occupational therapists, and medical social workers, to technical specialists often with an associate's degree, such as dental assistants, sonographers, and laboratory technicians.

Within public health, there is a growing array of health specialties. Some specialties require associate or bachelor's degrees, such as environmental health technicians, environmental health specialists, and health educators. However, many public health roles require graduate degrees that focus on disciplines including: epidemiology, biostatistics, environmental sciences, health administration and policy, and social and behavioral sciences.

Education and training are central to the development and definition of most health professions. Education implies that a student is pursuing a degree or certificate from an accredited educational institution. Training is often organized and directed outside of educational institution. Hospitals, health departments, and large group practices often have the responsibility of training new health professionals.

Before we take a look at specific health professions, let's step back and ask the more general question: how do education and training serve to define health professions?

HOW DO EDUCATION AND TRAINING SERVE TO DEFINE HEALTH PROFESSIONS?

Defining and enforcing educational requirements is central to creating and maintaining a profession. This can be accom-

plished using two basic approaches: **accreditation** and **credentialing**.

Accreditation implies a process of setting standards for educational and training institutions and enforcing these standards using a regularly-scheduled institutional self-study and an outside review. Accreditation is used by most health professions to define and enforce educational expectations. At times, these expectations may be laid out in detail down to the level of square footage per student for laboratory space and the number of hours devoted to specific subjects. In other health professions, educational subject areas may be outlined and institutions left to judge how to best implement the curriculum.

Credentialing implies that the individual, rather than the institution, is evaluated. Credentialing is a generic term indicating a process of verifying that an individual has the desirable or required qualifications to practice a profession. Credentialing often takes the form of **certification**. Certification is generally a profession-led process in which applicants who have completed the required educational process take an examination. Successful completion of formal examinations leads to recognition in the form of certification.

Certification also has come to define specialties and even subspecialties within a profession. Successful completion of a specialty or subspecialty examination may entitle a health professional to call themselves "board-certified." Certification is often a prerequisite for **licensure**, which is a state governmental function and usually requires more than certification. It may include residency requirements, a legal background check, continuing education requirements, etc. Licensure, when applicable, is usually required for practice of a health profession.

Thus, in order to understand what is meant by a particular health profession, it is important to understand the credentials that are expected or required. Let us take a look at the education required for specific health professions, such as physicians, nurses, and public health professionals.

WHAT IS THE EDUCATION AND TRAINING PROCESS FOR PHYSICIANS?

Physicians are a central part of what is called the practice of medicine. They can be categorized as allopathic and osteopathic physicians. Allopathic physicians graduate with an MD degree, while osteopathic physicians graduate from osteopathic medical schools and receive a DO degree. Graduates of both allopathic and osteopathic medical schools are eligible to apply for the same residency and fellowship programs for their postgraduate medical education. The number of osteopathic medical schools has grown rapidly in recent years and now totals approximately 30 nationwide. Allopathic medical schools number approximately 130 and have only recently begun to again grow in size and number.[a]

Within medicine, specialties and subspecialties continue to emerge. For instance hospice and palliative medicine has recently been added to the list of specialties and others such as hospitalists may be moving in that direction. Table 9-1 outlines many of the current specialties and subspecialties within the field of medicine.[2]

Box 9-1 discusses the process of medical education and the changes that have occurred in recent years and continue to evolve.[3]

Now let us take a brief look at the largest of the health professions—nursing.[4]

WHAT IS THE EDUCATION AND TRAINING PROCESS FOR NURSING?

Nursing as a profession dates from the middle of the 19th century, when it began to be organized as a profession in England. Florence Nightingale is often associated with the founding of nursing as a profession. In the United States, the nursing profession grew out of the Civil War and the essential role played by women in this conflict who performed what we would today call nursing functions. Nursing has long been organized as a distinct profession and is governed by its own set of laws often refer to as the "nursing practice acts."

Today, there are a wide range of health professionals that fall under the legal definition of nursing. Licensed practical nurses (LPNs) provide a range of services often under the direction of registered nurses (RN). An LPN's educational requirements vary widely from state to state, ranging from short-term education after high school to a two-year associate's degree.

Registered nurses are central to the nursing profession and they are usually responsible for hospital-based services. Each state defines its own requirements for RN licensure. Traditionally, many nurses graduated with a diploma which was offered through hospital-based programs. The move toward integrating nursing into the formal degree system has resulted in nurses with associate's degrees, bachelor's of science in nursing (BSN), as well as graduate degrees. Being a registered nurse (RN) requires a state license that, depending on the state, may or may not require a BSN degree.

Advanced nursing degrees are offered as masters of science in nursing, or as an academic research-based degree, the PhD and a clinical doctorate, the doctor in nursing practice (DNP).

Until recent years, there was little formal specialization within nursing, at least compared to physicians and other health professions. Nurse midwives and nurse anesthetists, however, are two traditional specializations within nursing. Graduate-level education and training of nurses has expanded rapidly in recent years. Nursing has added a series of advanced practice degrees including nurse practitioners, as well as specialists such as pediatric, geriatric, and intensive care nurses. The Doctor of Nursing Practice (DNP) degree is becoming recognized for a range of specialty areas within nursing. It is expected to replace many nursing master's degrees over the next decade.

Recent changes in nursing have opened up the option to pursue a bachelor's degree in a range of fields followed by a shorter degree program leading to a BSN or a nurse practitioner degree. As we will see later in the chapter, the shortage of nurses is often seen as the most critical workforce issue in the health field. Now, let us take a look public health professionals.[5, 6]

WHAT IS THE EDUCATION AND TRAINING PROCESS FOR PUBLIC HEALTH PROFESSIONALS?

In the United States, education in public health began as part of medicine in the late 19th century. Shortly before and after World War I, with the support of the Rockefeller Foundation, separate schools of public health were established. The aim of the initial schools of public health was to train physicians, nurses, and other professionals who sought to play lead roles in local and state health departments. Thus, for many years public health education was often combined with other professions. Box 9-2 discusses the roles of clinicians in public health.

Public health professionals today include those who specialize in a wide range of disciplines and work in a variety of settings from governmental public health to not-for-profit and for-profit institutions, as well as in educational and healthcare institutions. There are approximately 500,000 public health professionals in the United States and it is estimated that in coming years there will be a substantial shortage, especially in federal and state health departments.[5]

Public health is one of the last health fields to formalize educational and professional requirements. Today, many public health professionals are trained exclusively in public health and the process of formal credentialing is underway. The

---

[a] Osteopathic and allopathic medical education curricula are quite similar today. The prerequisite for admission are similar and both types of medical schools generally require the Medical School Admissions Test (MCAT). However, osteopathic medical education retains its focus on manipulation of the muscular skeletal system and sees itself as providing a holistic approach to medicine, including a greater focus on prevention. A substantially higher percentage of DOs go into primary care as compared to MDs.

TABLE 9-1 Selected Specialities and Subspecialities of Medicine

Example of specialty area	Example of subspecialty area	Example of specialty area	Example of subspecialty area
Anesthesiology	Critical Care Medicine Hospice and Palliative Medicine Pain Medicine	Otolaryngology	Neurotology Pediatric Otolaryngology Plastic Surgery within the Head and Neck Sleep Medicine
Emergency Medicine	Hospice and Palliative Medicine Medical Toxicology Pediatric Emergency Medicine Sports Medicine Undersea and Hyperbaric Medicine	PATHOLOGY Anatomic Pathology and Clinical Pathology Pathology—Anatomic Pathology—Clinical	Blood Banking/Transfusion Medicine Chemical Pathology Cytopathology Dermatopathology Forensic Pathology Hematology Medical Microbiology Molecular Genetic Pathology Neuropathology Pediatric Pathology
Family Medicine	Adolescent Medicine Geriatric Medicine Hospice and Palliative Medicine Sleep Medicine Sports Medicine		
Internal Medicine	Adolescent Medicine Cardiovascular Disease Clinical Cardiac Electrophysiology Critical Care Medicine Endocrinology, Diabetes, and Metabolism Gastroenterology Geriatric Medicine Hematology Hospice and Palliative Medicine Infectious Disease Interventional Cardiology Medical Oncology Nephrology Pulmonary Disease Rheumatology Sleep Medicine Sports Medicine Transplant Hepatology	Pediatrics	Adolescent Medicine Child Abuse Pediatrics Developmental-Behavioral Pediatrics Hospice and Palliative Medicine Medical Toxicology Neonatal-Perinatal Medicine Neurodevelopmental Disabilities Pediatric Cardiology Pediatric Critical Care Medicine Pediatric Emergency Medicine Pediatric Endocrinology Pediatric Gastroenterology Pediatric Hematology-Oncology Pediatric Infectious Diseases Pediatric Nephrology Pediatric Pulmonology Pediatric Rheumatology Pediatric Transplant Hepatology Sleep Medicine Sports Medicine
Obstetrics and Gynecology	Critical Care Medicine Gynecologic Oncology Hospice and Palliative Medicine[1] Maternal and Fetal Medicine Reproductive Endocrinology/Infertility	Physical Medicine and Rehabilitation	Hospice and Palliative Medicine Pain Medicine Neuromuscular Medicine Pediatric Rehabilitation Medicine Spinal Cord Injury Medicine Sports Medicine
Orthopaedic Surgery	Orthopaedic Sports Medicine Surgery of the Hand		

continues

TABLE 9-1 Selected Specialities and Subspecialities of Medicine (continued)

Example of specialty area	Example of subspecialty area	Example of specialty area	Example of subspecialty area
Plastic Surgery	Plastic Surgery within the Head and Neck Surgery of the Hand	RADIOLOGY Diagnostic Radiology Radiation Oncology Radiologic Physics	Diagnostic Radiological Physics Hospice and Palliative Medicine Medical Nuclear Physics Neuroradiology Nuclear Radiology Pediatric Radiology Therapeutic Radiological Physics Vascular and Interventional Radiology
PREVENTIVE MEDICINE- Aerospace Medicine Occupational Medicine Public Health and General Preventive Medicine	Medical Toxicology Undersea and Hyperbaric Medicine		
Psychiatry Neurology Neurology with Special Qualifications in Child Neurology	Addiction Psychiatry Child and Adolescent Psychiatry Clinical Neurophysiology Forensic Psychiatry Geriatric Psychiatry Hospice and Palliative Medicine Neurodevelopmental Disabilities Neuromuscular Medicine Pain Medicine Psychosomatic Medicine Sleep Medicine Vascular Neurology	Surgery Vascular Surgery Urology	Hospice and Palliative Medicine Pediatric Surgery Surgery of the Hand Surgical Critical Care Pediatric Urology

Source: Data from American Board of Medical Specialties http://www.abms.org/Who_We_Help/Physicians/specialties.aspx. Accessed December 15, 2008.

recognition of public health as a distinct professional field with its own educational process has been formalized through accreditation of public health schools and programs by the Council on Education for Public Health (CEPH). CEPH requires five areas of knowledge basic to public health: biostatistics; epidemiology; environmental health sciences; social and behavioral sciences; and health services management. Specific disciplines within public health, such as epidemiology and social and behavioral sciences, have provided recognition for specialized training through advanced degrees, such as the academically-oriented Doctor of Philosophy (PhD) degree and the practice-oriented Doctor of Public Health (DrPH) degree.

Specific technical areas have existed within public health for many years and have included competency examinations, especially in fields such as occupational and environmental health. Health educators in recent decades have formalized and standardized their education and increasingly taken on the structure of a profession including examinations, certifications, and continuing education requirements.

Formal certification as a public health specialist has only been available since 2008, when the first certifying examination was given. The examination covers the five areas expected for a professional master's degree, such as a Master's of Public Health (MPH). These are biostatistics, epidemiology, environmental health sciences, social and behavioral sciences, and health policy and management. In addition, new cross-cutting competencies have been defined and are being incorporated into the examination. These include: communications and informatics, diversity and culture, leadership, professionalism, program planning, systems thinking, and public health biology.

The certifying examination tests core competencies, rather than more advanced competencies that students frequently achieve as part of their education in a public health specialty. Certification is a voluntary process, though it is expected that many employers will look for certification as an important credential. Licensure of public health professionals is not yet an issue. Thus, public health, along with health care, has increasingly formalized its educational requirements, formal credentialing, and competencies.[5,6] This process is likely to continue.

BOX 9-1 Medical Education.

Medical education in 19th and early 20th century America was built upon the apprentice system. Future physicians, nearly all men, worked under and learned from practicing physicians. Medical schools were often moneymaking enterprises and primarily used lectures without patient contact or laboratory experiences. That changed with the introduction of the European model of science-based medical education, hospital-based clinical rotations, and a four-year education model. The 1910 Flexner Report formalized these standards, which soon became universal for medical education in the United States, in what came to be called the Flexner era of American medicine. This era extended into the 1980s, and at some institutions into the 21st century. It led to the growth and dominance of specialties and specialists within particular medical fields.

Hospital-based residency programs and fellowships leading to specialty and subspecialty training became the dominant form of clinical training. Emphasizing this trend, medical school education came to be called **undergraduate medical education**. Medical school was traditionally formally or informally divided into two years of basic science or preclinical training, followed by two years of hospital-based clinical rotations in specialty areas including surgery, internal medicine, obstetrics and gynecology, and psychiatry. This division of medical education is reflected in the examinations of the National Board of Medical Examiners, which traditionally included Part 1 after the second year of medical school, Part 2 prior to graduation, and Part 3 after the first year residency often called the "internship." Additional specialty and subspecialty board examinations were linked to completion of training that occurs after medical school.

Change began to accelerate in medical education during the mid-1980s with the increasing movement of health care outside of hospitals, the increased medical school enrollment of women and minorities, a broader view of what should be included in medical education, and a better understanding of how learning takes place. Specific changes have occurred in the last two decades at all stages of medical education and new proposals for change continue to be formally reviewed and implemented. These can be outlined as follows, starting with the pre-med college years and continuing through residency and fellowship training:

- Premedical training in the Flexner era was largely restricted to majors in the physical and biological sciences, plus specific social sciences such as psychology. Beginning in the early 1990s, medical schools encouraged a wider range of majors, while usually retaining biology, chemistry, and physics courses as prerequisites. Medical schools are increasingly receptive to a wide range of preparation for medical education, encouraging completion of courses in behavioral and social sciences including public health, and epidemiology. A comprehensive review of the Medical College Admissions Test (MCAT) is now underway and may greatly broaden the examination to cover disciplines beyond the natural sciences.
- Admission to medical school was dominated by white males throughout the Flexner era. In the last 20–30 years, the percentage of women applicants has increased steadily. Today, the majority of medical students at many institutions are females. Likewise, the increase in minority applicants has paralleled the changes occurring in other aspects of American education and society.
- The first two years of medical school in the Flexner era were dominated by lectures and laboratories. Basic sciences were the focus with little or no patient contact. An important change in the last two decades includes widespread use of Problem Based Learning (PBL). PBL is characterized by small-group, student-initiated learning centered on "cases" or patient-oriented problems. New curricula in medical education, including evidence-based medicine, interviewing skills, and ethics, have become a standard part of coursework. A new simulated patient interview and physical examination are now part of the examination process.
- Changes in the third and fourth years of medical school began in the 1960s, the era of student activism. Since then, the fourth year of medical school has been dominated by electives. Fourth-year students may choose formal courses, elective clinical experiences, or a wide array of other options. These usually include: options for laboratory or clinical research, international experiences, and clinical rotations at other institutions, often called "audition" rotations, designed to increase a graduate's potential for selection as a resident.
- The growing trend of patient treatment outside of the traditional hospital setting has increased the range of types and locations of clinical experiences available. Most medical schools now require primary care experiences, along with traditional specialty rotations.
- Residency training has paralleled the changes in medical school with greater outpatient and less inpatient, or hospital-based education. Fellowship training beyond residency is now a routine part of the process of specialization. The general move toward more and more specialization has led to longer postgraduate training. The rigors of residency training remain, but limits have now been placed on it by the Residency Review Committees (RRCs), which govern graduate medical education. An average of 80 hours per week and 30 hours at one time are now the maximum standards for residents.

(continues)

BOX 9-1 continued.

Further changes in medical education and residency programs can be expected in the near future. The increasing recognition that health care is a group, and not an individual enterprise, is leading to a focus on interprofessional education and practice. An appreciation that evidence is central to improving quality and controlling costs should continue to encourage the critical reading of clinical research as part of evidence-based medicine in medical school and in journal clubs as part of postgraduate education. The use of computer-based information systems should increase the sharing and coordination of information; the ability to monitor and control health care; and the ways that physicians communicate with colleagues and patients. Technology is also likely to have continued unexpected impacts on the ways that medicine is taught, learned, and practiced.

BOX 9-2 Roles of Clinicians in Public Health.

Public health is often distinguished from the clinical health profession by its focus on populations rather than individuals; public service rather than individual service; disease prevention and health promotion rather than disease diagnosis and treatment; and its broad perspective on the determinants of disease. However, at the professional level individuals have commonly combined the two approaches or moved from one to the other.

Clinicians have always played key roles in public health. From the early years of formal public health training nearly a century ago, until the 1960s and 1970s, the Master of Public Health (MPH) degree was aimed primarily at physicians and nurses who were expected to take up leadership roles in health departments. Today, public health professionals come from much more diverse backgrounds, many entering masters programs directly after receiving a bachelor's degree. The role of clinicians in public health is also far more varied. For instance, today's pharmacists—now educated as doctors of pharmacy or PharmDs—play an increasingly important public health role in providing education about drugs for patients and practitioners and controlling prescription drug abuse. Prevention of dental and gum disease and early detection of oral cancers have much improved due to the careful attention of dentists and dental assistants. The dental profession has been a long-standing advocate of fluoridation of public water systems and other population health interventions.

Primary care specialists, including allopathic and osteopathic physicians, nurse practitioners, and physician assistants, are on the front lines of clinical prevention. Their involvement in screening, behavioral counseling, immunization, and the use of preventive medication, is key to the success of these efforts. Primary care clinicians, as well as specialty care clinicians, also have important roles to play in being alert to new diseases or changes in well-known diseases; reporting adverse effects of drugs, vaccines, and medical devices; and coordinating case-finding efforts with public health agencies.

Within medicine, the field of preventive medicine has a long history. Formal specializations exist in public health and general preventive medicine, occupational medicine, as well as aerospace medicine.

Finally, all clinicians have the right and often the responsibility to advocate for improvements in patient care and of the health system as a whole. A few clinical specialties, such as pediatrics, regard advocacy as a core responsibility of the profession. Their work has had major impacts on child health policies ranging from the use of child car restraints, to advocacy for pediatric HIV/AIDS care, to universal coverage of childhood vaccinations, as well as provision of comprehensive insurance coverage for children.

Joint clinical and public health degrees are now widely available. Many schools in the fields of nursing, physician assistants, dentistry, social work, and the law, offer options to pursue both degrees simultaneously. The roles of clinicians in public health are likely to become every more varied in coming years as public health and health care systems and institutions become more closely coordinated.

Remember that we have only touched on three basic types of health professionals: physicians, nurses, and public health professionals. There are several hundred other types of professions in the healthcare realm. As you think about a career in health, you should take a look at a range of health professions using the concepts of education, training, and certification that we have discussed.

To understand the connections between the large number of diverse health professions, we need to look at how clinical care is organized into primary, secondary, and tertiary care.

WHAT IS MEANT BY PRIMARY, SECONDARY, AND TERTIARY CARE?

Primary, secondary, and tertiary care are traditional ways to categorize services delivered within the healthcare system.[7] **Primary care** traditionally refers to the first contact providers of care who are prepared to handle the great majority of common problems for which patients seek care. **Secondary care** often refers to specialty care provided by clinicians who focus on one or a small number of organ systems or on a specific type of service, such as obstetrics and gynecology or anesthesiology. **Tertiary care**, or subspecialty care, is usually defined in terms of the type of institution in which it is delivered, often academic or specialized health centers. Tertiary care may also be defined in terms of the type of problem that is addressed, such as trauma centers, burn centers, or neonatal intensive care units.

Primary care is widely seen as the foundation of a healthcare system and a strong primary care system is viewed as a prerequisite for maximizing the potential benefits of health care. Traditionally, primary care was considered the domain of physicians. Today, a range of health professionals are involved in primary, as well as secondary and tertiary care. In fact, the term "**medical home**" is becoming widely used, suggesting that primary care is increasingly viewed as a team effort.

Today, only about one-third of physicians in the United States practice primary care. Increasingly, primary care is being delivered by physician assistants (PAs) and nurse practitioners (NPs), who in most states have authority to diagnose disease and prescribe medication either under the supervision of a physician (in the case of PAs) or under a nursing practice act (as in the case of NPs). A team approach to primary care is becoming standard practice.

It is important to understand the ideals of primary care, as well as today's realities.[7] Primary care is key to the healthcare system because it is where most care is delivered and it is often the entry point for subsequent specialty care. In addition, primary care is critical to the delivery of clinical preventive services and to the connections between health care and public health. Ideal primary care has been described using 6 Cs: contact, comprehensive, coordinated, continuity, caring, and community.

- Contact implies first contact with patients as they present for health care.
- Comprehensive refers to the ability of primary care practitioners or primary care teams to completely or at least initially address most health issues.
- Coordinated relates to the concept that primary care teams should have the responsibility to ensure that the parts of the healthcare system work together for the good of patients.
- Continuity is the role that primary care teams see themselves playing to hold together the components of the system.
- Caring implies a personalized relationship with each patient.
- Community implies that primary care provides the link with the broader community, including with public health institutions and services.

Despite the fact that many primary care practitioners continue to see this model of primary care as a highly desirable way to deliver clinical care, the realities of today's healthcare system deviate substantially from this model. Table 9-2 outlines the 6 Cs and indicates ways that the current healthcare system differs from this primary care ideal.[7, b]

Thus, there is a large gulf between the ideals of primary care and their execution in practice. Part of the reason for this and other realities of health care can be better understood by looking at how health professionals are rewarded and compensated.

HOW ARE CLINICAL HEALTH PROFESSIONALS REWARDED AND COMPENSATED FOR THEIR SERVICES?

Physicians—and increasingly other health professionals—are compensated through a variety of mechanisms. Compensation levels depend on the site where care is delivered, the nature of the patient's insurance, and the type of institution in which the professional works or is employed.

---

[b] A new approach, often called **concierge practice**, is attempting to provide primary care based upon many of these principles. Concierge practices often limit the number of patients they serve, provide longer time for appointments and guarantee same or next-day access to appointments. However, to provide these services, concierge practices often charge several thousand dollars per patient as a yearly charge, which is not covered by insurance. Thus, concierge practices have been limited to those who can afford to pay for these services.

TABLE 9-2 Ideals and Realities of Primary Care—the 6 Cs

	Primary care ideals	Realities
Contact	The point of first contact with the healthcare system—the entry point	Patients enter the healthcare systems through many disconnected points including: ER, specialists, urgent care centers, nontraditional practitioners, etc.
Comprehensive	Primary care intends to be able to diagnose and treat the great majority of problems	Rapid increase in possible treatments and high-volume practices increase proportion of patient problems that are referred to specialists
Coordinated	Primary care intends to be the focal point for diagnosis and treatment with coordination through referral to specialists for consultation and feedback	Primary care physicians increasingly being replaced by "hospitalists," who are full time in the hospital and provide care for inpatients and direct patient access to specialists
Continuity	Patient followed over many years—continuous care provision	Patients increasingly required or encouraged to change physicians/providers for insurance purposes
Caring	Individualized care based on individual relationships	Primary care increasingly becoming an administrative entity without long-term individual relationships
Community	Primary care designed to connect the individual patient with community resources and community requirements (required examinations, reportable diseases, vaccinations, driver's licenses, etc.)	Healthcare professionals and public health have a long history of distant and—at times—contentious relationships

Source: Data from Institute of Medicine. *Defining Primary Care: An Interim Report.* Washington, DC: National Academies Press; 1994.

Complicating the issues of coordination of services and continuity of care is the fact that patients can and are often encouraged to change insurance coverage on a yearly basis. Thus, clinicians now live in a complex, changing, and often confusing world in which issues of compensation can get in the way of quality care. Despite the best of intentions, many clinicians find themselves having to address compensation as another "C." Table 9-3 outlines a number of methods of financial compensation to providers of health services and examines some of their advantages and disadvantages.

In addition to the mechanism of payment for services, another key factor that affects health professionals is the number of people in the profession. Let us look at how the right number makes a difference.

HOW CAN WE ENSURE THE SYSTEM HAS THE RIGHT NUMBER OF HEALTHCARE PROFESSIONALS?

Financial compensation is the fundamental market mechanism for regulating the supply of most professionals. This mechanism has not generally worked well in the health professions. The demand for positions in medical schools, for instance, far exceeds the supply. Thus, much of the control over the number of professionals that are trained has been made by the profession itself through policies that control the number and size of accredited degree-granting institutions. This control has had limited success. For instance, in the 1980s, dentists determined that there was an oversupply of dentists. A number of dental schools were closed and new dental schools were limited. Today, there is an undersupply of dentists. Balancing the supply and demand for health professionals is a complex undertaking, as illustrated by the current shortage of nurses.[8] The nursing shortage is discussed in Box 9-3.

We have now taken a look at the complex world of health care and public health professions, including the creation of health professions through education, training, and credentialing. We have also looked at issues of compensation and how we can try to ensure the right numbers of health professionals. Now, let us turn our attention to Chapter 10, which examines institutions in which health care is delivered.

TABLE 9-3 Method of Financial Compensation to Providers of Health Services

Compensation method	Meaning	Examples	Advantages	Disadvantages
Fee-for-service	Clinician paid for each covered service	Physicians often paid for medical visits and procedure, but may not be paid for counseling for prevention	Reward linked directly to work performed Encourages efficiency of delivery of services	May encourage delivery of unnecessary, as well as necessary services
Capitation	Clinician is paid a set amount per time period for each patient for whom they are responsible, regardless of level of use of services	Primary care physicians in health plans may be paid a set amount per patient per month and are expected to provide all primary care services	Discourages unnecessary care, may encourage preventive care, allows for predictable budgeting	May discourage necessary care, may encourage referral to specialists unless specialty care is financially discouraged
Episode of care	Institution or clinician is paid a set amount for providing comprehensive services, such as hospital treatment based on the patient's diagnosis	Medicare pays for hospital care based on Diagnosis Related Groups (DRGs) allowing defined number of days per condition	Encourages rapid and efficient delivery of care	May encourage discharge prior to ability to provide self-care
Salary	Set amount per time period	Governmental facilities generally pay clinicians on a seniority-based salary	May allow focus on quality	May discourage efficiency
Pay for Performance "P4P"	Compensation adjusted based on measures of the quality of care delivered	Additional compensation for adherence to evidence-based guidelines	Links income with quality providing strong incentive for quality	Difficult to measure quality, outcomes may be related to factors outside clinician's control

BOX 9-3 The Nursing Shortage and What Can Be Done About It?

The number of U.S.-trained registered nurses (RNs) has not kept up with demand. The shortage of nurses, especially those who work in the increasingly technical hospital environment, continues to grow. The projected size of the shortage is controversial, but estimates of a 20–30 percent shortage of RNs are commonly quoted. Everyone agrees that nursing is one of the most rapidly growing professions in terms of available job positions. The shortage is made worse by the fact that the average age of nurses is increasing because until very recently there was a decline in the number of newly-trained nurses. Why is there such a large and growing shortage? A number of factors contribute to this problem reflecting changes in nursing and American society. There is both a greater demand for nursing services and a supply that is not growing fast enough. Among the factors are:

- **Technology**—The increased availability and use of technology has increased the need for skilled nurses. Most of those who qualify for these technologically-oriented jobs are recent graduates and the number of recent graduates is very small compared to the demand.
- **More patients**—The aging baby boomer generation is expected to have a major impact on the need for nursing services. The large number of baby boomers born between 1946 and 1964 will need and expect increased nursing services.
- **Reduced supply**—Nursing has been viewed as a woman's profession, which has historically limited its attractiveness to men. In addition, many women leave the profession or practice part time, which may be accelerated by the increasingly stressful nature of the work.
- **Restrictions on entry**—Until recently, nursing education was self-contained—to become a nurse you needed to complete an undergraduate nursing degree and the only way to pursue a graduate nursing degree was to already have a bachelor's degree in nursing.
- **Shortage of nursing faculty**—A shortage of nursing faculty and teaching facilities has also contributed to the shortage of nurses and the ability to rapidly expand the size of Colleges of Nursing.

A national effort is now underway to increase the number of nurses in training. The approaches being used include:

- **Better compensation**—higher salaries and more flexible work schedules
- **Increased educational opportunities**—scholarships to encourage admissions to nursing schools and more flexibility in entering nursing after bachelor's degree training in other fields
- **Increase applicant pool**—encouraging male and underrepresented minority group enrollment
- **Raising status of nursing**—greater independence and recognition

Enrollment in Colleges of Nursing is now increasing. However, it will take many years before the supply of nurses meets the demand.

Key Words

- Accreditation
- Credentialing
- Certification
- Licensure
- Primary care
- Secondary care
- Tertiary care
- Medical home

Discussion Questions

Take a look at the questions posed in the following scenarios which were presented at the beginning of this chapter. See now whether you can answer them.

1. *Upon arrival at the hospital, the nurse specialist examines you and consults with the radiologists, the gastroenterologist, and the general surgeon. Your medication is reviewed by the PharmD, and your meals by the clinical nutritionist. Throughout the hospitalization you are followed by a hospitalist. Once you get back home, the home care team comes to see you regularly for the first two weeks and the physician assistant and registered nurse see you in the office. You realize that health care is no longer just about doctors and nurses. You ask yourself: what roles do all of these health professionals play in the healthcare system?*

2. *Jenna decides that after college she wants to become a doctor and practice medicine. "I thought there was only one kind of doctor who could diagnose disease and prescribe medicine," she mentions at a career counseling meeting. "Not so, anymore," says her advisor. "There are allopathic and osteopathic physicians. In addition, there are nurse practitioners who are authorized to diagnose and prescribe medications, and there are physician assistants who do the same under a physician's supervision. The universe of "doctors" now includes doctors of nursing practice, as well as other doctoral degree professionals, such as pharmacists and physical therapists." Understanding careers in health care can be as difficult for students as it is for patients, Jenna thinks to herself. Now she understands why her advisor asked: "what do you mean by 'practice'? What do you mean by 'doctor'?"*

3. *Sarah was about to begin medical school and was expecting two years of "preclinical" classroom lectures focusing on the basic sciences, followed by the study of*

clinical diseases. Then, as she'd heard from her physician father, she expected two years of clinical hospital "rotation and electives investigating specialties. She is surprised to find that medical school has changed. There are small group problem-based learning sessions where she needs to be able to locate and read the research literature. There is contact with patients and their problems right from the beginning. There is increasingly a four-year approach instead of a preclinical and clinical approach to medical education. She wonders: are these changes for the better? What else needs to be done to improve medical education?*

4. *You are interested in clinical care, as well as public health. need to make a choice," you think to yourself. "Not necessarily," your advisor says. "There are many ways to combine clinical care with public health." After a little investigation, you find out that undergraduate public health education is increasingly seen as preparation for clinical education and clinical prevention and population health are increasingly becoming part of clinical care. In addition, many careers from health administration, to health policy, to clinical research combine the individual orientation of clinical care with the population perspective of public health. So what's the best pathway to a public health career for you?*

REFERENCES

1. Shi L, Singh D. *Essentials of the US Health Care System.* Sudbury, M Jones and Bartlett Publishers; 2005.

2. American Board of Medical Specialties. Specialties and Subspecialties Available at: http://www.abms.org/Who_We_Help/Physicians/specialties.asp Accessed March 19, 2009.

3. Ludmerer KM. *Time to Heal: American Medical Education from the Turn of the Century to the Era of Managed Care.* New York: Oxford University Press 2005.

4. American Board of Nursing Specialties. Accredited Certification Programs. Available at: http://www.nursingcertification.org/exam_program. htm. Accessed March 19, 2009.

5. Association of Schools of Public Health. Public Health Workforce Crisis—What Can Be Done? Available at: http://www.asph.org/document. cfm?page=1039. Accessed March 19, 2009.

6. Gebbie K, Rosenstock L, Hernandez LM, eds. *Who Will Keep the Public Healthy? Educating Public Health Professionals for the 21st Century.* Washington DC: National Academy Press; 2003.

7. Institute of Medicine. *Defining Primary Care: An Interim Report.* Washington, DC: National Academy Press; 1994.

8. American Association of Colleges of Nursing. Nursing Shortage Fact Sheet. Available at: http://www.aacn.nche.edu/Media/FactSheets/Nursing Shortage.htm. Accessed March 19, 2009.

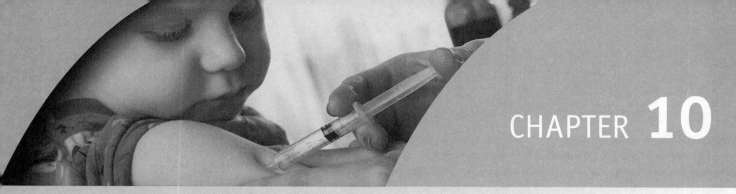

CHAPTER 10

Healthcare Institutions

LEARNING OBJECTIVES

By the end of this chapter, the student will be able to:

- identify a range of inpatient healthcare facilities that exist in the United States.
- identify a range of outpatient healthcare facilities that exist in the United States.
- describe approaches being used to define and measure the quality of health care.
- describe types of coordination of care and methods available to facilitate coordination of care.
- identify roles that may be played by electronic medical records in improving the delivery of health care.
- identify components of medical malpractice and disclosure of medical errors.

George didn't have health insurance and went to the emergency room whenever he needed care. They always treated him there, but then tried to get him connected to a primary care facility. He wasn't eligible for care at the Veterans Administration facilities. So, they sent him to the local community health center, which they called the "safety net" provider. George did go there and they tried to treat his problems and get him his medicines despite his not having insurance. When he got sick, however, George went back to the emergency department. Even George agreed that it wasn't the best way to get care, but he wondered: what is needed to make the system work better?

Laura had breast cancer and it had spread. Her medical records were on file at the hospital, at four doctor's offices, in two emergency rooms, and at an outpatient imaging facility. No one seemed to know how to put the system together. Whenever her old

records were essential, they asked her to go get a copy of them and bring them to her next appointment. That worked for a while, but when she ended up in the emergency room her records just weren't available. There must be a better way, Laura thought to herself. Hasn't the healthcare system discovered the Internet yet?

Fred ended his walk one day at the emergency room. He seemed confused about how to get home. "It looks like we are dealing with Alzheimer's," his doctor told Fred's wife, Sonya, at their next appointment. Taking care of Fred at home was not easy. Home health aides and occasional weekend relief called "respite care" eased the burden for a while. The new assisted-living facilities looked attractive, but Fred's family just couldn't afford one. When Fred fell and broke his hip, he required hospitalization for surgery. The hospital discharge planner arranged for a skilled nursing home for rehabilitation services paid for by Medicaid. After a few weeks there, the only alternative was long-term or custodial care in a nursing home. The care at the nursing home was not what the family had expected. The staff did clean Fred up before the announced family visits, but once when the family arrived unannounced, they were shocked to see Fred lying half-naked in his wheelchair. The end came almost two years from the day they moved him to the nursing home. Looking back, the family asked: can the healthcare system do better at addressing the needs of Alzheimer's patients?

These are the types of situations faced by many patients as they try to navigate through the institutions that provide health care in the United States. Let us take a look at these different institutions.

WHAT INSTITUTIONS MAKE UP THE HEALTHCARE SYSTEM?

The number and types of healthcare institutions are almost as diverse and complicated as the number and types of healthcare professionals. In recent years, the complexity has grown as a range of facilities have developed to serve new needs and new financial reimbursement approaches.[1,2] Nonetheless, it is possible to understand the scope of healthcare institutions by categorizing them as **inpatient facilities** and **outpatient facilities**, with inpatient facilities implying that patients remain in the facility for at least 24 hours.

Inpatient facilities include hospitals, skilled nursing and rehabilitation facilities, nursing homes, and institutional hospices. Outpatient facilities include those providing clinical services by one or more clinicians and those providing diagnostic testing or treatment. We will provide an overview of inpatient and outpatient facilities and then ask: do these facilities together provide a coordinated system of care? Let us begin by looking at inpatient facilities.

What Types of Inpatient Facilities Exist in the United States?

We can classify inpatient facilities as: 1) hospitals generally designed for short-term stays by patients; and 2) long-term care facilities. Let us first take a look at hospitals.

The history of hospitals in the United States goes back to the colonial period. However, prior to the middle of the 19th century, hospitals were generally institutions for those without other sources of care, which included the poor, the military, and those with communicable diseases. Hospitals generally provided little more than shelter and food and separated the sick—especially those with communicable diseases—from the healthy.[1]

Today, the American hospital is usually a modern high-tech enterprise that lies at the center of the healthcare system educationally, structurally, and psychologically. You can often identify the hospital from far away because it is frequently the largest and most modern facility in town. The psychological hold that the hospital has on American health care is symbolized by the term "house" and the concept of "housestaff," or residents who practically live full time in the hospital during their training.[3,a]

Hospitals share some common features including:

- Hospitals are licensed by the state and usually accredited by a national organization, such as The Joint Commission (formally called The Joint Commission on the Accreditation of Healthcare Organizations (JCAHO)).
- Hospitals have an organized physician staff and provide 24-hour-a-day nursing services.
- The hospital is governed by a governing board separate from the medical and nursing staff that has overall responsibility for the operation of the hospital consistent with state and federal laws.

The several types of hospitals in the United States differ in their purposes and organizational structures. Hospitals can be categorized as general hospitals and specialty hospitals. General hospitals attempt to serve a wide spectrum of patients and problems, though they may concentrate on serving only children or only those who qualify for services, such as a Veterans Administration (VA) hospital. In the past, specialty hospitals sought to serve the needs of patients who could not be accommodated in general hospitals, such as those with tuberculosis or severe mental illness. Today, these conditions are usually addressed in general hospitals. Today's specialty hospitals are more a result of the specialization of medical services. Institutions focused on cancer, heart disease, psychiatric illness, ophthalmology, and orthopedics, for instance, are rapidly developing.

Hospitals are often categorized today by their funding source and financial arrangements. They can be divided into nonprofit and for-profit, or investor-owned hospitals. Nearly 90 percent of the approximately 5000 hospitals in the United States are nonprofits. These include the broad category of private nonprofit hospitals, hospitals run by state or federal government, and hospitals run by institutions, such as universities.[b]

Approximately half of these 5000 hospitals are private nonprofit hospitals, many of which have affiliations with religious denominations, but accept patients of all faiths. State and local governments run nearly 20 percent of hospitals, many of which are described—along with private nonprofit hospitals—as community hospitals. Federal medical institutions include the Veterans Administration hospitals and the military hospital system. For-profit or investor-owned hospitals make up over 10 percent of all hospitals, many of which are owned by several large corporations specializing in providing healthcare services.

Hospitals today are often more than an inpatient facility. The most rapidly growing component of most hospitals is the

---

[a] The book *The House of God*, written in the 1960s, captured the mentality of the housestaff of the era and has been unofficial required reading by subsequent generations of residents. It portrays housestaff as having their own culture and portrays patients, as well as community physicians, in often disparaging ways.

[b] Hospitals are also categorized as teaching and nonteaching hospitals. A teaching hospital is one that has one or more accredited residency programs. Today, many community hospitals, as well as federal and state hospitals, have residency programs. The designation **academic health center** implies a medical school, one or more other health professions schools, and an affiliated hospital.

spectrum of outpatient services they provide. In addition to emergency departments, hospitals usually also provide outpatient surgical and medical services including diagnostic and treatment services and may provide facilities for routine office-type visits.

The hospital should no longer be viewed as one building. Hospital networks or systems are increasingly being created, some of which provide a range of services including skilled nursing and rehabilitative services, as well as long-term care.

We have classified inpatient facilities as including hospitals and long-term care facilities. Today, there are a range of long-term care facilities, some of which are not primarily operated as healthcare facilities.[1, 2] These facilities may include skilled nursing facilities, nursing homes, assisted living and dementia care, and at times, hospice care. To fully understand the provision of long-term care, you also need to appreciate the types of services that are increasingly being provided in an individual's home.

It is important to distinguish between skilled nursing and rehabilitative services in contrast to nursing home services. Skilled nursing and rehabilitative services, like hospital services, are generally short term and aimed at accomplishing specific objectives, such as recovery from a stroke or injury. Though these services may continue for many months, they are not designed to provide long-term care beyond the point at which improvement can no longer be expected.

Nursing homes, on the other hand, are designed for long-term or custodial care while also providing a limited amount of healthcare services. Individuals in nursing homes usually require care because of their inability to perform the activities of daily living, such as dressing, feeding, and bathing themselves. Nursing homes may provide routine medical care and some acute care, but this type of facility is not primarily designed to improve the medical status of its residents.[c]

Nursing homes are generally operated according to a specific set of nursing home regulations determined by and enforced by the states. Federal minimal standards are set as part of the requirements to receive payment through the Medicare and Medicaid systems. Most nursing homes, like most hospitals, are run as private nonprofit institutions. However, for-profit or investor-owned nursing homes provide approximately 15 percent of the beds nationally. There are over 16,000 nursing homes in the United States with over 1.5 million residents.

---

[c] Some states, such as California, have developed an additional long-term care model which is not part of the "medical model." That is, limited or no nursing care is provided and the facility is not obliged to provide services if the individual's health status changes substantially.

Most, but not all residents are elderly and over 80 percent need help with mobility, nearly two-thirds are considered incontinent, and nearly half require assistance with eating. Alzheimer's patients are the most rapidly growing population in the nursing home system of care.[1,2]

Although not strictly inpatient healthcare facilities, assisted-living facilities and home health care increasingly provide long-term care for those who have less severe impairments. Assisted-living facilities are not organized as healthcare facilities, but may provide or coordinate health care as part of their services. New concepts, such as continuing care retirement communities, attempt to provide a range of options including independent-living, assisted-living and nursing home facilities.

Most elderly and disabled individuals are not residents in long-term care institutions, rather they live on their own or with family members. Thus, much attention in recent years has been paid to providing and financing home healthcare services including home health aides, healthcare delivered at home, and respite care. Respite care provides short-term time away for primary caregivers such as family members.

The hospice movement today can be viewed as part of the long-term care system. It is care provided to those with a life expectancy of six months or fewer as determined by a physician. The goal of hospice care is to provide comfort, emotional support, and palliation—not to increase longevity. In some cases, hospice care may occur in a separate institution, but today it is more often provided in the patient's place of residence.

What Types of Outpatient Facilities Exist in the United States?

The variety of types of outpatient facilities is even more diverse and complicated than those of inpatient facilities. The basic distinction between clinical facilities and diagnostic testing or therapeutic facilities helps define the types of services provided.

Clinical services were traditionally viewed as being provided in "the doctor's office." None of these words—the/doctor's/office—does a good job of describing the current organization of clinical services. "The" implies one. Today, clinical services are rarely organized around one doctor or clinician. Group practice and multispecialty practices have become the rule. "Doctors" (or physicians) are by no means the only health professionals to organize and provide clinical services. Physical therapists, nurse practitioners, audiologists, optometrists, clinical psychologists, and a long list of other health professionals often provide their own office services. Rather than "doctor," the term **provider** is increasingly used to encompass this growing array of health professionals. Even the term "office" is no longer appropriate. In addition to the traditional office setting, many clinicians now provide services in shopping centers, work places, and even make house calls.

The average American has over three visits for clinical services per year. An increasing number of these visits are provided outside of "the doctor's office" in the traditional sense. These sites now include a growing network of community health centers designed to provide what is called the "safety net" services for those who cannot or do not wish to seek other types of clinical services. Box 10-1 provides an overview of community health centers.[4]

A key issue in the organization of health care is the delivery of quality services. Let us take a look at what we mean by quality and what mechanisms are being used to ensure the quality of healthcare services.

WHAT DO WE MEAN BY THE QUALITY OF HEALTHCARE SERVICES?

The quality of healthcare services may mean different things to different people. Administrators may focus on the structures, such as the availability of operating rooms or laboratory services. Clinicians may focus on the process, such as the technical competence of the practitioners. Patients may focus on different types of processes like the personal relationships and their personal satisfaction. External reviewers may focus on the outcome—lives saved or disabilities prevented.

Quality can be assessed using what are called **structure**, **process**, and **outcome measures**. Structure focuses on the physical and organizational infrastructure in which care is delivered. Process concentrates on the procedures and formal processes that go into delivering care—for example, systems for ensuring credentialing of health professionals and procedures to ensure timely response to complaints. Outcome measures implies a focus on the result of care from rates of infection to readmissions with complications.

Defining and measuring quality remains a controversial subject. However, the National Committee for Quality Assurance (NCQA) has developed a widely-recognized framework to assist with this challenge.[5] Table 10-1 outlines this framework.[d]

The complexity of inpatient and outpatient services in the United States has made the delivery of quality healthcare ser-

---

[d] Note that NCQA's framework emphasizes structure and process measures. These have little emphasis on the actual outcomes of care.

BOX 10-1   Community Health Centers.

Initially named neighborhood health centers, community health centers were established in 1965 as part of the Johnson administration's War on Poverty. The centers were designed based on a community empowerment philosophy that encouraged the flow of funds directly to nonprofit, community-level organizations, often bypassing state governments.

The Health Centers Consolidation Act of 1996 combined community health centers with healthcare services for migrants, the homeless population, and residents of public housing to create the consolidated health centers program under Section 330 of the Public Health Service Act. These centers are often called 330 grantees. To receive a 330 grant, a clinic must meet certain statutory requirements. It must:

- Be located in a federally-designated medically-underserved area (MUA) or serve a federally-designated medically-underserved population (MUP).
- Have nonprofit, public, or tax exempt status.
- Provide comprehensive primary healthcare services, referrals, and other services needed to facilitate access to care, such as case management, translation, and transportation.
- Have a governing board, the majority of whose members are patients of the health center.
- Provide services to all in the service area regardless of ability to pay and offer a sliding fee schedule that adjusts according to family income.

Community health centers have undergone rapid expansion in recent years and now serve over 15 million individuals annually at more than 4000 sites in all 50 states and the District of Columbia. Nearly half of the patients are uninsured and nearly the same number is eligible for Medicaid. Only a small number have private insurance. According to a recent review, "[h]ealth centers have proven to be an effective investment of federal funds, have garnered sustained goodwill and advocacy in the communities they serve, and, as a result, generally have enjoyed broad, bipartisan support."[4]

TABLE 10-1 Characteristics of Healthcare Quality—National Committee for Quality Assurance

Characteristic	Meaning	Examples	How measured?
Access and service	Access to needed care and good customer service	Enough primary care physicians and specialists Satisfaction of patients in terms of problems obtaining care	Patient satisfaction surveys, patient grievances and follow-up, interviews with staff
Qualified providers	Personnel licensed and trained and patients satisfied with services	System for checking credentials, sanctions Patient satisfaction with providers of care	Presence of system for checking credentials Patient satisfaction surveys
Staying healthy	Quality of services that help people maintain good health and avoid illness	Presence of guidelines for appropriate clinical preventive services Evidence that patients are receiving appropriate screening tests	Review of independently-verified clinical records Review of responses from patients
Getting better	Quality of services that help people recover from illness	Presence of method for evaluating new procedures, drugs, and devices to ensure that patients have assess to the most up-to-date care Providing specific services, such as smoking cessation	Review of independently-verified clinical records Interviews with staff
Living with illness	Quality of services that help people manage chronic illness	Programs to assist patients to manage chronic conditions like asthma Provision of specific services, such as eye examinations for diabetics	Review of independently-verified clinical records Interviews with staff

Source: Data from NCQA Health Plan Report Care. Available at: http://www.ncqa.org/. Accessed November 9, 2008.

vices very challenging. The complexity of the system raises two closely connected questions:

- How can the pieces of the system be coordinated to provide integrated care?
- How can we improve and ensure the quality of health care?

The coordination and integration of healthcare delivery is often considered key to both the efficiency and the quality of health care. Let us begin by taking a look at how healthcare delivery can be coordinated between institutions.

HOW CAN HEALTH CARE BE COORDINATED AMONG THE MULTIPLE INSTITUTIONS THAT PROVIDE HEALTHCARE SERVICES?

The types of institutions that deliver health care in the United States have continued to proliferate in recent years. Each type differs in its governance, finance, accreditation, and organizational structure. It is not surprising that most patients, policy makers, and even clinicians do not have a good overview of the system. Connecting the institutions to achieve an organized system has become a major challenge.

Healthcare delivery systems aim to connect inpatient and outpatient services, as well as short-term and long-term clinical services to provide a coordinated system of care. The desire for an integrated healthcare delivery system is not a new idea. For many years, the concept of "the patient's doctor" was seen as the mechanism to hold together the system. The doctor provided all care or coordinated the care with other clinicians. The doctor "followed" the patient into the inpatient facility and provided their "follow-up" care after they left.

Like the concept of "the doctor's office," the concept of "the patient's doctor" is no longer a reflection of reality. Once again "the" rarely reflects the reality of multiple providers of care. Primary care physicians are now far less likely to follow the patient into the hospital or the nursing home and far less likely to be aware of the patient's multiple sources of and approaches to care.

Efforts to integrate the system are underway. We will look at two basic approaches that are being used: the development of integrated healthcare delivery systems and the use of integrated electronic medical records. These approaches are likely to be used together and form the basis for a future integrated system of healthcare delivery. In order to understand the uses and potential of these two approaches, we first need to think about the types of coordination of care that we want to see occur and the purposes they serve.

WHAT TYPES OF COORDINATION OF CARE ARE NEEDED AND WHAT PURPOSES DO THEY SERVE?

As we have discussed, the traditional approach to coordination of care revolved around the clinician-patient or doctor-patient relationship. Traditionally, the concepts of continuity of care and coordination of care have been almost synonymous. This approach assumed that the relationship between one doctor and one patient would provide the individualized knowledge, trust, and commitment that would ensure the coordination of care by ensuring the continuity of care. The concepts of primary care that we have discussed were built in large part upon this concept of one-to-one continuity.

Today, there is an increasing emphasis on ensuring coordination rather than one-to-one continuity. Coordination is sought between institutions and settings where care is delivered. The approach that leaves continuity of information and continuity of responsibility for care to individual clinicians alone has often failed to produce the desired results. As we will see, efforts are underway to formally link institutions, services, and information between the various healthcare delivery sites and institutions.

Institutional coordination often relies on financial coordination. If services are covered by insurance in one setting but not another, the system is not likely to function efficiently or effectively. When services are not covered at all, patients may receive excellent care in one setting only to lose the benefits of that care when necessary preparation or follow-up is not paid for and not accomplished in another setting.

Coordination is not just an issue within the healthcare delivery system, it is also an issue that straddles healthcare delivery and public health functions. Communicable disease control and environmental protections, such as controlling antibiotic resistance and lead exposure, cannot be successful without effective and efficient coordination between healthcare and public health professionals and institutions. Table 10-2

outlines these types of coordination, their intended function, and the types of challenges that commonly occur with their implementation.

Let us take a look at the development of healthcare delivery systems as one approach to ensuring coordination of health care.

WHAT TYPES OF HEALTHCARE DELIVERY SYSTEMS ARE BEING DEVELOPED AND HOW CAN THEY HELP ENSURE COORDINATION OF HEALTH CARE?

We will use the term **healthcare delivery system** to imply a linkage of institutions and healthcare professionals that together take on the responsibility of delivering coordinated care.[e]

In a nation such as the United States, in which health care is provided by a range of providers and institutions, holding together one delivery system is not easy. A wide range of efforts are under way to connect the pieces. Let us take a look at some successful examples.

Care coordination challenges have been quite successfully met in the emergency response system. Today, there is a network of institutions, including government agencies and private emergency medical services providers, that cooperate with hospital emergency departments to facilitate and expedite the care of the seriously ill and injured. The emergency response system helps to quickly respond to emergencies, provide on-site assistance and information, and identify the healthcare institution that is best prepared to handle the emergency based on location, staffing, and capabilities. This system, while not perfect, demonstrates that coordination of care—at least urgent care—is possible.

Coordination of routine health care has proven to be a more difficult challenge. Healthcare systems are beginning to be developed often based on common ownership or governance. These integrated systems are designed to provide a wide range of services from outpatient clinical care, diagnostic testing and treatment services, to inpatient, home health, skilled nursing, nursing home and even hospice care.

Two of the longest standing and most developed healthcare systems are the Kaiser Permanente and Veterans Administration systems.[6, 7] These are discussed in Box 10-2. Many more healthcare systems are being formed by caregivers, such as multispecialty group practices, and by institutions, such as

---

[e] We will distinguish **healthcare delivery systems, healthcare system,** and **health systems.** Healthcare delivery systems include the delivery of healthcare services to a defined population. A healthcare system also includes the financial arrangements needed to pay for the care. A health system, the broadest of the three terms, includes the public health system, as well as the health care system.

TABLE 10-2 Type of Coordination of Care, Intended Functions, and Challenges with Implementation

Type of coordination	Intended function	Challenges with implementation
Clinician-patient relationship	Continuity as a mechanism for ensuring coordination Development of one-to-one relationships built on knowledge and trust over extended periods of time	Multiple clinicians involved in care Team rather than individual concept of primary care Frequent changes in insurance coverage require change in health professionals
Institutional coordination	Coordination of individual's information between institutions needed to inform individual clinical and administrative decision making	Different structures and governance often lead to lack of coordination between in-patient facilities and between inpatient and outpatient facilities
Financial coordination	Implies that a patient has comprehensive coverage for services provided by the full range of institutions Maximize the efficiency of the care received and minimize the administrative effort required to manage the payment system	Lack of comprehensive insurance coverage often means that essential services cannot be delivered or cannot be delivered at the most efficient or effective institutional site
Coordination between health care and public health	Coordination of services between clinical care and public heath requires communication to ensure follow-up and to protect the health of others	Lack of coordination of services between public health services and clinical care is often based on lack of communications

university medical centers. The coming years are likely to produce a number of successful models that will become examples that others will try to copy.

HOW CAN ELECTRONIC MEDICAL RECORDS BE USED TO FACILITATE COORDINATION OF CARE AND IMPROVE QUALITY?

There is widespread agreement that an electronic health record system could improve coordination of care, as well as achieve a number of other quality objectives. The Institute of Medicine (IOM) outlined the following potential roles for an electronic health information system. These roles aim in large part to provide the cornerstone for coordination of healthcare delivery.

- *Health information and data*—laboratory and pharmacy data, as well as records of a patient's history and findings on examination including past medical records

- *Results management*—integration of findings from multiple providers at multiple sites
- *Order entry/management*—electronic ordering of tests and prescriptions to maximize accuracy and speed implementation
- *Decision support management*—computer reminders and prompts to encourage timely follow-up and adherence to evidence-based guidelines
- *Electronic communication and connectivity*—facilitation of communications between providers and between providers and patients
- *Patient support*—tools for patient education and patient involvement in decision making
- *Administrative processes*—facilitation of scheduling, billing, and other administrative services to increase efficiency and reduce costs
- *Reporting and population health*—improvements in the efficiency and completeness of required reporting

BOX 10-2 Healthcare Delivery Systems: Kaiser Permanente and the Veterans Administration.

The Kaiser Permanente and the Veteran's Administration healthcare systems are two of the largest organized healthcare systems in the United States. They have very different histories, philosophies, and serve quite different populations. Nonetheless, they have both moved in the direction of developing an integrated set of healthcare delivery institutions linked together by an electronic health record and fostering evidence-based interventions. They share a common advantage in that they are financed by single sources, the Kaiser Permanente health plan and the federal government, respectively.

Kaiser helped introduce the concept of the health maintenance organization by offering a comprehensive package of preventive and curative services at a fixed monthly fee. The Kaiser Permanente health system has its roots in World War II when employers offered health benefits when they were prohibited from raising wages. In the subsequent decades, Kaiser Permanente grew from its California base, enrolling over 8 million individuals. It was created as a staff model prepaid health plan, enrolling patients who would receive all of their services directly from clinicians and institutions that were part of the plan. This allowed Kaiser Permanente to develop an integrated approach to healthcare delivery.

Kaiser, the management component, owns or contracts with hospitals, skilled nursing facilities, home healthcare systems, and a range of other institutions that provide care under their management. Permanente, the physician component, aims to provide an integrated set of inpatient and outpatient services. Kaiser Permanente competes actively in the market for healthcare services and often limits the amount and types of care that can be provided. Nonetheless, it has been able to develop an integrated healthcare delivery system, promote evidence-based interventions, and introduce an integrated electronic health record system.

The Veterans Administration healthcare system began as an outgrowth of World War I, though its roots go back to the Revolutionary War. After World War II, the Veterans Administration hospital system rapidly increased in size and developed strong relationships with medical schools and other health professional training schools for education and research. Today, the VA heath care system is part of the Cabinet-level Department of Veterans Affairs and serves over six million patients each year.

For many years, the VA system was accused of poor quality care and lack of coordination of care because it emphasized inpatient services and patients often went back and forth between the VA and other healthcare delivery sites. In the mid-1990s, the VA health system underwent a major "systems reengineering," designed to improve quality. The changes included the development of an integrated electronic health record and an emphasis on evidence-based interventions for preventive, acute, and chronic care.

In recent years, the VA health system has been organized into a series of networks, including inpatient and outpatient facilities. Many of the networks aim to provide comprehensive outpatient and inpatient services including skilled nursing and nursing home services, as well as outpatient and hospital services. Survey data collected a decade after the systems reengineering initiative began suggests that the VA health system provides an increasing quality of integrated care based upon evidence-based interventions.

The VA and Kaiser Permanente systems represent two of the largest healthcare systems in the United States. Both aim to serve a large number of patients and provide coordinated care utilizing evidence-based interventions and integrated healthcare records. The success of these two quite different healthcare systems suggests that an integrated system of care, patient information, and financing is possible and can be widely applied to improve the quality of health care.

and the speed and completeness of public health surveillance

The IOM also concluded that electronic record systems have the potential for helping achieve quality and efficiency objectives as outlined in Box 10-3.[8]

Efforts to implement a national system of electronic health records are underway. Nearly $20 billion has been allocated to this effort as part of the 2009–2010 stimulus plan. A federal plan envisions the widespread adoption of an integrated electronic record by 2014. Recent efforts to include patients as direct users of their health information may spur more rapid acceptance of the electronic records. The need for security of data and control by patients over who has access and for what purposes is critical to acceptance and use of an electronic system such as this. Assuming that security issues can be adequately addressed, you should expect to see widespread use of electronic records and an increased role for patients in accessing and managing their own medical records.[f]

---

[f] Despite the national commitment to implement electronic health records, the usage by physicians in their offices has remained low and far behind that of other developed countries. This is expected to change rapidly with the infusion of new funding.

BOX 10-3 **Use of Electronic Health Records to Improve Quality and Efficiency of Healthcare Delivery.**

The IOM report indicates that the electronic health record has the potential to improve quality and efficiency of patient care in the following ways:

- *Improve patient safety.* Safety is the prevention of harm to patients. Each year in the United States, tens of thousands of people die as a result of preventable adverse events due to health care. Electronic records containing information on prescribed drugs and other treatments are expected to improve patient safety.
- *Support the delivery of effective patient care.* Effectiveness is providing services based on scientific knowledge to those who could benefit and at the same time refraining from providing services to those not likely to benefit. Only about one-half (55 percent) of Americans receive recommended medical care that is consistent with evidence-based guidelines. Reminder systems that require clinicians to accept or reject the recommendations of a clinical guideline are expected to increase the use of evidence-based guidelines.
- *Facilitate management of chronic conditions.* More than half of those with chronic conditions have three or more different providers and report that they often receive conflicting information from those providers; moreover, many undergo duplicate tests and procedures, but still do not receive recommended care. Physicians also report difficulty in coordinating care for their patients with chronic conditions and believe that this lack of coordination produces poor outcomes. Electronic records can help inform clinicians of other care being given to their patients.
- *Improve efficiency.* Efficiency is the avoidance of waste, in particular, waste of equipment, supplies, ideas, and energy. Methods must be found to enhance the efficiency of healthcare professionals and reduce the administrative and labor costs associated with healthcare delivery and financing. Electronic records, if consistently and widely implemented in the healthcare arena, can be expected to reduce costs as they have in many other fields.

Electronic health records are only one of the many ways that technology is changing the delivery and quality of healthcare services in the United States.

HOW IS TECHNOLOGY BEING USED TO IMPROVE THE QUALITY OF CARE?

The United States is among the leaders in adoption of new healthcare technologies, especially those that allow for technological approaches to disease diagnosis and treatment. In comparison with most other nations, the United States has more rapidly developed and accepted the use of medical technologies ranging from magnetic resonance imaging (MRI), to invasive cardiac procedures, to surgery for weight loss.

This country has generally relied on market mechanisms to develop, introduce, and disseminate or diffuse technology. This has resulted in extremely rapid innovation in areas with high levels of financial compensation and slower innovation in areas with less financial support. For instance, high-tech procedures ranging from heart surgery to hip replacements have been well compensated and have seen rapid innovation and diffusion. Well-compensated preventive procedures, such as mammography, have likewise seen widespread use. Other tech-

nologies like telemedicine are likely to have widespread applications only after financial reimbursement is provided.

Longer term innovations in technology have been fueled by the long-term U.S. investment in basic and applied research through the National Institutes of Health (NIH). The budget for the NIH was doubled during the 1990s, but has been relatively flat in recent years when adjusted for inflation. New stimulus funding has again at least temporarily increased funding. The innovations in care and in technology pioneered by NIH have often led to new approaches and new health-related industries. In recent years, the NIH has begun to focus on translational research or efforts to bring the benefits of new knowledge and new technologies to individual patients and whole communities.

Increased knowledge of the human genome has laid the groundwork for new diagnostic and therapeutic approaches, as well as a better understanding of the causes of disease. Better understanding of brain function and better technology for measuring changes in the brain are leading to new strategies for dealing with diseases ranging from Alzheimer's to depression. Advances in technology continue to provide hope and new challenges to improving health care.

We have now looked at how the development of integrated healthcare delivery systems and electronic health records and other technologies are being used to try to improve the quality and efficiency of healthcare delivery. Now, let us take a look at mechanisms that are being developed to monitor and ensure quality of care.

WHAT MECHANISMS ARE BEING USED TO MONITOR AND ENSURE THE QUALITY OF HEALTH CARE IN THE UNITED STATES?

In Chapter 9, we looked at a variety of methods, such as academic accreditation and individual credentialing, to help monitor and attempt to ensure that health professionals are well educated and prepared for clinical practice. Increasing requirements for continuing education and often recertification are being used to help ensure maintenance of competence. Integrating financial compensation with quality of care through the use of pay-for-performance approaches is gaining momentum as an approach to ensuring quality.

In addition, we have discussed the development and use of evidence-based recommendations and guidelines. Today, these recommendations are often available to clinicians in the form of protocols or step-by-step advice on approaches to diagnosis and treatment of specific conditions. The complexity of clinical practice and the limits of current research, however, mean that evidence-based recommendations are available for only a small percentage of the problems that clinicians face on a daily basis.

In addition to these approaches, a series of other mechanisms attempts to address issues of quality. They include:

- hospital privileges and approval to perform specific procedures,
- accreditation of additional healthcare organizations including clinical practices,
- malpractice liability, not only for physicians, but increasingly for other health professionals, and
- disclosure of medical errors.

Hospital privileges imply that hospitals may set criteria for allowing clinicians to practice in their facility. The criteria may include specialty and/or subspecialty boards. Approval to perform specific procedures implies the need to demonstrate competence either by training or experience or both.

Accreditation of hospitals and long-term care facilities have been long-standing efforts. It is often linked to reimbursement, and thus essential to the survival of these institutions. Accreditation of clinical practices, especially large group practices, is a growing trend. The NCQA and the Joint Commission are encouraging this process and providing quality criteria that need to be met. While still a voluntary process, these new forms of accreditation are becoming a sign of quality that is useful when recruiting patients and dealing with insurance companies.

BOX 10-4 Medical Malpractice.

Medical malpractice is a body of state law, therefore it differs from state to state. It is part of the civil law, as opposed to criminal law, which means that a case may be decided by a jury based upon what is called the **preponderance of the evidence**. This implies that malpractice was more likely than not. Despite the differences that exist from state to state, malpractice law builds upon a tradition known as **negligence law**, which is intended to protect the individual from harm.

The occurrence of harm or a bad outcome resulting from health care is not the same as negligence or malpractice. Errors in judgment and unsuccessful efforts are only considered medical malpractice if the patient can establish all four of the following: 1) a duty was owed; 2) a duty was breached; 3) the breach caused an injury; and 4) damages occurred. Let us look at each of these requirements.[g]

1. A duty was owed—This implies that a healthcare provider undertook the care or treatment of a patient. This duty may stem from services provided ranging from a long-term relationship, a single visit, or a telephone call to a contractual relationship based upon an insurance agreement.
2. A duty was breached—This implies a failure of the healthcare provider to meet a relevant standard of care. The standard of care is defined in terms of the clinician's specialty. A healthcare provider is generally expected to possess the knowledge and skill and exercise the care and judgment expected of a reasonably competent clinician of the same specialty.
3. The breach caused the injury—The legal concept of causation is based on what is called proximal cause. In medical malpractice, responsibility for an injury lies with the last negligent act. Proximal cause asks whether the injury or other event would have occurred if the negligent act had not occurred. Causation can be divided between different "parties," including clinicians and institutions.

(continues)

BOX 10-4 **continued.**

4. Damages occurred—Damages can be divided into direct, indirect, and punitive categories. Direct damages include lost earnings, as well as current and future medical expenses. Indirect damages may include pain and emotional distress. Punitive damages may be awarded when conduct is intentionally harmful or grossly negligent.[h]

Instructions to a jury in a medial malpractice case include efforts to convey the meaning of each of these components of malpractice law. However, juries have a great deal of latitude when interpreting their meaning. For example, the concept of proximal causation used in the law may not conform to the jurors' understanding of causation. Assume a clinician refused to continue to provide prenatal care after the first 13 weeks. The jury may decide based upon their own understanding of causation that the clinician's refusal was the cause of a subsequent birth defect.

Medical malpractice is a complex and changing field. Many factors affect whether or not a malpractice suit is brought. These include the extent of damages, the relationship between the patient and the healthcare provider, and the standards of practice of both medicine and law in the community.

---

[g] Physicians are not the only providers of health care that can be sued under malpractice laws. Other clinicians such as pharmacists may be sued, especially those that do not work directly under the authority of physicians. In addition, healthcare facilities as institutions may be sued and are often included as additional defendants in malpractice cases. In this section, we will refer to the defendant in a malpractice suit as a healthcare provider.
[h] Indirect damages may include what has been called a "loss of consortium," which includes services provided by a domestic partner including companionship, homemaking, etc., and future reproductive capabilities of either sex. Gross negligence includes the intentional or wanton omission of care that would be proper to provide or alternatively doing of that which would be improper to do. Punitive damages are often justified as a method of deterring such conduct by other providers of care.

The United States healthcare delivery system has a unique body of law called **medical malpractice**. Medical malpractice is hailed by its supporters as the ultimate guarantor of quality. It is attacked by its detractor as leading to defensive medicine, increased costs, and shortages in vulnerable professions, such as obstetrics. Regardless of your view of malpractice, it has come to have a major impact on the relationship between clinicians and patients. Box 10-4 examines the criteria for malpractice so you can understand what it means.[9]

Malpractice is an inherently adversarial process. Increasingly, patients, clinicians, and healthcare institutions are looking for alternatives. One recent approach is the disclosure of medical errors.

CAN DISCLOSING MEDICAL ERRORS CONTRIBUTE TO QUALITY OF CARE AND SERVE AS AN ALTERNATIVE TO MALPRACTICE?

In its report, *To Error is Human*, the IOM documented the extent to which medical errors produce harm to patients—they estimated over 40,000 deaths per year.[10] This makes medical errors a slightly more common cause of death than either breast cancer or motor vehicles. Errors may be due to deficiencies in the diagnostic or therapeutic process on the part of clinician(s). They may also be due to what are called **system errors**, problems resulting from deficiencies in the system for delivering health care.

As we discussed in Chapter 3, clinicians in the not-too-distant past often withheld key information from patients, including a diagnosis of cancer and the potential harms of recommended treatment. Today, disclosure of these types of information is an expected part of clinical practice. However, until recently, disclosure of medical errors had not been an expected part of clinical practice.

Beginning in 2001, the Joint Commission requires that patients be informed of all outcomes of care including "unanticipated outcomes." Recent efforts to develop a system of disclosure have included a far more specific set of expectations including conveying to the patient:

- facts about the event
- presence of error or systems failure
- expression of regret
- a formal apology

In addition, institutions are expected to integrate the disclosure process with other aspects of patient safety and risk management activities, provide support for the process including educating clinicians, and keeping track of the use of disclosure at their institutions. Such formal efforts to disclose errors are becoming increasingly common in clinical care. It is still too early to determine the impact of these efforts on quality and their ability to reduce malpractice suits. However, there has already been an a growing acceptance of disclosure as a way of addressing medical errors.[11]

We have examined the structure of the U.S. healthcare delivery system, including the types of services that are provided in the inpatient and the outpatient settings. We have seen the need for and difficulty in developing a coordinated system to provide continuity of care. We have also seen how the U.S. system is developing models of coordination linking institutions and providers in new ways. The use of technology is a major strategy used by the U.S. healthcare delivery system to hold itself together through electronic medical records and innovative approaches to diagnosis and treatment. The development of the healthcare delivery system is closely tied to the way that health care is financed and services are paid for. Therefore, let us turn our attention directly to the issue of paying for health care in Chapter 11.

Key Words

- Inpatient facilities
- Outpatient facilities
- Academic health center
- Provider
- Structure, process, and outcome measures
- Healthcare delivery system
- Healthcare system
- Health systems
- Preponderance of the evidence
- Negligence law
- Proximal cause
- System errors

Discussion Questions

Take a look at the questions posed in the following scenarios which were presented at the beginning of this chapter. See now whether you can answer them.

1. *George didn't have health insurance and went to the emergency room whenever he needed care. They always treated him there, but then tried to get him connected to a primary care facility. He wasn't eligible for care at the Veterans Administration facilities. So, they sent him to the local community health center, which they called the "safety net" provider. George did go there and they tried to treat his problems and get him his medicines despite his not having insurance. When he got sick, however, George went back to the emergency department. Even George agreed that it wasn't the best way to get care, but he wondered: what is needed to make the system work better?*

2. *Laura had breast cancer and it had spread. Her medical records were on file at the hospital, at four doctor's offices, in two emergency rooms, and at an outpatient imaging facility. No one seemed to know how to put the system together. Whenever her old records were essential, they asked her to go get a copy of them and bring them to her next appointment. That worked for a while, but when she ended up in the emergency room her records just weren't available. There must be a better way, Laura thought to herself. Hasn't the healthcare system discovered the Internet yet?*

3. *Fred ended his walk one day at the emergency room. He seemed confused about how to get home. "It looks like we are dealing with Alzheimer's," his doctor told Fred's wife, Sonya, at their next appointment. Taking care of Fred at home was not easy. Home health aides and occasional weekend relief called "respite care" eased the burden for a while. The new assisted-living facilities looked attrac-*

tive, but Fred's family just couldn't afford one. When Fred fell and broke his hip, he required hospitalization for surgery. The hospital discharge planner arranged for a skilled nursing home for rehabilitation services paid for by Medicaid. After a few weeks there, the only alternative was long-term or custodial care in a nursing home. The care at the nursing home was not what the family had expected. The staff did clean Fred up before the announced family visits, but once when the family arrived unannounced, they were shocked to see Fred lying half-naked in his wheelchair. The end came almost two years from the day they moved him to the nursing home. Looking back, the family asked: can the healthcare system do better at addressing the needs of Alzheimer's patients?

REFERENCES

1. Shi L, Singh D. *Delivering Health Care in America: A Systems Approach.* 4th ed. Sudbury, MA: Jones and Bartlett Publishers; 2008.

2. Sultz HA, Young KM. *Health Care USA: Understanding Its Organization and Delivery.* 6th ed. Sudbury, MA: Jones and Bartlett Publishers; 2009.

3. Shem S. *The House of God: The Classic Novel of Life and Death in an American Hospital.* New York: Delta Trade Paperbacks; 2003.

4. Taylor J. *The Fundamentals of Community Health Centers, National Health Policy Forum.* Washington, DC: The George Washington University; 2004: 23.

5. National Committee for Quality Assurance. Report Cards. Available at: http://www.ncqa.org/. Accessed April 3, 2009.

6. Kaiser Permanente. Kaiser Permanente—More than 60 Years of Quality. Available at: http://xnet.kp.org/newscenter/aboutkp/historyofkp.html. Accessed April 3, 2009.

7. United States Department of Veterans Affairs. History of the Department of Veterans Affairs. Available at: http://www1.va.gov/opa/feature/history/index.asp. Accessed April 3, 2009.

8. Institute of Medicine Committee on Data Standards for Patient Safety. *Key Capabilities of an Electronic Health Record System: Letter Report.* Washington, DC: National Academies Press; 2004.

9. Louisville Law Kentucky Legal Resources on the Internet. Elements of Proof—Medical Malpractice. Available at: http://www.louisvillelaw.com/medical/malpractice/elements.htm. Accessed April 3, 2009.

10. Institute of Medicine. *To Error is Human: Building a Better Health Care System.* Washington, DC: National Academies Press; 1999.

11. The Joint Commission. Medical Errors Disclosure—Selected Bibliography. Available at: http://www.jointcommission.org/patientsafety/me_bibliography.htm. Accessed April 3, 2009.

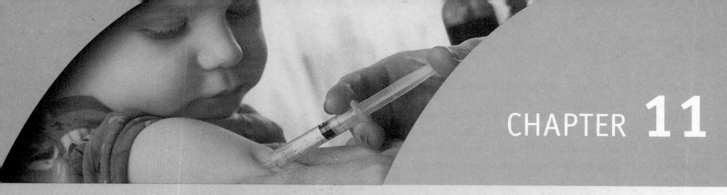

CHAPTER 11

Healthcare Systems

LEARNING OBJECTIVES

By the end of this chapter, the student will be able to:

- identify the largest insurance systems in the United States and explain the basic principles of their financing.
- identify the basic types of managed healthcare organizations and explain the principles of how they differ.
- illustrate how individual circumstances affect the most favorable type of employment-based insurance.
- describe the extent and consequences of being uninsured or underinsured in the United States.
- describe the basic structure and financing aspects of the healthcare systems in Canada and the United Kingdom and compare them to those of the United States.
- identify options for addressing the cost of health care in the United States.

The politicians seem to agree that health care is too expensive. However, some argue for greater regulation, while others argue for less. You ask yourself: what are the options for controlling costs and what are the consequences?

You take a job right out of college and need to select from among your company's healthcare options or alternatively choose not to be insured. The choices appear to be quite complicated and none of them seems just right for you. How can you go about choosing between health insurance options?

You decide to take your chances and refuse the expensive health insurance offered by your employer. What are the consequences of not having insurance?

Members of the Smith family live in the United States, Canada, and the United Kingdom. They have the same inherited disease. The recommended treatment is quite similar in the three countries and can be delivered as part of primary care. How might the delivery of care and the payment for care differ among the three countries?

You wonder how the United States ranks globally in terms of the performance of its healthcare system. You're surprised when you find out that its ranking is not #1 or even near the top. Why is that? you ask yourself.

These are the types of questions we are faced with when trying to understand and evaluate healthcare systems. Understanding healthcare systems requires us to understand the workforce and institutions that make up the system. It also requires us to examine the central measures of success: the issues of cost, quality, and access to health care.

We have already examined issues of the quality of health care. In this chapter, we will take a look at questions of access to and the costs of health care. Both of these issues are closely tied to issues of healthcare finance or paying for health care. As we will see, in the United States the ability to access health care is very much dependent on having health insurance. Thus, to better understand the U.S. healthcare system, we will begin by taking a look at the finances. We need to know how much money is spent and how it is spent. This will require us to look at health insurance—including insurance provided by government, employers, and issues of the uninsured and underinsured. Then, we will look at the overall features of the U.S. healthcare system and compare them to features of the systems in Canada and the United Kingdom.

Equipped with this understanding, we will see how health systems can be scored or graded and how the United States compares with other nations. Finally, we will examine the issue of controlling costs while maintaining or improving care quality—a major challenge facing the U.S. health system today. Let us start by looking at how much we currently spend on health care.

HOW MUCH MONEY DOES THE UNITED STATES SPEND ON HEALTH CARE?

The United States spends well over $2 trillion per year on health care. That represents over 16 percent of the gross domestic product or over $7000 per person per year. Dollars spent have been growing faster than inflation for over 40 years. At the current rate of growth, the United States is estimated to spend 20 percent of its gross domestic product on health care by the year 2020.

Continuing that rate of growth takes money away from other activities, which makes it more difficult for the United States to compete globally. Other developed countries, such as Canada, the United Kingdom, France, Germany, Japan, and Australia, spend about half as much per person and generally spend 10 percent or less of their gross domestic product on health care.

To understand how we spend so much of our money on health care, it is critical to know more about the U.S. health insurance system.[1,2] Much of the money spent on health care pays for insurance coverage with the majority of the remaining funds being spent to fill the holes in insurance coverage through direct payments by patients called out-of-pocket expenses.

Let us look at the basic types of insurance available in the United States. We start by examining government-financed insurance. We'll then take a look at employment-based insurance, and finally we'll examine the issue of having no insurance or being underinsured. Before getting started, however, it is important to understand the language of health insurance. Box 11-1 defines some important insurance terms.

WHAT TYPES OF GOVERNMENT-SUPPORTED HEALTH INSURANCE ARE AVAILABLE?

The two largest government programs of insurance are **Medicare** and **Medicaid**.[1,2] Both programs began in the mid

---

BOX 11-1 Important Insurance Definitions.

Cap—A limit on the total amount that the insurance will pay for a service per year, per benefit period, or per lifetime.

Copayment—An amount that the insured is responsible for paying even when the service is covered by the insurance. **Coinsurance**, in contrast, is the percentage of the charges that the insured is responsible for paying.

Covered service—A service for which health insurance will provide payment or coverage if the individual is eligible, i.e., any deductible has already been paid.

Customary, prevailing, and reasonable—These standards are used by many insurance plans to determine the amount that will be paid to the provider of services. Under many employer-based plans, the provider may bill patients above and beyond this amount. This is known as **balance billing.**

Deductible—The amount that an individual or family is responsible for paying before being eligible for insurance coverage.

Eligible—An individual may need to meet certain criteria to be eligible for enrollment in a health insurance plan. These may include: an income level for Medicaid, age and enrollment in the Social Security system for Medicare, or specific employment requirements for employer-based insurance. Health status is not generally a factor in eligibility or premium costs for these types of group insurance, but often is when applying for an individual policy.

Medical loss ratio—The ratio of benefit payments paid to premiums collected—indicating the proportion of the premiums spent on medical services. Lower medical loss ratios imply that a larger amount of the premium is retained by the insurance company for administrative costs, marketing and/or profit. *Obamacare 80% small group markets 85% large group*

Out-of-pocket cost—The cost of health care that is not covered by insurance and is the responsibility of the insured. These costs may be due to caps on insurance, deductibles, copayments, and/or balance billing.

Portability—The ability to continue employer-based health insurance after leaving a job—usually by paying the full cost of the insurance. A federal law, known as COBRA, generally ensures employees 18 months of portability.

Premium—The price paid by the purchaser for the insurance policy on a monthly or yearly basis.

1960s, but have very different funding sources, coverage, and populations served.[a]

Medicare began as a program for persons 65 and older. It was expanded to include disabled persons eligible for social security benefits and those with end-stage renal disease. Today, over 40 million Americans are eligible for Medicare and the number is expected to increase to 60 million by 2020.

When Medicare began it was designed primarily to cover hospital services and doctors' services. It did not cover drugs, most preventive services, or nursing home care. Drugs are now partially covered by Part D of Medicare. Preventive services are covered only when specifically approved by Congress or when it can be shown that they actually save the Medicare system money. Skilled nursing or rehabilitative care, but not nursing home or custodial care is covered by Medicare. Hearing aids and eyeglasses, perhaps the two most important medical devices for the elderly, are not covered by Medicare.

Medicare is a federal government program which means that eligibility and benefits are consistent throughout the United States. It is funded by a payroll tax of 1.45 percent from employees and 1.45 percent from employers. There is no income limit on this tax. That is, all income from employment is taxed. Self-employed individuals pay the employer, as well as the employee share. Medicare is a complicated program because there are four different parts: A, B, C, and D. The following describes the current basic costs and coverage of Medicare. The details are expected to change in coming years.

Part A covers hospital care, as well as follow-up skilled nursing care, home health care after a hospitalization, and hospice care. It is paid for primarily by the payroll tax and no premium is required. Currently, the annual deducible is approximately $1000.

Part B is a voluntary supplementary insurance that covers a wide range of diagnostic and therapeutic services provided by physicians, emergency departments, and other outpatient services. Seventy-five percent of Part B is funded by general tax revenues and 25 percent by a monthly premium, which is approximately $100 per month with additional payments by those with higher incomes. Copayments of 20 percent apply to most services, as well as a relatively small deductible. Health in-surance policies called **Medigap policies** offered by private insurance companies are often obtained by individuals to cover all or most of the 20 percent copayment.

Part C is a special program designed to encourage Medicare beneficiaries to enroll in prepaid health plans.

Part D is a relatively new prescription drug coverage plan. It is a complicated plan that is open to those who are enrolled in Parts A and B of Medicare. It requires a monthly premium of approximately $30 per month and an annual deductible of approximately $300. The exact terms depend on contracts through private plans which compete by offering lower costs or greater coverage. Standard coverage includes 75 percent of the costs of covered drugs once the deductible is satisfied up to approximately $2500 in drug costs. A gap or "doughnut hole" occurs above the $2500 limit. No coverage is provided for drug costs within the doughnut hole. Once an enrolled individual reaches a "catastrophic level" of total annual drug costs of about $5000, Medicare pays 95 percent of the additional cost of drugs.

Medicaid is a federal plus state program designed to pay for health services for specific categories of poor people and other designated categories of individuals. The federal government pays a variable amount of the cost ranging from 50–83 percent, depending on the per capita income of the state. All states have chosen to be part of the program and therefore must provide benefits for such groups as the disabled and children and pregnant women with a family income of less than 133 percent of the federal poverty level. The federal poverty level for a family of four is currently slightly more that $20,000 per year. Thus, there are a substantial number of poor and near-poor individuals, especially men, who are not eligible for Medicaid.

States at their discretion may include other categories of "medically needy" and may increase the eligible income level up to 185 percent of the federal poverty level. Most states cover custodial care in nursing homes for eligible individuals who have limited financial resources. As a result, Medicaid has become the largest source of insurance funds for nursing homes.[b]

In order to obtain federal funding through Medicaid, states which administer the program must provide basic services that include most inpatient and outpatient services, including preventive services. States may choose to offer these services and the federal government will provide matching funds for a wide range of services including drugs, eyeglasses, and transportation services. Thus, for those who are eligible

---

[a] The federal government also provides health care through the Veterans Administration, military health systems, and the Indian Health Service. The Veterans Administration is required to provide health care for military service-related conditions, but may—contingent upon resources—also provide care to veterans for nonservice-related conditions. The military health-care system provides care directly or contracts for care through the TriCare system for all active duty military and their families. American Indian and Alaskan Native members of federally-recognized tribes are eligible for comprehensive health services, as well as public health services provided or funded through the Indian Health Service.

[b] Medicaid requires that eligible individuals have very limited financial resources. Those with financial resources are generally expected to utilize most of these resources before becoming eligible. This process is known as "spending down." Complicated rules govern this process, including efforts to transfer the funds as gifts to others, including family members.

for Medicaid the coverage is usually quite comprehensive. However, the reimbursement rates to clinicians are often comparatively low and clinicians may choose not to participate in the Medicaid program.

A program begun in the late 1990s called the **State Child Health Insurance Program (SCHIP)** provides additional funds that states may use to enhance the Medicaid program for children. This may include raising the income level for eligibility, starting eligibility more rapidly, and ensuring longer periods of eligibility. In 2009 Congress expanded and made this program more flexible utilizing funds from an increase in the tax on cigarettes.

Medicaid now covers approximately 50 million individuals, about half of whom are children. Funds spent on the elderly, who constitute less than ten percent of Medicaid beneficiaries, exceeds that spent on children. The rising costs and increasing number of individuals eligible for the Medicaid program has led many states to require that Medicaid enrollees become members of a Medicaid managed care organization in an effort to reduce costs and improve continuity of care.

WHAT TYPES OF EMPLOYMENT-BASED HEALTH INSURANCE ARE AVAILABLE?

Employment-based insurance is the largest single category of insurance coverage in the United States. Over 50 percent of all Americans have the option to purchase some form of this type of insurance.

Employment-based insurance is in large part an accident of history. During World War II, employers were prohibited from raising wages. Instead, they offered healthcare benefits. Employment-based insurance grew rapidly in the 1950s and 1960s based on a principle known as **community rating**. Community ratings implied that the cost of insurance was the same regardless of the health status of a particular group of employees. Community rating has since been replaced by what is called **experience rating**. This concept means that employers and employees pay based on their groups' use of services in previous years.[c]

In the 1950s and 1960s and in many parts of the country well into the 1990s, employment-based insurance provided payments to clinicians and hospitals based almost entirely on **fee-for-service** payments. Fee-for-service, as its name implies, consists of charges paid for specific services provided and as a payment system, it encourages provision of as many services as possible. Thus, this system has been accused of increasing healthcare costs through overuse of services.

In 1973, the federal government began to encourage an alternative approach to employment-based insurance called Health Maintenance Organizations (HMOs). HMOs charged patients a monthly fee designed to cover a comprehensive package of services. Clinicians or their organizations were paid based upon the number of individuals that enrolled in their practice. Their compensation was based on what is called **capitation**, which is a fixed number of dollars per month to provide services to an enrolled member regardless of the number of services provided. Classic HMOs were traditionally "staff model" HMOs, like Kaiser Permanente, that directly or indirectly provided the entire package of services.

Capitation, as opposed to fee-for-service, has the potential for underuse of services in an effort to reduce costs. HMOs, in contrast to a fee-for-service system, generally covered preventive services and thus argue that they do a better job of keeping people healthy.[d]

Classic fee-for-service systems and staff model HMOs represent the two traditional models of employment-based health insurance in the United States. Beginning in the 1990s, both these systems began to change in ways that brought them closer together.

Fee-for-service systems often evolved into what are called **Preferred Provider Plans** or **PPOs**. Staff model HMOs developed options for what are called **Point of Service Plans (POSs)**. PPOs imply that the insurance system decides to work with only a limited number of clinicians called preferred providers. These providers agree to a set of conditions that usually includes reduced payments and other conditions. Patients may choose to use other clinicians, but if they do so, they typically will pay more out-of-pocket.

Point of Service Plans imply that patients in an HMO may choose to receive their care outside the system provided by the health plan. Like a PPO, patients who choose the POS option must expect to pay more out-of-pocket. PPOs and POSs are today the most common forms of employment-based insurance. They now come in a variety of forms and together can be called mixed models. An employer may offer its employees a number of complicated mixed model choices, as well as ones that are closer to the classic fee-for-service and HMO staff model, or HMO classic. To better understand the types of options faced by employees take a look at Box 11-2.

---

[c] It has been argued that community rating is a form of health insurance that is closer to the social justice approach to health care because individuals and groups with better health subsidize those with poorer health and greater expenses. This implies that experience rating has moved the system toward a market justice approach. Note that mental health services are now treated the same as services directed at physical health under all types of health insurance plans.

[d] It has been argued that the reason HMOs provided preventive services is related to the increased interest and use of these services by healthy individuals. Enrolling predominately healthy individuals has been called **skimming**. By enrolling these individuals, HMOs can reduce their overall costs because healthy individuals are far less likely to require large amounts of health care.

BOX 11-2   Prototype Health Insurance Options.

Let us imagine that you go to work for a large employer that offers a full range of health insurance options. The options fall into three basic categories: fee-for-service classic, mixed-model HMO, and HMO classic. Your employer offers the following chart (Table 11–1) comparing the benefits and costs of each of these three options. Employers often subsidize the cost of insurance for the employee but not for the rest of the family.

TABLE 11-1 Prototype Health Insurance Options

	Fee-for-Service Classic	Mixed Model	HMO Classic
Monthly cost to employee	$200 for employee $1200 Family of 4 $1000 yearly deductible per person	$100 for employee $600 Family of 4 $500 yearly deductible per person	$50 for employee $300 Family of 4 No yearly deductible
Choice of physician	No restrictions–full coverage Physicians paid "prevailing fee"	No restrictions, 20% copayment for out of network Physicians paid lower discounted fee for service	Staff physicians only Full coverage Physicians paid through capitation
Access to specialists including OB-GYN	Access without referral–full coverage	Access with referral–full coverage Access without referral–20% copayment	Access with referral only
Drugs	Full coverage as ordered	$20 copayment for generic or approved/formulary drugs	$10 copayment for generic or approved/formulary drugs
Hospital	Full coverage as authorized by physician	80% coverage if preauthorized by plan	100% coverage if preauthorized by plan
Skilled nursing	Full coverage if ordered by physicians	80% coverage if found necessary by plan	100% coverage if found necessary by plan
Hospice	100% coverage based on physician authorization	80% coverage based on plan authorization	100% coverage based on plan authorization
Preventive services	Not covered	100% coverage in network 20% copayment out of network	100% coverage in network
Emergency Department and out-of-area services	100% coverage	Requires prior authorization except in emergencies as defined by "reasonable person"	Requires prior authorization except in emergencies as defined by "reasonable person"

(continues)

BOX 11-2 continued.

Now, let us put ourselves in the position of those who might need to choose among these options and think about which option they might choose. Remember—there is a fourth option—to not to enroll in any of the heath insurance plans.

- *A healthy, single, 22–year-old male right out of college with an income of $30,000*—This person might choose not to be covered if they consider themselves at low risk of needing health care and are willing to take their chances in exchange for cost savings. However, they would need to be willing to take the substantial risks associated with being uninsured.

- *A healthy 30-year-old recently married professional who intends to start a family in the next year. Their family income is $60,000*—This person might choose the plan with the most comprehensive and flexible coverage for pregnancy—their most pressing health issue. Thus, they might choose a classic fee-for-service plan with the knowledge that they will receive full choice of services for the additional cost of coverage.

- *A 40-year-old married employee with a family of four with a family income of $80,000. Both husband and wife require ongoing treatments to prevent illness, including regular preventive care and expensive medications. They want to choose which clinicians to use while controlling the costs of care.*—This person might choose the mixed-model plan because it provides greater choice than the HMO classic model, while reducing the cost compared to the fee-for-service model.

- *A 35-year-old single parent of two young children and an income of $30,000. The mother and children need preventive care and the mother needs regular mental health care*—This person might favor the HMO classic model because it minimizes costs and maximizes benefits. However, they would need to be willing to accept the restriction on access to care built into the plan.

- *A 55-year-old single professional with an income of $250,000 and no current major medical problems*—This person might choose the fee-for-service model if they were concerned about future healthcare needs. However, they may choose not to enroll in any of these plans and to accept the risk of paying for health care out of pocket. They might be attracted to healthcare savings accounts, which allow them to put aside pretax earnings to pay for current and future health care. Despite their high income, they might become one of the uninsured.

Today these types of choices face most employees of large organizations. No one plan is likely to be the best plan for everyone. In reality, there are often far more choices and the best choice for each employee can be very difficult to determine. The classic models are rapidly disappearing and a wide range of mixed models are now the usual options facing employees.

In addition to those people with government and employment-based insurance, the other large category of individuals in the United States are those who are called uninsured or underinsured. Let's look at the extent and consequences of being uninsured and underinsured.

WHAT ARE THE EXTENT AND CONSEQUENCES OF BEING UNINSURED AND UNDERINSURED IN THE UNITED STATES?

Over 15 percent of all Americans do not have any form of health insurance. This percentage has increased in recent years even in years of economic growth and continues to grow. A national debate is now underway to address the issue of the uninsured and underinsured.

It is important to understand what types of people are uninsured and underinsured and to think about the consequences. Let us look first at the issue of the uninsured. The uninsured can be classified into the following quite different groups:

- Healthy, often young, individuals who choose not to purchase insurance through their employer
- Poor or near-poor individuals who do not qualify for Medicaid
- Self-employed persons or employees of small companies that despite substantial incomes decide not to purchase insurance because they must pay much higher premiums than those usually offered through large organizations

Approximately 20 percent of employed persons do not have health insurance. It may surprise you to learn that nearly 40 percent of the uninsured population comes from families that can be considered to have middle-class or higher incomes. The largest number of uninsured are in the 18–24 year-old age group with approximately 30 percent of this age group being uninsured.

In addition to the issue of the uninsured, we need to recognize the additional issue of underinsurance. A large number of individuals and families have health insurance that does not adequately cover expected or potential healthcare costs. The three models of health insurance discussed in Box 11-2 are representative of those offered by large employers. Despite their deductibles, copayments and caps on these insurance options are considered comprehensive coverage. It is estimated that for every two individuals who are uninsured, there is another American who has health insurance, but their coverage is not considered comprehensive. They are categorized as underinsured and often have large out-of-pocket expenses if they require extensive medical care.

Who are the underinsured? They are primarily individuals and families who have obtained health insurance through employment, especially employment at smaller firms, that often is not as comprehensive as those described. In addition, individuals may purchase less than comprehensive plans on their own.

The consequences of being uninsured and underinsured can be very great. The Institute of Medicine (IOM)[3] and the Henry J. Kaiser Family Foundation[4] have identified a series of consequences. Being uninsured, and to a lesser extent underinsured, harms individuals and families in at least the following ways:

- They receive less preventive care, are diagnosed at more advanced stages of disease, and receive less treatment once diagnosed.
- They are much less likely to have a usual source of health care and more likely to use the emergency department for routine care.
- They have an increased mortality rate—an estimated nearly 20,000 excess deaths per year.

Those without insurance can and often do use an emergency department to obtain care. Emergency departments are required to provide routine care, as well as life-threatening emergency care. However, after stabilizing an individual with a life-threatening emergency, they may transfer them to an institution that provides care for those without insurance. For other conditions, the uninsured and underinsured may delay care until it is too late to fully benefit. The Institute of Medicine has described the care of the uninsured as too little and too late.[3]

When the uninsured and underinsured do seek health care, clinicians and healthcare institutions often bill the individual undiscounted prices for the healthcare services provided. When these individuals require substantial amounts of outpatient or inpatient health care, they often find themselves faced with large debts and in some cases declare bankruptcy. When these individuals fail to pay their medical bills, the costs are often picked up by other patients with insurance, thus raising the costs of health care for all who purchase health insurance.

A number of approaches for addressing these issues have been put forward and extensive experimentation is underway. Box 11-3 outlines some of the approaches that have been suggested.

We have described the basic components of the U.S. healthcare system, including the health professionals and institutions that provide health care, and addressed issues of quality, cost, and access. We are now ready to compare the U.S. healthcare system to that of other developed countries. First, let us look at a framework that we can use to describe and compare healthcare systems.

HOW CAN WE DESCRIBE HEATHCARE SYSTEMS IN GENERAL AND THE U.S. HEALTHCARE SYSTEM IN PARTICULAR?

One approach to describing healthcare systems is to define their characteristics using the following categories:

- Method of financing
- Method of insurance and reimbursement
- Methods for delivering services
- Comprehensiveness of insurance
- Cost and cost containment
- Degree of patient choice
- Administrative costs

Table 11-2 uses these categories to describe the complex U.S. healthcare system.

The U.S. system is often compared to those of Canada and the United Kingdom. Despite the fact that these countries have much in common, their healthcare systems have evolved in very different ways.

HOW CAN WE DESCRIBE THE HEALTHCARE SYSTEMS IN CANADA AND THE UNITED KINGDOM?

Let us use the same chart we used to describe the U.S. system to outline the features of the Canadian[5] and United Kingdom[6] healthcare systems. Table 11-3 describes the Canadian healthcare system.

Now, take a look at Table 11-4 describing the healthcare system in the United Kingdom.

WHAT CONCLUSIONS CAN WE REACH FROM THESE DESCRIPTIONS OF THE U.S., CANADIAN, AND U.K. HEALTHCARE SYSTEMS?

These charts highlight key features of the three systems, while demonstrating substantial differences. When describing these characteristics we can ask: on the spectrum of market justice versus social justice, where do the United States, Canada, and the United Kingdom lie?

It can be argued that the United States relies most heavily on market justice, while the United Kingdom places the greater

BOX 11-3   Potential Approaches to Providing Health Insurance to the Uninsured and Underinsured.

A large number of approaches to providing at least basic coverage for all Americans have been put forth. A growing majority favors insuring all or the vast majority of individuals, which is called **universal coverage**. Considerable disagreement exists on the best way to accomplish this goal. Most of the approaches being advocated fall into one of the following categories.

- **Employer mandate**—Employers are required to provide comprehensive insurance coverage for all their employees. A number of variations on this approach have been put forward, some of which provide subsidies for small employers. Another option, called "play-or-pay," requires payments by employers who fail to provide comprehensive coverage.
- **Individual mandate**—Individuals are required to purchase individual health insurance policies which include at least standardized minimum coverage. Those with limited income may receive subsidies to allow them to pay for the insurance. Variations on this approach have been discussed including allowing individuals to refuse to purchase insurance, but then requiring them to pay when receiving services. Another variation encourages individuals to put aside funds in tax-free accounts referred to as "health savings accounts" to pay for health services.
- **Single-payer**—This approach is characterized by a single source of payment for all basic healthcare services usually provided by the government at the state or federal level. Funding may come entirely from taxes or premiums may be charged to individuals or employers.

For over half a century, employer-based health insurance has been the most common method for financing health care. These options above imply that the choice is either to expand this system or to move to a new system. The option of individual mandates retains the basic insurance structure, but puts the burden on individuals rather than employers. The single-payer system envisions a single entity, most likely the government, which directly or indirectly will pay all the bills. This system might be similar to the current Medicare system or to the health insurance system for federal employees including members of Congress.

The United States is in the process of healthcare reform. It is expected that one or more of the above approaches will form the basis for the emerging system. For updates on healthcare reform in the United Sates, see www.publichealth101.org.

---

emphasis on social justice. Canada lies somewhere in between. In describing these systems, it can also be useful to identify areas in which the United States has unique approaches and unique results. The following distinguish the U.S. healthcare system not only from that of Canada and the United Kingdom, but from the healthcare systems of most other developed countries:

- The United States spends considerably more per person and as a percentage of gross domestic product (GDP).
- The United States has far more uninsured and underinsured individuals.
- The U.S. healthcare system is more complex for patients and providers of care and costs far more to administer.
- The U.S. healthcare system places more emphasis on specialized physicians and on nurse practitioners and physician assistants to provide primary care.
- The United States encourages rapid adoption of technology, especially for diagnosis and treatment.
- The United States places greater emphasis on giving patients a wider choice of clinicians.
- The United States has a more complex system for ensuring quality and a unique system of malpractice law.

Equipped with all this information, we will now see if it is possible to grade or score the performance of the U.S. healthcare system compared to those of other developed countries.

HOW CAN A HEALTHCARE SYSTEM BE SCORED?

The Commonwealth Fund's Commission on a High Performance Health System (The Commission) has developed The National Scorecard on the U.S. Health System (National Scorecard).[7] The national scorecard uses a standardized set of measurements to try to objectively measure performance in 19 developed countries.[e] Box 11-4 outlines the criteria used to score these healthcare systems and the types of measurements that are used.

---

[e] The Commonwealth Fund describes itself as "a private foundation working toward a high performance health system." The national scorecard on U.S. Health Systems Performance was developed by a Commission appointed by the Commonwealth Fund made up of individuals who, according to the Commonwealth Fund, are "...a distinguished group of experts and leaders representing every sector of health care, as well as the state and federal policy arena, the business sector, professional societies, and academia..."

2:45

TABLE 11-2 Describing the U.S. Healthcare System

Category	Description
Financing	Cost over 16% of GDP and rising rapidly Complicated mix of federal, state, employer and self-pay
Type(s) of insurance and reimbursement	Employment-based insurance plus government insurance through Medicare and Medicaid provide most insurance Mix of fee-for-service, capitation, and salary with incentives are the most commonly used methods
Delivery of care	Mix of practice types with private practice dominant Physicians: $\frac{1}{3}$ Primary Care; $\frac{2}{3}$ Specialists Primary care increasingly based upon nurse practitioners and physician assistants Hospitalists increasingly coordinate inpatient care Need for better continuity of care between institutions and between clinicians
Comprehensiveness of insurance	15% uninsured plus half again as many underinsured Drug benefits included for elderly and those with comprehensive insurance Preventive services increasing, but not comprehensive
Cost and cost containment	Emphasis on competition as means of controlling costs, plus cost sharing by patients
Patient choice	Considerable choice of primary care and often direct access to specialty care Greatly increased access for those with comprehensive insurance
Administrative costs	High: 25–30% of total costs including administrative costs of health insurance, clinicians and institutions, but this does not include administrative time spent by patients and their families

Let us take a look at how the United States scores in comparison with other developed countries based upon the national scorecard.

USING THE NATIONAL SCORECARD, HOW DOES THE UNITED STATES' HEALTHCARE SYSTEM PERFORM COMPARED TO THOSE OF OTHER DEVELOPED COUNTRIES?

The Commission scored the performance of 19 developed countries, including the United States, 14 European nations, Canada, Japan, New Zealand, and Australia. It set benchmarks high, but established realistic levels of performance for each area using the score of the top three countries as the highest standard. Thus, high but realistic performance is given a score of 100.[f]

Table 11-5 summarizes the performance of the United States on each of the criteria as well as the overall score.

These scores for the United States in 2008 were actually slightly lower than the scores for 2006 with a substantial reduction of the access score from 67 in 2006 to 58 in 2008.

The scorecard leaves us with some fundamental questions including: how can access be improved, quality be increased, and costs be controlled. We have looked at the issues of quality in Chapter 10 and reviewed a series of current and proposed mechanisms for improving quality. In this chapter, we have looked at issues of access and outlined the options for obtaining universal or near-universal coverage. Perhaps the greatest negative aspect of the U.S. healthcare system is the issue of high and escalating costs. Let's complete our look at the U.S. healthcare system by examining the options for controlling costs.

[f] The Commission also used the performance of the top ten percent of states in the United States to make comparisons within the United States.

TABLE 11-3 Describing the Canadian Healthcare System

Category	Description
Financing	National policy to keep expenditures under 10% of GDP Combination of Provincial and Federal ~70% government through taxes ~30% private insurance payments by individuals
Type(s) of insurance and reimbursement	Government insurance for basic services, individual policies with subsidies for the poor for most other services Negotiated fee-for-service reimbursement with single payer for basic services
Delivery of care	Mix of practice types with private practice dominant—emphasis on physicians in primary care Physicians ~50% primary care and ~50% specialists Primary care physicians generally admit to the hospital and are responsible for continuity of care Concerns about access to high tech procedures
Comprehensiveness of insurance	Three-tiered: 1. Medically necessary basic services—Universal coverage. Government funded and guaranteed to all without any cost-sharing, including preventive services. No private insurance allowed for medically necessary services 2. Private insurance and government subsidized insurance for other medical services including drugs, long-term care, home care with government payment for needy. Negotiated bulk purchasing of drugs on formulary 3. Private insurance or self-pay for dental, vision, and many nonphysician services
Cost and cost containment	Capital purchases, such as of high-tech diagnostic equipment, are regulated Concern about waiting time for access Negotiated fees between providers and government with government as single payer having considerable negotiating power
Patient choice	Choice of primary care physician Referral often needed to see specialists
Administrative costs	Low—approximately 15% or less of total costs

HOW-CAN THE COSTS OF HEALTH CARE BE CONTROLLED IN THE UNITED STATES?

To understand the options for controlling costs, it is important to first understand the reasons that costs are increasing. The United States is not alone in facing increased costs for health care. There are a number of forces at work in most developed countries that increase and most likely will continue to increase the costs of health care, including the following:

- *The aging of the population:* The success of public health and healthcare efforts over the last century has produced a population that is living longer. Longer life is strongly associated with the development of chronic diseases, many of which require expensive care over many years or decades.

- *Technological innovations have greatly expanded treatment options:* A wide range of interventions are now possible, some of which can have dramatic impacts on longevity and the quality of life. However, many

TABLE 11-4 Describing the United Kingdom's Healthcare System

Category	Description
Financing	Budget about 7–8% of GDP has been rising Tax-supported comprehensive and universal coverage through National Health Service Private insurance system with overlapping coverage purchased as additional coverage by ~15% of the population with perception of easier access and higher quality
Type(s) of insurance and reimbursement	National Health Service is single payer with capitation, plus incentives for General Practitioners, i.e., physicians responsible for panel of patients Specialists generally salaried in National Health Service often earn substantial additional income through private insurance
Delivery of care	Governmental system of healthcare delivery in National Health Service including government-owned and administered hospitals Emphasis on physicians Primary care general practitioners ~2/3 Specialist physicians ~1/3 General practitioners generally do not admit to hospital
Comprehensiveness of insurance	National Health Service comprehensive with little cost sharing plus may cover transportation costs Incentives to provide preventive services and home care
Cost and cost containment	Overall limit on national spending ("Global budgeting") Negotiated rates of capitation and salary with government as single payer within National Health Service having considerable negotiating power
Patient choice	National Health Service provides limited choice of general practitioners Waiting lines for services in National Health Service especially specialists and high-tech procedures Referral to specialists generally needed Greater choice with private insurance
Administrative costs	Greater than Canada, less than U.S.

others produce very modest improvements at high costs. It may be difficult to distinguish these different types of results.

- *The successes of medical care over the last half century have raised the expectations of patients:* Greater expectations for access to technology, preventive interventions, individualized care, rapid access to care, privacy and protection of confidentiality, are now all possible, but often quite expensive.

Nearly all developed countries face these forces to a greater or lesser extent. Many countries in Europe, as well as Japan, face an even more rapidly aging population than the United States. How the healthcare systems respond to these challenges will determine in large part the overall costs of health care in each country.

The United States, however, also faces some issues to a far greater extent than other developed countries. The United States has a far more complex and changing structure. The sheer complexity of the system has led to a need for multiple levels of administration, which are not required in most other countries. In addition, patients are often expected to fill out and process complex insurance applications and claim forms. Clinicians are often required to bill for each service provided,

BOX 11-4 Criteria and Measurements Used in the Commonwealth Fund's Commission on a High Performance Health System.

The Commission's scorecard measures the following five areas of health system performance:

- *Healthy lives:* National health outcomes using such measures as: life expectancy, infant mortality, HALEs at age 60, limitations in activities among adults under 65, and missed school days by children due to illness or injury
- *Quality:* Quality of preventive, curative, and rehabilitative health care using such measures as: adults and children receiving recommended preventive services; control of chronic diseases; availability of services (including mental health) after hours and on an urgent basis; hospital quality of care including the ratio of observed to expected mortality; and preventive measures in nursing homes
- *Access:* Availability of care using such measures as insurance coverage including the percentage of uninsured and underinsured, as well as the impact of the cost of insurance
- *Efficiency:* Inappropriate, wasteful, or fragmented care using such measures as: emergency departments use for routine care, hospital admissions for preventable conditions, short-term readmission rates, and costs of administration
- *Equity:* Disparities in health services and health outcomes by racial/minority status and income using such measures as: access to preventive and acute services, control of chronic diseases, insurance coverage, and measures of healthy lives

The scores from each of these areas are added together to produce overall scores.

TABLE 11-5 Performance of U.S. Compared to Best Performing Countries

Area of performance	U.S. score (out of 100)
Healthy lives	72
Quality	71
Access	58
Efficiency	53
Equity	71
Overall score	65

Source: The Commonwealth Fund. Commission on a High Performance Health System. Available at: http://www.commonwealth fund.org/programs/programs_list.htm?attrib_id=11932. Accessed November 9, 2008.

justify the services provided, and in many cases obtain approval for payments prior to treating patients. Today, a clinician's office usually has far more individuals involved in administering the system compared to those directly delivering care to patients.

The United States also has a far more complex and changing system of quality control. As we have seen, healthcare quality is monitored and maintained via a system that includes accreditation, certification, licensure, and malpractice, to name a few. The direct and indirect costs of this system may them-

selves contribute to the large and escalating cost of health care. A variety of efforts have been and are being made to reduce costs in the United States. These include:

- *Cost control through reimbursement incentives:* The concept of capitation has been widely used as a mechanism for controlling or reducing costs. A special form of capitation, diagnosis-related groups (DRGs), have been successfully used to reduce the length of stay in hospitals. DRGs pay hospitals a set amount for a particular diagnosis regardless of the length of hospital stay. However, reimbursement systems at times have moved the costs from one part of the system to another. Restrictions on payment for procedures may increase the number of procedures performed. Restriction on inpatient reimbursement may encourage an increase in outpatient or home care services.
- *Cost sharing:* This involves efforts to shift the costs of health care to individuals on the assumption that individuals will spend less when the costs are coming out of their pockets. Measures, such as deductibles, copayments, and caps are all intended to reduce costs by shifting them to individual patients.
- *Regulation:* At times, efforts have been made to reduce costs by placing limits on how much care can be provided or how much compensation can be provided. Government-controlled health insurance, such as

Medicare and Medicaid, is targeted for regulation. National issue of rates of compensation for clinicians and hospitals have become part of the political process.

- *Restrictions on malpractice:* It has been argued that the U.S. malpractice system encourages clinicians to practice "defensive medicine," that is, to perform unnecessary tests to protect themselves against lawsuits. The extent of the problem and the impact of changes in malpractice are controversial, but efforts are being made to reduce the number of lawsuits that reach the court system and to restrict the amount of compensation that can be awarded beyond actual damages.

A more general approach to reducing costs favored by many in the United States is to increase competition between providers of health services including institutions and individual clinicians and groups of clinicians. To better understand the potential for competition to succeed and the changes that are occurring to encourage competition, take a look at Box 11-5.[8]

Understanding healthcare systems is a challenge for patients, as well as those who work in the system. Understanding the roles of healthcare professionals, institutions, and the issues of quality, access, and cost help us understand the system as a whole. **The United States is undergoing a major review and reform of the healthcare system. For an update on the United States healthcare system, see the student Web site for Public Health 101: Healthy People-Healthy Populations at www.publichealth101.org.**

A well-functioning healthcare system is essential to the public's health. An efficient system that works in concert with organized public health efforts and leaves adequate financial resources to invest in programs directed at the health of the entire population is a key goal. The population health approach thus needs to pay considerable attention to the workings of the public and private healthcare system, as well as that of the public health system. In Chapter 12, we will seek to better understand what we mean by public health institutions and the public health system.

BOX 11-5 Using Competition to Control Costs.

The healthcare system in the United States is perhaps the most market-oriented system of any major nation. To successfully control costs through market mechanisms, a number of characteristics of a well-functioning market need to be in place. It has been argued that, until recently, the U.S. healthcare system has not reflected most of these characteristics. Advocates of a market approach often share these concerns, but argue that it is possible to modify the U.S. healthcare system so that it functions as a better market system.

Let us take a brief look at key features of a well-functioning market, examine the extent to which the U.S. healthcare systems fulfills these conditions, and examine changes that are being made or considered to move the United States toward a more effective market-based system.

- **Informed purchaser:** An informed purchaser is a key requirement for a well-functioning healthcare market. In the U.S. healthcare system, the employer often serves an intermediary role in selecting the health plans from which their employees may choose. Until recent years employers paid little attention to the details of the health plans that they offered. However, that habit is changing rapidly. Cost information is now widely available to both employees and employers, and quality measures are also becoming available. Employers often rely on accreditation standards, such as those of the National Committee on Quality Assurance, which now accredits a range of types of health plans and group practices. In addition, data on outcomes for surgical and medical procedures are increasingly available at the level of the hospital and group practice.
- **Purchasing power:** The second requirement of a well-functioning market is the ability of those who need the product to have the purchasing power to obtain it. In the United States, approximately 15 percent of the population is uninsured and many more are underinsured. Thus, many cannot afford the available product. Any effort to make the U.S. healthcare market work better needs to ensure adequate purchasing power for those who need it to pay for health insurance and thereby participate in the system.
- **Multiple competing providers:** Well-functioning markets give purchasers a choice of service providers. Consumers' choices then generally favor providers who offer the services at reduced costs and/or increased quality. The availability of choices for employed individuals has increased in recent years, especially for those whose employers pay a substantial portion of the premiums. Employees of large firms and organizations typically have a range of choices and can choose their health plan based on

(continues)

BOX 11-5 continued.

criteria including cost, quality, and convenience. Many other consumers, however, have limited or no choice in healthcare coverage.

- **Negotiation:** Negotiation is the key to putting information, purchasing power, and competition together. These negotiations increasingly take place through the employer. However, labor unions are becoming more involved in issues related to health benefits as well because health insurance constitutes an increasing percentage of their current, as well as future, benefits. The individual employee often has little negotiating power and needs to rely on their employee representatives and/or their employers.

If the U.S. healthcare system continues to move in the direction of becoming a competitive healthcare market, it will need to ensure that these conditions are fulfilled as much as possible.

Key Words

- Medicare
- Medicaid
- Medigap
- State Child Health Insurance Program (SCHIP)
- Community rating
- Experience rating
- Fee-for-service
- Capitation
- Skimming
- Preferred Provider Organization (PPO)
- Point-of-Service Plan (POS)
- Universal coverage
- Employer mandates
- Individual mandates
- Single payer

Discussion Questions

Take a look at the questions posed in the following scenarios which were presented at the beginning of this chapter. See now whether you can answer them.

1. *The politicians seem to agree that health care is too expensive. However, some argue for greater regulation, while others argue for less. You ask yourself: what are the options for controlling costs and what are the consequences?*

2. *You take a job right out of college and need to select from among your company's healthcare options or alternatively choose not to be insured. The choices appear to be quite complicated and none of them seems just right for you. How can you go about choosing between health insurance options?*

3. *You decide to take your chances and refuse the expensive health insurance offered by your employer. What are the consequences of not having insurance?*

4. *Members of the Smith family live in the United States, Canada, and the United Kingdom. They have the same inherited disease. The recommended treatment is quite similar in the three countries and can be delivered as part of primary care. How might the delivery of care and the payment for care differ among the three countries?*

5. *You wonder how the United States ranks globally in terms of the performance of its healthcare system. You're surprised when you find out that its ranking is not #1 or even near the top. Why is that? you ask yourself.*

REFERENCES

1. Shi L, Singh D. *Delivering Health Care in America: A Systems Approach.* 4th ed. Sudbury, MA: Jones and Bartlett Publishers; 2008.

2. Sultz HA, Young KM. *Health Care USA: Understanding Its Organization and Delivery.* 6th ed. Sudbury, MA: Jones and Bartlett Publishers; 2009.

3. Institute of Medicine. Hidden Costs, Value Lost: Uninsurance in America. Washington, DC: National Academies Press; 2003.

4. The Henry J. Kaiser Family Foundation. Health Coverage and the Uninsured. Available at: http://www.kff.org/uninsured/index.cfm. Accessed April 3, 2009.

5. Health Canada. Health Care System. Available at: http://www.hc-sc.gc.ca/hcs-sss/index-eng.php. Accessed April 3, 2009.

6. National Health Service History. Chapter from "From Cradle to Grave: 50 Years of the NHS." Available at: http://www.nhshistory.net/envoi1.html. Accessed April 3, 2009.

7. The Commonwealth Fund. Commission on a High Performance Health System, Available at: http://www.commonwealthfund.org/programs/programs_list.htm?attrib_id=11932. Accessed April 3, 2009.

8. CATO Institute. Health Care Needs a Dose of Competition. Available at: http://www.cato.org/pub_display.php?pub_id=5070. Accessed April 3, 2009.

Section IV:
Cases and Discussion Questions

When Nursing Meets Medicine

Maureen felt she had no other choice but to let the hospital administrator know when a physician had repeatedly prescribed the wrong dose of medication. How many times could she double-check with Dr. George Ludwig just to be sure that she had understood his orders. "Orders, they still call them," she thought to herself, "that is certainly what they want them to be."

The days of obeying orders were over for Maureen. She had been through nursing school and after five years working in the hospital she went back to get her master's as a nurse specialist so she could work in an intensive care unit. Now she was doing the weekend 12-hour nursing shift to make ends meet and finish her degree. Nurses were in short supply so she could now for the first time speak her mind without fear of losing her job. Nursing, she realized, was by its very name designed to nurture and take care of patients, but that did not apply to physicians. Their arrogance was so deep she didn't think they saw it.

Hospital policy required nurses to follow the orders after first checking with the head nurse and then double-checking with a physician. Complaints could be filed with the hospital quality assurance committee, but the process took months and the nurse who initiated the process could be reprimanded if the committee found their complaints to be unfounded or trivial. Trivial, this wasn't, but when she confronted the hospital administrator, he confided, "Don't put me in the middle of this." The pharmacist finally agreed to call the doctor and check on whether he preferred the "standard dose" of medication or the "unusual dose" he had first ordered. Dr. Ludwig agreed that the standard dose was "worth a try," so Maureen went ahead and followed the doctor's new orders.

Not too many months later, Maureen found herself confronted with new decisions in her first job as a nurse

specialist in the intensive care unit. She now worked under "standing orders," which allowed her to make many a decision on her own. For the first time, she felt like she was calling the shots and making the decisions that made a difference for patients.

On one shift, late in her middle of the night, she was running from bed to bed covering the intensive care unit when she realized that she had given a patient the wrong medication. Fortunately, it was not a life-threatening mistake. She sighed with relief. Checking the chart carefully, however, she winced when her eyes fell upon the name of the attending physician, Dr. George Ludwig.

1. How is Maureen's situation affected by the structure of the nursing profession?
2. How is Maureen's situation affected by the changes in roles of women that have occurred in the United States in the last 30 years?
3. How is Maureen's situation affected by the changes that have occurred in the delivery of health care over the last 10–20 years?
4. What changes do you think are needed in the healthcare system to prevent the types of mistakes illustrated in this case?

Jack and Continuity of Care

Jack was told that he had high blood pressure and high cholesterol when he was in the army. Because the conditions didn't bother him, Jack paid little attention to them. His job did not provide health insurance, so he decided to take his chances. Anyway, he was strong and athletic. Over the years, Jack gained weight, exercised less, and developed a "touch of diabetes."

When the diabetes produced symptoms, he went to the emergency room where they did a good job of diagnosing his problem and sent him off with a prescription and a few pills to get started. The pills seemed to help, but Jack couldn't afford to fill the prescription or follow-up with his "family doctor" because he didn't have one. Jack didn't understand all the terms the doctors and nurses used to describe his condition, but he knew it was serious and could get worse.

It wasn't long before he was sick again, so this time he sought care at a free clinic. He didn't qualify for Medicaid, but the treatment was free. For a couple of months, he followed up and was feeling better, but on the next scheduled visit they told him, "you need to be in the hospital—you're getting worse." They got him to the hospital where he was admitted to the university service and assigned to a young resident who just graduated from a well-known medical school. The resident reviewed his condition, developed a treatment plan, and explained to Jack what needed to be done. He ordered a TB skin test and collected sputum to check for TB because of Jack's chronic cough. Unfortunately, before the treatment could be implemented the resident rotated to another service and Jack's new resident didn't seem to pay much attention to him.

Jack decided to leave the hospital against medical advice and left no forwarding address. His TB skin test was never read. When his positive sputum culture for TB came back, the laboratory alerted the local health department. Not knowing where Jack lived, the health department was not able to follow up.

Before he left, the hospital made sure that Jack had signed all the forms to receive Medicaid payments for the hospitalization. However, Jack didn't complete the forms because he didn't plan to get any more medical care. That changed one day when the pain was more than he could stand. He decided to try another emergency room. This time the place was very crowded and he had to wait hours to be seen. Once he was examined, the physicians and nurses tried to get information from him on his condition and treatment, but Jack couldn't provide much useful information.

He was prescribed pain medicine and sent home. He was told to follow up with a doctor in the next few days. By then it was too late. In the middle of the night, Jack had a terrible headache and lost his speech. He struggled to call 911. Despite the fact that he could not speak, the operator was able to send an ambulance by tracing his telephone location. The EMTs rushed to Jack's home and got him to the nearest hospital. Once again, the emergency room clinicians evaluated him, but this time it was too late to be of much help. Jack was admitted for a stroke.

He stayed in the hospital for a week and made some improvement, but he needed help with the activities of daily living and could only speak a few words. The hospital was able to place him in a rehabilitation center since Jack qualified for skilled nursing care. He was transferred to the facility and received intensive rehabilitation services for the next month until he no longer improved. At that point, Jack was no longer eligible for skilled nursing care. He was transferred to a facility closer to his only relatives. The new facility had a large number of patients needing "custodial care." It provided all the services required by law, but Jack soon realized that he was just another stroke patient.

1. How does this case illustrate the lack of institutional continuity?
2. How does this case illustrate the lack of continuity between the healthcare and public health systems?
3. How does this case illustrate the lack of financial continuity?
4. What role does the lack of information play in this case? How can information technology serve to reduce or eliminate these lapses in continuity? Which lapses require other types of interventions?

Susan and the System

"PAYMENT REJECTED" was stamped in large letters on the bill that Susan received from her health insurance. She didn't find out much more after waiting on the phone and being transferred three times. All she was told was that her assigned doctor had not followed the guidelines distributed by the plan.

Susan had been doing well until a small area of breast cancer was discovered at the site of her original mastectomy. She now wondered if she had made the right decision in deciding not to take the medication she was prescribed. She never admitted to anyone that she just couldn't afford the medication, but after the alimony checks stopped coming she had to make some hard choices. Her doctor told her that he now thought she should be aggressive. After a consultation with her oncologist, he prescribed what he called a "new approach using approved drugs."

When Susan's doctor finally got through the managed care system, he was told "we don't pay for promising new treatments—we only pay for established or proven treatments." The new emphasis on patients' rights had given Susan the right to appeal. But the issue was not whether or not she and her doctor had made a reasonable decision for her. The question was: did her managed care health insurance contract cover this type of promising new treatment?

It didn't look like she had a chance on appeal and she decided to pay for her care herself, or out-of-pocket, as they call it in insurance language. Actually, at first it was out of her modest savings and then when that dried up she began to use her credit cards. "What choice do I have?" she often cried out in frustration. It was death or bankruptcy and at least with bankruptcy she got a second chance.

The treatment worked, but as expected Susan ran out of savings and credit. For follow-up care, Susan ended up on Medicaid, the health insurance system designed for the poor. Her oncologist didn't take Medicaid—she was told she'd have to make other arrangements. That wasn't easy—the only oncologist she could find who accepted Medicaid was across town in an area she was afraid to be in after dark. But, she went ahead anyway and despite the initial fears, she was pleased when the doctor seemed to understand her situation medically and personally.

Susan's cancer finally was under control and she was determined to put herself back on her feet financially. Susan found a new job, but couldn't manage to work full time and thus could not afford her employer-sponsored health insurance. Being on Medicaid made her feel like a second-class citizen. Now, when she finally seemed to be getting back on her feet financially, they were going to take it away. "The safety net is sure full of holes. The only right in health care is the right of the doctors and hospitals to be paid," she thought to herself.

1. How did the structure and operation of her health insurance plan affect the care that Susan received?
2. How did the structure and operation of Medicaid affect the care that Susan received?
3. What other factors influenced the care that Susan received?
4. What changes would you make in healthcare financing to address the issues raised in this case?

Donna's Doctor—To Error Is Human

Donna's heart was racing again and there just didn't seem to be a reason for it. She wasn't upset and hadn't been exercising. She was only 48 and no one seemed to take her seriously when she told everyone that something was wrong with her heart. She knew it was more than her recent divorce and raising a couple of teenagers. Not even the diagnosis of menopause satisfied her.

She decided to change primary care doctors having heard that Dr. Stein actually listened. He did listen and examined her carefully, but didn't find anything. He ordered a 24-hour test to monitor her heart. Donna did her usual activity and the portable device recorded a basic electrocardiogram. She had one brief episode of racing heart. She recorded the time and length of the episode just as requested and sure enough she was having a brief episode of what the doctor called "atrial fibrillation" at the time.

A week later Donna got the results—episodes of atrial fibrillation. The upper chambers of her heart, called the atria, were beating very rapidly. Her lower chambers, called the ventricles which pumps the blood out of the heart, were doing just fine so she was not in immediate danger. "The real danger is blood clots and potentially a stroke," Dr. Stein told her, "and we should thin or anticoagulate your blood." The thought of a stroke was enough to convince Donna to go ahead.

Anticoagulation may require a drug called Warfarin often known by the brand name Coumadin she was told, but it has to be done carefully. It can cause bleeding if it is not checked often. Taking Coumadin, Donna felt protected. She went back for the tests to adjust the dose. She felt better and now had lots of energy, but she still had some of those episodes of rapid heart rate.

When the hot flashes began, she knew that menopause had in fact arrived, but she felt better than ever and found herself skipping her blood tests because she wanted to be sure that she had time for her exercise routine. She didn't realize that anything was wrong until she fell off her bike one day, hitting her head. Fortunately, she was wearing a helmet so the injury didn't seem too bad. However, she did feel dizzy afterwards. And then a few hours later, her son told her that her speech was slurred. "Have you been drinking, Mom?" he asked. The look of disdain on her mother's face was enough to worry her son who now insisted on taking her to the emergency room.

Dr. Stein met Donna and her son in the emergency room. He arranged an emergency MRI scan that showed evidence of a small bleed and the blood test showed her anticoagulation level was too high. The doctors rapidly reversed the level and over the next few days Donna's mental state returned to normal. "What a relief," she thought, "but there has to be a better answer than going back to anticoagulation." Her doctors in the hospital asked for a consultation. First, the medical student, then the resident, and finally the professor came to look her over, examined her carefully, and then talked about her just outside her door where she could hear bits and pieces of their conversation. "Dr. Stein sure missed the diagnosis,"…"If she had only been compliant, none of this would have happened,"…"An obvious case of hyperthyroidism,"… "No need for Coumadin."

"The blood tests confirm overactivity of your thyroid, which is a condition called hyperthyroidism," the resident told her. "This caused your atrial fibrillation and your increased energy. You need treatment, but we don't do that here—we'll give you a referral." Donna could hardly absorb everything and didn't get a chance to even ask questions.

She went back to Dr. Stein who told her how badly he felt about missing the hyperthyroidism—he too had learned a lesson and he apologized for what had happened. He told her that there was very good treatment for hyperthyroidism and he would be pleased to take care of her after consultation with a specialist. Donna knew that doctors make mistakes, but she didn't know that they admitted them. She knew that Dr. Stein was a good doctor and that he would pay extra attention to her. Donna hoped that things would go well and was confident that she was in good hands with Dr. Stein.

1. Did Dr. Stein's care fulfill the duty, breach, causation, and damages criteria for medical malpractice?
2. What additional aspects of Dr. Stein's care affected whether a malpractice case resulted?
3. What role do you think the disclosure of error played in preventing a malpractice suit?
4. What attitudes toward decision making in health care on the part of Donna influenced the approach she took to her healthcare?

Health Care in America—For Better or Worse?

The final hours came as no surprise to his wife and family, who made daily visits to the hospital where Sam had been treated on and off for the final year of his life. His doctor had spared no expense to give him the most effective treatments available. "But wouldn't it have been nice if he could have died at home," they thought to themselves as they gathered at the funeral. "At least he held out until after the baby was born."

Sam's diagnosis of colon cancer did not shock him. His father died of colon cancer and he had been thinking it was time to be checked. Surgery went well and he and his doctor were optimistic about the future. The surprise came about 18 months later, when during a follow-up examination, he was told that there might be a recurrence.

Chemotherapy seemed to do more harm than good. There didn't seem to be a good answer. Sam's physician sought out the newest treatment, but it didn't seem to help. The final shock to his system came after he received a dose of the wrong medicine administered by a nurse who was new to the unit. She was hired in response to the recent accreditation review, which criticized the hospital for understaffing.

Though his death was no surprise, the bills from the hospital and physician were an unexpected burden in the months and years that followed. The health insurance that was offered through Sam's employer did not pay for screening for the colon cancer that killed him. In addition, its loopholes, caps, and copayments left the family with bills that would require years to repay. It was not just the uncovered expenses that they had to pay out-of-pocket, it was the mountains of paperwork that arrived in the mail.

Nonetheless, the family understood. The doctors had done everything possible and treated Sam and them with respect and responded quickly to their calls and continuous questions. Maybe things weren't ideal, they concluded, but at least they did everything they could.

1. What strengths of the U.S. healthcare system are illustrated in this case?
2. What limitations of the U.S. healthcare system are illustrated in this case?
3. What steps would you recommend to improve the delivery of preventive and curative services to better serve patients like Sam?
4. How might Sam's health care have been different in other developed countries, such as Canada and the United Kingdom? In what ways might it have been better and in what ways might it have been worse?

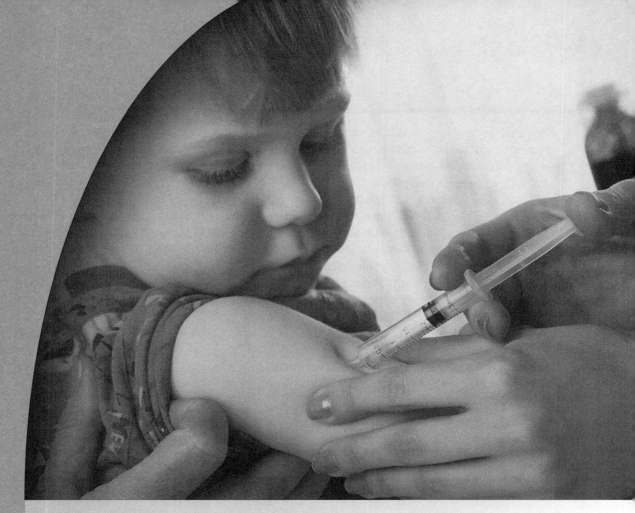

SECTION V

Public Health Institutions and Systems

Now that we have taken a look at the U.S. healthcare institutions and healthcare system, we need to turn our attention to the public health system. Treating healthcare and public health systems as separate systems is artificial because they have many points of overlap and collaboration. However, historically public health institutions and systems have developed from different philosophies, have different goals, and have organizational structures and lines of accountability different from those of the healthcare system.

We will begin by outlining the current goals and roles of public health agencies. Then, we will look at the current system of local/state, federal, and global public health institutions and examine how they are organized. We will explore why public health agencies need to coordinate with each other to achieve the goals of public health.

We will then return to our definition of population health—*the totality of all evidence-based public and private efforts to preserve and promote health and prevent disease, disability and death*. This broad 21st century definition requires public health agencies and professionals to collaborate with a range of government agencies and healthcare professionals and institutions.

In Chapter 13, the final chapter, we will turn our attention to the roles that public health needs to play in planning for the future. We will begin by examining its role in preparing for and responding to disasters. We will then take a look at what we can learn from the past that can help us predict and prepare for the future. Finally, we will examine and illustrate the emerging approach known as systems thinking which can help us see and address the big picture issue of health.

Thus, in this final chapter of *Public Health 101*, we will examine the complex puzzle that we call population health. We will look at frameworks for putting the pieces together to address the health issues that will inevitably be part of your future. Regardless of where your career leads, you will find that public health affects every corner of your lives and every corner of our world.

Let us turn our attention in Chapter 12 to the current public health institutions and public health systems.

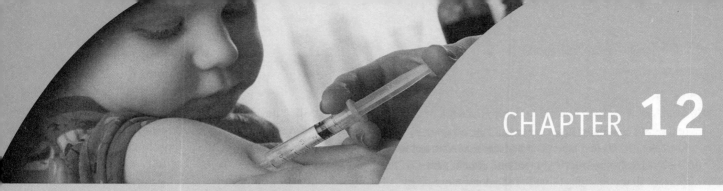

CHAPTER 12

Public Health Institutions and Systems

LEARNING OBJECTIVES

By the end of this chapter, the student will be able to:

- identify goals of governmental public health.
- identify the ten essential services of public health.
- describe basic features of local, state, and federal public health agencies in the United States.
- identify global public health organizations and agencies and describe their basic roles.
- identify roles in public health for federal agencies not identified as health agencies.
- illustrate the need for collaboration by governmental public health agencies with other governmental and nongovernmental organizations.
- describe approaches to connecting public health and the health-care system.

A young man in your dormitory is diagnosed with tuberculosis. The health department works with the student health service to test everyone in the dorm, as well as in his classes, with a TB skin test. Those who are positive for the first time are advised to take a course of a medicine called INH. You ask: is this standard operating procedure?

You go to a public health meeting and learn that many of the speakers are not from public health agencies, but from the Departments of Labor, Commerce, Housing, and Education. You ask: what do these departments have to do with health?

You hear that a new childhood vaccine was developed by the NIH, approved by the FDA, endorsed for federal payment by the CDC and recommended for use by the American Academy of Pediatrics. You ask: do all these agencies and organizations always work so well together?

A major flood in Asia leads to disease and starvation. Some say it is due to global warming, others to bad luck. Coordinated efforts by global health agencies, assisted by nongovernmental organizations (NGOs) and outside governmental donors, help get the country back on its feet. You ask: what types of cooperation are needed to make all of this happen?

A local community health center identifies childhood obesity as a problem in their community. They collect data demonstrating that the problem begins as early as elementary school. They develop a plan that includes clinical interventions at the health center and also at the elementary school. They ask the health department to help them organize an educational campaign and assist in evaluating the results. Working together, they are able to reduce the obesity rate among elementary school children by one-half. This seems like a new way to practice public health, you conclude. What type of approach is this?

These cases all reflect the responsibilities of public health agencies at the local, federal, and global levels. They illustrate public health working the way it is supposed to work. Of course, this is not always the case. Let us start by taking a look at the goals and roles of public health agencies.

WHAT ARE THE GOALS AND ROLES OF GOVERNMENTAL PUBLIC HEALTH AGENCIES?

Public health is often equated with the work of governmental agencies. The role of government is only a portion of what we mean by public health, but it is an important component. So important, in fact, that we often define the roles of other components in terms of how they relate to the work of governmental public health agencies.

In 1994, the United States Public Health Service put forth the "Public Health in America Statement," which provided the framework that continues to define the goals and services of governmental public health agencies.[1] These goals should already be familiar to you. They are:

- to prevent epidemics and the spread of disease
- to protect against environmental hazards
- to prevent injuries
- to promote and encourage healthy behaviors
- to respond to disasters and assist communities in recovery
- to ensure the quality and accessibility of health services

These are ambitious and complicated goals to achieve. To be able to successfully achieve them, it is important to further define the roles that governmental public health agencies themselves play, and by implication, the roles that other governmental agencies and nongovernmental organizations need to play.

The Public Health in America Statement built upon the Institute of Medicine's (IOM) 1988 report called The Future of Public Health.[2] The IOM defined three **core public health functions** that governmental public health agencies need to perform. The concept of "core function" implies that the job cannot be delegated to other agencies or to nongovernmental organizations. It also implies that the governmental public health agencies will work together to accomplish these functions because as a group they are responsible for public health as a whole—no one agency at the local, state, or federal level is specifically or exclusively responsible for accomplishing the essential public health services.[a]

The core functions defined by the IOM are: 1) assessment, 2) policy development, and 3) assurance.[2]

- **Assessment** includes obtaining data that defines the health of the overall population and specific groups within the population, including defining the nature of new and persisting health problems.
- **Assurance** includes governmental public health's oversight responsibility for ensuring that key components of an effective health system, including health care and public health, are in place even though the implementation will often be performed by others.

- **Policy development** includes developing evidence-based recommendations and other analyses of options, such as health policy analysis, to guide implementation including efforts to educate and mobilize community partnerships.

The three core functions, while useful in providing a delineation of responsibilities and an intellectual framework for the work of governmental public health agencies, were not tangible enough to provide a clear understanding or definition of the work of public health agencies. Thus, in addition to the goals of public health, the Public Health in America Statement defined a series of **ten essential public health services** that build upon the IOM's core functions, guide day-to-day responsibilities, and provide a mechanism for evaluating whether the core functions are fulfilled. These ten services have come to define the responsibilities of the combined local, state, and federal governmental public health system.

WHAT ARE THE TEN ESSENTIAL PUBLIC HEALTH SERVICES?

Table 12-1 outlines the ten essential public health services and organizes them according to which IOM core function they aim to fulfill.[1] A description of each service is presented in column two and examples of these essential services are listed in column three.

We have now looked at the core public health functions and the ten essential services of public health agencies. Figure 12-1 puts these together to allow you to see the connections.

These public health services are delivered through a complex web of local and federal agencies, as well as via increasing involvement of global organizations. Let us take a look at the work of public health agencies at each of these levels.

Figure 12-2 provides a framework to guide our review of the delivery of public health services. It diagrams the central role of governmental public health agencies and the complicated connections required to accomplish their responsibilities. We will begin by taking at look at the structure and function of governmental public health agencies at the local/state, federal, and global levels. Then, we will examine the key connections with other governmental agencies, community, and private organizations, and finally with the healthcare delivery system as a whole.

WHAT ARE THE ROLES OF LOCAL AND STATE PUBLIC HEALTH AGENCIES?

The United States Constitution does not mention public health. Thus, public health is first and foremost a state responsibility. States may retain the authority, voluntarily request or

---

[a] This does not imply that components of the work cannot be contracted to nongovernmental organizations. This activity is increasingly occurring. The concept of core function, however, implies that public health agencies remain responsible for these functions even when the day-to-day work is conducted through contracts with an outside organization.

TABLE 12-1 Ten Essential Public Health Services

Essential service	Meaning of essential service	Example
ASSESSMENT—Core function		
1. Monitor health status to identify and solve community health problems	This service includes accurate diagnosis of the community's health status; identification of threats to health and assessment of health service needs; timely collection, analysis, and publication of information on access, utilization, costs, and outcomes of personal health services; attention to the vital statistics and health status of specific groups that are at a higher risk than the total population; and collaboration to manage integrated information systems with private providers and health benefit plans.	Vital Statistics Health Surveys Surveillance, including reportable diseases
2. Diagnose and investigate health problems and health hazards in the community	This service includes epidemiologic identification of emerging health threats; public health laboratory capability using modern technology to conduct rapid screening and high-volume testing; active infectious disease epidemiology programs; and technical capacity for epidemiologic investigation of disease outbreaks and patterns of chronic disease and injury.	Epidemic investigations CDC–Epidemiology Intelligence Service State Public Health Laboratories
POLICY DEVELOPMENT—Core function		
3. Inform, educate, and empower people about health issues	This service includes social marketing and media communications; providing accessible health information resources at community levels; active collaboration with personal health care providers to reinforce health promotion messages and programs; and joint health education programs with schools, churches, and worksites.	Health education campaigns, such as comprehensive state tobacco programs
4. Mobilize community partnerships and action to identify and solve health problems	This service includes convening and facilitating community groups and associations, including those not typically considered to be health-related, in undertaking defined preventive, screening, rehabilitation, and support programs; and skilled coalition-building to draw upon the full range of potential human and material resources in the case of community health.	Lead control programs: testing and follow-up of children, reduction of lead exposure, educational follow-up, and addressing underlying causes
5. Develop policies and plans that support individual and community health efforts	This service requires leadership development at all levels of public health; systematic community and state-level planning for health improvement in all jurisdictions; tracking of measurable health objectives as a part of continuous quality improvement strategies; joint evaluation with the medical health care system to define consistent policy regarding prevention and treatment services; and development of codes, regulations, and legislation to guide public health practice.	Newborn screening program for PKU and other genetic and congenital diseases

continues

TABLE 12-1 Ten Essential Public Health Services (continued)

Essential service	Meaning of essential service	Example
ASSURANCE—Core function		
6. Enforce laws and regulations that protect health and ensure safety	This service involves full enforcement of sanitary codes, especially in the food industry; full protection of drinking water supplies; enforcement of clean air standards; timely follow-up of hazards, preventable injuries, and exposure-related diseases identified in occupational and community settings; monitoring quality of medical services (e.g. laboratory, nursing home, and home health care); and timely review of new drug, biological, and medical device applications.	Local: Fluoridation and chlorination of water State: Regulation of nursing homes Federal: FDA drug approval and food safety
7. Link people to needed personal health services and ensure the provision of health care when otherwise unavailable	This service (often referred to as "outreach" or "enabling" service) includes ensuring effective entry for socially disadvantaged people into a coordinated system of clinical care; culturally- and linguistically-appropriate materials and staff to ensure linkage to services for special population groups; ongoing "care management"; and transportation.	Community Health Centers
8. Ensure the provision of a competent public and personal health care workforce	This service includes education and training for personnel to meet the needs for public and personal health services; efficient processes for licensure of professionals and certification of facilities with regular verification and inspection follow-up; adoption of continuous quality improvement and lifelong learning within all licensure and certification programs; active partnerships with professional training programs to ensure community-relevant learning experiences for all students; and continuing education in management and leadership development programs for those charged with administrative/executive roles.	Licensure of physicians, nurses, and other health professionals
9. Evaluate effectiveness, accessibility, and quality of personal and population-based health services	This service calls for ongoing evaluation of health programs, based on analysis of health status and service utilization data, to assess program effectiveness and to provide information necessary for allocating resources and reshaping programs.	Development of evidence-based recommendations
ALL THREE IOM—Core function		
10. Research for new insights and innovative solutions to health problems	This service includes continuous linkage with appropriate institutions of higher learning and research and an internal capacity to mount timely epidemiologic and economic analyses and conduct needed health services research.	NIH, CDC, AHRQ other federal agencies

Source: Data from Public Health in America. Essential Public Health Services. Available at http://www.health.gov/phfunctions/public.htm. Accessed November 8, 2008.

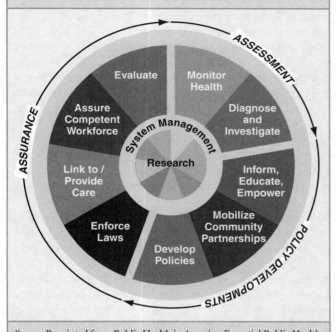

FIGURE 12-1 Essential public health services and IOM core functions

Source: Reprinted from Public Health in America. Essential Public Health Services. Available at http://www.health.gov/phfunctions/public.htm. Accessed November 8, 2008.

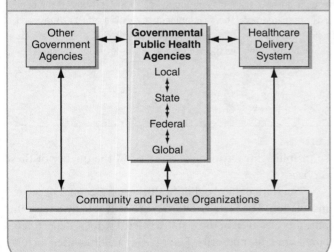

FIGURE 12-2 Framework for viewing governmental public health agencies and their complicated connections

accept help from the federal government, or delegate their responsibility and/or authority to local agencies at the city, county, or other local levels.[b]

Box 12-1 describes a brief history of public health agencies in the United States. It is a complex history and has resulted in more structures than there are states—more because large cities often have their own public health systems.[3] In addition, the District of Columbia and several U.S. territories have their own systems and often have authority to make public health system decisions as if they were states.

To understand the role of local health departments, it is useful to think of two models.[4] In the first model, which we will call the home rule or local autonomy model, authority is delegated from the state to the local health department. The local health department, or the local government, has a great deal of autonomy in setting its own structure and function and often raising its own funding.

In the second model, which we will call the branch office model, the local health department can be viewed as a branch office of the state agency with little or no independent authority or funding. Most health departments lie somewhere in between these two extreme models, however these models provide a framework for understanding the many varieties of department structures. Thus, when we speak of local public health, we may be speaking of a state agency with branch offices or a relatively independent local agency. Regardless of which model a state uses, many public health responsibilities of local public health departments are quite similar and they usually have authority and responsibility for at least the following:[4]

- immunizations for those not covered by the private system
- communicable disease surveillance and initial investigation of outbreaks
- communicable disease control, often including at a minimum tuberculosis and syphilis case finding and treatment
- inspection and licensing of restaurants
- environmental health surveillance
- coordinating public health screening programs, including newborn and lead screenings
- tobacco control programs
- public health preparedness and response to disasters

Health departments in many parts of the United States have also served as the healthcare provider for those without

---

[b] This delegation may occur at the discretion of the state government or it may be included in the state's constitution providing what is called **home rule authority** to local jurisdictions. In general, jurisdictions with home rule authority exercise substantially more autonomy.

BOX 12-1   Brief History of American Public Health Agencies.

An understanding of the history of American public health institutions requires an understanding of the response of local, state, and federal governments to public health crises and the complex interactions between these levels of government.

The colonial period in America saw repeated epidemics of smallpox, cholera, and yellow fever focused in the port cities. These epidemics brought fear and disruption of commerce, along with accompanying disease and death. One epidemic in Philadelphia in 1793 in what was then the nation's capital nearly shut down the federal government. These early public health crises brought about the first municipal Boards of Health, made up of respected citizens authorized to act in the community's interest to implement quarantine, evacuation, and other public health interventions of the day. The federal government's early role in combating epidemics led to the establishment in 1798 of what later became known as the U.S. Public Health Service.

Major changes in public health awaited the last half of the 19th century with the great expansion of understanding of disease and the ability to control it through community actions. The Shattuck Commission in Massachusetts in 1850 outlined the roles of state health departments as responsible for: sanitary inspections, communicable disease control, food sanitation, vital statistics, and services for infants and children. Over the next 50 years, the states gradually took the lead in developing public health institutions based upon delivery of these services.

Local health departments outside of the largest cities did not exist until the 20th century. The Rockefeller Foundation stimulated and helped fund early local health departments and campaigns in part to combat specific diseases, such as hookworm. There was no standard model for local health departments. Local health departments developed in at least 50 different ways in the 50 states and were chronically underfunded.

The federal government played a very small role in public health throughout the 1800s and well into the 20th century. An occasional public health crisis stimulated in part by media attention did bring about federal action. The founding of the Food and Drug Administration in 1906 resulted in large part from the journalistic activity known as "muckraking," which exposed the status of food and drug safety. The early years of the 20th century set the stage for expansion of the federal government's role in public health through the passage of the 16th Amendment to the Constitution authorizing federal income tax as a major source of federal government funding.

The Great Depression, in general, and the Social Security Act of 1935, in particular, brought about a new era in which federal funding became a major source of financial resources for state and local public health departments and nongovernmental organizations. The founding of the what was then called the Communicable Disease Centers (CDC) in 1946 led to a national and eventually international leadership role for the CDC which attempts to connect and hold together the complex local, state, and federal public health efforts and integrate them into global public health efforts.

The Johnson Administration's War on Poverty, as well as the Medicare and Medicaid programs, brought about greatly expanded funding for health care services and led many health departments to provide direct healthcare services especially for those without other sources of care. The late 1980s and 1990s saw a redefinition of the roles of governmental public health including the Institute of Medicine's definition of core functions and the development of the 10 Essential Public Health Services. These documents have guided the development of a broad population focus for public health and a move away from the direct provision of healthcare services.

As we will explore in Chapter 13, the terrorism of 9/11 and the subsequent anthrax scare moved public health institutions to the center of efforts to protect the public's health through emergency and disaster preparedness. The development of flexible efforts to respond to expected and unexpected hazards is now a central feature of public health institutions' roles and funding. The success of these efforts requires new levels of coordination of local, state, federal, and global public health agencies utilizing state-of-the-art surveillance, laboratory technology, and communications systems.

other sources of health care. This has been called the **healthcare safety net**. In recent years, many health departments have reduced or discontinued these services often transferring them to the healthcare system or integrating their efforts into community health centers. The concept of core functions holds that while these activities can be performed by other organizations or agencies, the public health agencies still retain re-

sponsibility for ensuring access to and the quality of these services.

The work of local public health agencies cannot be viewed in isolation. The State Health Department usually retains important roles even in those states where the local departments have home rule authority. These responsibilities often include: collecting vital statistics, running a public health laboratory, licensing of health professionals, administering nutrition programs, and regulation of health facilities, such as nursing homes. In addition, drinking water regulation, administration of the state Medicaid program, and the office of the medical examiner may also fall under the authority of the State Health Department.

Today, the federal government has a great deal of involvement in national and global issues of public health and often works closely with local agencies. Let us take a look at the structure and role of the federal government in public health.

WHAT ARE THE ROLES OF FEDERAL PUBLIC HEALTH AGENCIES?

As we saw in Chapter 5, the federal government's role in public health does not explicitly appear in the United States Constitution. It has been justified largely by the Interstate Commerce clause, which provides federal government authority to regulate commerce between the states. Federal public health authority often rests on the voluntary acceptance by the states of funding provided by the federal government. This funding may come with requirements for state action in order to qualify for the funding.

The Department of Health and Human Services (HHS) is the central public health agency of the federal government. It includes operating agencies each of which report directly to the cabinet-level Secretary of HHS. Table 12-2 outlines most of these agencies, their roles and authority, and their basic public health structure and activities.[5]

The National Institutes of Health (NIH) is far and away the largest agency within HHS with a budget of over $30 billion—as much as all the other six agencies' budgets combined. However, most of its efforts are devoted to basic science research and the translation of research into clinical practice. Some of the federal agencies, such as the Health Services and Resources Administration (HRSA), Substance Abuse and Mental Health Services Administration (SAMHSA), and the Indian Health Service, provide or fund individually-oriented health services in addition to population-oriented preventive services. The Indian Health Service is unique because it is responsible for both public health and healthcare services for a defined population.

The Centers for Disease Control and Prevention (CDC) is perhaps the agency most closely identified with public health at the federal level. Box 12-2 describes its first 50 years from 1946 to 1996 in a reprint of its official history first published in the *Morbidity and Mortality Weekly Report* (MMWR), a weekly publication of agency.[6]

Today, the CDC's role in connecting federal, state, and local governmental public health efforts is central to the suc-cess of the system. Approximately half of the CDC's current approximately $10 billion budget is channeled to state and local health departments. A key function of the CDC is to provide national leadership and to coordinate the efforts of local/state and federal public health agencies.

To understand the local/state and federal public health system, it is important to appreciate that only five percent of all health-related funding goes to public health and of that, less than half goes to population-based prevention as opposed to providing healthcare services as a safety net for individuals. In addition, the role of governmental public health is limited by social attitudes toward government. For instance, we have seen that there are constitutional limitations on the authority of public health and other government agencies to impose actions on individuals. These may limit public health agencies' abilities to address issues ranging from tuberculosis and HIV control to responses to emergencies. The social attitudes of Americans may also limit the authority and resources provided to public health agencies. Americans often favor individual or private efforts over governmental interventions when they believe that individuals and private organizations are capable of success. For instance, some Americans resist active efforts in the schools to provide information and access to contraceptives, while others resist the type of case-finding efforts for HIV/AIDS that have been used successfully in investigating and controlling other communicable diseases.

Today, governmental public health is a global enterprise. Let us take a look at the roles of global health organizations and agencies.

WHAT ARE THE ROLES OF GLOBAL HEALTH ORGANIZATIONS AND AGENCIES?

Public health is increasingly becoming a global enterprise. Global governmental efforts have grown dramatically in recent years. The World Health Organization (WHO) was created in 1948. Its impact has become more prominent in the 21st century with the increasing importance of global health issues. The WHO is a part of the United Nations organizations, which also include the United Nations Infant and Child Emergency Fund (UNICEF) and the Joint United Nations Programme on AIDS/HIV (UNAIDS).[7]

Today, the World Bank and other multilateral financial institutions are the largest funding source for global health efforts.[8] National governmental aid programs, including the United States Agency for International Development (USAID), also play an important role in public health. Table 12-3 outlines the structure/governance, roles, and limitations of global public health agencies.

TABLE 12-2 Key Federal Health Agencies of the Department of Health and Human Services

Agency	Roles/Authority	Examples of Structures/Activities
Centers for Disease Control and Prevention (CDC) and Agency for Toxic Substances and Disease Registry (ATSDR)	CDC is the lead agency for prevention, health data, epidemic investigation, and public health measures aimed at disease control and prevention. The CDC administers ATSDR, which works with the Environmental Protection Agency to provide guidance on health hazards of toxic exposures.	The CDC and ATSDR work extensively with state and local health departments. The CDC's Epidemiology Intelligence Service (EIS) functions domestically and internationally at the request of governments.
National Institutes of Health (NIH)	Lead research agency. Also funds training programs and communication of health information to the professional community and the public.	17 institutes in all—the largest being the National Cancer Institute. The National Library of Medicine is part of NIH Centers. The Centers include the John E. Fogarty International Center for Advanced Study in the Health Sciences. NIH is the world's largest biomedical research enterprise with intramural research at NIH and extramural research grants throughout the world.
Food and Drug Administration (FDA)	Consumer protection agency with authority for safety of foods and safety and efficacy of drugs, vaccines and other medical and public health interventions	Divisions responsible for food safety, medical devices, drug efficacy and safety pre- and post- approval
Health Resources and Services Administration (HRSA)	Seeks to ensure equitable access to comprehensive quality health care	Funds community health centers, HIV/AIDS services, scholarships for health professional students
Agency for Healthcare Research and Quality (AHRQ)	Research agenda to improve the outcomes and quality of health care, including patient safety and access to services	Supports U.S. Preventive Services Task Force, Evidence-based medicine research, and Guidelines Clearinghouse
Substance Abuse and Mental Health Services Administration (SAMHSA)	Works to improve quality and availability of prevention, treatment, and rehabilitation for substance abuse and mental illness	Research, data collection and funding of local services
Indian Health Service (IHS)	Provides direct health care and public health services to federally-recognized tribes	Services provided to 550 federally-recognized tribes in 35 states. Only comprehensive federal responsibility for health care, plus public health services

BOX 12-2 History of the CDC.

The Communicable Disease Center was organized in Atlanta, Georgia on July 1, 1946; its founder, Dr. Joseph W. Mountin, was a visionary public health leader who had high hopes for this small and comparatively insignificant branch of the Public Health Service (PHS). It occupied only one floor of the Volunteer Building on Peachtree Street and had fewer than 400 employees, most of whom were engineers and entomologists. Until the previous day, they had worked for Malaria Control in War Areas, the predecessor of CDC, which had successfully kept the southeastern states malaria-free during World War II and, for approximately 1 year, from murine typhus fever. The new institution would expand its interests to include all communicable diseases and would be the servant of the states, providing practical help whenever called.

Distinguished scientists soon filled CDC's laboratories, and many states and foreign countries sent their public health staffs to Atlanta for training....Medical epidemiologists were scarce, and it was not until 1949 that Dr. Alexander Langmuir arrived to head the epidemiology branch. Within months, he launched the first-ever disease surveillance program, which confirmed his suspicion that malaria, on which CDC spent the largest portion of its budget, had long since disappeared. Subsequently, disease surveillance became the cornerstone on which CDC's mission of service to the states was built and, in time, changed the practice of public health.

The outbreak of the Korean War in 1950 was the impetus for creating CDC's Epidemiological Intelligence Service (EIS). The threat of biological warfare loomed, and Dr. Langmuir, the most knowledgeable person in PHS about this arcane subject, saw an opportunity to train epidemiologists who would guard against ordinary threats to public health while watching out for alien germs. The first class of EIS officers arrived in Atlanta for training in 1951 and pledged to go wherever they were called for the next 2 years. These "disease detectives" quickly gained fame for "shoe-leather epidemiology" through which they ferreted out the cause of disease outbreaks.

The survival of CDC as an institution was not at all certain in the 1950s. In 1947, Emory University gave land on Clifton Road for a headquarters, but construction did not begin for more than a decade. PHS was so intent on research and the rapid growth of the National Institutes of Health that it showed little interest in what happened in Atlanta. Congress, despite the long delay in appropriating money for new buildings, was much more receptive to CDC's pleas for support than either PHS or the Bureau of the Budget.

Two major health crises in the mid-1950s established CDC's credibility and ensured its survival. In 1955, when poliomyelitis appeared in children who had received the recently approved Salk vaccine, the national inoculation program was stopped. The cases were traced to contaminated vaccine from a laboratory in California; the problem was corrected, and the inoculation program, at least for first and second graders, was resumed. The resistance of these 6- and 7-year-olds to polio, compared with that of older children, proved the effectiveness of the vaccine. Two years later, surveillance was used again to trace the course of a massive influenza epidemic. From the data gathered in 1957 and subsequent years, the national guidelines for influenza vaccine were developed.

CDC grew by acquisition....When CDC joined the international malaria-eradication program and accepted responsibility for protecting the earth from moon germs and vice versa, CDC's mission stretched overseas and into space.

CDC played a key role in one of the greatest triumphs of public health, the eradication of smallpox. In 1962 it established a smallpox surveillance unit, and a year later tested a newly developed jet gun and vaccine in the Pacific island nation of Tonga....CDC also achieved notable success at home tracking new and mysterious disease outbreaks. In the mid-1970s and early 1980s, it found the cause of Legionnaires disease and toxic-shock syndrome. A fatal disease, subsequently named acquired immunodeficiency syndrome (AIDS), was first mentioned in the June 5, 1981, issue of *MMWR*.

Although CDC succeeded more often than it failed, it did not escape criticism. For example, television and press reports about the Tuskegee study on long-term effects of untreated syphilis in black men created a storm of protest in 1972. This study had been initiated by PHS and other organizations in 1932 and was transferred to CDC in 1957. Although the effectiveness of penicillin as a therapy for syphilis had been established during the late 1940s, participants in this study remained untreated until the study was brought to public attention. CDC was also criticized because of the 1976 effort to vaccinate the U.S. population against swine flu, the infamous killer of 1918–1919. When some vaccinees developed Guillain-Barre syndrome, the campaign was stopped immediately; the epidemic never occurred.

As the scope of CDC's activities expanded far beyond communicable diseases, its name had to be changed. In 1970 it became the Center for Disease Control and in 1981, after extensive reorganization, Center became Centers. The words "and Prevention" were added in 1992, but, by law, the well-known three-letter acronym was retained. In health emergencies CDC means an answer to SOS calls from anywhere in the world, such as the recent one from Zaire where Ebola fever raged.

Fifty years ago CDC's agenda was non-controversial (hardly anyone objected to the pursuit of germs), and Atlanta was a backwater. In 1996, CDC's programs are often tied to economic, political, and social issues, and Atlanta is as near Washington as the tap of a keyboard.

Source: Reprinted from Centers for Disease Control and Prevention, MMWR 1996;45: 526–528.

TABLE 12-3 Global Public Health Organizations

Type of agency	Structure/Governance	Role(s)	Limitations
World Health Organization	United Nations Organization Seven "regional" semi-independent components, e.g., Pan American Health Organization covers North and South America	Policy development, e.g., tobacco treaty, epidemic control policies Coordination of services, e.g., SARS control, vaccine development Data collection and standardization, e.g., measures of health care quality, measures of health status	Limited ability to enforce global recommendations, limited funding and complex international administration
International organizations with focused agenda	UNICEF UNAIDS	Focus on childhood vaccinations Focus on AIDS	Limited agendas and limited financing
International financing organizations	The World Bank Other multilateral regional banks, e.g., InterAmerican and Asian Development Banks	World Bank is largest international funder. Increasingly supports "human capital" projects and reform of health care delivery systems and population and nutrition efforts Provides funding and technical assistance primarily as loans	Criticized for standardized approach with few local modifications
Bilateral governmental aid organizations	USAID Many other developed countries have their own organizations and contribute a higher percentage of their gross domestic product to those agencies than does the United States	Often focused on specific countries and specific types of programs, such as the United States' focus on HIV/AIDS, and maternal and child health	May be tied to domestic politics and global economic, political, or military agendas

The complexity of local, state, federal, and global public health agencies raises the question of whether or not these agencies can and do work together. It should not surprise you that close collaboration, while the goal, is often difficult to achieve with so many organizations involved. Thus, it is important to ask: how can public health agencies work together?

HOW CAN PUBLIC HEALTH AGENCIES WORK TOGETHER?

Coordination among public health agencies has been a major challenge that is built into our local, state, and federal system of governance. Increasingly, coordination also requires a global aspect as well. Efforts on all levels have a long way to go. There are signs of hope with the recent progress in such fields as tobacco control, food safety, and most notably, the response to SARS. Box 12-3 discusses the dramatic events of the 2003 SARS epidemic, providing an example of what can be done and what needs to be done to address future public health emergencies.[9]

Collaboration needs to be an everyday effort, and not just a requirement for emergencies or epidemics. Let us look at the relationships and needed collaboration among governmental

BOX 12-3 SARS and the Public Health Response.

The SARS epidemic of 2003 began with little notice, most likely somewhere in the heartland of China and then spread to other areas of Asia. The world took notice after television screens filled with reports of public health researchers sent to Asia to investigate the illness subsequently contracting and dying from the disease. Not an easily transmissible disease except for those in very close contact, such as investigators, family members, and healthcare providers, the disease spread slowly but steadily through areas of China. Among those infected, the case-fatality rate was very high especially without the benefits of modern intensive care facilities.

The disease did not respond to antibiotics and was thought to be a viral disease by its epidemiological pattern of spread and transmission, but at first no cause was known. The outside world soon felt the impact of the brewing epidemic when cases appeared in Hong Kong that could be traced to a traveler from mainland China. Fear spread when cases were recognized that could not be explained by close personal contact with a SARS victim.

The epidemic continued to spread jumping thousands of miles to Toronto, Canada, where the second greatest concentration of disease appeared. Soon, the whole world was on high alert, if not quite on the verge of panic. At least 8000 people worldwide became sick and almost 10 percent of them died. Fortunately, progress came quite quickly. Researchers coordinated by the World Health Organization (WHO) were able to put together the epidemiological information and laboratory data and establish a presumed cause, a new form of the coronavirus never before seen in humans leading to the rapid introduction of testing.

The WHO and the CDC put forth recommendations for isolation, travel restrictions, and intensive monitoring that rapidly controlled the disease even in the absence of an effective treatment aimed at a cure. SARS disappeared as rapidly as it emerged, especially after systematic efforts to control spread were put in place in China. Not eliminated, but no longer a worldwide threat, SARS left a lasting global impact. The WHO established new approaches for reporting and responding to epidemics—these now have the widespread formal acceptance of most governments.

Once the world could step back and evaluate what happened, it was recognized that the potential burden of disease posed by the SARS epidemic had worldwide implications and raised the threat of interruption of travel and trade. Local, national, and global public health agencies collaborated quickly and effectively. Infection control recommendations made at the global level were rapidly translated into efforts to identify disease at the local level and manage individual patients in hospitals throughout the world. It is a model of communicable disease control that will be needed in the future.

public health and other governemental agencies, nongovernmental organizations, and the healthcare delivery system.

WHAT OTHER GOVERNMENT AGENCIES ARE INVOLVED IN HEALTH ISSUES?

To address health issues, it is important to recognize the important roles that government agencies not designated as health agencies play in public health. Such agencies exist at the local/state, federal, and global levels. To illustrate the involvement of these agencies in health issues, let's begin with the roles of nonhealth agencies at the federal level.

A number of federal agencies serve public health functions even though they are not defined as health agencies. The roles they play are important especially when we take the population health perspective that includes the totality of efforts to promote and protect health and prevent disease, disability, and death.

Environmental health issues are an important part of the role of the Environmental Protection Agency (EPA). Reducing

injury and hazardous exposures in the workplace are key goals of the Occupational Safety and Health Administration (OSHA), which is part of the Department of Labor.

Protecting health as part of preparation and response to disasters and terrorism is central to the role of the Department of Homeland Security. The Department of Agriculture shares with the FDA the role of protecting the nation's food supply. The Department of Housing and Urban Development influences the built environment and its impacts on health. The Department of Energy plays important roles in setting radiation safety standards for nuclear power plants and other sources of energy.

The multiple federal agencies involved in health-related matters often means that coordination and collaboration are required across agencies. This is certainly the case with food safety and disaster planning and response. It is true as well for efforts to address problems that cut across agencies, such as lead exposure or efforts to reduce the environmental causes of asthma.

WHAT ROLES DO NONGOVERNMENTAL ORGANIZATIONS PLAY IN PUBLIC HEALTH?

Nongovernmental organizations play increasingly important roles in public health in the United States and around the world. The United States has a long tradition of private groups organizing to advocate for public health causes, delivering public health services, and providing funding to support public health efforts. In recent years, these efforts have been expanding globally as well.

The American Red Cross and its network of international affiliates represent a major international effort to provide public health services. The organization plays a central role in obtaining volunteers for blood donations and ensuring the safety and effectiveness of the U.S. and world supply of blood products in collaboration with the U.S. Food and Drug Administration. The ability of the Red Cross to obtain donations, mobilize volunteers, and publicize the need for disaster assistance has allowed it to play a central role in providing lifesaving public health services.

Many private organizations provide public health education, support research, develop evidence-based recommendations, and provide other public health services. Many of these are organized around specific diseases or types of disease, such as the American Cancer Association, the American Heart Association, the American Lung Association and the March of Dimes, which focuses on birth defects. Other private organizations focus primarily on advocacy for individuals with specific diseases, but these organizations also may advocate for specific public health interventions. For instance, Mothers Against Drunk Driving (MADD) has had a major impact on the passage and enforcement of drunk driving laws. HIV/AIDS advocacy groups have influenced policies on confidentiality, funding, and public education.

Globally, nongovernmental organizations (NGOs) increasingly play a key role in providing services and advocating for public health policies. CARE and OXFAM are examples of the types of organizations involved in global health-related crises. Physician groups, including Physicians for Social Responsibility and Doctors without Borders, have been active in advocating for public health efforts, seeking funding for public health needs, and addressing the ethical implementation of public health programs.

New combinations of governmental and nongovernmental organizations are increasingly developing to fill in the gaps. At the global level, the Global Fund to Fight AIDS, Tuberculosis and Malaria, a public-private effort, provides funding for evidence-based interventions to address these diseases. It is funded not only by governments, but also by private foundations, such as the Bill and Melinda Gates Foundation.

Private foundations have played major roles in funding public health efforts and also stimulating governmental funding. The Rockefeller Foundation's efforts were instrumental in developing local health departments and initiating Schools of Public Health in the United States during the early years of the 20th century. The Kellogg Foundation, the Robert Wood Johnson Foundation, and most recently the Gates Foundation have all played key roles in advancing public health efforts in areas ranging from nutrition to tobacco control to advancing new public health technologies.

Foundation funding has been the catalyst in initiating new funding efforts and sustaining those that are not adequately funded by governments. They cannot be expected, however, to provide long-term support for basic public health services. Thus, additional strategies are required. One key strategy is to link public health efforts with the efforts of healthcare professionals and the healthcare system.

HOW CAN PUBLIC HEALTH AGENCIES PARTNER WITH HEALTH CARE TO IMPROVE THE RESPONSE TO HEALTH PROBLEMS?

We have already seen a number of traditional connections between public health and health care. Clinicians and public health professionals increasingly share a common commitment to evidence-based thinking, cost-effective delivery of services, and computerized and confidential data systems. They also increasingly share a commitment to provide quality services to the entire population and eliminate health disparities. The potential for successful collaboration between public health and health care is illustrated by the National Vaccine Plan, which is discussed in Box 12-4.[10]

In the mid-1990s, a Medicine-Public Health Initiative was initiated to investigate better ways to connect public health with medicine, in particular, and health care, in general. Connecting these two fields has not always had easy or successful results. Additional structures are needed to formalize effective and efficient bonds. Models do exist and new ideas are being put forth to connect clinical care and public health. Box 12-5 discusses one such model called **community-oriented primary care (COPC)**.[11]

Despite efforts in the healthcare system to reach out to the community and address public health issues (such as COPC), it remains the primary responsibility of public health to organize and mobilize community-based efforts. Working with nongovernmental organizations and healthcare professionals and organizations is imperative to effectively and efficiently accomplish the goals of public health. But, how exactly can public health agencies accomplish these goals?

BOX 12-4 National Vaccine Plan.

In 1994, a National Vaccine Plan was developed as part of a coordinated effort to accomplish the following goals:
1. Develop new and improved vaccines.
2. Ensure the optimal safety and effectiveness of vaccines and immunizations.
3. Better educate the public and members of the health profession on the benefits and risks of immunizations.

A recent Institute of Medicine (IOM) report evaluated progress since 1994 on achieving the above goals and made recommendations for the development of a revised National Vaccine Plan.[10] The IOM highlighted a number of successes since 1994 in achieving each of the goals of the Plan. These successes illustrate the potential for improved collaboration between public health systems and healthcare systems.

In terms of the development of new and improved vaccines since 1994, over 20 new vaccine products resulting from the collaborative efforts of the National Institutes of Health (NIH), academic, and industry researchers were approved by the Food and Drug Administration (FDA). Novel vaccines introduced include vaccines against pediatric pneumococcal disease, meningococcal disease, and the human papillomavirus (HPV)—a cause of cervical cancer.

In terms of safety, vaccines and vaccination approaches with improved safety have been developed since 1994, including those directed against rotavirus, pertussis (whooping cough), and polio. The FDA Center for Biologics Evaluation and Research (CBER), which regulates vaccines, now has an expanded array of regulatory tools to facilitate the review and approval of safe and efficacious vaccines. The FDA and the Centers for Disease Control and Prevention (CDC) have collaborated on surveillance for and evaluation of adverse events. Efforts have also been made to increase collaboration with the Centers for Medicare and Medicaid, the Department of Defense, and the Department of Veterans Affairs to improve surveillance and reporting of adverse events following immunization in the adult populations these agencies serve.

In terms of better education of health professionals and the public, progress has also been made. The American Academy of Pediatrics (AAP) collaborates with the CDC for its Childhood Immunization Support. The American Medical Association (AMA) cosponsors the annual National Influenza Vaccine Summit, a group that represents 100 public and private organizations interested in preventing influenza.

Despite the growing collaboration and success in vaccine development and use, new issues have appeared in recent years. Vaccines are now correctly viewed by the health professionals and the public as having both benefits and harms. In recent years, the public has grown more concerned about the safety of vaccines, including the issue of the use of large numbers of vaccines in children. The limitations of vaccines to address problems, such as HIV/AIDS, have also been increasingly recognized. Hopefully, the new National Vaccine Plan will build upon these recent successes and address the new realities and opportunities.

HOW CAN PUBLIC HEALTH TAKE THE LEAD IN MOBILIZING COMMUNITY PARTNERSHIPS TO IDENTIFY AND SOLVE HEALTH PROBLEMS?

An essential service of public health is the mobilization of community partnerships and action to identify and solve health problems. These efforts by public health agencies are critical to putting the pieces of the health system together to protect and promote health and prevent disability and death.

Examples of successful collaboration include state tobacco control programs that have been led by public health agencies, but rely heavily on nongovernmental organizations, healthcare professionals and other governmental agencies. These efforts have been able to substantially reduce statewide cigarette smoking rates.

Efforts to organize coordinated programs for lead control have also met with some success. Collaborative efforts between public health and health care have identified and treated children with elevated lead levels. Cooperation with other agencies has provided for the removal of lead paint from homes and testing and control of lead in playgrounds, water, and most recently, toys.

It is possible to view the coordinated mobilization of public and private efforts as **community-oriented public health (COPH)**. We can see this as a parallel to COPC. In COPC, healthcare efforts are expanded to take on additional public health roles. In COPH, public health efforts are expanded to collaborate with healthcare delivery institutions, as well as other community and governmental efforts. Child oral health, an example of COPH, is illustrated in Box 12-6.[12]

BOX 12-5 Community Oriented Primary Care (COPC).

Community-oriented primary care (COPC) is a structured effort to expand the delivery of health services from a focus on the individual to also include an additional focus on the needs of communities. Serving the needs of communities brings healthcare and public health efforts together. COPC can be seen as an effort on the part of healthcare delivery sites, such as community health centers, to reach out to their community and to governmental public health institutions.

Table 12–4 outlines the six steps in the COPC process and presents a question to ask when addressing each of these steps. Notice the parallels between COPC and the evidence-based approach that we have outlined. In both cases, the process is actually circular because evaluation efforts often lead to recycling to move the process ahead.

TABLE 12-4 The Six Sequential Steps of Community-Oriented Primary Care (COPC)

Steps in the COPC process	Questions to ask
1. Community definition	How is the community defined based upon geography, institutional affiliation, or other common characteristics, e.g., use of an Internet site?
2. Community characterization	What are the demographic and health characteristics of the community and what are its health issues?
3. Prioritization	What are the most important health issues facing the community and how should they be prioritized based upon objective data and perceived need?
4. Detailed assessment of the selected health problem	What are the most effective and efficient interventions for addressing the selected health problem based upon an evidence-based assessment?
5. Intervention	What strategies will be used to implement the intervention?
6. Evaluation	How can the success of the intervention be evaluated?

Source: Data from District of Columbia Area Health Education Center. The Conceptual Framework for COPC. Available at: http://dcahec.gwumc.edu/education/session4/index.html. Accessed November 8, 2008.

A series of principles underlies COPC including:
- Healthcare needs are defined by examining the community as a whole, not just those who seek care.
- Needed healthcare services are provided to everyone within a defined population or community.
- Preventive, curative, and rehabilitative care are integrated within a coordinated delivery system.
- Members of the community directly participate in all stages of the COPC process.

The concept of COPC, if not the specific structure, has been widely accepted as an approach for connecting the organized delivery of primary health care with public health. It implies that public health issues can and should be addressed when possible at the level of the community with the involvement of healthcare providers and the community members themselves.

Developing community partnerships is a time-consuming and highly political process that requires great leadership and diplomatic skills. Central authority and command and control approaches are generally not effective in the complex organizational structures of the United States. New approaches and new strategies are needed to bring together the organizations and individuals who can get the job done.

We have now looked at the organization of the public health system and the challenges it faces in accomplishing its core functions and providing its essential services. The role of

BOX 12-6 Child Oral Health and Community Oriented Public Health (COPH).

The problem of childhood dental disease illustrates the potential for community-oriented public health (COPH). A lack of regular dental care remains a major problem for children in developed, as well as developing countries. The need for this type of care is often high on the agenda of parents, teachers, and even the children themselves.

Public health efforts to improve oral health go back to the late 19th- and early 20th centuries when toothbrushing and toothpaste were new and improved technologies. The public health campaigns of the early 20th century were very instrumental in making toothbrushing a routine part of American life. The history of public health interventions in childhood oral health is a story of great hope and partial success. The benefits of the fluoridation of drinking water were well grounded in evidence. The American Dental Association and the American Medical Association have supported this intervention for over half a century. Resistance from those who view it as an intrusion of governmental authority, however, has prevented universal use of fluoridation in the United States. After over a half century of effort, fluoridation has reached less than two-thirds of Americans through the water supply.

Today, new technologies from dental sealants to more cost-effective methods for treating cavities have again made oral health a public health priority. However, the number of dentists has not grown in recent years to keep up with the growing population. In addition, dental care for those without the resources to pay for it is often inadequate and inaccessible. Thus, a new approach is needed to bringing dental care to those in need. Perhaps a new strategy of COPH can make this happen.

Community-oriented public health can reach beyond the institutional and geographical constraints that COPC faces when based in a community health center or other institutions serving a geographically defined population or community. COPH as a governmentally led effort allows a greater range of options for intervention includes those that require changes in laws, incentives and governmental procedures. These might include: authorizing new types of clinicians, providing services in nontraditional settings such as schools, funding innovations to put new technologies into practice, and addressing the regulatory barriers to rapid and cost-effective delivery of services.

public health cannot be viewed only in its current form. Understanding public health also requires considering its future and how we can plan for the expected and the unexpected. Let us take a look at the role of public health in planning for the future in Chapter 13.

Key Words

- Core public health functions
- Assessment
- Assurance
- Policy development
- Ten essential public health services
- Home rule authority
- Healthcare safety net
- Community-oriented primary care (COPC)
- Community-oriented public health (COPH)

Discussion Questions

Take a look at the questions posed in the following scenarios which were presented at the beginning of this chapter. See now whether you can answer them.

1. *A young man in your dormitory is diagnosed with tuberculosis. The health department works with the student health service to test everyone in the dorm, as well as in his classes, with a TB skin test. Those who are positive for the first time are advised to take a course of a medicine called INH. You ask: is this standard operating procedure?*

2. *You go to a public health meeting and learn that many of the speakers are not from public health agencies, but from the Departments of Labor, Commerce, Housing, and Education. You ask: what do these departments have to do with health?*

3. *You hear that a new childhood vaccine was developed by the NIH, approved by the FDA, endorsed for federal payment by the CDC and recommended for use by the American Academy of Pediatrics. You ask: do all these agencies and organizations always work so well together?*

4. *A major flood in Asia leads to disease and starvation. Some say it is due to global warming, others to bad luck. Coordinated efforts by global health agencies, assisted by nongovernmental organizations (NGOs) and outside governmental donors, help get the country back on its feet. You ask: what types of cooperation are needed to make all of this happen?*

5. *A local community health center identifies childhood obesity as a problem in their community. They collect data demonstrating that the problem begins as early as elementary school. They develop a plan that includes clinical interventions at the health center and also at the elementary school. They ask the health department to*

help them organize an educational campaign and assist i evaluating the results. Working together, they are able to redu the obesity rate among elementary school children by on half. This seems like a new way to practice public health, yo conclude. What type of approach is this?

REFERENCES

1. Public Health in America. Essential Public Health Services. Availab at: http://www.health.gov/phfunctions/public.htm. Accessed April 3, 2009.

2. Institute of Medicine. *The Future of Public Health.* Washington, D National Academies Press; 1988.

3. Turnock BJ. *Public Health: What It Is and How It Works.* 4th e Sudbury, MA: Jones and Bartlett Publishers; 2009.

4. Turnock BJ. *Essentials of Public Health.* Sudbury, MA: Jones an Bartlett Publishers; 2007.

5. United States Department of Health and Human Services. Organiz tional Chart. Available at: http://www.hhs.gov/about/orgchart/. Accessed Ap 3, 2009.

6. Centers for Disease Control and Prevention. History of CD *Morbidity and Mortality Weekly Report.* 1996;45: 526–528.

7. World Health Organization. About WHO. Available at: http://ww who.int/about/en/. Accessed April 3, 2009.

8. The World Bank. Health, Nutrition and Population. Available http://web.worldbank.org/WBSITE/EXTERNAL/TOPICS/EXTHEALT NUTRITIONANDPOPULATION/0,,menuPK:282516~pagePK:149018~pi :149093~theSitePK:282511,00.html. Accessed April 3, 2009.

9. Duffin J, Sweetman A. *SARS in Context: Memory, History, Poli* Montreal: McGill-Queen's University Press; 2006.

10. Institute of Medicine. Initial Guidance for an Update of the Natior Vaccine Plan: A Letter Report to the National Vaccine Program Office. Availab at: http://www.nap.edu/catalog/12257.html. Accessed April 3, 2009.

11. District of Columbia Area Health Education Center. The Conceptu Framework for COPC. Available at: http://dcahec.gwumc.edu/educatio session4/index.html. Accessed April 3, 2009.

12. Pfizer Global Pharmaceuticals. *Milestones in Public Health: Accor plishments in Public Health over the Last 100 Years.* New York: Pfizer Glob Pharmaceuticals; 2006.

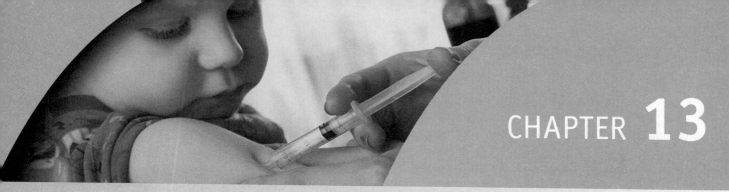

CHAPTER 13

The Future of Population Health

LEARNING OBJECTIVES

By the end of this chapter, the student will be able to:

- explain the basic uses of outbreak investigations.
- identify public health roles in disaster prevention and management.
- explain the basic public health roles in preventing and responding to bioterrorism.
- identify lessons for the future that can be learned from past public health mistakes.
- identify trends in public health that may have implications for the future.
- identify possible impacts of climate change.
- explain how principles of systems thinking can be used to address complex problems.
- explain the importance of an educated citizenry to the future of public health.

It is 2015 and you are working at a large organization with its own cafeteria where most employees eat lunch. An outbreak of an acute diarrhea occurs among your coworkers who eat there. The company calls in the local health department. To your surprise, they cannot identify a known cause and request help from the CDC's Epidemic Intelligence Service (EIS). You are quite impressed when the EIS detects a never-before-recognized strain of toxin-producing E.coli and sends out a worldwide alert. You wonder: could this be a bioterrorism attack or just a routine outbreak? The "all-hazards" team assures you that this is just routine and that we're making progress. Now that a systems approach is in place, only 10 percent of Americans suffers foodborne illnesses each year. Back in the early 21st century, it was closer to 25 percent.

It is 2025 and the worst predictions about infectious disease have come true. It seems like every day there is a new outbreak of drug-resistant infections. New technology has allowed us to get the word out instantly and mount rapid campaigns to control infections and develop vaccines to protect those at greatest risk. Clean water is increasingly scarce and infectious disease outbreaks are emerging throughout the world as nations compete for the remaining sources of clean water. You worry about your child who is about to be born into a new world of emerging infections.

It is 2035 and you are now middle-aged. The epidemic of obesity has reached your waistline—on top of that, you have high cholesterol, high blood sugar, and high blood pressure. Fortunately, cigarettes are history, but heart disease and strokes are making a comeback as the number one killers. It seems like everyone is having surgery to treat their obesity and look better, but you wonder if there just might be a better approach. In other ways, the world is beginning to come to grips with problems including the pressures of population growth and environmental deterioration. You begin to see hope for the future.

It is 2055 and at this point in your life, you thought you'd be getting ready for retirement. Now, you look ahead to working until you are 75 or maybe 80. Life expectancy at birth is now approaching 90, so the retirement age is going up, too. You're delighted that people are living longer, but you still hope that a cure for Alzheimer's will come along soon. It seems like people are living longer, but are they living better? The world has agreed to put a limit on what it spends for medical care on those over 85 and instead invests in new technology to deal with climate change.

It is 2076 and you are about to celebrate the 300th birthday of the United States. There is a lot to celebrate. Economic progress has spread throughout the world and the population health approach has greatly improved the quality, as well as the quantity, of life. Technology has produced a cure for Alzheimer's and many other diseases. Climate change turned out to be a real challenge, but the global cooperation that it produced has had positive side effects. HIV/AIDS is still with us, but we have learned how to effectively prevent its spread and it no longer needs to shorten how long people live. New challenges continue to face you as you look ahead. However, now that there is a health system that uses a systems thinking approach and an educated citizenry that understands public health problems and approaches, you are confident about the future.

All of these issues illustrate the roles of public health in preparing for and planning for the future. Let us start by taking a look at current and emerging efforts to deal with outbreaks of disease, as well as crises and disasters. Then we will examine how we can learn from the past to help us plan for the future. Finally, we will take a look at some approaches that should help us address the inevitable health crises we will face in coming years.

WHAT IS PUBLIC HEALTH'S ROLE IN ADDRESSING OUTBREAKS OF DISEASE?

Public health's role in emergencies and disasters has roots in responses to epidemics of infectious disease. In recent decades, perhaps the most visible role of public health agencies has been in outbreak investigations. The image of public health professionals, sometimes called "disease detectives," working in the field in big cities, as well as remote areas of the United States and around the world, has become a positive image often featured on television and in films. Box 13-1 discusses some of the successes health departments and the CDC have had in outbreak investigations.[1]

HOW ARE PUBLIC HEALTH AGENCIES INVOLVED IN PROTECTING AGAINST TERRORISM AND BIOTERRORISM?

Public health surveillance and investigation of outbreaks were well established as key public health functions well before the September 11, 2001 terrorism attacks and the subsequent anthrax bioterrorism episode. These events, however, had a major impact on the role of public health in society. Box 13-2 reviews the anthrax case and describes its impact on public health.[2]

BOX 13-1 Outbreak Investigations.

Outbreak investigations have been a key component of public health's effort to respond to epidemics and clusters of acute disease. These investigations are often successfully handled by local and state health agencies. The Centers for Disease Control (CDC), however, may be called in to assist with them. The CDC is involved in hundreds of outbreak investigations each year.

Famous investigations include the 1976 outbreak of what came to be called Legionnaires' disease. Hundred of military veterans, called Legionnaires, gathering in Philadelphia in July to celebrate the nation's bicentennial, were infected and many died from pneumonia. The CDC identified the cause as a previously-unrecognized bacteria—now called Legionella—that can grow in hot water and can be spread through the air. In the early 1980s, an outbreak of life-threatening cardiovascular shock, known as toxic shock syndrome (TSS), was traced to a new type of absorbent tampon. It brought to light the need for surveillance of new products, even those not suspected of causing disease. The most important outbreak of the late 20th century was investigated and brought to professional and public attention in 1981 by the CDC. It came to be called acquired immunodeficiency syndrome (AIDS).

Outbreak investigations are not limited to communicable diseases. In fact, the illnesses may originate, for example, from an environmental toxin, a food additive or supplement, or a drug reaction. For instance, eosinophilia-myalgia syndrome (EMS) is an incurable and sometimes fatal neurological condition that often presents with vague flu-like symptoms. It was traced by the CDC to poorly-produced L-trytophan, an amino acid widely used as a food supplement. Reye's syndrome, an often fatal acute liver disease of children, was traced to the use of "baby aspirin" for healthy children during acute viral infections.

Over 1000 outbreak investigations are conducted in the United States each year and are mostly handled by state and local health departments. These types of investigations can take months or even years to complete. Often the outbreak is over before the investigation can be completed. Outbreak investigations will remain an important part of public health. However, new technologies, new tracking systems, and better communications systems, will hopefully make these critical investigations more rapid and efficient. In addition, new forms of investigation are being developed to address the issues of terrorism and bioterrorism.

BOX 13-2 Bioterrorism.

Shortly after the terrorism attack on the United States on September 11, 2001, a second attack occurred which greatly altered the course of public health in the country. The attack occurred in the form of letters containing a powdered form of anthrax bacteria delivered through the U.S. mail to Congress and national news networks.

Anthrax is a bacteria long known for its occasional spread from cattle to humans by close contact and its potential to cause a life-threatening pneumonia. It is considered a particularly deadly agent for bioterrorism with the potential to kill tens of thousand of people. When prepared in the form of a weapon and delivered in quantity, it has the potential to widely disperse over an entire city or region. Early detection of the substance and treatment of its effects are key to controlling such an attack, including preventing the pneumonia through the early use of antibiotics.

The anthrax attack in 2001 made headlines for weeks temporarily shutting down Congress and much of Washington, killing five people and causing severe illness in 17 others. The episode also brought attention and funding to public health programs. It was soon recognized that even large health departments with extensive responsibilities and expertise were not prepared to address bioterrorism and ensure availability of public health laboratories to diagnose anthrax-related illness and other potential agents of bioterrorism.

Preparation for bioterrorism also focuses on the unique characteristics of bioterrorism and the specific organisms that may be involved with it. The anthrax episode highlighted how terrorism, in general, and bioterrorism, in particular, differ from the types of emergencies and disasters that have become familiar. First, they may involve the military, as well as law enforcement. Second, they require knowledge of agents that are often very rare. Little expertise exists in either the public health or medical communities about agents such as anthrax, botulism, smallpox, and plague. In addition, bioterrorism may not be easily detected, allowing the agent to spread widely before it is noticed and action can be taken. Finally, there is the potential for multiple simultaneous threats at multiple locations. Thus, bioterrorism requires special preparation above and beyond the evolving preparedness system for emergencies and disasters. Public health agencies, including the CDC and local health departments, were on the front lines of the anthrax attack and will continue to be part of the first response to bioterrorism attacks if they occur in the future.

In recent years, public health agencies have been increasingly integrated into a National Incident Management System (NIMS), which is part of the Department of Homeland Security (DHS).[3] A central feature of the NIMS is an incident command system (ICS), widely used by police, fire, and emergency management agencies. The ICS attempts to establish uniform procedures and terminology, and an integrated communications system with established and practiced roles for each agency. The goal is to integrate these approaches into ongoing operations and not reserve them solely for emergency situations. The DHS has established a color-coded hierarchy of response levels with corresponding increasing public health agency responsibility at each of these levels. These levels are:

Green—low
Blue—guarded
Yellow—elevated
Orange—high
Red—severe threat

Public health agencies have specific roles to play at each level of the process. When levels are orange and red, public health agencies' responsibilities include: active surveillance for disease and disease agents; organization of systems for triaging patients to hospitals and other healthcare facilities; and key roles in accurate and timely communication of information on hazards to the public.

The DHS has developed what is called an **all-hazards approach**. An all-hazards approach to public health preparedness uses the same approach to preparing for many types of disasters, including use of surveillance systems, communications systems, evacuations, and an organized healthcare response. The all-hazards approach has been widely endorsed by public health agencies and organizations in part at least because it recognizes the need for basic public health infrastructure to respond, not only to the dramatic crisis or emergency, but to day-to-day needs as well.

Preparing for and responding to emergencies and disasters is key to addressing the expected and unexpected crises that we will inevitably face in the future. Preparing for the future also requires that we learn from the past. We will therefore examine approaches that look at history in order to plan for the future.

The first approach looks at past mistakes to derive principles we can use in planning for the future. The second looks at past trends and uses them to better understand the problems that we can expect to face in the future. Finally, we will take a look at the approach known as systems thinking that focuses on how to connect the components of the healthcare system and the public health system to make for a more effective and efficient overall health system.

WHAT CAN WE LEARN FROM THE MISTAKES OF THE PAST?

Some of the most important lessons for the future come from learning from past mistakes. Learning from hindsight is easier than having foresight, but looking back can help us learn from our past mistakes. Let us take a look at some examples.

Avoid Implementing Interventions When Preparation Is Enough

In 1976, public health authorities moved rapidly to vaccinate the entire U.S. population against what was called the swine flu. They feared that a handful of new influenza cases contracted from pigs resembled the influenza of 1918 that caused over 40 million deaths worldwide. Unfortunately, the swine flu vaccine was associated with an unexpected number of cases of Guillain-Barré syndrome, a rapidly progressive potentially life-threatening neurological condition. Despite the early termination of the swine flu campaign, the disease never spread from human to human. Today we recognize that person-to-person spread needs to be established and the ease of transmission measured in order to assess the epidemic potential of influenza and other potential threats.

Another episode of acting rather than preparing occurred after 9/11 and the subsequent bioterrorism scare. The federal government developed and rapidly implemented a campaign to vaccinate healthcare providers and other first responders using the original smallpox vaccine. The vaccine produced a large number of side effects, including life-threatening effects on the heart. The campaign was ended before it moved into full-scale implementation. In retrospect, it was recognized that the smallpox vaccine has long been known to cause severe side effects, especially in adults. Preparation and research is often better than large scale interventions. We have hopefully learned from incidences like these to extensively prepare and carefully act.

Interventions Routinely Used on Large Numbers of People Need to Be Especially Safe

In the 1960s and 1970s, the widespread use of an intrauterine device to prevent pregnancies known as the Dalkon Shield caused a large number of cases of fallopian tube infections, infertility, as well as pregnancies in the fallopian tubes called ectopic pregnancies. This led to the regulation of medical devices by the FDA.

Estrogen therapy was widely used in the late 20th century for women beginning menopause. The treatment seemed to make sense as a replacement for the declining level of estrogen that occurs at this time in a woman's life. It took the Women's Health Study, a large randomized clinical trial, to demonstrate the risks of postmenopausal estrogen on the heart, as well as the increased risk of breast cancer.

While we often cannot anticipate adverse effects of interventions, we need to have a system to detect and address side effects, especially when they are used on large numbers of people. Safety cannot be guaranteed by biological plausibility or even by long-term use.

Control of a Disease Is Often Possible; Elimination Is Rarely Realistic

As we have seen, elimination of a disease requires special conditions and a concerted global effort. Putting forth a campaign to eliminate a disease when these conditions are not present can do more harm than good. In the 1950s, the World Health Organization set out to eliminate malaria, only to have it rebound in recent years. More recently, the United States proclaimed an intention to eliminate tuberculosis, an equally unattainable goal, before eventually turning attention to controlling increasingly resistant strains. Based upon what we know, it is important not to talk about the "end of AIDS," which seems well beyond reality at least for the immediate future. In addition to learning from the mistakes of the past, there is much to learn from the trends of the past.

WHAT CAN WE LEARN FROM PAST TRENDS?

A number of trends in the pattern of disease have been described in recent years that have implications for what we can expect to happen throughout the 21st century. We will call these the demographic, epidemiological, and nutritional transitions.

The **demographic transition** describes the impact of falling childhood death rates and extended life spans on the size and the age distribution of populations.[4] During the first half of the 20th century, the death rates among the young fell dramatically in today's developed countries. Death rates continued their dramatic decline in most parts of the developing world during the second half of the 20th century.

Birth rates tend to remain high for years or decades after the decline in deaths. High birth rates paired with lower death rates lead to rapid growth in population size, as we have seen in much of the developing world. This trend continues today and is expected to go on in many parts of the world well into the 21st century. Figure 13-1 illustrates how the population of the Nigeria is expected to grow during the first half of the 21st century due to a high birth rate and a lowered death rate.

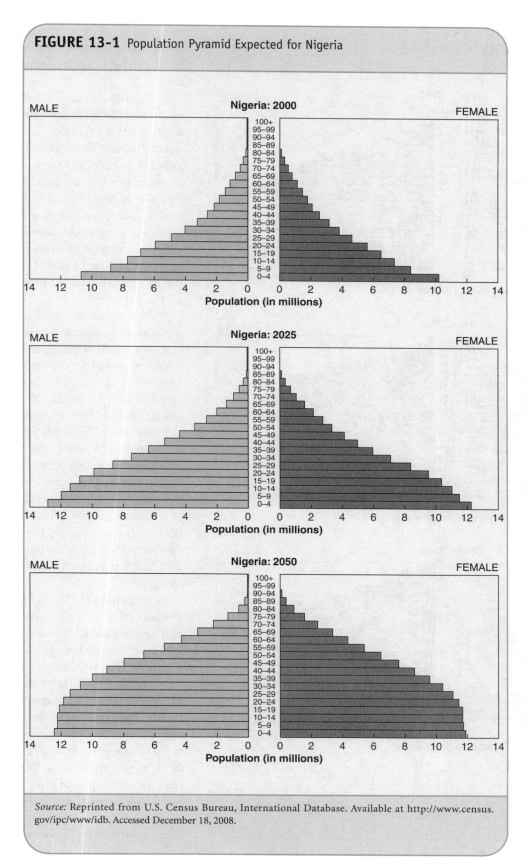

FIGURE 13-1 Population Pyramid Expected for Nigeria

Source: Reprinted from U.S. Census Bureau, International Database. Available at http://www.census.gov/ipc/www/idb. Accessed December 18, 2008.

Despite the delay, a decline in birth rates reliably occurs following the decline in childhood deaths. This decline in births gradually leads to aging of the population. We are now seeing societies in much of Europe and Japan with growing elderly populations. Improved health care and extended life spans for the elderly has magnified this trend. Take a look at Figure 13-2, which shows what is expected to occur in the coming years in much of Europe and Japan. Japan is used as an example of the emergence of an inverted population pyramid with a smaller young population and a larger older population.

The large number of immigrants to the United States and their generally higher birth rates has slowed this process in the United States, but the basic trend of a growing elderly population continues. The U.S. baby boom, which occurred between 1946 and 1964, is expected to have major impacts on the numbers of elderly in coming years, as illustrated in Figure 13-3.

As we saw in Section III, a second transition has been called the **epidemiologic transition**,[5] or public health transition. The epidemiologic or public health transition implies that as social and economic development occurs, different types of diseases become prominent. Deaths in less-developed societies are often dominated by epidemic communicable diseases and diseases associated with malnutrition and childhood infections. As a country develops, communicable diseases often come under

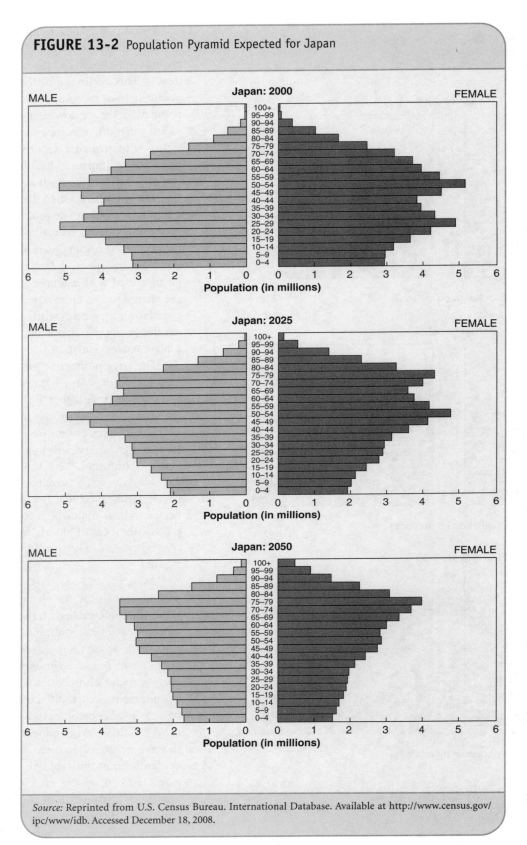

FIGURE 13-2 Population Pyramid Expected for Japan

Source: Reprinted from U.S. Census Bureau. International Database. Available at http://www.census.gov/ipc/www/idb. Accessed December 18, 2008.

control and non-communicable and chronic diseases, such as heart disease often predominate.

A related transition known as the **nutritional transition**[6] implies that countries frequently move from poorly balanced diets often deficient in nutrients, proteins, and calories to a diet of highly-processed food including fats, sugars, and salt. The consequences of both under- and overnutrition affect and will continue to affect the public's health well into the 21st century.

These trends can help us understand the great disparities that exist among countries and within countries in the early years of the 21st century. They can also help us predict the changes that are likely to occur in future years. Preparing for these predictable changes is a critical goal for public health in the 21st century. One clear trend that is likely to affect the health of everyone is the effect of climate change. Box 13-3 outlines some of the likely and possible health impacts of climate change.[7, 8]

Throughout *Public Health 101* we have used the population health approach to examine how traditional public health, health care, and social interventions can all contribute to improvements in the public's health. The key to our future successes may be knowing how to put these approaches together in the most effective and efficient ways. An approach to putting the pieces together, that we have called systems thinking, has great promise for the future.

FIGURE 13-3 Population Pyramid Expected for the United States

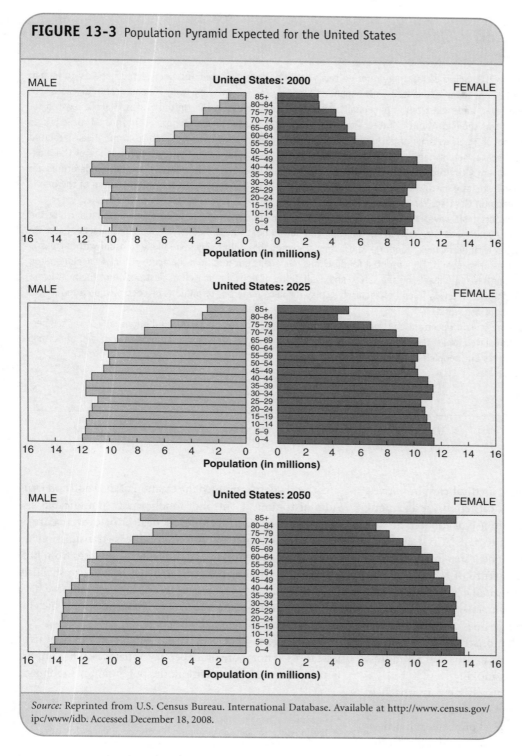

Source: Reprinted from U.S. Census Bureau. International Database. Available at http://www.census.gov/ipc/www/idb. Accessed December 18, 2008.

WHAT IS SYSTEMS THINKING AND HOW CAN IT IMPROVE PUBLIC HEALTH EFFORTS?

Systems thinking is a comprehensive strategy for thinking about a problem as part of an interrelated network or sys-

tem. In health, systems thinking is increasingly used to integrate public health and healthcare systems into an integrated health system. System thinking focuses on identifying **leverage points** or points in the system at which to intervene. It also looks at how to combine interventions to maximize their effectiveness and efficiency.[9]

The systems-thinking approach contrasts with traditional approaches that study problems by breaking them down into their separate elements. Systems thinking focuses on the connections between problems and the impacts of multiple interventions at key leverage or control points.

To begin to understand systems thinking, let us go back to where we began with a look at the problems of cigarette smoking and health. We will then look at an even more complex problem, the issue of food safety, and see how system-thinking approaches can help. We have seen that tobacco control efforts have been responsible for a reduction in tobacco use of approximately 50 percent compared to the 1950s. Nonetheless, tobacco remains the number one cause of preventable death. Recently, the National Cancer Institute (NCI) and the Institute of Medicine (IOM) have looked at tobacco control efforts and concluded: "We are long past the time that tobacco use is purely a matter of individual choice and its control dependent on a strategy of one-person-at-a-time. Tax policy, school interventions, clean indoor air regulations, agricultural

---

BOX 13-3   Climate Change.

Global warming, or climate change as it is being increasingly referred to, is likely to have expected and unexpected impacts on human health. The most predictable changes are those associated with expanded territory for currently existing communicable diseases. For instance, cases of malaria, dengue fever, and insect-borne encephalitis are likely to increase in the United States. Malaria existed for many years in the country as far north as the Mid-Atlantic states. The mosquitoes that transmit malaria are present in the United States and the disease could readily reestablish itself as a major pathogen. Dengue, or "breakbone fever" is a mosquito-borne disease related to yellow fever. One strain of the disease, hemorrhagic dengue fever, has a high case-fatality rate. The geographic range of the mosquito that carries dengue fever is currently limited because frost kills both the adult insects and their larvae. Rising temperatures are expected to allow the disease to move steadily northward in future decades. Outbreaks of acute encephalitis (inflammation of the brain) transmitted by mosquitoes are already on the rise. We can expect to see more frequent and severe outbreaks in the future.

In addition, more frequent and intense heat waves are likely to occur, especially in currently temperate climates covering much of the United States. Deaths among the very young and the very old can be expected during heat waves. Additional possible impacts of climate change on health are those associated with hurricanes, flooding, forest fires, and drought—all of which are likely to occur with increased frequency and severity in specific areas of the world. The potential for hurricane damage is not just from the acute storm. As demonstrated by Hurricane Katrina, there can be long-lasting impacts on the safety and availability of housing, as well as destruction of the healthcare and public health infrastructure. Rising ocean levels in and of themselves may displace hundreds of millions of people who currently live in low-lying river delta areas throughout the world.

The exact impacts of climate change remain uncertain and controversial. Alterations in ocean currents could potentially lower temperatures in Europe and other highly-populated areas. Despite the great uncertainties ahead, it is clear that climate change will affect not only the lives of today's college students but people's lives for centuries to come.

---

initiatives, advertising campaigns, medical care initiatives, community mobilization, and political action, are all among the elements at work to reduce the use of tobacco among Americans." NCI and IOM go on to say: "A systems-level focus on tobacco control is a logical next step in understanding and managing the complex nature of tobacco use, as both an epidemiological and a personal health issue."[10] Box 13-4 outlines a number of key principles that distinguish systems thinking from a traditional one issue at a time **reductionist approach**. It also demonstrates how systems thinking leads to new and different approaches to address health problems, such as cigarette smoking.

Thinking in systems is a relatively new approach in public health though it has already become a "crosscutting competency" expected of master's level public health professionals who pursue certification.[11] Systems thinking is often useful for the most challenging public health issues. One such issue is food safety.

Food safety is not a new issue in public health; it has a long history. Early 20th-century public health efforts to ad-

dress food safety prompted the creation of the Food and Drug Administration.[a] Control of foodborne communicable diseases has been central to public health for over a century. Knowledge of causes and patterns of disease transmission has led to successful efforts to control specific diseases from botulism due to canning processes to hepatitis A due to shellfish. Despite these successes, it has become apparent that we have much to learn about the spread of foodborne disease, which increasingly crosses national borders.

Food affects all of us every day—in fact, for most of us at least three, if not more times per day. What we eat has important implications for nutrition, the potential for foodborne

---

[a] As we saw in Chapter 1, the case of Typhoid Mary came to symbolize public health efforts to control communicable disease in the early years of the 20th century. Typhoid Mary was a chronic carrier of typhoid who transmitted the disease as she moved from restaurant to restaurant serving food to a large number of unsuspecting customers. Typhoid Mary, despite being a chronic carrier, remained in good health. A widely-publicized legal action eventually resulted in her being quarantined on a New York City island to prevent her from continuing to spread typhoid.

BOX 13-4 Systems Thinking versus Reductionist Thinking and Cigarette Smoking.

The work of the National Cancer Institute and the Institute of Medicine on tobacco control encourages a systems-thinking approach. Systems thinking is more easily understood by contrasting it with the traditional approach, which has been called the **reductionist approach**. The following three concepts are key to understanding the differences between systems thinking and reductionist thinking:

1. *One intervention at a time versus multiple simultaneous interventions*

   A reductionist approach attempts to look at one factor or intervention at a time. An intervention, such as a smoking cessation program, might be investigated to determine whether it works when used alone. Rather than looking at one intervention at a time, systems thinking asks about the best combination of interventions. Systems thinking might identify smoking cessation programs, social marketing, and higher taxes as three important compatible interventions that need to be effectively and efficiently combined.

2. *Straight-line or linear projections versus measuring complex interactions*

   A reductionist approach usually assumes a straight-line or linear relationship implying that increased levels of an intervention, such as increasing taxes on tobacco, will produce a straight-line decrease in the levels of tobacco use. However, it is possible that small increases in taxes have little effect, while slightly larger increases have dramatic effects. In addition, reductionist approaches do not look at how the impact of one intervention may be affected by connecting it with other interventions, whereas systems thinking looks at these interactions. Thus, systems thinking would ask questions about how to most effectively utilize cigarette taxes by combining them with other approaches, such as using the taxes to support tobacco education programs, or reduce exposure to radon, asbestos, or other causes of lung cancer.

3. *One-point-in-time or static analysis versus a changing or dynamic analysis*

   Reductionist approaches look at the relationships at one point in time. That is, they use **static models** and do not take into account changes that often occur over time. For instance, they would not look at how changes over time in social attitudes may alter the effectiveness of tobacco cessation programs or set the stage for enforcement of public smoking regulations or increased tobacco taxes. Rather than seeing interventions as static or at one point in time, systems thinking develops **dynamic models** that look at the feedback process, the changes that occur over time, and bottlenecks that slow down change. For instance, systems thinking might identify a need to train large numbers of clinicians in smoking cessation methods so that they can address the demand for smoking cessation services created by social marketing, increased cigarette taxes, and better drug treatments.

disease, and has become an effective vehicle for implementing public health interventions.[b]

Today, our food comes from all parts of the world, many times going through multiple levels of processing to create prepared food, and is often stored for long periods of time before reaching our dinner plate. The World Health Organization estimates that approximately 1.8 million people die worldwide from foodborne disease each year.[12] In the United States, the CDC estimates that the number is approximately 5000 per year. However, hospitalizations are estimated at over 300,000 per year, making it a major cause of disability.[13 c]

The complexity of issues related to food and food safety has resulted in a complicated mix of local/state, federal and global agencies involvement. Table 13–1 outlines many of the agencies involved and suggests the need for a great deal of coordination to successfully achieve food safety.

Because of the inherent complexity of the problems of food safety and the large number of organizations involved at every level, systems-thinking approaches are key to food safety.

---

[b]Supplementation of food with vitamins and minerals has been an effective method for addressing specific disease. The addition of iodine to salt beginning in the 1920s is credited worldwide with a dramatic reduction in goiters (enlargements of the thyroid). Supplementation of milk with vitamin D greatly reduced the incidence of rickets, a deforming bone disease of children.

[c] Supplementation of bread with niacin dramatically reduced pellagra, a disease characterized by the 4 Ds: dermatitis, diarrhea, dementia, and death. Most recently, the addition of folic acid to a variety of products generally consumed by pregnant women is credited with a nearly 50 percent reduction in spina bifida, a birth defect in which the spinal column fails to fuse.

TABLE 13-1 Levels of Public Health Coordination Needed for Successful Food Safety

Level	Organizations involved	Roles
Global	The Food and Agriculture Organization of the United Nations (FAO)	The United Nations agency with overall responsibility for the food supply with special emphasis on ensuring an adequate supply of food worldwide
	The World Health Organization (WHO)	Not a regulatory agency, but establishes policy and makes recommendations regarding the safety of the world food supply through its Food Safety Department (FOS)
	The Codex Alimentarius Commission (CAC)	Initiated as a joint program of FAO and WHO that develops food standards, guidelines, and codes of practice. These now form the basis for the rules of global trade under the jurisdiction of the World Trade Organization (WTO)
Federal	The United States Food and Drug Administration (FDA)	Overall regulatory responsibility for food safety regulation in the United States
	The United States Department of Agriculture (USDA)	Regulatory responsibilities for meat, poultry, and eggs in the United States
	The United States Environmental Protection Agency (EPA)	Regulation of pesticide usage and the establishment of water quality standards
	The Centers for Disease Control and Prevention (CDC)	Not a regulatory agency, but responsible for ongoing surveillance, as well as acute investigations in collaboration with state and local health department
State/Local	State and local health departments	Restaurant inspections
Consumer	Consumer protection agencies	Education in safe food purchasing, preparation, and storage

Source: Awofeso N. What's new about the "New Public Health"? *American Journal of Public Health.* 2004;94(5): 705–709.

HOW CAN SYSTEMS-THINKING APPROACHES BE APPLIED TO FOOD SAFETY?

Two basic systems-thinking approaches to food safety have been put forward in recent years. In the first strategy the focus is on one type of food at a time. This process has been called the Hazard Analysis and Critical Control Point (HACCP) system.[14, 15] In a second systems-thinking approach, the food's detailed location and time of production down to the level of the farm or factory is identified on the label, allowing officials to trace the food back to where and when the problem occurred. Putting these two approaches together is now seen as

key to a successful systems approach. Let us take a look at these two approaches.

HACCP is a systems approach that looks for key leverage or control points to manage food safety issues. It is built upon a series of prerequisite conditions designed to first ensure basic environmental and operating conditions. These include: facilities that maintain sanitary conditions; proper equipment construction, installation, and maintenance; personal hygiene by employees, etc.

Once these basic conditions of food safety are accomplished, HACCP looks for options for interventions at multiple leverage or control points and institutes a series of safeguards at these specific points, as illustrated for ground beef in Box 13-5.

Knowing the type of food that causes an outbreak is not enough if we do not know where the food came from and cannot trace it back to the point of contamination. This became clear in an often fatal U.S. outbreak of salmonella from peppers coming from Mexico because there was delay in resolving the cause of the outbreak and tracing the product across national boundaries.[16] It is key to an effective and efficient systems approach to be able to rapidly trace the source of contamination to avoid shutting down whole industries to solve the problem caused by a single source. Efforts are underway to label foods to be able to identify and trace their origins. This tracking system can then draw upon the data collected as part of the HACCP system. Putting these two strategies together should allow public health officials to more quickly and reliably respond to foodborne disease that occurs often thousands of miles from the source of the food.

Protection against foodborne communicable disease is an ongoing daily public health challenge that is not about to go away. Systems thinking is now a well-established approach to control this rapidly changing and challenging problem.

BOX 13-5 Foodborne Communicable Diseases and Systems Thinking.

The systems approach known as Hazard Analysis of Critical Control Points (HACCP) attempts to understand, monitor, and quickly respond to breakdowns in the food safety system. This methodology, originally developed for the U.S. space program, requires that food be monitored from the field to the consumer. HACCP is increasingly being adopted for such products as seafood, meat, poultry, and fruit juices. HACCP includes the following seven steps:

- **Analyze hazards.** Potential hazards associated with a food and potential interventions to control those hazards are identified. The hazard could be biological, such as a microbe; chemical, such as a toxin; or physical, such as ground glass or metal fragments.
- **Identify critical control points.** These are points in a food's production—from its raw state through processing and shipping to consumption by the consumer—at which the potential hazard can be controlled or eliminated. Examples are: cooking, cooling, packaging, and metal detection.
- **Establish preventive measures with critical limits for each control point.** For a cooked food, for example, this might include setting the minimum cooking temperature and time required to ensure the elimination of any harmful microbes.
- **Establish procedures to monitor the critical control points.** Such procedures might include determining how and by whom cooking time and temperature should be monitored.
- **Establish corrective actions to be taken when monitoring shows that a critical limit has not been met.** For example, reprocessing or disposing of food if the minimum cooking temperature is not met.
- **Establish procedures to verify that the system is working properly.** For example, testing time- and temperature-recording devices to verify that a cooking unit is working properly.
- **Establish effective recordkeeping to document the HACCP system.** This would include records of hazards and their control methods, the monitoring of safety requirements, and actions taken to correct potential problems. Each of these principles must be backed by sound scientific knowledge—for example, published microbiological studies on time and temperature factors for controlling foodborne pathogens.

Meat safety issues reflect this approach. Toxin-producing strains of E. coli are widespread in beef products and have been responsible for a number of fatal outbreaks of foodborne illness. The threats to health have led to a more coordinated systems-thinking approach using the HACCP system. Ground beef, which combines meat often leftover from multiple animals, has been identified as a high-risk product or potential hazard. Key control points at which ground beef may be contaminated in the meatpacking process have been identified. Monitoring by testing includes a random testing process on all batches of ground beef. The process uses rapid testing of a sample of the finished ground beef and holding up distribution until the results are available.

These are among the efforts to identify control points, establish interventions at these leverage points, and implement corrective actions to address the potential hazards of contaminated ground beef. This systems approach has already reduced the frequency and severity of outbreaks of life-threatening disease from toxigenic E. coli.

In *Public Health 101*, we have examined the population health approach to public health. We have viewed population health as putting together individual, at-risk group, and population approaches to address public health problems using an evidence-based approach. We have seen that the key to successful population health approaches in the future requires a systems-thinking approach combining these types of strategies to maximize the efficiency and effectiveness of our health system.[d]

Seeing the big picture and finding the most effective and efficient combination of interventions using a systems-thinking approach is key to the future of public health. Perhaps at least as important to the future of public health is the active engagement of an educated citizenry that understands what is meant by public health and supports its methods and interventions.

HOW CAN AN EDUCATED CITIZENRY MAKE THE 21ST CENTURY DIFFERENT FOR THE PUBLIC'S HEALTH?

The history of American public health is a history of crisis and response. From the yellow fever and cholera epidemics of the colonial period that produced the first Boards of Health, to the food and drug safety scares that produced the Food and Drug Administration to the terrorism of 9/11 and anthrax, we have repeatedly responded rapidly to crises with new funding, new structures, and new energy. Once each of these emergencies passed from the public mind and the media focused elsewhere, it becomes more difficult to support the efforts and implement the programs envisioned in the aftermath of crisis. Public health approaches require sustained attention and big-picture thinking. It requires an educated citizenry.

In 2003, the IOM recommended that all undergraduates have access to education in public health. This recommendation was supported by the contention that "public health is an essential part of the training of citizens."[18] That is, education in public health is important not just for the future health professional, but for all those who will participate in decision making, including all those who vote in local, state, and national elections.

The IOM recommendations lay the groundwork for what has become the Educated Citizen and Public Health movement. This movement aims to develop an educated citizenry that understands public health issues and supports population health approaches for addressing them. *If you have read this book, you are part of the Educated Citizen and Public Health movement.*

---

[d] Systems thinking principles are increasingly being applied to public health using what is called a **syndemic orientation**.[17] A syndemic orientation focuses attention on how specific health problems interact as parts of larger systems. For instance, what are the consequences of the spread of AIDS and the simultaneous spread of tuberculosis? Large-scale public health problems, such as health disparities, may also be better understood by focusing not on one disease or condition at a time, but on the connections among diseases and their relationships to socioeconomic, organizational, and cultural issues.

Key Words

- All-hazards approach
- Demographic transition
- Epidemiologic transition
- Nutritional transition
- Leverage points
- Reductionist approach
- Static models
- Dynamic models
- Syndemic orientation

Discussion Question

Write your own mini-scenarios for what the world of public health will look like in the years 2015, 2025, 2035, 2055, and 2076.

REFERENCES

1. Reingold RL. Outbreak Investigations—A Perspective. Available at: http://www.cdc.gov/ncidod/EID/vol4no1/reingold.htm. Accessed April 3, 2009.

2. Hugh JM, Gerberding JL. Anthrax Bioterrorism: Lessons Learned and Future Directions. Available at: http://www.cdc.gov/ncidod/EID/vol8no10/02-0466.htm. Accessed April 3, 2009.

3. United States Federal Emergency Management Administration. National Incident Management System. Available at: http://www.fema.gov/emergency/nims/. Accessed April 3, 2009.

4. U.S. Census Bureau. International Database. Available at: http://www.census.gov/ipc/www/idb/pyramids.html. Accessed April 3, 2009.

5. Omran AR. The epidemiologic transition: a theory of the epidemiology of population change. *The Milbank Memorial Fund Quarterly.* 1971; 49(4): 509–538.

6. Skolnik R. *Essentials of Global Health.* Sudbury, MA: Jones and Bartlett Publishers; 2008.

7. Sierra Club. Global Warming Impacts: Health Effects. Available at: http://www.sierraclub.org/energy/health/. Accessed December 17, 2008.

8. Science Daily. Global Warming and Your Health. Available at: http://www.sciencedaily.com/releases/2006/10/061023192524.htm. Accessed April 3, 2009.

9. Meadows H. *Thinking in Systems: A Primer.* White River Junction, Vermont: Chelsea Green Publishing; 2008.

10. National Cancer Institute–United States Department of Health and Human Services. *Greater than the Sum: Systems Thinking in Tobacco Control—Executive Summary.* Washington, DC: U.S. Department of Health and Human Services–National Institutes of Health; 2007.

11. Association of Schools of Public Health. MPH Core Competency Development Project. Available at: http://www.asph.org/document.cfm?page=851. Accessed April 3, 2009.

12. World Health Organization. Food Safety. Available at: http://www.who.int/foodsafety/en/. Accessed April 3, 2009.

13. Centers for Disease Control and Prevention. Foodborne Illness. Available at: http://www.cdc.gov/ncidod/dbmd/diseaseinfo/foodborneinfections_g.htm. Accessed April 3, 2009.

14. Hoffmann S. Mending our food safety chain. *Resources.* 2007; 166: 11–15.

15. United States Food and Drug Administration. HACCP: A State-of-the-Art Approach to Food Safety. Available at: http://www.cfsan.fda.gov/~lrd/bghaccp.html. Accessed April 3, 2009.

16. Consumer Reports. Country-of-origin labeling: A shopper's guide. Available at: http://www.consumerreports.org/health/healthy-living/health-safety/country-of-origin-labeling-tool/overview/country-of-origin-labeling-tool-ov.htm. Accessed April 3, 2009.

17. Centers for Disease Control and Prevention. Syndemics Overview—What Principles Characterize a Syndemic Orientation? Available at: http://www.cdc.gov/SYNDEMICS/overview-principles.htm. Accessed April 3, 2009.

18. Gebbie K, Rosenstock L, Hernandez LM, eds. *Who Will Keep the Public Healthy? Educating Public Health Professionals for the 21st Century.* Washington, DC: National Academies Press; 2003: 144.

Section V:
Cases and Discussion Questions

Public Health Departments—
Getting the Lead Out

A series of articles appears in your local newspaper investigating reports of elevated lead levels and reduced academic performance among students in a local grade school. The series ends with an editorial asking: "Where was the health department and what are they going to do now?"

The health department was aware of these reports and had sent a letter to each parent alerting them to the dangers of increased lead levels and letting them know of doctors and local clinics that could follow up and provide treatment through a health department-funded program. The mayor was not satisfied. He asked: "But isn't public health about prevention? How can we prevent this from happening again?" He asks the health department for a full report within a month.

The health department sets out to evaluate the range of potential sources of lead exposure in the community. They find the following contributing factors: a local factory releases fumes that contain lead; local playgrounds are still contaminated by lead from gasoline despite the fact that lead was removed from gasoline well over a decade ago; lead paint in older homes; possible exposure from lead used in water pipes; and lead from painted toys and glazes on homemade pottery. The health department's report to the mayor concluded that prevention of lead exposure requires not just the health department's role, but the cooperation of schools, parks, the environmental protection agency, the water system, the housing agency, as well as local industry and merchants. "We can't do it alone," the report concludes.

"Okay," says the mayor, "it sounds like this is a job for the whole city. I'm issuing an order requiring all city agencies to cooperate with the health department to find the sources of lead and develop a plan to reduce

them." Then, he turns to you, a new health department employee. "Work on this and write me a report by next month, but I want a press release out this afternoon."

1. How does this case reflect the role that the media and effective communications play in public health?
2. How does this case reflect the multiple collaborations that are needed to practice public health effectively?
3. How does this case reflect the relationship between public health agencies and clinicians?
4. How does this case illustrate the inherently political nature of public health?

Community-Oriented Primary Care (COPC)

A community-oriented primary care team was developed in a large Hispanic/Latino community defined by census tracks. The vast majority of the community is employed and over half of the working population receive minimum wage and have no health insurance. There are a large number of immigrants from Central America. Over 25 percent of the community is estimated to be undocumented aliens, most of whom live in crowded conditions. A high percentage of those over 18 are married with an average family size of 5—considerably larger than other communities in the same city. The population of the community is generally younger than surrounding more affluent communities. The vast majority of the community receives its health care at one community clinic.

The community's priority issues according to community residents include tuberculosis (TB), HIV/AIDS, a lack of recreational facilities for children, a lack of dental services, and a lack of Spanish-speaking healthcare professionals. The COPC team, consisting of health professionals, public health experts, a clinical administrator, and members of the community, identified tuberculosis for further study. They found CDC evidence-based guidelines that recommends the following:

- early and accurate detection, diagnosis, and reporting of TB cases leading to initiation and completion of treatment
- identification of contacts of patients with infectious TB and treatment of those at risk with an effective drug regimen

- identification of other persons with latent TB infection at risk for progression to TB disease and treatment of these persons with an effective drug regimen
- identification of settings in which a high risk exists for transmission of *Mycobacterium tuberculosis* and application of effective infection-control measures

To implement these recommendations, risk factors for tuberculosis were identified in the community including: crowded conditions, HIV infections, high numbers of recent immigrants from endemic areas, and poor follow-up of treatment.

The COPC team found data on the estimated prevalence of a positive skin test for TB, the prevalence of active TB, the percentage of HIV-positive patients among those with active TB, and the percentage of active TB patients who completed a full course of treatment. The team recommended interventions for those factors that are most amenable to change including intensive testing and follow-up of HIV-positive patients and special home health assistance to ensure completion of TB treatment.

The team recommended monitoring the percentage of HIV patients who were given tuberculosis skin tests and the percentage of TB patients who completed a full course of treatment. They also recommended measuring the prevalence of active TB before and after the interventions. Finally, they advised working closely with the local health department so that recommended TB follow-up practices are successfully performed. This included making sure that whenever active TB is diagnosed, all those in contact with the individual are offered TB skin testing and preventive treatments if they convert to positive.

1. Identify how the COPC team accomplished each of the six steps in the COPC process.
2. What factors would you consider in selecting a particular condition, such as tuberculosis, for special interventions efforts?
3. Identify one of the community's other priority issues and suggest interventions that you would use for addressing it and assessing, monitoring, and evaluating the impact of your intervention.
4. What are the strengths and limitations of the COPC approach?

Hurricane Karl and the Public Health Success in Old Orleans

Hurricane Karl, a Category 4 hurricane, made landfall last August 29th on the gold coast of the state of Good Fortune. The state was home to the town of Old Orleans, an historical community built below sea level and home to a large community from a range of socioeconomic backgrounds. Old Orleans has a model health department that seeks to provide the ten essential public health services.

Before Hurricane Karl made its impact on the community, preparation for hurricanes had been an ongoing activity of the health department, which worked closely with first responders to ensure safe evacuation and protection from fire and looting. The department also worked with the local TV and radio stations to advise citizens on the purchasing and storing of essential food, water, and first aid supplies. It organized a community-wide emergency care network to ensure that 911 calls were responded to as quickly as possible in the event of a hurricane and worked with local hospitals to ensure that a triage system was in place to allocate patients to available emergency facilities, while not overwhelming any one healthcare institution.

When Hurricane Karl did strike, the damage was more extensive than expected. Leaks in the public sewer system led to water contamination. A local chemical plant experienced a major chemical discharge. Almost 200 residents were stranded in their homes without adequate food. Nearly half of the homes experienced water damage and rapid growth of mold. Many older residents did not have access to their daily medications.

The local health department had prepared for disasters like Hurricane Karl. After testing the water for contamination, supplies of stockpiled bottled water were distributed to homes in the contaminated areas by the National Guard. The police department had purchased specially-equipped vehicles on the recommendation of the health department and were able, with the help of community organizations, to evacuate the stranded residents. The health department also sent out trained teams to diagnose the type and extent of hazards related to chemical contamination. With the help of the emergency radio system and cell phones, all individuals in the contaminated areas were notified and educated about methods for protecting themselves and their children.

Based on the emergency plan, the health department set up temporary healthcare sites and pharmacies staffed by nurses, physicians, and pharmacists who had been certified as emergency responders. The department also worked with representatives of the building industry to test water-exposed homes for mold and provided assistance to minimize the damage.

After the emergency, the health department joined with the local Schools of Public Health and Medicine to evaluate the response to Hurricane Karl and make recommendations for future emergencies. The data on infections, injuries, and deaths, as well as the use of services during the emergency was collected and published. A national network was set up as a result to coordinate efforts for future disasters and learn from the experience in dealing with Hurricane Karl.

1. Which of the ten essential services did the health department of Old Orleans fulfill?
2. What other efforts were needed to accomplish the ten essential public health services?
3. In addition to providing the ten essential public health services, to what extent are efforts required to deal with a disaster such as Hurricane Karl?
4. How does this case illustrate the complementary relationship between public health and medicine. What are the benefits of working together?

Glossary

Absolute risk–The actual chances or probability of developing the disease expressed as a probability such as 0.01 or a percentage such as 1%.

Academic Health Center–An organization that includes a medical school, one or more other health professions schools and an affiliated hospital.

Accreditation–A process applied to educational institutions, healthcare institutions, and proposed for governmental health departments to define and enforce required structures, processes, and outcomes.

Action phase–The fourth phase of the stages of change model in which the change in behavior takes place.

Actual causes of death–Modifiable factors that lead to major causes of mortality.

Administrative law–In the United States the type of law produced by executive agencies of federal, state, and local governments.

Age-adjustment–Taking into account age-distribution of a population when comparing population or when comparing the same population at two different points in time.

Age-distribution–The number of people in each age group in a population.

All hazard approach–An approach to public health preparedness that uses the same approach to preparing for many types of disasters including use of surveillance systems, communica-tions systems, evacuations, and an organized healthcare response.

Antibody–A protein produced by the body in response to a foreign antigen which can bind to the antigen and facilitate its elimination.

Artifactual association–An association observed in the data that is actually the result of the method of data collection.

Artifactual difference or changes–Differences between population or changes in a population over time due to changes in interest in identifying the disease, change in ability to recognize the disease or changes in the definition of the disease.

Assessment–A core public health function that includes obtaining data that defines the health of the overall population and specific groups within the population including defining the nature of new and persisting health problems.

Association–The occurrence together of two factors, such as a risk factor and a disease, more often than expected by chance alone.

Assurance–A core public health function that includes governmental public health's oversight responsibility for ensuring that key components of an effective health system including health care and public health are in place even though the implementation will often be performed by others.

Asymptomatic–Without symptoms. When referring to screening for disease, it implies the absence of symptoms of the disease being sought.

At-risk population–The group of people who have a chance or probability of developing a disease.

Attributable risk percentage–The percentage of the disease or disability that can potentially be eliminated, among those with the factor being investigated, assuming a contributory cause and assuming the impact of the "cause" can be immediately and completely eliminated (*Synonym:* percent efficacy).

Authoritative decision–A decision made by an individual or a group that has the power to implement the decision.

Balance billing–Billing of patients for charges above and beyond those covered by health insurance.

Belmont Report–The commonly used name for a report of The National Commission for the Protection of Human Subjects of Biomedical and Behavioral Research which established key principles upon which the current approach to protection of human subjects is based.

Beneficence–An ethic principle which states that persons are treated in an ethical manner not only by respecting their decisions and protecting them from harm, but also by making efforts to secure their well-being.

Benefits–The positive outcomes that occur with or without an intervention.

BIG GEMS–A mneumonic which summarizes the determinants of disease including behavior, infection, genetics, geography, environment, medical care, and socioeconomic status.

Bioethics–Lies at the intersection of health law and policy and attempts to apply individual and group values and morals to controversial issues.

Biological plausibility–An ancillary or supportive criteria for contributory cause in which the disease can be explained by what is currently known about the biology of the risk factor and the disease.

Block grants–A system of federal funding to states and local jurisdictions that consolidates overall funding for a number of categories. They provide greater flexibility and allow the states to allocate funds to coordinate the delivery of services and to areas of greatest perceived need.

Branding–A marketing concepts for creating identification with a product or service that is also used in social marketing.

Built environment–The physical environment constructed by human beings.

Burden of Disease–Generically an analysis of the morbidity and mortality produced by disease. Often used to refer to the use of DALYs to estimate the burden of morbidity and mortality.

Cap–A limit on the total amount that the insurance will pay for a service per year, per benefit period, or per lifetime.

Capitation–A system of reimbursement for health care based upon a flat payment per time period for each person for whom a provider of care assumes responsibility for providing healthcare services regardless of the services actually provided.

Case-control studies–A study that begins by identifying individuals with a disease and individual without a disease. Those with and without the disease are identified without knowledge of an individual's exposure or non-exposure to the factors being investigated (*Synonym:* retrospective study).

Case-Fatality–The chances of dying from a condition once it is diagnosed.

Case finding–As used in public health an effort to identify and locate contacts of individuals diagnosed with a disease and evaluate them for possible treatment.

Categorical funding–Providing funds for public health program based upon categories such as heart disease, tuberculosis, HIV/ AIDS, maternal and child health.

Cell mediated immunity–Immunological protection that is produced by t-lymphocytes and other white blood cells that combats intracellular pathogens and tumor cells.

Certainty effect–A risk-taking attitude in which the decision maker favors the status quo rather than a probability of obtaining a better or a worse outcome.

Certification–A nongovernmental process designed to ensure competence by individual health professionals based upon completion of educational requirement and performance on an examination or other evaluation procedure.

Cohort study–An investigation that begins by identifying a group that has a factor under investigation and a similar group that does not have the factor. The outcome in each group is then assessed (*Synonym:* prospective study).

Communicable disease–A disease due to an organism such as a bacteria or virus which is transmitted person-to-person or from animals or the physical environment to human by a variety of routes from air and water, to contaminated articles or fomites, to insect bites and animal bites. Here considered a subset of infectious disease.

Community Oriented Primary Care (COPC)–A structured six step process designed to move the delivery of health services from a focus on the individual to an additional focus on the needs of communities.

Community Oriented Public Health (COPH)—An effort on the part of governmental health agencies to reach out to the community and to the healthcare delivery system to address specific health issues.

Community rating—Insurance rates set the same for all eligible individuals and families based on the previous expenses in a defined community.

Concierge practice—A form of private practice of medicine that aims to provide personalized health care to those who can afford to pay for additional access and services out-of-pocket.

Confounding variable—A difference in the groups being compared that makes a difference in the outcome being measured.

Co-insurance—The percentage of the charges that the insured is responsible for paying.

Consistency—A supportive or ancillary criteria implying that the relationship has been observed in a wide range of populations and settings.

Constitutional law—In the United States a form of law based upon the United States constitution or the constitution of a state.

Contemplation phase—The second phase of the stages of change model in which an individual is actively thinking about the benefits and barriers to change.

Contributory cause—A definition of causation that is established when all three of the following have been established: (1) the existence of an association between the "cause" and the "effect" at the individual level; (2) the "cause" precedes the effect in time; and (3) altering the "cause" alters the probability of the "effect."

Co-payment—An amount that the insured is responsible for paying even when the service is covered by the insurance.

Core public health functions—Describes governmental public health functions that cannot be delegated and remain the responsibility of governmental public health. The Institute of Medicine has defined these functions as assessment, assurance, and policy development.

Cost effective—A measure of the cost of an intervention relative to its benefit. A cost effective intervention implies that any additional benefit is considered worth the cost. Cost effective can also imply that a large cost savings is worth a small reduction in net effectiveness.

Covered service—A service for which health insurance will provide payment if the individual is otherwise eligible.

Credentialing—A general term indicating a process of verifying that an individual has the desirable or required qualifications to practice a profession.

Customary, prevailing, and reasonable—These standards are used by many insurance plans to determine the amount that will be paid to the provider of services.

Data—Facts or the representation of facts as opposed to information.

Database—A collection of data organized in such a way that a computer program can select and compile the desired pieces of data.

Decision Analysis—A method of quantitative decision making that incorporates probabilities and utilities and the timing of events into the process of comparing options and making recommendations.

Decision Maker—A generic term that can be applied to a range of individuals and organizations that make health decisions including individuals, health professions and organizations ranging from non-profits to corporations to government agencies.

Deductible—The amount that an individual or family is responsible for paying before being eligible for insurance coverage.

Demographic transition—Describes the impact of falling childhood death rates and extended life spans on the size of populations and the age distribution of populations.

Determinants—Underlying factors that ultimately bring about disease.

Dietary supplements—A category within FDA law that includes vitamins, minerals, and many herbal remedies.

Diffusion of Innovation Theory—A theory that identifies stages of dissemination and types of adopters of new technology and other changes including behavioral change.

Disability Adjusted Life-Years (DALYs)—A population health status measure that incorporates measures of death and disability and allow for measurement of the impact of categories of diseases and risks factors.

Discounting—A process in which we place greater importance on events which are expected to occur in the immediate future than on events that are expected to occur in the distant future.

Distribution of Disease—How a disease is spread out in a population often using factors such as person, place, and time.

Dose-response relationship–A relationship which is present if changes in levels of an exposure are associated with changes in frequency of the outcome in a consistent direction.

Downstream factors–Factors affecting behavior that directly involve an individual and can potentially be altered by individual interventions such as an addiction to nicotine.

Dread effect–Perception of an increase in the probability of occurrence of an event due to its ease of visualability and its feared consequences.

Dynamic model–An approach to understanding a problem or system that looks at the components over a period of time.

Early adopters–Individuals categorized by Diffusion of Innovation theory as those who seek to experiment with innovative ideas.

Early majority adopters–Individuals categorized by Diffusion of Innovation theory as opinion leaders whose social status frequently influences others to adopt the behavior.

Ecological assessment–An assessment of the impact of an alteration of the physical environment on plants and animals.

Effectiveness–An intervention has been shown to increase the positive outcomes or benefits in the population or setting in which it will be used.

Efficacy–An intervention increased positive outcomes or benefits in the population on which it is investigated.

Eligible–An individual may need to meet certain criteria to be eligible for enrollment in a health insurance plan.

Employer Mandates–Employers are required to directly or indirectly provide comprehensive insurance coverage for all their employees.

Epidemiological transition–A concept indicating the change that has been historically observed as part of social and economic development from mortality and morbidity dominated by infections to morbidity and mortality dominated by what has been called non-communicable disease or degenerative and man-made diseases (*Synonym:* public health transition).

Epidemiological treatment–Treatment of contacts of an individual with a disease even in the absence of evidence of transmission of the disease.

Epidemiologists–An investigator who studies the occurrence and control of disease or other health conditions or events in defined populations.

Essential public heath services–The ten services that have come to define the responsibilities of the combined local, state, and federal governmental public health system.

Estimation–A statistical term implying a measurement of the strength of an association or the size of a difference.

Evidence–Reliable quantitative or qualitative information or data upon which a decision can be based.

Experience rating–Health insurance rates set on the basis of a group's past history of healthcare expenses (*Synonym:* Medical underwriting).

False negative–Individuals who have a negative result on a screening test but turn out to have the disease.

False positive–Individuals who have a positive result on a screening test but turn out not to have the disease.

Fee-for-service–A system of reimbursement for health services provided based on charges for health services actually provided to patients.

Group association–Two factors such as a characteristic and a disease occur together more often than expected by chance alone in the same group or population. Does not require that the investigator have data on the characteristics of the individuals that make up the group or population (*Synonym:* ecological association).

Harm–The negative outcomes that may occur with or without an intervention (see side effect).

Hazard–A measure of the inherent capability of a substance to produce harm.

Health Adjusted Life Expectancy (HALE's)–A population health status measure that combines life expectancy with a measure of the population's overall quality of health.

Healthcare delivery system–A linkage of institutions and healthcare professional that together take on the responsibility of delivering coordinated care.

Healthcare system–A healthcare delivery system plus the financial system that pays for the delivery of health care.

Health Communications–Method for conveying, interpreting, and utilizing health information as the basis for decision making.

Health Informatics–Methods for obtaining and compiling health information.

Health Related Quality of Life (HRQOL)–A health status measure that reflect the number of days of unhealthy days due to physical plus mental impairment. HRQOL provides an overall quality of health measure but it does not incorporate the impact of death.

Health system–The healthcare system plus the public health system.

Herd immunity–Protection of an entire population from a communicable disease by obtaining individual immunity through vaccination or natural infections by a large percentage of the population (*Synonym*: population immunity).

Heuristics–Rules of thumb for decision making that often allow more rapid decision making based on a limited amount of information.

Home rule–Authority granted to local jurisdictions such as cities or countries by state constitutions or state legislative actions.

Immunization–The strengthening of the immune system to prevent or control disease through exposure to antigens or administration of antibodies.

Inactivated vaccine–Injection of a nonliving organism or antigens from an organism designed to develop antibodies to protect an individual from the disease (*Synonym*: dead vaccine).

Incidence–Rates which measure the chances of occurrence of a disease or other condition over a period of time usually one year.

Incremental cost effectiveness–A measurement of the additional cost relative to the additional net-effectiveness (see net-effectiveness).

Individual mandates–Individuals are required to purchase individual health insurance policies which include at least standardized minimum coverage.

Infant mortality rate–A population health status measure that estimates the rate of death in the first year of life.

Infectious disease–A disease caused by an organism such as a bacteria or virus. Here used to include communicable diseases as well as other infections that are not communicable.

Infectivity–The ability of a pathogen to enter and multiply in a susceptible host.

Inference–A statistical term used to imply the drawing of conclusions about a population based upon data from a sample using statistical significance testing.

Inform of decision–A decision making approach in which a clinician is merely expected to inform the patient of what is planned.

Information–As used here, the compiling or presenting of data for a range of uses.

Informed consent–A decision making approach in which a clinician is expected to provide information and obtain agreement to proceed from the patient.

Inpatient facility–A healthcare facility in the United States in which an individual may remain for more than 24 hours. Examples include hospitals and nursing homes.

Institutional Review Board (IRB)–An institution-based group that is mandated by federal regulations to review human research conducted at the institution and determine whether it meets federally defined research standards.

Interaction analysis–An approach to environmental health assessment that looks at the consequences of two or more exposures.

Interventions–The full range of strategies designed to protect health and prevent disease, disability, and death.

Judicial law–Law made by courts when applying statutory or administrative law to specific cases (*Synonym*: case law, common law).

Justice–An ethical principle based on a sense of fairness in distribution of what is deserved.

Koch's postulates–Four postulates that together definitely establish a cause and effect for a communicable disease: the organism must be shown to be present in every case of the disease; the organism must not be found in cases of other diseases; once isolated the organism must be capable of replicating the disease in an experimental animal; and the organism must be recoverable from the animal (see Modern Koch's postulates).

Late adopters–Those identified by Diffusion of Innovation theory as in need of support and encouragement to make adoption as easy as possible (*Synonym*: laggard).

Lead time bias–The situation in screening for disease in which early detection does not alter outcome but only increases the interval, between detection of the disease and occurrence of the outcome such as death.

Legislative law–In the United States the type of law that includes statutes passed by legislative bodies at the federal, state, and local levels.

Leverage points–Points or locations in a system in which interventions can have substantial impacts (*Synonym*: control points).

License–A legal document granted by a governmental authority that provide permission to engage in an activity such as the practice of a health profession.

Life Expectancy–A population health status measure that summarizes the impact of death in an entire population utilizing the probability of death at each age of life in a particular year in a particular population.

Live vaccines–Use of a living organism in a vaccine. Living organism included in vaccines are expected to be attenuated or altered to greatly reduce the chances that they will themselves produce disease (*Synonym:* attenuated vaccine).

Long shot effect–A decision making attitude in which a decision maker perceives the status quo as intolerable and is willing to take an action with only a small chance of success and a large chance of making the situation worse.

Mainstream factors–Factors affecting behavior that result from the relationship of an individual with a larger group or population such as peer pressure to smoke or the level of taxation on cigarettes.

Maintenance–The fifth phase of the stages of change model in which the new behavior become a permanent part of an individual's lifestyle.

Market justice–The philosophy that market forces should be relied upon to organize the delivery of healthcare services.

Medicaid–A federal-state program which covers groups defined as categorically needed as well as groups that may be covered at the discretion of the state including those defined as medically needy such as those in need of nursing home care.

Medical Home–A term describing a concept of primary care that includes a team approach as part of a larger healthcare system.

Medical loss ratio–The ratio of benefits payments paid to premiums collected, indicating the proportion of the premiums spent on medical services.

Medical malpractice–A body of state civil law designed to hold practitioners accountable to patients for the quality of health care.

Medicare–A federal health insurance system that covers most individuals 65 and older as well as the disabled and those with end-stage renal disease.

Medigap–A supplemental health insurance linked to Medicare designed to cover all or most of the charges that are not covered by Medicare including the 20% co-payment required for many outpatient services.

Modern Koch's postulates–A set of criteria for establishing that an organism is a contributory cause of a disease requiring evidence of an epidemiological association, isolation, and transmissions (see Koch's postulates).

Morbidity–A public health term to describe the frequency of impairments or disability produced by a disease or other condition.

Mortality–A public health term to describe the frequency of deaths produced by a disease or other condition.

Multiple risk factor reduction–Simultaneous efforts to reduce more than one risk factor.

Multiplicative interaction–A type of interaction between two or more exposures such that the overall risk when two or more exposures are present is best estimated by multiplying the relative risk of each of the exposures.

Natural experiment–A change that occurs in one particular population but not another similar population without the intervention of an investigator.

Necessary cause–If the "cause" is not present the disease or "effect" will not develop.

Negative constitution–The principle that United States constitution allows but does not require government to act to protect public health or to provide healthcare services.

Negligence law–A body of law designed to protect individuals from harm.

Net effectiveness–A measure of the benefits minus the harms of an intervention (*Synonym:* Net benefit).

No-duty principle–The principle of United States law that healthcare providers, either individuals or institutions, do not have an obligation to provide health services.

Nutritional transition–Countries frequently move from poorly balanced diets often deficient in nutrients and calories to a diet of highly processed food including fats, sugars, and salt.

Odds ratio–A measure of the strength of the relationship that is often a good approximation of the relative risk. This ratio is calculated as the odds of having the risk factor if the disease is present divided by the odds of having the risk factor if the disease is absent.

Outcome measures–Measures of quality that imply a focus on the result of health care ranging from rates of infection to readmissions with complications.

Out-of-pocket expenses–Payments for health services not covered by insurance that are the responsibility of the individual receiving the services.

Outpatient facility–A healthcare facility in the United States in which patients can remain for less than 24 hours. These facilities include the offices of clinicians, general and specialty clinics, emergency departments and a range of new types of community-based diagnostic and treatment facilities.

Passive immunization–Administration of antibodies to provide short term protection against a disease.

P.E.R.I. Process–A mnemonic which summarizes the evidence-based public health process including problem description, etiology, recommendations based upon evidence, and implementation.

Phenotypic expression–The clinical presentation of a disease which may be quite variable despite the same genetic composition or genotype.

Point of Service Plans (POS)–A type of health plan that is a modification of staff model HMOs that allow enrollees to obtain care outside the HMO but require that the patient pay for a portion of the cost of the care received.

Police powers–Authority of governmental public health based on the power of state government to pass legislation and implement actions to protect the common good.

Policy development–A core public health function that includes developing evidence-based recommendations and other analyses of options such as health policy analysis to guide implementation including efforts to educate and mobilize community partnerships to implement these policies.

Population comparisons–A type of investigation in which groups are compared without having information on the individuals within the group (*Synonym:* ecological study).

Population health approach–As used here, a term used to describe an evidence-based approach to problem solving that considers a range of possible interventions including health care, traditional public health and social interventions (*Synonyms:* ecological approach, socio-ecological approach).

Population health status measures–Quantitative summary measures of the health of a large population such as life-expectancy, HALEs, and DALYs.

Portability–The ability to continue employment-based health insurance after leaving employment usually by paying the full cost of the insurance. A federal law known as COBRA generally ensures employees of 18 months of portability.

Potential risk factors–Factors that are thought to be associated with an increased probability of disease.

Precontemplation phase–The first phase of the stages of change model in which an individual has not yet considered changing their behavior.

Prediction rule–A quantitative formulae designed to increase the ability to predict the outcome of an condition and thereby guide the use of interventions.

Preferred Provider Plans (PPOs)–An insurance system that works with a limited number of clinicians. These providers agree to a set of conditions that usually includes reduced payments and other conditions. Patients may choose to use other clinicians but they often need to more pay more out-of-pocket.

Preparation phase–The third phase of the stages of change model in which the individual is developing a plan of action.

Preponderance of the evidence–A legal term implying that a trial is decided based upon the conclusion that the evidence is more supportive of the plaintive than the defendant or visa versa.

Prevalence–A measurement of the number of individuals who have a disease at a particular point in time divided by the number of individuals who could potentially have the disease.

Primary care–Traditionally refers to the first contact providers of care who are prepared to handle the great majority of common problems for which patients seek care.

Primary intervention–An intervention that occurs before the onset of the disease.

Procedural due process–A form of due process that prohibits governments from denying individuals a right in an arbitrary or unfair way.

Process measures–Measurement of quality that focus on the procedures and formal processes that go in delivering care from procedures to ensure credentialing of health professionals to procedures to ensure timely response to complaints.

Proportion–A fraction in which the numerator is made up of observations that are also included in the denominator.

Protective factor–A factor which is associated with a reduced probability of disease.

Provider–A term used to include a wide range of health professionals that provide health services.

Proximate cause–A legal concept of causation which asks whether the injury or other event would have occurred if the negligent act had not occurred.

Public health assessment–A formal assessment that incorporates risk assessment but also includes data on the actual exposure of a population to a hazard.

Public health surveillance–Collection of health data as the basis for monitoring and understanding health problems, generating hypotheses about etiology, and evaluating the success of interventions (*Synonym:* Surveillance).

Quality Adjusted Life Year (QALY)–A measurement that asks about the number of life-years saved by an intervention rather than the number of lives.

Quarantine–The compulsory physical separation of those with a disease or at high risk of developing a disease from the rest of the population.

Randomization–As part of a randomized clinical trial, assignment of participants to study and control groups using a chance process in which the participants are assigned to a particular group with a known probability (*Synonym:* Random assignment).

Randomized clinical trial–An investigation in which individuals are assigned to study or control groups using a process of randomization. (*Synonym*: experimental study).

Range of normal–The range of values on a test that is established by performing the test on those who are believed to be free of a disease. (*Synonym:* reference interval).

Rates–Used here as a generic term to describe measurements that have a numerator and a denominator.

Recommendations–Statements based upon evidence indicating that actions such as cigarette cessation will improve outcomes such a reducing lung cancer.

Reductionist approach–An approach to problem solving that looks at each of the components of a problem one at a time.

Relative risk–A ratio of the probability of the outcome if a factor known as a risk factor is present compared to the probability of the outcome if the factor is not present.

Respect for persons–An ethical principle that incorporates two ethical convictions: first, individuals should be treated as autonomous agents, and second, that persons with diminished autonomy are entitled to protection.

Revenue sharing–A system of allocating federal funding to states and local jurisdictions according to a specific formula with few restrictions on its use.

Reverse causality–The situation in which the apparent "cause" is actually the "effect."

Rights–Protections afforded individuals on the basis of the United States constitution, a state constitution, or legislative actions.

Ring vaccination–As used in the smallpox eradication program, immediate vaccination of populations in surrounding geographic areas after identification of a case of disease.

Risk assessment–A process used in environmental health to formally assess the potential for harm due to a hazard taking into account factors such as the likelihood, timing, and duration of exposure.

Risk avoider–A decision maker who consistently favors avoiding an action even when a decision analysis utilizing probabilities, utilities, and timing argues for the action.

Risk indicator–A characteristic such as gender or age that is associated with an outcome but is not considered a contributory cause (*Synonym:* risk marker).

Risk factor–A characteristics of individuals or an exposure that increases the probability of developing a disease. It does not imply that a contributory cause has been established.

Risk taker–A decision maker who consistently favors taking an action even when a decision analysis utilizing probabilities, utilitizes, and timing argues against the decision.

Risk taking attitudes–A decision making attitude in which an individual or group consistently favors taking action or avoiding action that differ from the recommendations of a decision analysis utilizing probabilities, utilities, and the timing of events.

Safety net–The provision of services for those who cannot afford to purchase the services.

Sample–A small subset drawn from a larger group or population.

Score–In the context of evidence-based recommendations, a measurement of the quality of the evidence and a measurement of the magnitude of the impact.

Screening–As used here, testing individuals who are asymptomatic for a particular disease as part of a strategy to diagnose a disease or identify a risk factor.

Secondary care–Refers to specialty care provided by clinicians who focus on one or a small number of organ systems or on a specific type of service such as obstetrics or anesthesiology.

Secondary intervention–Early detection of disease or risk factors and intervention during an asymptomatic phase.

Sensitivity–A measurement of how well a test performs in the presence of disease.

Sequential testing–A screening strategy that uses one test followed by one or more additional tests if the first test is positive (*Synonym:* two-stage testing).

Shared decision making–A decision making approach in which a clinician is expected to directly or indirectly provide information and options for intervention to a patient and then rely on the patient to synthesize the information and make their own decision.

Side effect–A negative outcome that may occur from an intervention.

Single Payer–A single source of payment for all healthcare services usually envisioned as government at the state or federal level as the payer for all basic healthcare services.

Simultaneous testing–A screening strategy that uses two tests initially with follow-up testing if either test is positive (*Synonym:* parallel testing).

Skimming–Enrolling predominating healthy individuals into a health plan to reduce the costs to the plan.

Social justice–A philosophy that aims to provide fair treatment and a fair share of the reward of society to individuals and groups.

Social marketing–The use of marketing theory, skills, and practice to achieve social change, e.g., in health promotion.

Socio-economic status–In the United States a measurement using scales reflecting education, income, and professional status.

Specificity–A measure of how well a test performs in the absent of disease. Equals 1 minus the false negative rate.

Stages of Change model–A model of behavioral change that hypothesizes five steps in the process of behavioral change including pre-contemplation, contemplation, preparation, action, and maintenance.

Standard population–The age distribution of a population that is often used as the basis for comparison with other populations. The age distribution of the United States population in the year 2000 is generally used.

State Child Health Insurance Program (SCHIP)–A federally funded health insurance program that provides funds to the states to use to expand or facilitate the operation of Medicaid or other uses to serve the health needs of lower income children.

Static model–An approach to understanding a problem or system that looks at the components at one particular point in time.

Statistical significance test–A method used to draw conclusions or inferences about populations from data on sample(s) of the population.

Strength of the relationship–A supportive or ancillary criteria implying that a measurement of the strength of an association such as a relative risk or odds ratio is large or substantial.

Structural measures–Measure of quality of health care focused on the physical and organizational infrastructure in which care is delivered.

Substantive due process–A type of due process in which state and federal governments must justify the grounds for depriving an individual of life, liberty, and property.

Sufficient cause–If the "cause" is present the disease or "effect" will occur.

Supportive criteria–Criteria that may be used to argue for a cause and effect relationship when the definitive requirements have not been fulfilled (*Synonym:* ancillary criteria).

Surrogate outcome–A measurement of outcome that looks at short term results such as changes in laboratory tests that may not reflect longer term or clinical important outcomes.

Syndemic–A systems thinking approach that focuses attention on how health problems interact as part of larger systems.

System error–Problems resulting from deficiencies in the system for delivering health care or other services.

Systems analysis–An approach to environmental exposures as well as other public health problems that examines the interconnections between exposures or components of larger networks.

Tertiary care–A type of health care often defined in terms of the type of institution in which it is delivered, often academic or specialized health center. This type of care may also be defined in term of the type of problem that is addressed such as trauma centers, burn centers, or neonatal intensive care.

Tertiary intervention–An intervention that occurs after the initial occurrence of symptoms but before irreversible disability occurs.

True rate–A measurement that has a numerator which is a subset of the denominator and a unit of time, such as a day or a year, over which the number of events in the numerator is measured.

Uncontrollability effect–Perception of increased probability of occurance of an event due to the perceived inability of an individual to control or prevent the event from occurring.

Under-5 Mortality–A population health status measure that estimates the probability of dying during the first 5 years of life.

Undergraduate medical education–Refers to the four years of medical school leading to a MD or DO degree despite the fact that an undergraduate or bachelors degree is generally required for admission.

Unfamiliarity effect–Perception of increased probability of an event due to an individual's absence of prior experience with the event.

Universal coverage–Provision of at least basic or medically necessary health insurance for an entire population.

Upstream factors–Factors affecting behavior that are grounded in social structures and policies, such as government-sponsored programs that encourage tobacco production.

Utility scale–A scale that goes from 0 to 1 with zero reflecting immediate death and 1 reflecting full health. This scale is used to measure the value or important that an individual or a group places on a particular outcome.

Victim blaming–Placing the responsibility or blame for a bad outcome on the individual who experiences the bad outcome due to their behavior.

Viral load–A measurement of the quantity of a virus such as HIV which is present in the blood.

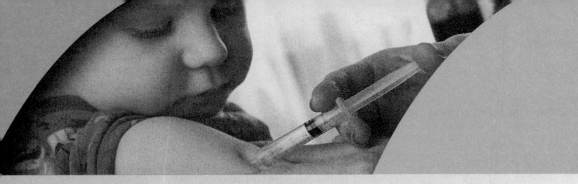

Index